JUSTICE DENIED

THE REALITY OF THE INTERNATIONAL CRIMINAL COURT

JUSTICE DENIED

THE REALITY OF THE INTERNATIONAL CRIMINAL COURT

David Hoile

The Africa Research Centre

Copyright © David Hoile 2014
First published in 2014 by The Africa Research Centre
Communications House, 26 York Street, LONDON W1U 6PZ

Distributed by Gardners Books, 1 Whittle Drive, Eastbourne,
East Sussex, BN23 6QH
Tel: +44(0)1323 521555 | Fax: +44(0)1323 521666

The moral right of David Hoile to be identified as the author of this work has been asserted in accordance with the Copyright Design and Patents Act 1988

All rights reserved. This book is sold subject to the condition that it shall not, by way of trade or otherwise, be lent, resold, hired out or otherwise circulated without the publisher's prior consent in any form of binding or cover other than that in which it is published and without a similar condition including this condition being imposed on the
subsequent purchaser.

British Library Cataloguing in Publication Data
A catalogue record for this book is available from the British Library.

ISBN 978-0-9928035-0-6

Typeset by Amolibros, Milverton, Somerset
www.amolibros.com
This book production has been managed by Amolibros
Printed and bound by T J International Ltd, Padstow, Cornwall, UK

"Imagine if there were a criminal court in Britain which only ever tried black people, which ignored crimes committed by whites and Asians and only took an interest in crimes committed by blacks. We would consider that racist, right? And yet there is an International Criminal Court which only ever tries black people, African black people to be precise, and it is treated as perfectly normal. In fact the court is lauded by many radical activists as a good and decent institution, despite the fact that no non-black person has ever been brought before it to answer for his crimes. It is remarkable that in an era when liberal observers see racism everywhere, in every thoughtless aside or crude joke, they fail to see it in an institution which focuses exclusively on the criminal antics of dark-skinned people from the 'Dark Continent'…. Liberal sensitivity towards issues of racism completely evaporates when it comes to the ICC, which they will defend tooth and nail, despite the fact that it is quite clearly, by any objective measurement, racist, in the sense that it treats one race of people differently to all others."

Brendan O'Neill, The Daily Telegraph, *15 March 2012*

Contents

Abbreviations	xi
About the Author	xiii
Introduction	1
Chapter One: The International Criminal Court	11
The funding of the ICC	15
One rule for Europe and another for everyone else	19
Illegal reservations to the treaty	20
The ICC is not a universal court	21
China's stance on the ICC	22
The Indian position on the ICC	24
The ICC is a political body	25
Chapter Two: A European Court	35
Political Support for the ICC	39
The Cotonou Agreement	39
EU Common Positions on ICC	42
The European Union, International Criminal Court and Japan: A case study	47
The EU European Neighbourhood Policy	48
The EU's funding of pro-ICC non-governmental organisations	49
The European Parliament	54
Chapter Three: The Court and the Security Council	56
Chapter Four: The United States and the Court	69
Chapter Five: The Court and Non-Governmental Organisations	84
Chapter Six: A Glaring Democratic Deficit	93
Chapter Seven: Judges Elected by Vote-Trading	99
Chapter Eight: The Office of the Prosecutor	115
The first chief prosecutor	116
The arrogance and prejudice of the Prosecutor	118
A record of incompetence and failure	120

The chief prosecutor's legal incompetence	129
The chief prosecutor's trial incompetence	133
The chief prosecutor's administrative incompetence	134
Allegations of sexual misconduct and breach of due process	136
The ICC and hijacking civilian airliners: European "extraordinary rendition"?	140
Chapter Nine: Avoiding the Crime of Aggression	144
Chapter Ten: Entrenching Impunity, Granting Immunity	150
Chapter Eleven: The European Guantánamo Bay?	159
Guantánamo military commissions and ICC similarities	163
Chapter Twelve: Inaction Over Iraq	167
Chapter Thirteen: An Afghan Case Study	176
The 4 September 2009 Kunduz massacre	179
Germany, Colonel Klein and the International Criminal Court	194
Two colonels: two standards	195
The abuses continue	197
Chapter Fourteen: The International Criminal Court and Africa	199
The African Union and the ICC	205
Effects on peace in Africa	209
Africa says no	212
The October 2013 extraordinary AU summit	216
Chapter Fifteen: The Fiction of African "Self-Referral"	219
Self-referrals are in contravention of the Rome Statute	221
Self-referral as a useful tool for the prosecutor	224
Self-referral by states – state self-interest	224
Chapter Sixteen: The Fiction of Deterrence	228
Uganda: A Case Study in Non-deterrence	230
Chapter Seventeen: The Fiction of a Victims' Court	236
Chapter Eighteen: The Court and Uganda	240
Impeding a peaceful settlement	246
The retributive European justice model	249
A lesson for Africa	250

Contents

Chapter Nineteen: The Court and the Democratic Republic of the Congo	252
The Prosecutor v. Thomas Lubanga Dyilo	252
The Prosecutor v. Germain Katanga and Mathieu Ngudjolo Chui	266
The Prosecutor v. Callixte Mbarushimana	267
The Prosecutor v. Jean Bosco Ntaganda	268
The Prosecutor v. Sylvestre Mudacumura	269
Chapter Twenty: The Court and the Central African Republic	274
Chapter Twenty-one: The Court and Sudan	278
The special criminal court on the events in Darfur	280
The Chief Prosecutor's application for an arrest warrant for President al-Bashir	283
Ocampo's mortality claims versus reality	286
Uganda and Darfur compared	288
Allegations of genocide in Darfur	291
The Sudanese position on the ICC and Darfur	296
More ICC double standards	300
The ICC v. the rest of world	305
The Prosecutor v. Bahar Idriss Abu Garda	308
The Prosecutor v. Abdallah Banda Abakaer Nourain and Saleh Mohammed Jerbo Jamus	309
The Prosecutor v. Abdel Raheem Muhammad Hussein	310
Chapter Twenty-two: The Court and Kenya	312
The Prosecutor v. William Samoei Ruto and Joshua arap Sang	317
The Prosecutor v. Francis Kirimi Muthaura and Uhuru Muigai Kenyatta	317
Chapter Twenty-three: The Court and the Ivory Coast	335
The Prosecutor v. Laurent Gbagbo	335
The Prosecutor v. Simone Gbagbo	343
The Prosecutor v. Charles Blé Goudé	343
Chapter Twenty-four: The Court and Libya	345
Chapter Twenty-five: The Court and Mali	369
Chapter Twenty-six: European Double Standards	374
Impunity and pensions for European human rights abusers	375
Britain's Darfur	377
Amnesty for some but not Africa	383

Chapter Twenty-seven: A Way Forward   387

Conclusion   397
   The "McDonaldization" of justice   399
   What has the International Criminal Court achieved?   400

Appendix One: Sudan's Notification of No Obligation to the ICC   406
Appendix Two: African Union decision regarding
   the International Criminal Court (ICC)   407
Appendix Three: Agreement between the International Criminal Court
   and the European Union on Cooperation and Assistance   410
Appendix Four: Full text of the Secret Human Rights Watch letter to the
   Office of the Prosecutor, International Criminal Court,
   dated 15 September 2008   419
Appendix Five: Speech by His Excellency Hon. Uhuru Kenyatta, CGH,
   President and Commander in Chief of The Defence Forces of the
   Republic of Kenya at the Extraordinary Session of the Assembly
   of Heads of State and Government of the African Union, Addis Ababa,
   Ethiopia, 12th October, 2013   423
Appendix Six: African Union decision regarding its relationship with the
   International Criminal Court (ICC)   430

Bibliography   433
Notes to chapters   473
Index   599

ABBREVIATIONS

ACP	African, Caribbean and Pacific Bloc of Nations
ASP	Assembly of States Parties
ASPA	American Servicemembers' Protection Act
AU	African Union
AUPD	African Union High Level Panel on Darfur
BIA	Bilateral Immunity Agreement
CAPP	Council of African Political Parties
CAR	Central African Republic
CICC	Coalition for the International Criminal Court
CPA	Comprehensive Peace Agreement
DPA	Darfur Peace Agreement
DRC	Democratic Republic of the Congo
ECOWAS	Economic Community of West African States
ECtHR	European Court of Human Rights
ENP	European Neighbourhood Policy
EU	European Union
FNI	Front des Nationalistes et des Intégrationnistes
FRPI	Force de Résistance Patriotique en Ituri
GI-Net	Genocide Intervention Network
HRW	Human Rights Watch
IBA	International Bar Association
ICC	International Criminal Court
ICG	International Crisis Group
ICID	International Commission of Inquiry into Darfur
ICJ	International Court of Justice
ICTJ	International Center for Transitional Justice
ICTR	International Criminal Tribunal for Rwanda
ICTY	International Criminal Tribunal for the Former Yugoslavia
IDP	Internally Displaced Person
ILO	International Labour Organisation
ISAF	International Security Assistance Force
IWPR	Institute for War & Peace Reporting
JEM	Justice and Equality Movement
LRA/M	Lord's Resistance Army / Movement
MONUC	Mission des Nations Unies en République Démocratique du Congo
MSF	Médecins Sans Frontières

NATO	North Atlantic Treaty Organisation
NGO	Non-Governmental Organisation
NTC	National Transitional Council
OPCD	Office of Public Counsel for the Defence
OTP	Office of the Prosecutor
SAF	Sudanese Armed Forces
SLA	Sudan Liberation Army
SCCED	Special Criminal Court on the Events in Darfur
SRRC	Social Sciences Research Council
UN	United Nations
UNICEF	United Nations Children's Fund
UNOHCHR	United Nations Office of the High Commissioner for Human Rights
UNSC	United Nations Security Council
UPC	Union des Patriotes Congolais
UPDF	Ugandan People's Defence Force

ABOUT THE AUTHOR

Dr. David Hoile is a public affairs consultant specialising in African and international affairs. He is an elected Fellow of the Royal United Services Institute for Defence and Security Studies, a member of the Royal Institute of International Affairs, the Royal African Society and the African Studies Associations of the United Kingdom and United States. He is the author of *The International Criminal Court: Europe's Guantánamo Bay?* (2010), *Darfur: The Road to Peace* (2008), *Images of Sudan: Case Studies in Propaganda and Misinformation* (2003), *Farce Majeure: The Clinton Administration's Sudan Policy 1993–2000* (2000), *Mozambique: A Nation in Crisis* (1989), *Mozambique, Resistance and Freedom: A Case for Reassessment* (1994) and the editor of *Mozambique 1962–93: A Political Chronology* (1994). David Hoile is a visiting professor at Sudan International University. He has commented on public policy issues on CNN, Al-Jazeera English and Arabic, BBC News 24, BBC TV News, BBC radio, France 24, Chinese Central TV, Press TV, Al-Arabiya and the Islam Channel.

Introduction

"Sentence first – verdict afterwards"

The Queen in Alice in Wonderland[1]

The pursuit of justice, in the wake of wrongdoing and especially in the face of crimes against humanity and war crimes, is one of mankind's most noble instincts. The International Criminal Court was embraced with understandable enthusiasm by a wide range of people, non-governmental organisations and governments when it came into being on 1 July 2002. Many of those who initially welcomed it were African. Despite an auspicious start, however, the ICC ran into considerable controversy within months of its establishment. With hindsight, it can be seen that the court clearly contained the seeds of its own destruction from the start. The ICC has turned out to be one of the nastier manifestations of globalisation with what appears to be an almost exclusive focus on Africa. The court that countries idealistically signed up for in 2002 is not the grubby, inept institution they found themselves with a decade or so later.

This study is both an examination and an indictment of the ICC. It has to be said from the start that the court is an ideological construct and like most if not all ideologies it bears a questionable connection with reality. Given the hallowed – almost sacred – claims made of the ICC, the court, its functionaries and its ideological adherents have assumed an automatic immunity to criticism. The reality is that the ICC was the most questionable concept to come down the ideological pipeline for quite some time. The concept's subsequent physical manifestation, heralded by mantras and slogans promising justice, has proved to be professionally inept, corrupt and racist. The court has shown itself to be a prisoner of several vested interests, notably permanent members of the United Nations Security Council most identified with the ultimate crime against humanity, waging wars of aggression.

The ICC has already been described as "Europe's Guantánamo Bay for Africans".[2] The comparisons are clear. The Guantánamo Bay and The Hague tribunals both claim international jurisdiction. Both claim that they exist in order to punish and deter the most serious of crimes. And both tribunals have a legally autistic approach that states that there is no alternative to what they are doing. Both the Guantánamo Bay and ICC tribunals have one more thing in common. Both are synonymous with judicial failure and imperial arrogance.

The British jurist Geoffrey Robertson QC, an internationally renowned human-rights lawyer, has dismissed the ICC as "the triumphalist nonsense [of] deluded propagandists".[3]

He presents a picture of a court that is little more than a backdrop for show trials against those involved in conflicts in countries like Rwanda and the former Yugoslavia where none of the combatants have superpower support.[4] Watching it in operation since 2003, he further noted the court's "crippling failure to work expeditiously and effectively".[5]

The intellectual premise underpinning the ICC was questionable from the start. Previous studies of human-rights treaties found that non-compliance with treaty obligations was commonplace. Treaty ratification is not infrequently associated with worse practices than otherwise expected. Because human-rights treaties tend to be weakly monitored and enforced, countries that ratify may enjoy the benefits of accession – including, perhaps, reduced pressure for improvements in practices – without bearing significant costs. The positive effects of human-rights treaties may sometimes be offset or even outweighed by treaties' less beneficial effects.[6] This was more than borne out in the decade since those studies. Terrence Chapman and Stephen Chaudoin have updated these earlier conclusions. They suggest caution towards arguments about the impact of the ICC on global practices and provide support for the notion that states strategically select themselves into supranational judicial agreements.[7]

There is very little doubt that international law, and international legal institutions such as the ICC, have been deliberately and cynically used by a range of governments as instruments of lawfare. David B. Rivkin Jr. and Lee A. Casey have summed up the deployment of "lawfare": "The term 'lawfare' describes the growing use of international law claims, usually factually or legally meritless, as a tool of war. The goal is to gain a moral advantage over your enemy in the court of world opinion, and potentially a legal advantage in national and international tribunals."[8]

The Lawfare Project has also defined the term: "Lawfare denotes the use of the law as a weapon of war, or more specifically, the abuse of the law and legal systems for strategic political or military ends."[9] US Major-General Charles Dunlap defined the concept as a "strategy of using – or misusing – law as a substitute for traditional military means to achieve an operational objective."[10] The above definitions clearly fit the United Nations Security Council's use of the ICC by way of referrals, as well as self-serving self-referrals by several African states.

Even its most avid supporters have admitted that the Rome Statute establishing the ICC was itself seriously flawed. And it is not hard to see the fault lines. Good law evolves over decades. The ICC statute was rushed through in four weeks, by Western non-governmental organisations, not lawyers, on a take-it-or-leave-it basis.[11] The ICC states "[t]he Court is an independent judicial institution".[12] The truth is that the ICC is as independent as the UNSC lets it be. Far from being an independent, impartial, international court, the ICC is inextricably tied to the UNSC. Articles 13(b) and 16 of the ICC's own statute grant special "prosecutorial" rights, to refer or defer an ICC investigation or prosecution, to the Security Council, or more specifically to the five permanent members of the Security Council.[13] Political interference was thus made part of the court's founding terms of reference. We have the deeply questionable situation whereby three of the five permanent members – the USA, China and the Russian Federation – who are not members of the court, claim to be able to refer another non-signatory to the

Rome Statute to the court when it is politically expedient for them so to do, something they have done on two occasions. The former UN Secretary-General Kofi Annan has admitted that "questions of credibility will persist so long" as three of the five permanent members of the Security Council are not parties to the statute.[14]

European control of the court is clear. Any examination of the ICC's budget clearly shows that the court is umbilically tied financially to the European Union, which provides almost sixty percent of its funding, with most of it coming from Britain, France, Germany, Italy and Spain. One of Africa's most distinguished academics, Professor Mahmood Mamdani has said the ICC is dancing to the "tune" of Western states.[15] Given Africa's traumatic experience with the very same colonial powers that now in effect fund and direct the ICC, it is an unfortunate *déjà vu*. This reality has been picked up on by Rwandan President Paul Kagame. He has dismissed the ICC as a new form of imperialism created by the West and "put in place only for African countries, only for poor countries". He said that the ICC reflected "colonialism, slavery and imperialism".[16] It is a simple fact that every single one of the thirty-two people the court has chosen to indict is African.

The distinguished international peace researcher and a past Senior Vice-Rector of the United Nations University, Professor Ramesh Thakur, reflects this growing consensus within the developing world: "[A]...troubling issue is how an initiative of international criminal justice meant to protect vulnerable people from brutal national rulers has managed to be subverted into an instrument of power against vulnerable countries. A court meant to embody and pursue universal justice is in practice reduced to imposing selective justice of the West against the rest."[17]

And while the ICC may aspire to be a universal court exercising universal jurisdiction, the simple fact is that it does not qualify on either count. Its members represent less than one third of the world's population: China, Russia, the USA, India, Pakistan and Indonesia are just some of the many countries that have remained outside of the court's jurisdiction.

Several other key claims made by the court have also proved to be inaccurate or deceptive. The court has claimed to be "economical", yet it has cost close to a billion euros to conclude one deeply flawed trial. The court has claimed to be victim-centred yet Human Rights Watch has publicly criticised the ICC's ambivalence towards victim communities. The court has claimed to bring "swift justice" but it took several years to bring the first accused to trial for allegedly using child soldiers. The Nuremberg trials, which addressed infinitely more serious charges, were over and done with within a year. The court claims to be fighting impunity, yet it has afforded *de facto* impunity to several serial abusers of human rights who happen to be friends of the EU and the USA, and granted *de jure* immunity to non-member states such as the USA.

In the ICC, one has a court whose judges are appointed not because they are the best legal minds in the world, but because of squalid vote trading. Some are appointed because it is a cosy retirement job; some are washed-up politicians; some are diplomats; some use the court as a waiting room before greater things; others are appointed because their governments pay the ICC a lot of money; and some don't even bother to show up for work because something better came along. *We have judges making critical rulings on very difficult issues of law who have never been lawyers, let alone judges.* We have judges who have pressed for legal indictments on the basis of what they have seen on CNN. We have judges who cite classical Greek mythology to justify prolonging Africa's civil wars rather than to put peace before selectively retributive European law. We have judges who are political activists with little practical experience beyond abstract sloganising. And we have judges who have taught law in classrooms without any courtroom experience whatsoever.

The ICC has produced witnesses in several trials who recanted their testimony when in the witness box, admitting that they were coached by non-governmental organisations as to what false statements to make. We have seen prosecutorial decisions that should have ended any fair trial because they compromised the integrity of any subsequent process. We have seen trials stopped because of judicial decisions to add new charges halfway through proceedings. And most telling of all, the court brought into being in 2002 to punish the most serious crimes in the world, the most grave of which being waging a war of aggression, has consciously avoided meaningfully addressing aggression – managing to postpone any action for at least another decade. It has turned a blind eye to the invasion and occupation of both Iraq and Afghanistan by Western military forces.

As reluctant as one is to fall back upon Anglo-Saxon popular culture in a study of such a daunting field as international justice, it is hard not to describe the ICC as the Keystone Kops meets *Alice in Wonderland*.[18] The ICC is increasingly becoming the target of derision. It has also been likened to the international equivalent of the disreputable "ambulance chaser" lawyers that give domestic lawyers a bad name.[19]

It is abundantly clear that the ICC was very badly served by its first Chief Prosecutor, an impetuous celebrity lawyer, Luis Moreno Ocampo In addition to having been a state prosecutor in his native Argentina, Ocampo had also been the *Judge Judy* of Argentine television, hosting his own legal reality show called *La Corte del Pueblo,* or *The People's Court.* Simply put, Ocampo was a gift to those forces opposed to the ICC. He accentuated and exemplified all the intrinsic flaws within the court.

To begin with, the court's chief prosecutor showed scant respect across the board for legal procedures and due process. In one extraordinary instance, he withheld hundreds of items of potentially exculpatory evidence not only from the defence but also from the judges in his first ever trial. In any Anglo-Saxon judicial system he may well have been disbarred for such behaviour. He demonstrated his contempt for the legal process by leaving his own courtroom halfway through the opening day of the ICC's first ever trial (at a cost of half a billion euros) to attend the Davos World Economic Forum to rub shoulders with fellow celebrities such as Brad Pitt and Angelina Jolie. Even when he was in court, observers noted that he spent time texting on his Blackberry. No self-respecting court should have allowed such behaviour. A change in chief prosecutor clearly hasn't improved standards. In 2013 an ICC judge actually requested to be removed from a case she was hearing citing "grave problems in the Prosecution's system of evidence review, as well as a serious lack of proper oversight by senior Prosecution staff".

Despite ICC claims that the Office of the Prosecutor would be a model for employer-employee relations, Ocampo's office hemorrhaged staff at all levels, experienced lawyers unable to put up with the prosecutor's questionable behaviour and unprofessionalism.

INTRODUCTION

And this is not to mention Ocampo's well-documented sexual misconduct while on ICC business in South Africa, and his subsequent related abuse of due process that cost the ICC hundreds of thousands of euros in compensation and costs. Indeed, it is claimed that the only reason Ocampo chose to escalate his claims about Darfur to allegations of genocide was in order to distract attention away from his predatory sexual misconduct at the time.

The ICC had a chief prosecutor who, while focused on the Darfur issue, had never been to Darfur, whose office had not investigated inside Sudan, and whose reliance on claims made by externally based partisan "advocacy" groups and NGOs repeatedly tripped him up – as they have also done in the Democratic Republic of the Congo and Kenya. His claims, for example, that 5,000 internally displaced people were dying per month in Darfur jarred with the real figures provided by the United Nations, the African Union, the joint UN-AU Mission in Darfur and even anti-Khartoum groups such as Genocide Intervention-Net, who reported spikes of between 100 to 200 fatalities (including soldiers, militiamen and civilians) per month from *all* causes (a figure that should perhaps be compared to estimates of 45,000 deaths per month in the DRC). It is not for nothing that Mamdani has warned that international NGOs have blown the Darfur conflict out of all proportion.[20] One would have expected a more professional and discerning approach from such a senior official of the court.

The ICC has all too obviously ignored crystal-clear cases of superpower and Western abuses of human rights, and human rights abuses by their client states. The ICC chief prosecutor has courageously gone after only those people he has seen as being weak and unprotected by the UNSC and its permanent members. The question has quite understandably been asked by reputable Africa experts: "[I]s the [ICC] Prosecutor a stormtrooper for judicial neo-colonialism, kicking down the doors of others' hard-won independent sovereignties, brushing aside the protests of peace mediators, to demand the unconditional surrender and handcuffing of those without the protection of a superpower?"[21]

As of September 2010, the Office of the Prosecutor reported having received 8,874 complaints from more than 130 countries.[22] From these almost 9,000 alleged instances of serious abuses of human rights, the ICC has acted in eight African "situations", to the exclusion of any complaints implicating white Europeans and North Americans or their *protégés*. The ICC, for example, has turned a blind eye to self-evident human-rights abuses well within its jurisdiction in Iraq and Afghanistan. The court has chosen instead to indict thirty-two Africans. And even in the eight African countries the court has selected for action, the Office of the Prosecutor has been politically selective as to which human-rights abuses it chose to pursue, ignoring well-documented, systemic war crimes by certain governments. In so doing, the court has made a mockery of its claims to bring about an end to impunity.

And when provided with the opportunity of addressing any of its many flaws at the court's first Review Conference in Kampala in 2009, it engaged in a little, light "housekeeping". It also continued to duck the issue of aggression, postponing any possible action until at least 2017.

It might come as no surprise that the ICC appears to have a questionable approach to the concept of presumption of innocence. The court's Chief Prosecutor has repeatedly ignored the presumption of innocence in respect of a number of people indicted by the court. Ocampo repeatedly stated without reservation at a wide variety of fora and in newspaper articles, for example, that President Omar al-Bashir of Sudan is guilty of genocide, crimes against humanity and war crimes, alleged crimes for which he has never been tried. The prosecutor also sought to freeze and seize the assets of the four Kenyans before the court months before their trial was scheduled to start.

What might come as more of a surprise is that for all their declared commitment to presumption of innocence, the USA and key EU countries have also turned a blind eye to the concept when it is politically convenient to do so. Article 6.2 of the *Convention for the Protection of Human Rights and Fundamental Freedoms* of the Council of Europe states: "Everyone charged with a criminal offence shall be presumed innocent until proved guilty according to law". This convention is binding on all Council of Europe members, which includes all members of the EU. This right is also enshrined in Article 48 of the *Charter of Fundamental Rights of the European Union*. Nevertheless, in the run-up to the Kenyan presidential election in 2013, the USA, EU, Britain and Germany all pointedly cautioned against electing anyone indicted by the ICC. Some of these governments stated they would not even meet with anyone indicted by the court. It fell to the High Court of Kenya to explain and uphold the presumption of innocence on 15 February 2013, when it ruled that Uhuru Kenyatta's presidential bid could go forward because the High Court had no jurisdiction to determine the qualifications of a person who has been duly nominated to run for president; the Rome Statue has no provision for the ICC to bar candidates; and, most importantly, under Article 50 of the Kenyan Constitution, there is a presumption of innocence until the contrary is proved.

The ICC's actions regarding the Darfur situation in Sudan have been particularly controversial, not least of which because Sudan, as a non-signatory of the Rome Statute, does not come under the ICC's jurisdiction. This flies in the face both of natural justice and international law as laid out in the 1969 *Vienna Convention on the Law of Treaties*, and the 1986 *Convention on the Law of Treaties Between States and International Organisations or Between International Organisations*. Quite simply a state cannot be made party to a treaty or agreement to which it was not a signatory. The situation in Darfur was referred to the court by the UNSC in 2005. More people died from gun violence in Washington DC in 2008 – the year the court sought to indict Sudan's President al-Bashir – than died from armed violence in Darfur. Four times as many Mexican civilians died in drug-related violence alone in 2008 than died in Darfur that year.[23] Yet the ICC Chief Prosecutor chose to intensify his focus on Darfur. In so doing, the ICC polarised international opinion on the court between, in effect, the EU and the Anglosphere, and the rest of the world, especially the non-aligned and developing world.[24]

Unfortunately for the ICC and Europe they are targeting Africa at a time when the continent is asserting its political and economic independence. *Time* magazine has noted "a renewed mood of self-assertion in Africa".[25] Despite the presence of one or two pro-ICC Uncle Toms, Africa and the AU has rejected European and ICC attempts at regime change by deeply questionable legal *diktat*. Former South African President Thabo Mbeki has forcibly stated: "We have a common responsibility as Africans to determine our destiny."

The ICC has emerged as a *de facto* European court, funded by Europe, directed by Europe and to date focused exclusively on the African continent, and thereby serving Western political and economic interests in Africa. The ICC was brought into being with the assistance of a range of EU-funded Western non-governmental organisations. Mamdani has observed that "The rule of law cannot be introduced from outside. We are not yet back into colonialism. These NGOs must be accountable to African governments." This Western, ivory-tower legal fundamentalism has had disastrous consequences in the real world. The ICC, through its stifling of peace initiatives, is itself indirectly responsible for thousands of deaths, and the suffering of many more civilians, on the continent of Africa. It has also betrayed victims across the African continent and beyond.

Wishful thinking has been a hallmark of adherents of the court. This has most clearly manifested itself with regard to the USA and its position regarding the ICC. The USA has made its position very clear. It has correctly stated that the court is an irretrievably defective institution subject to political manipulation and that none of its citizens would ever appear before it. Almost as if to prove its point the Bush Administration went from opposing even the very mention of the court at the UN, to cynically using the court for its own political purposes, for example with the Sudan referral, while of course immunising its citizens from any repercussions. The fact that the Obama Administration has continued – and even increased – Washington's political manipulation of the court, while paying lip service to notions of international justice, has somehow been portrayed as a positive development in The Hague. It clearly wouldn't pass *Judge Judy*'s informal legal test.[26]

The court has actually been described as a "kangaroo court" by a wide spectrum of disparate observers, ranging from US Supreme Court justices and legislators through to Zimbabwean ministers of justice.[27] A US Supreme Court Justice told UN Secretary-General Kofi Annan to his face: "I'll be damned if I'm going to let my son be dragged before some foreign kangaroo court to face judgment." His son had served as a US Army officer in Iraq.[28] In 2002, Representative Tom DeLay, the then US House of Representatives majority leader, described the ICC as a "kangaroo court...a shady amalgam of every bad idea ever cooked up".[29] This study consciously draws in large part upon the observations and commentary on, and analysis of, the ICC provided by international legal scholars, activists and organisations sympathetic to it, many of whom helped to create and shape the court. These include people such as Professors William Schabas, Philippe Sands QC, Benjamin Schiff and David Kaye. It also relies upon the views of distinguished international jurists such as Sir Geoffrey Nice QC, Geoffrey Robertson QC, Courtenay Griffiths QC, Antonio Cassese and Louise Arbour who have appeared before the court and other international criminal tribunals. The study is also based on the analysis of a number of acknowledged experts on the African situations within which the court has become involved. These include Dr. Adam Branch, Dr. Phil Clark, Dr. Lucy Hovil and Dr. Alex de Waal. Interestingly, the ICC prosecutor's own expert witness in the Lubanga trial, Dr. Gérard Prunier, stated: "I tend to trust people in the field more than people who have documents. Documents are a lot nicer and a lot more elegant. It's intellectually a lot more satisfying, but people in the field tend to base themselves on practical measurements."[30] He also warned against any "certitude of facts" in the African context[31] and cast doubt on UN reports and investigations.[32] The book also includes a range of comments by groups such as Human Rights Watch, Amnesty International and *Médecins Sans Frontières*. None of these people or organisations can be accused of being in favour of impunity or of being ideologically hostile to the court: they have nonetheless been damning of the institution, its professional shortcomings and the disastrous impact it has had on the war-affected communities in Africa in question.

This study also includes commentary by those who are intrinsically hostile to the ICC, people such as former US Ambassador John Bolton, John Rosenthal and Henry Kissinger. But more importantly, the study has sought to draw on the views of Africans and some of the many victims of war crimes that have been ignored or manipulated to its bureaucratic advantage by the ICC and the court's ideological friends in the West, safe and secure as they are in comfortable Western countries.

This study consciously includes detailed endnotes and references. This is for two reasons. Firstly, the reality of the court sometimes appears to be stranger than fiction. The endnotes document the body of open sources providing ample evidence of the political expediency and human weakness that is making the court an irrelevance. And secondly, this work is a work in progress and merely skims the surface of how corrupted the court has become. There will hopefully be others who may wish to build on the research presented in this work and available in the endnotes.

The ICC is a court that states that it is tasked with addressing the most serious of crimes – genocide, crimes against humanity and war crimes. Rather than investigating these crimes, however, it is presently investigating election violence in Kenya, the deaths of between 50 and 157 people in the course of a protest gathering in a stadium in Guinea, money laundering networks in Switzerland and the destruction of religious shrines in Mali.[33] These may all be against various laws, but they are not Nuremberg-level crimes, despite the attempts of the human-rights industry to deem them crimes against humanity.[34] The US Africa diplomat Jendayi Frazer was also drawn to note in 2013 that "the ICC, an organisation founded to bring those accused of the most heinous of crimes to account, was initially used (unsuccessfully) *as political leverage* to get Kenya's Parliament to set up a domestic special tribunal to address the post-election violence".[35] (Emphasis added.)

The ICC has been the subject of devastating criticism from both friend and foe in the ten years of its existence. Some of its friends have been very candid. The comments, for example, of Professor David Kaye, the founding executive director of the International Human Rights Law Program at the University of California School of Law and its International Justice Clinic, are telling.[36] A supporter of the ICC, Kaye has nevertheless said of the court that it "has not been a success"; "its reputation as a truly international tribunal is in question"; it was "an institution that is still struggling to find its footing almost a decade after its creation"; it had "a management and decision-making style that has alienated subordinates and court officials alike"; "many of its wounds have been self-inflicted"; "[i]nternal dissent at the court had been exposed"; "the court has also invited the charge that it is an agent for postcolonial Western interests", and "a target for charges of politicization". Kaye also noted "repeated judicial setbacks", "[m]anagement and personality clashes", "petty battles over turf and resources", "micromanaging", "erratic decision-making", and a "lack of legitimacy among some African leaders". Human Rights Watch, an avid institutional supporter of the ICC, has criticised the court's "seeming lack of impartiality", its "inconsistency", its "absence of coherent practice in selecting cases", behaviour that "has undermined local perceptions of the court's independence and impartiality", "significant flaws in prosecutorial policy", and stated that the court "can be seen as a tool to advance political objectives".[37] Human Rights Watch's International Justice Programme director, Richard Dicker, has gone so far as to state that "[t]he attitude in The Hague stinks".[38] A further keen supporter of the ICC, the International Crisis Group, criticised the ICC's first chief prosecutor, Luis Moreno Ocampo, stating that he risked "politicizing his office", and had taken a needlessly "confrontational" approach in cases before the court. Rony Brauman, the President of the legendary French humanitarian NGO of MSF from 1982 to 1994, dismissed some of Ocampo's assertions as "insane" and "intellectual incontinence".[39] *The Economist* described the court as "bumbling" in Africa, and reported that the court's "proceedings have been chaotic", highlighted by "near-farcical scenes".[40]

Another supporter of the court, Michael Ignatieff, an expert on international human rights and former Harvard professor, has also been reduced to scepticism about the ICC and international justice: "Creating an international court was supposed to rescue the possibility of universal justice from the revenge frenzies, political compromises, and local partialities of national justice. International justice turns out to be as much the prisoner of international politics as national justice is of national politics. Indeed, given the stakes, international justice may be more partial, that is, more politicized, than national justice."[41]

It is apparent that one decade later and despite expenditure to date of more than one billion euros, the ICC still lacks even the basic ability to properly conduct crucial investigations – a core function of any real court. In June 2012, ten years into the court's existence, *The Guardian* newspaper, an ideological supporter of the ICC, noted that the court had been identified with "reckless investigative techniques". It urged the court to "build its capacity to carry out independent, professional investigations on the ground", and to "independently investigate locally." *The Guardian* stated that "the ICC needs to avoid the over-reliance on NGOs, who…are not trained in interrogation and evidence gathering for legal purposes, and whose mandate and expertise mean they are no substitute for… trained investigators". *The Guardian* also noted that "The use of intermediaries – where witnesses never communicate directly with prosecutors but provide evidence through NGOs – is also deeply problematic and should be made more transparent".[42]

The reality is that the court has clearly failed in its fundamental claim to existence, to end human rights abuses within conflicts. Diana Johnstone, the author of *Fools Crusade: Yugoslavia, NATO and Western Delusions*, has observed: "Rather than a Court to keep the peace, the ICC could turn out to be – contrary to the wishes of its sincere supporters – an instrument to provide pretexts for war."[43] This is, of course precisely the role the court played in the Western military intervention in and bombing of Libya. It is also a simple fact that the court is responsible for the deaths of tens if not hundreds of thousands of Africans, and the displacement and suffering of hundreds of thousands more for the simple reason that it has destroyed delicate peace processes within Africa, starting with Uganda. For Kofi Annan and other transnational bureaucrats and international activists, safe, secure, comfortable and well-fed in their First World offices and comfortable lives, this is at best an abstract concern. Indeed, Annan can afford to note, almost absent-mindedly, that an "interesting question is whether international [ICC] involvement can actually undermine hopes for peace".[44] This may be merely an interesting question to him. The answer has been fatal for countless Africans.

There is a clear lesson for Africa: do not refer your country to the ICC. It is the equivalent of inviting a cancer into your system. The court does not have Africa's welfare at heart but only itself and its bureaucratic imperative – to exist, to please its European funders, to placate Washington whenever and wherever possible, to employ more Europeans and North Americans and to increase its budget. The ICC has shown itself to be the legal equivalent of those international banking institutions caught up in the sub-prime mortgage scandal that has resulted in the international banking crisis. The ICC provides sub-prime justice within the international legal system. In so doing it has either prolonged or in some cases provoked crises in Africa.

Mahmood Mamdani is correct when he warns that "[f]or Africa, a lot is at stake in Darfur". The same applies to Africa and the ICC. Mamdani's warning also rings true: "The future of our children is more important than the criminalisation of individuals."[45]

Chapter One

THE INTERNATIONAL CRIMINAL COURT

"The ICC is not a court set up to bring to book prime ministers of the United Kingdom or presidents of the United States."

Robin Cook, former British Foreign Minister[46]

"[T]he triumphalist nonsense [of] deluded propagandists."

Geoffrey Robertson QC[47]

The doyen of international jurists Georg Schwarzenberger, writing in the late 1940s, observed that international lawyers suffered from a "professional disease against which other members of the legal profession are remarkably immune". He said they suffered from an over-zealous legal evangelism that failed to distinguish between commendable values and existing realities; the most mistaken lawyers, he observed, were those who believe in the existence of an "international criminal law".[48] H. L. A. Hart's contribution to analytical jurisprudence has also shaped the landscape of legal philosophy in the Anglo-American sphere and beyond. For Hart, international law was problematic inasmuch as its ill-defined nature means that it does not have all the elements of a fully developed judicial system, especially with regard to procedural safeguards that ensure the due process of law.[49] Anyone seeking to come to terms with the disaster that is the ICC should read Scwarzenberger's warnings and Hart's commentary in conjunction with an observation from one of the ICC's most enthusiastic supporters, Professor William Schabas.[50] Schabas, a participant observer in the creation of the ICC, candidly admits that "[t]he final version of the Rome Statute [establishing the ICC] is not without serious flaws".[51] Here we have the irreparable hole in the heart of the ICC since its establishment in 2002. The combination of legal evangelism and a seriously flawed statute is a fatal one. And that is without taking the dismal quality of most of the judges and chief prosecutor into account. Quite why the enthusiasts of the ICC feel that the community of nations should make do with an institution intrinsically flawed from inception is unclear, all the more so given the incredibly delicate issues with which the ICC was expected to deal.

Respected international lawyer Philippe Sands QC has pointed to the deeply flawed nature of what passes for "international justice", and the supposed role of the ICC:

> The more serious concern is the danger of lopsided international justice, a world of laws that are "spider webs through which the big flies pass and the little ones get caught", as Balzac put it. Look on the website of the ICC and see who is in the dock. Every one of the faces and names is African. Yet Africa plainly does not have a monopoly on international crime, and this unhappy and lopsided picture tends to give force to the critique that international justice is pro-western and controlled by the victors. One wonders quite what it will take, for example, for a proper international investigation of the well-documented allegations of torture and other abuse at Bagram and elsewhere in Afghanistan, a country that has been a party to the ICC statute since 2003.[52]

The ICC would claim to trace its roots to the International Military Tribunal at Nuremberg that tried Nazi war criminals after World War II. The Nuremberg trials did lead to UN proposals for a permanent successor court, but the campaign stalled in the 1950s, in part because of the Cold War. The idea of an international criminal court was re-presented for consideration by Trinidad and Tobago at the forty-fourth session of the United Nations General Assembly in 1989. In 1993, the UNSC established an *ad hoc* court, the International Criminal Tribunal for the Former Yugoslavia (ICTY), which was then followed by the International Criminal Tribunal for Rwanda (ICTR), and then tribunals for East Timor, Sierra Leone and Cambodia. At its fifty-second session, the General Assembly decided to convene the "United Nations Diplomatic Conference of Plenipotentiaries on the Establishment of an ICC", which was held in Rome, Italy, from 15 June to 17 July 1998, "to finalize and adopt a convention on the establishment of an international criminal court".[53] This conference drafted a treaty for the ICC. On 17 July 1998, the *Rome Statute of the International Criminal Court* was adopted by a vote of 120 to 7, with 21 countries abstaining. Seven countries voted against the treaty: Iraq, Israel, Libya, the People's Republic of China, Qatar, the USA and Yemen. After receiving more than sixty ratifications by April 2002, the treaty became legal on 1 July 2002 for those who had signed up.

The ICC's real roots are clear. As Mahmood Mamdani points out, the new humanitarian order, driven by the EU and by largely EU-funded non-governmental organisations describing themselves as "civil society", and officially adopted at the UN's 2005 World Summit, claims responsibility for the protection of vulnerable populations. That responsibility is said to belong to "the international community", to be exercised in practice by the UN, and in particular by the Security Council. He has also pointed out that "[t]he era of the international humanitarian order is not entirely new. It draws on the history of modern Western colonialism." At the outset of colonial expansion in the eighteenth and nineteenth centuries, leading Western powers – Britain, France, Russia – claimed to protect "vulnerable groups".[54] And as Professor Mamdani has also made clear there is nothing new in legal concepts being used to serve the expedience of great powers.[55]

It is clear that the Rome Statute was rushed through the conference. While ostensibly a diplomatic conference, it was NGO-driven. Professor David Davenport has written about the tactics of the NGO activists at the Rome Conference, noting that one tactic:

> [W]as bundling the key elements of the court into a package that became a take-it-or-leave-it proposal, not subject in the end to further compromise...'the package'.... Additionally, the Rome Statute provided no possibility of a nation signing 'with reservations,' reflected in the Vienna Convention on the Law of Treaties as a standard part of international treaties.... As with the element of time deadlines, such a nonnegotiable approach is most out of character with the thorough, consensus-based processes of international law.[56]

Davenport also recorded that another tactic was to replace the consensus-based approach of customary international law with a straight vote of nations. He further noted:

> The bar for approval of the Rome Statute was set remarkably low, with the court to be approved upon ratification of only 60 nations out of 189 in the United Nations. For a court that purports to have worldwide jurisdiction, even over citizens of countries that do not sign the treaty, this is a narrow base of approval. Further, such a process takes no account of geographic representation, population base, or strategic considerations, but simply relies upon a one-nation-one-vote approach. The ICC went into effect on July 1 with fewer than half the nations of the world ratifying it, representing considerably less than half the population of the world. Strategic powers including not only the United States, but China, India, Japan, and Russia were all absent, while the total ratification number was padded with small states that traditionally play little part in international affairs.[57]

Geoffrey Robertson has been frank about the Rome Conference: "The Rome Conference was hardly an advertisement for wise global governance."[58] He stated that it was "not a resounding success.... Concessions were made throughout in an effort to keep the United States on side, and those flaws remained embedded in the Statute at the end after the US had denounced it."[59] The delegates, for example, "deliberately fudged the lawfulness of landmines and nuclear weapons as weapons of international law".[60]

Robertson was also critical of the double standards that undermined much of what was claimed for the conference: "For human rights campaigners...what was truly ironic was their zeal for a court so tough that it would actually violate the basic rights of its defendants.... Insouciance about the danger of miscarriages of justice was common among NGOs like Amnesty...when the defendants have for years been tried and convicted in the media and when prosecutors and judges are trying to carve out careers in a growth profession like international human rights."⁶¹ He concluded that "[t]he worst feature of the Rome Statute is that it makes no provision for the defence".⁶² Robertson is very clear about this flaw in the statute, stating that "unnecessarily, and indeed oppressively, the prosecution is also given a right of appeal against an acquittal, and the defendant may even be imprisoned pending such an appeal".⁶³ He also identified key flaws with regard to the disclosure of evidence, noting that there have been "serious problems in working out a disclosure regime which is fair to the defence".⁶⁴

On 11 March 2003, the ICC was officially established as a permanent tribunal to prosecute individuals for genocide, crimes against humanity, war crimes, and the crime of aggression, though it was unable to agree upon a definition of, and therefore exercise jurisdiction over, the crime of aggression. The court can only prosecute crimes committed on or after 1 July 2002, the date the Rome Statute of the ICC entered into force. The ICC was established by a multilateral treaty that states that it can only exercise territorial jurisdiction or personal jurisdiction in relation to states that are parties to the Rome Statute. The court "inherits" the jurisdiction of States Parties to the Rome Statute, which gives the court jurisdiction over crimes committed in the territory of a State Party and over crimes committed by nationals of a State Party. The ICC does not have universal jurisdiction of its own. The court claims to complement existing national judicial systems: it can only exercise its jurisdiction when it decides that national courts are unwilling or unable to investigate or prosecute the grave crimes in question. Primary responsibility to exercise jurisdiction over suspected criminals is therefore left to individual states. Article 13(b) of the court's statute enables the UNSC, acting under its Chapter VII authority, to refer a situation to the ICC for investigation and possible prosecution. Article 16 also enables the UNSC to delay prosecutions for a year at a time. One of the intrinsic flaws of the ICC is that for all its claims to usher in a new era of "accountability", the court is itself unaccountable to any public entity.

As of early 2013, the ICC had 121 States Parties.⁶⁵ The ICC's management oversight and legislative body is in theory the Assembly of States Parties (ASP), which consists of one representative from each State Party. Each State Party has one vote and "every effort" has to be made to reach decisions by consensus. If consensus cannot be reached, decisions are made by vote. The assembly is presided over by a president and two vice-presidents, who are elected by the members to three-year terms.

The first President of the ASP was Zeid bin Ra'ad Al-Hussein (Jordan) with as Vice-Presidents, Allieu Ibrahim Kanu (Sierra Leone) and Felipe Paolillo (Uruguay). In December 2011, the ASP to the Rome Statute elected Ambassador Tiina Intelmann (Estonia) as President of the Assembly and Markus Börlin (Switzerland) and Ken Kanda (Ghana) as Vice-Presidents for the tenth to twelfth sessions.⁶⁶

The assembly meets in full session once a year in New York or The Hague, and may also hold special sessions where circumstances require. Sessions are open to observer states and non-governmental organisations. The assembly elects the judges and prosecutors, decides the court's budget, adopts important texts, such as the *Rules of Procedure and Evidence*, and provides management oversight to the other organs of the court. The vast majority of representatives in the assembly are diplomats.⁶⁷

On 21 November 2012, the ASP to the Rome Statute of the ICC concluded its eleventh session in The Hague. The Assembly approved appropriations totalling €115,620,300 with €115,120,300 for the court's 2013 budget and €500,000 to replenish the contingency fund. The assembly approved a staffing level of 766 people.[68] This was an increase on the court's 2012 establishment. The ICC's 2012 budget was €108,800.000. As of 31 August 2012, the court included 696 staff on established posts (358 professional staff and 338 general services staff), 169 persons on general temporary assistance (GTA), 33 consultants or contractors and 77 interns or visiting professionals. On 31 August 2012, staff subject to geographical representation were distributed as follows (in comparison with target figures): 16.82 per cent from the Group of African States (target: 12.76 percent): 6.54 per cent from the Group of Asian States (target: 19.25 percent); 7.17 percent from the Group of Eastern European States (target: 8.08 per cent); 8.72 per cent from the Group of Latin American and Caribbean States (target: 14.46 per cent); 60.75 per cent from the Group of Western European and other States (target: 45.45 per cent).[69]

The judicial divisions consist of the eighteen judges of the court. Judges are elected to the court by the ASP. They serve nine-year terms and are not generally eligible for re-election. All judges must be nationals of States Parties to the Rome Statute, and no two judges may be nationals of the same state. They must be "persons of high moral character, impartiality and integrity who possess the qualifications required in their respective States for appointment to the highest judicial offices". The court has three chambers, the Pre-Trial Chamber (with seven judges), the Trial Chamber (with six judges) and the Appeals Chamber (with five judges). The Pre-Trial Chamber decides whether the prosecutor is allowed to start a formal investigation into a case. The Trial Chamber decides whether the accused person is guilty as charged and if they find him or her guilty, will assign the punishment for the crime and any damages to be paid to the victims. It also must ensure that a trial is fair and expeditious, and is conducted with full respect for the rights of the accused with regard for the protection of victims and witnesses. When the prosecutor or the convicted person appeals against the decision of the Pre-trial or Trial Chambers, the case comes to the Appeals Chamber. The Appeals Chamber may decide to reverse or amend a decision, judgment, or sentence. It can also order a new trial before a different Trial Chamber.

The funding of the ICC

The funding of the ICC is a critical issue in assessing the credibility and viability of the organisation. There are deep concerns not just about the ICC's acute financial dependence upon western European funding corrupting the court's legal independence but also on the all too obvious inefficiencies in how that money is used. American commentator John Rosenthal has gone to the heart of the ICC's claim to political independence while accepting money from major funding states accused of involvement in large-scale war crimes: "It is a self-evident principle that the independence and hence impartiality of a court is only as sure as the independence of its financing."[70]

The court states that it is financed by contributions from the States Parties. The amount payable by each State Party is determined using the same method as the UN: each state's contribution is based on the country's capacity to pay, which reflects factors such as a national income and population. The maximum amount a single country can pay in any year is limited to twenty-two per cent of the court's budget. The court spent €80.5 million in 2007.[71] The ASP approved a budget of €90,382,100 for 2008[72] and €101,229,900 for 2009.[73] The 2010 budget of the ICC totalled €102.98 million, of which €99.83 million (ninety-seven per cent) was for the court itself; and €3.15 million (three per cent) was for the Secretariat of the ASP. Within the court, the 2010 budget was apportioned as follows: €10.50 million (10.2 per cent) for the Judiciary (Presidency and Chambers); €27.09 million (26.3 per cent) for the Office of the Prosecutor; €60.22 million (58.5 per cent) for the Registry; €1.43 million (1.4 per cent) for the Secretariat of the Trust Fund for Victims; and €0.59 million (0.6 per cent) for the Project Office for the Permanent Premises. The ICC declared that this budget reflected an increase of €1.75 million or 1.7 per cent over 2009.[74]

There are two points of immediate concern regarding the ICC's budget. The first is that while the Rome Statute sets a cap on funding at twenty-two per cent of its budget from any one state, considerably more than fifty per cent of its funding comes from member countries of the EU, which is to all intents and purposes one state, especially after the ratification of the Lisbon Treaty in November 2009.[75] The 1933 Montevideo convention sets out the definition, rights and duties of statehood. The most important section is Article 1, which sets out the four criteria for statehood that are recognised as an accurate statement of customary international law:

> The state as a person of international law should possess the following qualifications: (a) a permanent population; (b) a defined territory; (c) government; and (d) capacity to enter into relations with the other states.[76]

The EU qualifies as a state in all four of these respects. It has a permanent population within a defined territory. As will be seen from the Cotonou Agreement, and many other international and bilateral agreements, the EU can and does enter into relations with other states. And the EU clearly has its own government. It has a president, a cabinet, a parliament, a flag, a constitution, a bill of rights, a central bank and single currency, a common passport, an anthem, a court system with the power to overrule the superior courts of every member state and an 80,000-page legal code, all the way through to a standard car licence plate. The EU also has a permanent 60,000-strong army (the *Eurocorps* rapid reaction force), which has deployed to Bosnia, Kosovo and Afghanistan, and a navy (the European Maritime Force, EUROMARFOR or EMF).[77] It is a state with a legal personality. The EU's contributions to the ICC's 2012 budget clearly illustrates the continuing European hold on the court's funding. The EU provided €62,867,105 of the 2012 budget, or 57.7 per cent. The biggest contributors to the ICC in 2012 were Germany, €12,927,484 (almost twelve per cent); UK, €10,647,681 (almost ten per cent); France, €9,872,161 (nine per cent); Italy, €8,059,927 (seven and a half per cent); and

Spain, €5,122,301 (almost five per cent). The five dominant EU countries alone paid forty-two per cent of the ICC budget, some €46,629,554.[78] The funding of the court is unlawful in terms of its own statute, with all the implications that flow from that fact.

If one includes those states associated with the EU, that is to say an EU acceding country, Croatia; candidate member countries the former Yugoslav Republic of Macedonia, Montenegro, Iceland and Serbia; the countries of the Stabilisation and Association Process; and potential EU member states Albania and Bosnia and Herzegovina; as well as Ukraine, the Republic of Moldova and Georgia, they provide an additional €353,095. This would then come to €63,220,200, or 58.1 per cent of the budget. If one also adds the budget contribution of the three other European states outside of the EU, Switzerland, Norway and Liechtenstein, which provided €1,821,908, €1,404,320 and €14,511 respectively (€3,240,739), Europe provides €66,460,939. This comes to some sixty-one per cent of the overall ICC budget.[79]

If one then adds on the Anglosphere of Canada, which paid €5,170,672, Australia, €3,116,592, and New Zealand, €440,160,[80] white nations provide €70,017,691, or some sixty-nine per cent of the budget of a court that is exclusively prosecuting black Africans. In 2009, that funding base provided seventy-one per cent of the ICC's budget. The biggest contributors to the ICC in 2009 were Germany, €12,955,434 (almost fourteen per cent); UK, €10,032,646 (ten per cent); Italy, €7,671,754 (eight per cent); France, €7,559,682 (eight per cent); and Spain, €4,483,121 (four per cent). The five dominant EU countries paid forty-four per cent of the ICC budget.

There is as always a direct relationship between levels of payment and control. Noting Germany's "ideological sponsorship of the court", and commenting on the inevitably political nature of the ICC, Rosenthal records that official German sources spoke early on of Germany alone assuming upwards of twenty per cent of the court's budget. He documents that in 2001, Hans-Peter Kaul, at the time an official of the German Foreign Office (and subsequently an ICC judge), cited a figure of twenty-two to twenty-five per cent for the German contribution.[81] Rosenthal notes: "In what amounted to an admission that it expected this financial support to translate into influence, the Foreign Office published a bulletin (reproduced in facsimile in the Kaul article) announcing that Germany would be able to 'fill' a more or less commensurate portion – 'around 20 percent' – of the court's administrative positions and providing a Foreign Office contact for potential candidates. A revised version of the bulletin dated November 2003 cited a more modest figure of 11 per cent, presumably referring only to Germany's assessed contribution, and stresses that it is merely an 'aim' of the Foreign Office to see that German citizens compose an equivalent portion of the court's personnel."[82] They had realised that they had possibly gone a little bit too far in public.

Secondly, in the section of the ICC's own website entitled "How is the Court funded?", the court interestingly reveals that it also receives money from "international corporations, individuals, and other entities". Article 116 of the Rome Statute provides for these voluntary contributions. No details are provided of this funding line and in its report of 13 May 2009, the ASP also makes no reference to these mysterious donors. The thought of private interests such as major multinational businesses helping to finance a judicial organisation is one that should be of great alarm to all those who believe in the rule of law. Rosenthal notes: "None of us would put faith in the impartiality of a local or national court if it depended upon the largesse of private individuals or corporations, who, by definition, might have an interest in the outcome of particular proceedings."[83]

Rosenthal points out that in this respect, the ICC follows the "bad precedent" set by the ICTY. "The claim of the latter to impartiality in trying Yugoslav officials has been compromised by the fact that it accepted contributions in money and materiel not only from private foundations, but also from states that openly supported secessionist forces in their battle against the federal authority or even intervened militarily on their behalf." Rosenthal also notes that as the statute of the ICTY makes no provision for such voluntary contributions, and states in its Article 32 that funds for the tribunal shall be borne by the regular UN budget. "The authors of the Rome Statute thus seem to have drawn their inspiration from a practice of the ad hoc tribunal that was, according to its own statute, illegal."

Rosenthal concludes: "Thus, the ICC's very statute openly invites contributions from a whole range of 'entities,' any of whom could have an interest in the outcome of proceedings and some of whom, notably 'Governments' might even have been parties to the hostilities in which the alleged crimes over which the court claims jurisdiction are supposed to have occurred." Rosenthal also points out that the ICC is clearly itself aware of how this might be read. In September 2002, the ICC's Assembly of States Parties passed a "remarkable resolution" which asked all such "entities" making such contributions to declare that their contributions "are not intended to affect the independence of the Court". Rosenthal notes that "much in the spirit of the statute itself, verbal assurances were here offered as the equivalent of substantive protections". He concludes: "The ICC is not merely a matter of good intentions gone awry in the face of stubborn political realities.... . The ICC... has been made to be abused."[84]

The ICC Chief Prosecutor has declared that the court is "proud to be economical".[85] This is yet another misleading statement. The funding of the court, and how it has been spent, has caused considerable controversy. Dr. Guénaël Mettraux is a respected practitioner, scholar, and teacher of international criminal law. He has appeared before or served as a consultant for all of the major international criminal tribunals in The Hague.[86] He has questioned the economic efficiency of the ICC, noting that:

> Since it was created, the International Criminal Court (ICC) has spent almost half a billion euro. Considering that only one trial – and a relatively minor one by international standards – has started before the ICC (after about 6 years of existence), this seems – and is – a staggering figure. What is equally staggering is the structure that is put in place around the beating heart of the ICC: its courtroom. With only one trial going on, the ICC now has a budget of 101,000,000€ and the ICC website tells us that as of January 2009, 285 women and 302 men worked for the ICC (i.e., 587 employees).[87]

Mettraux has compared the ICC to the ICTY, which had a biennium budget for 2008–09 of €238,000,000, approximately €120,000,000 per year,[88] which funded over 1,118 employees dealing with seven on-going trials, five appeals (plus contempt matters) and three cases in preparation at the pre-trial stage. He has made the point that with almost twice the staff and much greater judicial activity, the ICTY is costing almost the same as the ICC, and that even then, the ICTY has been criticised for being too expensive. Mettraux asks: "In those circumstances, what should be said of the ICC?"

Dr. Mettraux's criticism was at both macro and micro levels. He pointed out that the ICC had advertised in the 1–7 August 2009 issue of *The Economist*, purchasing a full one-page advert for administrative positions that it wished to fill in the "Executive Focus" section of the magazine. This cost £21,000. By comparison, the UN Habitat organisation advertised in the same section of the magazine for two – hierarchically superior positions – in a quarter of a page at a cost of £5,800. Mettraux asked whether the ICC should perhaps have advertised in the cheaper "Appointments" section of *The Economist* where bodies such as the European Investment Bank and the International Tribunal for the Law of the Sea consider it sufficient to advertise in a quarter of a page costing them £4,900. He also pointed out that the ICTY advertises its positions on free websites such as Reliefweb, the UN network or its own website.

Mettraux further notes:

> There comes a point…when the gap between what is being achieved judicially and what it costs to the international community should raise some serious concerns among those who foot the bill. Some indications are quite worrying…. Or it may be that the ICC suffers from institutional egomania? Whatever the answer, it is time for the ICC to promote transparency, not just financial/budgetary, but also in terms of allocations of those resources that are put at its disposal and to focus those resources onto its primary mandate, i.e., to investigate, prosecute and try criminal cases, not to create an inflated bureaucracy.

Mettraux concluded: "With only one trial to show for, half a billion euros is simply too much money to spend for a tribunal. £21,000 is just too much to recruit two administrators. Time perhaps for the court to reconsider its priorities and to spend our money more wisely."[89]

One rule for Europe and another for everyone else

At the same time that the ICC is dictating to Africa, and to countries that are not even members of the ICC, even those states that have signed up to the Rome Treaty are not fulfilling their obligations to the court. Amnesty International noted with concern in 2009: "More than seven years into the work of the court most states parties remain unprepared to cooperate fully with the Court: 69 of the 110 states parties have failed to enact legislation providing for cooperation with the Court."[90] Amnesty International also pointed out that 49 of the 110 States Parties had yet to ratify or accede to the Agreement on Privileges and Immunities of the ICC.[91] And only 2 of the 110 States Parties had then entered into agreements with the court to enforce sentences in their national facilities.[92] Amnesty also noted: "Although the statistical information and identity of countries is kept confidential, the Court has indicated on several occasions that only a small number of states have entered into agreements to relocate victims and witnesses." Additionally, Amnesty International states that it "is aware of instances of states parties failing to respond or declining to provide requested assistance, imposing conditions incompatible with the Rome Statute on the provision of assistance and failing to implement such requests promptly".[93]

It is also apparent that there has been a slowing down in ICC-related momentum within ICC member states. Amnesty documents that:

> Regrettably, most states have failed to inform the Assembly of their activities at the national level to ratify and implement the Rome Statute and their efforts to promote the implementation of the Plan by other states. Most states have failed to take even the basic step set out in the Plan to appoint a national contact point. Responses by states parties to the Secretariat's annual questionnaire on the Plan of Action have decreased from 24 in 2007, to 13 in 2008 and 8 currently three in 2009.

By 2009 only 44 of the then 110 States Parties had enacted complementarity legislation and Amnesty stated that much of the legislation that had been drafted and enacted fell short of what is required by the Rome Statute and other international law.[94] By 2010, only the UK had formally adopted all of its obligations under the 1998 Rome Statute, from witness protection to sentence enforcement and rules on privileges and immunities.[95]

Illegal reservations to the treaty

In addition to not fulfilling their obligations to the ICC, and while threatening African countries that do not do as the ICC demands, several European countries are themselves blatantly violating the Rome Statute. It is the case, for example, that several of the declarations made upon ratification by some states amounted to disguised reservations – despite the fact that Article 120 of the Rome Statute provides that no reservations may be made to the statute. Amnesty International identified several of these state members. In its 2005 report, *International Criminal Court: Declarations amounting to prohibited reservations to the Rome Statute*, Amnesty International examined declarations made by States Parties, including unilateral declarations made by Australia, Colombia, France, Malta, the UK and Uruguay, and concluded that a number of them amounted to reservations.[96] Uruguay withdrew its declaration on 26 February 2008.

It is significant that the two most enthusiastic supporters of the ICC, themselves permanent members of the UNSC, have in effect weakened the ICC right from the start with their questionable "declarations". It is once again one rule for some states and another rule for others. Upon its ratification of the Rome Statute, France declared under Article 124 that it would not recognise the court's jurisdiction for seven years over war crimes when they were alleged to have been committed by its nationals or on its territory. France also made eight declarations upon ratification, declarations that sought to alter or limit the definitions in the Rome Statute[97] Upon ratification, France also made seven interpretative declarations to Article 8 (war crimes) of the Rome Statute. Amnesty International observed "[t]hat these other declarations are intended to function as reservations is demonstrated by the fact that all of them are also found within the text of the eighteen statements made, ten months later, under the label of 'reservations and declarations' to the Protocol Additional to the Geneva Conventions of 12 August 1949, and relating to the Protection of Victims of International Armed Conflicts (Protocol I)".[98]

Amnesty International found France's Article 124 declaration "particularly worrying" considering that France "has failed to fulfill its obligations under the Geneva Conventions, Protocol I and the Rome Statute to define war crimes clearly under national law and further makes war crimes subject to a geographical and temporal limitation, thereby making a prosecution for war crimes in French courts difficult or impossible".[99] Thus, as Rosenthal succinctly noted, "in June 2000, France at one and the same time ratified the statute of the court and declared that it did not recognize its jurisdiction over war crimes – except when alleged to have been committed by non-French citizens or on non-French territories".[100]

Upon ratification of the Rome Statute, the UK made the following declaration:

> The United Kingdom understands the term "the established framework of international law", used in article 8 (2) (b) and (e), to include customary international law as established by State practice and opinio juris. In that context the United Kingdom confirms and draws to the attention of the Court its views as expressed, inter alia, in its statements made on ratification of relevant instruments of international law, including the Protocol Additional to the Geneva Conventions of 12th August 1949, and relating to the Protection of Victims of International Armed Conflicts (Protocol I) of 8th June 1977.

Amnesty International considers that this declaration in which the UK "confirms and draws to the attention of the Court" the statements it made upon the ratification of the Protocol Additional to the Geneva Conventions of 1949, is a prohibited reservation by virtue of Article 120.[101]

The ICC is not a universal court

As of 2013, 121 states were members of the court, and a further 32 countries had signed but not ratified the Rome Statute. However, a number of key states, including the USA, Russia, China, Indonesia, India and Pakistan are critical of the court and have not joined. The ICC's claim to be the international court is clearly undermined by the fact that its members represent less than one third of the world's population. Over seventy per cent of the world's population is outside the court's jurisdiction. Six out of ten of the world's most populous countries are not members of the court. They alone account for over half of the world's population.[102] This imbalance is highlighted by Rosenthal: "Seven of the ratifiers taken together (San Marino, Nauru, Andorra, Liechtenstein, Dominica, Antigua and Barbuda, and the Marshall Islands) have a population of roughly 347,000 – which is less than the population of New York's smallest borough of Staten Island. On the side of the non-ratifiers, by contrast, one finds India, with its billion inhabitants; China, one and a quarter billion; Indonesia, 230 million; Russia, 150 million; Japan, 125 million; and, of course, the United States."[103]

Additionally, for all the claims of those NGOs and activists that the Rome Statute and the ICC are a victory for people over governments, the simple fact is that the ICC was established by the votes of states and not people. As David Davenport states: "To impose a treaty on the world with less than half its people in support undercuts the very principles for which these organizations claim to stand."[104] The ICC Chief Prosecutor Luis Ocampo, in a startling moment of lucidity, stated the obvious himself: "I am not the world prosecutor."[105] The veteran international jurist David Tolbert, has confirmed this: "A fundamentally important question regarding international justice…is that the ICC's jurisdiction is not universal…there are many countries that are not covered by the ICC's jurisdiction…there are still vast areas of the world that are not covered by the ICC and this is a problem."[106]

For all its publicity and aspirations to universal jurisdiction the simple fact is that the ICC is little more than a European court. Even the EU has admitted that the ICC is not a truly international court. The EU ambassador to the UN, speaking in May 2009, noted that while a number of states were members of the ICC, it was "not yet beyond the critical mass to ensure universalisation".[107]

Significantly, following the ICC's decision to issue arrest warrants for the Sudanese president, the President of the UN General Assembly, Miguel D'Escoto Brockmann, the former foreign minister of Nicaragua, probably reflected much of the emergent world's opinion when he roundly criticised the ICC's decision: "I am sorry about this decision of the ICC and I think it's more a decision motivated by political considerations than really for the sake of advancing the cause of justice in the world. A few people with a very dubious past and with very little credibility pretend to know better than the whole African Union. This is absurd and really not an adequate way to deal with this issue."[108]

China's stance on the ICC

Chinese academics Lu Jianping and Wang Zhixiang have outlined the five main reasons for China's opposition to the ICC:

> First, its jurisdiction is not based on the principle of voluntary acceptance; furthermore, complementarity gives the ICC the power to judge whether a

state is able or willing to conduct proper trials of its own nationals. Secondly, also war crimes in internal armed conflicts fall under the jurisdiction of the ICC. Thirdly, crimes against humanity are prohibited in time of peace as well. Fourthly, the inclusion of the crime of aggression within the jurisdiction of the ICC weakens the power of the UNSC. Fifthly, the proprio motu power of the Prosecutor may make the ICC open to political influence.[109]

In 2003 China reiterated its commitment to international justice and the concept of an international court: "If the operation of the court can really make the individuals who perpetrate the gravest crimes receive due punishment, this will not only help people to establish confidence in the international community, but also will be conducive to international peace and security at long last. It was precisely based on this stand and understanding that the Chinese Government took an active part in the process of negotiations on the Rome Statute"[110]

The Rome Statute, however, did not satisfy Chinese doubts about the court's independence: "What was regrettable was that because some articles of the text of the statute agreed by Rome Conference could not satisfy some reasonable concern of the Chinese Government, the participating Chinese Delegation had to vote against the statute when it was adopted. This was also the reason why China could not sign the Rome Statute."[111] China expressly disagreed with the power given the prosecutor to initiate investigation or to prosecute proprio motu, which it considered to be exercisable "without checks and balances against frivolous prosecution", thus amounting to "the right to judge and rule on State conduct".[112]

The Chinese government noted that the court is "subject to influence of many factors whether the ICC can operate effectively in the time ahead". It called upon the court to "strictly follow relevant principles based on which the Court was established". China also made it clear that the performance of the court would influence possible Chinese membership: "As to the question of acceding to the Statute, the Chinese Government adopts an open attitude and the actual performance of the Court is undoubtedly an important factor for consideration."[113]

The Chinese government was subsequently very critical of the court's indictment of President al-Bashir, which it found was a political rather than legal move. In 2011, at the sixty-sixth Session of the United Nations General Assembly, the Chinese government restated its position regarding the ICC:

> China supports the establishment of an independent, impartial, effective and universally recognized institution of international criminal justice to complement national legal systems in punishing the most serious international crimes and promoting world peace and judicial justice. The work of the ICC should serve the purpose of promoting international peace and security and safeguarding the well-being of mankind, and it should operate in coordination and cooperation with other international mechanisms without impeding or jeopardizing the relevant peace processes. China will continue to pay close

attention to the work of the ICC, and *we hope that it will win the trust and respect of the international community by becoming objective and fair in its future conduct.*[114] (Emphasis added.)

The Indian position on the ICC

India has refused to join the ICC. That the world's largest democracy chose not to join the ICC was a significant blow to the organisation. The absence of India badly damages the ICC's claim to be the international court. India declared that it expected to join and "would have wanted to be one of the first signatories of the ICC". The position of the Indian government regarding the ICC, as articulated at the Rome Conference in 1998, foresees several of the problems that would subsequently emerge. Given India's size and political prominence internationally, it is important to explore India's concerns in some detail.

India noted at the time: "We have always had in mind a Court that would deal with truly exceptional situations where the State machinery had collapsed, or where the Judicial system was either so flawed, inadequate or non-existent that justice had to be meted out through an International Court, because redress was not available within the country..... That, however, has not happened." India attacked the Rome Statute's claim to universality: "[I]t was odd...that the draft adopted a definition of crimes against humanity with which the representatives of over half of humanity did not agree. And we are now about to adopt a Statute to which the Governments who represent two-thirds of humanity would not be a party. This is an unusual measure of success."[115]

India was very critical of the role given to the UNSC: "Firstly, the Statute gives to the Security Council a role in terms that violate international law...it is the power to refer, the power to block and the power to bind non-States Parties. All three are undesirable." India also suspected that "some members of the Council do not plan to accede to the ICC, will not accept the obligations imposed by the Statute, but want the privilege to refer cases to it. This too is unacceptable."

The Indian position clearly identified the legal flaw at the heart of the ICC:

> The power to bind non-States Parties to any international treaty is not a power given to the Council by the [UN] Charter. Under the Law of Treaties, no state can be forced to accede to a treaty or be bound by the provisions of a treaty it has not accepted. The Statute violates this fundamental principle of international law by conferring on the Council a power which it does not have under the Charter, and which it cannot and should not be given by any other instrument. This is even more unacceptable, because the Council will almost certainly have on it some non-States Parties to this Statute. The Statue will, therefore, give non-States Parties, working through the Council, the power to bind other non-States Parties.[116]

India also objected to the granting of these powers to the Security Council because it "provided escape routes for those accused of serious crimes but with clout in the U.N. body".[117] The Indian government also, correctly, noted "that the role for the Security Council built into the Statute of the ICC sows the seeds of its destruction". We are seeing precisely this happening with regard to the Security Council's illegal referral of the Darfur and Libyan situations to the ICC.

The Indian government warned of "zealots" and noted that: "Instead of legislating for the exception, the scope of the Statute has been broadened so much that it could be misused for political purposes or through misplaced zeal, to address situations and cases for which the ICC was not intended, and where, as a matter of principle, it should not intrude." India stated: "[W]e tried, unsuccessfully, to ensure that the Court would be free from political influence." India was very critical of the "the purists [who] resurrected and forced into the Statute the concept of universal or inherent jurisdiction, which too makes a mockery of the distinction between States Parties and those who choose not to be bound by a treaty". India was particularly critical of the ICC attempts to sideline and violate international law: "It is truly unfortunate that a Statute drafted for an institution to defend the law should start out straying so sharply from established international law. Before it tries its first criminal, the ICC would have claimed a victim of its own – the Vienna Convention on the Law of Treaties."

India, a state with nuclear weapons, was critical that the ICC statute did not explicitly ban the use of nuclear weapons. "Expediency has prevailed." India tabled a draft amendment to list nuclear weapons among those whose use is banned for the purposes of the Statute. "To our very great regret, this was not accepted." India noted that "the Statute does not list any weapon of mass destruction among those whose use is banned as a war crime.... What this final decision means is that the Statute of the ICC lays down, by clear implication, that the use of weapons of mass destruction is not a war crime. This is an extraordinary message to send to the international community."[118]

The ICC is a political body

All of Schwarzenberger's concerns have manifested themselves in subsequent attempts to introduce and enforce "international" criminal law. The ICTY and ICTR have both been severely criticised and the ICC has been mired in controversy since its inception, especially in light of its exclusive focus on African situations. Over-zealous evangelism has been caught up in double standards, hypocrisy, racial stereotyping and national and personal agendas.

The former British foreign minister Robin Cook was very frank about the unspoken political limitations of the ICC: "The ICC is not a court set up to bring to book prime ministers of the United Kingdom or presidents of the United States."[119] *The Economist* has been equally blunt: "The purpose of the ICC is to provide a permanent forum to put on trial...not Americans or, for that matter, Europeans."[120]

International jurist Judge Richard Goldstone has highlighted the political nature of the international criminal tribunals that preceded the ICC: "The problem with the Security Council is that it says no in the case of Cambodia, Mozambique, Iraq and other places where terrible war crimes have been committed, but yes in the case of Yugoslavia and Rwanda. That's a political way of deciding where international justice should be meted out."[121] He confirmed that the UNSC's involvement was clear: "[T]here has long been a concern that these tribunals 'politicize justice,'...it is noteworthy that no ad hoc tribunals were established to investigate war crimes committed by any of the five permanent members of the UNSC or those nations these powerful states might wish to protect."[122]

It is clear that the structural weaknesses of the international tribunals have been visited upon the ICC. John Lloyd, in a *Financial Times* article in which he interviewed many of the key lawyers involved in the ICTY, reported: "Nearly all those I spoke to, including Pocar [Fausto Pocar, Italian President of the Tribunal], noted that powerful nations against whose leaders a case might be made – Russia, China and the US – would never end up in court. *The International Criminal Court, which will continue after the ICTY ends and which was constructed partly on its model, is trying African cases only.*"[123] (Emphasis added.)

This is a point that has been drawn out by Mahmood Mamdani. He has outlined the ICC's careful relationship with the USA:

> The fact of mutual accommodation between the world's only superpower and an international institution struggling to get its bearings is clear if we take into account the four countries where the ICC has launched its investigations: Sudan, Uganda, Central African Republic, and Congo. All...are places where the United States has no objection to the course charted by ICC investigations. In Uganda...the ICC has charged only the leadership of the LRA [Lord's Resistance Army] but not that of the pro-United States government. In Sudan, too, the ICC has charged officials of the Sudan Government.... In Congo, the ICC has remained mum about the links between the armies of Uganda and Rwanda – both pro-United States – and the ethnic militias that have been at the heart of the slaughter of civilians.[124]

Mamdani notes further that "[t]he ICC's attempted accommodation with the powers that be has changed the international face of the ICC. Its name notwithstanding, the ICC is rapidly turning into a Western court to try African crimes against humanity. Even then, its approach is selective: It targets governments that are adversaries of the United States and ignores U.S. allies, effectively conferring impunity on them."[125] A prime example of this attempted accommodation is provided by ICC enthusiast Richard Goldstone. He has gone on record as stating that nothing the USA did in Iraq could ever constitute a war crime that could be prosecuted by the ICC: "I don't believe that any allegation that I have read or heard against the United States leaders comes anywhere near the sorts of crimes that the ICC has been set up to investigate. Genocide, crimes against humanity, serious war crimes – it just doesn't measure up."[126]

Writing in 2001, Henry Kissinger, the veteran American statesman, stated that the crimes detailed in the ICC treaty are "vague and highly susceptible to politicized application". Kissinger further asserted that the ICC prosecutor will have "discretion without accountability". He warned about "the tyranny of judges" and raised the danger of an international Kenneth Starr, the "Independent Counsel" who pursued the impeachment of President Clinton in the 1990s.[127] Kissinger's warnings, especially about Starr, proved to be uncannily accurate.[128] There has been considerable criticism of the ICC. John Rosenthal has noted another of its central failings:

> The failings of the Rome Statute are glaring. Its provisions flout the elementary principles of international law that have formed the express basis of the international system since the founding of the U.N. after World War II. Most gravely, they undermine the principle that has formed the very cornerstone of the U.N. system: namely, what the U.N. Charter in its article 1.2 calls the "principle of self-determination".[129]

It is naïve not to accept that the ICC is a political entity. Professor Tom Ginsberg has noted: "All courts by their nature do have political impact and are political institutions."[130] Professor Eric Leonard, a leading international criminal expert, and author of *The Onset of Global Governance: International Relations Theory and the International Criminal Court*, has pointed to this reality: "I think the ICC has to recognize, and what Ocampo has to recognize and I don't think he really did at first, is whether he likes it or not, the ICC is a political institution. I fully believe that there are no institutions, governmental, legal, etc., that are not political institutions. There is a political component to all aspects of the global community and the ICC is not exempt from that."[131]

The view of William Schabas, a keen supporter of the ICC, on the essentially political nature of the ICC, is stark:

> I would have held to the view in the 1990s that the Court should be totally separate from political debates and that there should be no possibility of political involvement in the work of the Court. As you know, in the final Statute, there's a bit of a compromise there, mainly with respect to Article 16, which allows the Security Council to temporarily halt the proceedings of the Court. The other places where you have quite a clear political involvement of the Court are the triggering mechanisms where you allow both the Security Council and states to trigger the Court. This is politics. These are political bodies that make their decisions politically. I'm increasingly of the view that politics is actually a part of international criminal law and that it's unavoidable.
>
> I see this increasingly in decisions about whom to prosecute: decisions about individuals who are prosecuted and also about the organizations that are targeted. In Uganda, for example, the prosecution has targeted the rebels and not the government. I think that's a political decision. The prosecutor has

couched it in a strange and ultimately unconvincing theory about prosecuting the most serious crimes, but he defines this in a purely quantitative way. So if the rebels kill more people than the government, then the rebels should be the focus. But the problem with that is you need a more qualitative approach when deciding who your targets should be. Most of us living in an orderly society would find it far more threatening that the government is committing crimes, even if the outlaws are committing more, because outlaws are supposed to commit crimes and governments aren't.[132]

The ICC's selectivity regarding cases has drawn criticism from even its keenest supporters. Human Rights Watch has warned: "There's a concern that the ICC is biased, or at least applying justice selectively."[133] Human Rights Watch have summed up one of the central issues affecting the court's credibility: "When officials from or supported by powerful states have been able to avoid international prosecutions, the legitimacy of international justice, and, in turn, the ICC as its flagship institution, is called into question."[134]

Nicholas Waddell and Phil Clark have noted: "[P]erceptions of the ICC on the ground have at times been damaged by insufficient efforts by the court to make clear the basis on which individuals have been the subject of warrants and of particular charges, while those of apparently equal culpability have not."[135] The American Congressional Research Service has confirmed that:

> The Prosecutor's selection of cases…has proven controversial…. Some have criticized ICC prosecutions in Uganda, the DRC, and CAR for focusing on alleged abuses committed by rebel fighters to the exclusion of those reportedly committed by government troops. In Uganda, some observers suggest that the ICC is locally seen as associated with the administration of President Museveni, as only LRA commanders have been targeted since the Prosecutor's investigation in northern Uganda began despite reported abuses by government troops. The decision to pursue DRC opposition leader Jean-Pierre Bemba Gombo has provoked accusations that the Prosecutor was swayed by political bias, as Bemba was seen as a leading opposition figure in DRC before he entered into exile and was arrested; or excessive pragmatism, since other Congolese political actors accused of similar abuses have not been pursued to date.[136]

Richard Goldstone has admitted that "[a]ll the court's cases, thus far, have been from Africa, leading some to suppose that the institution will provide 'international justice' only for those countries too weak to resist it. Indeed without expanding to other corners of the world, the ICC does risk being branded, at best, as a selective prosecutor, and at worst, as a purveyor of racially conscious justice."[137]

Jacqueline Geis and Alex Mundt have noted that "[a]lthough the ICC was established as an impartial arbiter of international justice, both the timing and nature of its indictments issued to date suggest that the intervention of the ICC in situations of ongoing conflict is influenced by broader external factors".[138] This selectivity is clear. The ICC's founding treaty, the Rome Statute, provides that individuals or organisations may submit information on crimes within the jurisdiction of the court. These submissions are referred to as "communications" or complaints to the ICC. In its first year of existence, 2002–03, the ICC received 472 requests that the ICC investigate war crimes.[139] By February 2006, the prosecutor had received 1,732 communications alleging crimes.[140] As of 4 October 2007, the Office of the Prosecutor had received 2,889 communications about alleged crimes in at least 139 countries.[141] These complaints were received from individuals or groups in at least 103 different countries but, as of 1 February 2006, sixty per cent of the communications originated in just four countries: the USA, the UK, France and Germany.[142] As of July 2009, the prosecutor reported that his office had "received over 8137 communications…from more than 130 countries".[143] As of September 2010, the court had received over 8,874 complaints.[144]

Despite almost 9,000 complaints about alleged crimes from more than 130 countries, the ICC began investigations in just 8 countries, all of them African: Uganda, the DRC, the Central African Republic, Sudan, Kenya, Ivory Coast, Libya and Mali; and has opened cases against thirty-two people, all of them Africans.

The court has gone through the pretence of claiming that it is investigating non-African situations. *The Economist* has punctured this assertion:

> The list of places where the court says it is carrying out preliminary investigations is broad enough: Afghanistan, Colombia, Georgia, Gaza, Honduras and the Korean peninsula, as well as Guinea and Nigeria. But the total number of staff involved in those initial probes is a bare handful. *The court's resources are overwhelmingly directed at a single continent.*[145] (Emphasis added.)

With regard to the ICC, Human Rights Watch noted:

> [The] uneven reach of international justice. Indeed, this unevenness increasingly poses a challenge to the credibility of international justice, and, in turn, to that of the ICC. Concerns that impunity is not being tackled consistently around the world have a factual basis. Officials from or supported by powerful states have been able to avoid international prosecutions. Victims of the most serious international crimes in Afghanistan, Burma, Chechnya, Gaza, Iraq, and Sri Lanka, for example, have lacked access to justice.[146]

The court's inaction regarding Iraq and Afghanistan is dealt with in separate chapters in this book, but even when the ICC has selectively chosen to investigate a "situation", it has not shown the due impartiality that is expected of any objective legal scrutiny. The legitimacy of the ICC depends on its ability to maintain an appearance of impartiality. In its 2006 draft policy on "Criteria for Selection of Situations and Cases", the Office of the Prosecutor articulated its "guiding principles": independence, impartiality, objectivity, and non-discrimination. In a further draft policy paper dealing with the selection of situations for investigation, the OTP reiterated the first three of these as "general principles."[147] In its 2009–12 strategy paper, OTP stated that "focused investigations and prosecutions" are one of four "fundamental principles" of the OTP's prosecutorial strategy in order to make efficient use of "limited resources". In selecting incidents for trial, the OTP's stated goal is "to provide a sample that reflects the gravest incidents and the main types of victimization".[148] This strategy paper specifically restates the fundamental ICC principle of "addressing the interests of victims".[149] As Allison Danner points out: "If the Prosecutor becomes identified with any political agenda other than seeking justice, the role of the Court in providing an impartial, independent forum for individuals accused of the most serious crimes will be severely compromised."[150] Louise Parrott has noted that this is a problem that has already arisen with regard to Uganda in that "only LRA rebels have been targeted, making the Court open to claims that its purpose is to selectively rid Uganda of the rebels rather than to impartiality prosecute the crimes committed."[151] She went on to observe that the Ugandan government hoped "that joining the ICC would help it prosecute the rebels... . These recent developments raise numerous issues, not least of which is the desirability of the ICC becoming involved in ongoing conflicts, particularly where the referring government is one of the parties. As a result, questions arise about the impartiality of the Prosecutor, the feasibility of enforcement and ultimately the prospects of peace."[152]

Human Rights Watch has also confirmed that the ICC's impartiality has come into question almost immediately regarding its involvement in Uganda: "The ICC badly needs to regain the confidence and trust of the people whose interests it is pursuing. It must correct the image it has acquired of an institution subject to manipulation by the Ugandan government for political expediency. It must restore the image of a credible international institution." Human Rights Watch felt it necessary to urge the ICC to "quickly act to demonstrate the court's impartiality", noting that "[c]ivil society remains concerned that the ICC is being manipulated by President Museveni, whose statements have not dispelled that impression".[153] These questions have also been voiced by Ugandan political leaders such as Norbert Mao: "When the ICC first came they said they would investigate both sides. In the eyes of many people the ICC is serving the interests of the Ugandan government, not justice."[154] *The Guardian* has also noted: "While the LRA's crimes have been widely exposed, the actions of the Ugandan army have not been subjected to the same scrutiny. It has been involved in wholesale forced removals, often brutally carried out, of hundreds of thousands of people from their homes to deny the rebels support. People in the area also accuse government soldiers of rape and killings."[155]

This was also the case in the second situation within which the court became involved, the DRC. In 2011 Human Rights Watch noted: "So far, however, the ICC's record in DRC has been mixed, at best... . The ICC's prosecutorial strategies in DRC have also raised questions as to the ICC's independence and impartiality."[156] Human Rights Watch concluded that the court's behaviour "may have caused irreparable damage to perceptions about the ICC's impartiality in the DRC."[157]

Human Rights Watch ultimately observed that "[i]n four situations – DRC, Uganda, CAR, and Darfur – the absence of more coherent and effective strategies has undermined perceptions of independence and impartiality, threatening the court's credibility".[158] Human Rights Watch provided details: "[I]n the DRC situation – as in Uganda and CAR – there have been no investigations leading to charges against [government] officials. In these three situations, a total of 11 arrest warrants have been issued, but the targets of these warrants are, in effect, all rebel leaders. The absence of charges against government officials has given credence to the perception that the ICC is powerless to take on those on whom it must rely for its investigations. Even if the problem is one of perception rather than actual compromised independence, it has nonetheless created a profound credibility gap for the ICC in each of the three situations."[159]

And yet, for all the ICC's bluster about impunity, principle and human rights, once the Chief Prosecutor had realised the damage that his indictment of President al-Bashir was causing to his reputation and that of the court, the court was not above trying to make deals. In September 2008, for example, the former foreign minister of a Pacific country that supports the ICC told the *Inner City Press* that Ocampo had been telling diplomats that he had offered to Bashir not to indict him, if he turned over the two previously indicted Sudanese nationals, Kushayb and Harun.[160] In so doing, Ocampo was clearly in line with the European powers also willing to play games: "It appears that the Europeans would like to use the court as a sort of negotiating stick to induce Bashir to behave better in Darfur."[161]

The new prosecutor, Fatou Bensouda, has in effect admitted the political instrumentalisation of the court: "What has to be recognized is that even though we are a judicial institution, we operate in a political environment, whether we like that or we don't. Those who do not understand the limitations of the I.C.C. jurisdiction – they are the ones who think the I.C.C. is picking and choosing."[162]

Are there alternatives to the legal fundamentalism of the ICC? The answer is yes. The case has been clearly made that amnesties and truth commissions, so long as their primary purpose is addressing and resolving conflict and not shielding a perpetrator from criminal responsibility, can qualify as valid attempts at "investigating crimes".[163] Although the peace-versus-justice issue is dealt with in detail in subsequent chapters it is useful to note the comments of Fabrice Weissman, the Head of Research for MSF, and a former MSF Head of Mission in Darfur, on the subject: "The expression 'no peace without justice' does not, however, reflect historical reality. All of human history gives lie to the assertion that judging war criminals is a necessary condition for peace. To take only a few recent examples, from Mozambique to Northern Ireland, from the Basque country to Angola and South Africa, it has been policies of amnesty, pardon or forgetting that have accompanied in the end of war."[164] Yet, as David Lanz notes: "[A]mong different means of justice – forgiveness, reconciliation, truth-telling, compensation, retribution, revenge, etc. – the ICC chooses only one, that is, punishment."[165] The ICC's institutional autism is evident. Rosenthal has summed up some of the other dangers of the ICC:

> If we consider the ICC's erosion of the classical U.N. principles, the contempt for due process written into its statute, and – last but by no means least – its mode of financing, what will become abundantly obvious is the risk it presents

of being an interventionary court subordinated to the geostrategic aims of its richest and most powerful member states, whether singular or in league. In short, the ICC's practice threatens to be nothing other than the continuation of war by quasi- or pseudo-judicial means.[166]

A dangerous precedent has also been set by the ICC. The court's co-option of the UN in an attempt to arrest LRA leaders in January 2006 in Garamba National Park was a disastrous failure, resulting in death and injury to scores of attackers and Africans. Eight UN peacekeepers were killed. This use of the UN to attempt to execute an arrest warrant, probably resulting in fatalities on both sides, places the UN in all its manifestations, from UN humanitarian agencies through to peacekeepers, in danger.

The ICC's political and legal autism with regard to the people and situations it is affecting so negatively has been outlined by Geis and Mundt:

> The issue of what impact the timing of indictments has on a conflict situation comes into sharpest relief in the debate over whether justice and peace can be pursued simultaneously. Many in the human rights community argue that peace and justice are mutually reinforcing, promoting reconciliation and ensuring the sustainability of peace by deterring future abuses and addressing abuses already committed in a non-violent manner. However, the four case studies presented here suggest that such logic oversimplifies the reality of peacemaking. There is an inherent tension in simultaneously pursuing a strategy that assigns criminal scrutiny and/or blame to a party in the midst of peace negotiations that depend on the full cooperation of those accused. Ocampo himself has conceded that his mandate may at times be in tension with the efforts of those seeking peace. A more pragmatic approach, some argue, is to recognize that tensions often exist between peace and justice and that pragmatism demands that justice sometimes take a backseat to achieving peace. The Ugandan Refugee Law Center and Acholi civil society organizations have advocated strongly for this "peace then justice" approach in the northern Uganda conflict, as have some members of the humanitarian community with respect to the situation in Darfur. Recent statements from the DRC government have alluded to favoring a similar sequencing with regard to the current situation in North Kivu.[167]

The ICC's subsequent, and selective, legal autism has jarred with the views of many of the international lawyers who helped to establish it. The distinguished British jurist and human rights activist Lord Peter Archer QC, a key British negotiator in the establishment of the court, has argued that the use of international tribunals in Africa needs to be pragmatic. He noted that, as with domestic law, two issues need to be considered. Firstly, "has a breach of the law occurred?" and, secondly, "is it in the public interest to prosecute?" For Archer, this meant that whether or not international law concerning war crimes should be applied should be decided on a case-by-case basis.[168]

The arrogance of the ICC and its first chief prosecutor is clear. Observers such as Nick Grono and Adam O'Brien state: "[I]t is difficult to tell victims of these conflicts that the prosecution of a small number of people should take precedence over a peace deal that may end the appalling conditions they endure and the daily risks they face."[169] This is especially the case if all that is motivating such a prosecution is a personal or bureaucratic imperative on the part of the court, its chief prosecutor and a self-serving Western élite.

The British parliamentarian Ian Paisley Jr., who has experience both as a peace envoy for the UN and the EU to Guinea-Bissau, and as a peace-process negotiator in his native Northern Ireland, has challenged the court's central mantra, that there cannot be peace without justice:

> Proponents of the I.C.C. say there cannot be peace without justice. Yet experience teaches us that this is not always the case. Reconciliation is not an easy option, but it does allow people to move forward with the hope of unity, and the potential for justice in the future. The experiences of Northern Ireland and South Africa show us that there is nothing more important than peace.[170]

The court had failed in almost every one of its objectives. William Schabas has observed that "[t]he International Criminal Court continues to plod along, consistently failing in the targets that it has itself set".[171] He has also noted, perhaps with Canadian understatement, that "[i]t is hardly a secret that in its early years the Court has struggled to find its way".[172] Schabas has become more focused about the failings of the ICC: "The Court lacks vision and leadership."[173] Schabas has compared the activity of the ICC with other international courts. He observed that nine years after the UNSC established the ICTY "it had issued 76 indictments, three times the number of the ICC". As Schabas documents: "Forty-six people were in detention in The Hague, compared with five for the ICC. The Tribunal was conducting six simultaneous trials, compared with three for the ICC. Perhaps most telling, the Yugoslav Tribunal had completed the trials of 25 accused persons. In 18 of these cases, even the appeals were finished."[174] Schabas also compared the work of the ICC to that of the ICTR, noting that the Rwanda tribunal's performance "is…rather stellar when set beside that of the ICC". He observed that "[n]ine years after its establishment, it had completed the trials of 13 accused. Several appeals had also been adjudicated." Schabas has also noted that within the same time frame, "the Special Court for Sierra Leone had completed three trials of nine defendants through to the appeals stage".[175]

Schabas has also pointed to an institutional malaise, observing that while the court is "[a]fflicted with a cumbersome and inflexible procedural regime, there is nevertheless resistance to contemplation of any reforms."[176] He has stated that the Rules of Procedure and Evidence and the Regulations of the court "provide the ICC with flexible instruments enabling adjustments as pitfalls are identified." Schabas states that at the UN tribunals the rules of procedure and evidence were "subjected to a constant process of fine-tuning and amendments as adjusted in light of experience and changes in the nature of the workload." He is obviously surprised to note that "[a]lthough the same should be possible at the ICC, in practice there is nothing of the sort." His frustration is evident when he goes on to observe that "[w]hen provided with the opportunity for changes, in the context of the Review Conference, the Court refused even to allow the discussion."[177]

Schabas notes that in the lead-up to the 2010 Kampala Review Conference, "it became clear that there was no stomach for any soul-searching" about the court's performance:

> The Court's institutions and the Assembly of States Parties agreed not to talk about any shortcomings. Some said it was out of concern that this would only nourish Africa's simmering malaise with the Court. But if anything feeds disappointment and cynicism, it is a refusal to acknowledge that the emperor has no clothes. The Review Conference indulged in some "stocktaking", but there was no introspection.[178]

Schabas is absolutely correct. The Emperor has no clothes. The court is a failure.

Chapter Two

A European Court

"The EU had been a strong supporter of the establishment of the ICC; we had worked for years to achieve its creation; Europe had adopted a common position on this."

Chris Patten, former EU Commissioner for External Relations[179]

"The financial contribution the EU has made to the ICC is so significant that it... has led to suspicions arising about a possible process of assimilation between the two organisations."

Vidal Martín[180]

"[T]he ICC is, more humbly and realistically, just a project of the European Union."

John Rosenthal[181]

The ICC is a *de facto* adjunct to, and instrument of, European foreign policy. The ICC has been openly described by European academics as an "EU Court"[182] The prominent American commentator George F. Will describes the ICC as "a facet of the European elites' agenda of disparaging and diluting the sovereignty of nations".[183] Courtenay Griffiths QC has been equally blunt: "The court acts as a vehicle for its primarily European funders, of which the UK is one of the largest, to exert their power and influence, particularly in Africa."[184] This view is shared within the emergent world. The Mozambican foreign minister Leonardo Simão, for example, has referred to the ICC as Europe's "brainchild".[185] The only question is whether the court is the EU's child by conception or adoption. The EU describes itself as "a staunch supporter" of the ICC.[186]

The EU's avid support for the court, from conception to statute and beyond, over almost two decades, is a matter of record. Belgian analyst Michael Bourguignon has observed that the EU has been "the international voice for the ICC". He also noted: "The EU can be seen to indirectly be the public diplomatic arm of the ICC."[187] The EU was seen as a coherent actor that advanced the case of the court both during the preparations for the Rome Conference and afterwards.[188] The reality is that one way or another the EU adopted the ICC as its offspring. Following the Rome Conference, the EU publicly pushed in the preparatory commission for state ratifications and a solution of all outstanding issues.[189] The EU's first Common Position on the court, issued on 11 June 2001, placed its approach to the court within the EU's Common Foreign and Security Policy.[190] The common position adopted an official position on the ICC that sought "to pursue and support an early entry into force of the Rome Statute and the establishment of the Court."[191] The EU pledged to "make every effort to further this process by raising the issue of the widest possible ratification...of the Statute in negotiations or political dialogues with third States, groups of States or relevant regional organizations, whenever appropriate". This was followed up by the EU's May 2002 action plan and subsequent updates. The EU established an ICC Focal Point in the Council Secretariat and instructed each of its member states to establish national Focal Points. The EU pushed then as now for other states – and particularly Third World countries – to join the court.

That the ICC is an extension of the EU is clear. Wikipedia, for example, has noted:

> The EU has been the strongest supporter of the ICC and has supported it in nearly every instance. In ways it has operated as a public relations branch of the ICC and encouraged states around the world to adopt the Rome Statute (including putting it in trade agreements, as mentioned above). Due to the difficulty of the court's work, and opposition from major powers such as the US, this support has been indispensable and, likewise, *the EU has been using the ICC as a tool to make its presence felt*.[192]

The Wall Street Journal noted that the Rome Treaty received the required ratifications to establish the court from at least sixty nations, "thanks to strong European support".[193] Judge Sang-Hyun Song, President of the ICC, in a keynote speech to European parliamentarians in October 2009, acknowledged the EU's pivotal role within the ICC: "The Parliament was instrumental in mobilising the forces that brought the ICC into existence."[194] Song also admitted the EU's political involvement: "In its external relations, the EU has provided the Court with important political support. This has included encouraging new ratifications and accessions to the Rome Statute. The Court has benefited from inclusion of ICC language in the Revised Cotonou Agreement and several country-specific Partnership and Cooperation Agreements." Song also acknowledged the EU's key funding of pro-ICC NGOs: "Beyond the assessed contributions of its Member States, the EU has provided critical financial backing for PGA and other effective civil society proponents of international criminal justice."[195]

Jan Wouters and Sudeshna Basu have noted the EU's unconditional support for the ICC:

> [T]he EU has not only rhetorically supported the Court from the off-set but has also confirmed its commitment through its diplomatic capital and

use of financial instruments. The EU has and continues to demonstrate an "unconditional attitude" of support for the ICC. This may be observed in its measures taken within the Union, in its external relations and also between the EU and ICC at the institutional level…the EU…holds a special position in the ICC's overarching system of international cooperation.[196]

The inter-relationship between the ICC and the EU is clear. The ICC is a treaty-based organisation, as is the EU: both founding treaties were signed in Rome. The EU is a political union of twenty-seven member states. Both the ICC and EU are superficially organisations made up of states of equal standing. In reality both are dominated by those governments that are their main funders. In both cases it is the same: Germany, France, Italy, Spain and Britain. The EU clearly dominates the ICC financially. The EU openly admits that "Since the set up of the ICC, EU Member States have been the main contributors to the ICC". Up to July 2007, EU member states provided 75.6 per cent of the ICC's funding. Funding by Japan, following its accession in July 2007, saw this EU contribution decrease to 57.4 per cent, but it remains pivotal.[197] In 2009, the EU, through its member states, paid sixty per cent of the ICC's budget of €94,175,008. If one includes – as the EU does in its statements regarding the ICC – those other European states that it says are candidate or potential candidate members of the EU and those other European states that associate themselves with the EU position, the European contribution in 2009 came to sixty-three per cent.[198]

The EU provided €62,867,105 of the 2012 budget, or 57.7 per cent. The biggest contributors to the ICC in 2012 were Germany, €12,927,484 (almost twelve per cent); UK, €10,647,681 (almost ten per cent); France, €9,872,161 (nine per cent); Italy, €8,059,927 (seven and a half per cent); and Spain, €5,122,301 (almost five per cent). The five dominant EU countries alone paid forty-two per cent of the ICC budget, some €46,629,554.[199] If one includes those states associated with the EU, that is to say an EU acceding country, Croatia, candidate member countries the former Yugoslav Republic of Macedonia, Montenegro, Iceland and Serbia, the countries of the Stabilisation and Association Process; and potential EU member states Albania and Bosnia and Herzegovina, as well as Ukraine, the Republic of Moldova and Georgia, they provide an additional €353,095. This would then come to €63,220,200, or 58.1 per cent of the budget. If one also adds the budget contribution of the three other European states outside of the EU, Switzerland, Norway and Liechtenstein, which provided €1,821,908, €1,404,320 and €14,511 respectively (€3,240,739), Europe provides €66,460,939. This comes to some sixty-one per cent of the overall ICC budget for 2012.[200]

It is also worth noting that while there are a large number of administrative positions and sinecures that are given to a wide range of nationalities, this is window dressing. The power remains within the big five funders. They dominate the court, they make the running, they make the decisions. It is their court, just as to all intents and purposes they dominate the EU. Western Europeans have been appointed to key jobs throughout the ICC. Even studies of the court by organisations sympathetic to it have been critical of the European dominance of the positions filled within the institution:

France once again has the highest number of nationals appointed to the Court. Between 2008 and 2012, there has been an 87.5% increase in the number of French nationals appointed to professional posts. The number of French nationals (45) in 2012 is 105% more than the top-end of the desirable range of country representation for France, as specified by the Committee on Budget and Finance (CBF).... The two countries with the second and third highest number of appointees are the United Kingdom and the Netherlands. Both of these countries are also overrepresented within the Court with the number of nationals appointed to professional positions exceeding the top-end of desirable level of representation per country as specified by the CBF. With 27 nationals appointed to professional posts within the Court against a desirable range of 17.42–23.57, the UK exceeds the top-end of the desirable range by three individuals (13%). In the case of the Netherlands, the current number of employees (17), exceeds the top-end of the desirable range of 5.60–7.58, by 9 individuals (113%).[201]

In the ASP the EU also plays a pivotal role as the largest player and biggest funder. Its role is also political. Bourguignon has noted that "in the ASP, the body inside the ICC equivalent to the General Assembly of the UN, the EU plays a pivotal role as the largest player."[202]

As the ICC follows the EU model, it is useful to examine the European experience. The dominance within Europe of Germany, France and Britain is an open secret. *The Economist* magazine, for example, has reported the comments of the Czech President, Vaclav Klaus, made in December 2008 about the forthcoming Czech presidency of the EU (the EU presidency rotates every six months). Speaking to EU ambassadors in Prague, Klaus stated that the Czech presidency was an insignificant event because the EU is dominated by its big founding nations. *The Economist* reported that President Klaus then turned to the envoy from Slovenia and remarked that everybody knew the Slovene presidency in the course of 2008 had been a charade, scripted by France and Germany.[203] Germany, France, Britain and Italy pay for the EU, and thereby dominate it.[204] In 2009 Germany paid the largest sum into the EU budget, a record $13 billion, followed by Italy and France, which paid about $6 billion each, and then Britain. It must be made very clear that when one refers to the "European Union", one is in effect referring to the small number of western European states that finance and dominate that grouping of European states that have come together as the EU. The same five European states dominate the ICC in the same way.

The Israeli researcher Seth Frantzman also noted the European dominance of the ICC:

[T]he court is primarily European run. Yet those it judges are not from Europe; they are usually kidnapped from their home countries, without the ability to appeal their extradition, and shipped to Europe to sit in a European prison where they have no access to legal protections that other Europeans enjoy.

This is at best an unfair system and at worst a colonialist one, which places even a former SS officer above suspects from Africa or elsewhere.²⁰⁵

Political Support for the ICC

EU support for the ICC is expressed first and foremost within the framework of the UN. Since the presentation of the "First Report" of the ICC to the UN General Assembly on 8 November 2005, all the current EU member states co-sponsor the annual resolution in support of the ICC. The EU has also issued numerous foreign minister conclusions in which the ICC is featured.²⁰⁶ The complex architecture of the EU – its three-pillar structure involving the first (Community), second (Common Foreign and Security Policy) and third (Police and Judicial Cooperation in Criminal Matters) – has seen roles accorded to all three pillars in supporting the ICC.

The Cotonou Agreement

The Cotonou Agreement, coming under pillar one, is a prime example of this approach. The Cotonou Agreement is the key trade, development and aid treaty between the EU and the group of African, Caribbean and Pacific (ACP) states. It was signed in June 2000 in Cotonou, in Benin, by seventy-nine ACP countries and the then fifteen member states of the EU. It entered into force in 2002 and is the latest agreement in the history of ACP-EU development cooperation. The revised Cotonou Agreement includes Article 11.6, which is a clear-cut provision that obliges States Parties to: "(a) Share experience on the adoption of legal adjustments required to allow for the ratification and implementation of the Rome Statute of the International Criminal Court and (b)…The parties shall seek to take steps towards ratifying and implementing the Rome Statute and related instruments." Commentators have remarked that Article 11.6 was contentious: "The negotiations had been in progress for some 8 months with a number of difficult issues in debate including the desire on the part of the EU to make participation in the International Criminal Court (ICC) an integral part of the agreement."²⁰⁷

The consequences of an ACP state not ratifying all of the Cotonou Agreement, including the ICC clauses, are clear:

> Sudan has chosen not to ratify the revised Cotonou Agreement by the legal deadline of 30th June 2009. This is due to a clause in the Agreement – which Sudan signed some time ago – encouraging the ACP to take "steps towards ratifying and implementing the Rome Statute and related instruments". The Rome Statute is the treaty that established the ICC; so far the revised Cotonou agreement is the only binding legal instrument including an ICC-related clause… . Since Cotonou provides the legal framework for relations between the EC and ACP states, non-ratification by Sudan prevents the EC

from implementing bilateral development cooperation in Sudan under our main financial instrument for development assistance to developing countries, the 10th European Development Fund (EDF). This means that the EC will not be able to disburse the €300 million pledged at the May 2008 Sudan consortium for the period 2008–2013.[208]

It should also be noted that the Sudan consortium funds were for the post-war development of Sudan, different from normal "development" funds and therefore was an even more egregious move on the part of the EU.

Any ACP state that chose not to ratify the Cotonou Agreement in its entirety and continue to play the ICC game would lose hundreds of millions of euros in "development" funds, a distinct financial disincentive. The EU was very critical, however, of American attempts to discourage cooperation with the ICC by imposing financial disincentives on those states that were members of the ICC. In 2005, for example, Dr. Benita Ferrero-Waldner, Commissioner for External Relations and European Neighbourhood Policy, complained:

> Another challenge to the Court has more recently come in the shape of the adoption in December 2004, by the US Congress, of the "Nethercutt Amendment", which extends to economic assistance the threat of US sanctions to the State Parties refusing to sign bilateral immunity agreements. On 10 December 2004, the EU publicly expressed concern about the adoption of this Amendment. *The Commission is particularly concerned that vulnerable countries, in Latin America, Africa or the Middle East, may see significant amounts of US economic aid withdrawn. The EU has expressed such concern to the US.*[209] (Emphasis added.)

The hypocrisy is obvious. To be clear then, the EU protested vehemently at the USA threatening to withhold economic assistance from those ICC members unwilling to sign bilateral immunity agreements. US Congressman George Nethercutt's so-called "Nethercutt Amendment" to the Foreign Operations, Export Financing, and Related Programs Appropriations Act sought to suspend Economic Support Fund assistance to ICC States Parties who refused bilateral immunity agreements with the USA or were not provided with a presidential waiver. The Nethercutt Amendment differed from other anti-ICC provisions, such as the American Servicemembers' Protection Act (ASPA), by imposing economic aid cuts instead of military aid cuts.

Yet the EU itself threatens similarly to withhold economic assistance from African, Caribbean and Pacific members of the Cotonou Agreement who do not agree to the pro-ICC clauses.

In commenting on the US actions aimed at poorer ICC State Parties, Richard Dicker, Director of the International Justice Program at Human Rights Watch, stated: "The U.S. is preying on small, vulnerable, impoverished states that are hugely dependent on assistance — military, economic, political — from the United States."[210] And yet with regard to the EU's political and economic blackmail of ACP countries into ratifying pro-ICC clauses in trade agreements, Human Rights Watch and other advocacy groups are silent.

The EU have also sought to introduce similar ICC clauses in Partnership and Cooperation Agreements (PCAs) with Indonesia, Thailand, Singapore, Brunei Darussalam, Malaysia, Vietnam and the Philippines, and in the Trade, Development and Cooperation Agreement (TDCA) with South Africa. The negotiating mandates for Iraq, China, Russia, Ukraine, the Andean Community and Central America also include an ICC clause. The EU Strategy for Central Asia, adopted by the European Council in June 2007, is another clear example of how the EU seeks to mainstream the ICC in its external policies. The EU is aware that Central Asia remains significantly underrepresented in the court's system, and thus has included ICC membership among the objectives to be pursued in any partnership with Kazakhstan, the Kyrgyz Republic, Tajikistan, Turkmenistan and Uzbekistan. To this end the EU is pushing for the adoption of the necessary legal adjustments required to join the ICC as well as seeking to provide technical assistance aimed at making the legislative and constitutional amendments required for accession to and implementation of the Rome Statute.[211]

In 2008, the EU clearly stated its pivotal involvement with the ICC:

> The EU will continue to use all means available to it to promote the ICC in its policies and the principles of international criminal justice. It will accordingly bring the ICC into its policies, particularly in development, conflict prevention, justice, freedom and security.[212]

In 2010, the EU summarised its policy of tying trade, cooperation and development agreements to membership of the ICC:

> The EU systematically seeks the inclusion of a clause supporting the ICC in negotiating mandates and agreements with third countries. So far, the revised Cotonou agreement of 2005, which applies to 75 African, Caribbean and Pacific countries and the EU, is the only binding legal instrument including an ICC-related clause. However, an ICC clause has been agreed to in the Partnership and Cooperation Agreements (PCAs), Trade Cooperation and Development Agreements (TDCAs) and Association Agreements (AAs) with Indonesia, South Korea, South Africa, Ukraine and Iraq. ICC clauses are currently being negotiated in the PCAs and AAs with Singapore, Thailand, Malaysia, The Philippines, Brunei Darussalam, Vietnam, China, Libya, Russia and Central America. The TDCA with South Africa was signed in September 2009 and the PCA with Indonesia in November 2009. Article 11 of the Cotonou Agreement forms the "standard clause" to be followed when negotiating other agreements, although it is of course necessary to adopt a case-by-case approach, taking into account the different positions on the ICC of the countries with which the EU enters into agreements.[213]

It has been noted, however, that the EU applies a "differentiated treatment, especially vis-à-vis less important countries". ICC clauses have not been included in agreements with the EU's strategic partners, such as the USA, China or Russia. The differentiated treatment of certain states has left the EU open to being "criticised for applying a double standard".[214] The EU's behaviour could also be described as that of a bully.

EU Common Positions on ICC

The EU Common Positions with regard to the ICC are adopted under the second pillar. They take the form of a declaration by the EU presidency on behalf of the EU, acceding countries, the associated countries, the European Free Trade Area countries and members of the European Economic Area. The first Common Position, released in June 2001, included a call for successive revisions of the position every six months.[215] The adoption of a Common Position on the ICC is significant at both the EU and international levels as it not only defines the approach of the union in regard to the court itself but places an obligation on EU member states to ensure that their national policies also conformed to the Common Position. There were revisions of the Common Position in June 2002 and June 2003, which strengthened the EU position regarding the ICC. The 2002 revision introduced a specific reference to the "universal support" the EU offers the court. It also called specifically for the collaboration of non-member states and the international community at large with the ICC, and outlined practical, technical, political and financial assistance in creating the legal framework necessary to put the Rome Statute into practice in non-member states. The revised 2003 Common Position tightened the EU-ICC relationship,[216] referring to the pro-ICC conclusions reached by the EU Council on 30 September 2002 regarding the ICC and the adherent guiding principles of the EU.[217] Member states were instructed to "support the effective functioning of the Court and to advance universal support for it by promoting the widest possible participation in the Rome Statute". The EU reiterated its strong commitment to support the effective functioning of the court and to promote the widest possible ratification of the Rome Statute. The document also demanded that EU member states become more involved in the advancement of the ICC, calling on them to "follow closely developments concerning effective cooperation with the Court".[218] In order to carry out and fulfil these three areas, the EU has had to apply instruments from all three pillars at its disposal.

The third pillar of the EU has sought to coordinate ICC legislation within the internal policies of member states. As early as 2001 the EU had also called for the EU-ICC relationship to be developed by means of an action plan. The *Action Plan to Follow-up on the Common Position on the ICC* was adopted by the EU in February 2004.[219] It outlined co-ordination of EU activities regarding the ICC; pushed the universality and integrity of the Rome Statute; and called for the more effective working of the ICC. The action plan detailed a wide range of initiatives directed at coordinating EU-ICC activities, including the setting up of EU and national focal points for the ICC. Wouters and Basu have elaborated on the EU-ICC "focal point" mechanism:

A key instrument in this regard is the EU and national ICC focal points. The EU-ICC Focal Point's responsibilities revolve around facilitating effective coordination and maintaining the consistency of information. This is to be achieved through a number of means, as outlined in the Annex of the Action Plan, such as: establishing appropriate contacts and exchanging information between the ICC, international organizations, third countries and NGOs; identifying opportunities for the inclusion of the ICC on the draft list of issues to be discussion in negotiations and political dialogues; and to liaise with the National Focal Points for the purpose of coordinating the activities of the Union and its Member States. The National Focal Points are established by each Member State to assist with the exchange of information that may be relevant in the implementation of the Common Position.[220]

The action plan also called on the EU to give technical assistance to third states in the ratification and implementation of the Rome Statute, and called for the EU to put political pressure on non-member states to ratify the Rome Statute by recommending the integration of an ICC clause into agreements and the negotiation of external agreements including recognition of the ICC as an essential prerequisite to the signing of international agreements.

Additionally, as but one example of the micro-level support for the ICC, EU member states support the "International Criminal Law Network's annual conference on the ICC and Arab States". In 2007 this was supported by the UK, Germany and Ireland. In 2006 it was sponsored by the UK, Belgium and Ireland. In 2005 it was supported by Denmark, Germany and Ireland. Another area of EU-ICC cooperation is the hosting by the European Institutions of ICC diplomatic debriefings in Brussels. The Council of the EU, for example, hosted the ninth and tenth ICC debriefings in 2006 and 2007. This level of support has continued.

The EU's ownership of the ICC is now palpable. On 21 March 2011, the Council of the European Union adopted a decision on the ICC that updated its 2003 Common Position.[221] The EU's July 2011 *Action Plan to follow-up on the Decision on the International Criminal Court*[222] fleshed out the EU's March 2011 decision, as outlined in Article 1.2 of that decision, "to advance universal support for the Rome Statute of the ICC...by promoting the widest possible participation in it".[223] The court has been incorporated into the EU's diplomatic service, the "European External Action Service". The EU's 2011 action plan stated "[t]he ICC should be further mainstreamed in EU external relations" and that "[t]he Service will mainstream the ICC across its different departments, including thematic and geographical directorates as well as crisis management structures and relevant CSDP missions and operations". EU member states were "encouraged to have an expert in their embassies in The Hague and in their missions in New York dealing also with specific ICC matters". EU embassies are instructed to "monitor developments on the ground in relation to countries under investigation by the ICC or under preliminary examination, as well as in relation to countries under a specific obligation to cooperate with the ICC".

The action plan states that "[t]he EU will provide political and diplomatic support to the ICC in the framework of political dialogues with third countries, regional organisations and other regional groups as well as in the conduct of the EU's action on the international scene, such as at the UN and other relevant fora". Article 2 of the decision addressed the issue of the universal participation in the Rome Statute, by committing the EU and its member states to furthering the process of its ratification, accession and implementation. The EU noted that the "above objectives will continue to be relevant until universal participation in the Rome Statute is attained". The extent to which the EU seeks to extend the court is clear:

> In some cases, the primary objective with regard to third countries is to maximise their political will for the ratification, accession and implementation of the Statute in order to achieve the desired universality. The realisation of this objective requires the use of a variety of means such as political dialogue, démarches, clauses in agreements, letters from the High Representative or other bilateral means, statements, including at the UN and other multilateral bodies, and support for the dissemination of the ICC principles and rules. It may also be important to assist countries which are willing but which may encounter difficulties with ratification, accession or implementation of the Statute. This could involve, inter alia, concrete expert assistance, financial support or access to data compiled by others.

The EU noted that various initiatives have been taken and continue to be taken, "ranging from political dialogue and bilateral démarches to the dissemination of the principles and rules of the ICC Statute through awareness-raising campaigns led by non-governmental organisations and to expert assistance in drafting relevant legislation", and that "[t]he EU and others have been involved, directly or indirectly, as providers of funds or technical assistance for these activities. This practice should continue in a coordinated manner."

The EU reiterated its policy of tying European economic and political agreements to membership of the ICC:

> [T]he ratification, accession and implementation of the Rome Statute should be addressed in the negotiation of EU agreements with third countries. The EU should follow up the implementation of ICC clauses included in agreements with third countries by, inter alia, reporting from Delegations, raising the matter in political and human rights dialogues, and through letters from the High Representative, as appropriate. Consideration should be given to these issues being brought up at summits and other high level meetings with third countries as appropriate. Whenever appropriate, the EU should continue to use other diplomatic means, including bilateral demarches, to encourage ratification of or accession to the Rome Statute and related instruments such as, in particular, the Agreement on Privileges and Immunities of the ICC.

Brussels outlined the work that must be done to follow up on its ICC outreach: The effect of démarches and other measures should be monitored; member states should raise the ICC in bilateral contacts with third countries, whenever appropriate, and should inform partners through the EU Focal Point of the outcome of such contacts; whenever appropriate, the EU should cooperate with interested third countries (including those that have developed a partnership in the framework of their bilateral cooperation with the EU such as Japan, Canada, Australia, Brazil and South Africa) and with international and regional organisations as well as non-governmental organisations in order to further the goal of the universality and integrity of the Rome Statute. Member states were also instructed to contribute when requested with technical and, where appropriate, financial assistance to the legislative work that may be needed for the ratification of or accession to the statute by third countries. The EU stated that it would, when requested, also contribute with such assistance that would include the use of non-governmental organisations. The EU also stated that it and its member states would facilitate technical assistance to interested states by supporting their participation in the ICC and their access to its instruments, as well as by facilitating their co-operation with the ICC.

An extensive pro-ICC outreach is available through the EU:

> Technical assistance to third states could be provided through different channels: the secondment or any other form of deployment of EU Member States' experts to the relevant administrations of the requesting state. Third states could also apply for exchange programmes of experts or the detachment of their own experts to Member States' relevant administrations, according to the relevant legislation; organization of technical consultations at expert level between the EU and target countries; EU development and cooperation programmes; and civil society projects, especially those funded by the EU and its Member States.

Even staunch supporters of the ICC such as Michael Bourguignon have warned of the ever closer relationship between the EU and ICC: "[T]he two organisations may need to be more independent in their outlook towards international justice… . The EU can be seen to indirectly be the public diplomatic arm of the ICC." Bourguignon has also touched on the essentially political interaction that has developed: "The willingness to globally support international justice through the ICC is a bold initiative that supports the EU's effectiveness as a diplomatic actor… . The EU has a priority in using the ICC as an instrument to make its presence felt as a player in international justice. In fact, this is an intelligent and useful method for both organizations." He also pointed to the ICC's dependence on the EU. "The reliance of the ICC on the EU will not let the court be able to develop the ability to fight its own battles."[224]

The reality is that the ICC has been made an integral part of EU policies. Rosenthal is clear about the fact that the ICC is a European project:

> In the form in which it emerged from Rome, the ICC is, more humbly and

realistically, just a project of the European Union, for which the EU has succeeded in rallying support among countries that, for the most part, due either to their small size or to their extreme poverty and large external debt, cannot seriously be regarded as independent players on the world stage. Alongside the world's smallest countries, the ratification registry also features many of its most highly indebted poor ones (Bolivia, Mali, Sierra Leone, Djibouti, etc.). Not surprisingly, on closer inspection, these turn out almost invariably to be privileged beneficiaries of European development aid. With very little to lose and significant financial reward to gain from demonstrating their political "worthiness" of EU assistance, more such countries can be expected to join the court in the future.[225]

The EU's political projection of the ICC has been massive, systematic and open-ended. To this end, since 2002 the EU has issued 342 démarches, approximately 60 per year, targeting more than 110 third countries and international organisations, to encourage the ratification and implementation of the Rome Statute, as well as ratification of the Agreement on Privileges and Immunities.[226] The ICC was raised in thirty-one separate démarches in the period from July 2007 to December 2008 alone.[227] This in and of itself provides irrefutable evidence that the EU is the political engine at the heart of the ICC and its promotion.

The EU has demanded inclusion of the ICC on the agenda of almost all major summits and ministerial meetings with third countries. Brussels admits that "EU initiatives include political dialogue, demarches and other bilateral agreements with third states".[228] In 2006, for example, language related to the ICC was included in the joint statements of the ninth China Summit (Helsinki, 9 September 2006) and the seventh EU-India Summit (Helsinki, 13 October 2006) and in the Asia-Europe summit chairman's statement (Helsinki, 10 November 2006). In 2007, the sixteenth EU-Japan summit joint press statement welcomed Japan's ratification of the Rome Statute (Berlin, 5 June 2007). During the 2007 UN General Assembly ministerial week, the ICC was raised in the meetings with the Non Aligned Movement and India. The EU has also stated that "Outreach does not only have an external dimension. Internally, the EU ensures that the ICC is also mainstreamed into the work of other Council preparatory bodies, targeting in particular areas where the ICC is underrepresented such as Asia, Central Asia and the Middle East."[229] The EU states that it "systematically pursues the inclusion of an ICC clause in negotiating mandates with third states. On the initiative of the Commission, the Cotonou Agreement with ACP countries (2005) includes a binding ICC clause. Under the European Neighborhood Policy, the Commission has also negotiated the insertion of ICC clauses into many related Action Plans."[230]

The EU has admitted that it serves as a recruiting sergeant for the ICC: "The ICC is mainstreamed into EU internal, as well as external, policies targeting areas where the Court is under-represented, such as Asia, Central Asia and the Middle East."[231] The EU also currently has nine "Special Representatives" promoting EU policies and interests in troubled regions of the world. Several are said by the EU to "have a clear mandate related to the ICC...and maintain regular contacts with, among others, the OTP of the ICC" and "play an important role in cooperating with and promoting the ICC in their respective areas of action". In 2009 the EU stated that it planned to engage its Special Representatives more intensively in the "promotion" of the ICC.[232]

The European Union, International Criminal Court and Japan: A case study

The EU had publicly lauded its own efforts to expand the ICC. It was particularly pleased with itself regarding Japan: "The intense work of the EU towards Japanese accession in the last two years could be mentioned as a successful example."[233] The extraordinary extent of the EU's proselytising role on behalf of the ICC was illustrated by a high-level, ICC-focused visit to Japan in December 2004. There were thirteen EU officials and one ICC representative in the delegation.[234] One would have expected any visit to Japan aimed at encouraging ICC membership to have included more than one ICC official. There had been a similar visit, in December 2002. The Japanese government noted:

> With regard to the previous event, it was held shortly after the entry into force of the Rome Statute (in July 1, 2002) and the work of the Court was yet to become visible. Accordingly, the public interest to the ICC in Japan remained at a general level. In contrast, the current visit took place when the public had increased and more specific interests on current activities as well as the future of the Court since in two years time the Court has commenced investigations in both Democratic Republic of Congo and northern Uganda. Because of such background, it can be said that this visit was organized at most opportune timing. It was also valuable to have had the presence of the senior official from the ICC's OTP.[235]

The EU's intense lobbying paid off, in more ways than one. On 17 July 2007, Japan became a member of the ICC. Japan subsequently made the maximum possible contribution to the ICC budget, the equivalent of twenty-two per cent of the whole budget. The EU voting bloc at the ASP subsequently ensured that a Japanese diplomat, Fumiko Saiga, Japan's then Ambassador to Norway and Iceland, and non-lawyer, was appointed as an ICC judge in December 2007, and re-elected in January 2009. A more clear-cut example of political vote-trading at the expense of legal integrity is hard to come by.

More disturbingly, the EU has admitted to engaging in secret intelligence sharing with regard to the ICC both in DRC and Sudan. On 10 April 2006, the EU and ICC signed *The EU-ICC Co-operation and Assistance Agreement*, which entered into force on 1 May 2006.[236] This was the first time a regional organisation has ever signed such an agreement with the court. This further cemented European control over the ICC and placed an obligation of co-operation and assistance between the EU and the ICC. It formalised the sharing of information, including classified information, regular EU-ICC meetings, testimony by EU personnel, security, immunity and training matters, as well as direct cooperation between the EU and the ICC's prosecutor. It placed a particular emphasis on the exchange of "classified information".[237] Indeed, the ICC states that: "It is hoped that the exchange of classified information will further strengthen the EU's relationship with the ICC."[238] Additionally, as a follow-up to the EU-ICC Cooperation and Assistance Agreement, an EU-ICC *Implementing Arrangements* agreement was finalised in March 2008 for the exchange of classified information.[239]

The EU has admitted that it has already assisted the ICC's OTP in the DRC by way of the EU delegation within the country, EU Special Representative for the Great Lakes, the EU Electoral Mission, EU Police Mission and EUFOR, the European Union Force rapid reaction force operated by the EU as part of its Common Security and Defence Policy. They all assisted in facilitating information and contacts locally. The EU states that it has supported NGOs working on the fight against impunity and for good governance and justice. In Sudan, the EU has provided the OTP with assistance from the EU Special Representative, and from military observers seconded by EU member states. The EU Satellite Centre has also provided the ICC with imagery and analyst reports on requested locations.[240]

The Common Position and Action Plan are the fundamental reference documents for EU policy towards the ICC. Vidal Martín notes: "The support offered by the EU in technical and economic resources remains a fundamental element in the development of the Court."[241] The German lawyer Alexandra Kemmerer also noted that "[t]he European Commission shouldered over 60% of the costs for the ICC's Advance Team, established in June 2002 as a planning unit in The Hague".[242]

The EU European Neighbourhood Policy

The EU's European Neighbourhood Policy (ENP) was developed in 2004, with the objective of imposing EU policy upon the EU's immediate neighbours by land or sea.[243] It also addresses the strategic objectives set out in the December 2003 European Security Strategy. The ENP agreements set out in concrete terms how the EU proposes to work more closely with these countries on its terms. It holds out the prospect of deeper political relationships and economic integration, which depends on the extent to which the EU's neighbours accept European positions including those regarding the ICC. The central element of the European Neighbourhood Policy is the bilateral ENP action plan agreed between the EU and each neighbour. Implementation is jointly promoted and monitored through sub-committees. In the sphere of the European Neighbourhood Policy, the Commission has negotiated the insertion of ICC clauses into action plans with Armenia, Azerbaijan, Georgia, Egypt, Lebanon, Jordan, Moldova and Ukraine.[244]

The EU's funding of pro-ICC non-governmental organisations

There has also been massive additional funding from the EU in support of the ICC. The EU has revealed that on top of direct contributions to the ICC, EU member states "also contribute individually to support the Court and its activities either contributing to the voluntary funds and/or funding ICC and international criminal justice related projects and programmes".[245] This "assistance" has been enormous. In addition to annual contributions to the budget, the EU has spent well over €40 million on projects supporting the ICC since 1995. Chris Patten, the former European Union Commissioner for External Relations, has openly admitted this funding: "The EU had been a strong supporter of the establishment of the ICC; we had worked for years to achieve its creation; we helped to fund organizations that themselves acted as advocates for the court. Europe had adopted a common position on this."[246] Alexandra Kemmerer has observed "[t]o accelerate the establishment of international criminal justice structures, the EU has actively contributed to the enhanced role of NGOs on a global level":

> [I]t can rightly be argued that without the support of the [European] Commission the leading NGO Coalition, the umbrella organisation ICCNOW, would probably not have been in a position to participate actively in all relevant meetings, to take substantial influence on State Delegations and to provide expertise especially to smaller State Delegations. The often acclaimed enhanced role of NGOs on a global level (and in international law) can thus partly be claimed as a European (Commission) success.[247]

The EU has reported that "[s]ignificant funds have been used to promote the ratification of the Rome Statute, particularly by funding global NGO activity through organisations such as the 'Coalition for the International Criminal Court' (CICC) and 'No Peace Without Justice' and promoting awareness-raising among parliamentarians through 'Parliamentarians for Global Action'".[248] The "Coalition for the International Criminal Court" received about €3.7 million in such grants between 2000 and 2008 alone. "Parliamentarians for Global Action" received just over €2 million; and "No Peace without Justice" €3.5 million over the same period. The EU also funds the ICC's "internship and visiting professionals program". A further grant of €2 million for this was budgeted for the period 2008–10.[249] In addition, the EU has drawn up a list of experts to facilitate ratification of the Rome Statute in third-party states.

The EU has used several mechanisms to fund pro-ICC activities. One such body has been the European Instrument for Democracy and Human Rights (EIDHR). The European Parliament has admitted that "[s]ince 1995 the international justice budget line of the EIHDR has been funding NGOs working to promote the adoption of the Rome Statute and its subsequent entry into force. Much of this funding has gone to support the global ratification campaigns of the Coalition of the International Criminal Court (CICC)."[250] Martín notes that "it's worth emphasising the healthy relationship between the ICC and non-governmental organisations working in the same field".²⁵¹ This may well be because so many NGOs have been receiving funding from the EU.

The essentially Western and Western-orientated, élitist nature of those who sought to create the ICC is clear. Even pro-ICC commentators such as Marlies Glasius have admitted as much: "In practice...participation still belongs primarily to an exclusive club: members of the English-speaking, university-educated, Internet-connected, plane-riding global élite will find it much easier to participate than others".²⁵² This Western élite and Western funding – from at least in large part the EU – was also used to fund NGOs within the developing world and fly in their employees to rubber stamp Western designs at set-piece gatherings such as the Rome Conference.

Glasius has also made clear the use of this European funding in the lead-up to and during the 1998 Rome Conference: "Much of the funding sought by the coalition for an ICC went into taking more southern NGOs and academic experts to the negotiations in New York and Rome. A number of countries, including Bosnia, Trinidad and Tobago, Sierra Leone, Senegal, Burundi, and Congo, relied on a technical assistance programme by the NGO No Peace Without Justice to augment the size and expertise of their delegations."²⁵³ It must also be pointed out that civil society, or "non-governmental organisation", involvement is itself fundamentally undemocratic because NGOs, and those who work for NGOs, are not elected. It is also self-evident that many of the key NGOs and their employees involved in the establishment of the ICC were funded in large part by the EU – an undemocratic influence on the proceedings.

The EU's financial support for the CICC provides a key insight into how the Europeans have massively funded pro-ICC advocacy organisations. The CICC, steered by a grouping of international human rights groups, claims to be a global network of over 2,000 NGOs said by the European Parliament to be "advocating for a fair, effective and independent ICC".²⁵⁴ As free, fair and independent as European pro-ICC funding will make it. The CICC acknowledges funding, among other sources, from "the European Commission...and the governments of Belgium, Canada, Denmark, Finland, Germany, Greece, Italy, Ireland, Liechtenstein, Luxembourg, the Netherlands, New Zealand, Norway, Portugal, Sweden, Switzerland and the United Kingdom".²⁵⁵ The European Parliament states that: "The CICC facilitates NGO access to negotiations on the ICC, including the meetings of the ASP, and enables NGOs to meet, become informed, and agree common strategies on issues related to the Court."²⁵⁶

From 1995 to 1999 the EIHDR provided ECU 935,000 to fund two pivotal CICC campaigns: "From the Preparatory Committee to the Diplomatic Conference", and "Final Preparations, CICC Coordination and NGO Participation in the Rome ICC Treaty Conference". In the same period the EIHDR funded CICC staff to the value of ECU 550,000. From 2000 to 2002 the EIHDR contributed an additional €2,9 million for further CICC campaigns: "Completing the Establishment of the ICC and Working to Ensure its Effectiveness", and "From Entry into Force to a Fully Functioning Court". In the same period the EIHDR also provided funding of €530,000 for a "Parliamentary Campaign for the Ratification and Implementation of the Rome Statute", organised by parliamentarians for Global Action, and €150,000 for the setting up of an International

Bar Association for the ICC. EIHDR funding has also gone to support the ICC-related work of the International Commission of Jurists and the Carnegie Endowment for International Peace in this field.

The UN asked the CICC coordinator to organise the accreditation of NGOs to the Rome Conference. In the words of Glasius, it was "a unique form of self-regulation not attempted before at international conferences."[257] The CICC produced a great deal of documentation relating to the ICC. These included articles, especially in legal journals by individuals and reports by NGOs. Both were aimed at informing and influencing specialist NGOs, academics, and government officials. NGOs also organised a range of conferences, seminars and meetings around the world, seeking to direct and influence the international debate on the ICC. The CICC's pivotal role in the 1998 conference is clear. They "had a highly developed system of twelve shadow teams to follow negotiations on different parts of the Statute, they debriefed friendly state delegates after closed meetings, and they kept 'virtual vote' tallies on crucial issues."[258]

From 2002 onwards, the EU funded a further twenty-one pro-ICC NGO projects to the value of more than €17 million. Much of this funding went to international ratification campaigns for the ICC, especially those organised by the CICC and Parliamentarians for Global Action. Other funding has included specific projects aimed at changing national legal systems, such as that being undertaken by *Avocats Sans Frontières* in the DRC. Recipients of EIHDR funding since 2002 have included: World Federalist Movement (CICC), Parliamentarians for Global Action, No Peace Without Justice, Gustav Stressemann Institute, FIDH, European University Institute, *Corporación de Desarrollo La Morada*, Academy of European Law, MOVIMONDO, *Avocats Sans Frontières*, Oxfam-UK, and the Institute for War and Peace.[259]

The role of NGOs is self-evidently institutionalised within the ICC. During a key visit in February 2007 to the ICC, by a group of European parliamentarians led by Ms. Hélène Flautre, Chairwoman of the European Parliament's Sub-Committee on Human Rights, the official programme included meetings with "specialized NGOs" such as the CICC, FIDH, *Avocats Sans Frontières* and the Centre for Justice and Reconciliation.[260] The EU has proudly reported on the activities of the EU-funded CICC:

> The Coalition and its members have also worked in a close alliance with the European Commission, in particular with the Directorates General for External Relations, Development and AidCo. From liaising with the Commissioners' cabinets to working with thematic and geographic desk officers, NGOs have helped to ensure that the ICC is mainstreamed into different EC policies and in bilateral relations with third countries. The Coalition also plays an important role in keeping all relevant actors informed in a timely manner on major developments relating to the ICC and international justice.

The EU also stated that:

> The Coalition and its members also maintain a high degree of cooperation

with the ICC Focal Point at the Council Secretariat, as well as with EU Presidencies and EU Member States. In particular, over the course of the years, NGOs have been providing to each Presidency, as well as to EU Member States and the Council Secretariat information and input on countries, regions or developments at the Court or on the U.S. position, thereby facilitating the coordination and implementation of common actions. Further, under the CICC umbrella, NGOs are invited to participate in the meetings of the Council Working Party COJUR ICC for an exchange of views with EU Member States on several ICC issues.[261]

The CICC remains as active as ever on ICC issues. The Coalition's seventeen-page strategy for 2009–11 states that it aims to focus on the following areas:

> Building targeted public awareness of the ICC.... Broadening and diversifying the Court's reach and impact by spearheading the next stage of national and regional campaigns to ratify and implement the Rome Statute (with a focus on major powers, potential situation countries, and underrepresented regions); Multi-level Advocacy for Cooperation: Securing and facilitating the cooperation of and among states, the Assembly of States Parties (ASP), the United Nations (UN) and the UN Security Council (UNSC), and other multilateral institutions (including the African Union (AU), European Union (EU), and the Arab League) in fully enforcing this new system of justice: Strengthening & Monitoring the Court: Engaging with the Court's operations.

The CICC also states that its 2009–11 strategy includes issuing press releases and media advisories to a network of more than 5,000 journalists around the world on important issues: "The CICC will generate media statements, press releases, and/or suggested talking points on the occasion of major Court and Coalition developments, for each of our monthly ratification target campaigns.... In each media statement, the CICC includes full contact information for civil society experts. These experts are then often called upon by prominent media outlets for on-the-record commentary about the Court."[262]

This European funding of pro-ICC non-governmental organisations has had other tangible effects. Benjamin Schiff, in his book *Building the ICC*, for example, has documented the pivotal role played by the European-funded CICC: "During the 2003 process of nominating and electing judges (and during the 2006 second round of elections) the CICC organized meetings between NGOs and those running for judgeships...quite likely influencing the votes that were eventually cast."[263] The CICC was founded on 10 February 1995 as "a broad-based network of NGOs and international law experts", whose main purpose was "to advocate the creation of [the] ICC". Several of the large Western international human rights organisations "all had full-time staff almost entirely devoted to the ICC". The ICC steering committee "consisted almost exclusively of these groups – including Amnesty International, Human Rights Watch [and] the Lawyers Committee for Human Rights".[264]

Kenneth Anderson and David Rieff have linked the rise of transnational and international NGOs, itself aided by considerable European funding, as "a movement seeking to universalise the ultimately parochial model of European Union integration".[265] They note that:

> [O]ne may admire the accomplishments of the EU without believing that it represents a universal model for humankind at the planetary level... . Why does this matter? Because it raises the possibility that what has been urged with such grandiosity as the universal condition of liberal internationalism is, instead simply the unjustified universalising of a particular historical and cultural experience, EU integration – a project, moreover, whose ultimate outcome is far from clear.[266]

The EU has also deliberately sought to influence younger people artificially, and professionals within regions such as Africa, Asia, Eastern Europe, Latin America and the Caribbean. The first EIHDR targeted project between the ICC and the European Commission was signed in 2003. It was entitled "Strengthening the International Criminal Court – enhancing its universality and increasing awareness on the national level with regard to complementarity". The EC's initial contribution was €747,000 over a twelve-month period from 1 April 2004. This project was the "Clerkship and Visiting Professionals Programme" and targeted university graduates or young people in the final stages of their studies as well as professionals who have already embarked on a career, and brought them to work within the ICC for a period of time. They are then expected to then "contribute" within national judiciaries, local and central government, local NGOs and academia. A second project concerned the dissemination of informational materials on the "rights of victims" as part of the External Communication Programme of the court. Funding for the "Clerkship and Visiting Professionals Programme" was renewed and funded to the value of €1,760,000 over a twelve-month period from 2005 to 2006. It has continued.

An EU evaluation of review of the 2003 and 2004 projects showed that the court had offered 221 interns and visiting professionals from both State and non-States Parties the chance of working in the court: "During this period, the programme had succeeded in building a network of contacts with the judiciary, central and local government, civil society and academia in the target countries concerned. The statistics showed that the majority of participants returned to their countries of residence upon the completion of their placement at the Court and continued working closely with their national authorities on ICC-related issues." The project deliberately targets "young talented and highly educated people": it noted that "[s]ince 2003 the number of applications from all over the world has increased, particularly from under-represented regions such as Africa, Asia, Eastern Europe, Latin America and the Caribbean".

The European Parliament

The European Parliament has been an enthusiastic supporter of the ICC. It has issued a flurry of pro-ICC resolutions that have sought to assert the ICC's position in international law. It has devoted part of its human rights activity to back the ICC. European Parliamentary resolutions have taken two forms: resolutions and recommendations focusing on the effective functioning of the ICC; and resolutions focusing on the EU policy on the ICC. Resolutions and recommendations belonging to the first category have urged the Council and Commission to promote universal ratification of the Rome Statute, indicated the EU bodies' measures to be undertaken when the ICC and its effective functioning come "under attack", urged the Council and the Commission to do whatever possible to convince the USA to change its attitude towards the ICC. The second category have pushed for an effective EU common policy on the ICC, and a monitoring role of the parliament regarding its implementation.

The European Parliament resolutions on the ICC have sought to be declarative of international law, reaffirming the legal strength of international norms and principles. A clear example in this respect is the 26 September 2002 resolution on the ICC in which the European Parliament recalls the obligations under the 1969 Vienna Convention on the Law of Treaties and states that they apply in the case of the Rome Statute. Other resolutions have claimed that international crimes trigger universal jurisdiction. Secondly, European Parliament resolutions have sought to support "current trends" in international law. These, of course, include resolutions claiming that the establishment of the ICC is a "breakthrough" in the field of international law, and that the establishment of the ICC are major "antidotes" addressing human rights abuses. Thirdly, European Parliament resolutions on the ICC also seek to push the parliament's claim to advocate the "development" of international law. There have also been resolutions which baldly state that countries wishing to join the EU should ratify the ICC statute as it is a "shared feature of the legal culture of the EU", part of the Copenhagen criteria, and "an essential component of the democratic model and value of the EU".[267] These resolutions on the part of the European Parliament are an attempt to assert a sort of "emerging *opinio juris*", expressing the belief that the ratification of the Rome Statute should form part of EU constitutional law. Early resolutions included: *Resolution on Ratification of the Rome Statute of the ICC*, 16 December 1999; *Resolution on Ratification of the Rome Statute of the ICC*, 18 January 2001; *Resolution on Entry into Force of the Statute of the ICC*, 28 February 2002; *Resolution on Draft American Servicemembers' Protection Act (ASPA)*, 4 July 2002; *Resolution on ICC*, 26 September 2002; *Resolution on General Affairs Council's Position Concerning the ICC*, 24 October 2002.

In conclusion, however, it has to be said that actions ultimately speak louder than words. For all the EU's much-heralded commitments to international justice, human rights, an end to impunity and common positions regarding the ICC, the reality is very different. France and the UK, the two permanent members of the UNSC, together with Germany, states at the heart of the EU and the ICC, have had no reservations about playing politics with the court and international law. This was brought into sharp focus in the lead-up to, and following, the 2012 UN vote recognising Palestine as a state.

Ostensibly committed by repeated EU common positions to actively encourage membership of the ICC, and its use to address serious abuses of human rights, France, Britain and Germany pressurised the Palestinian Authority not to join the court and not to initiate any action in respect of Israel before the court. The British government sought to tie its support for Palestinian statehood to the Palestinian Authority *not* seeking membership of, or any recourse, to the ICC. *The Guardian* newspaper reported: "Whitehall officials said the Palestinians were now being asked to refrain from applying for membership of the international criminal court or the international court of justice, which could both be used to pursue war crimes charges or other legal claims against Israel."[268] The British Foreign Minister William Hague said that the UK would not support the vote for Palestinian statehood unless the Palestinians agreed not to seek membership of the ICC: "[I]n the absence of these assurances, the UK would abstain on the vote."[269] Britain duly abstained.[270] Baroness Tonge, a British parliamentarian, asked the obvious question: "By making our government's support for the UN bid conditional on Palestine not pursuing Israel through the ICC, is the government not admitting Israel has committed war crimes in Gaza and the West Bank and is seeking impunity for that country?"[271] France had also warned the Palestinian Authority against taking action against Israel in the ICC should Palestine be granted observer state status at the UN. In a clear reference to the ICC, French Foreign Minister Laurent Fabius stated: "Speaking purely of the law, from the moment there is a recognition of a state, even as a non-member and observer, it would have the possibility of referring such-and-such a state to the court. However if we want to move toward negotiations and find a solution, it is obvious that elements should not be used."[272] It was also reported that Germany, a vocal advocate of "international justice", "called on Palestine not to use one of the rights gained by yesterday's vote – to be able to bring cases before the International Criminal Court".[273]

The position taken by France, Germany and Britain is particularly hypocritical. These countries insist on muzzling the court in the interests of "peace negotiations" and a political solution – "peace before justice" – in one particular conflict, the case of Israel, while vociferously denying any such approach in other situations. In short, therefore, retributive international justice for some, but not all.

Perhaps the final comment about the EU and the court can be left to Vidal Martín. Martín has broken the silence regarding the EU and the ICC: "[The EU] is seen as trying to 'appropriate' the ICC for itself. With greater or lesser steadfastness, the EU has demonstrated an unconditional attitude of support…making use of a range of different instruments to effectuate this backing."[274] It is also guilty of demanding adherence to international law that key members of the EU have systematically violated.

Chapter Three

THE COURT AND THE SECURITY COUNCIL

"[T]he role for the Security Council built into the Statute of the ICC sows the seeds of its destruction."

The Indian Government[275]

"The effect of Article 16 is to give the Security Council ultimate control over the Court through its power to order a deferral of any particular investigation or prosecution."

Geoffrey Robertson QC[276]

"The politicization of the ICC continues to threaten its legitimacy."

The Jurist, 2012[277]

The political institutionalisation of the ICC is amply illustrated by its relationship to the UNSC. Indeed, the court is seen by many in the developing world as an extension of the Security Council – itself widely perceived as a body ultimately dominated by the permanent five members, the USA, Britain, France, China and the Russian Federation. One clear example of this was that the government of Sudan received offers from the Bush Administration saying that it would halt ICC proceedings in return for Khartoum's consent to deploy UN troops in Darfur. The then Minister of State at the Sudanese Ministry of Foreign Affairs, Ali Karti, stated: "This shows this court has been formed for political purposes and not to serve justice."[278] Previous British and French hints at suspending ICC action regarding Darfur are also a matter of record.[279] Similar offers of Security Council deals ending ICC action were made to Muammar Gaddafi and Saif al-Islam Gaddafi by the Obama Administration, Britain and France during NATO's war in Libya.[280]

Columbia University Professor Samuel Moyn has observed with regard to the ICC: "[L]aw is just politics by other means, and glaringly so in the international realm... . The beginning of wisdom about the ICC, in short, is to acknowledge that it's a political enterprise, and moreover never an autonomous one, for it intersects other extant political agendas, especially great power politics, in incredibly complex ways."[281] The noted French legal expert Albert Bourgi has described the ICC as nothing more than an "executive branch for executing UNSC directives".[282]

The authority and credibility of the ICC was weakened from the very start by its formal and informal relationship with the USA as a permanent member of the Security Council. The USA has ensured that it is immune not just by virtue of not being a member of the ICC but also by specific immunities granted by the Security Council, on behalf of the court, something which fundamentally contradicts any ICC claim to judicial independence. The leading Indian newspaper, *The Hindu*, has focused on the hypocrisy at the heart of the ICC: "The wheeling-dealing by which the U.S. has managed to retain its exceptionalism to the ICC while assisting 'to end the climate of impunity in Sudan' makes a complete mockery of the ideals that informed the setting up of a permanent international criminal court to try perpetrators of the gravest of crimes against humanity."[283] Geoffrey Robertson describes the USA as "the nation which refuses to be bound by international human rights law [yet] demands the prosecution of foreigners who violate it".[284] He has also put it another way: "They are happy for the nationals of any other country to be tried and convicted but they won't support anything that has the power to touch a single American soldier."[285] Philippe Sands QC echoed Robertson's view, stating that the US position, the double standard "which says that international criminal courts are good enough for your citizens, but not for ours", "causes tremendous resentment".[286]

The reality is that the ICC will only be able to focus on alleged cases within the developing world. Western states and their citizens will to all intents and purposes be immune from prosecution. A South African analysis has succinctly observed, "we cannot ignore the global context of intervention, which is presently dominated by the apparent failure of international action in Iraq. How is the international community to play honest broker when images of the Middle East and the UN's particular inability to prevent violations of international law in Israel and Palestine feed local paranoia in Sudan?"[287]

Legal scholar Frédéric Mégret has described how "the irresistible attraction of power" leads the ICC to "gravitate towards the Security Council". The ICC has had "a tendency to gravitate towards the very power that [it is] supposed to constrain" and finds itself:

> Obsessed with the need to enlist power for [its] cause not only in the sense of needing immediate patrons for the purposes of having certain ideas endorsed, but because [the ICC] depend on power to be implemented in the long term. The irony...then, is a tremendous tendency to reinforce that which [the ICC claims] to transcend, sovereign states on the one hand, and the Security Council on the other.... . [T]he ICC's aspiration to international criminal justice...[is] exposed as ultimately weak and dependent on the very sort of power whose limitations [it] condemn[s].... . The Court thus ends up being highly subservient to the Security Council power logic that was supposed to be so lethal to the fundamental justice of international criminal justice...[288]

The truth is that the ICC is as independent as the UNSC (and some claim, by default, the USA) will allow it to be. David Tolbert notes that: "The Security Council referrals are obviously subject to the veto of the permanent five, so there are still vast areas of the world that are not covered by the ICC and this is a problem."[289] Professor Eric Leonard has confirmed this interpretation of the ICC's relationship with the ICC:

> Article 16 provides the Security Council with the opportunity to suspend the activities of the Prosecutor's office for 12 months and then renew the investigation more or less at their discretion. So this power of deferral of investigations and prosecutions is clearly a point at which authority resides in the Security Council and not the Prosecutor's office.[290]

Professor Hans Köchler has clearly illustrated the ICC's relationship with the UN.[291] There are two articles in the Rome Statute that completely undermine the independence of the ICC from politicisation. While the court claims to be totally independent of the UN organisation, Article 13(b) and Article 16 of its statute fundamentally tie the ICC to the Security Council. These articles open the ICC to political interference at the whim of permanent members of the Security Council. Article 13(b) gives authority to the Security Council to refer a "situation" to the ICC in cases where the court has no jurisdiction *per se* (for example where a state is not a member of the ICC). This assertion clearly violates the general principle of international law, which states that only states party to a treaty are bound by that treaty's provisions.[292]

The relationship between third parties and treaties is defined by a general formula *pacta tertiis nec nocent nec prosunt* (a treaty does not create either obligations or rights for a third state without its consent).[293] This principle is central in states' practice, and its existence has never been questioned. For states non-parties to a treaty, the legal doctrine of *res inter alios acta*, ("a thing done between others does not harm or benefit others") applies. This holds that a contract cannot adversely affect the rights of one who is not a party to the contract. The 1969 Vienna Convention on the Law of Treaties is a treaty concerning the international law on treaties between states. It is the pre-eminent "Treaty of Treaties". At the heart of the treaty is Article 34 of the 1969 Vienna Convention, which states: "A treaty does not create either obligations or rights of a third State without its consent." Article 34 of the 1986 Convention on the Law of Treaties Between States and International Organisations or Between International Organisations also states: "A treaty does not create either obligations or rights for a third State or a third organisation without the consent of that State or that organisation."[294] The 1969 Vienna Convention defines "third state" as a state not party to the treaty (Article 2 para. 1 lit.(h)); the 1986 convention defines "third state" and "third organisation" as a state or an international organisation not a party to a treaty (Article 2 para. 1 lit.(h)).

Köchler also pointed out the second fatal flaw in the Rome Statute of the ICC, which shows the Chief Prosecutor's claim to be an independent prosecutor to be untrue. Articles 13(b) and 16 grant special "prosecutorial" rights, to refer or defer an investigation or prosecution, to the UNSC, or more specifically the five permanent members. In so doing, as Köchler notes: "political interference is made part of the Court's terms of reference"[295]. He also notes that:

> It is very similar, in structural terms, to the power given, under the United Nations Charter (Art. 27[3]), to the five permanent members of the Security Council to veto any substantive (i.e. non-procedural) decision of the Council in matters of international peace and security, a provision which effectively has enabled, even encouraged, those countries to systematically violate international law, and which has allowed them to act in a climate of impunity – without fear of the consequences, even in cases of wars of aggression.[296]

Professor Köchler makes it clear that "[t]he political ('national') interests of any individual permanent member can effectively prevent the Council from referring a situation to the Court as they may prevent the Court from going ahead with an investigation or prosecution even in cases where the Court has genuine jurisdiction". Köchler goes on further to note that "[a] special irony of the Council's 'referral authority' (i.e. its competence to create jurisdiction for the ICC where it otherwise would not exist) lies in the fact that it is bound to the political will of states that are not even parties to the Rome Statute (at the moment three permanent members out of five, first and foremost among them the USA) and who, with their own and their allies' leaders and personnel being shielded from the Court's jurisdiction, can use the Court to advance their own political agenda".[297]

The simple reality is that no deferral can be ordered against the will of a permanent member.[298] As Schabas stated about Article 16 referrals and deferrals, they are "nakedly political considerations".[299] Bruce Broomhall has also clearly stated that the granting of control over court proceedings to the Security Council "would allow inequitable protection of the nationals of permanent members of the Council (as well as the nationals of their proxy and client states), and has thus been criticised for institutionalizing inequality before the law".[300]

Another example of political rather than legal considerations being paramount with regard to the ICC is that in a meeting between US and EU officials in Brussels in February 2005, to prepare for the spring meeting of the UN Commission on Human Rights, the EU presidency representative, Ambassador Julien Alex, was reported as stating that "the EU was waiting for a political signal from their internal political and security committee on how much the EU should push the ICC at Geneva or New York".[301] Signals not from legal advisers, but from political and security bureaucrats.

A participant at an international law meeting hosted by Chatham House and Parliamentarians for Global Action described the ICC as being "shaped as much by crude politics as by philosopher kings".[302] The brutally political nature of international justice *à la* superpower was made clear in February 2012, when US Secretary of State Hillary Clinton said that an argument could be made for declaring Syrian President Bashar al-Assad a war criminal. She also stated that such an action, however, could complicate a solution in Syria: "Based on definitions of war criminal and crimes against humanity, there would be an argument to be made that he would fit into that category. People have been putting forth the argument. But I also think that from long experience that can complicate a resolution of a difficult, complex situation because it limits options to persuade leaders perhaps to step down from power."[303] The Parliamentarians for Global Action have noted: "The selectivity with which the Council has made referrals has become a significant challenge facing the legitimacy of the ICC."[304] They placed on record that the court was being used for political objectives: "The finding by the Security Council that a situation constitutes a threat to international peace and security is not a judicial, but a political decision."[305] The Chatham House and Parliamentarians for Global Action meeting observed that:

> One of the strongest criticisms of the relationship between the ICC and the Security Council analysed in this meeting concerns the ability of the members of the Security Council, of which three of the five permanent members are not parties to the Rome Statute, to refer situations involving states not parties to the Court. This, it is argued, undermines the legitimacy of the ICC regime, if it is considered that its legitimacy is derived from its basis upon state consent. Furthermore, in principle, it is questioned how those states not parties, especially from among the permanent members of the Council (P5 member states), can justify their exceptionalism, namely of subjecting to the Court another state not party while they do not accept the Court's jurisdiction over themselves. Thus, many question whether, through Security Council referrals, the ICC becomes a policy tool to advance the political interests of those states represented on the Security Council.[306]

Superpower fingerprints were all over the ICC from the start, reflected in part by Articles 13 and 16 of the Rome Statute. In addition to sidelining the crime of aggression, the ICC has excluded weapons of mass destruction and terrorism from its jurisdiction. The Indian government, for example, expressed concern that "the Statute of the ICC lays down, by clear implication, that the use of weapons of mass destruction is not a war crime. This is an extraordinary message to send to the international community."[307] It is clear that this limitation of jurisdiction is very much in favour of the permanent members of the Security Council and those other Western countries who possess immense arsenals of such weapons.

The simple fact is that the ICC is closely identified with the Security Council. Geis and Mundt have pointed to how the ICC's relationship with the Security Council has compromised the court:

> The Security Council's referral of the Darfur crisis to the Court followed several years of failed diplomacy and peace negotiations, the imposition of sanctions, and an inability among the permanent five to find agreement over how and whether to effectively pressure the Sudanese government to curb the violence. By effectively outsourcing the role of "bad cop" to the ICC, the Council in effect made the Court a proxy for its own inaction and indecision

– an unenviable position for a nascent institution attempting to establish its authority and credibility.[308]

Schabas admits that the UNSC is "essentially a political body". He also touches on the key issue, the Security Council's right of referral: "[N]o Court can leave determination of such a central factual issue to what is essentially a political body."[309] In a landmark opinion in 1986, Judge Schwebel of the International Court of Justice noted that a Security Council determination of aggression is not a legal assessment, but is based on political considerations. The Security Council was not acting as a court.[310]

The court's relationship with the UNSC is not just laid down in the Rome Statute but is also a practical, logistical one. Judge Sang-Hyun Song has admitted that "The ICC does not have the tools to enforce its own decisions".[311] In 2009, the ICC restated its intimate relationship with the UN: "Cooperation with the United Nations continued to be essential to the court institutionally and in the different situations and cases. Logistical support from the United Nations greatly facilitated the work of the Court in the field."[312] As Louise Parrott notes, "Having no police force of its own, the ICC must rely on international cooperation in order to effect the arrests. Giving the ongoing nature of the conflict, this is likely to require security forces, which increases the control of states."[313] Human Rights Watch has also confirmed this: "Without its own police force, the ICC must rely on the cooperation of the international community to enforce its orders."[314] Certain nation states may well, for their own particular reasons, acquiesce in requests to militarily assist in ICC investigations or the enforcement of arrest warrants against its own nationals. This may adversely affect some national perceptions of the impartiality of the ICC. An example of this would be if the ICC used Ugandan government forces to execute its mission. And Parrott also points out that "while it may be more desirable…to rely on United Nations peacekeeping forces for enhanced security in undertaking investigations and efficiency in carrying out arrests, the use of UN forces also presents various problems. Not only could the neutrality of the forces be compromised if they were perceived as part of the operation that was building a case against a party to the conflict."[315] Should Sudan not cooperate with the ICC, the court could report this "non-compliance" to the UNSC, which in turn considers appropriate action. One is then back to the independence or otherwise of the Security Council.

Cooperation between the UN and the ICC is outlined in a formal agreement.[316] It is clear that there has been active support from the UN for the ICC. The ICC's 2006 report noted, for example:

> [T]he support of the United Nations was particularly beneficial in facilitating the Court's operations in the field. Positive cooperation continued between the Court and the Office for the Coordination of Humanitarian Affairs and the United Nations Mission in the Democratic Republic of the Congo…. . The Court established strong relationships with and received support in the field from several United Nations funds, programmes or other bodies, including the United Nations Development Programme, the Office of the

United Nations High Commissioner for Refugees and the United Nations Children's Fund.[317]

The ASP has highlighted the crucial role of the UN and enumerated a number of valuable ways to properly "root" the ICC into the UN machinery. It stated that States Parties should ensure that the ICC is adequately taken into account in Security Council action, including in relation to peacekeeping mandates, missions, and sanctions; the ICC should also be referenced in General Assembly and other resolutions where appropriate; States Parties should remind UN member states of their duty to cooperate and should request that states fulfil their obligations, in particular with respect to arrest and surrender; when considering candidacies for membership in UN organs, States Parties should consider willingness and capacity to ratify the Rome Statute and should cooperate with the court; regional groupings should keep the court's needs in mind as appropriate; States Parties should raise awareness and support for the ICC in appropriate UN fora, including in bilateral meetings with UN officials and in debates in the various UN committees.[318]

The close relationship between the UNSC and the ICC was borne out by the disastrous attempt by United Nations Mission in the DRC (MONUC) peacekeepers to arrest LRA leaders in Garamba National Park in the DRC in January 2006.[319] UN peacekeepers had been tasked with executing an ICC arrest warrant on Vincent Otti, the LRA's indicted Deputy Commander. A contingent of eighty Guatemalan Special Forces troops were deployed into the national park near the border with Sudan in which LRA forces were known to be operating. The mission, officially described as a "reconnaissance patrol", was a bloody failure. Eight Guatemalan soldiers were killed and upwards of forty others were said to have been wounded. It was the second deadliest loss in the history of the UN mission in Congo. The Guatemalan government demanded an inquiry into the deaths. Sergio Morales, Guatemala's human rights ombudsman, said that the Guatemalan troops were "doing the dirty work" of the UN – or more accurately, the ICC. A UN official admitted that "there will be lots of questions asked about what they (the Guatemalans) were doing. And yes, very few people knew about it."[320] In late 2008, Béatrice le Frapper du Hellen, the French diplomat who served as a deputy chief prosecutor at the ICC, admitted that the failed January 2006 attempt to arrest LRA leaders had been ICC-driven. She cited the incident as an example of how difficult the court's work was.[321] This ICC use of the UN to attempt to execute an arrest warrant, places the UN in all its manifestations, from UN humanitarian agencies through to peacekeepers, in danger throughout the region.

The use of UN forces in Garamba also had a negative effect on the Ugandan peace process. Very rare peace talks had been held outside of Uganda in Juba in southern Sudan. The ICG admitted that a major obstacle to peace in Uganda since the ICC arrest warrants were issued was "that Kony and Otti have said they will not attend the [Juba] talks while the ICC prosecutions are ongoing, for fear of the arrest". The ICG claimed that "Kony and Otti's fear is a misplaced one. With no independent enforcement mechanisms, the ICC is entirely dependent on others to execute its own arrest warrants. Juba is safe for the LRA leaders because the UPDF is not deployed there and the Sudan People's Liberation

Army (SPLA) has given firm assurances of protection." The United Nations Mission in Sudan (UNMIS) stated that they would not actively pursue the arrest warrants.[322] But after the failed and bloody attempt by MONUC in the DRC to arrest Otti in January 2006, the LRA's leaders' disinclination to attend meetings in South Sudan, with the presence of large numbers of UNMIS soldiers and policemen was understandable.[323]

The Security Council also controls the court in another way. A Parliamentarians for Global Action meeting stated that "one of the biggest scandals" regarding the ICC is the practice of the Security Council of making a referral to the court but then explicitly placing full financial responsibility for meeting the costs of that referral upon parties to the Rome Statute.[324] It was further observed:

> [T]hat one of the greatest dangers to the effectiveness of the Court is the failure of the Council to provide follow up support to the ICC once it has referred to it a situation. The failure of the Council to take any further measures or pursue in any way the Court's progress, aside from receiving the periodic reports by the Prosecutor concerning each situation, does not convincingly demonstrate an exemplary commitment to the Court and its pursuit of international accountability. At the most basic level of cooperation, it was questioned why the Security Council did not issue any kind of statement in relation to the arrest of Saif Al Islam Gaddafi, against whom the ICC has issued an arrest warrant in relation to the situation in Libya, referred by the Security Council.[325]

This issue has also been raised by Professor David Kaye:

> The Security Council, the very body that referred the Sudan situation to the ICC, has not stood firmly behind the arrest warrant against Bashir; it could have increased the cost of doing business with Bashir by imposing sanctions on fugitive Sudanese officials and governments that flout the arrest warrant. The Security Council may deserve credit for making the referral, but it appears uninterested in giving the court the kind of support it needs. And it is unclear whether when the time comes to back up the recent referral on Libya, the Security Council will once more undermine the court even as it seems to be empowering it.[326]

Not only is the ICC to all intents and purposes unaccountable but the Security Council's power to refer cases to the ICC, and to then postpone ICC actions for a year at a time, enshrined in the Rome Statute, adds an additional illegitimacy. This issue was one of the main reasons why India did not join the ICC. India's "basic objection was that granting powers to the Security Council to refer cases to the ICC, or to block them, was unacceptable, especially if its members were not all signatories to the treaty" because it "provided escape routes for those accused of serious crimes but with clout in the U.N. body". India also objected that "giving the Security Council power to refer cases from a non-signatory country to the ICC was against the Law of Treaties under which no country can be bound by the provisions of a treaty it has not signed".[327]

In 2012, the *Jurist* noted that "[t]he politicization of the ICC continues to threaten its legitimacy".[328] Addressing the problem of legitimacy in international criminal justice, a *Jurist* contributing editor focused upon the shortcomings at the heart of the ICC:

> The source of the danger lies in the Rome Statute of the ICC, which has a rather narrow prescription of jurisdiction, limiting it for the most part to specified international crimes either (i) occurring in States which are parties to the statute or in which a national of such a State is a Party or (ii) referred to it by the Security Council. To put the matter starkly, if China - not a member to the Rome Statute and with veto power in the Security Council - were to engage in a broad genocide of Tibet's population (no intention to suggest that this is at all within China's contemplation, and offered only by way of illustrative hypothetical), the ICC would lack jurisdiction entirely. The same would not be true if a government without a permanent seat in the Security Council were to kill dozens of protesters in a rally, and the Security Council were to refer the matter to the court for resolution. This disturbing discrepancy is scarcely defended by those earnestly engaged in the work of international criminal justice but rather justified as a necessary compromise to political realities.... To the extent that these courts are understood to be nothing more than the (well-intentioned) legal enforcement wing of the Security Council, less engaged in justice and more in pursuing selectively chosen political enemies for prosecution while ignoring allies whose crimes are no less great, the grave threat to legitimacy thereby arises.[329]

Human Rights Watch has echoed these concerns, stating that the West's double-standards have resulted in "a real danger that [the ICC] can be seen as a tool to advance political objectives. This risk is reinforced by the inconsistent support from states, especially the Western governments that champion accountability." The organisation has noted:

> The inconsistency can make the court seem less like a permanent institution of international justice and more like a light switch at the fingertips of a few permanent Security Council members. The patchy support fuels the argument of court opponents that the ICC is just another instrument in the diplomatic tool kit of the big powers.[330]

Michael Ignatieff has also put his finger upon the hollow claims that the ICC and UNSC are genuine in their pursuit of justice:

> International justice, above all, remains justice for criminals from defeated states or those too weak to deny jurisdiction. We will not have international justice in the true meaning of the term until one of the great powers allows

one of its citizens to face judgment at The Hague. None of the Security Council members with a veto – the US, Russia, China, France, and Britain – is willing to send one of its nationals to the ICC, should they be accused of crimes against humanity.[331]

Even US government cables have described the P-3, the USA, Britain and France, as "gaming the ICC".[332] An insight into this "gaming" was evident in attempts by the Western permanent members of the Security Council to politically exploit the ICC's actions on Sudan. A selection of cables released by WikiLeaks illustrated American, British and European thinking on the issue. In February 2009, for example, cables revealed that the British Prime Minister's special advisor for Africa and development, Brendan Cox, discussed the political use of the ICC arrest warrants with his American counterparts, stating that the indictment of Sudanese President al-Bashir presented new opportunities, and there might be scope for a "grand bargain" regarding the 2005 Comprehensive Peace Agreement and Darfur.[333] On another occasion, the British government was reported as saying that if "played right", an Article 16 deferral "has potential leverage for progress in Darfur and possibly in CPA implementation". The British government was said not to want to be seen as having "made a deal" or to be politicising the work of the ICC. The cable noted: "In [Her Majesty's Government] estimation, the time at which the international community has the maximum leverage is just before the pre-trial ruling on the ICC Chief Prosecutor's application for indictment." The British government was reported as expressing the view that the frequent review of the Article 16 deferral "would enable the international community to force progress in Sudan over the long-term and maintain leverage".[334] *The Economist* was critical of the British position: "At best, it seems, Britain sees [President al-Bashir's indictment] as a chip to be exchanged for setting south Sudan free and making peace in Darfur. That may be clever diplomacy, but it does nothing for the ICC's credibility to be seen as a pawn in a foreign power's chess game."[335]

Lionel Yee has pointed to the simple fact that in any case, due to the precedence of the UN Charter over other international agreements (Charter Articles 103 and 25), UN members are under an obligation to follow the Security Council rather than the court.[336] Morten Bergsmo and Jelena Pejic´ have also identified the basis of the Security Council's relationship with the ICC:

> *First*, political considerations were given as much, if not more, weight than legal arguments in the determination of the appropriate role for the Security Council in ICC proceedings. *Secondly*, the Security Council's deferral power confirms its decisive role in dealing with situations where the requirements of peace and justice seem to be in conflict. *Thirdly*, article 16 provides an unprecedented opportunity for the Council to influence the work of a judicial body.[337]

The German jurist Paulus notes that "the Council…symbolizes political intervention in an independent international judiciary. With the showdown in the Security Council over the submission of UN operations under the jurisdiction of the Court, the intricacies of this relationship have already tarnished the entry into force of the Statute."[338] Paulus has also stated that: "The adoption of SC Resolution 1422, which exempted UN personnel of non-member states from ICC jurisdiction for one year, confirms the primacy of the political over the legal, a primacy which was intended both by the Charter (Articles 103, 25) and the ICC Statute (Article 16)."[339] Paulus has also noted that "[t]he complicated interrelationship between the Court and Council should have led to a reciprocal reluctance to test the limits of the tension between law and politics. Regrettably, at least one Council member seems to have chosen the opposite path, not even shying away from blackmailing the rest of the international community into adopting resolutions of dubious legality."[340] Paulus noted that the board of editors of the key commentary on the Rome Statute had expressed a fear that Security Council deferrals would become a threat to the judicial independence of the court.[341] He had also stated that this fear was "realized even before the Court has tried its first case".[342]

Louise Arbour, the former Chief Prosecutor for the ICTY and the ICTR, has also been very concerned about the court's relationship with the Security Council:

> I have long advocated a separation of the justice and political agendas, and would prefer to see an ICC that had no connection to the Security Council. But this is neither the case nor the trend… . The increasing entanglement of justice and politics is unlikely to be good for justice in the long run. To make criminal pursuits subservient to political interests, activating and withdrawing cases as political imperatives dictate, is unlikely to serve the interest of the ICC which must above all establish its credibility and legitimacy as a professional and impartial substitute for deficient national systems of accountability. I'm not sure that partnership with the Security Council is the best way to attain these objectives.[343]

Victor Peskin has confirmed that: "The promise of the ICC as a legal body independent of and untarnished by international politics is…called into question by [Article 16]… . The politics currently surrounding and embedded in the fabric of the ICC and the Rome Statute presents a serious obstacle to the realization of the cosmopolitan ideals of fairness, autonomy, and universality that are so central to the Court's mission."[344]

This relationship was most recently manifested in the interaction between the Security Council and ICC in respect of the Libyan conflict. Having pressed the court to become involved with the Libyan situation – which it did with marked alacrity – the Western members of the Security Council then offered Gaddafi various political deals in which the ICC involvement would be circumvented, including one in which he would have been allowed to remain in Libya – directly contradicting the ICC arrest warrant. Richard Dicker, a director of Human Rights Watch, criticised the deal being offered at one stage by the UNSC referring to what he termed a "get-out-of-jail-free" card: "After setting the wheels of justice in motion, all Security Council members – and [Britain, France and the USA] in particular – should be reaffirming the message that impunity is no longer an option, instead of proffering a get out of jail free card to end a military stalemate."³⁴⁵ Mark Kersten has also pointed to the Security Council's political use of the ICC: "The Libyan experience demonstrates that the Council is willing to instrumentalize the Court but unwilling to lend it much in terms of political support. Together, these developments will have implications on the capacity of the ICC to contribute to the pursuit of conflict and post-justice for the foreseeable future."³⁴⁶ Benjamin Schiff described the Libyan referral as the court's "second poisoned chalice", the first having been the Darfur referral.³⁴⁷

In February 2012, Ambassador Christian Wenaweser, the former President of the ASP, noted that while the Security Council has referred two situations, Darfur and Libya, to the Council it had done little to support the referrals: "Why didn't the Security Council welcome the arrest of Seif Gaddafy and call on Libya to cooperate with the Court. There is little diplomatic political support from the Security Council on referrals and it is not likely to come."³⁴⁸ Ambassador Wenaweser also expressed dissatisfaction about the funding of the court's work when the situations were initiated by the Security Council. Both the Darfur and Libyan Security Council resolutions made it clear that the UN would not contribute to any ensuing costs: "We cannot have situations in which States (including non-party States) send things to the Court and then don't pay. In the future we have to think about the benefits for the Court [of Security Council referrals]."³⁴⁹

Human Rights Watch has echoed these views:

> The two Security Council referrals to the ICC, Resolutions 1593 and 1970, have included provisions that are damaging to the court, Human Rights Watch said. Both referrals imposed the entire financial burden of the new investigations and prosecutions on the court and its member countries. They also allowed exemptions for the nationals of non-member third countries should they be implicated in serious crimes committed in the referred country.³⁵⁰

There is a sense in which referrals by the Security Council and self-referrals by States Parties are possibly similar. When faced with an intractable problem there is a temptation to pass the buck. It was observed at a Parliamentarians for Global Action international law meeting, for example, that "[w]hat can be discerned from the initial practice of the Council regarding Darfur is that a referral may be considered by some as a measure of last resort, when other non-forcible measures have been exhausted".³⁵¹ This once again constitutes a political use of the court.

In conclusion, it is perhaps ironic that it has fallen to Human Rights Watch to very clearly outline the Security Council's instrumentalisation of the ICC:

> [UN Security] Council selectivity and double standards in making – and failing to make – referrals undermines the appearance of the court's independence. Indeed, the Council has referred situations only twice, in regards to the Darfur region of Sudan in 2005 and Libya in 2011. Meanwhile, the Council has failed to act in other situations where grave international crimes have

occurred. Until now, there is no apparent coherence in the practice of Council referrals. This perception is aggravated by the role of the Council's three permanent members, China, Russia, and the USA, that are not ICC states parties. Through their non-ratification and veto power as permanent Council members, they are in effect insulated from the court they have twice mandated to consider investigating crimes in other non state parties. Practically, these three powerful non states parties have also shielded some of their respective allies from the reach of the ICC, creating a virtual "accountability free zone" that includes Syria, Israel and the Occupied Palestinian Territories, and Sri Lanka, to name a few.

There have also been significant problems in the language of the Council's referrals. Both referrals (resolutions 1593 and 1970) contained provisions that imposed the entire financial burden of investigation and prosecution on the court and its states parties. Moreover, both resolutions allowed exemptions for the nationals of third non states parties should they be implicated in serious crimes committed in the country situation referred.... The danger of political taint for the court is further exacerbated by Council inaction following referral. When the Council has tasked the court to address mass atrocity crimes it has then failed to insist on full cooperation with the court. This "on again, off again" support makes the court seem like an ineffective instrument of short-term political interests at the Council.[352]

Perhaps the final comment about the ICC, the Security Council, and the court's independence, can be given to Geoffrey Robertson. Writing in 2012 he stated: "In short, the politicians and diplomats of the superpowers remain in the driving seat."[353]

Chapter Four

The United States and the Court

"[T]here is insufficient protection against politicized prosecutions or other abuses."

US Department of State[354]

"[T]he ICC...may be actively courting the U.S. military for assistance."

Dr. Adam Branch[355]

The USA is not a party to the Rome Statute. The USA has refused point-blank to become a member of the ICC, and has generally sought to oppose, obstruct and inconvenience the court for most of the institution's existence. Washington has very clearly stated that the ICC is a sub-standard body incapable of delivering justice and that it is subject to political instrumentalisation. This has not stopped the USA from cynically using the court when it suits American foreign policy interests. The Clinton Administration engaged in the negotiations in Rome in 1998, and was able to extract a number of concessions from those shaping the statute. Some would say these distorted the outline and procedure of the future court. The Clinton Administration signed the Rome Statute but was unable to ratify the treaty, encountering fierce opposition from the US Congress. In July 1998, for example, Senator Jesse Helms, Chairman of the US Senate Foreign Relations Committee, made the views of Congress very clear. Referring to "this fatally flawed treaty", he stated:

> The Rome Treaty is irreparably flawed.... In short, this treaty represents a very real threat to our soldiers, our citizens and our national security interests.... I must...be clear: Rejecting this treaty is not enough. The United States must fight this treaty...we must be aggressively opposed to this Court.... The United States shall not permit a U.S. soldier to participate in any NATO, U.N., or other international peacekeeping mission, until the United States has reached agreement with all of our NATO allies, and the U.N., that no U.S. soldier will be subject to the jurisdiction of this court.

Helms referred to the drafters of the ICC Statute as a "collection of ne'er-do-wells in Rome", and stated that any treaty, such as the Rome Statute, which undermined US constitutional protections, "will be dead-on-arrival at the Senate Foreign Relations committee. Let's close the casket right now".[356]

Michael Ignatieff has summed up the international legal aspects of what has been described as "American exceptionalism" central to the foreign policy of the USA:[357]

> [American] [e]xceptionalism also influences the practice of American policy, nowhere more so than in US approaches to international law and justice. Law, after all, constrains power, and the United States, like any great power, is likely to support a law-bound international order only if it ties up the power of its competitors more than it constrains its own. Other great powers have subscribed to this realist calculus in advancing international law. America is exceptional in combining standard great-power realism with extravagant idealism about the country's redemptive role in creating international order.[358]

Ignatieff notes further that "the US has promoted universal legal norms and the institutions to enforce them, while seeking by hook or by crook to exempt American citizens, especially soldiers, from their actual application. From Nuremberg onward, no country has invested more in the development of international jurisdiction for atrocity crimes and no country has worked harder to make sure that the law it seeks for others does not apply to itself."[359] Ignatieff concludes that "[i]n relation to international justice...all the great powers played a double game, but none more so than the United States".[360]

The Clinton Administration's Ambassador-at-Large for War Crimes Issues, David Scheffer, outlined some of Washington's early reservations, stating that the ICC's apparent jurisdiction over nationals of non-party states and the resultant binding nature of the Rome Statute on non-party states was the "single most fundamental flaw in the Rome Treaty".[361] Scheffer also told the US Senate Foreign Relations Committee that "the treaty purports to establish an arrangement whereby US armed forces operating overseas could be conceivably prosecuted by the international court even if the US has not agreed to be bound by the treaty.... This is contrary to the most fundamental principles of treaty law."[362]

Scheffer's memoir of his involvement as the US government's point man on international justice and human rights issues, *All the Missing Souls: A Personal History of the War Crimes Tribunals*, provides a black-and-white account of Washington's double standards on those matters.[363] Scheffer assisted Madeleine Albright on war-crimes issues while she was Ambassador to the UN between 1993 and 1997. Scheffer then served as the first US Ambassador for War Crimes throughout President Clinton's second term. Scheffer was involved in the establishment, as the result of UNSC resolutions, of every major international criminal tribunal since the 1990s Rwanda, Yugoslavia, Sierra Leone, Cambodia, and the ICC. Ignatieff notes that "[t]he central paradox is that none of them would have come into being without US leadership and yet all of them were crippled by American refusal to help them do their jobs".[364] Scheffer's job was "trying to advance the

American agenda on international justice, while simultaneously having to tell potential allies in other countries that the agenda did not apply to Americans".[365] Scheffer sought to support the tribunals, despite having to explain to furious international prosecutors why the USA could not supply them with the evidence they needed to convict war crimes suspects. The USA supported the establishment of the Yugoslav and Rwanda criminal tribunals in 1993 and 1994 and provided a quarter of their funding. Washington then refused to task US forces in Bosnia with arresting prominent war crimes suspects and the Clinton administration also refused to provide the tribunals with the satellite imagery, data intercepts and interviews the courts needed to prepare their cases. The US military, the Pentagon, the Defense Intelligence Agency and the CIA repeatedly refused to assist. Scheffer states they were "stubbornly lackadaisical".[366]

Washington's stated objections included a lack of adequate checks and balances on the powers of the ICC prosecutors and judges; lack of due process and the absence of juries; the perceived dilution of the role of the UNSC in maintaining peace and security; and the ICC's potentially chilling effect on America's willingness to project power in the defence of its interests. On 31 December 2000, when the USA signed the treaty, President Clinton made clear that his administration still had clear reservations about the Rome Statute:

> In signing, however, we are not abandoning our concerns about significant flaws in the treaty. In particular, we are concerned that when the court comes into existence, it will not only exercise authority over personnel of states that have ratified the treaty, but also claim jurisdiction over personnel of states that have not.... Given these concerns, I will not and do not recommend that my successor submit the treaty to the Senate for ratification until our fundamental concerns are satisfied.[367]

The Bush Administration made no secret of its opposition to the court. President George W. Bush and his administration shared Helms' views, stepped up opposition to the court and renounced any US obligations under the treaty. President Bush himself concluded: "[T]he United States can no longer be a party to this process. In order to make [U.S.] objections clear, both in principle and philosophy, and so as not to create unwarranted expectations of U.S. involvement in the Court, [he] believe[d] that he ha[d] no choice but to inform the United Nations…of [the U.S.] intention not to become a party to the Rome Statute…"[368] The US Ambassador to the UN, John Bolton, famously "de-signed" the treaty.[369]

The Bush Administration restated its objections to the court: "Under the Rome Statute, the ICC claims the authority to second guess the actions taken and the results reached by sovereign states with respect to the investigation and prosecution of crimes."[370] The danger of politicised prosecutions was again pointed to by the USA: "We are also concerned that there are insufficient checks and balances on the authority of the ICC prosecutor and judges. The Rome Statute creates a self-initiating prosecutor, answerable to no state or institution other than the Court itself. Without such an external check on the prosecutor, there is insufficient protection against politicized prosecutions or other abuses."[371]

There is considerable wishful thinking that but for Jesse Helms and a conservative Senate during the Clinton Administration, the Democrats would have willingly signed up to the ICC. This is clearly false. Human Rights Watch's Richard Dicker revealed that in May 1998, US Defence Secretary William Cohen told Human Rights Watch that he would not recommend that President Bill Clinton endorse the treaty without an "ironclad guarantee" that no US service member would be brought before the court.[372] David Scheffer reveals that in July 1998 Madeleine Albright, Clinton's Secretary of State, voiced "exceptionally negative views…about the International Criminal Court". He states she asked: "What can we do to blow up the entire [Rome] conference?" The two principal officers of state, therefore, were hostile to the court.[373]

From very early on in the court's existence, the USA threatened to veto the renewal of all UN peacekeeping missions unless its citizens were shielded from prosecution by the ICC. After considerable negotiation United Nations Security Council Resolution 1422 was adopted unanimously on 12 July 2002.[374] It granted immunity from prosecution by the ICC to UN peacekeeping personnel from countries that were not party to the ICC.[375] The USA insisted on the immunity provisions and Resolution 1422 was passed and came into effect on 1 July 2002 for a period of one year. It was renewed for twelve months by Security Council Resolution 1487, which was passed on 12 June 2003. However, the UN refused to renew the exemption again in 2004 after pictures emerged of US troops abusing Iraqi prisoners in the Abu Ghraib prison in Iraq, and the USA withdrew its demand. The USA then announced the withdrawal of its personnel from the UN peacekeeping mission in Ethiopia and Eritrea as well as US personnel from the UN peacekeeping mission in Kosovo because the countries involved had not signed bilateral immunity agreements with the USA to exempt US citizens from possible surrender to the ICC.

American opposition to the court extended to refusing to countenance any mention of the court in resolutions before the UN. On 26 August 2003, for example, the USA refused to support a UNSC resolution protecting humanitarian aid workers – even after the bombing in Baghdad that killed twenty-two UN workers – because it referred to the fact that the ICC has explicitly criminalised attacks against aid workers as war crimes. The version that passed, Security Council Resolution 1502, referred instead indirectly to "existing prohibitions under international law". This behaviour continued for several years. In September 2005, for example, at a world summit of member states meeting on the UN's sixtieth anniversary to discuss reform and the most important issues before it, the new US Ambassador to the UN demanded that all references to the ICC were deleted from sections of a resolution covering the struggle against impunity and for accountability in committing atrocities. This was refused and the resultant resolution did not contain any reference to impunity and accountability.

The USA moved beyond merely objecting to the premise of the ICC or any mention of the court in UN documents. Under President Bush, the USA increased its hostility to the ICC. The US Congress passed, and the President signed into law, several pieces of legislation intended to distance the USA from the ICC and thereby undermine the court. Several of them have either restricted US cooperation with or funding to the ICC, or punished other countries for not accepting the previous hostile US approach to the court. *The Admiral James W. Nance and Meg Donovan Foreign Relations Authorization Act*, Fiscal Years 2000 and 2001 prohibited funds from the *Foreign Relations Authorization Act* "or any other act" from being used by or for the support of the ICC, or to extradite a USA citizen to a foreign country obligated to cooperate with the ICC unless the USA received guarantees that that person will not be sent to the ICC. It also states that the USA "shall not become a party to the ICC except pursuant to a treaty made under Article II, section 2, clause 2 of the Constitution of the United States". *The Foreign Relations Authorization Act* (HR 3427) prevents any US funds from going to the ICC. The Obama Administration interprets this law as only permitting in-kind support to the court.

In July 2002 the *American Service-members' Protection Act* (ASPA), which became known unofficially as "The Hague Invasion Act", drafted by Senator Helms and Representative Tom Delay, was passed by both Houses of Congress as an amendment to the *2002 Supplemental Appropriations Act for Further Recovery From and Response To Terrorist Attacks on the United States* (HR 4775). The stated purpose of the amendment was "to protect United States military personnel and other elected and appointed officials of the United States government against criminal prosecution by an international criminal court to which the United States is not party". The legislation threatened to cut International Military Education and Training (IMET) and Foreign Military Funds (FMF) aid to nations unwilling to enter into a Bilateral Immunity Agreement (BIA), subject to waiver by the President. It also included an amendment by Senator Christopher Dodd incorporated into the text of ASPA: "Nothing in this title shall prohibit the United States from rendering assistance to international efforts to bring to justice Saddam Hussein, Slobodan Milosevic, Osama bin Laden, other members of Al Queda, leaders of Islamic Jihad, and other foreign nationals accused of genocide, war crimes or crimes against humanity." President Bush signed HR 4775 into law on 2 August 2002. This law also threatened American lawyers with legal action should they ever work on a case that could lead to a US citizen being put before the ICC. The US government is prohibited by law from assisting the ICC in its investigations, arrests, detentions, extraditions, or prosecutions of war crimes, under the *American Service-members' Protection Act*. The prohibition is comprehensive, covering, among other things, prohibiting assistance in investigations on US territory, participation in UN peacekeeping operations unless certain protections from ICC actions are provided to specific categories of people, the obligation of seizing appropriated funds, and the sharing of classified and law enforcement information. The legislation authorised the President to use "all means necessary and appropriate to bring about the release of any US or allied personnel being detained or imprisoned by, on behalf of, or at the request of the International Criminal Court", hence the act's unofficial name.

The USA also actively sought to penalise states that support the ICC. In an attempt to further distance the USA from the ICC, the Bush Administration sought to conclude bilateral immunity agreements, known as "Article 98 agreements" with most States Parties to exempt US citizens from possible surrender to the ICC. These agreements are named for Article 98(2) of the ICC Statute, which bars the ICC from asking for surrender of persons from a State Party that would require it to act contrary to its international obligations. Each State Party to an Article 98 agreement promises that it will not surrender citizens of the other State Party to international tribunals or the ICC, unless both parties agree in advance. An Article 98 agreement would prevent the surrender of certain persons to the ICC by parties to the agreement, but would not bind the ICC if it were to obtain custody of the accused through other means.

In July 2003, President Bush announced the suspension of military aid to thirty-five States Parties to the ICC. Waivers for the ASPA prohibition on US military assistance were provided to ICC States Parties that had concluded, or were in the process of concluding, BIA arrangements. In November 2003, President Bush partially waived military assistance cuts, as a result of their not signing BIAs, to Bulgaria, Estonia, Latvia, Lithuania, Slovakia, and Slovenia for certain specific projects the US government had decided were needed to support the integration of these countries into NATO, or to support the US-led post-invasion occupation of Iraq. It was the first time waivers were granted to countries that refused to sign bilateral immunity agreements.

In December 2004, President Bush signed *FY2005 Foreign Operations, Export Financing, and Related Programs Appropriations Act* (HR 4818). This general appropriations bill included the Nethercutt Amendment (HR 4818). This legislation was far more widereaching than the ASPA, and authorised, in addition to ASPA cuts in military aid, the loss of economic support funds (ESF) to all countries, including many key US allies, that had ratified the ICC treaty but had not signed a bilateral immunity agreement with Washington. It presented the threat of broad cuts in foreign assistance, including funds for cooperation in international security and terrorism. The amendment allowed presidential exemptions for NATO, MNNA (major non-NATO allies), and Millennium Fund countries. The American government continued to fine-tune its approach to the immunity agreements. The Nethercutt Amendment to the Fiscal Year 2006 Foreign Operations spending bill was renewed, continuing the USA policy to withhold economic assistance from nations that refused to sign BIAs. The amendment that year affected $326.6 million in US economic assistance to twelve nations. The withholding of military and security assistance to non-BIA countries did however raise questions from the US military. In its 2006 "Quadrennial Defense Review Report", the US Department of Defense observed that it would "[c]onsider whether the restrictions on the American Service Members Protection Act (ASPA) on IMET [International Military Education and Training] and other foreign assistance programs pertaining to security and the war on terror necessitate adjustment as we continue to advance the aims of the ASPA". In September 2006, the US Congress approved the *John Warner National Defense Appropriations Act for Fiscal Year 2007*, which included an amendment striking international military education and training sanctions from ASPA. Both foreign military funds restrictions under ASPA and economic support funds barred by the Nethercutt Amendment remain in place. In October 2006, President Bush directed the Secretary of State to waive ASPA IMET prohibitions with respect to twenty-one nations that had not signed BIAs. In April 2007, Montenegro became the last country to sign a BIA with the USA. President Bush subsequently directed the Secretary of State to waive prohibitions provided for in ASPA with respect to Montenegro.

In December 2007, the US Congress approved the *Consolidated Appropriations*

Act, 2008 (HR 2764), which reinstated the so-called Nethercutt provision cutting off economic support funds to states unwilling to enter into BIAs. The bill came into law on 26 December 2007. In January 2008 the US Congress approved the *National Defense Appropriations Act for 2008* (HR 4986), which ended restrictions on foreign military financing to nations unwilling to enter into BIAs. In June 2008, President Bush directed the Secretary of State to waive ESF restrictions with respect to fourteen nations unwilling to sign BIAs provided for in the Nethercutt Amendment.

As of March 2011, some 100 BIAs had been signed, while fifty-three countries had publicly refused to sign.[376] As early as October 2002, the EU reached an accommodation with the BIAs. They adopted a common position, permitting member states to enter into Article 98 agreements with the USA, but only in respect of US military personnel, US diplomatic or consular officials, and persons extradited, sent to their territories by the USA with their permission: the common position did provide that any person protected from ICC prosecution by such agreements would have to be prosecuted by the USA. This was said to be in agreement with the original position of the EU, that Article 98 agreements were allowed to cover these protected classes of persons but could not cover all the citizens of a state.[377] Others saw it differently. In the words of the former British Foreign Secretary Robin Cook, "the whole of Europe...buckled under".[378]

How did the ICC respond to this bullying by the USA? The court followed the lead of its European masters and similarly pursued a policy of accommodation. Branch has recorded the court's institutional soft-pedalling regarding Washington and its friends:

> In its early days, the ICC appeared to have calculated that it could best protect its viability and relevance by showing the United States that it would not challenge it or its allies, since alienating the United States could easily spell disaster for the Court. Since its inception, therefore, the ICC has made clear its lack of interest in pursuing U.S. allies, or simply to focus on issues that had little interest for the U.S. government.[379]

As we shall see, the court subsequently changed its position with regard to the USA from accommodation to seeking its approval.

With regard to Darfur and the ICC, the Bush Administration's actions have clearly illustrated the political nature of the court, and its susceptibility to political influence. Having claimed that it did not support the ICC because it was unsound and that politically motivated prosecutions would ensue – possibly against the USA – the USA had long shunned anything to do with it. Washington's subsequent decision not to veto a UNSC resolution purporting to give the ICC jurisdiction in Darfur, enabling the very action against a non-party state that it had long warned about, and its continuing support for subsequent ICC action against Sudan was itself clearly motivated by political pressures, domestically and internationally. Professor Noam Chomsky has very accurately described the motivation for the USA allowing the referral to go ahead: "[T]he administration found itself caught in a political dilemma. A large part of their voting base is ultra right Christian fundamentalists for whom Darfur is a huge issue. They had to offer something to them and for that they were willing to stand by while there was a reference made to the ICC."[380]

To be clear: The US government blocked and would continue to block even the mention of the ICC in UN resolutions, but on Darfur – a foreign policy hobby horse of the Bush Administration's conservative and neo-conservative hinterland – the US Administration did not block a questionable resolution referring the Darfur situation to the court. The hypocrisy goes even deeper as the USA acquiesced in the referral of a non-signatory state (a circumstance it had long pointed to as unacceptable) to a court Washington did not recognise, would never join and which it had accused of being little better than a kangaroo court.

On 31 March 2005, therefore, and with US acquiescence, the Security Council referred the situation of Darfur, Sudan to the ICC. Resolution 1593 was passed eleven to nil, with four members, including the USA, abstaining. While the USA stated it did not veto the referral because of the need for the international community to end "impunity" in Sudan, at the same time it demanded that the resolution included immunity clauses for US nationals from any investigation or prosecution. American hypocrisy regarding the court had come full circle. In 1999, Ambassador David Scheffer, who represented the USA at the Rome Conference, said that the referral of a third-party, non-signatory to Rome Statute to the court, was a particular concern of the USA: "A fundamental principle of international treaty law is that only states that are party to a treaty should be bound by its terms."[381] By 2005, this fundamental, principled objection to the credibility of the court had gone by the wayside as Washington saw the potential for politically manipulating the court to serve American domestic and foreign policy. It also distracted attention from the ongoing Iraqi fiasco. Nicholas Burns, the US Under Secretary of State for Political Affairs, said that Washington had "achieved precedent-setting assurances" that American citizens were exempt from the jurisdiction of the ICC. He added: "But that in no way implies that we think Americans are committing crimes." Burns also reiterated that the USA still has "fundamental objections to the Rome Statute and the International Criminal Court".[382] As Philippe Sands recounts, when Condoleezza Rice was asked to explain US support for the Darfur referral given that it would affect citizens of Sudan, which is not a party to the ICC, she "seemed a little flummoxed", reiterating that "we do believe that as a matter of principle it is important to uphold the principle that non-parties to a treaty are indeed non-parties to a treaty", before adding that "Sudan is an extraordinary circumstance."[383] It was, of course, an extraordinary circumstance that was to be followed by yet another extraordinary circumstance, that of Libya in 2011.

The USA continued to warm towards the ICC, albeit strictly on Washington's terms. In a November 2005 hearing, US Assistant Secretary of State for African Affairs Jendayi Frazer told the US House of Representatives International Relations Committee that if the ICC requires assistance in Darfur, the US stood ready to assist: "Ambassador Zoellick…has made very clear that if we were asked by the ICC for our help, we would try to make sure that this gets pursued fully." In a press interview at the end of December 2006, US Department of State legal adviser John B. Bellinger III told the Associated Press, "At least as a matter of policy, not only do we not oppose the ICC's investigation and prosecutions in Sudan but we support its investigation and prosecution of those atrocities." In December 2008, US Secretary of State Condoleezza Rice confirmed the intensity of the Bush Administration's focus on Sudan, stating that the USA has "been the country that's been the most active in resisting calls to interfere with the international criminal court investigation of the leadership [in Sudan], despite the fact that we're not members of the international court". Washington was now criticising criticism of the court by those articulating long-stated US objections to the institution.

Cables released into the public domain in 2007, however, revealed how the USA had sought to manipulate the court in the lead-up to the Darfur referral. In early January 2005, upon learning that the UN Commission of Inquiry was to recommend ICC referral, UN Ambassador John Danforth cabled Secretary of State Rice for instructions: should the US seek to block the ICC referral altogether, or secure a US exemption (wording in the resolution that would grant immunity to any Americans that might be caught up in the investigation)? Danforth recommended the latter course, saying that that was the easier option. The Bush Administration went for the first option, and for the next three months Washington attempted to block a resolution giving jurisdiction to the ICC, because in the words of a cable from the State Department, "We do not want to be confronted with a decision on whether to veto a court resolution in the Security Council." Rice directed the US mission to the UN to "position ourselves to table our text before any other member formally proposes language seeking accountability through the ICC". During these three months, the USA proposed creating an alternative "accountability venue" that would be an AU-UN hybrid court instead of the ICC. When EU members of the Security Council resisted the AU-UN hybrid option, the US Administration sought to circumvent them, with one cable reading: "The proposal might gain momentum…if the Africans supported it." Pierre-Richard Prosper, the then US Ambassador-at-Large for War Crimes Issues, travelled to Africa to press AU member states to agree to the American proposal for a hybrid AU-UN court. The USA failed to convince African countries. Under political pressure, from within the USA and internationally, the USA abstained from vetoing Resolution 1593, which gave the ICC jurisdiction, with immunities granted to American citizens, to investigate crimes in Darfur.[384]

Professor Hans Köchler, author of *Global Justice or Global Revenge? International Criminal Justice at the Crossroads*, criticised the UNSC for having granted immunity from prosecution by the ICC to USA citizens and nationals from other non-States Parties to the Rome Statute, operating in Sudan on Security Council or AU missions. He warned that this arbitrary measure has applied double standards in dealing with international crimes in Sudan and severely undermined the ICC's efficiency, credibility and legitimacy:

> In an inadmissible way, the Security Council has tied the referral of the situation in Sudan according to Art. 13 (b) of the Rome Statute to a deferral of investigation or prosecution according to Art. 16. While the Security Council, under the Court's Statute, has the right to refer a "situation" (not individual cases) in which crimes that fall under the jurisdiction of the Court appear to have been committed to

the Prosecutor of the Court, the Council has no authority to order a deferral of investigation or prosecution on a selective and at the same time preventive basis.

Köchler concluded that by linking the referral of a situation to a collective deferral in favour of certain categories of people, the council, under USA pressure, has not only undermined the authority of the ICC but introduced a "policy of double standards" into the practice of international criminal justice.

A key reason given by the USA for its refusal to become a member of the ICC is that they say the court is a political tool that will be used to pursue political agendas. In 1998, Ambassador Scheffer noted that the ICC statute "provides a recipe for politicization of the Court".[385] He elaborated further in comments before the US Senate:

> The prosecutor…will have to make judgments as to what he pursues and what he does not pursue for investigative purposes. In the end, those kinds of judgments by the prosecutor will inevitably be political judgments because he is going to have to say no to a lot of complaints, a lot of individuals, a lot of organizations that believe very strongly that crimes have been committed, but he is going to have to say no to them. When he says no to them and yes to others and he is deluged with these, he may find that he ends up making some political decisions. Even if he has to go to the Pretrial Chamber and get the approval of at least two of the three judges in the Pretrial Chamber, in the end you have three individuals making that decision.[386]

And yet, for all of Washington's early warnings about the court being used to pursue political vendettas, in allowing the Darfur referral by the UNSC, and its subsequent support for ICC actions against Sudan, the USA has itself used the ICC to pursue its own anti-Sudan political agenda – and in so doing has more than proved its own point. This amounts to little more than the sort of short-term politicised opportunism that Washington foresaw, criticised and sought to prevent in others.

Professor Mahmood Mamdani has accurately summarised the USA interaction with the ICC:

> [I]t began with Washington criticizing the ICC and then turning it into a useful tool. The effort has been bipartisan: the first attempts to weaken the ICC and to create US exemptions from an emerging regime of international justice were made by leading Democrats during the Clinton Administration…. When it came to signing the treaty, Washington balked. Once it was clear that it would not be able to keep the ICC from becoming a reality, the Bush Administration changed tactics and began signing bilateral agreements with countries whereby both signatories would pledge not to hand over each other's nationals – even those accused of crimes against humanity – to the ICC…. The Bush Administration's next move was accommodation, made possible by the kind of pragmatism practiced by the ICC's leadership.[387]

On taking office in January 2009 President Obama's Administration promised to discuss possible US membership of the ICC with legal and military advisers as well as pledging to assist the court on Darfur. The Obama Administration, however, has ruthlessly continued with a policy of American exceptionalism, a selective engagement with the ICC on its own terms. It should perhaps be noted that Obama's own position and that of his first Secretary of State, Hillary Clinton, with regard to the ICC had previously been confusing where not crassly two-faced and opportunistic. While serving as an Illinois state senator, for example, Obama voted on 25 February 1999 in favour of a non-binding resolution urging the Illinois Senate to reject US ratification of the ICC statute. Proposed by Patrick O'Malley, a conservative Republican state senator, the resolution stated that the ICC was an institution that would "diminish America's sovereignty, produce arbitrary and highly politicized 'justice,' and grow into a jurisdictional leviathan". Obama had voted as a member of the Illinois Senate's Judiciary Committee. The vote was ten to nil. One week after having voted against the ICC, Obama absented himself from the vote on the floor in the Senate itself. The resolution passed fifty-two to one.[388] For all her weasel words about the ICC once in office, Hillary Clinton as US Senator for New York voted for the *American Service-members' Protection Act*, and had actually voted against Senator Chris Dodd's amendment to limit the punitive measures of the act to one year. Her successor as Secretary of State, former Senator John Kerry, had similarly also voted for ASPA. In her confirmation hearing before the US Senate Foreign Relations Committee in January 2009, Secretary of State Hillary Clinton stated: "[W]e...look for opportunities to encourage effective ICC action in ways that promote U.S. interests by bringing war criminals to justice."[389] In March 2009, the then acting Assistant Secretary of State for International Organizations James B. Warlick said, in response to a question on the administration's position on joining the ICC: "There will be a policy process that will address this Administration's position on the International Criminal Court, so it's too early to say."[390] In the same month, the US Ambassador to the UN, Susan Rice, stated that the court is an "important and credible instrument for trying to hold accountable the senior leadership responsible for atrocities committed in the Congo, Uganda and Darfur".[391] On 12 August 2009, in a speech at New York University on a new US approach at the UN, Rice went on to state that the US would no longer oppose mentions of the ICC in UN statements and resolutions. And, the following month, UNSC Resolution 1888, addressing sexual violence in armed conflict, and drafted by the USA, departed from Washington's prior practice of opposing references to the ICC in UN resolutions, and included a reference to the Rome Statute and ICC.

In October 2009, US Ambassador-at-Large for War Crimes Issues Stephen J. Rapp stated that the US policy towards the ICC was under review and that the USA was beginning an approach of greater cooperation with the ICC. On 16 November 2009, Rapp announced that the USA would participate in that month's meeting of the ICC's ASP in The Hague, as well as the May-June 2010 ICC Review Conference in Kampala, Uganda, and the preparations for it. In January 2010, Ambassador Rapp stated that the US would not be joining the ICC in the "foreseeable future". At the Review Conference, the US government's legal adviser Harold Koh stated: "After 12 years, I think we have reset the default on the U.S. relationship with the court from hostility to positive engagement."[392]

And why should the USA need to join the court given that the institution is serving its national security and foreign policy objectives on a case-by-case basis? That its engagement was on American terms was made clear in May 2010, when President Obama stated in his annual National Security Strategy Report that the US government was "engaging with State Parties to the Rome Statute on issues of concern and are *supporting the ICC's prosecution of those cases that advance U.S. interests and values*, consistent with the requirements of U.S. law".[393] (Emphasis added.) The Obama Administration has not even included the Rome Statute on its treaty priority list.

It is true that the Administration has paid lip service to the ICC's actions in the DRC, Sudan, Uganda and Kenya. There has been much wishful thinking that the Obama presidency has somehow ushered in a positive engagement by Washington with the court. The reality is that while the Obama Administration has taken what may appear to be a new approach to the ICC, it is in reality a virtually seamless continuation of the previous American approach under Bush. The Obama Administration has continued with the Bush Administration's selective cooperation with the court on a carefully considered, case-by-case basis. The *2002 American Service members' Protection Act* and other legislation limiting US cooperation with the ICC remains in effect. This legislation also permits case-by-case cooperation with the court only when it serves American interests. This selective engagement has been cloaked by a January 2010 legal opinion from the US Justice Department's Office of Legal Counsel that US diplomatic or "informational" support for particular ICC investigations or prosecutions would not violate US law. In January 2010, Ambassador Stephen Rapp publicly stated that no US President was likely to present the Rome Statute to the US Senate for ratification in the "foreseeable future". Rapp stated that the fact the USA had a strong national court system together with American fears that US officials would be unfairly prosecuted were obstacles to Washington signing the Rome Statute. What was unspoken was the political impossibility of any administration obtaining the two-thirds vote in the Senate necessary for ratification. Furthermore, in March 2011, the USA told the UN Human Rights Council at the conclusion of its Universal Periodic Review of the USA that the USA did not accept the recommendations by a number of states that the USA ratify the Rome Statute. The Obama Administration has also shown no inclination whatsoever to introduce legislation to change US statutes and practices that are hostile to the ICC. Over 100 BIAs concluded by the Bush Administration remain in force, though the related military sanctions have been repealed and the related economic sanctions have expired. One cosmetic concession is that the USA may no longer oppose mentions of the ICC in UN statements and resolutions.

A conservative comment on the ICC by Brett D. Schaefer, of the influential US conservative think tank the Heritage Foundation, is telling:

> The consistency of U.S. policy toward the ICC, based on decidedly conservative views, is rather remarkable considering the Democratic majorities in Congress in recent years and the election of President Barack Obama. The most significant

policy change is that the U.S. now attends the meetings of the Assembly of States Parties of the International Criminal Court.... U.S. policy is already largely where they want it to be, and the Obama administration, thankfully, appears uninterested in changing it.[394]

William Schabas has a clear explanation for the "apparent warming of the United States to the Court", a warming which he correctly points out predates the election of the Obama Administration: "[T]he process was underway well before the 2008 election. It seems to be as much related to the fact that the Court's priorities correspond to the strategic interests of the United States as it is to the progressive multilateralism of President Obama and Secretary of State Clinton."[395] And for all the claims that the USA was engaging positively with the ICC, the reality was very different. In a re-run of the Bush Administration's notorious demands for a blanket immunity for its military personnel in UN peacekeeping operations in 2002–03, and in the 2005 Darfur referral (soft pedalled into immunity for all non-States Parties personnel), President Obama and Secretary of State Clinton demanded exactly the same immunity for US personnel during NATO's war in Libya.

Adam Branch has warned of the court's increasingly close engagement with the US government, and especially the new Obama Administration:

> [T]he ICC is no longer trying simply to avoid American censure, as it was in the early 2000s, but now may be actively courting the U.S. military for assistance.[396]

It is a matter of record that, as pointed out by Branch, "ICC intervention...provided the justification for increased American militarization of Uganda and military involvement in central Africa", the most significant example of which was Operation Lighting Thunder carried out with American military assistance against LRA rebels in the DRC in 2008.[397] Operation Lighting Thunder was a coordinated attack on what were believed to be LRA locations in the Garamba National Park in northeast DRC. In November 2008, President Bush had personally signed a directive to the USA Africa Command to provide financial and logistical assistance to the Ugandan government during this unsuccessful offensive.[398] It was claimed that no US. troops were directly involved, but US military advisers provided intelligence, equipment and logistical assistance to the Ugandan forces.

As has also been documented by Branch, in June 2009 the Chief Prosecutor of the ICC stated that the court had a need for "special forces" with "rare and expensive capabilities that regional armies don't have", and that "coalitions of the willing", led by the USA, were needed to enforce ICC arrest warrants.[399] It is of course a matter of record that the Bush Administration used the term "coalition of the willing" to refer to the countries who militarily supported the 2003 invasion of Iraq and subsequent military occupation of post-invasion Iraq. In 2010, Béatrice le Frapper du Hellen, then Head of the Jurisdiction, Complementarity and Cooperation Division of the OTP, and subsequently France's representative on the ASP, declared that "[w]e have our shopping list ready of requests for assistance from the U.S.". She added that the court needed American "operational support" for military action in the DRC, CAR and Uganda. Frapper stated that "the U.S. has to be the leader".[400]

In May 2010, President Obama signed into law the *Lord's Resistance Army Disarmament and Northern Uganda Recovery Act*. This legislation targeted Joseph Kony and the LRA. On 24 November 2010, Obama presented a strategy document to the US Congress, asking for funds for its LRA operations.[401] On 14 October 2011, the American government announced the deployment of 100 US Army Special Force advisors to further assist the Ugandan Army at a cost of approximately $4.5 million per month.[402] In April 2012, the US government announced that, following a 150-day review, it would maintain the presence of the military advisers in the affected countries beyond the initial six-month period initially envisaged.

Branch is clear about the danger of the direction in which the court is heading: "The result is that the United States may pose more of a threat to global justice, not by actively opposing the ICC, but by cynically engaging with it."[403]

Branch has been blunt about the implications of the ICC's fawning over the US government:

> The ICC's entreaties are a response to an apparent re-assessment of U.S.-ICC relations undertaken by the Obama administration and to the inception of a new U.S. policy of pragmatic, ad hoc engagement with the Court…. If the ICC comes to rely on the military capacity of the United States as its enforcement arm, in particular when the United States continues to declare itself above the very law it claims to enforce, the ICC will trade what little independence it retains in return for access to coercive force, a…bargain that will be made at the price of the Court's legitimacy, impartiality, and legality. However the price paid by the ICC will be trivial compared to the very dangerous possibility that this alliance could help justify and expand U.S. militarization in Africa…at a dramatic cost to peace and justice.[404]

American doublespeak with regard to the ICC was particularly evident in comments in 2013 by Deputy Assistant Secretary of Defence William Lietzau: "We fully support constructive engagement with the ICC, and we believe that bringing perpetrators to justice is in line with our national security interests. We do not, however, support ICC jurisdiction that is susceptible to political manipulation."[405] The Obama Administration was also not above blatant economic blackmail. In March 2012, the USA announced that it was suspending $350 million allocated to Malawi through the Millennium Challenge Corporation citing governance issues in the country. The MCC is a US government foreign aid agency. The $350.7 million MCC grant was meant to revitalise the country's faltering energy sector. The agency also stated that "Malawi's decision to allow Sudanese President Omar al-Bashir to attend a trade summit in Lilongwe, despite the International Criminal Court's (ICC) outstanding warrant for his arrest, further deepened MCC's concerns".[406]

In 2013, the Bush Administration's senior Africa diplomat, former US Assistant Secretary of State for African Affairs Jendayi Frazer, admitted the ICC's lack of credibility:

"[T]he West's often quiet role but strong political influence on who the court targets for indictment tarnishes the court as a tool of geopolitical influence, not balanced global justice." She added: "The ICC indeed has fallen far from the high ideals of global justice and accountability that inspired its creation."[407] She stated that "the ICC's very legitimacy has been fundamentally compromised by its first Prosecutor, Luis Moreno Ocampo, only finding cases of atrocities and crimes against humanity in Africa". Frazer very clearly pointed to the dangers of the American government continuing to use the ICC as a political mechanism while pretending it was an independent international court:

> My concern is with the credibility and effectiveness of US policy in Africa. I remain troubled by the not so subtle attempt to use the ICC politically to essentially threaten Kenyans about whom to vote for in their presidential elections. To base US foreign policy on the ICC is especially problematic since the US is not a signatory to the Rome Statute which established the International Criminal Court.... It is therefore especially reckless for the United States to tie its foreign policy towards Kenya on an ICC case against the President-elect that is unproven and based on hearsay, with the alleged sole eyewitness, on whom the case rested, now dropped by the Prosecutor for unreliability.[408]

Frazer should know. Her newly found concern about the political use of the court was somewhat off-key. She had been at the centre of Washington's ruthless and focused political instrumentalisation of the ICC within Africa for four years.[409]

In March 2013, Jendayi Frazer quite categorically summed up the American position that will be taken by any US administration: "We would never allow the ICC to interfere in our justice system."[410]

Chapter Five

THE COURT AND NON-GOVERNMENTAL ORGANISATIONS

"They were in on nearly every meeting. They were in on everything."

Chief Counsel of the Israeli Delegation in Rome[411]

"[T]he ICC's involvement in northern Uganda was met with immediate and widespread condemnation by Ugandan civil society."

International Refugee Rights Initiative[412]

As a political entity, the ICC is naturally prone to political influences. The court's relationship with non-governmental organisations is both politically unhealthy and opportunistic. Human Rights Watch has confirmed the ICC's unprecedented relationship with the NGO community: "The International Criminal Court has been uniquely open in its interaction with civil society."[413] In his *Prosecutorial Strategy 2009–2012*, Ocampo confirmed the ICC's relationship with NGOs, stating that the OTP aims to work with NGOs, in "[c]ontributing to the preliminary examinations, investigations and prosecutions; Promoting national activities to end impunity and prevent future crimes; Securing the cooperation of States and international organizations with the Court; Helping to communicate the work of the OTP to different audiences".[414] American conservative critics of the ICC, however, have unambiguously pointed to possible political manipulation of the court, including by non-governmental organisations:

> Unscrupulous individuals and groups and nations seeking to influence foreign policy and security decisions of other nations have and will continue to seek to misuse the ICC for politically motivated purposes. Without appropriate checks and balances to prevent its misuse, the ICC represents a dangerous temptation for those with political axes to grind. The prosecutor's proprio motu authority to initiate an investigation based solely on his own authority or on information

provided by a government, a nongovernmental organization (NGO), or individuals is an open invitation for political manipulation.[415]

The role of Western non-governmental organisations and activists in the establishment of the ICC is clear.[416] William Schabas noted in respect of the Rome Conference. that established the ICC, that "a well-organized coalition of non-governmental organizations" drove "the dynamism of the Conference".[417] Schabas also refers to "the phenomenal and unprecedented contribution of non-governmental organizations" in the establishment of the ICC.[418] Conservative commentators agreed. David Davenport stated that in Rome "a thousand nongovernmental organizations came together under a master ngo, the Coalition for the International Criminal Court ...the ngos were central players, involved in setting the agenda, drafting documents, and lobbying delegates".[419] Alan Baker, Chief Counsel to the Israeli Delegation, noted: "In all my years of international work, I've never seen the NGOs play a more powerful role.... They were in on nearly every meeting. They were in on everything."[420] This dominance raised concerns about "whether ngos are appropriate and reliable leaders. The typical ngo is a passionate, single-issue organization, often suffering from tunnel vision. Although by definition they are not seeking a profit, these ngos are nevertheless special-interest groups that would sacrifice a wide range of other international values to pursue their own agenda." Similarly, the way the NGOs went about their work in Rome had negative effects:

> The ngo methodology is also troubling. Unlike governments, ngos are really accountable to no one, which makes them potentially dangerous players in a political negotiation. They also, by their nature and history, tend to approach problems in an adversarial and rhetorical manner, contrasted with the consensual and legal nature of most treaty negotiations.... This makes them better advocates than leaders of a complex legal negotiation, with its give and take and need for consensus.[421]

It is also evident that there was considerable overlap between Western legal non-governmental organisations and activists and some of the developing world government delegations. Schiff confirms that NGO personnel were members of some state representations, "so in some cases NGO positions became state positions.... Observers and participants agreed in retrospect that the NGO role at the Statute Conference was more influential in the progress of the Conference than had NGO participation been at any prior large international negotiation."[422] Glasius confirms the presence of non-government organisation activists and "consultants" in delegations from the developing world. She states that they helped "to develop their legal arguments.... Bosnia, Trinidad and Tobago, Sierra Leone, Senegal, Burundi and Congo relied on a technical assistance programme by No Peace Without Justice to augment the size and expertise of their delegations." Glasius is candid enough to admit that they brought with them views that was not "entirely neutral" and "influenced the delegations from within".[423] As but three examples, Philippe Sands and Andrew Clapham attached themselves to the Solomon

Islands Delegation and the American activist Bart Brown was part of the Trinidad Delegation.[424] These activist lawyers would have been instrumental in visiting Western positions upon smaller delegations.

Benjamin Schiff has also stated that: "From the Statute to the budget, from referral to defense, NGOs have been crucial to the ICC."[425] He observed: "Perhaps more than for any other international organization, the ICC depends upon NGOs for its operations… and so [they] implicitly set an agenda for the future evolution of the ICC".[426] Schiff has also noted that the NGOs are "a prime constituency for the Prosecutor from the time of his selection through to current operations".[427]

Chris Patten, a former European Union Commissioner for External Relations, admitted that Brussels had long funded non-government organisations to work towards the establishment of the court: "The EU had been a strong supporter of the establishment of the ICC; we had worked for years to achieve its creation; we helped to fund organizations that themselves acted as advocates for the court."[428] The EU has itself stated that since 1995, the union "represented by the European Commission, has funded civil society organisations designed to help ensure the effective functioning of the International Court under the Instrument for Democracy and Human Rights (EIDHR)".[429] In 2010, the EU stated:

> Since 2003, after the Rome Statute came into force, the European Commission has provided funding of more than €20 million to global ratification campaigns undertaken by civil society coalitions and to projects of the ICC. The European Commission has been the principal financial supporter of many of these organisations, whose work has contributed to increasing the ratification rate of the Rome Statute, the awareness of the mandate of the Court and to promoting the complementarity principle and the principle of cooperation.[430]

The EU has also placed on record that "NGOs also enjoy an extraordinary level of cooperation with the rotating EU Presidencies, as well as with individual EU Member States." NGOs such as the CICC, Parliamentarians for Global Action, and Amnesty International are reported to provide each presidency in turn with a list of countries that could be targeted by the EU in its ratification and implementation démarches. Brussels has also stated that "under the umbrella of the CICC, NGOs are invited to exchange views with EU Member States in the framework of the Council Working Party COJUR ICC, to discuss implementation of the EU Common Position on the ICC, as well as developments related to the ICC and other international tribunals". This was said to have provided EU officials and EU member states with "insight and information on country and regional positions and developments at the Court, thereby increasing awareness on critical ICC matters and seeking to facilitate common actions".[431]

In his review of four key studies of the negotiations and activities that led to the Rome Statute and the formation of the ICC, the German jurist Andreas Paulus notes that they all "describe the role of NGOs, which can hardly be overestimated, in enthusiastic terms".[432] Paulus notes that NGOs were present not just as NGOs but were also "embedded" into governmental delegations. He also notes that NGOs often served "as representatives of small countries which were not able to set up a negotiating team of their own".[433] Paulus commented upon this involvement by NGOs: "If their involvement leads to the 'hijacking' of small states for activist agendas, this innovation might do more harm than good."[434] He cautions that one should not expect any critical assessment of the role of NGOs, if for no other reason than the fact that they were the ones recording events: "One might wonder, however, whether it was the best editorial decision in all these cases to let NGO representatives comment on their own role."[435]

The reality is that reliance on politically motivated advocacy groups and non-governmental organisations has badly damaged the court's credibility. It is a matter of record that the prosecutor has actively pursued allegations with regard to "genocide" in Darfur that have only really been articulated by non-governmental organisations and "advocacy" groups (or in the case of the Bush Administration, because of similar pressure upon it from similar NGOs and lobby groups). The danger of doing so is very clear. Even ICC investigators have pointed to the disparity between claims made and information provided by human-rights groups, and reality. Bernard Lavigne, a French magistrate and former police detective who headed the Congo investigation team revealed that "The gap between the assessment of the humanitarian groups and the evidence was sort of a surprise."[436] The former British Prime Minister Tony Blair, somebody who should know, observed of non-governmental organisations that "there's as much politics in NGOs as in politics – sometimes more – and they are treated as objective observers when they simply aren't. Partly they campaign for a cause and partly for vested interests."[437] He also stated:

> [T]he trouble with some of them is that while they are treated by the media as concerned citizens...they are also organisations, raising money, marketing themselves and competing with other NGOS in a similar field.... And they've learned to play the modern media game perfectly. As it's all about impact, they shout louder and louder to get heard. They also have their own tightly defined dogma and conventional wisdom which, if you challenge them, they defend fiercely – not usually on their merits, but by abusing your motives for challenging them.[438]

Kenneth Anderson and David Rieff, commentators with considerable experience of humanitarian work and international non-governmental organisations, have challenged several key claims made by international non-governmental organisations. Anderson and Rieff declared themselves to be sceptical of the claim made by international NGOs that they constitute "global civil society". Indeed, they find the very term "global civil society" to be "conceptually incoherent" and in reality an "inflated ideological" claim.[439] They state: "International NGOs may believe that they...aspire to the legitimacy of 'global civil society', they cannot and do not."[440] Anderson and Rieff echo Blair's comment about dogma, noting that a better way of viewing the rise of transnational or international NGOs is as a "quasi-religious movement, and as a revival of the post-religious of the earlier European and American missionary movements".[441] They have elaborated further on this analogy:

> It is worth noting that international NGOs can be understood as a social movement on very different models from that of global civil society…. One model is simply that of a contemporary secular, post-religious missionary movement. On this view, the NGO movement, rather than being global civil society…is simply an analogue of the Western missionary movements of the past, which carried the gospel to the rest of the world and sought in this way to promote truth, salvation, and goodness…it remains a powerful way of explaining the international NGO movement…it appeals to universal, transcendental, but ultimately mystical values… rather than to the values of democracy and the multiple conceptions of the good that, as a value, it spawns.[442]

They state that international NGO personnel "do indeed resemble missionary orders". They mention the ultra-Catholic Opus Dei movement as an example.[443]

Anderson and Rieff have also cut to the heart of the disconnection between the claim of international NGOs to be universal, and reality:

> As they fly effortlessly from place to place, continent to continent, capital to capital…they cannot grasp that "international" is not the same as "universal", and that even those who have apparently abandoned fidelity to location might still have interests, class interests to defend, the interests of, well, the interests of those who live in the jet stream. Nor can they grasp that there are those at the bottom who, without being moral relativists, nonetheless believe that they are just as capable of discerning the true universals, just as capable of identifying universal values, as those who take the overnight flight business class from New York to Geneva.[444]

Pace and Schense noted that the then Canadian foreign minister Lloyd Axworthy coined the term "new diplomacy"[445] for what Paulus describes as "the coordination between governments, inter-governmental and non-governmental organizations", as seen in the drafting of the Rome Statute.[446] The reality is that Western non-governmental organisations, unaccountable either to the public in their countries of origin or the public in the countries in which they wished to see the court operate, and not lawyers, were responsible in very large part for drafting the Rome Statute. The direct result of this NGO involvement in drafting law is that political compromises were made that sought to avoid the more difficult legal issues before any such international court.

It is also clear that the very same Western non-governmental organisations that brought the court into being have not always had the integrity to criticise the court when and where the court has gone wrong. Geoffrey Robertson has noted that "most NGOs that would usually offer criticisms of international institutions tend to be over-supportive of the Court".[447] Western NGOs and the Western-created court, while lauding the role of civil society in the creation and maintenance of the ICC, have consciously ignored those non-governmental organisations and manifestations of civil society – especially within Africa – that have questioned or come to question the activities of the court, especially when their concerns have proved to be inconvenient to the court.

For all its rhetoric about how the ICC cooperates with and respects civil society and non-governmental organisations, the court very clearly seeks to pick and chose the non-governmental organisations and the sections of civil society to which it listens.

The value of genuine civil society and non-government organisations is clear. The World Bank states that:

> Civil society's role in conflict-affected countries is now widely acknowledged, including at the global level. The latest and most prominent indication is the UNSC statement (September 2005) highlighting the comparative advantage of civil society in facilitating dialogue and providing community leadership. A recent UN-Civil Society conference on the role of civil actors in Peace building further established the issue on the international policy agenda.[448]

The World Bank has adopted a definition of civil society developed by a number of leading research centres:

> [T]the term civil society to refer to the wide array of non-governmental and not-for-profit organizations that have a presence in public life, expressing the interests and values of their members or others, based on ethical, cultural, political, scientific, religious or philanthropic considerations. Civil Society Organizations (CSOs) therefore refer to a wide of array of organizations: community groups, non-governmental organizations (NGOs), labor unions, indigenous groups, charitable organizations, faith-based organizations, professional associations, and foundations.[449]

The court's Western supporters have struggled to downplay the fact that the ICC has met a wall of criticism from African civil society – that is to say genuine civil society, not the artificial NGOs funded and directed by Western governments to serve as an echo chamber for Western support for the court. Schiff has confirmed that many Ugandan non-governmental organisations challenged the imposition of the court on their situation. He stated that they "argued that ICC involvement would make peace less likely".[450] These have included the Acholi Religious Leaders' Peace Initiative, whose negotiator Father Carlos Rodriquez warned that "[t]he issuing of [ICC] international arrest warrants would practically close once and for all the path to peaceful negotiation as a means to end this long war, crushing whatever little progress has been made during these years."[451] David Kaiza, the Director of the Refugee Law Project, affiliated with the Makerere University School of Law in Uganda, noted:

> The impact of the ICC has been to heighten the violence. The problem with the ICC is that it has arrogated itself the responsibility to judge the process of the peace talks. There have been accusations that although atrocities have also been committed by the UPDF, the ICC is going to investigate only the LRA.... . Sadly, the ICC is silent on what it would do with the UPDF.... . This conflict has

spanned two decades and a whole generation has been lost. I am not sure this is not the use of Africa as a guinea pig for the ICC.[452]

As the International Refugee Rights Initiative noted: "[T]he ICC's involvement in northern Uganda was met with immediate and widespread condemnation by Ugandan civil society."[453] Adam Branch observed that "[f]or perhaps the first time in the history of international law…those opposing the enforcement of humanitarian and human rights law were not self-interested government officials or rebel leaders. Instead, the protests came from the Ugandan human rights community itself, from activists, lawyers, and civil-society organisations working for peace in the North."[454]

The International Refugee Rights Initiative went on to record:

> An increasingly heated debate between national and international NGOs developed over the course of the following months, and seven years later many of the issues that lie at the heart of it remain unresolved. This debate highlighted the polarisation that was emerging between international understandings of the appropriateness of different forms of justice (as represented by the ICC…) and local understandings (as represented by the majority of local human rights and civil society organisations, and community leaders in the north).[455]

Dr. Lucy Hovil's detailed 2013 study of the ICC's intervention in Uganda provided a devastating critique of the court, its absolutist approach to "international justice", and its intimidation of civil society and especially non-conformist civil society in the country. Hovil, a Refugee Law Project worker with considerable first-hand experience of the Ugandan conflict, revealed the extent of the court's arrogance:

> The ICC, with support from its international justice constituency, seemed to be acting no differently than any external actor with money, power, and resources who forces its agenda onto local communities and organisations regardless of its efficacy. Instead, concerns voiced by civil society about the potential impact of the ICC's approach were condemned both by ICC staff members and officials of the Court and by a number of international human rights groups. Because the ICC's actions were being done in the name of promoting justice (the proverbial "fight against impunity"), anyone who spoke out against the Court was by implication labelled anti-justice.[456]

She correctly points out that:

> By questioning the ICC's involvement…in the conflict, those who criticised the intervention were not turning their backs on the promotion of justice. Rather, they were demanding more justice: justice that was robust and that genuinely engaged with the context; justice that would contribute to, or at least complement, the promotion of fair and equal governance; and justice that would deliver. Arrest

warrants that promised so much but were inevitably fated to deliver so little were seen as yet another unrealistic ideal, and a dangerous one at that, given the critical gap between the ICC's ability to talk about and realise justice.[457]

Hovil notes that "civil society in Uganda had not requested ICC involvement…members of Ugandan civil society – who were themselves living and working in the midst of the conflict – did not understand or support the rationale for this form of international intervention".[458] Hovil recorded that Ugandan civil society had formed a negative opinion of the ICC: "[T]he Court appeared to ignore the fact that the local population saw the government as a key perpetrator. Consequently, the Court's neutrality was seen by local observers to be compromised from the start." She stated:

> It was perceived to have become complicit in the political manoeuvring that has enabled President Museveni to maintain power for 25 years, and jeopardised the Court's own neutral stance as a result. The ICC's actions had effectively legitimised the government's military campaign in the north (and subsequent forays into eastern Democratic Republic of Congo (DRC), Sudan, and Central African Republic (CAR)) and reinforced its justification for continuing that campaign.[459]

Lucy Hovil provides a first-hand account of the pressure to conform placed upon Ugandan civil society by the court and its international supporters: "[T]he Court, with support from a powerful and articulate international justice community, appeared to be pushing an agenda that seemed to ignore local understandings of the conflict and the seriousness of the different crimes committed – and, therefore, of the right response to that conflict."[460] Hovil also documented some of the heavy-handed international pressure on local civil society organisations to stop speaking out against the ICC's actions, including pressure brought to bear on local employees of international non-governmental organisations:

> A number of field officers of international organisations based in Uganda initially voiced their concerns about the ICC's actions, but were soon silenced by head offices that took an official stance of support for the ICC, once again stifling debate. National voices that had previously been supported by international organisations were now being questioned by those same organisations because they were not showing unequivocal support for the Court's actions. Instead of healthy discussion, a major dispute developed which left everyone feeling bruised.[461]

Hovil also cited pressure she herself faced regarding her perspective on the court: "[T]he author was asked to remove any negative references to the ICC from a report for an international body, because it was 'against the interests of justice.'"[462]

Many Ugandan NGOs clearly felt themselves to have been ignored by the court's actions in Uganda. They included, among others, the Gulu-focused Human Rights Focus, Conciliation Resources, the Concerned Parents Association, the Ugandan peace initiative Kacoke Madit and Christian Aid.[463] The International Refugee Rights Initiative further notes that "local civil society actors had, and their decades of involvement in a war that had affected many of them personally, seemed to be effectively ignored…concerns voiced by civil society about the potential impact of the ICC's approach were condemned both by ICC staff members and officials of the Court".[464] And it is clear that these grassroots non-governmental organisations reflect genuine public opinion on the issue. For example, in a 2007 survey of 2,875 adults in northern Uganda, only three per cent of respondents indicated that justice was their top priority despite the protracted and brutal conflict.[465] Instead, they emphasised "resolving immediate needs for peace, food, and health"[466] and over eighty-one per cent of respondents said they believed amnesty would help achieve peace.[467]

It is a matter of record, therefore, that the ICC's relationship with non-governmental organisations and civil society has been deeply flawed. The role of Western and Western-funded non-governmental organisations and civil society in drafting the deeply flawed statute that brought the court into existence is very regrettable. The subsequent unwillingness or inability of Western NGOs to criticise the deeply flawed institution they had brought into being does no favour either for Western civil society or the court. The fact that the court and rich Western non-governmental organisations have then ridden roughshod over local civil society within Africa, within the very conflict-affected areas within which the court has chosen to involve itself, reflects very poorly on them.

The simple fact is that non-governmental organisations, accountable to no one except their funders, played a pivotal role in the establishment of the ICC. The indifference subsequently shown by well-funded, zealously pro-ICC, white non-governmental organisations in the First World to legitimate concerns about the court raised by black grassroots NGOs and civil society in Africa has mirrored that shown by the European government funders of the ICC to the concerns articulated by African States Parties.

Chapter Six

A Glaring Democratic Deficit

"[R]ules of international law in general, and the authority of international institutions in particular, cannot be imposed on states that have not consented to them.

Lee A. Casey and David B. Rivkin Jr.[468]

"Democracy confers legitimacy on a system of governance."

Eric Stein[469]

The American statesman John Bolton has said of the ICC that "the court is fundamentally illegitimate…in concept it violates basic democratic theory".[470] He was referring to the institution's lack of democratic accountability. Bolton is absolutely correct. The question of legitimacy and accountability has always been a source of considerable interest and great controversy among international legal scholars.[471] This controversy has also extended to international legal institutions. Douglas Lee Donoho has made the point that most major international organisations were created by sovereign states to serve sovereign interests.[472] Prominent international law scholars and lawyers such as Madeline Morris have confirmed that in crucial respects the ICC ultimately lacks democratic legitimacy.[473] This is quite simply because it is an international court that does not answer to a democratic body in a similar way to any of its domestic counterparts. Morris makes the argument that because of this "democratic deficit" the ICC lacks legitimacy and should not be engaged with by states that support democratic principles. Morris, who served as a legal advisor both to the US and Rwandan governments, points particularly to the fact that in its debatable jurisdiction over non-ICC States Parties nationals, as well as in some of its bureaucratic structures, the court is not accountable to any democratic political body. The ICC, for example, claims it is entitled by the Rome Statute to prosecute the nationals of certain states that are not State Parties to the ICC, in opposition to the democratic will of those states. Morris quite correctly points out that all of the relevant human-rights texts assert that there is a human right to democratic governance and the court quite simply violates the human rights of those it seeks to prosecute in those circumstances and therefore is illegitimate. Morris also correctly observes that this issue does not arise with regard to those states that are States Parties to the ICC. The issue also arises when the court seeks jurisdiction over citizens of democratic states, such as the USA, that are not signatories to the Rome Statute, if they are alleged to have committed war crimes on the territory of an ICC State Party.

The same argument applies to Sudan or Libya and their nationals as a result of UNSC referrals to the ICC. In all three examples the nationals of these countries may find themselves supposedly answering to a court that claims a jurisdiction over them to which their countries have pointedly not consented. Morris asks the key question: "What is the democratic basis for the ICC's power as applied to populations whose states have not consented on their behalf? Here the ICC's claim to democratic legitimacy breaks down."[474] Morris makes it clear that the court is therefore illegitimate in that there is no democratic relationship between the ICC and those non-party nationals over whom it seeks or would seek to exercise authority:

> What is ultimately at stake, beneath the heated controversy concerning ICC jurisdiction over non-party nationals, is a tension embodied in the Rome Treaty between the human rights embodied in humanitarian law (rights to freedom from genocide, war crimes, and crimes against humanity) and the human right to democratic governance.[475]

Casey and Rivkin similarly note:

> [R]ules of international law in general, and the authority of international institutions in particular, cannot be imposed – either by treaty or custom – on states that have not consented to them. Although that consent may be implied in certain instances (as when a new customary rule develops over a long period without dissent), under no circumstance can consent be dispensed with altogether. That, however, is precisely what the ICC states parties have done in their efforts to incorporate "universality" into the Rome Statute. Under that instrument, the ICC asserts jurisdiction over the nationals, including governmental officials, of non-parties. Such claims are unprecedented and unsupported by any established doctrine of international law.[476]

Morris points out an additional example of the ICC's "democratic deficit" that can be found in other non-democratic aspects of the court's structure, namely that the court can revise its jurisdiction and expand into areas such as "the crimes of terrorism and drug crimes" not explicitly outlined in the Rome Statute.[477] The ASP for the ICC, that is to say diplomats by and large, will ultimately decide these issues by way of a majority vote. What this means is that pivotal legal issues, including the framing of new crimes to be prosecuted, can be decided without the unanimous consent of States Parties or indeed without the consent of non-party states. Morris has also observed that the court will be able to adjudicate on cases of significant political importance relating to the ability of states and their nationals to conduct both military and peacetime policy. She concludes: "These are not thin questions. Each involves areas where the law is indeterminate and the politics are weighty. These questions do not require anything like the 'mere' 'application of laws to the facts.' These issues implicate the enormous political, and even moral issues and controversies."[478]

In his critique of the ICTY, Sir Geoffrey Nice, a leading international lawyer and the Chief Prosecutor in the ICTY trial of Slobodan Milosevic from 1998 to 2001, saw the ICTY's problem as a lack of accountability: "Domestic courts have governments, democratic parliaments and the media supervising them, and barristers and judges are very vulnerable to making a big mistake, which can ruin their careers. But the UN created this court for political purposes – nothing wrong with that, per se – and then set it loose. That meant that the chief prosecutor of the Tribunal has huge powers: ask any government for anything, make large claims, get publicity around the world."[479] Exactly the same criticism can and has been made of the ICC. It is a point that has also informed more conservative critiques of the ICC, such as that made by Marc Grossman, the US Under Secretary of State for Political Affairs in the Bush Administration, in May 2002:

> The U.S. system of government is based on the principle that power must be checked by other power or it will be abused and misused. With this in mind, the Founding Fathers divided the national government into three branches, giving each the means to influence and restrain excesses of the other branches. For instance, Congress confirms and can impeach federal judges and has the sole authority to authorize spending, the President nominates judges and can veto legislation, and the courts can nullify laws passed by Congress and overturn presidential actions if it judges them unconstitutional. The ICC lacks robust checks on its authority, despite strong efforts by U.S. delegates to insert them during the treaty negotiations. The court is an independent treaty body. In theory, the states that have ratified the Rome Statute and accepted the court's authority control the ICC. In practice, the role of the Assembly of State Parties is limited. The judges themselves settle any dispute over the court's "judicial functions." The prosecutor can initiate an investigation on his own authority, and the ICC judges determine whether the investigation may proceed. The U.N. Security Council can delay an investigation for a year – a delay that can be renewed – but it cannot stop an investigation.[480]

Grossman also noted:

> Under the UN Charter, the UNSC has primary responsibility for maintaining international peace and security. But the Rome Treaty removes this existing system of checks and balances, and places enormous unchecked power in the hands of the ICC prosecutor and judges. The treaty created a self-initiating prosecutor, answerable to no state or institution other than the Court itself.[481]

It is worth noting, when assessing attitudes within the USA towards the ICC, that even traditional international law is viewed with scepticism by conservative American legal minds. Judge Robert Bork, a leading conservative constitutional lawyer, has argued that international law is simply too elastic in its application and too prone to "non-legal" – political and diplomatic – criteria to be considered law. Bork has also attacked international law for its lack of accountability to any elected body that strips international law of the legitimacy inherently possessed by domestic law. As Judge Bork noted: "There can be no authentic rule of law among nations until nations have a common political morality or are under a common sovereignty."[482]

Morris states that the undemocratic character of the ICC is similar to that of the World Trade Organisation, the World Bank and the International Monetary Fund. She points out that many of those anti-globalisation forces within civil society, the legal profession and academia who are critical of these organisations because they greatly impact on large numbers of people without their consent are silent with regard to the ICC:

> Why…have we heard no clamor – indeed, no discussion – of democratic legitimacy in relation to the ICC? Why has there been virtually no discussion of democracy relative to the ICC, even while the "democratic deficit" of other institutions, like the WTO, has been a cause célèbre?[483]

A pillar of international law studies, Eric Stein, clearly states: "Democracy *confers* legitimacy on a system of governance."[484] (Emphasis added.) Laws and the legal system within which they function and are exercised are at the heart of governance. Jean d'Aspremont has also stated that "there is little doubt today that democracy [is] a prominent yardstick with which to assess the legitimacy of governments".[485] By extension it is also an important yardstick with which to assess the legitimacy of courts, and especially international courts.

The Pulitzer Prize-winning American journalist George F. Will, described by *The Wall Street Journal* as "perhaps the most powerful journalist in America", has been very critical of the court's democratic deficit: "Although the ICC is supposed to advance the rule of law around the world, it is potentially – even inherently – inimical to the rule of law. And it is retrograde – premodern, actually – because it affronts the principle that every institution wielding power over others should be accountable to someone…the ICC floats above accountability to representative institutions." Will has also stated that the problem is not just that the ICC is "above the law", but that "there is not much clear and pertinent law to be above. The rule of law must involve a body of controlling precedents that give due notice of what behavior is required or proscribed."[486] George Will was absolutely right. In the absence of such a framework a gathering of largely mediocre, self-serving jurists and in some cases non-lawyers, in The Hague, have made things up as they went along.

Kenneth Anderson and David Rieff have also clearly pointed to the democratic deficit, the lack of democratic legitimacy, at the heart of the "global civil society" that brought the ICC into being: "[T]he fact remains that democratic legitimacy – of a kind obtained only at the ballot box – *does* matter. It is simply a fact of contemporary life…the ballot box is indispensable. This is true both in fact and as a matter of perception."[487] They note of civil society institutions: "They do not stand for office. Citizens do not vote for this or that civil society organisation as their representatives because, in the end, NGOs exist to reflect their own principles, not to represent a constituency to whose interests and desires they must respond." It should go without saying that an extension of "global civil society", such as the ICC, is even further removed from any pretence of democratic legitimacy. Anderson and Rieff also stated that "[t]he 'democracy deficit' of the international system is buttressed rather than challenged by the global civil society movement".[488]

Lucy Hovil has placed on record the undemocratic and overbearing interference of unelected Western judicial institutions in Uganda:

> [T]he absolutist nature of international law and the justice it purports to generate were seen as ignoring or even negating the value of local understandings of justice. Local mechanisms of justice were demoted and written off as not meeting the demands of justice (as defined in international law via the interpretation of concepts such as complementarity and admissibility). Those who were promoting these local understandings – including religious and cultural leaders in the north – suddenly had their integrity and motivations questioned.[489]

Paul Valentine states that the democracy deficit controversy in inter-governmental international organisations hinges on the fact "that governments and not the electorate, select individuals who become the country's legal representative in the international community"[490] D'Aspremont has also made the closely related point that the constant reshuffling of governments further complicates the authority of those selected to represent their governments in inter-governmental international organisations.[491] Any democratic mandate that may have vaguely existed under one government decays even further with the election of subsequent governments.

As Valentine succinctly puts it: "Thus, governments act by proxy, leaving the electorate to act by proxy of a proxy."[492] D'Aspremont correctly points out: "The international legal order is consequently a legal order where legal persons act via proxies."[493] Peter Gerhart found that because transnational governance moves the decision-making away from the electorate, there is a perceived democracy deficit in inter-governmental international organisations.[494] Valentine notes: "The structural intent was never to represent the democratic values of the individual states. Therefore, by design, the interests of individual citizens are only indirectly and tenuously represented, if at all."

Many commentators believe that a state's acceptance of international law and inter-governmental international organisations fundamentally shifts a critical aspect of sovereignty – the right to prescribe and determine the scope and meaning of legal obligations.[495] Eric Stein noted that because democratic control over the executive is notoriously loose in matters of foreign affairs, lawmaking at inter-governmental international organisations is not subject to the usual checks and balances present in domestic legislation.[496] Valentine points out that global and transnational governance separate the sources of decision-making away from the people of a state in at least two ways. He points out that first of all, the transnational process dilutes the vote of the individual and has fewer procedural checks, such as democratic oversight. Secondly, he points out that the representatives conducting and approving the negotiations are rarely elected officials; instead the executive usually appoints these representatives. The ASP, for example, which oversees the ICC and which selects the judges and officials of the court, consists overwhelmingly of non-elected diplomatic representatives of the nations represented.

Stein has also observed that when a member state is out-voted, the democracy deficit becomes more palpable as the inter-governmental international organisation is imposing an international law upon a state against the express wishes of that state.[497] This is even more acute in the case of the ICC and Sudan. Sudan has not accepted the Rome Treaty, is not a State Party to the statute and does not fall under the jurisdiction of the ICC. Sudan's people have not voted to become part of the court and its government has quite clearly declared that it has no intention to acceding to the Rome Treaty. Yet, a court its people and government have never agreed to become party to has sought to violate Sudan's sovereignty and impose itself on the country. The circumstances become even more difficult to follow, and any pretence of a democratic paper trail all but invisible, given that the court's claim to jurisdiction is based on a referral from the UNSC, three out of five of whose permanent members are themselves not even States Parties to the court.

Those elected governments that seek to continue to force the ICC upon the government of Sudan, and other non-member states, clearly fail to respect the substantive elements of democracy. At face value such governments certainly qualify as illiberal democracies.[498]

Chapter Seven

JUDGES ELECTED BY VOTE-TRADING

"[V]ote-trading, campaigning, and regional politicking invariably play a great part in candidates' chance of being elected than considerations of individual merit."

Professor Philippe Sands QC[499]

"Unqualified judges...have been appointed to key positions because of highly politicised voting systems and a lack of transparency."

The *Guardian*[500]

The simple fact is that with a few exceptions the judges at the ICC have been lacklustre political appointees, very much the result of the very "vote trading" about which Human Rights Watch and others have so long warned. Yet these are the same people who are tasked with making very difficult decisions about some of the most complex situations in the world, decisions that quite literally affect life and death in Africa. They are manifestly not up to the task.

There is a related concern. Just as was the case in the ICTY and other projections of international "justice", the ICC is making things up as it goes along. Human Rights Watch has pointed to "a creeping discord in the interpretations and solutions offered by the court's Chambers to the issues before them. Differences in approach are evident from decisions (and dissents) on fundamental issues including victims' participation, witness protection, and disclosure practices in connection with a defendant's fair trial rights."[501] The ICC is perfectly willing to argue the case for universal jurisdiction but not for its own trial chambers. The Rome Statute does not make the decisions of chambers binding on one another.[502] Human Rights Watch has rationalised this: "As the Chambers confront various country situations with unique requirements, different approaches in the application of the law to the facts may be both expected and necessary."[503] Yet when peace advocates and peace negotiators within various African conflicts try to advance the same sort of argument by way of suggesting a more nuanced peace first approach because of "unique" circumstances, the ICC and Human Rights Watch are their most vocal critics.

In September 2010, *The Guardian* reported that "[u]nqualified judges, in some cases with no expertise on international law and in one case no legal qualifications, have been appointed to key positions because of highly politicised voting systems and a lack of transparency". The newspaper also stated that "[c]ritics say…the practices threaten the future of the international criminal court".[504] Geoffrey Robertson was unusually restrained when he described the ICC's judicial appointments as "problematic".[505] He drew a very clear link between the quality of the court and the quality of those people appointed as judges:

> The viability of the ICC ultimately depends more on the calibre and experience of its judges and prosecutors than on the fine print of its statute. International appointment systems are prone to thrown up mediocrities trusted to toe the line of their nominating governments… . Often missing are persons of real independence with first-class minds and imagination… . In this respect, the statutory arrangements for appointing the Court's eighteen full-time judges leave much to be desired.[506]

The relationship between international judicial appointments, and "deal-making" between states is an open secret.[507] The quality of such appointments has also been the subject of sometimes abrasive criticism. In 2008, for example, *The Economist* explored the issue of whether the selection processes to the international courts led to the appointment of "government hacks and lickspittles, with little or no judicial experience".[508] The ICC has no shortage of either. The distinguished British judge Iain Bonomy has noted that "[t]o many judicial minds, that system is basically unsound".[509]

A central criticism of the ICC is that the prosecutor and judges are unaccountable to anyone. It goes without saying that the allocation of such unqualified power is based on the belief that the ICC prosecutor and judges are beyond reproach, by way of qualifications, professionally, ethically and personally. This sadly is quite clearly not the case in respect of the ICC Chief Prosecutor or a number of the people appointed as ICC judges.

Selecting International Judges: Principle, Process, and Politics, a groundbreaking study of international judicial appointments, written by Philippe Sands QC, Professor Kate Malleson, Ruth Mackenzie and Penny Martin as part of Oxford University Press' International Courts and Tribunals Series, concluded that "the evidence leads unequivocally to the conclusion that merit is not the main driving factor in the election processes".[510] The study notes that "rules are meant to insulate nominations from political influence. In practice, a recurring theme across the interviews was the strong vested interest of governments in strictly controlling the nomination process in order to influence the composition of international courts."[511] The study recorded that "[t]he picture that emerges from the interviews…highlights the important, if not central, role played by political factors that are unrelated to the merits of any candidate".[512]

The study also noted that "the majority of the states studied used informal or semi-structured procedures. These processes were marked by their lack of transparency and accountability and a stronger likelihood of being informed by extraneous political considerations…political factors, rather than the individual selection criteria, could determine nominations."[513] The study also revealed that "[m]any individuals who participate in the ICC process believe it to be even more politicized than other international judicial elections".[514]

Benjamin Schiff, in his book *Building the ICC*, documented the role played by an unelected non-governmental organisation, the Coalition for the International Criminal Court, in selecting ICC judges: "During the 2003 process of nominating and electing judges (and during the 2006 second round of elections) the CICC organized meetings between NGOs and those running for judgeships...quite likely influencing the votes that were eventually cast."[515] He provides a telling example of the election of the only male ICC judge in 2003: "The single victorious male candidate described his campaigning as having been focused largely on NGO meetings, in contrast to some other competitors who spent no time with the NGOs. He believed that his selection was also aided by his experience in his home country as the head of a children's welfare-oriented NGO."[516]

The danger of vote-trading for judicial appointments to the ICC bench was obvious from the inception of the court. There was an attempt to discourage the practice of vote-trading in the election of judges before the first bench was even elected. At the first session of the ASP to the Rome Statute, on 9 September 2002, the President of the Bureau, Zeid Ra'ad Zeid Al-Hussein, appealed to assembly members to refrain from vote-trading. He clearly stated that "[i]n order to ensure the integrity of the electoral process, the Bureau... appealed to States Parties to refrain from entering into reciprocal agreements of exchange of support in respect of the election of judges of the Court".[517] *Selecting International Judges* confirmed that "[n]onetheless, vote-trading took place from the outset".[518] An early Centre for International Courts and Tribunals study of the election noted:

> The practice of ICC elections indicates that states have actively engaged in vote trading and have not responded to the appeal of the Bureau. This suggests that the practice of vote trading is considered by states to be integral to elections in political bodies. In general, it appears that most states are not willing to consider judicial posts to be qualitatively different to other expert and political posts.[519]

Ten years on, it is very clear that the appeals articulated in 2003 continue to fall on deaf ears. In 2005, three years after the first election of ICC judges, the Institute for War & Peace Reporting stated that "there has been a call for greater transparency in the nomination and election processes of future war crimes proceedings – specifically those held for the ICC". The CICC proposed that a reformed nomination and election process was established to end "deal brokering" during the ICC judicial elections. CICC's Caroline Baudot stated that "NGOs really think that there is something very wrong with [The Hague election procedure], especially the nomination process.... [Some] people are [being put forward] without any transparency, procedure or evaluation of qualifications. It is based on political deals and vote trading. We don't want this to happen at the ICC."

These concerns by ideological supporters of the ICC were once again restated in December 2011. At a press conference held during the ICC's December 2011 annual ASP to the Rome Statute meeting in New York, Women's Initiatives for Gender Justice board member María Solís García said she was dismayed that the CICC's independent panel of experts, formed to examine candidates, had not been used by the ICC to guide it in its selection of judges. She said that instead the election process was rife with vote-trading, disregarding the candidates' qualifications. Asked about what the ramifications should be for vote-trading during court elections, García said that the practice in the assembly had mirrored the same practices at the UN: "The great problem here is they are not respecting the Rome Statute. They are violating the Statute by trading votes."[520]

The vote-trading phenomenon was also documented by Benjamin Schiff: "Election depends more on campaigning, bargaining, and vote trading, than on the issue- or experience-based characteristics of the candidates." He noted that some ICC judges were also critical of flawed elections based on national interests rather than qualifications.[521]

The first bench of eighteen judges was elected by the ASP in February 2003. They were sworn in at the inaugural session of the court on 1 March 2003. The first president of the court, Philippe Kirsch, was a diplomat by profession. He joined the Canadian Foreign Ministry in 1972, has held a number of positions in the ministry, including Assistant Deputy Minister for Legal, Consular and Passport Affairs, Ottawa (1994–96); and Director General, Bureau of Legal Affairs, Ottawa (1992–94). He was Deputy Permanent Representative of Canada to the UN (1988–92), Deputy Representative to the Security Council (1989–90) and Canada's Ambassador to Sweden. From 1999 to 2002, he chaired the Preparatory Commission for the ICC. The second election was held in January 2006, and a third in January 2009. Elections for vacancies were conducted in November-December 2007 and November 2009. At its tenth session, in December 2011, the ASP elected judges Miriam Defensor-Santiago (the Philippines), Howard Morrison (UK), Anthony T. A. Carmona (Trinidad and Tobago), Olga V. Herrera Carbuccia (Dominican Republic), Robert Fremr (Czech Republic) and Chile Eboe-Osuji (Nigeria) to the court for a term of nine years. Their terms of office commenced on 11 March 2012. On 11 March 2012, Judge Sang-Hyun Song (Republic of Korea) was re-elected as President of the Court and Judge Sanji Mmasenono Monageng (Botswana) and Judge Cuno Jakob Tarfusser (Italy) were elected First and Second Vice-President, respectively. They will serve for a period of three years.

Sylviade Bertodano, an international lawyer with experience of the ICTY, ICTR and East Timor, has pointed to the political selection of ICC judges and the dangers to judicial independence:

> Judges in international tribunals have historically been subject to political pressures which might influence the independence of their position. The Rome Statute for the International Criminal Court has created a system in which judges are selected by political representatives of state parties, without any independent screening process. Furthermore, judges will have a high degree of control over the fundamental decisions as to who should be prosecuted, an area which normally falls in the province of the Prosecutor. There are legitimate

reasons to fear that this system will fail to provide the necessary safeguards to ensure that judicial independence is maintained.[522]

It is a matter of record that the legal competence of a number of the people appointed to become ICC judges has repeatedly been called into question. Sir Geoffrey Nice QC observed in his critique of the ICTY that the tribunal's judges were "generally not of the top flight…they are appointed by geographical spread – and some are dumped here; some are academics with little experience; some ex-diplomats with little experience of the law". One of the most controversial such appointees was Carla del Ponte, the former Swiss Attorney-General who was ICTY Chief Prosecutor from 1999 to 2007. Nice recorded that "[s]he had little interest in the details of a case. She was obsessed by publicity".[523] Other senior lawyers have expressed views similar to those of Geoffrey Nice. John Jones, a British former ICTY prosecutor – who has co-written the standard work on international criminal practice – said that "initially I was very much a believer: here, for the first time since Nuremberg, was international justice. Then I became cynical – I saw that the judges often didn't know what was happening, the trials were being ruined. And I saw that the UN, which is supposed to supervise, has no moral compass. It enjoins even-handedness, on ethnic grounds, not on grounds of justice."[524]

The comparisons with the ICC resonate. ICC judges are also generally "not of the top flight" and similarly appointed by an ethnic and geographical spread and in many cases lack relevant legal experience. Judges are selected by political representatives of state parties, without any independent screening process. With a few exceptions, the ICC judges have been a combination of former politicians, diplomats, academics and "human rights" activists. The Centre for International Courts and Tribunals' study of the first batch of ICC judges noted the candidates in the first elections were "a mix of diplomats who had been members of their states' delegations to the Preparatory Committees, academics with involvement in the drafting or ratification of the Rome Statute and national criminal judges". The study also revealed that "more than 50% had no prior experience or knowledge of a judicial process".[525] One interviewee said that the ICC judges who did not have a judicial background were "completely at sixes and sevens. They didn't know what a warrant was or what the originating procedure should be, or how you handle a trial…"[526] Examples abound. Judge Elisabeth Odio Benito of Costa Rica has been Minister of Justice and Vice President of her country, but she was never a judge before she was appointed as one for the ICTY. Judge Blattman of Bolivia is an ex-politician, a former law professor and activist. Judge Kuenyehia of Ghana was Dean of the Law Faculty at Ghana University before his appointment to the ICC bench. Judge Kaul of Germany was employed by the German Foreign Ministry before his appointment as an ICC judge.

The inexperience of the court's judges is self-evident. Stating that lengthy proceedings are the biggest problem of international criminal trials, Heidi Hansberry's study of the working practices at the ICC reveals unacceptable delays:

> Statistics reflect that an accused person spends an average of 2.3 years awaiting trial at the ICC while in custody. The average time period between custody

and a decision on charges, the first step toward a trial at the ICC, alone is 0.9 years. Similarly, the time period between Bahr Idriss Abu Garda's voluntary appearance and the decision on charges was 0.7 years. Thus, it is typical that an exceedingly long period of time elapses before the trial itself begins even for those defendants who appear voluntarily.[527]

Robert Heinsch has enumerated several reasons for the slow pace of international criminal trials. The inexperience of judges emerges as a key factor. He points out that judges are not proactive enough in encouraging cooperation between the parties, and that they are hindered by insufficient information on the background of cases. Most importantly, however, they even lack awareness of exculpatory material. Heinsch also states that the participation of victims distorts the holding of a typical trial, and, in the absence of a "proactive", for which read trial-experienced, bench, delays ensue. Quite simply, the picture Heinsch presents is one of judges who by and large either have no real trial or courtroom experience or if they had had some time in court, hadn't learnt much.[528] This shortfall is accentuated given that the ICC's rules allow hearsay evidence. Richard Ashby Wilson notes that "there is no hearsay rule, and the evidentiary regime allows most evidence to be admitted and trusts professional judges to separate the pertinent from the extraneous and the reliable from the implausible".[529] A generous assessment of the qualifications of the people appointed as ICC judges shows that very few have ever been professional judges. This shortfall in trial experience continues to manifest itself in the abysmal practice record of the court.

The distinguished American prosecutor, T. Markus Funk, has illustrated the substandard qualifications of many of the ICC judges: "What will – or at least should – be surprising to the uninitiated is that there is no requirement that ICC judges have any experience as a domestic judge. Indeed, there in fact is no general requirement that ICC judges have any practical in-court experience, or, for that matter, even have attended law school or obtained a law degree."[530] Funk finds the make-up of the ICC's judges a surprising one:

> [T]he judges of the ICC are split into an unexpected mix of experienced jurists, as well as individuals with no real criminal justice background, no trial experience, no judicial records, and indeed, in at least one case, no law degree or legal training. The somewhat surprising decision to on occasion transfer judicial laymen, with backgrounds in diplomacy, at NGOs, or in the academy, into practicing judges in a criminal court of the ICC's stature…is a difficult one to defend.[531]

He is clear that professional competence as a lawyer is not the main criteria for selection as an ICC judge: "The unwritten reality of the ICC…has been that judicial candidates in the end typically obtain their positions after surviving a gauntlet of negotiations, lobbying, and old-fashioned 'horse-trading'", something which "contributes little to ensuring that the judges are the 'best and brightest' of their profession".[532] Funk also makes the obvious point that "the ICC is arguably the worse place for judicial novices for the first time...to make their maiden appearances in a criminal court. Yet, this is precisely what has been done at the ICC".[533]

Hans Corell, the former UN Under-Secretary-General for Legal Affairs and the legal counsel of the UN from 1994–2004, who also served as the Representative of the UN Secretary-General at the Rome Conference for the establishment of the ICC, has shown similar reservations about ICC judges: "To elect persons to the ICC who have no courtroom experience is in my view simply not appropriate no matter what other qualifications these candidates may have... . Hearing complex criminal cases is an extremely demanding charge that requires a thorough knowledge of criminal court administration and the methodology."[534]

Even diehard supporters of the court, such as William Pace from the Coalition for the International Criminal Court, have acknowledged the presence of unqualified and unsuitable ICC judges. In 2005, he admitted: "We identified a number of very under-qualified candidates, including [some] that had not even read the Rome Statute." He said that greater public scrutiny was the best way forward for the new international court and the CICC establishing "something like an elections committee so that any improper nomination process is corrected before the [ballot is] allowed".[535] Five years later he was saying the same thing: "There are a number of judges who really shouldn't be there... . To elect a person to the ICC who doesn't even have a law degree for example, is a most unfortunate precedent to have set. We were facing the prospect of a defence lawyer appealing a case on the basis that the judge was not qualified."[536] In the meantime unqualified, unsuitable and incompetent appointees with no business being on the bench of any court, let alone one said to be as important as the ICC, continue to wreak havoc and prolong war in Africa. Some of these judges would be unable to hold their own in a traffic court.

There is ample evidence that the basic quality of ICC judges in many instances has been sub-standard. Philippe Sands, one of the authors of *Selecting International Judges*, has stated that the poor quality of judges "is deeply troubling for a court which is dealing with some of the most serious criminal cases and the deprivation of liberty for human beings".[537] Sands has said that "[t]he horse-trading and politicking is endemic". His book found that "vote-trading, campaigning, and regional politicking invariably play a great part in candidates' chance of being elected than considerations of individual merit".[538] William Schabas said that "[i]t is a very ugly process... . States campaign ferociously for their candidates. They can be quite aggressive and very competitive. There is a lot of horse-trading going on."[539]

The International Judge, a 2007 study of those people holding international judicial appointments, has confirmed that "International courts have often been criticized for the overly political nature of their judicial elections, and the ICC is no exception". The study also noted one of the other dimensions of that political interference: "The ICC is the first inter-national judicial institution that has striven for a gender balance on the bench."[540] The South African ICC judge Navanethem Pillay has also confirmed the huge influence NGOs have over who is elected as an ICC judge. She used the example of electing judges just because they are women: "Had it not been for the NGO movement in civil society *having such an influence over the structure of the ICC election process*, I don't think we would have gotten the seven women on our bench."[541] (Emphasis added.)

This sort of gender-based political interference in the selection of judges is as corrupting to the professionalism of the bench as vote-trading. Several of the people made judges for no other reason than they were female have clearly demonstrated legal shortcomings. Judge Elisabeth Odio Benito is a case in hand. Elected as a result of pressure by women's groups, Benito is said by the ICC to have "comprehensive practical and academic experience in the field of human rights and international humanitarian law". She was Second Vice-President of Costa Rica from 1998 to 2002, and served as Minister of Justice of Costa Rica from 1978 to 1982, and from 1990 to 1993.[542] She is the only person elected as an ICC judge without the support of his or her own country: Costa Rica refused to nominate her. Panama's President Mireya Moscoso, a prominent gender activist, nominated her instead. The 2007 study notes that "various women's rights NGOs mobilized to campaign in her support".[543] Benito clearly has a lot of political experience but she obviously does not have enough basic experience in a courtroom. The IBA cited Benito in its concerns over irregularities in basic legal procedures. The IBA has had to caution judges against questioning witnesses in a manner that may be unfair to the defendant: "[W]e urge that great care be taken in particular by the prosecution, the other participants and the judges to avoid leading questions." The IBA pointed to one particular exchange between Judge Benito and a witness. Judge Benito: "You said that the orders given by the commanders entailed taking girls by force that is, 'raping them and taking them to the place where we lived'. Could you explain to us a little bit more about that? That means that you took these women and girls and brought them to your camp? Could you explain a little bit?" A: "We would take them from their parents and take them to a place, a place that we would find where we could do those things, and after that we would free them." Judge Elisabeth Odio Benito: "Or perhaps *you also killed them*?" (Emphasis added.) A: "No, we didn't kill them."[544] Behaviour such as leading the witness, on the part of a judge, would be unthinkable in a British or American court.

This was the same Judge Benito who when she was a judge at the ICTY, described how upon reading some media reports alleging rape, had "urged" the prosecutor to amend an indictment to include rape charges. She was insistent that if it was mentioned by CNN the prosecution should act upon them.[545] A clearer case of media-driven "justice" at the expense of legal professionalism is difficult to imagine.

The ICC's two Japanese women judges provide further examples of the shortcomings of electing judges by way of gender-based vote-trading. A 2007 study of international judges found that of the 215 judges sitting in more than a dozen courts and tribunals in January 2006, only one did not have a degree in law or international relations. That person was a member of the World Trade Organization Appellate Body.[546] Within two years, the ICC added two more to that total. A Japanese judge, Fumiko Saiga, was appointed as an ICC judge in late 2007 after Japan became the biggest single contributor to the ICC, paying twenty per cent of the ICC budget. Between 2003 and 2007, Saiga had served as the Japanese Ambassador to Norway and Iceland. She also had considerable experience in Japan's relations with the UN. She had no legal training or judicial experience, but did have a degree in English studies. Joshua Rozenberg asked the question: "[S]urely someone who is going to have to give binding legal rulings in court without the assistance of a legal adviser needs some experience as a lawyer?"[547] Iain Bonomy, a real judge, has observed: "It is not easy to identify what particular expertise it is thought that former diplomats bring to the judicial process in international criminal law."[548]

Amazingly, Saiga's lack of legal training or experience did not in any way hinder her election: she received the highest number of votes, winning her appointment in the first round of what can only be described as carefully orchestrated vote-trading. Saiga died in April 2009. The Japanese government nominated Kuniko Ozaki as her replacement. Ozaki similarly has no experience as a judge or as a practising lawyer: she has an arts degree. Ozaki is a career civil servant. Her ICC CV described her as a "highly competent career diplomat". Up to her appointment as a full judge at the ICC, she served from 2006 to 2009 as Director of the Division for Treaty Affairs, United Nations Office on Drugs and Crime. She had also served as an ambassador to the UN Convention on Biological Diversity. She has taught at the National Graduate Institute for Policy Studies in Japan. Most of her career has been at the Japanese Ministry of Foreign Affairs. She has described her professional life as that of "a diplomat, a UN official or an academic".[549] There is no mention of law whatsoever. Ozaki's total lack of courtroom experience, either as a judge or lawyer, did not prevent her being appointed within two years as the presiding judge in Trial Chamber V, trying four Kenyan nationals for crimes against humanity in a very complex case.

Rozenberg reported that the reason for the lack of experienced Japanese judges is that "no Japanese judge is likely to speak English to the level required to operate in The Hague. The only people who can do the job are likely to be career diplomats." With regard to Japan's seat on the court, one of *Selecting International Judges*' judicial interviewees observed: "Japan is like Zsa Zsa Gabor – if Zsa Zsa wants something, Zsa Zsa gets it. So they, with their money and their efficiency, they go and they get it. They shouldn't have a permanent judge on the court."[550] Journalists have also pointed directly to the financial issue: "But there could be another factor as to why ICC rules allow non-lawyer Japanese diplomats such as Ozaki and Saiga tickets on this multilateral gravy train: Japan will provide about 20 per cent of the ICC budget this year. Perhaps if a DRC, or a Qatar, or an Israel provided a fifth of the court's budget, they too could have their non-lawyers appointed to transact justice on our behalf."[551] One academic analyst has observed that the election and re-election of candidates from countries such as Japan, based on the state's size or economic importance, puts political influence above merit, flying in the face of Article 2.[552]

The election of Miriam Defensor-Santiago of the Philippines as an ICC judge in December 2011 is a perfect example of how opportunistic vote trading and gender-based political interference by NGOs result in the election of lacklustre candidates. An added twist in her case is that after her election she has sought to put her domestic political career as a senator before her appointment as an ICC judge. The Philippines was rewarded with the judgeship because it had just joined the court from a region that the EU and

ICC bureaucrats had been avidly courting. On 23 August 2011 the Philippines' senate finalised the Philippines' membership of the ICC. On 26 August 2011 the government announced that it would nominate a politician, former minister and two-time failed presidential candidate, Miriam Defensor-Santiago, as an ICC judge at the December 2011 session of the ASP. On 1 November 2011 the Philippines became the 117th state party to the ICC. The Europeans rewarded the Philippines and their bloc vote ensured that Miriam Defensor-Santiago was duly elected in December 2011.[553] Miriam Defensor-Santiago has minimal experience as a lawyer. She served in the Philippines' Senate from 1995 to 2001. She was re-elected to the Senate in 2004, serving as the Chairperson of the Senate Subcommittee on the ICC. She has lots of experience in losing elections but virtually none as a courtroom lawyer.

Senator Santiago's commitment to her position at the ICC was lukewarm from the start. In January 2012, Santiago said she would prioritise her work as a senator in Supreme Court Chief Justice Renato Corona's impeachment trial.[554] She was absent during the March 2012 oath-taking of new ICC judges, citing medical reasons. On 1 March 2010, her office issued a statement saying she had to skip the oath-taking because of her high blood pressure and a condition known as "lazy bone marrow".[555] This was a very convenient circumstance. Santiago subsequently admitted, "In hindsight, it was fortuitous that I did not take my oath as judge, because it could have disqualified me from remaining as Senator."[556] The reality is that Santiago avoided the oath-taking in order to be present as a senator at Corona's ongoing impeachment trial. On the day of the oath-taking Santiago's press spokeswoman, having forgotten the medical excuse given to the court, told a Philippine journalist: "As much as possible she would want to see it (the Corona trial) through."[557]

Santiago later went on to reveal that she had written to the President of the ICC to request that she be the last of the six newly elected judges to take her post to allow her more time to fulfil her responsibilities as a senator to avoid disappointing those who elected her as senator for a six-year term.

In February 2013, Santiago was accused of illegally using senate funds, for among other things to put up a cock-fighting arena. One of her colleagues in the Philippines senate, Senator Lacson, has called Santiago a "crusading crook".[558] Santiago's prejudiced attitude towards homosexuality seems to have escaped those Western human rights activists that applauded her election. In an exchange with a male colleague in the senate, she warned him: "Be ready. I have parliamentary immunity. I'll expose all your sins. And it will include your sexuality."[559]

In August 2013, more than a year on from her having deliberately missed her oath-taking ceremony, Santiago produced further excuses for not having taken up her ICC seat, citing additional medical issues such as acute chronic fatigue, complicated by "heart palpitations" that produce shortness of breath. She stated that she had been taking "megadoses" of vitamin D to fight tiredness.[560] Senator Santiago was however still able to attend senate meetings including, for example, presiding over the public hearing of the Commission on Appointments Committee on Foreign Affairs on 4 September 2013.

A January 2012 editorial in the Philippines media provides an insight into how Santiago was seen in her own country:

> The Filipino people have just about had enough of Miriam Defensor-Santiago. She is loud, arrogant, and intolerant of anyone but herself.... Her arrogant and bullying...demeanor has turned her into a one-woman freak show that will ultimately be her undoing. She leaves in March of this year for a nine-year stint as a judge at the International Criminal Court (ICC). Let's keep our fingers crossed and hope she does not make herself too much of an embarrassment for the country.[561]

In an unprecedented move an online campaign was launched by Filipino citizens in March 2012 urging the rejection and removal of Senator Santiago as an ICC judge before she had even started her tenure. The petition cited her mental instability:

> We submit that a person who is emotionally or psychologically unstable, prone to fits of uncontrollable rage, lacking in patience and empathy, ruthless with the feelings of fellow human beings, bereft of civility and uncaring about decorum does not deserve a place in your honorable court.... We further submit that an individual who has admitted to having publicly lied and who has demonstrated partiality, prejudice, lack of principles and questionable integrity as a public official does not deserve to be a judge, much less a judge of the International Criminal Court.[562]

Amnesty International has been very blunt with regard to the quality of ICC judges. Amnesty has called for "all states parties to...identify the most highly qualified candidates from their countries to be put forward to the election of judges". In 2009, however, Amnesty publicly stated that it "is once again concerned that states parties are failing to meet their responsibility to ensure the nomination of highly qualified candidates". Amnesty noted in October 2009 that with regard to the election of two replacement judges at the eighth session of the ASP only 5 of the 110 states parties had nominated candidates, and that the deadline for nominations had had to be extended three times because Asian and Eastern European states parties failed to meet their regional minimum nomination requirements. No candidates had been nominated by African, Eastern European and Western European and other governments. Amnesty observed that "the small number of nominations not only limits the opportunity to identify the highest qualified candidates from the 110 states parties, but it may also have an impact on the overall expertise and geographical balance of the 18 Court judges". It is also the hallmark of "vote trading". What was even more disturbing is that Amnesty International had to admit that with regard to the election facing the ninth session of the ASP, "only one of the five nominated judges has established competence in criminal law and procedure, and the necessary experience, whether as a judge, prosecutor, advocate or in other similar capacity, in criminal proceedings" as opposed to experience in international law.[563]

Human Rights Watch has also repeatedly voiced concern at the quality of judges being appointed to the ICC. In its November 2009 memorandum to the ICC ASP, Human Rights Watch returned again to this theme: "[W]e have advocated in previous judicial elections [that] states parties should resist the practice of 'vote-trading'...vote-trading over ICC positions could lead to the election of poorly qualified judges, and hence to a bench that will not be the most skilled and representative. Human Rights Watch urges states parties to put aside narrow interests and vote only for the most highly qualified judges." This was all the more important, Human Rights Watch stated, because of "the growing visibility of the work of the pre-trial, trial, and appeals divisions". That is to say it would be increasingly difficult to hide how incompetent some of the judges were. The organisation once again strongly urged the states parties to "[e]lect only the most highly qualified judges to the ICC bench".[564]

Selecting International Judges reported that in some State Parties in the ICC candidate nomination process there could "barely be said to amount to a 'procedure' at all".[565] The study noted that "in most states in the study, the nomination decision was made by just one or two government officials with no broader consultation. This is surprising given the high hopes placed on the ICC, and its political significance." In one Western Europe and Other States group state, the study reported that the ICC nomination process was "conducted entirely by the Ministry of Foreign Affairs", without any input from the Ministry of Justice.[566] This was not atypical.

One of *Selecting International Judges*' interviewees noted with regard to one state that "[f]or the ICC nomination, the selection pool consisted of one person who was a diplomat, because national judges did not have sufficient language skills".[567] *Selecting International Judges*' interviewees stated that "regional quotas per se are rather bad for quality".[568] This was echoed by another interviewee who pointed out: "Equitable geographical representation can be problematic, for example, if you expect a dictatorship to come up with an independent candidate."[569] The same issue raises itself given that nominations made by State Parties also have to comply with Article 36(4)(a)(i), which states that nominations should be in accordance with the "procedure for nominations to the highest judicial offices of that state". The procedure for nomination to the highest judicial office in the UK may well be very different from the procedures for nomination in some of the ICC state members identified with questionable politics. And in any instance, as pointed out in *Selecting International Judges*, "[i]n practice, states vary widely in their criteria for membership of their highest courts, and some do not require any legal background".[570]

Selecting International Judges also found that judicial nominations were being used as "political tools: a state may wish to reward an individual or to banish an individual". The study reported that "in one instance it was said that an ICC candidate was nominated 'as a way to get him out of the country'".[571] The study also revealed that the process of "horse-trading" to secure votes for judicial nominations is not limited to guarantees of reciprocal vote-trading or agreeing to vote for each other's candidates in elections to international bodies. While "some states may suggest the possibility of support for international development aid or projects in exchange for votes...one interviewee...told us that cars were promised to those who voted for a particular candidate in an ICC election."[572]

The Rome Statute outlines several criteria to guide ICC States Parties in selecting judges. Article 36(3) provides that "judges shall be chosen from among persons of high moral character, impartiality and integrity who possess the qualifications required in their respective States for appointment to the highest judicial offices". "List A" candidates for election as an ICC judge must have established competence either in criminal law and procedure, and "List B" candidates established competence in relevant areas of international law. In addition, Article 36(8) mandates states parties to take into account the requirements such as gender, geography, and type of legal system represented, as well as the need to select judges with specific legal expertise on issues including violence against women and children.

In November 2011 Human Rights Watch once again stated "[a]s we have advocated in previous judicial elections, states parties…should resist the practice of 'vote-trading,' where states agree to support one another's candidates with minimal regard to the individual's qualifications".[573] The ASP was set to elect six new judges – one-third of the entire bench – and the next ICC prosecutor. With regard to these elections Human Rights Watch once again appealed for the ASP to "[p]ut aside narrow interests and vote only for the most highly qualified candidates".[574]

The ASP was clearly very sensitive to the claims about the quality of the judges being elected by the practice of vote-trading. In 2010, the ASP established a search committee to help in the selection of ICC judges. The ASP Search Committee was made up of the following individuals from each of the five UN regional groups: Zeid Ra'ad Zeid Al-Hussein, Jordanian Ambassador to the UN(Asian Group and Coordinator); Baso Sangqu, Permanent Representative of the Republic of South Africa to the UN (African Group); Miloš Koterec, Slovakian Ambassador to the UN (Eastern European Group); Joel Hernández García, legal adviser of the Ministry of Foreign Affairs of Mexico (Group of Latin American and Caribbean States); and Sir Daniel Bethlehem QC, former legal adviser to the Foreign and Commonwealth Office of the United Kingdom (Western European and Others Group).[575]

Human Rights Watch observed that the Search Committee "represents an effort to break with 'business as usual' to push merit to the forefront", creating "space for the search process to prioritize merit above other factors". It went on to note that: "By limiting the familiar practices of campaigning and 'vote trading' when it comes to high-level positions, use of the Search Committee may have encouraged candidates to come forward who might otherwise have been deterred by the perception such practices create that the breadth of support by states parties trumps merit."[576] The trouble was that this was in 2011, almost ten years after the court was established, and only after there had already been several elections of judges to nine-year terms.

The reality is that the vote-trading continues. In October 2011, for example, in the lead-up to the December 2011 election of six ICC judges, the *Inner City Press* revealed that "France offered to support a candidate found to be unqualified if his country would support the French candidate Bruno Cathala". The nineteen candidates for the six positions were reviewed by the Independent Panel on International Criminal Court Judicial Elections and several were found to be "unqualified". Nevertheless, when one of the "unqualified" candidates met with French officials to try to make his case, he told *Inner City Press* reporters "that he was surprised to be offered a deal: that if his country committed to vote for the French candidate, he could count on France's vote".[577] In November 2011, *The Economist* confirmed that ICC judges were still being elected through a process of "diplomatic back-scratching", "bargaining" and "canvassing".[578]

As the December 2011 elections ended, *Inner City Press* asked the outgoing ICC prosecutor Ocampo if the vote trading that had characterised the 2011 election was any way to choose ICC judges: "He said that as prosecutor he would not comment. The former and now current presidents of the ASP both condemned the practice. But a practitioner remains in the race, as it gets uglier with each round. It will continue."[579]

The Independent Panel on International Criminal Court Judicial Elections Panel was established by the Coalition for the International Criminal Court in December 2010, "in response to widespread criticism about the nomination procedures of governments by governments, non-governmental organisations, international justice officials and international judges".[580] The panel stated that it was aware of the expectation that "a number of the judges to be elected at the tenth session of the Assembly in December will not be called up for full-time service for some time after the start of their term".[581] They were still sitting as judges in other courts. The panel highlighted potential conflicts of interest with their future judicial duties, pointing to the text of Article 40 of the Rome Statute and Article 10 of the Code of Judicial Ethics, namely Rome Statute:

> Article 40: 1. The judges shall be independent in the performance of their functions. 2. Judges shall not engage in any activity which is likely to interfere with their judicial functions or to affect confidence in their independence. 3. Judges required to serve on a full-time basis at the seat of the Court shall not engage in any other occupation of a professional nature. 4. Any question regarding the application of paragraphs 2 and 3 shall be decided by an absolute majority of the judges. Where any such question concerns an individual judge, that judge shall not take part in the decision.

The ICC's Code of Judicial Ethics also states: "Article 10 Extra-judicial activity 1. Judges shall not engage in any extra-judicial activity that is incompatible with their judicial function or the efficient and timely functioning of the Court, or that may affect or may reasonably appear to affect their independence or impartiality. 2. Judges shall not exercise any political function." These concerns were glossed over by the ASP. And yet, a little over a year later, these concerns were borne out. Anthony T. Carmona, elected to a nine-year term as an ICC judge in December 2011, and assigned to the trial division, did not even bother to take up his seat before resigning as a judge after he was elected the President of Trinidad and Tobago.[582]

The ASP has been similarly dismissive of other concerns. The court's ability to handle its caseload has become a clear case for concern. Claude Jorda, a former ICTY judge and President of that tribunal, elected as an ICC judge in 2003 and sitting in Pre-Trial Chamber I, stated on the record in 2005 that "a trial should never last more than eighteen months total".[583] The Lubanga case lasted for six years. Geoffrey Robertson has stated that "the length of the proceedings – six years – for a crime that was relatively easy to prove, was wholly unsatisfactory".[584]

The court has also compromised itself administratively. In March 2009, following the swearing in of five new judges, ICC judges "elevated" two of their colleagues from Pre-Trial Chamber I to the Appeals Chamber. As Schabas pointed out: "There was a problem with this that was obvious to everyone: because the two judges had been sitting for several years on the Pre-Trial Chamber, they were 'contaminated' with respect to cases and situations that were already proceeding. In effect, they could only hear appeals concerning matters before the other Pre-Trial Chamber. It didn't seem to make much sense at a practical level, and we can only speculate as to why this was done." Both the Committee on Budget and Finance and the ASP asked the court to reconsider the decision. The ICC judges did so, and voted, by nine to seven, not to change their original decision. As Schabas noted: "The two judges who were named to the Appeals Chamber voted and, presumably, made up the majority. Without them, the vote would have been seven to seven." Schabas concluded: "This entire business is not a healthy development at the Court. It reflects a group of judges who appear themselves to be divided in a way that cannot contribute to the spirit of collegiality that the Court requires in these difficult times." In short, the judges were more focused on careerism, bureaucratic advancement and benefits than a functioning court.

Human Rights Watch was clearly appalled at this behaviour: "The decision of the ICC judges at their fifteenth plenary to organize themselves into divisions in a manner that will require frequent recusal of two judges from the Appeals Division did not reflect a priority on the welfare of the institution. States parties should also elect candidates who demonstrate an ethic of public service and commitment to the ICC's mandate and institutional development."[585] The *Opinio Juris* blog also expressed concern, noting "that two of the judges that ruled on Bashir's arrest warrant – Judge Kuenyehia and Judge Ušacka – are now in the Appeals Division. They will obviously have to recuse themselves from the Prosecution's appeal, which means that the [Sudan] genocide issue will be decided by a bare majority of the Division. That is unfortunate, because a decision by the full five-judge Appeals Chamber, whether yea or nea on genocide, would likely be seen as more fair than a three-judge decision, especially if the three judges don't reach a unanimous conclusion."[586]

Schabas has also pointed to the absolute waste of resources resulting from the bureaucratic incompetence of the court: "By the time the ICC completes its first full cycle of judicial elections, in early 2012, a full-time five-judge Appeals Chambers (together with professional assistants and secretarial help) will have occupied a floor of the Court's premises for nearly the entire period without ever engaging in the fundamental reason for its existence: appeal by an accused of a conviction."[587] Despite these criticisms, the then President of the ASP, Ambassador Wenaweser, rejected any tangible action about the judges' ability to manage their own cases: "We wrote to the judges and said it was a concern to us. But we have not concluded that we have to take it [the organisation of their workload] out of the hands of the judges."[588]

It is unlikely that things will change any time soon. The same concerns voiced in 2002 continued to be voiced ten years later. In 2011 the continuing issue of poorly qualified judges was again raised in the media.[589] Christian Wenaweser admitted there were concerns. He said that any independent oversight would be unwelcome: "Any situation where a group of representatives of States Parties would in any way comment on the quality of candidatures put forward by other States Parties is delicate, and must be approached with care." In the lead-up to the 2012 election of an ICC deputy prosecutor, Human Rights Watch still felt the need to "urge states parties to put merit first in their consideration of the nominees".[590]

Their competence already in doubt, the independence of the judges most recently elected in 2011 was also immediately called into question. When *Inner City Press* asked Judge Miriam Defensor-Santiago if she thought the ICC should indict at least some non-African leaders, to move away from the perception that only Africans are targeted by the court, Santiago replied: "I don't know…that remains to be answered by the major powers." As the *Inner City Press* noted, "this is a troubling answer".[591] According to a full ICC judge, therefore, critical legal decisions were to be made by "major powers" and not the court.

Chapter Eight

THE OFFICE OF THE PROSECUTOR

"There is every reason to believe that the careful and analytical lawyer that had been advertised was in so many ways anything but the truth...[he has been] an ineffective and seemingly megalomaniacal Prosecutor."

Professor Mark Gibney[592]

"Moreno Ocampo is a man who diminishes with proximity... . Lawyers and investigators who served in the OTP...say they believe the Court's reputation, and perhaps even its life, is at risk."

De Waal and Flint[593]

"There is strong argument that all current cases should be reviewed under a new Prosecutor."

Sir Geoffrey Nice QC[594]

The OTP, and those who hold that appointment, are central to the ICC. The ICC has itself stated that "the Prosecutor is a public face of the Court".[595] Human Rights Watch has observed: "[T]he public's first encounter with the institution will often come through the investigations of the prosecutor."[596] The UN Secretary-General Kofi Annan at the time of the establishment of the court rightly said that "the decisions and public statements of the prosecutor will do more than anything else to establish the reputation of the court".[597] As Benjamin Schiff put it: "Moreno Ocampo headed the engine of the Court."[598] It goes without saying that those elected to the position of Chief Prosecutor are expected to exemplify the highest professional, ethical and moral standards. Any shortcomings on their behalf reflect directly on the court itself. On the occasion of the swearing-in ceremony of the court's first judges in 2003, UN Secretary-General Kofi Annan stressed that the choice of the ICC's prosecutor was "crucial", adding:

We cannot exaggerate the importance of this position. The example of the International Tribunals for the former Yugoslavia and for Rwanda taught us that nothing carries more weight in affirming the Court's reputation – particularly in the first phases of its proceedings – than the decisions and public statements of the Prosecutor. That is why it is absolutely essential that we find a person with the highest moral standards to take on this heavy responsibility.[599]

It is no secret that the first Chief Prosecutor, Luis Moreno Ocampo, was a disastrous choice for the court, professionally, ethically and morally. It also has to be said that Ocampo's replacement, Fatou Bensouda, and the nature of her appointment, have also been controversial. Geoffrey Robertson, for example, noted of the court's second chief prosecutor:

> The search for his replacement lacked transparency and integrity: it was apparently decided – by whom it is not clear – that because most criticism of the Court was coming from African states, the successor should be an African, and preferably a woman. Without any proper advertising for candidates, it was simply decided that Fatou Bensouda, Ocampo's deputy, fitted the bill.[600]

While apologists for the ICC will doubtless attempt to identify the systemic failures within the court in general, and the OTP in particular, with Ocampo himself, the simple fact is that they are a reflection on the court itself and the ASP which appointed him and then allowed him to continue in office for nine years despite his track record of misconduct – professionally and personal – as well as prosecutorial irregularities that should have ended the court's first trial on the spot. Prosecutorial misconduct was also allowed to continue by incompetent ICC judges, possibly unaware of the reality of his inept behaviour because of their own inexperience in a real courtroom or institutional pressure.

The first chief prosecutor

Luis Moreno Ocampo was elected as the first chief prosecutor of the ICC on 21 April 2003. He was sworn in for a nine-year term on 16 June 2003. For all the claims made about the ICC's independence from political considerations, Ocampo's appointment was itself intensely political. Joshua Rozenberg states, for example, that Ocampo was appointed ICC Prosecutor because the EU-funded ICC did not want Africans to be prosecuted by a Western European. This is an interesting insight into the way in which the European states that dominate the ICC were thinking about their primary focus, Africa, even before the court was operational. Rozenberg also noted that Ocampo "has limited English and… no French" despite fluency in one of those two languages being mandatory.[601]

Ocampo is an Argentine lawyer who had been involved in the prosecution of Argentinean military officers in the 1980s. He resigned as a state prosecutor in 1992 and established a private law firm, Moreno-Ocampo & Wortman Jofre. He represented wealthy clients in disputes over family assets, filed shareholder suits and consulted on corporate accountability issues. He also defended several controversial figures, including celebrities such as Diego Maradona, and a priest accused of sexually abusing minors. During the late 1990s, Ocampo was the Judge Judy of Argentine television, starring in a reality television programme, *Fórum, la corte del pueblo*, in which he arbitrated private disputes. As Rozenberg reminds us, "Before taking the job in 2003, Moreno Ocampo was best known in his native Argentina as a 'celebrity' lawyer."[602] *The Wall Street Journal* also described Ocampo as "a legal celebrity", and cited him as promising that "[the ICC] will be a sexy court".[603]

Alex de Waal and British journalist Julie Flint have noted that Ocampo has indeed "focused on creating a 'sexy court' that for many critics is based on public opinion rather than justice for victims".[604] There is little doubt that Ocampo has embraced his celebrity status. He has sought publicity and attention at the expense of his legal responsibilities and justice for ICC prisoners. In January 2009, for example, on the very opening day of the first case the ICC had brought (at the expense of half a billion euros), he made his opening speech and then left the courtroom immediately without listening to the opening speech of the defence. He did so in order to travel to the Davos World Economic Forum in Switzerland to rub shoulders with the world's glitterati, including Bill Clinton, Angelina Jolie, Michael Douglas, Bono and Sir Richard Branson. He may also have found time to fit in some skiing. His commitment to his day job has been questioned. Even while Ocampo was in court on the opening day observers said the prosecutor appeared uninterested in his case, apparently texting on his mobile while Lubanga's "not guilty" plea was made.[605]

In 2008 *Inner City Press* noted that "Ocampo…drapes himself in the role of the last of the just, an objective man, a slave to justice."[606] Ocampo, however, has quite simply been a disaster in office, a disaster for international law, a disaster for the Europeans who have invested so much time and capital in the court, and, more poignantly, a disaster for Africa. Even Human Rights Watch has had to admit that the prosecutor's approach has had significant negative implications.[607] His legal, ethical and moral shortcomings have manifested themselves. He has come in for considerable, sustained and detailed criticism.[608] The focus on Ocampo should not have been unexpected. The integrity and competence of the ICC prosecutor is clearly outlined in the Rome Statute for the ICC. Article 42.3 states, for example: "The Prosecutor and the Deputy Prosecutors shall be persons of high moral character, be highly competent in and have extensive practical experience in the prosecution or trial of criminal cases." Legal commentators have also made the point that:

> The personal qualifications of the Prosecutor and the Deputy Prosecutors must not allow doubts as to their professional competence, integrity and independence. The credibility of the very idea of an independent ICC Prosecutor depends on the personal qualifications and qualities of the Prosecutor.[609]

Luis Moreno Ocampo proved himself to be an arrogant, legally incompetent bully, lacking in integrity and eager to please both Europeans and North Americans at the expense of those he saw as being weak, Africans.

The arrogance and prejudice of the Prosecutor

The chief prosecutor's arrogance was apparent from the start. *The Wall Street Journal* reported that in 2005 Ocampo stated that the ICC aimed to bring a different case each year, and to televise them across the globe from the ICC's high-tech courtroom: "The goal: swift justice that is comprehensible to often-uneducated victim populations."[610] He was seemingly oblivious to the fact that the "victim populations" of which he talked do not have access to CNN: his real target audience was the Western glitterati and legal *nomenklatura*. And when the ICC did broadcast the first day of the Lubanga trial it only screened the prosecution's opening statement and did not carry that of the defence. Even Ocampo's terminology points to a mindset of wishing to present "white man's justice" projected by "white man's magic" to an undeveloped and underdeveloped world that should be grateful. The prosecutor's grip on reality has also been shown as weak by his statement in January 2005 that he would have the LRA leadership in court within six months, and that he would start a trial in the DRC shortly afterwards.[611] The LRA leadership remained at large in Uganda and in the region, and his first ever trial, of an alleged Congolese militia commander, eventually began in 2009.

Both Ocampo's professional competence and personal integrity have also come into sharp focus. Both have been found wanting. Conor Foley, an international humanitarian aid worker and author of *The Thin Blue Line: How Humanitarianism Went to War*, had worked in northern Uganda and has written about the mistakes the ICC made in that country: "One of the most consistent criticisms I heard was about the manner in which Moreno Ocampo conducted himself. Terms such as arrogant, imperious, and out of touch were among the politer ones used."[612] Any assessment of the ICC and its prosecutions is made simple by the fact that Ocampo has micro-managed the investigations and prosecutorial strategy. One of Ocampo's European colleagues who worked with him for two years has noted that "he meddles with every decision and that causes delays".[613]

The chief prosecutor would come to be notorious for making inaccurate or inappropriate claims about the political and legal situations within which the court became involved. There was an early indication that Ocampo had a tendency for less than accurate assertions. As early as 2003, US government officials reported a discussion with ICC Registrar Bruno Cathala: "Cathala told an embassy legal officer that he has strongly advised Ocampo to speak very carefully in public and to be extraordinarily sensitive to the way even strictly accurate statements may be perceived. In the face of the media 'pushing and pushing' and under the watchful eyes of governments, the 'first wrong word,' Cathala said, could easily spell disaster for the court."[614] It was advice Ocampo clearly ignored.

In the ICC selection process for initiating court action, the chief prosecutor outlined the four principles that guided his office in the selection process: independence, impartiality, objectivity, and non-discrimination.⁶¹⁵ The prosecutor's stated policy in assessing the degree of participation in human rights abuses is to target "those bearing the greatest responsibility" for alleged crimes.⁶¹⁶

For all his puff and rhetoric, Ocampo was overtly discriminatory and far from objective in his selection process. He displayed little independence and no impartiality. As outlined in Chapter One, far from targeting "those bearing the greatest responsibility" for alleged crimes, that is to say the presidents and other senior military and political officials in Uganda and the DRC – as documented by the ICJ, Human Rights Watch, Amnesty International, etc., the court has focused on the little people, middle-ranking militia commanders who, in the case of the Congo, were themselves vehicles for those presidents. In the case of Uganda, Ocampo ignored proven involvement by the government at the highest level in grievous human rights abuses and the displacement of over a million civilians in northern Uganda into government-controlled camps (which in Uganda he ignored while he cited similar displacement in Sudan as evidence of genocide). He has turned a similarly blind eye to government complicity in abuses in the CAR and Ivory Coast. In addition, along with other international celebrity lawyers he was very reluctant to point any fingers at the USA or the UK on Iraq. He refused, for example, to initiate any investigation into the Iraq conflict claiming there were only an estimated four to twelve victims of wilful killing and a limited number of victims of inhuman treatment, totalling in all fewer than twenty persons, that would qualify for the court's attention during the Anglo-American invasion and occupation of Iraq.

Professor Rhona Smith has noted: "Initially focused on pursuing those highest up the command structure, Thomas Lubanga was an unusual first choice, selected by default rather than design, from an all-too-crowded global 'rogue's gallery'."⁶¹⁷ That Ocampo has responded to political pressure and calls from and non-governmental organisations to the detriment of law was also mentioned by Rhona Smith: "Indicting President al-Bashir responds partly to political and popular demands, rather than pure law (evidentiary issues abound)."⁶¹⁸

Even the ICC judges occasionally pulled Ocampo up on his attempts to avoid having to take action against governments with whom he had an understanding. In order to avoid having to refer to the Ugandan government's involvement in supporting militias in DRC allegedly involved in recruiting child soldiers, Ocampo tried to characterise the conflict as an internal rather than an international one, thus avoiding having to address the international, Ugandan, dimension. Responding to this attempted sleight of hand by Ocampo, Pre-Trial Chamber I changed the legal characterisation of the facts, replacing the prosecutor's charges under Article 8(2)(e)(vii) of the Rome Statute with crimes punishable under Article 8(2)(b)(xxvi). Although both articles make punishable the conscription, enlistment, and use of child soldiers, the charges brought by the prosecutor require their conscription and enlistment into armed forces or groups in the context of an armed conflict not of an international character. The charges substituted by the pre-trial chamber refer to conscription and enlistment into national armed forces in the context of an international armed conflict.⁶¹⁹ The pre-trial chamber denied the prosecutor leave to appeal its decision.⁶²⁰

Human Rights Watch has pointed to the prosecutor's professional failings: "Aspects of the policy of Luis Moreno-Ocampo, the first ICC prosecutor, tended to exacerbate rather than ameliorate accusations of bias and politicization in the court's work, for example, through charging strategies that too often appeared to favor one side or the other to a conflict."[621] It was not just the perception that Ocampo was exclusively focused on Africa that undermined his credibility and that of the court. Geoffrey Robertson had also pointed out that "[Ocampo] created a perception that the ICC is in favour of certain governments, and in the case of the Libyan rebels (whose uninvestigated war crimes include the murder of Gaddafi after he had surrendered), in favour of the side that had Europe's support".[622] Robertson also pointed out that "Ocampo had failed to investigate the DRC government for creating and arming Lubanga's militia, or to indict the Central African Republic generals whose forces have committed most of the war crimes."[623]

Even Schiff had to note that "[Ocampo] was criticized by some for seeking too political a role externally, preferring the bright lights of international exposure to the nitty-gritty of investigation and prosecution, and also for micromanaging his division internally, stifling initiative and orderly procedure".[624]

The fact that Ocampo had been playing political games while in office as the Chief Prosecutor was all too transparent. Professor Chandra Lekha Sriram outlined his double-standards:

> It appears that he willfully seeks to avoid, not politics, but rather an open acknowledgement of the political impact of his actions. His decision to announce investigations into crimes in northern Uganda alongside the President of Uganda, notwithstanding allegations of abuses by the country's army, may have heightened the perception of his politicization and apparently intentional ignorance of his political effects. In this, he is very much political and politicized, and his attempt to insist on his purely legal role is, not surprisingly, unconvincing, whether to international NGOs or his own legal staff.[625]

A record of incompetence and failure

When Schabas raised the differences in performance between the ad hoc tribunals and the ICC in person with the Chief Prosecutor, he noted that Ocampo was very defensive, claiming that the ICC had a more complex procedural system. Schabas did not buy this explanation: "The Lubanga trial…is a relatively minor matter, concerning one accusation of child soldier recruitment and a single defendant. The evidentiary phase of the proceedings took almost 30 months to complete. By that time, the accused had been in detention in The Hague for more than five years. Even if he is convicted, 'time served' will probably be an appropriate sentence."[626] He pointed out that the first trial at the Yugoslav Tribunal, involving multiple charges and multiple crimes, began on 7 May 1996 and the verdict was announced one year later. He also observed that the first Rwanda tribunal trial began on 9 January 1997 and ended twenty-one months later.[627]

Schabas also notes that "[t]he Prosecutor's dismissal of criticism about the Court's poor performance does not correspond to some of his own exceedingly optimistic forecasts".[628] As Schabas observed, one year after assuming office, the prosecutor outlined a budget that stated that "[i]n 2005, the Office plans to conduct one full trial, begin a second and carry out two new investigations".[629] The prosecutor anticipated that the first trial would be completed by August 2005.[630] No trials began, let alone completed, in 2005. The first trial would eventually begin in 2009. US government cables have documented further examples of Ocampo's poor analysis. In discussions with the US Ambassador to the UN in June 2009, for example, a cable reported that "Ocampo asserted that Bashir was quickly losing power".[631] Four years later President al-Bashir was still in power, and Ocampo was out of office.

In his *Report on Prosecutorial Strategy*, published in 2006, Ocampo outlined five strategic objectives for the then coming three years' work of the court. Firstly, the court would seek "to further improve the quality of the prosecution, aiming to complete two expeditious trials" by 2009. Secondly, the court would initiate between four and six "new investigations of those who bear the greatest responsibility in the Office's current or new situations". Thirdly, the court would seek "to gain the necessary forms of cooperation for all situations to allow for effective investigations and to mobilize and facilitate successful arrest operations". Fourthly, the court would improve its relations with victims. And fifthly, the court would establish "forms of cooperation with states and organizations to maximize the Office's contribution to the fight against impunity and the prevention of crimes".

It is very clear that the court and the OTP failed in all but one of these stated objectives, that being the opening of new investigations – by far the easiest thing to do. The reality is that the court's first trial only began in early 2009, and the court's second trial commenced in November of that year. As Schabas notes: "No reasonable observer would use the adjective 'expeditious' to describe its glacial pace."[632] He also observes that "[g]iven that holding trials is the core activity of the Court, these mistaken projections reflect an unrealistic assessment of the difficulties facing the institution".[633] The court has also conspicuously failed to secure cooperation in all of its "situations" to either investigate or arrest. The court's relationship with victims has been at best mediocre, with several groups of victims criticising its aloofness and decrying its role in destroying the peace process in Uganda. Schabas admitted that "[m]uch of the institutional energy of the Court in its first decade has been devoted to [victim representation and participation]". At the same time he noted that "it is not apparent that the right scheme for victim participation has been found.... . The continental procedural model of the *partie civile* on which victim participation was premised seems very remote from what we actually see in the Chambers of the ICC." He is also some cynical about how the court's resources have been spent with regard to victims: "One suspects that if the victims understood that many millions had been invested – mainly in professional salaries and international travel – in order to ensure the respect of their rights, they might ask if they could simply be given the money instead."⁶³⁴ And, far from fighting impunity, the court has itself entrenched impunity in several of the African countries within which it claims to operate. It has also not prevented crimes: its very involvement had dramatically increased both the scale and intensity of a range of crimes.

The court and its chief prosecutor continued to live in a world of make-believe. In 2010, for example, the Prosecutor made another set of promises. In its publication, *Prosecutorial Strategy 2009–12*, released in February 2010, the OTP stated that it would finish the three trials then in hand and begin "at least one new trial". The Prosecutor also stated that he was continuing with investigations in seven cases and that he intended to commence "up to four new investigations of cases".⁶³⁵ As Schabas reported in 2012, "[i]n fact, by early 2011 not even one trial was close to completion".⁶³⁶

The ICC Chief Prosecutor's judgment has been called into question on numerous occasions and by the full spectrum of observers, including his elders within the international justice system, his peers within the international justice system, his colleagues within the ICC, ICC staff members, international experts on Sudan who have known Darfur and other situations intimately for decades, humanitarian groups such as *Médecins Sans Frontières*, the biggest aid group in Darfur, by the AU, all the way through to the government of Sudan and the parties in opposition to that government, including the Sudanese Communist Party. Even doctrinal supporters of the ICC are critical of Ocampo. The Convenor of the Coalition for the International Criminal Court, William Pace, told *Inner City Press* that Ocampo could be an "egomaniac".⁶³⁷

Professor Chandra Lekha Sriram has also pointed to a range of other failings:

> Certainly, the mishandling of evidence in the Lubanga case suggests a failure of attention to legal detail in an attempt to complete a first prosecution, and rightly caused Human Rights Watch and others to raise concerns…the prosecutorial strategy – in terms of situations and individual cases, and in terms of timing of crucial steps and engagement with peace negotiations – illustrate an approach that is both highly political and strangely blind to its political impact.⁶³⁸

Chris Blattman has also confirmed the question marks about Ocampo: "The ICC's Ocampo has a reputation as a loose cannon and a publicity hound, and is said to have an eye on the Argentine presidency. This reputation accords with my impressions of the ICC's work in northern Uganda – a rash, risky, poorly informed and planned move that nearly backfired."⁶³⁹

A prime example of Ocampo's bumbling was evident in Ituri, in the east of the DRC, where his actions managed to enflame local ethnic tensions between the Hema and Lendu communities. Ocampo's attempts to "balance" his charge sheet (since when does "balance" equate with justice?) resulted in the ICC charging militia leaders from different ethnic communities. Because he chose to play a quick and safe hand with the Hema Lubanga, he charged him with the bare minimum, recruiting child soldiers – albeit he still managed to totally blunder with those charges and the resultant process. He then charged Lendu militiamen with a broader range of charges. The result has been very negative. As Marlies Glasius noted: "The subsequent warrants, including much wider charges, do not necessarily rectify the impression made by the first case. On the contrary, the fact that leaders of rival Ituri factions are accused on wider charges could further inflame ethnic tensions by allowing the interpretation that crimes perpetrated by Hema, historically the dominant ethnic grouping, are not as serious as crimes by other groups such as the Lendu."[640]

Ocampo's decision to charge President al-Bashir with genocide has been the focus of unprecedented criticism both of the ICC as an institution and of Ocampo in particular. Aside from the natural controversy about charging a serving head of state with genocide, much of the criticism has centred on the sheer weakness of the charge, the unthought-through implications for peace, and whether Ocampo's motive was based more on attracting publicity than it was on law.

The distinguished Italian jurist Antonio Cassese publicly criticised Ocampo's decision to request an arrest warrant against al-Bashir. He described Ocampo's request as puzzling for three reasons. First, if Ocampo intended to have al-Bashir arrested, he should have issued a sealed request to be made public only once al-Bashir travelled abroad. The request for a public warrant public would alert al-Bashir who could simply refrain from travelling abroad and thus avoid arrest. Just seven weeks before the July application, the Prosecutor secured the arrest of Jean-Pierre Bemba using a sealed warrant. Secondly, he could not understand why Ocampo inexplicably decided to indict only Sudan's president. And thirdly, he was critical of Ocampo's decision to accuse al-Bashir of the "crime of crimes" genocide, instead of filing charges what were more appropriate. Cassese pointed out "strict conditions must be met to prove genocide". He also believed that there was not enough evidence to infer genocidal intent as claimed by the prosecutor: "The arrest warrant...seems unlikely to produce the extra-judicial effects – the political and moral delegitimisation of the accused – that sometimes follow.... Instead, Moreno-Ocampo's request may have serious negative political repercussions."[641] He was also critical of Ocampo's classification of the three Darfur tribes in question.

Alex de Waal said that Ocampo's case was "so shoddy any reasonable judge would throw it out".[642] The charges have also been questioned by Andrew Cayley, Ocampo's former senior prosecuting counsel on Sudan: "[I]t is difficult to cry government-led genocide in one breath and then explain in the next why two million Darfuris have sought refuge around the principal army garrisons of their province."[643]

Dr. Christophe Fournier, President of the International Council of Médecins Sans Frontières, flatly contradicted Ocampo's hyperbole: "[C]ontrary to what the I.C.C. prosecutor stated to the U.N. Security Council in July 2008, the camps for displaced people in Darfur were not the ultimate instrument of 'genocide by attrition.' Despite the persistence of insecurity and localized episodes of great violence, international humanitarian aid has succeeded since 2005 in avoiding famine and lowering mortality and malnutrition rates to pre-war levels."[644]

Critics noted very basic mistakes being made by Ocampo. Sir Geoffrey Nice, in a submission to the ICC on behalf of the Sudan Workers Trade Unions Federation and the Sudan International Defence Group, raised a failure of judgment that went to heart of Ocampo's behaviour.⁶⁴⁵ He noted that the Chief Prosecutor "has been active in the political environment and at conferences around the world seeking to create a groundswell of public opinion adverse to Sudanese government in general and to President Bashir in particular. These actions are incompatible with the role of a Prosecutor acting fairly, impartially and recognising the presumption of innocence." He cited as an example of Ocampo's behaviour, his speech on 17 October 2008 to the Council of Foreign Relations in New York. At no stage in his address "did he pay even lip-service to the presumption of innocence" with regard to his Sudanese indictees, President al-Bashir, Ahmed Haroun and Ali Kushayb. On the contrary, Ocampo asserted as facts things that had been alleged in his applications but never tested before a court of law. Nice noted: "The only reason for travelling round the world addressing bodies in the way exemplified here (and he has made many addresses on similar lines) can have been to put pressure on the judges to accede to his application or to attract publicity for himself." He further observed that "in many or most domestic jurisdictions for a prosecutor to announce as conclusions facts that he wants to prove in the way done here would contravene various rights and be unacceptable for reasons of possible contempt of court or on grounds of privacy or defamation".

Nice stated that there may be:

> [G]ood grounds under Article 42 and Rule 34 to seek to disqualify the Prosecutor from participation in the Sudan cases by application to the Appeals Chamber pursuant to Article 42(8)(a) and Rule 103. Article 42(5) provides that the Prosecutor shall not "engage in any activity which is likely to interfere with his or her prosecutorial functions or to effect confidence in his or her independence". Article 42(7) states that the Prosecutor shall not 'participate in any matter in which their impartiality might reasonably be doubted on any ground'. Rule 34 provides that a ground for disqualification is: "Expression of opinion, through the communications media, in writing or in public actions that, objectively, could adversely affect the required impartiality of the person concerned."⁶⁴⁶

Ocampo's poor judgment continued to manifest itself. In an article in *The Guardian* newspaper on 15 July 2010, Ocampo called for international action to arrest Sudanese President Bashir:

> The genocide is not over. Bashir's forces continue to use different weapons to commit genocide: bullets, rape and hunger. For example, the court found that Bashir's forces have raped on a mass scale in Darfur. They raped thousands of women and used these rapes to degrade family and community members. Parents were forced to watch as their daughters were raped. The court also found that Bashir is deliberately inflicting on the Fur, Masalit and Zaghawa ethnic groups living conditions calculated to bring about their physical destruction.⁶⁴⁷

William Schabas pointed out that Ocampo's claims were "quite misleading". The court had "found" no such thing. They had ruled there was a possibility this may have happened. Schabas pointed to the April 2010 report on Darfur by the UN Secretary-General, which had preceded Ocampo's July 2010 article:

> 46. The humanitarian situation in the well-established camps for internally displaced persons remains stable. During the reporting period, food distributions carried out by the World Food Programme at some 300 points throughout Darfur regularly reached more than 95 per cent of the intended beneficiaries. Approximately 4.2 million vulnerable people continued to receive the direct food assistance of the Programme in this manner.
>
> 47. The continuous availability of a safe water supply was ensured for more than 1.2 million internally displaced persons through support for the operation and maintenance of more than 650 water systems, including the chlorination of the water supply. During the reporting period, a safe water supply was provided for 32,500 additional internally displaced persons and hosting communities through the construction of new water sources and was re-established for 26,000 through the rehabilitation of existing water sources.
>
> 48. Bilateral efforts are under way on the ground to provide assistance to internally displaced persons who are already returning voluntarily or who may decide to do so in the near future.[648]

Schabas asked the simple question: "Does this sound like ongoing genocide?"[649] He went on to point out: "The Court did not *find* 'that Bashir's forces have raped on a mass scale in Darfur'. The Court did not *find* 'that Bashir is deliberately inflicting on the Fur, Masalit and Zaghawa ethnic groups living conditions calculated to bring about their physical destruction'. The Court did not – and would not – do anything to suggest the issue of whether or not genocidal acts had taken place was actually decided. It merely issued an arrest warrant."[650] Ocampo's claims were described by another legal commentator as "not only inaccurate but…shocking in their inaccuracy". Writing on the *European Journal of International Law* blog, Oxford academic Dapo Akande stated:

> [W]hat is shocking is the Prosecutor's claim that the PTC found that Bashir's forces have committed the acts listed by the Prosecutor. This is just simply not true. No such finding was made. The decision by the Court was a decision to issue an arrest warrant. The standard applied under Art. 58 of the ICC Statute for such a decision is that there are "reasonable grounds to believe" that the crime has been committed. This is a low standard. It is lower than the "substantial grounds to believe" that the crime has been committed which is required for a confirmation of charges and lower than the standard of "beyond reasonable doubt" which is required for a conviction.[651]

The *European Journal of International Law* blog further noted:

> [S]aying that there are reasonable grounds to believe that the crime of genocide has been committed is very far from saying that the Court found that the crime had been committed. For the Court to have so found at this stage would have been a stunning reversal of the presumption of innocence and of the right of the accused to defend himself.[652]

The conclusion drawn is a disturbing one:

> Either the Prosecutor knows that his statements on this point in the Guardian pieces are inaccurate or he does not know. Either conclusion would be very troubling. If he does know his statements are inaccurate then he has willfully misrepresented what the Court said. If he doesn't know that his statements are inaccurate then this would suggest that he doesn't know what the relevant procedural standards are. This would be bad enough in general but doubly troubling given that it is this precise issue that has been the subject of the PTC and Appeals Chambers decision in the Bashir case.[653]

Schabas asked almost in despair: "Shouldn't the Prosecutor remind readers that the presumption of innocence continues to apply? Shouldn't he point out that this is only an arrest warrant, and that the issue as to whether the crimes took place and whether Bashir was responsible remains to be determined? Is this sort of statement really compatible with a Prosecutor who is supposed to show a measured neutrality and who should, according to article 54, 'investigate incriminating and exonerating circumstances equally'"?[654] Professor Kevin Jon Heller, a senior lecturer at Melbourne Law School, stated that the editorial demonstrated such poor judgment that the ASP should have considered removing the Prosecutor from office.[655]

The presumption of innocence until proven guilty, sometimes referred to by the Latin expression *Ei incumbit probatio qui dicit, non qui negat* (the burden of proof lies with who declares, not who denies), is the key, defining principle of all respected legal systems. Application of this principle is a legal right of the accused in a criminal trial, recognised in many nations. The Universal Declaration of Human Rights, Article 11, for example, states: "Everyone charged with a penal offence has the right to be presumed innocent until proved guilty according to law in a public trial at which they have had all the guarantees necessary for their defence." Ocampo cannot have been unaware of this central legal concept. It is enshrined in the ICC's own Statute. Article 66(1) of the Rome Statute, for example, states: "Everyone shall be presumed innocent until proved guilty before the Court in accordance with the applicable law." Article 66(2) states: "The onus is on the Prosecutor to prove the guilt of the accused." Article 66(3) states: "In order to convict the accused, the Court must be convinced of the guilt of the accused beyond reasonable doubt."

In December 2009, the chief prosecutor actually went beyond ignoring presumption of innocent. He made a case not just for denying the presumption of innocence but making it a war crime to *deny* the guilt of someone indicted but unconvicted by the court. The then Sudanese Ambassador to the UN denied that Sudanese President Omar al-Bashir was guilty of the crimes of which he had been accused by the court. The chief prosecutor warned that the "active denial" of an *alleged* crime could itself be an international crime: "My Office is considering the criminal responsibility of Sudanese officials who actively deny and dissimulate crimes." The New York-based *Inner City Press*, which reports on UN affairs, and is no friend of Sudan, wrote that "[t]o many this seems an abuse of power, as well as Kafka-esque. The prosecutor accuses a defendant of crimes, and then threatens to issue further indictments for any denial of the crime." The *Inner City Press* also asked the obvious question: "If controversial prosecutors like [former New York US District Attorney] Rudy Giuliani did this, civil libertarians and liberals would denounce it. What will be the reaction to Ocampo's statement?"[656] The answer was that there was a deafening silence.

Amazingly, in June 2012, Ocampo repeated this threat. He had called on the Security Council to take tougher action to detain President al-Bashir and other Sudanese officials indicted by the ICC. Sudan's new UN ambassador, Daff-Alla Elhag Ali Osman, said that Sudan rejected all of Ocampo's recommendations, accused the prosecutor of providing inaccurate information about the Darfur situation and stated that Ocampo's investigations were politically motivated: "There is no accountability system for the prosecutor which prompted him to deviate from credibility and legal professionalism." Ocampo was incensed and stated that his office would investigate the ambassador's comments. In a re-run of his 2009 threat, Ocampo stated that the ambassador's "activities denying the crimes in Darfur could be considered part of the crimes". Ocampo went on to state that the ICC will "investigate if Mr Daff-Alla Elhag Ali Osman's denial of the crimes committed could be considered a contribution to the perpetrators, acting with a common purpose". He warned that "appropriate measures" would be taken if investigators decided there was a case for a formal inquiry.[657] *Inner City Press* later asked Ocampo: "[W]ouldn't this theory chill even a defense lawyer?"[658] The newspaper asked: "Should a country under fire have no defense at all?"[659] Kevin Jon Heller referred to Ocampo's outburst as "idle and ridiculous". Heller went on to state: "I'm not even going to dignify Moreno-Ocampo's claims with a legal analysis. There is, quite simply, nothing to be gained by these kind of intemperate comments. They just make Moreno-Ocampo and – worse – the OTP seem childish and petty."[660]

The chief prosecutor's credibility went from worse to worse. The Sudan situation provided further examples. On 17 December 2010, for example, WikiLeaks published a US diplomatic cable giving details of a meeting he had had with the US Ambassador to the UN, Susan Rice, on 20 March 2009, at which the ICC prosecutor alleged that Sudanese President Omar al-Bashir had $9 billion in Lloyds Bank accounts in London.[661] Given that the British government owns a sixty-five per cent shareholding in Lloyds Banking Group in London, this was very easy to investigate. The seriousness of the claim resulted in written parliamentary questions asked in the British parliament about the veracity of the ICC's claim. In written parliamentary answers published in Hansard on 31 January and 28 February 2011, the British government clearly stated that the ICC claim was baseless. The British government has also cited internal enquiries by the Lloyds Banking Group and the Financial Services Authority, the British banking regulator.

On 31 January 2011, for example, the British government responded to questions asked in parliament about the steps "they have taken to investigate claims that President al-Bashir of Sudan has $9 billion in bank accounts held by the Lloyds Banking Group; and what were their conclusions", and what was "their assessment of the statement by Lloyds Banking Group that there is no evidence that President al-Bashir of Sudan has $9 billion in bank accounts held by the Lloyds Banking Group". The British government answer was that the "Lloyds Banking Group has conducted their own internal investigation into the claim that President al-Bashir holds accounts with the group, and is confident that the group does not hold any account for Mr al-Bashir or any individuals or entities associated with him. The Financial Services Authority has reviewed this report and has not raised any further concerns."

On 28 February 2011, in responding to a parliamentary question about "what steps they have taken to confirm that President al-Bashir or individuals or entities associated with him do not have $9 billion in bank accounts held by or known to the Lloyds Banking Group", the British government stated that "Lloyds Banking Group (LBG) has assured HM Treasury that it has conducted its own internal investigation into the claim that President al-Bashir holds accounts with the group and is confident that the group does not hold any account for Mr al-Bashir or any individuals or entities associated with him. The Financial Services Authority has reviewed LBG's internal investigation report and has not raised any further concerns."[662]

There was considerable backpedalling on this claim by Ocampo. When *Inner City Press* asked Ambassador Rice about the cable and what she and the US Mission to the UN had done after Moreno Ocampo had made the claim to her and her then deputy Alejandro Wolff, Rice denied any such meeting with Ocampo. She added: "I don't know if it was said to anyone else."[663] *Inner City Press* noted that "the cable may cause major problems for Ocampo with the ICC. This explains Ocampo's fast December 18 press release putting his spin on the cable. If the Court does not hold a hearing on it, credibility will again be at issue. What do the Court's supporters have to say?"[664] Perhaps needless to say, the court did not have a hearing on it, and Ocampo's wildly sensationalist claims were ignored for the lies that they were. When subsequently pressed on the issue again, Ocampo claimed that it was too early to discuss specifics, including where the secret accounts or the investments were held, other than to contradict himself, denying that the accounts were British banks: "We shall clarify this later."[665] Equally needless to say, the court never did clarify this extraordinary claim. Quite simply, this very serious allegation made by the chief prosecutor of the ICC was false. The professionalism, integrity and judgment of Luis Moreno Ocampo were once again shown to be deeply questionable.

There are four possible explanations for the chief prosecutor's actions regarding President al-Bashir. They may be NGO-driven (and given how ferociously "advocacy" groups have pushed the "genocide" claims this may well be the case). They may be media-driven, fuelled by the prosecutor's obvious obsession with his celebrity status and press attention. His behaviour may be explained in part by poor research and analysis and it may well be that Ocampo is just legally incompetent. In reality his deeply questionable stance, actions and claims about Sudan are probably a combination of all four.

Ocampo's pursuit of legally and morally flawed cases, in the face of the resultant negative impact on the peace processes and prospects for peace in those countries, is another example of the intransigence and arrogance of both the ICC and its prosecutor. Ocampo's actions and arrogance have probably led to the deaths of many hundreds if not thousands of Africans across the continent, and the displacement of hundreds of thousands of others.

The chief prosecutor's legal incompetence

The legal competence of the ICC's first chief prosecutor, and by default the OTP, was called into question by many of his colleagues – and indeed, many international lawyers senior to him – as well as experienced commentators. In 2012, Sir Geoffrey Nice summed up the questionable standards within the court: "It has to be asked whether the standards revealed in the court so far would be applied to Western country or would ever encourage US or UK to have their nationals tried before the international court on questionable evidence, with inadequate investigations."[666] He went on provide examples of the prosecution's lacklustre record, pointing to a "[l]ack of well-investigated cases is what stands out in Sudan, Kenya and Libya; and indeed in Lubanga – much OTP evidence was rejected and Judges had to convict on what they could piece together with what was left but unable to convict on sexual crimes of which there was evidence, but for which there were no charges!"[667] Alex de Waal and Julie Flint noted in 2009 that "three years into his tenure, many in the OTP (OTP) were questioning his ability to do the job. A further three years on, and the Court is in trouble – a trickle of resignations has turned into a hemorrhage, and cases under prosecution and investigation are at risk of going calamitously wrong."[668]

De Waal and Flint documented the growing concerns about Ocampo's legal competence. They state that "the first public signal of dissatisfaction with the Prosecutor" showed itself in July 2006, with regard to Darfur. The ICC Pre-Trial Chamber I, citing its responsibilities for protection under Articles 57(3)(c) and 68(1), as well as evidence preservation under Article 57(3)(c), invited the UN High Commissioner for Human Rights, Louise Arbour, and Antonio Cassese to review the ICC's work on Darfur and to make Rule 103 submissions on the protection of victims and on the preservation of evidence in Darfur.[669] De Waal and Flint reported that "[b]oth challenged Moreno Ocampo's performance". Human Rights Watch noted that "[b]oth Arbour and Cassese... made clear, public comments about the Darfur investigation, and their submissions disagreed on various grounds with the prosecutor's decision not to conduct his investigations within Darfur".[670] Cassese was described as having addressed "the Prosecutor like a teacher dressing down a particularly inept student". Cassese, naming Ocampo on thirty-six occasions, was critical of "every aspect of Moreno Ocampo's investigations but especially his failure to undertake even 'targeted and brief interviews' in Darfur".[671]

Ocampo had stated that he would not go to Darfur: "In the Darfur situation, the prosecutor had adopted a policy of conducting his investigation wholly outside of Darfur, citing security conditions that prohibited the establishment of a system of victim and witness protection there."[672] Cassese was very critical of Ocampo's claim that Darfur was too dangerous for investigations and that victims and witnesses could not be protected from the Sudan government. Cassese disagreed. He had himself led a comprehensive UN enquiry into Darfur in 2004 during which his commission had identified and interviewed many victims and witnesses in both Darfur and Khartoum. Arbour also thought that Ocampo had made questionable decisions. She agreed with Cassese, and called for "an increased visible presence of the ICC in Sudan". She also echoed Cassese's position on interviewing witnesses: "It is possible to conduct serious investigations of human rights during an armed conflict in general, and Darfur in particular, without putting victims at unreasonable risk."[673] Ocampo rejected these observations.[674]

With regard to Ocampo's indictment of President al-Bashir, Ocampo's decision to include genocide in the Bashir indictment, and pressing for genocide to be part of that indictment, was also seen as an error of judgment by distinguished supporters of the ICC such as William Schabas, who described it as:

> One more bad exercise of discretion by the prosecutor, one more bad call by Moreno Ocampo. He was chastened last year because of his decisions on gathering evidence that he could not then disclose to the defense and that led to a terrible and unnecessary delay in the Lubanga proceedings for more than six months. This was an error in judgment and I think seeking a warrant for genocide charges in Darfur was also an error in judgment.... The delay of six months in issuing the arrest warrant was due to the prosecutor insisting on trying to get a genocide charge, which was doomed to fail as shown by the Pre-Trial Chamber's ruling. These actions show a lack of good judgment on the prosecutor's part; it is a mistake, and not the first he's made.[675]

Schabas also reflected a more general criticism of Ocampo when he said in 2008 that it was incomprehensible that the chief prosecutor had not been able to build up a criminal case during the two years Lubanga had been in custody: "They are working incredibly slowly."[676] Human Rights Watch had also been disappointed in the prosecutor: "[W]e note that the prosecutor announced the opening of an investigation in Congo in July 2004; Lubanga was arrested in March 2006. After nearly two years of investigation, it is disappointing that there was not enough evidence to include more charges in the initial arrest warrant."[677] *The Economist* has stated that the Lubanga case "was mishandled from the start". It also wrote of "missteps" and "dithering" on the part of the court.[678]

Ocampo was actually very lucky that the ICC's first trial ever started. In an extraordinary development, in June 2008 the ICC Trial Chamber stayed Thomas Lubanga's trial because of the prosecutor's failure to disclose exculpatory evidence (or in normal language evidence that showed that the accused was innocent), to the defence. Ocampo had admitted to the court that he was holding 204 such items. He claimed he was entitled to rely on an exception to the normal disclosure rules in Article 54(3)(e) of the ICC, which provides that "[t]he Prosecutor may: agree not to disclose, at any stage of the proceedings, documents or information that the Prosecutor obtains on the condition of confidentiality and solely for the purpose of generating new evidence, unless the provider of the information consents". This was meant to be resorted to only in exceptional circumstances, not over 200 times. What made matters worse was that Ocampo sought to hide these 200-plus documents not only from the defence, but even from the judges themselves.

It was clear from the court's inception that Ocampo intended to dominate the court and its activities. One of the three organs of the court, the Registry has a range of duties, including the responsibility to record all transactions between the prosecution and the chambers. This includes the transmission of documents. In early 2006, as the Lubanga case started, the Registry and the OTP clashed with regard to evidence disclosure. The Registry believed that all evidence to be disclosed to the defence should go first to the Registry for recording and then to the defence. The prosecutor objected, clearly seeking to minimise the role of the Registry, proposing that the materials be handed directly to the defence with a record handed to the Registry. The OTP's subsequent involvement in serious irregularities in the disclosure of evidence would come to scar the reputation of the court and delay its proceedings in the Lubanga case for several months.

Three-quarters of the exculpatory items held back by the prosecutor came from the UN, which has a peacekeeping mission on the ground in the DRC. Of these pieces of evidence, the UN had actually agreed that fifty-three could be disclosed unconditionally and a further eighty-three with sections blanked out. The UN had no objection to the court, but not the defence, viewing the redacted sections and all remaining material. A further fifty or so documents had been supplied by six non-governmental organisations. The UN's agreement notwithstanding, Ocampo offered Lubanga and his lawyers access to just 3 of these 200 and more documents – and even those were redacted.

The judges correctly stated that Ocampo's behaviour "constitutes a wholesale and serious abuse" of an exception that allows prosecutors to receive evidence that is not, in itself, admissible – but that could to lead, in turn, to usable evidence.[679] The judges stated: "the trial process has been ruptured to such a degree that it is now impossible to piece together the constituent elements of a fair trial".[680] *Inner City Press* revealed that it had been told by sources inside the UN Secretariat and its Congo peacekeeping mission, MONUC, "that they never expected Ocampo to base his prosecution on the hearsay material they provided him, but he did. Now that material must be disclosed, and they are unhappy. Neither they nor the Western members of the permanent five, however, will criticise Ocampo in public. That would be politically incorrect."[681]

The trial chamber categorically rejected the prosecutor's attempt to justify his actions: "The prosecution has given Article 54(3)(e) a broad and incorrect interpretation: it has utilised the provision routinely, in inappropriate circumstances, instead of resorting to it exceptionally, when particular, restrictive circumstances apply." The judges stated further:

> [T]he prosecution's general approach has been to use Article 54(3)(e) to obtain a wide range of materials under the cloak of confidentiality, in order

to identify from those materials evidence to be used at trial (having obtained the information provider's consent). This is the exact opposite of the proper use of the provision, which is, exceptionally, to allow the prosecution to receive information or documents which are not for use at trial but which are instead intended to "lead" to new evidence. The prosecution's approach constitutes a wholesale and serious abuse, and a violation of an important provision which was intended to allow the prosecution to receive evidence confidentially, in very restrictive circumstances. The logic of the prosecution's position is that all of the evidence that it obtains from information-providers can be the subject of Article 54(3)(e) agreements.[682]

The trial chamber was especially critical of the prosecutor's refusal to disclose the confidential information to the bench. As the chamber pointed out, it – not the prosecutor – is ultimately responsible for ensuring that the defendant receives a fair trial. Even the President of the ICC ASP, Ambassador Christian Wenaweser, noted that the exculpatory evidence affair was being cited by some as evidence that Ocampo "is incompetent and doesn't know how to write an indictment".[683] The *Christian Science Monitor* noted that "the legal body's performance in the court of world opinion remains an issue. The ICC has a staff of 745 people that has worked six years – only to find its first case nearly thrown out in June."[684]

The trial chamber thus held that it had no other choice but to stay the proceedings. It stated that its judges:

> are enjoined to ensure that the accused receives a fair trial. If, at the outset, it is clear that the essential preconditions of a fair trial are missing and there is no sufficient indication that this will be resolved during the trial process, it is necessary – indeed, inevitable – that the proceedings should be stayed. It would be wholly wrong for a criminal court to begin, or to continue, a trial once it has become clear that the inevitable conclusion in the final judgment will be that the proceedings are vitiated because of unfairness which will not be rectified.

On 2 July 2008, the court ordered Lubanga's release, on the grounds that "a fair trial of the accused is impossible, and the entire justification for his detention has been removed".[685] Ocampo desperately asked the judges to lift the suspension of the trial, and also appealed against the trial chamber's decision, requesting that Lubanga did not go free. On 3 September 2008, Trial Chamber I rejected the prosecutor's plea to lift the stay, because the judges decided that the problem affecting Lubanga's rights to a fair trial still had not been remedied: the prosecutor had not secured guarantees from the organisations with confidentiality agreements that would allow the judges to see all the relevant documents, nor had he ensured that the judges would have access to the documents throughout the course of Lubanga's trial, to make sure Lubanga's rights were being protected. The partial fix that the prosecutor had proposed would still, according to the judges, "infringe fundamental aspects of the accused's right to a fair trial". Because there was an appeal in progress, Lubanga had to remain in jail while the appeal was being decided. On 21 October 2008, the appeals chamber decided to maintain the trial's suspension, but to keep Lubanga in jail.

Acknowledging his grave error, the prosecutor eventually agreed to make all the confidential information available to the court. On 18 November 2008, the trial chamber, despite having previously declared that a fair trial was "impossible", then reversed its decision and ordered that the trial could go ahead.[686] All in all a cripplingly embarrassing chain of events for any court and any prosecutor.

In the opinion of ICC Watch Director Marc Glendening, Ocampo's action could have been investigated by police in Britain and other Western societies: "By withholding key evidence from Thomas Lubanga's defence team, Luis Moreno-Ocampo is possibly guilty of attempting to pervert the course of justice. This outrageous behaviour, combined with the continued illegitimate detention of the defendant, demonstrates that the ICC is flouting basic liberal, civilised legal principles and is therefore incapable of providing a genuinely fair trial." He pointed out, however, that "[t]he officials of the ICC enjoy immunity from prosecution (Article 48, Rome Statute) and the court is not answerable to any democratic, higher authority. It has given itself the right to hold its proceedings in camera and to accept anonymous hearsay testimony."[687]

The ICC was also accused of institutionalising a further imbalance in the process. Lubanga's defence team have pointed out that there has been a huge discrepancy between the financial resources the ICC has made available to the prosecution compared to the defence. In the run-up to the trial, the prosecutor's office had twenty researchers working in the DRC seeking to discover evidence, whereas the defence could only afford one researcher.[688] As Phil Clark also pointed out, the Congolese authorities had themselves carried out extensive investigations beforehand regarding the Lubanga case prior to his arrest and while he was in Congolese custody before his transfer to The Hague, all of the results of which would have been made available to Ocampo.

The chief prosecutor's trial incompetence

The legal competence of the ICC's chief prosecutor in the preparations for the Lubanga case has clearly been questioned across the board. The ICC has made a series of legal blunders and abuses of due process. Given Ocampo's well documented obsession with micromanaging every detail of every case, he was clearly responsible for them. This pattern of errors continued into the trial phase.

In September 2011, Human Rights Watch stated that: "The ICC's investigations and prosecutions, however, have failed to demonstrate coherent and effective strategies for delivering justice…the absence of such strategies has undermined perceptions of the ICC's independence and impartiality."[689] In 2012, Human Rights Watch noted:

> There have been problematic past practices by the Office of the Prosecutor, Human Rights Watch said. For instance, in the Democratic Republic of

Congo (DRC), Uganda, and Central African Republic (CAR) situations, the absence of charges against government officials without a clear explanation has undermined perceptions of the court's independence, Human Rights Watch said. The perceived failure to pursue allegations against all sides in these countries has fed concerns that the prosecutor is yielding to pressure for "victor's justice," damaging the court's credibility.[690]

Other problematic practices are equally clear. It is extraordinary, for example, that despite the fact the court has for ten years focused in depth on the Great Lakes region of Africa, that its first two situations were Uganda and the DRC, that more than one third of its indictees are from those two countries, and that investigations and trials are ongoing, the ICC has only one dedicated research analyst specialising in the Great Lakes region. That is to say one employee out of 717 members of staff who has any real idea of what may or may not be going on in a region allegedly under the court's intense legal focus on life-and-death issues. This is despite recommendations in an official advisory document highlighting the importance of having such analysts. As Richard Wilson notes, an analytical capacity "facilitates an independent investigative culture".[691] Instead, the court has chosen to rely upon non-governmental organisations and various intermediaries, often with their own self-serving financial and political agendas, who have produced questionable analysis of the situations as well as a number of subsequently discredited witnesses.

This in large part explains the court's disastrous track record in several of its trials. The presiding judge at the Lubanga trial tried to end the trial on two separate occasions because of witness and evidentiary malpractice: on both occasions an appeals chamber, with more of a bureaucratic eye to the court's continuing existence than concerns about ensuring a fair trial, reversed Sir Adrian Fulford's decision. The case against Mathieu Ngudjolo Chui was dismissed because of almost identical legal malpractice to that seen in the Lubanga trial. The Ngudjolo trial judges were particularly critical of the prosecutor's inability to independently investigate its cases.

The chief prosecutor's administrative incompetence

Schiff has noted that "[t]he Strategic Plan demonstrated that the Court is largely fixated on organization building – the majority of its objectives were in its category of being a 'model of public administration'".[692] The reality is that the court has failed spectacularly both as a judicial entity and as a "model of public administration". Schabas has confirmed that the court's "employees exude frustration and even demoralization".[693]

There were administrative difficulties within the court virtually from the start. In March 2004, the ASP Committee on Budget and Finance reported "concern over a certain fragmentation between the three organs" of the court.[694] Ocampo was at the heart of these issues. Schiff pointed to the "fractious nature of the Court's structure".[695] He noted: "The Registry and OTP clashed on numerous occasions, leading to relations between the Chief Prosecutor and the Registrar that some observers described as poisonous."[696]

Schiff further noted that "[a]mong NGOs, it was reputedly the case that, for long periods of time, Moreno Ocampo and Cathala were not on speaking terms".[697] As early as 2004, ICC President Philippe Kirsch admitted that bureaucratic infighting among the Registry, chambers and the OTP was rampant.[698] The Registry has overall responsibility for recruitment, something that the OTP challenged. The two offices clashed until the ASP's Committee on Budget and Finance found in favour of the Registry, with the final decisions being made by the OTP. As Schiff has observed, "[o]ther matters have been more difficult to resolve".[699]

It is obvious that the working environment within the ICC, and particularly within the OTP, has been deeply questionable. The ICC itself addresses the working environment within which its staff is expected to work. The ICC's separate strategic plan for the OTP states that it "fully subscribes" to the goal of being a "model of public administration", and commits to "nurtur[ing] a working environment with minimal bureaucracy, where diversity and initiative are celebrated, and in which staff feel responsible and valued".[700] It appears that the total opposite was the case within Ocampo's office for the nine years he was the Chief Prosecutor.

Human Rights Watch was forced to address this issue in a secret letter to the ICC. It noted that they were aware that many experienced investigators have left the OTP since 2005, and that this was due "at least in part to the failure to develop a sufficiently supportive work environment".[701] This is a clear understatement. There have been several reports that many senior staff, especially in the chief prosecutor's office, have left in frustration at the ICC's actions, and especially those of Ocampo, actions often delaying the functioning of the court. Schabas has referred to former colleagues of Ocampo's who stated that "the delay is largely due to the prosecutor's authoritarian and unpredictable management style".

De Waal and Flint noted further:

> Moreno Ocampo's staff found it difficult to agree with their own Prosecutor, whose penchant for publicity and extravagant claims rather than fine detail was the polar opposite of their own work ethic.... As internal criticism grew louder, Moreno Ocampo listened less and took closer personal charge than ever. Many in the Investigations Division felt sidelined; in the Prosecutions Division, insufficiently consulted. A senior team member said the Prosecutor was 'the most complicated and difficult' manager he had ever worked for, emotionally volatile and obsessed with micromanaging. Some tried to raise concerns, privately deploring the absence of "a culture in which objectivity and a critical review of the evidence with all its shades drives the institution." A key member of the OTP left, saying privately that he was fearful of having to defend an indefensible position a few years down the line. A second followed, saying the Prosecutor ran the OTP like a medieval kingdom. A third told us the OTP was run "like a police state," with a "culture of fear" that was "very real," and "sapping." He quit too.

Richard Dicker warned that with many of the court's top staff having left in recent years, the ICC runs the risk of being unable to meet the rigorous demands of investigations.[702] Other legal commentators have also noted the administrative and investigative crisis within the ICC:

> Citing organizational and management problems under Moreno Ocampo, countless ICC Office of the Prosecutor staff have left the institution, and many blame Moreno Ocampo for its limited success. Additionally, some high level UN officials fear that if left to his own devices, Moreno Ocampo will continue to undermine the progress of the ICC, and more specifically, its promise of achieving international justice and accountability.[703]

Among those who left were Silvia Fernandez de Gurmendi, Ocampo's first chief-of-staff; his chief administrative officer Paulo Rajao; his spokesman Yves Sorokobi; senior legal adviser Morten Bergsmo; legal adviser Gilbert Bitti; DRC team leader Bernard Lavigne; Uganda team leader Martin Witteveen; Sudan senior trial lawyer Andrew Cayley; external relations adviser Darryl Robinson; chief analyst Paul Seils; trial lawyer Christine Chung, a former assistant US attorney from New York; and the head of the appeals section, Fabricio Guariglia. A particularly prominent example of the departure of ICC staff was that of the ICC's Deputy Chief Prosecutor and Investigations Chief, Serge Brammertz, in 2007. Belgium's former Federal Prosecutor, Brammertz had been at the court since 2003. He had been very critical of Ocampo's close identification with the Ugandan government, advising him to distance himself from Museveni. *The Wall Street Journal* reported that when Ocampo stated that he planned to announce the ICC's involvement in Uganda in a joint news conference with Museveni, several ICC staff members objected, citing the Ugandan government's reputed involvement in atrocities in eastern Congo. A court source revealed that Brammertz "was going bananas telling Luis not to do this, and he did it anyway".[704] This negatively impacted on the working relationship between Ocampo and his deputy. Brammertz resigned.[705]

Ocampo also chose to remove the chief trial attorney on the Lubanga trial, Ekkehard Withopf, an experienced trial lawyer, a month before the trial opened. Withopf had been a former judge at the Würzburg and Nuremberg regional courts and former public prosecutor in Karlsruhe. He had also worked at the ICTY. Withopf had spent five years preparing the Lubanga case. Sources at the court said that Withopf had also clashed with Ocampo on how the case should be handled.[706]

Allegations of sexual misconduct and breach of due process

In a somewhat unusual turn of events, in October 2006 the ICC chief prosecutor was accused of sexual misconduct, abusing his position and of breaching due process internally within the ICC itself. In October 2006, Christian Palme, a staff member in the prosecutor's office, citing Regulation 119.1 of the Regulations of the Court and Rule 23 of the Rules of Procedure and Evidence of the Court,[707] submitted an internal staff complaint alleging that on 28 March 2005 Ocampo had committed "the crime of rape, or sexual assault, or sexual coercion, or sexual abuse" against a female South African reporter "who had traveled to Cape Town for a pre-agreed interview with Moreno-Ocampo on this day". Palme alleged that "the crime was committed in a guest suite of Lord Charles Hotel in the town Somerset West in the Western Cape Province of South Africa", in the course of an official visit to South Africa by the prosecutor. Ocampo was said to have forced the journalist to have sex in return for her car keys.[708]

Palme stated that Ocampo had "committed serious misconduct, either in the course of his official duties, which is incompatible with official functions, and causes or is likely to cause serious harm to the proper administration of justice before the court or the proper internal functioning of the Court; or of a grave nature outside the course of his official duties that causes or is likely to cause serious harm to the standing of the Court". Palme stated in his complaint that he found it "deplorable that the Prosecutor of the International Criminal Court, one of the highest legal officials in the world, performs acts such as those of 28 March 2005, when he forced or coerced a woman into sexual intercourse, in a manner that would most likely have merited a prison term in most highly developed countries of the world. I am not willing to live with the knowledge of this crime being unreported and the perpetrator being able to continue working in high office."[709] Palme's 52-page complaint was supported by an audio recording of telephone conversations on 28 March 2005 between Ocampo's alleged victim and one of Palme's colleagues, Ocampo's press spokesman Yves Sorokobi.

A panel of three judges from the court reviewed Palme's complaint. It noted: "The alleged victim sounded distressed and denied that she had been forced to have sexual intercourse but did not deny that she had consented in order to regain possession of her keys. She indicated unambiguously that the prosecutor 'took [her] keys' and that she had consented to sexual intercourse 'to get out of [the situation]…'" The panel's ruling in December 2006 nevertheless dismissed Palme's complaint. Perhaps unsurprisingly, the ICC judges asked Palme "to obtain all copies of taped conversations between Ms. [...] and Mr Sorokobi and hand them to the President for destruction".

Despite the fact that the panel made no finding that the press officer had acted in bad faith or with malicious intent, in January 2007 Ocampo suspended Palme for three months and then in April 2007 the prosecutor summarily dismissed him for "serious misconduct". He claimed that Palme had "falsely alleged, with obvious malicious intent to damage the professional and personal reputation of the prosecutor, that…he 'committed the crime of rape'". Palme appealed to the ICC's internal disciplinary advisory board. The board ruled that Ocampo's decision regarding Palme was unsound and that it had not been established that Palme had acted "with obvious malicious intent". The appeals panel recommended that Palme should have his job back. Ocampo rejected the recommendation and confirmed Palme's dismissal.

Palme then filed a complaint with the Administrative Tribunal of the International Labour Organisation in Geneva for unfair dismissal. Having reviewed all the evidence, the tribunal set aside Palme's dismissal. It said the evidence available to Palme had come primarily from a colleague who knew the alleged victim and to whom she had apparently turned for support: "The colleague's evidence was secondary evidence but, depending on the circumstances, it may have been probative in criminal proceedings." The tribunal stated that there was nothing to suggest that this colleague was unreliable or untrustworthy: "In these circumstances, there is no basis for concluding that [Mr Palme] did not believe on reasonable grounds the truth of what he put in his internal complaint."

The tribunal noted that Palme's characterisation of "the Prosecutor's alleged conduct as 'rape, or sexual assault, or sexual coercion or sexual abuse'; which given differing national laws, is tolerably accurate." The tribunal rejected Ocampo's attempts to justify dismissing Palme, finding that "the material on which the International Criminal Court relies does not justify a finding that the complainant acted with malicious intent".

The tribunal also touched on Ocampo's own involvement in Palme's sacking: "It is a fundamental aspect of due process that a person should not take a decision in a matter in which he or she has a personal interest. The prosecutor had a direct personal interest in establishing that the internal complaint against him had been made falsely and maliciously." This "breach of due process" was a "serious infringement" of Palme's rights. This breach was "compounded by the prosecutor's action in maintaining his decision in the face of the internal memorandum from the presidency [of the court] indicating that there had been no finding of bad faith or malice and contrary to the recommendation of the disciplinary advisory board".

The ILO tribunal awarded Palme €25,000 in "moral damages", €5,000 costs, as well as compensatory damages approaching €160,000.[710] An ICC spokesman stated: "The International Criminal Court respects the decision of the tribunal and will implement it accordingly." These damages and costs were not paid by the prosecutor but by the ICC itself. Palme, who worked closely with Ocampo for two and a half years as his personal spokesman, concludes: "I am extremely disillusioned with Moreno-Ocampo. [He] is a mediocre lawyer and everything but the person of high moral standards that a prosecutor with the ICC should be, according to its statutes."[711]

It should be noted that the UN High Commissioner for Refugees, Ruud Lubbers, had resigned in February 2005 following allegations of sexual harassment considerably less serious than those against Ocampo.[712] Palme also pointed to the silence of international human rights groups: "[I]t is very remarkable that one of the most important prosecutors in the world can be accused of sexual crimes without any reaction from human rights organisations such as Amnesty and Human Rights Watch."[713] Indeed, rather than address the rape issue at the heart of the tribunal's ruling, Human Rights Watch showed more interest in bureaucratic procedural issues, stating that they were "disturbed by findings that the prosecutor had ignored the recommendation of the court's Disciplinary Advisory Board and involved himself directly even though the individual's alleged misconduct meriting dismissal concerned the prosecutor personally. The poor management practices we see in this case not only incur economic costs to the court - already under strain to account responsibly for its budget to states parties - but, more importantly, costs to the morale of staff, who are entitled to have their due process rights respected in an employment dispute."[714]

Ocampo's arrogance on the matter continued. He dismissed the ILO tribunal ruling as "manifestly unfounded". This prompted journalists to note that "[s]uch a dismissive attitude to judicial findings, and such misleading statements about a ruling, Moreno Ocampo would be sure to criticize in any of his indictees. How then does he engage in them? And how could this behavior by the ICC's chief prosecutor be curtailed? Or is he above the law? Moreno Ocampo's behavior, including that underlying the ILO's 190,000 Euro judgment, injure the reputation and integrity of the international criminal justice system."[715]

The chief prosecutor's judgment can only be called into question again by the simple fact that Palme's contract was to end in any instance in June 2007: Ocampo sought to have him fired in May 2007. His vindictiveness got the better of him.

It is also outrageous that the then head of the ICC's Jurisdiction, Complementarity and Cooperation Division, and deputy prosecutor, French diplomat Beatrix le Frapper du Hellen, sought to reject the allegations of sexual misconduct by claiming that "his opponents are obsessed with his sex life". In claiming there is a culture clash between the "white, very European" lawyers and their South American colleagues, she came very close to pleading some sort of Latin American "exceptionalism" for "macho" sexual behaviour.[716] This is the same court that is adamant that there can be no African "exceptionalism", especially with regard to crimes and especially sexual crimes.

Ocampo's case attracted considerable international attention. Dutch radio, for example, noted:

> The ILO ruling is damaging to Mr Moreno Ocampo, particularly the way in which he dealt with a complaint directed against himself. It can be expected of a chief prosecutor for the International Criminal Court that he should exercise the utmost discretion in cases in which he is personally involved. He has not only damaged his own reputation, but also that of the court. He has handed many of the ICC's opponents an extra trump card. It was not Christian Palme who damaged the chief prosecutor's reputation but the prosecutor himself. The ILO's pronouncement puts additional pressure on Mr Moreno Ocampo's position at the court. ICC-watchers say that, for some time now, there has been serious criticism of his methods within his own department, resulting in the departure of several employees. They accuse him of operating too much on his own and of paying little attention to any criticism of his policies.[717]

Joshua Rozenberg concluded: "The role of a prosecutor is to assess accurately the available evidence. The duty of a decision-maker is to withdraw from a case in which he has a personal interest. On the tribunal's findings, Mr Moreno-Ocampo has failed to meet these two fundamental responsibilities. A prosecutor who seeks to bring a president to justice must have judgment of the highest order. On the strength of these findings, Mr Moreno-Ocampo does not...he should resign immediately."[718]

The ILO judgment against Ocampo and the ICC led to pressure on the ICC to introduce an independent means of oversight. The Women's Initiatives for Gender Justice project urgently recommended to the ICC ASP that "[t]he Bureau should progress, with urgency, the development of a comprehensive, independent Oversight Mechanism and staff rules. These should address serious issues of misconduct, including fraud, corruption, waste, sexual harassment, exploitation, and abuse committed by ICC staff in the course of their work, especially in the field, and should include the waiving of immunity and strict disciplinary accountability for staff that violate these rules (including termination of employment). 'Serious misconduct' should be defined to expressly include sexual violence/abuse and sexual harassment. All staff should be provided with training on these rules." The project said that in the light of the "well publicized" ILO Administrative Tribunal decision against Ocampo for the unlawful termination of Palme "it would be timely for the Court to undertake a review of its internal complaints procedures to ensure they are sufficiently robust, are transparent, provide adequate protection for staff, are an effective mechanism for accountability, uphold the rights of employees and ensure the positive reputation and good standing of the Court as a whole".[719]

The ICC and hijacking civilian airliners: European "extraordinary rendition"?

Ocampo's judgment was also brought into sharp focus in June 2008, when the ICC revealed that it had encouraged the capture of the Sudanese government minister Ahmed Haroun, the subject of an ICC arrest warrant, by way of the hijacking of a civilian airliner, something the Bush Administration would have referred to as "extraordinary rendition".[720] Extraordinary rendition and irregular rendition are terms used to describe the illegal apprehension and transfer of a person from one state to another.[721]

An ICC spokeswoman stated that the ICC had planned to divert Haroun's plane away from its destination, Mecca, Saudi Arabia, and force it to land in an ICC member state where Haroun would be arrested and turned over to The Hague. It was believed that Haroun had been planning to go on a Muslim pilgrimage to Mecca. The spokeswoman declined to name the countries involved and gave no further details of how the operation would have worked.[722] Legal commentators have asked whether such a diversion was not "tantamount to hijacking?" They have also stated "it is hardly different from the U.S. claiming similar pragmatic reasons to seize and render suspected terrorists".[723] Haroun said of the ICC effort: "It is the ICC which is committing crime and practicing airplane hijacking.... The court is not worthy of respect and is using criminal methods."[724]

One of the registered counsels at the ICC, the Libyan-born French counsel Dr. al-Hadi Shalluf, described the would-be ICC attempt to divert a plane carrying Haroun as "illegal". He noted that diverting planes "is a violation of international law because of the negative impact it has on civil aviation. Even if it was done for the purpose of applying the law it is still considered a criminal act." Shalluf said that he is "very surprised that the court would resort to something disgraceful and immoral like this. I condemn this act." He said that the operation would have been legal only if the plane landed at its destination and then the ICC could have asked for extradition of Haroun. He also said that countries that may have been part of the plan "are in violation of civil aviation treaties signed in Montreal and New York and any other international conventions regarding safety of passengers".

Shalluf noted further that: "The court's mandate does not include arresting suspects directly. The ICC can ask countries to execute arrest warrants in accordance with Rome Statue. Otherwise the court becomes a hijacking institution and a police institution." Shalluf also noted that if the plan had been successful it would have created a "regional conflict and even war" between Sudan and the countries that were enlisted for help in this operation: "The ICC and its prosecutor bear the full responsibility for this and the UNSC must investigate how that was allowed to happen."[725]

By way of comparison the European Parliament launched its own investigation into the reports of the American use of extraordinary rendition and European complicity in these acts. In April 2006, MEPs leading the investigations expressed concerns that there had been a large number of secret flights over European territory since 2001, some to transfer suspects from one country to another. In a resolution passed on 14 February 2007 the European Parliament approved a report that criticised the extraordinary rendition programme and concluded that several European countries tolerated illegal secret flights over their territories. The report stated, *inter alia*, it "Regrets that European countries have been relinquishing control over their airspace and airports by turning a blind eye or admitting flights...being used for illegal transportation of detainees".[726]

Ocampo was seen in 2003 as the brightest star in the international legal world. The shine has gone off the star. De Waal and Flint concluded that "Moreno Ocampo is a man who diminishes with proximity". Despite all the fanfare, the ICC was always going to be controversial for a range of reasons relating to jurisdiction, doctrine, judicial competence, funding and politicisation to name but a few. For all those difficulties, the biggest threat to the court's credibility and even existence has been the ICC's first chief prosecutor. Ocampo showed himself to be a professionally and legally incompetent bully, whether it was of African governments or his office staff. He was more concerned with his celebrity status and his place on the celebrity circuit than with the day-to-day issues of legal ethics and professionalism. Ocampo claimed to be an enemy of impunity yet he granted impunity to some of the world's worst abusers of human rights. He promised swift justice yet managed to complete a single, flawed, trial. He claimed to uphold the law yet he was guilty of sexual misconduct while on ICC business. He was deceptive and clearly incapable of accepting that he was in any way to blame for the shortcoming or ineffectuality of his office or the court in general.

Rather than blame himself in any way for the manifest shortcomings of the ICC, Ocampo claimed that "oil and other interests" stopped the states that set up the ICC from doing enough to support the ICC in getting fugitives arrested.[727] In May 2009, Ocampo chose to blame the British government for the fact that President al-Bashir had not been arrested and delivered to The Hague. He claimed that Britain's "complex agenda" was preventing it from doing more to ensure the arrest of the Sudanese president and called on Britain to show "unity and leadership" on the issue.[728] For Ocampo, it was always someone else's fault.

And from the start there have been concerns about his honesty and integrity. In an interview with Aljazeera television, Ocampo denied getting any help or information from NGOs with regard to his Sudan indictments.[729] This must be set against Ocampo's dissembling regarding evidence during the Lubanga case, when he sought to hide hundreds of items of evidence from the UN, its agencies and other NGOs. Conor Foley confirms that Ocampo "has repeatedly stated that he is obtaining information from aid agencies".[730] Indeed, for all his denials, it is a matter of record that the ICC has accepted hundreds of items of "evidence" from NGOs, including more than 500 children's drawings provided by the UK-based Darfur group "Waging Peace" that were accepted by ICC as evidence in any trial.[731] On 8 March 2009, a statement by the spokesman for the SLA/M Abdel Wahid Darfur rebel movement, Issa Ibrahim Suleiman, was published on the Sudaneseonline website, thanking and commending NGOs in the camps for their help, including the information and evidence they collected and that helped in the case before the ICC.[732]

In 2009, de Waal and Flint placed the blame for the malaise at the heart of the ICC squarely on Ocampo:

> Six years after he became Prosecutor, the priceless human capital invested in his office is draining away. Lawyers and investigators who served in the OTP, and who count among the brightest and the best of their profession, say they believe the Court's reputation, and perhaps even its life, is at risk.[733]

In December 2008, *Inner City Press* asked Ocampo if he had learnt anything "from the ILO's criticism, and from the suspension of the cases against Thomas Lubanga of the Congo, for failure to turn over exculpatory evidence". It noted that Moreno Ocampo would not admit any error in either case: "in fact, he laughed at the finding of retaliation". *Inner City Press* stated that Ocampo said on camera that despite the ILO's clear finding, the charges against him had been "manifestly unfounded".[734]

If the ICC continues to have problems regarding its credibility it is in large part because of the behaviour of Luis Ocampo during his tenure as the court's first chief prosecutor. He was the best possible asset of those opposed to the ICC. Ocampo's grip on reality appeared to be in question to the very end. When asked in 2012 about his record in his ten years in office, Ocampo replied without hesitation: "Mission more than accomplished!"[735]

It also has to be noted that the initial behaviour in office of his successor Fatou Bensouda does not provide much confidence that she will be any more focused, competent or realistic. *The New York Times* has observed of Bensouda that "she is not universally admired". President Paul Kagame of Rwanda, familiar with Bensouda because of her work on the 1994 Rwanda genocide prosecutions, has suggested she is little more than a disciple of Ocampo, who appointed Ms. Bensouda as his deputy in 2004. *The New York Times* reported that lawyers who have worked with Ms. Bensouda say she is not noted for her skills "as a trial lawyer": she is known more as an affable organiser.[736] The newspaper has also reported that Bensouda "has done little to dispel the impression that the court works too slowly". It added that a short time into her tenure "her office lost its first case…an inauspicious mark on Ms. Bensouda". Matters went from bad to worse as her Kenyan cases began to implode due to prosecution witnesses admitting they had perjured themselves. The court's deeply flawed dependency on questionable intermediaries and non-governmental organisations has continued under Bensouda.[737]

A lacklustre lawyer and a fawning courtier of the first chief prosecutor, in reality Bensouda is nothing more than convenient window dressing, appointed for no better reason than she was African.

Eleven years, and one billion euros, after the court was established, and ten years after it began its work, the OTP, the engine of the court, continues to lurch from one disaster to another while prolonging and rekindling conflict in Africa. The IWPR, a pro-ICC organisation, reported in March 2013 that "international justice experts say ICC prosecutors need to review the way they investigate cases". It cited the Lubanga trial judgment in March 2012, which observed: "A series of witnesses have been called during this trial whose evidence, as a result of the essentially unsupervised actions of three of the principal intermediaries, cannot safely be relied on." The Institute noted that of "the 14 cases that have come before the ICC, five have lacked enough evidence to go forward to trial, and of the two that were completed, Lubanga was convicted but Ngudjolo acquitted". Ngudjolo was freed after the supposed witnesses were deemed to be similarly unreliable. IWPR observed that "[i]n the wake of previous judgements, there are questions about the court's use of eyewitness testimony, something that can be notoriously unreliable compared with other forms of evidence". William Schabas observed after the dismissal of the charges against Francis Muthaura, also as a consequence of perjured witness testimony presented by the prosecution, "I hope they are going through a lot of soul-searching, and they had better solve the problem [of securing convictions] soon. I think more and more people realise that there is something very unsatisfactory about the performance of the court."[738]

In March 2013, Schabas suggested that ICC prosecutors could move away from the type of cases they are currently investigating. He pointed out that it has been the court's choice to prosecute cases stemming from rebel conflicts in the DRC and electoral violence in Kenya. The IWPR noted: "He argues that the ICC could equally select other crimes in other parts of the world, on the basis that stronger evidence is available."[739]

Chapter Nine

AVOIDING THE CRIME OF AGGRESSION

"[T]he parties to the ICC have funked a universal law against unilateral military intervention."

Geoffrey Robertson QC[740]

"It may be decades before there are any prosecutions for the crime of aggression."

William Schabas[741]

At the heart of the credibility of the ICC is whether or not it is truly independent, and will genuinely pursue without fear or favour those who commit genocide, crimes against humanity and war crimes. For all the ICC's attempts to claim legal descent from the Nuremburg tribunal, that the court is independent and that it will prosecute the gravest of crimes, it has already failed in all three respects. It has failed and continues to fail regarding the crime that was front and centre at Nuremburg, the crime of aggression. The Nuremburg court referred to the crime of aggression as a supreme crime or harm committed against humanity. The Nuremberg judgment stated that "to initiate a war of aggression...is not only an international crime; it is the supreme international crime differing only from other war crimes in that it contains within itself the accumulated evil of the whole".[742]

While accepting aggression to be a major crime subject to its jurisdiction, the ICC initially deferred from defining "aggression". The ICC's 1998 deferral on the crime of aggression was all the more shallow given that a clear definition of aggression had been adopted by the UN General Assembly in 1974.[743] Geoffrey Robertson observed that "the major state parties at the Rome Conference were nervous about incriminating their political and military leaders if they went to war without Security Council cover.... A compromise was reached: the crime of aggression was placed within the jurisdiction of the ICC by Article 5, but it was left undefined and would be operational only after a definition had been approved at the first review conference."[744] As Loru Sinanyan also points out: "This opt-out for aggression was written into the statute solely to assuage U.S. fears."[745] This was itself the first clear indication that the court lacked the independence so avidly claimed of it as in so doing it bowed from the outset to Western political pressure.

Robertson has also described the current situation regarding the court and the legal issues surrounding the crime of aggression:

> The worst war crime of all – declaring and waging aggressive wars in which millions of combatants and civilians may be killed – is absent from Article 8, because the Rome Conference could not agree on a definition. As a compromise, the ICC was given a provisional jurisdiction over the crime of aggression (by Article 5(1)(d)) which will operate after 2017 when a majority of states accept the definition agreed at the Kampala Review Conference. This is unsatisfactory.[746]

Robertson also pointed to further delays in seeing legislation against aggression in action:

> [T]here can be no prosecution for the crime at least until after 1 January 2017…but there has been a remarkable lack of interest in endorsing the new crime – three years after the Kampala Conference, only Liechtenstein has bothered to ratify the amendment. It is therefore unlikely that the ICC will be equipped to prosecute crime aggression until well after 2017.[747]

William Schabas has also conceded that "[i]t may be decades before there are any prosecutions for the crime of aggression".[748]

The Rome Statute specifically provided that the ICC would not exercise jurisdiction over the crime of aggression until the ASP developed a suitable definition and appropriate conditions.[749] As Philippe Kirsch, the first President of the ICC, stated, this was "[i]n accordance with the principle *nullum crimen sine lege* [no crime without law]… . The definition must be consistent with the UN Charter."[750] It was agreed that no amendment would be considered until seven years after the treaty's entry into force; and even then "[t]he definition must be accepted by 7/8 of States Parties, and…will bind only those who accept it".[751] It should be noted that this in itself contradicted the rest of the ICC statute, which states that the core crimes apply whether or not a state is a party to the statute. Almost ninety per cent of those states that ratify the ICC statute must also ratify the definition of aggression before the ICC can exercise jurisdiction. In addition, even if the required number of states accepts a definition that the remainder do not find acceptable, those states are given the opportunity to refuse jurisdiction of the court over aggression. Therefore even if Washington did not approve of the definition of aggression ratified by seven eighths of the states, it still would not be subject to the court for aggression if it opted out. The USA could simply opt out of a definition of aggression that it did not agree with and be *immune* from prosecution for that crime.[752]

It is obvious that there was considerable pressure on the Rome Conference by the permanent members of the UNSC not to include the term. Schabas noted that the reference in Article 5(2) of the Rome Statute to the fact that the definition of aggression "shall be consistent with the relevant provisions of the Charter of the United Nations", was a "carefully constructed phrase" that was "understood as a reference to the role the Council may or should play". He pointed out that the underlying issue is the fact that Article 39 of the Charter of the UN declares that determining situations of aggression is a prerogative of the Security Council: "If the Security Council is the arbiter of situations of aggression, would this mean that the Court can only prosecute aggression once the Council has pronounced on the subject. Such a view seems an incredible encroachment upon the independence of the Court, and would mean, for starters, that no permanent member of the Security Council would ever be subject to prosecution for aggression."[753]

The two issues seen to be at the centre of the debate around the crime of aggression were how to translate what was essentially an act of state into individual liability; and the UNSC role in determining the filter for prosecutions of the crime of aggression by the ICC. Of the two the latter was the most intractable. The two main issues regarding the crime of aggression were said to have been "the definition of the crime and the conditions of exercise of jurisdiction by the Court".[754] The permanent members of the Security Council would only support a provision that called for the Security Council to make a determination of whether an act of aggression has been committed before the court would be able to step in.[755]

In its closing plenary session the 1998 Rome Conference adopted Resolution F, establishing a preparatory commission to prepare proposals in regard to the crime of aggression, including its definition and elements, and the conditions under which the court could exercise jurisdiction in regard to that crime. Resolution F also stated that: "The Commission shall submit such proposals to the ASP at a Review Conference, with a view to arriving at an acceptable provision on the crime of aggression for inclusion in this Statute."[756] Article 121 of the ICC Statute stipulated that the ICC Statute would not be amended for a period of seven years from the date upon which the ICC Statute entered into force, which was on 1 July 2002. The ICC had effectively fudged the issue of the supreme crime against humanity for seven years.

In the period 2002–10, defining the crime of aggression and determining the circumstances under which the ICC would be competent to prosecute the crime was considered by a special working group on the crime of aggression of the ASP, of which membership was open to all member states of the UN.[757]

The 2010 ICC Review Conference agreed to insert Article 8 *bis*, into the ICC Statute. This article provides the following definition of the crime of aggression and an act of aggression:

> (1) For the purpose of the Statute, "crime of aggression" means the planning, preparation, initiation or execution, by a person in a position effectively to exercise control over or to direct the political or military action of a State, of an act of aggression which, by its character, gravity and scale, constitutes a manifest violation of the Charter of the United Nations.

(2) For the purpose of paragraph (1), "act of aggression" means the use of armed force by a State against the sovereignty, territorial integrity or independence of another State, or in any other manner inconsistent with the Charter of the United Nations. Any of the following acts, regardless of a declaration of war, shall, in accordance with United Nations General Assembly resolution 3314 (XXIX) of 14 December 1974, qualify as an act of aggression:

(a) The invasion or attack by the armed forces of a State of the territory of another State, or any military occupation, however temporary, resulting from such invasion or attack, or any annexation by the use of force of the territory of another State or part thereof;

(b) Bombardment by the armed forces of a State against the territory of another State or the use of any weapon by a State against the territory of another State;

(c) The blockade of the ports or coast of a State by the armed forces of another State;

(d) An attack by the armed forces of a State on the land, sea or air forces, or marine and air fleets of another State;

(e) The use of armed forces of one State which are within the territory of another State with the agreement of the receiving State, in contravention of the conditions provided for in the agreement or any extension of their presence in such territory beyond the termination of the agreement;

(f) The action of a State in allowing its territory, which it has placed at the disposal of another State, to be used by that other State for perpetrating an act of aggression against a third State;

(g) The sending by or on behalf of a State of armed bands, groups, irregulars or mercenaries, which carry out acts of armed force against another State of such gravity as to amount to the acts listed above, or its substantial involvement therein.[758]

It is worth noting that the definition of "act of aggression" simply repeats General Assembly Resolution 3314 (XXIX) of 14 December 1974. The article also included a phrase requiring that the act of aggression must "by its character, gravity and scale, constitute a manifest violation of the Charter of the United Nations".

The text of Articles 15 *bis* and 15 *ter* set out the conditions for the court's exercise of jurisdiction over the crime of aggression. These articles outlined when the ICC prosecutor can initiate an investigation into a crime of aggression. Where a "situation" is referred to the prosecutor by the UNSC, Article 15 *ter* of the statute provides that the court's jurisdiction is triggered in the same manner as with the other crimes in the statute, meaning the prosecutor may proceed with an investigation into the crime of aggression.

Article 15 *bis* states that the prosecutor may only proceed with his (*proprio motu*) investigation or an investigation based on a state referral of a situation into the crime of aggression: after first ascertaining whether the Security Council has made a determination of the existence of an act of aggression (under Article 39 of the UN Charter) and waiting for a period of six months; where that situation concerns an act of aggression committed between States Parties; and after the Pre-Trial Division of the court has authorised the commencement of the investigation.

Article 15 *bis* also provides that States Parties may opt-out of the court's jurisdiction under the article by lodging a declaration of non-acceptance of jurisdiction with the court's Registrar. Such a declaration can be made at any time (including before the amendments enter into force) and shall be reviewed by the State Party within three years. It is noteworthy that non-State Parties have been explicitly excluded from the court's jurisdiction into a crime of aggression under this article when committed by that state's nationals or on its territory.

The amendments were adopted by consensus in accordance with Article 5(2) of the statute and will enter into force under Article 121(5). However, the provisions of both Article 15 *bis* and Article 15 *ter* provide that the court will not be able to exercise its jurisdiction over the crime of aggression until at least thirty States Parties have ratified or accepted the amendments; and a decision is taken by two-thirds of States Parties to activate the jurisdiction at any time after 1 January 2017.

Schabas was obviously surprised by the stance taken by human rights groups regarding finalising the definition of the crime of aggression within the Rome Statute:

> The major international human rights NGOs, generally highly devoted to the creation and work of the International Criminal Court, were surprisingly indifferent to the issue of the crime of aggression. Although present at the Kampala Conference, they concentrated their attention on the "stock-taking" sessions…[when the] Conference shifted its attention to the main act, which was the crime of aggression, most of the NGOs retreated. Many of them simply returned to their homes in Europe or America…[759]

Schabas asked how the main human rights NGOs arrived at their positions regarding the crime of aggression. Amnesty explained that it had not:

> [T]aken a stance on the definition of the crime of aggression because its mandate – to campaign for every person to enjoy all of the human rights (civil and political and economic, social and cultural rights) enshrined in the Universal Declaration of Human Rights and other international human rights standards – does not extend to the lawfulness of the use of force.[760]

Human Rights Watch explained that its "institutional mandate includes a position of strict neutrality on issues of jus ad bellum...or jus in bello..... Consistent with this approach, we take no position on the substance of a definition of the crime of aggression."[761] Schabas posed the key question: "Isn't the issue of the legitimate aim or purpose in human rights law fundamentally the same as determining the lawfulness of the conflict?"[762]

The decision on aggression made by the Review Conference was summed up by the US delegation, which was self-evidently satisfied with the result:

> The court cannot exercise jurisdiction over the crime of aggression without a further decision to take place sometime after January 1st, 2017. The prosecutor cannot charge nationals of non-state parties, including U.S. nationals, with the crime of aggression. No U.S. national can be prosecuted for aggression as long as the U.S. remains a non-state party. And if we were to become a state party, we'd still have the option to opt out from having our nationals prosecuted for aggression. So we ensure total protection for our Armed Forces and other U.S. nationals going forward.[763]

Robertson has made the court's new timetable regarding the crime of aggression very clear: "There can...be no prosecutions for 'aggression' until after 2017, the earliest date that a majority of states can endorse the definition of the crime agreed at the Kampala Review Conference in 2012."[764]

The reality is that the court and its supporters have continued to fudge the issue of the ultimate crime against humanity, waging wars of aggression. Robertson has also made this very clear: "Because the crime cannot be prosecuted until two thirds of the state parties agree, it may not ever come into operation, and even if it does, member states will be entitled to opt out. In this way, the parties to the ICC have funked a universal law against unilateral military intervention."[765]

Chapter Ten

Entrenching Impunity, Granting Immunity

"Impunity is no longer an option."

Luis Moreno Ocampo[766]

"The ICC…has not helped to check a prevailing culture of impunity for crimes committed at the hands of government forces, both in northern Uganda and in more recent operations elsewhere."

Human Rights Watch[767]

"It appears that the ICC has effectively granted the Ugandan government impunity for its legacy of violence in northern Uganda."

Dr. Adam Branch[768]

The ICC has made much of its claim to seek to end impunity. Impunity is defined as exemption or freedom from punishment, harm, or loss.[769] Immunity is defined as exemption from legal prosecution.[770] Writing in 2009, the court's Chief Prosecutor Luis Moreno Ocampo declared: "Impunity is no longer an option." He wrote: "In 1998, more than 100 states adopted the Rome Statute to end impunity for those crimes that we had thought, over and over, would never happen again, only to see them occur, again and again: genocide, crimes against humanity and war crimes." He also noted: "Together, we had to transform the idea of ending impunity into a reality."[771] In 2012, the court actually incorporated the claim "10 Years Fighting Impunity" into its logo on a range of its documents.[772] Ocampo's successor as Chief Prosecutor, Fatou Bensouda, also made the court's position clear with regard to immunity, declaring that "[t]here is no immunity for International Crimes at the ICC".[773]

These claims are false. The reality is that the ICC has deliberately granted immunity from prosecution and has also knowingly entrenched impunity within several of the situations within which it has become involved. Lord Robertson, a former British defence secretary, who also served as NATO Secretary General, let the cat out of the bag early on when he suggested that most defendants at the ICC would probably come "from countries with no super power support".[774]

The British international lawyer Courtenay Griffiths QC has addressed both impunity and selectivity issues: "[T]here is a need for an end to impunity in Africa. But it's the way the West is going about it in a selective fashion. A selectivity of denunciation, a selectivity of investigation, a selectivity of prosecution, and even within Africa, a selectivity of indictment."[775] He has also noted:

> Despite all this talk of an end to impunity, it turns out that all of the ICC indictments have been issued against Africans. Yet even within Africa this selectivity is nuanced, in that it carefully excludes some presidents with much blood on their hands, but immune from prosecution, because they are highly valued clients of the West. Likewise, when one looks at the West's response to the "Arab Spring", one sees a marked divergence of attitude towards Libya as contrasted with Egypt, Bahrain (supported by a reactionary Saudi Arabia), Yemen and Syria.[776]

Ocampo tried to take the high ground with regard to impunity, claiming to be applying the law without fear or favour: "I apply scrupulously one standard – the law."[777] In his more gushing moments he went further: "I am putting a legal limit to the politicians. That's my job. I police the borderline and say, if you cross this you're no longer on the political side, you are on the criminal side. I am the border control."[778] He claimed to be pursuing a crusade against impunity, additionally declaring: "The days of fearing a frivolous court are over."[779] This was simply untrue. Far from scrupulously applying the law, the court and its chief prosecutor have been extraordinarily selective and partisan. They have chosen cases that they knew would not antagonise their EU funders or the USA. They have also clearly avoided cases that would embarrass the governments in whose countries, Uganda, DRC and the CAR, the ICC was physically present and active. The examples of this hypocrisy abound.

It is a matter of record that the ICJ, the world's foremost international legal institution, has itself pointed conclusively to Ugandan government involvement in war crimes and crimes against humanity. In a 2005 judgment in a landmark case, *Armed Activities on the Territory of the Congo* (DRC v. Uganda), first filed at the UN's highest court in 1999, the ICJ adjudicated on claims by the DRC that its neighbour Uganda had invaded Congolese territory, plundering its natural resources and massacring its civilians. The ICJ unanimously found:

> [A]dmissible the claim submitted by the Democratic Republic of the Congo relating to alleged violations by the Republic of Uganda of its obligations under international human rights law and international humanitarian law in

the course of hostilities between Ugandan and Rwandan military forces in Kisangani; found by sixteen votes to one, that the Republic of Uganda, by the conduct of its armed forces, which committed acts of killing, torture and other forms of inhumane treatment of the Congolese civilian population, destroyed villages and civilian buildings, failed to distinguish between civilian and military targets and to protect the civilian population in fighting with other combatants, trained child soldiers, incited ethnic conflict and failed to take measures to put an end to such conflict; as well as by its failure, as an occupying Power, to take measures to respect and ensure respect for human rights and international humanitarian law in Ituri district, violated its obligations under international human rights law and international humanitarian law.[780]

Human Rights Watch confirmed that "[t]he International Court of Justice found that the Ugandan army committed massive human rights violations and grave breaches of international humanitarian law in DRC, and cited some incidents that would fall within the ICC's temporal jurisdiction".[781] It could not have been any easier for the ICC, had the court been genuinely interested in applying the law. It would have been impossible for the ICC not to have been aware of this detailed investigation over several years, including a period post-July 2002, from which time the court could take action, by truly objective lawyers. The ICJ held that both international humanitarian law and human rights obligations were binding on the Ugandan troops then occupying the DRC, and that the Ugandan government was liable under the doctrine of responsibility for those acts:

> The Court thus concludes that Uganda is internationally responsible for violations of international human rights law and international humanitarian law committed by the UPDF and by its members in the territory of the DRC and for failing to comply with its obligations as an occupying Power in Ituri in respect of violations of international human rights law and international humanitarian law in the occupied territory.

The ICJ also outlined exactly which human rights laws had been abused by the Ugandan forces:

> [T]he Court finds that the acts committed by the UPDF [Ugandan People's Defense Force] and officers and soldiers of the UPDF (see paragraphs 206–211 above) are in clear violation of the obligations under the Hague Regulations of 1907, Articles 25, 27 and 28, as well as Articles 43, 46 and 47 with regard to obligations of an occupying Power. These obligations are binding on the Parties as customary international law. Uganda also violated the following provisions of the international humanitarian law and international human rights law instruments, to which both Uganda and the DRC are parties: Fourth Geneva Convention, Articles 27 and 32 as well as Article 53 with regard to obligations of an occupying Power; International Covenant on Civil and

Political Rights, Articles 6, paragraph 1, and 7; First Protocol Additional to the Geneva Conventions of 12 August 1949, Articles 48, 51, 52, 57, 58 and 75, paragraphs 1 and 2; African Charter on Human and Peoples' Rights, Articles 4 and 5; Convention on the Rights of the Child, Article 38, paragraphs 2 and 3; Optional Protocol to the Convention on the Rights of the Child, Articles 1, 2, 3, paragraph 3, 4, 5 and 6.

The African Commission on Human and Peoples' Rights had also found for the DRC and against Uganda in relation to Ugandan military violations of human rights law and international humanitarian law on its territory.[782]

The issue was crystal clear. This massive violation of law by the Ugandan government occurred in Ituri district, the same area in which the ICC would become active. It is inconceivable that the ICC Chief Prosecutor and his researchers would not have known of the ICJ's detailed case against Uganda, or that of the African Commission on Human and Peoples' Rights. While the ICC scrupulously ignored the ICJ's comprehensive case and did not itself undertake any investigation of the Uganda government abuse, it did indict and eventually convict a minor Congolese rebel commander, Thomas Lubanga, of recruiting and using child soldiers in the district. It ignored his relationship with Uganda.

For all the Chief Prosecutor's claims of scrupulously upholding the law and policing the borderline of criminality he consciously shirked his clear responsibility and duty. And if that was not bad enough, not only did Ocampo not do his job with regard to Ugandan involvement in the Ituri bloodbath, he deliberately attempted to classify the situation as a "non-international (internal) armed conflict". This meant that Ocampo could proceed with a case against Lubanga while not having to investigate the clear Ugandan involvement in the conflict. Human Rights Watch had also documented that the Ugandan government was an occupying force in Ituri between August 1998 and May 2003 and implicated in human rights abuses[783] and criticised Ocampo for having an inaccurate classification.[784] The ICC judges, in an unusual moment of clarity, also added to this criticism.

Just to recap. The ICC has been invited in as an international court to investigate serious crimes against humanity and war crimes in both Uganda and the DRC. Despite having declared that "I apply scrupulously one standard – the law," the ICC and its then chief prosecutor blatantly ignored clear instances of the most serious crimes imaginable in both Uganda and DRC, and specifically a range of war crimes committed by Ugandan military forces in DRC – crimes that could clearly be tied to the Ugandan President Yoweri Museveni, his ministers and military commanders. These crimes were unambiguously documented by the ICJ, and having occurred in large part after the establishment of the court thus came within the ICC's brief. It was exactly the sort of case for which the court had been established: bringing to justice an otherwise unaccountable head of state and government engaging in the most serious of crimes. What did the ICC do? Nothing. In fact, less than nothing: the Chief Prosecutor sought to play around with the classifications of war crimes and their jurisdictions in order to avoid having to in any way deal with the Ugandan war crimes. Despite the ICJ's detailed listing of serious war crimes, the ICC chose instead to indict Lubanga for allegedly using child soldiers. And, of course, similarly, the ICC has not indicted any Ugandan officer or official for involvement in the large-scale crimes against humanity for which they have been responsible within Uganda itself – choosing only to charge Ugandan rebels. It would be difficult to imagine clearer examples of the Ugandan government, a close US ally and darling of the EU, being accorded "exemption or freedom from punishment" by the ICC.

Ironically, the ICC's blundering in Uganda has led to renewed Ugandan military intervention in the DRC and other countries in the region – as outlined by Dr. Adam Branch, an expert on Uganda and its conflict:

> Museveni has used the arrest warrants to justify the UPDF's reentry into eastern DRC, where their prior intervention led to massive looting and atrocities against Congolese civilians. The UPDF now has a justification it uses for maintaining its troops in South Sudan and throughout central Africa with dangerous consequences for regional stability.[785]

The obscenity of the court's warm relationship with the Ugandan government is perhaps also best described by Branch:

> This unashamed public support the ICC gives the Ugandan government has seen a number of highlights, from the initial joint press conference announcing the investigation between Luis Moreno-Ocampo and President Museveni, to ICC investigators occasionally being accompanied by UPDF officers, including the notorious divisional commander, when carrying out interviews with potential witnesses in Acholiland, to the 2010 ICC Review Conference held in Kampala and the tragi-comic spectacle of the War Victim's Day football match, held in the conference, in which President Museveni led a team of war victims named "Dignity" against a team led by Ban Ki-Moon named "Justice".[786]

Branch is also clear about the consequences of this engagement:

> It appears that the ICC has effectively granted the Ugandan government impunity for its legacy of violence [in] northern Uganda in a case of double standards and the politicized use of complementarity, whereby international mechanisms are used to deal with the state's enemies, whereas the state is allowed to prosecute – and absolve – itself.[787]

The ICC has also afforded *de facto* impunity to the government of the DRC. Ocampo and the ICC, for example, cannot be unaware of the ninety-six-page Human Rights Watch report, entitled *We Will Crush You': The Restriction of Political Space in the Democratic Republic of Congo*, published in 2008, which documented the Kabila government's use of violence and intimidation to eliminate political opponents. Human Rights Watch found that Kabila himself set the tone and direction by giving orders to "crush" or "neutralize" the "enemies of democracy", implying it was acceptable to use unlawful force against them.[788] The government's armed forces have been accused of savage abuses of human rights. On 9 April 2009, for example, the USA newspaper *Inner City Press* asked the UN Mission in DRC (MONUC) chief Alan Doss about detailed reports of rapes in March 2009 by the Congolese Army. Doss confirmed the rapes, and even knew which DRC Army unit committed the crimes, naming the 85th Brigade. This is yet another instance where the ICC could step in, given its jurisdiction "by referral", and its campaign against "impunity".[789] It has not. Human Rights Watch has also specifically stated that the DRC government was involved in creating, supporting, and arming Lubanga's militia – including the child soldiers for which he was indicted and charged, and called on the court to bring cases against its officials. The ICC has not.

One of the four DRC militia leaders the ICC has managed to indict, Jean Bosco Ntaganda, was at large within the country until 2013 when he handed himself over to the US Embassy in Rwanda. Far from arresting Bosco, the DRC government promoted him to the rank of Major-General and to the position of Deputy Commander of an anti-rebel offensive that was being supported by MONUC. The *Inner City Press* questioned the UN's Special Envoy to the Great Lakes, Olusegun Obasanjo, about the UN collaborating with Jean Bosco Ntaganda. Obasanjo acknowledged that Bosco is "not out of circulation". *Inner City Press* also asked Secretary-General Ban Ki-moon's spokesperson Michele Montas, what the UN is doing to ensure that it does not work even indirectly with the indicted war criminal, and whether it might even help to apprehend him. Ms. Montas responded that that is the job of the Congolese authorities.[790] The *Inner City Press* also noted "The UN's shifting answers, first that they wouldn't work with an army that included Bosco, then that they wouldn't work with operations in which Bosco has a formal role, finally only that no pictures will be taken with Bosco." This, the paper stated, "cast a different light on the UN and war criminals".[791] On 10 November 2009, Howard Wolpe, US Envoy to the Great Lakes, also called on the DRC to arrest Jean Bosco Ntaganda.[792] On the same day, however, a DRC government spokesman stated that the arrest of Ntaganda was "not possible for the time being". The spokesman added that squabbles about bringing legal proceedings straightaway could inflict a "cure worse than the illness" on an already fragile country.[793]

The ICC turned a blind eye to all this behaviour by the DRC government, thus according impunity to the government. In the case of Ntaganda, the double standards of the ICC were once again very evident. In January 2008 the ICC initiated an operation using MONUC military personnel to try to arrest Ugandan rebels subject to an ICC arrest warrant: this attempt was a bloody failure with the deaths of a number of MONUC personnel. Ntaganda was a serving DRC general for several years following his indictment, with regular contact with MONUC, yet the ICC and MONUC did nothing to arrest him. He eventually surrendered himself to the court.

In 2009 the ICC Chief Prosecutor tried to explain away the court's inability to bring Ntaganda into custody: "Some individuals sought by the court are enjoying the protection of their own militias, such as Jean Bosco Ntaganda in Congo."[794] Ocampo was characteristically disingenuous. He knew full well that it was the Congolese government that was protecting Ntaganda, the very government to which the ICC had accorded impunity. It continued to publicly refuse the ICC indictment until late 2012.[795] In July 2009, Ocampo visited Uganda and DRC. In both countries he declared that the ICC's mission was to "end impunity". In Bunia, Moreno Ocampo told Congolese civilians: "We are prosecuting those most responsible for the crimes committed in Ituri, but our mission is also to end impunity to prevent the commission of future crimes."[796] The dishonesty of this claim by the ICC is all too clear.

In 2011, Human Rights Watch pointed to the court's entrenching of impunity in the country in situations it has become involved in:

> [I]n the DRC situation – as in Uganda and CAR – there have been no investigations leading to charges against [government] officials. In these three situations, a total of 11 arrest warrants have been issued, but the targets of these warrants are, in effect, all rebel leaders. The absence of charges against government officials has given credence to the perception that the ICC is powerless to take on those on whom it must rely for its investigations. Even if the problem is one of perception rather than actual compromised independence, it has nonetheless created a profound credibility gap for the ICC in each of the three situations.[797]

Human Rights Watch warned:

> In the absence of clearer, more widely available public explanations, it is easy to understand how some have reached the conclusion that the prosecutor has deliberately chosen not to target Ugandan military and civilian authorities for prosecution for political reasons. Considerable damage has been done to the ICC's reputation in Uganda due to these perceptions.[798]

Human Rights Watch returned to the issue a year later, pointing to the ICC's granting of *de facto* immunity and impunity to government forces in its target countries:

> There have been problematic past practices by the Office of the Prosecutor, Human Rights Watch said. For instance, in the Democratic Republic of Congo (DRC), Uganda, and Central African Republic (CAR) situations, the absence of charges against government officials without a clear explanation has undermined perceptions of the court's independence, Human Rights Watch said. The perceived failure to pursue allegations against all sides in these countries has fed concerns that the prosecutor is yielding to pressure for "victor's justice," damaging the court's credibility.[799]

Human Rights Watch further noted that "The ICC's relative silence about possible investigation of UPDF crimes has not helped to check a prevailing culture of impunity for crimes committed at the hands of government forces, both in northern Uganda and in more recent operations elsewhere."[800]

Human Rights Watch has noted: "[s]ignificant gaps in accountability for serious crimes by government officials remain, which have done little to reverse a decline in human rights protection". The organisation has also placed on record the ICC's *de facto* granting of impunity to Uganda government forces: "This ongoing and longstanding impunity for high-ranking members of the Ugandan military who have led operations, particularly in the war with the LRA, continues to undermine the reputation of the court. Furthermore, it is unclear whether the government will seek to institute prosecutions against state actors for crimes committed in the war in northern Uganda before the newly established International Crimes Division (ICD), although officials have indicated that members of the Ugandan military will not be tried before the ICD, but could face trials before the military courts."[801] Human Rights Watch has repeatedly urged the OTP to provide an account of the status of its investigations into the actions of the Uganda government.[802]

The ICC has also knowingly and officially granted immunity from prosecution for crimes against humanity, war crimes and genocide to a number of countries in conflict situations. Shortly after the court came into being in 2002, the court immunised personnel from the USA and other non-States Parties from ICC jurisdiction in the course of UN peacekeeping operations. The UNSC passed Resolutions 1422, 1487 and 1497, which granted immunity from prosecution by the court for crimes against humanity and war crimes for American personnel and those of other non-ICC states during their service in UN peacekeeping operations. The USA threatened to veto the renewal of the UN mission in Bosnia and Herzegovina, which was to expire on 15 July 2002, if the council did not grant immunity from prosecution by the ICC for its personnel. Resolution 1422 was adopted unanimously, exempting personnel from non-party states from ICC jurisdiction. Resolution 1487, adopted on 12 June 2003, again at the insistence of the USA, granted a one-year extension for immunity from prosecution by the ICC to UN personnel from countries that were not party to the ICC, beginning on 1 July 2003. UN Security Council Resolution 1497, adopted on 1 August 2003, authorised a multinational force to intervene in the Liberian conflict in support of a ceasefire agreement using "all necessary measures". The USA once again ensured that the resolution exempted soldiers from countries not party to the ICC. A number of states objected vociferously to the passage of these resolutions, stating that the UN resolutions violated the Rome Statute.[803] There is a considerable body of legal opinion that these states may have been correct. Professor Neha Jain is typical in her observation that "SC Resolutions 1422, 1487 and 1497 are inconsistent with the Rome Statute and ultra vires the powers of the Security Council."[804] The Security Council subsequently refused to renew the exemption again in 2004 after pictures emerged of US troops abusing Iraqi prisoners in Abu Ghraib Prison, and the US withdrew its demand.

In March 2005, the USA allowed the adoption of UN Security Council Resolution 1593 (2005). This resolution referred "the situation in Darfur since 1 July 2002 to the Prosecutor of the International Criminal Court". The resolution, following US pressure, also provided immunity from prosecution to nationals from non-ICC States Parties that might become involved in operations in Sudan:

> Decides that nationals, current or former officials or personnel from a contributing State outside Sudan which is not a party to the Rome Statute of the International Criminal Court shall be subject to the exclusive jurisdiction of that contributing State for all alleged acts or omissions arising out of or related to operations in Sudan established or authorized by the Council or the African Union, unless such exclusive jurisdiction has been expressly waived by that contributing State.[805]

On 26 March 2008, President Bush certified for the purposes of American Servicemembers' Protection Act, that US service members participating in the UN-AU Darfur Mission (UNAMID) were immunised from criminal prosecution by the ICC due to an exemption by the Security Council under Resolution 1593.

The ICC repeated the Darfur wording and also immunised American and other non-State Party military personnel from prosecution for their actions during the war in Libya in 2011. UN Security Council Resolution 1970 (2011) stated that the UNSC:

> Decides that nationals, current or former officials or personnel from a State outside the Libyan Arab Jamahiriya which is not a party to the Rome Statute of the International Criminal Court shall be subject to the exclusive jurisdiction of that State for all alleged acts or omissions arising out of or related to operations in the Libyan Arab Jamahiriya established or authorized by the Council, unless such exclusive jurisdiction has been expressly waived by the State.

The British *Daily Telegraph* newspaper made it clear that "the US insisted that the UN resolution was worded so that no one from an outside country that is not a member of the ICC could be prosecuted for their actions in Libya". American diplomats had been under strict instructions to have the paragraph included. The paragraph was added by the USA to prevent any of its citizens being held accountable for any crimes committed during the UN operation in Libya. The French Ambassador to the UN, Gerard Araud, described the paragraph as "a red line for the United States…. It was a deal-breaker, and that's the reason we accepted this text to have the unanimity of the council."[806]

Ironically perhaps, the former US Assistant Secretary of State for African affairs Jendayi Frazer has accused the court itself of acting with impunity: "[T]he ICC begins to look like an organisation that is behaving with impunity in international affairs, rather than a court that is respectful of victims or the principle of presumption of innocence."[807] The ICC's claim to be working to end impunity and immunity is simply false. It has entrenched both.

Chapter Eleven

THE EUROPEAN GUANTÁNAMO BAY?

"Assuming arguendo *that the ICC's rules satisfy international jurisprudential norms, it follows that [Guantánamo Bay] military commissions also do – and that there is every reason to conclude that they will be fair."*

Colonel Frederic Borch, Acting Chief Prosecutor Guantánamo Bay[808]

For all the claims made by, about and on behalf of the ICC, the simple fact is that in its assertion to have legal jurisdiction over persons over whom it has no jurisdiction – for example over Sudanese nationals – it is no more legitimate or legal than the US military commissions sitting at Guantánamo Bay in Cuba.[809] In fact the case has been made that the Guantánamo Bay detainees enjoy more rights than those offered by the ICC. And the comparisons are not limited to questionable legal claims but also to the ethos and mentality of the organisations. Human Rights Watch, for example, has reported that in the DRC, some non-governmental organisation representatives in April 2007 referred to the ICC there as "Guantánamo" because of its secrecy, isolation, and a perceived bunker mentality.[810]

Following the terrorist attacks within the USA on 11 September 2001, President Bush invoked his powers as President and Commander-in-Chief, citing the *Uniform Code of Military Justice* (UCMJ) and congressional authorisation, to issue his Military Order of 13 November 2001 authorising the use of military commissions to try suspected foreign terrorists. This instrument stated that the 11 September 2001 attacks were carried out "on a scale that has created a state of armed conflict that requires the use of the United States Armed Forces".[811]

The order also stated that "individuals shall not be privileged to seek any remedy or maintain any proceeding, directly or indirectly, or to have any such remedy or proceeding sought on the individual's behalf, in (i) any court of the USA, or any State thereof, (ii) any court of any foreign nation, or (iii) any international tribunal". This was a suspension of the writ of *habeas corpus*.[812] President Bush's Military Order was supported by two subsequent memoranda by the US Government Office of Legal Counsel in December 2001 and January 2002, which stated, respectively, that al-Qaeda and Taliban members could not claim *habeas corpus* privileges in a US court and were not protected by the Geneva Conventions.[813]

In accordance with his Military Order of 13 November 2001, the president must determine if an individual is subject to his Military Order. This decision is the jurisdictional basis for prosecution. Until the president determines that an individual is subject to his Military Order, no prosecution is possible. However, this determination does not require that criminal charges be brought against the individual; that decision is made by the appointing authority after the chief prosecutor recommends that charges be approved.

The Guantánamo military commissions brought into being in November 2001 are made up of military officers and are directly subordinate to the US Department of Defense. The commissions were to consist of a presiding officer (a lawyer), at least four other officers (between eight and eleven in capital cases), and one alternate. The commissions are tasked with trying non-US citizens whom the president has reason to believe are or have been members of al-Qaeda; have engaged in, aided or abetted or conspired to commit acts of international terrorism; or have harboured such people.[814] The US government supplemented the original 2001 Military Order with six orders and ten instructions governing rules and procedures at Guantánamo Bay from 2001 to 2006.[815] On 30 April 2003, the US government issued eight "Military Commission Instructions", further establishing the structure and regulations for the trials of individuals designated as subject to trial by military commission.[816]

Since January 2002, 779 persons from forty-two different countries have been detained by the USA at Guantánamo Bay in Cuba. Many of those detained were captured by the USA on battlefields in Afghanistan in late 2001. Others have been detained across the world.

Military commissions have a long history in the USA.[817] The Guantánamo military commissions are war courts (as opposed to occupation courts and martial law courts). The Guantánamo military commissions derive their authority from Articles I and II of the US Constitution and are based on the 1950 *Uniform Code of Military Justice*, the foundation of US military law.[818] Military commissions must be authorised by an Act of Congress or through the common law of war, and their jurisdiction is "limited to offenses cognizable during time of war". They do not require a state of war to have been declared by the US Congress. Military commissions are authorised to try any "persons not otherwise subject to military law", for "violations of the laws of war and for offenses committed in territory under military occupation".[819] Prior to 2001 the Supreme Court had supported the US government's position whenever the jurisdiction of US military commissions was challenged.

Since their introduction in 2001, the military commissions at Guantánamo Bay have been vigorously tested in the USA federal court system. Federal legal rulings have also shaped the way in which the commissions are presently constituted. In June 2004, in *Hamdi v. Rumsfeld*, for example, the Supreme Court established that detainees at Guantánamo Bay had the right to challenge their detention in US courts. As a result, the US government established the Combatant Status Review Tribunals (CSRTs) to determine whether detainees had been correctly identified as "enemy combatants". Later that year, the Administrative Review Board was established to conduct annual status reviews of those still detained and to decide whether a detainee still poses a threat to the USA and its allies. Ninety-three per cent of the detainees who appeared before the 572 tribunals held between August 2004 and 15 June 2007, were ruled to be "enemy combatants".[820]

In 2005 the US Congress passed the *Detainee Treatment Act* (DTA). This act sought to prohibit inhumane treatment of prisoners, including prisoners at Guantánamo Bay. It requires military interrogations to be performed according to the US Army Field Manual for Human Intelligence Collector Operations; and strips federal courts of jurisdiction to consider *habeas corpus* petitions filed by prisoners in Guantánamo, or other claims asserted by Guantánamo detainees against the US government, as well as limiting appellate review of decisions of the Combatant Status Review Tribunals and military commissions.

A 2006 Supreme Court ruling, *Hamdan v. Rumsfeld*, presented the administration with a choice between operating the military commissions as regular courts martial or seeking congressional approval for the military commissions as outlined in the 2001 Military Order. President Bush chose the congressional route and presented a bill for a *Military Commissions Act* (MCA) to Congress on 6 September 2006. The act became law on 17 October 2006, thus legalising the military commissions as they were constituted, and provided procedural guidelines for the conduct of the commissions and clearly defines what constitutes an "unlawful enemy combatant".[821] The act lays out exactly how the military commissions are convened, and what procedural safeguards must be in place. These include a presumption of innocence, proof of guilt beyond a reasonable doubt, the right of the accused to represent himself, provides for a right to call and cross-examine witnesses, lawyer/client privilege, no presumption of guilt from remaining silent, representation by a military defence counsel and the inadmissibility of statements obtained through torture. The legislation also confirms that, in accordance with the Supreme Court ruling, Common Article 3 of the Geneva Conventions applies to military commissions. The act states, however, that "as provided by the Constitution…and by this section [of the act], the President has the authority for the United States to interpret the meaning and application of the Geneva Conventions". According to President Bush the MCA was "one of the most important pieces of legislation in the war on terrorism". Bush also stated that "These military commissions are lawful, they are fair, and they are necessary."[822]

After the military panel has delivered its verdict and imposed a sentence there is a clear review process. All records of trial must be reviewed by the appointing authority who may return the case to the military commission for further proceedings if he determines it is not administratively complete. A three-member Review Panel of Military Officers, one of whom must have prior experience as a judge, will review all cases for material errors of law, and may consider matters submitted by the prosecution and defence. Review panel members may be civilians who were specifically commissioned to serve on the panel. If a majority of the review panel members believe a material error of law has occurred, they may return the case to the military commission for further proceedings. The Secretary of Defense will review the record of trial and, if appropriate, may return it to the military commission for further proceedings, or forward the case to the President with a recommendation as to disposition. The President may either return the case to the military commission for further proceedings or make the final decision as to its disposition.

The President may delegate final decision authority to the Secretary of Defense, in which case the secretary may approve or disapprove the findings or change a finding of guilty to a finding of guilty to a lesser-included offence, or mitigate, commute, defer, or suspend the sentence imposed, or any portion thereof. A finding of not guilty as to a charge shall not be changed to a finding of guilty. Under the *Detainee Treatment Act* of 2005, the USA Circuit Court of Appeals for the District of Columbia had the exclusive jurisdiction to determine the validity of any final decisions of a military commission case. Review shall be "as of right" for capital cases or cases with a sentence of ten years or more. Review for all other cases shall be at the discretion of the US Circuit Court of Appeals for the District of Columbia.

Invoking the *Military Commissions Act*, President Bush issued an executive order on 14 February 2007 establishing military commissions to try "alien unlawful enemy combatants". On 12 June 2008, the USA Supreme Court ruled in *Boumediene v. Bush* that the Guantánamo captives were entitled to the protection of the United States Constitution. Justice Anthony Kennedy, writing for the majority, described the Combatant Status Review Tribunals as "an inadequate substitute for habeas corpus" although "both the DTA and the SCRT process remain intact."[823]

The Obama Administration introduced and signed into law the *Military Commissions Act* of 2009, which was included in the *National Defense Authorization Act* (NDAA). This act significantly improves upon the Bush Administration's system of military commissions. The new legislation excludes statements obtained through torture or through cruel, inhuman, or degrading treatment, while empowering the Secretary of Defense to enact rules permitting admission of coerced statements and hearsay evidence. It allows for defendants to have the right to attend their entire trial and examine all evidence presented against them, to cross-examine witnesses against them, and to call their own witnesses. Defendants may be excluded from a commission proceeding for being disruptive, but not to prevent them from being present during the presentation of classified evidence. Military prosecutors are required under the new law to disclose the existence of any exculpatory evidence as well as any evidence that might impeach the credibility of a government witness. Defendants are allowed to appeal in the first instance to the US Court of Military Commission Review, with further appeals to the Federal Appeals Court in Washington and ultimately to the US Supreme Court. It allows government prosecutors to file appeals before or during the trial, but it limits a defendant's appeals until after the commission has concluded. Military commissions are allowed jurisdiction over thirty-two crimes including pillaging, denying quarter, taking hostages, torture, mutilation, and rape. The new law also authorises military commissions to try individuals for conspiracy and providing material support for terrorism. The legislation also makes provision for defendants to receive good legal assistance: "The fairness and effectiveness of the military commission system…will depend to a significant degree on the adequacy of the defense counsel and associated resources for individuals accused, particularly in the case of capital cases… . Defense counsel in military commission cases, particularly in capital cases…should be fully resourced."

Guantánamo military commissions and ICC similarities

While the ICC may well seek to distance itself from the Guantánamo Bay military commissions, the American military definitely sees similar legal standards. Colonel Frederic Borch, a senior USA military lawyer, writing in *The Army Lawyer*, favourably compared the Guantánamo Bay military commissions to the ICC.[824] Borch noted that President Bush mandated in his Military Order that all commissions be "full and fair". He states that:

> Military Commission Order No. 1 provides the following safeguards for an accused – all of which are similar to those protections enjoyed by an accused at courts-martial: (1) the presumption of innocence; (2) proof of guilt beyond a reasonable doubt; (3) the right to call and cross-examine witnesses (subject to rules regarding production of witnesses and protection of information); (4) access to all evidence the prosecution intends to introduce at trial and any exculpatory evidence known to the prosecution; (5) no statements made by an accused to his attorney, or anything derived from those statements, may be used against him at trial; (6) the right to remain silent at trial, with no adverse inference from such silence; (7) the right to military defense counsel at no cost to the accused; (8) the right to civilian defense counsel at no cost to government (provided counsel is a U.S. citizen and obtains a security clearance); and (9) the right to have any findings and sentence reviewed by an appellate panel.[825]

Borch then stated that American courts martial should not be the measure of fairness. He stated that the public should use similar standards to evaluate the fairness of Guantánamo Bay, and compared the procedures of the military tribunals to "the rules governing prosecutions before the new International Criminal Court", which provide for the following: "(1) a presumption of innocence; (2) proof beyond a reasonable doubt; (3) choice of counsel at no cost; (4) right to cross-examine witnesses against him; (5) right against self-incrimination; and (6) a right to appeal any findings or sentence to an 'Appeal Chamber'".[826]

Borch points out that "While the United States is not a party to the Treaty of Rome, and while the ICC does not apply to our armed conflict with al Qaida and the Taliban, a comparison of its rules with the regulations governing military commissions shows that there is no difference between the rights enjoyed by an accused at either proceeding. Assuming *arguendo* that the ICC's rules satisfy international jurisprudential norms, it follows that military commissions also do – and that there is every reason to conclude that they will be fair."

In all formal contexts the US government has carefully sought to position its actions in terms of existing international law. For example, in March 2002, the Organization of American States' Inter-American Commission on Human Rights issued a call for the USA to take "urgent measures" to determine whether the detainees were prisoners of war. The USA replied that "Under Article 4 of the Geneva Convention...Taliban detainees are not entitled to prisoner of war status... . The Taliban have not effectively distinguished themselves from the civilian population of Afghanistan... . Al-Qaeda is an international terrorist group and cannot be considered a state party to the Geneva Convention." According to the USA, all Taliban and al-Qaeda members rounded up worldwide are, by default, "unlawful combatants" rather than prisoners of war.

The USA would argue that all law, either implicitly or explicitly, carries with it recourse to exceptional situations. Exceptions to the rule have in fact defined the rule of the laws of war, as can be demonstrated through close examination of the Geneva Conventions.

Riddhi Dasgupta, the author of *Changing Face of the Law: A Global Perspective*, has also compared the Guantánamo Bay military commissions with the ICC.[827] He has examined whether or not "the ICC could be considered superior to the Guantánamo military Commissions". He notes that the ICC is a formal institution with rules and procedures entrenched in the Rome Statute, while the Guantánamo commissions were the USA government's *ad hoc* response to the events of 11 September 2001, a legal response subsequently shaped by US Supreme Court pronouncements in *Hamdi v. Rumsfeld* (2004) and *Rasul v. Bush* (2004). These cases opened USA courts to detainee challenges from Guantánamo and required a "neutral decision-maker" to decide culpability. A third case, Hamdan v. Rumsfeld (2006), referenced Common Article 3 of the Geneva Conventions and the *Uniform Code of Military Justice* (UCMJ) (rights protected by US federal law) in criticising the Guantánamo military commissions' trial procedures.

Gupta states that "suggesting...that the ICC inherently is a better alternative [to the Guantánamo military commissions] is an oversimplification. Certain protections at the core of an American criminal trial and considered fundamental judicial guarantees are not secured to an ICC defendant."

Gupta notes five issues that highlight the differences between the American legal system and the ICC, differences that undermine the legal legitimacy of the ICC when compared to US law: the ICC's Rules of Procedure and Evidence ("ICC Rules") do not guarantee the defendant a speedy trial (a right preserved by the Sixth Amendment to the US Constitution) nor is there a stipulation about the maximum length of time that a prisoner may be detained, thus causing significant delay in the commencement of a trial; Rule 150 allows prosecutors to appeal a criminal defendant's acquittal (in the USA, the Fifth Amendment to the Constitution categorically forbids such double jeopardy); Rule 74 enables the ICC to require witnesses to provide self-incriminating testimony, only if the court itself privileges the testimony as classified and secretive, including from the defence itself (the Fifth Amendment to the US Constitution expressly rules out all judicial or governmental efforts to compel self-incrimination); Rules 81 and 82, either individually or in tandem, allow secret trials, the use of hearsay or anonymous testimony, or narrow the rights of defendants to confront their accusers (in contrast, the US Constitution guarantees the right to a public trial, bans hearsay or anonymous testimony and promises the actual confrontation by the accusers in court; and the ICC trials are adjudicated by judges (in the USA the constitutional rights to jury trial and due process have been construed to require a unanimous vote to convict by the jury of one's peers, not judges).

As proof that the ICC proceedings are not necessarily superior to American criminal trials, Gupta points to the differences inherent in Anglo-American versus the continental European legal system: trials by judges rather than juries, regulations weakening the defendant's right to cross-examine witnesses, and no prohibition against double jeopardy.

Gupta also points to structural reasons that "militate against summarily preferring the ICC structure over the Guantánamo commissions". He notes that the Rome Statute's six-year precedential history is far from time-tested: "On the other hand, unlike the ICC, the body of caselaw (*stare decisis*) germane to Guantánamo is substantial." He notes that the legal bases for the Guantánamo challenges were the Geneva Conventions and the *Uniform Code of Military Justice:*

> The UCMJ's roots run even deeper [than the Geneva Conventions], before the founding of the American Republic and before the Declaration of Independence. In 1775, the Continental Congress passed 69 Articles of War to govern military conduct; in 1806, Congress first enacted 101 Articles of War into federal law; and in 1951 the modern-day UCMJ became effective. The Rasul-Hamdi-Hamdan line of precedent traced the American court cases that have helped develop this strain of jurisprudence.

Gupta was particularly concerned about the ICC not being "strong enough to deter prosecutorial overreach", especially with regard to his judgment as to the admissibility of evidence obtained in a manner contrary to universal human rights if the violation would mar the integrity of the proceedings.

He also questioned what would be the case if the admissibility criteria regarding evidence were "opaque, malleable and susceptible to insider manipulation by experts versed in the field". As a prime example he cites the text of the ICC prosecutor's application for an arrest warrant against Sudanese President al-Bashir given that the application presents "[d]ata from refugee camps in Chad and camps for internally displaced persons…within Darfur". Gupta makes the point that:

> Simply owing to the difficult situation on the ground, the reliability of this data is likely to be imperfect. Yet there might be pressure to admit this or other forms of evidence, including anecdotal testimony, in order to make a morally compelling case against al-Bashir. Similarly, there might be international insistence from many quarters to ignore rules concerning hearsay as well as victim impact statements which, in ordinary cases, are scrutinised rigorously before being admitted into a criminal proceeding.

Gupta states that there are concerns regarding "what, according to the international legal norms, is the remedy if an intolerable conflict of interest or other deviation from lawful prosecutorial behaviour is uncovered". He concludes that "In short, what went 'wrong' (at least through the often clouded lens of international law) in Guantánamo could recur [at the ICC]."

Gupta sees a direct comparison between Guantánamo Bay and The Hague. He warns that the ICC "evidence" rules may well replicate events at Guantánamo Bay: "In al-Bashir's case, this panacea might have the unintended effect of supplanting demanding rules of evidence entirely with anecdotes, hearsay and otherwise questionable testimony – concerns familiar to the military commissions at Guantánamo." He is clear that the admissibility of evidence is crucial: "This is especially problematic given that the data accumulated by the ICC prosecutor is almost entirely secondary, and based on evidence from the Sudanese diaspora rather than independent investigations on the ground."[828]

The comparisons between Guantánamo Bay and the ICC are clear. Both courts are made up of judges not juries. Both have been very slow in bringing the accused to trial. Both tribunals have been accused of using hearsay testimony and anonymous evidence in trials. As Gupta points out, Guantánamo Bay detainees are now entitled to rights under the US Constitution which are not available to ICC prisoners.

Chapter Twelve

INACTION OVER IRAQ

"The information available at this time supports a reasonable basis for an estimated 4 to 12 victims of wilful killing and a limited number of victims of inhuman treatment, totaling in all less than 20 persons."

ICC Chief Prosecutor Luis Moreno Ocampo[829]

"A lawyer representing Iraqi civilians who claim they were abused by British soldiers in Iraq, has said there are 'tens of thousands' of allegations of mistreatment from 'hundreds and hundreds of people'."

ITV News[830]

In 2003 Iraq was attacked and invaded by USA and British military forces. The invasion concluded with the capture of the Iraqi capital by American forces and resulted in the overthrow of the government of Saddam Hussein. The invasion was followed by an insurgency fought between Iraqi insurgents and American-led occupation forces supporting a newly constituted US-installed Iraqi government. The USA completed its withdrawal of military personnel in December 2011: British forces ended their military involvement in April 2009. The insurgency continues. Thirty-six other countries were militarily involved as occupation forces in the aftermath of the invasion and during the insurgency. The occupation forces, designated "Multi-National Force – Iraq", more commonly referred to as coalition forces, were responsible for conducting and handling military operations during much of the insurgency. A significant number of States Parties to the ICC were among them, including Britain, Australia, Poland, Italy, the Netherlands, Spain, Denmark, Norway, Hungary, Portugal, Romania, Estonia, Bulgaria, Czech Republic, Slovakia, Lithuania, South Korea, Georgia, El Salvador, New Zealand, Honduras, Dominican Republic and Nicaragua.

The invasion and occupation precipitated a humanitarian disaster. The human cost has been staggering. There are an estimated 1.3 million internally displaced persons in Iraq.[831] The *Lancet* is the world's leading general medical journal. In 2006 it published a study of civilian mortality following the 2003 invasion.[832] The study estimated that "as a consequence of the coalition invasion of March 18, 2003, about 655,000 Iraqis have died above the number that would be expected in a non-conflict situation, which is equivalent to about 2.5% of the population in the study area.⁸³³ About 601,000 of these excess deaths were due to violent causes."⁸³⁴ The *Lancet* study's figure of 654,965 excess deaths through to the end of June 2006 was based on household survey data. The estimate was for all excess violent and non-violent deaths, and included deaths as a result of damaged infrastructure and poorer healthcare, a direct consequence of the invasion and occupation. The study estimated that of the 601,027 deaths due to violence, thirty-one per cent were attributed to coalition forces, twenty-four per cent to others and forty-six per cent were unknown. That is to say coalition forces were said to have been responsible for the violent deaths of over 186,000 Iraqi civilians. The study stated that a copy of a death certificate was available for a high proportion of the reported deaths (ninety-two per cent of those households asked to produce one). The study noted that:

> The proportion of violent deaths attributed to coalition forces might have peaked in 2004; however, the actual number of Iraqi deaths attributed to coalition forces increased steadily through 2005. Deaths were not classified as being due to coalition forces if households had any uncertainty about the responsible party; consequently, the number of deaths and the proportion of violent deaths attributable to coalition forces could be conservative estimates.⁸³⁵

The invasion of Iraq, the country's subsequent occupation by foreign armies and the resultant humanitarian and human-rights disaster were precisely the sort of issues many ICC States Parties, non-governmental organisations and individuals believed the ICC had been established to address. It was in many respects the litmus test for the new court. While it was unable to act with regard to the planning and waging of a war of aggression by the USA and the UK because of the cynical fudging of the issue at the Rome Conference, there were nevertheless countless examples of crimes against humanity and war crimes during the invasion and subsequently – many of them committed by ICC States Parties and their citizens. Interestingly, in March 2005, the Iraqi government announced that it was considering becoming a party to the ICC. Michael Scharf stated that the day after the announcement, "bowing to intense pressure by the United States, the Iraqi government reversed course".⁸³⁶

It is worth noting that ICC Prosecutor Luis Ocampo declared that the court would be evenhanded in its work: "I cannot allow that we are a court just for the Third World. If the First World commits crimes, they have to investigate, if they don't, I shall investigate. That's the rule and we have one rule for everyone."⁸³⁷ Except that it was a rule the court conspicuously failed to follow. The court quite simply failed to address the Iraq issue. The OTP of the ICC reported in February 2006 that it had received 240 communications in connection with the invasion of Iraq in March 2003, which alleged that various war crimes had been committed. Many of these complaints concerned the British participation in the invasion, as well as alleged British responsibility for the mistreatment of civilians and torture and deaths of Iraqis while in detention in British-controlled areas.⁸³⁸ On 9

February 2006, Ocampo published his response to all those who had raised the issue of Iraq.[839] The prosecutor explained that the complaints involved issues concerning the legality of the invasion itself, and complaints concerning the conduct of hostilities between March and May 2003, which included allegations in respect of the targeting of civilians or clearly excessive attacks and wilful killing or inhuman treatment of civilians. Ocampo correctly stated that he did not have authority to consider the complaint about the legality of the invasion. Although the ICC statute included the crime of "aggression", at that stage the court had chosen not to define the crime. Ocampo then also stated that there was insufficient evidence for proceeding with an investigation of the complaints in connection with targeting of civilians or clearly excessive attacks. He concluded that the situation in Iraq did not appear to meet the "gravity" threshold necessary to initiate any such investigation. *Ocampo stated that there was a reasonable basis for believing that there had been an estimated four to twelve victims of wilful killing and a limited number of victims of inhuman treatment, totalling in all fewer than twenty persons.* The American lawyer Alan Dershowitz has stated that the armed forces of the USA and the UK have "caused the deaths of thousands of civilians in Iraq and Afghanistan".[840] The ICC and Ocampo ignored all of these deaths as well as a catalogue of thousands of other human-rights abuses.

Although it finally formally announced its decision about Iraq in 2006, it is now clear that as early as July 2003 the ICC was going to ignore the human-rights disaster in Iraq. US government diplomats noted that in semi-private forums and in private conversations reported to embassy legal officers, "Ocampo has indicated consistently that his initial investigative interests will [not] focus...on Iraq." The American diplomats reported that "Ocampo has said that he wishes to dispose of Iraq issues (i.e., not investigate them), much in line with what Registrar Cathala is urging." ICC Registrar Bruno Cathala's views were documented in the same cable. Cathala told American diplomats that it will be crucial for the ICC to dispose easily of "silly things like Iraq", stating: "We're not going to run all over the world." Cathala stated that he personally wanted relations with the American government to be smooth.[841]

In addition to simply not investigating involvement in alleged war crimes by British citizens, the ICC also chose not to investigate whether or not the UK, its leaders or personnel might be answerable to charges of acting with a common purpose with the USA, and thereby also accountable for any alleged war crimes attributable to the American forces with which they were in coalition. "Common purpose" is a legal doctrine stating that all participants in a crime are responsible for its consequences, even if it wasn't the original intention. Article 25 of the Rome Statute states:

> [A] person shall be criminally responsible and liable for punishment for a crime within the jurisdiction of the Court if that person: (a) Commits such a crime, whether as an individual, jointly with another or through another person, regardless of whether that other person is criminally responsible; (b) Orders, solicits or induces the commission of such a crime which in fact occurs or is attempted; (c) For the purpose of facilitating the commission of such

a crime, aids, abets or otherwise assists in its commission or its attempted commission, including providing the means for its commission; (d) In any other way contributes to the commission or attempted commission of such a crime by a group of persons acting with a common purpose. Such contribution shall be intentional and shall either: (i) Be made with the aim of furthering the criminal activity or criminal purpose of the group, where such activity or purpose involves the commission of a crime within the jurisdiction of the Court; or (ii) Be made in the knowledge of the intention of the group to commit the crime.[842]

Nicholas Wood has put an alleged relationship between the US and Britain in Iraq in layman's terms: "In a crude legal comparison, the US is the armed robber, and the UK provides the getaway car."[843]

While the ICC claimed that there were fewer than twenty instances of human-rights abuses by British forces in Iraq, the British government has itself admitted that its forces had been party to human-rights abuses involving hundreds of Iraqi civilians. There are at the very least 1,000 additional cases in the public domain. In January 2013, for example, British lawyers headed by Phil Shiner from the Public Interest Lawyers group, representing almost 200 Iraqis, requested an independent judge-led public inquiry into unlawful killings and British detention practices between 2003 and 2008, alleging that British troops carried out "terrifying acts of brutality" against Iraqi civilians.[844] A total of 1,051 sworn statements were entered into the proceedings. It was claimed that these British human-rights abuses were "systemic". Women, the elderly and children were among the victims. The lawyers said that there were hundreds of further claims. It was revealed that the British government had already paid out more than £15 million to settle over 200 claims of mistreatment and unlawful detention, with many more cases being negotiated.[845] In January 2013, *The Guardian* revealed that a further £1.1 million had been paid to twenty-two more people; payments to about 180 more former prisoners were being negotiated, and a further 700 cases were said to be in the pipeline.[846] Shiner said there were "tens of thousands" of allegations of mistreatment from "hundreds and hundreds of people". He stated that "some of the cases are truly shocking", and listed as examples the unlawful killing of a sixty-two-year-old grandmother, an eight-year-old girl playing with friends, and a man shot as he slept. Michael Fordham QC, representing the Iraqis, told the court: "We are saying enough is enough and there must be a public inquiry in relation to the credible and prima facie cases of human rights violations perpetrated by the British military in Iraq."[847] The trial lawyers, led by Fordham, said that while the Baha Mousa inquiry "may have shone a torch into a dark corner", the case before the court was more like "a stadium in which we will switch on the floodlights".[848]

The Observer newspaper has described the behaviour by British military forces, which the ICC either ignored or of which the court was ignorant:

[A]n orgy of sadism, outlawed interrogation methods and unlawful killings by soldiers and intelligence officers against Iraqi civilians and prisoners of war between 2003 and 2008.... Civilians say they were subjected to hooding, beating, threats of rape and execution, forced nakedness and maintaining stress positions, violence against wives and children, ritual humiliation. And they claim that others...were beaten to death. They say walls of noise were used to drive the prisoners mad and cover the sounds of abuse and pain.[849]

Professor Andrew Williams, the author of *A Very British Killing: the Death of Baha Mousa*, a study of the most infamous case to date of British war crimes in Iraq, the torture to death in British Army custody of an innocent hotel receptionist, Baha Mousa, has written of "a culture of callous indifference that infected a whole battalion and permeated far up the command chain, both military and governmental". A public inquiry into Mousa's death, chaired by retired Lord Justice of Appeal Sir William Gage, concluded on 8 September 2011 after three years of investigation. The final 1,400-page report stated that a "large number" of soldiers assaulted Mousa and that many others including officers must have known about the abuse. The report called his death an "appalling episode of serious gratuitous violence". The inquiry condemned the Ministry of Defence for "corporate failure" and the regiment involved for a "lack of moral courage to report abuse". Seven members of the British Army were ultimately tried on charges relating to this case. On 19 September 2006, Corporal Donald Payne pleaded guilty to a charge of inhumane treatment to persons, making him the first member of the British armed forces to plead guilty to a war crime.[850] He was jailed for one year and dismissed from the service. The BBC reported that the six other soldiers were cleared of any wrongdoing.[851] *The Independent* reported that the charges had been dropped, and that the presiding judge, Justice Ronald McKinnon, stated that "none of those soldiers has been charged with any offence, *simply because there is no evidence against them as a result of a more or less obvious closing of ranks*".[852] (Emphasis added.)

Williams' book detailed the flawed investigation and prosecutions that followed Baha Mousa's murder. The British government subsequently claimed that the Baha Mousa inquiry, which investigated the killing of Mousa and the torture of several other civilians, addressed the issues of detention and interrogation generally. The government also claimed that its own Iraq Historic Allegations Team, established in 2010, would be a sufficient response to the allegations. This unit consists of Royal Military Police officers appointed to internally investigate unlawful killing and torture in Iraq by British forces. Its unsuitability for the task, however, was obvious. The British appeal court ruled in November 2011 that because its own personnel were involved in much of the behaviour in question, the RMP was itself "substantially compromised". Williams makes the following point directly relevant to the ICC:

> The international principle in criminal law is that you look at the connection between commanders and what happens on the ground. Responsibility is supposed to rest with those at the top. It's no excuse for ministers and officials to say they didn't know what was happening. These are international obligations. This is what we demand of others, but we do not demand it of

ourselves. What kind of message does that give to the world about who we are?[853]

The Observer newspaper noted that:

> The legal issue at stake is whether the other abuses were isolated incidents of which commanders were unaware, as the government insists, or systemic and authorised as policy. With these cases comes the contention that the violations were systemic and thereby illegal – with responsibility reaching senior command level – which would put the state in breach of international law and necessitate an independent public inquiry.

Shiner stated that the evidence presented to the court established several illegal "state practices" by British forces, adding that "[w]e've got the training materials [and] we've got the policy documents". He observed: "Violence was endemic to the state practices and part of the state practices." One "state practice" was "the use of trained coercive interrogation techniques, as a matter of policy… . They knew full well that what was happening was unlawful, right to the top." Shiner stated that second "state practice" was "an unlawful detention and internment regime which did not meet international obligations" with regard to tribunals, combatant status for prisoners of war and obligations to civilian suspects during arrest and detention. A third "state practice" was a "rolling programme of strike operations" to arrest civilians that entailed "blowing doors off so that 20 soldiers can run into houses at one or two in the morning while women and children are sleeping, men dragged from bed and rifle-butted – one man was simply shot in bed – women and children abused". Shiner stated that "a lot of people were killed".[854] The victims' claim before the court asserted: "No Iraqi appeared to be exempt from ill-treatment from arrest onwards."

The abuses in question took place in facilities named by the British forces as Battlecamp Main, Camp Stephen, Camp Bucca and Camp Breadbasket and also at the Shaibah logistics base, a contingency operations base, and other holding facilities. Many abuses also occurred in people's homes and in public. Shiner claimed that the government knew about the behaviour: "What we're dealing with are the widespread abuses… . We say to the ministry and government: 'Don't say you didn't know – what you can do is explain why you failed to do anything about it'." In the case before the court, he stated that "[a]ll of these allegations involve circumstances in which it can be said that the UK state knew, or ought to have known" about breaches of international law. He added the government's "response, or lack of one, is highly pertinent". He has further stated that "[m]ilitary facilities at which abuse occurred were under the command of the relevant commanding officer" and that "each detainee was medically examined at various points by doctors… . It is inconceivable that senior officers did not witness what was happening, or otherwise be aware of these incidents and practices."[855]

The ICC has stood idly by in the face of these detailed accounts of grave and systemic abuses of human rights. Schabas has demolished the court's self-serving justifications for not investigating crimes against humanity and war crimes committed by the military personnel of ICC States Parties during and after the 2003 invasion of Iraq. He has confirmed that the court was in a position to initiate prosecutions: "[T]he Prosecutor is enabled with the authority to investigate and prosecute war crimes attributable to British troops in Iraq, because Britain is a State Party to the Rome Statute."[856] Ocampo's reluctance to do so is also clear. Schabas, for example, points to the US diplomatic cable written at about the same time as the prosecutor's decision to do nothing regarding Iraq, and subsequently released by WikiLeaks.

As can be seen from their website, Phil Shiner's group, Public Interest Lawyers, is a very small legal firm with five employees, three of whom are lawyers.[857] This very small team has managed to document and bring to court well over 1,000 separate cases involving tens of thousands of alleged abuses of human rights by British forces. The ICC has had a budget of a billion euros over ten years and has 800 staff members. The ICC's investigation of abuses by British forces claimed that it could find fewer than twenty instances of human-rights abuses. And this by a court that constantly extolled its commitment to victims and victims' justice. This is quite simply a scandalous state of affairs.

It is clear that for political reasons the ICC and its chief prosecutor did not wish to adequately investigate alleged human rights abuses by British government forces in Iraq. In his attempt to justify the court's deliberate inaction regarding Iraq, Ocampo invoked the term "gravity". Schabas has explored and challenged the Prosecutor's contradictory and self-serving reliance of this term. It is worth citing him at length:

> The term "gravity", which appears in the Statute in two places relevant to the selection of cases and situations, had not figured in any significant manner in the early pronouncements of the Office of the Prosecutor. Up to that time, academic writers on the Rome Statute had generally failed to view the concept of "gravity" as being particularly relevant to the exercise of prosecutorial discretion. The two main Commentaries on the Rome Statute published at the time virtually ignored the matter. That changed in late 2005, when the Prosecutor discovered the gravity criterion in order to explain his decision to proceed against the leadership of the Lord's Resistance Army in Uganda rather than against those of the government forces.[858]

Ocampo came under a barrage of criticism from human-rights organisations and civil society groups internationally and within Uganda for focusing only on one side in the Uganda Civil War – as a result of the deal he had made with the Ugandan government. Schabas notes that "[i]n reply, the Prosecutor invoked 'gravity' and said that the Lord's Resistance Army had killed many more people than the soldiers of the Ugandan People's Defence Forces".[859] Schabas then went on to document the prosecutor's subsequent deployment of the "gravity" issue: "Within a few months the Prosecutor used the same gravity argument to resist entreaties that he investigate the conduct of British troops in Iraq." Schabas correctly states that while the ICC could not look at the legality of the war – the crime of aggression had been placed on hold – "there was no shortage of evidence that British soldiers had been engaged in various atrocities, including murder of civilians, and these were war crimes in the classic sense. Because the United Kingdom was a State Party to the Rome Statute, the Court had jurisdiction over war crimes perpetrated by British nationals."[860]

Schabas went on further to analyse the Chief Prosecutor's use of the "gravity" argument to justify inaction regarding the Iraq situation:

> The sum of these violations, he reasoned, was "of a different order" than the number of victims in other situations being investigated or analysed by the Office of the Prosecutor, notably northern Uganda, the Democratic Republic of the Congo and Darfur. He said that each of the latter situations involved thousands of wilful killings as well as intentional and large-scale sexual violence and abductions. The explanation was unconvincing, because any reasonable observer knows that since the invasion by the United Kingdom and the United States in 2003, and largely as a consequence, Iraq has been the scene of massive human rights violations. At a minimum, tens of thousands of innocent civilians have been killed and perhaps millions have been displaced. By setting specific acts attributable to British troops of which he had evidence, rather than the war as a whole, alongside general reports of victimization in other conflicts in central Africa, the Prosecutor was comparing apples and oranges. Or rather, he was comparing cases to situations.
>
> The fallacy of the comparison between Iraq and central Africa became clear within a matter of days, when Moreno-Ocampo announced the arrest of the Court's first prisoner, Thomas Lubanga. A Congolese warlord, Lubanga was not charged with the massive murders, abductions, and sexual violence that the Prosecutor had cited in his comparison with the British conduct in Iraq. Lubanga was accused only of the recruitment of child soldiers within the context of a civil war. Was that more serious than the murder and ill-treatment of civilians by British soldiers engaged in a war of aggression?[861]

For all of Ocampo's attempts to be clever and disguise the politics at the heart of the court's inaction over Iraq, Schabas concludes:

> All that the Prosecutor's decision did was confirm suspicions that the Court was not the politically neutral body its proponents had bragged about. In addition to being an influential member of the Court, the United Kingdom is also a permanent member of the Security Council. In contrast, Uganda and the Democratic Republic of the Congo were soft targets for the Court's activities. And they were compliant ones, in a sense, to the extent that the Prosecutor appeared to be interested only in rebel groups rather than government forces. The contrived reasoning about gravity also kept the Prosecutor sweet with the

Americans, who would not have been keen on prosecutions relating to the behaviour of their principal military ally in the Iraq invasion.[862]

Schabas notes that those responsible within the OTP for the "gravity" argument "have undoubtedly convinced themselves that they have found a legalistic formula enabling themselves to do the impossible, namely, to take a political decision while making it look judicial".[863] Schabas, however, has cut away the court's cynical use of the "gravity" argument: "The 'gravity' language strikes the observer as little more than obfuscation, a laboured attempt to make the determinations look more judicial than they really are."[864]

Schabas robustly challenged the court's excuse for inaction: "The explanation was unconvincing, because the evidence of massive death in Iraq was notorious…if the Democratic Republic of the Congo was inherently more serious than Iraq, because of the number of deaths, why was the Prosecutor not dealing with murder rather than the arguably less important crime of recruitment."[865] Schabas concluded of Ocampo: "In 2006 he appeared to decide that murder and torture of civilians by a foreign army following an illegal invasion was not as serious as the recruitment of child soldiers by a rebel militia. Others might be inclined to reverse the order."[866] Ocampo's selectivity and hypocrisy could not be more clear. Schabas has admitted that the prosecutor preferred to go for "soft targets" rather than "investigate the behaviour of…the British in Iraq."[867]

Hans Köchler has noted the dangers of the ICC's selectivity: "Selectively prosecuting cases from formerly colonized countries of sub-Saharan Africa while choosing not to use prosecutorial authority in cases that affect the interests of influential States Parties – and non-States Parties – to the Rome Statute is definitely not the way to convince the international public of the worthiness of the goals pursued by the International Criminal Court."[868]

To be clear then. The ICC refused to investigate British involvement in war crimes in Iraq or that the UK might through acting in a common purpose be jointly accountable for the alleged war crimes and crimes against humanity committed by its American ally: The *Lancet*'s mortality study indicated that American and British forces may have been responsible for the violent deaths of over 186,000 Iraqi civilians. There is a telling footnote to this decision by the court. When the Sudanese Ambassador to the UN stated that the Sudanese President was not guilty of the alleged crimes of which he was accused – and not convicted – the Chief Prosecutor of the ICC announced that the court will "investigate if…denial of the crimes committed could be considered a contribution to the perpetrators, acting with a common purpose". He warned that "appropriate measures" would be taken if investigators decided there was a case for a formal inquiry.[869] The legal doctrine of common purpose would not be examined by the ICC in respect of the uninvestigated violent deaths of hundreds of thousands of civilians, but is then invoked by the same court to justify the investigation of a simple denial of guilt for charges that had not even been proven.

Chapter Thirteen

An Afghan Case Study

"Several events have taken place under Mr. Obama's watch that could bring charges for war crimes."

The Washington Times[870]

"War crimes are not investigated in Afghanistan."

Afghanistan Independent Human Rights Commission[871]

Afghanistan provides a further example of a developing world nation invaded and occupied by Western states. It also provides another clear example of the ICC's disinclination, for political reasons, to deal with blatant war crimes allegedly committed and unaccounted for by Western military forces, including prominent European States Parties to the Rome Statute, in the territory of another State Party. The occupation of Afghanistan and the military operations that have been conducted and continue to be carried out in that country fall under the control of two international missions. The first international mission is Operation Enduring Freedom, a joint USA, UK and Afghan military operation. The operation began in 2001, following the 9/11 terrorist outrages in the USA. By the winter of 2001, the USA had unseated the Taliban government. The operation continues against a subsequent insurgency being fought against both the occupation forces and the new Afghan government the USA installed in Kabul, with military direction mostly coming from United States Central Command. The second mission is the International Security Assistance Force (ISAF), a NATO-led mission in Afghanistan that was established by the UNSC in December 2001 by Resolution 1386, as envisaged by the Bonn Agreement.[872] ISAF was set up as a UN-mandated international force to assist the new Afghan interim authority to provide security in and around the capital, Kabul, and to support the reconstruction of Afghanistan. On 11 August 2003, NATO assumed leadership of the ISAF operation, and from January 2006 onwards ISAF also assumed some combat duties from the ongoing Anglo-American mission, Operation Enduring Freedom. NATO became responsible for the command, coordination and planning of the force, including the provision of a force commander and headquarters on the ground in Afghanistan. ISAF is made up of military forces from the USA, UK and other NATO member states. ISAF falls under the command of NATO's Joint Force Command in the Dutch town of Brunssum. The two missions run in parallel. Their personnel are generally known as the coalition forces.

Afghanistan is a member of the ICC. William Schabas has confirmed that the court is able to initiate prosecutions of war crimes and crimes against humanity committed in Afghanistan: "[The Prosecutor] may...proceed with respect to war crimes committed by American troops in Afghanistan, which is a State Party to the Rome Statute, because there is jurisdiction over all crimes committed on Afghan territory."[873] Philippe Sands QC has confirmed this jurisdiction exists and has outlined the broad extent of the behaviour that could trigger ICC action: "A CIA officer who conducted an abusive interrogation at Bhagram air base could be tried before the court."[874] If this applies to non-lethal human-rights abuses by a citizen of a non-State Party to the ICC in an ICC State Party, how much stronger is the court's jurisdiction in the case of murder/attempted murder by a citizen of an ICC member state on the territory of an ICC member state?

Even *The Washington Times* has stated that "[s]everal events have taken place under Mr. Obama's watch that could bring charges for war crimes", actions that come under the ICC's remit.[875] There have been numerous incidents amounting to crimes against humanity and war crimes since Afghanistan was invaded in 2001, and since the court acquired jurisdiction in 2002. These grave abuses of human rights have implications for both the Bush and Obama Administrations, and for several ICC States Parties who have acted in coalition with US forces in ISAF/NATO operations. Professor Mark Herold has pointed to one incident among many that qualifies as a war crime but that has never been taken up by the ICC. On the evening of 29 June 2007, American warplanes killed between 50 and 130 innocent Afghan civilians in a night-time aerial assault upon the village of Haydarabad, about fifteen kilometres northeast of the town of Gereshk. The village was bombed for at least two hours, killing men, women and children.[876] Another major incident occurred on 4 May 2009, in what may be the single deadliest US attack in Afghanistan since the 2001 invasion, when American bombers killed as many as 147 Afghan civilians, 93 of them children, in an airstrike in western Afghanistan that locals call the Farah Massacre. With regard to this incident, US Central Command officials stated that US airstrikes in Afghanistan's Farah Province had killed only "20 to 30" civilians. A member of Farah's Provincial Council, Abdul Basir Khan, said he collected the names of the 147 individuals who died in the attack. Relatives of the victims showed mass graves to investigators, along with the remains of bombed-out buildings and homes. The International Red Cross reported that women and children were among the dozens of dead.[877] The UN reported that in 2008, US, NATO and Afghan forces were responsible for over 828 civilian deaths. Most of these deaths were the result of US and NATO airstrikes. In November 2008, for example, US troops bombed a wedding party in the Shah Wali Kot area in southern Afghanistan, killing about forty civilians – mainly women and children. NATO rejected the UN figure of 828 deaths, saying its forces were responsible for only 237 civilian deaths in 2008.[878]

In his study of war crimes in Afghanistan, *Afghanistan War Crimes: Government, ICC and NGOs*, Akbar Nasir Khan has written of the "culture of impunity ingrained in the country's legal system".[879] Khan pointed out that there are several indications that the Afghan government has no interest in addressing crimes against humanity and war crimes in Afghanistan: "The Government of Afghanistan has made no concrete efforts to deal with the issue of war crimes…" Khan has pointed to evidence that the government "is not interested in fulfilling its international obligations and participating against impunity". These include the fact that suggested draft legislation to make domestic laws conform to Article 68 of the Rome Statute has been ignored by the government; Afghanistan's seat is still vacant in the ASP of the ICC, and nobody has been appointed to the body yet; and that Afghanistan has never invited the ICC to conduct any investigations of past crimes.[880] In March 2009, the government let an action plan to implement a national "Action Plan for Peace, Reconciliation and Justice", prepared by the Afghanistan Independent Human Rights Commission in 2005, lapse.

In January 2007, both the lower and upper houses of the Afghan parliament passed a national stability and reconciliation resolution, which granted blanket amnesty to "[a]ll the political wings and hostile parties who had been in conflict before the formation of the interim administration". This was enacted as legislation in early 2010, in the Amnesty, National Reconciliation and Stability Law in the *Official Gazette* (No. 965). Section 3, Clause 2, of the amnesty law extends immunity from prosecution by the government to "armed people who are against the government of Afghanistan, after the passing of this law, if they cease from their objections, join the national reconciliation process, and respect constitutional law and other regulations of the Islamic Republic of Afghanistan, they will have all the perquisites of this law". Khan notes: "Legally, this law contradicts Afghanistan's 'duty to prosecute' norm which has been established under different instruments of international laws including Genocide Convention, Convention against Torture, and all four Geneva Conventions."

Khan noted further that "[h]uman rights abusers continued to enjoy almost complete impunity". He observed: "The Afghan parliament is made up largely of lawmakers who once belonged to armed groups, some of which have been accused of war crimes by human rights groups and the general public."[881] Afghanistan Human Rights Organization researcher Maghferat Samimi stated that the warlords and their militia commanders continue to commit crimes with impunity, protected by their alliances with foreign nations and comfortable positions within the Afghan government.[882]

Impunity, amnesty, warlords, militias and alleged war crimes in Africa are at the top of the ICC's agenda. In Afghanistan they barely rate a footnote in ICC reports, let alone a full investigation, despite the hundreds of thousands of victims of human-rights abuse and forced displacement. It is not as if the Chief Prosecutor does not have documentary evidence with which to work regarding war crimes in Afghanistan. Much of the investigative work has already been done for the ICC. The *Report of the United Nations Special Rapporteur on Extrajudicial, Summary or Arbitrary Executions* in 2009, for example, stated that:

> [T]here have been chronic and deplorable accountability failures with respect

to policies, practices and conduct that resulted in alleged unlawful killings – including possible war crimes – during the United States' international operations. The Government has failed to effectively investigate and punish lower-ranking soldiers for such deaths, and has not held senior officers responsible under the doctrine of command responsibility. Worse, it has effectively created a zone of impunity for private contractors and civilian intelligence agents by failing to investigate and prosecute them."[883]

In addition, in July 2010 WikiLeaks released a set of documents called the "Afghan War Diary", a compendium of over 91,000 reports covering the war in Afghanistan from 2004 to 2010.[884] Christopher Hall, a legal adviser for Amnesty International, said the WikiLeaks material, together with data collected previously, contained enough evidence of atrocities for the ICC prosecutor to seek permission to launch a full probe on Afghanistan:

It is not an issue at this stage whether the leaked information, whose authenticity has not been denied, is admissible evidence in a trial in the ICC. Coupled with all the other reliable information that the office of the prosecutor has been compiling since 2007, concerning all parties to the conflict, the office has more than sufficient information to determine whether to seek authorisation from the ICC pre-trial chamber to open a formal criminal investigation designed to obtain sufficient admissible evidence for the trial of individuals for war crimes and crimes against humanity.[885]

Harold Koh, the US State Department's legal adviser, said the ICC prosecutor should investigate "more immediate" concerns than acts by US forces in Afghanistan. Koh, predictably, said that the WikiLeaks data dump was unreliable as evidence. He added, "frankly I don't think a prosecutor conducts his business as a serious prosecutor by not first doing investigations in which he gathers evidence, as opposed to things on the web, and determine whether there is basis for a case".[886] (Interestingly, it emerged in July 2011 that while the ICC prosecutor was not interested in using the huge WikiLeaks material release regarding Afghanistan, he would be relying on one or two leaked American cables released by WikiLeaks as part of his evidence in Kenyan cases before the court.[887])

The 4 September 2009 Kunduz massacre

A particularly infamous and well-documented incident occurred on 4 September 2009 when a German officer serving with the NATO-led ISAF in Afghanistan, Colonel Georg Klein, called in an airstrike by two US F-15E Strike Eagle fighter bombers on two immobilised fuel tankers, seven kilometres southwest of Kunduz in northern Afghanistan, near the hamlet of Omar Kheil on the border of the Char Dara and Aliabad districts. It was the bloodiest German military action since the end of the Second World War.[888] It was also the largest airstrike that had ever been launched in northern Afghanistan.

The German Bundestag lower house of parliament would come to describe the Kunduz massacre as "one of the most serious incidents involving the German army since the Second World War".[889] A political advisor to the German Army, Timo Noetzel, stated that "It was, by far, the most aggressive and in its consequences most deadly operational decision for which a German soldier had been responsible since the end of the Second World War."[890]

The fuel tankers, each carrying some 50,000 litres of petrol, had been hijacked and were stuck on a small island in the middle of the Kunduz River, then a dry river bed. *Der Spiegel* noted that "the trucks were obviously going nowhere, and had been stuck for four hours".[891] The US warplanes dropped two GBU-38 bombs, each weighing approximately 250 kilograms (500 pounds), and reported "weapons impact". The GBU-38 is a highly accurate weapon system, thanks to a GPS guidance system. On the ground, the fuel tankers exploded in a gigantic fireball. The attack killed as many as 140 civilians, many of them burned alive. Many of the victims were women and children trying to siphon fuel. *Der Spiegel* stated: "It was an unnecessary air strike, that much is certain."[892] The then Bundeswehr Chief of Staff Wolfgang Schneiderhan, stated: "Now we have lost our innocence."[893] Afghan President Hamid Karzai was fiercely critical of the attack: "Targeting civilian men and women is not acceptable."[894] He went on to observe: "What a miscalculation! More than 90 dead for a simple fuel tanker that was stuck in a river bed. Why didn't they send ground troops to get the tankers back?" Karzai also revealed that in a telephone call to apologise for the tragedy, General McChrystal had distanced himself from the incident, stating that he had not ordered the attack.[895] *Der Spiegel* reported that Germany:

> "[C]ame under strong international pressure because of the attack. An informal meeting of European Union foreign ministers in Stockholm on the weekend of Sept. 5–6 turned into an indictment of the German deployment. French Foreign Minister Bernard Kouchner said that the bombing was "a big mistake" and it needed to be thoroughly investigated. His British counterpart David Miliband called for an "urgent investigation" and said it was important to "make sure that it doesn't happen again".[896]

The German government and ISAF initially said that all those killed in the bombing were Taliban fighters. Defence Ministry spokesperson Captain Christian Dienst told journalists in Berlin on the day of the attack that "According to our knowledge at present, no civilian was injured" and that the attack was ordered because the military was in possession of data "which allowed the conclusion that no uninvolved civilians would be harmed in the attack". Dienst claimed that German soldiers were "completely in the know" about "what they are allowed to do and what they are not allowed to do".[897] Dienst also stated: "Had civilians been present, the air strikes could not have been called in."[898] These claims were all false.

In the days that followed the attack, the German government continued to claim that no civilians had died and that only insurgents had been killed. The Defence Ministry then went on to lie about the circumstances of the attack, claiming German use of reconnaissance drones and reconnaissance vehicles during the night to gather information about the situation in the riverbed before the attack. When questions were asked about the questionable circumstances of the attack, the ministry then claimed on 7 September that there was a "further intelligence source that we are not discussing publicly". The following day, at a special meeting of the Bundestag's defence committee, this "third source" was revealed to be nonexistent.[899] The German Defence Minister at the time, Franz Josef Jung, told the *Bild am Sonntag* newspaper on 6 September that "the air strike was absolutely necessary" and that no civilians were killed.[900] In the interview with *Bild am Sonntag* – two days after the airstrike – Jung said: "According to all the information I currently have, only Taliban terrorists were killed in the operation carried out by US aircraft." On 8 September, in comments to the Bundestag, Jung stated that Klein "had clear intelligence indicating that those involved were exclusively enemies of the state".[901] These were blatant lies. On the evening of 4 September, the German Regional Military Command in Masar-i-Sharif sent clear reports back to Berlin that there had been civilian casualties, something confirmed in a subsequent German military police report.

When the claim that no civilians had been killed became untenable, the new German and ISAF position later in September was that seventy of those killed were Taliban and that only thirty were civilians.[902] As Neta Crawford noted: "ISAF forces eventually acknowledged that most of those killed were civilians."[903] When it was obvious that their previous positions were indefensible and that civilians may have died, Berlin's new claim was that the bombing had still been militarily appropriate. Karl-Theodor zu Guttenberg, Jung's successor as Defence Minister following national elections, assumed office on 28 October 2009. On 6 November he stated: "I myself have concluded that I have no doubts with regard to the assessment of the Inspector General (of the German military), namely that the military strikes and the airstrikes, given the overall threat environment, must be viewed as militarily appropriate." He said that a NATO report into the incident had only uncovered "procedural errors".[904] Guttenberg's version, an unsustainable falsehood, nevertheless remained the official position for four weeks. On 3 December, in the German parliament, Guttenberg reversed this position. He stated that the airstrike was "from today's objective viewpoint, and in light of all of the documents that were withheld from me at the time, militarily inappropriate".[905] The Defence Minister's new position was also based on a clear lie: he had had unfettered access to the papers he claimed had been withheld from him. Attempts to cover-up the affair became public knowledge. This led to three high-profile resignations. The Defence Minister at the time of the attack, Franz Josef Jung, was forced to resign from his subsequent government position.[906] His resignation followed those of State Secretary Peter Wichert, one of his deputies while he was Defence Minister, and Germany's top military officer, General Wolfgang Schneiderhan.[907] In December 2009, in an unprecedented action by a German army officer, Schneiderhan accused Guttenberg of outright lying.[908]

Bild has demonstrated the German government's immediate dishonesty about the attack:

For days after the attack, then-Defence Minister Franz Josef Jung claimed there had been no civilian casualties. But he must have known better, according to documentation he would have had access to at the time.... Top secret videos and an up-till-now secret army report seemingly prove that Jung's Ministry from the outset had clear knowledge of civilian casualties as well as the unclear intelligence before the strike.[909]

One year later, the German newspaper *Bild* reported that officials in the Defence Ministry had been aware almost immediately that there had been civilian deaths, and that information about civilian casualties had been withheld from parliament and from prosecutors. On the afternoon of 4 September, for example, about seventeen hours after the bombing, a German news agency, citing the Defence Ministry, reported that the bombing had averted a Taliban attack and quoted Deputy Defence Minister Thomas Kossendey as saying that the reaction was warranted, because it was a case of "imminent danger". *Der Spiegel* reported that the German Foreign Ministry was already aware that the statement was false: "One of the diplomats involved in the case wrote in an e-mail, not without irony: 'If this attempt to clear up the case is completely logical and reasonable, cows will be flying soon.... In my opinion, Kossendey is completely on the wrong track here. Very irritating!'"[910] *Der Spiegel* reported further that on 6 September, the highest-ranking military official at the Chancellery, Erich Vad, noted to Merkel's foreign policy advisor, Christoph Heusgen, that "contrary to the current press releases" by the Defence Ministry, "civilian dead cannot be categorically ruled out". The German Bundesnachrichtendienst (BND) intelligence service had been intercepting mobile telephone calls both during the attack and in its aftermath. They recorded a conversation between two villagers, one of whom lamented that "our villagers are all dead! They have taken 10 to 15 bodies to Isa Khel alone. Every house has lost two or three people!" Another intercepted call spoke of "about 150 dead village residents" and complained: "Oh God, oh God, what a huge catastrophe this is." The person he was speaking to called it an "unbelievable disaster". *Der Spiegel* reports that "The BND intercepted many dozens of similar conversations and sent copies to Berlin, where they now remain in the agency's top-secret archives."[911] There may also have been additional evidence available to the German government. It emerged that as well as having access to real-time video feeds from the US warplanes as they circled the target area, Klein may also have had access to a separate live German military video feed of the stranded vehicles and the civilians gathered around them.[912]

That civilians had died was a conclusion the *Financial Times Deutschland* had reached within days of the attack: "The air strike clearly violated NATO's mission guidelines. Air strikes may only be ordered if there's imminent danger. And that is hard to see when two fuel tankers are stuck in the sand.... The disturbing aspect is how Franz Josef Jung is dealing with this disaster...someone who denies there were civilian casualties even if there's overwhelming evidence to the contrary is no longer suitable for the job."[913]

On 8 September 2009, the German Chancellor Angela Merkel personally promised a full investigation into the murderous bombing. In late August 2010, *Der Spiegel* noted: "One year on, questions about the bombing in Afghanistan are still unanswered and many of the details remain classified... . The Kunduz air strike was covered up, kept quiet and downplayed as much as possible. Even today, little has changed."[914] One year after the attack, internal documents from the German Chancellery dealing with the issue were still classified as secret. *Der Spiegel* reported: "There is no sign of the promised full investigation."[915] In fact quite the opposite had been the case. In March 2010, for example, *Der Spiegel* published documents that showed that the German military and the Defence Ministry in Berlin made more concerted efforts at covering up the truth after the airstrike than was previously known: "Confidential documents...show that the Defense Ministry set up a special working group composed of at least five officials to influence the NATO investigation into the incident...'Group 85,' as the task force was known, was charged with creating a 'positive image' of the events in Kunduz through a targeted communication strategy in a bid to deflect criticism of the Bundeswehr, Germany's military."[916] This included attempts to downplay a forty-two-page German military police report on its investigation into the incident that documented rule violations by Klein, violations subsequently confirmed by NATO. The military police report concluded that "the evaluation of the information to hand at the PRT (German military police base) in Kunduz made it clear that the air strike would and did lead to many dead and injured, and that the events prior to and after the incident was not adequately handled."[917]

The work of two journalists, *Stern* magazine editor Christoph Reuter and photographer Marcel Mettelsiefen, in documenting the Kunduz bombing was presented from 2–20 February 2011 in an exhibition entitled "Kunduz—September 4, 2009: Looking for clues" at Munich's House of Literature and published in a book under the same name.[918] The exhibition, which told the story of each victim, has been described as "a harrowing documentation of the greatest war crime committed by German officers since the fall of Hitler's Third Reich in 1945".[919] Christoph Reuter noted that "Neither Klein nor any other section of the army bothered to find out exactly who and how many they had actually killed. The NATO commission of inquiry and even the Red Cross spent only a few hours at the location, without trying to determine the exact number of victims or identify them."[920] The official NATO report cynically noted that there were "between 17 and 142 casualties".[921]

Der Spiegel had sight of NATO and German military transcripts and documents dealing with the Kunduz bombing, which gave "the impression that in dealing with the incident the Germans and also the NATO officials were more concerned with their own reputations than in working out what really happened". NATO also initially tried to downplay the incident. ISAF commander General Stanley McChrystal's intelligence chief in Afghanistan, Major-General Mike Flynn, stated that "[t]he most important thing is for local official to refute CIVCAS (civilian casualties)". Brigadier-General Jörg Vollmer, commander of all German troops in Afghanistan, was asked by his ISAF colleagues about the scope and nature of the contact with the enemy that led to the airstrike. He replied: "Very short." *Der Spiegel* noted that Vollmer's claim "provoked astonishment among the ISAF representatives. Contact with the enemy was a central precondition for an air strike, and Vollmer was fully aware of that. The ISAF rules are very clear... . Bombs should only be dropped in the cases of acute danger to ISAF soldiers... . The Kunduz air strike did not fit into this picture at all."⁹²² Vollmer's statement was in any case untrue. General McChrystal was said to be furious. *Der Spiegel* reported that "[h]e had just tightened up the rules for air strikes in the Afghanistan conflict". McChrystal stated he was "deeply disappointed" with the German response and that the first statements from the Germans had been "foolishness". *Der Spiegel* reported that McChrystal said he "had doubts that the rules of engagement had been followed".⁹²³

It is worth noting that both NATO and ISAF continued to downplay the Kunduz affair. Crawford notes that while the UN noted the Kunduz deaths in their database of civilian casualties, the "ISAF CIVCAS database does not record any civilian deaths due to close air support for September 2009 in northern Afghanistan, and only eight deaths in the South West despite the fact that this is one of the most well-known incidents of civilian killing by ISAF forces in the war".⁹²⁴

A secret NATO report into the Kunduz incident seen by *Der Spiegel* subsequently revealed that Klein had lied repeatedly about the incident. The American pilots asked Klein's air controller twice whether German forces had "troops in contact" with the enemy. The response was: "Confirmed." Klein eventually admitted that he had deliberately lied to ensure the bombing took place. For an airstrike to be launched Klein had to create the impression that there were German "troops in contact", or TIC, and that there was a serious threat to German soldiers. *Der Spiegel* reported that: "According to the NATO report's summary of Klein's interrogation, 'his problem was that he knew that they did not have a TIC in reality…'. He believed that by declaring a 'TIC he would get the air support he wanted', even though everyone knew that Klein's TIC claims were in fact untrue. One untruth led to another. Klein knew that if there was no contact with the enemy, then there was no imminent threat, either."⁹²⁵

The NATO report makes it clear that Klein was primarily interested in killing the people who had gathered around the tankers in an effort to siphon off fuel. The NATO report states that the US pilots who ultimately carried out the airstrike asked their wing commander whether they were to target the vehicles or the people. *Der Spiegel* reports that "They were told, on Klein's authority, to target the people. When the pilots asked if German troops had had contact with the enemy, they received the response, 'confirmed'. Yet no German troops had approached the scene from their nearby base." *Der Spiegel*'s conclusion is stark: "Should that version of events be true, then Klein's order to attack countermanded both NATO's mandate in Afghanistan and the German military's mandate as provided by German parliament. Targeted killings, whether carried out against Taliban insurgents or civilians, are not allowed."⁹²⁶ *Der Spiegel* notes that "Even more problematic, according to the NATO report, Klein likely knew at the time he gave the order that at least one civilian was present at the site." A translator working with the German military told NATO investigators that he told the German soldiers that one of the two tanker drivers was still alive; the other driver had been killed by the Taliban.⁹²⁷

The NATO report makes it abundantly evident that Klein broke every standing order on the night of the attack. The report states that Klein relied upon only one person for "intelligence gathering", which, even when combined with the aerial video images, was "inadequate to evaluate the various conditions and factors in such a difficult and complex target area". The report also makes it clear that Klein "isolated himself from the checks and balances", and that he "failed to declare the specific rules of engagement he was using". There was also said to have been a "lack of understanding" by the German commander and his forward air controller, "which resulted in actions and decisions inconsistent" with ISAF procedures and directives. Moreover, the report concludes, intelligence summaries and specific intelligence "provided by HUMINT (human intelligence) did not identify a specific threat" to the camp in Kunduz that night. This was the mandatory condition for an airstrike: Klein claimed he acted because of such a threat.[928]

Klein would have been very familiar with the ISAF rules for deploying fighter jets. There is a binding set of rules that must be followed to avoid "collateral damage", that is to say unintended civilian casualties or destruction of civilian property, in ISAF attacks. These include the general Rules of Engagement (ROE) for the Afghanistan mission and the Standing Operation Procedures (SOP), in this case specifically SOP 311, which applies to close air support. In addition to these rules and procedures, there was also the revised Tactical Directive, issued by ISAF Commander General Stanley McChrystal in August 2009. The directive also clearly states that troops must establish a "pattern of life" to ensure that no civilians are in the target area.[929] It is made clear that if there is a risk of civilian casualties, ISAF commanders should call off air support at the last minute and allow the enemy to escape. Commanders require at least two mutually independent sources before they can request airstrikes. The target categories are described in these rules. Air support can be requested when there are "troops in contact", when the operation would hit "time sensitive targets", or if specific persons or objects would be eliminated. These are known as deliberate targets.[930] The directive clearly states that NATO forces cannot bomb residential buildings based on a sole source of information.[931] These guidelines were to apply to all uses of air power, except when troops were in imminent danger.

Klein did not consult his legal adviser, as is customary for important decisions, nor his superiors. If there were no "troops in contact", and in the absence of an acute threat, Klein lacked the authority to order the airstrike by himself. In the absence of such a threat, the commander is required to consult with ISAF headquarters in Kabul before ordering an airstrike. And if there is a risk of civilian casualties, an airstrike can only then be authorised by NATO's Joint Force Command in the Dutch town of Brunssum.[932]

The US Air Force pilots involved in the incident said that they "could tell the ground commander was really pushing to go kinetic" – in other words, to bomb. One of the pilots said that because of this behaviour by Klein they even considered breaking off the operation altogether. The warplanes' camera pods beamed live images to Klein's command centre, showing the trucks and a lot of people around them. The pilot repeatedly suggested that he and the pilot of the second F-15 fighter fly low over the gathered crowd to frighten away civilians, should any be present. *Der Spiegel* reported: "The response from the German base was clear: 'Negative... . I want you to strike directly.'"[933] In so doing the German government admitted that Klein ignored another of the escalation levels that, according to NATO procedures, need to precede an airstrike. The secret NATO report, subsequently leaked to the *Sueddeutsche Zeitung* newspaper, reported that Colonel Klein, "wanted to attack the people, not the vehicles."[934] *Der Spiegel* also revealed that:

> At 1:46 a.m., the American pilots asked the Germans one more time whether the people on the ground truly constituted an "imminent threat." Under the NATO rules of engagement, only an imminent threat justified an attack. Absent such a threat, the pilots would have been required to leave the area. But Klein was apparently intent on having the airstrike go forward, and his forward air controller, acting on Klein's orders, replied: "Yes, those pax (people) are an imminent threat." He said that the insurgents were trying to tap the gasoline from the trucks, and when they had finished, they would "regroup and we have intelligence information about current operations" and they would probably be "attacking Camp Kunduz." … The investigation report soberly concludes that there was no "specific information" or "hard intelligence" to indicate the Taliban "were either preparing or had a plan for attacking" the German forces that night.[935]

Klein subsequently tried his best to keep investigators from the site of the bombing. A NATO fact-finding team, led by a senior British RAF officer, Air Commodore Paddy Teakle, the NATO mission's Director of Air Operations, arrived in Kunduz. They wanted to visit the bombing site, which was just six kilometres south of Kunduz Airport, where they had landed. Klein urged them not to go, claiming it would be dangerous. Klein also said that a visit to the hospital would be too dangerous. Instead, they received briefings at the nearby German base from Klein and his subordinates. It is worth noting that General McChrystal would himself later arrive in Kunduz to investigate the incident. He drove to the bombing site – calling into question self-serving German claims that the area was too dangerous.[936]

In the immediate aftermath of the attack, Afghanistan Rights Monitor, a non-governmental group funded by domestic human rights campaigners, stated: "Preliminary reports received…indicated 60–70 non-combatants died." The group said it had reached the figure based on interviews with residents in the area. The Taliban said they had set up their own commission to investigate the incident and released a list of seventy-nine civilians they said were killed in the attack: the list included the names of victims, fathers' names and ages and included details of twenty-four children under eighteen. The victims were said to have been from Char Dara and Aliabad districts.[937] Amnesty International reported that village elders provided it with "a list of 83 people killed in the incident who the elders identified as having no affiliation with the Taleban". The list included their names, their fathers' names, their age, village and district.[938] Some eyewitnesses reported seeing more than 100 dead civilians at the site.[939] Dr. Safi Sidique was on duty in Kunduz Hospital on the Friday morning when the wounded came from Omar Kheil, and treated many of them. He stated: "Simple village people were killed. They were not Taliban."[940] A "strictly confidential" report by the International Committee of the Red Cross examining the Kunduz attack concluded that the attack had been unlawful. In the annex to the report, the ICRC listed the names of seventy-four dead civilians, including a number of children.⁹⁴¹ The ICRC had sent a medical team to support Kunduz Provincial Hospital immediately after the incident. ICRC delegates had spoken to families who were mourning their dead in nearby villages.

Karim Popal, a German lawyer in Bremen who grew up in Afghanistan, and who has represented many of the families of the victims, has stated that the number of victims is significantly higher than that admitted by the German authorities.⁹⁴² Popal proposed compensation for projects that could provide a livelihood for the survivors, most of them women and children. Having carried out his own investigations on the ground in Afghanistan, Popal asserts that the attack claimed 169 civilian victims – 139 dead, 20 wounded and 20 missing. As a result of the attack, there are 163 orphans and 91 women have lost their husbands.⁹⁴³ More details continue to emerge of the numbers and identify of victims.

Amnesty International stated that its research showed that NATO did not provide civilians in the area with effective warning that they were going to launch an attack, thus endangering the lives of people in the area. Eyewitnesses to the attack told Amnesty International that they did not see NATO aircraft engage in any warning action prior to the Kunduz airstrike. Amnesty International recorded that a local villager, Omera Khan, told the organisation that: "The Germans could have responded differently to the hijacking and prevented the civilian casualties. People were there to take the free fuel offered by the Taleban and at the time of the attack there was no warning." Amnesty stated: "An urgent and transparent investigation needs to be launched by the German government into what happened in Kunduz. NATO, and the German government, must show accountability for the loss of civilian life and prove that it has the will and mechanism in place to investigate civilian casualties."⁹⁴⁴

Despite calls such as that by Amnesty International, the German government dragged its feet in all aspects of the Kunduz attack and its consequences, legal and humanitarian. To date, there has been no official apology by Germany to the victims. The Bundeswehr did its best to avoid taking any action on the case and – contrary to clear NATO regulations – did nothing to investigate the results of the airstrike. *Der Spiegel* reported that "the Bundeswehr behaved for months as if there had been no civilian casualties".⁹⁴⁵ When faced with a legal case over the killings, it did not have a clear overview of the situation. *Der Spiegel* reported that "The case has revealed a woeful lack of local knowledge on the part of the Bundeswehr. Indeed, the German army ultimately had to rely on the help of journalists to determine the number and the names of the civilian victims." The Defence Ministry had to contact Christoph Reuter for details of the Afghan casualties. Christoph Reuter and Marcel Mettelsiefen read through the 500 pages of NATO's official report with dismay. Reuter recalled: "There were so many exact details, including every communication between soldiers and commanders… . But then we saw the numbers, between 17 and 142 casualties. We thought this gap was unacceptable." Mettelsiefen stated: "We were astonished. Everyone was talking about who did what, and who knew what when. But they had forgotten the victims."⁹⁴⁶

In August 2010, *Der Spiegel* reported that the German military had gone behind the back of the legal team that had opened the legal case against the German government, unilaterally agreeing to pay compensation to the families of over 100 civilian victims of the Kunduz airstrike in Afghanistan. The victims' lawyers noted: "The way in which the Bundeswehr went behind our backs and negotiated directly with our clients is strange."[947] The German army reluctantly admitted to the deaths of ninety-one people in the attack. Lawyers for the families say at least 137 were killed.[948] *Der Spiegel* has reported that up to 142 people died.[949] The German government based its figure of 102 victims, 91 dead and 11 seriously injured civilians, on the work by Reuter.[950] Reuter's figures formed the basis for the compensation that was offered. The Bundeswehr offered payments of €3,800 (US$5,000). The government refused to admit any liability, stating that it was a one-off, *ex gratia* payment.

In October 2010, *Der Spiegel* focused on the legal quest for compensation: "For now, it is the last act in a months-long dispute over a single question: How much is a human life worth? More specifically, how much is an Afghan life worth? This question is the source of a dispute between the German Defense Ministry and the families of the victims who are represented by a team of German attorneys." *Der Spiegel* reported that "At the Defense Ministry in Berlin, the burly man [the military's lawyer] smiles. 'We're not terribly worried about a lawsuit or a trial.'" The magazine concluded that "it seems that the incident is being downplayed and portrayed as something of a minor offence. A $5,000 case, if you will. It was a year in which German authorities failed to find a way to react, quickly and appropriately, to the fatal mistake of a German colonel."[951] The German government clearly felt that Afghan lives were becoming cheaper by the year. *Der Spiegel* noted:

> In the past, Germany has paid $20,000 to the family of an Afghan woman who was shot at a checkpoint, and $33,000 for a dead Afghan boy. The price has apparently gone down since then.... The Kunduz bombing, Germany's war trauma, its big case, is now a $5,000 case. Little more than a wartime fender bender, if you will.[952]

It is perhaps worth putting the German approach into context. The following are compensation settlements for *non-lethal* injuries within the jurisdictions of two of Germany's NATO allies. In 2012 a girl injured at birth in a British hospital received £11 million in compensation.[953] An American lawyer who injured his shoulder while lifting and inspecting the underbelly of his leather office chair received $107,913 in compensation. Another lawyer received $95,000 for an injury when trying to lift his briefcase out of his car trunk.[954] In 2013, a San Diego college student who had been accidentally left for four days inside a drug enforcement administration holding cell was paid $4 million as compensation.[955]

The German government was clearly aware of the possible wider legal implications of the bombing. In February 2010, German Foreign Minister Guido Westerwelle told the German parliament that the German mission in Afghanistan was to be redefined as an "armed conflict within the parameters of international law". *Der Spiegel* pointed out that the reclassification of the German military involvement in Afghanistan would serve two purposes. The first is that it would protect German soldiers based in Afghanistan from the risk of being prosecuted under German law. *Der Spiegel* noted that "[t]he statement should allow German soldiers based in the country to act without fear of being prosecuted back home under the German penal code". It reported further that "[t]he legal gray-area in which the Bundeswehr has been operating was laid bare last September after a German-ordered airstrike left 142 people dead, many of them Afghan civilians. It was unclear whether Col. Georg Klein, the officer who ordered the strike, was operating under international or German law."[956] And secondly, the magazine observed it would negatively affect the legal rights of victims of the Kunduz attack: "Bundeswehr lawyers...believe that the German government's recent reclassification of the mission in Afghanistan as a 'non-international armed conflict' – in other words, a war – means that the victims of the bombardment no longer have any legal claims."[957]

The coverage of the German government's move to immunise their servicemen from German law led to interesting analyses in the German media. German papers welcomed the clarification of the legal position protecting German service personnel. The *Frankfurter Allgemeine Zeitung* stated: "[U]ndoubtedly the air strike ordered by Col. Georg Klein in Kunduz, which is now the subject of a parliamentary enquiry, has contributed to the mission being seen in this new light. It remains to be seen what affect the new evaluation of the mandate by the government will have on the orders to the soldiers, as well as on their behavior and their legal responsibility. The case of Kunduz may also be affected retrospectively." The center-left *Süddeutsche Zeitung* newspaper wrote: "The new legal evaluation of the conflict in Afghanistan...places the responsibility for the mission there where it belongs: with the politicians. Soldiers should not have to worry about the legitimacy of their actions, they should not have to weigh up which laws might be broken with every small decision. In the future international law will create the framework, not German law." *Die Tageszeitung* correctly noted that "[t]he German government was... doing its bit to exonerate Col. Klein and the Bundeswehr".

In April 2010, German state prosecutors announced they would not be charging Klein with any offences under either international or German law. The prosecutor said ordering the airstrike did not in any way qualify as an illegal act.[958] He received an absolute acquittal. The German authorities denied Klein's guilt at any level, going so far as to state that even if Klein had anticipated civilian casualties, the attack would have still have been proportionate. It is an example of the sort of impunity the German government and the ICC vigorously condemn in African situations. In June 2010, the German government announced it would pay US$5,000 to each of the families of the victims, as an *ex gratia* payment without admitting liability.[959] The former Afghan Commerce Minister Amin Farhang described the US$5,000 as a "laughable" sum.[960]

To say that the German investigation into the Kunduz massacre was a whitewash would be an understatement. Murder is defined very narrowly in German law as an intended killing that the perpetrator committed, for example, "*out of a lust for killing*".[961] The NATO report on the massacre said Klein "wanted to attack the people, not the vehicles". It is also clear that Klein would have known that there were large numbers of unarmed people in the target area. The Berlin-based European Center for Constitutional and Human

Rights stated that at the very least Klein had committed offences under German criminal law, such as wilful or negligent homicide. The German law of homicide distinguishes between voluntary and involuntary killings.[962] Voluntary homicide[963] is defined as "[…] any killing of a human being carried out with an intention to kill which is not murder".[964] The Federal Prosecutor did not even consider trying Klein on a charge of negligent homicide.[965] Negligent homicide applies when death is caused by the negligent conduct of another. One of the most important cases of negligent homicide in German law was the crash and derailment of the suspension railway in Wuppertal.[966] It has a clear bearing on the Klein case. On 12 April 1999, the first train of the morning ran into a metal claw left on the railway line and fell into the River Wupper. Five people died, and over forty others were injured. The German courts established that the claw had been forgotten by a building team that had been modernising the railway construction. The suspension railway operator WSW was responsible for supervising the work. The ARGE company was responsible for construction. Four ARGE workers had failed to remove the claw from the railway after the work had been finished. The ARGE construction manager and two supervisors from WSW failed to check the railway before services restarted. These checks were necessary according to a safety system that had been devised by a representative of WSW, but which was in several respects unclear and thus likewise faulty.[967] A German court convicted each of the three supervisors of negligent homicide due to their failure to undertake the necessary checks. The four workers were on appeal convicted of negligent homicide by nonfeasance, the intentional failure to perform a required duty or obligation.[968] German criminal law focuses on individual liability. Neither of the companies involved was prosecuted.

Klein had a clear and unambiguous duty to perform several checks before finally authorising the use of lethal force in the Kunduz airstrike. He self-evidently failed to do so. It is also clear that his was an intentional failure to perform the checks he was obliged to carry out. NATO's report into the incident stated that Klein's behaviour "resulted in actions and decisions inconsistent" with ISAF procedures and directives, and that he had "isolated himself from the checks and balances" he should have followed before authorising lethal force. Klein ignored obligations outlined in NATO's general Rules of Engagement for the Afghanistan mission, Standing Operation Procedures, specifically SOP 311, which applies to close air support, and ISAF's Tactical Directive. The NATO report stated that Klein "failed to declare the specific rules of engagement he was using". NATO forces are not authorised to call in airstrikes based on a sole source of information. Klein was obligated to seek two mutually independent sources about the prospective target. He did not. The report made it clear that Klein relied on only one person for "intelligence" about the target, who himself was not at the location of the incident. The information available to Klein was therefore "inadequate to evaluate the various conditions and factors in such a difficult and complex target area". Klein claimed the airstrike was necessary because of a clear threat to German forces on the evening of the airstrike. This was a mandatory regulating condition for an airstrike. The NATO report stated that intelligence summaries and specific intelligence "did not identify a specific threat" to German forces that night. Klein ignored the Tactical Directive's stipulation that NATO forces had to establish a "pattern of life" to ensure that no civilians are in the target area before calling in an airstrike. Live video links from the American warplanes that Klein would have seen showed numerous, unarmed people around the road tankers over a long period of time: Klein did not ensure that no children or civilians were present at the time of the attack. If there were no "troops in contact", and in the absence of an acute threat, Klein lacked the authority to order the airstrike by himself. In the absence of such a threat, Klein was required to consult with ISAF headquarters in Kabul before ordering an airstrike. Klein lied and claimed there were troops in contact. And if there was a risk of civilian casualties, Klein was obliged to have the airstrike he wanted authorised by NATO's Joint Force Command in Brunssum.[969] They were not contacted.

A German court convicted each of the three supervisors in the Wuppertal case of negligent homicide due to their failure to undertake required and necessary checks. The four workers were similarly convicted of negligent homicide due to their intentional failure to perform a required duty or obligation. Colonel Klein's guilt was no less obvious. As documented by the European Centre for Constitutional and Human Rights, Klein ignored standing orders, rules of engagement and operating procedures and deliberately misinformed the US pilots present at the scene.[970] At the very least Article 57(2)(c) of Additional Protocol I to the Geneva Conventions, incorporated into German law, clearly states the obligation that "effective advance warning shall be given of attacks which may affect the civilian population, unless circumstances do not permit". A violation of this obligation amounts to criminal liability as an act of negligence under ordinary criminal law. Klein repeatedly refused suggestions by the US pilots on the scene that they do fly-bys to warn any civilians in the area before dropping any bombs.

The announcement that the investigation into Colonel Klein had been dropped was welcomed by Defence Minister Guttenberg. He said it provided "the greatest possible legal security" for German soldiers in Afghanistan.[971] This came from a minister who had previously described Klein's behaviour as "militarily inappropriate". The German government's decision not to proceed with any case against Klein was controversial. The European Centre for Constitutional and Human Rights, which has followed the incident from the beginning, concluded:

> The criminal investigations conducted so far have been insufficient.... The Federal Prosecutor terminated his investigations in April 2010 regarding the alleged commission of war crimes, after having received statements by the suspects and others involved in the air strike. As stated in the press release of the Federal Prosecutor, *only the perspective of the suspect was considered according to the relevant provisions in the German Code of Crimes against International Law.*" [Emphasis added.]

Lawyers following the case for victims of the attack were denied the opportunity to make representations to the relevant authorities:

> The lawyers in this case, who had announced their representation to the Federal Prosecutor, never received a formal notice of the termination of the

investigations. Without this notice, no appeal and judicial review of the Federal Prosecutor's decision is possible. Furthermore, the lawyers were denied access to the files and they were not allowed to file their own statement before the decision to terminate the investigations was made. They only were informed about the termination of investigations through the press release. The Federal Prosecutor never gave reasons why the investigation was terminated, although he is obliged under German law to give reasons... . But in the end the file was closed without hearing any statement from the victims and without allowing access to the files. At the very latest upon the decision not to have any victims testify, access to the files should have been granted – also following their own reasoning – but was again denied. Procedural rights have hence been violated continuously.[972]

Much of the investigation and the evidence was classified as secret, as were parts of the dismissal decree itself. The centre stated that the "secret proceedings" in this case sidestepped "both democratic and juristic controls. The rights of those affected are being severely violated."[973]

On 17 March 2011, a constitutional complaint by a father who lost his two sons in the attack challenged the April 2010 decision to terminate any further investigation of Klein's involvement in the Kunduz attack; it also called for public charges and investigations against Colonel Klein and others regarding the air attack. The legal pleading outlined the inadequacy of investigations carried out to date by the General Federal Prosecutor, and included substantial amounts of evidence. According to German proceedings to force criminal prosecution (the so-called *Klageerzwingungsverfahren*), those injured by a criminal act are entitled to call for a legal examination of any decision to suspend investigations. The complaint addressed numerous procedural mistakes made during the investigative proceedings. The case also argued that the accused failed to take adequate information measures before giving the order to attack. Marco Sassòli, an international law professor, and Anne-Laurence Brugère (University of Geneva) supported this argument in an expert legal opinion submitted as part of the petition. The opinion describes safety measures for conducting attacks as stipulated by international humanitarian law, and traced the relationship between such measures and the principle of proportionality. Another expert legal opinion by Professor Florian Jeßberger (University of Hamburg) supported the request for further investigations, because the German Federal Prosecutor is not able to suspend the investigations completely. The constitutional complaint submitted in March 2011 primarily addressed the right of access to the courts to bring about an examination of the Federal Prosecutor's dismissal decision. The German prosecuting authority's handling of victims connected to the bombing also came under the spotlight. The motion also pointed out that the German government has violated its duty under the European Convention on Human Rights to effectively investigate deaths caused by state officials.[974]

The European Centre for Constitutional and Human Rights observed that the decision taken by the Office of the Federal Prosecutor to dismiss the criminal proceedings against Klein "appears to be politically motivated". A culture of impunity, the very thing so often criticised by the German government abroad, is thus created. The centre noted: "When one remembers that Germany is a key player in the international prosecutions of the most serious crimes, the behavior of the Office of the Federal Prosecutor with regards to such procedure is more than simply inappropriate." It went on to state:

> [T]his decision creates a clear precedent in the way in which the criminally relevant conduct of German soldiers in missions abroad is dealt with. Such decisions send out a message to soldiers and – by no means less important – to the western allies that Germany does not impose serious legal penalties for the murder of civilians in armed conflict.[975]

The centre added: "Should this way of proceeding provide a precedent for future cases, it would signal a carte blanche for war crimes committed by German soldiers in overseas operations."[976]

The German army announced in August 2010 that its investigation into Klein's actions had ended. The investigation concluded that Klein had not violated any provisions of the German military code, and that he would not be the subject of any disciplinary measures. Amazingly, the German military investigation concluded that Klein could not have known about civilians and that neither he nor any of the other officers present were in a position to know that civilians were present at the time.[977] This was a blatant lie. The Head of the German Mission Command and the German Defence Press Officer on duty, who had described the Kunduz incident as a "successful mission against insurgents in the Kunduz area", still have their jobs.[978] Klein did not even receive as much as an official warning about his conduct. In fact shortly afterwards the government actually promoted Klein to General Officer rank.[979]

Given the obstacles to any domestic criminal prosecution for the civilian deaths, a civil case with regard to the Kunduz situation was opened in the regional court in Bonn in March 2013 before Judge Heinz Sonnenberger. Two relatives of the victims were listed as lead plaintiffs against the German government. They sought a ruling on whether the German government could be held liable for the deaths. A criminal lawsuit against Colonel Klein was suspended earlier by the Federal Public Prosecutor General. The victims' legal team has lodged an appeal and intends to take the matter to the German Constitutional Court.[980]

The victims' representatives have requested between €20,000 and €75,000 ($26,000–$98,000) in compensation for each of the 137 reported casualties, claiming Klein killed the civilians premeditatedly. The case was based on Paragraph 839 of the German Civil Code, according to which officials who intentionally violate their duty are obliged to provide compensation for resulting damages. The victims' lawyers stated that Klein acted on behalf of the German government, which, therefore, should be held liable for the damage caused. The victims' lawyer Karim Popal stated that "Mr. Klein acted erroneously.... He made the decision himself, and he saw the civilians. Despite this, he consciously and intentionally issued the command for an airstrike, even though the pilots at first refused."[981]

The defendant was the German Ministry of Defence on behalf of the Federal Republic of Germany. The government's lawyer, Mark Zimmer, denied any liability. The German government disingenuously denied any responsibility on their part: "In this case, Col. Klein wasn't acting primarily on behalf of the Federal Republic of Germany but was integrated in a NATO system. Because of this, his superiors were NATO officers and not German army officers." The government also disputed any liability claim by civilian victims of the airstrike, asserting that as the incident was part of an armed conflict the law concerning officials could not be applied to the case: "In war, there are different laws." The government's lawyer also claimed that because the criminal lawsuit against Klein was dropped by the Federal Public Prosecutor General, Klein had not acted illegally.[982]

It should be noted that Judge Sonnenberger had dealt with a similar situation in 2003 during the Kosovo conflict. Ten civilians had been killed and seventeen injured during a NATO airstrike on a bridge near the Serbian town of Varvarin in 1999. Thirty-five Serbians claimed compensation ranging from €5,000 and €100,000. Sonnenberger dismissed the claim, stating that "neither in international law nor in government liability law is there a legal basis" that allows an individual to sue a state "for the consequences of war".[983]

The reality is that all we have seen so far as a result of the Kunduz massacre are resignations and attempts by the German government to retrospectively protect their servicemen from any prosecution in Germany for war crimes. The German government was clearly able but unwilling to prosecute Klein. It is a textbook example of the circumstances in which the ICC is meant to intervene.

Germany, Colonel Klein and the International Criminal Court

To recap then, the death of up to 140 Afghan civilians, and the injury to dozens more, in a military airstrike (one of many such airstrikes resulting in civilian fatalities) in a situation in which the ICC clearly has jurisdiction is ignored by the ICC. Yet, the death of 57 to 157 protestors during a demonstration in Guinea, many of whom may have been accidentally trampled to death, possible Columbian money-laundering and the destruction of religious shrines in Mali are the subjects of official ICC investigations.[984] With regard to its investigations in Afghanistan, the ICC stated in 2012:

> The Office of the Prosecutor continued to gather and analyse information from multiple sources relating to alleged crimes committed in Afghanistan since 1 May 2003. The Office sought to verify the seriousness of information received relating to a large number of alleged crimes, including killings, torture, attacks on humanitarian targets and the United Nations, attacks on protected objects and the recruitment of child soldiers. The Office has encountered challenges in obtaining the detailed information required to conduct a proper legal assessment of each reported incident and to attribute responsibility to specific perpetrators.[985]

Ten years of investigations in Afghanistan have resulted in no action whatsoever by the

ICC. Yet, as Louise Arbour has noted, the speed of the court's investigation in Libya in 2011 was "unprecedented...in this case, it took only four days".[986]

The case against Colonel Klein is clear. It is difficult to see any credible defence of his actions. Crawford points out that "foreknowledge of incidental harm to non-combatants may be criminal even if that harm is unintended".[987] The Rome Statute is clear on the issue: "Intentionally launching an attack in the knowledge that such attack will cause incidental loss of life or injury to civilians or damage to civilian objects or widespread, long-term and severe damage to the natural environment which would be clearly excessive in relation to the concrete and direct overall military advantage anticipated."[988]

Any excuse by the court that its prosecutors have "encountered challenges in obtaining the detailed information required to conduct a proper legal assessment" of the Kunduz massacre would be untrue. The Kunduz case could not be more clear-cut for ICC investigators. General Klein has admitted his responsibility. There are NATO and ISAF reports that provide more than enough evidence of Klein's culpability. Those German and American servicemen responsible for the deaths of well over 100 civilians in the Kunduz incident are subject to the ICC's jurisdiction, the Germans because they are a member of the ICC, and Germans and Americans both because the actions have been carried out in Afghanistan, an ICC signatory state.

In a reversal of circumstances of the ICC's hallowed concept of complementarity, in the Kunduz case we have a court, the ICC, which is more than able to prosecute a serious example of an unpunished war crime, but which is unwilling to do so. Article 17(1)(a) of the Rome Statute triggers the court in cases that demonstrate the "unwillingness...of the State genuinely to prosecute". Article 17(2) of the Rome Statute states:

> In order to determine unwillingness in a particular case, the Court shall consider, having regard to the principles of due process recognized by international law, whether one or more of the following exist, as applicable: (a) The proceedings were or are being undertaken or the national decision was made for the purpose of shielding the person concerned from criminal responsibility for crimes within the jurisdiction of the Court... . (b) There has been an unjustified delay in the proceedings which in the circumstances is inconsistent with an intent to bring the person concerned to justice; (c) The proceedings were not or are not being conducted independently or impartially, and they were or are being conducted in a manner which, in the circumstances, is inconsistent with an intent to bring the person concerned to justice.

Not only has the ICC not initiated a case regarding the Kunduz massacre, it hasn't even initiated an investigation.

Two colonels: two standards

It is useful to compare the ICC's inaction regarding Colonel Klein with its action against

Colonel Mathieu Ngudjolo Chui. In 2007, the ICC issued sealed arrest warrants for Ngudjolo, a commander of the rebel *Front des Nationalistes et Intégrationnistes* movement in the DRC. He was charged with allegedly having "acted in concert to mount an attack targeted mainly at Hema civilians" in Ituri in 2003.[989] He was accused by the ICC of being responsible for the deaths of 200 civilians, many of them women and children. The judicial system of the DRC had not charged him in connection with this alleged crime. He was transferred by Congolese authorities to ICC custody in February 2008, and his trial began on 24 November 2009. Ngudjolo stated that he was innocent of the crime of which he was accused. Three years later, Ngudjolo was acquitted of all charges in December 2012.[990] The court clearly had jurisdiction in the Ngudjolo case.

Colonel Klein is alleged to have been responsible for the deaths of up to 140 Afghan civilians, including women and children, in Kunduz in 2009. NATO's own report indicates that he deliberately lied about and misrepresented the circumstances on the ground in order to secure an airstrike that killed the civilians, many of whom were burnt alive. Many others were injured. Klein does not deny that he was responsible for the deaths of several dozen Afghan civilians. Klein has publicly described his actions as "appropriate".[991] The German legal system did not bring any charges against him in connection with their deaths.

Given that the German legal system has failed to proceed with a prosecution of Klein, there is a *prima facie* case that the ICC should investigate Klein for some of the same crimes of which Ngudjolo was accused. These would include the crime against humanity of murder under Article 7(1)(a) of the Rome Statute, and the following war crimes under the statute: wilful killing under Article 8(2)(a)(i); wilfully causing great suffering, or serious injury to body or health under article 8(2)(a)(iii); intentionally directing attacks against the civilian population as such or against individual civilians not taking direct part in hostilities under Article 8(2)(b)(i); and wilfully causing great suffering, or serious injury to body or health under Article 8(2)(b)(iii). It is clear that Klein went out of his way to deliberately kill in the attack he directed, ordering an airstrike without providing any prior warning to civilians on the ground; Klein intentionally directed an attack against the civilian population, against individual civilians not taking direct part in hostilities and posing no military threat to him or his colleagues; he self-evidently intentionally directed attacks against civilian objects that were not military objectives. Klein's actions certainly fall under Article 8(2)(b)(iv) of the Rome Statute, which outlines the crime of "[i]ntentionally launching an attack in the knowledge that such attack will cause incidental loss of life or injury to civilians or damage to civilian objects or widespread, long-term and severe damage to the natural environment which would be clearly excessive in relation to the concrete and direct overall military advantage anticipated".

Colonel Mathieu Ngudjolo Chui was indicted in 2007, taken into ICC custody in 2008, eventually brought to trial in 2009, and underwent a three-year trial for allegedly being responsible for the deaths of 200 civilians in the Congo. Colonel Klein has admitted responsibility for the deaths of almost 100 civilians in Afghanistan. There were significant attempts by German government ministers to cover up the incident. Two ministers and an army commander-in-chief had to resign as a result. Klein, however, was not arrested or taken into custody. He was not reprimanded, demoted or dismissed from the service. He is still in the German army, and has been promoted to General.⁹⁹²

It is clear that the ICC has jurisdiction regarding the Kunduz massacre. Klein is a German citizen and Afghanistan is a State Party. It is also clear that the Afghan government is either unwilling or unable to prosecute Klein. It is self-evident that the German government, while perfectly able to do so, is unwilling to prosecute Klein for any of the several crimes he committed under German military or civil law. The Rome Statute allows the court to intervene when the domestic jurisdictions of States Parties are not seeking or unable to prosecute relevant cases. The Prosecutor himself was clear about the state's obvious disinclination to proceed being the most important factor in triggering action by the court: "As a general rule, the policy of the OTP will be to undertake investigations only where there is a clear case of failure to act by the State or States concerned…where States fail to act, or are not 'genuinely' investigating or prosecuting, as described in article 17 of the Rome Statute."⁹⁹³ This is a classic ICC case. Yet, while even the *Washington Times* has pointed to both the Kunduz and Farah incidents as qualifying for investigation as Western war crimes, the ICC remains silent. The Kunduz incident provides yet another example of the ICC granting *de facto* immunity to yet another government. This time the government in question is not an African state but is instead a European government at the political and financial heart of the court.

The abuses continue

The former British Ambassador to Afghanistan, Sir Sherard Cowper-Coles, provides yet another example of a large-scale massacre of civilians. He reported that US and Afghan forces were involved in "a massacre of civilians at a village called Azizabad in Shindand district in western Afghanistan in late August 2008".⁹⁹⁴ These forces had called in an airstrike on the village, which "flattened" it. The US and Afghan forces initially claimed that only half a dozen Taliban insurgents had died. Cowper-Coles states that "some ninety civilians had in fact been killed". He also reported that many of these civilians had been in the village for a wedding party. The ambassador revealed that far from being Taliban, some of the dead civilians actually worked for a British-owned security company protecting a local US base. The UN Secretary-General's Special Representative for Afghanistan, Kai Eide, presented evidence of the massacre both to the American Commander of ISAF, and Cowper-Coles. The ambassador described the material as "shocking". The US government initially denied the gravity of the affair. After weeks of pressure, the American military authorities eventually admitted the scale of the civilian casualties and sought to pay compensation. Cowper-Coles reveals that Eide was "under tremendous pressure to drop the whole thing, from some very angry and upset Americans in denial about what their Special Forces had done".⁹⁹⁵ Given that the Afghan government is obviously unwilling or unable to investigate and prosecute the killing of these civilians, at face value another war crime as outlined within the Rome Statute, it is a clear-cut case for the ICC. The court continues to be silent on this and numerous other similar atrocities.

NATO airstrikes, with or without German controllers, have continued to kill Afghan civilians on a regular basis. The deaths reached such a level that in February 2013, following yet another airstrike that resulted in the deaths of five children and four women, Afghan President Hamid Karzai banned any more NATO airstrikes in Afghanistan. Speaking at Kabul's National Military Academy he said: "I will issue a decree stating that under no conditions can Afghan forces request foreign air strikes on Afghan homes or Afghan villages during operations."[996] In the same month the Afghan government barred American special forces from operating in a strategic province adjoining the capital Kabul, citing complaints that Afghans working for American Special Operations forces had tortured and killed villagers in the area. Afghan officials said they had tried for weeks to get the coalition to cooperate with an investigation into claims that civilians had been killed, abducted or tortured by Afghans working for American Special Operations forces in the area. They stated that the coalition was not responsive. Attaullah Khogyani, a spokesman for the provincial government, stated: "There have been lots of complaints from the local people about misconduct, mistreatment, beating, taking away, torturing and killing of civilians by Special Forces and their Afghan associates." Khogyani cited a raid on a village on 13 February when American troops and Afghans working with them detained a veterinary student: "His dead body was found three days later in the area under a bridge." An Afghan presidential spokesman Aimal Faizi said that villagers in the province had reported a number of similar episodes in recent months, including the disappearance of nine men in a single raid: "People from the province, elders from villages, have come to Kabul so many times, and they have brought photographs and videos of their family members who have been tortured." He said that Afghan officials have provided the coalition with pictures and videos of the men thought responsible for the abuses. They appeared to be Afghan, but could be Afghan-American. The US forces were not responsive.[997]

Needless to say, the ICC has shown no intention of investigating these actions either.

Chapter Fourteen

THE INTERNATIONAL CRIMINAL COURT AND AFRICA

"[T]he Court's focus on Africa has stirred African sensitivities about sovereignty and self-determination – not least because of the continent's history of colonisation and a pattern of decisions made for Africa by outsiders."

Nicholas Waddell and Phil Clark[998]

"The court focuses on Africa because African countries are weak."

Professor Eric Posner[999]

It was Alexander Murdoch Mackay, the Scottish Presbyterian missionary to Uganda, who observed in 1889: "In former years, the universal aim was to steal Africans from Africa. Today the determination of Europe is to steal Africa from the Africans."[1000] A hundred and twenty years later Europe appears still to be trying to steal both Africa and Africans. They are now using their new creation, the ICC, to steal Africans from Africa to appear before show trials in western Europe. This has been seen as a means of destabilising the African continent – something that then makes the political domination of Africa and the subsequent exploitation of African minerals and resources that much easier. The simple fact is the court reinforces anti-African stereotypes more in keeping with the Victorian era, as illustrated by Adam Branch: "[The ICC] framework is characterised by...the 'savage-victim-savior' structure. The savage is the African violator of human rights, whether a state or nonstate entity...leaving it up to the ICC to save the victim and apprehend the savage."[1001]

The reason for a flawed Western interventionist approach content with demonising Africa is apparent. British international lawyer Courtenay Griffiths QC has provided an in-depth analysis of the Western focus on Africa, and the involvement of the ICC as part of that focus:

> There's a new scramble for Africa going on at this point in the twentieth-first century. And I think the West is seeking to use the tool of international criminal law to facilitate its penetration into that market. It seems somewhat coincidental that in virtually every situation where the ICC has intervened, a major economic interest is at stake. Darfur – there just happened to be oil. In northern Uganda and the great lakes region – they've discovered oil there. In Libya, [ex-British prime minister Tony] Blair made some major deals for oil there before Gaddafi was killed. Congo – one of the most minerally rich countries on the planet, a place where certain rare minerals used in mobile phones and laptops can only be found. Why only in those places?[1002]

The AU agrees: "The abuse and misuse of indictments against African leaders have a destabilising effect that will negatively impact on political, social and economic development of member states and their ability to conduct international relations…"[1003]

Griffiths has said that his critique "is based on my love and respect for the law and my disgust at the way in which international criminal justice is currently being practised".[1004] He has challenged the racist overtones of this European interference, stating that the West's "persistent idea of Africa being the Dark Continent [and] uncivilised" provides the perfect stage for Western nations, through the ICC, to demonstrate their moral superiority. He observes that the ICC "is in part…a civilising mission by the West. 'Let's teach these darkies about the rule of law.' I find this quite offensive, as if Africans don't understand what this rule of law is all about unless told and taught by the West."[1005] He concluded:

> Africa has suffered enough…there is a need for an end to impunity. But in my mind, the push against impunity has to come from African people themselves, from the bottom up. The idea that the white man comes to Africa as he did during the nineteenth century – bearing the White Man's Burden – to bring the benefits of international justice to black people…I reject that totally. It's for black people to do it for themselves in Africa. That's the start [of an end to impunity].[1006]

Not content with having been party to a series of public miscarriages of justice across the African continent, and at a time of budgetary constraint, in August 2013 the ICC signalled a continuing interest in Nigeria, announcing with regard to the Boko Haram insurgency in northern Nigeria that there was a "reasonable basis" to believe that the militia had committed crimes against humanity.[1007] This would be the tenth African situation it was examining or involved in. Once again this attention was selective and skewed. The court has not paid any attention to the alleged widespread abuses by the Nigerian military. It is one more example of the court focusing exclusively on rebels. Kevin Jon Heller noted: "At the moment the ICC investigation is great for the Nigerian government as it's just about [Boko Haram]. But the court is going to be essentially useless if it becomes the ICC for rebels. The biggest challenge for the court is how to investigate government officials and military officials that are associated with government when that government is still in power."¹⁰⁰⁸ Heller was puzzled at the court's interest in Nigeria:

> Nothing is preventing Nigeria from prosecuting members of [Boko Haram] other than their inability to get their hands on them. Nigeria has a functioning judicial system and has every interest in capturing and prosecuting high-level members of BH so why should the ICC waste its precious resources on prosecutions that the government is perfectly willing to do?¹⁰⁰⁹

That Africa is becoming increasingly assertive in challenging arbitrary Western intervention and stale Western stereotypes is clear. In a landmark lecture at the University of South Africa in August 2013, the former South African President Thabo Mbeki called on Africa to reject with one voice the West's contempt for Africa: "We have a common responsibility as Africans to determine our destiny...we are concerned about our own renaissance, our own development, and we must as indigenous people make sure that we have control of our development, our future, and that includes our resources.... We stand up as Africans to say [there must be] an end, and really an end, to that contempt for African thought! We have to. If we don't, this development we are talking about will not happen."¹⁰¹⁰

The British journalist Brendan O'Neill has quite simply asked if the ICC is racist, pointing out that "to have a war crimes court which only investigates blacks really is as perverse as it would be to have a court in Britain that investigated black burglaries and ignored white ones":

> Imagine if there were a criminal court in Britain which only ever tried black people, which ignored crimes committed by whites and Asians and only took an interest in crimes committed by blacks. We would consider that racist, right? And yet there is an International Criminal Court which only ever tries black people, African black people to be precise, and it is treated as perfectly normal. In fact the court is lauded by many radical activists as a good and decent institution, despite the fact that no non-black person has ever been brought before it to answer for his crimes. It is remarkable that in an era when liberal observers see racism everywhere, in every thoughtless aside or crude joke, they fail to see it in an institution which focuses exclusively on the criminal antics of dark-skinned people from the "Dark Continent".... Liberal sensitivity towards issues of racism completely evaporates when it comes to the ICC, which they will defend tooth and nail, despite the fact that it is quite clearly, by any objective measurement, racist, in the sense that it treats one race of people differently to all others.¹⁰¹¹

Avoiding the race issue, *The Guardian* has instead noted that the "ICC's overemphasis on the African continent" has "pushed relations with the African Union to breaking point".¹⁰¹² It added that "many Africans...feel that the court is an imperialist vehicle, controlled by the West and intent on undermining sovereignty on the continent".[1013] The ICC's interference in sub-Saharan Africa can only but recall the long history of foreign intervention on the continent. The ICC's exclusively African indictments include the cases of, among others, four heads of state, a vice-president, a former vice-president from a fourth country and several other political leaders. The ICC's actions have provoked furious debates over the court's potential impact, its exclusive focus on Africa over other parts of the world, its selection of cases, and the effect of its indictments and prosecutions on peace processes on the African continent. It is jeopardising the settlement of long-running civil wars in the pursuit of an often abstract, "hegemonic", European "justice" – a "justice" selectively foisted upon Africa by Western governments and Western, "ivory tower" non-governmental organisations pursuing their own narrow agendas.

To this one must also add international jurists musing about Greek mythology. An article in the German periodical, *Der Spiegel*, provides a crystal-clear example of how out of touch the self-selecting international law élite is with the reality on the ground. *Der Spiegel* asks the question peace or justice – which comes first? The magazine then cites the response of the Bolivian judge René Blattmann, the second Vice-President of the ICC. He once served as the Justice Minister in his home country – a nation with a weak legal system. Blattmann is emphatic, justice comes first. His reason: "In Greek mythology, Irene was the daughter of Themis, the goddess of justice." And the Greek name Irene means peace. There one has it. A classical Greek myth is cited in support of an abstract need to impose Western justice on Africa, which is more important than ending savage civil wars in Africa by mediation and negotiation.[1014] Quite what relevance quoting classical Greek mythology has for a victim of civil war in Africa praying for peace, and who has never heard of Themis or Irene or the Rome Statute, is unclear.

The European use of the court to intimidate Africa was clear from the start. Rosenthal documents quite clearly the French government's threatened use of the ICC at the January 2003 French-African summit in Paris. This was even before the ICC was established. The then French President Chirac warned the perpetrators of political violence, including the representatives of legitimate national governments combating rebel movements, that they "will have from now on to fear the judgment of the International Criminal Court, which extends its protection to all the citizens of the world". As Rosenthal points out Chirac "did not mention that France had itself largely opted out of the court's jurisdiction and, hence, that the some 2,500 French soldiers deployed to the Ivory Coast at the time (their number [subsequently] increased to nearly 4,000) needed, in fact, to 'fear' very little from the ICC". Rosenthal noted that "the immediate target of Chirac's remarks was no doubt Laurent Gbagbo, the President of the Ivory Coast, who just weeks before had been put under pressure by Paris to accept a peace agreement bringing into the national government representatives of rebel forces who had been seeking its violent overthrow".[1015] A decade later, Gbagbo would find himself in ICC custody in the wake of a French military intervention.

As of July 2009, the ICC prosecutor reported that his office had "received over 8137 communications…from more than 130 countries".[1016] He had opened investigations into just four situations, all of them in Africa: Uganda, the DRC, the CAR and Sudan. By early 2013, the court had initiated cases in eight African countries, the previous four plus Kenya, Ivory Coast, Libya and Mali. The court is also investigating Guinea and Nigeria. There have additionally been calls for an ICC investigation into human-rights abuses reportedly committed by government forces in Zimbabwe.[1017]

The ICC has charged thirty-two people to date. They are all Africans: Joseph Kony, Vincent Otti, Raska Lukwiya, Okot Odhiambo, Dominic Ongwen (Uganda); Thomas Lubanga, Germain Katanga, Mathieu Ngudjolo Chui, Jean Bosco Ntaganda, Sylvestre Mudacumura and Callixte Mbarushimana (DRC); Jean-Pierre Bemba (CAR); Ahmed Harun, Ali Kushayb, Omar al-Bashir, Bahr Idriss Abu Garda, Abdallah Banda Abakaer Nourain, Saleh Mohammed Jerbo Jamus, Abdel Raheem Muhammad Hussein (Sudan); William Ruto, Joshua Sang, Francis Muthaura, Uhuru Kenyatta, Henry Kiprono Kosgey and Mohammed Hussein Ali (Kenya); Laurent Gbagbo, Simone Gbagbo and Charles Blé Goudé (Ivory Coast); Muammar Gaddafi, Saif al-Islam Gaddafi and Abdullah Al-Senussi (Libya). In October 2013 the ICC charged a Kenyan citizen, Walter Osapiri Barasa, with three counts of corruptly influencing a witness, stating that Kenya must now arrest Barasa.[1018]

The simple fact is that it is reputable international observers, not just Africans themselves, who are pointing to the ICC's exclusive focus on Africa. Professor Eric Leonard, an American international law expert, has noted that "[p]erception often creates reality and this is a problem that the Court has to work on. The perception at this point is that the Court is focusing on Africa and that it has a Western bias and that this is why it is looking at these particular cases."[1019] *The Guardian* has placed on record that "the fact remains that the ICC has failed to pursue any cases in other regions, despite the fact that equally serious atrocities have occurred in Arab, Asian and Latin American states".[1020]

Schabas is commendably sceptical about the court's choice of "situations" within which to become active:

> The first six "situations" investigated by the Prosecutor concern geographically contiguous countries in central Africa: Uganda, Sudan, Central African Republic, Democratic Republic of the Congo, Kenya and Libya. Is it really conceivable that an objective application of the gravity criterion, as proposed in materials from the Office of the Prosecutor, leads inexorably to this result? Is this simply a coincidence... . There must surely be a strong presumption that some sort of policy determination is involved, absent any convincing explanation to the contrary.[1021]

Schabas observes that the USA "seem very comfortable with the Prosecutor's focus on central Africa".[1022]

The Council on Foreign Relations has also recorded that:

> Human rights organisations have criticised the ICC for a lack of transparency in how cases are chosen. So far all have come from Africa. Four situations have been publicly referred to the Prosecutor of the ICC: Three state parties

(Uganda, Democratic Republic of the Congo and Central African Republic) have referred situations occurring on their territories, and the UNSC has referred the situation of Darfur, Sudan. While prosecutor Moreno-Ocampo has defended his choices as the "gravest admissible situations" within his jurisdiction, potential ICC action over US actions in Iraq was dismissed in 2006.[1023]

US Government cables provide an interesting insight into European attitudes towards the USA, Sudan and the ICC:

> In Paris (and also in Norway), the Europeans raised the International Criminal Court (ICC) with the Sudanese. French [Foreign Minister] Kouchner was particularly aggressive telling [Sudanese ministers] Ismail and Alor that "Sudan must cooperate with the ICC. We are serious about this, you are challenging the world and we will not let you get away from this." Kouchner reportedly went on to add that "who does Al-Bashir think he is, President Bush? There is only one superpower. *We have to accept that America ignores the ICC, but we won't accept it from you.*"[1024] [Emphasis added.]

The above exchange is very instructive. So much for universal jurisdiction. Supporters of the court often hide behind the claims that they speak for the international community. Despite the fact that neither the USA nor Sudan are members of the ICC, the Europeans accept that the USA will ignore the court, but are outraged that an independent, poor African country should also have the courage to do so. In the absence of the USA on the issue and the hostility of the AU, Arab League, Organisation of the Islamic Conference, Non-Aligned Movement and the G-77, the "international community" to which Kouchner refers must in essence be the EU and an assortment of national camp followers.

Human Rights Watch has been candid in admitting the criticisms of the ICC regarding its African focus: "[T]he court's exclusive focus on Africa at present has led to criticism among some African states and ICC observers that the continent is the court's main target, with the prosecution strategy being intentionally geographically-based. Underlying this criticism is the perception that the ICC is a European court designed to try African perpetrators because they are believed to be politically and economically 'weak'. Among these critics, the ICC is perceived as a biased institution."[1025] In September 2008, Lord Malloch Brown, the British Minister for Africa, acknowledged that President al-Bashir's indictment did not have the support of African leaders whom he said feel that the ICC:

> [I]s real intrusion of [a] Western institution into Africa's affairs where you can start indicting African leaders while in office. They [African leaders] say who is next? It is not that they think Bashir is not guilty of things. But they could imagine circumstances that some smooth well spoken opposition leader fooling Westerners into thinking that they were human right abusers right or wrong and then suddenly there was an indictment against them.[1026]

Die-hard supporters of the ICC have tried to explain the ICC focus away. When asked in 2005 about the fact that the ICC's only referrals up to then had been African, the ICC enthusiast Judge Richard Goldstone replied that "it is a coincidence that the first four cases have come from Africa".[1027] He would doubtless find the fact that the subsequent twenty-eight cases were also exclusively from African states to be equally coincidental. Unsurprisingly, Goldstone is also very Africa-focused in his views as to where the ICC should go next. In March 2009 he suggested that the ICC should indict President Robert Mugabe of Zimbabwe.[1028]

The African Union and the ICC

On 21 July 2008, at its 142nd meeting, the Peace and Security Council of the AU requested that the Security Council used Article 16 of the Rome Statute to defer the investigations of the ICC on Darfur:

> The approval by the Pre-Trial Chamber of the application by the ICC Prosecutor could seriously undermine the ongoing efforts aimed at facilitating the early resolution of the conflict in Darfur and the promotion of long-lasting peace and reconciliation in the Sudan as a whole and, as a result, may lead to further suffering for the people of the Sudan and greater destabilization with far-reaching consequences for the country and the region.[1029]

Ten days later, during the debate establishing the UNAMID peacekeeping mission in Darfur, Libya argued at the Security Council in support of the AU Peace and Security Council's request. In Resolution 1828 (2008), the Security Council acknowledged the request and decided to consider the matter further. In February 2009, the AU Assembly decided at its twelfth session to reinstate its request to the council to defer the process initiated by the ICC against the President of Sudan.[1030] On 1 July 2009, the AU Assembly at its thirteenth session moved to reinstate its request to the council to defer the process initiated by the ICC against the President of Sudan.[1031] On 3 July 2009, the AU made its position regarding the ICC and its decision to indict President al-Bashir very clear. It called upon all AU member states not to cooperate in the arrest of President al-Bashir.[1032]

In preparation for the Kampala Review Conference, South Africa on behalf of the States Parties to the Rome Statute that are also members of the AU circulated a proposal to the Working Group on the Review Conference to amend Article 16 of the Rome Statute. The proposal reaffirmed the powers of the Security Council for deferral, sought to grant the state concerned the capacity to request a Security Council deferral, and regulate how the General Assembly, under the Uniting for Peace Resolution procedure, could make a decision concerning a deferral. The proposal was not considered by the Review Conference.

On 2 February 2010, the AU Assembly decided again at its fourteenth session to reinstate its request to the council to defer the process initiated by the ICC against the

President of Sudan.¹⁰³³ This request was renewed during the AU Assembly's fifteenth session to reinstate its request to the council to defer the process initiated by the ICC against the President of Sudan.¹⁰³⁴ On 29 August 2010, the African Commission of the AU rejected the decision of the Pre-Trial Chamber of the ICC to call upon the Security Council and the Assembly of States parties to the Rome Statute to condemn President al-Bashir's visits to the Republic of Chad and the Republic of Kenya. On 31 January 2011, the AU Assembly at its sixteenth session renewed its request to the Security Council to defer the process initiated by the ICC against the President of Sudan and in Kenya.¹⁰³⁵ Meeting in Kampala on 27 July 2010, six weeks after the conclusion of the ICC Review Conference, the Assembly of Heads of States of the AU, reiterated their decision of June 2009 instructing AU members not to cooperate with the ICC.¹⁰³⁶ The assembly was also very critical of the ICC prosecutor, stating that he "has been making egregiously unacceptable, rude and condescending statement[s]" in the case against President al-Bashir and "other situations in Africa".¹⁰³⁷

There is very much a feeling within the AU that the Security Council has disrespected Africa and its institutions by failing to respond either positively or negatively to its deferral request. This has been reflected in AU statements. The July 2009 AU decision on the ICC states that the AU: "Deeply regrets that the request by the African Union to the UNSC to defer the proceedings initiated against President Bashir...has neither been heard nor acted upon.... Decides that in view of the fact that the request by the African Union has never been acted upon, the AU Member States shall not cooperate pursuant to the provisions of Article 98 of the Rome Statute of the ICC relating to immunities, for the arrest and surrender of President Omar El Bashir of The Sudan."¹⁰³⁸ The July 2010 AU decision stated that the AU: "Expresses its disappointment that the United Nations Security Council (UNSC) has not acted upon the request by the African Union to defer the proceedings initiated against President Omar Hassan El-Bashir...and reiterates its request in this regard; Reiterates its Decision that AU Member States shall not cooperate with the ICC in the arrest and surrender of President El-Bashir of The Sudan."¹⁰³⁹

In January 2012, the African Union Commission criticised the ICC in very strong terms, noting the court's decisions ICC-02/05-01/09-139 and ICC-02/05-01/09-140 of 12 and 13 December 2011, respectively, of Pre-Trial Chamber I on the alleged failure of Malawi and Chad to comply with the cooperation requests issued by the ICC with respect to visits to those countries by President al-Bashir.¹⁰⁴⁰ The AU noted that in its decision on Malawi, and *mutatis mutandis* on Chad, the chamber asserts to have found, "in accordance with article 87(7) of the Rome Statute, that the Republic of Malawi has failed to comply with the cooperation requests contrary to the provisions of the Statute and has thereby prevented the court from exercising its functions and powers under this Statute. The Chamber decides to refer the matter both to the United Nations Security Council and to the ASP." With respect to the immunity of heads of state in relation to requests for arrest and surrender, the court claimed:

> [T]here is an inherent tension between articles 27(2) and 98(1) of the Statute and the role immunity plays when the Court seeks cooperation regarding

the arrest of a Head of State. The Chamber considers that Malawi, and by extension the African Union, are not entitled to rely on article 98(1) of the Statute to justify refusing to comply with the Cooperation Requests.[1041]

The AU observed with deep regret that this claim has the effect of:

> (i) Purporting to change customary international law in relation to immunity ratione personae; (ii) Rendering Article 98 of the Rome Statute redundant, non-operational and meaningless; (iii) Making a decision per incuriam by referring to decisions of the African Union while grossly ignoring the provisions of Article 23 (2) of the Constitutive Act of the African Union, to which Chad and Malawi are State Parties, and which obligate all AU Member States "to comply with the decisions and policies of the Union".[1042]

The AU Commission pointed out that while Article 27(2) of the statute provides that "[i]mmunities or special procedural rules which may attach to the official capacity of a person, whether under national or international law, shall not bar the Court from exercising its jurisdiction over such a person", Article 27 appears under the part of the statute setting out "general principles of criminal law" and applies only in the relationship between the court and the suspect. In the relationship between the court and states, Article 98(1) unambiguously states: "The Court may not proceed with a request for surrender or assistance which would require the requested State to act inconsistently with its obligations under international law with respect to the State or diplomatic immunity of a person or property of a third State, unless the Court can first obtain the cooperation of that third State for the waiver of the immunity."

The AU also stated that as a general matter, the immunities provided for by international law apply not only to proceedings in foreign domestic courts but also to international tribunals: states cannot contract out of their international legal obligations vis-à-vis third states by establishing an international tribunal. Indeed, contrary to the assertion of the ICC Pre-Trial Chamber I, Article 98(1) was included in the Rome Statute establishing the ICC out of recognition that the statute is not capable of removing an immunity that international law grants to the officials of states that are not parties to the Rome Statute. This is because immunities of state officials are rights of the state concerned and a treaty only binds parties to the treaty. The AU noted:

> A treaty may not deprive non-party States of rights which they ordinarily possess. In this regard, it is to be recalled that the immunity accorded to senior serving officials, ratione personae, from foreign domestic criminal jurisdiction (and from arrest) is absolute and applies even when the official is accused of committing an international crime. The International Court of Justice made this clear in the Arrest Warrant Case (Democratic Republic of Congo v. Belgium).[1043]

The AU pointed out that the ICJ had stated that "it has been unable to deduce… that there exists under customary international law any form of exception to the rule according immunity from criminal jurisdiction and inviolability to incumbent Ministers for Foreign Affairs, where they are suspected of having committed war crimes or crimes against humanity". The AU also noted that the Security Council has not lifted President Bashir's immunity either: "[A]ny such lifting should have been explicit, mere referral of a 'situation' by the UNSC to the ICC or requesting a state to cooperate with the ICC cannot be interpreted as lifting immunities granted under international law. The consequence of the referral is that the Rome Statute, including article 98, is applicable to the situation in Darfur."

Additionally, the African Union Commission expressed its total disagreement with the decisions of Pre-Trial Chamber I, which did not take cognisance whatsoever of the obligations of AU member states arising from Article 23(2) of the Constitutive Act of the African Union, to which Chad and Malawi are State Parties, and which obligate all AU member states "to comply with the decisions and policies of the Union". Moreover, by decision Assembly/AU/Dec. 245(XIII) adopted by the thirteenth Ordinary Session of the Assembly of Heads of State and Government, the assembly "Decide[d] that in view of the fact that the request by the African Union has never been acted upon (by UNSC), the AU Member States shall not cooperate pursuant to the provisions of Article 98 of the Rome Statute of the ICC relating to immunities, for the arrest and surrender of President Omar El Bashir of The Sudan". The AU made clear that the decision adopted by the AU policy organs pursuant to the provisions of Rule 33 of the Rules of Procedure of the Assembly is binding on Chad and Malawi and it would be wrong to seek to coerce them to violate or disregard their obligations to the AU.

The African Union Commission also challenged the ICC on the issue of impunity. It stated that by virtue of their membership of the AU, Chad and Malawi, and indeed all other African States Parties to the Constitutive Act, have committed themselves under Article 4 of the Constitutive Act to "condemnation and rejection of impunity" and voluntarily negotiated the Rome Statute and joined the ICC with a view to enhancing the fight against impunity. The AU stated that it will "continue to fight against impunity as required by Article 4 of the Constitutive Act and the relevant Assembly decisions". The AU declared that it would:

> [O]ppose any ill-considered, self-serving decisions of the ICC as well as any pretensions or double standards that become evident from the investigations, prosecutions and decisions by the ICC relating to situations in Africa. Indeed, the African Union believes that the fight against impunity is too important to be left to the ICC alone. The African Union believes that issues of peace and justice should be addressed comprehensively and in a holistic manner and will continue to pursue in respect of The Sudan the interconnected, mutually interdependent and equally desirable objectives of peace, justice and reconciliation.[1044]

The commission also requested all AU member states and friends of Africa to "reject any draft resolution that may be tabled before the UNSC as well as the Assembly of the States Parties to the Rome Statute with the intention of sanctioning the Republic of Malawi and Chad".[1045] Later that month, the eighteenth Summit of the African Union concluded with a decision on the progress report of the commission on the implementation of the assembly decisions on the ICC. In it, the AU stressed the need to explore means to secure the deferral of proceedings against Omar al-Bashir, but also regarding the situation in Kenya, and reiterated its request for deferrals to the UNSC. Moreover, the AU affirmed that the republics of Malawi, Djibouti, Chad and Kenya in refusing to arrest President al-Bashir were implementing AU Assembly decisions on non-cooperation with the ICC regarding the arrest and surrender of Omar al-Bashir.[1046] The AU urged all its members to comply with the assembly's decisions on non-cooperation with respect to the warrants of arrest issued by the ICC.[1047] On 23 May 2012, the Chadian minister of foreign affairs responded to the ICC in relation to the judicial finding on non-cooperation. The Chadian government stated that its actions were justified on the basis of the AU Decisions and on the need to balance the imperatives of peace and justice.

Effects on peace in Africa

The ICC is not just being criticised on grounds of selectivity. Richard Dowden, director of the Royal African Society, has argued that the intrusion of "international law" into African conflicts such as Uganda and the DRC, can cause problems for local peace deals, as in Africa peace deals have usually included losers in government and tying them into a peaceful settlement rather than punishing combatants for the conflict. Dowden has stated that concerns that the ICC's Western-inspired, universalist idea of justice might come into conflict with local forms of law, jeopardising the process of reconciliation "may turn out to have been justified".[1048] He has warned that a global justice system "must have its ideas of justice informed by cultures other than our own. The ICC cannot hand out justice in Sudan as if it were Surrey... If the ICC cannot bring peace and reconciliation to the victims of war, what is the point of its justice?" As Dowden has stated: "If the ICC is going to step into Africa's complex wars, it must understand the local contexts and think through the effects of its actions. Local input and outcomes based on peace and reconciliation must be as close to the heart of the ICC's mission as justice."[1049] Dowden further states that it is Western, not African, imperatives that push for international courts: "Who is it for? I suspect it is for us, watching these wars on television.... The court may be a salve for our consciences for doing nothing about the wars in the first place."[1050] Even keen supporters of "international law" such as South African Judge Richard Goldstone appear to confirm that such a process can impede peace: "If you have a system of international justice you've got to follow through on it. If in some cases that's going to make peace negotiations difficult, that may be the price that has to be paid."[1051] That is, of course, easy for Goldstone to say from the safety and comfort of his judges' chambers and residence.

Academic studies of peace and conflict note that:

> When a conflict is ongoing, the immediate concern will be to bring an end to the bloodshed. Although the pursuit of justice can potentially contribute to long-lasting peace through the imposition of the rule of law...punishment has the potential to reinforce hostility and impede efforts to encourage rival parties to agree. For those most at risk in the conflict, it is more than likely that it will be peace and not justice that is of greatest concern.[1052]

There is no doubt that the ICC has deliberately sought out Africa. All its cases are situated on the African continent. This is quite simply because the western European states and non-governmental organisations at the heart of the ICC see Africa as a "free-fire zone" in which to experiment with a questionable – some would say an alien – European legal model, established by a flawed statute. Others dismiss the ICC as part of a cynical campaign to continue and even intensify the destabilisation of Africa for political, economic or energy reasons.

Justice before peace? Snyder and Vinjamuri document the fact that more than two-thirds of peace agreements since the end of the Cold War, including, for example, the very relevant cases of South Africa and Mozambique, were signed without prosecuting those accused of human-rights abuses in the course of those conflicts.[1053] Even John Bolton, the die-hard US conservative ideologue, has counselled that "accumulated experience strongly favors a case-by-case approach, politically and legally, rather than the inevitable resort to adjudication. Circumstances differ, and circumstances matter."[1054]

What then is the alternative to the sort of retributive Western "justice" advocated by the ICC for Africa? President Paul Kagame of Rwanda, who came to power in the wake of the 1994 Rwandan genocide, has highlighted both the complexity of justice and politics and an African solution. Speaking before the UN high-level meeting on the rule of law during the sixty-seventh session of the United Nations General Assembly at the UN headquarters in New York, President Kagame initially warned of the dangers of politicising issues of justice:

> One can begin with the important principle of universal justice, an ideal which I believe we all would like to see realised. The rule of law internationally is premised on the principle that equality before the law is universal. This, however, is not always the case. What many countries can attest to, in actual fact, is that in application, "justice" is often not pursued fairly or without favour – what may be overlooked in one situation is aggressively sanctioned in another.[1055]

He then highlighted the Rwandan experience and the Rwandan solution. He noted that Rwanda's experience following the genocide was a clear example of the challenges. From a purely legal perspective, there were hundreds of thousands of perpetrators, and a strong case for a punitive approach: "But to best serve our priorities of both justice and social harmony, we sought to balance the strict application of punitive provisions of the law with restorative alternatives." He pointed to the semi-traditional *gacaca* courts, which tried nearly 2,000,000 genocide suspects within ten years: "This home-grown solution through our Gacaca court process, has served us better than any other system could… . We have been able to strengthen the rule of law in our country, particularly through universal access to quality justice, so that citizens are not hindered by financial constraints or long distances to judicial centres."[1056] The courts wound up their activities in June 2012.

Kagame accused some quarters of "politicising issues of justice":

> As a global community, we should be alert to the dangers of politicising issues of justice, both at the national and international level, because ultimately, this undermines the rule of law. We see principles such as universal jurisdiction being used many times selectively and in one direction as a political tool in the arena of international affairs for the purposes of control and domination.[1057]

The Rwandan President warned that punitive Western retributive justice could have unintended consequences: "A purely punitive course of action is not always the best, even when grievances are legitimate and obvious. In fact, the singular pursuit of either justice or political imperatives may aggravate the situation."[1058]

Mahmood Mamdani's solution is also one that has worked for Africa: to step back from the violence and examine the politics of violence: "The way to address violence is not by criminalising perpetrators. We need to analyse why people are fighting. Find out the issues behind the endless civil wars and address them."[1059] He noted that: "The founding movement of every state is a huge crime. How do you make it a pre-history? By the South African model of non-accountability as happened in South Africa." In the case of South Africa when no military victory was possible, Mamdani said that there was a change in focus. The decision was made to put the country's violent past behind it and reach an internal settlement, to "deglobalise" the issues and make no one accountable for past crimes: "Forgive but do not forget." In this way, Mamdani observes, the state begins with something close to a blank slate with an emphasis on non-violence. New rules can be established that focus on solving problems without being burdened by the responsibility of having to judge crimes that were committed in a completely different socio-political situation. Mamdani also pointed to the example of Mozambique where, after years of civil war, there has been growth and peace with the Liberation Front of Mozambique (FRELIMO) and Mozambique National Resistance (RENAMO) turning from guerilla warfare to governance. He also notes "that same choice was made in ending the civil war in South Sudan. Why not in Darfur?"[1060] He does point out that this comes at "a big cost" but it was the only model that brought an end to bloodletting.[1061]

In a surprising meeting of minds John Bolton shares Mamdani's view about the South African model. Bolton suggested that one alternative to the ICC is the kind of Truth and Reconciliation Commission created in South Africa in the aftermath of apartheid. He pointed out that the new government chose not to prosecute perpetrators of human-rights abuses, but instead opted for a different model. The commission made public more of the truth of the apartheid regime and then permitted "society to move ahead without the prolonged opening of old wounds that trials, appeals, and endless recriminations might bring". Bolton further noted that "I do not argue that the South African approach should be followed everywhere, or even necessarily that it was correct for South Africa. But it is certainly fair to conclude that that approach is radically different from the ICC, which operates through vindication, punishment, and retribution."[1062] Bolton also pointed to the circumstances within many former communist countries where the "secret police activities of the now-defunct regimes" were so extensive that some societies have chosen "amnesia" because "it is simply too difficult for them to sort out relative degrees of past wrongs, and because of their desire to move ahead. One need not agree with these decisions to respect the complexity of the moral and political problems they address."[1063]

Africa says no

The shift in attitude towards the ICC by Senegal and Senegalese President Abdoulaye Wade has been very significant. Senegal was the first state to accede to the Rome Statute. President Wade had been one of the court's most enthusiastic advocates, but grew increasingly concerned at the court's focus on Sudan. In July 2008, President Wade asked the ICC to freeze its Darfur investigation for a year.[1064] In 2009, following the court's issuing of arrest warrants for President al-Bashir, President Wade stated:

> The accusations of President Bashir by the International Criminal Court have come to complicate things, because the rebels now say, how can we now negotiate with a president who's going to go to prison, so that's what caused a setback in negotiations with the rebels. The problem is that today many Africans have the impression that this tribunal is only there to judge Africans and this wasn't my intention when I signed for it.[1065]

He also subsequently observed at a press conference that he is "disturbed to see that the ICC only judges Africans".[1066] President Wade, who was also the then sitting Chairman of the Organisation of the Islamic Conference, called for the ICC to abandon its genocide charges against President al-Bashir. He said that there was no genocide in that country.[1067] In his address to the United Nations General Assembly in September 2010, he returned to the theme, saying that the ICC would never be a credible body if Sudan's President was the only one to be pursued with suspicious haste.[1068]

The President of Burundi, Pierre Nkurunziza, was the first to meet with President al-Bashir after his indictment by the ICC. He made his country's position clear: "The problems of the African continent must be solved in the internal framework."[1069] The President of Benin, Thomas Boni Yayi, has accused the ICC of targeting African nations in its investigations: "Curiously, this international body – is it just a coincidence? – ... doesn't stop harassing African statesmen, only Africans. We have the feeling that this court is chasing Africa." Benin is of the original signatories of the Rome Statute that as a then non-permanent member of the UNSC in 2005 voted in favour of Resolution

1593, which referred the situation in Darfur to the ICC. This made Benin's criticism of the court all the more powerful.[1070]

The former Nigerian President Olugun Obasanjo criticised the ICC for drifting towards politics in its investigations: "When I was President of Nigeria, I supported ICC but I supported ICC – we signed – because we believe that it can serve some good for the world. I wonder today whether we have taken the right decision in supporting ICC because some of what I have personally seen, smack of more of politics than criminality and if ICC continues along that line, its repetition will be costly, endangered and undermined." Obasanjo suggested that Bashir should not be held liable for crimes committed in the war-ravaged region of Darfur:

> I have been a military leader in the field and I have been a political leader also running the affairs of my country.... For what reason should a political leader who has to fight a war to save his country, be held responsible for the atrocities committed by the soldiers in the field, unless there is conclusive evidence that he have given instruction for those atrocities to be committed? We all know that the situation in war is not a picnic situation.... I fought [in the] Nigerian Civil War.... If any of them [soldiers] was found not to have acted according to that code of conduct, should General Gowan in Lagos be arrested or shall I in Port Harcourt be arrested?

The former president also hinted that the decision to indict Al-Bashir was to satisfy unspecified parties. Obasanjo questioned the motivation for the arrest warrants: "Are these arrests criminal arrests or political arrests that have been recommended and if they are political arrests to satisfy who? And we must watch what we do and what we allow to do."[1071]

As early as 2009, several African leaders began to make the case that African States Parties to the ICC should withdraw from the Rome Statute.[1072] President Paul Kagame of Rwanda, which is not a state party to the court, has portrayed the ICC as a new form of "imperialism" that seeks to "undermine people from poor and African countries, and other powerless countries in terms of economic development and politics".[1073] The *Christian Science Monitor* newspaper notes that "now there's a growing African political backlash against a wholesale acceptance of global justice, and the ICC specifically.... African lawyers, scholars, and human rights advocates...say that concerns of anti-African bias, are rising." African commentators describe the Western position as one of "double standards" and that "international justice" is a neo-colonial project. African judicial authorities are also questioning the mostly hands-off approach to the ICC taken by the USA, saying this has undercut their moral authority as legal torchbearers.[1074]

This has dramatically slowed the whole ICC process within Africa itself: "The perception of an anti-African ICC bias is thwarting efforts by UN and justice advocates for African states to take the next step to implement the Rome Statute. This process requires states to reform and conform their judiciary to international rule of law standards.... But 'implementation' in Africa may be grinding to a halt for now."[1075]

In May 2013, the AU backed a motion to refer Kenyan President Uhuru Kenyatta's case back to Kenya.[1076] The AU also dramatically upped its criticism of the ICC when it accused the court of "hunting" Africans because of their race. Speaking at the end of an AU summit in Ethiopia's capital, Addis Ababa, Ethiopia's Prime Minister Hailemariam Desalegn said that African leaders were concerned that out of those indicted by the ICC, "99% are Africans". Hailemariam added: "This shows something is flawed within the system of the ICC and we object to that. The Ethiopian leader observed that the ICC had been formed more than a decade ago to end the culture of impunity, but "now the process has degenerated into some kind of race hunting".[1077]

Senior AU officials have also pointed to the double standards being imposed upon Africa. The AU Peace and Security Council head Ramtane Lamamra stated that it was unreasonable for the UNSC to refer the Sudanese president to the ICC when three of its five permanent members – the USA, Russia and China – had either not signed up to or not ratified the Rome Statute which established the ICC: "How could you refer the cases of others while you don't feel compelled to abide by the same rule?"[1078]

In August 2013, the Council of African Political Parties (CAPP), a pan-African coalition of African political parties, stated that the ICC was a tool targeted at African leaders for regime change. In a communiqué issued after a two-day executive meeting in Lusaka, the Zambian capital, CAPP's secretary-general said the ICC was not adjudicating matters between African countries in an impartial way, adding that any conflict in Africa only served the interest of those outside: "It's not by accident that some countries supporting the ICC didn't sign the statute law. All indictees have been African leaders, yet we know what is going on in the Western world… . If those countries were part of the ICC, they would have been at the Hague." The communiqué recorded that African political parties were "gravely concerned" that the ICC seemed to be selective in its work as it was only targeting African leaders while turning a blind eye to atrocities and horrendous crimes committed by leaders of powerful Western nations.[1079]

Wynter Kabimba, Zambia's Minister of Justice, Secretary General of the ruling Patriotic Front and President of the Council of African Political Parties, told journalists during the CAPP meeting in Lusaka that the time had come for African countries to reject the ICC and other Western influences meant to humiliate Africans: "We support Kenya for pulling out of the ICC and urge other African countries to follow suit."[1080]

On 8 September Uganda and Rwanda asked President Uhuru Kenyatta to stop Deputy President William Ruto from flying to The Hague for the start of his trial. The request was made of President Kenyatta in a meeting with Uganda's Foreign Affairs Minister Sam Kutesa and Rwanda's Foreign Minister Louise Mushikiwabo in Nairobi. President Kenyatta insisted on his deputy attending court, arguing that failure to appear before the ICC could trigger a warrant of arrest and "the argument of whether they are innocent would be lost". The request was said to be part of the behind-the-scenes efforts by the AU to stop the prosecution of President Kenyatta and his deputy by the ICC in The Hague.[1081] African states, led by the AU, were reported to be "pursuing an aggressive diplomatic effort" to halt the trials. The strategy involved mobilising support across the continent "to turn a trial of two Kenyan politicians, into a trial of the African people".

A senior African diplomat stated: "If they ignore us, we will need to find alternatives because the ICC has become a theatre of a witch-hunt of Africans. We haven't heard of any prosecutions of people from Syria, from Burma, from Iraq; we want them to be fair and for the court to work for all people."[1082]

The Permanent Secretary in the Ugandan Foreign Affairs Ministry James Mugume challenged the need for trials at The Hague: "Now Uganda has domesticated the Rome Statute and opened a special court to try war crimes, meaning Kony can be tried here. That is in line with the principles of the Rome Statute; of delivering justice for impunity but also fostering peace and reconciliation. If Kony were tried by the ICC and imprisoned in The Hague, it would make some Western and a few other countries happy, but would that deliver justice to the people in Acholi who were victims of LRA atrocities?" He added: "For some of us who participated in formulation of the Rome Statute, there were two key principles: Justice and impunity on the one hand and peace and reconciliation on the other. It seems some people have forgotten this. The West says it was Kenyans who in the first place took the case to ICC; yes, Kenya took the case there because they did not have structures [to try suspects and deliver justice at home]. But now they have. So why can't they be allowed to handle the case at home?"[1083]

In a 10 September letter to the ICC, signed by AU Chairperson Hailemariam Desalegn and by AU Commission Chairperson Nkosazana Dlamini-Zuma, and copied to the UNSC, the AU made the case for the ICC cases against President Uhuru Kenyatta, his deputy William Ruto and journalist Joshua arap Sang to be stopped until its application to have the cases brought back home was heard and determined. The AU argued that the court should first determine the referral application before commencing the cases: "In addition, the prosecution has ignored several procedural requirements having the effect of eroding the principles on natural justice. The court's attention has been drawn to this aspect on two occasions by its own judges. This leaves the African Union with no option but to ask that until the request of the AU is considered and clearly responded to, the cases should not proceed."[1084]

The letter also referred to an appeal that has been filed by ICC Prosecutor Fatou Bensouda against allowing Ruto to attend part of the sessions, arguing that the judges should not have forced the deputy president to attend all the sessions before the appeal was determined: "The Trial Chamber in its earlier decision had taken cognisance of the Deputy President's constitutional responsibilities on which basis the court permitted him to attend only some sessions. On these grounds the court should have upheld its decision pending the determination of the Prosecutor's appeal."[1085]

In September 2013, Okello Oryem, Uganda's deputy foreign minister, announced that an upcoming summit of the AU would debate the possible exit of some African countries from the ICC. He said that Uganda would be compelled to quit the Rome Statute that created the court if a "summit-level" recommendation is made in solidarity with the leaders of Kenya who face criminal charges at The Hague. Oryem cited concerns about the credibility of the witnesses in the trials of Kenyan President Uhuru Kenyatta and his deputy, William Ruto, and stated that Ugandan President Yoweri Museveni "is doing everything possible" to stop the criminal trials in Europe of Kenya's leaders.[1086]

Uganda's President Yoweri Museveni returned to the theme in his speech before the United Nations General Assembly in New York in September 2013. He heavily criticised the ICC, accusing it of making serious mistakes regarding Africa: "[T]he ICC in a shallow, biased way has continued to mishandle complex African issues. This is not acceptable. The ICC should stop." Museveni accused the court of arrogance in its dealings with Kenyan President Uhuru Kenyatta and his deputy William Ruto: "The latest manifestation of arrogance is from the ICC in relation to the elected leaders of Kenya." Museveni said the ICC should listen to African leaders: "Many African countries supported the setting up of ICC because we abhor impunity. Our advice to them is from very capable actors who know what they are doing and saying. Kenya is recovering. Let her recover. We know the origin of the past mistakes. The ICC way is not the right one to handle those mistakes."[1087]

The October 2013 extraordinary AU summit

On 12 October, an extraordinary summit of heads of state and government of the AU unanimously agreed to a resolution that no sitting African president should be tried in international courts while in office. The AU also called on the ICC to postpone the trial of Kenyan president Uhuru Kenyatta. If the court failed to do so, the AU agreed that Kenyatta ought to refuse to attend. The meeting was specially convened to discuss the role of the ICC on the continent. Hailemariam Desalegn, Prime Minister of Ethiopia and the current AU chairman, noted that "The unfair treatment that we have been subjected to by the ICC is completely unacceptable."[1088] He also stated that the ICC was showing "double standards".[1089] Ethiopia's Foreign Minister, Tedros Adhanom, said at the summit that the court had become a "political instrument". He went on to state: "We should not allow the ICC to continue to treat Africa and Africans in a condescending manner.... Far from promoting justice and reconciliation, and contributing to the advancement of peace and stability in our continent, the court has transformed itself into a political instrument targeting Africa and Africans."[1090] President Robert Mugabe of Zimbabwe had also recently stated that "selective justice has eroded the credibility of the ICC on the African continent". President Kenyatta told the summit that "The ICC has been reduced into a painfully farcical pantomime."[1091] Kenyatta welcomed the decision and further criticised the court: "It stopped being the home of justice the day it became the toy of declining imperial powers. Africa is not a third-rate territory of second-class peoples. We are not a project, or experiment of outsiders."[1092]

The closing remarks of Ethiopian Prime Minister and AU Chairman Hailemariam Desalegn at the end of the summit showed just how far the African continent had moved with regard to the ICC. They are worth citing at length:

> I am very glad to note that we conducted our discussion in a manner that ensures our unity and solidarity. We have also adopted our decision speaking with one voice and sending a strong political message on Africa's relationship

with the ICC. In this regard, we have reaffirmed the principles deriving from national laws and international customary law by which sitting Head of State or Government and other Senior State officials are granted immunities during their tenure of office. Accordingly, we have agreed that no charges shall be commenced or continued before any international court or tribunal against any serving Head of State or Government or anybody acting or entitled to act in such capacity during his/her term of office. To safeguard the constitutional order, stability and integrity of member States, we have resolved that no serving AU Head of State or Government or anybody acting or entitled to act in such capacity, shall be required to appear before any international court or tribunal during his term of office. Furthermore, we have decided to set up a Contact Group of the Executive Council to be led by its Chairperson, composed of five (5) members from each region plus Kenya to undertake consultations with the members of the United Nations Security Council, in particular its five Permanent members with a view to engaging with them on all concerns of the AU in its relationship with the ICC, including the deferral of the Kenyan and the Sudan cases in order to obtain their feedback before the beginning of the trial on 12 November 2013. If our request for deferral does not get a response until then, we have agreed to request for postponement of the trial.

In our decision, we have stressed that the ICC is a Court of last resort and noted the efforts being made to expand the African Court on Human and People's Rights to try international crimes such as genocide, crimes against humanity and war crimes. We have, therefore, requested the Commission to expedite this process to deal with international crimes in accordance with the relevant decisions of the Policy Organs of our Union.

We have also requested African States Parties to the Rome Statute to introduce amendments to the Statute with a view to ensuring recognition to the African regional Judicial mechanisms dealing with international crimes in accordance with the principle of complimentarity. Particularly, we requested members of the Bureau of the Assembly of State Parties to inscribe on the agenda of the forthcoming sessions of the Assembly the issue of indictment of African sitting Heads of State and Government by the ICC and its consequences on peace, stability and reconciliation in African Union member States.

Above and beyond this, we have agreed that any member State that wishes to refer a case to the ICC may inform and seek the advice of the African Union. We have also agreed that Kenya should send a letter to the United Nations Security Council requesting for deferral, in conformity with Article 16 of the Rome Statute, of the proceedings against the President and Deputy President of Kenya that would be endorsed by all African States Parties.[1093]

The ICC has not just lost credibility within Africa. Geis and Mundt have noted how the ICC's Africa focus is fragmenting international opinion: "[T]he broad international consensus in favor of the Rome Statute has begun to fray as the court pursued justice in some of the worlds most politically-charged and complex crises, all of which happened to fall within Africa. At the same time, other states, such as Burma or North Korea, have so far eluded potential ICC investigations, most likely for geopolitical reasons and/or deference to regional interests."[1094] Other commentators allege that the Prosecutor has limited investigations to Africa because of geopolitical pressures, either out of a desire to avoid confrontation with major powers or as a tool of Western foreign policy.[1095]

It is clear that the ICC has made a fatal mistake in issuing an arrest warrant for African heads of state, including one whose country was not even subject to the ICC treaty. There are welcome signs that Africa is not going to accept the disastrous European-prescribed "White Man's magic" in the shape of the ICC. African problems must be solved by Africans.

Chapter Fifteen

THE FICTION OF AFRICAN "SELF-REFERRAL"

"Why focus on cases in Africa? Because...the leaders requested our intervention."

Luis Moreno-Ocampo[1096]

"[T]o argue that Moreno-Ocampo is only responding to requests is no longer tenable."

Inner City Press[1097]

When pressed on the fact that all the ICC cases and indictments have been in Africa and nowhere else, the court's Chief Prosecutor has always defended this narrow focus by claiming that they were all "self-referrals" by the African countries themselves, or in the case of Sudan and Libya, referrals from the UNSC. Ocampo claimed that the court was merely responding to spontaneous referrals from African state members of the ICC: "Why focus on cases in Africa? Because...the leaders requested our intervention."[1098] On another occasion, Ocampo elaborated: "[T]he law says I need a State which signed the treaty to apply the law in that country. So I can work in the Congo because the President of the Congo requested me to do it. I can work in Uganda and the Central African Republic because in both cases the Presidents signed the treaty and requested me. That's why I'm working with them."[1099] This is deceit on the behalf of the prosecutor. The ICC brought considerable pressure to bear on both Uganda and DRC to refer themselves to the court.

There are compelling theoretical, practical, legal and political objections to state "self-referrals", whether forced or voluntary. William Schabas has said that state referrals are an "invention of the Office of the Prosecutor".[1100] The Prosecutor sought to justify self-referrals as early as 2003: "[T]here may be cases where inaction by States is the appropriate course of action. For example, the court and a territorial State incapacitated by mass crimes may agree that a consensual division of labour is the most logical and effective approach. Groups bitterly divided by conflict may oppose prosecutions at each others' hands and yet agree to a prosecution by a Court perceived as neutral and impartial."[1101] The reality is that when it came to self-referrals the court was neither. Schabas has also made the case that state referrals allow states to manipulate the court; that they seek to focus attention on non-state actors rather than governments; and that they can result in governments passing the buck with regard to prosecuting crimes against humanity and war crimes. Benjamin Schiff somewhat diplomatically observed that Ocampo's concept of "self-referrals" constituted "a novel view of the ICC's relationship with states", and that it "provoked widespread scepticism among the ICC 'old hands'".[1102] By "old hands" Schiff probably means those people who designed the court and brought it into being.

As pointed out by Darryl Robinson,[1103] Schabas states that such referrals "[flow] from a creative interpretation of Article 14 of the Rome Statute that was not seriously contemplated by the 1998 Diplomatic Conference and during the prior negotiations".[1104] Schabas has also observed further that self-referrals are based on a "novel interpretation of Article 14...of which there is not a trace in the travaux préparatoires",[1105] and that self-referrals are an "interpretative deviation" and an "opportunistic construction"[1106] on the part of the Prosecutor driven by a need to generate activity.[1107] Schabas goes on further to note that these "flawed sophomoric experiments"[1108] present a "trap" for the ICC[1109] that "distort[s] the proper role of the Court".[1110]

An active participant in the discussions that shaped the Rome Statute, Schabas states that "a consensual relationship between the State of territorial jurisdiction and the international body...was not what was contemplated when the Rome Statute was drafted".[1111] Schabas noted that in addition to not appearing in any of the *travaux préparatoires*, there was also no trace "in the various commentaries by participants in the drafting process to suggest that a State referring a case against itself was ever contemplated".[1112] Schabas has reiterated that "there had never been even the slightest suggestion, in the drafting history of the Statute, that a State might refer a case 'against itself'".[1113] The commentaries were authored by participants in the negotiations leading to the Rome Statute. Schabas states that "in other words, the drafting history of article 14 of the *Rome Statute* leaves little doubt that what was considered was a 'complaint' by a State party against another State".[1114] Mueller and Stegmiller have echoed this statement: "[T]he mechanism has not operated as intended", and that self-referral "was not foreseen by the delegates at Rome".[1115] Mahnoush Arsanjani and W. Michael Reisman confirm that "before and during the Rome negotiations, no one...assumed that governments would want to invite the future court to investigate and prosecute crimes that occurred in their territory", and that "there is no indication that the drafters ever contemplated that the Statute would include voluntary state referrals to the Court of difficult cases arising in their own territory".[1116]

Schiff has sought to explain the Prosecutor's somewhat tortured justification for seeking the self-referrals. The OTP termed it "positive complementarity". "Negative complementarity", which had originally been envisaged as triggering the complementarity issue, was described by Schiff as follows: "[S]uspecting that a state is not pursuing prosecutions in good faith, the Court carries out investigations, issues warrants, gains custody, and prosecutes suspects."[1117] "Positive complementarity" was said to envisage providing legal training, capacity building and monitoring local judicial processes. Schiff points out that "positive complementarity" has been criticised for turning the court into a judicial development assistance organisation.[1118] Another view would be that the Prosecutor was making things up as he went along.

Schabas has publicly warned that self-referrals "distort the vision of those who struggled so hard to create the Court".[1119] Arsanjani and Reisman also warned that "the innovative allowance of voluntary referral...may take the ICC into areas where the drafters of the Rome Statute had not wished to tread"[1120] and that such referrals "could open the way to...selective externalization of difficult cases".[1121] This view was echoed by Mueller and Stegmiller who warned that self-referrals are not a "panacea" but a "patient" and should be avoided.[1122]

Self-referrals are in contravention of the Rome Statute

The OTP's acceptance of self-referrals, which it had itself actively sought, is in direct contravention of the Rome Statute. Article 42(1) states:

> The Office of the Prosecutor shall act independently as a separate organ of the Court. It shall be responsible for receiving referrals and any substantiated information on crimes within the jurisdiction of the Court, for examining them and for conducting investigations and prosecutions before the Court. A member of the Office shall not seek or act on instructions from any external source.

Schabas has made the important general point that even when a referral is legitimate, let alone remotely questionable, it is still absolutely within the Prosecutor's right not to proceed with the issue: "[E]ven when States Parties or the Security Council refers a situation, the Prosecutor still has the power to refuse to proceed if he or she judges that this is not in the 'interests of justice'."[1123]

It is now common knowledge that Ocampo actively sought the state "self-referrals" by Uganda and the DRC. Phil Clark has stated that "Prosecutor Ocampo approached President Museveni in 2003 and persuaded him to refer the Uganda case to the ICC. The referral suited both parties, providing the ICC with its first state referral of a case and the Ugandan government with another stick with which to beat the [Lord's Resistance Army]."

On 17 July 2003, Ocampo announced that he had analysed the 500 complaints the ICC had then received since the Rome Statute had entered into force on 1 July 2002.[1124] Of all these complaints, he said that he chose to "follow closely" the situation in the DRC and that of all the situations it was "the most urgent situation to be followed" with a view to possible further action.[1125] Ocampo made it very clear to the presidents of both the DRC and Uganda that he had been "closely analyzing the situation in the DRC since July 2003.... In September 2003 the Prosecutor informed the States Parties that he was ready to request authorization from the Pre-Trial Chamber to use his own powers to start an investigation, *but that a referral and active support from the DRC would assist his work.*" (Emphasis added.) In autumn 2003, the prosecutor said he was ready to act but pointed out that he preferred to wait for the Congolese government to ask him to intervene. Pro-ICC sources confirmed the pressure on Uganda: "In July 2003, Prosecutor Ocampo identified Uganda as an area of concern."[1126] Museveni was forced to "refer" the situation in his country to the ICC in December 2003. Under similar pressure, the DRC government "welcomed" the ICC involvement, and in March 2004 the DRC "referred" the situation in the country to the court.[1127] The reality is that Ocampo hectored them: "I invited them to refer the case to me and they did it, so in Uganda and the Congo, I invited them but then the president of the countries invited the Court to intervene. So it's not an intrusion."[1128] *The Wall Street Journal* revealed that "[a]t a July 2003 news conference, Mr. Moreno-Ocampo announced out of the blue that he 'believed' atrocities in the DRC could qualify for an ICC investigation".[1129] The Congressional Research Service confirmed that "[a]ccording to an Office of the Prosecutor official, referrals by the governments of Uganda and DRC followed moves by the Office of the Prosecutor to open investigations under its discretionary power".[1130] Human Rights Watch baldly confirmed that "the Office of the Prosecutor actively sought the referrals in the DRC and Uganda".[1131] On the 17 July 2008, the ICC Chief Prosecutor admitted that he had invited Uganda and DRC to refer their situations to the ICC. As the *Inner City Press*, which closely monitors the UN and ICC, subsequently noted: "After this admission, to argue that Moreno-Ocampo is only responding to requests is no longer tenable."[1132]

The Rome Statute allows the court to intervene when the domestic jurisdictions of States Parties are not seeking or unable to prosecute relevant cases. The Prosecutor himself was clear about the state's obvious disinclination to proceed being the most important factor in triggering action by the court: "As a general rule, the policy of the OTP will be to undertake investigations only where there is a clear case of failure to act by the State or States concerned…where States fail to act, or are not 'genuinely' investigating or prosecuting, as described in article 17 of the Rome Statute."[1133] Clark has pointed out several difficulties with Ugandan self-referral. He has referred to "the unusual grounds on which the ICC has opened the LRA cases. These grounds appear to contradict the OTP's own stated investigative and prosecutorial policies."[1134] As Clark makes clear, the ICC's acceptance of the Uganda referral undermines the court's guiding policy of complementarity: "The Ugandan judiciary – one of the most proficient and robust in Africa – is unquestionably able and willing to prosecute serious cases such as those involving the LRA."[1135] Geoffrey Robertson has also noted that "it is difficult to see how the complementarity principle could apply: Uganda has an effective court system".[1136] Schiff observed that the OTP's excuse for involvement, claims that the referring states were unable to prosecute was seen as "problematic".[1137] The Ugandan government admits the competence and capacity of its own legal system to bring LRA rebels to trial in its own self-referral to the ICC: "[t]he Ugandan judicial system is widely recognised as one of the most independent, impartial and competent on the African continent…. There is no doubt that Ugandan courts have the capacity to give captured LRA leaders a fair and impartial trial."[1138] The ICC Pre-Trial Chamber agreed. Schiff writes that they "viewed skeptically the OTP's argument that the case was admissible on the grounds that the DRC justice system was inadequate to provide appropriate judicial measures for the crimes under the Statute".[1139] In February 2006, the Pre-Trial Chamber confirmed that the judicial system in the DRC, and especially within Ituri, was fit for purpose:

> [F]or the purpose of the admissibility analysis of the case against Mr Thomas Lubanga Dyilo, the Chamber observes that since March 2004 the DRC national justice system has undergone certain changes, particularly in the region of Ituri where a *Tribunal de Grande Instance* has been re-opened in Bunia. This has resulted *inter alia* in the issuance of two warrants of arrest by the competent DRC authorities for Mr Thomas Lubanga Dyilo in March 2005 for several crimes, some possibly within the jurisdiction of the Court, committed in connection with military attacks from May 2003 onwards and during the so-called Ndoki incident in February 2005. Moreover, as a result of the DRC proceedings against Mr Thomas Lubanga Dyilo, he has been held in the *Centre Pénitentiaire et de Rééducation de Kinshasa* since 19 March 2005. Therefore, in the Chamber's view, the Prosecution's general statement that the DRC national judicial system continues to be unable in the sense of article 17(1)(a) to (c) and (3) of the Statute does not wholly correspond to the reality any longer.[1140]

Pre-Trial Chamber I clearly believed that the Congolese justice system was not suffering from "a total or substantial collapse or unavailability of its national judicial system", to use the words of Article 17.

Clark makes that case that "even if it is considered justifiable for the ICC to open investigations on the basis that Uganda's military and police (rather than judicial) capacity is insufficient to address serious crimes, the fact remains that the ICC itself has neither military nor police capacity."[1141] The Uganda-based International Refugee Rights Initiative has also asked the key question: "Where was the gap that the ICC needed to fill in the armoury of tools that were available to pursue accountability and end the war? It seemed clear to those on the ground that the issue was not whether Kony and his senior commanders could be *tried*; it was whether they could be *caught*."[1142]

This also applied to the Congo self-referral. Geoffrey Robertson observed that the ICC's Lubanga indictment which followed the DRC self-referral was "criticized on the basis that they charge crimes committed in the province of Ituri, which has the best-functioning courts in the country (thanks to a $20 million EU grant) where Lubanga was already facing much more serious charges than the single offence levelled at him by the ICC, namely that of recruiting child soldiers".[1143]

Clark has concluded that the ICC "opened the case in northern Uganda on grounds for which it is not adequately equipped to respond".[1144] Clark states that the ICC accepted the referral "not on the basis of the unwillingness or inability of the Ugandan judiciary to prosecute serious cases but rather on the inability of government forces to capture and arrest the LRA leadership".[1145] The court's position with regard to Uganda can be tested, for example, in a simple analogy to the USA and the UK. Let us assume for a moment that the USA was an ICC State Party: using the court's own criteria, the USA would have failed Ocampo's complementarity test because it had not been able to prosecute those responsible for the attack on the Twin Towers, not because of any unwillingness or inability on the part of the American judiciary to proceed but because it was unable to apprehend those involved. Similarly, the UK would have previously failed the complementarity test because it was unable to bring to justice those responsible for thousands of murders and attempted murders in Northern Ireland. The American and British analogies place the court's rationale for its self-serving intervention in Uganda – and the DRC – in focus.

Referring to the situation in DRC and Uganda Clark states "the ICC has been fundamentally motivated by self-interested pragmatic concerns, avoiding the fraught task of investigating and prosecuting sitting members of government who are responsible for grave crimes, while also overlooking the capacity of domestic jurisdictions to address the atrocities concerned".[1146]

Self-referral as a useful tool for the prosecutor

It is clear that the ICC Chief Prosecutor sought to use self-referrals to suit his own institutional and political needs. Geoffrey Nice has pointed very clearly to the politics behind the DRC referral:

> Was this in fact pushed by the Prosecutor? It appears that the Prosecutor had himself requested [the self-referral] and encouraged it by declaring that – absent a referral by the DRC – he was ready to use his proprio motu powers. The Prosecutor would have been likely to receive the required authorization from the Pre-Trial Chamber without great difficulty but may the Prosecutor have had a political motive? At the Rome Conference that established the court, many of these countries strongly opposed giving the Prosecutor power to initiate an investigation proprio motu. Pushing for, and gaining, a self-referral brought the advantage of not wielding his proprio motu powers in a way to worry other countries, as well as providing some guarantee of cooperation that is required to bring a case to trial with an investigation that may proceed smoothly with the appropriate the necessary level of protection for investigators and witnesses.[1147]

Self-referral by states – state self-interest

Even assuming that the self-referrals were genuine – which they were not – they lack credibility given that they are obvious attempts to manipulate the court. Schabas warns that "self-referral, far from being an expedient to provide a fledgling institution with some cases, is actually a trap. If a State refers a situation against itself, that is, against its rebels, it is doing so with a result in mind."[1148] Schabas makes this motivation clear: "When a State is actively engaged in initiation of the process, there is potential for manipulation.

In effect, the state quite predictably uses the international institution to pursue its enemies."¹¹⁴⁹ Sir Geoffrey Nice states:

> It appears that the Ugandan referral was a military strategy and international reputation campaign and may have been initiated in the Ministry of Defence, as a research interview with a government minister revealed; the referral could also rally international assistance for the arrest of the government's military opponents.¹¹⁵⁰

Refugee Law Project researcher Lucy Hovil has also questioned the Ugandan government's motivation for self-referral: "Could it be that the decision to refer the case was taken in order to shift international attention onto a group of 'lunatics' committing heinous crimes across the north and away from growing criticism of the regime's hold on power – and international armed forays – which were coming under increasing scrutiny?"¹¹⁵¹

Phil Clark confirms "the view that Museveni has instrumentalised the ICC".¹¹⁵² Schiff also used the term "instrumentalisation" in connection with the Ugandan self-referral, going on to note that "President Museveni's referral to the ICC appeared to serve his own political objectives.¹¹⁵³ Geoffrey Robertson shares these views: "The Court has… convincingly, been upbraided for ignoring allegations of war crimes committed by the Uganda Defence Force, and for allowing itself to be used as a political instrument by Museveni."¹¹⁵⁴ Schiff has observed that "[l]ike Museveni, Kabila's decision to refer the DRC situation to the Court appears to have been motivated significantly by his own political calculations… . His referral to the ICC apparently came about because he saw that he could gain from it both domestically and internationally."¹¹⁵⁵ Jendayi Frazer also noted instrumentalisation of the court: "A review of ICC cases also reveals that some African officials have instrumentally cooperated with the Prosecutor to indict their political opponents, further diminishing the impartiality of the Court."¹¹⁵⁶ She neglected to mention that the administration she had served had been at the heart of the very use of the ICC that she subsequently saw fit to criticise.

It is evident that part of the Prosecutor's attempts to secure self-referrals was an implicit understanding that the court would focus only on one side of the conflict, the rebel side. Darryl Robinson has noted that "the prospect of improper understandings attached to territorial state referrals has graduated in the literature from speculation to presumed fact".¹¹⁵⁷ Schabas argues that self-referrals entail an "implied compact with governments" or a "degree of complicity" between the state and the OTP.¹¹⁵⁸ Mueller and Stegmiller assert as a simple matter of fact that self-referrals "will often be accompanied and burdened by 'understandings' between The Hague and the referring state that can taint the subsequent proceedings".¹¹⁵⁹ As the International Refugee Rights Initiative succinctly noted: "The ICC, therefore, had appeared to sidestep the one area of chronic injustice (the actions of the government and its armed forces) that was least likely to be reached by the domestic courts, which were subject to state control."¹¹⁶⁰ It is also evident that the court acquiesced to American demands not to focus on the Ugandan government. Branch reported:

[I]n a closed-door meeting between ICC officials and the U.S. representative in charge of central Africa in the U.S. State Department, the U.S. representative expressed American support for the execution of the arrest warrants against the LRA, but reportedly warned the ICC Prosecutor not to pursue UPDF activities.[1161]

At a Pre-Trial Chamber hearing on 3 February 2006, the experienced French judge Claude Jorda asked the following pointed question: "Where is the office of the Prosecutor heading? We are at the beginning of these proceedings and this is a very central issue. Do you intend to prosecute individuals with national level responsibilities? Or do you intend to limit your action to individuals who are leaders of militias?"[1162]

There is a further fiction surrounding claims about "self-referral". All the self-referrals were asking the court to take action against rebel groups within the referring states. This includes the most recent, that of Mali.[1163] As Schabas notes: "When the first Prosecutor launched the 'self-referral' cases in 2004 and 2005, there was much concern about the danger of directing the Court towards rebel groups." He is also clear about the argument used in response by the court and its adherents:

> In reply, it was argued then that this would ensure cooperation by the State Party and thereby contribute to the effectiveness of the Court. Eight years of practice have shown that State Party cooperation adds very little to the process. The Ugandan arrest warrants remain unenforced. Bosco Ntaganda is still at large in the Democratic Republic of the Congo. A single prosecution has resulted from the Central African Republic, of an individual who miscalculated by travelling to Belgium. In other words, some of the compelling arguments invoked several years ago in support of self-referrals have proven to be rather hollow."[1164]

The fourth "self-referral" was that by Mali in July 2012. The government of Mali referred "the situation in Mali since January 2012" to the ICC. As with the other three referrals the government was asking the court to prosecute rebel groups rather than do it themselves. Even ICC-apologist Darryl Robinson had admitted that "[u]p to the present, the OTP has yet to bring charges against agents of a referring state".[1165] Schabas also confirms that "[t]he profound flaw in the 'self-referral' model is that it flies in the face of 'positive complementarity'. If Mali wants to ensure that its rebels are prosecuted, the Court should encourage it to do so by itself. Referring the situation to the Court doesn't do anything to bring the rebels into custody. And if perchance they are captured, why can't Mali prosecute the cases?"[1166]

The legal commentator Dov Jacobs has stated that:

> It is not really in the spirit of complementarity for States to so easily delegate prosecutions to the ICC, when the end goal of the system, at least in the rhetoric, is that States be the first in line in the fight against impunity, with

the ICC coming in when the system does not work, or is used to shield the perpetrators from actual justice.... . But the fact remains that this is what the legal framework says. Complementarity in practice resembles nothing like the nice philosophy that is sold to us.[1167]

It is clear that state self-referrals should never have been accepted by the court. Arsanjani and Reisman go so far as to challenge the basic premise of "self-referrals", stating that "such a referral does not seem to meet the requirement of admissibility".[1168] As pointed out by several respected international lawyers and commentators, in the case of Uganda there was nothing more that the ICC could add, except in a negative sense of destroying a peace process and precipitating a worsening humanitarian situation.

In 2011 Schabas expressed the hope that the court would grow out of the phase of pursuing and accepting self-referrals.[1169] This does not seem to be the case, with Mali's self-referral of the situation in Mali since January 2012 to the ICC continuing this flawed process.[1170] The fact that the new prosecutor accepted the self-referral does not bode well – it appears that the manipulation of the court continues, with the incumbent prosecutor willing to play along.

Chapter Sixteen

The Fiction of Deterrence

"Deterrence is the most important goal of the ICC."

Luis Moreno Ocampo[1171]

"I disagree with the point...that somehow the ICC will deter things that have happened in the past from happening in the future. I see no reason why that should be the case."

Lord Lamont[1172]

The issue of the claims made with respect to deterrence in relation to the ICC is important for two reasons. Firstly, it is claimed to be a core tenet of the Rome Statute. And secondly, in the absence of any tangible progress in executing the Ugandan arrest warrants, apologists for the ICC have then sought to justify the ICC's intervention by claiming that if nothing else the ICC has deterred violence, the peace process has been stable and that Uganda has been more peaceful since the arrest warrants were issued. The claim of deterrence has also been extended to other conflicts.

On the claim that deterrence is at the heart of the court, ICC functionaries sing from the same song sheet. Philippe Kirsch has stated that "[b]y putting potential perpetrators on notice that they may be tried before the court, the ICC is intended to contribute to the deterrence of these crimes".[1173] Christine Chung, the first senior trial attorney to work in the ICC's OTP, has stated that "[d]eterrence is the most important goal of the ICC".[1174] Ocampo claimed that deterrence is at the heart of the Rome Statute and that the ICC has indeed been an effective deterrent.[1175] In its decision regarding the arrest warrant for Lubanga, the Pre-Trial Chamber spoke of "maximizing" the "deterrent effects of the activities of the Court".[1176] The court cited the "deterrent function" to justify the "key role" of the gravity threshold in determining whether a case was admissible.[1177] Fans of the ICC also promised a lot. Amnesty International, for example, boldly stated that "[The ICC] will serve as a permanent deterrent to people considering these crimes."[1178] The ICC-friendly ICG asserted in 2006 that deterrence had worked in Uganda: "[T]he

ICC's investigation played a direct role in spurring the current peace initiative."¹¹⁷⁹ In fact there is a considerable body of empirical evidence that shows the exact opposite is true. There is, as always, a big difference between aspirations, institutional propagandising and reality.

By its own account it is self-evident that the ICC and its actions have failed to deter what the court would term war crimes and crimes against humanity. As of 2013, seventeen cases in eight African countries have been brought before the ICC since its establishment in 2002. The ICC has publicly indicted thirty-two people, proceedings against twenty-four of whom are ongoing. The ICC has issued arrest warrants for dozens of individuals and summonses to nine others. The 2009 "Report of the International Criminal Court" stated that the ICC was "seized of four situations" and that six "other situations" were under analysis by the OTP.¹¹⁸⁰ Interestingly, in his "Proposed Programme Budget for 2010 of the International Criminal Court", Ocampo increased that number to eight – probably for budgetary reasons.¹¹⁸¹ The reality is that the court has had to open cases in seven more countries *since* its original involvement in Uganda. Of the thirty-two people indicted by the court, twenty-seven of the indictments were issued since the original five indictments in respect of Uganda.

Commentators, academics and peace practitioners have challenged the claims made about the deterrent effect of court action. They point to the fact that evidence for the deterrent effect of modern war-crimes courts cannot be shown by way of case study.¹¹⁸² In a noted article in 2006, Helena Cobban stated that "it is time to abandon the false hope of international justice".¹¹⁸³ In making her case, which was focused on the International Criminal Tribunal for the Former Yugoslavia (ICTY) and Kosovo, she stated that there was very little evidence that war-crimes prosecutions deter future atrocities: "There is important evidence against the proposition that war crimes prosecutions deter atrocities."¹¹⁸⁴ The case she made applies equally to the ICC.¹¹⁸⁵ In their study of international criminal courts and deterrence Julian Ku and Jide Nzelibe have stated "we believe [international criminal tribunal] prosecutions will be unlikely to have any meaningful deterrence effect".¹¹⁸⁶ They said that this is also the case where those courts have full international backing "even when there is support for [international criminal tribunals] by powerful countries like the USA, it is still very likely that ICTs will play a marginal, if not counterproductive, role in deterring humanitarian atrocities in the weak or failing states where such atrocities are most likely to be committed".¹¹⁸⁷ Geis and Mundt have noted that "there is little empirical evidence to suggest that the possibility of international criminal indictments for mass atrocity crimes serve as a deterrent or moderating force on government and rebel leaders".¹¹⁸⁸ Nick Grono, the Deputy President of the ICG, has also noted that "there are plenty of examples in which the threat of criminal prosecution failed to deter perpetrators of atrocity crimes, and it is difficult to point to cases of successful deterrence".¹¹⁸⁹ The distinguished Columbian human-rights lawyer Gustavo Gallón pointed out the obvious fault lines in the deterrence argument even before the establishment of the ICC:

> Deterrence can also be a dangerous illusion if it leads us to assume that no more

violations will be committed after the actual establishment of an international criminal court. Or if it leads us to assume that most heinous crimes that humanity has known so far will not be repeated, because of the deterrent effect of such a court. Unfortunately, such an effect is not attainable. No legal system can ensure the elimination of criminal activity. On the contrary, the existence of criminal legal systems is related to the conviction that crimes will continue to take place and will need to be dealt with, not to the expectation of the disappearance of criminal activity.[1190]

An experienced analyst such as Paul van Zyl, Country Programme Director at the International Center for Transitional Justice, has also noted: "It is important for advocates of international justice and strong proponents of the ICC not to overstate the deterrence argument."[1191] Ignatieff has noted that any observer should "be skeptical of the claim by the Court's current president that international justice serves a useful deterrent function".[1192]

Daniel Sutter has argued that punishment of regime leaders guilty of crimes against humanity is not always beneficial, since the prospect of punishment provides a disincentive for regime leaders to step down from power. He also states that the crucial factor in deterrence is the probability that the court's punishments will actually be imposed. Since the Rome Statute establishing the court has few effective measures to allow punishments to be imposed, he concludes that the ICC is unlikely to have a major deterrent effect.[1193]

Uganda: A Case Study in Non-deterrence

It is apparent that regarding the LRA the prospect of ICC punishment has waned in the face of the military offensives being undertaken against the organisation. ICC indictments have not deterred the LRA. LRA activity has in fact increased dramatically. In October 2010, AU member states met in Bangui, the capital of CAR, where they agreed on a number of joint military and communications initiatives. Participants also agreed to appoint a special envoy on the LRA issue and to designate the LRA as a "terrorist" group.[1194] Francisco Madeira, a Mozambican official, was appointed as the AU envoy.[1195] The AU's military initiative on the LRA involved a joint coordination mechanism body composed of the ministers of defence of the four LRA-affected countries, with a secretariat in Bangui and chaired by the African Union Commissioner for Peace and Security – whose task is dealing with the general political aspects, providing strategic direction and coordinating with all stakeholders in the fight against the LRA. The AU had put a military force into the field with a headquarters in Yambio, South Sudan; and three operational sectors, in Nzara in South Sudan, Dungu in the DRC, and Obo in the CAR. The AU initiative also included a "Joint Operations Center" made up of thirty officers responsible for "integrated planning and operation".[1196] This comprised military officers from the AU regional task force headquarters. The United Nations Office to the African Union, the EU and the USA were also involved in assisting the military effort. In July 2011, for example, the Security Council commended "the important efforts that are being undertaken by the militaries of the Central African Republic, the Democratic Republic of the Congo, the Republic of South Sudan and Uganda to address the threat posed by the LRA, and emphasized the importance of sustained coordinated action by these Governments to bring an end to the LRA problem".[1197]

In March 2012, the AU announced that the militaries of the four LRA-affected countries would contribute a total of 5,000 troops for a counter-LRA offensive. The AU force would be commanded by – and made up largely of – the UPDF.[1198]

Dr. David Lanz is very blunt about claims that the ICC action has in any way deterred continuing conflict and violence in Uganda: "[C]onsidering the tripling of IDP numbers from 2002 to 2006 as well as the red flag-raising by humanitarian organizations working in Northern Uganda, this argument seems unconvincing, if not intellectually dishonest. Indeed, the reasoning that the ICC has a preventative impact in Northern Uganda seems to be wishful thinking, rather than reality."[1199] These figures have themselves doubled and trebled again in the years since Lanz's statement. Grassroots feelings in the DRC echo those in Uganda. Alex Losinu, a community elder in Ituri, has urged the ICC to arrest also those in power in DRC: "The ICC must also arrest members of the government who are implicated in various crimes in Ituri. The ICC trial has no deterrent effect because the real criminals are exempt from charges and are integrated in communities."[1200]

Deterrence has not worked. The ICC's own 2009 report amply illustrated the ICC's impotence with regard to the Lord's Resistance Army, in the Ugandan conflict, its first "situation", one in which it has been involved for nine years and in which its involvement has made matters considerably worse. It is useful to cite the report at length:

> According to information received by the Office, the incidence of alleged crimes rose sharply from September 2008, as the Lord's Resistance Army, operating increasingly freely across a wide area between Garamba National Park in the Democratic Republic of the Congo and border areas of southern Sudan close to the Central African Republic, put into operation plans to expand their numbers by several hundred through the abduction of civilians, primarily children. The Office received reports of particularly savage attacks taking place in December 2008 and January 2009, with the killing and abduction of several hundred people in a series of raids on towns and villages across a broad area of the Democratic Republic of the Congo and southern Sudan. The reports indicated that there may have been more than 1,000 deaths, more than 1,500 abductions and more than 200,000 persons internally displaced as a result of Lord's Resistance Army activity in the period covered by the present report [12 months].[1201]

In 2010 Human Rights Watch noted that:

> Between December 14 and 17, 2009, the Lord's Resistance Army...carried out a horrific attack in the Makombo area of Haut Uele district in northeastern Democratic Republic of Congo, near the border with Sudan. In a well-planned

operation, the LRA killed more than 321 civilians and abducted more than 250 others, including at least 80 children... . The attack was one of the largest single massacres in the LRA's 23-year history.¹²⁰²

Human Rights Watch further observed that: "The Makombo massacre is part of a longstanding practice of horrific attacks and abuses by the LRA committed in four countries in the central African region: Uganda, southern Sudan, CAR, and Congo. *Initially restricted to northern Uganda, the LRA has evolved into a regional threat.*" (Emphasis added.) The UN Office for the Coordination of Humanitarian Affairs reported that in 2009 "the LRA killed 1,096 civilians and abducted 1,373 adults and 255 children in Haut and Bas Uele districts of northern Congo.... [I]t is clear that the LRA maintains its capacity to kill, abduct, and terrorize the civilian population." OCHA has estimated that by January 2010, 282,661 people were displaced from their homes in these districts, including 224,594 people in Haut Uele and another 58,067 in Bas Uele.¹²⁰³ The extent of the LRA's post-indictment threat to the region was evident when on 11 March 2010, the US Senate unanimously passed the Lord's Resistance Army Disarmament and Northern Uganda Recovery Act, requiring the USA government to develop a regional strategy to protect civilians in central Africa from attacks by the LRA.

In September 2011, Human Rights Watch reported that since 2006 the LRA has "become a regional threat operating in the remote border areas between South Sudan, DRC, and CAR" and that since September 2008, "the LRA has killed nearly 2,400 civilians and abducted about 3,400 others, according to documentation by Human Rights Watch and the UN... . In the first four months of 2011, the LRA carried out at least 120 attacks, killing 81 civilians and abducting 193, many of them children. Ninety-seven of these attacks were in Congo, representing nearly half the total number of attacks reported in 2010. More than 38,000 Congolese civilians were newly displaced in 2011 due to LRA attacks, adding to the hundreds of thousands in the region who had already fled their homes."¹²⁰⁴

A year later Human Rights Watch noted further that "[t]he failure to arrest Joseph Kony and other senior commanders of the Lord's Resistance Army (LRA) has left the LRA free to export atrocities across the borders of central Africa, creating new generations of LRA victims in DRC, South Sudan, and Central African Republic".¹²⁰⁵ The LRA was said to have killed more than 2,400 civilians in the DRC, CAR and South Sudan between 2008 and December 2011.¹²⁰⁶ As of December 2011, the LRA were said to have been responsible for the displacement of 438,504 civilians in the DRC, CAR and South Sudan. There were also said to have been 28,390 refugees due to LRA violence in DRC, CAR, and South Sudan, as of December 2011.¹²⁰⁷ More than 3,400 civilians are also said to have been abducted by the LRA in the DRC, CAR and South Sudan since 2008, including over 1,500 children as of March 2011.¹²⁰⁸

This violence continued into 2012 and 2013. It was reported that attacks and abductions attributed to the LRA doubled in the first six months of 2012 relative to the latter half of 2011. There was a seventy-three-per-cent increase in killings attributed to the organisation in the same time period. A vast majority of the almost 200 reported LRA attacks occurred in northern DRC (155), with concentrations west and south of

Garamba National Park. LRA attacks also increased significantly in the southeast of the CAR, with as many reported attacks in the first half of 2012 as in all of 2011. Reported LRA abductions increased by 127 per cent in the latter half of 2011 in comparison with the first half of 2012.[1209]

The metastasisation of the violence that has been associated with the LRA into the DRC, CAR and South Sudan is all too evident. Rather than acknowledge that the responsibility for this explosion in violence and human rights abuse is in large part attributable to the ICC because the court derailed and destroyed a promising peace process in Uganda, apologists for the court have sought to spin a different story out of this tragedy. Adam Branch has captured this spin perfectly:

> ICC supporters' blanket identification of peace with criminal justice gives rise to a self-serving reading of history, in which anything good that happens in situations where the ICC has intervened is caused by the ICC's intervention, while anything that goes wrong demonstrates the high cost of impunity and the need for further ICC intervention. This is how ICC supporters can, for example, give credit to the Court for driving the LRA out of northern Uganda and bringing peace there, while refusing responsibility for the violence used by the LRA against civilians in DRC, which instead is chalked up to continued impunity.[1210]

There are numerous other examples of how the claims of deterrence made in defence of the court are false. One more may well suffice. The ICC has been the direct cause of escalating violence in the DRC besides that of the LRA. On 23 March 2009, the *Congrès national pour la défense du peuple* (CNDP, National Congress for the Defence of the People) signed a peace treaty with the government of the DRC. CNDP became a political party, and its military forces became part of the government's armed forces. The M23 rebellion began in April 2012 in the North Kivu province of the DRC when nearly 300 soldiers, most of them previously affiliated with the CNDP, took up arms against the DRC government. They claimed that the government was reneging on the 23 March 2009 peace agreement, and that conditions in the army were unsatisfactory. There had been a move to redeploy former CNDP soldiers away from their home area. An ICC indictee, General Jean Bosco Ntaganda, was believed to be behind the rebellion. On 11 April 2012, under considerable pressure from the ICC and Western countries, President Kabila eventually called for Ntaganda's arrest.[1211] Human Rights Watch has pointed to a direct relationship between the ICC and the violence in eastern DRC: "General Ntaganda led the mutiny following Congolese government attempts to weaken his control and increased calls for his arrest and surrender to the ICC."[1212] Heavy fighting ensued between M23 rebels and government forces in North Kivu, especially in Rutshuru and Masisi. Almost 3,000 members of the Congolese Army and police forces switched sides in Goma on 20 November and joined the rebellion, which picked up momentum. M23 fighters threatened to overthrow the government in Kinshasa. A government offensive against the rebels was defeated and the rebels captured the provincial capital of Goma in November 2012. The

UN Secretary-General Ban Ki-moon alleged that the M23 rebels were responsible for human-rights violations in the attack on Goma. *The New York Times* reported the M23 action raised "serious questions about the stability of Congo as a whole".[1213] As part of a subsequent peace deal, M23 forces withdrew from Goma. Human Rights Watch has alleged that "[t]he M23 rebels are committing a horrific trail of new atrocities in eastern Congo", and that they are "responsible for widespread war crimes, including summary executions, rapes, and forced recruitment".[1214]

In addition to disproving any claims made about the deterrent effect of the ICC the fighting that followed the M23 rebellion also provided yet another black-and-white example of the ICC continuing to turn a blind eye to systematic human-rights abuses by *Forces armées de la République démocratique du Congo*. On 22 November 2012 thousands of Congolese Army troops entered the town of Minova in eastern DRC following fighting with M23 forces. *The Guardian* reported that "When they arrived in Minova they were drunk, hungry and violent. The locals suffered two nightmarish days of looting, rape and murder.... Hundreds of women were raped."[1215] On 18 December 2012 *Inner City Press* reported that "the number of rapes by Congolese forces in Minova, covered up and stonewalled by top UN Peacekeeper Herve Ladsous, rose on Tuesday to 126 rapes, between November 20 and 30. So far a grand total of two Congolese soldiers have been arrested."[1216] One year on, one more soldier had been arrested. *The Guardian* noted:

> To date there have been few concrete developments. Military justice personnel told the Guardian they did not want to be involved in the case if it would lead to charges against officers, as they feared a backlash from powerful army figures. So far only three soldiers have been arrested.... Until significant arrests are made, however the women of Minova remain sceptical that justice will be done or that impunity will end.[1217]

The UN MONUSCO mission's May 2013 report on human-rights violations perpetrated near Sake, Goma and Minova on the Minova situation confirmed the atrocities committed by the army, the *Forces armées de la République démocratique du Congo*.[1218] *The Guardian* quoted the head of the victim refuge centre in Minova: "'The government says it will arrest these soldiers and officers. They may arrest some, but then later they will just set them free again.' Unfortunately it is the gloomy predictions of the sceptics that have so far proved correct."[1219]

Two units of the Congolese Army implicated in the murders and rapes, the 41st and 391st Commando Battalions, were units to which the UN provide support. This relationship was said to be an issue on which the UN peacekeeping mission has been "far less than transparent".[1220] Such involvement contravenes the UN Secretary-General's human rights due diligence policy cited in applicable UNSC resolutions.[1221] The 41st Battalion has been linked with the Hutu genocidaires-linked FDLR militia. The 391st Commando Battalion was trained by the USA in 2010.[1222] The French Permanent Representative to the UN, Gerard Araud, stated that the 391st is the "best unit" of the Congolese Army, "which doesn't have many good units".[1223] UN Peacekeeping Chief Herve

Ladsous continued UN support to the 391st Battalion even after the unit's involvement in well over 100 rapes in Minova in November 2012. Even more embarrassingly for the UN, the 391st battalion was also subsequently implicated in the mistreatment of prisoners and desecration of corpses.[1224]

The atrocious abuses of human rights outlined above are powerful evidence of at least two things. Firstly, that the ICC continues to ignore well-documented crimes against humanity that are being committed within the territory of a State Party in which it has accepted a referral and is duty bound to investigate human-rights abuses, and in which the government has clearly opted not to prosecute offenders who happen to form part of its armed forces – precisely the circumstances for which the court claims to exist. Secondly, the presence of the court, and its self-publicised activities within the DRC, has very clearly served no deterrent effect whatsoever. The much vaunted deterrence value claimed of the court, a value claimed in lieu of any tangible contribution to peace, is less than zero.

In November 2012, Human Rights Watch further highlighted the lie of the ICC's claim to have deterred alleged further human-rights abuses: "Bosco Ntaganda…has left an unbroken record of new abuses. Since the ICC issued a first arrest warrant for Ntaganda in August 2006 (a second arrest warrant on a new set of charges was issued in July 2012), Human Rights Watch's research has documented his repeated involvement in human-rights abuses, violations of the laws of war, and mass atrocities."[1225] Human Rights Watch claimed that Ntaganda commanded troops accused of massacring 150 civilians in Kiwanja in North Kivu province in November 2008,[1226] as well as "a wave of forced recruitment, including of children, by Ntaganda and officers loyal to him between September and December 2010, marking a repeat of the same crimes for which Ntaganda has been sought by the ICC since 2006".[1227]

Legal commentators noted that this increase in violence in the Democratic Republic of the Congo coincided with the announcement of the judgment in the Lubanga case:

> [I]t was a sobering coincidence to see how the rendering of [the Lubanga] judgment came on the same day as news that M23, a group rumoured to be allied to Bosco Ntaganda marched on Goma in the DRC. M23 broke away from the FARDC in late March 2012 and in an added twist of bitterness, is also accused of the using of child soldiers…Bosco Ntaganda was allowed to move freely in Goma despite the ICC arrest warrant against him. The continuing impunity for Bosco Ntaganda – and his continued involvement in the same crimes listed on his outstanding arrest warrant before the ICC – threaten the message achieved by the Lubanga trial.[1228]

Amazingly, in March 2013, the court was still trying to justify its poor performance with the "we may be useless in what we do but we do deter crime" defence. A spokesman self-servingly stated: "Justice is not just about securing convictions. There are various facets to justice." The spokesman claimed that there was also "the court's preventative role and its capacity to defuse potentially tense situations that could lead to violence".[1229]

Chapter Seventeen

THE FICTION OF A VICTIMS' COURT

"[T]he ICC's investigations and prosecutions have failed to demonstrate coherent and effective strategies for delivering meaningful justice to affected communities."

Human Rights Watch[1230]

It was claimed that under the Rome Statute, for the first time before an international criminal tribunal, victims had been granted access to the proceedings and the possibility of presenting their views and concerns in court. The ICC trumpets its involvement with victims: "One of the great innovations of the Statute of the International Criminal Court and its Rules of Procedure and Evidence is the series of rights granted to victims. For the first time in the history of international criminal justice, victims have the possibility under the Statute to present their views and observations before the Court."[1231] The term "victim" features in the Rome Statute no fewer than thirty-eight times. At the opening of the Rome Conference in 1998, UN Secretary-General Kofi Annan stated that "the overriding interest must be that of the victims".[1232] The ICC further asserted that the participation of victims in proceedings represented a landmark development in international criminal justice:

> [T]he victims participation regime established by the drafters of the Statute ensued from a debate that took place in the context of the growing emphasis placed on the role of victims by the international body of human rights law and by international humanitarian law…the Statute grants victims an independent voice and role in proceedings before the Court. It should be possible to exercise this independence, in particular, vis-à-vis the Prosecutor of the International Criminal Court so that victims can present their interests.[1233]

Rule 85 of the ICC Rules of Procedure and Evidence defines those seen as being "victims":

> (a) "Victims" mean natural persons who have suffered harm as a result of the commission of any crime within the jurisdiction of the Court; (b) Victims may include organizations or institutions that have sustained direct harm to any

of their property which is dedicated to religion, education, art or science or charitable purposes and to their historic monuments, hospitals and other places and objects for humanitarian purposes. In order to fall within the definition, a person has to show that he or she "suffered harm as a result of the commission of any crime within the jurisdiction of the Court". There is no requirement that the crime directly targeted him or her, or that the harm suffered was directly caused by the crime. The definition should therefore be interpreted to include victims' families and dependants, referred to as 'indirect victims'…

Human Rights Watch has noted however that "[t]here…have been long-standing problems in giving effect to the Rome Statute-guaranteed right of victims to participate in proceedings before the court". The organisation felt duty-bound to recommend to the ASP that "states parties should…[e]xpress concern for the court's ability to have real impact in affected communities".[1234] In selecting incidents for trial, the OTP's 2009–12 strategy paper stated that its objective was "to provide a sample that reflects the gravest incidents and the main types of victimization".[1235] This strategy paper also specifically restates the fundamental ICC principle of "addressing the interests of victims".[1236]

The court has simply failed in this claim. The reality is very different. *The Guardian* newspaper noted that the Prosecutor has instead "alienated" victims groups.[1237] In 2012, for example, Human Rights Watch admitted: "[T]he first prosecutor's approach…did not always prioritize the experience of affected communities." The organisation went on to observe:

> Moving international justice forward at the ICC should [mean]…a real and operative concern to place affected communities at the heart of the court's work. This is a vision of the court that has yet to be realized, however. In fact, if anything it appears that the ICC and its states parties over time may be settling for a much more reductive view of its mandate…. The court's Trust Fund for Victims is currently implementing its assistance mandate in only two of seven country situations, Uganda and Democratic Republic of Congo.[1238]

Writing about the wars in Uganda and DRC, Julian Ku and Jide Nzelibe have stated that "the victims of these conflicts likely have very different visions of the relationship between the ICC and their governments. Perhaps that is why most of the representatives of the LRA victims in northern Uganda, as well as the mediators in that conflict, have accused the ICC of turning a blind eye to their concerns in that region's crisis."[1239] *Der Spiegel* provides a snapshot of the views of the very victims on whose behalf the court claims to act and yet whose visceral concerns it ignores. The magazine cites the example of Calvin Ocora from village of Lukodi in northern Uganda. Ocora's family, including his mother, sister, brothers and daughter were killed in an attack by the LRA. The magazine reports: "Every night, the man who lost his family is plagued by nightmares – and every day he rails against Luis Moreno-Ocampo." It quoted Ocora: "Western criminal justice doesn't bring us any closer to peace. We could have had peace a long time ago without

The Hague."[1240] Ocora states that justice must prevail nevertheless, and that in Uganda they have their own methods: "We have to forgive – even the perpetrators deserve a chance." Ocora sometimes sees his family's murderers in the neighborhood: "We even chat sometimes. Now they find their actions infinitely shameful. God will pass judgment on them one day."[1241] A 2010 Victims' Rights Working Group report has also noted an additional dimension of concern to victims:

> In Uganda, many victim communities negatively perceived the ICC as biased because it has only issued arrest warrants against the LRA (Lord's Resistance Army) without equally holding government forces to account: "The ICC looks at only the LRA as the perpetrators of insecurity and yet forces like the UPDF did the same and the ICC has not handled them." Some state that "there is evidence in some parts in Northern Uganda to prove that UPDF victimised people and witnesses are ready to testify in court".[1242]

This feeling was also summed up by international refugee worker and lawyer Katherine Southwick who has reported that the ICC in Uganda is "widely opposed by those groups the Rome Statute is designed to serve: the victims".[1243] *The Economist* has reported that the court has also "raised and then dashed expectations among victims" in the CAR.[1244] The Kenyan cases have also demonstrated the court's inability to live up to its claims. A panel of political analysts and former legislators, including the Centre for Multi-Party Democracy Chairman Omingo Magara, concluded that the Kenyan trials at The Hague have not done much to address the suffering of victims of the 2007–08 post-election violence. The panel accused the ICC of hypocritically claiming to champion the rights of the victims who have lived as internally displaced persons since the court's involvement in Kenya. The head of the Africa Police Institute, Professor Peter Kagwanja, was very critical of ICC claims:

> The kind of hang 'em high justice you see at the ICC has absolutely nothing to do with the victims. For the last five years IDPs have been in camps rain come, rain go. Children who were born when they were displaced are now five years. What has the ICC done to ensure these kids go to school? What has ICC done to ensure that these people are resettled as it pursues this other kind of justice.[1245]

In a startling example of self-serving cognitive dissonance, when pressed about the court's interaction with victims, Ocampo responded, "from the victims, we have had full support".[1246] Ocampo's successor, Fatou Bensouda, has continued with this false mantra: "It is the victims we are representing, so in these cases we are representing African victims."[1247]

Human Rights Watch have themselves had to highlight the court's ambivalence to victim communities:

> We have also stressed how important it is for the court – including the

prosecutor – to more proactively engage with affected communities to make its work meaningful and relevant to them. *This will require a complete and deeply rooted shift from the ICC's prior ambivalence to doing so, which was evident in the court's early approach to outreach and field operations, and the prosecutor's investigations.*[1248] (Emphasis added.)

Helena Cobban's critique of the fiction of international justice has highlighted the contradictions between First World theory and what is actually the reality within emergent, conflict-prone countries, especially with regard to victims: "When people in rich, secure countries advocate the prosecution of war criminals, they often claim to be acting in the interests of victims. But the actual preferences articulated by survivors of atrocities are varied, and often differ from what many activists suppose."[1249] Cobban has clearly challenged the need for ICC intervention in these circumstances:

> Is the cumbersome machinery of an expensive international court operating in The Hague what the people of war zones need most? Of course, there are some victims who demand prosecutions, and activists from rich countries often echo their demands to anyone who will listen. But those who want to help the survivors of atrocities should first ask broad sections of society in an open-ended way how they define their own needs and how they define justice. The international community should be guided by the answers to those questions rather than by the simple assumption that prosecutions are always helpful.[1250]

In trying to be all things to all men, the drafters of the Rome Statute saddled the court with very clear design faults that rapidly became apparent during the court's first trial. *The Guardian* noted "a system which allows victims an active role in undermining a prosecutor's discretion", that "[v]ictims are likely to want as many charges as possible to be brought; prosecutors must limit an indictment to make trials manageable and may sometimes accept guilty pleas to lesser charges to avoid the expense and risk of a contested hearing. The two interests are bound to be in conflict."[1251]

The reality is that by doing backroom deals with, among others, the governments of Uganda, the DRC and the CAR, whereby the ICC agreed only to pursue alleged crimes by anti-government forces, and in turning a blind eye to British military excesses in Iraq and Afghanistan, the court has deliberately ignored hundreds of thousands and possibly millions of victims of government human-rights abuse in those countries.

Chapter Eighteen

THE COURT AND UGANDA

"[I]n the case of Northern Uganda, the actions of the Office of the Prosecutor are increasingly seen by the local population as prolonging the conflict."

Jacqueline Geis and Alex Mundt[1252]

"[T]he ICC's investigations into LRA and not UPDF crimes create a perception of the ICC as one-sided and heavily politicised."

Dr. Phil Clark[1253]

The Ugandan government, a State Party to the ICC treaty, referred "the situation concerning the Lord's Resistance Army" to the court in December 2003, the first state referral that the ICC had received since its inception.[1254] This was after the ICC Chief Prosecutor had hinted he would commence an investigation himself should he not be invited in. On 29 January 2004, the Chief Prosecutor participated in a joint press conference in London with President Museveni to announce the referral.

A savage civil war between the Ugandan government and a largely Acholi-based rebel movement calling itself the Lord's Resistance Army (LRA) has raged in northern Uganda for several decades.[1255] Western commentators state that: "The LRA is primarily composed of former soldiers from the north who left the army after a southern president, Yoweri Museveni, came to power in a guerrilla offensive waged by his own southern-dominated rebel National Resistance Army in 1986."[1256] The LRA leader, Joseph Kony, declared to *The Times* of London newspaper: "I'm a freedom fighter who is fighting for freedom in Uganda. I am not a terrorist."[1257] Tens of thousands of civilians have died and millions more have been displaced into government-controlled IDP camps. The prospect of a peaceful solution to the war came sharply into focus from November 2004 onwards when Ugandan President Yoweri Museveni announced a unilateral ceasefire in parts of northern Uganda. The initial ceasefire period was extended, amnesty laws were passed and a major breakthrough seemed imminent.

The ICC referral was itself questionable from the start. This has already been examined in a previous chapter. Arsanjani and Reisman enquired: "What contribution to the settlement of the dispute accrues from transferring the problem, at this juncture, to the International Criminal Court, a body that was neither intended nor equipped to resolve, through judicial means, a longstanding political problem of a government."[1258] They have also asserted that Uganda's referral of the situation to the ICC amounts to "washing its own hands of an insoluble internal problem" and sets a bad example as it is "a move that could encourage [other] governments to externalize to the court the domestic problems they are unable or unwilling – because they do not wish to invest the necessary resources – to manage or resolve".[1259]

Sarah Nouwen has outlined some of the questionable aspects of the referral:

> No OTP document addressed the statutorily relevant question of admissibility, namely, whether Uganda had genuinely investigated or prosecuted crimes within the Court's jurisdiction. The OTP never mentioned existing Ugandan arrest warrants for Joseph Kony and other senior LRA members. The sole ground for inability that Uganda had advanced, namely inability to arrest, was not subject to critical reflection, the ICC's own inability on this front notwithstanding. No attention was paid to the irony that in many other ways, too…the OTP would rely heavily on the services of the "unable" state.[1260]

The *Harvard Human Rights Journal* posed another key question: "Uganda is known to have a competent and functioning judicial system. This begs the question: can a state with a judicial system that is both willing and able to carry out an investigation or prosecution voluntarily confer jurisdiction to the ICC?"[1261] Phil Clark has also drawn attention to this issue, noting: "the unusual grounds on which the ICC has opened the LRA cases. These grounds appear to contradict the OTP's own stated investigative and prosecutorial policies. They centre not on the basis of the unwillingness or inability of the Ugandan judiciary to prosecute serious cases but rather on the inability of government forces to capture and arrest the LRA leadership."[1262]

This leads on to another, related, issue. What was it that the ICC thought it might be able to achieve? This has been articulated by the ICG's Nick Grono and Adam O'Brien: "In Uganda, the Ugandan army has failed to defeat the LRA for more than 20 years." They admit that this means "that the ICC cannot arrest those it wishes to prosecute". They also note that: "The threat of prosecution…can have a salutary effect…but only if there is a real likelihood that [those indicted] may face the consequences of their policies."[1263] Ugandans have also asked themselves this question. Betty Bigombe, a former Ugandan cabinet minister and veteran peace negotiator who has held peace negotiations with the LRA since the early 1990s, enquired: "Now what difference does it make for ICC to give the Ugandan army just a piece of paper? The Ugandan army has tried for the last 19 years to kill or capture Kony."[1264] What can a court in the Netherlands achieve without any army, police or enforcement mechanism of its own?

The question that has to be asked is why did the ICC and the Ugandan government agree to a referral? The answer is simple. Referral of the situation in northern Uganda to the ICC was politically beneficial for both Museveni and Ocampo. Museveni was able both to bask in the international legal limelight, acclaimed as he was at the time by Western governments and the Western human rights industry, and to further de-legitimise and criminalise the insurgency in northern Uganda. For Ocampo, the benefit was equally clear: it gave him the ICC's first state referral of a case, albeit one that he had actively solicited.

On 29 July 2004, the ICC announced that it would undertake a full investigation of the situation in northern Uganda. Ocampo's naivety was obvious from the start. In August 2004, he stated that he expected to commence the trial of LRA suspects within six months and that this would swiftly end the conflict in northern Uganda.[1265] In 2006, *The Wall Street Journal*, among many others, noted: "In January 2004, Mr. Moreno-Ocampo predicted arrests by year's end and a trial in 2005... . Today, not a single suspect is in custody and no trial date is in sight."[1266] Ocampo was either lying or he was hopelessly naïve – neither of which reflects well on his judgment, or the people who put him into office.

In May 2004, peace negotiator Betty Bigombe revitalised the peace process in northern Uganda. In late 2004, the government declared a unilateral ceasefire in a part of northern Uganda. A range of stakeholders, including the government, local politicians, religious leaders, civil society representatives, international observers, and rebel commanders began discussions on a ceasefire agreement. Delegations of senior northern Ugandan leaders travelled to The Hague in February and April 2005 to urge the ICC not to issue arrest warrants while peace negotiations were ongoing.[1267] The leaders were afraid that the ICC's vow to prosecute [Kony] left the rebel leadership little incentive to negotiate – and every reason to fight on. David Onen Acana II, the paramount chief of the Acholi, asked if the ICC was "able to provide peace, or only justice? We want peace by any means."[1268] Following renewed contacts, in September 2005, Bigombe outlined a detailed peace proposal. This was accepted as a basis for discussion by the Ugandan government. Nonetheless, in October 2005, the ICC unsealed arrest warrants – the first issued by the court – for five LRA leaders, LRA commander Joseph Kony and his deputies, Vincent Otti, Okot Odhiambo, Dominic Ongwen, and Raska Lukwiya.[1269] Bigombe complained that the ICC "rushed too much".[1270] The Ugandan rebels withdrew from the peace process and the conflict continued. One of the LRA leaders indicted by the ICC, Vincent Otti, pointed out the obstacle it posed to the Ugandan peace process: "The ICC remains a big stumbling block to peace in Uganda. If ICC indictments are not lifted, we shall not come out. It's simple. No." In a previous interview, Otti had said the LRA leaders would surrender to the ICC only if the court charged the Ugandan Army on similar counts of war crimes: "If the UPDF [Ugandan People's Defence Force] are included on the list of indicted commanders, I will definitely go to The Hague. Short of that, I will never go." Otti said that the ICC's decision to indict only members of the LRA was "very one-sided": "It's not only the LRA who committed atrocities in northern Uganda. It's both the LRA and the UPDF. Why did ICC indict us alone?"[1271]

The ICC's involvement in Uganda has been heavily criticised. Even avid supporters of the ICC have been critical of the court's work. William Pace, head of the coalition for the ICC, made up of advocacy groups such as Amnesty International and Human Rights

Watch, that promoted the creation of the tribunal, has stated: "In Uganda, they have not done well."[1272] The ICC's aloof approach alienated it from the Ugandan population. Claudia Perdomo, the head of the ICC public-information office, admitted as much: "What we have heard from Ugandans is: 'We need you to explain what the court is about. You are behaving in a way as the guerrillas do, in a very clandestine way.'" Perdomo also revealed that prosecutors rebuffed her suggestions for reaching out more aggressively to communicate with Ugandans.[1273]

The ICC action in Uganda has been criticised for three main reasons: selectivity and bias on the part of the ICC and its prosecutor; severely damaging the peace process; and trying to impose a retributive European model of justice on Africans.

Questions were raised almost immediately about the selectivity of the ICC's work in Uganda. The announcement of the referral, for example, was by means of a joint press conference held by Ocampo and President Yoweri Museveni. Ocampo's own senior staff counselled against a joint appearance. International transitional justice experts Paul Seils and Marieke Wierda noted that: "This caused the perception that the Prosecutor was being manipulated by the government, which is itself party to the conflict."[1274] Michael Otim and Marieke Wierda also stated that "[s]ubsequent to the Prosecutor's joint appearance with President Museveni, many felt that the ICC was associating too closely with one party to the conflict, thus undermining perceptions of the Court's impartiality". Otim and Wierda additionally noted: "The absence of investigation of the UPDF has often been presumed to be the result of bias rather than as the consequence of the ICC's application of its criteria for case selection."[1275] The ICG records that one Acholi camp resident at the Anaka camp outside Gulu, put it more simply: "[T]he ICC is Museveni's dog."[1276]

The Ugandan government's involvement in terrible, systematic abuses of human rights is clear.[1277] Phil Clark has stated that "[l]ocal and international human rights groups have reported regular and grave atrocities committed by the UPDF in northern Uganda, particularly the forced displacement of around 1.5 million civilians into IDP camps".[1278] Grono and O'Brien have described the Ugandan government's clear involvement in the abuse of and mortality within the Acholi community: "Unfortunately, the Ugandan government's response has been little better than the problem it purports to address. The government herded over a million of the north's inhabitants (predominantly Acholi) into squalid, insecure camps – condemning them to a life removed from their fertile land, with little hope for a productive future. Every week, according to the government's own statistics, a thousand people on average die from conflict-related disease and malnutrition."[1279]

H. Abigail Moy, an American international lawyer noted:

> [M]any organizations expressed concern for the ICC's failure to take broader action against human rights violations perpetrated on the other side of the conflict, by the UPDF and Ugandan government officials. In its attempts to flush out the LRA, for instance, the UPDF bombed and burned down villages, thus fueling the displacement of the Acholi. Organizations such as the Refugee Law Project and the Acholi Religious Leaders Peace Initiative have

documented numerous accounts of rapes and sexual attacks against women by UPDF soldiers. Other alleged UPDF abuses include overzealously killing any civilian found outside IDP camps, effectively holding people captive within their protected villages.[1280]

Human Rights Watch has noted that: "The International Court of Justice found that the Ugandan army committed massive human rights violations and grave breaches of international humanitarian law in DRC, and cited some incidents that would fall within the ICC's temporal jurisdiction."[1281] Human Rights Watch documented that "soldiers of the Uganda Peoples' Defence Forces (UDPF) committed serious human-rights violations…government forces carried out deliberate killings, routine beatings, rapes, and prolonged arbitrary detentions of civilians. In addition, through a combination of a government policy of forced displacement and the actions of the LRA, by 2005, nearly the entire rural population of the three Acholi districts of northern Uganda – some 1.9 million people – were living in internally displaced persons camps. For many years, those living in camps were without basic services, such as education and health, and the camps were far from secure; they remained vulnerable to attacks and abuses by both the LRA and the Ugandan military."[1282]

When challenged that the ICC was only focusing on abuses by the rebels, and ignoring well-documented government abuses of human rights, the ICC Prosecutor said that he could investigate crimes wherever he found them. He has of course not done so. Humanitarian commentators, Jacqueline Geis and Alex Mundt, have pointed this out:

> While the Prosecutor made a point to note that once a situation is referred to the ICC, he can investigate crimes committed by all parties to the conflict, Ocampo's office…focused its investigation on crimes committed by the LRA… . However, the fact that indictments have been issued only against the LRA has further entrenched the perception that the ICC was being used as a tool by the Ugandan government against the LRA.[1283]

Geis and Mundt have further noted:

> [T]he impartiality of the prosecutor has been called into question by national observers, as has his perceived deference to state power. And, in the case of Northern Uganda, the actions of the Office of the Prosecutor are increasingly seen by the local population as prolonging the conflict and attempting to institute a form of justice at odds with local culture.[1284]

Phil Clark concludes that: "[T]he ICC's investigations into LRA and not UPDF crimes create a perception of the ICC as one-sided and heavily politicised. A common view among community leaders and members of the political opposition in Kampala and northern Uganda is that, as one politician argued, 'the ICC has become Museveni's political tool'."[1285]

Human Rights Watch has repeatedly urged the ICC to provide a public explanation of the status of its investigations into the actions of UPDF forces.[1286] In 2011 Human Rights Watch once again called upon the court to "Provide – as a matter of priority – an explanation of the decisions taken with regard to investigation of Ugandan government forces and the prospects of future cases against government officials."[1287] Human Rights Watch has made clear the consequences of this prevarication: "For many in Uganda and other observers of the ICC, however, oft-repeated assurances that the Uganda investigations have not ended or are not limited to the LRA arrest warrants have worn thin. The lack of justice for crimes by both sides to the conflict seriously compromises perceptions of the ICC's independence and has undermined its credibility among affected communities in Uganda."[1288]

William Schabas has challenged the ICC's excuse for not pursuing government crimes against humanity:

> Even assuming that the Ugandan People's Defence Forces have killed significantly fewer innocent civilians than the Lord's Resistance Army, is not the fact that the crimes are attributable to the State germane to the gravity of the case? …With respect to the government forces, on the other hand, we are confronted with the classic impunity paradigm: individuals acting on behalf of a State that shelters them from its own courts. But in a domestic justice setting involving ordinary crime, would we countenance a national prosecutor who ignored clandestine police death squads on the grounds that gangsters were killing more people than the rogue officials?[1289]

In 2011, Human Rights Watch also pointed out that there is very little chance of another phase of investigations in Uganda by the court:

> Resources allocated to the OTP for the Ugandan situation have dropped from €3.5 million and 27 staff members in 2006 to a request of €111,200 and one staff member for 2012…the drop in resources, coupled with public statements that investigations are "ongoing" without an accessible and substantive explanation of the status or nature of those investigations, raises questions about the rigor with which allegations against Ugandan forces continue to be pursued by the ICC prosecutor.[1290]

A year later Rebecca Hamilton, a former Special Assistant to the Prosecutor, outlined the implications of this reduction in focus by the court:

> As of the time of writing [May 2012], there is one full-time staff member left on a team that was originally 15 strong. According to the OTP this is explainable by the fact that the earliest stages of an investigation invariably demand more resources than the later stages because the OTP builds institutional knowledge of a situation over time. But even taking that appropriate level of attrition into account, it is hard to see how just one full-

time staff member can be responsible for what the OTP still officially describes as an ongoing investigation. In the absence of either an acknowledgment by the prosecutor that he has closed the Uganda investigation or, if he has not closed it, an explanation as to why there have been no arrest warrants since those sought against LRA members in 2005 despite claims by his office that Ugandan government forces are being investigated, allegations of partisanship seem certain to continue.[1291]

Impeding a peaceful settlement

The second major criticism is that the ICC action is directly impeding a peaceful, negotiated settlement by the government and the LRA of the conflict. Even ICC fans such as the ICG admit that the "the commonly held belief that the ICC is the single greatest barrier to a successful resolution of the 20-year old conflict" predominates Ugandan peace talks.[1292] For a number of years the Museveni government ruthlessly sought a military solution to the rebellion in northern Uganda. It begrudgingly was forced to explore a political solution – a negotiated end to the conflict. Concern about the effect the ICC is having on that process has been articulated by countless voices in Uganda and elsewhere.[1293] Religious and community leaders in war-affected northern Uganda criticised the ICC's arrest warrants. The day after the UN announced the ICC indictments, Uganda's Roman Catholic Church warned that the threat of legal action could put the peace process in the north at risk. Archbishop John Baptist Odama stated: "The peace process has been put in jeopardy...we do feel that the presence of the court here and its activities are in danger of jeopardising efforts to rebuild the rebels' confidence in peace talks. How can we tell the LRA soldiers to come out of the bush and receive amnesty when at the same time the threat of arrest by the ICC hangs over their heads?"[1294] Monsignor Matthew Odongo, the Vicar-General of the Roman Catholic diocese of the northern district of Gulu, at the epicentre of the conflict, said: "This is like throwing a stone in water that had settled. Any move that adds to the suffering of the people will not be good." Odongo, speaking on behalf of the Acholi Religious Leaders Peace Initiative, an inter-faith peace group, said he was also concerned about the timing of the announcement, coming as it did just as the LRA had announced its commitments to peace talks.[1295]

Peter Onega, Head of the Uganda Amnesty Commission, a statutory body set up by the government to encourage the peace process, said the decision by the international court had left their work in "total confusion". Onega warned that the indictments would provide rebel hardliners with the tools to consolidate the rebel ranks: "They will be at liberty to tell these people that 'this is just the beginning, don't think we are the only ones wanted by the ICC – your turn is coming' and very few will come out [of the bush] if such a message was driven home." Onega expressed the fear that the ICC indictments could only encourage more atrocities because the LRA leadership could act as "desperately as a wounded buffalo". He also warned of the negative effect on reconciliation:

The ICC should have known all the consequences before they issued the warrants. They should have also considered another issue in all this – reconciliation. Does the taking of only five people for prosecution at The Hague bring about reconciliation among the divided Acholi [northern ethnic group] people? The warrants are not any good for national unity if you have people who will go to testify against others.[1296]

The Uganda Program Development Officer for Conciliation Resources stated that "the ICC has committed a terrible blunder" by initiating "war crimes investigations for the sake of justice at a time when northern Uganda sees the most promising signs for a negotiated settlement".[1297] Even supporters of the ICC admit general Ugandan unease with the involvement of the ICC, and their government's initial invitation to the ICC: "Interviews with Ugandans reveal that many do not support ICC involvement and view the government's referral as a threat to a peaceful resolution of the conflict."[1298] Civil society groups such as the Acholi Religious Leaders Peace Initiative have condemned the ICC for hindering the peace process.[1299]

The Guardian reported in January 2007 on the local opposition in northern Uganda to the ICC: "[H]ostility to the ICC in Gulu is so widespread that Norbert Mao, the chief elected representative for about 300,000 people in the district around the town and a member of the opposition Democratic party, has warned the court's investigators that their lives are at risk." He stated: "What would be the point in taking these LRA leaders to a prison in Stockholm? Would that be a definition of justice for us? I think this is the ICC grandstanding as it's its first case."[1300]

Reuters, reporting in April 2007, stated: "Since peace talks started, a wave of popular opposition to the ICC amongst northern Ugandans – the main victims of Kony's cult-like rebel group – has dismayed rights groups. Northerners say only a lifting of the indictments will bring lasting peace."[1301] Senior UN officials such as Jan Egeland, the UN Under Secretary-General for Humanitarian Affairs, for example, have been confronted by northern Ugandan leaders on the issue. The leader of a camp of 25,000 displaced persons – victims of the conflict – told him to his face, "We don't want the International Criminal Court. We want peace… . Will the court really bring peace, or fuel the war again?"[1302] Even the Ugandan government, faced with the prospect of continuing conflict, has indicated that it wishes to approach the ICC to drop indictments against the LRA leadership if a peace deal is signed. In September 2007, the Ugandan Defence Minister, Ruth Nankabirwa, stated Uganda had contacted the ICC "to request them to relax or to withdraw the warrants of arrest to enable Uganda to handle the culprits".[1303]

A renewed peace process, the Juba Process, was begun in June 2006: this resulted in the signing of five protocols leading up to an expected final peace agreement. The Juba peace talks were described by Jan Egeland as "the best chance ever to end [the] war".[1304] The ICG also believed the Juba negotiations to be the most promising in the history of the conflict.[1305] The agreement has been abandoned. It remains unsigned, in very large part because of the ICC indictments, which the LRA insist must be withdrawn before the final agreement. Delegates to the Juba peace process were clear about the need to challenge the ICC's actions. Otim and Wierda reported that: "Besides agreements about traditional justice, delegates concurred that there should be a national approach to accountability and reconciliation and that this would require the government to challenge the jurisdiction of the ICC under the Rome Statute."[1306]

The Juba process saw the government and LRA sign an annexure to the agreement on 19 February 2008. The annexure outlined the mechanisms that will be established for transitional justice in Uganda. These include a special division of the High Court to try persons responsible for serious crimes, as well as the establishment of a "Commission of inquiry into the past and related events" with functions similar to those of a truth commission. The annexure also states that "traditional justice will play a central part of the alternative justice and reconciliation framework referred to in the Agreement". Unsurprisingly, Western human rights groups have been critical of the annexure. For instance, Amnesty International declared: "It is not acceptable for the Ugandan government and the LRA to make a deal that circumvents international law" and that Uganda would still need to hand senior LRA leaders over to the ICC. The International Federation for Human Rights (FIDH) also stated that "Uganda is…under an absolute obligation to cooperate with the ICC and to hand over the LRA leaders."[1307]

Key foreign participants in the Ugandan peace process, such as Bishop Tutu of South Africa and Britain's UN Ambassador Emyr Jones Parry, have acknowledged that the ICC's role in Uganda has probably worsened the chances for any peaceful resolution of the Ugandan conflict.[1308] Their views have been echoed by Adam Branch, who has seen the ICC's involvement in Uganda used by President Museveni to justify repression of legitimate political grievances.

> The Ugandan government has also used the ICC intervention to justify its repression of domestic political dissent. Designating political opposition as international criminals helps legitimate the use of force against them.… . The ICC intervention has…intensified the national political crises in Uganda, thus entrenching the conditions for possible future conflict.[1309]

Branch has highlighted the extent of the ICC's undermining of peace in Uganda:

> [T]he Chief Prosecutor himself acted in ways that appeared to be intended to undermine and foreclose peace negotiations between LRA and the Ugandan government, particularly through his repeated dismissals of the LRA's commitment to negotiations and accusations that the rebels were engaging in peace talks only to buy time and rearm so as to commit more atrocities… . If the ICC Prosecutor is going to actively work against peace negotiations, then the ICC is going to be a danger to peace wherever it intervenes and should be held accountable for the consequences of its actions…the ICC's one-side prosecution has had…consequences that are incontrovertibly antithetical to long-term and sustainable peace.[1310]

Branch is also clear about the depth of the court's interference in Ugandan domestic politics:

> The first major instance of the ICC silencing alternative approaches to justice was seen in its dismissal of the Ugandan Amnesty Act of 2000. There was a broad understanding in Acholiland that the war would not end until the LRA leadership abandoned the rebellion, which provided the impetus behind the mobilization for the act.... Despite this popular support, however, the ICC demanded the Amnesty Act's amendment.... The ICC irresponsibly frames the Amnesty Act, not as the product of mobilization by the Acholi trying to find peace and duly promulgated by the Ugandan Parliament, but as a gift from the Ugandan executive, to be withdrawn by President Museveni at his convenience.[1311]

The Refugee Law Project in Uganda was clear about the value of the amnesty law to the Ugandan peace process:

> The findings suggest that...the Amnesty Law is perceived as a vital tool for conflict resolution, and for longer-term reconciliation and peace within the specific context in which it is operating. Furthermore, numerous respondents emphasised the fact that it resonates with specific cultural understandings of justice: amnesty is taking place within societies in which the possibility of legal and social pardon is seen to better address the requirements for long-term reconciliation than more tangible forms of punishment meted out within the legal structures.[1312]

The retributive European justice model

Thirdly, and directly related to the impediment to the peace process posed by the ICC, many Ugandans believe that the ICC is ignoring African victims by imposing a European concept of retributive justice, which is at odds with local mechanisms and a desire for traditional restorative justice and Acholi traditions of forgiveness, such as *mato oput* among those most affected by the conflict, the Acholi communities in northern Uganda. This has been summed up by international refugee worker Katherine Southwick who has reported that the ICC in Uganda is "widely opposed by those groups the Rome Statute is designed to serve: the victims".[1313]

Christian Aid's Gemma Houldey has claimed that a tension exists between retributive and restorative justice: "The people of the North would prefer restorative justice.... That is rooted in their culture and they would argue that the ICC have no grounding with what is going on in the region if it thinks the answer is to pull out a whole lot of rebels."[1314] The Council on Foreign Relations has also noted: "Ugandans are increasingly dissatisfied with the ICC, which they say fails to respect their desire for traditional reconciliation and is undermining efforts for genuine peace in their country."[1315] The *Harvard Human Rights Journal* has further noted that "[Archbishop] Odama and other Acholi religious and political leaders continue to press for traditional justice, a process involving confessions of guilt, cleansing rituals, and the eventual acceptance of LRA members back into communities."[1316]

The ICG has summed up the criticism that the ICC has faced in Uganda:

> The ICC has come under intense criticism in northern Uganda since the announcement in January 2004 that the Ugandan government had made the first state party referral to the ICC. The Court has been condemned by a wide range of international NGOs, academics, mediators and northern Ugandans. These critics argued that the threat of international prosecutions would undermine fragile local peace initiatives; would prolong the conflict by obliterating the LRA's incentive to negotiate; and would make displaced northern Ugandans even more vulnerable to LRA attacks... . The ICC's intervention, opponents argued, would ultimately perpetuate rather than prevent conflict.[1317]

A lesson for Africa

It is a matter of record that shortly after having brought the ICC in, it would seem that President Museveni may have had second thoughts about the referral.[1318] Even before the warrants were issued, Museveni asked the ICC to drop the charges.[1319] The government subsequently stated that traditional justice would be a more effective tool for dealing with the LRA and its crimes, with a special chamber in Uganda's High Court to deal with the leaders of the LRA.[1320] The Western response was immediate. And the response was arrogant. The London-based Amnesty International immediately declared this could not be done.[1321] Judge Goldstone has also alluded to Museveni's political use of the ICC. In a lecture to the UN, following Museveni's attempts to reverse the ICC action in Uganda, Goldstone noted that "Museveni [was] now wanting to turn off the tap having used the ICC to rein in Koni".[1322] A conference in the USA, chaired by Judge Goldstone, stated: "The Ugandan government may believe it can simply retract the referral, and nullify the work of the ICC, if the UPDF is implicated. It is not clear that the government understands that once an investigation is launched, it can only be delayed by the UN; it cannot be revoked."[1323] The ICG states: "Uganda cannot revoke its referral to the ICC at this point even if it wanted to... . However, the ICC's Statute provides no formal way for the Ugandan government to force the ICC to close the case, short of demonstrating that it is willing and able to prosecute the indicted commanders domestically."[1324]

The Guardian newspaper has reported on Museveni's continuing insistence on trying to ignore the ICC action that he initiated, and that critics have accused Museveni of misusing the international criminal court indictments as a bargaining tool to pressure Kony into a peace settlement: "Under international law, the Ugandan government is obliged to send the accused men for trial at The Hague. But the issue has opened a rift between African governments, which believe trials should be subordinated to local peace deals and reconciliation, and countries such as Britain, which back the ICC as establishing international justice. Museveni told journalists his government had the right to pull Kony out of the clutches of the ICC because it had requested the court to investigate in the first place."[1325]

The American legal expert, Professor Tom Ginsberg, has clearly stated the case: "A government that wants to make a decision to forgive cannot do so, once it has signed the Rome Statute". It is clear: "Under the Rome Statute…there is no way for a government to withdraw a request."[1326]

The lesson therefore is a clear one for any government considering referring a situation to the ICC. However cosy the arrangement may have been at the start, however much the Prosecutor may have wooed or blackmailed the government in question for a referral, once in play it has had a life of its own – and when stopping proceedings is against the personal ambitions of the Prosecutor the action will not end. In Ocampo's own words: "I can do nothing else than prosecute Kony now. When the court requests an arrest warrant, it's a judicial activity. The judges decide. It's not my decision. And the judges cannot take into account political factors, the judges consider evidence and it has to be lawyers presenting evidence… . The judges cannot review an arrest warrant based on political considerations. It's a court."[1327]

Ocampo was, of course, being characteristically disingenuous. The ICC is political, the judges continue to make political decisions and it is not a real court.

Chapter Nineteen

THE COURT AND THE DEMOCRATIC REPUBLIC OF THE CONGO

> *"[The ICC] may have caused irreparable damage to perceptions about the ICC's impartiality in the DRC."*
>
> Human Rights Watch[1328]

The government of the DRC, a state signatory to the Rome Statute, referred "the situation of crimes within the jurisdiction of the court allegedly committed anywhere in the territory of the DRC" to the Prosecutor in April 2004.[1329] This followed considerable pressure by the ICC Prosecutor to do so. The DRC's five-year civil war had ended in 2003. A transitional government led to national elections in 2006. There has nevertheless been ongoing armed conflict in the eastern part of the DRC, along its borders with Rwanda, Uganda, and Burundi.

The ICC has opened five cases into, and issued arrest warrants for, crimes allegedly committed in the DRC's eastern district of Ituri, the centre since 2003 of an inter-ethnic war reportedly also involving neighbouring governments. These were *The Prosecutor v. Thomas Lubanga Dyilo*; *The Prosecutor v. Jean Bosco Ntaganda*; *The Prosecutor v. Germain Katanga*; *The Prosecutor v. Mathieu Ngudjolo Chui*; *The Prosecutor v. Callixte Mbarushimana*; and *The Prosecutor v. Sylvestre Mudacumura*. Thomas Lubanga has been convicted.[1330] Mathieu Ngudjolo Chui was acquitted. In the case *The Prosecutor v. Callixte Mbarushimana*, on 16 December 2011, the Pre-Trial Chamber I decided by majority to decline to confirm the charges against Mbarushimana. Mbarushimana was released from the ICC's custody on 23 December 2011. Germain Katanga remains in custody and Jean Bosco Ntaganda surrendered to the US Embassy in Rwanda in early 2013.

The Prosecutor v. Thomas Lubanga Dyilo

The ICC issued a sealed arrest warrant in February 2006 for Thomas Lubanga, the founder and leader of the *Union des Patriotes Congolais* (UPC) in Ituri and its military wing, the *Forces Patriotiques pour la Libération du Congo* (FPLC). At the time, Lubanga was in Congolese custody, having been arrested and charged by the DRC authorities with several crimes.[1331] Lubanga was transferred to ICC custody by the Kinshasa government in March 2006. The ICC charged Lubanga with three counts of war crimes related to the recruitment and use of child soldiers.[1332] Lubanga pleaded not guilty.

A bare chronology of the proceedings is useful. From 9–28 November 2006, Pre-Trial Chamber I held hearings to confirm charges against Lubanga; four victims were authorised to participate. On 29 January 2007, the Pre-Trial Chamber confirmed the charges against Lubanga and sent the case to trial. On 13 June 2008, Trial Chamber I indefinitely stayed the proceedings due to a failure by the OTP to disclose exculpatory material. On 18 November 2008 Trial Chamber I decided to resume proceedings after problems with disclosure of evidence to Lubanga had been resolved. On 26 January 2009 the Lubanga trial commenced; ninety-three victims were authorised to participate. From 28 January to 14 July 2009 the ICC Prosecutor presented its case, calling twenty-five witnesses. On 22 May 2009 victim participants filed an application claiming that existing evidence presented by the prosecution warranted the addition of charges of sexual slavery and cruel and inhuman treatment, notably against girl child soldiers. On 14 July a majority of judges in Trial Chamber I ruled that additional charges should be added. The decision was appealed. In October 2009 Trial Chamber I decided to suspend the trial pending resolution of this issue. On 8 December 2009, the Appeals Chamber reversed the Trial Chamber's decision to add charges. On 7 January 2010 the trial recommenced with the hearing of two expert witnesses called by the chamber and testimony of three victim participants. The defence presented its case from 27 January 2010 to 15 April 2011. The defence called twenty witnesses. On 8 July 2010 Trial Chamber I ordered the proceedings stayed for a second time because of the prosecution's failure to disclose the name of one of its intermediaries to the defence.[1333] In October 2010, the Appeals Chamber reversed the decision to stay proceedings. In December 2010, Lubanga's defence requested that the case be thrown out, arguing that the OTP had engaged in an "abuse of the process" that affected Lubanga's right to a fair trial. This application was rejected on 23 February 2011. The evidence phase of the trial ended on 20 May 2011. Final submissions were heard on 25 August 2011: 123 victims are authorised to participate. On 14 March 2012, Lubanga was convicted of committing, as co-perpetrator, war crimes, namely:

> Enlisting and conscripting of children under the age of 15 years into the Force patriotique pour la libération du Congo [Patriotic Force for the Liberation of Congo] (FPLC) and using them to participate actively in hostilities in the context of an armed conflict not of an international character from 1 September 2002 to 13 August 2003 (punishable under article 8(2)(e)(vii) of the Rome Statute).

On 10 July 2012, Lubanga was sentenced to a total period of fourteen years of imprisonment. The time he spent in the ICC's custody was to be deducted from this sentence.

To say that Lubanga's trial before the ICC was a farce would be an understatement.

Geoffrey Robertson has stated that "the length of the proceedings – six years – for a crime that was relatively easy to prove, was wholly unsatisfactory".[1334] The legitimacy of the proceedings was marred from the start by serious irregularities regarding the prosecution's investigation, its use of intermediaries and the credibility of the witnesses it presented.[1335]

The court was actually very lucky that its first ever trial even started. In an extraordinary development in June 2008 the ICC Trial Chamber stayed Thomas Lubanga's trial because of the Prosecutor's failure to disclose exculpatory evidence (or in normal language evidence that showed that the accused was innocent), to the defence. Ocampo had admitted to the court that he was holding 204 such items. He claimed he was entitled to rely on an exception to the normal disclosure rules in Article 54(3)(e) of the ICC, which provides that "The Prosecutor may: agree not to disclose, at any stage of the proceedings, documents or information that the Prosecutor obtains on the condition of confidentiality and solely for the purpose of generating new evidence, unless the provider of the information consents." This was meant to be resorted to only in exceptional circumstances, not over 200 times. What made matters worse was that Ocampo sought to hide these 200-plus documents not only from the defence, but also from the judges.

Three-quarters of the exculpatory items held back by the Prosecutor came from the UN, which has a peacekeeping mission on the ground in the DRC. Of these pieces of evidence, the UN had actually agreed that fifty-three could be disclosed unconditionally and a further eighty-three with sections blanked out. The UN had no objection to the court, but not the defence, viewing the redacted sections and all remaining material. A further fifty or so documents had been supplied by six non-governmental organisations. Lubanga and his lawyers had been offered access to just *three* of their documents — and even those would be redacted.

The judges correctly stated that Ocampo's behaviour "constitutes a wholesale and serious abuse" of an exception that allows prosecutors to receive evidence that is not, in itself, admissible – but that could lead, in turn, to usable evidence.[1336] The judges stated: "[T]he trial process has been ruptured to such a degree that it is now impossible to piece together the constituent elements of a fair trial."[1337] *Inner City Press* revealed that it had been told by sources inside the UN Secretariat and its Congo peacekeeping mission, MONUC, "that they never expected Ocampo to base his prosecution on the hearsay material they provided him, but he did. Now that material must be disclosed, and they are unhappy. Neither they nor the Western members of the permanent five, however, will criticise Ocampo in public. That would be politically incorrect."[1338]

The Trial Chamber categorically rejected the Prosecutor's attempt to justify his actions: "The prosecution has given Article 54(3)(e) a broad and incorrect interpretation: it has utilised the provision routinely, in inappropriate circumstances, instead of resorting to it exceptionally, when particular, restrictive circumstances apply." The judges stated:

> [T]he prosecution's general approach has been to use Article 54(3)(e) to obtain a wide range of materials under the cloak of confidentiality, in order to identify from those materials evidence to be used at trial (having obtained the information provider's consent). This is the exact opposite of the proper

use of the provision, which is, exceptionally, to allow the prosecution to receive information or documents which are not for use at trial but which are instead intended to "lead" to new evidence. The prosecution's approach constitutes a wholesale and serious abuse, and a violation of an important provision which was intended to allow the prosecution to receive evidence confidentially, in very restrictive circumstances. The logic of the prosecution's position is that all of the evidence that it obtains from information-providers can be the subject of Article 54(3)(e) agreements.

The Trial Chamber was especially critical of the Prosecutor's refusal to disclose the confidential information to the bench. As the chamber pointed out, it – not the Prosecutor – is ultimately responsible for ensuring that the defendant receives a fair trial. Even the then President of the ICC ASP, Ambassador Christian Wenaweser, noted that the exculpatory evidence affair was being cited by some as evidence that Moreno Ocampo "is incompetent and doesn't know how to write an indictment".[1339] The *Christian Science Monitor* noted that "the legal body's performance in the court of world opinion remains an issue. The ICC has a staff of 745 people that has worked six years – only to find its first case nearly thrown out in June."[1340]

The Trial Chamber thus held that it had no other choice but to stay the proceedings. It stated that its judges:

> [A]re enjoined to ensure that the accused receives a fair trial. If, at the outset, it is clear that the essential preconditions of a fair trial are missing and there is no sufficient indication that this will be resolved during the trial process, it is necessary – indeed, inevitable – that the proceedings should be stayed. It would be wholly wrong for a criminal court to begin, or to continue, a trial once it has become clear that the inevitable conclusion in the final judgment will be that the proceedings are vitiated because of unfairness which will not be rectified.

On 2 July 2008, the court ordered Lubanga's release, on the grounds that "a fair trial of the accused is impossible, and the entire justification for his detention has been removed".[1341] Ocampo desperately asked that the judges lift the suspension of the trial, and also appealed against the Trial Chamber's decision, requesting that Lubanga did not go free. On 3 September 2008, Trial Chamber I rejected the Prosecutor's plea to lift the stay, because the judges decided that the problem affecting Lubanga's rights to a fair trial still had not been remedied: the Prosecutor had not secured guarantees from the organisations with confidentiality agreements that would allow the judges to see all the relevant documents, nor had he ensured that the judges would have access to the documents throughout the course of Lubanga's trial, to make sure Lubanga's rights were being protected. The partial fix that the Prosecutor had proposed would still, according to the judges, "infringe fundamental aspects of the accused's right to a fair trial". Because there was an appeal in progress, Lubanga had to remain in jail while the appeal was being decided. On 21

October 2008, the Appeals Chamber decided to maintain the trial's suspension, but to keep Lubanga in jail.

Acknowledging his grave error, the Prosecutor eventually agreed to make all the material available to the court. On 18 November 2008, the Trial Chamber, despite having previously declared that a fair trial was "impossible", then reversed its decision and ordered that the trial could go ahead.[1342] This was, of course, a very convenient decision by a bureaucracy that realised that to end the court's first trial in this way would have done immeasurable damage to the institution.

The landmark, first-ever trial held by the ICC finally began on 26 January 2009, after several years of preparation and at much expense. Trial Chamber I, comprising Judges Sir Adrian Fulford, Elisabeth Odio Benito and René Blattmann, commenced *The Prosecutor v. Thomas Lubanga Dyilo*. Much of Ocampo's opening statement at the trial wasn't about child soldiers, but focused more on rape and other sex crimes – "Lubanga's group recruited, trained and used hundreds of children to kill, pillage and rape" – overlooking the fact that he had not been charged with those allegations. The charges he was facing were recruiting and deploying child soldiers. Lisa Clifford noted that Ocampo's presentation reminded her of "a student who hadn't prepared properly for his final exam".[1343] Lubanga's defence lawyer immediately complained pointing out that rape was not included in the charge sheet of her client; Clifford agreed, observing that it was "unreasonable for Lubanga to answer charges that were never issued". Ocampo then left the courtroom, and indeed The Hague, without listening to the defence's opening statement, to attend the World Economic Forum in Davos. Lubanga's defence counsel *Maître* Catherine Mabille quite rightly complained at Ocampo's disrespect by not attending court that day and protested that the defence still had no access to the exculpatory evidence Ocampo had sought to withhold. She also complained that the defence and the public had been excluded from about half of the pre-trial hearings, which prevented her client from defending himself adequately. She laid the blame squarely with Ocampo: "How can we have a fair trial under [these] conditions? ...There has been a wholesale abuse of the rules by the office of the prosecutor."[1344]

The Chief Prosecutor, therefore, was not present in court to witness his prosecution being tripped up almost immediately when their first witness, a former child soldier known as Dieumerci, giving testimony from behind a screen and with his voice distorted, said that he had lied: "What I said earlier, was not what I intended to say." The young man told the court that a humanitarian aid group had coached him on what to lie about. Deputy Prosecutor Fatou Bensouda asked him: "Did you attend the training camp?" He answered no. The presiding judge, Adrian Fulford, then asked the witness if his original story was true or false. The witness replied: "It's not true." The *Christian Science Monitor* reported that "Ms. Bensouda, who replaced another prosecutor only six weeks ago, could not seek counsel from Moreno-Ocampo, who had decamped to the celebrity economic forum at Davos, Switzerland, according to a court spokeswoman."[1345] The court then went into closed session and dismissed the witness. The defence complained at this, arguing that the young man should be allowed to testify, since his reversal could benefit Lubanga.[1346] Dieumerci was not the only witness to change his story once he took the stand. Another witness, identified as "number 15", told the court that he had provided a false name and statement to prosecutors. Adrian Fulford said that a fresh statement should be obtained from the witness "setting out what he says is the truth". The statement was taken in the presence of defence lawyers, but "witness 15" did not return to testify before the prosecution rested.

Things did not get much better for Ocampo. The ICC's communication strategy for the trial had stated an intention to "publicise the first trial at the ICC and to make the proceedings accessible to the general public and to the communities most affected by the crimes committed". While the Prosecutor's opening statement was duly broadcast in the DRC, the defence counsel's opening speech, however, was not broadcast. The outreach unit of the Registry later claimed that while arrangements had been made for a live public screening of the proceedings to be held in Bunia, the capital of Ituri in the DRC, it was not anticipated that the opening of the proceedings would have gone beyond the first day.[1347] The IBA stated that "the failure to broadcast the defence speech was regrettable as it reportedly led to concerns about the partiality of the Court among Mr Lubanga's supporters on the ground".[1348]

The trial then very quickly hit another obstacle, again one of Ocampo's own making. Legal commentators had noted Ocampo's obsession with rape and sex, seemingly at the expense of the Lubanga's alleged crime of recruiting child soldiers. Rozenberg stated that Ocampo "seemed unable to confine the evidence to the allegations against the defendant. Instead, in his opening statement, he introduced allegations that young girl soldiers had been treated as "sexual slaves"'.[1349] However, Lubanga was not charged with rape or crimes relating to sexual violence. This is where "victim participation" comes into the picture. As of late 2008, the ICC reported that 960 victims had applied to participate in judicial proceedings in one of the situations or cases before the court.[1350] By late 2009, in the DRC situation these numbered 102 in the Lubanga case, and 350 in the Katanga and Ngudjolo case. In the Darfur Abu Garda case seventy-eight victims had been accepted.[1351]

The Lubanga case was the first time that alleged victims have been able to present their views and concerns before an international court. A total of 102 victims represented by seven lawyers participated in the Lubanga trial at the ICC. The lawyers were present in the courtroom each day, where they were able to question witnesses and put their clients' views. Kevin Jon Heller has confirmed the impact this procedure had on the trial: "The trial has been undeniably altered by the influence of the victims."[1352] On 22 May 2009, probably because of Ocampo's obvious obsession with sexual misconduct, their lawyers asked for rape and other sexual crimes to be added to the indictment. On 14 July, the court then ignored all established procedures and norms and ruled that it was possible to add new charges *after* a trial had commenced, and also said that the new charges could be based on fresh evidence – not only on existing facts. The presiding judge, Adrian Fulford, delivered a twenty-eight-page dissenting opinion in which he said that the court should not add, substitute or amend the charges.[1353] In his view, and quite correctly, the Prosecutor could request such changes only before a trial begins. Fulford suggested that the trial should be allowed to continue on the basis of the existing charges while any appeal by the defence was being considered. Appeals were lodged by the defence. The

Appeals Chamber took a long time to rule and defence lawyers quite correctly stated that they could not proceed until they knew whether Lubanga would face further charges. On 2 October 2009 the trial reconvened for the defence. *Maitre* Mabille, Lubanga's lead lawyer, told judges: "The defense is unable to continue with this trial if we don't know the charges brought against the accused." The Trial Chamber agreed and adjourned the trial until the Appeals Chamber delivered its ruling:

> The Chamber is persuaded that a necessary precondition for the "effective preparation" of the accused's defence, at this stage in the trial…now that the prosecution has concluded its evidence, and before the evidence proceeds further, the accused should have certainty as regards these issues…. If the case continues…the defence will be placed in [an] unfair position…. It follows that if the Chamber continues to hear evidence in the case prior to the decision of the Appeals Chamber on the substantive issue, there is too great a risk that the defence will proceed, as least for part of the trial, on a significantly false basis.

Maitre Mabille was very critical of the judges' 14 July decision: "What is the [point] of having the preliminary chamber [decide on the charges] if you can change the charges after the end of the prosecutor's case?" Mabille also noted that the addition of new charges would also cast doubt on the fairness of the proceedings and the right of the accused to be tried in a reasonable amount of time: "We would have to call back all the prosecution witnesses, because we didn't do any cross examination of crimes that didn't exist at that time. The defense will have to ask for lots of time to re-prepare its case." Mabille made the point that the victims' role should be in the reparations phase – not during the trial: "At the moment, their role is too close to the role of the prosecutor. We have to face the prosecutor, and then the victims. For us, it's exactly the same."[1354]

Heller expressed considerable concern about the idea that victims could simply ask for brand new charges midway through the trial. He warned that if the judges' 14 July decision had been upheld and the Lubanga case required to be re-investigated this would have set a dangerous precedent: "When would a defendant ever be safe, if at any point during a trial…the chamber can just re-characterise the facts to add new charges? You can never be certain that your defence is adequate or adequately tailored to the charges, because you'll never know what the charges are."[1355]

The Economist noted that "impressions that the judges and prosecutor were making the rules up as they went along were often accurate".[1356] Even the IBA, a pro-ICC body supportive of the concept of victim participation, acknowledged that the timing of the victims' request in the Lubanga case was "unfortunate" given how far the trial had progressed: "It really does put the defence in a difficult position. What is important going forward is that we don't have a situation where the presence of victims ends up being unfair."[1357]

Heller criticised the confusion at the ICC regarding the new charges at the Lubanga trial: "Victims have an absolute right to lobby, submit briefs, argue in the court of public opinion, but it is the prosecutor's final decision to bring charges. It is not the role of victims at trial to be deciding what charges are brought."[1358] As Rozenberg also noted of the addition of new charges in the middle of a trial: "A criminal trial is not a public inquiry into every crime that may have been committed. It is method of establishing whether a defendant is guilty of the charges brought against him. This case should have been over by now." He attributed full responsibility to Ocampo: "More than six years after Luis Moreno-Ocampo became prosecutor of this ill-fated court, he has not achieved a single conviction. He is nowhere near completing his first trial. He should never have been appointed."[1359]

With regard to "victims participation", Human Rights Watch also described this as a "significant" challenge for the ICC:

> Decisions of the pre-trial chambers...may come under review by the appellate division after a final judgment in the case, or, in certain circumstances, through interlocutory appeal. Indeed, the substantial efforts of the pre-trial chamber in working out the scope and modalities of victims' participation have been revised by the trial chamber in one case and are now under review in a number of respects by the appeals division.[1360]

The IBA's ICC monitoring programme documented several other major concerns about the Lubanga trial. It stated, for example, that: "A major challenge of the trial to date has been that so much of the proceedings is held in closed session...the number of closed session hearings arguably impinges on Lubanga's right to open, transparent public proceedings...the IBA is concerned that the defendant's right to open justice and the public perception of the trial are being affected by the fact that much of the proceedings is conducted in closed session."[1361] The Prosecutor was also said to have been unprofessional with regard to the issue of self-incrimination with regard to witnesses. The IBA noted that this "was not fully explored prior to the commencement of the trial. Indeed, it is unclear why this was not done... . Clear judicial and policy determinations ought to have been made at this earlier stage such that legal representatives of victims, the VWU, the Office of the Prosecutor (OTP) and any other relevant organs of the Court would be suitably apprised of their responsibilities in that regard."[1362]

The case recommenced only to hit another serious problem. On 8 July 2010 ICC Trial Chamber I ordered a second stay in the Lubanga case, stating that the fair trial of the accused was no longer possible due to the Prosecutor's non-compliance with the chamber's orders. The chamber had ordered the OTP to confidentially disclose to the defence the identity of intermediary 143, who had provided witnesses for the prosecution. It was clear that the Prosecutor was attempting to conceal questionable behaviour on the part of the prosecution regarding the sourcing of witnesses subsequently seen to be unreliable. On 15 July 2010, ICC Trial Chamber I ordered Lubanga's release. The judges stated:

> No criminal court can operate on the basis that whenever it makes an order in a particular area, it is for the Prosecutor to elect whether or not to implement it, depending on his interpretation of his obligations. The judges, not the

Prosecutor, decide on protective measures during the trial, once the Chamber is seized of the relevant issue, as regards victims, witnesses and others affected by the work of the Court, and the prosecution cannot choose to ignore its rulings.... The Prosecutor now claims a separate authority which can defeat the orders of the Court, and which thereby involves a profound, unacceptable and unjustified intrusion into the role of the judiciary.... [The Prosecutor] cannot be allowed to continue with this prosecution if he seeks to reserve to himself the right to avoid the Court's orders whenever he decides that they are inconsistent with his interpretation of his other obligations. In order for the Chamber to ensure that the accused receives a fair trial, it is necessary that its orders, decisions and rulings are respected, unless and until they are overturned on appeal, or suspended by order of the Court.... Whilst these circumstances endure, the fair trial of the accused is no longer possible, and justice cannot be done, not least because the judges will have lost control of a significant aspect of the trial proceedings as provided under the Rome Statute framework.[1363]

The prosecution appealed the decision and Thomas Lubanga remained in detention pending a decision. Ralph Henham and Mark Findlay confirmed the background to the second stay of the proceedings in the Lubanga case:

ICC trials have recently been plagued with questions about the integrity and truthfulness of witnesses during proceedings at The Hague. In the Lubanga case for instance some witness testimony has been accurate; some of the witnesses have been accused of coming to The Hague with intention of providing false testimony. Some have claimed to have lied as to their names, age or as to being child soldiers.... In addition, there are accusations of "intermediaries" inducing witnesses to supply false statements to ICC investigators.[1364]

"Intermediaries" were organisations and individuals said to serve as liaisons between the ICC, including the OTP, and individuals and communities in the field with regard to cases before the court. They were said to have assisted the prosecutor in identifying and contacting witnesses for prosecution. The prosecution used seven intermediaries to contact approximately half of the witnesses that testified against Lubanga in this case.[1365]

Joshua Rozenberg has put Ocampo's behaviour into a British context:

Imagine that the Director of Public Prosecutions had been found guilty of contempt of court for deliberately flouting the orders of an Old Bailey judge. Imagine, further, that the prosecutor's disobedience was so fundamental that, in the court's view, it was no longer possible for the defendant to receive a fair trial. There would be two consequences. First, the defendant would be acquitted. And, second, the prosecutor would resign.[1366]

As Rozenberg noted further, however, "that's not the way the International Criminal Court [chose] to deal with just such a case".[1367] On 8 October 2010, the ICC Appeals Chamber reversed the Trial Chamber's July 2010 decision to stay proceedings. Appeals judges stated that although the prosecutor did not comply with the Trial Chamber's orders relating to protection issues, the judges should first have tried applying sanctions before imposing a stay of proceedings. The Appeals Chamber found that the Prosecutor's non-compliance was deliberate. The Appeals Chamber stated that it found "that such wilful non-compliance constituted a clear refusal to implement the orders of the Chamber" and there was "a more profound and enduring concern", which was that the Prosecutor appeared to wish to decide whether or not to implement the Trial Chamber's orders depending on his interpretation of his obligations under the statute.[1368]

The Appeals Chamber was also critical of the prosecution's choice of team members and its sourcing of witnesses:

> The Chamber is particularly concerned that the prosecution used an individual as an intermediary with such close ties to the government that had originally referred the situation in the DRC to the Court. He not only introduced witnesses to the investigators, but he was also involved in the arrangements for their interviews. Given the likelihood of political tension, or even animosity, between the accused and the government, it was wholly undesirable for witnesses to be identified, introduced and handled by one or more individuals who, on account of their work or position, may not have had, to a sufficient degree or at all, the necessary qualities of independence and impartiality. Whilst it is acceptable for individuals in this category to provide information and intelligence on an independent basis, they should not become members of the prosecution team.[1369]

There was further related and equally deserved criticism of the prosecution by the Appeals Chamber following a 15 March 2010 interview given by Béatrice le Frapper du Hellen, a deputy prosecutor and the Head of the Jurisdiction, Complementarity and Cooperation Division of the OTP, to an organisation called Lubangatrial.org. This interview claimed that the prosecution's intermediaries in question were credible without providing any evidence in support. The interview suggested that the Prosecutor was to decide if facts were proven in the case. The chamber's criticism stressed that "as a matter of professional ethics a party to proceedings is expected not to misrepresent the evidence, to misdescribe the functions of the parties or the chamber, or to suggest or imply without proper foundation that anyone in the case, including the accused, has misbehaved". It stated further that "it was inappropriate for the prosecution representative to state in unequivocal terms that they are fantastic, committed people, who support international justice, and that they are admired by the prosecution".[1370]

Clear questions arose soon after the opening of the prosecution case in January 2009 as to whether intermediaries influenced witness testimony.[1371] The first prosecution witness, presented as an alleged former child soldier, recanted his testimony and stated that an intermediary had instructed him on its contents.[1372] Similar allegations of fabricated witness testimony instigated by intermediaries led to the defence filing for abuse of process in December 2010, requesting a permanent stay of proceedings and the immediate release of the accused.[1373] In its March 2011 ruling, the Trial Chamber rejected the application for a stay, while reaffirming its right to reserve judgment on the credibility of witnesses in its judgment.[1374] In the final judgement, the Trial Chamber found all but one of the alleged former child soldiers called as witnesses by the prosecution to be unreliable.

The chamber also pointed to the prosecution's negligent supervision of intermediaries and failure to verify the resultant "evidence". It found that the prosecution's undue reliance upon intermediaries created the significant possibility that they improperly influenced witnesses to falsify their testimony, rendering most of it unreliable.[1375]

In its 31 May 2010 ruling on the prosecution's relationship with intermediaries, the Trial Chamber stated that this relationship had "become an issue of major importance in the trial", and directed that the prosecution produce representatives "to testify as to the approach and the procedures applied to intermediaries".[1376] Ocampo called two investigators, Bernard Lavigne and Nicolas Sebire to give evidence. Lavigne was the team leader of the investigation. The chamber found both witnesses to be "essentially reliable", though "not necessarily accurate on every issue". Lavigne stated that he had established a twelve-strong team. Deputy Prosecutor Serge Brammertz, and his assistant Michel De Smedt, Deputy Head of the Investigation Division, were Bernard Lavigne's direct supervisors. Chief Prosecutor Luis Ocampo directly supervised Brammertz and De Smedt.[1377] A parallel structure, described as "joint teams", reported directly to the Prosecutor and the Executive Committee, which was itself composed of Ocampo and the three heads of division (Investigations, Jurisdiction and Complementarity and Cooperation).[1378]

The investigators noted that the OTP admitted to "inconsistent requests" being made of the investigators and that "the OTP hesitated in formulating its objectives and the steps to be taken to attain them".[1379] Lavigne testified that during the early investigations, "UN agencies had received information to the effect that some individuals were falsely presenting themselves at demobilisation centres as former child soldiers from the militias in order to join the reintegration programme." He also noted that "it became known in Bunia that a threatened witness might be relocated and some individuals treated this as an opportunity to secure free re-housing".[1380] Lavigne also noted that because of the security situation, the investigators did not seek to corroborate witness accounts by contacting their families or checking school records regarding alleged child soldiers.[1381] He stated that this policy was applied to all witnesses and it was only varied on an exceptional basis. Lavigne testified that it was also difficult to establish age from documents as the civil administration was dysfunctional and that "as an investigation leader, [he] was not alone in considering that a prosecution forensic expert should be instructed immediately, in order to provide at least an approximate idea of age". He revealed however that "the Executive Committee within the [OTP] was of the view that the statements given by the witnesses sufficiently indicated that the relevant individuals were below 15 years of age".[1382] The chamber concluded that, while acknowledging the difficulties faced by investigators in the field, "this failure to investigate the children's histories has significantly undermined some of the evidence called by the prosecution".[1383]

The chamber noted that "many – although by no means all – of the evidential difficulties in this case as far as the prosecution is concerned have been the result of the involvement of three particular intermediaries (P-0143, P-0316 and P-0321)".[1384] Intermediary 143 provided the ICC with many "witnesses", including five of the alleged former child soldiers whom the Trial Chamber found lacking in credibility, and one of the other intermediaries in question. The Trial Chamber concluded that there was "a risk" that intermediary 143 "persuaded, encouraged or assisted witnesses to give false evidence".[1385] It should also be noted that the prosecution's failure to immediately comply with the chamber's order to disclose the identity of intermediary 143 was the subject of the second stay of proceedings in this case in July 2010.[1386]

Intermediary 321 provided the prosecution with its opening witness in the trial, a witness who then immediately recanted his testimony while in the witness box.[1387] A number of alleged former child soldiers and defence witnesses also stated that intermediary 321 had encouraged and assisted them to give false evidence. The chamber also noted that intermediary 321 was also party to discrepancies indicating that the intermediary did not utilise lists provided by the OTP in setting up interviews between investigators and the children; eight of the eleven children whom the investigator met with in 2007 were not on the original list provided by the prosecution. The chamber concluded that "a real possibility exist[ed]" that intermediary 321 "encouraged and assisted witnesses to give false evidence".[1388]

The prosecutor's relationship with intermediary 316, and the intermediary's contact with numerous witnesses, was also very questionable.[1389] At the same time as working for the ICC he was also employed by the Congolese intelligence services, the *Agence Nationale de Renseignement*.[1390] The chamber expressed its concern "that the prosecution used an individual as an intermediary with such close ties to the government that had originally referred the situation in the DRC to the Court". The chamber also found that intermediary 316 had falsely claimed that Congolese police services had threatened witnesses. The UN confirmed that the harassment had not occurred.[1391] It was also determined that the intermediary had lied about the fact that his assistant and his family had been murdered, and that the killers were pursuing him.[1392] The chamber was especially concerned about the prosecution's relationship with intermediary 316, stating that there were "strong reasons to believe" that he "persuaded witnesses to lie as to their involvement as child soldiers within the UPC".[1393] More than 100 of the judgment's 593 pages recounted the problems that the use of intermediaries had caused.

In its trial judgment, the Trial Chamber concluded:

> The prosecution should not have delegated its investigative responsibilities to the intermediaries…notwithstanding the extensive security difficulties it faced. A series of witnesses have been called during this trial whose evidence, as a result of the essentially unsupervised actions of three of the principal intermediaries, cannot safely be relied on. The Chamber spent a considerable

period of time investigating the circumstances of a substantial number of individuals whose evidence was, at least in part, inaccurate or dishonest. The prosecution's negligence in failing to verify and scrutinise this material sufficiently before it was introduced led to significant expenditure on the part of the Court. An additional consequence of the lack of proper oversight of the intermediaries is that they were potentially able to take advantage of the witnesses they contacted. Irrespective of the Chamber's conclusions regarding the credibility and reliability of these alleged former child soldiers, given their youth and likely exposure to conflict, they were vulnerable to manipulation.[1394]

During the trial the prosecution presented eleven witnesses who claimed to have been former child soldiers. The chamber found that, with one exception, all of these alleged former child soldiers provided contradictory evidence regarding their ages, education, their family members and recruitment.[1395] In conclusion the chamber found that it could only rely upon the testimony of one of these prosecution witnesses.[1396] In fact, the chamber found that with respect to former child soldiers, defence witnesses were generally more credible than the prosecution witnesses.[1397] The chamber subsequently withdrew the victim status it had previously granted to several of the prosecution's witnesses.

The Lubanga trial resumed but was again put on hold for six weeks in early 2011 due to various challenges brought by the defence, once again because of irregularities in the disclosure of the identity of witnesses and participating victims. On 23 February 2011, Trial Chamber I rejected another defence application for a stay of proceedings and the trial resumed on 21 March 2011.

It is clear that Lubanga had been severely disadvantaged at all levels by ICC procedure during his trial. The IBA confirmed that "the late disclosure of the potentially exculpatory confidential material which initially led to the stay of proceedings in the Lubanga case may have affected the defendant's ability to properly prepare his case and conduct an effective defence. Indeed, given the imminence of the trial the defence may not even have had a full opportunity to decide whether to seek leave to appeal the Chamber's decision to retain some redactions and impose what in its view were appropriate counter-balancing measures." The IBA also pointed out that the related "residual effect of the Article 54(3)(e) confidentiality issue may yet create challenges for the defence at a later stage in the trial. The defence may wish to rely on the evidence, seek additional information or question witnesses based on the confidential material but would however be prohibited from doing so under Rule 82 of the Rules of Procedure and Evidence, which could have a significant impact on its case."[1398] The IBA was also concerned about the use of leading questions during the questioning of witnesses. The IBA cautioned against questioning witnesses in a manner that may inadvertently be unfair to the defendant and urged that great care be taken in particular by the prosecution, the other participants and the judges to avoid leading questions.[1399]

The Lubanga trial was also marred by translation errors. In February 2010 proceedings were stopped because of discrepancies between the French and English versions of the testimony being offered by prosecution witnesses. Lubanga's lawyers pointed out that in the French transcript, for example, there were two names mentioned by the witness, whereas in the English transcript there was only one name. The trial was adjourned and the bench asked the various parties to consult with transcribers. When the hearing resumed, Lubanga's lawyers said that the defence team had found that "there are very serious interpretation problems" and that the defence found it difficult to continue. The trial continued nevertheless.[1400]

It is also very noteworthy that in January 2010, as part of the court's much heralded commitment to victims, three designated victims, authorised to appear as witnesses upon request by their legal representatives, were afforded the opportunity to testify as witnesses against Lubanga. The chamber noted both their "evasiveness" and inconsistencies in their testimony and subsequently withdrew their victim participation status.

The behaviour of the Chief Prosecutor was criticised by the judges to the very end of the trial. Following Lubanga's conviction Ocampo had sought a thirty-year sentence for him and urged the judges to consider aggravating circumstances, including the alleged sexual abuse of female recruits to Lubanga's militia. *Foreign Policy* noted of the verdict that "[t]he court's decision was as notable for the harsh words directed at former ICC prosecutor Luis Moreno-Ocampo…as for its discussion of Lubanga's crimes". The Chairman of the Trial Chamber, Sir Adrian Fulford, placed on record that:

> The Chamber strongly deprecates the attitude of the former Prosecutor in relation to the issue of sexual violence. He advanced extensive submissions as regards sexual violence in his opening and closing submissions at trial, and in his arguments on sentence he contended that sexual violence is an aggravating factor that should be reflected by the Chamber. However, not only did the former Prosecutor fail to apply to include sexual violence or sexual slavery at any stage during these proceedings, including in the original charges, but he actively opposed taking this step during the trial when he submitted that it would cause unfairness to the accused if he was convicted on this basis. Notwithstanding this stance on his part throughout these proceedings, he suggested that sexual violence ought to be considered for the purposes of sentencing.[1401]

The chamber noted that the defendant had been subject to "some particularly onerous circumstances" as a result of the prosecution's behaviour. The chamber listed these circumstances as including: (i) the fact that the prosecution had gathered information under confidentiality agreements which led to a failure to disclose exculpatory material, and which led to a stay of proceedings and a provisional order to release Mr. Lubanga; (ii) the prosecution's repeated failure to comply with the chamber's disclosure orders, leading to a second stay of proceedings and a second provisional order releasing Lubanga; and (iii) the prosecution's use of a public interview, given by a member of the prosecution office, to make misleading and inaccurate statements to the press about the evidence in the case and Mr. Lubanga's conduct during the proceedings. According to the chamber, the "conduct of the prosecution" in this respect placed Mr. Lubanga under "considerable unwarranted pressure". It was noted that "the Chamber's frustration with the Prosecutor's conduct of the trial is palpable".[1402]

Lest there be any doubt, the trial of Thomas Lubanga before the ICC was a travesty of justice. The almost unbelievable catalogue of legal, procedural and investigative errors in the course of the Lubanga trial would have seen the case thrown out of any reasonable court.

The Prosecutor v. Germain Katanga and Mathieu Ngudjolo Chui

The ICC issued sealed arrest warrants for Germain Katanga, the alleged commander of the *Force de Résistance Patriotiqueen Ituri* (FRPI) and Mathieu Ngudjolo Chui, a commander of the *Front des Nationalistes et Intégrationnistes* (FNI), in July 2007. They were charged with allegedly having "acted in concert to mount an attack targeted mainly at Hema civilians" in Ituri in 2003.[1403] They were transferred by Congolese authorities to ICC custody in October 2007 and February 2008 respectively. The trial in the case *The Prosecutor v. Germain Katanga and Mathieu Ngudjolo Chui* began before Trial Chamber II on 24 November 2009. They were both charged with three crimes against humanity: Murder under Article 7(1)(a) of the Rome Statute; sexual slavery and rape under Article 7(1)(g) of the statute; and seven war crimes: Using children under the age of fifteen to take active part in hostilities under Article 8(2)(b)(xxvi) of the statute; deliberately directing an attack on a civilian population as such or against individual civilians or against individual civilians not taking direct part in hostilities under Article 8(2)(b)(i); wilful killing under Article 8(2)(a)(i) of the statute; destruction of property under Article 8(2)(b)(xiii) of the statute; pillaging under Article 8(2)(b)(xvi) of the statute; sexual slavery and rape under Article 8(2)(b)(xxii) of the statute.

On 21 November 2012, Trial Chamber II severed the charges of the two defendants, Katanga and Ngudjolo. It announced that Ngudjolo's case would be adjudicated first, with the verdict against Katanga issued later and based on separate charges.[1404] The case against Mathieu Ngudjolo Chui was ended in December 2012 by Presiding Judge Bruno Cotte, who acquitted him of all charges, saying the prosecution had "not proved beyond reasonable doubt that Mathieu Ngudjolo Chui was responsible" for the crimes of which he had been accused. He said the decision was unanimous, and that witness testimony had been "too contradictory and too hazy". The court ordered Ngudjolo's immediate release, and rejected prosecutor Fatou Bensouda's attempts to have him detained pending an appeal: "The chamber dismisses the prosecution's application for further detention." Judge Cotte stated that there were "no exceptional circumstances" to continue to detain Mr Ngudjolo.[1405]

William Schabas observed of the trial that "[i]t's pretty bad when, as in the Ngudjolo case, judges don't believe the witnesses".[1406] The fault lines in the prosecution case were clear. The judges complained of prosecutors failing to check out their witnesses' stories and of using intermediaries who may have had agendas of their own. Reuters reported that under cross-examination, the credibility of a key witness, P-279, ebbed away because of long silences during his testimony, most often "when faced with contradictions he couldn't resolve".¹⁴⁰⁷ In the trial, witness P-279 testified that he had seen Ngudjolo and his co-accused Germain Katanga enter a school near a military camp. When judges visited the site, however, they found it was impossible to see the school from where the witness had been standing, and criticised the prosecution for not checking this: "It would have been desirable for the Prosecutor, before the debate about the facts of the matter began, to have been able to visit the places where the accused lived." The OTP claimed that "[a]ll visits by investigators from the prosecutor's office were advised against by all authorities, including the UN which was in a position to assist with our movements in Ituri". While this would have been a convenient excuse, the court's claim was contradicted by the United Nations Department for Safety and Security, which said it was not aware of any specific advisory to ICC prosecutors in the case.¹⁴⁰⁸ Rather than visit the site – as the judges did – and do their own on-site investigations, the OTP chose instead to rely on intermediaries to source convenient "witnesses", such as witness P-279, who appeared to be making things up as they went along.

The self-serving claim that "[a]ll visits by investigators from the prosecutor's office were advised against" is all the more surprising given that Ocampo himself visited Ituri district in July 2009. There is carefully choreographed television footage of Ocampo arriving in Ituri. The opening scene of *Prosecutor*, a film made about the Prosecutor and the court, shows him disembarking from a UN helicopter and striding towards a remote African village, wearing a white linen suit, ready to assume the court's self-assumed role of shouldering the white man's burden of bringing justice to black Africa.¹⁴⁰⁹ It was excellent public relations work by the Prosecutor and his highly paid team of public relations advisers. Regrettably while he was there Ocampo clearly failed to do any of the prosecutorial work at the heart of his day job, actually investigating alleged war crimes. As Alex de Waal has so aptly observed of the Prosecutor and the court: "In the absence of law and evidence, we have the theatrics."¹⁴¹⁰

The Prosecutor v. Callixte Mbarushimana

In the case *The Prosecutor v. Callixte Mbarushimana*, the Prosecutor alleged that Callixte Mbarushimana was the Executive Secretary of the Democratic Forces for the Liberation of Rwanda or *Forces Démocratiques pour la Libération du Rwanda* (FDLR), the rebel group operating in eastern DRC. Ocampo alleged that after the arrest of the FDLR's president in 2009, Mbarushimana assumed many of the president's powers and was guilty of crimes against humanity. Mbarushimana was arrested on 11 October 2010 after the ICC unsealed a warrant for his arrest issued in September 2010. The prosecution had applied for the arrest warrant under Article 58 of the Rome Statute in August 2010. In its decision granting the application for the warrant of arrest, Pre-Trial Chamber I at the ICC found that there were reasonable grounds to believe that between January and September 2009, several attacks were directed by the FDLR against the civilian population of the North Kivu and South Kivu provinces in the DRC. In addition, the chamber found reasonable grounds to believe that Mbarushimana was criminally responsible under Article 25(3)(d) of the Rome Statute for five counts of crimes against humanity (murder, torture, rape, inhumane acts, persecution) and six counts of war crimes (attacks against a civilian population, destruction of property, murder, torture, rape, inhuman treatment). On 3 November 2010, a Paris court approved Mbarushimana's extradition to the custody of the ICC in The Hague. Mbarushimana was the fourth person to be brought before the ICC in relation to the situation in the DRC, but the first to face charges in relation to crimes committed in the Kivu provinces. On 25 January 2011, Mbarushimana was transferred by the French judicial authorities to the ICC detention centre.

On 16 December 2011 the Pre-Trial Chamber I decided by majority to decline to confirm the charges against Mbarushimana.[1411] On 30 May 2012 the Appeals Chamber dismissed the prosecution's appeal against the decision.[1412] Mbarushimana was released from the ICC's custody on 23 December 2011.

The Prosecutor v. Jean Bosco Ntaganda

In the case of the *Prosecutor v. Jean Bosco Ntaganda*, the court issued a sealed warrant for the arrest of Ntaganda, a senior commander in Thomas Lubanga's FPLC, in August 2006: it was unsealed in April 2008. The ICC Prosecutor charged Ntaganda with three counts of war crimes related to the alleged recruitment and use of child soldiers in 2002 and 2003.[1413] Ntaganda reportedly led the *Congrès National pour la Défense du Peuple* (CNDP) in the DRC's North Kivu province. Ntaganda agreed to be integrated into the Congolese military, where he was promoted to the rank of Major-General. The DRC authorities had cited peace efforts in the Kivu region as their reason for not detaining Ntaganda on behalf of the ICC.[1414] On 13 July 2012, the Pre-Trial Chamber accepted additional charges against Ntaganda in a second arrest warrant issued following an application by the Prosecutor.

In February 2009, the government of the DRC officially refused to hand over Jean Bosco Ntaganda on the grounds that domestic peace was best served by his remaining free. DRC's Justice Minister Emmanuel-Janvier Luzolo stated that "in the judicial practice of any state, there are moments when the demands of peace override the traditional needs of justice".[1415] When the New York-based *Inner City Press* asked what Ocampo was doing to bring about the arrest of the ICC-indicted Ntaganda, given that he was openly serving with the Congolese Army and indirectly with the UN Mission in the DRC, MONUC, Ocampo merely replied he was "talking" to the government.[1416] The complicity of Western human rights organisations on this issue is also clear. When *Inner City Press* raised the Bosco issue with Richard Dicker of Human Rights Watch, he said that the Prosecutor needed to make "affirmative" statements "on this issue". As *Inner City Press* noted "But why…doesn't HRW, and groups like it, affirmatively critique Ocampo for his silence, rather than waiting for Press questions in order to do so?"[1417]

On 11 April 2012 under pressure from the ICC and certain Western countries, President Kabila called for Ntaganda's arrest.[1418] As predicted, a direct result of this was a resurgence of conflict in eastern DRC. Human Rights Watch pointed to the direct relationship between the ICC and the violence: "General Ntaganda led the mutiny following Congolese government attempts to weaken his control and increased calls for his arrest and surrender to the ICC."[1419] Heavy fighting ensued between M23 rebels and government forces in North Kivu, especially in Rutshuru and Masisi, which led to a renewed humanitarian crisis in the DRC.

In March 2013, Jean Bosco Ntaganda surrendered himself to US diplomats and he was transferred to ICC custody.

The Prosecutor v. Sylvestre Mudacumura

Sylvestre Mudacumura is alleged to be the Commander of the FDLR. On 14 May 2012, the OTP filed an application for a warrant of arrest for Mudacumura, whom it referred to as "one of the main leaders of the FDLR", for five counts of crimes against humanity and nine counts of war crimes.[1420] On 31 May 2012, Pre-Trial Chamber II issued a decision dismissing the Prosecutor's application in its entirety.[1421] Even the unredacted version of the Prosecutor's application proved unsatisfactory to the chamber: it did not contain some of the crucial pieces of information required by the chamber. The chamber noted that Article 58(2)(b)(c) of the Rome Statute requires that the Prosecutor's application for a warrant of arrest should contain both "a specific reference to the crimes within the jurisdiction of the Court which the person is alleged to have committed" and "a concise statement of the facts which are alleged to constitute those crimes".[1422] The Pre-Trial Chamber stated that "it is beyond controversy that the fundamental principles of fair trial do not allow the Chamber to establish on its own any of the connections which are missing in the Prosecutor's Application".[1423]

The OTP made a second application for a warrant of arrest on 13 June 2012.[1424] This was granted by Pre-Trial Chamber II on 13 July 2012.[1425] The Prosecutor alleged that Mudacumura was criminally responsible for committing nine counts of war crimes, from 20 January 2009 to the end of September 2010, in the context of the conflict in the Kivus, in the DRC on the basis of his individual criminal responsibility (Article 25(3)(b)) including: attacking civilians, murder, mutilation, cruel treatment, rape, torture, destruction of property, pillaging and outrages against personal dignity. It is worth noting that the court made the following observation with regard to this case:

> The Chamber notes that the Prosecutor's Application bears some similarities with the case presented in The Prosecutor v. Callixte Mbarushimana, a case where Pre-Trial Chamber I, by majority, declined to confirm the charges. This decision was upheld on appeal. However, the Chamber is of the view that the findings from Pre-Trial Chamber I in the Mbarushimana confirmation decision should not, in principle, affect the outcome of the present assessment, as this is a distinct case before a new Chamber involving a different person and a lower standard of proof.[1426]

As with the Ugandan issue, a central question with regard to the DRC was why the ICC, as a court of last resort, chose to become involved in Ituri. Phil Clark has noted that of all the conflict-affected provinces of the DRC:

> Ituri has the best-functioning local judiciary, which has already shown adeptness at investigating serious crimes, including those committed by Lubanga, Katanga and Ngudjolo. It is therefore unclear whether the ICC can adequately justify its involvement in Ituri, given the capacity of domestic institutions to investigate and prosecute major crimes. Since July 2003, the EU's Ituri-focused investment of more than US$40m. towards reforming the Congolese judiciary has seen considerable progress in local capacity.[1427]

It is also a matter of record that the major militia leaders were already in police custody and "significant evidence of crimes had already been gathered by the local civilian and military courts, working closely with MONUC".[1428] Clark concludes that "This has led observers to question the validity of the ICC's strategy in Ituri, asking why a global court has focused its energies where the judicial task is more straightforward due to substantial local capacity, while mass atrocities continue in provinces where judicial resources are severely lacking."[1429]

Clark has pointed to the blatant selectivity on several levels that is at the heart of the ICC involvement in DRC. This selectivity sought to ignore well-documented and large-scale human-rights abuses by President Kabila and his government in DRC, and by President Museveni and the Ugandan state. The ICC's choice of the Ituri district as the focus of its activities was transparently pragmatic. Clark has stated that while Ituri has seen considerable human-rights abuses, the ICC's investigations and prosecutions in Ituri were unlikely to implicate the current government: "[T]here is less clear evidence to connect President Kabila to atrocities committed in Ituri, although it is suspected that he has previously supported various rebel groups in the province, including Germain Katanga's FRPI." Clark notes that there was considerable violence in other provinces, particularly North and South Kivu and Katanga, "where government forces and Mai Mai militias backed by Kabila are directly implicated in serious crimes". The ICC chose not to pursue these abuses: "This was a crucial consideration for the ICC, as it needed to maintain good relations with Kinshasa to ensure the security of ICC investigators and other personnel working in the volatile eastern provinces." Clark was clear in his analysis of this ICC intransigence: "The ICC also wanted to avoid implicating government officials in the lead-up to Congo's first post-independence elections, held in July 2006… . This sends a message to major perpetrators that their senior political or military status will insulate them from prosecution. For the Congolese population, this spells continued impunity for the leaders most responsible for the immense harm they have suffered."[1430]

The ICC also chose to let Museveni and Uganda off the hook: "The OTP has resisted investigating the wider dimensions of Lubanga's crimes, notably the alleged training and financing of Lubanga's UPC by the Ugandan and Rwandan governments. Such investigations could implicate key figures in Kampala and Kigali, including Salim

Saleh, Ugandan President Yoweri Museveni's half-brother and a former Ugandan People's Defence Force (UPDF) commander."[1431] This policy has caused controversy within the ICC itself. In the wake of Lubanga's confirmation hearing, the Pre-Trial Chamber's 29 January 2007 ruling included an unprecedented statement that the Prosecutor's charges against Lubanga were insufficient as they failed to recognise the "international" nature of the Ituri conflict, implying the role of Uganda and Rwanda. The Prosecutor appealed to the Pre-Trial Chamber, requesting that references to crimes in the "international" conflict dimension be removed from the charges against Lubanga, as the OTP's evidence related only to crimes committed in the "internal" conflict.

Marc Glendening, the Director of ICC Watch, has also pointed this out:

> The Lubanga trial also highlights a key charge made against the ICC, namely that it is a politically motivated body and is incapable of upholding the rule of law. Mr Lubanga was referred to the ICC by DRC president Joseph Kabila, a political opponent. Officials from the Kabila regime have been active in the case against Mr Lubanga. The ICC chief prosecutor has shown no interest in investigating the numerous accusations of human rights abuses directed at the DRC government and military.[1432]

Clark has summarised the ICC's deeply questionable involvement in the DRC:

> In the Lubanga, Katanga and Ngudjolo cases, domestic authorities and MONUC had done most of the hard work of capturing the suspects and investigating their crimes. The Lubanga case, while addressing grave crimes, does not address the gravest of Lubanga's crimes for fear these would greatly complicate the judicial process. The Lubanga, Katanga and Ngudjolo cases also represent the ICC's attempts to maintain good working relations with the Congolese government in order to facilitate ICC investigations during ongoing conflict and to maintain the support of the Court's principal donors in the context of the Congolese elections and their direct aftermath. This highlights a fundamental dilemma for the ICC, which often operates in fraught political and military environments. However, the ICC's responses to this dilemma so far in the DRC have significantly undermined the Court's legitimacy among affected populations, which had hoped it would finally hold accountable those most responsible for mass atrocities.[1433]

Human Rights Watch has also noted: "Our research in Congo, covering the period from 1998 to this writing, suggests that key political and military figures in Kinshasa, as well as in Uganda and Rwanda, also played a prominent role in creating, supporting, and arming Lubanga's Union of Congolese Patriots, Katanga's Nationalist and Integrationist Front, and Ngudjolo's Ituri Patriotic Resistance Forces… . We, therefore, urge the prosecutor to investigate senior officials in Kinshasa, Kampala, and Kigali and, evidence permitting, to bring cases against them."[1434]

Clark concluded that: "Overall, it is clear that self-serving pragmatism rather than pragmatism geared to the needs of the Congolese population has been the primary consideration in the ICC's case selection to date in the DRC." It has also not escaped the attention of commentators that the ICC had brought essentially minimalist charges against Lubanga. In prosecuting Lubanga on three counts of war crimes involving children, and ignoring Lubanga's alleged involvement in a host of other serious crimes, the ICC had gone for what it saw as the easiest, softest option. Ocampo wanted a quick trial on lesser crimes rather than risk a longer, more complicated process. This was hardly the victim-orientated justice that the ICC and its many Western liberal supporters had promised victims of war crimes in particular and the international community at large. As Marlies Glasius notes: "[T]he Congolese people must marvel at the apparent priorities of international justice, putting the use of child soldiers above mass murder, torture and rape as the only one deserving of immediate prosecution."[1435]

Impartiality aside, there have also been questions about whether or not the ICC is able to offer a fair trial. These questions arose from the very start in the ICC's first case, that of Thomas Lubanga. The court has been accused of unfair treatment. Resources allocated to the defence were inadequate; his evidence and witness statements were slow to arrive and many documents are impossible to read because they were so heavily redacted by the ICC. The IBA supported concerns raised by Dyilo's legal defence team.[1436] The Council on Foreign Relations has also noted that "some in Africa are questioning the court's ability to provide justice".[1437]

The ICC's Lubanga action had negative consequences in the DRC's conflict zones. Human Rights Watch noted that militia leaders in Ituri were changing their approach to child soldiers because of the charges against Lubanga. Previously, these leaders openly admitted approximate numbers of children in their ranks and handed children over to MONUC and UNICEF as part of the demobilisation process:

> Following the confirmation of charges against Lubanga, however, many denied having any children under their command.... Children were hidden or chased from the ranks, and some were abandoned rather than being brought to the demobilization ceremonies, which is concerning. The children themselves appeared to have been briefed by their commanders to claim to be older than they actually were. One source from a child protection organization whom we interviewed reported that many children refused to admit that they were under age 18, saying "we know that you want to try our commander like you tried Lubanga." Child protection officials working in this area refer to this phenomenon as the "Lubanga syndrome." There were also threats against child protection workers by armed group leaders following Lubanga's arrest. These developments pose significant challenges to agencies working for child welfare in the region.[1438]

Even committed ICC supporters have had to concede grave mistakes on the part of the court in the DRC. Human Rights Watch: "So far...the ICC's record in DRC has been mixed, at best... . The ICC's prosecutorial strategies in DRC have also raised questions as to the ICC's independence and impartiality."[1439] Human Rights Watch went on to note that the court's behaviour "may have caused irreparable damage to perceptions about the ICC's impartiality in the DRC".[1440] The court's blunderings in the Congo may have even worse repercussions. Louis Michel, the Foreign Minister of Belgium and one of the key participants in the Congo peace process, has additionally expressed concern that the ICC's investigation could "run the risk of causing the [peace] process to implode".[1441]

The question that must be asked at the end of the day is whether justice was served by focusing on Lubanga. Commenting on Lubanga's conviction, the Prosecutor said that "[f]orcing children to be killers jeopardises the future of mankind".[1442] However, as Schabas has noted, "arguably, the justice system of the Democratic Republic of Congo was doing a better job than the Court itself, because it was addressing crimes of greater gravity".[1443] The legacy of the court's selective actions in DRC is a negative one. Far from bringing peace to the eastern Congo, its actions have most recently rekindled conflict in the east of the country.

Chapter Twenty

THE COURT AND THE CENTRAL AFRICAN REPUBLIC

"The damage to perceptions of the ICC's independence and impartiality has been compounded by the absence, so far, of ICC scrutiny of crimes committed by [CAR government forces]."

Human Rights Watch[1444]

The government of the CAR, a State Party to the ICC, referred "the situation of crimes within the jurisdiction of the Court committed anywhere on [CAR] territory" to the ICC Prosecutor in January 2005.[1445] Almost two and half years later, in May 2007, the ICC Prosecutor opened an investigation into the situation in CAR.[1446] On 23 May 2008, the ICC issued a sealed warrant of arrest for Jean-Pierre Bemba, a commander of the *Mouvement de Libération du Congo* (MLC), one of two main rebel groups active during the civil war in the DRC. He is a former vice-president of the DRC.

On 24 May 2008, Bemba was arrested by Belgian authorities and transferred to the ICC's detention centre in The Hague in July 2008. Bemba appeared for the first time before the court on 4 July. The confirmation of charges hearing began on 12 January 2009. On 15 June 2009 the court confirmed two counts of crimes against humanity (rape and murder) and three counts of war crimes (rape, murder and pillaging) against Bemba, and sent his case to trial. The crimes were allegedly committed in the CAR from 26 October 2002 to 15 March 2003. The Bemba trial opened on 22 November 2010. On 20 March 2012, the last of forty prosecution witnesses was presented. On 1 May 2012, victims party to the case began to testify. On 14 August, Bemba's legal team began to present its defence, commenced the presentation of its evidence and called its first witnesses. Proceedings were suspended for several weeks in September and October 2012 due to the non-appearance of two witnesses.

The court's approach in the Chad situation has been very questionable. Aprodec asbl, a Belgian organisation that defends Congolese citizens, officially complained to ICC judges with regard to the Bemba case, citing "conflicts of interest, biased behavior and selective and discriminatory criminal proceedings" on the part of the ICC Prosecutor. The organisation was particularly shocked at the manner in which the Prosecutor sought to collect victim stories: "upon arriving in the Central African Republic, the investigators of the prosecutor's office have sought out exclusively victims for evidence against the MLC soldiers...radio and TV spots called on people who had been victims of the MLC soldiers to come forward. The Prosecutor should instead look out for all victims testimonies from all belligerents involved, without any a priori, keeping a neutral approach without exceptions or exclusions."[1447]

In 2002–03, local human rights organisations affiliated with the International Federation for Human Rights alleged widespread violence committed by all parties and called for the investigation of serious crimes in the capital.[1448] The ICC alleged that Bemba had directed attacks on civilians in CAR territory between October 2002 and March 2003, having reportedly been invited into CAR by then President Ange-Félix Patassé to help quell a rebellion led by François Bozizé. Bemba had served from 2003 to 2006 as one of four vice-presidents in the DRC transitional government. In the 2006 presidential elections Bemba won forty-two per cent of the vote, losing to the incumbent President Joseph Kabila. Elected to the senate in 2007, Bemba left the DRC to live in exile in Europe. His trial began in The Hague in November 2010.[1449] President Kabila and the ICC have been suspected of political collusion in Bemba's arrest. Human Rights Watch reported that some of those it had interviewed "were of the opinion that the prosecutor's decision to open an investigation in the CAR in May 2007, nearly three years after the CAR referred the situation there to the ICC, was to pursue Jean-Pierre Bemba, a political rival of President Kabila who had been defeated in the 2006 presidential elections".[1450] This would support claims that the ICC had a secret working relationship with the governments of the DRC and the CAR.

Human Rights Watch noted:

> [T]here is a perception in the DRC that the prosecutor targeted Bemba because he wanted the cooperation of Congolese President Joseph Kabila in the ICC's investigations in DRC. Bemba was Kabila's chief political rival in DRC at the time of his arrest, which closely followed attacks against him and his supporters in Kinshasa. The damage to perceptions of the ICC's independence and impartiality has been compounded by the absence, so far, of ICC scrutiny of crimes committed by Bozizé's own troops. This echoes the shortcomings of the ICC's approach to DRC and Uganda, where security forces affiliated with the referring government appear to have avoided ICC scrutiny.[1451]

The ICC's involvement in CAR attracted concern and criticism from the start. Credible observers noted that "CAR's president François Bozizé...is inextricably linked with the violence the ICC is investigating, having led a failed coup against then-president Ange-Felix Patassé in 2002. Bozizé...won power in 2003 after a protracted and bloody struggle, which involved civilians in and around the capital Bangui being killed and raped, with a pattern of widespread sexual violence, perpetrated by armed men, a central feature of the conflict."[1452] Human Rights Watch has also confirmed that government troops – particularly those in the presidential guard – have carried out hundreds of unlawful killings and have burned thousands of homes in their anti-rebel activities. These government actions have forced tens of thousands to flee their villages.[1453] Human Rights Watch has noted that "[t]he majority of these crimes were allegedly committed by forces affiliated with the government that voluntarily referred crimes to the ICC".[1454]

Amnesty International also felt it necessary to note with reference to the ICC in the CAR that "prosecutors must investigate individuals in the current government who continue to commit atrocities with impunity. The ICC has so far failed to demonstrate that being in power is not a basis for enjoying impunity. This has been the case in DRC and Uganda, with regard to suspects in positions of power."[1455] Human Rights Watch noted that in the ICC's decision to open an investigation in the CAR, "the prosecutor stated that his office continues to monitor violence and crimes being committed in the northern areas of the country bordering Chad and Sudan". Despite these assurances, the only person facing trial for abuses within the CAR was Jean-Pierre Bemba. Indeed, during Bemba's trial and shortly before Patassé's death, the Prosecutor-General of CAR, Firmin Feindiro, testified at Bemba's trial that a national investigation had implicated both Bemba and Patassé in war crimes, though neither was tried in the country itself.[1456] There was considerable pressure for the ICC to investigate government officials.[1457]

Human Rights Watch said that the ICC's involvement in the CAR "has added to concerns about the court's independence and impartiality, and its commitment to do meaningful justice for crimes committed in both CAR and DRC". The organisation called on the ICC to "revisit its strategy for CAR and begin additional investigations, or communicate clearly to the affected communities and the broader public its reasons for concluding that no further cases should be brought at this time".[1458]

Through its inaction the ICC has afforded *de facto* impunity for those committing crimes against humanity and war crimes. In June 2010, for example, the International War Crimes Report Project stated with regard to the CAR that "[t]he population continues to suffer widespread human rights abuses on a systematic scale". It added that "human rights abuses including summary executions and unlawful killings, beatings, house burnings, rape, extortion and unlawful taxation and the recruitment and use of child soldiers are still widespread" in the CAR, and that there is "little action to ensure accountability for the crimes committed has been taken".[1459] The report placed on record that:

> In Bangui and a number of other towns, civilians find themselves at the mercy of brutal and ill-trained security forces. The Presidential Guard in particular has been implicated in a number of cases of rape, arbitrary arrest, and assault. Outside of Bangui, human rights violations are intertwined with the conflict… the Central African Armed Forces and the Presidential Guard are responsible for the majority of the abuses, in particular the burning of houses in retaliation for rebel attacks, as well as summary executions and unlawful killings, looting and forced displacement. Rape has also become quasi institutionalised within militia groups and the military.

The report also noted:

[A]rmed forces present in the country are often some of the worst human rights offenders. Despite their training by the FOMUC (Force of the Economic and Monetary Community of Central Africa), the FACA (Forces Armées Centrafricaines) and the GP (Garde Présidentielle) remain renowned for their abusive behaviour and habit of attacking civilians in retaliation for rebel advances. The FACA and GP in particular seem immune from prosecution as they are left to carry out beatings, lootings and summary killings of civilians in total impunity. The absence of prosecution for rape by the FACA and GP is particularly worrying. While a number of cases have been brought to court, they have systematically been dismissed. Unless the Government takes immediate action to put an end to this culture of impunity, human rights violations will continue to take place on a widespread scale.[1460]

The ICC remains both silent and selective in its approach to "justice" in the CAR.

The ICC's claim that its involvement in Africa serves to deter violence continues to ring hollow. The CAR is no exception. In March 2013, for example, an alliance of rebel groups known as Seleka forced President Francois Bozizé and his forces out of the capital. Justin Kombo Moustapha, Secretary-General of Seleka, announced that the "Central African Republic has just opened a new page in its history. The political committee of the Seleka coalition, made up of Central Africans of all kinds, calls on the population to remain calm and to prepare to welcome the revolutionary forces of Seleka."[1461] Rebel leader Michel Djotodia declared himself President on 25 March. Djotodia had already served as Defence Minister since the formation of the national unity government in January 2013.[1462] In July the UN declared CAR's entire 4.6 million population to be victims and the country among its most dangerous destinations.[1463] By October 2013, at least 440,000 people – nearly ten per cent of the country's population – were said to have been displaced in the violence following Bozizé's overthrow.[1464]

Chapter Twenty-one

THE COURT AND SUDAN

"There's one big problem with [the ICC and Darfur]: Most of the perpetrators in Darfur can't be tried before the ICC because Sudan hasn't ratified the court's founding statute. The panel's failure to admit this limitation is staggering."

Stéphanie Giry, international lawyer[1465]

"In the absence of law and evidence, we have the theatrics."

Alex de Waal[1466]

The one country that has become most associated with the ICC has been Sudan, with a particular focus on the conflict in Sudan's western region of Darfur. Given the resultant international attention on this conflict and the ICC's claims of genocide it is useful to examine the situation in some detail. The war in Darfur began in February 2003, when two armed groups, the Justice and Equality Movement (*harakat al-adil walmusawah*, JEM) and the Sudan Liberation Army (*jeish tahrir as-sudan*, SLA), launched attacks on policemen, government garrisons and civilians in the area. Darfur presents a very complex situation with very complex problems.[1467] Rebel claims that the war is simply about marginalisation of their communities have been contradicted by reputable, independent observers such as Ghazi Suleiman, Sudan's most prominent human rights activist. He has been described by Reuters as "a prominent non-partisan political figure".[1468] Suleiman has stated: "The conflict in Darfur has nothing to do with marginalisation or the inequitable distribution of wealth. Inherently it is a struggle between the two factions of the Sudanese Islamist movement, the (opposition) Popular Congress party and the ruling National Congress (party)."[1469]

The Darfur conflict has been fought between the government of Sudan and a number of rebel groups, initially two and now perhaps up to twenty-four different factions.[1470] It has been described by Alex de Waal in the following terms:

> Darfur is a typical north-east African civil war, consisting of multiple overlapping conflicts interspersed with large-scale offensives by the

government army and its proxies and rebels. During 2001–2003, local disputes were exacerbated by the breakdown of local governance and combined with the ambitions of a frustrated provincial elite to fuel an insurgency, which escalated more quickly and bloodily than either side anticipated.[1471]

Sadly, what de Waal is saying is that the war itself is nothing out of the ordinary. It is a typical civil war. While there can be no simple analysis of the conflict, the issue has also been caught up in the inevitable propaganda war invariably associated with all war, and particularly civil war. Simply put, this propaganda war has clouded and distorted international perspectives on Darfur. This in turn has unjustifiably pushed governments into corners and continues to hinder international attempts to negotiate an end to the crisis. A clear example of this is the action by the ICC. As one British commentator has observed, "There is no civil war so bad that it cannot be made worse by the intervention of Western liberals."[1472] The government has stated that 10,000 people have been killed in the fighting. The ICC claims that there have been 35,000 violent deaths.[1473]

By 2006 the Darfur conflict had slowed down considerably – certainly when compared to the deaths per month being recorded in 2004. The conflict had changed from a war of manoeuvre into banditry, inter-tribal raiding and hit-and-run rebel attacks on aid convoys. Mortality levels in Darfur, especially within the IDP camps, have dramatically improved since the early day of the conflict. The *Los Angeles Times* reported in August 2007, for example, that UN figures showed the mortality rate in Darfur at about 0.35 deaths daily per 10,000 people, a rate that is "near, or perhaps even below, the region's pre-conflict level. In sub-Saharan Africa, 0.44 deaths daily per 10,000 people is a common baseline." A *Médecins Sans Fontières* doctor noted "[p]eople in Darfur are now getting better healthcare than people in other parts of Sudan, such as the east and central regions", and better than in Khartoum.[1474] This improvement was because of an unprecedented effort by the international community, UN agencies and non-governmental organisations. De Waal and Julie Flint, another long-time critic of the Khartoum government, observed in 2007 that "for the past two years, mortality rates among people reached by international aid have been lower than they were before the war. That's a tremendous achievement."[1475] Flint further noted that Darfur mortality levels are lower than in the Sudanese capital, and that "in southern Sudan, where conflict is stilled, children have higher death rates and lower school enrolment".[1476]

The *Los Angeles Times* reported, for example, UN figures that showed violence-related casualties in 2007 averaged 100 to 200 per month: civilian casualties were down seventy per cent in the first half of 2007, compared with the same period last year.[1477] And 2007's casualty figures in turn were much less than 2006's and vastly reduced in comparison with 2004. The respected British journalist Jonathan Steele noted: "Far more civilians are dying from Nato airstrikes in Afghanistan."[1478] In August 2009, General Martin Agwai, the outgoing Head of UNAMID, said Darfur now suffered more from "security issues" than full-blown conflict. "Banditry, localised issues, people trying to resolve issues over water and land at a local level. But real war as such, I think we are over that," he said. General Agwai said that the real problem in Darfur was political.[1479]

Due in large part to pressure from anti-Sudanese domestic lobby groups within the USA, the US administration pushed for action against the Sudanese government. American pressure at the UNSC saw the creation of the International Commission of Inquiry on Darfur (ICID) pursuant to Security Council Resolution 1564 (2004), adopted on 18 September 2004. The five-member body, chaired by Italian jurist Antonio Cassese, was appointed by the Secretary-General in October 2004. The commission was tasked "to investigate reports of violations of international humanitarian law and human rights by all parties" and "to determine also whether or not acts of genocide have occurred". It was requested to report back to the Secretary-General by January 2005. The commission reported that while there had been serious violations of human rights in Darfur, genocide had not occurred.[1480]

The Sudanese government established its own national commission of inquiry into human-rights violations in Darfur in 2004. This commission also published its report in January 2005. Established by presidential decree and chaired by a former chief justice of Sudan, the commission visited Darfur on several occasions and spent several months taking evidence from hundreds of witnesses. The national commission also found that there was no evidence to support allegations of genocide in Darfur. The commission found that there had been grave violations of human rights and recommended the establishment of a judicial commission to investigate, indict and try those responsible for crimes in Darfur. It also recommended the setting up of compensation and administrative commissions to assist with reconciliation within Darfur.[1481]

The special criminal court on the events in Darfur

On 7 June 2005, the Chief Justice and President of the Supreme Court in Sudan established by decree the Special Criminal Court on the Events in Darfur (SCCED). The court was created following the recommendation of the Sudanese National Commission of Inquiry. Its mandate was to investigate and prosecute crimes committed in the course of the conflict in Darfur. The Sudanese government stated that they refused to extradite Sudanese nationals to be tried abroad, and that Sudan's judiciary has sole jurisdiction over crimes in Darfur.[1482] The special criminal court was originally established as a single court sitting in al-Fashir, the capital of North Darfur (the court would subsequently sit in all three Darfur state capitals, Nyala, al-Fashir and Geneina, the capitals respectively South Darfur, North Darfur and West Darfur). The decree establishing this court gave it jurisdiction over the following: "(a) Acts which constitute crimes in accordance with the Sudanese Penal Code and other penal codes; (b) Any charges submitted to it by the Committee established pursuant to the decision of the Minister of Justice No. 3/2005 of 19 January 2005 concerning investigations into the violations cited in the report of the [Sudanese government's] Commission of Inquiry; (c) Any charges pursuant to any other law, as determined by the Chief Justice."[1483] The special court's jurisdiction was subsequently broadened in late November and December 2005 to include "international humanitarian law".

Additionally, on 18 September 2005, the government established a Special Prosecution for Crimes against Humanity Office in Khartoum. This office is tasked with "exercising the powers provided for in the Criminal Procedures Act, 1991, the international humanitarian law, the international conventions to which the Sudan is party and any other relevant law in relation to crimes against humanity and any other crimes stated in any other law and which infringes upon (constitutes a threat to) the security and safety of humanity".[1484] While based in Khartoum it has worked closely with the special courts in Darfur. The government announced that 160 people were to appear before the special court.[1485] The trials have progressed.

It is worth noting that Human Rights Watch complained in 2006 that after one year of existence, "only a small number of people have been brought before the SCCED".[1486] Yet, the same sort of criticism by Human Rights Watch has been noticeably absent with regard to the ICC. The ICC's first case, for allegedly recruiting child soldiers – a charge less serious than many of the cases that have been prosecuted by the SCCED – was only completed in 2012. It took three years for the ICC's first case to even come to trial. Once again, the double-standards of the Western human rights industry are all too clear.

On 31 March 2005, following on from a recommendation by the Cassese commission, the fact that Sudan is a non-state party notwithstanding, the UNSC passed Resolution 1593 (2005) referring the prosecution of those allegedly responsible for atrocities committed in Darfur to the ICC.[1487] The resolution was adopted by a vote of eleven in favour, none against, and with four abstentions – the USA, China, Algeria, and Brazil.[1488] Hans Köchler noted that "Resolution 1593…has once more documented that the Security Council's decisions are mainly shaped by international power politics and that the Council's statutory relations with the International Criminal Court are prone to abuse in favour of the political agenda of the most powerful member state."[1489]

In recommending that the Security Council refer the situation in Darfur to the ICC, the UN Commission of Inquiry on Darfur claimed that there would be several benefits from such a referral: the prosecution of the crimes would be conducive to peace and security in Darfur; the ICC, as the "only truly international institution of criminal justice" would ensure justice is done because the ICC sits in The Hague, far from the alleged perpetrators' spheres of influence; the cumulative authority of the ICC and the Security Council would be required to compel those leaders responsible for atrocities to acquiesce to investigation and potential prosecution; the court was the "best suited organ for ensuring a veritably fair trial of those indicted by the Court Prosecutor" owing to its international composition and established rules of procedure; it was claimed that the work of the ICC would not necessarily involve a significant financial burden for the international community; and, finally, it was also claimed as a benefit that the ICC could be activated immediately, without any delay.[1490] Of all of these, only the last assertion might go without challenge. Far from being conducive to peace, it endangers and obstructs peace; the authority and legitimacy of the ICC and the UNSC has been fatally undermined by the behaviour of the court and its first Chief Prosecutor; the ICC has also become a byword for legal incompetence and at a cost of half a billion euros had by then already become an expensive white elephant.

The ICC Chief Prosecutor informed the UN General Assembly in October 2006 that the court had started pre-trial investigations, including more than fifty visits to fifteen countries and the screening of almost 500 potential witnesses. The ICC had also visited Khartoum on three occasions to assess national proceedings, although it must be noted that they never left the Hilton Hotel. Ocampo claimed that the ICC was unable to open an office in Darfur, and its office in Chad had been temporarily closed in 2006 due to violence.

On 27 February 2007, Ocampo announced that he would ask the pre-trial chamber of the ICC to issue summonses against two Sudanese nationals, Ahmed Muhammad Haroun, a former minister of state for the interior of the government of Sudan, subsequently Minister of State for humanitarian affairs and then Governor of South Kordofan, and Ali Muhammad Ali Abd-Al-Rahman, also known as Ali Kushayb, an alleged militia leader. The application stated that the OTP had concluded that there were reasonable grounds to believe that these two persons bore criminal responsibility for crimes against humanity and war crimes committed in Darfur in 2003 and 2004. The summonses were ignored.

On 27 April 2007, the court issued warrants of arrest for alleged crimes against humanity and war crimes for Haroun and Ali Kushayb.[1491] The allegations in the Prosecutor v. Ahmad Muhammad Harun ("Ahmad Harun") and Ali Muhammad Ali Abd-Al-Rahman ("Ali Kushayb") claimed that Haroun was criminally responsible for forty-two counts on the basis of his individual criminal responsibility under Articles 25(3)(b) and 25(3)(d) of the Rome Statute, including: twenty counts of crimes against humanity: murder (Article 7(1)(a)); persecution (Article 7(1)(h)); forcible transfer of population (Article 7(1)(d)); rape (Article 7(1)(g)); inhumane acts (Article 7(1)(k)); imprisonment or severe deprivation of liberty (Article 7(1)(e)); and torture (Article 7(1)(f)); and twenty-two counts of war crimes: murder (Article 8(2)(c)(i)); attacks against the civilian population (Article 8(2)(e)(i)); destruction of property (Article 8(2)(e)(xii)); rape (Article 8(2)(e)(vi)); pillaging (Article 8(2)(e)(v)); and outrage upon personal dignity (Article 8(2)(c)(ii)). The court alleged that Kushayb was criminally responsible for fifty counts on the basis of his individual criminal responsibility under Articles 25(3)(a) and 25(3)(d) of the Rome Statute, including: twenty-two counts of crimes against humanity: murder (Article 7(1)(a)); deportation or forcible transfer of population (Article 7(1)(d)); imprisonment or other severe deprivation of physical liberty in violation of fundamental rules of international law (Article 7(1)(e)); torture (Article 7(1)(f)); persecution (Article 7(1)(h)); and inhumane acts of inflicting serious bodily injury and suffering (Article 7(1)(k)). The court also listed twenty-eight counts of war crimes: violence to life and person (Article 8(2)(c)(i)); outrage upon personal dignity, in particular humiliating and degrading treatment (Article 8(2)(c)(ii)); intentionally directing an attack against a civilian population (Article 8(2)(e)(i)); pillaging (Article 8(2)(e)(v)); rape (Article 8(2)(e)(vi)); and destroying or seizing property (Article 8(2)(e)(xii)).

By way of response, Sudan's Justice Minister Mohamed Ali al-Mardi stated: "We do not recognize the International Criminal Court…and we will not hand over any Sudanese even from the rebel groups who take up weapons against the government."[1492]

The Chief Prosecutor's application for an arrest warrant for President al-Bashir

On 14 July 2008, the ICC Prosecutor accused Sudanese President Omar al-Bashir of genocide, crimes against humanity and war crimes.[1493] Ocampo had trailed this indictment for some time before the announcement. Even before the indictment of President al-Bashir, Julie Flint and de Waal noted that "Chief prosecutor Luis Moreno-Ocampo's approach is fraught with risk – for the victims of the atrocities in Darfur, for the prospects for peace in Sudan and for the prosecution itself."[1494] While addressing the Security Council on 5 June 2008, Ocampo spoke of Darfur being a vast, single crime scene where "the entire Sudanese state apparatus" has been mobilised "to physically and mentally destroy entire communities". Flint and de Waal stated that in so doing Ocampo described a Darfur "we do not recognise". They disagreed with his comparison of Sudan with Nazi Germany. While they saw "grave continuing violations of human rights" in Darfur, they said that they did "not see evidence for the two-stage plan Ocampo described".[1495]

The Chief Prosecutor's public application for an arrest warrant against Sudanese President Omar al Bashir was on ten counts: three of genocide, five of crimes against humanity and two of war crimes. Ocampo's application dwelt on the genocide charges: the other seven counts against Bashir were dealt with almost in passing. The genocide charges were said to cover the entire period of the conflict since early 2003 until the present and specifically referred to the Fur, Masalit and Zaghawa tribes. Ocampo claimed not only genocidal intent but also a central genocidal plan.[1496] He claimed a criminal conspiracy within the Sudanese government to destroy the Fur, Masalit and Zaghawa tribes of Darfur, the first stage of which being the fighting in 2003–04, and the second the destruction of the IDP camps that subsequently housed these communities. William Schabas referred to Ocampo's genocide charge as "spectacular and extravagant".[1497] Commenting on the Prosecutor's 14 July 2008 press conference at which Ocampo announced his public application for an arrest warrant against President al-Bashir, de Waal was also aghast at the inclusion of the genocide charges:

> I came out of the press conference in a state of shock. He painted a picture no scholar would recognise. He was basically calling for regime change, making a political statement, which is surprising coming from the chief prosecutor of the ICC. By presenting his case in such stark terms, the prosecutor has made it easy for his critics to dismiss him as ill-informed and driven by a desire for publicity, and has made it harder for the advocates of justice in Darfur to pursue the challenge of calling to account those responsible for crimes no less heinous than genocide.[1498]

He further noted that "[i]n the absence of law and evidence, we have the theatrics".[1499] Alex de Waal went on to produce the most detailed critique yet of the public application. The Prosecutor claimed that President Bashir has headed a government that has been responsible for crimes committed by those who profess their loyalty to him and yet "Moreno Ocampo succeeded in accusing Bashir of the crime for which he is not guilty. That is a remarkable feat."[1500] De Waal states that the public application was "a document that shows the hallmarks of having been hastily put together and poorly edited". He also referred to the "poor technical quality of the document, purely in terms of the extent to which it has been copy-edited and fact-checked. Although the Prosecutor announced the Application at a press conference on 14 July, the document itself was not released to the public until September. In the meantime, many pages of errata were added. This indicates that the document was not ready in final version at the time when the Application was announced."[1501]

De Waal points out that "some rudimentary ethnographic errors mar the text and raise the question of the OTP's competence in this regard".[1502] One ethnographic issue not addressed by Ocampo is that the Fur, Masalit and Zaghawa tribes are just three of a number of African tribes that have been caught up in the Darfur conflict. Would an anti-African genocide not have included all African tribes and not just three of them? De Waal also points to factual mistakes in the public application. One example were allegations made at paragraph 233 that on 5 May 2008, the Sudanese armed forces launched an aerial attack on the town of Shigeg Karo: "They dropped approximately 30 bombs on the market and near the primary school, killing 11 civilians, including 7 children and wounding 27 civilians, including 4 children and 2 women." De Waal notes: "The bombing of Shigeg Karo on 5 May 2008 was initially but erroneously reported by activists and the media as an aerial attack on a school in which schoolchildren were killed and injured. Subsequent UN investigations discovered, first, that the intended target for the attack might have been a JEM armed column that was in the vicinity (and which participated in the attack on the national capital five days later), and second, that the school was not in fact hit and children were not among the badly wounded, who were only adults." He further points out that the Prosecutor's use of the incorrect version of events, indicated "the Prosecutor's reliance on quick turnaround reports from advocacy organizations rather than more rigorous investigations. The incident may be a war crime (use of excessive force and failure to take precautions to prevent civilian fatalities), but it did not occur as described by the Prosecutor."[1503] Conor Foley supports de Waal's claims: "[Ocampo] gives the impression of someone who may cut corners on legal preparation, fails to think strategies through to their logical conclusion and is influenced by the media rather than evidence-driven."[1504]

Ocampo's theory of state-directed genocidal intent immediately ran up against facts. One immediate difficulty was that it had been previously discounted by the UN Commission of Inquiry into Darfur, which had noted in 2005 that "one central element appears to be missing, at least as far as the central Government authorities are concerned: genocidal intent. Generally speaking the policy of attacking, killing and forcibly displacing members of some tribes does not evince a specific intent to annihilate, in whole or in part, a group distinguished on racial, ethnic, national or religious grounds."[1505]

And as de Waal points out, the application cites as evidence for the genocide of African communities that General Ismat al-Zain said that during military operations "numerous small villages would be overrun".[1506] Yet this is the same General Ismat who as Officer commanded the Western Command armed volunteers from *all* tribes to try to counter the rebellion on a non-ethnic basis. This is confirmed by Darfurian commentator Ali Haggar, who noted, "Shortly after the SLA attacked al Fashir in April 2003, the Sudan Armed Forces began a major recruitment drive for the Popular Defence Forces. Both Arab and non-Arab tribes were targeted."[1507] Julie Flint has also noted: "In the first months [of the Darfur conflict], General Ismat al-Zain, head of western command, armed Arabs and non-Arabs alike."[1508] It is somewhat unbelievable that those committing genocide would have actively sought to militarily train and arm the very communities it was intending to exterminate. The question that must be asked, given Ocampo's comparison, is did the Nazis arm Jewish civilian communities? Did the Hutu extremists arm Tutsi communities before they attacked them with genocidal intent? Short of saying that the vast majority of Darfurians are suffering from some sort of collective "false consciousness", it is impossible for Ocampo and the ICC to explain away this simple fact.

Geoffrey Nice observed that "the labelling of genocide for what happened in Darfur is highly controversial…whatever else it was…it wasn't genocide".[1509] Conor Foley was sceptical about Ocampo's motivation for the genocide claim: "I fear that the prosecution of Sudan's president has more to do with politics and media strategy than evidence of genocide." He has also questioned the timing of the genocide allegations, pointing out that the ILO judgment regarding Ocampo's abuse of procedure following allegations of sexual misconduct was released on 9 July 2008. The following day, 10 July 2008, Ocampo told the *Washington Post* that he intended to "seek an arrest warrant Monday for Sudanese President Omar Hassan al-Bashir, charging him with genocide and crimes against humanity". Foley states that "[t]he timing of these two announcements could be entirely coincidental".[1510] Chris Blattman, a political scientist with extensive experience in northern Uganda, and hostile to the Sudanese government, has also queried the motivation for the indictments: "[They] are a blunt instrument wielded by a narrowly focused and unelected body, the ICC, fighting for its existence and relevance (and trying to make up for a number of bungles)."[1511]

Several credible commentators were very critical of Ocampo's claims that the displacement of Fur, Masalit and Zaghawa ethnic groups into internally displaced persons (IDP) camps constituted a genocidal attempt to destroy them through "causing serious bodily and mental harm – through rapes, tortures and forced displacement in traumatizing conditions – and deliberately inflicting on a substantial part of these groups conditions of life calculated to bring about their physical destruction, in particular by obstructing the delivery of humanitarian assistance". This assertion was first publicly aired by the Prosecutor in his December 2007 statement to the UNSC, repeated in June 2008 and then incorporated into his application.

De Waal responded to Ocampo's claim about the IDP camps being the focus of genocide: "Those with even a passing familiarity with one of the world's largest humanitarian operations laugh off the idea that we are seeing the continuation of a policy of eradication."[1512] He points out that "The target groups are, of course, assisted in the IDP camps in what has been for several years the largest humanitarian operation in the world.

The fact of this assistance would seem to contradict any eliminationist agenda. This was also pointed out in the ICID report authored by Antonio Cassese."[1513] De Waal stated that should the case come to court, one would expect the defence to put the argument: "[W]hy should a man with genocidal intent allow such a huge humanitarian operation to assist the targets of his destruction? Since 2005, data for mortality and nutrition indicate near-normal levels in the majority of the camps.... Much of the credit for this can go to the 12,000 humanitarian workers (most of them Sudanese, including government officials) who work in Darfur, chiefly in the camps." De Waal concluded: "Comparisons with the Warsaw Ghetto would not be appropriate."[1514]

Rony Brauman, the President of the French NGO *Médecins Sans Fontières* from 1982 to 1994, has also been very critical of Ocampo's statement that the refugee camps were sites where the genocide was being perpetrated. *Médecins Sans Fontières* were active throughout Darfur for most if not all of the conflict. Brauman dismissed Ocampo's claim as "insane" and "intellectual incontinence".[1515] Brauman also challenged Ocampo's claim that there had been an intention on the part of the Sudanese government to exterminate the peoples of Darfur: "If it was the case, how is one to understand the fact that two million Darfuris have sought refuge around the principal army garrisons of their province? How is one to understand the fact that one million of them live in Khartoum, where they have never been bothered during the entire course of the war? How is one to understand the fact that an enormous humanitarian apparatus has been put in place that has permitted thousands of lives to be saved? Can one seriously imagine Tutsis seeking refuge in areas controlled by the Rwandan army in 1994 or Jews seeking refuge with the Wehrmacht in 1943?"[1516] It is unfortunate for the ICC and its reputation that its Chief Prosecutor was given to such obvious hyperbole. It has gone hand-in-hand with similar exaggerations. In June 2008, for example, Ocampo once again compared the Sudanese state to the Nazi regime in Germany: "We've seen it before. The Nazi regime invoked its national sovereignty to attack its own population, and then crossed borders to attack people in other countries."[1517]

The ICC Pre-Trial Chamber declined to include genocide charges when it issued the first arrest warrant for al-Bashir. The Prosecutor appealed the decision on the basis that the Trial Chamber had used an inappropriate standard of proof in declining to include the genocide charges. In a March 2010 ruling, the Appeals Chamber agreed and instructed the Pre-Trial Chamber to reconsider the charges. On 12 July 2010, the Pre-Trial Chamber issued a second arrest warrant on charges of genocide.[1518]

Ocampo's mortality claims versus reality

In December 2008, speaking before the UNSC, Ocampo claimed that 5,000 Darfurians were dying per month in IDP camps. This was presented as evidence of a "continuing" genocide.[1519] Two months later, on 6 February 2009, Ocampo publicly repeated this claim at Yale University. Not only did Ocampo's claims simply not match reality, but they continued to reflect the shallowness of his Darfur genocide claims in general.

Coincidentally, in the same month as Ocampo's claims at Yale, the Genocide

Intervention Network (GI-Net) – a particularly active critic of the Sudanese government – published its analysis of fatalities due to violence in Darfur, based on available reports from 1 January to 8 September 2008.[1520] Working with GI-Net, Alex de Waal cross-checked the GI-Net figures with the UNAMID incident dataset, and extended the analysis up to the end of 2008. He noted that there was a very good match between the two datasets, and that all major incidents had been included: he stated that the level of monitoring in most areas of Darfur was sufficiently good that few deaths escaped notice. GI-Net gave a total figure of 1,211 violent deaths between 1 January and 8 September 2008, an average of 150 per month. The UNAMID dataset had a total figure of 1,551 reported violent deaths for the 2008 calendar year, an average of 130 per month. These figures included the deaths of hundreds of combatants. The UNAMID dataset indicated that sixty IDPs were killed in fighting in the course of 2008.[1521]

The October 2009 Darfur report published by the AU's high-level panel on Darfur also contained an analysis of data for violent fatalities in Darfur. It stated that "two independent sources of data were used to produce a merged dataset". The sources were the UNAMID Joint Mission Analysis Centre and the other an open source search in the public realm. The data provided estimates for total fatalities between January 2008 and July 2009 "in the range of 2,112 – 2,429". The open source data produced a higher figure. The AU figures showed that ninety IDPs had died in the nineteen months studied, which amounted to a month average of 4.7 fatalities.[1522] This contrasts somewhat with Ocampo's claim of 5,000 deaths per month.

The comparison is a clear one to make. By virtue of his own arithmetic Ocampo cites as evidence for his allegation of genocide in Darfur that 64,000 people were killed by the government in 2008. UNAMID, the joint UN-AU peace-keeping mission in Darfur, however, states that 1,551 people died in 2008, several hundred of whom were combatants, dozens were bandits and some were civilians. The UNAMID figures are also very similar to figures produced by the Genocide Intervention Network.

In a cable on 11 December 2008, the US Embassy in Sudan reported a meeting with UNAMID's Joint Special Representative Rodolphe Adada. In a section headlined "Ocampo's imaginary numbers", the cable stated that Adada poured scorn on the "wildly inaccurate" statements of ICC Prosecutor Luis Moreno Ocampo that "5,000 people were being killed each month in Darfur". He asked who would be so naive and ill-informed to believe such a thing? "He mused that such patently absurd and false information put out by Ocampo doesn't make him look very credible in the eyes of those who actually know something about the reality of Darfur."[1523]

It is useful to examine the Darfur mortality issue in some depth. Observers are fortunate that there has been an unprecedented focus on the humanitarian situation in Darfur. The crisis in Darfur peaked in 2004, and mortality levels were stabilised shortly afterwards. In its 2004 year-end report, the Office of the United Nations Resident and Humanitarian Coordinator for the Sudan reported that the ninety-day humanitarian action plan, from June to August 2004, coordinated with the government, had been a success. It further reported that "by 31 December 2004 the humanitarian situation for most of the 2.2 million people affected…stabilized… . The catastrophic mortality figures predicted by some quarters have not materialised."[1524] The UN reported that a June 2005 mortality survey showed that "the crude mortality rate was 0.8 deaths per 10,000 people per day in all three states of Darfur". This was "below the critical threshold" of one death per 10,000 people per day. A year earlier, a similar survey showed crude mortality rates three times higher. As of September 2005 there were 184 fixed health centres in Darfur with an additional 36 mobile centres. The UN noted: "75% of accessible hospitals had been rehabilitated, providing free access to 70% of the IDPs and conflict affected population."[1525] The situation continued to improve with UN agencies and UNAMID have documented that war-related deaths in 2008–09 were perhaps 150 per month. Ocampo's claims were incontrovertibly false.

Uganda and Darfur compared

It is perhaps useful by way of testing the intellectual consistency of Ocampo's claims about "genocide" in Darfur to compare the conditions in IDP camps in Darfur with those in northern Uganda. Both are the consequence of insurgency and counter-insurgency, they are in neighbouring countries, and they have been the focus of the international humanitarian community. The ICC states that it has also focused on both situations. And as both crises have overlapped chronologically one can also make direct time-line comparisons. At the beginning of 2003 there were over 2.6 million people in IDP camps in the north of Uganda: there are currently over 1.7 million people still languishing in these IDP camps.[1526]

The Rt. Rev. Macleord Baker Ochola II was the Anglican Bishop of Kitgum in the heart of northern Uganda. In 2006 he referred to "the genocide that has been unfolding in Northern Uganda for the last 20 years, while the whole world turns a blind eye to it". Bishop Ochola quite clearly accused President Museveni's government of genocide by way of attrition within the IDP camps in northern Uganda: "The Government of Uganda has also used violence to force a majority of the population into the Internally Displaced People's (IDP) camps. The harassment and forcing of the people into the IDP camps started in 1996 in Gulu. As result, many people have lost their lives due to the conditions of congestion in the IDP camps." Bishop Ochola was clear about what had been happening in northern Uganda:

> As for what is happening in Northern Uganda for the last 20 years, it is nothing less than genocide in the truest sense of the word.... It is genocide against humanity.... The question is, why such an unspeakable, unbelievable, and unimaginable situation has been allowed to prevail in Northern Uganda for the last 20 years? The fact that inhuman and appalling conditions in the IDP camps have been killing the children of Northern Uganda at the rate of over 1000 children per week for over a decade, is clear evidence of deliberate genocide against humanity in Northern Uganda by the NRA/M Government in power in Uganda today.

Ochola stated that "the Government of Uganda has been unable and unwilling to improve the inhuman conditions it has created for the children of Northern Uganda in the IDP camps for over a decade now. The Government of Uganda deliberately refused to implement a unanimous resolution passed by Parliament of Uganda in 2004 to declare Northern Uganda a disaster area. On many occasions the Government of Uganda deliberately derailed the peace process in Northern Uganda at critical points." Ochola also cited the Ugandan journalist Elias Biryabarema, who has written that "there is no justification for the sickening human catastrophe that has been going on in Lango and Acholiland for the last 20 years. People have been subjected to degradation, desolation, and the horrors, all resulted into killing off generation after generation." Biryabarema described what he saw in the IDP camps as "a slow extinction facing the peoples of Acholi and Lango".[1527]

Bishop Ochola's claims clearly have a basis in fact. In mid-2005, the World Health Organisation (WHO) led a multi-agency survey of health and mortality in northern Uganda, the focus of the conflict between the Ugandan government and the LRA. The survey's assessment of health conditions was peer-reviewed. Francesco Checchi coordinated this multi-agency survey. He noted that "The methodology was standard, and had been used in other settings, including Darfur and the Democratic Republic of Congo." The survey estimated crude and under-five mortality rates greatly in excess of emergency thresholds corresponding to between 19,000 and 30,000 excess deaths between January and July 2005 alone, depending on assumptions of baseline mortality. This amounted to a figure of 1,000 excess deaths per week.

Checchi was also able to compare the Acholi IDP camps to those in Darfur. He noted that at face value "everything would seem to place Darfur at a disadvantage with respect to Northern Uganda", including greater insecurity, the immense size of Darfur compared to Acholiland, distances from supply centres; a hostile climate; and approximately twice as many affected people. Checchi notes: "Yet Darfur, at least from a humanitarian 'effectiveness' perspective, is mostly a success story.... Indeed, 33 out of 35 region-wide or site-specific mortality surveys – 94% of the total – conducted since 2005 consistently report mortality rates below the emergency threshold, and about half the rates measured in Acholi in 2005 (0.4 – 0.9 versus 1.54 per 10,000 per day)." He states that "the Acholi camps provide an almost textbook example of how not to mitigate the effects of forced displacement."[1528]

One can draw a number of conclusions from these assertions and hard facts. The selectivity of Ocampo's approach is clear. The ICC chose to claim that circumstances within IDP camps in Darfur constituted genocide while ignoring circumstances in neighbouring countries in similar conflict situations. Independent humanitarian experts have, however, been able to compare and contrast the two situations at the time period in question.

Having raised the issue of genocide and provided the international community with his criteria for genocide (albeit one which manifestly failed with regard to Darfur), one is duty bound to test his criteria in Uganda, a country in which the ICC does have jurisdiction for genocide and other crimes against humanity. In Uganda, however, the

ICC and Ocampo clearly turn a blind eye to circumstances that more than match their own criteria for genocide. They turn a blind eye to well-documented WHO surveys that do show 1,000 civilians, mainly children, dying per month as the result of Ugandan government policies and intransigence – described by Anglican bishops as a policy of genocide.

A comparison between the ICC's approach to Darfur and the DRC is also instructive. A survey by the International Rescue Committee stated that 5.4 million civilians had died in the DRC as a consequence of the war and its lingering effects since 1998, and that 45,000 people continue to die every month. The survey also noted that the national mortality rate is nearly sixty per cent higher than the sub-Saharan average.[1529] It was estimated that twice as many people died in the Congo in 2007 alone as may have died in the entire Darfur conflict since it began in 2003.[1530] If a case for genocide might be made then these sorts of figures could well support it. The death toll in the DRC, as the result of ethnic conflict, is approaching that of the Holocaust in Europe. What had the ICC done in this case of the DRC by 2009? It had put one middle-ranking militia leader on trial for allegedly recruiting child soldiers. In the instance of Darfur, where Ocampo claims that 35,000 civilians may have been killed, and that between 80,000 and 265,000 people may have died from conditions during displacement and in IDP camps – claims that were manifestly absurd[1531] – Ocampo charges the head of state with genocide.

There were other obvious contradictions in the Prosecutor's public application. Ocampo claimed, for example, that President al-Bashir "used the Ministry for Humanitarian Affairs to deny domestic humanitarian assistance to IDPs in Darfur".[1532] This claim simply jars with reality. The UN reported that the number of foreign and national aid workers in Darfur had increased from 200 in March 2004 to 8,500 by the end of 2004.[1533] In September 2005 the number of humanitarian workers in Darfur had grown further to around 13,500. They were working for eighty-one NGOs and thirteen UN agencies.[1534] By January 2009, the number of humanitarian workers in the region had increased to a record 17,700, working for some eighty-five NGOs and Red Cross/Crescent Movement and sixteen UN agencies, making it the largest humanitarian operation in the world.[1535] President al-Bashir's government could have prevented a single humanitarian worker or NGO from entering the region had it wished to do so.

Ocampo also claimed in his application that President al-Bashir "used his control of the state apparatus to cover up and allow for continuation of crimes" by way of "a campaign to deny, downplay and hide the crimes", and "by preventing the truth about the genocide from being revealed". This claim stumbles somewhat given that President al-Bashir's government has allowed hundreds of foreign reporters into Darfur. These have included journalists from virtually every Western nation, and have included reporters from the BBC, Reuters, *The Times*, *The New York Times*, the *Washington Post*, the *Chicago Tribune*, *Financial Times*, *The Christian Science Monitor*, *The Daily Telegraph*, *The Sunday Telegraph*, *The Independent*, *The Guardian*, Sky, CNN, Time, Knight Ridder news service and *The Economist*. A number of these journalists spent several weeks, and some several months, in Darfur. Most governments involved in a programme of genocide go out of their way to prevent any outsiders, especially journalists, from roaming around the area in question.

Allegations of genocide in Darfur

The genocide issue is central to Ocampo's credibility. It should be examined in some detail. There has been unprecedented criticism of Ocampo's claims of genocide in Darfur. Ocampo cannot have been unaware of how controversial claims of genocide had been in Darfur. The only government to have alleged genocide in Darfur has been that of the USA. The Bush Administration had come under considerable domestic pressure to do so.

Marc Gustafson has studied how Washington came to claim genocide in Darfur. He noted the only investigation that eventually "concluded" that "genocide" had occurred in Darfur was the one conducted by the USA and led by the then Secretary of State, Colin Powell, in the summer of 2004. Gustafson observed that "The evolution of this study, however, was peculiar. Immediately following the investigation and before the results were finalised, Powell announced on National Public Radio that genocide had not occurred."[1536] Powell made a clear statement that genocide had not taken place in this interview on 30 June 2004.[1537] Gustafson then notes that "After two months of intense pressure and protests from activists, particularly from the Sudan Campaign Coalition and the Congressional Black Caucus, Powell changed his mind and declared in front of the Senate Foreign Relations Committee, on 9 September 2004, that genocide had occurred." He now stated "genocide has been committed in Darfur...and that genocide may still be occurring".[1538] Gustafson observed that given the "vociferous calls from activists, it is easy to see why Congress, shortly after Powell's speech, unanimously passed Senate Concurrent Resolution 133 to use the word 'genocide' to describe the situation in Darfur. No congressperson wanted to be identified with voting against fighting genocide."[1539]

That the Bush Administration in essence caved in to domestic political pressure was confirmed by Senator John Danforth, President Bush's Special Envoy to Sudan and subsequently US Ambassador to the UN. In a July 2005 BBC interview he stated that the use of the genocide label "was something that was said for internal consumption within the United States". When asked whether he meant the Christian Right, Danforth agreed.[1540] The *Financial Times* has also noted that Powell was under intense domestic pressure, notably from Christian lobby groups, to use the genocide word.[1541]

Gustafson noted further:

> In 2004 and 2005, use of the term "genocide" was an essential part of the marketing strategy for the Save Darfur Coalition and the Genocide Intervention Network, which are the two largest American activist campaigns for Darfur. By the end of 2006, these groups had reached out to tens of millions of Americans and collected almost $100 million dollars in contributions, according to publicly available reports from the Internal Revenue Service.[1542]

Ocampo, nevertheless, chose to repeat what can only be described as politicised, marketing- and "advocacy"-driven claims of genocide in Darfur. When asked how many victims of genocide there were, Moreno Ocampo answered "2.5 million", noting that it is not necessary to be killed to be a victim of genocide. Rony Brauman was particularly critical of Ocampo's "judicial inflation" in using the term "genocide". He said that the use of this term was inaccurate: "In practice, it meant that any war could henceforward be regarded as genocidal – unless we can somehow imagine 'good' armed conflicts in which the two sides make an appointment to fight at a given time and place as in a duel. If one applies the logic of the ICC, the Spanish Civil War, the Algerian War of Independence, the Vietnam War and the Afghanistan War – to name just a few – should be regarded as genocidal in character: since these wars as well have involved massacres of civilians, the use of militias, torture, and forced transfers of population."[1543]

That Ocampo would prostitute reality to please Western activists, anti-Sudan lobby groups and the human-rights industry in his claim of "genocide" in Darfur came as no surprise. It is an indication of how highly politicised and judicially mediocre the court's judges were that they went along with Ocampo's convenient, activist-friendly fiction.

The USA's claim of genocide was seen at the time for what it was, political posturing, by the rest of the international community. The then UN Secretary-General, Kofi Annan, contradicted allegations of genocide: "I cannot call the killing a genocide even though there have been massive violations of international humanitarian law."[1544] The AU's position was clearly outlined by its Peace and Security Council in July 2004: "Even though the crisis in Darfur is grave, with unacceptable levels of death, human suffering and destruction of homes and infrastructure, the situation cannot be defined as a genocide."[1545] The then AU Chairman, Nigerian President Olusegun Obasanjo, also stated in early December 2004 that events in Darfur did not constitute genocide: "Now, what I know of Sudan it does not fit in all respects to that definition. The government of Sudan can be condemned, but it's not as…genocide." Obasanjo stated that "the real issue of Darfur is governance. It is a political problem which has mushroomed into a military (one) when the rebels took up arms."[1546] Speaking at a press conference at the UN Headquarters in New York on 23 September 2004, President Obasanjo had previously stated: "Before you can say that this is genocide or ethnic cleansing, we will have to have a definite decision and plan and program of a government to wipe out a particular group of people, then we will be talking about genocide, ethnic cleansing. What we know is not that. What we know is that there was an uprising, rebellion, and the government armed another group of people to stop that rebellion. That's what we know. That does not amount to genocide from our own reckoning. It amounts to of course conflict. It amounts to violence." It should also be noted that the AU had hundreds of observers on the ground throughout Darfur, whose first-hand observations would have shaped President Obasanjo's conclusions.

Similarly, the EU's fact-finding mission concluded that, although there was widespread violence, there was no evidence of genocide. A spokesman for the mission stated: "We are not in the situation of genocide there."[1547] The Arab League took the position that events in Darfur were neither genocide nor ethnic cleansing and accused the Bush Administration of seeking to exploit the crisis for electoral gain. Even Israel, a state founded in large part by survivors of a genuine holocaust, has perhaps indirectly demurred from Washington's claim in publicly turning away Darfurian refugees.[1548]

Of particular significance is the fact that claims of genocide have been pointedly criticised by well-respected humanitarian groups such as *Médecins Sans Fontières*.[1549] In

2004, *Médecins Sans Fontières* pointedly criticised the unfounded use of words such as genocide: "By screaming 'the crime of all crimes', mixing military with humanitarianism... to justify intervention, words do have concrete implications and often serve political interests." The organisation also noted of the allegations of genocide in Darfur: "Resorting to this terminology says much about the racist representation of African conflicts in the West (the conflict in Darfur reduced to an inevitable antagonism between Blacks and Arabs). It also demonstrates, as if it were necessary, that words are used by States, not for what they mean but for the political objectives that they might serve." *Médecins Sans Fontières* cautioned that to continue with its job would entail "distancing ourselves from propaganda and resisting this era of confusion".[1550] MSF-France President Dr. Jean-Hervé Bradol subsequently described claims of genocide in Darfur as "obvious political opportunism".[1551] Dr. Bradol had previously stated that the use of the term genocide was inappropriate: "Our teams have not seen evidence of the deliberate intention to kill people of a specific group. We have received reports of massacres, but not of attempts to specifically eliminate all the members of a group."[1552] Dr. Mercedes Taty, *Médecins Sans Fontières*' Deputy Emergency Director, who worked with twelve expatriate doctors and 300 Sudanese nationals in field hospitals throughout Darfur at the height of the emergency, has also warned: "I don't think that we should be using the word 'genocide' to describe this conflict. Not at all. This can be a semantic discussion, but nevertheless, there is no systematic target – targeting one ethnic group or another one. It doesn't mean either that the situation in Sudan isn't extremely serious by itself."[1553]

Médecins Sans Fontières is an exceptionally credible observer with regard to allegations of genocide for three reasons. Firstly, *Médecins Sans Fontières* was among the first humanitarian groups to establish a presence in Darfur as the conflict unfolded. *Médecins Sans Fontières* is very heavily involved in the provision of medical and emergency services in all three of the states that make up Darfur, deploying 2,000 staff.[1554] It has been actively assisting hundreds of thousands of people displaced by fighting throughout the region. *Médecins Sans Fontières* is also present and engaged in Chad. *Médecins Sans Fontières*, therefore, has a unique institutional awareness of events in Darfur. Secondly, *Médecins Sans Fontières*' reputation is quite simply beyond reproach. *Médecins Sans Fontières* was the recipient of the Nobel Peace Prize in 1999. It has also received numerous other awards recognising its outstanding humanitarian work throughout the world.[1555] And, thirdly, and most significantly, *Médecins Sans Fontières*' record with regard to genocide is also unambiguous. Dr. Bradol, cited above, headed *Médecins Sans Fontières*' programmes in Rwanda in 1994, and spent several weeks assisting the surgical team that struggled to remain in Kigali during the genocide. Dr. Bradol and *Médecins Sans Fontières* called for armed intervention in Rwanda stating "doctors can't stop genocide". Dr. Bradol has stated that "genocide is that exceptional situation in which, contrary to the rule prohibiting participation in hostilities, the humanitarian movement declares support for military intervention. Unfortunately, an international military intervention against the genocide never came to pass and the Rwandan Patriotic Front did not win its military victory until after the vast majority of victims were killed." Given the clear position with regard to genuine genocide taken by Dr. Bradol and *Médecins Sans Fontières*, their unambiguous position in pointedly criticising allegations of genocide in Darfur is all the more powerful.

Dr. Bradol has also criticised the way in which the truth was twisted in order to claim genocide in Darfur: "The need to revive the notion of race to support the premise of genocide in Darfur is not the only point of weakness in the genocide argument. Public statements of the intent to destroy a human group have been no more obvious than the existence of distinct races. No traces of this intent can be found in statements by the Sudanese dictatorship or in the country's laws. In short, the alleged intent to destroy a human group is not obvious, and the definition of the group of victims is based on a category that was rightly invalidated many years ago."[1556] Interestingly, *Médecins Sans Fontières*' comments about allegations of genocide were echoed by other medical organisations. Interviewed in April 2005, Dr. Gino Strada, a war surgeon and founder of Emergency, a humanitarian NGO that had worked through the Rwandan genocide, and in Darfur, stated that "I will say there is no genocide at all in Darfur. There is a big humanitarian disaster, and the problem is to act toward that humanitarian disaster." Dr. Strada further noted that "All this business of genocide in Sudan…I think has come up as an idea to sort of pave the ground for a possible military intervention. And next door there is the…Democratic Republic of Congo, where four million people have died because of the conflict, and no one has ever thought about mentioning genocide… . A country comes to the light of the media when there are some political agendas from very powerful nations behind them."[1557]

There has also been criticism of the questionable claim of genocide from American elder statesmen such as the former President Jimmy Carter. Speaking during a visit to Darfur in 2007, Carter, whose charitable foundation, the Carter Center, worked to establish the ICC, said that the use of the term "genocide" was both legally inaccurate and "unhelpful". He went on to say that: "There is a legal definition of genocide and Darfur does not meet that legal standard. The atrocities were horrible but I don't think it qualifies to be called genocide. If you read the law textbooks…you'll see very clearly that it's not genocide and to call it genocide falsely just to exaggerate a horrible situation I don't think it helps."[1558] Carter also noted that: "Rwanda was definitely a genocide; what Hitler did to the Jews was; but I don't think it's the case in Darfur."[1559]

Perhaps the most telling contradiction of claims of genocide in Darfur was the simple fact pointed to by several observers that victims of genocide do not move towards those engaged in their slaughter. Jews within Germany in the 1930s and 1940s were seeking to flee Germany not move towards Berlin or other urban centres within the Third Reich. Jews elsewhere in Europe were not moving towards Germany. Similarly, during the Rwandan genocide, Tutsis were not heading towards Kigali or other Hutu government-controlled centres; they were fleeing into the countries neighbouring Rwanda. During the fifty-year civil war in southern Sudan, however, at least half of the southern population voluntarily trekked northwards – often in difficult circumstances – to seek refuge in northern Sudan, and particularly Khartoum. They could more easily have gone to live in Uganda, Kenya, Ethiopia or the Congo, often among their own extended tribal kin. Many thousands more chose to live within government-controlled cities and towns in southern Sudan. Similarly, most of those displaced in Darfur have chosen not to flee to Chad, to live among their extended kin, but have chosen instead to move to government-controlled urban areas such as al-Fasher, Nyala and al-Geneina. Most people do not flee toward "genocidal" assaults. Flint and de Waal have observed: "Many crimes have been committed in Sudan. The systematic eradication of communities today is not one of them."[1560]

This has been pointed out by several commentators. *Guardian* journalist Jonathan Steele reported that: "Grim though it has been, this was not genocide or classic ethnic cleansing. Many of the displaced moved to camps a few kilometers from their homes. Professionals and intellectuals were not targeted, as in Rwanda. Darfur was, and is, the outgrowth of a struggle between farmers and nomads rather than a Balkan-style fight for the same piece of land. Finding a solution is not helped by turning the violence into a battle of good versus evil or launching another Arab-bashing crusade."[1561] Marc Lavergne, of the French National Centre for Scientific Research in Paris, has made the similar observation that the violence has not been aimed at Darfurian identity: "Darfurians who live in Khartoum are not targeted."[1562]

Given Ocampo's attempt to present the Darfur conflict as a genocidal plot by the "Arab" government in Khartoum to exterminate Darfur's "African" communities, it is also interesting to note that the three Sudanese that he claims have been actively engaged in this "plot" are themselves African. De Waal points out Ahmed Haroun is of Borgu, i.e. "African" origin and that Ali Kushayb is "also of Borgu lineage, though he calls himself 'Arab'".[1563] The most active critic of President al-Bashir in the USA is Nicholas Kristof. Kristof has pointed out that President al-Bashir's family "appears to come from an African tribe". This has led to Kristof then choosing to disingenuously claim political rather than racial roots for his claims of genocide in Darfur.[1564] These facts cut away the very heart of the claims made by Ocampo about an "Arab", anti-"African" genocide in Darfur.

The misuse of the genocide term is very regrettable. Crying wolf on genocide in Darfur can only but denigrate the memory of the reality of the Holocaust in Europe during the Second World War and encourage Holocaust deniers. As and when it becomes increasingly apparent that Ocampo's claims about genocide in Darfur were opportunistic and false it will further discredit a court already in considerable trouble.

On 4 March 2009, Pre-Trial Chamber I, made up of judges Akua Kuenyehia, Sylvia Steiner and Anita Ušacka, issued a warrant of arrest against President al-Bashir.[1565] Al-Bashir became the first sitting head of state to be indicted by the ICC. The chamber claimed that there were grounds to believe he had committed crimes within the jurisdiction of the court, namely five counts of crimes against humanity (murder, extermination, forcible transfer, torture and rape) and two counts of war crimes (attacking civilians and pillaging). The chamber found that there was not sufficient evidence to sustain the three charges of genocide.[1566] On the instruction of the chamber, the registrar transmitted requests for cooperation for the arrest and surrender of President al-Bashir to the Sudan, to all States Parties to the Rome Statute and to all Security Council members not party to the Rome Statute. In issuing the decision, the chamber claimed that, according to Security Council Resolution 1593 (2005), taken together with Article 25 of the Charter of the United Nations, the Sudan was obligated to cooperate with the court, including by arresting and surrendering President al-Bashir. On 10 March 2009, the prosecution applied for leave to appeal in relation to the genocide charges. On 24 June, Pre-Trial Chamber I granted leave to appeal on the issue of whether the chamber had applied the wrong legal test in relation to the correct standard of proof required for issuing a warrant of arrest. On 6 July 2009, the prosecution submitted its appeal.

President al-Bashir's response was unambiguous: "Any decision by the International Criminal Court has no value for us, it will not be worth the ink it is written with." Regarding the warrant itself he suggested that "they can eat it".[1567] The Sudanese government's response was to also expel thirteen Western non-governmental organisations that it believed had provided information to the ICC.[1568]

The Sudanese position on the ICC and Darfur

The Sudanese government stated from the start that it did not recognise the ICC. Khartoum correctly asserted that the court has no jurisdiction over its sovereignty or nationals. One of the principles of international law is that a treaty does not create either obligations or rights for third states. Sudan has not ratified the Rome Treaty and is a non-state party. The Sudanese government signed the Rome Statute on 8 September 2000, but did not ratify it. On 26 August 2008, Sudan notified the Secretary-General of the UN, as depositary of the Rome Statute of the ICC, that Sudan "does not intend to become a party to the Rome Statute. Accordingly, Sudan has no legal obligation arising from its signature on 8 September 2000."[1569]

The ICC's action runs up against other legal norms. Customary international law states that certain government officials, such as a head of state, cannot be tried abroad for any crimes whatsoever.[1570] The Rome Statute's Article 27(2) waives this immunity for member states that have ratified the statute and therefore gives the court jurisdiction over high-ranking government officials. It does not, however, waive this immunity for non-member states. Article 98(1) asserts that the ICC cannot request a member state "to act inconsistently with its obligations under international law". One of these obligations is the responsibility to respect a head of state's immunity. Article 98(1) clarifies that a member state cannot arrest or even assist in the arrest of an official with immunity from a state that has not ratified the Rome Statute. The head of the International Commission of Inquiry into Darfur, Antonio Cassese, observed that since Sudan has not signed the statue of the court, Bashir can claim immunity: "[The ICC's] warrant can be carried out only if Bashir himself orders his guards to arrest him. Outside Sudan, the warrant has virtually no legal weight."[1571]

Professor Hans Köchler has stated that "it is obvious that the arrest warrant against the President of Sudan is without legal basis, and states, whether parties to the Rome Statute or not, are not obligated to implement it. Similarly, states' obligations under the United Nations Charter do not force them to honour the warrant either since…the Security Council resolution contains contradictory norms and is itself ultra vires. The international rule of law requires that no state or intergovernmental body, not even the

United Nations Security Council, puts itself above the law."[1572]

President al-Bashir has unambiguously stated on several occasions that Sudan will not hand over any Sudanese national, even a rebel, to a foreign court. There have also been very large popular demonstrations within Sudan against any idea of such a legal action.[1573] When the arrest warrant was issued for Ahmed Haroun, President al-Bashir refused to relieve him of his duties as a government minister, stating that Haroun "will not resign or be fired and will not be interrogated.... The former secretary of state for interior was only performing his duty to defend the citizens and their property from the aggressors at the time of the events (in 2003–2004)." The then Sudanese Foreign Minister Lam Akol also stated that the ICC "has no right to put any Sudanese citizen on trial" for alleged war crimes in Darfur.[1574] On 8 May 2009, in a continuing snub to the ICC, Haroun was appointed to the key position of Governor of South Kordofan state. He was re-elected as Governor in 2010.

The simple fact is that in claiming jurisdiction over Darfur, the ICC is acting beyond its legal powers. The South African think tank, the Institute for Security Studies, has noted that the Darfur case "is a monumental moment for the court as it steps beyond its classical treaty-based constraints to exercise jurisdiction over a non-party state, Sudan".[1575] This has also been recognised by international legal experts. Commenting on the recommendations made by the UN Commission of Inquiry into Darfur to refer the situation in Darfur to the ICC, Stéphanie Giry, an international lawyer formerly with the UN Office of Legal Affairs, noted:

> There's one big problem with it: Most of the perpetrators in Darfur can't be tried before the ICC because Sudan hasn't ratified the court's founding statute. The panel's failure to admit this limitation is staggering. It is so staggering, in fact, that coming from a group of respected experts, it may not be an oversight at all. More likely, it's a daring strategy to expand the court's ambit over one of the world's worst humanitarian crises. Unfortunately, it's also a losing strategy.[1576]

The fact that Sudan has not signed the statute is an insurmountable impediment to any ICC action. Rosenthal has also pointed to the fact that "The Rome Statute is a treaty. It is a self-evident principle of the law of treaties – one explicitly confirmed by article 34 of the 1969 Vienna Convention – that treaties create no obligations per se for states that are not parties to them."[1577] South African legal experts have also pointed out the difficulties of the ICC position: "Sudan is not a state party to the ICC and, as such, owes no treaty obligations to the court. This is an inevitable problem with the referral of situations involving non-party states to the ICC, as the referral extends the court's jurisdiction beyond the parameters of the Rome Treaty, but does not concomitantly extend the court's power to enforce that jurisdiction."[1578]

The impact on peace within Sudan of the Darfur indictments is clear. The ICC actions have had a very negative effect on the Darfur peace process, serving to radicalise both sides to the conflict. They bolster the fragmented rebel movements, who may think all they have to do is sit tight, continue the conflict and wait for regime-change by indictment. On the other government side, as pointed out by Christopher Caldwell of *The Weekly Standard*, "Threatening leaders with life sentences in the Hague turns a situation that might conceivably be resolved by diplomacy into a fight to the death."[1579]

The actions of the ICC, the ICC's subsequent issuing of an arrest warrant for the Sudanese head of state had clear implications for peace in Sudan in general, and Darfur in particular. The two are closely linked. For a better understanding of the issue it is important to examine briefly the Comprehensive Peace Agreement (CPA) signed in 2005. This was an internationally mediated agreement between the government of Sudan and southern Sudanese rebels, which ended a conflict in southern Sudan that had been fought off and on since 1955. The CPA settled issues of power and wealth-sharing between the north and the south, and agreed on a government of national unity and elections in the lead-up to a referendum in 2011 on unity or separation for southern Sudan. The south chose separation and South Sudan became independent. The CPA was very much the product of the international community – in the shape of the UN, USA, UK, the EU and Norway among others – which also agreed to be a partner for peace. The CPA consisted of a complex security and political architecture involving the UN, Western countries and the government of national unity. Similarly, the Darfur peace process involved the UN, the AU, the USA and Britain – all of whom mediated and guaranteed the 2006 Darfur Peace Agreement between the Sudanese government and one faction of the rebel SLA. Edward Thomas, a leading independent expert on Sudan, has said of the CPA, it "remains the most thoughtful, considered and far-reaching document in Sudanese history. Its ideas for sharing wealth and power address the core problems of mismanaged diversity and unequal development, and offer a model for other countries in the Horn of Africa."[1580]

The ICC actions threatened peace in Sudan in two vital respects. First of all it severely undermined Sudanese confidence in the UN and its institutions as a partner for peace in Sudan. The ICC is seen by many Sudanese and others throughout Africa and the developing world, rightly or wrongly, as an extension of the UN. This impression was also reinforced by the fact that the UNSC referred the Darfur situation to the ICC, itself a distinctly political act. Similarly, the simple fact is that the ICC is a political entity with a political, not a legal, agenda.

To the extent that the UNSC has itself long been seen as an extension of Western political interests, the ICC action has also undermined Sudanese confidence in a number of Western countries. European support for the UNSC referral was also followed by demands that the ICC indictments and arrest warrants be followed through, something also echoed by the USA. It is hard to see what confidence was left with regard to Sudan's relationship with elements of the Western community with regard to the CPA.

It is a matter of fact that President al-Bashir is at the head of three major institutions in Sudan. He is first and foremost the President of Sudan; secondly, he is the head of the ruling National Congress Party, the then senior partner within the government of national unity; and thirdly he is the leader of perhaps the most important political party within Sudan, as Commander-in-Chief of the Sudanese armed forces. He headed the government of national unity in Sudan through a key referendum and the secession of southern Sudan, all this in the teeth of considerable opposition from nationalist, religious and rightwing elements in the country. President al-Bashir was the cornerstone of the CPA. Given that the political and security architecture of the CPA hinged on the role, position and status of President al-Bashir, active Western involvement in, and support for, the very ICC action that sought to remove him from that position left question marks about the West's then commitment to the CPA and peace in southern Sudan, let alone the Darfur peace process. Geis and Mundt state that: "Diplomats from across the political spectrum argued that an indictment of Bashir would be counterproductive to achieving peace in Sudan and could jeopardize the fragile comprehensive peace agreement that ended the 20 year north-south conflict."[1581] Western countries continued nevertheless to push for the arrest of President al-Bashir.

The political relationship between the then government of national unity and its Western partners in the CPA was very badly weakened, perhaps fatally so, as a direct consequence of the ICC and its actions. To many Sudanese, the ICC is pursuing a badly thought-out Western policy of regime change by indictment. These sorts of concerns undoubtedly undermined and continue to undermine the peace process in Darfur.

Unsurprisingly, in addition and as a consequence of the ICC's close relationship with the UN, and the ICC's repeated calls on members of the UN to arrest President al-Bashir, UN military peacekeeping personnel in Sudan – whether they had been in southern Sudan as part of the CPA or as part of UNAMID in Darfur – were viewed with understandable suspicion by the Sudanese government and people. The ICC has no police or military forces of its own – it is reliant upon the UNSC and UN member states for enforcement of any of its actions. Armed UN military personnel in Sudan, especially from those Western countries committed to the arrest of President al-Bashir, can clearly been seen as posing a threat to the Sudanese government. This suspicion understandably may well lead to the expulsion of Western elements from UN forces based in Sudan, something that may weaken or distort UNAMID forces in Darfur. The ICC indictments have also caused concern for the safety of UN personnel in general within Sudan.

Rather than speeding up resolution of the Darfur conflict, therefore, the ICC involvement will have the opposite effect. In the short term it is often cited as a reason why the Sudanese government will not entertain the idea of UN military forces in Darfur. International observers have noted, for example, that "the media has often talked about the threat of the ICC hanging over the dominant National Congress Party as a possible reason for its intransigence on the question of a UN deployment in Darfur".[1582] Such concerns would have been fuelled by statements by senior American officials, cited by the Council on Foreign Relations: "Ambassador David Scheffer, who led the U.S. delegation in UN talks to establish the ICC, says the investigation won't be able to have a presence in Darfur until there are UN peacekeepers on the ground. Analysts say this is one of the main reasons behind the Sudanese government's opposition to a UN-only force."[1583] UN radio reported that "The UN mission in Sudan has expressed fears for the security of its staff after the ICC accused two Sudanese officials of war crimes in Darfur." The acting UN special envoy to Sudan confirmed that the mission had warned its staff: "There could be reactions from people. Yes, the ICC is seen as part of the UN system. But we have no mandate on what the ICC does."¹⁵⁸⁴ It is a matter of record that the UN mission in the DRC, UNOMOC, has provided hundreds of items of information to the ICC.

The second major way in which ICC action endangers peace in Sudan is that it brings an almost unbearable aspect of uncertainty to all Sudanese affairs. Uncertainty destabilises and eats away at any peace process. If it is unclear whether those engaged in negotiating a delicate and complex peace process will be present at the end of the negotiating process, this uncertainty distorts that process in several ways.

Why should rebel factions seek to negotiate a deal with someone who may be out of the equation by the time any deal is struck? It is also self-evident that rebel negotiators will adopt a more hard-line position, hoping to capitalise on this very uncertainty. Brauman has also warned that the ICC actions will encourage continuing cycles of violence in Darfur: "Moreover, it is a good bet now that the protagonists of the Darfur conflict will become more intransigent. The rebel movements will be justified in thinking that they have won a battle and they have no reason to stop there.... This encouragement to them to fight could set in motion a new cycle of violence and reprisals, both the humanitarian and political consequences of which would be disastrous."¹⁵⁸⁵ Ramesh Thakur has also warned of the negative consequences of ICC action: "Many argue that this will jeopardize prospects for peace, as Bashir has less, not more, reason to give up power. Conversely, why would opposition rebel groups agree to negotiations with an alleged war criminal?"¹⁵⁸⁶

Having spent several years painstakingly negotiating the CPA with President al-Bashir and the political forces he represents, why did the West then acquiesce in questionable attempts to remove him and risk unravelling the CPA? Every official US foreign policy paper and briefing has warned of the danger of failed states. Why did Washington, in its tacit support for ICC actions seeking to remove a crucial head of state at a critical time within the volatile Sahel area, risk creating another failed state in Africa? Had they simply not thought things through? Can it really be true that Western foreign policy towards Sudan is in reality being made by autistic legal fundamentalists and anti-Sudanese pressure groups, and not by their foreign ministries? And the simple answer to all these questions is yes. What confidence can Sudan have in these Western countries when their Sudan policy can be written or changed by self-serving lobby groups such as "Save Darfur", the same sort of pressure groups that dragged the USA and Britain into the humanitarian disasters in Iraq and Afghanistan? Pressure groups that want the ICC to look at Darfur, but not Iraq or Afghanistan.

More ICC double standards

The ICC's actions against the Sudanese President also encouraged rebel intransigence within the Darfur peace process in other ways. While indicting President al-Bashir, the ICC has very publicly ignored the clear involvement of several Darfur rebel movements in a myriad of war crimes and crimes against humanity. The hypocrisy of the court and its prosecutor, for example, was clearly demonstrated by the case of child soldiers held by the rebel Justice and Equality Movement. In May 2008 JEM forces attacked the

Sudanese capital. More than 220 people were killed when the rebels thrust more than 1,000 kilometres from western Sudan's region of Darfur to Omdurman. Over 100 JEM child soldiers were captured during the attack. JEM's use of child soldiers has been confirmed by the UN and numerous other non-governmental organisations. The UN Secretary-General, in his February 2009 report on children and armed conflict in the Sudan, stated that:

> The majority of cases were reported from Western Darfur State. This includes many of the 99 children who have been confirmed as recruited and used by JEM during their attack on Omdurman in May 2008.... Following the arrest of some 110 children, aged from 11 to 17 years, in the aftermath of the JEM attack on Omdurman on 10 May 2008, concerted advocacy was undertaken by the National Council for Child Welfare on behalf of the children.... Towards the end of the reporting period, almost all detained children had been pardoned by Presidential decree and released and reunified with families and communities, including a number of children reunified with their families in Chad.[1587]

Paradoxically, despite the ICC's focus on child soldiers in the DRC, being at the heart of the ICC's first-ever trial – and in the face of black and white evidence of JEM's systematic use of child soldiers – and the fact that senior UN officials have flagged the case, the ICC refused to examine the issue.[1588] In late November 2008, for example, a spokesman for the ICC stated that the court had no plans for investigating the assault by Darfur Justice and Equality Movement on the Sudanese capital in May 2008.[1589] In the Lubanga trial, the ICC struggled to identify a handful of alleged child soldiers as part of their case: all but one of the "child soldiers" presented by the prosecutor were dismissed as unreliable. In the Darfur case, in the Omdurman attack alone, the UN and UNICEF were able to comprehensively document over ninety JEM child soldiers. The UN Under-Secretary-General and Special Representative for Children and Armed Conflict, Radhika Coomaraswamy, confirmed that the UN were aware of ninety-one JEM child soldiers, and that JEM is on the list of child-soldier recruiters:

> We are aware the Omdurman/JEM case...Child protection partners including UNICEF are following the case on the ground.... Please note also that we are aware of ongoing recruitment of children by JEM. They are listed in the annexes of the SG report and monitored under resolution 1612 monitoring and reporting mechanism. They could therefore be subject to targeted measures by the Security Council.

The UN is itself saying that JEM should be sanctioned by the Security Council for recruiting and using child soldiers.[1590] The ICC has pointedly ignored the issue. The court's double-standards have not gone unnoticed. Marc Glendening, Director of ICC Watch, in a letter to the ICC Chief Prosecutor, noted:

> It is extraordinary that you have failed to launch an investigation into the horrific activities of JEM in using child soldiers and other forces operating in Darfur in using child soldiers given the current prosecution of Thomas Lubanga for precisely this crime. Your failure to indicate any interest whatsoever in relation to the very serious accusations made by the United Nations and Waging Peace concerning the use of child soldiers in Darfur leaves the ICC open to the charge that it is motivated by highly selective, partisan political motivations in relation to what is taking place in the region. The ICC is not an organisation whose activities can currently be said to be consistent with the rule of law. Despite your frequently made allegations against the government of Sudan, you have failed to demonstrate any serious inclination to hold JEM to account for the human rights violations that they have been inflicting on children and other Darfurians.[1591]

Rather than focus on internationally documented, black and white instances of JEM's systematic use of child soldiers, served up to him on a plate, Ocampo has gone for a far less clear-cut option. On 20 November 2008, the ICC Prosecutor brought an application for arrest warrants for three Darfur rebel commanders, rebels including Abu Garda, Head of the insurgent United Resistance Front faction, on charges that they orchestrated an attack at the Haskanita AU camp in September 2007.

The war in Darfur continues because the West allows it to continue. Some would say it continues because some Western countries and interests wish it to continue. If Western governments and pressure groups spent even a tenth of the time they have spent on focusing on the symptoms of the war and pushing the ICC on governments instead of focusing on its cure, peace, the war would have ended years ago. So far, the West has been part of the problem and not the solution to the Darfur crisis. The ICC and its recent actions once again prove this point.

The ICC's attempt to claim jurisdiction in Darfur falls at the very first hurdle. Sudan has not ratified the Rome Statute and is therefore not a member of the ICC. As outlined in previous chapters, any action by the ICC is therefore simply illegal. The pressure-group-driven claims of genocide and crimes against humanity made by Ocampo against the Sudanese government have made for great publicity for the Prosecutor but have been inaccurate and divorced from reality. And additionally, the ICC's action has obstructed and destabilised two peace processes in Sudan. The ICC's indictments have backfired. Geis and Mundt have noted that:

> Whatever leverage could be derived from an indictment has likely been lost, as the divisions within the international community have only increased since Ocampo filed his charges in July 2008. African states and members of the Arab League have lined up firmly behind Bashir in condemning the indictment, and much of Sudan's political class, even opponents of the president, feel that Bashir has been unfairly charged. Whether or not the Security Council votes to suspend an indictment under Chapter XVI, the

ICC has little political space in which to operate and arguably has more at stake than Bashir.[1592]

One commentator has made the clear point that Ocampo has a bureaucratic reason for intensifying his grudge with President al-Bashir: "[I]f the ICC does not succeed in bringing President Bashir to account, the institution will be weakened and lose credibility. This is the likely outcome and Mr. Bashir knows it."[1593]

That the ICC has gone out of its way to focus on Sudan, rather than any number of other conflicts internationally and in Africa, has led to many questions regarding its true motivation in doing so. The fact that the action is being taken against an oil-rich Islamic and African country, and that the first head of state to be indicted by the ICC is a Muslim from Africa, has not been lost on its people and many within the developing world. These suspicions have not been allayed by the numerous double standards on the part of the ICC that have accompanied its actions against Sudan.

De Waal concluded that "Moreno Ocampo's political misjudgments have made life easier for Bashir and commensurately more difficult for the ICC…the Prosecutor has made it easy for his critics to dismiss him as ill-informed and driven by a desire for publicity".[1594]

The AU has taken an increasingly firm position with regard to the ICC and Sudan. On 21 July 2008, following the ICC's indictment of President Omer al-Bashir, the AU issued a communiqué that stated that any Pre-Trial Chamber approval of the al-Bashir warrant application would undermine peace prospects and requested an Article 16 deferral of the "process initiated by the ICC".[1595] Following the ICC's issuing of arrest warrants for President al-Bashir, the AU declared that it was "deeply concerned at the far reaching consequences of this decision, which comes at a critical juncture in the process to promote lasting peace, reconciliation and democratic governance in the Sudan".[1596]

On 3 July 2009, the Assembly of the African Union adopted a "Decision on the Meeting of African States Parties to the Rome Statute of the International Criminal Court".[1597] This stated that "AU Member States shall not cooperate pursuant to the provisions of Article 98 of the Rome Statute of the ICC relating to immunities, for the arrest and surrender of President Omar El Bashir of The Sudan". The declaration voiced Africa's frustration at the UNSC's failure to consider a request to suspend the warrant for one year. It was also particularly significant given that the AU includes thirty-one states parties and thirteen signatories to the Rome Statute. The then Chairman of the AU said that the ICC represented a "new world terrorism" and that it was unfairly targeting Africans. The then AU Secretary-General, Jean Ping, stated that Africa's leaders are "showing to the world community that if you don't want to listen to the continent, if you don't want to take into account our proposals…if you don't want to listen to the continent, as usual, we also are going to act unilaterally".[1598] Ghana's Foreign Minister Alhaji Muhammad Mumuni noted that African leaders "have been a little unhappy about the whole process, how this matter came before the ICC. The AU actually addressed a resolution to the security council asking the SC to defer the warrant for one year, and it was virtually ignored. That we thought was a slap. We thought that as Africans, and having a clear understanding and a clear interest in the interest of peace in the Sudan and in Darfur, we thought that was a matter (where) the Security Council should have listened to Africa, at the very minimum."[1599]

Following on from the ICC's indictment of President al-Bashir, the AU established a high level panel on Darfur chaired by former South African President Thabo Mbeki. The other panel members were General Abdulsalami Abubakar, former President of Nigeria; Mr. Pierre Buyoya, former President of Burundi; Hon. Justice Florence Mumba, Judge of the Supreme Court of Zambia; Ms. Rakiya A. Omaar, Director, African Rights; Mr. Mohammed Kabir, a Nigerian lawyer; and Mr. Ahmed Maher El Sayed, former Foreign Minister of Egypt. The panel's mandate was to examine the situation in Darfur in depth and to submit recommendations on how best the issues of accountability and combating impunity, on the one hand, peace, healing and reconciliation, on the other, could be effectively and comprehensively addressed. It was to take into account the AU position that there is a complementary relationship between peace and justice, and that neither should be pursued at the expense of the other.

The AU high-level panel on Darfur presented its report in October 2009.[1600] It called for a Sudanese political solution. In his introduction to the report, President Mbeki writes of "the Sudanese crisis in Darfur". The report establishes that the Sudanese people are the principal actors in the situation. As de Waal states, the report's message is clear: "The task of solving Sudan's crisis in Darfur is first and foremost a challenge for the Sudanese, next for Africa, and finally for the international community." He notes that the report "shifts the international debate on Sudan from the politics of condemning atrocities (where the UNSC has found itself stuck) to the politics of constructing political solutions". The AU report looks at the ICC issue alongside several other options, including a hybrid court and a Truth, Justice and Reconciliation Commission. De Waal states that the report "puts the ICC in its place as one possible part of comprehensive package – perhaps useful, possibly not, depending on the views of the Sudanese themselves".[1601]

AU leaders, meeting in the Nigerian capital Abuja on 30 October 2009, recommended the establishment of a new court for Darfur as outlined in the Mbeki report. The hybrid court would consist of Sudanese and foreign judges appointed by the AU in consultation with the Khartoum government. The summit set up another team of experts – including Mbeki, former President of Burundi Pierre Nkurunziza, and General Abdulsalami Abubakar – to help in the implementation of the recommendations. The team had a one-year mandate. The Sudanese government formally expressed reservations on the proposed hybrid court. In November 2009, the Sudanese government stated that it was considering accepting the AU hybrid court suggestion under certain conditions.[1602] It ultimately declined to pursue the option any further.

Professor Mamdani has touched on what is at stake for Africa with regard to Darfur. What he says about the "Save Darfur" movement, a Washington DC-based advocacy group, applies equally to the ICC:

> For Africa, a lot is at stake in Darfur. Foremost are two objectives, starting with the unity of Africa: The Save Darfur lobby in the United States has turned the tragedy of the people of Darfur into a knife with which to slice

Africa by demonizing one group of Africans, African Arabs.... At stake also is the independence of Africa. The Save Darfur lobby demands, above all else, justice, the right of the international community – really the big powers in the Security Council – to punish "failed" or "rogue" states, even if it be at the cost of more bloodshed and a diminished possibility of reconciliation. More than anything else, "the responsibility to protect" is a right to punish but without being held accountable – a clarion call for the recolonization of "failed" states in Africa. In its present form, the call for justice is really a slogan that masks a big power agenda to recolonize Africa.[1603]

The ICC v. the rest of world

The actions of the ICC have had a range of unintended consequences, both within Sudan and internationally. In Sudan even President al-Bashir's arch political opponents opposed the moves by the court. The indictments dramatically enhanced domestic support for al-Bashir, support that saw him win the international-monitored 2010 elections in Sudan, polling sixty-eight per cent of the vote. *The Economist*, no fan of President al-Bashir, had to ask how it was that he was poised to win presidential elections in Sudan, "How did it come to this?": "Mr Bashir, a former field-marshal, will be the undoubted favourite to win the presidency of Africa's biggest country. He may even be elected without a serious opponent. That would be an extraordinary...feat for someone indicted as a war criminal by the international court at The Hague."[1604]

The response of the non-Western world to the ICC actions regarding President al-Bashir and Sudan has been equally unambiguous. *The Guardian* newspaper reported: "The African Union (AU), the Arab League, the Organisation of the Islamic Conference, and an influential UN bloc of developing nations known as the Group of 77 and China have all backed Sudan's calls for the ICC prosecution to be dropped, with some officials arguing that it smacks of 'white man's justice'."[1605] The Chinese government said that any request by ICC Prosecutor for an arrest warrant against President al-Bashir would be "irresponsible".[1606] The Russian government was very critical of the ICC action. The Russian Presidential Envoy for Sudan, Mikhail Margelov, stated: "The untimely decision of the International Criminal Court creates a dangerous precedent in the system of international relations and could have a negative effect both on the situation inside Sudan and on the general regional situation."[1607] The Libyan representative at the UN at the time observed: "This decision [of the ICC] did not take into consideration the views of the African Union, the Arab League, the OIC and the Nonaligned Movement. The African Union, the Arab League and the OIC have all voiced opposition to the ICC ruling, warning it would undermine the stability of Sudan and leave the ongoing peace process in a fragile state."[1608]

The twenty-two-member Arab League, in a special summit meeting in Doha in March 2009, condemned the ICC action and voiced total support for President al-Bashir. The Arab League pointed to the West's double standard in dealing with Arabs by indicting

President al-Bashir while taking no action against what they saw as war crimes committed by Israel during its offensive in Gaza. They also stated that the indictment undermined efforts at bringing about a negotiated settlement by inflaming the situation. *The New York Times* reported that "[t]he Arab consensus on Mr. Bashir has partly been attributed to a feeling of resentment in a region that is still sensitive to what it views as Western colonial arrogance".[1609]

The comments of the Algerian Foreign Minister, Mourad Medelci, regarding the ICC, following this Arab League summit are informative. Medelci stated that Arab leaders at Doha were unanimous in opposing the ICC arrest warrant for Sudanese President Bashir. Medelci said the consensus view in Doha favoured giving Sudan an opportunity to resolve the crisis through reconciliation, a process in which Medelci said the Sudanese government was already engaged. Medelci also underlined the fact that the assembled leaders contrasted the court's readiness to endorse a warrant for a serving Arab head of state with the complete lack of accountability for Israel's actions in Gaza. He also added that no leaders at Doha accepted that someone from outside could tell a people that their elected president was no good. Medelci stated: "Opposition to the ICC warrant was a matter of principle for many of us." He said that to fail to punish those responsible for the "abominable" aggression in Gaza while placing Bashir in prison was unrealistic. The Algerian position also saw the Sudanese issue as political. Medelci noted: "In Doha we said 'enough'. We are not going to enter into an arcane discussion of international law to resolve a political problem. There needs to be a rational approach."[1610]

The response of Mauritanian parliamentarians to the indictment of President al-Bashir was typical of many Africans. In a statement released on 4 March 2009, they condemned the ICC and expressed their support for President al-Bashir. They labelled the arrest warrant "an injustice", stating that it is "eloquent proof that the ICC is nothing but another tool of American foreign policy – a policy characterized by double standards, particularly in the areas of African and Arab Affairs". The parliamentarians accused the ICC of seeking to destabilise Sudan while "refusing to even think about looking into war crimes commited by Israel in Gaza or Lebanon or by the Bush administration in Iraq and Afghanistan". The deputies observed that the ICC action highlights the degree of politicisation of the court, which in their view had lost all credibility. They called on all Arab and African nations to suspend their ICC membership and declared their unconditional solidarity with the President.[1611]

The Secretary General of the Cooperation Council for the Arab States of the Gulf, Abdul Rahman Al-Attiya, said that its members are opposed to the "double standards" of the ICC accusations against Sudanese President Omar al-Bashir.[1612] The Organisation of the Islamic Conference (OIC) similarly condemned the ICC action as "unwarranted" and "totally unacceptable". The Head of the OIC, Ekmeleddin Ihsanoglu of Turkey, rejected the move as "void and lacking sound reasoning".[1613] The OIC has fifty-seven member states, from the Middle East, Africa, Central Asia, Caucasus, Balkans, Southeast Asia and South Asia.

The support for President al-Bashir extended far beyond Africa, the Middle East and the Islamic world. In April 2009, for example, the Cambodian Prime Minister Hun Sen criticised the ICC's decision to issue arrest warrants for the Sudanese President, stating that it would hinder international efforts to end the Darfur conflict: "The arrest warrant for the Sudanese President issued by The Hague court will remain without effect as you can wait and see."[1614]

Significantly, in September 2008, following and clearly in direct response to the ICC's July 2008 indictment of President al-Bashir, Sudan was elected as Chairman of the G77, the largest intergovernmental organisation of developing states in the UN (originally 77 founding nations but now 130 strong). This clearly indicated an unprecedented level of solidarity and support in the wake of the ICC actions.[1615] The public support for al-Bashir by the prominent Latin America leader, Venezuela's Hugo Chavez, was typical of the G77's stance.[1616] Most recently, President al-Bashir was invited to chair part of the Sixteenth Summit of the Non-Aligned Movement, held from 26–31 August 2012 in Tehran, Iran. The summit was attended by leaders of 120 countries, including twenty-four presidents, three kings, eight prime ministers and fifty foreign ministers.

Criticism of the ICC is not limited to emergent countries. It has attracted adverse commentary from all sides of the political spectrum in both the developed and developing world. This has ranged from conservative American presidents, conservative British cabinet ministers and liberal international jurists, through to the Australian Communist Party. Steven Fake and Kevin Funk, prominent American leftist activists, have highlighted the view from the non-establishment left:

> That Bashir is on the ICC docket, while Clinton and other white-skinned, Western leaders are not, has done tremendous damage to the court – and its promise to end impunity around the world for human rights violations. Recognising the clear double standard, many across the globe, including those sympathetic to the ICC's stated aims, have come to regard it as little more than a tool of imperialism – and one that only sees human rights abuses if they are committed by poor countries not allied to the West. The ICC has done little to disprove this thesis.[1617]

Far-left critiques of the ICC are equally stark. The Australian Communist Party has said that "[t]he ICC could well stand for Imperialist Crimes Cover-up", adding:

> It certainly does not deserve its official title, since it studiously ignores truly "international" crimes, such as US and NATO aggression or the many massacres of civilians that result. Rather, so far the only alleged crimes it has undertaken to prosecute have all been the result of internal conflicts taking place in countries on the African continent. In short, the ICC so far acts mainly as a way of putting political pressure on, or justifying military action against, weaker governments the Western powers want to replace with leaders of their choice.[1618]

The communist commentators have highlighted the court's two-faced approach to "international justice":

The ICC has developed into one of the most blatant illustrations of double standards. The United States manipulates the ICC without recognising its jurisdiction, and having further protected itself by bilateral agreements with a long list of countries that provide immunity for United States citizens as well as by Congressional laws to protect US citizens from the ICC. Other NATO countries have recognized ICC jurisdiction, but there is no sign that they will ever be troubled by the international court.[1619]

Much to the annoyance of the ICC and its Chief Prosecutor – and a manifestation of the court's perceived lack of legitimacy – the Sudanese President travelled almost immediately after the ICC arrest warrants, within both the Gulf and Africa.[1620] As the ICC supporter Professor David Kaye has had to admit: "Bashir...has managed to travel around Africa and the Arab world, including to states that are parties to the Rome Statute, such as Chad and Kenya."[1621] *The Economist* noted that President al-Bashir "remains firmly in office and seems free to travel to a good number of countries".[1622] President al-Bashir has visited numerous countries in Africa and the Middle East since the court issued indictments and arrest warrants. These countries included Chad, Malawi, Djibouti, Ethiopia, Egypt, Turkey, Qatar and China. President al-Bashir visited Qatar at least five times in the last few years. He has also most recently visited China, Libya, Egypt, Eritrea, Ethiopia, Iran and Saudi Arabia.[1623]

The ICC has issued further indictments with regard to the situation in Darfur.

The Prosecutor v. Bahar Idriss Abu Garda

Bahar Idriss Abu Garda was said by the ICC to be the Chairman and General Coordinator of Military Operations of one of the Darfur rebel movements, the United Resistance Front. The court claimed that he was responsible for an attack carried out against African Union Mission in Sudan (AMIS) peacekeeping personnel, installations, material, units, and vehicles stationed at the Haskanita Military Group Site (MGS Haskanita) at Umm Kadada in North Darfur, Sudan. The Prosecutor alleged that splinter forces of the Justice and Equality Movement, under the command of Abu Garda, jointly with the troops of another armed group, attacked the AMIS base at Haskanita. The attackers, approximately 1,000 persons armed with anti-aircraft guns, artillery guns and rocket-propelled grenade launchers, allegedly killed twelve and severely wounded eight AMIS soldiers. They allegedly destroyed communication installations, dormitories, vehicles and other materials and appropriated property belonging to AMIS, including seventeen vehicles, refrigerators, computers, cellular phones, military boots and uniforms, fuel, ammunition and money during and after the attack.

A court summons for Abu Garda to appear was unsealed on 17 May 2009, and he voluntarily appeared before Pre-Trial Chamber I. This was the first voluntary appearance by a suspect before the court. The ICC held a confirmation hearing from 19–29 October 2009, and Pre-Trial Chamber I found that there were reasonable grounds to believe that

Garda was criminally responsible as a co-perpetrator or as an indirect co-perpetrator for three war crimes under Article 25(3)(a) of the Rome Statute: violence to life in the form of murder, whether committed or attempted, within the meaning of Article 8(2)(c)(i) of the statute; intentionally directing attacks against personnel, installations, material, units or vehicles involved in a peacekeeping mission within the meaning of Article 8(2)(e)(iii) of the statute; and pillaging within the meaning of Article 8(2)(e)(v) of the statute.

On 8 February 2010, Pre-Trial Chamber I refused to confirm the charges against Abu Garda. They ruled that there was not enough evidence to support a trial.[1624] On 23 April 2010, Pre-Trial Chamber I issued a decision rejecting the Prosecutor's application to appeal the decision declining to confirm the charges. Bahar Idriss Abu Garda was appointed the Sudanese Minister of Health in late 2011 as part of international and Sudanese attempts to end the conflict in Darfur.[1625]

The Prosecutor v. Abdallah Banda Abakaer Nourain and Saleh Mohammed Jerbo Jamus

This action is against two Darfur rebel commanders: Abdallah Banda Abakaer Nourain was the Commander-in-Chief of the Justice and Equality Movement Collective-Leadership, one of the components of the United Resistance Front rebel movement; and Saleh Mohammed Jerbo Jamus had been the former Chief of Staff of the SLA-Unity rebel movement, and was subsequently integrated into the Justice and Equality Movement. Banda and Jerbo are allegedly criminally responsible as co-perpetrators for three war crimes under Article 25(3)(a) of the Rome Statute: violence to life, whether committed or attempted, within the meaning of Article 8(2)(c)(i) of the statute; intentionally directing attacks against personnel, installations, material, units or vehicles involved in a peacekeeping mission within the meaning of Article 8(2)(e)(iii) of the statute; and pillaging within the meaning of Article 8(2)(e)(v) of the statute. Banda and Jerbo are alleged to have led an attack on the compound of the African Union Mission in Sudan at Haskanita, which killed twelve AU peacekeepers and left eight others severely wounded.

In March 2011, the Pre-Trial Chamber I confirmed the charges of war crimes brought by the Prosecutor against Banda and Jerbo, thereby committing them to trial by Trial Chamber IV. In January 2012 the defence filed a request for a stay in proceedings arguing that the accused could not receive a fair trial since adequate facilities to investigate and to obtain the attendance of witnesses could not be secured because of the situation in Sudan: "[T]he defence [contended] that severe restrictions on investigations have made an effective defence impossible and that these restrictions by the Government of Sudan... have been absolute." In October 2012, the Trial Chamber rejected this request for a stay, stating that judicial policy "favours deferring decisions on stay applications until the completion of the evidence, when the Trial Chamber is best able to take all factors of possible unfairness of trial, including their origins, into account in the ultimate outcome in the case". On the completion of the evidence, the chamber would then be in a position to either allow the request for a stay in proceedings or submit a verdict for acquittal on grounds of unfair trial. The judges also requested submissions regarding the start date of the trial.

The ICC terminated its case against Saleh Mohammed Jerbo Jamus, on 4 October 2013 following evidence it had received that pointed towards the death of Jerbo on 19 April 2013.[1626]

The Prosecutor v. Abdel Raheem Muhammad Hussein

On 1 March 2012, the ICC issued a warrant of arrest for Lieutenant-General Abdel Raheem Muhammad Hussein, the Minister of National Defence in Sudan and former Minister of the Interior and the Sudanese President's former Special Representative for Darfur. The warrant of arrest for Abdel Raheem Muhammad Hussein lists thirteen counts on the basis of his individual criminal responsibility under Article 25(3)(a) of the Rome Statute as an indirect (co) perpetrator including: Seven counts of crimes against humanity: persecution (Article 7(l)(h)); murder (Article 7(1)(a)); forcible transfer (Article 7(1)(d)); rape (Article 7(1)(g)); inhumane acts (Article 7(l)(k)); imprisonment or severe deprivation of liberty (Article 7(l)(e)); and torture (Article 7(1)(f)). There were also six counts of war crimes: murder (Article 8(2)(c)(i)); attacks against a civilian population (Article 8(2)(e)(i)); destruction of property (Article 8(2)(e)(xii)); rape (Article 8(2)(e)(vi)); pillaging (Article 8(2)(e)(v)); and outrage upon personal dignity (Article 8(2)(c)(ii)).

The ICC indictments have not stopped the Defence Minister from making routine ministerial visits. He has made trips to Libya, Ethiopia, South Sudan and Saudi Arabia.[1627]

The ICC's interaction with Sudan has been a case study in the court's flaws: the political instrumentalisation of the court, most starkly shown in the UNSC's "referral" of the situation in Darfur to the court; the professional ineptitude and arrogance of the OTP and the Chief Prosecutor himself; and the reliance by the court upon very questionable claims made by even more questionable non-governmental organisations, intermediaries and "advocacy" groups.

Ambassador Abdalmahmood Abdalhaleem Mohamed, Permanent Representative of Sudan at the UN in 2009, very clearly stated the Sudanese position regarding ICC:

> For us the ICC doesn't exist. We are not bound by its decisions and we are in no way going to cooperate with it.... It is an insult to justice and it is a demonstration of the Euro-American justice which caused destruction in Iraq, Afghanistan and Gaza.[1628]

Sudan has taken the ICC head on. It has challenged both the legitimacy of the court and its political agenda. In so doing, Khartoum led the way in reasserting African independence. In 2013, Ocampo admitted: "Bashir changed the narrative."[1629]

Tellingly, in July 2013, the former United Nations High Commissioner for Human

Rights Louise Arbour admitted that referring the Darfur case to the ICC was a wrong move given subsequent lack of international support for the Hague-based court on the issue: "I participated in the [UN] Commission of Inquiry [on Darfur]. I appeared before the [United Nations] Security Council (UNSC) so that we refer the matter to the ICC, but in retrospect, I realize that it was a very bad idea."[1630]

Chapter Twenty-two

THE COURT AND KENYA

"As far as I am concerned those cases have no merit and I have made my position clear before."

ICC Judge Hans Peter Kaul[1631]

"[T]here are grave problems in the Prosecution's system of evidence review, as well as a serious lack of proper oversight by senior Prosecution staff."

ICC Judge Christine Van den Wyngaert[1632]

Kenya has been a State Party to the Rome Statute since 1 March 2005. This allows the ICC jurisdiction over war crimes, crimes against humanity, and genocide committed by Kenyan nationals on Kenyan territory after 1 July 2002, in cases where the court decides that the government is unwilling or unable to investigate and prosecute those crimes.

The Kenyan situation provided the first example of the Prosecutor invoking the *proprio motu* powers granted to him under Article 15(3) of the Rome Statute to initiate an investigation at his own instigation, without a referral from the State Party or the UNSC. Kenya also provides a clear example of a sovereign nation's parliament deciding – as the UK had done in the case of Northern Ireland – to put peace before a judicial process, only in this instance to be challenged by an autistic European legal fundamentalism not applied to European countries.

On 27 December 2007, presidential, parliamentary and municipal elections were held in Kenya. The incumbent President, Mwai Kibaki, the Party of National Unity (PNU) candidate, and Raila Odinga, from the opposition Orange Democratic Movement (ODM), were the leading candidates. While early indications showed that Odinga was likely to win the election, the Kenyan Electoral Commission announced that Kibaki had been re-elected. He was sworn in as President. Odinga rejected the result, claiming widespread, systematic electoral fraud. Violence erupted and continued until a peace deal and power-sharing agreement was reached between Kibaki and Odinga under the mediation of former UN Secretary-General Kofi Annan. Kibaki remained as President and Odinga assumed the newly created office of Prime Minister. In the period from the 27

December 2007 election to 28 February 2008, when the power-sharing deal was agreed, more than 1,000 people died in the violence, which also uprooted 300,000 others.[1633]

The ICC Prosecutor alleged that the post-election violence was coordinated and targeted civilians. The Prosecutor argued that ODM opposition supporters were initially mobilised to attack ethnic Kikuyu and others perceived to have voted for President Kibaki and his PNU party. The prosecution then further alleged that as a consequence retaliation was then targeted at the Kalenjin, Luo, and Luhya ethnic communities, groups seen as being affiliated with the ODM opposition party.

The government of Kenya established an international Commission of Inquiry on Post Election Violence in February 2008. This was chaired by Kenyan Court of Appeals Judge Philip Waki, and became known as the Waki Commission. The Waki Commission recommended that the government establish a special tribunal of national and international judges to investigate and prosecute perpetrators of the post-election violence. Although both Kibaki and Odinga voiced support for a local tribunal, the idea was rejected by the Kenyan parliament. In February 2009, the Kenyan parliament voted against a bill to establish the special tribunal, and no further action was taken by the government. Waki passed his report back to Kofi Annan with instructions that it be passed to the ICC if progress with a local tribunal was not made. On 5 November 2009, the Chief Prosecutor of the ICC notified the court of his intention to submit a request for the authorisation of an investigation into the situation in Kenya pursuant to Article 15(3) of the Rome Statute, namely the post-election violence in Kenya in 2007–2008. On 6 November 2009, the court assigned the situation to Pre-Trial Chamber II, composed of Judge Ekaterina Trendafilova, Judge Hans-Peter Kaul and Judge Cuno Tarfusser. On 3 March 2010, the Prosecutor provided the court with a list of twenty names of persons alleged to bear the gravest responsibility for the post-election violence. Among the names were said to be senior Kenyan politicians and businessmen accused of allegedly organising and financing ethnic attacks.

On 31 March 2010, Pre-Trial Chamber II of the ICC granted the prosecution's request to open an investigation into alleged crimes against humanity in Kenya. In its decision, the majority stated that there was a reasonable basis to believe that crimes against humanity had been committed on the territory of Kenya. The court also held that jurisdictional requirements had been satisfied, and the threshold for opening an investigation had been met. The investigation would examine events in Kenya between 1 June 2002 and 26 November 2009. Judge Hans-Peter Kaul entered a dissenting opinion in the judgment, but the judgment was passed by a two-to-one majority. In his dissent he wrote: "In essence, the main reason for this position is the following: both, my interpretation of article 7(2)(a) of the [Rome] Statute, which sets out the legal definition of 'attack directed against any civilian population' as constitutive contextual element of crimes against humanity, and my examination of the Prosecutor's Request and supporting material, including the victims' representations, have led me to conclude that the acts which occurred on the territory of the Republic of Kenya do not qualify as crimes against humanity falling under the jurisdictional ambit of the Court."[1634]

The new Kenyan government continued with a range of legal and political reforms.

On 4 August 2010, a referendum overwhelmingly approved a new Kenyan constitution. The constitution was officially promulgated on 26 August. Reforms notwithstanding, on 15 December 2010 the Prosecutor requested that Pre-Trial Chamber II of the ICC issue summonses to appear for six prominent Kenyans on the basis that there existed reasonable grounds to believe that they were criminally responsible for crimes against humanity, pursuant to Article 7 of the Rome Statute. The men were the Kenyan Deputy Prime Minister, Minister of Finance and chairman of the KANU political party (which was part of President Kibaki's Party of National Unity), Uhuru Kenyatta; the Head of the Public Service, Cabinet Secretary and Chairman of the National Security Advisory Committee, Francis Muthaura; the Chief Executive of the Postal Corporation of Kenya, and former Commissioner of the Kenya Police, Major-General Muhammed Hussein Ali; the Minister for Higher Education, Science and Technology and ODM member of the National Assembly for the Eldoret North Constituency, William Ruto; the Head of Operations at the Kalenjin language radio station KASS FM, radio journalist Joshua arap Sang; and Chairman of the opposition Orange Democratic Movement and Minister for Industrialisation, Henry Kiprono Kosgey.

The indictments of the six Kenyans provided a clear-cut example of the court's political tailoring of its involvement in the situation. *The Economist* reported: "The ICC has shown some sensitivity to local politics in its handling of the Kenyan case – by indicting an equal number from the two groups."[1635] One does not have to be an expert in jurisprudence to know that justice does not equate to political balance.

The Prosecutor requested that the six Kenyans appear before the court in two separate cases. On 8 March 2011, ICC Pre-Trial Chamber II issued summonses to appear to the six men.[1636] On 7 April 2011, Ruto, Kosgey and Sang made their initial appearance at the ICC. The Confirmation of Charges hearing was scheduled for 1 September 2011. On 8 April 2011, Kenyatta, Ali and Muthaura made their first appearance before the court. On 23 January 2012, Pre-Trial Chamber II dismissed the charges against two of them, Henry Kosgey and Muhammed Hussein Ali. The Pre-Trial Chamber found that the Prosecutor's evidence failed to satisfy the evidentiary threshold required under the Rome Statute to bring Kosgey and Ali to trial. With regard to Kosgey, the chamber found that the Prosecutor relied on one anonymous and insufficiently corroborated witness. The chamber also determined that Kosgey suffered prejudice due to the redaction of certain dates related to a number of meetings that he allegedly attended, which proved to be essential for his defence and for the finding on his criminal responsibility. With regard to Ali, the chamber found that there was not sufficient evidence to connect the Kenyan Police to attacks carried out in the areas where perceived ODM supporters resided. The Prosecutor had alleged Ali, a former police chief, contributed to the crimes through directing the Kenyan Police to not prevent attacks carried out by PNU supporters. Without sufficient evidence of police involvement, however, the chamber declined to confirm charges.

Judge Kaul once again issued a dissenting opinion in both cases. In these opinions he stated that he continued to believe that the court lacked jurisdiction *ratione materiae* over the situation in Kenya. His assertion was that although crimes were committed they were not of a nature that constitute crimes against humanity within the jurisdiction of the ICC. This was the third time that Judge Kaul had entered a dissent opposing the prosecutions.

The British parliamentarian Ian Paisley Jr. pointed to the practical dangers of ICC intervention in Kenya:

> In Kenya, where one of the court's most high-profile cases is taking place, the I.C.C. has focused on bringing to trial those accused of inciting post-election violence in 2007–8. This risks fueling divisions in a country where tribal loyalties and factionalism still dominate politics. Kenya, often seen as a great African success story, is now heading toward a dangerous impasse. The court's determination to bring to trial several defendants accused of fomenting violence has enabled Prime Minister Raila Odinga to call for the arrest of his main political opponent, Deputy Prime Minister Uhuru Kenyatta, son of the country's founding president, who now faces I.C.C. charges. Mr. Odinga and Mr. Kenyatta are both leaders in a coalition government that came together with the support of the international community precisely in order to reconcile Kenya's opposing political and tribal groupings. Yet the I.C.C.'s intervention is increasingly likely to drive this government and the country further apart, allowing a political leader from one ethnic group to try to remove an opponent from another ethnic group from the scene. This is particularly perilous when the root of the post-election violence in Kenya is tribal conflict.[1637]

On 9 March 2011, Justice Minister Mutula Kilonzo stated that Kenya would challenge the right of the ICC to try the cases involving post-election violence, and on 22 March President Kibaki said that Kenya will fast-track laws to implement its new constitution, set up a supreme court and reform its judiciary to strengthen accountability of the courts to handle the trials of suspects. Nevertheless, on 30 August 2011, the ICC dismissed Kenya's bid to stop a probe into post-election violence, saying Kenya had failed to show it was conducting its own investigation of the suspects. This was in the face of Kenya's adoption of a new constitution and other reforms that showed the government's commitment to carry out its own prosecutions. The new constitution incorporated a bill of rights, which strengthened fair trial rights and procedural guarantees within the Kenyan criminal justice system. The constitution also introduced a comprehensive range of judicial reforms that transformed the administration of justice in Kenya. The Kenyan government stated:

> Deficiencies and weaknesses from the past have been specifically targeted to guarantee the independent and impartial dispensation of justice. National courts will now be capable of trying crimes from the post-election violence, including the ICC cases, without the need for legislation to create a special tribunal, thus overcoming a hurdle previously a major stumbling block. The new Constitution guarantees the independence of the State's

investigative organs and ushers in wide-ranging reforms to the police services. An independent Commission for the Implementation of the Constitution is established to monitor, facilitate and oversee the development of legislation and administrative procedures required to implement the Constitution.[1638]

Kenya pointed to the consequences of the court challenging Kenya's right to put its own citizens before its own courts:

> To challenge Kenya's right to try its own citizens in the present circumstances would send out the wrong message to countries that are seeking to strengthen their national jurisdictions to fulfil their obligations under the Rome Statute as well as to those States that are considering becoming parties to the Rome Statute. It could even be regarded as sending an inappropriate message to those major countries – including some permanent members of the Security Council – that have not ratified the Rome Statute.[1639]

The constitution established an independent Judicial Services Commission (JSC), chaired by the Chief Justice, to "promote and facilitate the independence and accountability of the judiciary and the efficient, effective and transparent administration of justice" (Articles 171-172). It is charged with responsibility of recommending persons for appointment as judges, including the Chief Justice. The Chief Justice is appointed by the President in accordance with the recommendation of the JSC, and subject to the approval of the National Assembly. All other judges shall be appointed by the President on the recommendation of the JSC (Article 166(1)). The *Judicial Services Act 2011* was enacted to give effect to these provisions. The act increases the personnel of the judiciary, streamlines organisational aspects, and manages all disciplinary matters. The act established the National Council on the Administration of Justice, which is charged with formulating policy for and monitoring the administration of justice. The Judicial Services Commission was enacted under Part III of the act. The act sets out a competitive, open and transparent procedure for the appointment of judges. A crucial new change is that the JSC has the power to vet judicial officers. A separate act, the *Vetting of Judges and Magistrates Act 2011*, has been passed to provide for the vetting of judges as well, whether already appointed or to be appointed.

A vital new post for the purpose of progressing the investigative process was created under the new constitution to direct and oversee all investigations and prosecutions, namely the Director of Public Prosecutions (DPP). This position had previously been filled by the Attorney General. Under the new constitution it has been separated from the Attorney General's office to create a new office entirely independent of government with all the necessary safeguards to guarantee independence of investigations and prosecutions at all levels. The new constitution established an independent office of the Director of Public Prosecutions, which "shall have the power to direct the Inspector-General of the National Police Service" to investigate any information or allegation of criminal conduct and the Inspector-General shall comply with any such direction" (Article 157(4)). The DPP shall have secure tenure of office for a term of eight years (Article 157(5)) and may only be removed from office on petition to the Public Service Commission and by an appointed tribunal in accordance with the procedure set out in Article 158. The DPP shall exercise state powers of prosecution and may "institute and undertake criminal proceedings against any person before any court…in respect of any offence alleged to have been committed" (Article 157(6)). The DPP "shall not require the consent of any person or authority for the commencement of criminal proceedings and in the exercise of his or her powers or functions, shall not be under the direction or control of any person or authority" (Article 157(10)). The DPP must exercise his powers having regard to "the public interest, the interests of the administration of justice, and the need to prevent and avoid abuse of the legal process" (Article 157(11)).

The issue of witness protection, which had been identified as a major concern by the Waki Report, was also comprehensively addressed in the *Witness Protection Amendment Act 2010* (which amended the *Witness Protection Act 2008*). The 2010 act established an independent and autonomous Witness Protection Agency (WPA) to deal with all witness protection matters arising in investigations and trials.

The ICC ignored all these developments and the trial of the four men was set for April 2013.

The Prosecutor v. William Samoei Ruto and Joshua arap Sang

Ruto was alleged to be an indirect co-perpetrator of crimes against humanity of murder, forcible transfer, and persecution allegedly committed against supporters of the PNU. Sang is alleged to have contributed to the commission of the crimes. Both were members of the Orange Democratic Movement, the opposition party at the time of the elections. The crimes were crimes against humanity of murder, Article 7(l)(a); deportation or forcible transfer of population, Article 7(l)(d); and persecution, Article 7(l)(h). The victims of these alleged crimes were PNU supporters as part of a plan to gain power in northern parts of Rift Valley Province by driving out PNU supporters.

The Prosecutor v. Francis Kirimi Muthaura and Uhuru Muigai Kenyatta

Muthaura and Kenyatta, members of the PNU, then the incumbent party, were alleged to be indirect co-perpetrators of the crimes against humanity of murder, forcible transfer, rape, persecution, and other inhumane acts, allegedly committed against ODM supporters, partly in retaliation against attacks against the PNU supporters. These crimes against humanity were murder, Article 7(l)(a); deportation or forcible transfer, Article 7(l)(d); rape, Article 7(l)(g); persecution, Articles 7(l)(h); and other inhumane acts, Article 7(l)(k). These crimes were allegedly committed to ensure that the PNU remained in power, and as part of orchestrated revenge attacks against ODM supporters in Nakuru and

Naivasha in the central Rift Valley. Muthaura and Kenyatta were accused of mobilising the Mungiki, a Kikuyu-led gang, to attack perceived ODM supporters.

Kenyatta and Muthaura resigned their posts of Finance Minister and Cabinet Secretary respectively on 26 January 2010: Kenyatta retained his position of Deputy Prime Minister. Both Uhuru Kenyatta and William Ruto declared their candidacy in the 2013 Kenyan presidential election.

On 22 December 2010, a week after the ICC Prosecutor made public the identities of the individuals he was seeking to prosecute, the Kenyan parliament passed a motion seeking to withdraw Kenya as a State Party to the Rome Statute, the treaty which established the ICC. The motion, introduced by assembly member Isaac Ruto, had previously been disallowed by Deputy Speaker Farah Maalim who ruled it was unconstitutional; however an amended version was introduced the following day and passed.[1640] During the debate, the Minister for Energy Kiraitu Murungi claimed the ICC was a colonialist, imperialist court. This motion mandated ministers to move to repeal Kenya's *International Crimes Act*, which ratified the Rome Statute and had amended Kenya's criminal code.[1641]

In February 2011, Kenya appealed to the UNSC, asking it to defer the trials at The Hague. Some critics in Kenya also questioned the constitutionality of the Rome Statute, arguing that it is incompatible with the Constitution of Kenya, which was passed by the 2010 referendum.[1642] The Kenyan government's attempt to defer the cases at the ICC by appealing to members of the UNSC failed without being voted on. The Western P-3 permanent members had indicated it simply would not happen.

On 31 March 2011, the Kenyan government, represented by British lawyers Sir Geoffrey Nice QC and Rodney Dixon, subsequently applied directly to the ICC. The Kenyan government challenged the admissibility of the cases before the ICC. It argued that the adoption of Kenya's new constitution and associated legal reforms had opened the way for Kenya to conduct its own prosecutions relating to the post-election violence. Kenya's application to Pre-Trial Chamber II that the two cases were inadmissible was rejected by the court.[1643] Judge Anita Ušacka entered a dissenting opinion, observing that the Pre-Trial Chamber "did not completely account for the sovereign rights of Kenya and the principle of complementarity. Instead, the Chamber, on the basis of its understanding of what constitutes a 'case' in terms of article 17(1)(a) of the Statute, gave too much weight to considerations of expeditiousness."[1644] On 30 August 2011, the ICC Appeals Chamber confirmed the Pre-Trial Chamber's decision on the admissibility of the cases.[1645]

On 26 November 2012, the Kenyan Chief Justice Willy Mutunga announced the establishment of a special division of the High Court to try post-election violence cases. The new institution's remit will include a range of international and transnational offences such as crimes against humanity, terrorism, money laundering, and narcotics, human and body-parts trafficking.

In another example of the ICC's questionable position on presumption of innocence, Ocampo, while still the Prosecutor, demanded that the assets of the four Kenyans before the court be frozen and made available to compensate victims of post-election violence in case they are jailed. The Kenyan Attorney General Githu Muigai categorically stated that it would not cooperate with identifying their assets. In a three-page letter sent to the

ICC, Githu said the government believed that the request had no basis: "This request cannot be acceded to without a court order and further our interpretation of the law is that Article 75(4) (of the Rome Statute) makes it clear that a request for cooperation in identifying and freezing assets for purposes of reparations (rather than forfeiture) may only take place after a person is convicted." The Attorney General stated that Article 77(2) provides for forfeiture of proceeds, assets and property but only after it is clear that they have been derived from the crime: "Please note that Article 93 of the Rome Statute enjoins states to provide certain forms of cooperation including requests for freezing of assets in accordance with national laws. Accordingly Article 40 of the Kenyan constitution prohibits the arbitrary deprivation of a person's property."

As with the case of the ICC and Sudan, the AU endorsed the position of the Kenyan government in seeking to delay or postpone the ICC proceedings.[1646]

Fatal flaws in the prosecution case soon began to emerge. A central prosecution claim was that in preparation for the post-election violence a meeting took place at the State House in Nairobi on 26 November 2007 between Muthaura, Kenyatta, Mungiki representatives and President Kibaki. A prosecution witness, "OTP-4", subsequently identified as James Maina Kabutu, was key to the prosecution's case at the pre-trial hearing in trying to establish that Kenyatta and Muthaura had met and were involved with the Mungiki, who were said have been a secretive group of organised criminals inspired by Kenya's Mau-Mau fighters who were used in the violence. OTP-4 was said to be one of the Mungiki representatives present at the meeting. It was also said that he witnessed Francis Muthaura giving money to Mungiki leaders. On 6 February 2013, Steven Kay QC, representing Kenyatta, told the court that this key prosecution witness had admitted lying. He said that without his testimony, the cases would not have been confirmed. Kay asked that Kenyatta's case should be referred back to the Pre-Trial Chamber for dismissal to "avoid a serious miscarriage of justice". Kay informed the court: "After the confirmation hearing, on 25 May 2012, OTP-4 resiled from his evidence and admitted he had lied and was not present at the meeting as alleged. OTP-4 has also admitted lying about another meeting at which he alleged he was present with Mr. Kenyatta and Mungiki personnel on 17 November 2007." The Prosecutor had also dropped OTP-4 from her list of proposed witnesses. *The Guardian* reported that "[t]he witness had admitted in 2010 that he was not present at the meeting but his statement was kept from defence lawyers for two years and not disclosed until after the confirmation hearing".[1647] The prosecution had misled the Pre-Trial Chamber in order to strengthen its case for the case to go forward to trial. In a re-run of the Lubanga trial, the prosecution had also prevented defence lawyers from having access to "significant exculpatory evidence necessary for the proceedings". The defence quite simply accused the prosecution of concealing critical exonerating evidence with the help of the pre-trial judges. Kay stated that if the Pre-Trial Chamber had had all the information it would not have confirmed the case for trial. He asked the Trial Chamber to refer the case back to the Pre-Trial Chamber for reconsideration and to "reprimand the prosecution for acting in bad faith".

The case of prosecution witness number four, OTP-4, had emerged some time earlier. Kabutu admitted that he had lied in his testimony to both the Waki Commission and the

ICC. Kabutu is said to have provided a written affidavit disclaiming his testimony before a notary public on 25 February 2009, at the Radisson Hotel in New York, and to have read a similar affidavit before a notary public at the Stanford Park Hotel in Palo Alto, California, on 28 July 2009.[1648] In March 2012, Kabutu was reported to have written to the Appeal Chamber of the ICC seeking to end his involvement with the case.[1649] Kabutu stated that the evidence he provided was not correct and that his request to withdraw his evidence and place as an ICC prosecution witness was denied by the OTP without informing the pre-trial chamber judges.[1650] The Ugandan journalist Dr. David Matsanga had produced a booklet on witness number four. In his publication, *Did He Investigate Kenyan Cases?*, Matsanga put Ocampo on the spot, publishing interviews with Kabutu. The publication was handed over to the Appeals Chamber of the ICC along with a cover letter dated 22 February 2012.[1651] In the letter, Matsanga stated that he arranged a meeting with Kabutu after being contacted by Kabutu's attorney: "[A]s an international investigative journalist who has done several other assignments in the media and the UK and the world, I was contacted by the attorneys of Mr. James Maina Kabutu. I did not know him or the attorney and after a brief exchange of telephone calls my investigation team fixed an appointment to meet them in the USA."[1652] Matsanga informed the judges that the prosecution was relying on false testimony: "[T]he testimony of witness number 4 forms the core fallacy on the chief prosecutor's case that is before you. It is imperative that the world knows whether a reputable international court of justice will rely on fake witnesses paraded to the court to put on the trial innocent people."[1653] In a typical display of arrogance, the ICC Chief Prosecutor threatened to request the arrest of David Matsanga. A statement from Ocampo's office stated: "We will investigate who is trying to tamper with potential witnesses and we will request appropriate measures, including arrests. Do not expect us to debate these issues in the media."[1654]

The new Chief Prosecutor, Fatou Bensouda, did not address the specific points raised by Kay in February 2013. She maintained that the conditions in the summons issued against Kenyatta were "adequate for the purpose of trial".[1655] *The Guardian* concluded: "Prosecutors must act in good faith. Moreno-Ocampo did not seem to understand his duty to disclose exculpatory evidence until it was explained to him by the court. Bensouda has inherited this case, along with many others, from her predecessor. If Kay's allegations of bad faith are made out, Bensouda should distance herself from an approach that did great damage to the court's reputation in its first decade."[1656] She chose not to do so and continued with a deeply flawed case.

In March 2013, Uhuru Kenyatta's lawyer Steven Kay stated that the case against Uhuru was now based on two other witnesses – OTP-11 and OTP-12 – whose evidence was based on what they had been told by OTP-4 who had subsequently been dropped from the court's witness list as unreliable. A Kenyan newspaper reported a statement by Kenyatta that described these two witnesses as "extortionists who had attempted to secure money from [Uhuru]" before they were adopted as prosecution witnesses:[1657]

> Bensouda also has serious questions to answer as to why she insists on saying OTP-11 and OTP-12 can still be considered to provide evidence to confirm

charges against Kenyatta, when these witnesses attempted to extort money from the Defence to testify in their favour, before their extortion demands were rebuffed and they became Prosecution witnesses funded by the witness protection scheme.[1658]

Steven Kay argued that the prosecution had for over two years been in possession of a second contradictory statement issued by Kabutu, but had instead gone ahead to use the first statement to gain confirmation of the charges against Uhuru. Kay claims that the ICC Pre-Trial Chamber decided to send Uhuru's case to trial based on what the prosecution knew at the time was "fraudulent evidence". In her filing in response, Bensouda admitted that the prosecution was wrong for failing to inform the Pre-Trial Chamber before it made its decision to confirm the charges against Uhuru, and that Kabutu's testimony could not be relied on due to inconsistencies. Bensouda argued that she could not refer Uhuru's case back to the pre-trial because she had additional evidence from witnesses 11 and 12. Uhuru's lawyers responded by pointing out that they had presented the court with evidence that the two witnesses only had corroborative value as their testimony was based on what they were told by Kabutu.[1659]

The comparisons with the Lubanga trial are clear and disturbing. In *The Prosecutor v. Thomas Lubanga Dyilo*, Ocampo hid items of exculpatory evidence from Lubanga's defence. The trial chamber in that case, headed by Sir Adrian Fulford, threw out many of Ocampo's witness statements, finding that they were at best deeply flawed and at worst perjury. The judge also warned the intermediaries who provided the witnesses that they may be prosecuted for their actions. The Prosecutor was also caught up in serious procedural irregularities with regard to the discredited witnesses. Sir Adrian twice sought to end the Lubanga case because of the withholding of exculpatory evidence and questionable witnesses, only to be reversed on appeal. Ocampo's successor, Fatou Bensouda, has now also found herself at the heart of a similar and equally serious scandal involving the withholding of vital exculpatory evidence and witnesses giving false testimony. Luckily for Bensouda the judges in the Kenya case were not as experienced as Adrian Fulford: one was a Japanese diplomat without any background whatsoever in law.

The use of intermediaries proved to be deeply flawed in the Lubanga case. Only one of the alleged witnesses produced by intermediaries was judged to be reliable in the trial. Yet, investigative journalist Elliot Wilson, who writes for *The Spectator*, *The Observer* and other international publications, has reported that "Ocampo has employed precisely the same methods in gathering evidence for the Kenyatta case in Nairobi". Wilson has pointed out that "[t]here is simply no personal, practical or legal reason why Ocampo and his inner circle could not have gathered witness statements directly, on the ground, in Kenya". In Kenya, the court has instead used local European funded non-governmental organisations such as the Kenya Human Rights Commission, and the Kenya National Commission on Human Rights. As with their counterparts in the DRC, these groups were said to have been particularly helpful in sourcing "witnesses". Wilson reported that "[o]ne such witness, incidentally, has proven himself to be utterly unreliable, having changed his statement on no fewer than four occasions, including attempting once to retract his statement completely". Courtenay Griffiths QC has reported an added dimension to the issue: "In the Kenya case, these intermediaries happened to be well known associates of Raila Odinga, the current prime minister of Kenya, and Mr. Kenyatta's long-term political opponent."[1660] Wilson has also asked the question: "Surely, you would think a witness who has changed his statement on multiple occasions, having been assisted by an intermediary whose intentions were so palpably political, should be dismissed by any reasonable provincial court, let alone the ICC. Yet the answer to that question would currently seem to be a resounding 'No'."[1661]

The court has also been party to a further, and related, abuse of process. The very late disclosure of prosecution materials by ICC Prosecutor Fatou Bensouda, possibly because of a reluctance on the part of the Prosecutor to expose yet more faulty evidence and questionable witnesses, made it very difficult for the defence teams to conduct an adequate defence when the trial was initially scheduled to begin in April 2013. Ruto's lawyer, David Hooper, stated: "It is submitted that such extensive late disclosure, which is still continuing, was anticipated by neither the defence team nor the Chamber. In those circumstances, the defence invites the Chamber to consider providing it with more time to prepare its case."[1662]

The court was also involved in another abuse of process. Defence teams accused the prosecution of introducing new allegations as a "patch up" once they had realised their case had been dramatically weakened after withdrawal of key witness testimony. In any functional court new allegations can only be introduced if they reinforce the confirmed case. Karim Khan QC, the lawyer for Francis Muthaura, has made this clear: "Mr Muthaura has been called to answer a case which bears no resemblance to the one confirmed against him, which is manifestly unfair."[1663] Khan stated further:

> The pre-trial brief contains new allegations that were not previously made against ambassador Muthaura. The pre-trial brief is based upon new and untested evidence obtained by the Office of the Prosecutor (OTP) post-confirmation. On any view, the case now advanced by the OTP has undergone a metamorphosis from that confirmed by the PTC in January 2012.[1664]

The ICC's involvement with Kenya is very interesting for several reasons. It was the first time that the Prosecutor had invoked the *proprio motu* powers granted to him under Article 15(3) of the Rome Statute. The Prosecutor chose to intervene in a situation of post-election violence in the country. The Prosecutor and Pre-Trial Chamber moved with undue speed, without affording the post-election coalition government sufficient time to investigate the violence, something the government had pledged to do. The court ignored the comprehensive raft of constitutional and political changes and reforms the government had introduced in order to expedite the investigation of what had happened. The court has ignored Kenyan government requests to try those alleged to have been responsible for the post-electoral violence in Kenya – despite an established judicial system, and comprehensive reforms to the system since 2007. At the same time, the court was bending over backwards to entertain Libyan transitional government requests to try two Libyan ICC indictees in Libya, despite a questionable and imperfect legal system. The court's involvement in Kenya has also been useful in that it has demonstrated that serious procedural irregularities – judicial misbehaviour that should terminate any legal proceedings forthwith – were not just limited to the situation in the DRC and other situations, but were repeated in Kenyan cases. And, quite simply, the prosecution has been making things up as the case has progressed.

What has also become clear is that the ICC intervention in Kenya has had unintended consequences. *New African* reported in January 2013 that "the Netherlands-based court has become propaganda fodder for Kenyan politicians":

> When former deputy premier and finance minister Uhuru Kenyatta, agriculture minister William Ruto, and two others appeared before a pre-trial session of the ICC in 2011, and were confirmed to stand trial, it was as if their political epitaphs had been written. Yet, today both Kenyatta and Ruto have managed to not only make the ICC an election campaign tool, but they have also swayed the majority of the public to their side. The two men have turned the ICC into a blessing and reinvented their political careers. They have used every available opportunity to score political points and effectively turn their ICC-debacle into a sympathy-seeking platform.[1665]

In January 2012, Ruto defied Raila Odinga, the head of Orange Democratic Movement, and set up his own party, the United Republican Party (URP). According to Ruto, one of the two main reasons that made him leave the ODM was the ICC charge with which he viewed Odinga to have been involved. Four months later, in May 2012, Uhuru Kenyatta left the Kenya African National Union to launch his own party, The National Alliance (TNA). The TNA immediately began to win parliamentary by-elections. Separate to Kenyatta's TNA victories, Ruto undercut Odinga's political appeal in the ODM's crucial Rift Valley constituencies. Kenyatta and Ruto subsequently formed a TNA-URP coalition. In January 2013, *New African* noted: "Amazingly, 'the ICC effect' which was initially thought to benefit Prime Minister Odinga is now turning out to be his worst nightmare, as Kenyatta and Ruto have succeeded in making the ICC an election issue at the expense of Odinga. The confirmation of Ruto for trial by the ICC significantly eroded Odinga's support in the Rift Valley province."[1666] The BBC observed that "anecdotal evidence suggests Mr Kenyatta re-branded the indictment in such a supremely intuitive way that the ICC label actually worked in his favour."[1667]

One month later, Chatham House noted that "Kenyatta and Ruto have both gained popularity since the ICC's charges against them were announced." A Chatham House analysis has noted of this popularity that:

> This is partly due to a commonly expressed opinion that the ICC's intervention is a political ploy by Odinga and his purported "Western allies" to ensure the electoral victory of [Odinga's coalition] CORD. In this narrative, President Kibaki and Prime Minister Odinga are seen to bear greater responsibility for

the 2007–08 post-election crisis. The idea that Kenyatta and Ruto have been targeted by the ICC as the result of malign political influences both within and outside Kenya draws strength from dissenting opinions at the ICC, and has placed great emphasis on the Luo background that US President Barack Obama's shares with Odinga.[1668]

Chatham House documented that "[s]trong narratives have also developed at a community level":

> Within the Kalenjin community, for example, prominent arguments cast the ICC's charges against Ruto and Sang as an indictment of the whole community based on a disputed claim that the violence in the Rift Valley was organized prior to the 2007 election by a "Kalenjin network". References to the existence of such a network were made by the ICC's prosecutor when charges against Ruto and Sang were confirmed, but have been rejected by many at the local level as being at odds with individual and collective experiences of the post-election crisis.[1669]

Chatham House also reported that "many in the Kikuyu community" maintain that "Kenyatta's alleged actions helped to end the violence and to force the principals to the negotiating table". Simply put, Kenyatta was seen as a peacemaker. Punitive ICC measures are thus seen to be invalid.[1670]

The Kenyan election also showed the extent of foreign attempts to interfere with the sovereignty and internal affairs of Kenya. Firstly, EU control over the ICC was strongly hinted at when the EU stated that it might back local trials if Kenya revamped its courts: Kenya did modernise its courts, but the EU chose to continue nevertheless with the action by the ICC. Secondly, the EU chose to make much more overt attempts to influence events in Kenya by directly interfering in the Kenyan electoral process. *New African* has observed:

> Worried by the surging popularity of Kenyatta and Ruto, foreign diplomats accredited to Kenya have waded in on the ICC issue. The possibility that the URP-TNA coalition could win the March polls has irked the diplomats who have warned Kenyans against electing "suspects", as it would compromise the country's international standing.[1671]

For all the pretence of respect for legal due process, the European countries controlling the ICC clearly share the former Chief Prosecutor's disregard for presumption of innocence. *New African* quotes the German Minister for Economic Co-operation and Development, Dirk Niebel, as saying while visiting Kenya in August 2012: "Though the suspects are innocent until proven guilty, Kenya could face difficulties if one of them was elected and later found guilty of crimes committed during the trial." The British High Commissioner to Kenya, Christian Turner, had earlier stated: "The electoral matter is a Kenyan affair. *But neither myself nor other government ministers talk to or engage with indictees.*"[1672] (Emphasis added.) Turner was also reported as stating: "The policy of my government remains that we do not have contact with ICC indictees unless it is essential. That is not only the policy of my government but also the policy of all the EU and indeed most other international partners."[1673] Kenyatta's Jubilee Alliance openly stated that it was "deeply concerned about the shadowy, suspicious and rather animated involvement of the British High Commissioner in Kenya's election."[1674] The French Ambassador Etienne De Poncins, said: "There will be consequences based on characters elected. Many programmes and international relations will be determined by who Kenyans choose. It is not a surprise the choice of leaders to be elected will greatly determine the place of Kenya with other countries within and outside the continent. France will have limited contact with Kenya as it is the policy of other countries who are signatories to the [ICC's] Rome Statute."[1675] The former UN Secretary-General Kofi Annan, and the US Secretary of State, Hillary Clinton, also expressed similar sentiments. Commentators noted that when Assistant US Secretary of State for African Affairs Johnnie Carson stated that "choices have consequences", he "triggered a wave of indignation" in Kenya.[1676]

Interestingly, Jendayi Frazer, the former US Assistant Secretary of State for African Affairs during the Bush Administration,[1677] and Carson's predecessor in office, criticised him for what he had said. In comments made in a public discussion at the Brookings Institution, she urged pragmatism in Western approaches to Kenya. Frazer said that she was "troubled" by Carson's "very reckless and irresponsible" statement, which she called "essentially meddling in Kenya's election". She stated that the ICC case against Kenyatta "is a weak one and is based on hearsay", and added that the ICC was "a very manipulated institution, particularly by the West".[1678] Frazer stated that "the ICC was politicised when used to warn Kenyans about whom to vote for in their 2013 elections". She noted: "[O]n the eve of the election, several Western countries were seen as using the ICC indictment to pre-emptively 'try and convict' Uhuru Kenyatta in the court of public opinion, presumably to tank his electoral prospects."[1679] She said that the statement by her successor as US Assistant Secretary of State for African Affairs that "choices have consequences…contradicted President Obama's appropriate statement that 'the choice of who will lead Kenya is up to the Kenyan people. The USA does not endorse any candidate for office.'"[1680] In so doing, Frazer herself displayed the double standards the American government applied to the ICC. When in office Frazer had not hesitated to ensure that the Bush Administration manipulated the court within African situations.

New African reported that the Western position was interpreted as "'foreign interference' in Kenya's affairs, and an application of double standards".[1681] Kenya's Attorney General Githu Muigai zeroed in on American criticism insinuating that Kenya was not committed to the ICC, while the USA itself has refused to sign the ICC's Rome Statute that established the court: "Kenya is among the founding members of the Rome Statute and among the first in the world to domesticate the Statute, yet non-members continue to speak loudest on its matters." The chairman of the influential Constitutional Implementation Committee, Charles Nyachae, also criticised Hillary Clinton's position: "[Her] position that Uhuru Kenyatta and William Ruto should not run for the presidency is unnecessary and unhelpful."[1682] Ruto has been equally critical of the American stance: "The US secretary of state has told the government that Mr. Kenyatta and I are not supposed to run. She has also hinted that America will impose sanctions on us if we participate in the polls and win. This is dictatorship. When she visited Chief Justice Willy Mutunga at the Supreme Court and commented on the ICC cases involving us, she was clearly interfering. We did not finance any chaos or beat anybody in the 2007 polls."

Kenyatta was himself critical of Western attempts to interfere in Kenyan domestic politics: "My focus is on Kenya, the region, and the continent. No Kenyan or African has said Uhuru should not vie for the presidency, so the rest can stay away if they don't want to associate with us." He dismissed the Western diplomats as "tourists": "We welcome them to continue visiting Kenya because tourists help our economy to grow, but I am not looking to be president in the UK or US. I am democratically seeking the presidency of Kenya. I am not forcing anyone to vote for me."[1683]

The Kenyatta and Odinga camps found themselves opposing each other in the 2013 Kenyan presidential and general elections. They were the first elections held under the new Kenyan constitution, passed during the 2010 referendum. They were also the first general elections run by Kenya's Independent Electoral and Boundaries Commission. In late January 2013, Kenya's electoral authority confirmed the registration of eight candidates for the Kenyan presidency elections in March 2013.[1684] Uhuru Kenyatta and William Ruto headed the Jubilee Alliance, a four-party coalition made up of the TNA, National Rainbow Coalition, United Republican Party and Republican Congress. Raila Odinga and Kalonzo Musyoka headed CORD, the Coalition for Reforms and Democracy, a coalition of political parties, including the Orange Democratic Movement, Wiper Democratic Movement, FORD-Kenya, Kenya Social Congress, The Independent Party, KADDU-Asili, Peoples Democratic Party, Mkenya Solidarity Movement, Chama Cha Uzalendo, Muungano Development Movement Party of Kenya, United Democratic Movement, Chama Cha Mwananchi, Federal Party of Kenya, Labour Party of Kenya.

Given the pending election it was announced that the ICC had postponed the Kenyan trials for several months.[1685]

Mahmood Mamdani stated that the ICC was the single most influential factor in the 2013 Kenyan election.[1686] Mamdani noted that "Jubilee presented itself as a party of a grand national reconciliation, and CORD as the party of vengeance. This was not an election for Jubilee to win. It was an election for CORD to lose." He also stated that if CORD lost, "the credit for that loss must go to human rights fundamentalists in its ranks".[1687]

In February 2013, the EU once again stated that while it was up to Kenyans to elect the leaders they warned that Kenyans would have to be prepared for negative consequences if they chose a leader accused of crimes before the ICC. Kenyan Foreign Minister Sam Ongeri criticised EU governments for meddling in Kenya's internal affairs: "The remarks made by EU envoys are clearly inflammatory and could have the effect of polarising the country."[1688]

The perception of foreign involvement, particularly by the UK, in Kenyan affairs has also been flagged by Ian Paisley Jr.:

> The I.C.C. must never be an instrument that can fuel the potential for division. And where the court intervenes it must be an exemplar of justice at its best, with standards that are above question. This has not always been the case: The Kenyan case rests on a main witness who has changed his statements several times, and is under a witness protection plan partly funded by the British government, which has publicly supported the trial. This has fuelled the erroneous belief among some Kenyans that the Western powers that fund the court are seeking to divide and rule the country themselves.[1689]

Chatham House has also touched on the continuing international interference in Kenyan domestic affairs:

> The ICC's intervention has also prompted much public debate about the role of foreign diplomats, international political commentators, media and international election observers in Kenya. The perception of some that such actors, along with the ICC, represent illegitimate external interference in Kenya's domestic politics has important implications for the way in which the involvement of international players might be received during the 2013 elections and beyond.[1690]

Chatham House stated that "[o]ne unintentional but potentially positive consequence of the ICC's intervention has been the increase in Kenya's engagement with regional and international bodies. For example, the government has used the AU to lobby other African states on the issue of non-cooperation with the ICC, and has also used its strong position within the Intergovernmental Agency for Development (IGAD)."[1691] The billion-euro court, with hundreds of lawyers, members of staff and analysts, continues, in the words of an American commentator, "to bumble in its assessment of regional politics".[1692]

The American journalist Dayo Olopade described the ICC involvement in Kenya as having been the elephant in the room during the 2013 elections.[1693] Kenyatta's campaign was in part "an assault on the Court's legitimacy". He framed the prosecutions "not as justice, but as western menace".[1694] For Kenyatta the ICC in Kenya was a zero-sum issue: "I am not saying that international justice doesn't have a purpose. But if Kenyans do vote for us, it will mean that Kenyans themselves have questioned the process that has landed us at the International Criminal Court."[1695] It is clear that whatever support there may have been for the ICC within Kenya plummeted. *Time* magazine reported that "a central message of most candidates' campaigns was strident, patriotic self-determination. Kenyatta and Ruto...managed to convert a Kenyan public...into one that viewed the ICC as a representative of unwarranted Western interference in African affairs."[1696] By the end of 2011, only thirty-eight per cent of the public were said to support the ICC. Western commentators noted: "[N]o one wanted to be seen as supporting a process suddenly tarred as neo-imperial."[1697]

In March 2013, the Kenyan people elected Uhuru Kenyatta as the President of Kenya. William Ruto was elected as Vice-President.[1698]

Time magazine noted that Kenyatta's victory represents:

> [T]he most stunning articulation to date of a renewed mood of self-assertion in Africa. Half a century ago, Africa echoed with the sound of anticolonial liberation. Today, 10 years of dramatic and sustained economic growth and a growing political maturity coinciding with the economic meltdown in the West and political dysfunction in Washington and Europe have granted Africa's leaders the authority and means to once again challenge Western intervention on the continent, whether it comes in the form of foreign diplomatic pressure, foreign aid, foreign rights monitors or even foreign correspondents.[1699]

In his victory speech, Kenyatta said: "We expect the international community [to] respect the sovereignty and democratic will of the people of Kenya. The Africa star is shining brightly and the destiny of Africa is now in our hands."[1700] This was a clear message to the ICC and its European masters.

In an interesting postscript to the election of Uhuru Kenyatta, the Prosecutor announced a decision that had obviously been forced upon her. Lawyers for both Muthaura and Kenyatta had filed motions earlier in the year asking the Trial Chamber to refer their cases back to the Pre-Trial Chamber so that it could reassess the confirmation of the charges given the questionable evidence upon which the original confirmation had been based. Schabas noted that "some of the materials on which the Pre-Trial Chamber based its decision confirming the charges were not reliable or plainly untrue".[1701] In late February 2013, the Prosecutor had to concede that Muthaura's motion was well-founded:

> The witness whose statement is at issue was essential on the issue of Mr. Muthaura's criminal responsibility and, in fact, was the only direct witness against him. Hence, the confirmation decision, if stripped of references to the witness' evidence, might not establish substantial grounds as a matter of law. The Prosecution also acknowledges that its disclosure error limited the Defence's ability to challenge the critical witness' testimony, which appears to have been the principal evidence relied upon by the Pre-Trial Chamber in its decision to confirm the charges against Mr. Muthaura. In the particular circumstances of Mr. Muthaura's case, and given that he has elected to waive his Article 67(1)(c) right to go to trial without undue delay, the Prosecution does not oppose new confirmation proceedings with respect to him, should the Trial Chamber determine that there is a legal basis for such relief.[1702]

Before the Pre-Trial Chamber was able to reconsider the issue, however, on 11 March 2013 the Prosecutor dropped the charges against Francis Muthaura. She stated: "Having considered the totality of the evidence, the Prosecution considers that, at this stage, it has no reasonable prospect of conviction were it to proceed to trial against Mr. Muthaura on the charges as confirmed." The Prosecutor also noted that a critical witness against

Muthaura had "recanted a significant part of his incriminating evidence after the confirmation decision was issued".[1703]

Following the court's dropping of the indictments, Francis Muthaura issued a personal statement dealing with his "awful odyssey" at the ICC. He stated that he believed in the rule of law and that law "is the only means by which humanity can co-exist and resolve disputes peacefully. Protection under the law and equality before the law is the only way by which the rights of the oppressed, the weak and the vulnerable can be safeguarded in the interests of advancement of civilization. The rule of law helps ensure that the hope of tomorrow can be ensured by action and protection today." Muthaura went on to note that as the Kenyan Ambassador to the UN, as Chair of the Fourth Committee and Chair of the Charter Review Committee of the UN, he had always supported international law and worked to advance the cause of the ICC and helped bring it to a reality resulting in Kenya signing and ratifying the Rome Statute. He then stated that his indictment by the ICC had given him "a unique insight into how the Prosecution and the ICC which I supported, even prior to its creation, actually operates in practice". He stated that he "submitted to the ICC even though the case against me was always baseless and unfair. I never thought I would be a target of the ICC or any court because I have always lived my life under the law. Never did I think that false allegations uttered against me would be accepted as truth by the ICC." Muthaura said that he was deeply saddened "because I have seen justice abused and manhandled by those whose primary duty it was to respect it and safeguard it at all costs. It is an injustice that charges were brought by the Prosecutor. It is a tragedy that safeguards to prevent abuse of the ICC mechanism so clearly and so obviously failed."[1704]

One week after the charges against Muthaura were dropped, it was reported that a key ICC witness against the Deputy President-elect William Ruto, referred to as OTP-8, had also withdrawn his testimony. He had written to the ICC Prosecutor in February 2013 withdrawing each and every piece of evidence attributed to him and asked to have his name removed from the list of prosecution witnesses. In a sworn affidavit the witness explained that during the 2007 general election he was a PNU official but after the election he was induced and enticed to be an ICC witness. He withdrew his claim to have visited the home of the Deputy President-elect: "I have never personally visited any of the homes of William Ruto and I did not witness any event and cannot vouch for the truth or otherwise of any allegation that has been made or attributed to me against him." The would-be witness claimed in the affidavit that he was promised that he would be rewarded and resettled in Europe, America or Australia if he testified before the ICC, and that his standard of living would improve tremendously. The court responded to Paul Gicheru, the lawyer acting for the witness, acknowledging receipt of the witness letter but rejecting the accusation that the ICC had been involved in inducing witnesses to provide false testimony. The court threatened legal action against the witness should his affidavit be made public: "[We are] sure you will be aware that should this affidavit be made public in any way and the accusations directed against individuals in the OTP are proven to be false your client might as a result be subjected to criminal and civil liability proceedings."[1705]

Gicheru stated that the witness had recorded many statements in which he was alleged to have said that the 2007–08 post-election violence in Rift Valley Province was planned, organised and financed by the Kalenjin community leaders, including Ruto. The witness affirmed: "I would like to state solemnly and swear that all the allegations that are attributed to me in the said interviews and statements are not true. To the best of my knowledge the 2007-2008 violence was spontaneous and was not planned or financed by anybody in Rift Valley including Henry Kosgei, Joshua Sang and William Ruto." The witness claimed he acted because of animosity between his political party PNU and ODM in his home area. The intermediaries who interviewed and presented him to the ICC included the EU-funded Kenya National Commission on Human Rights. He claimed that upon agreeing to be a witness for the ICC, the Kenya National Commission for Human Rights and the EU-funded International Medical Legal Unit were involved in moving him to Nairobi and then looking after him. In August 2010 he was flown to Arusha, Tanzania, by the ICC, where he was confined in a room at a facility that he later learnt belonged to the ICTR. The court then relocated him and his family to the Netherlands in early 2011: "During my stay in the Netherlands my ID, Passport, photographs and all other documents belonging to me and my family members were confiscated." He received periodic payments from the OTP. The witness stated that he was flown back to Kenya at his own request on 26 October 2012, had engaged in deep soul-searching and that his conscience could no longer allow him to stand by his false testimony.[1706] The witness subsequently accused the OTP of harassment. He alleged that court officials had made frantic telephone calls trying to get him to stand by his testimony. He further claimed that the evidence he gave was obtained from him through coercion and that some of it was falsified by the prosecutors.[1707]

The witness said: "Recent developments and dealings by the ICC has forced me to break my silence and go public as the dealings are bordering on harassment, intimidation and intruding into my private life." He added "[d]espite my having instructed my lawyer that the ICC prosecutor or his officers should contact me through him, they have breached this, and in the last 24 hours they have made concerted efforts to physically contact me without the knowledge of my lawyer... ." The witness provided gave two local telephone numbers from which he said he had received eighteen calls and two other numbers from a concealed number: "I have told them that I stand by my sworn affidavits and no amount of persuasion or harassment will make me recant from my position."[1708]

In April 2013, the Prosecutor had to admit that three other witnesses in the Kenyatta case, OTP witnesses 2, 9 and 10, had informed the court the previous year that they would not be testifying against Kenyatta. The Prosecutor, for example, stated: "When the prosecution contacted prosecution witness 2 on November 3, 2012 to confirm his availability to testify, he said he was rethinking his decision. The prosecution made several attempts to persuade witness 2 to testify, either as a prosecution or as a court witness, but on November 20, 2012, he informed the prosecution that his decision not to testify was final."[1709]

On the broader issue of Africa, Kenya and the ICC, the BBC has correctly noted that "[t]he Kenyan elections, to some extent [turned]…into a referendum on the ICC and in turn the West 'meddling' in Kenyan affairs".[1710] The response of the Kenyan people – and through them Africa at large – is clear. The Kenyan journalist Binyavanga Wainaina is one such person. He spoke for many Kenyans and even more Africans when he admitted that he thought initially that "[t]he idea of global justice was heroic". He now notes: "How naive." Wainaina has become very sceptical of the court:

> Today, there is a real possibility that none of the cases will go anywhere. We have come to see the track record of the ICC and doubt it. Bungled Congo. More bungled Sudan.... Now, it seems toothless. More than anything, it seems to want to use the Kenya cases to make itself legitimate as a meaningful global institution. We are not keen at all to be playing that sort of experiment.[1711]

He further observed: "I and many others no longer have any serious moral investment in its progress as an institution. I propose they go and build their court properly, and then come back and talk to us when it is grown up, when there are a few convictions of people who are not Africans."[1712] He declared: "We are not, and have never been, a CNN African country, held together by Western pins and glue, pity, bananas and paternal concern."[1713] Wainaina was very aware of the European arrogance epitomised by the ICC, and Kenya's response to pressure by the court:

> Gone are the days when a bunch of European ambassadors speak in confident voices to the Kenyan public about what we should do, why we should do it. Naughty boys and girls, we are not happy. We look forward to making stronger ties with India, to trading more with China and Brazil. We look forward to being no longer the nice beach-and-safari kind of country we have allowed ourselves to be for too long. The west should expect more defiance from an Uhuru government – and more muscular engagement. That is part of the reason he has won this election. No Côte-d'Ivoireing here thank you. You see what happens to the good-boy countries who do what they are told?[1714]

The Dean of Students and a sociology lecturer at the University of Nairobi, Father Dr. Dominic Wamugunda wa Kimani also spoke for many who had initially welcomed the attention of the ICC: "All the hype that Luis Moreno-Ocampo and his prosecution team created around the Kenyan ICC Cases is falling apart; what kind of investigations were done; who really carried out those investigations; and what did Ocampo, really, come to do in Kenya, other than to adopt a cheetah? Whatever one says and no matter how important the ICC process is; it is now abundantly clear in my mind that those cases were based on a cooked up process!"[1715]

In another crushing blow to the ICC's credibility, in April 2013 Judge Christine Van den Wyngaert requested to be excused from the case being brought against Uhuru Kenyatta.[1716] While citing her workload as the reason for her request, parts of her official written request were redacted. Even in the sections that were not redacted Van den Wyngaert was scathing about the credibility of the Prosecutor and the prosecution's Kenyan cases. In an opinion dated 26 April 2013 she stated:

[T]here are serious questions as to whether the Prosecution conducted a full and thorough investigation of the case against the accused prior to confirmation. I believe that the facts show that the prosecution had not complied with its obligations at the time when it sought confirmation and that it was still not even remotely ready when the proceedings before this Chamber started…the Prosecution offers no cogent and sufficiently specific justification for why so many witnesses in this case were only interviewed for the first time post-confirmation. The mere invocation by the Prosecution of generic problems with the security situation in Kenya, without explaining how this situation affected each of the individuals involved, does not adequately justify the extent and tardiness of the post-confirmation investigation…

[T]here can be no excuse for the Prosecution's negligent attitude towards verifying the trustworthiness of its evidence. In particular, the incidents relating to Witness 4 are clearly indicative of a negligent attitude towards verifying the reliability of central evidence in the Prosecution's case. This negligent attitude is particularly apparent in relation to Witness 4's evidence because, as the Prosecution concedes, "the Office as a whole was on notice, prior to the confirmation hearing, of the inconsistencies in the account Witness 4 gave during his [second] screening". The Prosecution offered a number of explanations for overlooking the problems with Witness 4's evidence. However, what all these explanations reveal is that there are grave problems in the Prosecution's system of evidence review, as well as a serious lack of proper oversight by senior Prosecution staff. Clearly, thorough and comprehensive due diligence with regard to the reliability of the available evidence is an ongoing obligation of the Prosecution under article 54(1)(a), which is as important as the collection of that evidence itself.

Based on the foregoing considerations, I find that the Prosecution failed to properly investigate the case against the accused prior to confirmation in accordance with its statutory obligations…. . In sum, whilst the application of the principles set out in the decision to the Prosecution's conduct in this case in my view results in a finding of a violation by the Prosecution of several of its obligations and the infringement by the Prosecution upon various rights of the accused…

Van den Wyngaert agreed with Kenyatta's argument that the prosecution introduced evidence and witnesses that had not been disclosed before: "I stress the concerns expressed in the decision about the overwhelming number of post-confirmation witnesses and the quantity of post-confirmation documentary evidence, as well as the very late disclosure of the latter." She noted that the prosecution had not justified how so many witnesses were interviewed after charges against Kenyatta were confirmed.

The legal commentator Kevin Jon Heller noted that "'Workload' strikes me as little more than a convenient excuse... ." He went on to say that he found it "difficult to believe that there is no connection between the Judge's criticisms and her decision to withdraw. She certainly could have withdrawn from a different case – one in which she had not savagely criticized the prosecution – instead."[1717]

Heller stated that "most obviously, Judge van den Wyngaert's withdrawal casts the prosecution in an extremely unflattering light. I cannot imagine that the Judge would have withdrawn unless she was profoundly concerned by the prosecution's actions." He also makes the point that Van den Wyngaert's withdrawal "is significantly unfair to the defence, because it deprives Kenyatta of a judge who was clearly willing to question the strength of the prosecution's evidence".[1718] Heller subsequently observed: "Even if Witness 4 will not appear at trial, the Judge's concerns were in no way limited solely to that witness. On the contrary, she uses her specific concerns about Witness 4 to indict the entire OTP system for assessing the reliability of evidence."[1719]

In October 2013 the ICC charged a Kenyan citizen, Walter Osapiri Barasa, with three counts of corruptly influencing a witness, stating that Kenya must now arrest Barasa.[1720] In response Barasa said the ICC had issued the arrest warrant against him in retaliation to his refusal to cooperate with the court. He claimed he had been working with ICC investigator Paul Irani, whom he met last year, but Barasa had refused to provide evidence implicating Deputy President William Ruto in the withdrawal of a witness from his case: "[Irani] told me he was going to engineer to have a warrant of arrest issued against me and that I could be jailed for five years, but added that, as a friend, he did not want me jailed and that the best option was for me to implicate the deputy president."[1721]

In early September 2013, the Kenyan National Assembly passed a motion to withdraw Kenya from the Rome Statute, to "suspend any links, co-operation and assistance" to the court and repeal the International Criminal Act that obliges the country to cooperate with the ICC. Garissa township MP Aden Duale, the majority leader from Kenyatta's Jubilee Coalition who moved the motion, justified it by saying that Kenya's independence was at threat by the workings of the ICC: "The sovereignty of Kenya with a working judiciary and a vibrant democracy is under threat." He told the Kenyan parliament that US Presidents Bill Clinton and George W. Bush both argued against becoming a party to the ICC to protect US citizens and soldiers from potential politically motivated prosecutions: "I am setting the stage to redeem the image of the republic of Kenya. Let us protect our citizens. Let us defend the sovereignty of the nation of Kenya."[1722] Duale added that the constitution of Kenya promulgated in 2010 was above any other law whether local or foreign. Mukurweini MP Kabando Wa Kabando, who rose in support of the motion, urged members of the National Assembly to approach the motion as Kenyans and not along party lines: "It comes a time irrespective of political divide to work for the good of Kenya." He noted that the motion to repeal the Rome Statute and withdraw from the ICC was a continuation of a motion that had been tabled in the tenth parliament.[1723] Senators in Kenya's second chamber supported the National Assembly's decision to withdraw from the ICC. Senate Majority Leader Kithure Kindiki said Kenya's withdrawal from the ICC was necessary to avoid engagement with the court's so-called political agenda: "The ICC has been turned into a vehicle to pursue international politics in a very rudimentary and capricious manner."[1724]

The reality is that the 2013 Kenyan elections dramatically changed the circumstances of the ICC involvement in the country. Charles Stith, the Director of Boston University's African Presidential Center, and a former US Ambassador to Tanzania, has focused on the contradictions at the heart of the ICC's Kenyan cases: "This trial could well sound the death knell for the ICC…Kenya is a fully functioning democracy, more than capable of prosecuting violators of its laws. Not only have no charges been brought against Kenyatta and Ruto in Kenya, they were recently elected in a free and fair election to run the country. That should be the only verdict that matters." Kenyan Foreign Minister Amina Mohamed has also noted that while President Kenyatta "has cooperated fully with the court up until now…. Are the circumstances different? Absolutely. Totally. Completely different. Before he wasn't the head of state of the republic… . It's going to be the first time that a sitting head is brought before any court of any time, not just here but anywhere in the world."[1725]

Chapter Twenty-three

THE COURT AND THE IVORY COAST

"Laurent Gbagbo's confirmation of charges hearing at The Hague started today. However, the ICC runs the risk of producing one-sided justice."

Think Africa Press[1726]

The Ivory Coast has experienced considerable political unrest in its history, most notably an armed conflict in 2002–03, fought between the rebel-controlled north and the government-controlled south, a schism that re-emerged after the 2010 presidential election. The Ivory Coast, also known as Côte d'Ivoire, ratified the Rome Statute on 15 February 2013. Although it had not ratified the treaty at that time, in April 2003 the government of Côte d'Ivoire under then President Laurent Gbagbo submitted a declaration under Article 12(3) of the Rome Statute accepting the ICC's jurisdiction beginning 19 September 2002.[1727] President Gbagbo called on the ICC to open an investigation into the grave abuses committed by then rebel leader Alassane Ouattara's *Forces Nouvelles* insurgents back in 2003. The court visited Côte d'Ivoire in 2006 but took no further action, possibly because Ouattara was seen to be close to the French government. On 14 December 2010, the Western-supported and Western-proclaimed President of Côte d'Ivoire Alassane Ouattara sent a letter to the OTP reaffirming the Côte d'Ivoire government's acceptance of the court's jurisdiction.[1728] On 3 May 2011, President Ouattara reiterated his wish that the court open an investigation into the situation in the Ivory Coast. There are clear indications that the court is once again being manipulated by participants in the situation, not least of which in its decision that the human rights abuses from 2002–10, abuses which would have implicated Ouattara, did not warrant further action.

The Prosecutor v. Laurent Gbagbo

Former President Laurent Gbagbo was taken into ICC custody on 30 November 2011 facing charges of four counts of crimes against humanity: murder, rape and other forms of sexual violence, other inhumane acts, and persecution.[1729] The crimes were allegedly committed by forces under his control during post-election violence in Côte d'Ivoire, between 28 November 2010 and mid-May 2011. He has been charged as being responsible for these crimes as an indirect co-perpetrator or, in the alternative, because he contributed to the commission or attempted commission of crimes "by a group of persons acting with a common purpose".

In November 2010, following bitterly contested elections, Gbagbo refused to step down when the Independent Electoral Commission and international observers proclaimed his rival, Alassane Ouattara, the putative winner of the presidential runoff election on 28 November 2010. Italian journalist and filmmaker Nicoletta Fagiolo has pointed out the irregularities surrounding the declaration by Youssouf Bakayoko, the Head of the Independent Electoral Commission (IEC), that Ouattara was the winner of the national elections. She noted that according to the Ivorian constitution, this commission is allowed to declare only the provisional results. Ouattara's victory was declared at Ouattara's election campaign headquarters — "in the absence, and therefore without the approval of the Constitutional Council, which is responsible, according to the Ivorian constitution, for declaring final election results... . Thus the provisional results, unapproved by all IEC members and without the presence of the representatives of the respective candidates, were declared as final election results."[1730] The Gbagbo coalition, *La majorité présidentielle* (the presidential majority), called for an annulment of the vote. They noted that observers in a number of Ouattara-dominated areas had reported death threats, murders, intimidations, physical violence, kidnappings of personnel and aggression against Gbagbo activists.

Fagiolo states that "It is still a mystery who actually won the elections in the run-off on 28 November 2010." Thabo Mbeki, the former South African President, who had worked as a mediator from 2004 onwards, and who had visited Côte d'Ivoire from 5–7 December 2010, concluded in his mission report that the elections could not be considered valid.[1731] Nonetheless, the questionable results were approved by the Special Representative of the United Nations for Côte d'Ivoire, Choi Young-Jin, although this was outside his mandate.

Nicoletta Fagiolo observed:

> What followed were four months of crisis that saw two presidents and two governments, where the UN and the European Union, breaching their mandates of political impartiality, had decided to support Ouattara. From December 2010 to March 2011, the UN, the EU, France and the United States carried out a policy of diplomatic and financial asphyxia against the Gbagbo government – which included an embargo on medicinal supplies, cocoa, international mandates, freezing of private funds and property and the closure of the local branches of French and American banks – followed in April 2011 by what the political scientist Michel Galy called a French-UN coup d'état.

Violence between followers of the presidential candidates ensued and lasted until mid-May 2011.

As international pressure increased on Gbagbo to step down, the violence intensified. In March 2011, in a move clearly coordinated with the French government, Ouattara's

Forces Nouvelles militias launched an offensive from the north and occupied the capital Abidjan.[1733] The French air force then bombed the presidential palace and other targets in April 2011. Gbagbo was subsequently arrested. India denounced the "regime change" policies of the UN peacekeepers in Ivory Coast; Russia denounced the illegality of French and UN military actions.

At least 3,000 people were said to have been killed by armed forces on both sides along political, ethnic, and religious lines during the fighting. Hundreds of people from both sides were killed in the Ivorian capital, Abidjan, and the far west of the country between February and April 2011. Gbagbo has been charged as being responsible for a series of alleged war crimes and crimes against humanity that were carried out during the post-electoral period.

Pro-Ouattara forces were also accused of grave abuses of human rights after they began a military offensive in March 2011 to seize control of the country. In village after village in the far west, Ouattara militias killed civilians from ethnic groups associated with Gbagbo and burned villages to the ground. In Duékoué, Ouattara forces and militias massacred several hundred people, including unarmed men from pro-Gbagbo ethnic groups. The *Inner City Press* reported in April 2011 that forces loyal to Alassane Ouattara were reported to have killed hundreds of civilians in Duékoué. Caritas put the death toll at 1,000, and the Red Cross at 800.[1734] Ouattara forces were also accused of executing and torturing men from ethnic groups aligned with Gbagbo when they seized Abidjan.

By the conflict's end, several human-rights groups had documented war crimes and likely crimes against humanity by both sides. A UN-mandated international commission of inquiry presented a report to the UN Human Rights Council in mid-June 2011 that found that both pro-Gbagbo and pro-Ouattara forces committed war crimes and likely crimes against humanity. In August 2012, a national commission established by President Ouattara released a report that also documented serious abuses of human rights committed by forces on both sides. It said the Côte d'Ivoire Republican Forces rebels were responsible for 727 deaths while Gbagbo's forces killed 1,452 people.[1735]

The then ICC Prosecutor Moreno Ocampo engaged in his characteristic assault on presumption of innocence. Although duty bound to be impartial, as early as 21 December 2010 Ocampo was seen to be taking sides, citing Blé Goudé, the Youth Minister in the Gbagbo government, as an ICC target. On 8 April 2011 – before he announced his intention to investigate events in Côte d'Ivoire – he stated "in December we put Gbagbo and others at notice".[1736] He was criticised at the time for undermining attempts to negotiate a resolution to the crisis.

After announcing that he had conducted a preliminary examination of the situation in Côte d'Ivoire, the Prosecutor concluded that there was a reasonable basis to believe that crimes within the jurisdiction of the court had been committed in Côte d'Ivoire since 28 November 2010. On 23 June 2011, the Prosecutor requested authorisation from ICC judges to open an investigation in Côte d'Ivoire in relation to war crimes and crimes against humanity allegedly committed following the disputed presidential election of 28 November 2010. On 3 October 2011, Pre-Trial Chamber III granted the Prosecutor's request for authorisation to open investigations *proprio motu* into the situation in Côte d'Ivoire with respect to alleged crimes within the jurisdiction of the court committed since 28 November 2010, as well as with regard to crimes that may be committed in the future in the context of this situation. On 23 November 2011, Pre-Trial Chamber III issued a warrant of arrest under seal for Gbagbo in the case of *The Prosecutor v. Laurent Gbagbo* for four counts of crimes against humanity.[1737] The arrest warrant against Gbagbo was unsealed on 30 November 2011, and he was transferred to the court's detention centre in The Hague by the Ivorian authorities.[1738] On 5 December 2011, Pre-Trial Chamber III held an initial appearance hearing.

The Ivory Coast became the seventh situation under investigation by the OTP. Pre-Trial Chamber III asked the Prosecutor to revert to the chamber with any additional relevant information that was available to him on potential crimes committed between 2002 and 2010 in Côte d'Ivoire, which the Prosecutor did on 3 November 2011. On 22 February 2012, ICC judges extended the authorisation for the Côte d'Ivoire investigation to include crimes within the jurisdiction of the court allegedly committed between 19 September 2002 and 28 November 2010. All were to be considered as a single situation. Gbagbo appeared before Pre-Trial Chamber III on 5 December 2011 at which time the chamber verified his identity, informed him of the charges he was facing and his rights under the Rome Statute.

On 12 June 2012, Pre-Trial Chamber I postponed the commencement of a confirmation of charges hearing to 13 August 2012. On 3 August, the hearing was postponed for a second time to allow a medical evaluation of Gbagbo's fitness to take part in the case. On 2 November, judges ruled that he was fit to take part in the proceedings and the hearing would be rescheduled. Following a case status hearing on 11 December 2012, pre-trial judges decided on a key confirmation-of-charges hearing to decide whether the case against Gbagbo would begin in February 2013. Professors Tim Zwart, a human rights expert, and Alexander Knoops, a criminal law specialist, have challenged the attitude and actions taken by the court:

> When Gbagbo was still being detained in Côte d'Ivoire, prior to being transferred to The Hague, he suffered ill-treatment at the hands of his guards. Such a breach of fundamental rights should normally have led to termination of proceedings against him, but the Court proved unwilling to go down that road. The Court made it clear that since it had no responsibility for his detention in Côte d'Ivoire, such violations of Gbagbo's rights could not be attributed to it. This position is difficult to maintain, since the prosecutor at that stage was already cooperating with the Ivorian authorities to secure his transfer to the ICC. The ill-treatment to which Gbagbo was subjected, resulted in a deterioration of his health.[1739]

Zwart and Knoops reported that "[a]ccording to medical experts hired by the Court, Gbagbo suffers from post-traumatic stress disorder, which would render him unfit to stand trial. But again the Court did not regard this as a valid reason to discontinue the proceedings."[1740]

The pre-trial hearing opened on 19 February 2013. The evidence produced by the new Chief Prosecutor Fatou Bensouda as usual relied heavily on NGO and UN reports, as well as newspaper articles and hearsay witness testimonies – the sort of "evidence" that has compromised almost every other ICC investigation. Gbagbo stated that during the previous fifteen months, the Prosecutor did not once call upon him to ask his point of view on the charges he was facing. Gbagbo pointed out at the pre-trial hearing that such an exchange would have given the trial a "fluidity of reasoning", allowing for a focus on what is essential, and leaving out simple errors on which some of the charges were based.[1741] The hearing revealed a number of basic errors on the part of the Prosecutor. Gbagbo's defence claimed that the Prosecutor had "blamed Gbagbo for misdoing of his adversaries".[1742] One example they cited was a handwritten document seized in Gbagbo's residence saying that on 29 May 2010 a minister was given 1,000,000 FCA francs to recruit forty Liberian mercenaries. The reality actually exonerated him. The defence established at the pre-trial hearing that this minister was in fact a pro-Ouattara minister appointed in the 2005 coalition government. False evidence was also included in the Prosecutor's evidence list. The defence also established that a video claimed to have been of a massacre, the fourth charge against Gbagbo, said to have been carried out in Youpougon, a suburb of Abidjan, in May 2011, was actually filmed in Kenya – something that should have been evident to the Prosecutor's investigators given that the people in it were in fact speaking Swahili. Quite how that simple fact escaped the supposedly professional investigators in the OTP was not addressed by the court. Despite the fact that the "witness" provided a clearly faked video as his evidence to the court, the Prosecutor stated that "The authenticity of this video...has no bearing on the credibility of this witness and on the probative value of the rest of his evidence."[1743]

Fagiolo challenged the Prosecutor's most basic claims:

> When reading the Prosecutors final Document Containing the Charges (DCC) in the brief statement of facts – *exposé des faits* – one is baffled by the sloppiness in describing the historical events in the first few pages: for example in the very first paragraph it states that Laurent Gbagbo made no effort to investigate into the crimes committed during the post-electoral crisis. Yet a UN Human Rights report dated February 2011 specifies that Gbagbo called as early as the 20 of December 2010 for a national regional and international evaluation commission into the post electoral crisis and on 7 January 2011 Gbagbo, by presidential Decree No. 2011-06, established an international commission of inquiry with a mandate to investigate human rights violations related to the post electoral crisis.[1744]

When the defence pointed out simple factual inaccuracies in the ICC's account of events, ICC OTP official Pascal Turlan was asked if he had changed his mind about the court's claims. He responded that "the Prosecutors' office stands to what they wrote in their DCC, we are not here to write history, that is up to historians". The question left answered is who writes the history?[1745] It is perhaps worth noting Edward Said's comment that "history is made by men and women, just as it can also be unmade and rewritten, always with various silences and elisions".[1746]

Human Rights Watch reported that Ivorian civilian and military prosecutors have together charged more than 150 people from the Gbagbo camp with crimes committed during the post-election crisis. It noted: "No member of the pro-Ouattara forces has been charged with such crimes." Human Rights Watch added:

> Many defendants from the Gbagbo camp have been in detention for nearly two years. Côte d'Ivoire's civilian prosecutor initially charged the civilian detainees – primarily the political elite from the Gbagbo camp, including Gbagbo's wife, Simone – with economic crimes and crimes against the state. Violent crimes (crimes de sang) have been added to the charge sheets of at least 55 defendants, including a number of people, among them Simone, who have been charged with genocide. The Ivorian government has indicated that other civilian defendants will likewise face charges of violent crimes related to the post-election crisis.[1747]

In January 2013 Nicoletta Fagiolo asked the following question:

> Why is there no trial for the serious crimes committed by the rebels who attacked Côte d'Ivoire in 2002 in the Central, North and West regions…which remained under their control until 17 March 2011 when Ouattara appointed them as the national military force renaming them the Republican Forces of Côte d'Ivoire (FRCI)?[1748]

Writing in May 2013, she further noted that in the five months from December 2010 to May 2011, the only period the Prosecutor decided to review in its case against Gbagbo, the activities of the *Forces Nouvelles* are conspicuous by their absence from his investigation. She pointed to the ICC's one-dimensional approach to alleged war crimes in Côte d'Ivoire:

> To date not a single case has been brought against pro-Ouattara forces for atrocities committed from 2002 to 2010, nor for the post electoral crisis period which saw one of the worst massacres of the conflict, with 1,000 people losing their lives in one day, committed by the *Forces Nouvelles* in Duékoué at the end of March 2011. Is the ICC not exasperating the crisis by repeating on an international level a one-sided justice system already deplorable at the national level, which currently has over 150 people from the former Gbagbo regime in prison or facing trial and no rebels? This seems to be a clear case that does not meet the criteria of "serving the interest of justice," a ICC statutory criteria for considering the opening of an investigation.[1749]

When the government did initiate legal proceedings against its own armed forces, the results were predictable. A trial of thirty-three FRCI troops opened in the capital Abidjan: two soldiers were handed prison sentences on 2 May.[1750]

The international lawyer and legal commentator Dov Jacobs has pointed to the manipulation of the ICC by the anti-Gbagbo regime:

> [The] Ivory Coast explicitly announced throughout 2011 that they were not prosecuting international crimes against former president Gbagbo, to allow the ICC to do so and avoid admissibility problems, with the OTP kindly complying, whereas everybody else belonging to the pro-Gbagbo camp has since been indicted locally with war crimes, crimes against humanity and even genocide since. If that is not a case of manipulation, I don't know what is.[1751]

Zwart and Knoops have also commented on the double standards undermining the credibility of the ICC with regard to Côte d'Ivoire:

> NGOs like Human Rights Watch have issued reports containing evidence indicating that the Quattara side may have engaged in serious crimes. This evidence is backed up by academic assessments and also a report submitted by the Ivorian government-initiated Commission on Post-Electoral Violence, referred to as the Badjo Report, which implicates people on both sides of the political divide. Thus, by issuing an arrest warrant for Gbagbo's wife, Simone, the ICC has done its legitimacy a disservice.[1752]

They conclude that "[s]ince 'not only must justice be done, it must also be seen to be done', the ICC should take the high road...and release President Gbagbo from custody". Such a move, they state, "may be a tough call for the Court, but is a sacrifice worth making, to safeguard its legitimacy as a court of law in Africa".[1753]

Africa analysts have noted that the UN and NGOs have been equally critical of both sides of the conflict: "Evidence has shown both sides acted inhumanely. Yet their treatment in the courts has, thus far, been vastly different." They cite the example of Guillaume Soro, once described by the BBC as "Ivory Coast's Charming Rebel":

> The single largest massacre during the five months of violence happened in the western town of Duékoué. Some 800 people were killed, and Soro's Republican Forces of the Ivory Coast (FRCI) were heavily implicated as the UN called on them to show restraint after reports emerged of "serious human rights violations". Other reports have claimed that ethnic groups considered loyal to Gbagbo, such as the Guere, were specifically targeted. But rather than being in the dock like Gbagbo and his allies, Soro is currently serving as President of the National Assembly. Meanwhile Ouattara has been praised by the international community, while only Gbagbo faces legal action.

The analysts stated that the ICC runs the risk of producing dangerously one-sided justice: "The current approach will considerably hinder healing the wounds after a tumultuous decade of division. It will foster mistrust on both sides. But, crucially, it will also risk reproducing rather than addressing the root causes of the fighting in the first place: if victors are allowed to escape judicial action, it could simply justify Gbagbo's win-at-all-costs attitude."[1754]

In April 2013 Human Rights Watch published a seventy-three-page report, *Turning Rhetoric Into Reality: Accountability for Serious International Crimes in Côte d'Ivoire*. This report examined Côte d'Ivoire's questionable efforts to hold to account those responsible for serious international crimes committed following the November 2010 presidential election. The report was based on research in Abidjan in September 2012 and follow-up interviews with government officials, lawyers, civil society members, UN representatives, diplomats, and officials from donor agencies.[1755] Param-Preet Singh, senior international justice counsel at Human Rights Watch, observed:

> President Ouattara's expressed support for impartial justice rings hollow without more concrete action to bring justice for victims of crimes committed by pro-government forces. If Côte d'Ivoire is going to break from its dangerous legacy in which people close to the government are beyond the reach of the law, it needs credible prosecutions of those responsible for crimes on both sides of the post-election conflict.[1756]

Human Rights Watch noted that the ICC only intervenes when national courts are unable or unwilling to do so. Its report sets out evidence that Côte d'Ivoire's key international partners such as the EU, while extolling the virtues of justice, have only made limited efforts toward securing justice in Côte d'Ivoire. Based on interviews with numerous Ivorian civil society activists Human Rights Watch concluded that the ICC's one-sided approach has legitimised the same approach by Ivorian judicial authorities and undermined perceptions of the ICC's impartiality: "The ICC should swiftly investigate crimes committed by those on the Ouattara side and, based on the evidence, seek arrest warrants. This is essential to restore the ICC's legitimacy in Côte d'Ivoire and to put pressure on the Ivorian authorities to deliver credible, impartial results."[1757]

A case may well be made that Laurent Gbagbo engaged in post-election violence that resulted in civilian deaths (although up until June 2013 the court had not been able to do so). Since November 2011 Gbagbo has been detained at the ICC accused of being an "indirect co-perpetrator" of crimes against humanity. At the same time there is a case that Alassane Ouattara, along with Guillaume Soro, the current President of the National Assembly, and the militiamen and paramilitaries they commanded, were direct and indirect co-perpetrators of violence on a scale similar to that alleged of Gbagbo. There are calls for Ouattara to be made to answer for his alleged involvement in war crimes and crimes against humanity in the Ivory Coast.[1758] Not only did the court turn a blind eye to the post-electoral violence allegedly carried out by Ouattara forces, in the pre-trial proceedings the judges took a decision on 22 February 2012 stating that "in light of the limited information provided by the Prosecutor the Judges are unable to assess whether crimes against humanity may also have been committed by any of the rebel forces" between 2002 and 2010.[1759]

Why is Gbagbo in The Hague and not Ouattara and Soro? The most obvious explanation is that Gbagbo was intellectually and politically opposed to continuing French involvement in his country. Fagiolo states that "Gbagbo is…considered a sociological phenomenon as he represents the birth of a nation-state and an intellectual middle class that had as its reference point Abidjan, and not Paris."[1760] There have been at least 122 French military interventions in sub-Saharan Africa since 1954. It is very obvious that the French government opted to augment its 2012 military coup in Côte d'Ivoire with a politicised judicial intervention by the ICC in its role as an adjunct of European foreign policy.

In June 2013, the judges appeared to support the concerns articulated by observers such as Fagiolo. They found the prosecution's case was inadequate and ruled that there was insufficient evidence to proceed to trial. The case was postponed till November 2013.[1761]

The Prosecutor v. Simone Gbagbo

Rather than focusing any attention on clearly documented instances of war crimes and crimes against humanity committed by pro-Ouattara forces in the post-election violence, the court turned instead to a very soft target, Laurent Gbagbo's wife, Simone Gbagbo. On 22 November 2012, Pre-Trial Chamber I unsealed a warrant of arrest issued against Simone Gbagbo, for four charges of crimes against humanity (murder, rape and other forms of sexual violence, other inhumane acts and persecution) allegedly committed in Côte d'Ivoire between 16 December 2010 and 12 April 2011.[1762] Madame Gbagbo is reported to be under house arrest in northwest Côte d'Ivoire since April 2011 and is also reportedly set to face trial before a national court for a number of charges, including genocide.

The Prosecutor v. Charles Blé Goudé

In October 2013 the ICC unsealed a warrant for the arrest of Charles Blé Goudé accusing him of working with Laurent Gbagbo to coordinate the wave of post-election violence. He was charged with four counts of crimes against humanity, including murder and rape, committed in Ivory Coast between December 2010 and April 2011.[1763]

The situation in Côte d'Ivoire is a good example of the manipulative, political use of the ICC. Soon after the court came into existence France threatened President Gbagbo with action by the court, clearly as political pressure of some sort. When Gbagbo requested ICC involvement in the Ivory Coast with regard to alleged rebel human-rights abuses, the court declined to get involved. When the French-supported rebel leader came to power and referred Côte d'Ivoire to the ICC, the court indicted former President Gbagbo, his wife and one of his supporters. In so doing the court ignored any alleged war crimes and human-rights abuses by Ouattara and his forces from 2002 onwards and including the post-electoral violence in 2011. Zwart, Knoops and Jacobs, among others, have pointed to further manipulation of the ICC. Once the court had served its purpose in indicting Gbagbo – and removing him from Côte d'Ivoire – the Ouattara government has subsequently snubbed any further requests by the court.

Chapter Twenty-four

The Court and Libya

"[T]he authority and legitimacy of the ICC seem likely to suffer in the wake of its intervention in Libya."

Mark Kersten[1764]

"[T]he ICC cannot even protect its own lawyers in Libya."

Geoffrey Robertson QC[1765]

In March 2011, led by France and the UK, NATO, the world's most powerful military alliance, made up of twenty-eight member states from North America and Europe, went to war with an African country, Libya, to remove Colonel Muammar Gaddafi and his government from power. The war in Libya ended in late October 2011, following the overthrow of the regime and Gaddafi's summary execution by rebel forces on 20 October.[1766] On 27 October, the Security Council voted to end NATO's mandate for military action on 31 October 2011. NATO attempts to cloak its actions in Libya with a legal veneer extended to using Europe's legal adjunct, the ICC. UN Security Council Resolution 1970 (2011) referred the situation in Libya from 15 February 2011 onwards to the ICC.[1767] On 3 March 2011, the ICC Prosecutor decided to open a formal investigation into alleged crimes against humanity in Libya. The following day the ICC assigned the Libya situation to Pre-Trial Chamber I. On 16 May 2011, the Prosecutor requested that Pre-Trial Chamber I issue arrest warrants for alleged crimes against humanity in Libya from 15 February onwards by three Libyan leaders, Muammar Gaddafi, his son Saif al-Islam Gaddafi and Abdullah Al-Senussi, the then Head of Libyan Intelligence. On 27 June 2011, ICC Pre-Trial Chamber I issued the requested arrest warrants for crimes against humanity of murder and persecution. By ICC standards it was a lightning-fast investigation.

For all the claims made about the integrity of the ICC and its single-minded pursuit of international justice, UNSC Resolution 1970 (2011) could not have more clearly demonstrated the Security Council's political instrumentalisation of the ICC. This manifested itself in three ways.

Firstly, the court was made to grant immunity from prosecution for action in Libya to the nationals of non-ICC states – that is to say, the USA. The sixth paragraph of resolution 1970 stated that the UNSC:

> Decides that nationals, current or former officials or personnel from a State outside the Libyan Arab Jamahiriya which is not a party to the Rome Statute of the International Criminal Court shall be subject to the exclusive jurisdiction of that State for all alleged acts or omissions arising out of or related to operations in the Libyan Arab Jamahiriya established or authorized by the Council, unless such exclusive jurisdiction has been expressly waived by the State.

The Daily Telegraph made it clear that "[t]he US insisted that the UN resolution was worded so that no one from an outside country that is not a member of the ICC could be prosecuted for their actions in Libya". American diplomats had been under strict instructions to have the paragraph included. The paragraph was added by the USA to prevent any of its citizens being held accountable for any crimes against humanity or war crimes committed during the UN operation in Libya. The French Ambassador to the UN, Gerard Araud, described the paragraph as "a red line for the USA… . It was a deal-breaker, and that's the reason we accepted this text to have the unanimity of the council"[1768]. *Inner City Press* noted that countries had to notify the UN if they intended to take military action in Libya under Security Council Resolution 1973:

> [T]he first twelve countries…have provided notice to the UN under Security Council Resolution 1973, several beyond the United States are not ICC members. That is, if they dropped bombs on civilians – even intentionally – they would be exempt from any referral to or prosecution by the ICC, thanks to the loophole the US demanded for itself.[1769]

Secondly, the referral included a reference to Article 16 of the Rome Statute, which enables the Security Council to suspend an investigation or prosecution by the court for twelve months, renewable yearly. Although it was not invoked during the intervention, its presence in the text of the resolution clearly sought to leave the Security Council with room for manoeuvre politically, whatever legal position may have been arrived at by the court.

Thirdly, the referral restricted the ICC's temporal jurisdiction in Libya to events that occurred after 15 February 2011. The exact wording was that the Security Council "Decides to refer the situation in the Libyan Arab Jamahiriya since 15 February 2011 to the Prosecutor of the International Criminal Court". This restriction on the court contradicted the Rome Statute itself, which states that the ICC can investigate any alleged crimes under its jurisdiction back to 1 July 2002. Geoffrey Nice has also pointed to the time selectivity within the Security Council's Libya referral: "The UNSC Referral's temporal limitation suggests shielding the West's relations with Gaddafi during investigations."[1770] Mark Kersten was more pointed: "[t]he restriction means, above all, that the cozy economic, political and intelligence relationships between Western states and the Gaddafi regime may never come to light during an investigation."¹⁷⁷¹

Some would say that the court prostituted itself at the behest of the Security Council. In any event it was a tawdry transaction for which once again the court wasn't even paid. As was also the case with the Darfur referral, the Libya resolution included a paragraph that ensured the Security Council would not be paying for the court's specialised services:

> [iv]...none of the expenses incurred in connection with the referral, including expenses related to investigations or prosecutions in connection with that referral, shall be borne by the United Nations and that such costs shall be borne by the parties to the Rome Statute and those States that wish to contribute voluntarily.¹⁷⁷²

Michael Ignatieff, an expert on the use and abuse of claims of a "responsibility to protect", has also pointed to conclusions by some that the ICC had not just been politically instrumentalised regarding Libya but had even been weaponised as a precursor to military intervention by Western countries: "The unresolvable question is whether the ICC indictment played a part, inadvertently or not, in driving the Libyan operation beyond its original UN mandate of protecting civilians into full-scale 'regime change'."¹⁷⁷³

Time magazine concluded at the time that the ICC action would have the probable effect of "burying any hope of a ceasefire deal or an arrangement for quiet exile for Gaddafi and his family as a way of ending the war".¹⁷⁷⁴ The court's involvement in Libya only served to make the Libyan situation more difficult to settle peacefully. The BBC also noted at the time that "any deal for Col Gaddafi to step aside would be even harder to achieve if these arrest warrants – also for his son, Saif, and his intelligence chief Abdullah Senussi – are approved". The BBC quoted a senior Gaddafi aide: "What options does he have? Even if he did resign, then he gets arrested and taken to the Hague."¹⁷⁷⁵ The ICG also noted: "To insist that he both leave the country and face trial in the International Criminal Court is virtually to ensure that he will stay in Libya to the bitter end and go down fighting."¹⁷⁷⁶ Even the American government had to admit: "It is a complicating factor."¹⁷⁷⁷

In May 2011, the ICC Prosecutor admitted that his office had not taken any evidence or accounts from witnesses inside Libya but claimed nevertheless that the court was "almost ready for trial".¹⁷⁷⁸ Experienced lawyers, such as former UN ICTY prosecutor Mark Ierace, were sceptical about this assertion:

> If Moreno Ocampo was correctly reported, a statement that he considered his Office to be virtually trial-ready without having visited the crime scenes is troubling. There is no substitute for investigators and prosecuting lawyers visiting crime scenes and interviewing local witnesses in situ, pointing out where they were at relevant times, and so on.¹⁷⁷⁹

Louise Arbour, the former UN High Commissioner for Human Rights, a former justice of the Supreme Court of Canada and a former chief prosecutor of the International Criminal Tribunals for the former Yugoslavia and Rwanda, expressed considerable surprise at the pace of the court's involvement:

> [T]he Libya referral is noteworthy for the speed with which it was made. In the case of Darfur…it took two years and an international inquiry before the Security Council made its referral. Another two months would pass before the ICC formally opened its investigation. In comparison, the Libya process has, so far, progressed at great speed. The decision to refer the situation to the ICC was taken less than two weeks after Gaddafi's crackdown began, and without waiting for the results of a Human Rights Council inquiry, announced just the day before. The ICC seems similarly keen to forge ahead: on 2 March, the ICC Prosecutor announced that, following a preliminary investigation, he believed that there was sufficient evidence to begin a full-scale investigation. The speed of this response is unprecedented: it normally takes months for a preliminary investigation to be concluded – in this case, it took only four days.[1780]

Arbour outlined some of the contradictions in the hurried approach to Libya:

> The Human Rights Council examined the case of Libya under the Universal Periodic Review in November 2010. While the massive protests that shook North Africa were not easily predictable last fall, the comments made regarding Libya's human rights performance were hardly indicative of what we are now hearing of the homicidal nature of the Gadaffi regime. The report of the UPR proceedings (A/HRC/16/15, 4 January 2011) notes that 46 delegations made comments; several noted with appreciation Libya's commitments to upholding human rights on the ground. For instance, Qatar praised Libya's legal framework for human rights protection; Australia and Canada welcomed improvements in human rights protection in Libya before expressing some concerns regarding specific issues. Numerous recommendations were made and accepted by Libya, ranging from adopting legislation to abolish torture to adopting a national strategy to combat discrimination against women. Nothing in that document would have given any serious reason to believe that the Libyan population had cause to rise in rebellion against oppression, nor that such an uprising would be met by deadly force and illegal reprisals.[1781]

The implication was that political considerations rather than human-rights factors were the driving force in the moves by NATO and the UNSC, including the deployment of the ICC to discredit the Gaddafi regime. Philippe Sands QC hit the nail on the head when he noted of the referral that "the effect has been more significant, in delegitimising the Gaddafi regime and paving the way to UN resolution 1973, that authorised 'all necessary measures' to protect Libyan civilians".[1782] The use of the court as a political instrument has continued. In June 2012, even Human Rights Watch was drawn to observe that "[o] ver the last year we have seen the court enter a particularly fragile period as its higher profile has attracted increased efforts to use the court for political ends – including in the Libya situation – rather than to support its work as an independent institution."[1783]

While the UK and France publicly proclaimed their commitment to the international rule of law, and deliberately deployed the ICC as added pressure on the Libyan government, ostensibly to investigate war crimes, crimes against humanity and other serious offences in Libya, at the same time both countries sought the defection of the then Libyan Foreign Minister, Musa Kusa, guaranteeing him immunity from prosecution for his alleged complicity in crimes during the crisis itself and crimes stretching back more than two decades. His presence for some time in Britain after he defected caused considerable controversy. He was still wanted in connection with the 1988 Lockerbie bombing and a 1984 shooting of a British policewoman. The *Daily Mail* described Kusa as Gaddafi's "Fingernail-Puller-in-Chief".[1784] In Britain the government deliberately allowed him to leave the country before he could be questioned in connection with these issues. The British government was obviously conscious of Musa Kusa's legal status. *The Independent* newspaper noted that "Mr. Hague assures us that Gaddafi's foreign minister, recently arrived in the UK, will not receive immunity from any prosecution, before an accusation of a crime has even been made!"[1785] The *Washington Post* reported that the French government had also guaranteed him immunity from prosecution.[1786]

Having demanded that Gaddafi remove himself from office, leave Libya and surrender to the ICC in The Hague, France and Britain then performed a U-turn. In the NATO panic in late July 2011, during a lull in the conflict, the British and French governments ignored the ICC altogether, effectively offering Gaddafi an amnesty if he agreed to step down. French Foreign Minister Alain Juppé explained: "One of the hypotheses envisaged is that he stays in Libya, but on condition, that he very clearly removes himself from Libyan political life."[1787] William Hague supported the new French position, stating: "What happens to Gaddafi is ultimately a question for the Libyans. It is for the Libyan people to determine their own future."[1788] *The Independent* pointed to the British government's U-turn on the ICC issue: "The Foreign Secretary has already retreated on his aim of bringing Col Gaddafi to justice in an international court, suggesting he could remain in the country if that was what the Libyan people wanted."[1789] Saif al-Islam Gaddafi also revealed at the time that the Americans and Europeans were offering a deal on the ICC: "It's a fake court. Under the table they are trying to negotiate with us a deal. They say if you accept this deal, we will take care of the court. What does that mean? It means this court is controlled by those countries which are attacking us every day! It is just to put psychological and political pressure on us. That's it. Of course, it won't work. The court is a joke here in Libya."[1790] Commentators have noted that this "raises a serious question about Europe's commitment to the international justice system" and that it is a "blow on the credibility of our already fragile international institutions".[1791]

Questions about the ICC's claims and Ocampo's professionalism regarding Libya arose almost immediately. The Prosecutor, for example, claimed at the UN on 8 June 2011 that hundreds of women in rebel areas had been raped by Libyan government forces as a punishment. Ocampo said rape was a new tactic for the Libyan regime: "Apparently,

[Gaddafi] decided to punish, using rape."[1792] Ocampo's claims were taken at face value by much of the world's media.[1793] Real lawyers were more cautious. Cherif Bassiouni, the distinguished UN Egyptian war crimes expert, often called "the Godfather of International Criminal Law", who had headed the UN inquiry into human-rights abuses in Libya, said his investigators had been unable to verify these rape allegations. Bassiouni, a long-standing critic of Gaddafi, voiced his doubts about the story, believing it to have been based on the claims of a doctor, one Dr. Sergewa, who was unable to substantiate her claims: "But she's going around the world telling everybody about it…she got that information to Ocampo and Ocampo is convinced that here we have a potential 259 women who have responded to the fact that they have been sexually abused."[1794] Bassiouni noted that as of that moment his team had only heard of three cases of rape.[1795] Summing up the ICC's claims of large-scale rape Bassiouni stated: "Can we draw a conclusion that there is a systematic policy of rape? In my opinion we can't."[1796] *The Independent* reported that "Amnesty International and Human Rights Watch have not found evidence of such mass government-ordered rape despite extensive investigations."[1797]

Amnesty International's crisis researcher Donatella Rovera was present in Libya throughout the crisis. She spent the period from 27 February to 29 May in Misrata, Benghazi, Ajabiya and Ras Lanouf in eastern Libya. With regard to the rape claims, she noted: "We have not spoken to any victims or anybody who has met victims, except for the one doctor who has spoken a lot to the media. We approached her to see if there was anything more to learn from her, on this particular issue; she couldn't put us in touch with any victims."[1798]

Amnesty International also noted that the doctor in question, Dr. Sergewa, was unable to provide documentary evidence for her claims.[1799] In a further report Rovera stated that "we have not found any evidence or a single victim of rape or a doctor who knew about somebody being raped".[1800] She was quoted in *Time* magazine as stating that in three months in Libya, she had not met one woman who said she had been raped. Rovera observed that "Normally the situation is the reverse – you don't get many people to focus on it in society, but you can get the victims to talk. Here everyone's talking about it, but despite our best efforts, we've not been able to meet a single victim."[1801] Diana Eltahawy, Amnesty International's Libya expert, echoed Rovera's conclusions. She told *The Independent* that Amnesty researchers in Libya had found no evidence of such a policy.[1802] Ms. Eltahawy says: "We spoke to women, without anybody else there, all across Libya, including Misrata and on the Tunisia-Libya border. None of them knew of anybody who had been raped. We also spoke to many doctors and psychologists with the same result."[1803]

Human Rights Watch found it similarly difficult to match the mass rape claims to evidence. Liesel Gerntholtz, Human Rights Watch's Director of Women's Rights, stated: "We have not been able to find evidence. We have not been able to verify it."[1804]

The ICC Chief Prosecutor Ocampo then built on his claims of systematic rape by stating that there was evidence that the government had been handing out Viagra to soldiers to encourage the sexual attacks. He stated: "There's some information with Viagra. So, it's like a machete. It's new. Viagra is a tool of massive rape."[1805] Cherif Bassiouni also challenged these claims made by the ICC, stating they were part of a "massive hysteria".[1806] Amnesty International also subsequently failed to find evidence to support allegations of premeditated Viagra-fuelled rape, findings which challenged Ocampo's claims.[1807] Such claims were almost immediately discredited by American military and intelligence officials, then engaged in a war with the Libyan government. NBC reported that there was no evidence that Libyan military forces had been given Viagra and had engaged in systematic rape of women in rebel areas.[1808] The *Christian Science Monitor*'s Dan Murphy noted that he was sceptical from the start, describing it as a story "that's being reported with entirely too much certainty: the claims that Muammar Qaddafi sent out thousands of soldiers with pockets full of Viagra and condoms to mass rape Libyan women". Murphy observed that "it's an extraordinary tale that has little hard information to back it. I was told the story repeatedly when I was in Libya in February and March, but could never verify any of it, so didn't report it." The award-winning investigative reporter Russ Baker also challenged the Viagra rape claims, asking: "Is massive rape a tool of Qaddafi – or of war propagandists?" He described the claim as seeming "too crazy" and found that the Western media's dissemination of these questionable claims was unacceptable:

> After all the other fake stories used to whip up public support for wars, you'd think we had learned something. Apparently not, judging from the media's unquestioning spreading of claims that Qaddafi ordered Viagra-fueled rapes – claims that look dubious under even a little scrutiny.[1809]

The *Belfast Telegraph*'s Eamonn McCann, no stranger to civil war, perhaps voiced many observers' scepticism regarding the Viagra claims:

> I don't believe that Libyan soldiers were supplied with Viagra to ensure they would be capable of raping women opponents of the Gaddafi regime. I think the story was made up to prepare the way for further escalation of a military operation which has already gone beyond the limits of the UN resolution underpinning its legality…as it stands, the account rings too many discordant bells to be taken at face-value.[1810]

The *Christian Science Monitor* described the Viagra claims as "stunning but unproven". It also confirmed that "independent researchers who have sought to corroborate the claim in Libya now say they have found no evidence to back it whatsoever".[1811] The *Christian Science Monitor* concluded: "There is plenty for Qaddafi to answer for. On balance, mass rape with Viagra doesn't appear to be on the list."[1812] Guy Martin, a British war photographer in Libya, reported coming across a doctor who claimed to have a packet of cocaine or Viagra that the doctor said had "been pulled off a mercenary". Martin stated: "It felt staged, a bit weird. How do you separate fact from fiction?"[1813] The reality is that Ocampo and the ICC simply didn't bother to try.

Sara Flounders, Co-Director of the International Action Center, criticised the allegations of rape used in Libya:

Without presenting a shred of reliable evidence, NATO and International Criminal Court conspirators are charging the Libyan government with conspiracy to rape – not only rape as the "collateral damage" of war, but rape as a political weapon. This charge of an orchestrated future campaign of rape was made at a major press conference called by the lead prosecutor of the International Criminal Court on June 8. The even wilder, unsubstantiated ICC charge that Libya plans to mass distribute Viagra to its troops confirms this as the most tawdry and threadbare form of war propaganda. It is important to understand that NATO countries, with the full complicity of the corporate media and the ICC, are spreading this Big Lie in order to win support for and close down all opposition to a ground assault of Libya – something that would otherwise be unpopular in both Europe and the United States.[1814]

The credibility of the ICC was further brought into question by the ease with which ICC judges found that the materials presented by the Prosecutor provided "reasonable grounds" to believe that Muammar Gaddafi had either directly or through the state apparatus taken "steps to recruit foreign nationals as mercenaries in support of the Security Forces". The judges also accepted allegations that the security forces had shot at civilians gathered in public places with "heavy lethal weapons". The judges also found "reasonable grounds to believe that" in Tripoli a helicopter belonging to security forces, armed with machine guns, fired on demonstrators", and that on 20 February 2011, Libyan security forces had shot at civilians using anti-aircraft guns.[1815]

These claims by the court and its Chief Prosecutor were also immediately challenged by reputable human-rights organisations. Both Amnesty International and Human Rights Watch have stated that there was no evidence to support claims that the Gaddafi regime had engaged thousands of foreign mercenaries to fight against the rebels. Amnesty's Rovera extensively investigated the mercenary allegations. She concluded they were unfounded: "Those shown to journalists as foreign mercenaries were later quietly released. Most were sub-Saharan migrants working in Libya without documents."[1816] In a July interview with Austria's *Der Standard*, Rovera added:

> We examined this issue in depth and found no evidence. The rebels spread these rumours everywhere, which had terrible consequences for African guest workers: there was a systematic hunt for migrants, some were lynched and many arrested. Since then, even the rebels have admitted there were no mercenaries, almost all have been released and have returned to their countries of origin, as the investigations into them revealed nothing.[1817]

In March 2011, Human Rights Watch, with three investigators on the front line, similarly stated it had seen no evidence of mercenaries being used in eastern Libya. The *Los Angeles Times* reported that "Human Rights Watch has not confirmed a single instance of a foreign mercenary having been brought in to fight in eastern Libya."[1818] Peter Bouckaert, Emergencies Director for Human Rights Watch in Libya, reported that there had been "widespread and systematic attacks" on Africans and black Libyans by rebels and their supporters because of the "mercenary" allegations: "Thousands of Africans have come under attack and lost their homes and possessions during the recent fighting.... A lot of Africans have been caught up in this mercenary hysteria."[1819] It was hysteria promulgated by the ICC. Nonetheless, although the mercenary allegations had been discredited on 19 April 2012, the Prosecutor persisted in claims that his office had "evidence linking [Saif al-Islam Gaddafi] to supervising and planning recruitment of mercenaries to fight the uprising".[1820]

Amnesty International also investigated the claims made by the ICC that aircraft were used against protestors. The organisation found that there was no evidence that aircraft or heavy anti-aircraft machineguns were used against crowds of civilians. Spent cartridges picked up after protesters were shot at came from Kalashnikovs or similar calibre weapons.[1821] The ICG also challenged claims that the Libyan government used its air force to attack unarmed protestors: "[T]here are grounds for questioning the more sensational reports that the regime was using its air force to slaughter demonstrators."[1822] ICG noted that two senior Western journalists interviewed on their return from eastern Libya told the ICG that "none of their Libyan interlocutors in Benghazi or other towns under the opposition's control had made any mention of the regime's supposed use of airpower against unarmed demonstrators in the first few days of the protests".[1823]

In an extraordinary turn of events, in June 2011, in the midst of the conflict, the Chief Prosecutor met with the head of the executive council of the rebel Transitional National Council, Mahmoud Jebril.[1824] Jebril was the then leader of a rebel movement that had been closely identified with allegations of systematic abuses of human rights in eastern Libya and elsewhere in the country. These had included the murder of prisoners of war and political opponents, the shooting, lynching and beating to death of large numbers of black Libyans and sub-Saharan migrants falsely accused of having been mercenaries fighting for the Libyan government and the illegal detention of Libyan civilians.[1825] Ocampo's meeting with Jebril was all the more jarring given that rebel forces had been accused of using child soldiers, a clear war crime under the Rome Statute. Weeks before their meeting, *The New York Times* had reported child soldiers, including thirteen-year-olds, with rebel forces.[1826] The *Daily Mail* subsequently documented seven-year-old children being trained by the rebels to fight against government forces.[1827] Photographs of Libyan rebel child soldiers were also published in several Western newspapers, including the *Los Angeles Times*, *The New York Times* and *The Daily Telegraph*.[1828] The ICC's relationship with a rebel movement clearly using child soldiers was ironic given that the court's premier case had been against a rebel leader in the DRC for using child soldiers.[1829]

The ICC Chief Prosecutor was party to another stunning example of unprofessionalism – once again accepting unsubstantiated rumours about one of his indictees as fact. Ocampo stated in August 2011 that the ICC had solid intelligence that Saif al-Islam Gaddafi had been detained by "rebel special forces". He said that "Saif was captured in Libya. We have confidential information from different sources that we have within Libya confirming this."[1830] The day after Ocampo's statement, the ICC said it was talking to the Transitional National Council about transferring Gaddafi to The Hague: "We're discussing his surrender."[1831] The only trouble with this claim was that like the al-Bashir nine-billion-dollars-in-British-bank-accounts claim, it was false. Saif al-Islam Gaddafi had not been captured: he was not in rebel hands.[1832] Once again the ICC lost considerable credibility. *The Guardian* newspaper reported that Sir Menzies Campbell, a senior British politician and former Liberal Democrat leader, said that the credibility of the ICC had been damaged by its decision to endorse the claim that Saif al-Islam had been captured: "It doesn't say very much, I'm afraid as someone who supports the international criminal court, for the credibility of that organisation that it should have apparently endorsed the information that the son had been taken into custody."[1833]

Despite claims that it is conducting enquiries, the ICC has not seriously investigated the death of Libyan civilians in NATO airstrikes. Warplanes from France, Belgium, Denmark, Italy, Sweden and the UK, all ICC States Parties, participated in the bombing of Libya. The Libyan government stated that as of early August 2011 NATO attacks had killed over 1,000 civilians.[1834] That was an increase in the figures as of 1 June 2011, when NATO bombings were said to have killed 718 civilians and injured another 4,067 since the commencement of bombing on 19 March. Four hundred and thirty-three people were then said still to be in hospitals, with their conditions described as critical.[1835] On 15 September 2011 Gaddafi spokesman Moussa Ibrahim declared that recent NATO airstrikes killed 354 civilians and wounded 700 others, while 89 other civilians are supposedly missing. He stated that over 2,000 civilians had been killed by NATO airstrikes since 1 September.[1836]

These are just some examples of the deaths of civilians. In May 2011, a NATO airstrike killed eleven Muslim clerics and wounded forty-five other civilians in a Brega guesthouse. The group of imams had travelled to Brega on a peace mission from across Libya. They had appeared on state-run television and had planned to travel further to Ajabiya and then to Benghazi. Christian priests joined Muslim leaders in condemning the deaths. NATO claimed that the guesthouse had been a "command and control centre" for the Libyan military but were unable to elaborate further. The building was a guesthouse popular with Western oil-company employees.[1837] On 6 June 2011, at 2.30 a.m. the central administrative complex of the Higher Committee for Children in central Tripoli, was hit with a total of twelve missiles. The complex housed the National Downs Syndrome Center, including its records and vital statistics office, the Crippled Women's Foundation, the Crippled Children Center, and the National Diabetic Research Center. On 16 June 2011 at five a.m. NATO bombed a private hotel in central Tripoli, killing three people and destroying a restaurant and shisha smoking bar.

Agence France-Presse reported that NATO admitted carrying out an airstrike in the early hours of 20 June on a target west of Tripoli that the Libyan regime alleged killed fifteen people. Eight American missiles destroyed the home of Khaled al-Hamedi, his parents and family. NATO had reversed an initial denial but insisted the target was military and that it was a precision airstrike against a "high-level" command and control point. AFP noted: "If Libyan government claims are true, it would be the second attack to cause civilian deaths in 24 hours." The Libyan government said fifteen people, including Mr. al-Hamedi's pregnant wife and three children, were killed in the attack, which he slammed as a "cowardly terrorist act which cannot be justified". Witnesses, neighbours and independent observers deny there was ever any military installation or troop presence on the property. Reporters were taken to Sabratha Hospital and an AFP correspondent saw nine bodies, including those of two children. The new Libyan claim of civilian deaths came just hours after NATO admitted that one of its missiles had gone astray on Sunday, hitting a residential neighbourhood of Tripoli. Reporters were shown the bodies of five of the nine civilians said to be killed in that strike, including a woman and two toddlers.

In late June 2011 on the main road west of Tripoli, a public bus with twelve passengers was hit by a NATO missile, killing all the passengers. NATO claimed that public buses were being used to transport military personnel.[1838] In early August NATO admitted carrying out an airstrike in the coastal town of Zliten, 160 miles east of Tripoli, where a mother and two children were killed. The attack killed the wife and two children of Mustafa Naji, a physics teacher.[1839] Associated Press reported NATO's July 2011 attack on the studios of the civilian Libyan state television network. Libyan officials say the airstrike killed three people and injured fifteen others.[1840] The Head of the International Federation of Journalists, Beth Costa, denounced NATO for the attack, "which targeted journalists and threatened their lives in violation of international law". Costa said that the use of "violence to stifle dissident media spell catastrophe for press freedom".[1841] *The Daily Telegraph* reported that the attack on the television transmitters was justified by NATO as an attempt to "reduce the regime's ability to oppress civilians" – noting that it was "a justification that is unlikely to please critics who argue that Nato has already exceeded its UN mandate".[1842]

On 9 August 2011, the Libyan government claimed that eighty-five civilians were killed in a NATO airstrike in Majer, a village near Zliten.[1843] A NATO spokesman confirmed that NATO bombed Zliten at 2.34 a.m. on 9 August, stating that he was unable to confirm the casualties. The Canadian commander of the NATO military mission, Lieutenant General Charles Bouchard, stated: "I cannot believe that 85 civilians were present when we struck in the wee hours of the morning, and given our intelligence. But I cannot assure you that there were none at all."[1844] In May 2012, *Inner City Press* reported that "[t]he International Criminal Court under Luis Moreno Ocampo has seemed engaged in two-stage justice, if that." It noted:

> In Libya it issued indictments of the Gaddafi side, but…Ocampo told Inner City Press that even in the case of NATO's bombing of Majer, which reportedly killed rescue workers, he is merely seeking more information. He declined to say much about immunity offered by the new Libyan government to its own fighters. Inner City Press asked about Law 37, which threatens life in prison for praising Gaddafi. Couldn't that hinder defense lawyers? Ocampo shrugged.[1845]

Even if NATO or the ICC refused to do so, the Italian government clearly acknowledged the deaths of civilians, warning that NATO's killing of civilians was endangering the alliance's standing. The Italian Foreign Minister Franco Frattini said at the time that "NATO's credibility is at risk."[1846] In March 2011, Russia urged Western nations to stop the indiscriminate use of force in Libya: "The reports say that during air raids on Libya strikes were also delivered on non-military facilities.... As a result, 48 civilians are reported dead and over 150 wounded. In this connection, we are calling on the respective states to halt the indiscriminate use of force."[1847]

The warrant of arrest against Muammar Gaddafi was terminated by the ICC on 22 November 2011, following his death. Saif al-Islam Gaddafi was arrested in Libya on 19 November 2011 and remains in the custody of militias in Zintan. Abdullah al-Senussi was arrested in Mauritania and a request for his surrender to the court was transmitted to the Mauritanian authorities on 17 March 2012. He was subsequently extradited to Libya.

The National Transitional Council (NTC) that succeeded the Gaddafi government has taken some steps towards re-establishing a justice system, which included the passing of a number of laws and preparing to initiate local trials.[1848] In December 2011, the NTC passed a law establishing the National Council for Civil Liberties and Human Rights, which was empowered to receive complaints on human-rights violations and to file cases in court.[1849] The NTC also passed transitional-justice legislation examining violations that occurred during the Gaddafi regime, as well as during the revolution of 2011. Part of the legislation established a fact-finding and reconciliation commission, investigating incidents of human-rights violations and disappeared persons. It also created a compensation fund to provide reparations for victims.[1850] The NTC also passed Law 38, which grants a blanket amnesty to those who committed crimes during the civil war if their actions were aimed at "promoting or protecting the revolution" against the Gaddafi government. However, Law 35, passed the same day, excludes certain crimes from amnesty, including torture and rape.[1851]

On 22 November 2011, the ICC Prosecutor paid an official visit to Libya. During this visit, the Prosecutor participated in a joint press conference with the Minister of Justice on 23 November 2011, during which the minister announced that "the Libyan authorities would conduct the trial in Libya but would coordinate with the ICC".[1852] In this press conference in Libya, the Prosecutor referred to Libya's right to try Gaddafi in Libya, and stated that if they did so, the court would not intervene.[1853] The Prosecutor also made several statements to the media in Tripoli. These were reported as the Prosecutor supporting the right of Libya to try Gaddafi in Libya.[1854]

On 25 November 2011, the Prosecutor filed submissions in which he noted, *inter alia*, that the Libyan authorities had informed the Prosecution that they wished to try Gaddafi in Libya. The Prosecutor also further informed the chamber that the NTC had communicated with the court setting out their position that the Libyan judiciary had primacy to try Gaddafi and therefore the court's request for his arrest and surrender would be discussed with the court and "the latter will be officially informed of the Council's decision later".[1855]

On 2 February 2012, the Office of Public Counsel for the Defence (OPCD), part of the ICC, filed the "OPCD Observations on Libya's Submissions Regarding the Arrest of Saif al-Islam", requesting that the chamber order the Libyan authorities to implement Gaddafi's rights immediately under Articles 55 and 59 of the Rome Statute and to submit reports verifying the implementation of these rights. A joint Registry-OPCD delegation visited Libya from 29 February 2012 to 4 March 2012. They visited Gaddafi as part of this trip. On 7 March 2012, the Pre-Trial Chamber rejected Libya's request to postpone Gaddafi's surrender, and ordered Libya to make its decision concerning the surrender request within seven days of the notification of the decision.[1856] On 22 March 2012, the Libyan authorities notified the Pre-Trial Chamber of their intention to challenge admissibility, and further requested the suspension of the surrender request pursuant to Article 95 of the statute.[1857] On 4 April 2012 the ICC Prosecutor gave interviews in which he stated *inter alia* that "one year ago, Saif Gaddafi was threatening people".[1858] On 5 April 2012, the Prosecutor was quoted by CNN as stating: "According to the rules, Libya has the primacy to prosecute Saif, so if they present this to the International Criminal Court judges, probably they will get an approval. That's the system. The system is the primacy for the national judges."[1859]

On 12 April 2012 Xavier-Jean Keïta, Head of the OPCD, called on the court to make a formal complaint to the Libyan authorities over Libya's refusal to hand over Saif al-Islam Gaddafi. On 17 April 2012, the Pre-Trial Chamber appointed Keïta and Melinda Taylor as counsel for Gaddafi.[1860] These counsel complained to the court that press coverage generated by Ocampo had created an appearance of a lack of independence and impartiality.[1861] On 18 April 2012, the Prosecutor visited Libya again. A joint press conference was conducted with the Chairman of the NTC, Mustafa Jalil, during which the chairman insisted that Libya would try Gaddafi.[1862] The Prosecutor also announced that "Libya has now established its government. They have the right to prosecute Saif and Senussi here. According to our role, the primacy is for national jurisdictions. If they conduct proceedings, the Court will not intervene."[1863]

The ICC Prosecutor is obliged to provide an independent and impartial presentation and assessment of the facts of the cases before him. In April 2012, the OPCD officially complained about the Prosecutor's behaviour: "The Prosecutor has recently issued several statements, which create the impression that certain issues before the International Criminal Court (ICC) are predetermined, and which undermine the appearance of the independence of the Prosecution."[1864] The OPCD noted:

> These statements have also prejudiced the rights of the Defence by conveying an impression that firstly, the ICC has already found that the defendant engaged in certain behavior, secondly, that the question of the admissibility of the case is predetermined, and thirdly, that judicial orders, which are central to the rights and security of the defendant, can be 'debated' by national authorities rather than implemented.
>
> The impact which these statements have had on the proceedings is exemplified by the fact that the Libyan authorities subsequently announced that they had no intention to transfer Mr. Saif Al Islam Gaddafi to the ICC, that Mr. Gaddafi had committed crimes, and that the ICC Prosecutor supported the position of the Libyan authorities.

> There is also a public perception that a deal has been done between the ICC
> and the Libyan authorities, to the effect that the Libyan authorities have been
> given the green light to try Mr. Saif Al Islam Gaddafi in Libya.[1865]

The OPCD stated that "Article 42 imposes a strict requirement that the Prosecutor should adopt a consistent and impartial position to legal and factual issues, and should not be seen to change or vary his stance, depending on the wishes or views of particular States."[1866] The OPCD pointed out "The adoption of inconsistent prosecutorial strategies directly conflicts with the obligation of the Prosecutor to act as an independent and impartial minister of justice."[1867] The comments, rulings or judgments of, *inter alia*, the United Nations Human Rights Committee, the African Commission on Human and Peoples' Rights and the European Court of Human Rights all state that relevant authorities, including prosecutors, must respect the presumption of innocence in their public statements and must "refrain from prejudging the outcome of a trial".[1868] The European Court of Human Rights has recalled that the presumption of innocence will be violated if "a statement of a public official concerning a person charged with a criminal offence reflects an opinion that he is guilty before he has been proved so according to law".[1869] Bergsmo and Harhoff have observed that "[e]ven activity which is *likely to affect confidence* in the independence is prohibited. The perception of independence is recognized as being important."[1870]

The OPCD motion made the point that "[p]rosecutorial independence from the executive is also an essential element of the right to a fair and impartial trial. Any perception of political interference could impact on the integrity and legitimacy of the prosecutorial decision making process." It also noted that according to the standard applied by the ICC, the presidency has concluded that an assessment of the appearance of bias should be determined by reference to a "consideration of whether the circumstances would lead a reasonable observer, properly informed, to reasonably apprehend bias".[1871] Article 54(1)(c) obliges the prosecution to "fully respect the rights of persons arising under this Statute". If someone is subject to an ICC arrest warrant, the prosecution should at the very least afford him the protections of the presumption of innocence. Similarly Articles 55 and 59 of the statute mandated the right not to be subject to arbitrary detention, the right to legal representation, and the right to be brought before a judge to challenge the legality of his detention.

On a number of occasions following Saif al-Islam Gaddafi's indictment the Prosecutor gave high-profile media interviews in which he has described Gaddafi, without any qualification, as "lying", as having committed a "crime against humanity", being "involved in the recruitment of soldiers from outside", "personally hiring people…financing the operations", being "ready to crush the demonstration", and "involved in the operation to kill the civilians on the street".[1872] He also stated that Gaddafi had been party to "threatening people".[1873] Ocampo also claimed that Gaddafi had personally committed crimes "some (where) he was involved with his own hands.[1874] In several of his interviews Ocampo commented on the strength of the Libyan challenge to admissibility, actually claiming there was "great evidence".[1875] The Prosecutor informed journalists that the Libyan authorities had a strong case against Saif Gaddafi, that he had been informed that Gaddafi had not been mistreated, and that issues such as his location and well-being fell within the prerogative of national authorities.[1876]

The law is clear. The Appeals Chamber of the Special Court for Sierra Leone noted that the publication of predetermined views concerning the criminal responsibility of a defendant could lead a reasonable bystander to conclude that the official in question lacks the requisite appearance of impartiality.[1877] With respect to the impartiality of the proceedings, the European Court of Human Rights has recalled that the presumption of innocence will be violated if "a statement of a public official concerning a person charged with a criminal offence reflects an opinion that he is guilty before he has been proved so according to law".

The defence motion noted that:

> The Prosecutor appears to be unwilling or unable to contemplate the possibility of a counter-narrative to the Prosecution theory. The Prosecutor categorically refutes the possibility that Mr. Gaddafi was not involved in the planning of the events in February or that the protestors may have been confrontational, and point blank calls Mr. Gaddafi a liar.[1878]

The motion stated that this interview was given in August 2011 – only a couple of months after the Security Council referral, and noted that:

> It would not have been feasible for the Prosecution to have conducted a comprehensive investigation at this point in time. Any reasonable bystander would understand from this interview that rather than exploring the possibility that there may be exculpatory lines of inquiry, the person who was ultimately responsible for directing the investigations in this case was denying the possibility that such lines of inquiry could exist.

The defence also pointed out that in many press statements, there was also no clear demarcation between the position of the ICC Prosecutor, and that of the Libyan authorities. For example, the Prosecutor has stated that "They will show they are able to prosecute Saif (al-Islam Gadhafi), who they believe is today the face of the old regime... . The rebellion in Libya started as a fight for justice, so they want to show they can do justice in the Saif case."[1879] The defence also noted that: "Issues concerning the merits of the protests and uprising in Libya have not yet been litigated or adjudicated before the ICC. Such categorical statements concerning the nature of the uprising and protests also conflicts with the Prosecutor's duty to remain impartial and independent, in particular, as concerns any parties to a conflict, which is being litigated before the Court."

The defence stated that the appearance that the Prosecutor identifies with or endorses a particular regime is also problematic as the Prosecutor has sole responsibility under the statute for investigating offences against the administration of justice. It is therefore imperative that the prosecution is willing to take positive steps concerning problems with the security of defence witnesses, even if they are attributable to government authorities.

The OPCD motion concluded:

> [A] reasonably informed observer would have a reasonable apprehension that the Prosecutor: a. has not and will not conduct his obligations under Article 54 in accordance with the standards of impartiality required for such a position b. has a preconceived notion concerning Mr. Gaddafi's responsibility and the nature of the uprising in Libya, c. will not actively take steps to investigate either exculpatory evidence or allegations that persons associated with or under the control of the Libyan government may be committing offences against the administration of justice against the defendant or defence witnesses; and d. will not take into consideration the rights of the defendant or defence witnesses when exercising his powers under the Statute.[1880]

The Prosecutor gave the clear impression of having implicitly endorsed the position of the NTC stating that "[t]hey are proud, they say to me that for them it's a matter of national pride to show that Libyans can do the case… . They will show they are able to prosecute Saif (al-Islam Gadhafi)."[1881] The Prosecutor also announced that "Libya has now established its government. They have the right to prosecute Saif and Senussi here. According to our role, the primacy is for national jurisdictions. If they conduct proceedings, the Court will not intervene." The Libyan Coordinator for the ICC, Dr. Gehani, stated that the "Prosecutor was totally in support of the Libyan judicial system and defends it and praises it. This trust stems from his visit to Tripoli on 23 November 2011, and what he was able to observe and witness in Libya."[1882] The Prosecutor subsequently admitted that due to confidentiality concerns, he had not actually seen the evidence of the Libyan authorities.[1883] The defence motion made the point that if this was the case then "it would not have been feasible for the Prosecutor to have reached an informed position based on an impartial appreciation of the evidence".

The defence motion also stated that the particular positions advanced by the Prosecutor in the Libyan case stand in stark contrast to the positions advocated in relation to similar circumstances in previous cases. In this regard, in the Bemba case, the prosecution advanced the position that the authorities of the CAR should be considered to be unable to conduct a genuine investigation due to the fact that security considerations had prevented the investigating magistrate from being able to conduct interviews with witnesses in particular crime scenes. Although the Libyan authorities have cited security concerns as a reason for the non-compliance with orders of the chamber,[1884] the ICC Prosecutor has made no reference to the impact of such in his filings in the case or in public statements.

Furthermore, in Ruto et al., the Prosecutor submitted that "holding the hearing in Kenya will further intimidate OTP witnesses, their families and potential witnesses […] The Prosecution has a legal duty to protect its witnesses against all foreseeable risks."[1885] The Prosecutor also asserted that "[Kenya's] interests are divergent with the Court in this case since it also insists that the prosecution should not continue" and as such "is impossible to assume that the Government of Kenya will provide the essential cooperation and substantial protection to enable an effective continuation of the hearings in situ".[1886]

As the defence motion also pointed out, "In the Kenya situation, the Prosecution repeatedly emphasized that any cooperation provided to national authorities was subject to the overriding requirement that the country has adequate security structures in place to guarantee that that witnesses would not be subject to threats or intimidation."[1887] The Prosecutor also declared that "the Prosecution disagrees that the Court is obligated to assist the Government of Kenya in order to promote complementarity and the State's effort to establish that the ICC prosecutions are inadmissible".[1888] The Prosecutor also stated that no assistance should be provided to national authorities, who are taking efforts to derail the possibility of convening proceedings before the ICC.[1889]

Yet, in the case of Libya, the court reversed itself on all these positions.

The defence pointed out that "in contradistinction" to his previous positions regarding Kenya and other situations, the Prosecutor announced in the course of his first visit to Libya that the prosecution would assist the Libyans to "do justice".[1890] The Prosecutor "made no mention of issues concerning the security and safety of witnesses, notwithstanding the fact that there have been credible reports of torture, arbitrary detention, and mistreatment of persons allegedly associated with the Gaddafi regime, or persons wrongly believed to be mercenaries".[1891] The Defence motion noted the contradictions in the Prosecutor's position:

> By publicly qualifying the future Libyan challenge to admissibility as being "very strong", and predicting that it was likely to succeed, the Prosecutor has also appeared to place his official imprimatur on their admissibility challenge. Such a stance is at odds with the prosecutorial stance adopted in the Kenya situation that it would be highly inappropriate to assist a State, which is not complying with its obligations under the Rome Statute.
>
> The apparent adoption of such inconsistent prosecutorial strategies directly conflicts with the obligation of the Prosecutor to act as an independent and impartial minister of justice. The ICTY has therefore underscored that the adoption of different prosecution policies in relation to the same facts was a "matter of concern", which could give rise to inferences concerning the credibility of the position advanced by the Prosecutor, and "serious internal policy concerns for the Prosecutor".
>
> The adoption of a position in the current case, which is so blatantly different from all previous cases, would also lead a reasonable observer to have a reasonable apprehension that there is an appearance that the Prosecutor is not applying legal and factual criteria to his assessment of the admissibility of this case in an independent and impartial manner.

The defence motion requested that the ICC Appeals Chamber disqualified "the Prosecutor from participating in the case against Mr. Saif Al Islam Gaddafi; and…pending the issuance of a determination on the present request, temporarily suspend the Prosecutor from conducting any prosecutorial activities related to the case against Mr. Saif Al Islam Gaddafi".[1892] The Office of Public Counsel for the Defence requested that the court:

> (i) deprecate any statements of the Prosecution, which create an impression that pending judicial matters concerning the admissibility of the case or the responsibility of Mr. Gaddafi are in any way predetermined or that judicial findings and orders can be "debated"; and (ii) request the Prosecutor to refrain from making any public pronouncements, which impact on the appearance of the independence and impartiality of the Prosecution, the presumption of innocence, and the integrity of judicial orders and pronouncements.[1893]

On 25 April 2012, the Appeals Chamber dismissed the appeal filed by the Libyan authorities, and rejected the request for suspensive effect of the order to immediately surrender Gaddafi to the ICC. On 1 May 2012, the government of Libya filed its challenge to the admissibility of the case against Gaddafi on the basis of the principle of complementarity pursuant to Article 19(2)(b) of the Rome Statute, arguing that it was investigating the same and additional crimes and the same underlying conduct as the OTP.

On 2 May 2012, the NTC promulgated Law Number 37, entitled "Criminalizing the glorification of the Tyrant". The law states in part

> [I]t is deemed inciteful advertising to glorify Mohammed Muammar Abu Abed el salam el Minyar KADDAFI, his regime, his ideas and his children, to glorify them and show them as being good people or heroes or loyal to the country, and equally so to invert the truth, mislead people about their behavior, and all that they have committed against the country and its citizens, or to advertise in support of the regime or its members in any form whatsoever. In cases where inciteful news or press releases or advertisements cause harm to the country, the penalty shall be life imprisonment.[1894]

The law makes it a criminal offence to speak in favour of Muammar Gaddafi or his sons. Ronda Hauben, a journalist working for the German *Die Tageszeitung* newspaper, notes: "Thus there is no possibility for a court to consider that Saif Al Islam Gaddafi is innocent. This law threatens to make any lawyer who defends Saif Al Islam Gaddafi subject to criminal prosecution."[1895] On 1 June 2012, the ICC allowed the postponement of the request of surrender of Saif Al-Islam Gaddafi pending the final determination on Libya's challenge to the admissibility of the case.

On 3 May 2012, Xavier-Jean Keïta, counsel for Gaddafi, presented a further clear-cut case to disqualify Ocampo from further participation in the case against Gaddafi, making the following points about the Prosecutor's behaviour:

> [T]here is a reasonable basis for concluding that there is an objective perception that the ICC Prosecutor's lacks the requisite impartiality to direct the investigations and prosecutions of this case, in a manner consistent

with his obligations under the Statute. This objective lack of impartiality is manifested by a repeated failure to respect the presumption of innocence and rights of the defendant under the Statute, and an objective appearance that the Prosecutor is affiliated with both the political cause and legal positions of the NTC government. This objective lack of impartiality clearly prejudices the right of the defendant to a fair and impartial trial, either before the ICC or Libyan courts, and could have implications concerning his personal security in Libya.[1896]

On 16 May 2012, Ocampo presented his third report to the UNSC on the action of the ICC on the referral of Libya to the court under UN Security Council Resolution 1970.[1897] His report dealt in part with the actions of the court regarding the detention of Saif al-Islam Gaddafi. Hauben challenged the accuracy of this report. She stated that "[t]he report...failed to mention important aspects of the case", and instead merely restated the position of the NTC on Libya rather than anything ascertained by the ICC itself, which provided the UNSC with "a false picture of the situation that exists regarding Saif Al Islam Gaddafi's detention." In his report to the Security Council and a subsequent press conference, the Prosecutor repeated the Libyan NTC's claims of "adequate conditions of detention", "access to ICC lawyers", "visits" to Saif Al-Islam Gaddafi by the ICRC, "NGOs", and "family members".[1898]

Hauben reported that according to reports by the ICC Registry and the ICC's Office of the Public Counsel for the Defence, Gaddafi has been held mostly incommunicado and denied access to a lawyer by his captors. The ICC officials who visited the defendant reported on the poor conditions and noted that he has only received two visits, one by the ICRC and one by Human Rights Watch.[1899] It should be noted that the Prosecutor was repeating previous character traits – accepting unconfirmed claims. Although obliged to present information confirmed by the ICC, he in fact repeated unconfirmed information from the Libyan officials of the NTC, something he has done in general with regard to the Libyan issue. As Hauben pointed out Gaddafi was not in the custody of the NTC. He is being held by a rebel group referred to as the Zintan militia.[1900]

On 18 May 2012, the OPCD filed a motion explaining how the order of the judges "has been met with a combination of stony silence and prevarication". The OPCD requested that the ICC officially "i. report the non-compliance of the Libyan authorities to the Security Council; ii. stay the Chamber's consideration of the admissibility proceedings due to Libya's non-compliance with the implementation of fundamental rights of the Defence; and iii. draw adverse inferences concerning the implementation of Mr. Gaddafi's rights in detention and the willingness and ability of the Libyan authorities to genuinely investigate the case in accordance with internationally recognized standards of due process."[1901]

For obvious political, bureaucratic and institutional reasons the ICC Appeals Chamber was unable to dismiss Ocampo. It failed to uphold the defence's 3 May 2012 appeal against the Prosecutor's behaviour. In its ruling on 12 June the Appeals Chamber did manage to show some backbone regarding Ocampo's misconduct. It stated:

> [T]he Prosecutor's behaviour was clearly inappropriate in light of the presumption of innocence. Such behaviour not only reflects poorly on the Prosecutor but also, given that the Prosecutor is an elected official of the Court and that his statements are often imputed to the Court as whole, may lead observers to question the integrity of the Court as a whole.[1902]

The ICC Appeals Chamber was particularly critical of Ocampo for statements in an interview in the August 2011 edition of *Vanity Fair*:

> [T]he Prosecutor did not exercise sufficient caution, either in the manner in which the interview was conducted or in the content of his statements. The Prosecutor discussed the case in depth and specific evidence against Mr Gaddafi. For nearly three hours, the Prosecutor and Mr Sands reviewed and analysed a 38 minute speech of Mr Gaddafi, with the Prosecutor frequently commenting on the veracity of Mr Gaddafi's statements or on the evidence against him. The Appeals Chamber considers that this detailed discussion of evidence was inappropriate in the context of a media interview. The in-depth discussion of evidence should generally be left to the courtroom. In relation to the content of the Prosecutor's statements, the Appeals Chamber notes that, on several occasions, the Prosecutor stated, as fact, material elements of the allegations against Mr Gaddafi or Mr Al-Senussi, saying, for example, "There was no battle. It was people going to a funeral. That's a crime against humanity". On other occasions, the Prosecutor passed judgment on the credibility of Mr Gaddafi's statements, stating, point blank, "He's lying". The Appeals Chamber finds that the Prosecutor's statements on these sub judice matters were inappropriate in that they gave the impression that factual issues yet to be determined by the judges had been determined or could not be contested?

The Appeal Chamber stated that Ocampo gave the impression that he and not ICC judges would decide Gaddafi's fate. The chamber noted that it was:

> [C]oncerned with the way in which the Prosecutor's statements and the interview are recounted in the Vanity Fair Interview. There is no indication that the Prosecutor clarified that the case was at an early stage or that it would be up to the Pre-Trial Chamber to decide whether to confirm charges and, if charges were confirmed, for the Trial Chamber to decide on Mr Gaddafi's criminal responsibility. To the contrary, the Vanity Fair Interview says that it is the Prosecutor "who may decide [Mr Gaddafi's] fate"...the Appeals Chamber considers that it appears that the Prosecutor failed to exercise due caution in how his interview was reported to the Court as whole, may lead observers to question the integrity of the Court as a whole.[1903]

In June 2012, in accordance with an ICC decision, dated 27 April 2012, an ICC delegation travelled to Libya to meet with Saif al-Islam Gaddafi in Zintan. This meeting was to be a privileged visit by Melinda Taylor, a lawyer within the ICC's Office of Public Counsel for the Defence, appointed to represent Gaddafi in the case brought against him. Following the meeting, Ms. Taylor and her interpreter were detained by the Libyan authorities on grounds of Libyan national security. Two other staff members remained with them out of solidarity. On 12 June 2012, the ICC President informed the Security Council of the detention of four ICC staff members in Libya.[1904] Three days later, the President of the Security Council expressed concern over the detention in Libya of the ICC staff members, and urged Libyan authorities at all levels and all concerned to work towards their immediate release. The Security Council emphasised that it is the legal obligation of Libya under the UN Security Council Resolution 1970 (2011) to cooperate fully with and provide any necessary assistance to the ICC pursuant to that resolution. On 2 July 2012, the four ICC staff members were released by the Libyan authorities. The ICC President confirmed that the information reported by the Libyan authorities on the visit's circumstances would be fully investigated in accordance with ICC procedures following the return of the ICC staff members to The Hague. The Prosecutor was surprisingly unsupportive of his imprisoned colleagues: "It's not what we would expect of the court, of the defence."[1905]

Ms. Taylor said that her actions in Libya were "consistent with my legal obligations" under ICC rules: "Irrespective of any issues concerning my own personal conduct, the rights of my client, Mr Saif al-Islam, were irrevocably prejudiced during my visit." She added that recent events had "completely underscored that it will be impossible for Mr Gaddafi to be tried in an independent and impartial manner in Libyan courts". She stated that Libyan officials had "deliberately misled the defence concerning whether the visit with Mr Gaddafi would be monitored". Ms. Taylor also claimed they seized confidential documents.[1906]

On 7 July 2012, Libya's NTC held democratic elections for a General National Congress (GNC). The 200-seat congress is tasked with drafting and ratifying a constitution for the country and will remain in existence for eleven months. At the end of this period, there will be general elections for a new legislature and the GNC will be dissolved.[1907] On 11 July 2012, the Security Council issued a statement welcoming the holding of elections in Libya, describing them as a "milestone for Libya's democratic transition". The statement made no reference to the ICC and consequences and obligations of Libya arising from Resolution 1970. On 8 August 2012, the NTC formally transferred power to the GNC, which elected Mohammed Magarief of the National Front Party as President on 9 August 2012.[1908]

Ronda Hauben notes failings by the UNSC, the ICC and the Libyan authorities with regard to the Gaddafi referral:

> The UNSC which made the referral of Saif Al Islam Gaddafi to the ICC has failed to oversee the criminal prosecution it has set in motion. The Security Council seems unaware or unconcerned that the OPCD has presented motions

to the ICC judges about the problems and that the ICC has failed to discipline the Prosecutor so as to protect the integrity of the Court's processes. Thus the action of the ICC, with the exception of the OPCD motions to the Court, have demonstrated the incapacity not only of the NTC, but more importantly of the ICC, to provide any semblance of an impartial and independent judicial process to a defendant referred to it by the UNSC.[1909]

She was particularly critical of the inaction on the part of the Security Council:

The Security Council and the ICC have already demonstrated an inability to provide any semblance of due process to an accused referred to it by the Security Council. Such a change in the Security Council processes would allow even more of the kind of abuse that Saif Al Islam Gaddafi has been subjected to as a result of the lack of any oversight by the UNSC of the cases they refer to the ICC.[1910]

Mark Kersten has also pointed to the damage the Libyan referral has caused to the ICC's credibility:

[T]he authority and legitimacy of the ICC seem likely to suffer in the wake of its intervention in Libya. Of course, this is in large part due to the failure of the international community, particularly the members of the U.N. Security Council that put the ICC's intervention into Libya in motion, to support the Court's work in Libya. But the ICC's own decision-making may also have significant ramifications on its future capacity to function effectively in conflict and post-conflict contexts. First, the Court's apology to Libya is likely to affect the capacity of ICC staff to operate in similar environments in the future. The ICC's apology to Libya in the Taylor affair appeared to send the message that the illegal arrest and detention of ICC staff was, at least in part, the fault of the Court. The danger is that this could set a precedent and encourage states to abuse the rights of ICC staff. Second, the OTP's leniency toward Libya and its currying favor with the NTC is something that must be more critically addressed as it has diminished the Court's perception as an impartial and independent institution. Third, the bitter divisions that have emerged within the Court must be resolved. To ultimately be an effective, independent and impartial Court, the ICC must have a well-functioning OTP *and* OPCD.[1911]

Geoffrey Robertson has been very critical of the ICC's actions with regard to the Libyan situation:

Libya was under an international duty to surrender Saif to The Hague. Foolishly however, the ICC Prosecutor rushed to Tripoli and announced that the ICC would lend assistance to local authorities if they wanted to put him on trial. This was a serious error, because the decision about whether any indictee in these circumstances should be tried in the Hague had to be made by the court, and not prematurely by an announcement from its prosecutor. As should have been obvious at the time (and became very obvious afterwards) the Libyan justice system was dysfunctional.[1912]

He was particularly scathing of the ICC double standards with regard to complementarity:

> The ICC has acted to indict and remove indictees from countries such as Uganda and DRC with perfectly functional judicial systems and courts, but seems content to indict and then abandon indictees in countries with non-existent or virtually non functional legal systems… . The…president of the ICC…failed to condemn the Libyans…and chose to negotiate in secret for the release of their lawyers. This incident illustrates the risk of the "complementarity principle" being turned into an excuse for abandoning indictees to the untender mercy of local lynch law.[1913]

Robertson has said of the Senussi and Gaddafi cases:

> These cases expose a design fault in the ICC. It is meant to be a court of last resort, leaving international criminals to their fate in their own country unless trial there is impossible. After a revolution, trial is always possible but fair trial usually is not. New governments want to execute old leaders as quickly as possible. There is overwhelming prejudice, usually a new set of judges hand-picked by the victors, and a public eager to see their past tormentors on the gallows. When the ICC indicts a political or military leader it contributes to their fall (as it did in the cases of Milosevic and Colonel Gaddafi) and has a moral duty to protect them from an unfair local trial and consequent death sentence. But the ICC cannot even protect its own lawyers in Libya.[1914]

Robertson has been very critical of the position taken by the UK with regard to its obligations: "So what did the British government do to ensure that international justice ran its proper course? Absolutely nothing… . As a permanent member of the security council, the UK had a duty to make sure Libya complied with resolution 1970, which places upon it an obligation to co-operate with the ICC prosecutor."[1915]

Human Rights Watch's Richard Dicker noted: "The status of Libya's ICC suspects reflects another glaring failure of [Security Council] support for the court." He also observed of the Western members of the Security Council:

> The Security Council's unanimous vote on Feb. 26, 2011, to refer Libya to the court generated a palpable sense of pride among the ambassadors in the council chamber. The resolution imposed a binding obligation on Libya to surrender Saif al-Islam al-Qaddafi and former intelligence chief Abdullah Senussi to the

court. *Yet, for the United States, Britain, and France, this obligation has vanished from official talking points. The word from Washington, London, and Paris is that justice for past crimes "is in the hands of the Libyan people."*[1916] (Emphasis added.)

Having used the ICC as a political weapon in an attempt to legitimise its military intervention in Libya, the Western members of the UNSC, and European funders of the ICC simply walked away from any of the consequences of their actions once their objective of overthrowing the Gaddafi regime had been achieved.

On 11 October 2013, judges at the ICC ruled that Libya was able to try Abdullah Senussi. The judges said that as Libya was able and willing to give Senussi a fair trial on similar charges to those for which he had been indicted by the ICC there was no need to transfer him to the court's custody. Ben Emmerson, Senussi's lawyer before the ICC called the decision "shocking", stated that "The country is sliding into wide-scale lawlessness where the law of the gun rules and armed militias do as they please. The effect of this decision is to condemn Mr. al-Senussi to face mob justice…in which the inevitable outcome is the death penalty."[1917]

Chapter Twenty-five

THE COURT AND MALI

"There should be little doubt that the Malian government has calculated using the ICC as a weapon to achieve its political aims."

Mark Kersten[1918]

"A decision to investigate Mali...will simply reinforce the perception that the ICC is the African Criminal Court, not the International Criminal Court."

Kevin Jon Heller[1919]

For several decades after independence from France in 1960, Mali experienced a turbulent political history. This included twenty-three years of military dictatorship until democratic elections were held in 1992. An insurgency among nomadic Tuareg communities in northern Mali over land and cultural rights began in the 1990s, and has continued to this day. The insurgency intensified as a result of weapons and fighters from Libya, following the 2011 Libyan Civil War, and made significant gains in January 2012. The Tuareg rebel movement, the *Mouvement national de libération de l'Azawad* (National Movement for the Liberation of Azawad, MNLA) attacked a military base in the town of Menaka in the Gao region on 17 January 2012. Dissatisfied with what they claimed was the government's mishandling of the rebellion in the north, Malian military officers led by Captain Amadou Haya Sanogo staged a *coup d'état* in March 2012 overthrowing President Amadou Toumani Touré, and forcing him into exile. Military units occupied the presidential palace, state television, and military barracks. A National Committee for the Restoration of Democracy and State was formed by the mutineers. There was blanket international condemnation of the coup. In the political turmoil that ensued northern Mali fell to rebel forces.

Under considerable international pressure from the international community, especially from the AU and the Economic Community of West African States (ECOWAS), the military junta promised a swift return to civil rule and a transition towards elections. As a result of ECOWAS mediation at the beginning of April 2012, President Touré resigned. Parliamentary speaker Dioncounda Traoré was elected interim President. On 5 July and on 2 October 2012, the UNSC adopted Resolution 2056 and 2071 respectively, stressing that the perpetrators of human-rights violations and international humanitarian law would be held accountable. At a meeting in Nigeria in November 2012 ECOWAS, with UN support, agreed to launch a coordinated military expedition to recapture the north. On 11 December 2012, President Traoré appointed Diango Cissoko as Prime Minister. On 20 December 2012, the Security Council adopted Resolution 2085 under Chapter VII of the UN Charter authorising the deployment of the African-led International Support Mission in Mali (AFISMA) to support national authorities to recover the north. The resolution called "upon AFISMA, consistent with its mandate, to support national and international efforts, including those of the ICC, to bring to justice perpetrators of serious human rights abuses". Before any ECOWAS forces could be deployed Malian rebels seized the initiative and began to advance towards the government heartland in the southwest of the country. The government in Bamako asked France for military assistance and French troops deployed in the country, rapidly retaking rebel strongholds in early 2013.

Mali signed the Rome Statute on 17 July 1998, and deposited its instrument of ratification on 16 August 2000. As such, the ICC has jurisdiction over crimes against humanity, war crimes and genocide committed on the territory of Mali or by its nationals from 1 July 2002 onwards. On 18 July 2012, a delegation from the government of Mali led by the Minister of Justice Malick Coulibaly transmitted a letter by which the government of Mali, as a State Party to the court, referred "the situation in Mali since January 2012" to the OTP and requested an investigation to determine whether one or more persons should be charged for crimes committed. The government of Mali claimed that the Malian courts were unable to prosecute or try the perpetrators. The Malian delegation also provided documentation in support of the referral. The referral by the government of Mali followed a 30 May 2012 decision by the Malian cabinet to refer the situation to the court. The Prosecutor instructed her office to immediately proceed with a preliminary examination of the situation in order to assess whether the Rome Statute criteria stipulated under Article 53(1) for opening an investigation were fulfilled.

The possibility of the court opening yet another formal investigation following a self-referral provoked considerable debate among legal scholars. Mark Kersten was blunt about the politics behind the Mali referral: "There should be little doubt that the Malian government has calculated using the ICC as a weapon to achieve its political aims."[1920] The court would be on old, bitterly contested ground. Any intervention in Mali would also inevitably focus once again on the rebels, and not the referring government, within another African state. Headlines such as "Mali asks Hague court to investigate rebel crimes" have already shaped how the story unfolded.[1921] Kersten observed that the Mali referral was "reminiscent of the referral by the Ugandan government in 2003, which referred the LRA to the ICC…. It is worth noting that the Court has still never managed to escape the perception that it was biased in favour of the Government of Uganda."[1922]

William Schabas asked the immediate question about any such referral: "[D]oes the Court really need yet another situation in Africa?"[1923] Kevin Jon Heller elaborated slightly more: "A decision to investigate Mali, especially as the first act of the new Prosecutor, will simply reinforce the perception that the ICC is the African Criminal Court, not the International Criminal Court."[1924] Kersten confirmed that there is no question over Mali's "ability or willingness to prosecute rebels". The only question was "its inability to arrest them".[1925] The US State Department "Country Reports on Human Rights Practices for 2011" stated that Mali had a functioning judicial system:

> The constitution provides for the right to a fair trial, and the judiciary generally enforced this right. Defendants are presumed innocent and have the right to confront witnesses, to present witnesses and evidence on their behalf, and to appeal decisions to the Supreme Court. Except in the case of minors, trials generally were public and juries were used. Defendants have the right to be present and have an attorney of their choice. Court-appointed attorneys are provided for the indigent without charge. Defendants have the right to consult with their attorney, but administrative backlogs and an insufficient number of lawyers, particularly in rural areas, often prevented prompt access. Defendants and attorneys have access to government evidence relevant to their cases.[1926]

Another reason for the court not to get involved in Mali was that the conflict is ongoing. The court should have learnt that intervening in ongoing situations could be very dangerous both to local populations as well as to the credibility of the court itself. The fiction that by intervening the court would act as a deterrent is just that, fiction – and all the more so given that the conflict involves Islamist rebels. Heller addressed another key issue – regarding the court's funding: "[W]hy should the ICC spend its limited resources on investigating crimes that Mali can prosecute itself if/when it prevails in the conflict?"[1927]

Nonetheless, despite all these concerns, on 16 January 2013 ICC Prosecutor Fatou Bensouda formally opened an investigation into alleged crimes committed on the territory of Mali since January 2012. This decision was said to have been the result of the preliminary examination of the situation in Mali that the office had been conducting since July 2012:

> Since the beginning of the armed conflict in January 2012, the people of Northern Mali have been living in profound turmoil. At each stage during the conflict, different armed groups have caused havoc and human suffering through a range of alleged acts of extreme violence. I have determined that some of these deeds of brutality and destruction may constitute war crimes as defined by the Rome Statute.[1928]

Prosecutor Bensouda stated that her office had determined that there was a reasonable basis to believe the following crimes were committed: (i) murder; (ii) mutilation, cruel treatment and torture; (iii) intentionally directing attacks against protected objects; (iv) the passing of sentences and the carrying out of executions without previous judgment pronounced by a regularly constituted court; (v) pillaging, and (vi) rape. She promised that her "[o]ffice will ensure a thorough and impartial investigation and will bring justice to Malian victims by investigating who are the most responsible for these alleged crimes".

The court stated that "[b]ased on the information gathered to date, the investigation will focus on crimes committed in the three northern regions of Mali".[1929]

Phil Clark has doubted the capacity of the court to investigate issues in Mali: "There are serious questions to be asked of the new prosecutor as to whether it is a drastic overstretch to have eight African countries being dealt with simultaneously with essentially the same level of staff and the same level of finance as her office was operating on before. Is it really feasible for the office to be dealing with so many cases?" Kevin Jon Heller has raised similar concerns: "They are really at the edge of what they can do with their resources.... It isn't like anyone from the ICC is going to Mali anytime soon."[1930]

There have been numerous reports of incidents of murders and mob lynching and looting of properties belonging to Arab and Tuareg communities in Mali, who have reportedly been accused of supporting armed groups based on their ethnicity. The UN Special Adviser on the Prevention of Genocide, Adama Dieng, stated: "I am deeply disturbed by reports of violations committed by the army, and by reports that the armed forces have been recruiting and arming proxy militia groups to instigate attacks against particular ethnic and national groups in northern Mali."[1931] The question is whether or not the court will investigate alleged war crimes by all sides to the conflict. IRIN has observed that "instances of alleged extra-judicial killings carried out by the Malian armed forces...and documented by human rights groups such as the International Federation of Human Rights, and Human Rights Watch, risk remaining untouched by the ICC."[1932] The French weekly magazine *L'Express* also reported a mass execution of captured Islamist fighters in Sevare.[1933] Erwin van der Borght, Amnesty International's Africa Programme Director: "[I]t's crucial that the Court looks at the full scope of alleged crimes across the country, including those carried out by Malian security forces." Amnesty International reported that "Malian security forces have also committed violations of international human rights and humanitarian law, including the extrajudicial executions of Tuareg civilians."[1934]

The reality is that – as in every instance to date of self-referrals – the court will not actively pursue the involvement of government forces in war crimes and crimes against humanity.

Africa and international law commentator Blake Evans-Pritchard was blunt about the effect that the ICC involvement will have in Mali: "Action by the ICC – already perceived as a Western institution in some parts of the world – could be a gift to Islamic extremist propagandists." He also cited Liaquat Ali Khan, a law professor at Washburn University in Kansas with particular expertise in Islam, who has also expressed reservations about how effective the ICC can be in Mali: "The ICC is making an almost symbolic gesture – that it dislikes or wants to discourage extremist violence, but its actual impact on these groups is going to be minimal." Madeline Morris, an international lawyer and expert on counterterrorism law and policy at Duke University School of Law in Durham, USA:

> I would be surprised if the ICC for some reason has an impact on extremist groups in Mali, whilst it has consistently failed to have an impact on atrocity

crimes in other regions where religious motivations were not even present. Why would a person who is willing to risk life and limb in committing widespread atrocities suddenly find himself deterred by the prospect of a prosecution in The Hague?¹⁹³⁵

Chapter Twenty-six

EUROPEAN DOUBLE STANDARDS

"To those who say there is no peace without justice, I reply, as a Brit, with two words: Northern Ireland. Human life is more precious than mantras."

British journalist Julie Flint[1936]

Given that the ICC is European-driven, and that the EU is at the front and centre of self-proclaimed attempts to "end impunity" and impose "law" on Africa, the European record with regard to peace, justice, impunity and amnesty is worth examining. There have been repeated claims that the Europeans have been imposing double standards in their approach to the ICC. It is all too clear that there is one rule for them and quite another for Africans.

Half of Europe has only in the very recent past emerged from the grip of some of the most vicious totalitarian regimes imaginable. Germany, at the heart of the ICC and an advocate of unfettered retributive international justice, is but one example. The German Democratic Republic (DDR) with its all-pervasive Stasi (*Ministerium für Staatssicherheit* or Ministry for State Security) secret police and the original Iron Curtain that divided Europe for so long is a case in point. The scale of the human-rights abuse was clear. Hundreds of thousands of deaths, millions of civilians displaced, hundreds of thousands of people detained and imprisoned from 1949 onwards. The previous Nazi state had controlled a population of about 80,000,000 Germans with a 40,000-strong Gestapo secret police. The East German state under Erich Honecker had 102,000 Stasi officers for just 17,000,000 East Germans. Taken together with those believed to have informed for the Stasi there was one Stasi for every six citizens.[1937] The renowned Nazi hunter Simon Wiesenthal noted that "[t]he Stasi was much, much worse than the Gestapo".[1938] John Koehler, the author of *Stasi: The Untold Story of the East German Secret Police*, noted further that "[o]ne might add that the Nazi terror lasted only twelve years, whereas the Stasi had four decades in which to perfect its machinery of oppression, espionage, and international terrorism and subversion."[1939] More than 72,000 people were arrested, interrogated and imprisoned by the Stasi just for trying to leave the country by "illegal" means.[1940] *Euronews* has reported that the Stasi operated a network of seventeen prisons where dissidents and those deemed criminals were subjected to systematic torture. Some were said to have been exposed to radiation to induce cancer.[1941] As one example of the extent of the East German prison system, the West German government literally bought 33,000 political prisoners from the German Democratic Republic between 1963 and 1989 at a price of nearly US$3 billion. In the words of one of the Stasi's prisoners: "It was like modern-day slave trade; they were soul sellers."[1942]

Chief Prosecutor Heiner Sauer, former Head of the West German Central Registration Office for Political Crimes, reported that the final figure of all political prosecutions was about 300,000. Koehler noted of these political trials: "In every case, the Stasi was involved either in the initial arrest or in pretrial interrogations during which 'confessions' were usually extracted by physical or psychological torture, particularly between the mid-1940s and the mid-1960s."[1943] Political prisoners could seek no redress in the post-unification dispensation. By the end of 1991, Sauer had registered 4,444 cases of actual or attempted killings by state officials. At least 825 people had been shot and killed while trying to escape to the West.[1944]

Impunity and pensions for European human rights abusers

With the collapse of the Iron Curtain, the DDR ceased to exist. Given the European mantra about the need for justice, one would have imagined this was the time to prosecute those many people who had kept the dictatorship in place and who had been guilty of so many human-rights abuses. Instead, however, there were one or two very superficial attempts to place those at the heart of the East German dictatorship on trial. The simple fact is that Erich Honecker and Erich Mielke, the last head of the Stasi, were not convicted of any crimes relating to abuses during the dictatorship: Mielke was eventually convicted of murdering two policemen in 1931: he served less than two years. Honecker was allowed to slip off to live in Chile. Barbara Miller, a historian of the Stasi and the East German dictatorship it served, noted "Many former Stasi victims were disappointed to discover that the criminal justice system would not necessarily guarantee justice for the crimes which had been committed in the dictatorship."[1945]

Koehler reported that "[a]fter the Berlin wall came down, the victims of the DDR regime demanded immediate retribution".[1946] This was painfully slow in coming where not simply non-existent. Koehler cites Rupert Scholz, a member of parliament and Professor of Law at the University of Munich, who stated that many East Germans felt there is little determination among their Western compatriots to bring the Stasi criminals to trial. "In fact, we already have heard many of them say that the peaceful revolution should have been a bloody one instead so they could have done away with their tormentors by hanging them posthaste."[1947]

In his study of the post-Wall situation in Eastern Germany, Koehler noted that "[b]efore unification, Germans would speak of *Vergangenheitsbewältigung* ('coming to grips with the past') when they discussed dealing with Nazi crimes. In the reunited Germany, this word came to imply the communist past as well. The two were considered comparable especially in the area of human rights violations."[1948] He noted:

> [T]he communists' brutal oppression of the nation by means including murder alongside legal execution put the SED leadership on a par with Hitler's gang. In that sense, Walter Ulbricht or Erich Honecker (Ulbricht's successor as the party's secretary-general and head of state) and secret police chief Erich Mielke can justifiably be compared to Hitler and Himmler, respectively.[1949]

Koehler notes that "In 1945, Nazis holding comparable or lesser positions were subject to automatic arrest by the Allies. They spent months or even years in camps while their cases were adjudicated. Moreover, the Nürnberg Tribunal branded the Reich and its Corps of Political Leaders, SS, Security Service (SD), Secret State Police (Gestapo), SA (Storm Troopers), and Armed Forces High Command criminal organizations. Similarly sweeping actions against communist leaders and functionaries such as Stasi officers were never contemplated, even though tens of thousands of political trials and human rights abuses have been documented."

Steven Ratner and Jason Abrams have noted that "supporters of the prosecutions have been disappointed by the number of defendants who have escaped punishment", and that "most of those convicted have successfully challenged their convictions on appeal, received light or suspended sentences, or avoided punishment due to illness".[1950] Reinhard Dobrinski, Chairman of victim's group the Forum for Education and Rehabilitation, has said that the legal action to date is simply not enough for hundreds of thousands of victims of "persecution, false imprisonment, perversion of justice and countless other crimes".[1951]

To add insult to injury, as with all former East German civil servants, Stasi officials receive regular state pensions from the unified Germany from the very government that demands justice before peace everywhere else. Rather than punish or imprison systematic violators of human rights, the German government actually pays them. In 2008, for example, the bill for retired army, customs and Stasi officers totalled €1.6 billion. The *Irish Times* had revealed that in the meantime many of their former victims, with only limited social welfare entitlements, live in often shocking poverty.[1952] The above examples are drawn from only one of the eastern European countries that languished under a brutal dictatorship. There were several others, now members of the EU and the ICC, and much the same can be reported from them. One has to ask those European international law exponents of no peace without justice where is the justice for the hundreds of thousands of Europeans whose human rights were so systematically abused for so long, or for those non-Europeans whose human rights have been abused by Europeans.

This chapter is also a tale of two countries. Both fought vigorous counter-insurgency campaigns against armed insurrections in their westernmost provinces, provinces with a history of armed ethnic unrest and with porous borders; the rebels in both instances were supported by their kith and kin across the border; both conflicts saw massive population displacement, at least some of which was enforced; both conflicts saw many thousands of civilians killed or injured; both conflicts saw the murder of hundreds of policemen and armed criminality; both conflicts saw the government use its security forces and pro-government militias within and against rebel communities; in both cases the rebels attacked the nation's capital; one country is in Europe and the other is African; in one case the conflict was brought to an end by putting peace before justice; in the other case, the insistence of a foreign court on "justice" before peace endangers an ongoing peace process and risks escalating the conflict.

The above analogy between Darfur and the UK's province of Northern Ireland, like all analogies, is far from perfect. It is also not in any way meant to deflect the seriousness of either conflict. It is hoped that it is an analogy that might focus British and continental European minds on some of the complexities of the Darfur conflict and the double standards and hypocrisy implicit in the differing approaches taken to it and the Northern Ireland conflict by the British government – especially with regard to its position on the ICC – hypocrisy that is all too easy to exploit within Africa and other countries within the developing world. It echoes repeated accusations that the ICC has only ever focused on African conflicts, consciously choosing not to pursue any white, NATO country for alleged involvement in war crimes or crimes against humanity in Iraq or Afghanistan.

Given that the British government was party to the ending of its war in Northern Ireland with a formula based on peace before justice enshrined in the "Good Friday Accord"[1953], its subsequent position regarding the recent ICC demands in respect of Darfur, that "justice" must supersede peace, can be described only as blatant, and arguably racist, double standards. Britain is insisting that Sudan recognise the ICC and accede to the court's 3 March 2009 demands that Sudan surrender up its president, Omar al-Bashir, and other citizens to The Hague to answer allegations of involvement in war crimes and crimes against humanity in relation to the conflict within its westernmost province of Darfur.[1954] This insistence ignores the fact that there are multiple peace processes progressing within Sudan (one having ended Africa's longest-running civil war in southern Sudan in 2005 and the current process within Darfur) and that the arrest of Sudanese President al-Bashir would stall or destroy them. ICC supporters, British ministers among them, repeat the mantras, "justice must take its course", an "end to impunity" and "no hiding place".

It seems to many observers within the developing world that there is one law for white Europeans and another for black Africans. White Europeans, whether they be prime ministers, government ministers, soldiers or militiamen, can act with impunity (whether it be in their own countries in the case of Northern Ireland or internationally in the cases for example of Iraq and Afghanistan) and then be awarded amnesties and immunity from prosecution for murder, attempted murder, crimes against humanity, war crimes etc., arising from armed insurrection and counter-insurgency, as part of a process resulting in peace, while black Africans having found themselves in very similar circumstances are to be prosecuted by a self-imposed European court while the conflict continues and probably intensifies.[1955]

Britain's Darfur

Whether it is uncomfortable or not for the British state, there are a number of convincing similarities between the Northern Irish and Darfur conflicts. It is matter of record that the British state aggressively resisted an armed rebellion in its westernmost province, Northern

Ireland, for over thirty years, from 1969 onwards.[1956] The Darfur rebellion began in 2003. The Irish rebellion was fought between the British state and two ethnically based armed movements, initially the Official Irish Republican Army and then the Provisional IRA (PIRA), and the Irish National Liberation Army (INLA), established within and recruited from Irish Catholic nationalist communities in Northern Ireland. The Darfur rebellion is being fought between the Sudanese government and the two main armed movements, the Justice and Equality Movement and the Sudan Liberation Army, both of which are recruited from the Zaghawa, Fur and Masalit communities in Darfur. PIRA and INLA claimed that their violence was in defence of their community and against violations of civil rights and political and economic marginalisation within their region. The Darfur rebels claimed to be fighting against the political and economic marginalisation of their communities. It is a matter of record that the British Army, assisted by locally recruited paramilitary police reserve forces, responded with a military and security crackdown that further polarised the communities. The Sudanese government responded in a similar fashion. There were allegations that sympathetic Irish nationalists across the border from Northern Ireland were providing their kinsmen with weapons and other logistical support. In the case of Darfur, the rebel movements have been actively supported by their fellow-tribesmen in Chad.

It is also a matter of history that well over 100,000 British citizens in Northern Ireland were internally displaced, and many thousands more left the region never to return. Tens of thousands of British citizens were killed or injured in what was euphemistically called "the troubles". The conflict saw 47,000 injuries, 37,000 shootings, 22,500 armed robberies, 16,200 bombings or attempted bombings, and 2,200 incidents of arson. By March 1995, the British government had paid over one and a half billion dollars in personal injuries compensation and half a billion dollars for damages to property as a result of the conflict.[1957] The death rate due to the conflict was on a par with the Middle East and South Africa and worse than in Argentina.[1958] All this within a province one thirty-fifth the size of Darfur, within a comparatively densely populated and well-policed first-world community in Western Europe.

Almost from the start of the conflict, the British state and military intelligence chiefs were accused of using pro-government, Protestant "Loyalist", militias against the nationalist rebels as an instrument of its counter-insurgency, either initially as members of official police reserve formations such as the "B Specials", locally recruited army units such as the Ulster Defence Regiment or within Loyalist paramilitary groups such as the Ulster Defence Association or Ulster Volunteer Force.[1959] In 2003, the Irish republican political party, Sinn Fein, now part of the government of Northern Ireland, stated that:

> For 30 years, the British government, through its agencies – MI5, British Military Intelligence and RUC/PSNI Special Branch – has been involved in the murder of its citizens. Together, they directed the activities of various loyalist death squads. This was much more than simply passing on information. This was about the deliberate and orchestrated targeting and assassination of

citizens. What has been allowed to happen, to borrow a phrase from former British Lord Chief Justice Denning, represents an 'appalling vista'.[1960]

The Sudanese state recruited local supporters into units such as the Popular Defence Forces (PDF), Border Intelligence Guard, Popular Police and Nomadic Police. Sympathetic communities also recruited their own militias. Irish republican leaders also alleged torture was routinely used on their community.[1961] As was the case in Darfur, a consequence of the initial violence was civilian displacement. Between 1969 and 1971 there was a huge forced movement of Catholic civilians in a number of areas of Northern Ireland, including the provincial capital, Belfast. Tom Hadden reported on nationalist civilian displacement: "in 1969 83% of the total moves were Catholic", and that as late as 1971 that figure was still at sixty per cent.[1962] It is clear that this forced movement was the result of activities by loyalist communities and loyalist militias, very possibly in official or informal collusion with government security forces. As Desmond Hamill's study of the early days of the Northern Ireland crisis made clear "the overall position was made worse by the wholesale movement of very frightened people. In Belfast some 30–40,000 people left their homes because of intimidation and went to areas among their co-religionists where they could feel safe. It was the largest movement of a civil population since WWII." David Holloway's study cited a larger number: "Between August 1969 and February 1973, around 60,000 Belfast people (around 10% of the population) were forced to leave their homes." As Steve Bruce also noted at the time: "It is also the case that most people were forced out of their houses not by violence so much as by the fear of violence. Irrespective of how they got on with their neighbours, they…concluded that what was happening elsewhere could soon be happening to them unless they moved to secure areas."[1963] This is precisely what also happened in large areas of Darfur.[1964]

This forced displacement was happening under the noses of the government security forces even in the provincial capital, Belfast, itself. Darby and Morris estimated "[o]ur estimate of the total…in the Belfast area between August 1969 and February 1973 is between 8,000 families (minimum) and approximately 15,000 families (maximum)… roughly between 6.6% and 11.8% of the population of the Belfast Urban area".[1965] Ten per cent of the population of one of the UK's biggest cities were forcibly displaced.

There are, of course, clear differences between these two westernmost provinces. Darfur is the size of France. Ulster is the one thirty-fifth the size of Darfur. Some would say that that would have made the job of the British state in protecting its citizens much easier. It chose instead to resort to military force, internment without trial, and the use of pro-government militias over which it may have lost some control. The militias killed or injured thousands of nationalists and were party to the biggest displacement of civilians in Western Europe since the Second World War – all this on the watch of the British government. Set against the Rome Statute, these actions would have constituted a host of crimes against humanity and war crimes. The highest-ranking British serviceman convicted of "war crimes" was a corporal.

The war in Ulster was brought to an end by the Good Friday Agreement, which put peace before justice. The Darfur conflict continues in part because of Western demands of justice before peace. The Northern Irish analogies are not lost on long-time British commentators on Darfur. Julie Flint, a fierce critic of the Sudanese government, and co-author of one of the definitive studies of the conflict, *Darfur: A New History of a Long War*, has noted: "To those who say there is no peace without justice, I reply, as a Brit, with two words: Northern Ireland. Human life is more precious than mantras."[1966] Convicted PIRA and INLA killers and bombers were released; other paramilitaries were not prosecuted and amnestied; government ministers and military officers who could be said to have exercised a command responsibility up to and including present and past prime ministers were not prosecuted.

The Times correspondent Rob Crilly has also written about the timing of the ICC arrest warrants for President Bashir, coming as they did just as the most coherent Darfur rebel movement, the Justice and Equality Movement, was holding unprecedented peace talks with the government:

> With peace talks between the Sudanese government and rebels of the Justice and Equality Movement starting in Qatar today, why do anything to disrupt the faint chance of peace in Darfur? (A bit like arresting Martin McGuinness during talks that led to the Good Friday agreement, is how one western diplomat in Khartoum put it)…criminalising a head of state can only raise temperatures in an already volatile country, putting peacekeeping operations at risk and forcing aid agencies on to a defensive footing. A shaky peace deal with the south, signed in 2005 ending more than 20 years of civil war, will weaken further under the pressure. And the Darfuri rebels could become sufficiently emboldened to have another crack at the capital, Khartoum.[1967]

Using the same logic that he used regarding Darfur, the ICC Prosecutor could have indicted several previous British prime ministers and a number of generals and intelligence chiefs with the following crimes – murder, extermination, forcible transfer and torture – as well as intentionally directing attacks against a civilian population as such or against individual civilians not taking direct part in hostilities, and pillaging. Lord Lamont added that genocide could also be added if the court was so inclined. In the face of the same sort of ICC demands made of Sudan, what would the British government have done? Would it have ignored the demand by a foreign court to turn over its leaders, ministers and soldiers? Perhaps, even though Britain is a signatory to the court. Would there have been a peace agreement in Northern Ireland had the British prime ministers and/or their predecessors as well as other senior politicians and generals been arrested and sent to The Hague? The chances are not, as it would have emboldened PIRA militants.

The British parliamentarian Ian Paisley Jr., who represents a constituency in Northern Ireland, has also outlined the case for putting peace before justice:

> If the I.C.C. had been in existence during the Northern Ireland peace process…there would no doubt have been calls for it to intervene and prosecute

those accused of violence. This would have driven old enemies even further apart in recrimination and hostility, hobbling the chance for peace.[1968]

Lord Lamont outlined the double standards at the heart of the ICC in this regard:

> The fact is that in the name of politics we have set aside the due process of law in order to achieve a political settlement. We are so high and mighty that we think we can deny that to other countries but we do it to ourselves. That is the flaw in this whole international court: its inflexibility will apply only to the weak, to the small. When it comes to the large and powerful country, it will not apply to them.... When we want the court to be flexible, when it has to be flexible, it will be made flexible. But when there are little countries to be bullied and we can go round meddling in the name of justice, with support from the NGOs, then we shall interfere anywhere, even if that means that a civil war will last longer and lives will be lost as a result.[1969]

The key question is how did the UK end its long-running war? Quite simply it put peace before justice. The British government sat down with its rebel gunmen, and signed a power-sharing agreement with the rebels in Northern Ireland. A general amnesty was signed and hundreds of rebel gunmen and bombers were released from prison. Peace before justice. This was something with which many people in Britain were unhappy, but which was accepted. Peace before justice. As Alex de Waal notes, however:

> It is inconceivable that the British Government would permit the ICC to investigate crimes committed in Northern Ireland, either by the IRA or the security forces. Some might argue that the ICC should have jurisdiction because the UK is a State Party to the Rome Statute and it shows no interest in prosecuting these crimes – having extended a de facto amnesty that the ICC cannot in law recognize. The interests of peace in Northern Ireland mean that the victims of these abuses will never see their perpetrators brought to a British court.[1970]

Ian Paisley Jr. has also outlined the case for putting peace before justice:

> During the height of the Troubles in the 1970s and 1980s, the British government used the courts to prosecute its opponents in Northern Ireland. People with blood on their hands were portrayed as martyrs by their supporters. But through a peace process that was backed by the international community – not driven by it – two hostile communities were able to come together to share power in our common home. People on both sides have committed violence, yet we now sit in government together, determined to put the past behind us for the common good.[1971]

Yet on Darfur (and Uganda and DRC), the same British government is insisting that Sudan must somehow put "Justice before Peace", despite the fact that this will prolong the war in Darfur – and would also have prolonged the war in southern Sudan. To the outside observer, there would seem to be one rule for the UK and another for Sudan. There seems to be one rule for white Europeans and another for black Africans. This is not lost on commentators within the developing world.

Ramesh Thakur makes the point that Europeans, members of the ICC, have committed human-rights abuses with impunity: "Africans are being held to international accountability for domestic acts of war crimes, but Westerners seem to escape international judgment." He makes an interesting point about "extraordinary rendition", with which both the USA and, more saliently, several members of the EU have been associated:

> Unlike Bashir or any other Africans in the dock, whose alleged atrocities were limited to national jurisdictions, the Bush administration asserted and exercised the right to kidnap suspected enemies in the war on terror anywhere in the world and take them anywhere else, including countries known to torture suspects. Many Western allies colluded in this distasteful practice of "rendition." No Westerner has faced criminal trial for it. In a surreal twist worthy of Kafka, Western governments send terror suspects to be tortured to countries that the same governments then brand as human rights abusers.[1972]

In January 2005, Swiss Senator Dick Marty, the representative at the Council of Europe in charge of the European investigations, concluded that 100 people had been kidnapped by the CIA in Europe – thus qualifying as ghost detainees – and then rendered to a country where they may have been tortured. *The Guardian* reported on 5 December 2005 that the British government is "guilty of breaking international law if it knowingly allowed secret CIA 'rendition' flights of terror suspects to land at UK airports, according to a report by American legal scholars".[1973]

The European Parliament launched its own investigation into the reports. In April 2006, MEPs leading the investigations expressed concerns that there had been more than 1,000 "rendition" flights over European territory since 2001, some to transfer terror suspects to countries that used torture. Investigators said that the same US agents and planes were involved over and over again. In a resolution passed on 14 February 2007 the European Parliament approved a report that criticised the rendition programme and concluded that many EU states tolerated illegal CIA activities including secret flights over their territories. The countries named were: Austria, Belgium, Cyprus, Denmark, Germany, Greece, Ireland, Italy, Poland, Portugal, Romania, Spain, Sweden and the UK.[1974] Given the number of EU countries involved it is hard not to believe that it has been an EU-sanctioned policy – the very same EU that is at the heart of the ICC demanding an end to impunity elsewhere but not in Europe.

The European Parliament report went on to denounce "the lack of co-operation of many member states and of the Council of the EU with the investigation; Regrets that

European countries have been relinquishing control over their airspace and airports by turning a blind eye or admitting flights operated by the CIA which, on some occasions, were being used for illegal transportation of detainees". The report also uncovered the use of secret detention facilities used in Europe, including Romania and Poland.[1975]

Manfred Nowak, the UN special rapporteur on torture, published a fifteen-page report, presented to the UN General Assembly, which stated that the UK, France, and Sweden, among other countries, were violating international human rights conventions by deporting terrorist suspects to countries where they may have been tortured.[1976] It can safely be said that several prominent members of the EU, prominent and vocal members of the ICC, have abused human rights with impunity.

Thakur also examines the nature of Western "international justice" within Europe itself: "consider the ad hoc International Criminal Tribunal for former Yugoslavia. It has tried several Serbs, but no NATO national. Might it have something to do with the tribunal's being located in a NATO country, its budget being paid mostly by NATO countries and its reliance on NATO for collection of evidence and enforcement of warrants?"[1977] These issues and others highlight the contradictions in the European and ICC position regarding Africa and African situations: one rule for Europe, another for Africa.

Amnesty for some but not Africa

There is an additional dimension to the focus on Africa, another manifestation of Western double standards, which is Western acceptance of the concept of amnesty within conflict and post-conflict situations – except in Africa. Dr. Louise Mallinder points out that much of the legal scholarship on the use of amnesty and international law does not document or explain the continued international use of amnesty laws that she and other scholars have highlighted.[1978] She states: "In recent years, international jurists and scholars have increasingly made proclamations on the status of amnesty laws under customary international law, but few have based their assertions on extensive comparative studies of state practice. Indeed, by relying on a small number of cases, many of these analyses have overlooked the continued prevalence and endurance of amnesties around the world."[1979] Mallinder observes that "Amnesty laws have played a central role in addressing political crises and violent conflicts for millennia."[1980]

Lord Lamont has also focused on the value of amnesty: "A national criminal justice system always provides a safety valve – a recourse to a pardon or an amnesty issued by political Ministers to stay the effect of a prosecution in the courts. There is no provision for that in the ICC."[1981] Lord Lamont referred specifically to the Northern Irish example:

> [M]y point is logical and correct. If we are prepared to have an amnesty in Northern Ireland and believe that no one should interfere with that from outside, why do we think that it is right for the International Criminal Court to interfere in other countries that have decided to put aside strict legal justice

and make a political settlement to advance peace and reconciliation? That is an important point.[1982]

The ICC's focus on Africa, its prohibition of any process short of Western retributive justice for alleged crimes within Africa, and its fervent objection to any amnesty in African situations flies in the face of reality, and seems to be aimed solely at Africa. As of late 2011, the amnesty law database contains information on 537 amnesty laws in 129 countries that were introduced between 1945 and June 2011.[1983] Between 1979 and 2011, there were a total of 398 amnesty laws enacted in 115 countries. Between January 1979 and December 2010, an average of 12.25 amnesty laws were enacted each year, and from January 2011 to June 2011 a further 6 amnesties were introduced.[1984] While the majority of amnesty laws enacted from 1979 to 2010 were introduced in sub-Saharan Africa (thirty-three per cent), a region with a large number of states, there is very little difference between the proportions of amnesty laws enacted in the Americas (sixteen per cent), Asia (eighteen per cent), and Europe and Central Asia (nineteen per cent) during this period.[1985] As Mallinder points out: "This is particularly remarkable considering Europe and the Americas have more developed regional human rights monitoring mechanisms than Asia."[1986]

Almost half of all amnesties enacted over the past thirty years were related to conflicts, and many were declared when the conflict was ongoing or during peace negotiations. If the data is restricted to the years from 1999 to 2011, the proportion of amnesties related to conflict rises to slightly over fifty per cent.[1987]

What is remarkable given Western insistence on a no-amnesties-for-insurgents policy – or governments, for that matter – within Africa, is that there are notable cases of strong international support for amnesty processes elsewhere. For example, during the final stages of the conflict between the Sri Lankan government and the "Liberation Tigers of Tamil Eelam" (LTTE or "Tamil Tigers") insurgents in 2009, Western states were at the forefront of endorsing an amnesty towards the end of the war in that country. The USA, EU, Japan and Norway all urged LTTE fighters to surrender and accept a government offer of amnesty.[1988] These statements of support did not refer to the need to prosecute serious war crimes and crimes against humanity committed during the conflict. The LTTE can be seen as an Asian equivalent of the LRA in Uganda. The former UN spokesman in Sri Lanka, Gordon Weiss, has documented the LTTE's "record of appalling violence".[1989] He records that the LTTE Chief Velupillai Prabakharan gave orders "to bomb buses full of women and children…murder monks and kill prisoners",[1990] and that "[t]hey hacked, bludgeoned, shot, burned and hanged civilians in a long series of massacres… . Children were slaughtered alongside the elderly in dozens of small-scale incidents."[1991] The LTTE "planted bombs on trains, aircraft and buses".[1992] Weiss also points out that between 1983 and May 2009, "there were around 200 individual Tiger attacks on civilian targets, in which between 3,700 and 4,100 civilians were killed".[1993] Weiss also notes that "[t]his figure does not include the number of Tamils allegedly killed by the Tigers in the areas they controlled, nor the many hundreds of prisoners thought to have been killed in Tamil Tiger gulags. The University Teachers for Human Rights, a respected Sri Lankan human rights organisation, estimates that the latter figure is as high as 7,000."[1994] Weiss also confirms that the LTTE "systematised the use of suicide bombers...and child soldiers".[1995] *The Economist* noted that "The Tigers were as vicious and totalitarian a bunch of thugs as ever adopted terrorism as a national-liberation strategy."[1996] The USA designated the LTTE as a foreign terrorist organisation in October 1997: it was named as a "Specially Designated Global Terrorist movement" on 2 November 2001. The US Federal Bureau of Investigation described the LTTE as "among the most dangerous and deadly extremists in the world".[1997] The EU listed the LTTE as a terrorist organisation on 17 May 2006. In 2006, the UK listed the LTTE as a proscribed terrorist group under the 2000 Terrorism Act.[1998] Canada had since 2006 listed the movement as a terrorist group, and does not grant residency to LTTE members on the grounds that they have participated in crimes against humanity. The State Department had similarly listed the Ugandan LRA on its "Terrorist Exclusion List" in 2001.[1999] In August 2008, the US Treasury Department placed LRA leader Joseph Kony on its list of "Specially Designated Global Terrorists".[2000]

The EU was in favour of amnesty for the LTTE, but not for the LRA. Western powers – the same countries in very large part who actively support the ICC's autistic demands for a strictly "retributive justice", "no amnesty" approach in Africa – clearly adopted a diametrically opposite stance in Asia. The double standard is clear and eats like acid into the credibility of Western attempts to impose "justice" in Africa.

The amnesty issue is the elephant in the room in international law, clearly present but an inconvenience to proponents of an international law fundamentalism. Mallinder has noted that "states have consistently failed to prohibit amnesty laws in international conventions". She also pointed out that during the 1998 Rome Conference that established the ICC, "delegates debated a range of proposals relating to amnesty laws, but were ultimately unable to reach a consensus on prohibiting them in the ICC Statute. As a result, the ICC Statute contains no reference to amnesty legislation."[2001]

Michael Freeman's groundbreaking study of amnesties and their relationship with peace supports Mallinder's case. He made two points about the ICC, international law and amnesties. He noted firstly that "it is important to recall that neither the Rome Statute nor its Rules of Procedure and Evidence refers to amnesties. Indeed, the Rome Statute does not prohibit, discourage, or encourage amnesties. Reference to them is simply absent." He also pointed out that it was "well known" that at the ICC Preparatory Commission that preceded the adoption of the Rome Statute, a number of delegations took up the issue of amnesty: "The discussion was sparked by a U.S. nonpaper on the subject in which concern was expressed that the Court could end up preventing amnesties essential to restore peace and half human rights violations." The nonpaper asserted "that a responsible decision by a democratic regime to allow an amnesty was relevant in judging the admissibility of a case". Freeman makes the point that "the example was not an abstract one". He notes further that "[t]he issue of amnesty was unaddressed at the first ASP, which was held during the height of the peace-versus-justice debates surrounding the ICC's arrest warrants against Ugandan rebel leaders".[2002]

The reality is that to date the only international convention to discuss amnesty laws explicitly is the Additional Protocol II to the Geneva Conventions, which states in

Article 6(5): "At the end of hostilities, the authorities in power shall endeavour to grant the broadest possible amnesty to persons who have participated in the armed conflict, or those deprived of their liberty for reasons related to the armed conflict, whether they are interned or detained."[2003]

The Commentary on the Additional Protocol states that this provision is "to encourage gestures of reconciliation which can contribute to re-establishing normal relations in the life of a nation which has been divided".[2004] The reality of amnesty arrangements was acknowledged by the UN Secretary-General in 2004: "In the end, in post-conflict countries, the vast majority of perpetrators of serious violations of human rights and international humanitarian law will never be tried, whether internationally or domestically."[2005] Mallinder points out that this could be for a number of reasons "including a lack of evidence, a lack of judicial and penal capacity, limited financial resources, the ongoing political and military strength of the offenders, or a decision by the government to prioritize other policies such as development and security over the pursuit of justice".[2006]

Mallinder states that her research casts doubt:

> [O]n the existence of the global accountability norm, particularly where the enactment of amnesty laws receives diplomatic and financial support from international organizations and donor states. Although such support has yet to be systematically documented, it seems that it is particularly forthcoming where the amnesty is enacted in the midst of ongoing conflict to encourage combatants to surrender and disarm. This suggests that despite the development of international criminal law and transitional justice, a belief persists within states and the international community that in times of extreme violence, amnesty may be a necessary compromise to achieve peace.[2007]

Mallinder's studies clearly illustrate that while amnesty is still a viable option in international conflict resolution, it appears to be denied to Africa. This is but one of the many European double standards applied to Africa and its people. Philippe Sands has openly admitted the amnesty issue is controversial:

> This will be one of the very real challenges to be faced by the ICC's judges in coming years. The Statute is silent on the question of national amnesties or processes of truth and reconciliation. The court is bound to be faced with arguments that it should not interfere with a legitimate and effective national consensus which decides that criminal proceedings are not the right way to redress past wrongs.[2008]

Chapter Twenty-seven

A Way Forward

"Court isn't necessarily... the best way to deal with some of these conflicts. They have social, economic and political roots, which the use of the law is never going to address."

Courtney Griffiths QC[2009]

The illegitimacy of the ICC is clear at all levels. Lady Justice, in Latin, *Justitia*, the Roman goddess of justice, is an allegorical personification of the moral force in judicial systems. Justice is depicted as wearing a blindfold, which represents objectivity, in that justice should be impartial, and meted out objectively, without fear or favour, regardless of identity, money, power, or weakness. The ICC's very selectivity fatally discredits the institution. This selectivity is common knowledge. Theodor Meron, the President of the ICTY and Presiding Judge of the Appeals Chambers of the ICTR and the ICTY, admitted in an interview in early 2013 that the ICC "is still...selective".[2010] He was responding to a comment by BBC journalist Stephen Sackur about the ICC that "it is actually justice imposed on the weak but never applied to the strong".[2011]

The court's own record also clearly documents its own incompetence at a practical level. The need for the court to review every one of its cases is a clear one. The dysfunctional nature of the court's OTP and its first chief prosecutor is quite literally a matter of record. The judges in the Lubanga case went out of their way to criticise the Chief Prosecutor and his conduct and behaviour before and during the trial. The court's use of questionable intermediaries and witnesses appears to have been institutionalised, with implications for all the cases before it. The withholding of exculpatory evidence from the defence and other serious irregularities have been documented in several situations, starting with the court's very first case in 2006. Judge Christine Van den Wyngaert's 2013 condemnation of the prosecution's behaviour demonstrates the continuing systemic malpractice within the court. A different way of dealing with allegations of serious crimes in Africa must be outlined.

Mahmood Mamdani has pointed to the poisoned chalice of "international law" pushed upon Africa by the ICC:

> Everyone knows that the worst thing to do in a contest is to leave your opponent without an escape route. If you do that, you turn the contest into

a life-and-death struggle. You transform adversaries into enemies... . The judicial process tends to be a winner take all process. In the court of law, you are either right or wrong, innocent or guilty; both parties cannot be guilty in a court of law. In a civil war, however, both parties often bear some share of the guilt. The judicial process criminalises one side, which is then politically disenfranchised...those who want to reform the political process need to assure all adversaries are represented in the political process, and none ruled out as enemies. Targeting leaders of political parties in a civil war-type situation in courts of law, and thereby excluding them from the political process, is a recipe for rekindling...civil war.[2012]

In the face of the moral, procedural and practical failure of the European-funded and European-based ICC and its flawed attempts to impose its jurisdiction on African situations, the case for an African solution – which had always been strong – has become overwhelming: African solutions for Africans. Nobel Peace Prize Laureate Archbishop Desmond Tutu, who served as the Chairman of the South African Truth and Reconciliation Commission, argues that Western-style justice does not fit with traditional African jurisprudence. It is too impersonal. He has stated that the African view of justice is aimed at "the healing of breaches, the redressing of imbalances, the restoration of broken relationships. This kind of justice seeks to rehabilitate both the victim and the perpetrator, who should be given the opportunity to be reintegrated into the community he or she has injured by his or her offence."[2013]

One option is a legal one. Both the Organisation of African Unity and subsequently the AU have sought to ensure justice for the victims of human and peoples' rights violations within Africa. Both established legal structures. The Constitutive Act of the African Union has specifically addressed this need.[2014] It envisaged an African court of justice, an institution that will be merged with the present African Court on Human and Peoples' Rights to form the African Court of Justice and Human Rights.

The African Court on Human and Peoples' Rights is a continental court established by African countries to ensure protection of human and peoples' rights in Africa. The court was established by virtue of Article 1 of the Protocol to the African Charter on Human and Peoples' Rights on the Establishment of an African Court on Human and Peoples' Rights, which was adopted by member states of the then Organisation of African Unity in Ouagadougou, Burkina Faso, in June 1998.[2015] The protocol came into force on 25 January 2004, after it was ratified by more than fifteen countries. Twenty-six states have now ratified the protocol: Algeria, Burkina Faso, Burundi, Côte d'Ivoire, Comoros, Congo, Gabon, Gambia, Ghana, Kenya, Libya, Lesotho, Mali, Malawi, Mozambique, Mauritania, Mauritius, Nigeria, Niger, Rwanda, South Africa, Senegal, Tanzania, Togo, Tunisia and Uganda. Until the new African Court of Justice and Human Rights is ratified and comes into existence, the African Court on Human and Peoples' Rights remains in place.

The court complements and reinforces the functions of the African Commission on Human and Peoples' Rights. The court has jurisdiction over all cases and disputes submitted to it concerning the interpretation and application of the African Charter on

Human and Peoples' Rights, the protocol and any other relevant human-rights instrument ratified by the states concerned.

The African Court on Human and Peoples' Rights is made up of eleven judges who are nationals of AU member states. On 22 January 2006, the Eighth Ordinary Session of the Executive Council of the African Union elected the first eleven judges of the court. Under Articles 11 to 14 of the protocol establishing the court, the judges are elected by secret ballot by the Assembly of the Heads of State and Government of the African Union, from among jurists of high moral character and of recognised practical, judicial or academic competence and experience in the field of human and peoples' rights. The current president of the court is Justice Sophia A. B. Akuffo (Ghana); the Vice-President is Justice Fatsah Ouguergouz (Algeria). The other judges in order of precedence are Justices Bernard Makgabo Ngoepe (South Africa), Gérard Niyungeko (Burundi), Augustino S. L. Ramadhani (United Republic of Tanzania), Duncan Tambala (Malawi), Elsie Nwanwuri Thompson (Nigeria), Sylvain Oré (Côte d'Ivoire), El Hadji Guissé (Senegal) and Ben Kioko (Kenya). The bench was sworn in before the Assembly of Heads of State and Government of the African Union on 2 July 2006, in Banjul, the Gambia. The judges are elected for a six-year or four-year term renewable once. The judges of the court elect a president and vice-president of the court among themselves who serve a two-year term. They can be re-elected only once. The President of the court resides and works on a full-time basis at the seat of the court, while the other ten judges work on a part-time basis. The President is assisted by a Registrar who performs registry, managerial and administrative functions of the court.

The court has competence to decide "all cases and disputes submitted to it concerning the interpretation and application of the Charter, this Protocol and any other relevant Human Rights instrument ratified by the States concerned",[2016] and to provide an opinion on any legal matter relating to the charter or any other relevant human rights instrument.[2017] According to the protocol (Article 5) and the rules (Rule 33), the court may receive complaints and/or applications submitted to it either by the African Commission of Human and Peoples' Rights or state parties to the protocol or African intergovernmental organisations. Non-governmental organisations with observer status before the African Commission on Human and Peoples' Rights, and individuals from states that have made a declaration accepting the jurisdiction of the court can also institute cases directly before the court. The court's first two decisions were: *Yogogombaye v. the Republic of Senegal*, delivered on 15 December 2009 and *African Commission on Human and Peoples' Rights v. Great Socialist People's Libyan Arab Jamahiriya*, delivered on 25 March 2011. The Libyan case was brought by the African Commission on Human and Peoples' Rights and concerned an order for provisional measures in respect of the violence that erupted in Libya in early 2011. The court ordered Libya to "immediately refrain from any action that would result in loss of life or violation of physical integrity of persons", and to report to the court within fifteen days on "measures taken to implement the Order". The court made this order *proprio motu* (of its own accord) in the course of its deliberations. As of June 2012, the court had received twenty-four applications. It had already finalised twelve cases and delivered decisions.

The court began its work in Addis Ababa, Ethiopia, in November 2006, and in August 2007 it moved to its permanent seat in Arusha in Tanzania. Between 2006 and 2008, the court dealt principally with operational and administrative issues, including the development of the structure of the court's Registry, preparation of its budget and drafting of its interim rules of procedure. In June 2010, the court adopted its final Rules of Court.

On 1 July 2008, at the AU Summit in Sharm El Sheikh, Egypt, the AU Assembly of Heads of State and Government signed and adopted the Protocol on the Statute of the African Court of Justice and Human Rights to merge the African Court on Human and Peoples' Rights with the African Court of Justice of the African Union.[2018] The Court of Justice of the African Union had been established by the AU's Constitutive Act. In 2003, the AU adopted the Protocol of the Court of Justice of the African Union defining the statute, composition and functions of the Court of Justice.[2019]

The decision to merge the two institutions had been taken by AU member states at a June 2004 AU summit. The merger was on organisational and financial grounds. The costs of maintaining two courts would have been prohibitive. The AU also wished to avoid the overlap within the European context between the European Court of Human Rights and the European Court of Justice. The new court will be known as the African Court of Justice and Human Rights and will be based in Arusha, Tanzania. The protocol on the new court will enter into force thirty days after the deposit of the instrument of ratification by fifteen member states of the AU. The African Court of Justice and Human Rights will be the main judicial organ of the AU.[2020] It shall have jurisdiction over all cases and legal disputes that relate to "the interpretation and application of the Constitutive Act, Union treaties and all subsidiary legal instruments, the African Charter and any question of international law".[2021]

The protocol establishing the African court will replace the existing protocols establishing both the African Court of Justice and the African Court on Human and Peoples' Rights. Until the required ratifications, technically Africa's principal judicial organ is the African Court of Justice and Human Rights. In practice, however, this task remains the responsibility of the African Court on Human and Peoples' Rights.

At the February 2009 AU summit, the heads of state and government requested "the (African Union) Commission, in consultation with the African Commission on Human and Peoples' Rights and the African Court on Human and Peoples' Rights, to examine the implications of the court being empowered to try international crimes such as genocide, crimes against humanity and war crimes and report thereon to the Assembly in 2010".[2022] Pursuant to the follow-up decision at the January 2010 summit, the AU Commission contracted the Pan African Lawyers Union (PALU) to produce a detailed study with comprehensive recommendations and a draft legal instrument amending the Protocol on the Statute of the African Court of Justice and Human Rights.

PALU submitted its first draft report and draft legal instrument to the Office of the Legal Counsel (OLC) of the AU Commission in June 2010, proposing amendments to the existing protocol as well as its statute. PALU followed this up in August 2010 with a second draft report and draft legal instrument, incorporating the directives and suggestions of the OLC. In August and in October-November 2010, the commission and the legal counsels or advisors of all relevant AU organs and institutions, as well as the legal counsels or advisors of the regional economic communities met in South Africa under the auspices of the African Union Pan-African Parliament to consider the draft report and draft legal instrument. These documents were amended, incorporating directives and suggestions from the meetings.

In March, May and October-November 2011 government experts came together at the commission in Addis Ababa to once again examine and where necessary amend the draft report and draft legal instrument. At the end of 2011, government delegations provisionally adopted the draft protocol and statute. The draft was then placed before a meeting of ministers of justice and attorneys general for approval and forwarded to the Assembly of Heads of State and Government and finally before the assembly for formal adoption and signature. When fifteen ratifications are secured, the protocol and statute will come into force, binding the first fifteen states. Other states will begin to be bound on the dates on which they accede to the protocol and statute.

The new merged court will have three sections: a general affairs section, a human and peoples' rights section, and an international criminal law section. The human and peoples' rights section "shall be competent to hear all cases relating to human and peoples' rights". These cases are those relating to "the interpretation and the application of the African Charter, the Charter on the Rights and Welfare of the Child, the Protocol to the African Charter on Human and Peoples' Rights on the Rights of Women in Africa; or any other legal instrument relating to human rights, ratified by the States Parties concerned". The general affairs section will hear cases submitted to it under Article 28 of the protocol, except those cases assigned to the human and peoples' rights section and the international criminal law section as specified. The protocol states that the international criminal law section "shall be competent to hear all cases relating to the crimes specified in this statute".

The AU is close to bringing the African Court of Justice and Human Rights into existence. The funding for this project should come from Africa itself. If Europe and the EU is as concerned as they claim to be about justice and judicial systems within Africa, then Europe could assist Africa in bringing this court into existence. The existent African Court on Human and Peoples' Rights should also be assisted in the meantime before the new court is ratified and established. One thing is sure. In comparison with the ICC, the African Court on Human and Peoples' Rights is a credible and hard-working institution, which has achieved considerably more in fewer years than the ICC, and with less than five per cent of its budget.

While African courts may well be able to play constructive roles in dispensing justice on the continent, it should never be at the expense of peace or by rejecting viable, alternative structures. Despite the relentless bullying of the ICC, the EU, the scores of European-funded non-governmental organisations and Western media, foisting Euro-centric justice models upon Africa and Africans, the case for African solutions to African problems is loud and clear.

Courtenay Griffiths QC has observed that "Court isn't necessarily, even though I'm a lawyer, the best way to deal with some of these conflicts. They have social, economic and political roots, which the use of the law is never going to address."[2023]

Griffiths has reached the following conclusions with regard to Western attempts to instrumentalise international law:

> (a) The West's appeal to the supposed universal principles of international justice is hypocritical. (b) NATO and the US, in the post-Cold War world, have embarked on a project to establish themselves as the global enforcer of international legal norms. (c) This role, as "world policeman", has been adopted to protect what are seen as vital Western interests, particularly in the new scramble for Africa. (d) "Humanitarian intervention" is the fig leaf behind which the US and NATO (…the "international community"), masks its true intentions and goals, utilising, where necessary, the legitimising function of the UNSC. The enforcement of these legal norms is: (i) mediated by relationships of relative power; (ii) selective in its application; and (iii) in some circumstances unsuited to the historical, social, cultural and other practical realities present in many of the societies in which they are sought to be imposed.[2024]

Restorative and procedural justice are alternatives to Europe's punitive and retributive models, although it should also be noted that the European approach to post-conflict situations has not always followed a punitive justice. This chapter presents two African voices articulating African approaches to the peace and justice debate. Professor Bereket Habte Selassie is a pan-Africanist academic and lawyer who has experienced both conflict and peace at first hand. He has commented on both the Rwandan and South African examples:

> In Rwanda, in the face of the enormity of the problem following the 1994 genocide, the government of Paul Kagame modified the demands of justice in two ways. First, in place of following the ICC criminal process, they resorted to traditional processes of justice – the *gacaca* – which places a high premium on peace, reconciliation and a consequent social harmony. Secondly, they let many of the minor offenders in the genocide go free, or with minimal punishment. Then there is the much celebrated South African model of Truth and Reconciliation. Perpetrators of crimes committed during the apartheid regime were forgiven on condition of a plea of guilty accompanied by remorse and apology to the victims of the crime, or to their surviving relatives. In these cases, the demand of justice was sacrificed in the interest of the imperative of peace and national reconciliation. In both the *gacaca* judicial process of Rwanda and the South African Truth and Reconciliation, a traditional African concept of justice is at work in a process that substitutes rehabilitation and restitution of social harmony for punishment. But remorse of the culprit and a ritual of apology and readiness to make amends is a precondition for forgiveness,

whereas in the ICC and Eurocentric judicial process in general, punishment is the governing concept.[2025]

Since the mid-1970s, at least fourteen states on four continents have declared amnesty, or enacted amnesty laws granting immunity to past regimes from accountability and liability.[2026] Ian Paisley Jr., a legislator with considerable experience of peace and reconciliation within communities in conflict, has pointed to the failure of the ICC in a crucial respect:

> The I.C.C. was intended as an instrument for delivering peace. In this respect it has not been a success. It will continue to falter because its current methods go against the experience of many places in Africa and around the world where peace has been delivered through political negotiations and reconciliation efforts, not the imposition of international justice. Over the past 20 years, countries divided by ethnicity and political turmoil, from South Africa to Liberia, from Sierra Leone to Rwanda, have been brought together through reconciliation.[2027]

The South African-based African Centre for the Constructive Resolution of Disputes has pointed to the experience and value of South Africa's Truth and Reconciliation Commission, and the role played by both it and the amnesty it provided in preventing further conflict in South Africa:

> The protective shield of amnesty creates a fertile environment in which truths can emerge. For example, South Africa's Truth and Reconciliation Commission, which granted amnesties for past crimes and resolved the dilemma of justice and peace by both easing the exit of the apartheid regime and recognising past atrocities committed, helped satisfy the need for justice and created the foundation for reconciliation. Amnesty in South Africa created the space for reconciliation, bringing former adversaries safely into contact and allowing uncomfortable truths to emerge. Amnesty facilitated reconciliation, whereas just retribution or punishment for all apartheid era crimes would have separated perpetrators from victims, and genuine reconciliation would have been impossible. South Africa turned away from civil war during the transitional negotiations, and slid peacefully into democracy. The truth set South Africans free, and amnesty helped facilitate the truth and the opportunity for reconciliation and, ultimately, freedom.[2028]

Professor Bereket Habte Selassie has also seen the use of amnesty at first hand:

> I am of the persuasion that amnesty and forgiveness is the best policy. There are always demands for justice, and all those who commit crimes must be brought to justice. But, take the case of Rwanda, which is an extreme case.

> It would take years – hundreds of years – to prosecute all those who were guilty of crimes. The Rwandan body politic would be affected by the strong divide that would be maintained. Instead, they used a traditional form of justice. People who knew the perpetrators could ask them questions publicly, and they would often have to pay penance, but they would be allowed back into society. I don't think they could have found a better system for Rwanda. The South Africa model was better in the context of South African history. The leaders, headed by Nelson Mandela, decided that it would be better to forgive. I was in South Africa in 2003, and at Robben Island I interviewed some members of government. They told me that Mandela decided to forgive even before his release.[2029]

As Barahona De Bito *et al.* point out, the South African amnesty was declared over 10,000 killings, and allegations of gross human-rights violation contained in about 21,298 statements. The report states that although apartheid is a crime against humanity not one of the perpetrators was charged. This crime is one of the most serious in the Rome Statute.[2030] Traggy Maepa has also pointed out that applicants granted amnesty would no longer be liable for prosecution or any civil claim for the actions in question.[2031]

Apologists for the ICC have sought to downplay the concerns of Africans about the legitimacy of the court by claiming that this criticism is merely Africans trying to prevent judicial scrutiny of their own actions. The reality is very different. Many of the claims made by Africa about the ICC echo similar criticism of other international courts, such as the European Court of Human Rights. The similarities are clear. A 2009 analysis of the European Court of Human Rights could have been speaking about the ICC:

> Judges on international courts are less subject to peer pressure and less steeped in a domestic judicial culture; and their selection is not always based on merit but sometimes seem to stem from an opaque mix of nepotism and diplomatic strategy. Abuse of judicial power is more likely when legislation is more indeterminate... . The judges are left with too much discretion. In addition, the ECtHR is known for its judicial activism in the form of "dynamic" interpretation, reading far more into the ECHR than what the signatories could plausibly have intended in the 1950s.[2032]

The analysis also noted the fundamental weakness at the heart of both the European Court of Human Rights and the ICC – the flawed judicial selection process leading to an "activist" bench without the courtroom experience essential to any credible legal process. The judicial nomination process for the European Court of Human Rights is as flawed as that of the ICC. Each member state nominates one judge. The state nominates three persons, from which the Parliamentary Assembly selects one by majority vote after a brief interview by a sub-committee:

This procedure has been challenged on several grounds, including its lack of transparency at both stages. Some national nominations are rumored to reflect political nepotism rather than merit. Members of the sub-committee often lack training in human rights law, and their decision sometimes seems influenced by party considerations... . Some recommend that State nominees be identified by independent national bodies staffed by independent representatives knowledgeable in international law and human rights. The Parliamentary Assembly recommends that governments nominate candidates that were either practitioners in the field of human rights law or activists in NGOs.[2033]

In April 2009, the second most senior judge in the UK, Lord Hoffmann, said the European Court had been unable to resist the temptation to "aggrandise its jurisdiction" by laying down a "federal law of Europe", and that the court should not be allowed to intervene in the detail of domestic law.[2034] He was also critical of the way in which the court worked, and the manner in which its judges are elected. Lord Hoffmann said that the behaviour of the European Court on Human Rights could be said to "trivialise and discredit the grand ideals of international human rights."[2035] His views were echoed in 2010 by Marc Bossuyt, President of the Constitutional Court of Belgium, who also criticised the European Court, stating that it had "assumed four functions, only one of which belonging to its core duty"; that it had adopted a "rather activist manner"; and that one could even describe its activism as a "judicial revolution".[2036] In 2011, the British Prime Minister David Cameron also warned that the European Court of Human Rights needs "consistently strong" judges, rather than the political appointments imposed by some countries. Cameron said that the court needs to be reformed "so that it is true to its original purpose". This legal criticism was also echoed within the British parliament. In January 2012, a group of British parliamentarians directly attacked the European Court stating that there was a need to "end rule by judges and reinstate Parliamentary democracy". The parliamentarians stated that "[t]he main problem with current human rights law is that we all have to accept judges' interpretations of human rights, even when those interpretations strike us as a gross distortion of such rights". The report called for the UK parliament to be given the power to overturn European Court judgments. Should this not prove possible, the report said that "the only viable option would be for Britain to extract itself from the jurisdiction of the Strasbourg court altogether". A recent report estimated that almost half of the court's judges have no judicial experience.[2037]

The British parliamentarian Douglas Carswell has called for the UK to "quit the jurisdiction of this foreign court". He stated that the question is "whether this supranational quango has the right to be making these decisions in the first place".[2038] A senior British government source was quoted as saying that "There is a once-in-a-generation opportunity for reform and we currently have it. We cannot have the current system of this panel of European judges being the final court of appeal on issues directly affecting our national security." Such a move "would be backed by a large number of Tory MPs and some Cabinet ministers, who have complained that the human rights convention and the Human Rights

Act, the British law which gives it force in this country, make it impossible to do their jobs".[2039]

Africa's objections to the ICC are not unfounded. As can be seen from the above discourse they all too clearly echo objections heard in Britain and elsewhere outside of Africa about similar "activist" courts made up of incompetent judges. The one pivotal difference between the other courts and the ICC is that the ICC is prolonging war in Africa and is indirectly responsible for thousands of deaths on the continent, and the suffering and displacement of hundreds of thousands of others. The way ahead for Africa must be separate from the ICC and its Eurocentric remedy – a remedy that even major European countries find immoral, difficult and dangerous to swallow. The way ahead must be one of African solutions to African problems.

Conclusion

"In reality, international criminal justice is governed by the law of gravity – it always travels from top to bottom, from north to south."

Courtenay Griffiths QC[2040]

There has been a certain natural flow to this study of the ICC. Having started with Georg Scwarzenberger's post-1945 warning about over-zealous legal evangelism in international law, one can conclude this book with the comment sixty years later by Dr. Adam Branch, an expert on the Ugandan conflict, that for Western judicial activists to jeopardise a peaceful resolution of one of Africa's most savage civil wars, in an attempt to impose "white man's justice", is tantamount to "international law fundamentalism."[2041] The ICC has come full circle.

Apart from vindicating Scwarzenberger's warnings, what has the ICC done in the first ten years or so of its existence? It has managed to spend a billion euros, employ hundreds of white Europeans and North Americans, fund hundreds of first-and-business-class flights all over the world, and provide a wonderful platform for the publicity-seeking celebrity lawyer appointed as the court's first Chief Prosecutor. It has become a showcase for mediocrity. It managed to see its first case suspended because of malpractice and incompetence before it even reached the trial stage. The trial eventually started only to be suspended once again and virtually collapse because of more irregularities, before eventually limping to a questionable completion in what was a six-year odyssey. Any real court would have thrown the case out before it came to trial. Some of its almost 800 staff have managed to arrange for the transfer from the DRC to the European Guantánamo Bay in The Hague of five Africans (who were already in someone else's custody), which presumably involved buying more business-class tickets and hiring some handcuffs (at the rate of arrests it hardly seems worth buying them), and one African from Belgium (not then in custody, but a sitting duck). This has also entailed turning a blind eye to the fact that while the court has focused on minor rebel leaders accused of relatively minor crimes, it has ignored massive crimes against humanity committed by the governments in whose countries the court has chosen to work and with whom it had made secret deals. And all this has also been done while ignoring any white European or North American alleged war criminals whose countries actually control the court and have disproportionately contributed to its billion-euro budget. While meant to be a court of last resort, it has nonetheless imposed itself upon countries with perfectly functional legal systems ready, willing and able to prosecute the crimes the ICC claimed to be addressing. It also managed to achieve the impossible. The ICC's "investigation" found that following the Anglo-American invasion of Iraq there may have been an estimated four to twelve victims of wilful killing and that fewer than twenty other people may have been subject to inhuman treatment, when even the British government has admitted to hundreds of instances of inhuman abuse and worse. This, of course, kept both the UK and USA very happy. It has been similarly myopic with regard to abuses in Afghanistan, itself a State Party, by European States Parties and the United States.

The self-set targets that the court has failed to reach are many and they are self-evident. That the court has failed is an open secret. Professor Eric Posner has stated: "The court has been a failure.... It is too weak to deter atrocities, end impunity or keep the peace, but it is strong enough to serve as an irritant to international relations."[2042] The ICC partisan Benjamin Schiff noted that the court could be considered successful "[i]f it deters criminality", and that "[The court] may be deemed irrelevant if potential perpetrators don't recognize it as a threat, if its efforts are thwarted by noncooperation or lack of resources, or if victims regard it as useless in their search for justice."[2043] If nothing else, this study provides example after example of the court's inability to "deter" alleged war crimes, non-cooperation by both the UNSC, numerous States Parties and those non-member states it has sought to focus upon, as well as the wall of criticism by victims and war-affected communities decrying the actions of the court. Ocampo himself provided a test for the court's success or failure: "[T]he absence of trials before this Court, as a consequence of the regular functioning of national institutions, would be a major success."[2044] The number of cases, thirty-two in eight countries, would therefore indicate failure. In 2011, Human Rights Watch pointed unambiguously to the manifest failure of the ICC:

> [T]he ICC's investigations and prosecutions have failed to demonstrate coherent and effective strategies for delivering meaningful justice to affected communities.... Gaps remain in delivering on the ICC's mandate in situations where the court is pursuing investigations and prosecutions. In four situations – DRC, Uganda, CAR, and Darfur – the absence of more coherent and effective strategies has undermined perceptions of independence and impartiality, threatening the court's credibility.[2045]

Other commentators have been equally blunt. In October 2013, eleven years after the establishment of the ICC, Dr. Phil Clark noted: "I think the court's had a problem with legitimacy right from the start of its work in Africa."[2046] The court's dysfunction was not just because of its fixed interest in Africa however: it was also the nature of that involvement. In the same month, for example, *Inner City Press* observed that the credibility of the court continued to be called into question for another key reason: "To many, the ICC is viewed as politicized, not only because of its over-focus on Africa but also because it dispenses victor's justice. Where are the prosecutions of the supporters of Ouattara in Cote d'Ivoire? Of extremists among those who overthrew Gaddafi?"[2047]

The ICC is also self-evidently a political institution at all levels. No clearer examples can be provided of the politics at play within the ICC than those provided by its own deliberate behaviour right from its inception. Joshua Rozenberg noted that Ocampo was appointed ICC Prosecutor simply because the European funders of the court did not want Africans to be seen to be prosecuted by a European from one of Africa's former colonial powers.[2048] European concern about the Africa issue then extended to further window dressing in holding the ICC Review Conference in Africa, and then went into hyperdrive with their appointment of an African surrogate, Fatou Bensouda, as the court's new Chief Prosecutor, replacing Luis Ocampo. The political instrumentalisation of the court by both the Security Council and several Western State Parties has also become clear. In the most recent example, Libya, the court was blatantly used as judicial cover for NATO military intervention.

The "McDonaldization" of justice

An argument can be made that the ICC is tantamount to the "McDonaldization" of justice. Professor Robert Bohm has written of the "McDonaldization" of justice with regard to American justice.[2049] Several of his observations would apply to the ICC. "McDonaldization", as outlined by sociologist George Ritzer, refers to "the [bureaucratic] process by which principles of the fast-food restaurant are coming to dominate more and more sectors of American society as well as of the rest of the world".[2050]

As Bohm points out, the principal problem with McDonaldised institutions, and another characteristic of the process, is irrationality. Ritzer calls this phenomenon the "irrationality of rationality."[2051] Bohm states that McDonaldisation does not always benefit all of the participants in the process or society in general and actually has several important costs or dangers associated with it. According to Ritzer, McDonaldised institutions inevitably produce irrationalities "that limit, eventually compromise, and perhaps even undermine their rationality".[2052] They can be inefficient because of excess red tape and other problems.[2053] They can produce poor-quality work and a decline in employee effort because of the emphasis on quantification (the substitution of quantity for quality and the resulting mediocrity of both the process and the product), the often mind-numbing routine, and the absence of meaningful employee job input.[2054] Bohm also states that "McDonaldized institutions can be unpredictable because employees, no matter how well trained and supervised, sometimes are confused, unsure about what they are supposed to do, inefficient, and apt to make mistakes."[2055] Ritzer points out that McDonaldised institutions can also be dehumanising.[2056] Ritzer also remarked that Max Weber noted what he called the "iron cage" of rationality in which people get trapped in bureaucracies that deny them their basic humanity[2057] "as, for example, when crime victims are ignored or mistreated by criminal justice officials".[2058]

All the above observations about the negative costs of the "McDonaldization" of justice clearly apply to the ICC. Bohm notes that accepting McJustice is not only supporting the status quo with all of its irrationalities, it is also rejecting viable, especially systemic, alternatives. He concludes: "McJustice, like McDonaldization generally, is a political enterprise in which definitions of rationality and irrationality are contested."[2059] Of one thing there is no doubt. Taking their behaviour and almost laughable ineptitude in office into account, within any "McDonaldization" analogy, both of the Chief Prosecutors of the ICC, Ocampo and Bensouda, would easily qualify for the role of the clown, Ronald McDonald.

What has the International Criminal Court achieved?

The question that must be asked is what has the ICC actually managed to do since it came into being in 2002? The answers are not ones the court and its fundamentalist supporters would like to hear.

Firstly, the court has squandered a vast amount of good will. African states were among the most enthusiastic signatories to the 1998 Rome Statute: they are now the most disillusioned, and a number would probably have left the ICC were it not for European economic-aid blackmail. And the disillusionment is not just Africa-focused. Much of the developing world has now been forced to re-evaluate the ICC, and the behaviour of the court's prosecutors, in the light of its exclusive focus on the Third World – which of course excluded those war crimes and crimes against humanity committed by the First World in the Third World – and its disastrous legal fumbling and bumbling in Africa. The fact, for example, that in September 2008, following and clearly in direct response to the ICC's July 2008 issuing of arrest warrants for President al-Bashir, Sudan was elected as Chairman of the G77, the largest intergovernmental organisation of developing states in the UN (originally 77 founding nations but now 130 strong), indicated an unprecedented level of solidarity and support for al-Bashir following the ICC actions.[2060]

Secondly, the ICC and Ocampo clearly demonstrated the institution's European centre of gravity. The ICC has proved itself to be a European court, in effect a political extension of the EU, held in place by blatant economic blackmail. In a stark flashback to empire, it is in effect a European court for Africa.

Thirdly, the appointment of Luis Ocampo and then Fatou Bensouda as ICC Chief Prosecutors, as well as most of its judges, has managed to confirm – if confirmation was ever necessary – that the age-old UN tradition of vote-trading for high office produces mediocrity. For all the First World media hype that accompanied his appointment, Ocampo proved to be legally and professionally lacklustre and morally bankrupt. In June 2009, for example, the *Washington Post* noted that: "Today, Moreno-Ocampo appears to be the one on trial, with even some of his early supporters questioning his prosecutorial strategy, his use of facts and his personal conduct."[2061] One of these supporters is Marlies Glasius: "Luis Moreno-Ocampo has a good eye for publicity. On the eve of the ten-year anniversary of the Rome statute...he indicted his first head of state. This announcement has trumped the news emerging a few weeks ago, that the prosecutor's first suspect in custody, Congolese warlord Thomas Lubanga, may have to be released without trial because of prosecutorial errors."[2062] And, of course, the bigger the alleged crime – and one gets no bigger than genocide – the more publicity and celebrity for the Prosecutor. Bensouda appears to be following in Ocampo's footsteps. A personal achievement of

Ocampo as Chief Prosecutor was his resilience. While an incompetent lawyer he has clearly been an accomplished politician – in the sense of managing to stay in office. He managed to shrug off both gross professional and sexual misconduct, lesser instances of which have seen more honorable men resign. He has also done a lot for the concept of exceptionalism. While denying any sort of African "exceptionalism" (the view that Africa should not be treated any differently to the rest of the world), he doggedly ring-fenced the case for European and American "exceptionalism": alleged American, British and European war crimes and crimes against humanity in Iraq and Afghanistan were not on his radar: only alleged African crimes are in focus. His spokesperson has also managed to introduce a Latin American exceptionalism into sexual misconduct. An incident that would qualify as rape under several European laws apparently did not qualify as rape to him.

Fourthly, the ICC has managed to impact negatively on several peace processes in Africa. The court has delayed peace in northern Uganda, rekindled war in the DRC, and has managed to hinder not one but two peace processes in Sudan. Even ICC enthusiasts have become increasingly realistic. Glasius admitted: "It is doubtful whether the indictment of al-Bashir on 14 July 2008…will have any immediate practical implications. Hence…in the current situation the arrest-warrants have only symbolic significance."[2063] That means that for an action of only "symbolic significance" – albeit one guaranteed to win him status on the international celebrity circuit – Ocampo endangered not just the Darfur peace process but also the Comprehensive Peace Agreement that ended Africa's longest running civil war, the conflict in southern Sudan. Publicity and celebrity first: peace, justice and professionalism a distant second.

Fifthly, despite having declared that "I apply scrupulously one standard – the law," and for all the ICC's repeated assurances and claims with regard to ending "impunity", far from ending impunity, Ocampo and the court have entrenched it. Leaving aside the court's studied lack of interest in ongoing Western human-rights abuses in Iraq and Afghanistan, this is nowhere more clearly shown than in Uganda, DRC, the CAR, and the Ivory Coast, on the very continent and in the very situations that the ICC has chosen to single out. The ICC has turned a blind eye to the clear and well-documented, alleged involvement of the governments of those countries in systematic and wide-scale human-rights abuses and crimes against humanity. In Uganda's case these abuses by government forces have been in both Uganda itself and in DRC and have been extensively documented by the International Court of Justice. And for the ICC to very publicly prosecute one Congolese militia leader for using child soldiers and then to ignore the very well-documented use of child soldiers – in the gaze of the world's media – by a rebel leader in a neighbouring country can only but be seen as political bias, double standards, disinterest and professional incompetence.

The sixth achievement of the ICC is that it has also managed to discredit the court's oft-repeated claims to be "victim"-centred. The reality is very different. Human Rights Watch have themselves had to point this out to the ICC: "We have…stressed how important it is for the court – including the prosecutor – to more proactively engage with affected communities to make its work meaningful and relevant to them. *This will require a complete and deeply rooted shift from the ICC's prior ambivalence to doing so, which was evident in the court's early approach to outreach and field operations, and the prosecutor's investigations."*[2064] (Emphasis added.) That is to say that far from being "victim"-focused, the ICC was aloof and arrogant. The court has simply ignored millions of victims in Afghanistan, Iraq, the DRC, Uganda and elsewhere.

A particular achievement of the ICC is that it managed to set a new low in international legal competence. Despite having had Thomas Lubanga in custody since March 2006, his trial for relatively minor alleged crimes only began in early 2009 – held up by unbelievable breaches in legal ethics on the part of the Prosecutor – only to be delayed by yet more procedural irregularities. It finally ended in 2012. The hallmark of most justice systems is the right to a speedy trial. In the heavily criticised trial of Slobodan Milosevic, the prosecution took two years to present its case; the court has taken longer in the Lubanga case. Nuremburg took one year.

The ICC has also very effectively managed to make the case for both African courts for Africa and for alternatives to retributive justice pushed by The Hague. For all the white, Western, Euro-centric disdain for black African courts (usually with the excuse of Africa not having the resources), if the ICC is the best that Europe has to offer, African courts can only but shine in comparison.

And, perhaps most upsetting of all for those liberal, internationalist supporters of the ICC, the court has managed to vindicate so much of what John Bolton said, and warned about the ICC. Bolton has been perhaps the ICC's most vocal critic and an opponent of the ICC for well over a decade.[2065] In 1998 Bolton warned that the ICC will be overbearing, unaccountable, powerless and ineffectual.[2066] While this may have seemed a contradictory combination, the ICC has indeed managed to be all four. The ICC has been overbearing and hectoring, threatening African leaders. The ICC and its Chief Prosecutor have also been powerless and ineffectual: Ocampo promised to have the indicted Ugandan rebel leaders on trial by mid-2005, and to have a trial going in the DRC in 2006. The Ugandans are still at large and his Congo trial began in 2009 before limping to a very questionable conclusion in 2012.

Bolton noted that "the ICC has almost no political accountability". The court has certainly been unaccountable to any meaningful professional oversight or democratic body. Bolton articulated the American belief in "checks and balances": he pointed out that the ICC lacks any such restraints, has an "unaccountable prosecutor" and that the court is simply "out there" in the international system. Ocampo has himself boasted of his *proprio motu* powers under the Rome Statute as conferring on him the status of a "new autonomous actor on the international scene".[2067] Bolton warned that the ICC's authority is vague and excessively elastic: "This is most emphatically not a Court of limited jurisdiction." Set up as a court of last resort to deal with crimes such as genocide, crimes against humanity and war crimes, the ICC is now involving itself with allegations of riot-related violence, Latin American money laundering in Europe, election violence in Kenya, and the destruction of religious shrines in Mali.

Bolton noted that "the ICC…carries an enormous risk of politicization". And in 2002 he warned of circumstances that one can subsequently quite clearly see come to pass in

Uganda: "[W]ith a permanent ICC, one can predict that one or more disputants might well invoke its jurisdiction at a selfishly opportune moment, and thus, ironically, make an ultimate settlement of their dispute more complicated or less likely."[2068] This is, of course, precisely what President Museveni did, which resulted in a continuing and more complicated conflict. The DRC, CAR and Mali have followed suit. And for its own bureaucratic imperatives the ICC has been a more than willing partner in these referrals.

Bolton also warned of the "politicization" of the day-to-day politics of the court: "Even at this early stage in the Court's existence, there are concerns that its judicial nomination process is being influenced by quota systems and backroom deals."[2069] This can clearly be seen in the "vote trading" by ICC state members that would come to fatally flaw the competence and workings of the ICC bench. Ironically, Bolton's warnings were subsequently also echoed by Human Rights Watch and Amnesty International.

In 2002 Bolton also pointed to the misguided view of ICC deterrence: "The most basic error is the belief that the ICC will have a substantial deterrent effect against the perpetration of crimes against humanity. Behind their optimistic rhetoric, ICC proponents have not a shred of evidence supporting their deterrence theories. Recent history is filled with cases where even strong military force or the threat of force failed to deter aggression or gross abuses of human rights." Yet again, Bolton has been proved right. The simple fact that the ICC reported that it had ten situations in its sights in 2009 – up from one in 2004 – would seem to indicate that the much-heralded deterrent effect is noticeably absent. Its own reports document how the intensity of alleged LRA violence has increased dramatically since its leadership was indicted. A new conflict in eastern Congo has been sparked by ICC interference. Bolton also pointed out that "deterrence ultimately depends on perceived effectiveness, and the ICC fails badly on that point.... Why should anyone imagine that bewigged judges in The Hague will succeed where cold steel has failed?" That the LRA leadership is still at large, and the Ugandan conflict and other conflicts continue in the other "situations" several years after the ICC's bewigged and robed judges issued their arrest warrants has more than proved Bolton's point.

And in an unexpected juxtaposition, Bolton has emerged as a liberal pragmatist with regard to ending civil wars, and the ICC as ideological zealots. Bolton counselled that "[a]ccumulated experience strongly favors a case-by-case approach, politically and legally, rather than the inevitable resort to adjudication. Circumstances differ, and circumstances matter." It is Ocampo, Bensouda and the ICC that present themselves as being inflexible ideologues. It is manifestly evident that peace is possible without the sort of "justice" pushed by the ICC. The kindest that can be said of the ICC in this regard is that it is selectively and institutionally autistic. As David Lanz notes: "among different means of justice – forgiveness, reconciliation, truth-telling, compensation, retribution, revenge, etc. – the ICC chooses only one, that is, punishment."[2070]

It is particularly ironic that the court has also proved one particular law to be true: the law of unintended consequences. Branch points to the Ugandan example, but it is also applicable to several of the court's other "situations": "[I]n the Ugandan case, the invocation of the ICC by President Museveni has only increased the discretionary power of his government, since the politicization of the ICC intervention serves the state's interests against those of the Ugandan people. In this way, global criminal law, although premised upon overcoming sovereignty, can paradoxically end up promoting the most dangerous aspect of sovereignty: unaccountable state power over the population."[2071] And on a sadly much more violent note, rather than deter human-rights abuses the indictment of the LRA leadership resulted in an explosion in alleged war crimes and violence in Uganda and three other neighbouring countries.

For all Europe's studied disdain for the US Guantánamo Bay process, the Guantánamo Bay courts and the ICC have similarities. They have both in many ways been arbitrary in their choice of people to indict. Guantánamo Bay detainees were often just people in the wrong place at the wrong time that happened to be Muslim. In the case of the ICC, its detainees are people who may have been in the wrong place at the wrong time but whose main shortcoming was that they definitely did not have the right friends – especially among the ICC, its European funders or in Washington DC. And, of course, both the Guantánamo Bay tribunal and the ICC share the same interest in "extraordinary rendition", defined as the apprehension and illegal transfer of a person from one state to another – with the added frisson that the ICC sought to add hijacking commercial airliners to the mix.

There is a central difference between the two tribunals, which is that Guantánamo Bay, despite being an American court, is truly global, detaining and trying nationals from across the world, whereas despite its name the ICC is only interested in putting black Africans on trial.

The Northern Irish parliamentarian Ian Paisley Jr. spoke for a great many people involved in the most delicate negotiations imaginable, the ending of civil wars, when he stated: "[T]he pursuit of justice should not replace or undermine ongoing national reconciliation efforts. The foremost challenge facing the [ICC] is to determine whether its intervention will help or hinder the cause of peace.... If this means the International Criminal Court does not always intervene or deliver justice, it may be a price that is worth paying."[2072] It is also clear that the court is in any instance simply not fit for purpose, intrinsically flawed as it is by European arrogance, double standards, incompetent judges and procedural irregularities.

The ideological supporters of the ICC are themselves blinded by arrogance and wishful thinking. German diplomat Hans-Peter Kaul, one of the founders of the court and subsequently a full ICC judge, stated that the ICC was the "first court that is based on the free will of the international community". Kaul went on to state that the "beauty of the court" is actually its independence from the UN and the resolutions of the Security Council.[2073] The reality is blindingly different. One quarter of all the court's situations, for example, is the direct result of a Security Council resolution. The court is not universal; it does not represent the international community; it is not based on the free will of the international community; and it is clearly not independent of the UNSC, upon which it has conferred special prosecutorial powers. ICC Prosecutor Ocampo's pronouncements have been no less fanciful. He sounded somewhat like the comic book hero Judge Dredd's "I am the law", with his declarations that "I apply the law and implement it in a world without justice," and "I have to apply and implement the law." Self-centred arrogance is one thing: crass dishonesty is another. He went on to state "I can't make allowances for politics. I have to apply and implement the law" and "We help in Africa, we protect Africa's victims, Africa has called on us for aid."[2074] The reality could not be more different. Instead, the ICC has bullied Africa, entrenched impunity, granted *de facto* immunity to killers, repeatedly played politics with the law and both betrayed – and created many more – victims. William Schabas has very aptly used the Emperor's clothes analogy for the court. The Emperor is surrounded by fawning courtiers, lickspittles, careerists, international bureaucrats, ideologues, incompetent lawyers, cynical politicians, accountants, profiteers and assorted hangers-on desperately trying to prevent the outside world from glimpsing his naked body. But naked it is.

It is perhaps useful to end with a solution to the situation within which Africa presently finds itself, a perspective from someone who has seen conflict on the continent at first hand. In 2011, Adam Branch called for a new approach:

> The very discourse of global justice needs to be taken back from the ICC, back from the focus on criminal justice and toward social and political justice, back from the obsession with spectacular atrocities committed by Africans, and instead toward contesting the massive transnational forms of inequality, oppression, and violence of which the West is the perpetrator and beneficiary, not the supposed redeemer.[2075]

Even the court's most avid supporters admit it is an imperfect institution, based upon an imperfect statute. Africa appears to be a laboratory for a disastrous European experiment in sub-prime justice. Africa must reject the sub-prime justice being foisted upon it and solve its own problems in its own way.

APPENDIX ONE

(XVIII.10)

UNITED NATIONS NATIONS UNIES

POSTAL ADDRESS—ADRESSE POSTALE: UNITED NATIONS, N.Y. 10017
CABLE ADDRESS—ADRESSE TELEGRAPHIQUE: UNATIONS NEWYORK

Reference: C.N.612.2008.TREATIES-6 (Depositary Notification)

ROME STATUTE OF THE INTERNATIONAL CRIMINAL COURT
ROME, 17 JULY 1998

SUDAN: NOTIFICATION

The Secretary-General of the United Nations, acting in his capacity as depositary, communicates the following:

The above action was effected on 26 August 2008.

<u>(Original: English)</u>

"I, Deng Alor Koul, Minister for Foreign Affairs of the Republic of Sudan, hereby notify the Secretary-General of the United Nations, as depositary of Rome Statute of the International Criminal Court, that Sudan does not intend to become a party to the Rome Statute. Accordingly, Sudan has no legal obligation arising from its signature on 8 September 2000."

27 August 2008

Attention: Treaty Services of Ministries of Foreign Affairs and of international organizations concerned. Depositary notifications are currently issued in both hard copy and electronic format. Depositary notifications are made available to the Permanent Missions to the United Nations at the following e-mail address: missions@un.int. Such notifications are also available in the United Nations Treaty Collection on the Internet at http://untreaty.un.org, where interested individuals can subscribe to directly receive depositary notifications by e-mail through a new automated subscription service. Depositary notifications are available for pick-up by the Permanent Missions in Room NL-300.

Appendix Two

AFRICAN UNION DECISION REGARDING THE INTERNATIONAL CRIMINAL COURT (ICC)

Doc. Assembly/AU/13(XIII)
Assembly/AU/Dec.245(XIII)

Adopted by the Thirteenth Ordinary Session of the Assembly in Sirte, Great Socialist People's Libyan Arab Jamahiriya on 3 July 2009

The Assembly,

1. TAKES NOTE of the recommendations of the Executive Council on the Meeting of the African States Parties to the Rome Statute of the International Criminal Court (ICC);

2. EXPRESSES ITS DEEP CONCERN at the indictment issued by the Pre-Trial Chamber of the ICC against President Omar Hassan Ahmed El Bashir of the Republic of The Sudan;

3. NOTES WITH GRAVE CONCERN the unfortunate consequences that the indictment has had on the delicate peace processes underway in The Sudan and the fact that it continues to undermine the ongoing efforts aimed at facilitating the early resolution of the conflict in Darfur;

4. REITERATES the unflinching commitment of Member States to combating impunity and promoting democracy, rule of law and good governance throughout the continent, in conformity with the Constitutive Act of the African Union;

5. REQUESTS the Commission to ensure the early implementation of Decision Assembly/Dec.213(XII), adopted in February 2009 mandating the Commission, in consultation with the African Commission on Human and Peoples' Rights and the African Court on Human and Peoples' Rights to examine the implications of the Court being empowered to try serious crimes of international concern such as genocide, crimes against humanity and war crimes, which would be complementary to national jurisdiction and processes for fighting impunity;

6. ENCOURAGES Member States to initiate programmes of cooperation and capacity building to enhance the capacity of legal personnel in their respective countries regarding the drafting and security of model legislation dealing with serious crimes of international concern, training of members of the police and the judiciary, and the strengthening of cooperation amongst judicial and investigative agencies;

7. FURTHER TAKES NOTE that any party affected by the indictment has the right of legal recourse to the processes provided for in the Rome Statute regarding the appeal process and the issue of immunity;

8. REQUESTS the Commission to convene a preparatory meeting of African States Parties at expert and ministerial levels (Foreign Affairs and Justice) but open to other Member States at the end of 2009 to prepare fully for the Review Conference of States Parties scheduled for Kampala, Uganda in May 2010, to address among others, the following issues:

(i) Article 13 of the Rome Statute granting power to the UNSC to refer cases to the ICC;

(ii) Article 16 of the Rome Statute granting power to the UNSC to defer cases for one (1) year;

(iii) Procedures of the ICC;

(iv) Clarification on the Immunities of officials whose States are not party to the Statute;

(v) Comparative analysis of the implications of the practical application of Articles 27 and 98 of the Rome Statute;

(vi) The possibility of obtaining regional inputs in the process of assessing the evidence collected and in determining whether or not to proceed with prosecution; particularly against senior state officials; and

(vii) Any other areas of concern to African States Parties.

9. DEEPLY REGRETS that the request by the African Union to the UNSC to defer the proceedings initiated against President Bashir of The Sudan in accordance with Article 16 of the Rome Statute of the ICC, has neither been heard nor acted upon, and in this regard, **REITERATES ITS REQUEST** to the UNSC;

10. DECIDES that in view of the fact that the request by the African Union has never been acted upon, the AU Member States shall not cooperate pursuant to the provisions of Article 98 of the Rome Statute of the ICC relating to immunities, for the arrest and surrender of President Omar El Bashir of The Sudan;*

11. EXPRESSES CONCERN OVER the conduct of the ICC Prosecutor and **FURTHER DECIDES** that the preparatory meeting of African States Parties to the Rome Statute of the ICC scheduled for late 2009 should prepare, *inter alia*, guidelines and a code of conduct for exercise of discretionary powers by the ICC Prosecutor relating particularly to the powers of the prosecutor to initiate cases at his own discretion under Article 15 of the Rome Statute;

12. UNDERSCORES that the African Union and its Member States reserve the right to take any further decisions or measures that may be deemed necessary in order to preserve and safeguard the dignity, sovereignty and integrity of the continent;

13. FINALLY REQUESTS the commission to follow-up on the implementation of this Decision and submit a report to the next Ordinary Session of the Assembly through the Executive Council in January / February 2010 and in this regard **AUTHORIZES** expenditure for necessary actions from arrears of contributions

Adopted by the Thirteenth Ordinary Session of the Assembly in Sirte, Great Socialist People's Libyan Arab Jamahiriya on 3 July 2009

* Reservation entered by Chad

Appendix Three

AGREEMENT BETWEEN THE INTERNATIONAL CRIMINAL COURT AND THE EUROPEAN UNION ON COOPERATION AND ASSISTANCE

Date of signature: 10 April 2006
Date of entry into force: 1 May 2006
Publication of the Official Journal

THE INTERNATIONAL CRIMINAL COURT, Hereinafter the Court , of the one part, and **THE EUROPEAN UNION**, hereinafter the EU , represented by the Presidency of the Council of the European Union, of the other part, hereinafter referred to as the Parties,

CONSIDERING the fundamental importance and the priority that must be given to the consolidation of the rule of law and respect for human rights and humanitarian law, as well as the preservation of peace and the strengthening of international security, in conformity with the United Nations Charter and as provided for in Article 11 of the Treaty on European Union;

NOTING that the principles of the Rome Statute of the International Criminal Court, as well as those governing its functioning, are fully in line with the principles and objectives of the European Union;

EMPHASISING the importance of the administration of justice in accordance with the rule of law and procedural fairness with particular reference to the rights of the accused provided in the Rome Statute;

NOTING the special role of victims and witnesses in proceedings before the Court and the need for specific measures aimed at ensuring their security and effective participation in accordance with the Rome Statute;

RECALLING that the European security strategy, adopted by the European Council on 12 December 2003, supports an international order based on effective multilateralism;

BEARING IN MIND Council Common Position 2003/444/CFSP of 16 June 2003 on the International Criminal Court as well as the Council's Action Plan to follow-up on such Common Position and particularly the essential role of the International Criminal Court for the purpose of preventing and curbing the commission of the serious crimes falling within its jurisdiction;

CONSIDERING that the European Union is committed to supporting the effective functioning of the International Criminal Court and to advance universal support for it by promoting the widest possible participation in the Rome Statute;

RECALLING THAT this Agreement must be read in conjunction with and subject to the Rome Statute of the International Criminal Court and the Rules of Procedure and Evidence;

RECALLING THAT Article 87(6), of the Rome Statute provides that the Court may ask any intergovernmental organisation to provide information or documents, and that the Court may also ask for other forms of cooperation and assistance which may be agreed upon with such an organisation and which are in accordance with its competence or mandate;

CONSIDERING THAT this Agreement covers terms of cooperation and assistance between the International Criminal Court and the European Union and not between the International Criminal Court and the Member States of the European Union;

CONSIDERING THAT, to that effect, the International Criminal Court and the European Union should agree on terms of cooperation and assistance in addition to Common Position 2003/444/CFSP, as well as to the EU Action Plan in follow-up to that Common Position,

HAVE AGREED AS FOLLOWS:

ARTICLE 1 Purpose of the Agreement

This Agreement, which is entered into by the European Union (EU) and the International Criminal Court (the Court) pursuant to the provisions of the Treaty on European Union (EU Treaty) and the Rome Statute of the International Criminal Court (the Statute) respectively, defines the terms of cooperation and assistance between the EU and the Court.

ARTICLE 2 Definition of terms

1. For the purposes of this Agreement, EU shall mean the Council of the European Union (hereinafter Council), the Secretary General/High Representative and the General Secretariat of the Council, and the Commission of the European Communities

(hereinafter European Commission). EU shall not mean the Member States in their own right. 2. For the purposes of this Agreement, the Court shall mean: (a) the Presidency, (b) an Appeals Division, a Trial Division and a Pre-Trial Division, (c) the Prosecutor's Office, (d) the Registry, (e) the Secretariat of the Assembly of States Parties.

ARTICLE 3 Member State Agreements

1. This Agreement, including any agreements or arrangements concluded under Article 11, shall not apply to requests for information from the Court which relate to information, other than EU documents including EU classified information, originating from an individual Member State. In such circumstances, any request shall be made directly to the relevant Member State. 2. Article 73 of the Statute shall be applied, mutatis mutandis, to requests made by the Court to the EU under this Agreement.

ARTICLE 4 Obligation of cooperation and assistance

The EU and the Court agree that, with a view to facilitating the effective discharge of their respective responsibilities, they shall cooperate closely, as appropriate, with each other and consult each other on matters of mutual interest, pursuant to the provisions of this Agreement while fully respecting the respective provisions of the EU Treaty and the Statute. In order to facilitate this obligation of cooperation and assistance, the Parties agree on the establishing of appropriate regular contacts between the Court and the EU Focal Point for the Court.

ARTICLE 5 Attendance at meetings

The EU may invite the Court to attend meetings and conferences arranged under its auspices at which matters of interest to the Court are under discussion in order to give assistance with regard to matters within the jurisdiction of the Court.

ARTICLE 6 Promotion of the values underpinning the Statute

The EU and the Court shall cooperate, whenever appropriate, by adopting initiatives to promote the dissemination of the principles, values and provisions of the Statute and related instruments.

ARTICLE 7 Exchange of information

1. The EU and the Court shall, to the fullest extent possible and practicable, ensure the regular exchange of information and documents of mutual interest in accordance with the Statute and the Rules of Procedure and Evidence. 2. With due regard to its responsibilities and competence under the EU Treaty, the EU undertakes to cooperate with the Court and to provide the Court with such information or documents in its possession as the

Court may request pursuant to Article 87(6), of the Statute. 3. The EU may, at its own initiative and in accordance with the EU Treaty, provide information or documents, which may be relevant to the work of the Court. 4. The Registrar of the Court shall, in accordance with the Statute and the Rules of Procedure and Evidence, provide information and documentation relating to pleadings, oral proceedings, judgements and orders of the Court, which may be of interest to the EU.

ARTICLE 8 Protection of safety or security

Should the cooperation, including the disclosure of information or documents, provided for in this Agreement endanger the safety or security of current or former staff of the EU or otherwise prejudice the security or proper conduct of any operation or activity of the EU, the Court may order, particularly at the request of the EU, appropriate measures of protection.

ARTICLE 9 Classified information

Provisions relating to the release of EU classified information by the EU to an organ of the Court are set out in the Annex to this Agreement, which is an integral part thereof.

ARTICLE 10 Testimony of staff of the European Union

1. If the Court requests the testimony of an official or other staff of the EU, the EU undertakes to cooperate fully with the Court and, if necessary and with due regard to its responsibilities and competencies under the EU Treaty and the relevant rules thereunder, to take all necessary measures to enable the Court to hear that person's testimony, in particular by waiving that person's obligation of confidentiality. 2. With reference to Article 8, the Parties recognise that measures of protection might be required should an official or other staff of the EU be requested to provide the Court with testimony. 3. Subject to the Statute and the Rules of Procedure and Evidence, the EU shall be authorised to appoint a representative to assist any official or other staff of the EU who appears as a witness before the Court.

ARTICLE 11 Cooperation between the European Union and the Prosecutor

1. While fully respecting the EU Treaty: (i) the EU undertakes to cooperate with the Prosecutor, in accordance with the Statute and the Rules of Procedure and Evidence, in providing additional information held by the EU that he or she may seek; (ii) the EU undertakes to cooperate with the Prosecutor, in accordance with Article 54(3)(c) of the Statute; (iii) the EU shall, in accordance with Article 54(3)(d) of the Statute, enter into such arrangements or agreements, not inconsistent with the Statute, as may be necessary to facilitate the cooperation of the EU with the Prosecutor. 2. The Prosecutor shall address requests for information in writing to the Secretary General/High Representative. The

Secretary General/High Representative shall provide a written reply no later than one month. 3. The EU and the Prosecutor may agree that the EU provide the Prosecutor with documents or information on condition of confidentiality and solely for the purpose of generating new evidence and that such documents or information shall not be disclosed to other organs of the Court or third parties, at any stage of the proceedings or thereafter, without the consent of the EU. The rules on classified information of Article 9 shall apply.

ARTICLE 12 Privileges and immunities

If the Court seeks to exercise its jurisdiction over a person who is alleged to be criminally responsible for a crime within the jurisdiction of the Court and if such person enjoys, according to the relevant rules of international law, any privileges and immunities, the relevant institution of the EU undertakes to cooperate fully with the Court and, with due regard to its responsibilities and competencies under the EU Treaty and the relevant rules thereunder, to take all necessary measures to allow the Court to exercise its jurisdiction, in particular by waiving any such privileges and immunities in accordance with all relevant rules of international law.

ARTICLE 13 Personnel arrangements

Pursuant to Article 44(4) of the Statute, the EU and the Court agree to determine, on a case by case basis, under which exceptional circumstances the Court may employ the expertise of gratis personnel offered by the EU, to assist with the work of any of the organs of the Court.

ARTICLE 14 Services and facilities

Upon request of the Court, the EU shall, subject to availability, provide for the purposes of the Court, such facilities and services as may be required, including, where appropriate, support at the field level. The terms and conditions on which any such facilities, services or support of the EU may be provided shall be, as appropriate, the subject of prior supplementary arrangements.

ARTICLE 15 Training

The EU shall endeavour to support, as appropriate and in consultation with the Court, the development of training and assistance for judges, prosecutors, officials and counsel in work related to the Court.

ARTICLE 16 Correspondence

1. For the purpose of this Agreement: (a) as regards the EU: all correspondence shall

be sent to the Council at the following address: Council of the European Union Chief Registry Officer Rue de la Loi/Wetstraat, 175 B-1048 Brussels; all correspondence shall be forwarded by the Chief Registry Officer of the Council to the Member States, to the European Commission and to the EU Focal Point for the Court subject to paragraph 2; (b) as regards the Court, all correspondence shall be addressed to the Registrar or the Prosecutor, as appropriate. 2. Exceptionally, correspondence from one Party which is only accessible to specific competent officials, organs or services of that Party may, for operational reasons, be addressed and only be accessible to specific competent officials, organs or services of the other Party specifically designated as recipients, taking into account their competencies and according to the need to know principle. As far as the EU is concerned, this correspondence shall be transmitted through the Chief Registry Officer of the Council.

ARTICLE 17 Implementation

1. The Office of the Prosecutor and the Registry of the Court and the Secretary-General of the Council and of the European Commission shall oversee the implementation of this Agreement, in accordance with their respective competencies. 2. The Court and the EU may, for the purposes of implementing this Agreement, enter into such arrangements as may be found appropriate.

ARTICLE 18 Settlement of Disputes

All differences between the EU and the Court arising out of the interpretation or application of this Agreement shall be dealt with through consultation between the Parties.

ARTICLE 19 Entry into force and review

1. This Agreement shall enter into force on the first day of the first month after the Parties have signed it. 2. This Agreement may be reviewed for consideration of possible amendments at the request of either Party. It shall be reviewed no later than five years after its entry into force. 3. Any amendment to this Agreement shall only be made in writing and by common agreement of the Parties.

ARTICLE 20 Denunciation

One Party may denounce this Agreement by written notice of denunciation given to the other Party. Such denunciation shall take effect six months after receipt of notification by the other Party, but shall not affect obligations already contracted under the provisions of this Agreement. In particular, all classified information provided or exchanged pursuant to this Agreement shall continue to be protected in accordance with the provisions set forth herein.

IN WITNESS WHEREOF the undersigned, respectively duly authorised, have signed this Agreement. Done at Luxembourg on the tenth day of April in the year two thousand and six.

ANNEX

1. Should EU classified information be requested by an organ of the Court within the meaning of Article 34 of the Statute, it may be released only in accordance with the Council's security regulations (1). For the purposes of this Agreement, classified information shall mean any information (namely, knowledge that can be communicated in any form) or material determined to require protection against unauthorised disclosure and which has been so designated by a security classification (hereinafter referred to as classified information). In particular: (i) the Court shall ensure that EU classified information released to it keeps the security classification given to it by the EU and shall safeguard such information, in accordance with an equivalent level of protection to that foreseen in the Council's security regulations. In this respect, the Court shall ensure that it provides the protection required by the EU in accordance with the rules, measures and procedures to be established pursuant to paragraph 4; (ii) the Court shall not use the released EU classified information for purposes other than those for which those EU classified information and documents have been released to the Court; (iii) the Court shall not disclose such information and documents to third parties without the prior written consent of the EU in accordance with the principle of originator consent as defined in the Council's security regulations; (iv) the Court shall ensure that access to EU classified information released to it will be authorised only for individuals who have a need to know ; (v) the Court shall ensure that all persons who, in the conduct of their official duties require access, or whose duties or functions may afford access to information classified CONFIDENTIEL UE and above, are appropriately security cleared before they are granted access to such information, in accordance with arrangements to be established on the basis of objective criteria pursuant to paragraph 4; (vi) the Court shall ensure that, before being given access to EU classified information, all individuals who require access to such information are briefed on and comply with the requirements of the protective security regulations relevant to the classification of the information they are to access; (vii) taking into account their level of classification, EU classified information shall be forwarded to the Court by diplomatic bag, military mail services, secure mail services, secure telecommunications or personal carriage. The Court shall notify in advance to the General Secretariat of the Council of the EU the name and address of the body responsible for the security of classified information and the precise addresses to which the information must be forwarded and will ensure that the addressees are security cleared; (viii) the Court shall ensure that all premises, areas, buildings, offices, rooms, communication and information systems, and the like, in which EU classified information is stored and/or handled, is protected by appropriate physical security measures, in accordance with the arrangements to be established pursuant to paragraph 4; (ix) the Court shall ensure that EU classified documents released to it are, on their receipt, recorded in a special register.

APPENDIX THREE

The Court shall ensure that copies of EU classified documents released to it, which may be made by the recipient body, their number and distribution, are recorded in this special register. The Court shall notify to the EU the date of return of those documents to the EU or provide a certificate of their destruction; (x) the Court shall notify to the General Secretariat of the Council of the EU any case of compromise of EU classified information released to it. In such a case, the Court shall initiate investigations and take appropriate measures to prevent a recurrence, in accordance with the arrangements to be established pursuant to paragraph 4. 2. In implementing paragraph 1, no generic release shall be possible unless procedures are established and agreed between the Parties regarding certain categories of information. 3. EU classified information may be downgraded or declassified in accordance with Council's security regulations before being released to the Court. Any EU classified document containing national classified information may be consulted only by appropriately cleared Court staff or downgraded or declassified and released to the Court with the express written consent of the originator. 4. In order to implement this Agreement, security arrangements shall be established between the three authorities designated below in order to lay down the standards of the reciprocal security protection for classified information subject to this Agreement: (a) the Security Office of the Court shall be responsible for developing security arrangements for the protection and safeguarding of classified information provided to the Court under this Agreement; (b) the Security Office of the General Secretariat of the Council, under the direction and on behalf of the Secretary General of the Council, acting in the name of the Council and under its authority, shall be responsible for developing security arrangements for the protection and safeguarding of classified information provided to the EU under this Agreement; (c) the European Commission Security Directorate, acting in the name of the European Commission and under its authority, shall be responsible for developing security arrangements for the protection of classified information provided or exchanged under this Agreement within the European Commission and its premises; (d) for the EU, these standards shall be subject to approval by the Council Security Committee. 5. The Parties shall provide mutual assistance with regard to security of classified information subject to this Agreement and matters of common interest. Reciprocal security consultations and inspections shall be conducted by the authorities defined in paragraph 4 to assess the effectiveness of the security arrangements within their respective responsibility to be established pursuant to paragraph 4. 6. The Parties shall have a security organisation and security programmes, based upon such basic principles and minimum standards of security which shall be implemented in the security systems of the Parties to be established pursuant to paragraph 4, to ensure that an equivalent level of protection is applied to classified information subject to this Agreement. 7. Prior to the initial provision of classified information subject to this Agreement, the responsible security authorities referred to in paragraph 4 must have agreed that the receiving party is able to protect and safeguard the information subject to this Agreement in a way consistent with the arrangements to be established pursuant to paragraph 4. 8. Nothing in this Agreement shall prejudice the possibility of the EU making available to the Court information with the highest level of classification subject to the Court ensuring an equivalent level of protection to that foreseen in the Council's security regulations. (1 Council Decision 2001/264/EC of 19 March 2001, adopting the Council's security regulations)

APPENDIX FOUR

FULL TEXT OF THE SECRET HUMAN RIGHTS WATCH LETTER TO THE OFFICE OF THE PROSECUTOR, INTERNATIONAL CRIMINAL COURT, DATED 15 SEPTEMBER 2008

Confidential

Executive Committee
Office of the Prosecutor
International Criminal Court

September 15, 2008

Dear Executive Committee:

We are writing to request a meeting to discuss management practices within the Office of the Prosecutor (OTP).

As you know, our organizations are deeply invested in the mission of the International Criminal Court (ICC) and were instrumental in its creation. Through dialogue with court officials on matters of policy, and intense advocacy with states parties and the broader international community to foster support for international justice, we have sought ever since to ensure the court's success. This should be evident in our current efforts to defend the independence of the OTP and the court from those who would seek to undermine your important efforts to bring justice in Darfur.

In this regard, we note that some recent media articles have raised criticisms about the management of the office with an apparent intention to weaken the court and its authority. We wish to disassociate ourselves clearly from any such agenda.

At the same time, however, we are very concerned that your increased attention to management practices within the office is needed, and seek this opportunity to discuss these concerns directly with you.

As you know, the court's strategic plan identifies establishing the ICC as a model of public administration as one of its three central goals. [1] The separate strategic plan for your office fully subscribes to this goal, and commits to nurtur[ing] a working environment with minimal bureaucracy, where diversity and initiative are celebrated, and in which staff feel responsible and valued. [2]

Meeting these goals is challenging, but nonetheless essential to the success of the court and of your office. Expectations of the world's first permanent criminal tribunal run high. So too do those placed on its staff who confront inordinate difficulties in bringing to justice those accused of the world's worst crimes. Support and incentives for initiative are necessary if staff members are to perform at the very high levels the court's important work demands. And as a permanent institution, every effort should be made to ensure that good policies and practices are in place to carry forward a supportive environment in successive years.

We would like to discuss with you whether more could be done to meet the management goals you have set for yourself. Our concerns are underscored by at least two recent developments.

First, we are aware that many experienced investigators have left the OTP since 2005. One reason commonly provided for these departures is that many investigators experienced burn out because there were simply not enough of them to handle the rigorous demands for conducting investigations. But another reason commonly provided is the perception that the input of investigators is not sufficiently valued within the OTP, leading to dissatisfaction.

The departure of senior staff – and the loss of their experience, knowledge of the country situation under investigation, and overall institutional memory – has a direct impact on the efficiency of investigations, and is particularly regrettable where due at least in part to the failure to develop a sufficiently supportive work environment. We note as well that the position of deputy prosecutor for investigations – who could help to share some of the burdens of providing good management and supervision of investigators – has remained vacant since 2007.

Second, we were concerned by findings in a recent decision of the administrative tribunal of the International Labour Organization of due process violations in the prosecutor's summary dismissal of an OTP staff member. The tribunal ordered the ICC to pay compensation. [3]

Sound management, of course, may require taking disciplinary measures. In this case, however, we were disturbed by findings that the prosecutor had ignored the recommendation of the court's Disciplinary Advisory Board and involved himself directly even though the individual's alleged misconduct meriting dismissal concerned the prosecutor personally. The poor management practices we see in this case not only incur economic costs to the court – already under strain to account responsibly for its budget to states parties – but, more importantly, costs to the morale of staff, who are entitled to have their due process rights respected in an employment dispute.

In our meeting with you, we would like to put forward for discussion the following recommendations addressed to these concerns.

First, the OTP's strategic plan, dating to September 2006, highlights that performance indicators and evaluation processes were to be developed to measure the office's performance against the goals identified in that plan. We would like to discuss whether your office has undertaken a comprehensive assessment of its activities to date, particularly with regard to establishing sound management practices. To the extent it has not, we would urge you to consider undertaking such an assessment, and implementing changes in management policy and practice it may indicate.

Second, we would ask you to consider whether the management responsibilities of the office's Executive Committee could be bolstered to provide additional support for cultivating the working environment envisioned in the strategic plans. Expanding the role and input of the Executive Committee could also ground concern for sound management in the structure of the office itself, helping to ensure that good practices established now are carried forward into the future. We would also like to encourage you to consider further augmenting the management resources within your office by raising plans for recruiting a deputy prosecutor for investigations with states parties in advance of the Assembly of States Parties' upcoming seventh session.

We would very much welcome the opportunity to discuss our concerns and recommendations at a meeting between the Executive Committee and representatives of our organizations. It is our firm belief that urgent attention to enhancing management practices within your office will increase its capacity to carry out its important work.

We look forward to hearing from you at your earliest convenience.

Sincerely,

Human Rights Watch

[1] Assembly of States Parties, Strategic Plan of the International Criminal Court, ICC-ASP/5/6, August 4, 2006, http://www.icc-cpi.int/library/asp/ICC-ASP-5-12_English.pdf (accessed August 25, 2008), pp. 9–12.

[2] Office of the Prosecutor, ICC, Report on Prosecutorial Strategy , September 14, 2006, http://www.icc-cpi.int/library/organs/OTP/OTP_Prosecutorial-Strategy-20060914_

English.pdf (accessed August 25, 2008), paras. 9, 12.

[3] Palme v. ICC, International Labour Organisation Administrative Tribunal, judgement no. 2757, July 9, 2008.

Appendix Five

SPEECH BY HIS EXCELLENCY HON. UHURU KENYATTA, CGH, PRESIDENT AND COMMANDER IN CHIEF OF THE DEFENCE FORCES OF THE REPUBLIC OF KENYA AT THE EXTRAORDINARY SESSION OF THE ASSEMBLY OF HEADS OF STATE AND GOVERNMENT OF THE AFRICAN UNION, ADDIS ABABA, ETHIOPIA, 12th OCTOBER, 2013

Chair of the African Union, Prime Minister Hailemariam Desalegn, Chair of the Commission of the African Union, Dr. Nkosazana Dlamini-Zuma, Colleagues Head of State and Government, Distinguished Ladies and Gentlemen, It gives me special pleasure to join your Excellencies at this Special Summit, where we have assembled to reflect on very significant matters relating to the welfare and destiny of our nations and peoples.

I thank you for the honour of addressing you today, because as it happens, I crave my brother and sister Excellencies' views on some issues. We are privileged to lead the nations of a continent on the rise.

Africa rests at the centre of global focus as the continent of the future. Although we have been relentlessly exploited in the past, we remain with sufficient resources to invest in a prosperous future.

Whilst we have been divided and incited against one another before, we are now united and more peaceful.

Even as we grapple with a few regional conflicts, as Africans, we are taking proactive measures to ensure that all our people move together in the journey to prosperity in a peaceful home.

Even though we were dominated and controlled by imperialists and colonial interests in years gone by, we are now proud, independent and sovereign nations and people. We are looking to the future with hope, marching towards the horizon with confidence and working in unity.

This is the self evident promise that Africa holds for its people today. As leaders, we are the heirs of freedom fighters, and our founding fathers. These liberation heroes founded the Organisation of African Unity, which was dedicated to the eradication of ALL FORMS OF COLONIALSM.

Towards this end, the OAU defended the interests of independent nations and helped the cause of those that were still colonised. It sought to prevent member states from being controlled once again by outsider powers.

The founding fathers of African Unity were conscious that structural colonialism takes many forms, some blatant and extreme, like apartheid, while others are subtler and deceptively innocuous, like some forms of development assistance.

It has been necessary, therefore, for African leaders to constantly watch out against threats to our peoples' sovereignty and unity.

In our generation, we have honoured our fathers' legacies by guaranteeing that through the African Union, our countries and our people shall achieve greater unity, and that the sovereignty, territorial integrity and independence of our States shall not be trifled with.

More than ever, our destiny is in our hands. Yet at the same time, more than ever, it is imperative for us to be vigilant against the persistent machinations of outsiders who desire to control that destiny. We know what this does to our nations and people: subjugation and suffering.

Your Excellencies, The philosophies, ideologies, structures and institutions that visited misery upon millions for centuries ultimately harm their perpetrators. Thus the imperial exploiter crashes into the pits of penury. The arrogant world police is crippled by shambolic domestic dysfunction.

These are the spectacles of Western decline we are witnessing today. At the same time, other nations and continents rise and prosper. Africa and Asia continue to thrive, with their promise growing every passing day.

As our strength multiplies, and our unity gets deeper, those who want to control and exploit us become more desperate. Therefore, they abuse whatever power remains in their control.

The Swahili people say that one ascending a ladder cannot hold hands with one descending. The force of gravity will be compounded and the one going up only loses.

The International Criminal Court was mandated to accomplish these objectives by bringing to justice those criminal perpetrators who bear greatest responsibility for crimes.

Looking at the world in the past, at that time and even now, it was clear that there have always been instances of unconscionable impunity and atrocity that demand a concerted international response, and that there are vulnerable, helpless victims of these crimes who require justice as a matter of right.

This is the understanding, and the expectation of most signatories to the Rome Statute. The most active global powers of the time declined to ratify the Treaty, or withdrew somewhere along the way, citing several compelling grounds.

The British foreign secretary Robin Cook said at the time, that the International Criminal Court was not set up to bring to book Prime Ministers of the United Kingdom or Presidents of the USA. Had someone other than a Western leader said those fateful words, the word "impunity" would have been thrown at them with an emphatic alacrity.

An American senator serving on the foreign relations committee echoed the British sentiments and said, "Our concern is that this is a court that is irreparably flawed, that is created with an independent prosecutor, with no checks and balances on his power, answerable to no state institution, and that this court is going to be used for politicized prosecutions."

The understanding of the States which subscribed to the Treaty in good faith was two-fold. First, that world powers were hesitant to a process that might make them accountable for such spectacularly criminal international adventures as the wars in Iraq, Syria, Libya, Afghanistan and other places, and such hideous enterprises as renditions and torture.

Such states did not, therefore, consider such warnings as applicable to pacific and friendly parties. Secondly, it was the understanding of good-faith subscribers that the ICC would administer and secure justice in a fair, impartial and independent manner and, as an international court, bring accountability to situations and perpetrators everywhere in the world. As well, it was hoped that the ICC would set the highest standards of justice and judicial processes.

Your Excellencies, As has been demonstrated quite thoroughly over the past decade, the good-faith subscribers had fallen prey to their high-mindedness and idealism. I do not need to tell your Excellencies about the nightmare my country in particular, and myself and my Deputy as individuals, have had to endure in making this realisation.

Western powers are the key drivers of the ICC process. They have used prosecutions as ruses and bait to pressure Kenyan leadership into adopting, or renouncing various positions. Close to 70 per cent of the Court's annual budget is funded by the European Union.

The threat of prosecution usually suffices to have pliant countries execute policies favourable to these countries.

Through it, regime-change sleights of hand have been attempted in Africa. A number of them have succeeded.

The Office of the Prosecutor made certain categorical pronouncements regarding eligibility for leadership of candidates in Kenya's last general election. Only a fortnight ago, the Prosecutor proposed undemocratic and unconstitutional adjustments to the Kenyan Presidency.

These interventions go beyond interference in the internal affairs of a sovereign State. They constitute a fetid insult to Kenya and Africa. African sovereignty means nothing to the ICC and its patrons. They also dovetail altogether too conveniently with the warnings given to Kenyans just before the last elections: choices have consequences.

This chorus was led by the USA, Britain, EU, and certain eminent persons in global affairs. It was a threat made to Kenyans against electing my Government. My Government's decisive election must be seen as a categorical rebuke by the people of Kenya of those who wished to interfere with our internal affairs and infringe our sovereignty.

Now Kenya has undergone numerous problems since its birth as a Republic 50 years ago. Yet over the same period, Kenya has also made tremendous progress. It is the same in all countries of Africa. At our Golden Jubilee, we look forward to a rebirth characterising the next 50 years, not a ceaseless harkening to our history.

I must make the point that we do not intend to forget, or discount the value of our history. Rather, we do want to learn from it, not live in it. As Kenya's President, it gives me a feeling of deep and lasting pride to know that I can count on the African Union to listen and help in trying times. Africa has always stood by our side.

When we faced violent disagreements over the 2007 election result, my distinguished predecessor, Mwai Kibaki came to you with a request for help, and you did not stint. You instituted a high-level team of Eminent Persons who came to our assistance.

Because of that, we were able to summon the confidence to speak to each other and agree. As a result, we put in place a 4-point plan, which not only put Kenya back on track, but formed the basis of the most rapid political, legal and social reform ever witnessed in our country.

Through it, we successfully mediated the dispute surrounding the 2007 election and pacified the country. A power-sharing coalition was formed with a mandate to undertake far-reaching measures to prevent future violent disputes, entrench the rule of law, prevent abuses of legal power and entrench equity in our body politic while also securing justice for the victims of the post-election violence.

We enacted a new, progressive constitution which instituted Devolution of power and resources, strengthened the protection of fundamental rights, and enhanced institutional and political checks and balances. It also provided the legal foundation for the national economic transformation roadmap, Vision 2030.

The project of national transformation presently underway in Kenya was given tremendous impetus by your Excellencies' needful intervention. On the basis of this constitution we have instituted legislation and established institutions to realise the people's basic rights, ensure transparency and accountability and protect the popular sovereignty of Kenyans.

A new Judiciary and electoral commission have ensured that we have credible elections and dispute resolution.

Your Excellencies, The people of Ethiopia warn against the deplorable presumption of chopping up meat for a lion; I cannot teach you your work, nor force you to accept my position.

Please institute a mechanism to empirically verify what I have told you. My part is to thank you on behalf of the people of Kenya for your help.

After the successful mediation of the post-election controversy in 2008, there was disagreement over the best way to bring the perpetrators of post-election violence to account and secure justice for the victims.

One proposal was to set up a local tribunal to try the cases, while another was to refer the matter to the ICC. The Mediator who had been appointed by your Excellencies referred the matter to the ICC when the disagreement persisted.

On the basis of this referral, the Prosecutor stated that he had launched investigations which, he claimed, established that 6 persons had committed crimes against humanity. According to the Prosecutor, your Excellencies, I fall among those men.

Your Excellencies, From the beginning of the cases, I have fully cooperated with the Court in the earnest expectation that it afforded the best opportunity for me to clear my name. I have attended court whenever required and complied with every requirement made of me in connection with my case.

Other Kenyans charged before that court have similarly cooperated fully. The Government has cooperated to the maximum; the Court itself found that Kenya's Government has fully complied in 33 out of 37 instances, and was only prevented from cooperating 100 per cent by legal and constitutional constraints.

After my election, we have continued to fully cooperate. As earlier stated, we see it as the only means to achieve personal vindication, but also to protect our country from prejudice. As I address your Excellencies, my deputy is sitting – in person – in that Court.

Proceedings continue revealing the evidence against us to be reckless figments and fabrications every passing day. I cannot narrate quite accurately the calculated humiliation and stigma the prosecution has inflicted on us at every turn, within and outside the proceedings.

It is all consistent with a political agenda, rather than a quest for justice. For 5 years I have strained to cooperate fully, and have consistently beseeched the Court to expedite the cases.

Yet the gratuitous libel and prejudice I have encountered at the instance of the Prosecution seeks to present me as a fugitive from justice who is guilty as charged. All I have requested as President is to be allowed to execute my constitutional obligations as the forensic side of things is handled by my lawyers.

Even as we maintain our innocence, it has always been my position, shared by my deputy, that the events of 2007 represented the worst embarrassment to us as a nation, and a shock to our self-belief.

We almost commenced the rapid descent down the precipitous slope of destruction and anarchy. Its aftermath was similarly an unbearable shame.

We are a people who properly take pride in our achievements and our journey as a nation. The fact that over that time we had lost direction, however briefly, was traumatising.

That is the genesis of our rebirth. Until our ascension to the Presidency of Kenya, thousands of internally-displaced persons remained in camps.

It is generally difficult to resettle many people owing to scarcity of land and sensitivity to their preference. But we have undertaken to ensure that no Kenyan will be left behind in our journey to progress.

Resettling the IDP therefore was a particularly urgent assignment for us. Within 6 months of assuming office, we resettled all of them, and closed the displacement camps for good. Our efforts at pacifying the main protagonists in the PEV have similarly borne fruit.

So much so, that the reconciliation efforts gave birth to a successful political movement which won the last general election. This not only speaks to the success of reconciliation, but also testifies to its popular endorsement by the majority of the people of Kenya.

We certainly do not bear responsibility at any level for the post-election violence of 2007, but as leaders, we felt it incumbent upon us to bear responsibility for reconciliation and leadership of peace.

Our Government wants to lead Kenya to prosperity founded on national stability and security. Peace is indispensable to this aspiration. Reconciliation, therefore was not merely good politics; it is key to everything we want to achieve as a Government.

Your Excellencies, America and Britain do not have to worry about accountability for international crimes. Although certain norms of international law are deemed peremptory, this only applies to non-Western states. Otherwise, they are inert. It is this double standard and the overt politicisation of the ICC that should be of concern to us here today.

It is the fact that this court performs on the cue of European and American governments against the sovereignty of African States and peoples that should outrage us. People have termed this situation "race-hunting". I find great difficulty adjudging them wrong.

What is the fate of International Justice? I daresay that it has lost support owing to the subversive machinations of its key proponents. Cynicism has no place in justice. Yet it takes no mean amount of selfish and malevolent calculation to mutate a quest for accountability on the basis of truth, into a hunger for dramatic sacrifices to advance geopolitical ends.

The ICC has been reduced into a painfully farcical pantomime, a travesty that adds insult to the injury of victims. It stopped being the home of justice the day it became the toy of declining imperial powers.

This is the circumstance which today compels us to agree with the reasons US, China, Israel, India and other non-signatory States hold for abstaining from the Rome Treaty.

In particular, the very accurate observations of John R. Bolton who said, "For numerous reasons, the United States decided that the ICC had unacceptable consequences for our national sovereignty. Specifically, the ICC is an organization that runs contrary to fundamental American precepts and basic constitutional principles of popular sovereignty, checks and balances and national independence."

Our mandate as AU, and as individual African States is to protect our own and each other's independence and sovereignty. The USA and other nations abstained out of fear. Our misgivings are born of bitter experience.

Africa is not a third-rate territory of second-class peoples. We are not a project, or experiment of outsiders. It was always impossible for us to uncritically internalise notions of justice implanted through that most unjust of institutions: colonialism.

The West sees no irony in preaching justice to a people they have disenfranchised, exploited, taxed and brutalised.

Our history serves us well: we must distrust the blandishments of those who have drunk out of the poisoned fountain of imperialism.

The spirit of African pride and sovereignty has withstood centuries of severe tribulation. I invoke that spirit of freedom and unity today before you. It is a spirit with a voice that rings through all generations of human history. It is the eternal voice of a majestic spirit which will never die.

Kenya is striving mightily, and wants to work with its neighbours and friends everywhere to attain a better home, region and world. Kenya seeks to be treated with dignity as a proud member of the community of nations which has contributed immensely, with limited resources, to the achievement of peace, security and multilateralism.

Kenya looks to her friends in time of need. We come to you to vindicate our independence and sovereignty. Our unity is not a lie. The African Union is not an illusion.

The philosophy of divide-and-rule, which worked against us all those years before, cannot shackle us to the ground in our Season of Renaissance. Our individual and collective sovereignty requires us to take charge of our destiny, and fashion African solutions to African problems.

It will be disingenuous, Excellencies, to pretend that there is no concern, if not outrage, over the manner in which ICC has handled not just the Kenyan, but all cases before it. All the cases currently before it arise from Africa.

Yet Africa is not the only continent where international crimes are being committed. Out of over 30 cases before the court, NONE relates to a situation outside Africa. All the people indicted before that court, ever since its founding have been Africans.

Every plea we have made to be heard before that court has landed upon deaf ears. When Your Excellencies' resolution was communicated to the Court through a letter to its president, it was dismissed as not being properly before the Court and therefore ineligible for consideration.

When a civil society organisation wrote a letter bearing sensational and prejudicial fabrications, the Court took urgent and substantial decisions based on it. Before the ICC, African sovereign nations' resolutions are NOTHING compared with the opinions of civil society activists.

The AU is the bastion of African sovereignty, and the vanguard of our unity. Yet the ICC deems it altogether unworthy of the minutest consideration. Presidents Kikwete, Museveni, Jonathan and Zuma have pronounced themselves on the court's insensitivity, arrogance and disrespect.

Leaders in my country have escalated their anxiety to the national Parliament, where a legislative process to withdraw altogether from the Rome Treaty is under consideration. As I said, it would not be right to ignore the fact that concern over the conduct of the ICC is strong and widespread.

There is very little that remains for me to say about the slights that the ICC continue to visit upon the nations and people of Africa. We want to believe in due process before the ICC, but where is it being demonstrated?

We want to see the ICC as fair and even-handed throughout the world, but what can we do when everyone but Africa is exempt from accountability? We would love nothing more than to have an international forum for justice and accountability, but what choice do we have when we get only bias and race-hunting at the ICC? Isn't respect part of justice?

Aren't our sovereign institutions worthy of deference within the framework of international law? If so, what justice can be rendered by a court which disregards our views?

Our mandate is clear: sovereignty and unity. This is the forum for us to unite and categorically vindicate our sovereignty.

Excellencies, I turn to you trusting that we will be faithful to our charge, to each other, and to our people.

I have utmost confidence that this Assembly's voice will be clear to the entire world. Like other African countries, Kenya did not achieve its independence with ease.

Blood was shed for it.

Your Excellencies,

I thank you. God Bless you. God Bless Africa. (PSCU)

Appendix Six

AFRICAN UNION DECISION REGARDING ITS RELATIONSHIP WITH THE INTERNATIONAL CRIMINAL COURT (ICC)

Ext/Assembly/AU/Dec.1(Oct.2013)

Adopted by the Extraordinary Summit of the African Union in Addis Ababa, Ethiopia, on 12 October 2013

The Assembly,

1. TAKES NOTE of the Progress Report of the Commission on the Implementation of Decision Assembly/AU/Dec.482(XXI) on the International Jurisdiction, International Justice and the International Criminal Court (ICC) and the Presentation made by the Republic of Kenya as well as the recommendations of the Executive Council thereon;

2. REITERATES, in accordance with the Constitutive Act of the African Union (AU), the AU's unflinching commitment to fight impunity, promote human rights and democracy, and the rule of law and good governance in the continent;

3. REAFFIRMS its previous Decisions on the abuse of the principles of Universal Jurisdiction adopted in Sharm El Sheikh in July 2008 as well as the activities of the ICC in Africa, adopted in January and July 2009, January and July 2010, January and July 2011, January and July 2012, and May 2013 wherein it expressed its strong conviction that the search for justice should be pursued in a way that does not impede or jeopardize efforts aimed at promoting lasting peace;

4. REITERATES AU's concern on the politicization and misuse of indictments against African leaders by ICC as well as at the unprecedented indictments of and proceedings against the sitting President and Deputy President of Kenya in light of the recent developments in that country;

5. UNDERSCORES that this is the first time that a sitting Head of State and his deputy are being tried in an international court and **STRESSES** the gravity of this situation which could undermine the sovereignty, stability, and peace in that country and in other

Member States as well as reconciliation and reconstruction and the normal functioning of constitutional institutions;

6. RECOGNIZES that Kenya is a frontline state in the fight against terrorism at regional, continental and international levels and, in this regard, **STRESSES** the threat that this menace poses to the region in particular and the continent in general, and the proceedings initiated against the President and the Deputy President of the Republic of Kenya will distract and prevent them from fulfilling their constitutional responsibilities, including national and regional security affairs;

7. RECALLS that following the 2007 Post Election Violence (PEV), the mediation process in Kenya was initiated by AU, which led to the enactment of the National Accord and Reconciliation Act and the Agreement establishing the coalition government, and **EXPRESSES** concern that the ongoing process before the ICC may pose a threat to the full implementation of the National Accord of 2008 and prevent the process of addressing the challenges leading to the post-election violence;

8. EXPRESSES its deep appreciation for the full cooperation that the President and Deputy President of Kenya have demonstrated to the ICC process and **CALLS UPON** the ICC to show the same level of cooperation in the process;

9. REAFFIRMS the principles deriving from national laws and international customary law by which sitting Heads of State and other senior state officials are granted immunities during their tenure of office;

10. NOW DECIDES:

(i) That to safeguard the constitutional order, stability and, integrity of Member States, no charges shall be commenced or continued before any International Court or Tribunal against any serving AU Head of State or Government or anybody acting or entitled to act in such capacity during their term of office;

(ii) That the trials of President Uhuru Kenyatta and Deputy President William Samoei Ruto, who are the current serving leaders of the Republic of Kenya, should be suspended until they complete their terms of office;

(iii) To set up a Contact Group of the Executive Council to be led by the Chairperson of the Council, composed of five (5) Members (one (1) per region) to undertake consultations with the Members of the United Nations Security Council (UNSC), in particular, its five (5) Permanent Members with a view to engaging with the UNSC on all concerns of the AU on its relationship with the ICC, including the deferral of the Kenyan and the Sudan cases in order to obtain their feedback before the beginning of the trial on 12 November, 2013;

(iv) To fast track the process of expanding the mandate of the African Court on Human and Peoples' Rights (AfCHPR) to try international crimes, such as genocide, crimes against humanity and war crimes;

(v) That the Commission expedites the process of expansion of AfCHPR to deal with international crimes in accordance with the relevant decision of the Policy Organs and INVITES Member States to support this process;

(vi) That African States Parties propose relevant amendments to the Rome Statute, in accordance with Article 121 of the Statute;

(vii) To request African States Parties to the Rome Statute of the ICC, in particular the Members of the Bureau of the Assembly of States Parties to inscribe on the agenda of the forthcoming sessions of the ASP the issue of indictment of African sitting Heads of State and Government by the ICC and its consequences on peace, stability and reconciliation in African Union Member States;

(viii) That any AU Member State that wishes to refer a case to the ICC may inform and seek the advice of the African Union;

(ix) That Kenya should send a letter to the United Nations Security Council requesting for deferral, in conformity with Article 16 of the Rome Statute, of the proceedings against the President and Deputy President of Kenya that would be endorsed by all African States Parties;

(x) Pursuant to this Decision, to request the ICC to postpone the trial of President Uhuru Kenyatta, scheduled for 12 November 2013 and suspend the proceedings against Deputy President William Samoei Ruto until such time as the UNSC considers the request by Kenya, supported by the AU, for deferral;

(xi) That President Uhuru Kenyatta will not appear before the ICC until such time as the concerns raised by the AU and its Member States have been adequately addressed by the UNSC and the ICC;

(xii) To convene, an Extraordinary Session, towards the end of November 2013, to review the progress made in the implementation of this Decision of the AU Assembly (Ext/Assembly/AU/Dec.1(Oct.2013)).

11. FINALLY REQUESTS the Commission to report on the implementation of this Decision to the next Ordinary Session of the Assembly in January 2014.

Bibliography

A Note About the Bibliography, Videography, Blogography and Online Resources

This study has relied upon a variety of sources, legal, academic and media, including newswire services and the UN Integrated Regional Information Network. A comprehensive online bibliographic catalogue for the ICC is available at the Peace Palace Library in The Hague, <www.ppl.nl>. Other online bibliographic sources include The Hague Justice Portal, <www.haguejusticeportal.net/>. The University of Chicago Library's online ICC bibliography, *International Criminal Court: Resources in Print and Electronic Format*, <http://www2.lib.uchicago.edu/~llou/icc.html>, has a particular focus on the early history of the Rome Statute and court up to 2003. And the ICC's own website, <www.icc-cpi.int>, is mandatory viewing if for no other reason than to see how much paperwork can be generated in an attempt to account for its billion-euros-plus expenditure to date.

A select number of scholars and commentators have taken it upon themselves to follow the ICC closely. There is a growing body of literature that has examined the history, activities and politics of the ICC. While many of the studies have been produced by legal scholars, international relations scholars and political scientists have also added considerably to the literature. William Schabas and Benjamin Schiff, among others, have both written accessible accounts of the court. In addition to this body of literature, the blogosphere has produced a number of sites that have focused on the ICC. William Schabas' blog, <humanrightsdoctorate.blogspot.com>, is interesting and objective in its criticism of the court. Other useful and sometimes questioning blogs include *Opinio Juris*, <opiniojuris.org>, and Mark Kersten's *Justice in Conflict* <www.justiceinconflict.org>. The International Criminal Law Bureau provides a useful online service, available at <www.internationallawbureau.com>. The *Lubanga Trial at the International Criminal Court* website, <www.lubangatrial.org>, is a joint project of the Open Society Justice Initiative and the IWPR. It has documented several of the ICC's glaring mistakes and legal shortcomings during a trial process that lasted several years. The Oxford Transitional Justice Research Group, based at Oxford University's Centre for Socio-Legal Studies, hosts the *ICC Observers* blog <www.iccobservers.wordpress.com>, which has sought to "provide an integrated interdisciplinary repository of news information, interviews, commentaries, and site-visit reports documenting the activities of the International Criminal Court and other major international legal tribunals". The group has published a range of research working papers focused on the ICC, <www.csls.ox.ac.uk/otjr>. It also published *Collected Essays, 2008–2010: Debating International Justice in Africa*, available at <otjr.csls.ox.ac.uk/materials/papers/122/Justice_in_Africa.pdf>.

The London-based ICC Watch provides a very sceptical perspective on the court at <www.iccwatch.org>. The *Facts about Morenogate* website, <www.article42-3.org>, also links to a blog, <comment.article42-3.org>, which is described as "[t]he real story of the International Criminal Court" and states it is dedicated to providing the full facts about the Morenogate scandal surrounding the ICC's Chief Prosecutor. The website contains a range of interesting articles and papers. The New York-based *Inner City Press*, and especially its reporter Matthew Russell Lee, have produced some very insightful, first-hand coverage of the ICC, its first Chief Prosecutor and their interaction with the UN in New York. Its blog, <innercitypress.blogspot.com>, has a number of relevant articles.

Videography

The Reckoning: The Battle for the International Criminal Court, Skylight Productions, New York, 2009.
The Court, Filmperspektive GmbH, Stuttgart, in co-production with: C-Films, SWR, NDR and ARTE, 2013.
Prosecutor, White Pine Pictures, Toronto, in co-production with the National Film Board of Canada, 2010.
In Search of International Justice, Bullfrog Films, Oley, in co-production with the Canadian Television Fund, 2009.
Ambassador Amina Mohamed – Foreign Minister, Kenya, BBC *HARDtalk*, 18 September 2013, available at <http://www.youtube.com/watch?v=8d2eUFHdVjs>.
Sir Geoffrey Nice QC – Barrister, BBC *HARDtalk*, 4 September 2012, available at <http://www.youtube.com/watch?v=MJIuK_n94TM>.
Africa and the permanent International Criminal Court – Sir Geoffrey Nice QC, Gresham College, 27 November 2012, available at <http://www.youtube.com/watch?v=IkN1A4VOV-k>.

Bibliography

Abass, Ademola, "The Competence of the Security Council to Terminate the Jurisdiction of the International Criminal Court", *Texas International Law Journal*, Volume 40, Number 2 (2005), pp. 263–97.
African Business, "Europe, Masters Behind The ICC", available at <http://www.africanbusinessmagazine.com/special-reports/sector-reports/icc-vs-africa/europe-masters-behind-the-icc>.

African Union, "Decision on the Meeting of African States Parties to the Rome Statute of the International Criminal Court (ICC)", 14 July 2009, Addis Ababa, available at <http://www.africa-union.org/root/au/Conferences/2009/july/Press%20Release%20-%20ICC.doc>.
—, "On the decisions of Pre-Trial Chamber I of the International Criminal Court (ICC) pursuant to Article 87(7) of the Rome Statute on the alleged failure by the Republic of Chad and the Republic of Malawi to comply with the cooperation requests issued by the Court with respect to the arrest and surrender of President Omar Hassan Al Bashir of the Republic of the Sudan", Addis Ababa, 9 January 2012.
Akhavan, Payam, "Beyond Impunity: Can International Criminal Justice Prevent Future Atrocities?", *American Journal of International Law*, Volume 95 (2001), pp. 7–31.
—, "The Lord's Resistance Army Case: Uganda's Submission of the First State Referral to the International Criminal Court", *American Journal of International Law*, Volume 99, Number 2 (2005), pp. 403–21.
—, "Self-Referrals Before the International Criminal Court: Are States the Villains or the Victims of Atrocities", *Criminal Law Forum*, Volume 21 (2010), pp. 103–20.
Al-Bulushi, Samar and Adam Branch, "AFRICOM and the ICC: Enforcing International Justice in Africa", *Pambazuka News*, Number 483, 27 May 2010.
Allen, Tim, *Trial Justice: The International Criminal Court and the Lord's Resistance Army*, Zed Books, London, 2006.
Alter, R. T., "International criminal law: a bittersweet year for supporters and critics of the International Criminal Court", *The International Lawyer*, Volume 37, Number 2 (2003), pp. 541–50.
Amnesty International, Library, "Africa: Uganda Concerns about the International Criminal Court Bill", 27 July 2004, available at <http://web.amnesty.org/library/Index/ENGAFR590052004?open&of=ENG-UGA>.
Andò, S., "The organization of the Court: the international campaign in support of an ICC", *Mediterranean Journal of Human Rights*, Volume 2, Number 1 (1998), pp. 159–62.
Andreasen, Scott W., "The International Criminal Court: Does the Constitution Preclude Its Ratification By the United States?", *Iowa Law Review*, Volume 85, Number 2 (2000), pp. 697–733.
Annan, Kofi, "Advocating for an International Criminal Court", *Fordham International Law Journal*, Volume 21, Number 2 (1997), pp. 363–66.
Anonymous, "The Controversial Actions of the ICC Prosecutor: a Crisis of Maturity?", The Hague Justice Portal, 15 September 2008, available at <http://www.haguejusticeportal.net/Docs/Commentaries%20PDF/Anonymous_Lubanga_EN.pdf>.
Antoniadis, Antonis and Bekou, Olympia, "The European Union and the International Criminal Court: an Awkward Symbiosis in Interesting Times", *International Criminal Law Review*, Volume 7, Number 4 (2007), pp. 621–65.
Apuuli, Kasaija Phillip, "The ICC Arrest Warrants for the Lord's Resistance Army Leaders and Peace Prospects for Northern Uganda", *Journal of International Criminal Justice*, Volume 4 (2006), pp. 179–87.

Arbour, Louise, "The need for an independent and effective prosecutor in the permanent International Criminal Court", *The Windsor Yearbook of Access to Justice*, Volume 17 (1999), pp. 207–20.

Arieff, Alexis, Margesson, Rhoda and Browne, Marjorie Ann, "International Criminal Court Cases in Africa: Status and Policy Issues", in Harry P. Milton (editor), *International Criminal Court: Policy, Status and Overview*, Nova Science, 2009.

Arsanjani, Mahnoush H., "The Rome Statute of the International Criminal Court", *American Journal of International Law*, Volume 93, Number 1 (1999), pp. 22–43.

Arsanjani, Mahnoush H. and Reisman, W. Michael, "The Law-in-Action of the International Criminal Court", *American Journal of International Law*, Volume 99, Number 2 (2005), pp. 385–403.

Austin, W. Chadwick and Kolenc, Antony Barone, "Who's afraid of the Big Bad Wolf? The International Criminal Court as a weapon of asymmetric warfare", *Vanderbilt Journal of Transnational Law*, Volume 39, Number 2 (2006).

Babiker, Mohamed Abdel Salam, "The International Criminal Court and the Darfur crimes: The dilemma of peace and supra-national criminal justice", *International Journal of African Renaissance Studies – Multi- Inter- and Transdisciplinarity*, Volume 5, Issue 1, June 2010, pp. 82–100.

Baines, E., "The haunting of Alice: Local approaches to justice and reconciliation in Northern Uganda", *International Journal of Transitional Justice*, Volume 1, Number 1 (2007), pp. 91–114.

Bass, Gary Jonathan, *Stay the Hand of Vengeance: The Politics of War Crimes Tribunals*, Princeton University Press, Princeton, 2000.

Bassiouni, M. Cherif, "Enforcing Human Rights through International Criminal Law and through an International Criminal Tribunal", in Louis Henkin and John Lawrence Hargrove (editors), *Human Rights: An Agenda for the Next Century*, American Society of International Law, Washington DC, 1994.

—, "Establishing an International Criminal Court: A Historical Survey", *Military Law Review*, Volume 149 (1995), pp. 49–63.

—, "Searching for Peace and Achieving Justice: The Need for Accountability", *Law and Contemporary Problems*, Volume 59, Number 4 (1996), pp. 9–28.

—, "From Versailles to Rwanda in 75 Years: The Need to Establish a Permanent International Criminal Court", *Harvard Human Rights Yearbook*, Volume 10 (1997), pp. 11–62.

—, "Policy Perspectives Favoring the Establishment of the International Criminal Court", *Journal of International Affairs*, Volume 52, Number 2 (1999), pp. 795–810.

—, "Negotiating the Treaty of Rome on the Establishment of the International Criminal Court", *Cornell International Law Journal*, Volume 32, Number 2 (1999), pp. 443–69.

—, "Universal Jurisdiction for International Crimes: Historical Perspectives and Contemporary Practice", *Virginia Journal of International Law*, Volume 42, Number 1 (2001), pp. 81–162.

—, (editor), *The Statute of the International Criminal Court and Related Instruments: Legislative History 1994–2000*, Transnational Publishers, Ardsley, New York, 2002.

—, "The Universal Model: The International Criminal Court" in M. Cherif Bassiouni (editor), *Post-Conflict Justice*, Transnational Publishers, Ardsley, New York, 2002, pp. 813–25.

—, "The ICC – Quo Vadis?" *Journal of International Criminal Justice*, Volume 4 (2006), pp. 421–27.

Baum, Lynne Miriam, "Pursing Justice in a Climate of Moral Outrage: An Evaluation of the Rights of the Accused in the Rome Statute of the International Criminal Court", *Wisconsin International Law Journal*, Volume 19, Number 2 (2001), pp. 197–229.

Bell, Christine, *Negotiating Justice? Human Rights and Peace Agreements*, International Council on Human Rights Policy, Geneva, 2006.

—, *On the Law of Peace: Peace Agreements and the Lex Pacificatoria*, Oxford University Press, 2008.

—, "Peace Settlements and International Law: From Lex Pacificatoria to Jus Post Bellum", Edinburgh School of Law Research paper no. 2012/16, 17 May 2012, available at *Social Science Research Network*, <http://ssrn.com/abstract=2061706> or <http://dx.doi.org/10.2139/ssrn.2061706>.

Benedetti, Fanny and Washburn, John L., "Drafting the International Criminal Court Treaty: Two Years to Rome and an Afterword on the Rome Diplomatic Conference", *Global Governance*, Volume 5 (1999), pp. 1–37.

Benedetti, Fanny, Bonneau, Karine and Washburn, John L., *Negotiating the International Criminal Court*, Martinus Nijhoff, 2013.

Benison, Audrey I., "International Criminal Tribunals: Is there a Substantive Limitation on the Treaty Power?" *Stanford Journal of International Law*, Volume 37, Number 1 (2001), pp. 75–115.

—, "War Crimes: A Human Rights Approach to a Humanitarian Law Problem at the International Criminal Court", *Georgetown Law Journal*, Volume 88 (1999), pp. 141–76.

Bergsmo, Morten, "Occasional Remarks on Certain State Concerns about the Jurisdictional Reach of the International Criminal Court, and Their Possible Implications for the Relationship between the Court and the Security Council", *Nordic Journal of International Law*, Volume 69 (2000), pp. 87–113.

Bickley, Lynn Sellers, "U.S. resistance to the International Criminal Court: is the sword mightier than the law?", *Emory International Law Review*, Volume 14, Number 1 (2000), pp. 213–76.

Bild, "Deadly Afghanistan air strike killed 142: Top secret Bundeswehr bomb video – was the truth hidden? Defence Minister Guttenberg forces German general and secretary of state to resign", 27 November 2009, available at <http://www.bild.de/news/bild-english/news/top-secret-bundeswehr-bomb-video-jung-klein-10587654.bild.html>.

Black, Tim, "The court where the West judges the Rest. The ICC metes out 'justice' to poor countries while denying them any say in their own affairs", *Spiked*, 15 March 2011, available at <http://www.spiked-online.com/site/article/10289/>.

—, "'Let's teach these darkies about the rule of law': Courtenay Griffiths, lead counsel for ex-Liberian president Charles Taylor, tells spiked about the racial bias in international criminal justice", *Spiked*, 29 May 2012, available at <http://www.spiked-online.com/site/article/12494/>.

Blakesley, Christopher L., "Obstacles to the Creation of a Permanent War Crimes Tribunal", *Fletcher Forum of World Affairs*, Volume 18 (1994), pp. 77–102.

Blanchet, C. R., "Some troubling elements in the Treaty language of the Rome Statute of the International Criminal Court", *Michigan Journal of International Law*, Volume 24, Number 2 (2003), pp. 647–62.

Blumenson, Eric D., "National Amnesties and International Justice", *Eyes on the ICC*, Volume 2, Number 1 (2005).

Boeving, James Nicholas, "Aggression, International Law, and the ICC: an Argument for the Withdrawal of Aggression from the Rome Statute", *Columbia Journal of Transnational Law*, Volume 43, Number 2 (2005), pp. 557–611.

Bohm, Robert M., "'McJustice': On the McDonaldization of Criminal Justice", *Justice Quarterly*, Volume 23, Issue 1, March 2006, pp. 127–46.

Boister, Neil, "The Exclusion of Treaty Crimes from the Jurisdiction of the Proposed International Criminal Court: Law, Pragmatism, Politics", *Journal of Armed Conflict Law*, Volume 3, Number 1 (1998), pp. 27–43.

Boldt, Martin, *Die Akte Kunduz: Der Luftangriff auf zwei Tanklaster am 4. September 2009 nahe der afghanischen Stadt Kunduz*, Grin Verlag, Munich, 2013.

Bolton, John, "Courting Danger: What's Wrong with the International Court", *The National Interest*, Number 54 (1998), pp. 60–71.

—, "The Global Prosecutors: Hunting War Criminals in the Name of Utopia", *Foreign Affairs*, Volume 78 (1999).

—, "Toward an International Criminal Court? A Debate", *Emory International Law Review*, Volume 14, Number 1 (2000), pp. 159–97.

—, "The Risks and Weaknesses of the International Criminal Court from America's Perspective", *Law and Contemporary Problems*, Volume 64, Number 1 (2001), pp. 167–80.

—, "The United States and the International Criminal Court", remarks at the Aspen Institute, Berlin, Germany, 16 September 2002, available at <http://www.state.gov/t/us/rm/13538.htm>.

—, "Courting Danger: What's Wrong with the International Criminal Court", in R. James Woolsey (editor), *The National Interest on International Law & Order*, Transaction Publishers, 2003, pp. 93–108.

—, "Signing of Article 98 Agreement of the Rome Statute: Remarks at the Romanian Foreign Ministry, Bucharest, Romania, August 1, 2002", in William Driscoll, Joseph Zompetti and Suzette Zompetti (editors), *The International Criminal Court: Global Politics and the Quest for Justice*, International Debate Education Association, 2004, pp. 158–60.

—, "The United States and the International Criminal Court: Remarks to the Federalist Society, Washington DC, November 14, 2002", in William Driscoll, Joseph Zompetti and Suzette Zompetti (editors), *The International Criminal Court: Global Politics and the Quest for Justice*, International Debate Education Association, 2004, pp. 160–69.

Bork, R. H., "Judicial Imperialism", *The Wall Street Journal*, 17 June 2003.

Bosco, David, *Rough Justice: The International Criminal Court's Battle to Fix the World, One Prosecution at a Time*, Oxford University Press USA, 2013.

Bourguignon, Michael, "The EU and the ICC: Wedding bells?", <theeuros.eu>, 6 January 2008, available at <http://www.theeuros.eu/The-EU-and-the-ICC-Wedding-bells,1109.html?lang=fr>.

Branch, Adam, "International Justice, Local Injustice: The International Criminal Court in Northern Uganda", *Dissent*, Volume 51, Number 3 (2004), pp. 22–26.

—, "The ICC should stop its African experimental investigations now", *The Monitor* (Uganda), 13 January 2005.

—, "Uganda's Civil War and the Politics of ICC Intervention", *Ethics & International Affairs*, Volume 21, Issue 2 (2007), pp. 179–98.

—, "What the ICC Review Conference can't fix", Oxford Transitional Justice Research Working Paper Series, 2010, available at <http://www.csls.ox.ac.uk/documents/AdamBranchICC_Final.pdf>.

—, *Displacing Human Rights. War and Intervention in northern Uganda*, Oxford University Press, New York, 2011.

Brown, Bartram S., "Primacy or Complementarity: Reconciling the Jurisdiction of National Courts and International Criminal Tribunals", *Yale Journal of International Law*, Volume 23 (1998).

—, "U.S. Objections to the Statute of the International Criminal Court: A Brief Response", *New York University Journal of International Law and Politics*, Volume 31, Number 4 (1999), pp. 855–91.

—, "Unilateralism, Multilateralism and the International Criminal Court", in Stewart Patrick and Shepard Forman (editors), *Multilateralism and U.S. Foreign Policy: Ambivalent Engagement*, Lynne Rienner, 2001, pp. 494–528.

Brauman, Rony, "The ICC's Bashir Indictment: Law against Peace", *World Politics Review*, 23 July 2008, available at <http://www.worldpoliticsreview.com/Article.aspx?id=2471>.

Bravin, Jess, "Justice Delayed. For Global Court, Ugandan Rebels Prove Tough Test", *The Wall Street Journal*, 8 June 2006.

Brems Knudsen, T., "Grotian Visions on Trial! The EU, the ICC and the Non-Humanitarian Intervention in Darfur", paper presented at the annual meeting of the International Studies Association Forty-eighth Annual Convention, Hilton Chicago, USA, 28 February 2007, available from <http://www.allacademic.com/meta/p180182_index.html>.

Brody, Reed, "Playing it firm, fair and smart: The EU and the ICC's indictment of Bashir", *ISS Opinion*, March 2009, p. 2, available at <http://www.iss.europa.eu/uploads/media/EU_ICC_Bashir.pdf.>.

Broomhall, Bruce, *International Justice and the International Criminal Court: Between Sovereignty and the Rule of Law*, Oxford University Press, Oxford, 2003.

—, "Toward U.S. Acceptance of the International Criminal Court", *Law and Contemporary Problems*, Volume 64, Number 1 (2001), pp. 141–51.

—, "Towards the Development of an Effective System of Universal Jurisdiction for

Crimes under International Law", *New England Law Review*, Volume 35, Number 2 (2001), pp. 399–420.

—, *Transitional Justice & The International Criminal Court*. Oxford University Press, Oxford, 2003.

Bruer-Schafer, Aline, *Der Internationale Strafgerichtshof: die Internationale Strafgerichtsbarkeit im Spannungsfeld von Recht und Politik*, Peter Lang, Frankfurt am Main, 2001.

—, Albin Eser, Giorgio Gaja, Philip Kirsch, Alain Pellet, and Bert Swart (editors), *International Criminal Law: A Commentary on the Rome Statute for an International Criminal Court*, Oxford University Press, Oxford, 2001.

Burke-White, W. W., "Protecting the Minority: A Place for Impunity? An Illustrated Survey of Amnesty Legislation, Its Conformity with International Legal Obligations, and Its Potential as a Tool for Minority-Majority Reconciliation", Harvard Law School, 2000, available at <http://www.ecmi.de/uploads/tx_lfpubdb/JEMIE03BurkeWhite30-07-01.pdf>.

Cakmak, Cenap, "Transnational Activism in World Politics and Effectiveness of a Loosely Organised Principled Global Network: The Case of the NGO Coalition for an International Criminal Court", *The International Journal of Human Rights*, Volume 12, Issue 3, June 2008, pp. 373–93.

Caldwell, Christopher, "It is best to stay out of Darfur", *Financial Times* (London), 16 December 2006.

Carpenter, Ted Galen, "No Civil Liberties at the International Criminal Court", the Cato Institute, Washington DC, 27 December 2000, available <http://www.cato.org/pub_display.php?pub_id=4416>.

Casey, Lee A., "The Case against the International Criminal Court", *Fordham International Law Journal*, Volume 25, Number 3 (2002), pp. 840–72.

Casey, Lee A. and Rivkin Jr., David R., "The International Criminal Court vs. the American People", Heritage Foundation Paper Number 1249, 5 February 1999.

—, "Court Dismissed: The ICC is a Snare and a Monstrosity - with No Standing", *National Review*, 11 November 2002.

—, "The limits of legitimacy: the Rome Statute's unlawful application to non-state parties", *Virginia Journal of International Law*, Volume 44, Number 1 (2003), pp. 63–89.

Cassese, Antonio, "Flawed International Justice for Sudan", Project Syndicate, n.d., available at <http://www.project-syndicate.org/commentary/cassese4short/English>.

—, "Is the ICC Still Having Teething Problems?", *Journal of International Criminal Justice*, Volume 4 (2006), pp. 434–441.

—, "The International Criminal Court five Years on Andante or Moderato?", in Carsten Stahn and Göran Sluiter (editors), *The Emerging Practice of the International Criminal Court*, Nijhoff, 2009.

—, *Realizing Utopia: The Future of International Law*, Oxford University Press, Oxford, 2012.

Cassese, Antonio *et al.* (editors), *The Rome Statute of the International Criminal Court – A Commentary*, Volume I and II, Oxford University Press, Oxford, 2002.

Castillo, Pablo, "Rethinking Deterrence: The International Criminal Court in Sudan", *UNISCI Discussion Papers*, Number 13 (January 2007), pp. 167–84.

Cayley, Andrew T., "The Prosecutor's Strategy in Seeking the Arrest of Sudanese President Al Bashir on Charges of Genocide", *Journal of International Criminal Justice*, Volume 6, Number 5 (2008), pp. 829–40, available at Social Science Research Network, <http://ssrn.com/abstract=1360573 or doi:mqn071>.

Chandler, David, "Making and breaking the rules. The USA v Europe clash over the new International Criminal Court is less about legalities than about competing interests", *Spiked*, 4 July 2002, available at <http://www.spiked-online.com/Articles/00000006D96E.htm>.

—, "Limits of the ICC", *Spiked*, 28 August 2002, available at <http://www.spiked-online.com/site/article/8386/>.

—, "The loaded scales of 'international justice'. Trials and tribulations at the International Criminal Court", *Spiked*, 29 June 2004, available at <http://www.spiked-online.com/Articles/0000000CA5B1.htm>.

—, "International tribunals: not fit for purpose?", *Spiked*, 6 June 2007, available at <http://www.spiked-online.com/index.php?/site/article/3447/>.

—, "Born Posthumously: Rethinking the Shared Characteristics of the ICC and R2P", *Finnish Yearbook of International Law*, Volume 21, 2010.

Clark, Phil, "Hybridity, Holism, and 'Traditional' Justice: The Case of Gacaca Courts in Post-Genocide Rwanda", Centre for Socio-Legal Studies, University of Oxford, 2007.

—, "Law, Politics and Pragmatism: The ICC and Case Selection in the Democratic Republic of Congo and Uganda", in Nicholas Waddell and Phil Clark (editors), *Courting Conflict? Justice, Peace and the ICC in Africa*, Royal African Society, London, March 2008.

Clark, Roger S., "Creating a statute for the International Criminal Court: a jurisdictional quandary", *Suffolk Transnational Law Review*, Volume 22, Number 2 (1999), pp. 461–80.

—, "Rethinking Aggression as a Crime and Formulating Its Elements: The Final Work-Product of the Preparatory Commission for the International Criminal Court", *Leiden Journal of International Law*, Volume 15, Number 4 (2002), pp. 859–90.

Clarke, Kamari Maxine, *Fictions of Justice. The International Criminal Court and the Challenge of Legal Pluralism in Sub-Saharan Africa*, Cambridge University Press, Cambridge, 2009.

Clifford, Lisa, "Uganda: ICC Policy under Scrutiny", Institute for War & Peace Reporting, 13 April 2007, available at <www.iwpr.net/?p=acr&s=f&o=334879&apc_state=henh>.

—, "ICC Risks Losing the Plot in Congo", Institute for War & Peace Reporting, 21 November 2008, available at <http://www.iwpr.net/?p=acr&s=f&o=347941&apc_state=heniacr200811>.

—, "Ocampo Underwhelms in Landmark Trial", Institute for War & Peace Reporting, 29 January 2009, available at <http://www.iwpr.net/?p=acr&s=f&o=349621&apc_state=heniacr2009>.

Cobban, Helena, "Think Again: International Courts", *Foreign Policy*, February 2006,

available at <http://www.foreignpolicy.com/articles/2006/02/17/think_again_international_courts>.
—, "Moreno-Ocampo and the future of the ICC", *Just World News*, 14 December 2008, available at <http://justworldnews.com/?p=2757>.
Cogan, Jacob Katz, "International Criminal Courts and Fair Trials: Difficulties and Prospects", *Yale Journal of International Law*, Volume 27 (Winter 2002).
—, "The Problem of Obtaining Evidence for International Criminal Courts", *Human Rights Quarterly*, Volume 22, Number 2 (2000), pp. 404–27.
Condorelli, L. and Villalpando, S., "Can the Security Council extend the ICC's jurisdiction", in Antonio Cassese, Paola Gaeta and John R. W. D. Jones (editors), *The Rome Statute of the International Criminal Court: a commentary*, Volume 1 (2002), pp. 571–82.
—, "Referral and deferral by the Security Council", in Antonio Cassese, Paola Gaeta and John R. W. D. Jones (editors), *The Rome Statute of the International Criminal Court: a commentary*, Volume 1 (2002), pp. 627–64.
Conso, G., "The Basic Reasons for US Hostility to the ICC in Light of the Negotiating History of the Rome Statute", *Journal of International Criminal Justice*, Volume 3, Number 2 (2005), pp. 314–22.
Constantine, Gus, "Scholar disputes 'genocide' term for Darfur", *The Washington Times*, 11 June 2009, available at < http://www.washingtontimes.com/news/2009/jun/11/scholar-disputes-genocide-term-for-darfur-region/?page=all>.
Corrigan, Patrick, "Why the ICC Must Stop Impeding Juba Process", *Monitor* (Kampala), 27 July 2007, available at <http://www.globalpolicy.org/component/content/article/164/28641.html>.
Council on Foreign Relations, "Africa and the International Criminal Court", New York, 17 November 2006.
Crawford, Neta, *Accountability for Killing: Moral Responsibility for Collateral Damage in America's Post-9/11 Wars*, Oxford University Press USA, 2013.
Crilly, Rob, "Darfur and the International Criminal Court", *Huffington Post*, 9 February 2009, available at <http://www.huffingtonpost.com/rob-crilly/darfur-and-the-internatio_b_165095.html>.
Crossette, Barbara, "World Criminal Court Having Painful Birth", *New York Times*, 13 August 1997.
Cryer, Robert, *Prosecuting International Crimes: Selectivity and the International Criminal Law Regime*, Cambridge University Press, Cambridge, 2005.
Curabba, Nicholas S., *The Rome Statute of the International Criminal Court: Selected Legal and Constitutional Issues*, Congressional Research Service, Washington DC, 22 February 1999.
Currie, Robert J., "Abducted Fugitives before the International Criminal Court: Problems and Prospects", *Criminal Law Forum*, Volume 18, Numbers 3–4 (2007).
Danilenko, Gennady, "The Statute of the International Criminal Court and third states", *Michigan Journal of International Law*, Volume 21, Number 3 (2000), pp. 445–94.

Danner, Allison Marston, "Navigating Law and Politics: The Prosecutor of the International Criminal Court and the U.S. Independent Counsel", *Stanford Law Review*, Volume 55 (2003).

Darnstädt, Thomas, Zuber, Helene and Puhl, Jan, "A Dangerous Luxury. The International Criminal Court's Dream of Global Justice", *Der Spiegel International*, 14 January 2009, available at <http://www.spiegel.de/international/world/0,1518,601258-2,00.html>.

David, Marcella, "Grotius Repudiated: The American Objections to the International Criminal Court and the Commitment to International Law", *Michigan Journal of International Law*, Volume 20, Number 2 (1999), pp. 337–412.

Davies, Thomas E., "How the Rome Statute Weakens the International Prohibition on Incitement to Genocide", *Harvard Human Rights Journal*, Volume 22, Number 2 (2009), pp. 245–70.

Dawson, Grant M., "Defining Substantive Crimes within the Subject Matter Jurisdiction of the International Criminal Court: What Is the Crime of Aggression?", *New York Law School Journal of International and Comparative Law*, Volume 19, Number 3 (2000), pp. 413–52.

de Waal, Alex, "Sudan and the International Criminal Court: a guide to the controversy", openDemocracy, 14 July 2008, available at <http://www.opendemocracy.net/article/sudan-and-the-international-criminal-court-a-guide-to-the-controversy>.

—, "Moreno Ocampo's Coup de Theatre", *Making Sense of Darfur*, 29 July 2008, available at <http://blogs.ssrc.org/darfur/2008/07/29/moreno-ocampos-coup-de-theatre/>.

—, "A Critique of the Public Application by the Chief Prosecutor of the ICC for an Arrest Warrant against Sudanese President Omar al Bashir", *Making Sense of Darfur*, Social Science Research Council, 25 January 2009, available at < http://blogs.ssrc.org/darfur/wp-content/uploads/2009/01/bashir-public-application-critique-d6-250109.pdf>

Deen-Racsmony, Zsuzsanna, "The Nationality of the Offender and the Jurisdiction of the International Criminal Court", *American Journal of International Law*, Volume 95, Number 3 (2001), pp. 606–23.

Dempsey, Gary T., "Reasonable Doubt: The Case against the Proposed International Criminal Court", the Cato Institute, Washington DC, 16 July 1998, available at <http://www.cato.org/pub_display.php?pub_id=1170>.

—, "Courting Disaster", the Cato Institute, Washington DC, 19 August 1998, available at <http://www.cato.org/pub_display.php?pub_id=5836>.

—, "America Leads by Leaving the ICC", the Cato Institute, Washington DC, 10 May 2002, available at <http://www.cato.org/pub_display.php?pub_id=3467>.

Der Spiegel, "'A Dangerous Luxury'. The International Criminal Court's Dream of Global Justice", 14 January 2009.

—, "Dozens Dead in Afghanistan UN Calls for Investigation into Air Strikes", 4 September 2009, available at <http://www.spiegel.de/international/world/0,1518,647084,00.html>.

—, "Aftermath of Afghan Air Strike Germany Pledges Full Probe as Pressure Mounts on Defense Minister", 7 September 2009, available at <http://www.spiegel.de/international/world/0,1518,647398,00.html>.

—, "The End of Innocence in Afghanistan 'The German Air Strike Has Changed Everything'", 14 September 2009, available at <http://www.spiegel.de/international/world/0,1518,648925,00.html>.

—, "Civilian Deaths in Afghanistan Did the German Government Misinform the Country?", 26 November 2009, available at <http://www.spiegel.de/international/germany/0,1518,663696,00.html>.

—, "Civilian Casualties in Afghanistan Germany's Top Soldier Resigns over Air Strike Accusations", 26 November 2009, available at <http://www.spiegel.de/international/germany/0,1518,663582,00.html>.

—, "Merkel Cabinet Reshuffle Minister Jung Resigns amid Afghanistan Airstrike Scandal", 27 November 2009, available at <http://www.spiegel.de/international/germany/0,1518,663820,00.html>.

—, "How Much Did The Chancellor Know? Pressure Mounts on Merkel Over Afghan Air Raid Debacle", 30 November 2009, available at <http://www.spiegel.de/international/germany/0,1518,664353,00.html>.

—, "Bundestag Debate on Afghanistan Defense Minister Calls Kunduz Air Strike 'Inappropriate'", 4 December 2009, available at <http://www.spiegel.de/international/germany/0,1518,665132,00.html>.

—, "Guilt and Compensation Did German Defense Minister Know More than He Let On?", 7 December 2009, available at <http://www.spiegel.de/international/germany/0,1518,665680,00.html>.

—, "Letter from Berlin. Details on Afghanistan Bombing Have Merkel on the Defensive", 14 December 2009, available at <http://www.spiegel.de/international/germany/0,1518,667011,00.html>.

—, "Interview with Eyewitness to Kunduz Bombing 'It Looked Like the Ground Was Spitting Up Fire'", 15 December 2009, available at <http://www.spiegel.de/international/world/0,1518,667231,00.html>

—, "The Dilemma of the Kunduz Bombing How Much Is a Human Life Worth?", 15 December 2009, available at <http://www.spiegel.de/international/world/0,1518,667123,00.html>.

—, "SPIEGEL Exclusive How ISAF Sought to Play Down the German Air Strike", 16 December 2009, available at <http://www.spiegel.de/international/world/0,1518,667476,00.html>.

—, "The World from Berlin 'The Public Wants to Know Who Lied' About Kunduz Bombing", 17 December 2009, available at <http://www.spiegel.de/international/germany/0,1518,667733,00.html>.

—, "NATO's Secret Findings: Kunduz Affair Report Puts German Defense Minister Under Pressure", 19 January 2010, available at <http://www.spiegel.de/international/germany/nato-s-secret-findings-kunduz-affair-report-puts-german-defense-minister-under-pressure-a-672468.html>.

—, "Deadly Bombing in Kunduz: German Army Withheld Information from US Pilots", 1 February 2010, available at <http://www.spiegel.de/international/germany/deadly-bombing-in-kunduz-german-army-withheld-information-from-us-pilots-a-675229.html>.

—, "Testimony to Parliamentary Inquiry: German Officer Defends Controversial Afghanistan Air Strike", 10 February 2010, available at <http://www.spiegel.de/international/germany/a-677109.html>.

—, "The World from Berlin: 'New Evaluation on Afghanistan Long Overdue'", 11 February 2010, available at <http://www.spiegel.de/international/germany/the-world-from-berlin-new-evaluation-on-afghanistan-long-overdue-a-677289.html>.

—, "Kunduz Bombing in Afghanistan: German Defense Ministry Sought to Obscure the Truth", 18 March 2010, available at <http://www.spiegel.de/international/germany/kunduz-bombing-in-afghanistan-german-defense-ministry-sought-to-obscure-the-truth-a-684411.html>.

—, "Civilian Deaths in Afghanistan Germany Clears Way to Compensate Kunduz Bombing Victims", 10 May 2010, available at <http://www.spiegel.de/international/germany/0,1518,693964,00.html>.

—, "Aftermath of an Afghanistan Tragedy Germany to Pay $500,000 for Civilian Bombing Victims", 6 August 2010, available at <http://www.spiegel.de/international/germany/0,1518,710439,00.html>.

—, "Aftermath of a Deadly Airstrike Misguided Esprit de Corps Lets Officer Off the Hook", 20 August 2010, available at <http://www.spiegel.de/international/germany/0,1518,712843,00.html>.

—, "Kunduz Bombing Victim 'The Germans Lied to All of Us'", 30 August 2010, available at <http://www.spiegel.de/international/world/0,1518,714552,00.html>.

—, "Slow Wheels of Justice: The ICC's Disappointing Track Record", 14 December 2011, available at <http://www.spiegel.de/international/world/slow-wheels-of-justice-the-icc-s-disappointing-track-record-a-803796.html>.

Deutsche Welle, "German court to rule on Kunduz airstrike", 20 March 2013, available at <http://www.dw.de/german-court-to-rule-on-kunduz-airstrike/a-16680014>.

Diaz, Pablo Castillo, "The ICC in Northern Uganda: Peace First, Justice Later?", *Eyes on the ICC*, Volume 2, Number 1 (2005).

Dicker, Richard, "Issues facing the International Criminal Court's Preparatory Commission", *Cornell International Law Journal*, Volume 32, Number 3 (1999), pp. 471–75.

—, "The Court of Last Resort", *Foreign Policy*, 29 June 2012, available at <http://www.foreignpolicy.com/articles/2012/06/29/ICC_the_court_of_last_resort?page=full>.

Diehl, D., "Zur Einstellung des Ermittlungsverfahrens gegen Oberst Klein und Hauptfeldwebel Wilhelm durch die Bundesanwaltschaft", *BOFAXE* Nr. 343D, Institut für Friedenssicherungsrecht und Humanitäres Völkerrecht, Ruhr University, 11 May 2010.

Dolan, Chris, "Imposed Justice and the need for Sustainable Peace in Uganda", Refugee Law Project, 18 July 2008, available at <http://www.beyondjuba.org/Conference_presentations/Imposed_Justice_and%20the_need_for_Sustainable_Peace_in_Uganda.pdf>.

Doria, José, "The ICC and the Peace vs. Justice Dilemma", *International Studies Journal*, Volume 5, Number 1 (2008), pp. 1–76.

Dowd, Alan W., "ICC: A Well-Intentioned but Flawed Court", *World Politics Review*, 1 July 2008, available at <http://www.worldpoliticsreview.com/article.aspx?id=2367>.

Dowden, Richard, "ICC in the Dock", *Prospect*, London, May 2007, available at <http://www.prospectmagazine.co.uk/2007/05/iccinthedock/>.

du Plessis, Max and Gevers, Christopher, "Darfur Goes to the International Criminal Court (Perhaps)", *African Security Review*, Institute for Security Studies, Tshwane (Pretoria), Volume 14, Number 2 (2005).

du Plessis, Max and Ford, Jolyon (editors), *Unable or Unwilling? Case Studies on domestic implementation of the ICC Statute in selected African Countries*, Institute for Security Studies, Tshwane (Pretoria), March 2008, available at <http://www.issafrica.org/dynamic/administration/file_manager/file_links/MONO141FULL.PDF?link_id=3&slink_id=5725&link_type=12&slink_type=13&tmpl_id=3>.

Dugard, John, "Obstacles in the Way of an International Criminal Court", *The Cambridge Law Journal*, Volume 56 (1997), pp. 329–42.

Dunn, Kevin C., "Uganda: The Lord's Resistance Army", in Kevin C. Dunn and Morten Bøås (editors), *African Guerrillas: Raging Against the Machine*, Lynne Rienner Publishers, Boulder CO, 2007, pp.131–49.

Durham, Helen, "The International Criminal Court and State Sovereignty", in Linda Hancock and Carolyn O'Brien (editors), *Rewriting Rights in Europe*, Ashgate Publishing, Aldershot, 2000, pp. 169–90.

Economist, The, "A Dilemma Over Darfur: Calculating the Consequences of Indicting Sudan's President, Omar al-Bashir, for Genocide and More", 15 July 2008, available at <http://www.economist.com/world/ international/displaystory.cfm?story_id=11737170>.

—, "Dim prospects. The International Criminal Court loses credibility and co-operation in Africa", 17 February 2011, available at <http://www.economist.com/node/18176088>.

—, "Cosy club or sword of righteousness?", 26 November 2011, available at <http://www.economist.com/node/21540230?zid=317&ah=8a47fc455a44945580198768fad0fa41>.

Edwards, George E., "International Human Rights Law Challenges to the New International Criminal Court: The Search and Seizure Rights to Privacy", *Yale Journal of International Law*, Volume 26, Number 2 (2001), pp. 323–412.

Ekeno, Augustine, *The International Criminal Court and African Conflicts: Transitional Justice in Kenya after the 2007/8 Post-Election Violence*, Lambert Academic Publishing, 2013.

Essoungou, André-Michel, "Uganda. Justice or Peace?", *The International Herald Tribune*, 21–22 April 2007.

European Center for Constitutional and Human Rights, *Stellungnahme zur strafrechtlichen Verantwortlichkeit im Fall Kundus*, 10 June 2010.

—, "German Air Strike near Kunduz – A Year After. Evaluation of judicial reactions and further information", 30 August 2010, available at <http://www.humanrightsblog.org/reports/kunduz.pdf>.

European Commission, "The International Criminal Court & the fight against impunity", available at <http://ec.europa.eu/external_relations/human_rights/icc/index_en.htm>.
—, "The Cotonou Agreement", available at <http://ec.europa.eu/development/geographical/cotonouintro_en.cfm>.
European Union, "International Criminal Court", available at <http://www.europa-eu-un.org/articles/ articleslist_t35_en.htm>.
—, "EU Presidency declaration on the EU Common Position on the ICC", European Union, Ref: CL03-232EN, Brussels, 24 June 2003, available at < http://www.europa-eu-un.org/articles/en/article_2475_en.htm>.
—, "Action Plan to Follow-up on the Common Position on the ICC", 4 February 2004, available at <www.consilium.europa.eu/uedocs/cmsUpload/ICC48EN.pdf>.
—, *The European Union and the International Court*, Council of the European Union, General Secretariat of the Council, Brussels, November 2007.
—, "The European Union and the International Criminal Court", February 2008, General Secretariat of the Council, Brussels available at <http://www.consilium.europa.eu/uedocs/cmsUpload/ICC_internet08.pdf>.
—, "Security arrangements for the protection of classified information exchanged between the EU and the ICC", Council of the EU, Brussels, 15 April 2008 (8349/1/08 REV 1).
—, "The Relationship between the EU Institutions and the ICC", Speech by Fernando Valenzuela, Head of the Delegation of the European Commission to the United Nations, 19 May 2009, New York, available at <http://www.europa-eu-un.org/articles/en/article_8743_en.htm>.
Fernandez de Gurmendi, Silvia A., "The Working Group on Aggression at the Preparatory Commission for the International Criminal Court", *Fordham International Law Journal*, Volume 25, Number 3 (2002), pp. 589–605.
Fichtelberg, Aaron, "The International Criminal Court and the Ethics of Selective Justice", in Beth A. Griech-Polelle (editor), *The Nuremberg War Crimes Trial and Its Policy Consequences Today*, Nomos, 2009.
Fletcher, G. P., "Against Universal Jurisdiction", *Journal of International Criminal Justice*, Volume 1 (2003), pp. 580–84.
Flint, Julie and de Waal, Alex, "Justice Off Course in Darfur", *Washington Post*, 28 June 2008, available at <http://www.washingtonpost.com/wp-dyn/content/article/2008/06/27/AR2008062702632_pf.html>.
—, "This Prosecution Will Endanger the People We Wish to Defend in Sudan", *The Observer*, 13 July 2008, available at <http://www.guardian.co.uk/world/2008/jul/13/sudan.humanrights>.
—, "Case Closed: A Prosecutor without Borders", *World Affairs*, Spring 2009, available at <http://www.worldaffairsjournal.org/2009%20-%20Spring/full-DeWaalFlint.html>.
Foley, Conor, "Darfur: a disaster for justice", *The Guardian*, 20 April 2009, available at <http://www.guardian.co.uk/commentisfree/2009/apr/20/sudan-war-crimes>.
Foundation for Law, Justice and Society, in collaboration with the Centre for Socio-Legal Studies, University of Oxford, *Collected Essays, 2008–2010: Debating International Justice in Africa*, Oxford, 2010.

Frantzman, Seth, "Terra Incognita: Strange justice: The ICC, Europe and the world", *The Jerusalem Post*, 22 September 2009, available at <http://www.jpost.com /servlet/ Satellite?cid=1253627541039&pagename=JPArticle%2FShowFull>.

Frye, Alton *et al.*, *Toward an International Criminal Court?: Three Options Presented as Presidential Speeches*, Council on Foreign Relations, New York, 1999.

Funk, T. Markus, *Victims' Rights and Advocacy at the International Criminal Court*, Oxford University Press, USA, 2010.

Gaeta, Paola, "The Defence of Superior Orders: The Statute of the International Criminal Court versus Customary International Law", *European Journal of International Law*, Volume 10 (1999).

—, "Is the Practice of 'Self-Referrals' a Sound Start for the ICC?", *Journal of International Criminal Justice*, Volume 2, Number 4 (2004), pp. 949–52.

Galbraith, J., "The Bush administration's response to the International Criminal Court", *Berkeley Journal of International Law*, Volume 21, Number 3 (2003), pp. 683–702.

Gallavin, Chris, "The Security Council and the ICC: Delineating the Scope of Security Council Referrals and Deferrals", *New Zealand Armed Forces Law Review*, Volume 5 (2005), pp. 19–39.

Gargiulo, P., "The controversial relationship between the International Criminal Court and the Security Council", in Flavia Lattanzi and William A. Schabas (editors), *Essays on the Rome Statute of the International Criminal Court*, Volume 1, 1999.

Gavron, Jessica, "Amnesties in the Light of Developments in International Law and the Establishment of the International Criminal Court", *International & Comparative Law Quarterly*, Volume 51, Number 1 (2002), pp. 91–117.

Geiger, Rudolf, "The German Border Guard Cases and International Human Rights", *European Journal of International Law*, Volume 9 (1998).

Geis, Jacqueline and Mundt, Alex, *When to Indict? The Impact of Timing International Criminal Indictments on Peace Processes and Humanitarian Action*, the Brookings Institution-University of Bern Project on Internal Displacement, paper to the World Humanitarian Studies Conference, Groningen, the Netherlands, February 2009, available at <http://reliefweb.int/rw/RWFiles2009.nsf/FilesByRWDocUnidFilename/ RWST-7RAQ9A-full_report.pdf/$File/full_report.pdf>.

Gibney, Mark, "The International Criminal Court", *Human Rights Human Welfare*, an online journal published through the Josef Korbel School of International Studies, University of Denver, 4 May 2009, available at <http://www.hrhw.org/2009/05/ editors-introduction-may-2009.html>.

Ginsberg, Tom, "The Clash of Commitments at the International Criminal Court", *Chicago Journal of International Law*, Public Law Working Paper Number 251, Center on Law and Globalization Research Paper No. 09-03, University of Chicago, 18 November 2008.

Giry, Stéphanie, "A Losing Strategy on War Crimes", *The International Herald Tribune*, 12–13 February 2005.

Glassborow, Katy, "DRC: ICC Investigative Strategy Under Fire", Institute for War & Peace Reporting, 17 October 2008, available at <http://www.ictj.org/en/news/ coverage/article/2075.html>.

Glasius, Marlies, "How Activists Shaped the Court", *Crimes of War Project*, December 2003, available at <http://www.crimesofwar.org/print/icc/icc-glasius-print.html>.
—, *The International Criminal Court: A Global Civil Society Achievement*, Routledge, London, 2006.
—, "What is global justice and who is it for? The ICC's first five years", Opendemocracy, 22 July 2008, available at <http://www.opendemocracy.net/article/globalisation/international_justice/the-iccs-first-five-years>.
Goldsmith, Jack, "The Self-Defeating International Criminal Court", *The University of Chicago Law Review*, Volume 70, Number 1 (2003).
Goldstone, Richard, "The role of the United Nations in the prosecution of international war criminals", *Washington University Journal of Law and Policy*, Volume 5 (2001), pp. 119–27.
Goldstone, Richard and Fritz, Nicole, "In the Interests of Justice and the Independent Referral: The International Criminal Court Prosecutor's Unprecedented Power", *Leiden Journal of International Law*, Volume 13 (2000).
Gowlland-Debbas, Vera, "The Relationship Between the Security Council and the Projected International Criminal Court", *Journal of Armed Conflict Law*, June 1998, pp. 97–119.
Griffiths, Courtenay, "The Politics Of International Criminal Law", *New African*, March 2012, available at <http://www.newafricanmagazine.com/special-reports/sector-reports/icc-vs-africa/the-politics-of-international-criminal-law>.
—, "The International Criminal Court is hurting Africa", *The Daily Telegraph*, 3 July 2012, available at <http://www.telegraph.co.uk/news/worldnews/africaandindianocean/kenya/9373188/The-International-Criminal-Court-is-hurting-Africa.html>.
Groenleer, Martijn and van Schaik, Louise G., "United we Stand?: the European Union's International Actorness in the Cases of the International Criminal Court and the Kyoto Protocol", *Journal of Common Market Studies*, Volume 45, Number 5 (2007), pp. 969–98.
Groenleer, Martijn and Rijks, David, "The European Union and the International Criminal Court: The Politics of International Justice", in K. Jørgensen (editor), *The European Union and International Organizations*, Routledge, London, 2009.
Grono, Nick, "The Role of the ICC in African Peace Processes: Mutually Reinforcing or Mutually Exclusive?", Institute for Public Policy Research, 28 November 2006.
Grono, Nick and O'Brien, A., "Justice in Conflict? The ICC and Peace Processes", in Nicholas Waddell and Phil Clark (editors), *Courting Conflict? Justice, Peace and the ICC in Africa*, Royal African Society, 2008.
Guardian, The, "5 things Fatou Bensouda should do at the ICC", 14 June 2012, available at <http://www.guardian.co.uk/law/2012/jun/14/fatou-bensouda-international-criminal-court1>.
Guffey-Landers, Nancy E., "Establishing an International Criminal Court: Will It Do Justice?", *Maryland Journal of International Law and Trade*, Volume 20 (1996), pp. 199–234.
Gurule, Jimmy, "United States opposition to the 1998 Rome Statute establishing an International Criminal Court: is the court's jurisdiction truly complementary to

national criminal jurisdictions?", *Cornell International Law Journal*, Volume 35, Number 1 (2001).

Gustafson, Carrie, "International Criminal Courts: Some Dissident Views on the Continuation of War by Penal Means", *Houston Journal of International Law*, Volume 21 (1998).

Hafner, Gerhard, "The Issue of Reservations and Declarations to the Rome Statute of the International Criminal Court", in Marcelo G. Kohen (editor), in *Promoting Justice, Human Rights and Conflict Resolution through International Law*, Nijhoff, 2007.

Hajar, Lisa, "Alternatives to an International Criminal Court", *Middle East Report*, Middle East Research and Information Project, Summer 1998.

Halperin, Morton and Dempsey, Gary, "Is the Permanent War-Crimes Tribunal Worthy of U.S. Support?", *Insight on the News*, September 1998.

Hannan, Daniel, "The International Criminal Court is a threat to democracy", *The Daily Telegraph* blog, 16 July 2008, available at <http://blogs.telegraph.co.uk/news/danielhannan/4628251/The_International_Criminal_Court_is_a_threat_to_democracy/>.

—, "Americans can now be tried by the International Criminal Court", *The Daily Telegraph* blog, 6 March 2009, available at <http://blogs.telegraph.co.uk/news/danielhannan/9105767/Americans_can_now_be_tried_by_the_International_Criminal_Court/>.

Hansberry, Heidi L., "Too Much of a Good Thing in Lubanga and Haradinaj: The Danger of Expediency in International Criminal Trials", *Northwestern Journal of International Human Rights*, Volume 9, Issue 3 (2011), available at <http://www.law.northwestern.edu/journals/jihr/v9/n3/6/Hansberry.pdf>.

Harlacher, Thomas, "Traditional Ways of Coping with Consequences of Traumatic Stress in Acholiland. Northern Ugandan ethnography from a Western psychological perspective", Intersoft Business Services Ltd., Kampala, 2006, available at <http://ethesis.unifr.ch/theses/downloads.php?file=HarlacherT.pdf>.

Harrelson-Stephens, Julie and Callaway, Rhonda L., "'The Empire Strikes Back': The US Assault on the International Human Rights Regime", *Human Rights Review*, Volume 10, Number 3 (2009).

Hayner, Priscilla, *Unspeakable Truths: Facing the Challenge of Truth Commissions*, Routledge, New York, 2002.

Heinsch, Robert, "How to achieve Fair and Expeditious Trial Proceedings before the ICC: is it Time for a More Judge-dominated Approach?", in Carsten Stahn and Göran Sluiter (editors), *The Emerging Practice of the International Criminal Court*, Nijhoff, 2009.

Heller, Kevin and Simpson, Gerry (editors), *The Hidden Histories of War Crimes Trials*, Oxford University Press, 2013.

Helms, Jesse, "We Must Slay This Monster: Voting Against the International Criminal Court Is Not Enough. The U.S. Should Try to Bring It Down", *Financial Times* (London), 31 July 1998.

Hoile, David, *Darfur: The Road to Peace*. European-Sudanese Public Affairs Council, London 2008.
—, *The International Criminal Court: Europe's Guantánamo Bay?*, Africa Research Centre, 2010.
—, "ICC Vs Africa. Is The ICC Fit For Purpose?", *New African*, March 2012, available at <http://www.newafricanmagazine.com/special-reports/sector-reports/icc-vs-africa>.
—, "Court Rise, Enter Your Honours!", *New African*, March 2012, available at <http://www.newafricanmagazine.com/special-reports/sector-reports/icc-vs-africa/court-rise-enter-your-honours>.
Hovil, Lucy, "Challenging International Justice: The Initial Years of the International Criminal Court's Intervention in Uganda", *Stability: International Journal of Security & Development*, Volume 2, Number 1 (2013).
Hovil, Lucy, and Okello, M. C., "Only peace can restore the confidence of the displaced": update on the implementation of the recommendations made by the UN Secretary General's Representative on internally displaced persons following his visit to Uganda, Internal Displacement Monitoring Centre/Norwegian Refugee Council Geneva, 2006.
Human Rights Watch, *World Report 1999*, Special Issues and Campaigns, "The International Criminal Court", including section on NGO role, available at <http://www.hrw.org/worldreport99/special/icc.html>.
—, "ICC: Investigate All Sides in Uganda Chance for Impartial ICC Investigation into Serious Crimes a Welcome Step", Human Rights Watch, New York, February 2004, available at <http://www.hrw.org/de/news/2004/02/04/icc-investigate-all-sides-uganda>.
—, "Courting History. The Landmark International Criminal Court's First Years", New York, July 2008, available at < http://www.hrw.org/en/reports/2008/07/10/courting-history>, pp. 184–91.
—, "Human Rights Watch Memorandum for the Tenth Session of the International Criminal Court Assembly of States Parties", November 2011, available at <http://www.hrw.org/sites/default/files/related_material/2011_Memo_tenth_%20session_ASP.pdf>.
—, *Turning Rhetoric Into Reality: Accountability for Serious International Crimes in Côte d'Ivoire*, 4 April 2013, available at <http://www.hrw.org/node/114480>.
Hunt, D., "The International Criminal Court: high hopes, creative ambiguity and an unfortunate mistrust in international judges", *Journal of International Criminal Justice*, Volume 2, Number 1 (2004), pp. 56–70.
Huyse, L. and Salter, M., *Traditional Justice and Reconciliation after Violent Conflict: Learning from African Experiences*, Stockholm International Institute for Democracy and Electoral Assistance, Stockholm, 2008.
ICC Watch, "New Group calls for police to investigate International Criminal Court Prosecutor", 8 December 2008, available at <http://www.iccwatch.org/pressrelease_dec08.html>.
—, "ICC Prosecutor Accused of Child Soldier Hypocrisy", 25 February 2009, available at <http://www.iccwatch.org/pdf/Press%20Release%2025Feb09.pdf>.

—, "Sudan Applauded for Standing up to ICC", 4 March 2009.
—, "Latest ICC Report reveals that Court is under European and Western Control", 23 June 2009.
—, "Lubanga Trial casts doubt over ICC's Capacity to provide Fair Trials", 2 July 2009.
—, "Why Won't the ICC Move Against Tony Blair on War Crimes?", 4 February 2010.
—, "ICC Echoes discredited Neo-Con Darfur 'Genocide' allegations against Sudan", 11 February 2010.
—, "ICC in New Threat to Human Rights. Chief Prosecutor wants to limit freedom of speech", 19 February 2010.
—, "The ICC: Half a Billion Euros, For What?", 3 March 2010.
—, "Why is Botswana behaving as a European Puppet?", 19 March 2010.
—, "ICC Chief Prosecutor challenged to account for 'partisan' refusal to take action against Museveni regime", 10 June 2010.
—, "Anti-colonialist group celebrates decision not to sack 'Buffoon' ICC Chief Prosecutor", 11 June 2010.
—, "ICC Conference wants jurisdiction over Wars of Aggression...except for members of UN Security Council!", 17 June 2010.
—, "Ocampo goes, a corrupt & incompetent court remains", 15 August 2012.
—, "Change of ICC Chief Prosecutor changes nothing", 1 September 2012.
—, "New ICC Prosecutor repeats old Prosecutor's mistakes", 17 January 2013.
Ierace, Mark, "Complexities in prosecuting international crimes: the ICC Libyan warrants", in Gideon Boas, William A. Schabas and Michael P. Scharf (editors), *International Criminal Justice: Legitimacy and Coherence*, Edward Elgar Publishing, 2012.
Igwe, Chikeziri Sam, "The ICC's favourite Customer: Africa and International Criminal Law", *Comparative and International Law Journal of Southern Africa*, Volume 41, Number 2 (2008), pp. 294–323.
Iijun, Y., "Some Critical Remarks on the Rome Statute of the International Criminal Court", *Chinese Journal of International Law*, Volume 2 (2003), pp. 599–622.
Inner City Press, "At UN, Doubts Grow of ICC's Moreno-Ocampo, on Lubanga and Uganda Abuses", 16 September 2008, available at <http://www.innercitypress.com/icc3ocampo091608.html>.
—, "As Indictment of Bashir Arises at UN, Moreno-Ocampo Accused of Ego and Errors", 22 September 2008, available at <http://www.innercitypress.com/icc4ocampo092208.html>.
—, "At UN, Ocampo Turns O-Kafka, Threatens Any Denier With ICC Prosecution, Sri Lanka Silence", 4 December 2009, available at <http://www.innercitypress.com/icc1okafka120409.html>.
—, "For ICC, France Offered to Support Unqualified Judge Quid Pro Quo for Cathala", 29 October 2011, available at <http://www.innercitypress.com/icc1cathala102911.html>.
—, "French Deal to Support Unqualified ICC Candidate for Cathala Nears Consummation", 9 December 2011, available at <http://www.innercitypress.com/icc2cathala120911.html>.
—, "For ICC, DR Gets In, Regional Solution Stalled on Mauritius & Cathala of France",

15 December 2011, available at <http://www.innercitypress.com/icc5cathala121511.html>.
—, "Ocampo Says Speech Can Be Crime, Steps Back from Sri Lanka Mapping", 5 June 2012, available at <http://www.innercitypress.com/ocampo1srispeech060512.html>.
Integrated Regional Information Networks, "Uganda: ICC indictments to affect northern peace efforts, says mediator", UN Office for the Coordination of Humanitarian Affairs, Nairobi, 10 October 2005, available at <http://www.irinnews.org/report.asp?ReportID=49453&SelectRegion=East_Africa&SelectCountry=UGANDA>.
—, "Uganda: Give peace a chance, northern leaders tell ICC", UN Office for the Coordination of Humanitarian Affairs, Nairobi, 2 June 2006.
Institute for War & Peace Reporting, "Will ICC prosecutions threaten Ugandan peace process?", Institute for War & Peace Reporting, Africa Report Number 46, 16 November 2005.
International Bar Association, *Balancing Rights: The International Criminal Court at a Procedural Crossroads*, IBA/ICC Monitoring and Outreach Programme, May 2008.
—, *The ICC under Scrutiny: Assessing Recent Developments at the International Criminal Court*, IBA/ICC Monitoring and Outreach Programme, November 2008.
International Center for Transitional Justice, *Forgotten Voices: A Population-Based Survey on Attitudes about Peace and Justice in Northern Uganda*, ICTJ, New York, July 2005.
International Criminal Court, "Rome Statute of the International Criminal Court", 1998, available at <http://www.un.org/law/icc/index.html>, and <http://www.icc-cpi.int/NR/rdonlyres/ADD16852-AEE9-4757-ABE7-9CDC7CF02886/283503/RomeStatutEng1.pdf>.
—, "Agreement between the ICC and EU on Cooperation and Assistance", 10 April 2006, available at <www.icc-cpi.int/library/about/offi cialjournal/ICC-PRES-01-01-06_English.pdf>.
—, "Delegations to the tenth session of the Assembly of States Parties to the Rome Statute of the International Criminal Court New York", *12–21 December 2011*, Assembly of States Parties, 27 March 2012, ICC-ASP/10/INF.1.
ICG, "Northern Uganda: Understanding and Solving the Conflict", Africa Report Number 77, 14 April 2004.
—, "Northern Uganda: Seizing the Opportunity for Peace", Africa Report Number 124, 26 April 2007.
International Labour Organisation, Palme v. ICC, Judgment No. 2757, 105th Session, International Labour Organisation Administrative Tribunal, 9 July 2008, available at <http://www.haguejusticeportal.net/Docs/ICC/ILO_Palme_9-7-2008.pdf>.
International Refugee Rights Initiative, "In the Interests of Justice? Prospects and Challenges for International Justice in Africa", New York, November 2008.
—, "Just justice? Civil society, international justice and the search for accountability in Africa", Series Background Paper, New York, November 2011,
Jain, Neha, "A Separate Law for Peacekeepers: the Clash between the Security Council and the International Criminal Court", *European Journal of International Law*, Volume 16, Number 2 (2005), pp. 239–54.

Jalloh, Charles C., Akande, Dapo and du Plessis, Max, "Assessing the African Union Concerns about Article 16 of the Rome State of the International Criminal Court", *African Journal of Legal Studies*, Volume 4 (2011), University of Pittsburgh Legal Studies Research Paper No. 2011-14, Oxford Legal Studies Research Paper No. 6/2011.

Jeu, Cassandra, "A successful, permanent International Criminal Court...'isn't it pretty to think so?'", *Houston Journal of International Law*, (2004).

Jianping, Lu and Zhixiang, Wang, "China's Attitude Towards the ICC", *Journal of International Criminal Justice*, Volume 3, Issue 3 (2005).

Jooma, Mariam Bibi, "The International Criminal Court and Sudan – Opening a Pandora's Box", *ISS Today*, Institute for Security Studies, Tshwane (Pretoria), 6 March 2007.

Kahn, Paul, "Why the United States Is So Opposed", *Crimes of War Magazine*, December 2003, available at <www.crimesofwar.org/print/icc/icc-kahn-print.html>.

Kaleck, W., Schüller, A., and Steiger, D., "Tarnen und Täuschen, die deutschen Strafverfolgungsbehörden und der Fall des Luftangriffs bei Kundus", *Kritische Justiz*, 2010, Heft 2, pp. 270–86.

Kalivretakis, E. I., "Are nuclear weapons above the law? A look at the International Criminal Court and the prohibited weapons category", *Emory International Law Review*, Volume 15, Number 2 (2001), pp. 683–732.

Kastner, Philipp, "The ICC in Darfur: Savior or Spoiler?", *ILSA Journal of International and Comparative Law*, Volume 14, Number 1 (2007), pp. 145–88.

Kaul, Hans-Peter, "Towards a Permanent International Criminal Court: Some Observations of a Negotiator", *Human Rights Law Journal*, Volume 18 (1997).

Kaye, David, "Who's Afraid of the International Criminal Court?", *Foreign Affairs*, May/June 2011, available at <http://www.foreignaffairs.com/articles/67768/david-kaye/whos-afraid-of-the-international-criminal-court>.

Keatts, Brian D., "The International Criminal Court: Far from Perfect", *New York Law School Journal of International and Comparative Law*, Volume 20, Number 1 (2000).

Keitner, C., "Crafting the International Criminal Court: Trials and Tribulations in Article 98(2)", *UCLA Journal of International Law and Foreign Affairs*, Volume 6 (2001).

Keitner, C. and Oosterveld, V., "Negotiating an Institution for the Twenty-First Century: Multilateral Diplomacy and the International Criminal Court", *McGill Law Journal*, Volume 46, Number 4 (2001), pp. 1141–60.

Kelley, Judith G., "Who Keeps International Commitments and Why? The International Criminal Court and Bilateral Non-Surrender Agreements", *American Political Science Review*, Volume 3, Number 101 (2007).

Kemmerer, Alexandra, "Like Ancient Beacons: The European Union and the International Criminal Court – Reflections from afar on a Chapter of European Foreign Policy", *German Law Journal*, Volume 5, Number 12 (2004).

Kersten, Mark, "Between Justice and Politics: The International Criminal Court's Intervention in Libya", available at <http://www.academia.edu/1558775/Between_Justice_and_Politics_The_International_Criminal_Courts_Intervention_in_Libya>.

—, "No winners in ICC-Libya standoff", *Foreign Policy*, 2012, available at <http://mideast. foreignpolicy.com/posts/2012/10/08/no_winners_in_icc_libya_standoff>.
Kimani, Mary, "International Criminal Court: Justice or racial double standards?", 16 December 2009, Afrik.com, available at <http://en.afrik.com/article16657.html>.
Kirsch, Philippe and Robinson, Darryl, "Referral by States Parties", in A. Cassese, P. Gaeta and J. R. W. D. Jones (editors), *The Rome Statute of the International Criminal Court: A Commentary*, Volume 1, Oxford University Press, Oxford, 2002, pp. 619–25.
Kissinger, Henry, "The Pitfalls of Universal Jurisdiction", *Foreign Affairs*, Volume 80 (2001), pp. 86–96.
Klabbers, Jan, "The Spectre of International Criminal Justice: Third States and the ICC", in Andreas Zimmermann and Ursula E. Heinz (editors), *International Criminal Law and the Current Development of Public International Law*, Duncker and Humblot, Berlin, 2003, pp. 49–72.
Köchler, Hans, *Global Justice or Global Revenge? International Criminal Justice at the Crossroads*, Springer: Vienna/New York, 2003, available at <http://i-p-o.org/global_justice-springer-2003.htm>.
—, "Sudan: Double Standards in International Criminal Justice. Security Council Resolution Violates Statute of International Criminal Court", International Progress Organization, P/RE/19140c-is, Vienna, 2 April 2005, available at <http://www.i-p-o.org/nr-sudan-icc-02apr05.htm>.
—, "Global Justice or Global Revenge? The ICC and the Politicization of International Criminal Justice", lecture delivered at the World Conference for International Justice "United against the politicization of justice", organized by the General Sudanese Students Union, Khartoum, Sudan, 6 April 2009, available at <http://www.i-p-o.org/IPO-Koechler-ICC-politicization-2009.htm>.
Kress, Claus, "'Self-Referrals' and 'Waivers of Complementarity'", *Journal of International Criminal Justice*, Volume 2 (2004), pp. 944–48.
Kriksciun, Alex K., "Uganda's Response to International Criminal Court Arrest Warrants: A Misguided Approach?", *Tulane Journal of International & Comparative Law*, Volume 16 (2007), pp. 213–14.
Ku, Julian and Nzelibe, Jide, "Do International Criminal Tribunals deter or exacerbate humanitarian atrocities?, *Washington University Law Review*, Volume 84, Number 4 (2006).
Kuehn, Tomas A., "Human 'wrongs'?: The U.S. takes an unpopular stance in opposing a strong International Criminal Court, gaining unlikely allies in the process", *Pepperdine Law Review*, Volume 27, Number 2 (2000), pp. 299–321.
Kurth, Michael E., "Anonymous Witnesses before the International Criminal Court: Due Process in Dire Straits", in Carsten Stahn and Göran Sluiter (editors), *The Emerging Practice of the International Criminal Court*, Nijhoff, 2009.
Lacey, Marc, "Victims of Uganda Atrocities Choose a Path of Forgiveness", *New York Times*, 18 April 2005.
Lahiri, D., "Explanation of India's Vote on the Adoption of the Statute of the International Criminal Court: United Nations Diplomatic Conference of Plenipotentiaries on

the Establishment of an International Criminal Court", in William Driscoll, Joseph Zompetti and Suzette Zompetti (editors), *The International Criminal Court: Global Politics and the Quest for Justice*, International Debate Education Association, (2004), pp. 42–45.

Lanham, Krissa, "A Paradox of Prediction: The ICC's Effect on US Humanitarian Policy in The Sudan", *Eyes on the ICC*, Volume 2, Number 1 (2005).

Lantto, Megan E., "The United States and the International Criminal Court: a Permanent Divide?", *Suffolk Transnational Law Review*, Volume 31, Number 3 (2008), pp. 619–46.

Lanz, David, "The ICC's Intervention in Northern Uganda: Beyond the Simplicity of Peace vs. Justice", the Fletcher School of Law and Diplomacy, May 2007, available at <http://www.reliefweb.int/rw/RWFiles2007.nsf/FilesByRWDocUnidFilename/PANA-78VKGJ-full_report.pdf/$File/full_report.pdf>.

Laughland, John, "Forget the rhetoric, this court is just another excuse for superpower bullying", *The Times* (London), 29 August 2000.

—, "This is not justice. The Hague has replaced Nuremberg's jurisprudence of peace with a licence to the west to kill", *The Guardian*, 16 February 2002.

—, *Travesty: The Trial of Slobodan Milosevic and the Corruption of International Justice*, Pluto Press, 2006.

—, *A History of Political Trials: From Charles I to Saddam Hussein*, Peter Lang, Oxford, 2008.

—, "The ICC and Universal Jurisdiction. 'Ubi lex voluit, dicit; ubi noluit, tacit'", ICC Watch, March 2009, available at <http://www.iccwatch.org/pdf/article_Mar09.pdf>.

Leigh, Monroe, "The United States and the Statute of Rome", *The American Journal of International Law*, Volume 95, Number 1 (2001).

Lerner, Ben, "Citizen-Defendants of the World", *The American Spectator*, 23 March 2009, available at <http://spectator.org/archives/2009/03/23/citizen-defendants-of-the-worl/print>.

—, "Ambulance Chasing - From Kabul to Gaza", *The American Spectator*, 8 October 2009, available at <http://spectator.org/archives/2009/10/08/ambulance-chasing-from-kabul-t/print>.

Lietzau, William, K., "International Criminal Law after Rome: Concerns from a U.S. Military Perspective", *Law and Contemporary Problems*, Volume 64, Number 1 (2001), pp. 119–40.

—, "The United States and the International Criminal Court: Concerns from a US Military Perspective", *Law and Contemporary Problems*, (2001).

Lohr, Michael F. and Lietzau, W. K., "One road away from Rome: concerns regarding the International Criminal Court", *Journal of Legal Studies*, USAFA, Volume 9 (1999), pp. 33–57.

Lomo, Z. and Hovil, Lucy, "Behind the violence: Causes, consequences and the search for solutions to the war in Northern Uganda", Refugee Law Project Working Paper 11, 2004.

Magliveras, Konstantinos and Sourantonis, Dimitris, "Rescinding the signature of an international treaty: the United States and the Rome statute establishing the international criminal court", *Diplomacy & Statecraft*, Volume 14, Issue 4, December 2003, pages 21–49.

Mail and Guardian, "Top Prosecutor a 'Sex Molester'" (South Africa), 25 July 2008, available at <http://article42-3.org/Mail%20&%20Guardian%2025%20July%202008.pdf>.

Mallinder, Louise, "Can Amnesties and International Justice be Reconciled?", *The International Journal of Transitional Justice*, Volume 1 (2007), pp. 208–30, available at <http://eprints.ulster.ac.uk/2263/1/Mallinder_IJTJ.pdf>.

—, "Indemnity, Amnesty, Pardon, and Prosecution Guidelines in South Africa", Working Paper Number 2, in *Beyond Legalism: Amnesties, Transition and Conflict Transformation*, Institute of Criminology and Criminal Justice, Queen's University, Belfast, 2009, available at <http://www.qub.ac.uk/schools/SchoolofLaw/Research/InstituteofCriminologyandCriminalJustice/Research/BeyondLegalism/filestore/Filetoupload,152146,en.pdf>.

—, "Amnesties' Challenge to the Global Accountability Norm? Interpreting Regional and International Trends in Amnesty Enactment", in Leigh A. Payne and Francesca Lessa (editors), *Amnesty in the Age of Human Rights Accountability: Comparative and Perspectives*, Cambridge University Press, Cambridge, 2012; Transitional Justice Institute Research Paper Number 10-14, 22 January 2012. Available at Social Science Research Network <http://ssrn.com/abstract=1680768> or <http://dx.doi.org/10.2139/ssrn.1680768>.

Maogoto, Jackson Nyamuya, "The International Criminal Court Goes to Bat on African Terrain: A Snapshot of Jurisdictional Hurdles Posed by the Situations in Sudan & Uganda", 8 December 2009, available at Social Science Research Network <http://ssrn.com/abstract=1520463>.

Marquand, Robert, "Global court starts with a fumble. Warlord grins. Witness recants testimony during start of Congo militia leader Thomas Lubanga's trial", *Christian Science Monitor*, 30 January 2009, available at <http://www.csmonitor.com/World/2009/0130/p01s01-wogn.html>.

Martín, Vidal, "The two faces of impunity: the EU and the International Criminal Court", Fundación para las Relaciones Internacionales y el Diálogo Exterior, Madrid, December 2007.

McAdams J., "Transitional justice: The issue that won't go away", *International Journal of Transitional Justice*, Volume 5, Number 2 (2011), pp. 304–12.

McCarthy, Conor, *Reparations and Victim Support in the International Criminal Court*, Cambridge University Press, 2012.

McConnell, Tristan, "Uganda: Peace vs. Justice", openDemocracy, 14 September 2006, available from <http://www.opendemocracy.net>.

McCormack, Timothy L. H., "Selective Reaction to Atrocity: War Crimes and the Development of International Criminal Law", *Albany Law Review*, Volume 60 (1997).

McDermott, Yvonne, "Some are More Equal than Others: Victim Participation in the ICC", *Eyes on the ICC*, Volume 5, Number 1 (2009).

McDoom, Opheera, "Analysis: Justice Clashes with Peace on Darfur Bashir Warrant", Reuters, 14 July 2008.

McDougall, Carrie, *The Crime of Aggression under the Rome Statute of the International Criminal Court*, Cambridge University Press, 2013.

McGreal, Chris, "African search for peace throws court into crisis. Uganda fears first crucial test for tribunal could prolong brutal 20-year civil war", *The Guardian*, 9 January 2007, available at <http://www.ictj.org/en/news/coverage/article/1117.html>.

McNerney, Patricia, "The International Criminal Court: issues for consideration by the United States Senate", *Law and Contemporary Problems*, Volume 64, Number 1 (2001), pp. 181–91.

Megret, Frederic, "Three Dangers for the International Criminal Court: A Critical Look at a Consensual Project", *Finnish Yearbook of International Law*, Volume 12 (2001), pp. 195–247, available at <http://ssrn.com/abstract=1156086>.

Menkel-Meadow, C., "Accomplishments of the TRC. Restorative Justice: What Is It and Does It Work?", Georgetown University Law Center, Washington DC, 2007, available at <http://www.judgesandmagistrates.org/CMM.Restorative%20Justice%20-%20What%20is%20it%20&%20does%20it%20work.pdf>.

Meron, Theodor, "Defining Aggression for the International Criminal Court", *Suffolk Transnational Law Review*, Volume 25, Number 1 (2001).

Mertens, Mitja, "The International Criminal Court: A European Success Story?", EU Diplomacy Papers 1/2011, College of Europe, 2011, p. 15, available at <http://aei.pitt.edu/15478/1/EDP_1_2011_Mertens.pdf>.

Mettelsiefen, Marcel and Reuter, Christoph, *Kunduz, 4. September 2009: Eine Spurensuche*, Rogner und Bernhard Verlag, Berlin 2010.

Moorcraft, Paul, "Bashing Omar al-Bashir", *The American Spectator*, 29 May 2009, available at <http://spectator.org/archives/2009/05/29/bashing-omar-al-bashir>.

Morris, Madeleine, "The jurisdiction of the International Criminal Court over nationals of non-party states", *ILSA Journal of International & Comparative Law*, Volume 6, Number 2 (2000), pp. 363–69.

—, "High Crimes and Misconceptions: The ICC and Non-party States", *Law and Contemporary Problems*, Volume 64, Number 1 (2001), pp. 13–66.

—, "The Disturbing Democratic Deficit of the International Criminal Court", *Finnish Yearbook of International Law*, Volume 12 (2001), pp. 109–18.

—, "The Democratic Dilemma of the International Criminal Court", *Buffalo Criminal Law Review*, Volume 5 (2002), pp. 591–600.

—, "Judgment without Democracy", *Washington Post*, 24 July 2002.

Moschetta, Teresa Maria, "Cooperation between the European Union and the International Criminal Court", in Mauro Politi and Federica Gioia (editors), *The International Criminal Court and National Jurisdictions*, Ashgate, 2008.

Moy, H. Abigail, "The International Criminal Court's Arrest Warrants and Uganda's Lord's Resistance Army: Renewing the Debate over Amnesty and Complementarity", *Harvard Human Rights Journal*, Volume 19 (2006).

Mueller, Andreas and Stegmiller, Ignaz, "Self-Referrals on Trial: From Panacea to Patient", *Journal of International Criminal Justice*, Volume 8 (2010), pp. 1267–94.

Müller-Schieke, Rina Kaye, "Defining the Crime of Aggression Under the Statute of the International Criminal Court", *Leiden Journal of International Law*, Volume 14, Number 2 (2001), pp 409–30.

Mwaniki, David and Wepundi, Manasseh, *The Juba Peace Talks – The Checkered Road to Peace in Northern Uganda,* Institute for Security Studies, Tshwane (Pretoria), 28 March 2007.

Nee, A. and Uvin, P., "Silence and Dialogue: Burundians' Alternatives to Transitional Justice", in R. Shaw and L. Waldorf (editors), *Localizing Transitional Justice,* Stanford University Press, 2010, pp.158–80.

New African, "What's the ICC up to?", *New African,* 1 May 2009.

—, "Who Pays For The ICC?", March 2012, available at <http://www.newafricanmagazine.com/special-reports/sector-reports/icc-vs-africa/who-pays-for-the-icc>.

—, "African Union vs The ICC", March 2012, <http://www.newafricanmagazine.com/special-reports/sector-reports/icc-vs-africa/african-union-vs-the-icc>.

—, "Europe, Masters Behind The ICC", March 2012, available at <http://www.newafricanmagazine.com/special-reports/sector-reports/icc-vs-africa/europe-masters-behind-the-icc>.

—, "Is Africa On Trial? The Role Of The ICC Examined", July 2012, available at <http://www.newafricanmagazine.com/features/politics/is-africa-on-trial-the-role-of-the-icc-examined>.

—, "Black Groups Challenge The ICC", September 2012, available at <http://www.newafricanmagazine.com/features/diaspora/black-groups-challenge-the-icc>.

—, "ICC's Long Shadow Over Impending Elections", 8 January 2013, available at <http://www.newafricanmagazine.com/features/politics/iccs-long-shadow-over-impending-elections>.

New Europe, "German court will examine Kunduz airstrike", 18 April 2013, available at <http://www.neurope.eu/article/german-court-will-examine-kunduz-airstrike>.

Ni Aoláin, Fionnuala and Gross, Oren (editors), *Guantánamo and Beyond: Exceptional Courts and Military Commissions in Comparative Perspective,* Cambridge University Press, 2013.

Nice, Sir Geoffrey, "International Criminal Tribunals: Experiments? Works in progress? Institutions that are here for good, or maybe not?", Gresham College Lectures, 12 September 2012, available at <http://www.gresham.ac.uk/lectures-and-events/international-criminal-tribunals>.

—, "The Permanent International Criminal Court and Africa", Gresham College Lectures, 31 October 2012, available at <http://www.gresham.ac.uk/lectures-and-events/the-permanent-international-criminal-court-%E2%80%93-the-icc-and-africa>.

Nindorera, A., "Ubushingantahe as a Base for Political Transformation in Burundi", Boston Consortium on Gender, Security and Human Rights, Working Paper Number 102, 2003, available at <http://www.genderandsecurity.umb.edu/Agnes.pdf>.

Noetzel, Timo, "The German politics of war: Kunduz and the war in Afghanistan", *International Affairs,* Volume 87, Issue 2 (2011), pp. 397–417.

Nouwen, Sarah, "The ICC's Intervention in Uganda: Which Rule of Law Does It Promote?", in Michael Zürn, André Nollkaemper and R. Peerenboom (editors), *Rule of Law Dynamics,* Cambridge University Press, New York, 2012.

—, *Complementarity in the Line of Fire: The Catalysing Effect of the International Criminal Court in Uganda and Sudan*, Cambridge University Press, 2013.

Nouwen, Sarah and Werner, Wouter, "Doing Justice to the Political: The International Criminal Court in Uganda and Sudan", *The European Journal of International Law*, Volume 21, Number 4 (2010), pp. 941–65, available at <http://ejil.oxfordjournals.org/content/21/4/941.full>.

NRC Handelsblad, "International court plagued by in-fighting", *NRC Handelsblad*, 19 November 2008, available at <http://www.nrc.nl/international/Features/article2066177.ece>.

O'Brien, Adam, "The Impact of International Justice on Local Peace Initiatives: The Case of Northern Uganda", International Crisis Group, available at <www.crisisgroup.org/home/index.cfm?id=4927&l=1>.

O'Callaghan, Declan, "Is the International Criminal Court the Way Ahead?", *International Criminal Law Review*, Volume 8, Number 3 (2008), pp. 533–56.

Odero, Steve, "Politics of International Criminal Justice: The ICC's Arrest Warrant for Al Bashir and the African Union's Neo-Colonial Conspirator Thesis", in Chacha Murungu and Japhet Biegon (editors), *Prosecuting International Crimes in Africa*, Pretoria University Law Press, 2011.

O'Neill, Brendan, "The International Criminal Court is, by any objective measurement, racist. So why do liberals love it?", *The Daily Telegraph*, 15 March 2012, available at <http://blogs.telegraph.co.uk/news/brendanoneill2/100144112/the-international-criminal-court-is-by-any-objective-measurement-racist-so-why-do-liberals-love-it/>.

Okello, M. C., "The false polarisation of peace and justice in Uganda", Presentation at Building a Future on Peace and Justice, Nuremberg, Germany, 2007.

Oketch, B., "Negotiators Try Again: Northern Ugandans Say They Prefer Talk of Peace to Talk of War", Institute of War and Peace Reporting, 11 July 2008, available at <www.iwpr.net/?p=acr&s=f&o=345650&apc_state=henh>.

Okuk, James, "ICC justice is useless if it destroys peace", *Sudan Tribune*, 19 July 2008, available at <http://www.ictj.org/en/news/coverage/article/1888.html>.

Olopade, Dayo, "Who's Afraid of the International Criminal Court? In Kenya, the answer is no one at all", *New Republic*, 9 March 2013, available at <http://www.newrepublic.com/article/112629/kenya-election-results-whos-afraid-icc#>.

Onana, Charles, *Al-Bashir & Darfour, La Contre-Enquête, Menaces sur le Soudan et révélations sur le Procureur Ocampo*, Editions Duboiris, 2010.

O'Neill, Timothy, "Dispute Settlement under the Rome Statute of the International Criminal Court: Article 119 and the Possible Role of the International Court of Justice", *Chinese Journal of International Law*, Volume 5, Number 1 (2006), pp. 67–78.

Opolot, Deogratius O., "The International Criminal Court Versus Peace Agreements: Juba Peace Talks Between the LRA Rebels and the Government of Uganda", *Journal of African and International Law*, Volume 2, Number 1 (2009), pp. 39–50.

Orentlicher, Diane F., "Politics by other means: the law of the International Criminal Court", *Cornell International Law Journal*, Volume 32, Number 3 (1999), pp. 489–97.

Otim, Michael and Wierda, Marieke, "Justice at Juba: International Obligations and Local Demands in Northern Uganda", in Nicholas Waddell and Phil Clark (editors), *Courting Conflict? Justice, Peace and the ICC in Africa*, Royal African Society, London, March 2008.

Pace, William and Thieroff, Mark, "Participation of Non-Governmental Organizations", in Roy S. Lee (editor), *The International Criminal Court – The Making of the Rome Statute*, Kluwer Law International, The Hague, 1999.

Pace, William and Panganiban, R., "The Power of Global Activists Networks: The Campaign for an International Criminal Court", in Peter I. Hajnal (editor), *Civil Society in the Information Age*, Ashgate Publishing, 2002, pp. 109–25.

Pace, William and Schense, Jennifer, "The Role of Non-Governmental Organizations", in Antonio Cassese, Paola, Gaeta and John R. W. D. Jones (editors), *The Rome Statute of the International Criminal Court: A Commentary*, Volume 1, Oxford University Press, Oxford, 2002.

—, "International lawmaking of historic proportions: civil society and the International Criminal Court", in Paul Gready (editor), *Fighting for Human Rights*, Routledge, New York, 2004.

Paisley, Ian, "Peace Must Not Be the Victim of International Justice", *The New York Times*, 16 March 2012, available at <http://www.nytimes.com/2012/03/17/opinion/peace-must-not-be-the-victim-of-international-justice.html?_r=0>.

Pallister, David, "Human rights: Growing clamour to remove the Hague prosecutor who wants Sudanese president arrested", *The Guardian*, 18 August 2008, available at <http://www.guardian.co.uk/world/2008/aug/18/humanrights.sudan>.

Palme, Christian, "Complaint against ICC Prosecutor Luis Moreno-Ocampo concerning serious misconduct", 20 October 2006, available at <http://www.innercitypress.com/ocampocomplaint.pdf>.

Parrott, Louise, "The Role of the International Criminal Court in Uganda: Ensuring that the Pursuit of Justice does not come at the price of peace", *The Australian Journal of Peace Studies*, Volume 1 (2006).

Pearson, Zoe, "Non-Governmental Organizations and the International Criminal Court: Changing Landscapes of International Law", *Cornell International Law Journal*, Volume 39, Number 2 (2006), pp. 243–84.

Pejic, Jelena, "The United States and the International Criminal Court: one loophole too many", *University of Detroit Mercy Law Review*, Volume 78, Number 2 (2001), pp. 267–97.

—, "Creating a Permanent International Criminal Court: The Obstacles to Independence and Effectiveness", *Columbia Human Rights Law Review*, Volume 29 (1998).

Petit, Franck, "The Small Steps' Strategy of the ICC in Darfur", *International Justice Tribune*, 5 March 2007.

Pittman, Thomas Wayde and Heaphy, Matthew, "Does the United States Really Prosecute Its Service Members for War Crimes?: Implications for Complementarity before the International Criminal Court", *Leiden Journal of International Law*, Volume 21, Number 1 (2008), pp. 165–83.

Posner, Eric, "The Absurd International Criminal Court. After 10 years and hundreds of millions of dollars, it has completed precisely one trial", *The Wall Street Journal*, 10 June 2012, available at <http://online.wsj.com/article/SB10001424052702303753904577452122153205162.html>.

Rabkin, Jeremy, "A Dangerous Step Closer to an International Criminal Court", *On the Issues*, American Enterprise Institute for Public Policy Research, January 2001.

—, "The Politics of the Geneva Conventions: Disturbing Background to the ICC Debate, *Virginia Journal of International Law*, Volume 44 (2003), pp. 169–205.

—, "No Substitute for Sovereignty: why International Criminal Justice has a Bleak Future, and deserves it", in Edel Hughes, William A. Schabas and Ramesh Thakur (editors), *Atrocities and International Accountability: Beyond Transitional Justice*, United Nations University Press, 2007.

Ralph, Jason, "International Society, the International Criminal Court and American Foreign Policy", *Review of International Studies*, Volume 31, Number 1 (2005), pp. 27–44.

—, *Defending the Society of States. Why America Opposes the International Criminal Court and its Vision of World Society*, Oxford University Press, Oxford, 2007.

Refugee Law Project, Position Paper on the ICC. Refugee Law Project, Kampala, July 2004.

—, "Whose Justice? Perceptions of Uganda's Amnesty Act 2000: The Potential for Conflict Resolution and Long-Term Reconciliation". Refugee Law Project, Kampala, February 2005.

Reeves, T. Y., "A Global Court? U.S. Objections to the International Criminal Court and Obstacles to Ratification", *Human Rights Brief*, Volume 8, Number 1 (2000).

Reisman, W. Michael, "The Definition of Aggression and the ICC", *American Society of International Law Proceedings*, Volume 96 (2002).

—, "Learning to deal with rejection: the International Criminal Court and the United States", *Journal of International Criminal Justice*, Volume 2, Number 1 (2004), pp. 17–18.

—, "On Paying the Piper: Financial Responsibility for Security Council Referrals to the International Criminal Court", *American Journal of International Law*, Volume 99, Number 3 (2005), pp. 615–18.

Roach, Steven C., *Politicizing the International Criminal Court. The Convergence of Politics, Ethics, and Law*, Rowman & Littlefield Publishers, Plymouth, 2006.

—, "The Turbulent Politics of the International Criminal Court", *Peace Review*, Volume 23, Issue 4, October 2011, pp. 546–51.

—, "Legitimising negotiated justice: the International Criminal Court and flexible governance", *The International Journal of Human Rights*, Volume 17, Issue 5–6, August 2013, pp. 619–32.

Roberts, Guy, "Assault on sovereignty: the clear and present danger of the new International Criminal Court", *American University International Law Review*, Volume 17, Number 1 (2001), pp. 35–77.

—, "US Foreign Policy and the International Criminal Court: Towards a Third Way of Strategic Accommodation", *International Politics*, Volume 43, Number 1 (2006), pp. 53–70.

Robinson, Darryl, "The Controversy over Territorial State Referrals and Reflections on ICL Discourse", *Journal of International Criminal Justice*, Volume 9, Number 2 (2011), pp. 355–84, available at <http://jicj.oxfordjournals.org/content/9/2/355.full.pdf+html>.

Rodman, Kenneth A., "Is Peace in the Interests of Justice? The Case for Broad Prosecutorial Discretion at the International Criminal Court", *Leiden Journal of International Law*, Volume 22 (2009), pp. 99–126.

Rodriguez, Cara Levy, "Slaying the monster: why the United States should not support the Rome Treaty", *American University International Law Review*, Volume 14, Number 3 (1999), pp. 805–44.

Roggemann, Herzwig and Sarcevic, Petar, *National Security and International Criminal Justice*, Kluwer Law International, The Hague, 2002.

Rosenne, Shabtai, "Poor drafting and imperfect organization: flaws to overcome in the Rome Statute", *Virginia Journal of International Law*, Volume 41, Number 1 (2000), pp. 164–85.

Rosenthal, John, "A Lawless Global Court: How the International Criminal Court Undermines the U.N. System", *Policy Review*, Hoover Institution, February-March 2004.

Rotberg, R. I. and Thomson, D., *Truth v. Justice*, Princeton University Press, Princeton, 2000.

Rothe, Dawn and Mullins, Christopher W., "The International Criminal Court and United States opposition. A Structural Contradictions Model", *Crime, Law and Social Change*, Volume 45, Number 3 (2006).

Roth, Kenneth, "The Court the U.S. Doesn't Want", *The New York Review of Books*, 19 November 1998.

Royal United Services Institute, *Prosecuting Presidents: The Challenges of International Indictments of African Leaders*, Royal United Services Institute for Defence and Security Studies, London, 27 March 2009, available at <http://www.rusi.org/downloads/assets/Prosecuting_Presidents.pdf>.

Rozenburg, Joshua, "Courting controversy", *The Law Gazette* (UK), 7 August 2008, available at <http://www.lawgazette.co.uk/opinion/columnists/courting-controversy>.

—, "Why the world's most powerful prosecutor should resign: Part 1 The International Criminal Court's first trial has been suspended because the prosecutor failed to disclose evidence that could have helped the defendant", *The Daily Telegraph* (London), 14 September 2008, available at <http://www.telegraph.co.uk/news/newstopics/lawreports/joshuarozenberg/2236288/Why-the-worlds-most-powerful-prosecutor-should-resign-Part-1.html>.

—, "Why the world's most powerful prosecutor should resign: Part 2 Sexual misconduct allegations against Luis Moreno-Ocampo have been dismissed as manifestly unfounded but he is held personally responsible for a breach of due process", *The Daily Telegraph* (London), 14 September 2008, available at <http://www.telegraph.co.uk/news/newstopics/lawreports/joshuarozenberg/2446064/Why-the-worlds-most-powerful-prosecutor-should-resign-Part-2.html.

—, "Why the world's most powerful prosecutor should resign: Part 3 Luis Moreno-Ocampo wants the president of Sudan arrested for genocide. But the chances of a conviction are slim", *The Daily Telegraph* (London), 14 September 2008, available at <http://www.telegraph.co.uk/news/newstopics/lawreports/joshuarozenberg/2700862/Why-the-worlds-most-powerful-prosecutor-should-resign-Part-3.html>.

—, "Why the world's most powerful prosecutor should resign: Part 4 In latest of four hard-hitting commentaries, Joshua Rozenberg argues that Luis Moreno-Ocampo still does not understand the concept of a fair trial", *The Daily Telegraph* (London), 14 September 2008, available at <http://www.telegraph.co.uk/news/newstopics/lawreports/joshuarozenberg/2700448/Why-the-worlds-most-powerful-prosecutor-should-resign-Part-4.html>.

—, "Lubanga Trial: More Delays", *Standpoint*, 3 October 2009, available at <http://www.standpointmag.co.uk/node/2256>.

—, "Okafka Creates New Offences", *Standpoint*, 13 December 2009, available at <http://www.standpointmag.co.uk/node/2505>.

—, "Contempt for Court", *Standpoint*, November 2010, available at <http://standpointmag.co.uk/node/3520/full>.

—, "Prosecutor Luis Moreno-Ocampo is the best asset of those opposed to the international criminal court", *The Guardian*, 21 April 2011, available at <http://www.guardian.co.uk/law/2011/apr/21/moreno-ocampo-international-criminal-court?intcmp=239>.

—, "Delay in Lubanga judgment demonstrates ICC weaknesses", *The Guardian*, 14 March 2012, available at <http://www.guardian.co.uk/law/2012/mar/14/delay-lubanga-weaknesses-icc-model>.

—, "ICC case against Kenya's deputy PM proceeds despite claim that witness lied. Uhuru Kenyatta's QC claims prosecutor Fatou Bensouda acted in bad faith in bringing the case based on fraudulent evidence", *The Guardian*, 7 February 2013, available at <http://www.guardian.co.uk/law/2013/feb/07/icc-case-kenya-deputy-pm>.

Rubin, Alfred P., "A Critical View of the Proposed International Criminal Court", *The Fletcher Forum of World Affairs*, Volume 139, Number 2 (1999).

—, "Challenging the Conventional Wisdom: Another View of the International Criminal Court", *Journal of International Affairs*, Volume 52, Number 2 (1999), pp. 783–93.

—, "The International Criminal Court: a Skeptical Analysis", in Michael N. Schmitt (editor), *International law across the spectrum of conflict: essays in honour of Professor L. C. Green on the occasion of his eightieth birthday*, 2000, pp. 421–38.

—, "The International Criminal Court: Possibilities for Prosecutorial Abuse", *Law and Contemporary Problems*, Volume 64, Number 1 (2001), pp. 153–65.

—, "Legal Response to Terror: An International Criminal Court?", *Harvard International Law Journal*, Volume 43, Number 1 (2002), pp. 65–70.

—, "Some Objections to the International Criminal Court", *Peace Review*, Volume 12, Issue 1, March 2000, pp. 45–50.

Ruegenberg, Guido, "The Independence and Accountability of Prosecutor of a Permanent International Criminal Court", *Zeitschrift für Rechtspolitik*, Volume 68 (1999).

Ryngaert, Cedric, "Universal Jurisdiction in an ICC Era: a Role to Play for EU Member States with the Support of the European Union", *European Journal of Crime, Criminal Law and Criminal Justice*, Volume 14, Number 1 (2006), pp. 46–80.

Sadat, Leila, *The International Criminal Court and the Transformation of International Law: Justice for the New Millennium*, Transnational Publishers, Ardsley, NY, 2002.

Sadat, Leila and Scharf, Michael P., *The Theory and Practice of International Criminal Law*, Martinus Nijhoff Publishers, Leiden, 2008.

Safferling, C. and Kirsch, S., "Die Strafbarkeit von Bundeswehrangehörigen bei Auslandseinsätzen: Afghanistan ist kein rechtsfreier Raum", *Juristische Ausbildung*, February 2010, p. 81 *et seq.*

Sarooshi, D., "The peace and justice paradox: the International Criminal Court and the UN Security Council" in Dominic McGoldrick, Peter Rowe and Eric Donnelly (editors), *The Permanent International Criminal Court*, Hart Publishing, 2004.

Schabas, William, *An Introduction to the International Criminal Court*, Cambridge University Press, Cambridge, 2001.

—, "International Criminal Court: The Secret of its Success", *Criminal Law Forum*, Volume 12, Number 4 (2001), pp. 415–28.

—, "United States Hostility to the International Criminal Court: it's all About the Security Council", *European Journal of International Law*, Volume 15, Number 4 (2004), pp. 701–20

—, "The Unfinished Work of Defining Aggression: How Many Times Must the Cannonballs Fly, before they are Forever Banned?", in Dominic McGoldrick and Erick Donnelly (editors), *The Permanent International Criminal Court: Legal and Policy Issues* (Studies in International Law), Hart Publishing, 2004, pp. 123–39.

—, "Prosecutorial Discretion v. Judicial Activism at the International Criminal Court", *Journal of International Criminal Justice*, Volume 6, Number 4 (2008), pp. 731–61.

—, "Complementarity in Practice: Creative Solutions or a Trap for the Court?", in Mauro Politi and Federica Gioia (editors), *The International Criminal Court and National Jurisdictions*, Ashgate, Aldershot, 2008, pp. 25–48.

—, "Prosecutorial Discretion and Gravity", in Carsten Stahn and G. Sluiter (editors), *The Emerging Practice of the International Criminal Court*, Martinus Nijhoff Publishers, Leiden, The Netherlands, 2009, pp. 229–46.

—, "'Complementarity in Practice': Some Uncomplimentary Thoughts", *Criminal Law Forum*, Volume 19 (2009), pp. 5–33.

—, "The Rise and Fall of Complementarity", in Carsten Stahn and M. M. El Zeidy (editors), *The International Criminal Court and Complementarity: From Theory to Practice*, Cambridge University Press, Cambridge, 2011.

—, *Unimaginable Atrocities. Justice, Politics, and Rights at the War Crimes Tribunals*, Oxford University Press, Oxford, 2012.

Schabas, William and Williams, S., "Article 17", in Otto Triffterer (editor), *Commentary on the Rome Statute of the International Criminal Court, Observers' Notes, Article-by-Article*, Hart Publishing, Portland, OR, 2008, pp. 605–25.

Schaefer, Brett D., "The International Criminal Court: Threatening U.S. Sovereignty and Security", Executive Memorandum Number 537, Heritage Foundation, 2 July 1998.

—, "The International Criminal Court: Threatening U.S. Sovereignty and Security", Executive Memorandum Number 537, Heritage Foundation, Washington DC, 2 July 1998, available at <http://www.heritage.org/Research/InternationalOrganizations/EM537.cfm>.

—, "Overturning Clinton's Midnight Action on the International Criminal Court", Executive Memorandum Number 708, Heritage Foundation, 9 January 2001, available at <http://www.heritage.org/Research/InternationalOrganizations/EM708.cfm>.

—, "The New World Court: Out of Order", Heritage Foundation, Washington DC, 10 January 2001, available at <http://www.heritage.org/Press/Commentary/ED011001.cfm>.

—, "Justice by Fiat", Heritage Foundation, Washington DC, 21 June 2004, available at <http://www.heritage.org/Press/Commentary/ed062104e.cfm>.

—, "The Bush Administration's Policy on the International Criminal Court Is Correct", Backgrounder Number 1830, Heritage Foundation, Washington DC, 8 March 2005, available at <http://www.heritage.org/Research/InternationalOrganizations/bg1830.cfm>.

—, "Crimes Need To Be Punished, But Is The ICC The Right Means?", Heritage Foundation, Washington DC, 13 February 2009, available at <http://www.heritage.org/Press/Commentary/ed021209b.cfm>.

—, "Beating the ICC", Heritage Foundation, Washington DC, 18 February 2013, available at <http://www.heritage.org/research/commentary/2013/2/beating-the-icc>.

Scharf, Michael P., "The Jury is Still Out on the Need for an International Criminal Court", *Duke Journal of Comparative & International Law*, Volume 1 (1991), pp. 135–68.

—, "The Politics of Establishing an International Criminal Court", *Duke Journal of Comparative & International Law*, Volume 6, Number 1 (1995), pp. 167–73.

—, "The Case for a Permanent International Truth Commission", *Duke Journal of Comparative and International Law*, Volume 7 (1997), pp. 375–410.

—, "The Politics Behind the U.S. Opposition to the International Criminal Court", *New England International and Comparative Law Annual*, 1999.

—, "The amnesty exception to the jurisdiction of the International Criminal Court", *Cornell International Law Journal*, Volume 32, Number 3 (1999), pp. 507–27.

—, "The United States and the International Criminal Court: A Recommendation for the Bush Administration", *Journal of International and Comparative Law* (2001).

—, "The ICC's jurisdiction over the nationals of non-party states: a critique of the U.S. position", *Law and Contemporary Problems*, Volume 64, Number 1 (2001), pp. 67–117.

—, "The United States and the International Criminal Court: A Recommendation for the Bush Administration", *ILSA Journal of International & Comparative Law*, Volume 7, Number 2 (2001), pp. 385–89.

Scharf, Michael P. and Dowd, Patrick, "No Way Out? The Question of Unilateral Withdrawals or Referrals to the ICC and Other Human Rights Courts", *Chicago Journal of International Law*, (2009).

Scheffer, David J., "Challenges Confronting International Justice Issues", *New England International and Comparative Law Annual*, Volume 4, (1998).
—, "The U.S. Perspective on the International Criminal Court", *MacGill Law Journal*, Volume 46, Number 1 (2000), pp. 269–80.
—, "The United States and the International Criminal Court", *American Journal of International Law*, Volume 93 (1999), pp. 12–22.
—, "Staying the Course with the International Criminal Court", *Cornell International Law Journal*, Volume 35 (2001).
Scheuerman, S., "International Law as Historical Myth", *Constellations: An International Journal of Critical and Democratic Theory*, Volume 11, Number 4 (2004), pp. 537–50.
Schiff, Benjamin, *Building the International Criminal Court*, Cambridge University Press, New York, 2008.
—, "Universalism meets Sovereignty at the International Criminal Court", in Noha Shawki and Michaelene Cox (editors), *Negotiating Sovereignty and Human Rights: Actors and Issues in Contemporary Human Rights Politics*, Ashgate publishing, 2009.
Seguin, John, "Denouncing the International Criminal Court: An Examination of U.S. Objections to the Rome Statute", *Boston University International Law Journal*, Volume 18, Number 1 (2000), pp. 85–109.
Sewall, Sarah and Kaysen, Carl (editors), *The United States and the International Criminal Court. National Security and International Law*, Rowman and Littlefield Publishers, 2003.
Shaw, Malcolm N., "The International Criminal Court – Some Procedural and Evidential Issues", *Journal of Armed Conflict Law*, Volume 3, Number 1 (1998), pp. 65–96.
Shukri, M. A., "Will aggressors ever be tried before the ICC?", in Mauro Politi and Giuseppe Nesi (editors), *The International Criminal Court and the Crime of Aggression*, 2004, pp. 33–42.
Simons, Marlise, "For International Criminal Court, Frustration and Missteps in First Trial", *The New York Times*, 22 November 2010.
Sinanyan, Loru, "The International Criminal Court: Why the United States should sign the statute (but perhaps wait to ratify)", *Southern California Law Review*, Volume 73 (2000).
Sirleaf, Matiangai V. S., *Regional or International Criminal Justice in Africa: The International Criminal Court and Africa Which Way Forward?*, 15 July 2013, available at SSRN <http://ssrn.com/abstract=2293988>.
Skidelsky, Robert, "A Warrant of Hypocrisy", Project Syndicate, 13 March 2009, available at <http://www.skidelskyr.com/site/article/a-warrant-of-hypocrisy/>.
Smidt, M., "The International Criminal Court: An Effective Means of Deterrence?", *Military Law Review*, Volume 167 (2001), pp. 156–240.
Smith, Stephen Eliot, "Inventing the Law of Gravity: the ICC's Initial Lubanga Decision and Its Regressive Consequences", *International Criminal Law Review*, Volume 8, Number 1-2 (2008), pp. 331–51.
Smith, T. W., "Moral hazard and humanitarian law: the International Criminal Court and the limits of legalism", *International Politics*, Volume 39, Number 2 (2002), pp. 175–92.

Snyder, Jack and Vinjamuri, Leslie, "Trials and Errors: Principle and Pragmatism in Strategies of International Justice", *International Security*, Volume 28, Number 3 (2003), pp. 5–44.

Song, Sang-Hyun, "International Criminal Court and the European Union: Challenges for the Promotion of International Justice and the Fight Against Impunity", address to European Parliament Group of Parliamentarians for Global Action, European Parliament, Brussels, 15 October 2009.

Southwick, Katherine, "Investigating War in Northern Uganda: Dilemmas for the International Criminal Court", *Yale Journal of International Affairs*, Volume 1, Number 1 (2005), pp. 105–19.

Spencer, Jack, "Bold & Appropriate: Withholding Military Aid Over ICC Waivers", WebMemo Number 310, Heritage Foundation, Washington DC, 10 July 2003, available at <http://www.heritage.org/Research/InternationalOrganizations/wm310.cfm>.

Sriram, Chandra Lekha, "Conflict Mediation and the ICC: Challenges and Options for Pursuing Peace with Justice at the Regional Level", in *Building a Future on Peace and Justice*, Springer, Berlin, 2009.

—, "The Prosecutor of the ICC: Too Political, Not Political Enough, or Both?", *Human Rights Human Welfare*, an online journal of the Josef Korbel School of International Studies, University of Denver, 4 May 2009, available at <http://www.hrhw.org/2009/05/prosecutor-or-icc-too-political-not_04.html>.

Sriram, Chandra Lekha and Pillay, Suren (editors), *Peace vs Justice? The Dilemma of Transitional Justice in Africa*, University of KwaZulu Natal Press, 2009.

Ssenyonjo, Manisuli, "The International Criminal Court and the Lord's Resistance Army Leaders: Prosecution or Amnesty?", *International Criminal Law Review*, Volume 7, Numbers 2–3 (2007), pp. 361–89.

—, "The International Criminal Court and the Warrant of Arrest for Sudan's President Al-Bashir: a Crucial Step Towards Challenging Impunity or a Political Decision?", *Nordic Journal of International Law*, Volume 78, Number 3 (2009), pp. 397–431.

Stahn, Carsten, "The Ambiguities of Security Council Resolution 1422 (2002)", *European Journal of International Law*, Volume 14 (2003).

—, "The Future of International Criminal Justice", The Hague Justice Portal, 9 October 2009, available at <http://www.haguejusticeportal.net/eCache/DEF/11/106.html#_edn14#_edn14>.

Stahn, Carsten and Sluiter, Göran (editors), *The Emerging Practice of the International Criminal Court*, Nijhoff, 2009.

Steele, Jonathan, "The ICC should not indict Omar al-Bashir. The list of practical problems that would flow from an indictment of Sudan's president is long and far outweighs the benefits", *The Guardian*, 11 July 2008, available at <http://www.guardian.co.uk/commentisfree/2008/jul/11/sudan.unitednations>.

Steiger, D., and Bäumler, J., "Die strafrechtliche Verantwortlichkeit deutscher Soldaten bei Auslandseinsätzen: an der Schnittstelle von Strafrecht und Völkerrecht", *Archiv des Völkerrechts*, 2010, pp. 189–225.

Stein, Mark S., "The Security Council, the International Criminal Court, and the Crime of Aggression: How Exclusive is the Security Council's Power to Determine Aggression?", *Indiana International & Comparative Law Review*, Volume 16, Number 1 (2005), available at Social Science Research Network <http://ssrn.com/abstract=888201>.

Struett, Michael J., *The Politics of Constructing the International Criminal Court: NGOs, Discourse, and Agency*, Palgrave Macmillan, 2008.

Stuart, Heikelina Verrijn, "Arbour and Cassese Criticize the ICC in Darfur", *International Justice Tribune*, Number 55, 23 October 2006.

—, "The ICC in Trouble", *Journal of International Criminal Justice*, Volume 6 (2008), pp. 409–17.

Suarez, Carla, *Addressing New Security Threats Through Justice: The International Criminal Court's Intervention in Uganda*, Dalhousie University, Halifax, March 2006.

Supple, Shannon K., "Global Responsibility and the United States: The Constitutionality of the International Criminal Court", *Hastings Constitutional Law Quarterly*, Volume 27 (1999).

Swoboda, Sabine, "The ICC Disclosure Regime – A Defence Perspective", *Criminal Law Forum*, Volume 19, Numbers 3–4 (2008).

Szasz, Paul C. and Ingadottir, Thordis, "The UN and the ICC: The Immunity of the UN and Its Officials", *Leiden Journal of International Law*, Volume 14, Number 4 (2001), pp 867–85.

Taulbee, James L., "A call to arms declined: the United States and the International Criminal Court", *Emory International Law Review*, Volume 14, Number 1 (2000), pp. 105–57.

Teitel, R. G., "Transitional Justice Genealogy", *Harvard Human Rights Journal*, 2003, available at <http://www.law.harvard.edu/students/orgs/hrj/iss16/teitel.pdf>.

Thakur, Ramesh, "Perks of the warring states", *The Japan Times*, 27 March 2009, available at <http://search.japantimes.co.jp/cgi-bin/eo20090327rt.html>.

Thynne, Kelisiana, "The International Criminal Court: A Failure of International Justice for Victims?", *Alberta Law Review*, Volume 46, Number 4 (2009).

Triffterer, Otto (editor), *Commentary on the Rome Statute of the International Criminal Court*, Beck/Hart, 2008, available at <http://article42-3.org/Triffterer3.pdf>.

Trombetta-Panigadi, F., "NGOs and the Activities of the International Criminal Court", in Tullio Treves *et al.* (editors), *Civil Society, International Courts and Compliance Bodies*, Asser Press, 2005, pp. 121–28.

United States Government, The International Criminal Court: Protecting American Servicemen and Officials from the Threat of International Prosecution, hearing before the Committee on Foreign Relations, US Senate, 106th Congress, Second Session, S. Hrg. 106-769, 14 June 2000, US Government Printing Office, Washington DC, 2000.

—, Is the U.N. ICC in the U.S. National Interest?, hearing before the Subcommittee on International Operations of the Committee on Foreign Relations, US Senate, S. Hrg. 105-724, 23 July 1998, US Government Printing Office, Washington DC, 2000.

—, The International Criminal Court, hearing before the Committee on International

Relations, House of Representatives 106th Congress, Second Session, No. 106-176, US Government Printing Office, Washington DC, 25–26 July 2000.

—, *U.S. Policy Regarding the International Criminal Court*, Congressional Research Service, Library of Congress, Washington DC, 3 September 2002.

—, "International Criminal Court Cases in Africa: Status and Policy Issues", Congressional Research Service, Washington DC, 12 September 2008, available at <https://www.policyarchive.org/bitstream/handle/10207/20071/RL34665_20080912.pdf?sequence=2>.

Vagias, Michail, *The Territorial Jurisdiction of the International Criminal Court*, Cambridge University Press, 2014.

Valentine, Paul J., "People in glass houses should not throw stones: Why the Democracy Deficit Argument against intergovernmental international organisation carries little weight in the United States of America", *Phoenix Law Review*, Volume 2, Number 1 (2009).

Van Acker, Frank, "Uganda and the Lord's Resistance Army: The New Order No One Ordered", *African Affairs*, Volume 103, Number 412 (2004), pp. 335–57.

Van Boven, Theodoor C., "The European Union and the International Criminal Court", *Maastricht Journal of European and Comparative Law*, Volume 5, Number 4 (1998), pp. 325–27.

Van Der Vyver, Johan D., "American Exceptionalism: Human Rights, International Criminal Justice, and National Self-righteousness", *Emory Law Journal*, Volume 50, Number 3 (2001), pp. 775–832.

Villa-Vincencio, Charles, "Why perpetrators should not always be prosecuted: where the International Criminal Court and truth commissions meet", *Emory Law Journal*, Volume 49, Number 1 (2000), pp. 205–22.

Vinci, Anthony, "Existential Motivations in the Lord's Resistance Army's Continuing Conflict", *Studies in Conflict & Terrorism*, Volume 30, Number 4 (2007), pp. 337–52.

Vinck, Patrick, Phuong, Pham, Stover, Eric, Moss, Andrew, Marleke, Wierda and Bailey, Richard, "When the War Ends: a New Population-Based Survey on Attitudes About Peace, Justice, and Social Reconstruction in Northern Uganda", Human Rights Center, University of California, Berkeley, 2007.

Vinck, Patrick, Phuong, Pham, Baldo, Suliman and Shigekane, Rachel, "Living With Fear: a Population-Based Survey on Attitudes About Peace, Justice, and Social Reconstruction in Eastern Democratic Republic of Congo", Human Rights Center, University of California, Berkeley, 2008.

Voeten, Erik, "The Impartiality of International Judges: Evidence from the European Court of Human Rights", *American Political Science Review*, Volume 102 (2008), pp. 417–33.

Volqvartz, Josefine, "ICC Under Fire Over Uganda Probe", CNN, 23 February 2005, available at <http://www.cnn.com/2005/WORLD/africa/02/23/uganda>.

von der Groeben, C., "Criminal Responsibility of German Soldiers in Afghanistan: The Case of Colonel Klein", *German Law Journal*, 2010, pp. 469–92.

Vreeland, James R., "Global Horse Trading: IMF Loans for Votes in the United Nations Security Council", *European Economic Review*, Volume 53, Number 7 (2009), pp. 742–57.

Waddell, Nicholas and Clark, Phil (editors), *Courting Conflict? Justice, Peace and the ICC in Africa*, Royal African Society, London, March 2008, available at <http://www.crisisstates.com/download/others/ICC%20in%20Africa.pdf>.

—, *Justice & the ICC in Africa. Meeting Series Synopsis*, Royal African Society, 2007, available at <http://www.royalafricansociety.org/images/stories/pdf_files/peacejusticeandtheicc-synopsis.pdf>.

Wallis, Daniel, "New World Court Faces Unexpected Trials in Uganda", *Reuters*, 25 July 2005, available at <http://www.alertnet.org/thenews/newsdesk/L25649571.htm>.

Wartanian, Annie, "The ICC Prosecutor's Battlefield: Combating Atrocities While Fighting for States' Cooperation – Lessons From the UN Tribunals Applied to the Case of Uganda", *Georgetown Journal of International Law*, Volume 36 (2005), pp. 1289–316.

Washington Times, "Obama in handcuffs", Editorial, 2 December 2009, available at <http://www.washingtontimes.com/news/2009/dec/02/obama-in-handcuffs/>.

Weber, Wolfgang, "Munich exhibition documents German army atrocity in Afghanistan", World Socialist Web Site, 8 February 2011, available at <http://www.wsws.org/en/articles/2011/02/kund-f08.html>.

Wedgwood, Ruth, "Fiddling in Rome: America and the International Criminal Court", *Foreign Affairs*, Volume 77, Number 6 (1998).

—, "The International Criminal Court: An American View", *European Journal of International Law*, Volume 10 (1999).

—, "The Irresolution of Rome", *Law and Contemporary Problems*, Volume 64 (2001).

Weller, M., "Undoing the Global Constitution: UN Security Council Action on the International Criminal Court", *International Affairs*, Volume 78, Number 4 (2002), pp. 693–712.

White, Nigel and Cryer, Robert, "The ICC and the Security Council: an Uncomfortable Relationship", in José Doria, Hans-Peter Gasser and M. Cherif Bassiouni (editors), *The Legal Regime of the International Criminal Court: Essays in Honour of Professor Igor Blishchenko: In Memoriam Professor Igor Pavlovich Blishchenko (1930–2000)*, Nijhoff, 2009.

Will, George F., "U.S. must not surrender sovereignty to International Criminal Court", *Pittsburgh Tribune-Review*, 11 July 2002, available at <http://triblive.com/x/pittsburghtrib/opinion/columnists/will/s_80658.html#axzz2ONjM3Lzi>.

Williams, Paul R., "The Role of Justice in Peace Negotiations", in M. Cherif Bassiouni (editor), *Post-Conflict Justice*, Transnational Publishers, Ardsley, New York, 2002, pp. 115–33.

Williamson, Cécile Aptel, "Justice empowered or justice hampered: The International Criminal Court in Darfur", *African Security Review*, Volume 15, Issue 1, January 2006, pp. 20–31.

Wilson, Richard Ashby, "Through the Lens of International Criminal Law: Comprehending the African Context of Crimes at the International Criminal Court", *Studies in Ethnicity and Nationalism*, Volume 11, Number 1 (2011).

—, *Writing History in International Criminal Trials*, Cambridge University Press, 2011.
Wirth, Steffen, "Immunities, Related Problems, and Article 98 of the Rome Statute", *Criminal Law Forum*, Volume 12, Number 4 (2001), pp. 429–58.
Wise, Edward M., "The International Criminal Court: a budget of paradoxes", *Tulane Journal of International and Comparative Law*, Volume 8 (2000), pp. 261–81.
Wolf, J., "Die ISAF – Luftschläge in Kunduz vom 4. September 2009 – eine humanitär – völkerrechtliche Analyse", *BOFAXE* Nr. 339D, Institut für Friedenssicherungsrecht und Humanitäres Völkerrecht, Ruhr University, 26 April 2010.
Wolters, S., "Selective Prosecutions Could Undermine Justice for Congo", Institute of War and Peace Reporting, 7 March 2007, available <www.iwpr.net/?p=acr&s=f&o=333874&apc_state=henh; and ICG, supra note 93, at 21–2>.
Women's Initiatives for Gender Justice, *Gender Report Card on the International Criminal Court*, The Hague, 2008.
—, *Gender Report Card on the International Criminal Court 2011*, The Hague, 2009.
—, *Gender Report Card on the International Criminal Court 2010*, The Hague, 2009.
—, *Gender Report Card on the International Criminal Court 2009*, The Hague, 2010.
—, *Gender Report Card on the International Criminal Court 2008*, The Hague, 2011.
Wouters, Jan and Basu, Sudeshna, "The Creation of a Global Criminal Justice System: the European Union and the International Criminal Court", in Cedric Ryngaert (editor), *The Effectiveness of International Criminal Justice*, Intersentia, 2009.
Wright, Daniel V., *Strategic Implications of U.S. Non-Support for the International Criminal Court*, US Army War College, Carlisle Barracks, Pa., 1999.
Yee, Lionel, "The International Criminal Court and the Security Council: Articles 13(b) and 16", in Roy S. Lee (editor), *The International Criminal Court: The Making of the Rome Statute*, Kluwer Law International, 2002.
Zappala, S., "Are some peacekeepers better than others?: UN Security Council Resolution 1497 (2003) and the ICC", *Journal of International Criminal Justice*, Volume 1, Number 3 (2003), pp. 671–78.
Zwanenburg, Marten, "The Statute for an International Criminal Court and the United States: Peacekeepers under Fire?", *European Journal of International Law*, Volume 10, Number 1 (1999), pp. 124–43.
—, "The Statute of an International Criminal Court and the United States: Peace without Justice?", *Leiden Journal of International Law*, Volume 12, Number 1 (1999), pp. 1–8.
Zwart, Tim and Knoops, Alexander, "Who is persecuting Laurent Gbagbo?", *New African*, April 2013, pp. 16–17.

Notes to Chapters

Notes to Introduction

1. "Alice in Wonderland Quotes. The Philosophy of Life Revealed in These Alice in Wonderland Quotes", About.Com: Quotations, available at <http://quotations.about.com/od/moretypes/a/alice1.htm>. *Alice's Adventures in Wonderland,* published in 1865, and best known as "Alice in Wonderland", is a novel written by English author Charles Dodgson under the pseudonym Lewis Carroll. The Queen of Hearts is a character in the book, quick to order death sentences at the slightest offence.
2. See, for example, Dr. Paul Moorcraft, "Bashing Omar al-Bashir", *The American Spectator,* 29 May 2009, available at <http://spectator.org/archives/2009/05/29/bashing-omar-al-bashir/print>.
3. Geoffrey Robertson, *Crimes Against Humanity. The Struggle for Global Justice,* Penguin Books, First Edition, 1999, p. 341. Geoffrey Robertson QC is founder and the joint head of Doughty Street Chambers. He is a 'distinguished jurist' member of the United Nations Justice Council, having served as the first President of the Special Court in Sierra Leone. He has argued many landmark cases in media, constitutional and criminal law in the European Court of Human Rights, the British House of Lords, the Privy Council and Commonwealth courts. He has appeared in the Court of Final Appeal for Hong Kong, the Supreme Court of Malaysia, the Fiji Court of Appeal, the High Court of Australia and the International Criminal Tribunal for the former Yugoslavia.
4. Geoffrey Robertson, *Crimes Against Humanity. The Struggle for Global Justice,* p. 304.
5. *Ibid.,* p. 793.
6. See, for example, Oona A. Hathaway, "Do Human Rights Treaties Make a Difference", *Yale Law Journal,* Vol. 111 (2002), available at <http://yalelawjournal.org/the-yale-law-journal/article/do-human-rights-treaties-make-a-difference?/>.
7. Terrence L. Chapman and Stephen Chaudoin, "Ratification Patterns and the International Criminal Court", *International Studies Quarterly,* 2012.
8. David B. Rivkin Jr. and Lee A. Casey, "Lawfare", *The Wall Street Journal,* 23 February 2007, available at <http://online.wsj.com/article/SB117220137149816987.html>. See, also, "Is Lawfare Worth Defining?", *Case Western Reserve Journal of International Law,* Vol. 43, No. 1 (2010).
9. David B. Harris and Aaron Eitan Meyer, "Lawfare: A Supporting Arm in Modern Conflict", The Lawfare Project, 4 April 2011, available at <http://www.thelawfareproject.org/Articles-by-LP-Staff/lawfare-a-supporting-arm-in-modern-conflict.html>.
10. "Lawfare Today", *Yale Journal of International Affairs,* Winter 2008, p. 146. Major General Dunlap was the Deputy Judge Advocate General of the US Air Force.
11. For an analysis of the role of non-governmental organisations see, for example, the chapter "Negotiations: NGOs Shape Terms of the ICC Debate 1995–1998", in Michael J. Struett, *The Politics of Constructing the International Criminal Court: NGOs, Discourse, and Agency,* Macmillan, 2008.

12   "Report of the International Criminal Court", A/64/356, General Assembly, 17 September 2009, available at <http://www.icc-cpi.int/NR/rdonlyres/1BC01710-9C42-44AC-8B18-85EE2A8876EB/281210/A_64_356_ENG2.pdf>.
13   The Security Council has fifteen members, of which five, China, France, the Russian Federation, the UK and the USA, are permanent, and ten non-permanent, elected by the General Assembly for two-year terms and not eligible for immediate re-election. The permanent five members have a veto vote over substantive matters. The USA, China and the Russian Federation are not members of the ICC. They are variously referred to as the P-5, or in the case of the three Western members acting together, the P-3.
14   Kofi Annan, *Interventions: A Life in War and Peace*, Penguin, New York, 2012, p. 153.
15   See, "Mamdani, Raps Bashir Indictment", *New Vision*, 26 August 2009, available at <http://allafrica.com/stories/printable/200908270286.html>. Ugandan-born Mahmood Mamdani, is the Director of the Makerere Institute of Social Research at Makerere University. He is also Herbert Lehman Professor of Government in the Departments of Anthropology and Political Science at Columbia University in the USA, and the Director of Columbia's Institute of African Studies. He is a former President of the Council for Development of Social Research in Africa (CODESRIA) in Dakar, Senegal. Mamdani,'s reputation as an expert in African history, politics and international relations has made him an important voice in contemporary debates about Africa. His book *Citizen and Subject: Contemporary Africa and the Legacy of Late Colonialism* won the 1998 Herskovits Award of the African Studies Association of the USA. In 2001, he was one of nine scholars to present at the Nobel Peace Prize Centennial Symposium. He has been named as one of the top 100 public intellectuals in the world by the US magazine *Foreign Policy* in May 2008, and the UK magazine *Prospect* in July 2008.
16   "Rwanda's Kagame says ICC targeting poor, African countries", *Agence France-Presse*, 31 July 2008, available at <http://afp.google.com/article/ALeqM5ilwB_Zg00Jx3N9hSX-Wu8zEyQGig>.
17   Ramesh Thakur, "Perks of the warring states", *The Japan Times*, 27 March 2009, available at <http://search.japantimes.co.jp/cgi-bin/eo20090327rt.html>. Professor Ramesh Thakur is a political scientist and peace researcher. He is a Distinguished Fellow at the Centre for International Governance Innovation and Professor of Political Science at the University of Waterloo, Canada. He has previously served as Senior Vice-Rector of the UN University at the Assistant Secretary-General level. He was in charge of the university's peace and governance programme.
18   The Keystone Kops was a series of silent film comedies about a totally incompetent group of policemen noted for their bungling inefficiency. The movies were produced by Mack Sennett, for his Keystone Film Company, between 1912 and 1917. The term has since come to be used to criticise any organisation for bungling ineptitude and mistakes, particularly if the mistakes went hand-in-hand with a great deal of energy and activity. Wikipedia uses the example of Senator Joseph Lieberman's criticism of the US Department of Homeland Security's response to Hurricane Katrina, in which be claimed that emergency workers under DHS chief Michael Chertoff "ran around like Keystone Kops, uncertain about what they were supposed to do or uncertain how to do it" ("Chertoff castigated over Katrina", BBC News, 15 February 2006, available at <http://news.bbc.co.uk/1/hi/world/americas/4717916.stm>). It is also an urban term for ineffective, bungling law enforcers who have nothing better to do than to stake out parties and arrest underage drinkers.
19   Ben Lerner, "Ambulance Chasing - From Kabul to Gaza", *The American Spectator*, 8 October 2009, available at <http://spectator.org/archives/2009/10/08/ambulance-chasing-from-kabul-t/print>.
20   Mahmood Mamdani, *Saviors and Survivors: Darfur, Politics, and the War on Terror*, Pantheon, 2009.

21 Alex de Waal, "The ICC, Sudan, and the Crisis of Human Rights", *African Arguments*, 5 March 2009, available at <http://africanarguments.org/2009/03/the-icc-sudan-and-the-crisis-of-human-rights/>.
22 ICC, "Policy Paper on Preliminary Examinations", OTP, 4 October 2010, available at <http://www.icc-cpi.int/NR/rdonlyres/9FF1EAA1-41C4-4A30-A202-174B18DA923C/282515/OTP_Draftpolicypaperonpreliminaryexaminations04101.pdf>.
23 The death toll in Mexico's drug-related violence has been put at more than 60,000 since late 2006. The Mexican government has been accused of involvement in massive human rights abuses and has not been able to adequately address this violence through its judicial system. Mexican activists have asked the ICC to investigate Mexico's President Felipe Calderon over the torture and killing of civilians in the war on drugs. Human rights lawyer Netzai Sandoval filed a complaint with the ICC in The Hague, asking it to investigate the deaths of hundreds of civilians at the hands of the security forces and drugs gangs, as well as alleged torture and rape: "The violence in Mexico is bigger than the violence in Afghanistan, and bigger than the violence in Colombia. We want the prosecutor to tell us if war crimes and crimes against humanity have been committed in Mexico, and if the president and other top officials are responsible." See, "Q&A: Mexico's drug-related violence", BBC News, 24 December 2012, available, <http://www.bbc.co.uk/news/world-latin-america-10681249>, and "Mexico activists seek ICC investigation of drugs war", BBC News, 25 November 2011, available at <http://www.bbc.co.uk/news/world-latin-america-15899687>.
24 This international support for Sudan on the ICC issue has been constant, from 2008 until the present. In September 2008, for example, in direct response to the ICC's July 2008 indictment of President al-Bashir, Sudan was elected as Chairman of the G77, the largest intergovernmental organisation of developing states in the UN (originally 77 founding nations but now 130 strong), a clear indication of an unprecedented level of solidarity and support following the court's actions. Most recently, President al-Bashir was invited to chair the second day of the sixteenth Summit of the Non-Aligned Movement, which was held from 26 to 31 August 2012 in Tehran, Iran. The summit was attended by leaders of 120 countries, including twenty-four presidents, three kings, eight prime ministers and fifty foreign ministers.
25 "Kenya's Election: What Uhuru Kenyatta's Victory Means for Africa", *Time*, 9 March 2013, available at <http://world.time.com/2013/03/09/kenyas-election-what-uhuru-kenyattas-victory-means-for-africa/>.
26 Judge Judy Sheindlin's test is a simple one encapsulated in the title of one of her books. See Judy Sheindlin, *Don't Pee on My Leg Tell Me it's Raining: America's Toughest Family Court Judge Speaks out*, HarperCollins, New York, 1998.
27 "No to the International Kangeroo Court", <antiwar.com>. 3 January 2001, available at <http://www.antiwar.com/justin/j010301.html>; Jeremy Rabkin, "The International Kangaroo Court", *The Weekly Standard*, 29 April 2002, available at <http://staging.weeklystandard.com/Content/Public/Articles/000/000/001/153kycni.asp>; John Perazzo, "International Kangaroo Court", *FrontPageMagazine*, 30 July 2003, available at <http://archive.frontpagemag.com/readArticle.aspx?ARTID=17001>; "The Hague, Kangaroo Court of the world", *Pravda*, 10 March 2009, available at <http://english.pravda.ru/opinion/columnists/10-03-2009/107212-hague_kangaroo_court-0/>; "ICC – 'Western kangaroo court'", *Southern Times* (South Africa), 15 March 2009, available at <http://www.globalresearch.ca/icc-western-kangaroo-court/12721>; "Alex Jones: 'ICC is a kangaroo court'", *Russia Today*, 27 June 2011, available at <http://rt.com/usa/jones-icc-court-gaddafi/>; "ICC, Glorified Kangaroo Court – Chinamasa", *The Herald* (Harare), 3 March 2012; "Justice Antonin Scalia on International Criminal Court: 'ICC a kangaroo court'", UNDP Watch, 3 August 2012, available at <http://undpwatch.blogspot.co.uk/2012/08/justice-antonin-scalia-on-international.html>.

28   Annan, *op. cit.*, pp. 147–48.
29   "Let the Child Live", *The Economist*, 27 January 2007.
30   ICC, Prosecutor v. Thomas Lubanga Dyilo, ICC-01/04-01/06, trial transcript, 26 March 2009, p. 20. Dr. Gérard Prunier is a noted Africanist. He is the author of more than 200 scholarly articles and a dozen books in four languages, including *The Rwanda Crisis: History of a Genocide* (Columbia University Press, 1995), *Darfur: The Ambiguous Genocide* (Hurst, 2005), and *Africa's World War: Congo, the Rwandan Genocide, and the Making of Continental Catastrophe* (Oxford University Press, 2008). He has worked as a senior researcher at the Centre National de la Recherche Scientifique, France's largest government research organisation, and as a professor at the University of Paris. From 2001 to 2006, he was seconded to the French Ministry of Foreign Affairs and served as the Director of the Centre Français des Études Éthiopiennes in Addis Ababa. Prunier has served as an advisor to the French government, the US State and Defense Departments, various European and African governments, as well as private companies.
31   ICC, Prosecutor v. Thomas Lubanga Dyilo, ICC-01/04-01/06, trial transcript, 26 March 2009, p. 14.
32   *Ibid.*, p. 41.
33   In September 2009, Ocampo said he had sent a letter to the Swiss government stating that the ICC may open a formal investigation into possible Columbian money laundering networks in Switzerland and could issue arrest warrants if the Swiss government did not conduct its own investigation: WikiLeaks, US Government cable, "Subject: ICC Prosecutor Moreno's Visit to Colombia", 4 September 2008, available at <http://cablegatesearch.WikiLeaks.org/cable.php?id=08BOGOTA3304&q=court%20criminal%20international%20ocampo>.
34   See, for example, Human Rights Watch, "Guinea: Stadium Massacre, Rape Likely Crimes against Humanity. Government, International Community Should Ensure Perpetrators Held Accountable", 17 December 2009.
35   "ICC has fallen from high ideals of global justice, accountability", *Daily Nation* (Nairobi), 16 March 2013, available at <http://www.nation.co.ke/oped/Opinion/-/440808/1722100/-/k4rufnz/-/index.html>.
36   David Kaye, "Who's Afraid of the International Criminal Court?", *Foreign Affairs*, May/June 2011, available at <http://www.foreignaffairs.com/articles/67768/david-kaye/whos-afraid-of-the-international-criminal-court>. Kaye's support for the court is clear. See, for example, "Feature: Prof. Kaye rallies global leaders to seek wider support of International Criminal Court", University of California at Irvine School of Law, available at <http://www.law.uci.edu/faculty/feature_d_kaye.html>. Professor Kaye presently teaches law at the University of California, Irvine.
37   See, for example, Richard Dicker, "The Court of Last Resort", *Foreign Policy*, 29 June 2012, available at <http://www.foreignpolicy.com/articles/2012/06/29/ICC_the_court_of_last_resort?page=full>. Dicker is Director of the International Justice Program at Human Rights Watch.
38   "The Hague struggles to find judges", *Financial Times*, 14 September 2011, available at <http://www.ft.com/cms/s/0/ecbbe978-dede-11e0-9130-00144feabdc0.html#axzz2Pn7xxcoG>.
39   Rony Brauman, "The ICC's Bashir Indictment: Law Against Peace", *World Politics Review*, 23 July 2008, available at <http://www.worldpoliticsreview.com/Article.aspx?id=2471>. He is the author of numerous volumes on humanitarian assistance and conflict situations, including *Aider, sauver: Pourquoi, comment?*
40   "Cosy club or sword of righteousness?", *The Economist*, 26 November 2011, available at <http://www.economist.com/node/21540230?zid=317&ah=8a47fc455a44945580198768fad0fa41>.
41   Michael Ignatieff, "We're So Exceptional", *The New York Review of Books*, 5 April 2012. Michael Ignatieff is a Canadian author, academic and former politician and noted expert on

international human rights. He was the leader of the Liberal Party of Canada and Leader of the Official Opposition from 2008 until 2011. Ignatieff has held senior academic posts at the University of Cambridge, the University of Oxford, Harvard University and the University of Toronto. Ignatieff served as the director of the Carr Center for Human Rights Policy at the John F. Kennedy School of Government at Harvard University. He also helped to prepare the report "The Responsibility to Protect" for the International Commission on Intervention and State Sovereignty.

42 "5 things Fatou Bensouda should do at the ICC", *The Guardian*, 14 June 2012, available at <http://www.guardian.co.uk/law/2012/jun/14/fatou-bensouda-international-criminal-court1>.

43 Diana Johnstone, "A Pretext for War. Do We Really Need an International Criminal Court?", *Counterpunch*, weekend edition 6–8 May 2011, available at <http://www.counterpunch.org/2011/05/06/do-we-really-need-an-international-criminal-court-2/>.

44 Annan, *op. cit.*, p. 155.

45 "Mamdani, Raps Bashir Indictment", *New Vision*, 26 August 2009, available at <http://www.newvision.co.ug/D/8/13/692558>.

Notes to Chapter One

46 Cited in Dr. John Laughland, "Forget the rhetoric, this court is just another excuse for superpower bullying", *The Times* (London), 29 August 2000.

47 Geoffrey Robertson, *Crimes Against Humanity: The Struggle for Global Justice*, p. 341.

48 Cited in Nehal Bhuta, "How Shall We Punish the Perpetrators? Human Rights, Alien Wrongs and the March of International Criminal Law", *Melbourne University Law Review*, Vol. 27, No. 1 (2003), available at Social Science Research Network: <http://ssrn.com/abstract=1143493>. Professor Georg Scwarzenberger was an eminent international lawyer and legal scholar. He was appointed to the Faculty of Laws at University College London in 1938 where he remained until his retirement in 1975. He was then appointed Professor Emeritus of International Law at the University of London. In international law he used an inductive approach, convinced that the practice of states and the jurisprudence of courts, both international and national, were more significant than doctrine and theory. His greatest contribution to international law is the four-volume work *International Law as Applied by International Courts and Tribunals* (1945–1986); however, the philosophy behind his approach is to be found in his *Inductive Approach to International Law* (1965). Among other works of major significance are his *International Law and Totalitarian Lawlessness* (1943); *A Manual of International Law* (sixth edition, with E. D. Brown, 1976); *The Legality of Nuclear Weapons* (1958); *The Frontiers of International Law* (1962); *International Law and Order* (1971); and *The Dynamics of International Law* (1976). In addition, he was a prolific writer of learned papers, which appeared in a variety of journals, including the *American Journal of International Law*.

49 See, for example, H. L. A. Hart, *The Concept of Law*, Oxford University Press, 1965, p. 209. See, also, H. L. A. Hart, *Essays in Jurisprudence and Philosophy*, Oxford University Press, 1984. Hart was Professor of Jurisprudence at Oxford University and the Principal of Brasenose College, Oxford. *The Concept of Law* is one of the seminal works of English-language jurisprudence.

50 Professor William Schabas is an established author and academic in the field of international criminal and human rights law. He is a professor of international law at Middlesex University in London and has been the Director of the Irish Centre for Human Rights at the National University of Ireland, Galway. He specialises in the study of human rights law, genocide, and the death penalty. In 2009 he was elected President of the International Association

of Genocide Scholars. He attended the 1998 Rome Conference. at which the statute of the ICC was adopted, as a representative of the International Centre for Criminal Law Reform. He had also been present at the preparatory committee and commission which led up to the Rome Conference.

51 William Schabas, *An Introduction to the International Criminal Court*, Cambridge University Press, 2001, vii.
52 Philippe Sands, "International justice is needed – even if it takes 100 more years to perfect it. ICC may seem Africa-centric, but hopefully this will come to be seen as teething." *The Guardian*, 6 May 2012, available at <http://www.guardian.co.uk/law/2012/may/16/international-justice-needed-expert-view>. Philippe Sands QC is a professor of law and Director of the Centre on International Courts and Tribunals, and a member of staff in the Centre for Law and the Environment at University College London. His teaching areas include public international law, the settlement of international disputes (including arbitration), and environmental and natural resources law. He is a member of the Advisory Boards of the *European Journal of International Law* and *Review of European Community and International Environmental Law* (Blackwell Press). As a practising barrister, he has extensive experience litigating cases before the International Court of Justice, the International Tribunal for the Law of the Sea, the International Center for the Settlement of Investment Disputes, and the European Court of Justice. He frequently advises governments, international organisations, NGOs and the private sector on aspects of international law. In 2003 he was appointed a Queen's Counsel.
53 For a list of all the participants in the Rome Conference, see "Final Act of the United Nations Diplomatic Conference of Plenipotentiaries on the Establishment of an International Criminal Court", Annexes II–IV, U.N. Doc. A/CONF.183/10 (1998). There were 160 states, the UN, eight UN programmes and bodies, sixteen international governmental organisations and other entities, five specialised agencies and related organisations, and 130 non-governmental organisations present at the conference.
54 Mahmood Mamdani, "Darfur, ICC and the new humanitarian order: How the ICC's 'responsibility to protect' is being turned into an assertion of neocolonial domination", *Pambazuka News*, 17 September 2008, Issue 396, available at <http://pambazuka.org/en/category/features/50568>.
55 *Ibid.*
56 David Davenport, "The New Diplomacy", *Policy Review*, No. 116, December 2002/January 2003, available at <http://www.hoover.org/publications/policyreview/3458466.html>. Professor Davenport is a research fellow and also counsellor to the director of the Hoover Institution at Stanford University. His research and writing focus on international law and treaties and federalism. From 1985 to 2000, he served as President of Pepperdine University, where he was also a professor of public policy and law.
57 *Ibid.*
58 Geoffrey Robertson, *Crimes Against Humanity. The Struggle for Global Justice*, Penguin Books, fourth edition, 2012, p. 507.
59 *Ibid.*, p. 505.
60 *Ibid.*, p. 519.
61 *Ibid.*, pp. 505–06.
62 *Ibid.*, p. 536.
63 *Ibid.*, p. 545.
64 *Ibid.*, p. 551.
65 These States Parties are the following. *African States*: Benin (22 January 2002), Botswana (8 September 2000), Burkina Faso (30 November 1998), Burundi (21 September 2004), the Central African Republic (3 October 2001), Cape Verde (11 October 2011), Chad (1 January 2007), Comoros (18 August 2006), Congo (3 May 2004), the Democratic Republic

of the Congo (11 April 2002), Djibouti (5 November 2002), Gabon (20 September 2000), Gambia (28 June 2002), Ghana (20 December 1999), Guinea (14 July 2003), Kenya (15 March 2005), Lesotho (6 September 2000), Liberia (22 September 2004), Madagascar (14 March 2008), Malawi (19 September 2002), Mali (16 August 2000), Mauritius (5 March 2002), Namibia (20 June 2002), Niger (11 April 2002), Nigeria (27 September 2001), Senegal (2 February 1999), Sierra Leone (15 September 2000), Seychelles (10 August 2010), South Africa (27 November 2000), Tunisia (22 June 2011), Uganda (14 June 2002), United Republic of Tanzania (20 August 2002), and Zambia (13 November 2002). *Asia-Pacific States*: Afghanistan (10 February 2003), Bangladesh (23 March 2010), Cambodia (11 April 2002), Cook Islands (18 July 2008), Cyprus (7 March 2002), Fiji (29 November 1999), Japan (17 July 2007), Jordan (11 April 2002), Maldives (21 September 2011), Mongolia (11 April 2002), Marshall Islands (7 December 2000), Nauru (12 November 2001), Philippines (30 August 2011), the Republic of Korea (13 November 2002), Samoa (16 September 2002), Tajikistan (5 May 2000), Timor-Leste (6 September 2002), Vanuatu (2 December 2011). *Eastern European States*: Albania (31 January 2003), Bosnia and Herzegovina (11 April 2002), Bulgaria (11 April 2002), Croatia (21 May 2001), Czech Republic (21 July 2009), Estonia (30 January 2002), the Former Yugoslav Republic of Macedonia (6 March 2002), Georgia (5 September 2003), Hungary (30 November 2001), Latvia (28 June 2002), Lithuania (12 May 2003), Montenegro (3 June 2006), Poland (12 November 2001), Republic of Moldova (12 October 2010), Romania (11 April 2002), Serbia (6 September 2001), Slovakia (11 April 2002), and Slovenia (31 December 2001). The *Latin American and Caribbean Group*: Antigua and Barbuda (18 June 2001), Argentina (8 February 2001), Barbados (10 December 2002), Brazil (20 June 2002), Belize (5 April 2000), Bolivia (27 June 2002), Chile (29 June 2009), Colombia (5 August 2002), Costa Rica (30 January 2001), Dominica (12 February 2001), Dominican Republic (12 May 2005), Ecuador (5 February 2002), Grenada (19 May 2011), Guatemala (2 April 2012), Guyana (24 September 2004), Honduras (1 July 2002), Mexico (28 October 2005), Panama (21 March 2002), Paraguay (14 May 2001), Peru (10 November 2001), Saint Kitts and Nevis (22 August 2006), Saint Lucia (18 August 2010), Saint Vincent and the Grenadines (3 December 2002), Suriname (15 July 2008), Trinidad and Tobago (6 April 1999), Uruguay (28 June 2002), and Venezuela (7 June 2000). *Western Europe and others group*: Andorra (30 April 2001), Australia (1 July 2002), Austria (28 December 2000), Belgium (28 June 2000), Canada (7 July 2000), Denmark (21 June 2001), France (9 June 2000), Finland (29 December 2000), Germany (11 December 2000), Greece (15 May 2002), Iceland (25 May 2000), Ireland (11 April 2002), Italy (26 July 1999), Liechtenstein (2 October 2001), Luxembourg (8 September 2000), Malta (29 November 2002), the Netherlands (17 July 2001), New Zealand (7 September 2000), Norway (16 February 2000), San Marino (13 May 1999), Spain (24 October 2000), Sweden (28 January 2001), Switzerland (12 October 2001), Portugal (5 February 2002), and the United Kingdom (4 October 2001).

66 UN, "Report of the International Criminal Court", 14 August 2012, A/67/308, available at <http://www.icc-cpi.int/en_menus/icc/reports%20on%20activities/court%20reports%20and%20statements/Documents/A67308EN.pdf>.
67 See, for example, ICC, "Delegations to the tenth session of the Assembly of States Parties to the Rome Statute of the International Criminal Court New York, 12–21 December 2011", ASP, 27 March 2012, ICC-ASP/10/INF.1.
68 ICC, "Assembly of States Parties concludes its eleventh session", 23 November 2012, Press Release, ICC-ASP-20121123-PR858, available at <http://www.icc-cpi.int/en_menus/asp/press%20releases/press%20releases%202012/Pages/pr858.aspx>.
69 ICC, "International Criminal Court. Figures from Registry", available from <http://www.icc-cpi.int/en_menus/icc/reports%20on%20activities/court%20reports%20and%20statements/Documents/RegistryFigures31August2014.pdf>.

70 John Rosenthal, "A Lawless Global Court. How the International Criminal Court Undermines the U.N. System", *Policy Review*, Hoover Institution, February–March 2004, available at <http://www.hoover.org/publications/policyreview/3439981.html>. John Rosenthal's writings on international politics have appeared in English, French and German in such publications as *Policy Review*, *Newsday*, *The Opinion Journal*, *Les Temps Modernes*, *Le Figaro*, and *Merkur*, as well as numerous scholarly journals and collective volumes. He has taught political philosophy and history of European philosophy at, among other institutions, New York University, Rutgers University and the École Normale Superieure of Lyon.

71 ASP, "Report on programme performance of the International Criminal Court for the year 2007", 26 May 2008.

72 ASP, "Resolution: Programme budget for 2008, the Working Capital Fund for 2008, scale of assessments for the apportionment of expenses of the International Criminal Court and financing appropriations for the year 2008", 14 December 2007.

73 ASP, "Resolution: Programme budget for 2009, the Contingency Fund, the Working Capital Fund for 2009, scale of assessments for the apportionment of expenses of the International Criminal Court and financing appropriations for the year 2009", 21 November 2008.

74 ICC, "Proposed Programme Budget for 2010 of the International Criminal Court", ICC-ASP/8/10, The Hague, 18 November 2009.

75 See, for example, "The New EU: Definitely a Superstate", *The Brussels Journal*, 4 January 2008, available at <http://www.brusselsjournal.com/node/2831>.

76 *League of Nations Treaty Series*, Vol. 165 (1936), pp. 20–43.

77 See, for example, "EU Navy says spotted yacht close to Somali coast", Reuters, 27 October 2009, available at <http://uk.reuters.com/article/idUKLR504888>.

78 ICC, ASP, "Report of the Committee on Budget and Finance on the work of its eighteenth session", The Hague, 14–22 November 2012, ICC-ASP/11/5, pp. 15–16, available at <http://212.159.242.181/iccdocs/asp_docs/ASP11/ICC-ASP-11-5-ENG-CBF18-Report.pdf>.

79 *Ibid.*

80 *Ibid.*

81 See Hans-Peter Kaul, "Der Aufbau des internationalen Strafgerichtshof", *Vereinte Nationen*, December 2001.

82 Rosenthal, *op. cit.*, Note 15.

83 *Ibid.*

84 *Ibid.*

85 Jess Bravin, "Justice Delayed. For Global Court, Ugandan Rebels Prove Tough Test", *The Wall Street Journal*, 8 June 2006.

86 Dr. Guénaël Mettraux is a member of the International Criminal Law Bureau undertaking international legal cases and providing advice, consultancy and training services to governments, international organisations and private clients. Dr. Mettraux has represented political and military leaders from Europe and Asia. He has published extensively in the field of international criminal law. He has lectured on international criminal law at top law schools in The Netherlands, Switzerland, Italy, the United States, and Bosnia-Herzegovina. The American Society of International Law awarded him the prestigious Francis Lieber Prize for outstanding scholarship in the field of armed conflict by a young author for his book *The Law of Command Responsibility* (Oxford University Press), 2009.

87 Dr. Guénaël Mettraux, "The Cost of Justice – Is the ICC living beyond its means?", International Criminal Law Bureau, 6 August 2009, available at <http://www.internationallawbureau.com/blog/?p=503>.

88 "The Cost of Justice", International Criminal Tribunal for the former Yugoslavia, available at <http://www.icty.org/sid/325>.

89 Dr. Guénaël Mettraux, "The Cost of Justice – Is the ICC living beyond its means?", *op. cit.*

90 These ICC States Parties are Afghanistan, Albania, Andorra, Antigua and Barbuda, Barbados, Belize, Benin, Bolivia, Botswana, Brazil, Burkina Faso, Burundi, Cambodia, Central African Republic, Chad, Chile, Columbia, Congo, Cook Islands, Costa Rica, Côte d'Ivoire (although not a state party, it has made a declaration under Article 12(3) to accept all cooperation obligations under the Rome Statute), Cyprus, Czech Republic, Democratic Republic of Congo, Djibouti, Dominica, Dominican Republic, Ecuador, Fiji, Gabon, Gambia, Ghana, Greece, Guinea, Ghana, Guyana, Honduras, Hungary, Italy, Jordan, Kenya, Lesotho, Liberia, Luxembourg, Madagascar, Malawi, Mali, Marshall Islands, Mauritius, Mexico, Mongolia, Namibia, Nauru, Niger, Nigeria, Panama, Paraguay, Portugal, San Marino, Serbia, Sierra Leone, St Kitts and Nevis, St Vincent and the Grenadines, Suriname, Tajikistan, Timor Leste, Uganda, United Republic of Tanzania, Venezuela and Zambia.

91 Afghanistan, Antigua and Barbuda, Australia, Barbados, Bosnia and Herzegovina, Brazil, Burundi, Cambodia, Chad, Chile, Comoros, Congo, Cook Islands, Costa Rica, Côte d'Ivoire (although not a state party, it has made a declaration under Article 12 (3) to accept all cooperation obligations under the Rome Statute), Czech Republic, Djibouti, Dominica, Fiji, Gabon, Gambia, Georgia, Ghana, Guinea, Japan, Jordan, Kenya, Madagascar, Malta, Marshall Islands, Mauritius, Mongolia, Nauru, Niger, Nigeria, Peru, Samoa, San Marino, Senegal, Sierra Leone, South Africa, St Kitts and Nevis, St Vincent and the Grenadines, Suriname, Switzerland, Tajikistan, Tanzania, Timor Leste, Venezuela and Zambia.

92 Austria and the UK.

93 Amnesty International, "International Criminal Court Concerns at the Eighth Session of the Assembly of States Parties", London, October 2009, available at <http://www.amnesty.org/en/library/asset/IOR40/011/2009/en/fdf3fc92-6273-41a2-8dda-6771fcf49f11/ior400112009en.pdf>, p.6.

94 *Ibid.*

95 See, "Courting disaster? At its forthcoming review, the International Criminal Court has things to celebrate, things to improve and pitfalls to avoid", *The Economist*, 27 May 2010, available at <http://www.economist.com/node/16219717>.

96 "International Criminal Court: Declarations amounting to prohibited reservations to the Rome Statute", AI Index: IOR 40/32/2005, November 2005 (also available in French and Spanish), available at <http://web.amnesty.org/library/index/engior400322005>.

97 The "interpretative declarations" made by France were: 1. The provisions of the Statute of the International Criminal Court do not preclude France from exercising its inherent right of self-defence in conformity with Article 51 of the Charter. 2. The provisions of Article 8 of the Statute, in particular paragraph 2 (b) thereof, relate solely to conventional weapons and can neither regulate nor prohibit the possible use of nuclear weapons nor impair the other rules of international law applicable to other weapons necessary to the exercise by France of its inherent right of self-defence, unless nuclear weapons or the other weapons referred to herein become subject in the future to a comprehensive ban and are specified in an annex to the Statute by means of an amendment adopted in accordance with the provisions of Articles 121 and 123. 3. The Government of the French Republic considers that the term 'armed conflict' in Article 8, paragraphs 2 (b) and (c), in and of itself and in its context, refers to a situation of a kind which does not include the commission of ordinary crimes, including acts of terrorism, whether collective or isolated. 4. The situation referred to in Article 8, paragraph 2 (b) (xxiii), of the Statute does not preclude France from directing attacks against objectives considered as military objectives under international humanitarian law. 5. The Government of the French Republic declares that the term 'military advantage' in Article 8, paragraph 2 (b) (iv), refers to the advantage anticipated from the attack as a whole and not from isolated or specific elements thereof. 6. The Government of the French Republic declares that a specific area may be considered a 'military objective'

as referred to in Article 8, paragraph 2 (b) as a whole if, by reason of its situation, nature, use, location, total or partial destruction, capture or neutralization, taking into account the circumstances of the moment, it offers a decisive military advantage. The Government of the French Republic considers that the provisions of Article 8, paragraph 2 (b) (ii) and (v), do not refer to possible collateral damage resulting from attacks directed against military objectives. 7. The Government of the French Republic declares that the risk of damage to the natural environment as a result of the use of methods and means of warfare, as envisaged in Article 8, paragraph 2 (b) (iv), must be weighed objectively on the basis of the information available at the time of its assessment. France's Declaration under Article 124 read as follows: "Pursuant to Article 124 of the Statute of the International Criminal Court, the French Republic declares that it does not accept the jurisdiction of the Court with respect to the category of crimes referred to in Article 8 when a crime is alleged to have been committed by its nationals or on its territory."

98   Amnesty International, "International Criminal Court: Declarations amounting to prohibited reservations to the Rome Statute", Index Number: IOR 40/032/2005, 24 November 2005, available at <http://www.amnesty.org/en/library/info/IOR40/032/2005>.
99   *Ibid.*, p. 32.
100 Rosenthal, *op. cit.*
101 Amnesty International, "International Criminal Court: Declarations amounting to prohibited reservations to the Rome Statute", Index Number: IOR 40/032/2005, 24 November 2005, available at <http://www.amnesty.org/en/library/info/IOR40/032/2005>, p. 39.
102 "List of countries by population", Wikipedia, available at <http://en.wikipedia.org/wiki/List_of_countries_by_population>, accessed 28 February 2013.
103 Rosenthal, *op. cit.*
104 David Davenport, "The New Diplomacy", *Policy Review*, No. 116, December 2002/January 2003, available at <http://www.hoover.org/publications/policyreview/3458466.html>.
105 "Interview: Luis Moreno-Ocampo, ICC Prosecutor", *The Africa Report*, 21 September 2009, available at <http://www.theafricareport.com/index.php?option=com_content&view=article&id=3281793&catid=54>.
106 "Exclusive Interview: David Tolbert, Deputy ICTY Prosecutor and Senior Fellow, Jennings Randolph Fellowship Program at the United States Institute of Peace", ICC Observers Project-Oxford Transitional Justice Research, 20 March 2009, available at <http://iccobservers.wordpress.com/2009/03/20/icc-observers-exclusive-interview-david-tolbert-deputy-icty-prosecutor-and-senior-fellow-jennings-randolph-fellowship-program-at-the-united-states-institute-for-peace/>. David Tolbert served as UN Assistant Secretary-General and Special Advisor to the UN Assistance at the Khmer Rouge Trials (UNAKRT). From 2004 through March 2008, he was the Deputy Prosecutor of the International Criminal Tribunal for the former Yugoslavia. Tolbert has extensive experience in international law. Prior to his position as Deputy Prosecutor, Tolbert was the Deputy Registrar of the ICTY.
107 "The Relationship between the EU Institutions and the ICC", Speech by Fernando Valenzuela, Head of the Delegation of the European Commission to the United Nations, 19 May 2009, New York, available at <http://www.europa-eu-un.org/articles/en/article_8743_en.htm>.
108 "UN Assembly chief says sorry for Bashir warrant", ABC News (Australia), 6 March 2009, available at <http://www.abc.net.au/news/stories/2009/03/06/2508819.htm>.
109 Lu Jianping and Wang Zhixiang, "China's Attitude Towards the ICC", *Journal of International Criminal Justice*, Vol. 3, Issue 3 (2005), pp. 608–20. Lu Jianping is a professor at the Renmin University's Law School and Research Centre of Criminal Jurisprudence; he has also served as Deputy Secretary-General of the International Association of Penal Law.

NOTES TO CHAPTERS

Wang Zhixiang is a professor at Hebei University's Law School and was a post-doctoral fellow of the Law Institute of China, Academy of Social Sciences.

110 "China and the International Criminal Court", Ministry of Foreign Affairs of the People's Republic of China, Beijing, 28 October 2003, available at <http://www.mfa.gov.cn/eng/wjb/zzjg/tyfls/tyfl/2626/2627/t15473.htm>. See, also, Zhu Wenqi, "The Prospect of a Chinese Accession to the International Criminal Court", in Gao Mingxuan, Zhao Bingzhi and Wang Xiumei (editors), *The International Criminal Court: the Choices Faced by China*, Chinese Public Security University Press, Beijing, 2005; Lu Jianping, "A Cultural Assessment of China Joining the ICC", in Zhao Bingzhi and Chen Hongyi (editors), *Issues of International Criminal Law and International Crimes*, Chinese Public Security University Press, Beijing, 2003; and Lijun Yang, "Some Critical Remarks on the Rome Statue of the International Criminal Court", *Chinese Journal of International Law*, Vol. 2 (2003).
111 *Ibid*.
112 See, A/CONF.183/SR.9, para. 39 and A/CONF.183/SR.10, para. 9, 22 June 1998.
113 "China and the International Criminal Court", *op. cit.*
114 "Position Paper of the People's Republic of China At the 66th Session of the United Nations General Assembly", Ministry of Foreign Affairs of the People's Republic of China, Beijing, 9 September 2011, available at <http://www.fmprc.gov.cn/eng/wjdt/wshd/t857763.htm>.
115 Government of India, "Explanation of Vote by Mr. Dilip Lahiri, Head of Delegation of India, on the Adoption of the Statute of the International Court", United Nations Conference of Plenipotentiaries on the Establishment of an International Criminal Court, Ninth Plenary Meeting, 17 July 1998, available at <http://www.un.org/icc/speeches/717ind.htm>.
116 *Ibid*.
117 See, for example, "Duplicity on Darfur", *The Hindu*, 12 April 2005, available at <http://www.thehindu.com/2005/04/12/stories/2005041204151000>.
118 Government of India, "Explanation of Vote by Mr. Dilip Lahiri, Head of Delegation of India, on the Adoption of the Statute of the International Court", *op. cit.*
119 Cited in Dr. John Laughland, "Forget the rhetoric, this court is just another excuse for superpower bullying", *The Times* (London), 29 August 2000.
120 "Right to the brink", *The Economist*, 4 July 2002, available at <http://www.economist.com/node/1217747>.
121 Richard Goldstone, "Crimes Against Humanity – Forgetting the Victims", the 2001 Ernest Jones Lecture, the Institute of Psychoanalysis, London, 25 September 2001.
122 Richard Goldstone and Adam M. Smith, *International Judicial Institutions: The Architecture of International Justice at home and abroad*, Routledge, London, 2008, p. 102.
123 "International Law on Trial", *Financial Times*, 25 July 2008.
124 Mahmood Mamdani, *Saviors and Survivors: Darfur, Politics, and the War on Terror*, Pantheon, 2009, pp. 283–84.
125 *Ibid.*, p. 284.
126 "Could ICC prosecute US for Iraq crimes?", Radio Netherlands Worldwide, 18 June 2009.
127 Henry Kissinger, "The Pitfalls of Universal Jurisdiction", *Foreign Affairs*, New York, July–August 2001.
128 Kenneth Starr, a former United States Federal Court of Appeals judge and Solicitor General, was appointed Independent Counsel during the presidency of Bill Clinton. He was initially tasked with investigating the suicide death of Deputy White House Counsel Vince Foster and Clinton's real estate investments. Starr subsequently used his broad investigative powers under the Independent Counsel Act to expand the inquiry into numerous areas including Clinton's extra-marital affair with Monica Lewinsky. After several years of investigation Starr published the "Starr Report", which alleged that Bill Clinton had lied about existence of the affair during a sworn deposition. The allegation opened the door for the impeachment

of Bill Clinton: the President was acquitted in the subsequent trial before the United States Senate and was not removed from office.
129 Rosenthal, *op. cit.*
130 "ICC Observers Exclusive Interview: Tom Ginsberg, Professor of Law University of Chicago", ICC Observers, 15 March 2009, available at <http://iccobservers.wordpress.com/2009/03/15/icc-observers-exclusive-interview-tom-ginsburg-professor-of-law-univeristy-of-chicago/>. Professor Ginsberg focuses on comparative and international law from an interdisciplinary perspective. He holds BA, JD, and PhD degrees from the University of California at Berkeley. One of his books, *Judicial Review in New Democracies* (Cambridge University Press, 2003) won the C. Herman Pritchett Award from the American Political Science Association for best book on law and courts. He currently co-directs the Comparative Constitutions Project, an effort funded by the National Science Foundation to gather and analyse the constitutions of all independent nation-states since 1789. Before entering law teaching, he served as a legal adviser at the Iran-US Claims Tribunal, The Hague, Netherlands, and consulted with numerous international development agencies and foreign governments on legal and constitutional reform.
131 "ICC Observers Exclusive Interview: Eric Leonard, Professor of Political Science Shenandoah University", ICC Observers, 14 April 2009, available at <http://iccobservers.wordpress.com/2009/04/14/icc-observers-exclusive-interview-eric-leonard-professor-of-political-science-shenandoah-university/>. Professor Leonard is Associate Professor of Political Science and the Henkel Family Endowed Chair in International Affairs at Shenandoah University in Winchester, VA. He has published several articles, case studies and a book on such issues as the ICC, US foreign policy, humanitarian law, theoretical conceptualisations of sovereignty, and global governance. His book is entitled, *The Onset of Global Governance: International Relations Theory and the International Criminal Court.*
132 "ICC Observers Exclusive Interview: William Schabas, Professor of Human Rights Law and Director of the Irish Centre for Human Rights at the National University of Ireland, Galway", ICC Observers, 26 March 2009, available at <http://iccobservers.wordpress.com/2009/03/26/icc-observers-exclusive-interview-william-schabas-professor-of-human-rights-law-and-director-of-the-irish-centre-for-human-rights-at-the-national-university-of-ireland-galway/>.
133 Stephanie Hanes, "ICC path to justice tested in Congo. Investigations for the International Criminal Court's first trial face serious logistical and security obstacles as well as charges of selective justice", *Christian Science Monitor*, 24 May 2007, available at <http://www.csmonitor.com/2007/0524/p06s02-woaf.html>.
134 Human Rights Watch, "Human Rights Watch Memorandum for the Eighth Session of the International Criminal Court Assembly of States Parties", November 2009, available at <http://www.hrw.org/sites/default/files/related_material/Memo%20for%20the%208th%20Session%20of%20the%20ASP%2011.09.09.pdf>.
135 Nicholas Waddell and Phil Clark (editors), *Courting Conflict? Justice, Peace and the ICC in Africa*, the Royal Africa Society, London, March 2008. Dr. Phil Clark is a political scientist specialising in conflict and post-conflict issues in Africa, particularly transitional justice. His current work focuses on international, national and community-based responses to mass violence in Rwanda, Uganda and the Democratic Republic of Congo. He lectures in comparative and international politics at the School of Oriental and African Studies, is a Golding Research Fellow at Brasenose College, and is the convenor of Oxford Transitional Justice Research. He is the editor, with Zachary D. Kaufman, of *After Genocide: Transitional Justice, Post-Conflict Reconstruction and Reconciliation in Rwanda and Beyond.*
136 "International Criminal Court Cases in Africa: Status and Policy Issues", Congressional Research Service, 14 July 2009 available at <http://www.fas.org/sgp/crs/row/RL34665.pdf>.

137 Richard Goldstone and Adam M. Smith, *International Judicial Institutions: The Architecture of International Justice at Home and Abroad*, Routledge, London, 2008, p. 113.
138 Jacqueline Geis and Alex Mundt, "When to Indict? The Impact of Timing International Criminal Indictments on Peace Processes and Humanitarian Action", the Brookings Institution-University of Bern Project on Internal Displacement, paper to the World Humanitarian Studies Conference, Groningen, the Netherlands, February 2009, p. 13, available at <http://reliefweb.int/rw/RWFiles2009.nsf/FilesByRWDocUnidFilename/RWST-7RAQ9A-full_report.pdf/$File/full_report.pdf>.
139 ICC, "Communications Received by the Prosecutor since July 2002", OTP, 2003.
140 ICC, "Update on communications received by the Office of the Prosecutor of the ICC", OTP, 10 February 2006.
141 ICC, "Report on the Activities of the Court", 18 October 2007.
142 ICC, "Update on communications received by the Office of the Prosecutor of the ICC", *op. cit.*
143 See, for example, American Society of International Law, Independent Task Force, "US Policy Toward the International Criminal Court: Furthering Positive Engagement", March 2009, p. 18, available at <http://www.asil.org/files/ASIL-08-DiscPaper2.pdf>, and ICC, OTP, "Communications, Referrals and Preliminary Analysis", available at <http://www2.icc-cpi.int/Menus/ICC/Structure+of+the+Court/Office+of+the+Prosecutor/Comm+and+Ref>.
144 ICC, "Policy Paper on Preliminary Examinations", OTP, 4 October 2010, available at <http://www.icc-cpi.int/NR/rdonlyres/9FF1EAA1-41C4-4A30-A202-174B18DA923C/282515/OTP_Draftpolicypaperonpreliminaryexaminations04101.pdf>.
145 "Cosy club or sword of righteousness?", *The Economist*, 26 November 2011, available at <http://www.economist.com/node/21540230?zid=317&ah=8a47fc455a44945580198768fad0fa41>.
146 Human Rights Watch, "Human Rights Watch Memorandum for the Eighth Session of the International Criminal Court Assembly of States Parties", November 2009, available at <http://www.hrw.org/sites/default/files/related_material/Memo%20for%20the%208th%20Session%20of%20the%20ASP%2011.09.09.pdf>.
147 See, ICC, "Policy Paper on Preliminary Examinations (DRAFT)", OTP, 4 October 2010, paragraphs 33–44, available at <http://www.icc-cpi.int/NR/rdonlyres/E278F5A2-A4F9-43D7-83D2-6A2C9CF5D7D7/282515/OTP_Draftpolicypaperonpreliminaryexaminations04101.pdf>; "Unfinished Business. Closing Gaps in the Selection of ICC Cases", Human Rights Watch, September 2011, available at <http://www.hrw.org/sites/default/files/reports/icc0911webwcover.pdf>.
148 ICC, "Prosecutorial Strategy 2009–2012", OTP, 1 February 2010, paragraphs 18–21, available at <http://www.icc-cpi.int/NR/rdonlyres/66A8DCDC-3650-4514-AA62-D229D1128F65/281506/OTPProsecutorialStrategy20092013.pdf>. See, also, "Unfinished Business", p. 7.
149 ICC, "Prosecutorial Strategy 2009–2012", *op. cit.*, paragraph 22.
150 Allison Danner, "Enhancing the Legitimacy and Accountability of Prosecutorial Discretion at the International Criminal Court", *American Journal of International Law*, No. 97 (2003).
151 Louise Parrott, "The Role of the International Criminal Court in Uganda: Ensuring that the Pursuit of Justice does not come at the price of peace", *The Australian Journal of Peace Studies*, Vol. 1 (2006).
152 *Ibid.*
153 See, for example, President Museveni's interview with Integrated Regional Information Networks, on 9 June 2005: "The involvement of the ICC in hunting Kony is very important, mainly because it enables us to deal with Khartoum. Khartoum is fully aware of the consequences of dealing with somebody under the ICC's indictment. If Kony is in Uganda or in the areas of Sudan where Khartoum has allowed us to operate, then we do

not need assistance – we shall catch him ourselves. But if Kony goes deeper into Sudan, beyond where Sudan has allowed us to pursue him, we need the ICC's assistance to get the Sudanese government to cooperate with us and help us to get him. That is why we need the ICC"; "Uganda: Interview with President Yoweri Museveni", IRIN, Kampala, 9 June 2005, available at <http://www.irinnews.org/S_report.asp?ReportID=47569>.

154 "African Search for Peace Throws Court into Chaos", *The Guardian* (London), 9 January 2007.
155 Ibid.
156 Human Rights Watch, "Unfinished Business. Closing Gaps in the Selection of ICC Cases", September 2011, p. 11, available at <http://www.hrw.org/sites/default/files/reports/icc0911webwcover.pdf>.
157 Ibid.
158 Ibid.
159 Ibid.
160 "ICC's Moreno Ocampo Learned Nothing from Lubanga Case, Laughs at Retaliation Finding", *Inner City Press*, 3 December 2008, available at <http://www.innercitypress.com/icc5ocampo120308.html>.
161 "ICC Observers Exclusive Interview: Tom Ginsberg, Professor of Law University of Chicago", ICC Observers, 15 March 2009, available at <http://iccobservers.wordpress.com/2009/03/15/icc-observers-exclusive-interview-tom-ginsburg-professor-of-law-univeristy-of-chicago/>.
162 "A Lifelong Passion Is Now Put to Practice in The Hague", *New York Times*, 18 January 2013, available at <http://www.nytimes.com/2013/01/19/world/africa/challenging-start-for-bensouda-as-chief-prosecutor-in-the-hague.html?pagewanted=all&_r=0>.
163 Naomi Roht-Arriaza, "Amnesty and the International Criminal Court", in Dinah Shelton (editor), *International Crimes, Peace, and Human Rights: The Role of the International Criminal Court*, Transnational Publishers, 2000.
164 Fabrice Weismann, "Humanitarian aid and the International Criminal Court: Grounds for divorce (2)", Making Sense of Darfur, Social Science Research Council, 21 July 2009, available at <http://blogs.ssrc.org/darfur/2009/07/21/humanitarian-aid-and-the-international-criminal-court-grounds-for-divorce-2/>. Weismann is the Director of Research at MSF Foundation in Paris, France. His work with MSF started in 1995 and has taken him to Liberia, southern Sudan, eastern Sudan, Kosovo, Eritrea, Guinea-Conakry, and the Darfur region of Sudan where he was MSF's Head of Mission from September 2005 to June 2006. He has published several articles and edited a volume of articles and essays entitled, *In The Shadow of Just Wars*.
165 David Lanz, "The ICC's Intervention in Northern Uganda: Beyond the Simplicity of Peace vs. Justice", the Fletcher School of Law and Diplomacy, May 2007, available at <http://www.reliefweb.int/rw/RWFiles2007.nsf/FilesByRWDocUnidFilename/PANA-78VKGJ-full_report.pdf/$File/full_report.pdf>. David Lanz has worked in Khartoum and Darfur as a researcher with the United Nations Mission in Sudan (UNMIS) and as a trainer for the Swiss Section of Amnesty International. He is currently with the Mediation Support Project at the Swiss Peace Foundation in Bern.
166 Rosenthal, *op. cit.*
167 Jacqueline Geis and Alex Mundt, "When to Indict? The Impact of Timing International Criminal Indictments on Peace Processes and Humanitarian Action", the Brookings Institution-University of Bern Project on Internal Displacement, paper to the World Humanitarian Studies Conference, Groningen, the Netherlands, February 2009, p. 13, available at <http://reliefweb.int/rw/RWFiles2009.nsf/FilesByRWDocUnidFilename/RWST-7RAQ9A-full_report.pdf/$File/full_report.pdf>.
168 See, for example, Lord Archer, "The Responsibility to Protect", presentation and discussion at the World Disarmament Campaign Annual General Meeting, Wesley's Chapel, London,

	31 March 2007. Lord Archer QC was a distinguished British lawyer and parliamentarian, a former Solicitor General, and a vigorous campaigner for human rights. He was a founding member of Amnesty International.
169	Nick Grono and Adam O'Brien, "Justice in Conflict? The ICC and Peace Processes", in *Courting Conflict? Justice, Peace and the ICC in Africa*, Royal African Society, London, March 2008.
170	Ian Paisley Jr., "Peace Must Not Be the Victim of International Justice", *The New York Times*, 16 March 2012, available at <http://www.nytimes.com/2012/03/17/opinion/peace-must-not-be-the-victim-of-international-justice.html?_r=0>.
171	William Schabas, *Unimaginable Atrocities. Justice, Politics, and Rights at the War Crimes Tribunals*, Oxford University Press, Oxford, 2012, p. 92.
172	*Ibid.*, p. 17.
173	William Schabas, "The International Criminal Court: Struggling to Find its Way", in Antonio Cassese (editor), *Realizing Utopia: The Future of International Law*, Oxford University Press, Oxford, 2012, p. 251.
174	*Ibid.*
175	*Ibid.*, pp. 251–52.
176	*Ibid.*
177	*Ibid.*, p. 253.
178	*Ibid.*

Notes to Chapter Two

179	Chris Patten, *Not Quite the Diplomat*, Penguin Books, London, 2006, p. 309. Patten is a British and European politician. A former British cabinet minister, in 1999 he was appointed as one of the UKs two members of the European Commission. He served as Commissioner for External Relations where he was responsible for the EU's development and cooperation programmes from 23 January 2000 until 22 November 2004.
180	Vidal Martín, "The two faces of impunity: the EU and the International Criminal Court", *Fundación para las Relaciones Internacionales y el Diálogo Exterior* (FRIDE), Madrid, December 2007. Vidal Martín runs the International Criminal Justice & Post-Conflict Project at FRIDE. He is also the FRIDE project coordinator of the Transnational Terrorism, Security and Rule of Law Consortium project, co-funded by the European Commission. He previously worked at the Irish Centre for Human Rights at the National University of Ireland (Galway).
181	Rosenthal, *op. cit.*
182	Martijn Groenleer and David Rijks, "The European Union and the International Criminal Court: The Politics of International Justice", in K. Jørgensen (editor), *The European Union and International Organizations*, Routledge, London, 2009, p. 167.
183	George F. Will, "U.S. must not surrender sovereignty to International Criminal Court", *Pittsburgh Tribune-Review*, 11 July 2002, available at <http://triblive.com/x/pittsburghtrib/opinion/columnists/will/s_80658.html#axzz2ONjM3Lzi>.
184	"Is ICC recolonising Africa?", *The Southern Times*, 10 June 2013, available at <http://www.southerntimesafrica.com/news_article.php?id=8422&title=Is%20ICC%20recolonising%20Africa%20&type=81>.
185	WikiLeaks, US Government Cable, "Subject: Mozambique: FM Simao on a Sudan Tribunal and Iraq Elections", 26 January 2005, available at <http://wikileaks.org/cable/2005/01/05MAPUTO128.html>. See, also, "Europe, Masters Behind The ICC", *African Business*, available at <http://www.africanbusinessmagazine.com/special-reports/sector-reports/icc-vs-africa/europe-masters-behind-the-icc>.
186	*The European Union and the International Criminal Court*, General Secretariat of the Council, European Union, May 2010, p. 5.

187 Michael Bourguignon, "The EU and the ICC: Wedding bells?", <theeuros.eu>, 6 January 2008, available at <http://www.theeuros.eu/The-EU-and-the-ICC-Wedding-bells,1109.html?lang=fr>.
188 Stefan Oltsch, "Konflikthafte Partnerschaft: Das transatlantische Verhältnis und die Schaffung des Internationalen Strafgerichtshofs", ESH Working Paper, No. 8, 2004, Hanover.
189 Martijn Groenleer and Louise van Schaik, "The EU as an 'Intergovernmental' Actor in Foreign Affairs. Case Studies of the International Criminal Court and the Kyoto Protocol", CEPS Working Document No. 228, 2005.
190 See, European Union, "Council Common Position", 2001/443/CFSP, 11 June 2001, available at <www.consilium.europa.eu/uedocs/cmsUpload/ICC25EN.pdf>.
191 See, for example, Luc Reydams and Jan Wouters, "The Politics of Establishing International Criminal Tribunals", in Luc Reydams, Jan Wouters and Cedric Ryngaert (editors), *International Prosecutors*, Oxford University Press, Oxford, 2012.
192 "European Union and the International Criminal Court", Wikipedia, available at <http://en.wikipedia.org/wiki/European_Union_and_the_International_Criminal_Court>.
193 Jess Bravin, "Justice Delayed. For Global Court, Ugandan Rebels Prove Tough Test", *The Wall Street Journal*, 8 June 2006.
194 Judge Sang-Hyun Song, "International Criminal Court and the European Union: Challenges for the Promotion of International Justice and the Fight against Impunity", address to European Parliament Group of Parliamentarians for Global Action, European Parliament, Brussels, 15 October 2009, available at <http://www.pgaction.org/uploadedfiles/Remarks%20by%20ICC%20President%20Judge%20Song%20at%20the%20European%20Parliament%2015%20OCT%202009%20-%20PGA.pdf>.
195 *Ibid.*
196 Jan Wouters and Sudeshna Basu, "The Creation of a Global Criminal Justice System: The European Union and the International Criminal Court", Working Paper No. 26, Leuven Centre for Global Governance Studies, June 2009.
197 *The European Union and the International Court*, General Secretariat of the Council, Brussels, November 2007. Jan Wouters is Professor of International Law and International Organizations, and the Director of the Leuven Centre for Global Governance Studies and the Institute for International Law, at the University of Leuven; Sudeshna Basu is a member of the Leuven Centre for Global Governance Studies and Institute for International Law, University of Leuven.
198 "EU Presidency Statement – United Nations General Assembly: Report of the International Criminal Court (ICC)", statement on behalf of the European Union by Mr. Carl Henrik Ehrenkrona, Director-General for Legal Affairs, Swedish Ministry for Foreign Affairs, in the General Assembly on the Report of the International Criminal Court (Agenda item 75), UN, New York, 29 October 2009, available at <http://www.europa-eu-un.org/articles/en/article_9183_en.htm>. In presenting the EU Presidency Statement on the ICC Report in October 2009, Ambassador Ehrenkrona stated he was speaking on behalf of the European Union, and that the EU candidate countries Croatia, the former Yugoslav Republic of Macedonia, Iceland, the countries of the Stabilisation and Association Process and potential candidates Albania, Bosnia and Herzegovina, Montenegro, Serbia, as well as Ukraine, the Republic of Moldova and Georgia aligned themselves with this statement.
199 ICC, ASP, "Report of the Committee on Budget and Finance on the work of its eighteenth session", The Hague, 14-22 November 2012, ICC-ASP/11/5, pp. 15-16, available at <http://212.159.242.181/iccdocs/asp_docs/ASP11/ICC-ASP-11-5-ENG-CBF18-Report.pdf>.
200 *Ibid.*

201 See, "Gender Report Card on the International Criminal Court", Women's Initiatives for Gender Justice, The Hague, 2012. See, also, ICC, Report of the Committee on Budget and Finance on the work of its eighteenth session, ICC-ASP/11/5, 9 August 2012, p. 25.
202 Michael Bourguignon, "The EU and the ICC: Wedding bells?", <theeuros.eu>, 6 January 2008, available at <http://www.theeuros.eu/The-EU-and-the-ICC-Wedding-bells,1109.html?lang=fr>.
203 "The next EU presidency", *The Economist*, 4 December 2008. See, also, "Mr Obama escapes dinner with Vaclav Klaus", *The Economist*, March 2009.
204 "Germany gives most to 2008 EU budget", UPI, 23 September 2009.
205 Seth Frantzman, "Terra Incognita: Strange justice: The ICC, Europe and the world", *The Jerusalem Post*, 22 September 2009, available at <http://www.jpost.com /servlet/Satellite?cid=1253627541039&pagename=JPArticle%2FShowFull>.
206 See, for example, EU, "The European Union and the International Criminal Court", February 2008, available at <http://www.consilium.europa.eu/uedocs/cmsUpload/ICC_internet08.pdf>, annex 2 (collecting relevant Council of the European Union conclusions).
207 "Revised Cotonou Treaty Agreed", *Europa World*, 2 February 2005, <http://www.europaworld.org/week213/revised25205.htm>.
208 "Non-ratification of the revised Cotonou Agreement by Sudan FAQ", August 2009, available at <http://ec.europa.eu/development/icenter/repository/sudan_final_non-ratification_faq_200908.pdf>.
209 Speech by Commissioner Ferrero-Waldner on "The ICC, Transatlantic Relations and Co-operation with Third Parties to Promote the Rule of Law", at the Parliamentarians for Global Action - ICC Round Table, Strasbourg, 14 April 2005.
210 Karen Kleiss, "Countries Must Choose: ICC or U.S. Dollars", *The Toronto Star*, 29 June 2003.
211 European Union, *The European Union and the International Criminal Court*, General Secretariat of the Council, Brussels, February 2008. See, also, "EU keen to bring international criminal court to Central Asia", *EU Observer*, 14 June 2007.
212 EU, "Declaration by the Presidency on behalf of the EU to mark the 10th anniversary of the Rome Statute of the International Criminal Court", 16 July 2008, Brussels.
213 EU, *The European Union and the International Criminal Court*, General Secretariat of the Council, May 2010, p. 5.
214 See, for example, Reed Brody, "Playing it firm, fair and smart: The EU and the ICC's indictment of Bashir", *ISS Opinion*, March 2009, p. 2, available at <http://www.iss.europa.eu/uploads/media/EU_ICC_Bashir.pdf.>; and Mitja Mertens, "The International Criminal Court: A European Success Story?", EU diplomacy papers 1/2011, College of Europe, 2011, p. 15, available at <http://aei.pitt.edu/15478/1/EDP_1_2011_Mertens.pdf>.
215 EU, "Council Common Position", 2001/443/CFSP, 11 June 2001, available at <www.consilium.europa.eu/uedocs/cmsUpload/ICC25EN.pdf>.
216 EU, "Council Common Position", 2003/444/CFSP, 16 June 2003, available at <www.consilium.europa.eu/uedocs/cmsUpload/ICC25EN.pdf>.
217 EU, "Conclusions on the ICC by the EU General Affairs and External Relations Council", 30 September 2002, available at <ue.eu.int/ueDocs/cms_Data/docs/pressData/en/gena/72321.pdf>.
218 EU, "Council Common Position", 2002/474/CFSP, 20 June 2002, available at <www.consilium.europa.eu/uedocs/cmsUpload/ICC25EN.pdf>.
219 EU, "Action Plan to Follow-up on the Common Position on the ICC", 4 February 2004, available at <www.consilium.europa.eu/uedocs/cmsUpload/ICC48EN.pdf>.
220 Jan Wouters and Sudeshna Basu, "The Creation of a Global Criminal Justice System: The European Union and the International Criminal Court", Working Paper No. 26, Leuven Centre for Global Governance Studies, June 2009.

221   EU, "COUNCIL DECISION 2011/168/CFSP of 21 March 2011 on the International Criminal Court and repealing Common Position 2003/444/CFSP", *Official Journal of the European Union*, 22 March 2011.
222   EU, "Action Plan to follow-up on the Decision on the International Criminal Court", Council of the European Union, 12080/11, Brussels, 12 July 2011.
223   EU, "COUNCIL DECISION 2011/168/CFSP of 21 March 2011 on the International Criminal Court and repealing Common Position 2003/444/CFSP", *op. cit.*
224   Michael Bourguignon, "The EU and the ICC: Wedding bells?", 6 January 2008, *Eurosduvillage*, available at <http://www.theeuros.eu/The-EU-and-the-ICC-Wedding-bells,1109>.
225   John Rosenthal, "A Lawless Global Court. How the International Criminal Court Undermines the U.N. System", *op. cit.*
226   EU, *The European Union and the International Criminal Court*, General Secretariat of the Council, May 2010, p. 5. A *démarche* is defined as a political initiative or manoeuvre and/or a petition presented through diplomatic channels.
227   EU, "The Relationship between the EU Institutions and the ICC", speech by Fernando Valenzuela, Head of the Delegation of the European Commission to the United Nations, 19 May 2009, New York, available at <http://www.europa-eu-un.org/articles/en/article_8743_en.htm>.
228   *Ibid.*
229   EU, *The European Union and the International Court*, Council of the European Union, General Secretariat of the Council, Brussels, November 2007.
230   EU, "The Relationship between the EU Institutions and the ICC", *op. cit.*
231   *Ibid.*
232   EU, *The European Union and the International Court*, *op. cit.*
233   *Ibid.*
234   See, "[Annex 1] List of EU and ICC officials visiting Japan", "Visit of EU and ICC Officials to Japan (Overall Assessment)", Ministry of Foreign Affairs of Japan, December 2004, available at <http://www.mofa.go.jp/policy/i_crime/icc/visit0412.html>. From the Netherlands (current EU Presidency); (1) Ambassador Edmond. Wellenstein, Director-General, ICC Task Force, Ministry of Foreign Affairs, (2) Mr. Gerritjan Van Oven, former Member of Parliament, currently Senior Legal Expert for the EU Just-Themis Rule of Law Mission in Georgia, (3) Dr. J. A. C. Bevers, Legal Advisor, Department of Criminal and Sanction Law, Ministry of Justice, (4) Ms. Lizzy Bansnobre, ICC Task Force, Ministry of Foreign Affairs. Other EU members: (5) Mr. Hans-Werner Bussmann, Commissioner for the ICC, Federal Foreign Office, Germany, (6) Mr. Roberto Bellelli, President, Military Tribunal in Turin/Counsellor, Ministry of Foreign Affairs, Italy, (7) Ms. Claire d'Urso, Magistrat, Chef du Bureau des Questions Institutionelles, Juridiques et Contentieux, Ministère de la Justice, France, (8) Mr. Olivier Barrat, Chargé de mission auprès du directeur des Affaires Juridiques, Ministère des affaires étrangères, France, (9) Mr. Håkan Friman, Deputy Director, Swedish Ministry of Justice, Division of Penal Law, Sweden, (10) Mr. Jacque Thill, Chargé de mission Direction des Affaires Politiques, Luxemburg (next EU Presidency), (11) Mr. Franc Miksa, State Undersecretary, International Law Department, Slovenia European Commission and the Council Secretariat, (12) Ms. Sybilla Fries, Legal Service, European Commission, (13) Mr. Paulo Oliveira, Council Secretariat, UN Division, ICC Focal Point. From the ICC, (14) Ms. Silvia A. Fernández de Gurmendi, Chef de Cabinet, OTP, ICC.
235   "Visit of EU and ICC Officials to Japan (Overall Assessment)", Ministry of Foreign Affairs of Japan, December 2004, available at <http://www.mofa.go.jp/policy/i_crime/icc/visit0412.html>.
236   See, EU, "Agreement between the ICC and EU on Cooperation and Assistance", 10 April 2006, available at <www.icc-cpi.int/library/about/officialjournal/ICC-PRES-01-01-06_English.pdf>.

237 EU, "The International Criminal Court & the fight against impunity", European Commission, European Union, available at <http://ec.europa.eu/external_relations/human_rights/icc/index_en.htm>. (accessed 22 October 2009).
238 EU, "The Relationship Between the EU Institutions and the ICC", *op. cit.*
239 EU, "Security arrangements for the protection of classified information exchanged between the EU and the ICC", Council of the EU, Brussels, 15 April 2008 (8349/1/08 REV 1).
240 EU, *The European Union and the International Criminal Court*, General Secretariat of the Council, May 2010, p. 5.
241 Vidal Martín, "The two faces of impunity: the EU and the International Criminal Court", Peace, Security and Human Rights, FRIDE, Madrid, November 2007.
242 Alexandra Kemmerer, "Like Ancient Beacons: The European Union and the International Criminal Court – Reflections from afar on a Chapter of European Foreign Policy", *German Law Journal*, Vol. 5 No. 12 (2004).
243 See, for example, EU, "European Neighbourhood Policy", European Commission, available at <http://ec.europa.eu/world/enp/policy_en.htm>.
244 See, for example, A. Rettman, "EU keen to bring international criminal court to Central Asia", *EU Observer*, 14 June 2007.
245 EU, *The European Union and the International Court*, General Secretariat of the Council, Brussels, November 2007.
246 Chris Patten, *Not Quite the Diplomat, op. cit.*
247 Alexandra Kemmerer, "Like Ancient Beacons: The European Union and the International Criminal Court – Reflections from afar on a Chapter of European Foreign Policy", *German Law Journal*, Vol. 5, No. 12 (2004), p.16.
248 EU, "The International Criminal Court & the fight against impunity", European Commission, European Union, available at <http://ec.europa.eu/external_relations/human_rights/icc/index_en.htm>. (accessed 22 October 2009).
249 EU, "The Relationship between the EU Institutions and the ICC", speech by Fernando Valenzuela, Head of the Delegation of the European Commission to the United Nations, 19 May 2009, New York.
250 "Visit to the International Criminal Court, The Hague, led by Ms. Hélène Flautre, Chairwoman of the Sub-Committee on Human Rights", European Parliament, 8 February 2007.
251 Vidal Martín, "The two faces of impunity: the EU and the International Criminal Court", Peace, Security and Human Rights, FRIDE, Madrid, November 2007.
252 Marlies Glasius, "How Activists Shaped the Court", Crimes of War Project, December 2003, available at <http://www.crimesofwar.org/icc_magazine/icc-glasius.html>. Marlies Glasius is a researcher with the Centre for the Study of Global Governance, London School of Economics and Political Science. She is the author of *The International Criminal Court: A Global Civil Society Achievement*. She is managing editor of the *Global Civil Society Yearbook*.
253 *Ibid.*
254 The informal steering group includes Amnesty International, Human Rights Watch, World Federalist Movement, Lawyers Committee for Human Rights, International Commission of Jurists, National Association for Public Interest Lawyers, Women's Caucus for Gender Justice, World Order Models Project, No Peace Without Justice, Asociacion Pro Derechos Humanos, European Law Students Association, International Centre for Human Rights and Democratic Development.
255 "About the Coalition for the International Criminal Court (CICC)", Coalition for the International Criminal Court, 8 May 2007, available at <http://www.iccnow.org/documents/CICCFS-AboutCICC_8May071.pdf>.
256 "Visit to the International Criminal Court, The Hague, led by Ms. Hélène Flautre, Chairwoman of the Sub-Committee on Human Rights", *op. cit.*

257 Marlies Glasius, *The International Criminal Court: A Global Civil Society Achievement*, Routledge, London, 2005.
258 Marlies Glasius, "How Activists Shaped the Court", *op. cit.*
259 "Visit to the International Criminal Court, The Hague, led by Ms. Hélène Flautre", Chairwoman of the Sub-Committee on Human Rights, European Parliament, 8 February 2007.
260 *Ibid.*
261 EU, *The European Union and the International Criminal Court*, General Secretariat of the Council, Brussels, February 2008.
262 See, for example, "CICC Three-Year Strategy & Plan as of July 7, 2009", discussion paper by William Pace, Convenor of the Coalition for the International Criminal Court prepared for the Consultative Conference on International Criminal Justice 9–11 September 2009, UN Headquarters, New York, available at <http://www.internationalcriminaljustice.net/papers/Session3.pdf>/.
263 Benjamin Schiff, *Building the ICC*, Cambridge University Press, New York, 2008. Schiff is Professor of Politics at Oberlin College.
264 Marlies Glasius, *The ICC: A Global Civil Society Achievement*, *op. cit.*, p.30.
265 Kenneth Anderson and David Rieff, "'Global Civil Society': A Sceptical View", *Global Civil Society 2004/5*, Sage Publications, London, 2005, p. 26. Kenneth Anderson is a professor of law. He teaches and writes in the areas of domestic and international law and economics, international organisations, human rights, and the laws of war. Professor Anderson's book, *Returning to Earth: What Multilateral Engagement Means in UN-US Relations*, was published in 2011. He actively blogs at *Opinio Juris*. He is a contributor to the *Times Literary Supplement*, *Revista de Libros*, *The Wall Street Journal*, *Weekly Standard*, *New York Times* magazine, *Financial Times*, *Policy Review*. Anderson has also worked as General Counsel for the Open Society Institute-Soros Foundations and as Director of the Human Rights Watch Arms Division. David Rieff is an American commentator and policy analyst. His books have focused on international conflict and humanitarianism. He is a senior fellow at the World Policy Institute at the New School, a fellow at the New York Institute for the Humanities at New York University, a member of the Council on Foreign Relations, a board member of the Arms Division of Human Rights Watch and a board member of the Central Eurasia Project of the Open Society Institute. His books include *Slaughterhouse: Bosnia and the Failure of the West; Crimes of War: What the Public Should Know* (with Roy Gutman) and *A Bed for the Night: Humanitarianism in Crisis*. Rieff has published numerous articles in *The New York Times*, *The Los Angeles Times*, *Washington Post*, *The Wall Street Journal*, *Le Monde*, *El Pais*, *The New Republic*, *World Affairs*, *Harper's*, *The Atlantic Monthly*, *Foreign Affairs*, *The Nation*, and other publications.
266 Kenneth Anderson and David Rieff, "'Global Civil Society': A Sceptical View", *op. cit.* p. 32. See, also, for example, Marcus Höreth, "The unsolved legitimacy problem of European governance", *Journal of European Public Policy*, Vol. 6 (1999); Lee A. Casey and David B. Rivkin, "Europe in the Balance: The Alarmingly Undemocratic Drift of the European Union", *Policy Review*, Hoover Institute, No. 107, 2001; "An undemocratic economic governance?", Corporate Europe Observatory, 14 April 2011, available at <http://corporateeurope.org/blog/undemocratic-economic-governance>; Janet Daley, "Europe's democratic deficit grows wider by the day", *The Daily Telegraph*, 5 November 2011, available at <http://www.telegraph.co.uk/news/worldnews/europe/eu/8871980/Europes-democratic-deficit-grows-wider-by-the-day.html>; "The Euro elite are totally out of touch with the modern world", *The Daily Telegraph*, 5 November 2011, available at <http://www.telegraph.co.uk/news/worldnews/europe/eu/8871973/The-Euro-elite-are-totally-out-of-touch-with-the-modern-world.html>; "Is the EU 'undemocratic'?", BBC Radio 4 *Today* programme, 11 November 2011, available at <http://news.bbc.co.uk/today/hi/

today/newsid_9636000/9636954.stm>; Kübra Dilek Azman, "The Problem of 'Democratic Deficit' in the European Union", *International Journal of Humanities and Social Science*, Vol. 1 No. 5 (2011), available at <http://www.ijhssnet.com/journals/Vol._1_No._5;_May_2011/27.pdf>.

267 The Copenhagen criteria are the rules that define whether a country is eligible to join the European Union.

268 "Britain ready to back Palestinian statehood at UN", *The Guardian*, 27 November 2012, available at <http://www.guardian.co.uk/world/2012/nov/27/uk-ready-to-back-palestine-statehood?INTCMP=SRCH>.

269 "William Hague says UK may abstain in Palestinian UN vote", BBC News, 28 November 2012, available at <http://www.bbc.co.uk/news/uk-politics-20524115>.

270 Canada, another ostensible godfather of "international justice", also demonstrated blatant double standards with regard to the ICC. In March 2013, Canadian Foreign Minister John Baird warned that if the Palestinian Authority engaged with the court with regard to Israeli actions, this would result in "consequences in the conduct of our relations with the Palestinian Authority". It was suggested that Canada would block Canadian aid to Palestine. Canada had voted against Palestinian statehood. See, "Palestinians will face 'consequences' if they pursue Israel at the ICC, says Baird", *The Globe and Mail* (Ottawa), 5 March 2013, available at <http://www.theglobeandmail.com/news/politics/palestinians-will-face-consequences-if-they-pursue-israel-at-the-icc-says-baird/article9324145/>.

271 "William Hague says UK may abstain in Palestinian UN vote", *op. cit.*

272 "France: Criminal Court 'Should Not Be Used' If PA Bid Granted", *Arutz Sheva* (Tel Aviv), 28 November 2012, available at <http://www.israelnationalnews.com/News/News.aspx/162630#.UR548mc2R7k>.

273 "EU votes favour Palestine", EuropeanVoice.com, 30 November 2012, available at <http://www.europeanvoice.com/article/2012/november/eu-votes-favour-palestine/75865.aspx>. See, also, "Germany confirms it won't support Palestinian statehood bid, UK to abstain", *Times of Israel*, 28 November 2012, available at <http://www.timesofisrael.com/germany-confirms-it-wont-support-palestinian-statehood-bid/>.

274 Vidal Martín, "The two faces of impunity: the EU and the International Criminal Court", Peace, Security and Human Rights, *Fundación para las Relaciones Internacionales y el Diálogo Exterior*, Madrid, December 2007.

Notes to Chapter Three

275 Government of India, "Explanation of Vote by Mr. Dilip Lahiri, Head of Delegation of India, on the Adoption of the Statute of the International Court", United Nations Conference of Plenipotentiaries on the Establishment of an International Criminal Court, Ninth Plenary Meeting, 17 July 1998, available at <http://www.un.org/icc/speeches/717ind.htm>.

276 Geoffrey Robertson, *Crimes Against Humanity. The Struggle for Global Justice, op. cit.*, p. 528.

277 "International Criminal Court", *Jurist*, University of Pittsburgh School of Law, 2 July 2012, available at <http://jurist.org/feature/2012/07/international-criminal-court.php>. *Jurist* is a web-based legal news and real-time legal research service powered by a mostly-volunteer team of over thirty part-time law-student reporters, editors and web developers led by Law Professor Bernard Hibbitts at the University of Pittsburgh School of Law in Pittsburgh, Pennsylvania, USA.

278 Cited in "Sudan Morning News", 28 February 2007, Public Affairs Section, US Embassy, Khartoum.

279 See, for example, "French official offers Sudan a deal to settle ICC row", *Sudan Tribune*, 4 September 2008; "French stance on ICC Darfur indictments comes under fire",

280   *Sudan Tribune*, 19 September 2008, available at <http://www.sudantribune.com/spip.php?article28692>; "France says ceasefire is not enough to suspend ICC indictment", *Sudan Tribune*, 13 November 2008, available at <http://www.sudantribune.com/spip.php?article29255>.

280 "US looks on Libya as McDonald's – Gaddafi's son", *Russia Today*, 1 July 2011, available at <http://rt.com/news/interview-gaddafi-libya-usa/>. See, also, "Muammar Gaddafi could stay in Libya, William Hague concedes", *The Guardian*, 25 July 2011, available at <http://www.guardian.co.uk/world/2011/jul/25/gaddafi-libya-william-hague-plan>.

281 Samuel Moyn, "For a political theory of the International Criminal Court (ICC, pt. 2)", *Humanity*, 29 January 2013, available at <http://www.humanityjournal.org/blog/2013/01/political-theory-international-criminal-court-icc-pt-2>.

282 See, Albert Bourgi, "*Quand le droit est mis au service de la politique: Albert Bourgi démasque la CPI*", abidjan.net, 19 December 2012, available at <http://news.abidjan.net/h/447151.html>, and Albert Bourgi, "*Les dérives de la CPI hypothèquent son avenir*", *Africa Nouvelles*, 17 December 2012, available at <http://www.africanouvelles.com/nouvelles/italie/4491-justice-internationale-albert-bourgi-les-derives-de-la-cpi-hypothequent-son-avenir.html>. Bourgi is Professor of Public Law and International Relations at the University of Rheims. He has also been a columnist for *Jeune Afrique* and *Radio France Internationale*. He is the author or co-author of several books, including *La Politique française de coopération en Afrique, le cas du Sénégal* (Editions LGDJ Paris) and *Le Printemps de l'Afrique* (Editions Hachette, Paris).

283 See, for example, "Duplicity on Darfur", *The Hindu*, 12 April 2005, available at <http://www.thehindu.com/2005/04/12/stories/2005041204151000>.

284 Geoffrey Robertson, *Crimes Against Humanity. The Struggle for Global Justice, op. cit.*, p. 386.

285 Cameron Woodhead, "Geoffrey Robertson QC: Interview", Behind The Critical Curtain, June 30, 2011, available at <http://cameronwoodhead.com/archives/geoffrey-robertson-qc-interview/>.

286 Philippe Sands, *Lawless World: The Whistle-Blowing Account of How Bush and Blair Are Taking the Law Into Their own Hands*, Penguin Books, 2006, p. 48.

287 Mariam Bibi Jooma, "The International Criminal Court and Sudan – Opening a Pandora's Box", *op. cit.*

288 Frédéric Mégret, "ICC, R2P, and the International Community's Evolving Interventionist Toolkit", 23 December 2010, Social Science Research Network, available at <http://ssrn.com/abstract=1933111> or <http://dx.doi.org/10.2139/ssrn.1933111>.

289 "Exclusive Interview: David Tolbert, Deputy ICTY Prosecutor and Senior Fellow, Jennings Randolph Fellowship Program at the United States Institute of Peace", ICC Observers Project-Oxford Transitional Justice Research, 20 March 2009, available at <http://iccobservers.wordpress.com/2009/03/20/icc-observers-exclusive-interview-david-tolbert-deputy-icty-prosecutor-and-senior-fellow-jennings-randolph-fellowship-program-at-the-united-states-institute-for-peace/>.

290 "ICC Observers Exclusive Interview: Eric Leonard, Professor of Political Science Shenandoah University", ICC Observers, 14 April 2009, available at <http://iccobservers.wordpress.com/2009/04/14/icc-observers-exclusive-interview-eric-leonard-professor-of-political-science-shenandoah-university/>.

291 See, for example, Professor Hans Köchler, "Global Justice or Global Revenge? The ICC and the Politicization of International Criminal Justice", lecture delivered at the World Conference for International Justice "United against the politicization of justice", organised by the General Sudanese Students Union, Khartoum, Sudan, 6 April 2009, available at <http://www.i-p-o.org/IPO-Koechler-ICC-politicization-2009.htm>. See, also, Hans Köchler, "Sudan: double standards in international criminal justice. Security Council resolution violates Statute of International Criminal Court", International Progress Organization, P/RE/19140c-is, Vienna, 2 April 2005, available at <http://www.i-p-o.org/

nr-sudan-icc-02apr05.htm>. Professor Köchler is Professor of Philosophy at the University of Innsbruck, Austria; Life Fellow, International Academy for Philosophy; and President of the International Progress Organization. He is the author of *Global Justice or Global Revenge? International Criminal Justice at the Crossroads*, Springer, Vienna/New York, 2003, available at <http://i-p-o.org/global_justice-springer-2003.htm>.

292 Professor Köchler has pointed to the following authorities with further comments: the Vienna Convention on the Law of Treaties (1969), entered into force on 27 January 1980, Article 34: "A treaty does not create either obligations or rights for a third State without its consent." It could further be argued that subjecting a state to obligations resulting from a treaty it has not acceded to violates the principle of sovereign equality of all UN member states (Article 2[1] UN Charter), a peremptory norm of general international law. On sovereign equality as peremptory norm see e.g. Rafael Nieto-Navia, Judge of the Appeals Chamber for the International Criminal Tribunals for the former Yugoslavia and Rwanda: "International Peremptory Norms (*jus cogens*) and International Humanitarian Law", published by the Coalition for the International Criminal Court, at <www.iccnow.org/documents/WritingColombiaEng.pdf>, p. 13. In view of Article 53 of the Vienna Convention, this has serious consequences for the Rome Statute of the International Criminal Court: "A treaty is void if, at the time of its conclusion, it conflicts with a peremptory norm of general international law." The problem of the validity of the Rome Statute under existing international law can only be resolved if the ASP amends the statute and removes those provisions that entitle the Security Council to "create" jurisdiction over citizens of or on the territory of non-States Parties.

293 See, for example, Lord McNair, *The Law of Treaties*, Clarendon Press, Oxford, 1961, p. 309; Harvard Research article 18: "(a) a treaty may not impose obligations upon a State which is not party thereto". See, also, Ronald Roxbourgh, *International Conventions and Third States*, Longmans, London, 1917, p. 453.

294 Vienna Convention on the Law of Treaties, Vienna 1969, available at <http://untreaty.un.org/cod/avl/ha/vclt/vclt.html>; Vienna Convention on the Law of Treaties between States and International Organizations or between International Organizations, Vienna, 1986, available at <http://untreaty.un.org/ilc/texts/instruments/english/conventions/1_2_1986.pdf>. The convention was adopted on 22 May 1969 and opened for signature on 23 May 1969 by the United Nations Conference on the Law of Treaties. The conference was convened pursuant to General Assembly Resolutions 2166 (XXI)1 of 5 December 1966 and 2287 (XXII) of 6 December 1967. The conference held two sessions, both at the Neue Hofburg in Vienna, the first session from 26 March to 24 May 1968 and the second session from 9 April to 22 May 1969. In addition to the convention, the conference adopted the Final Act and certain declarations and resolutions, which are annexed to that act. By unanimous decision of the conference, the original of the Final Act was deposited in the archives of the Federal Ministry for Foreign Affairs of Austria. The text of the Final Act is included in document A/CONF.39/11/Add.2.

295 Köchler, *Global Justice or Global Revenge? The ICC and the Politicization of International Criminal Justice, op. cit.*

296 *Ibid.* With regard to the UN voting procedure, see, for example, Hans Köchler, *The Voting Procedure in the United Nations Security Council. Examining a Normative Contradiction and its Consequences on International Relations*, Studies in International Relations, XVII, International Progress Organization Vienna, 1991.

297 Köchler, *Global Justice or Global Revenge? The ICC and the Politicization of International Criminal Justice, op. cit.*

298 There is a further irony surrounding Articles 13 and 16 in that these two provisions were written into the Rome Statute at the insistence of the USA during the negotiation process, a country that subsequently did not join the ICC.

299   William Schabas, *Unimaginable Atrocities. Justice, Politics, and Rights at the War Crimes Tribunals*, Oxford University Press, Oxford, 2012, p. 90.
300   Bruce Broomhall, "Toward U.S. Acceptance of the International Criminal Court", *Law and Contemporary Problems*, Vol. 64, No. 1 (2001), pp. 141–151, available at <http://scholarship.law.duke.edu/cgi/viewcontent.cgi?article=1203&context=lcp>.
301   WikiLeaks, US Government Cable, "Subject: US/EU Human Rights Consultations: Prepping for CHR", 10 February 2005, available at <http://cablegatesearch.wikileaks.org/cable.php?id=05BRUSSELS585&q=icc>.
302   "The UNSC and the International Criminal Court", International Law Meeting summary, with Parliamentarians for Global Action, International Law and Human Rights Programme, Parliamentarians for Global Action, Royal Institute of International Affairs, 16 March 2012, available at <http://www.pgaction.org/pdf/activity/Chatham-ICC-SC.pdf>.
303   "Calling Assad war criminal could complicate things: Clinton", *Agence France-Presse*, 28 February 2012.
304   "The UNSC and the International Criminal Court", *op. cit.*, p. 4.
305   *Ibid.*
306   *Ibid.*, p. 3.
307   Government of India, "Explanation of Vote by Mr. Dilip Lahiri, Head of Delegation of India, on the Adoption of the Statute of the International Court", United Nations Conference of Plenipotentiaries on the Establishment of an International Criminal Court, Ninth Plenary Meeting, 17 July 1998, available at <http://www.un.org/icc/speeches/717ind.htm>.
308   Jacqueline Geis and Alex Mundt, "When to Indict? The Impact of Timing International Criminal Indictments on Peace Processes and Humanitarian Action", the Brookings Institution-University of Bern Project on Internal Displacement, paper to the World Humanitarian Studies Conference, Groningen, the Netherlands, February 2009, p. 19, available at <http://reliefweb.int/rw/RWFiles2009.nsf/FilesByRWDocUnidFilename/RWST-7RAQ9A-full_report.pdf/$File/full_report.pdf>.
309   William Schabas, *An Introduction to the International Criminal Court*, Cambridge University Press, 2001, p. 27.
310   "Military and Paramilitary Activities in and Against Nicaragua" (Nicaragua v. United States), Merits, [1986] ICJ Reports 14, at 290).
311   Judge Sang-Hyun Song, "International Criminal Court and the European Union: Challenges for the Promotion of International Justice and the Fight against Impunity", address to European Parliament Group of Parliamentarians for Global Action, *op. cit.*
312   "Report of the International Criminal Court", A/64/356, General Assembly, 17 September 2009, available at <http://www.icc-cpi.int/NR/rdonlyres/1BC01710-9C42-44AC-8B18-85EE2A8876EB/281210/A_64_356_ENG2.pdf>.
313   Louise Parrott, "The Role of the International Criminal Court in Uganda: Ensuring that the Pursuit of Justice does not come at the price of peace", *The Australian Journal of Peace Studies*, Vol. 1 (2006).
314   Human Rights Watch, "Courting History. The Landmark International Criminal Court's First Years", New York, July 2008, available at < http://www.hrw.org/en/reports/2008/07/10/courting-history>, p.6.
315   *Ibid.*
316   International Criminal Court, "Negotiated Relationship Agreement between the International Criminal Court and the United Nations", adopted October 4, 2004, ICC-ASP/3/Res.1, available at <http://www.icc-cpi.int/library/asp/ICC-ASP-3-Res1_English.pdf>.
317   ASP, "Report of the International Criminal Court", A/62/314, 31 August 2007, available at <http://www.icc-cpi.int/library/organs/presidency/ICC_Report_to_UN_2006_2007_English.pdf>, para. 44.
318   *Ibid.*

319 The United Nations Organization Stabilization Mission in the Democratic Republic of the Congo or MONUSCO (until 2010 known as United Nations Mission in the Democratic Republic of Congo or MONUC, or *Mission de l'Organisation des Nations Unies en République démocratique du Congo*), is a UN peacekeeping force in the Democratic Republic of the Congo which was established by the UNSC in Resolutions 1279 (1999) and 1291 (2000) to monitor the peace process of the Second Congo War, though much of its focus subsequently turned to the Ituri conflict, the Kivu conflict and the Dongo conflict.

320 David Lewis, "Guatemalan blue helmet deaths stir Congo debate", Reuters, 31 January 2006, available at <http://www.reliefweb.int/rwarchive/rwb.nsf/db900sid/ABES-6LKL3W?OpenDocument&Click=>.

321 See, for example, "International court under fire for prosecution policy", *NRC Handelsblad* (the Netherlands), 20 November 2008, available at <http://www.nrc.nl/international/Features/article2067475.ece/International_court_under_fire_for_prosecution_policy>.

322 Nick Grono and Adam O'Brien, "Exorcising the Ghost of the ICC", *The Monitor* (Uganda), 31 October 2006, available at <http://www.crisisgroup.org/home/index.cfm?id=4483&l=1>.

323 The Security Council, by its Resolution 1590 (2005) of 24 March 2005, established the United Nations Mission in the Sudan (UNMIS) to support implementation of the Comprehensive Peace Agreement signed by the government of Sudan and the Sudan People's Liberation Movement/Army on 9 January 2005. It was made up of 10,000 military personnel including some 750 military observers; up to 715 police, and a civilian component. This UN mission ended on 9 July 2011 when South Sudan became independent. The UN military presence in South Sudan has continued. Security Council Resolution 1996 (2011) established a successor to UNMIS, the United Nations Mission in the Republic of South Sudan (UNMISS) for an initial period of one year, starting from 9 July 2011.

324 "The UNSC and the International Criminal Court", International Law Meeting summary, with Parliamentarians for Global Action, International Law and Human Rights Programme, Parliamentarians for Global Action, Royal Institute of International Affairs, 16 March 2012, available at <http://www.pgaction.org/pdf/activity/Chatham-ICC-SC.pdf>, p. 7.

325 *Ibid.*, p. 9.

326 "Who's Afraid of the International Criminal Court?", *Foreign Affairs*, May/June 2011, available at <http://www.foreignaffairs.com/articles/67768/david-kaye/whos-afraid-of-the-international-criminal-court>.

327 "Duplicity on Darfur", *The Hindu, op. cit.*

328 "International Criminal Court", *Jurist*, University of Pittsburgh School of Law, 2 July 2012, available at <http://jurist.org/feature/2012/07/international-criminal-court.php>.

329 Haider Ala Hamoudi, "*The Problem of Legitimacy in International Criminal Justice*", *Jurist*, 7 July 2011, available at <http://jurist.org/forum/2011/07/haider-hamoudi-libya-legitimacy.php>.

330 Richard Dicker, "The Court of Last Resort", *Foreign Policy*, 29 June 2012, available at <http://www.foreignpolicy.com/articles/2012/06/29/ICC_the_court_of_last_resort?page=full>.

331 Michael Ignatieff, "We're So Exceptional", *The New York Review of Books*, 5 April 2012.

332 WikiLeaks, US Government cable, "Subject: Sudan: P-3 Discuss way forward on ICC Indictment Coordination, Darfur Peace Process", 21 January 2009, available at <http://www.telegraph.co.uk/news/wikileaks-files/london-wikileaks/8305120/SUDAN-P-3-DISCUSS-WAY-FORWARD-ON-ICC-INDICTMENT-COORDINATION-DARFUR-PEACE-PROCESS.html>.

333 WikiLeaks, US Government Cable, "Subject: Africa: HMG's Priorities to discuss with the Obama Administration, Scope for Influence", 19 February 2009, available at <http://cablegatesearch.wikileaks.org/cable.php?id=09LONDON435&q=icc>.

334 WikiLeaks, US Government Cable, "Subject: Sudan: P-3 Discussions on Sudan-ICC issues", 27 August 2008, available at <http://cablegatesearch.wikileaks.org/cable.php?id=08LONDON2195&q=ocampo>.
335 "Dim prospects. The International Criminal Court loses credibility and co-operation in Africa", *The Economist*, 17 February 2011, available at <http://www.economist.com/node/18176088>.
336 See Yee, "The International Court and the Security Council: Articles 13(b) and 16", in Roy S. Lee (editor), *The International Criminal Court. The Making of the Rome Statute. Issues, Negotiations, Results*, Kluwer Law International, The Hague, 1999, at p. 152 note 31. Lionel Yee Woon Chin SC is a Singaporean jurist. He was appointed as the Second Solicitor-General of Singapore on 1 January 2011. He had previously served as the Director-General of the Attorney-General's Chambers' International Affairs Division. From December 2000 to March 2001, he was attached to the Ministry of Foreign Affairs where he served as Legal Adviser to the Permanent Mission of Singapore to the UN in New York. He is a graduate of the University of Cambridge and New York University.
337 Morten Bergsmo and Jelena Pejic´, "Deferral of investigation or prosecution", in Otto Triffterer (editor), *Commentary on the Rome Statute of the International Criminal Court, Observers' Notes, Article by Article*, Nomos, Baden-Baden, 1999.
338 Andreas L. Paulus, "Legalist Groundwork for the International Criminal Court: Commentaries on the Statute of the International Criminal Court", *European Journal of International Law*, Vol. 14, No. 4 (2003), p. 853.
339 *Ibid.*, pp. 843–60.
340 For details, see Carsten Stahn, "The Ambiguities of Security Council Resolution 1422", *European Journal of International Law*, Vol. 14 (2003), p. 85.
341 See, board of editors, "The Rome Statute: A Tentative Assessment", in Antonio Cassese, Paola Gaeta and John R. W. D. Jones (editors), *The Rome Statute of the International Criminal Court: A Commentary*, Oxford University Press, Oxford, 2002, p. 1907.
342 For details, see Carsten Stahn, "The Ambiguities of Security Council Resolution 1422", *European Journal of International Law*, Vol. 14 (2003), p. 85.
343 Louise Arbour, "The Rise and Fall of International Human Rights", lecture by Louise Arbour, President and CEO of the ICG, on the occasion of the Sir Joseph Hotung International Human Rights Lecture 2011, at the British Museum, 27 April 2011, available at <http://www.crisisgroup.org/en/publication-type/speeches/2011/the-rise-and-fall-of-international-human-rights.aspx>.
344 Victor Peskin, "An ideal becoming real? The International Criminal Court and the limits of the cosmopolitan vision of justice", in Roland Pierik and Wouter Werner (editors), *Cosmopolitanism in Context: Perspectives from International Law and Political Theory*, Cambridge University Press, Cambridge, 2010, p. 199.
345 Richard Dicker, "Handing Qaddafi a Get-Out-Of-Jail-Free Card", *The New York Times*, 1 August 2011, available at <http://www.nytimes.com/2011/08/01/opinion/01iht-eddicker01.html>.
346 Mark Kersten, "No winners in ICC-Libya standoff", *Foreign Policy*, 8 October 2012, available at <http://mideast.foreignpolicy.com/posts/2012/10/08/no_winners_in_icc_libya_standoff>.
347 Cited in Mark Kersten, "Between Justice and Politics: The International Criminal Court's Intervention in Libya", available at <http://www.academia.edu/1558775/Between_Justice_and_Politics_The_International_Criminal_Courts_Intervention_in_Libya>. Schiff's remarks were made at International Studies Association 2011 annual convention, "Global Governance: Political Authority in Transition", Montreal.
348 William Schabas, "The International Criminal Court at Ten", PhD studies in human rights blog, 15 February 2012, available at <http://humanrightsdoctorate.blogspot.co.uk/2012/02/international-criminal-court-at-tenw.html>.

349 *Ibid.*
350 Human Rights Watch, "UNSC: Address Inconsistency in ICC Referrals", 16 October 2012.
351 "The UNSC and the International Criminal Court", International Law meeting summary, with Parliamentarians for Global Action, International Law and Human Rights Programme, Parliamentarians for Global Action, Royal Institute of International Affairs, 16 March 2012, available at <http://www.pgaction.org/pdf/activity/Chatham-ICC-SC.pdf>, p. 5.
352 Human Rights Watch, "Letter on the October 17 Thematic Debate at the Security Council on the Council's Relationship with the ICC. ICC States Parties Should Urge a Principled Relationship Between the Security Council and the Court", 16 October 2012, available at <http://www.hrw.org/news/2012/10/16/letter-october-17-thematic-debate-security-council-councils-relationship-icc>.
353 Geoffrey Robertson, *Crimes Against Humanity. The Struggle for Global Justice*, Penguin Books, fourth edition, 2012, p. 527.

Notes to Chapter Three

354 "Frequently Asked Questions About the U.S. Government's Policy Regarding the International Criminal Court (ICC)", Fact Sheet, Bureau of Political-Military Affairs, US Department of State, Washington-DC, 30 July 2003, available at <http://www.state.gov/t/pm/rls/fs/23428.htm>.
355 Adam Branch, *Displacing Human Rights. War and Intervention in northern Uganda*, Oxford University Press, New York, 2011, p. 201. Dr. Branch is Assistant Professor of Political Science, San Diego State University. He is the author of "The Roots of LRA Violence: Political Crisis and Politicized Ethnicity in Acholiland", in Tim Allen and Koen Vlassenroot (editors), *The Lord's Resistance Army: War, Peace and Reconciliation*, Zed Press/African Arguments, London, 2010; "Gulu Town in War…And Peace? Displacement, Humanitarianism, and Post-War Crisis", in *Cities and Conflict*, LSE Crisis States Book Series, Hurst, London, 2010; "Fostering the Transition in Northern Uganda: From War to Peace, Camps to Home", report for the Ford Foundation for Eastern Africa, published by Human Rights Focus (Uganda), 2007; "The ICC Should Stop its Experimental African Investigation Now", *The Monitor* (Kampala), 13 January 2005.
356 Senator Jesse Helms, Subcommittee on International Operations of the Senate Committee on Foreign Relations of the United States Senate, 23 July 1998, 105th Cong., 2d Sess., S. Rep. No. 105.
357 See Michael Ignatieff (editor), *American Exceptionalism and Human Rights*, Princeton University Press, 2005. See also, Stephen Walt, "The Myth of American Exceptionalism", *Foreign Policy*, November 2011; and Jerome Karabel, "'American Exceptionalism' and the Battle for the Presidency", *The Huffington Post*, 22 December 2011.
358 Michael Ignatieff, "We're So Exceptional", *The New York Review of Books*, 5 April 2012.
359 *Ibid.*
360 See Michael Ignatieff (editor), *American Exceptionalism and Human Rights*, Stephen Walt, "The Myth of American Exceptionalism", and Jerome Karabel, "'American Exceptionalism' and the Battle for the Presidency", *op. cit.*
361 David Scheffer, "International Criminal Court: The challenge of jurisdiction", speech to the American Society of International Law, 26 March 1999, cited in Michael P. Scharf, "The United States and the International Criminal Court: The ICC's Jurisdiction over Nationals of Non-party States: A Critique of the US Position", *Law and Contemporary Problems*, No. 64 (2001), p. 68.

362 David Scheffer, Subcommittee on International Operations of the Senate Committee on Foreign Relations of the United States Senate, 23 July 1998, 105th Cong., 2d Sess., S. Rep. No. 105, cited in Scharf, *op. cit.*, p. 68.
363 David Scheffer, *All the Missing Souls: A Personal History of the War Crimes Tribunals*, Princeton University Press, 2012.
364 Ignatieff, "We're So Exceptional", *op. cit.*
365 *Ibid.*
366 See Michael Ignatieff (editor), *American Exceptionalism and Human Rights*, Stephen Walt, "The Myth of American Exceptionalism", and Jerome Karabel, "'American Exceptionalism' and the Battle for the Presidency", *op. cit.*
367 President Clinton, Statement on the Rome Treaty on the International Criminal Court, 31 December 2000, *Weekly Comp. Pres. Doc.*, 8 January 2001, available in Sean D. Murphy, *United States Practice in International Law*, Volume 1, 1999–2001, p. 384.
368 Marc Grossman, Under Secretary of State for Political Affairs, American Foreign Policy and the International Criminal Court, remarks to the Center for Strategic and International Studies, Washington DC, 6 May 2002, available at <http://www.iccnow.org/documents/USUnsigningGrossman6May02.pdf>.
369 Letter from John R. Bolton, US Under Secretary of State for Arms Control and International Security, to Kofi Annan, UN Secretary General, 6 May 2002 available at <http://2001-2009.state.gov/r/pa/prs/ps/2002/9968.htm>.
370 "Frequently Asked Questions About the U.S. Government's Policy Regarding the International Criminal Court (ICC)", Fact Sheet, Bureau of Political-Military Affairs, US Department of State, Washington DC, 30 July 2003, available at <http://www.state.gov/t/pm/rls/fs/23428.htm>.
371 *Ibid.*
372 Richard Dicker, "The Court of Last Resort", *Foreign Policy*, 29 June 2012, available at <http://www.foreignpolicy.com/articles/2012/06/29/ICC_the_court_of_last_resort?page=full>.
373 David Scheffer, *All the Missing Souls: A Personal History of the War Crimes Tribunals*, *op. cit.*
374 "Security Council requests International Criminal Court not to bring cases against peacekeeping personnel from states not party to statute", United Nations Press Release, 12 July 2002.
375 Resolution 1422 requests "that the ICC, if a case arises involving current or former officials or personnel from a contributing State not a Party to the Rome Statute over acts or omissions relating to a United Nations established or authorized operation, shall for a twelve-month period starting 1 July 2002 not commence or proceed with investigation or prosecution of any such case, unless the Security Council decides otherwise".
376 See, "Africa and the International Criminal Court", Council on Foreign Relations, New York, 17 November 2006, and the American Non-Governmental Coalitions for the International Criminal Court, "Chronology of US Actions Related to the International Criminal Court", 4 March 2011, available at <http://www.amicc.org/docs/US%20Chronology.pdf>.
377 "The EU's Human rights & Democratisation Policy: September 30, 2002: International criminal court (ICC) – Council Conclusions", General Affairs and External Relations Council of the European Commission, 2002.
378 Robin Cook, *Point of Departure*, Simon & Schuster, London, 2003, p. 229.
379 Adam Branch, *Displacing Human Rights. War and Intervention in northern Uganda*, Oxford University Press, New York, 2011, p. 185.
380 "Rights and reconciliation in a new era of international law Part II", "Justice for a Lawless World? Rights and reconciliation in a new era of international law", IRIN, June 2006, p. 3, available at <http://www.irinnews.org/pdf/in-depth/RightsAndReconciliationPart2.pdf>.
381 "The United States and the International Criminal Court", *American Journal of International Law*, Vol. 93, No. 1 (1999), p. 18.

382 "Countries not party to the ICC can be referred to the tribunal – US", *Washington Times*, 2 April 2005.
383 Philippe Sands, *Lawless World: The Whistle-Blowing Account of How Bush and Blair Are Taking the Law Into Their own Hands*, Penguin Books, 2006, p. 249. See also, "World Briefings", *New York Times*, 2 April 2005.
384 See, for example, "ICC, Darfur and a Flawed U.S. Foreign Policy", Partnership for a Secure America, available at <http://blog.psaonline.org/2007/08/02/icc-darfur-and-a-flawed-us-foreign-policy/>, 2 August 2007. Mark Goldberg, writer in residence of the United Nations Foundation had put in a Freedom of Information Act request for cable traffic and other items relating to the State Department's Darfur policy.
385 David Scheffer, "America's Stake in Peace, Security and Justice", American Society of International Law newsletter, September-October 1998, p. 9.
386 David Scheffer, statement before the US Senate Committee on Foreign Relations, "Is a U.N. International Criminal Court in the U.S. National Interest?": hearing before the Subcommittee on International Operations of the Senate Committee on Foreign Relations, 105th Congress. Vol. 2 (1998), p. 14.
387 Mahmood Mamdani,, "Darfur, ICC and the new humanitarian order: How the ICC's 'responsibility to protect' is being turned into an assertion of neocolonial domination", *Pambazuka News*, 17 September 2008, No. 396, available at <http://pambazuka.org/en/category/features/50568>.
388 David Freddoso, *The Case Against Barack Obama: The Unlikely Rise and Unexamined Agenda of the Media's Favorite Candidate*, Regnery Publishing, 2008, pp. 169–71.
389 Walter Pincus, "Clinton's Goals Detailed", *Washington Post*, 19 January 2009.
390 US State Department, "U.S. Reengagement with the U.N.", 20 March 2009, Foreign Press Center briefing transcript.
391 "Barack Obama May Subject US Troops to International Criminal Court", *The Daily Telegraph*, 6 March 2009.
392 "Koh and Rapp's Remarks on U.S. Engagement in the International Criminal Court and the Outcome of the ICC Assembly of States Parties Conference, June 2010", primary sources, Council on Foreign Relations, New York, 15 June 2010, available at <http://www.cfr.org/international-criminal-courts-and-tribunals/koh-rapps-remarks-us-engagement-international-criminal-court-outcome-icc-assembly-states-parties-conference-june-2010/p22454>.
393 "National Security Strategy", The White House, Washington DC, May 2010, available at <http://www.whitehouse.gov/sites/default/files/rss_viewer/national_security_strategy.pdf>.
394 Brett D. Schaefer, "Beating the ICC", Heritage Foundation, 18 February 2013, available at <http://www.heritage.org/research/commentary/2013/2/beating-the-icc>. Schaefer is the Jay Kingham Fellow in International Regulatory Affairs at the Heritage Foundation.
395 William Schabas, *Unimaginable Atrocities. Justice, Politics, and Rights at the War Crimes Tribunals*, Oxford University Press, Oxford, 2012, p. 89.
396 Adam Branch, *Displacing Human Rights. War and Intervention in northern Uganda*, Oxford University Press, New York, 2011, p. 201. For a longer examination of this theme, see Samar Al-Bulushi and Adam Branch, "AFRICOM and the ICC: Enforcing International Justice in Africa", *Pambazuka News*, No. 483, 27 May 2010.
397 Adam Branch, *Displacing Human Rights. War and Intervention in northern Uganda, op. cit.*, p. 191.
398 "U.S. Aided a Failed Plan to Rout Ugandan Rebels", *The New York Times*, 6 February 2009.
399 See, "How it Ends", video clip, Invisible Children website, available at <http://www.invisiblechildren.com/videos/5429085>, cited in Branch, *Displacing Human Rights*, p. 201.

400 "Ambassador: U.S. moving to support international court", CNN, 24 March 2010.
401 "Obama Administration Asks for Funds to Boost Uganda's Fight Against Rebels", Bloomberg, 25 November 2010.
402 "Obama orders U.S. troops to help chase down African 'army' leader", CNN, 14 October 2011.
403 Adam Branch, *Displacing Human Rights. War and Intervention in northern Uganda, op. cit.*, p. 201.
404 *Ibid.*, p. 202.
405 "Washington's Growing Ties With International Court. US steers clear of joining International Criminal Court, but it is now much more aligned with the court's goals than ever before", *ACR* Issue 337, Institute for War & Peace Reporting, 23 January 2013, available at < http://iwpr.net/report-news/washingtons-growing-ties-international-court>.
406 "US suspends aid to Malawi over governance and receiving Sudanese president", *Sudan Tribune*, 23 March 2012, available at <http://www.sudantribune.com/spip.php?article42015>.
407 "ICC has fallen from high ideals of global justice, accountability", *Daily Nation* (Nairobi), 16 March 2013, available at <http://www.nation.co.ke/oped/Opinion/-/440808/1722100/-/k4rufnz/-/index.html>.
408 *Ibid.*
409 Jendayi Frazer was the Assistant Secretary of State from 2005 to 2009 and is presently a distinguished service professor at Carnegie Mellon University, and Adjunct Senior Fellow for Africa Studies at the Council on Foreign Relations.
410 "Inside Story - Heavy is the head...", Al-Jazeera, 10 March 2013, available at <http://www.youtube.com/watch?v=CKof8bKtvrg&hd=0>.

Notes to Chapter Five

411 Cited in *The Monitor*, journal of the Coalition for the International Criminal Court, Issue No. 36, May–October 2008, available at <http://www.iccnow.org/documents/Monitor36_final.pdf>; *The Wall Street Journal*, 24–25 July 1998; and William Pace and Jennifer Schense, "The Role of Non-Governmental Organizations", in Antonio Cassese, Paola Gaeta and John R. W. D. Jones (editors), *The Rome Statute of the International Criminal Court: A Commentary*, Oxford University Press, Oxford, 2002, p. 125.
412 "A Poisoned Chalice? Just Justice? Civil Society, International Justice and the Search for Accountability in Africa", International Refugee Rights Initiative, Discussion Paper 1, October 2011, available at <http://www.refugee-rights.org/Assets/PDFs/2012/PoisonChaliceFINAL.pdf>.
413 Human Rights Watch, "Courting History. The Landmark International Criminal Court's First Years", New York, July 2008, available at < http://www.hrw.org/en/reports/2008/07/10/courting-history>, p. 8.
414 ICC, "Prosecutorial Strategy 2009–2012", OTP, The Hague, 18 August 2009, available at <http://www.grotiuscentre.org/cms/ACE/files/Prosecutorial%20Strategy%202009-2012.pdf>.
415 Brett D. Schaefer and Steven Groves, "The U.S. Should Not Join the International Criminal Court", Executive Summary No. 2307, Heritage Foundation, Washington DC, 17 August 2009.
416 William Pace and Mark Thieroff, "Participation of Non-Governmental Organizations", in Roy S. Lee (editor), *The International Criminal Court - The Making of the Rome Statute*, The Hague, Kluwer Law International, 1999; William Pace and Jennifer Schense, "The Role of Non-Governmental Organizations" in Chapter 2 of Antonio Cassese, Paola Gaeta

and John R. W. D. Jones (editors), *The Rome Statute of the International Criminal Court: A Commentary – Volume 1*, Oxford University Press, Oxford, 2002; William Pace and Jennifer Schense, "International lawmaking of historic proportions: civil society and the International Criminal Court", in Paul Gready (editor), *Fighting For Human Rights*, Routledge, New York, 2004; Marlies Glasius, "How Activists Shaped the Court", Crimes of War Project, December 2003, available at <http://www.crimesofwar.org/print/icc/icc-glasius-print.html>; Marlies Glasius, *The International Criminal Court: A Global Civil Society Achievement*, Routledge, London and New York, 2006; Human Rights Watch, *World Report 1999*, Special Issues and Campaigns, "The International Criminal Court" including section on NGO role, available at <http://www.hrw.org/worldreport99/special/icc.html>; transcript, "The New Court: Civil Society Victory", Common Ground, 6 October 1998.

417   William Schabas, *An Introduction to the International Criminal Court*, Cambridge University Press, 2001, p. 15.
418   *Ibid.*, p. 15, note 52. For an insider's account of the role of NGOs in Rome, see William R. Pace and Mark Thieroff, "Participation of Non-Governmental Organizations", in Roy Lee (editor), *The International Criminal Court: The Making of the Rome Statute, Issues, Negotiations, Results*, Kluwer Law International, 1999, pp. 391–98; William Bourdon, "Rôle de la société civile et des ONG", in *La Cour pénale internationale*, La Documentation française, Paris, 1999, pp. 89–96.
419   David Davenport, "The New Diplomacy", *Policy Review*, No. 116, December 2002/January 2003, available at <http://www.hoover.org/publications/policyreview/3458466.html>.
420   Cited in *The Monitor*, journal of the Coalition for the International Criminal Court, Issue No. 36, May/October 2008, available at <http://www.iccnow.org/documents/Monitor36_final.pdf>, and *The Wall Street Journal*, 24–25 July 1998.
421   David Davenport, "The New Diplomacy", *Policy Review*, *op. cit.*
422   Benjamin Schiff, *Building the ICC*, Cambridge University Press, New York, 2008, p. 149.
423   Marlies Glasius, *The International Criminal Court: A Global Civil Society Achievement*, Routledge, London, 2005, pp. 42–43.
424   Philippe Sands, *Lawless World: The Whistle-Blowing Account of How Bush and Blair Are Taking the Law Into Their own Hands*, Penguin Books, 2005, pp. 55–56.
425   Benjamin Schiff, *Building the ICC*, Cambridge University Press, New York, 2008.
426   *Ibid.*, p.154.
427   *Ibid.*, p.163.
428   Chris Patten, *Not Quite the Diplomat*, Penguin Books, London, 2006, p. 309.
429   See, "European Instrument for Democracy and Human Rights", available at <http://ec.europa.eu/europeaid/how/finance/eidhr_en.htm>.
430   EU, *The European Union and the International Criminal Court*, General Secretariat of the Council, May 2010, p. 5.
431   *Ibid.*
432   Andreas L. Paulus, "Legalist Groundwork for the International Criminal Court: Commentaries on the Statute of the International Criminal Court", *European Journal of International Law*, Vol. 14, No. 4 (2003), pp. 843–60. The four studies he reviewed were Antonio Cassese, Paola Gaeta and John R. W. D. Jones (editors), *The Rome Statute of the International Criminal Court: A Commentary*, Oxford University Press, Oxford, 2002; Knut Dörmann, *Elements of War Crimes Under the Rome Statute of the International Criminal Court: Sources and Commentary*, Cambridge University Press, Cambridge, 2003; Roy S. Lee (editor), *The International Criminal Court. The Making of the Rome Statute. Issues, Negotiations, Results*, Kluwer Law International, The Hague, 1999; and Otto Triffterer (editor), *Commentary on the Rome Statute of the International Criminal Court, Observers' Notes, Article by Article*, Nomos, Baden-Baden, 1999. Andreas Paulus is a justice of the Federal Constitutional Court of Germany (*Bundesverfassungsgericht*). He also holds the

Chair in Public and International Law at the Georg-August-University, Göttingen, where he teaches public law, international and European law, constitutional history and legal philosophy. In 2003/04, Justice Paulus taught at the University of Michigan Law School as a visiting assistant professor. From 1999–2006, he was Assistant Professor at the Ludwig-Maximilians-University, Munich. He studied law in Göttingen, Geneva, Munich and at Harvard Law School. Justice Paulus served as Counsel and Adviser to the Federal Republic of Germany before the International Court of Justice in the LaGrand (Germany v. United States) and Certain Property (Liechtenstein v. Germany) cases. Justice Paulus is a widely published authority on a variety of public law topics. He is an associate editor of the definitive *Commentary on the United Nations Charter* and co-editor of the third edition.

433 See Pace and Schense, "The Role of Non-Governmental Organizations", in Antonio Cassese, Paola Gaeta and John R. W. D. Jones (editors), *The Rome Statute of the International Criminal Court: A Commentary*, Oxford University Press, Oxford, 2002, p. 118.

434 Andreas L. Paulus, "Legalist Groundwork for the International Criminal Court: Commentaries on the Statute of the International Criminal Court", *op. cit.*, p. 849.

435 *Ibid.*, p. 849.

436 Jess Bravin, "Justice Delayed. For Global Court, Ugandan Rebels Prove Tough Test", *The Wall Street Journal*, 8 June 2006.

437 Tony Blair, *A Journey*, Hutchinson, London, 2010, p. 560.

438 *Ibid.*, p. 559.

439 Kenneth Anderson and David Rieff, "'Global Civil Society': A Sceptical View", *Global Civil Society 2004/5*, Sage Publications, London, 2005, p. 26.

440 *Ibid.*, p. 30.

441 *Ibid.*, p. 26.

442 *Ibid.*, pp. 31–32.

443 *Ibid.*, p. 32.

444 *Ibid.*, p. 34.

445 Pace and Schense, "The Role of Non-Governmental Organizations", in Antonio Cassese, Paola Gaeta and John R. W. D. Jones (editors), *The Rome Statute of the International Criminal Court: A Commentary*, Oxford University Press, Oxford, 2002, p. 107.

446 Andreas L. Paulus, "Legalist Groundwork for the International Criminal Court: Commentaries on the Statute of the International Criminal Court", *op. cit.*, pp. 848–49.

447 Geoffrey Robertson, *Crimes Against Humanity. The Struggle for Global Justice, op. cit.*, p. 551.

448 World Bank, "Civil Society and Peace Building: Potential, Limitations and Critical Factors", 2006, Social Development Department and Sustainable Development Network. Report No.36445-GLB, p. 7, available at <http://siteresources.worldbank.org/EXTSOCIALDEVELOPMENT/Resources/244 362-1164107274725/3182370-1164110717447/Civil_Society_and_Peacebuilding.pdf>.

449 World Bank, "Defining Civil Society", 2010, p. 1, available at <http://web.worldbank.org/WBSITE/EXTERNAL/TOPICS/CSO/0,,contentMDK:20101499~menuPK:244752~pagePK:220503~piPK:220476~theSitePK:228717,00.html>.

450 Benjamin Schiff, *Building the ICC*, Cambridge University Press, New York, 2008, p. 201.

451 "Probe Army Too, Amnesty Tells ICC", *New Vision*, 4 February 2004.

452 "Uganda: Engaging ICC Will Worsen the Conflict in Northern Uganda", *East African*, 25 April 2005.

453 "A Poisoned Chalice? Just Justice? Civil Society, International Justice and the Search for Accountability in Africa", International Refugee Rights Initiative, Discussion Paper 1, October 2011, available at <http://www.refugee-rights.org/Assets/PDFs/2012/PoisonChaliceFINAL.pdf>.

454 Adam Branch, "International Justice, Local Injustice: The International Criminal Court in Northern Uganda", *Dissent*, Summer 2004, available at <http://www.dissentmagazine.org/menutest/articles/su04/branch.htm>.
455 "A Poisoned Chalice? Just Justice? Civil Society, International Justice and the Search for Accountability in Africa", *op. cit.*
456 Lucy Hovil, "Challenging International Justice: The Initial Years of the International Criminal Court's Intervention in Uganda", *Stability: International Journal of Security & Development*, Vol. 2, No. 1 (2013). Dr. Hovil is the Senior Researcher for a research and advocacy project initiated by the International Refugee Rights Initiative and the Social Science Research Council, Citizenship and Forced Migration in the Great Lakes Region. She is also the managing editor for the *International Journal of Transitional Justice*. She was formerly the Senior Research and Advocacy Officer at the Refugee Law Project, Faculty of Law, Makerere University, Uganda, where she founded the organisation's research department and oversaw their working paper series. She obtained her doctorate (1999) from the School of Oriental and African Studies, University of London, in which she explored the relationship between violence and identity in South Africa during the period of conflict that preceded the country's first inclusive election in 1994.
457 *Ibid.*
458 *Ibid.*
459 *Ibid.*
460 *Ibid.*
461 *Ibid.*
462 *Ibid.*
463 See, for example, Schiff, *op. cit.*, pp. 202–03, and Josefine Volqvartz, "ICC under fire over Uganda probe", CNN, 23 February 2005.
464 "A Poisoned Chalice? Just Justice? Civil Society, International Justice and the Search for Accountability in Africa", *op. cit.*, pp. 4–5.
465 P. Pham, P. Vinck, M. Wierda, E. Stover and A. Di Giovanni, *Forgotten Voices: A Population-Based Survey of Attitudes About Peace and Justice in Northern Uganda*, International Center for Transitional Justice, 2005; P. Pham, P. Vinck, M. Wierda, E. Stover and A. Di Giovanni and R. Bailey, *When the War Ends: A Population-Based Survey on Attitudes about Peace, Justice and Social Reconstruction in Northern Uganda*, International Center for Transitional Justice, 2007.
466 Pham, *et al.*, *op. cit.*, p. 22.
467 Ibid., p. 39.

Notes to Chapter Six

468 Lee A. Casey and David B. Rivkin Jr., "The Limits of Legitimacy: The Rome Statute's Unlawful Application to Non-State Parties", *Virginia Journal of International Law*, Vol. 44 (2003).
469 Eric Stein, "International Integration and Democracy: No Love at First Sight", *American Journal of International Law*, Vol. 95 (2001), pp. 489, 494. Professor Eric Stein was regarded as an eminent scholar in international and comparative law. He was the Hessel E. Yntema Professor of Law Emeritus at the University of Michigan Law School. He served in the US Department of State and was adviser to the US Delegation to the UN General Assembly and to the US representatives at the UNSC and the International Court of Justice. He has taught and lectured widely at American, European, and Asian universities and at The Hague Academy of International Law. Stein was a member of editorial boards of a number of American and European periodicals including the *American Journal of International Law*. He died in 2011.

470 See, "International Criminal Court | John Bolton | Oxford Union", 13 February 2013, available at <http://www.youtube.com/watch?v=eYJW7CcWPbs>.
471 See, for example, Brad R. Roth, *Governmental Illegitimacy in International Law*, Oxford University Press, USA, 1999.
472 Douglas Lee Donoho, "Democratic Legitimacy in Human Rights: The Future of International Decision-Making", *Wisconsin International Law Journal*, Vol. 21, No. 1 (2003), p. 16. Donoho is Professor of Law at the Nova Southeastern University Shepard Broad Law Center, where he teaches international human rights, international law and constitutional law.
473 Madeline Morris, "The Democratic Dilemma of the International Criminal Court", *Buffalo Criminal Law Review*, Vol. 5 (2002), p. 596. See also, Morris, "The Disturbing Democratic Deficit of the International Criminal Court", *Finnish Yearbook of International Law*, Vol. 12 (2001), pp. 109–18 and "Judgment without Democracy", *Washington Post*, 24 July 2002, A19. See, also, Morris, "High Crimes and Misconceptions: The ICC and Non-Party States", *Law and Contemporary Problems*, Vol. 64 (2001), pp. 13–66. Madeline Morris is an expert in international criminal law, the law of war, transnational jurisdiction, and public international law. She has served as a member of the US Secretary of State's Advisory Committee on International Law; as an adviser on justice to the President of Rwanda; as a special consultant to the US Secretary of the Army; as senior legal counsel, OTP, Special Court for Sierra Leone; as an adviser to the Special Prosecutor, Republic of Serbia; and as a witness before the US Senate Committee on Foreign Relations. Morris has also served as Chief Counsel to the Office of the Chief Defense Counsel for Military Commissions, US Department of Defense. In 2005, Morris founded the Guantánamo Defense Clinic, which she directs. Morris has written extensively on issues pertaining to the detention and trial of suspected terrorists. She is the author of *Terror and Integrity: Preventive Detention in the Age of Jihad* (Oxford University Press, 2010).
474 Madeline Morris, "The Democratic Dilemma of the International Criminal Court", *op. cit.*, pp. 109–18 and "Judgment without Democracy", *Washington Post*, 24 July 2002, A19. See, also, Morris, "High Crimes and Misconceptions: The ICC and Non-Party States", *Law and Contemporary Problems*, Vol. 64 (2001), pp. 13–66.
475 Morris, "The Democratic Dilemma", *op. cit.*, p. 593.
476 Lee A. Casey and David B. Rivkin Jr., "The Limits of Legitimacy: The Rome Statute's Unlawful Application to Non-State Parties", *Virginia Journal of International Law*, Vol. 44 (2003).
477 See, Final Act of the United Nations Diplomatic Conference of Plenipotentiaries on the Establishment of an International Criminal Court Done at Rome, 17 July 1998.
478 Morris, "The Democratic Dilemma", *op. cit.*, p. 598.
479 "International Law on Trial", *Financial Times*, 25 July 2008.
480 Marc Grossman, "American Foreign Policy and the International Criminal Court", remarks to the Center for Strategic and International Studies, Washington DC, 6 May 2002, at <http://www.iccnow.org/documents/USUnsigningGrossman6May02.pdf>.
481 *Ibid.*
482 Robert Bork, "The Limits of 'International Law'", *The National Interest*, Winter 1989/9, p. 10.
483 Morris, "The Democratic Dilemma", *op. cit.*, p. 496.
484 Eric Stein, "International Integration and Democracy: No Love at First Sight", *American Journal of International Law*, Vol. 95 (2001), pp. 489, 494.
485 Jean d'Aspremont, "Legitimacy of Governments in the Age of Democracy", *New York University Journal of International Law and Politics*, Vol. 38 (2006), p. 878. Jean d'Aspremont is Chair of Public International Law at the University of Manchester. He is affiliated with the Amsterdam Centre for International Law. He is Editor-in-Chief of the *Leiden Journal*

of *International Law*. He acted as counsel in proceedings before the International Court of Justice.
486 George F. Will, "U.S. must not surrender sovereignty to International Criminal Court", *Pittsburgh Tribune-Review*, 11 July 2002, available at <http://triblive.com/x/pittsburghtrib/opinion/columnists/will/s_80658.html#axzz2ONjM3Lzi>.
487 Kenneth Anderson and David Rieff, "'Global Civil Society': A Sceptical View", *Global Civil Society 2004/5*, Sage Publications, London, 2005, p. 33.
488 *Ibid.*, p. 29.
489 Lucy Hovil, "Challenging International Justice: The Initial Years of the International Criminal Court's Intervention in Uganda", *op. cit.*
490 Paul J. Valentine, "People in glass houses should not throw stones: Why the Democracy Deficit Argument against intergovernmental international organisation carries little weight in the United States of America", *Phoenix Law Review*, Vol. 2, No. 1 (2009), p. 90.
491 Jean d'Aspremont, "Legitimacy of Governments in the Age of Democracy", *op. cit.*, p. 878.
492 Paul J. Valentine, "People in glass houses should not throw stones: Why the Democracy Deficit Argument against intergovernmental international organisation carries little weight in the United States of America", *op. cit.*, p. 90.
493 Jean d'Aspremont, "Legitimacy of Governments in the Age of Democracy", *op. cit.*
494 Peter M. Gerhart, "The Two Constitutional Visions of the World Trade Organization", *University of Pennsylvania Journal of International Economic Law*, Vol. 24 (2003), pp. 1, 6, 53.
495 See, Valentine, *op. cit.*, p. 90, and Anupam Chander, "Globalization and Distrust", *Yale Law Journal*, Vol. 114 (2005), pp. 1193, 1197–98.
496 Eric Stein, "International Integration and Democracy: No Love at First Sight", *American Journal of International Law, op. cit.*, p. 490.
497 *Ibid.*, pp. 491–92.
498 Fareed Zakaria, "The Rise of Illiberal Democracies", *Foreign Affairs*, Vol. 76, No. 6 (1997), pp. 22–43.

Notes to Chapter 7

499 See, "Election shines light on war crimes court", *Financial Times*, 14 September 2011.
500 "System for appointing judges 'undermining international courts'. Politicised voting and a lack of transparency has led to unqualified judges taking key positions, study claims", *The Guardian*, 8 September 2010.
501 Human Rights Watch, "Courting History. The Landmark International Criminal Court's First Years", New York, July 2008, available at < http://www.hrw.org/en/reports/2008/07/10/courting-history>, p.28.
502 Rome Statute of the International Criminal Court (Rome Statute), A/CONF.183/9, 17 July 1998, entered into force 1 July 2002, Art. 21(2).
503 Human Rights Watch, "Courting History. The Landmark International Criminal Court's First Years", *op. cit.*
504 "System for appointing judges 'undermining international courts'. Politicised voting and a lack of transparency has led to unqualified judges taking key positions, study claims", *The Guardian*, 8 September 2010.
505 Geoffrey Robertson, *Crimes Against Humanity. The Struggle for Global Justice, op. cit.*, p. 531.
506 *Ibid.*, p. 530.
507 M. Wood, "The Selection of Candidates for International Judicial Office: Recent Practice", in T. M. Ndiaye and R. Wolfrum (editors), *Law of the Sea, Environmental Law and Settlement of Disputes: Liber Amicorum Judge Thomas A. Mensah*, Martinus Nijhof Publishers, The Hague, 2007.

508 "Wanted: Better Judgment, fewer crowd-pleasers and lickspittles", *The Economist*, 22 November 2008, pp. 78–9.
509 Iain Bonomy, "Making war crimes trials work – balancing fairness and expedition", in Gideon Boas, William Schabas and Michael P. Scharf (editors), *International Criminal Justice: Legitimacy and Coherence*, Edward Elgar, 2012, p. 50. Iain Bonomy is a former Senator of the College of Justice, a judge of the Supreme Courts of Scotland, sitting in the High Court of Justiciary and the Inner House of the Court of Session from 2010 to 2012. From 2004 to 2009, he was a Judge of the International Criminal Tribunal for the former Yugoslavia.
510 "The Selection of Candidates for International Judicial Office", *op. cit.*, p. 134.
511 Ruth Mackenzie, Kate Malleson, Penny Martin and Philippe Sands, *Selecting International Judges: Principle, Process, and Politics*, International Courts and Tribunals Series, Oxford University Press, Oxford, 2010, p. 65.
512 *Ibid.*, *Selecting International Judges*, *op. cit.*, p. 101.
513 *Ibid.*, p. 95.
514 *Ibid.*, p. 101.
515 Benjamin Schiff, *Building the International Criminal Court*, Cambridge University Press, New York, 2008.
516 *Ibid.*, p. 154.
517 See, for example, Assembly of States Parties, "Proceedings", Official Records of the Assembly of States Parties to the Rome Statute of the International Criminal Court, first session, New York, September 3–10, 2002, ICC-ASP/1/3, Part I, para. 27 ("In order to ensure the integrity of the electoral process, the Bureau also appealed to States Parties to refrain from entering into reciprocal agreements of exchange of support in respect of the election of judges of the Court."), and "Selecting International Judges: Principle, Process and Politics", discussion paper, Centre for International Courts and Tribunals, University College London, 2008.
518 *Selecting International Judges*, *op. cit.*, p. 123.
519 "Selecting International Judges: Principle, Process and Politics", discussion paper, Centre for International Courts and Tribunals, University College London, 2008.
520 Press Conference on Annual Assembly of States Parties to International Criminal Court, UN Department of Public Information, New York, 16 December 2011, available at <http://www.un.org/News/briefings/docs//2011/111216_ICC.doc.htm>.
521 Benjamin Schiff, *Building the International Criminal Court*, Cambridge University Press, 2008, p. 107.
522 Sylviade Bertodano, "Judicial Independence in the International Criminal Court", *Leiden Journal of International Law*, Vol. 15, No. 2 (2002), pp. 409–30. Bertodano is a criminal barrister in the UK. He represented defendants before the ICTY and ICTR and has worked with No Peace Without Justice for the Public Defenders' Unit in East Timor; and also provided advice and representation for East Timor at the Preparatory Commission for the International Criminal Court.
523 "International Law on Trial", *Financial Times*, 25 July 2008.
524 *Ibid.*
525 Interview T24, 10, "Selecting International Judges: Principle, Process and Politics", discussion paper, Centre for International Courts and Tribunals, University College London, 2008.
526 Interview T24, 11, "Selecting International Judges: Principle, Process and Politics", discussion paper, Centre for International Courts and Tribunals, University College London, 2008, p. 55.
527 Heidi L. Hansberry, "Too Much of a Good Thing in Lubanga and Haradinaj: The Danger of Expediency in International Criminal Trials", *Northwestern Journal of International Human*

Rights, Vol. 9, Issue 3 (2011), available at <http://www.law.northwestern.edu/journals/jihr/v9/n3/6/Hansberry.pdf>.
528 Robert Heinsch, "How to achieve fair and expeditious trial proceedings before the ICC: Is it time for a more judge-dominated approach?", in Carsten Stahn and Göran Sluiter (editors), *The Emerging Practice of the International Criminal Court*, 2009.
529 Richard Ashby Wilson, *Writing History in International Criminal Trials*, Cambridge University Press, 2011, p. 196.
530 T. Markus Funk, "Victims' Rights and Advocacy at the International Criminal Court", *op. cit.*, p. 74.
531 *Ibid.*, p. 74.
532 *Ibid.*, p. 75.
533 *Ibid.*, p. 73.
534 Corell in Luc Reydams, Jan Wouters and Cedric Ryngaert (editors), *International Prosecutors*, Oxford University Press, Oxford, 2012, ix–x. During his time at the UN, he was involved in the establishment of the ICTY, the ICTR, the Special Court for Sierra Leone and the Extraordinary Chambers in the Courts of Cambodia.
535 Lauren Etter, "Call for ICC to Learn ICTY Election Lessons", Institute for War & Peace Reporting, 9 November 2005, available at <http://iwpr.net/print/report-news/call-icc-learn-icty-election-lessons>.
536 "System for appointing judges 'undermining international courts'. Politicised voting and a lack of transparency has led to unqualified judges taking key positions, study claims", *The Guardian*, 8 September 2010.
537 *Ibid.*
538 "Election shines light on war crimes court", *Financial Times*, 14 September 2011.
539 Lauren Etter, "Call for ICC to Learn ICTY Election Lessons", Institute for War & Peace Reporting, 9 November 2005, available at <http://iwpr.net/print/report-news/call-icc-learn-icty-election-lessons>.
540 Daniel Terris, Cesare P. R. Romano and Leigh Swigart, *The International Judge: An Introduction to the Men and Women Who Decide the World's Cases*, Oxford University Press, 2007, p. 47.
541 *Ibid.*, p. 48.
542 Official International Criminal Court profile, available at <http://www.icc-cpi.int/menus/icc/structure%20of%20the%20court/chambers/the%20judges/the%20judges/judge%20elizabeth%20odio%20benito/judge%20elizabeth%20odio%20benito?lan=en-GB>.
543 Daniel Terris, Cesare P. R. Romano and Leigh Swigart, *The International Judge: An Introduction to the Men and Women Who Decide the World's Cases*, p. 263, note 2.
544 "First Challenges: An examination of recent landmark developments at the International Criminal Court", International Bar Association ICC Monitoring and Outreach Programme, June 2009. See, also, Lubanga trial transcript 138, p. 21, lines 14–23, available at <http://www.icc-cpi.int/iccdocs/doc/doc649086.pdf>.
545 Cited in Vladimir Tochilovsky, "Globalizing Criminal Justice: Challenges for the International Criminal Court", *Global Governance*, Vol. 9 (2003).
546 Daniel Terris, Cesare P. R. Romano and Leigh Swigart, *The International Judge: An Introduction to the Men and Women Who Decide the World's Cases*, *op. cit.*, p. 262, note 7.
547 "Controversial Japanese judge dies in office", Joshua Rozenberg blog, 24 April 2009, available at <http://www.rozenberg.net/weblog/archives/2009/04/controversial_j.html>.
548 Iain Bonomy, "Making war crimes trials work – balancing fairness and expedition", in Gideon Boas, William Schabas and Michael P. Scharf (editors), *International Criminal Justice: Legitimacy and Coherence*, Edward Elgar, 2012, p. 49.
549 Coalition for the International Criminal Court, "Questionnaire to ICC Judicial Candidates

550 Interview T81, 10–11, Ruth Mackenzie, Kate Malleson, Penny Martin and Philippe Sands, *Selecting International Judges: Principle, Process, and Politics, op. cit.*, p. 33.
551 Eric Ellis, "Room for Everyone at The Hague", *The Global Mail*, 8 February 2012, available at <http://www.theglobalmail.org/feature/room-for-everyone-at-the-hague/42/>.
552 C. F. Amerasinghe, "Judges of the International Court of Justice – Election and Qualifications", *Leiden Journal of International Law*, Vol. 14, No. 2 (2001), p. 348.
553 An expert on international law interviewed by a Filipino journalist described Miriam Santiago's election as "a tribute to Philippine diplomacy". He noted that the government of the Philippines had for several years tried to secure a judgeship for Santiago. The previous administration of President Gloria Macapagal-Arroyo had tried but failed to get her a seat at the International Court of Justice. President Benigno Aquino III the sought to get her elected to the ICC instead of the ICJ. She was elected as a judge by way of the second list of specialists on public international law, which also happened to have "gender balance" as an additional requirement. The expert said that gave her an edge. See, "Judge Miriam skips ICC oath-taking as Asia's first woman judge for Corona trial", "Raissa Robles: inside Philippine politics and beyond" blog, 9 March 2012, available at <http://raissarobles.com/2012/03/09/judge-miriam-skips-icc-oath-taking-as-asias-first-woman-judge-for-corona-trial/>.
554 "Miriam: No available ICC seat for me in near future", *Rappler* (Manila), 28 June 2012, available at <http://www.rappler.com/nation/7738-miriam-icc-says-no-available-seat-in-near-future>.
555 "Miriam would have been ICC judge by now", *Rappler* (Manila), 3 October 2010, available at <http://www.rappler.com/nation/2293-miriam-would-have-been-icc-judge-by-now>.
556 "Why Miriam can't resign from Senate yet", ABS-CBNnews.com, 7 April 2012, available at <http://www.abs-cbnnews.com/-depth/07/04/12/why-miriam-cant-resign-senate-yet>.
557 "Judge Miriam skips ICC oath-taking as Asia's first woman judge for Corona trial", "Raissa Robles: inside Philippine politics and beyond" blog, 9 March 2012, available at <http://raissarobles.com/2012/03/09/judge-miriam-skips-icc-oath-taking-as-asias-first-woman-judge-for-corona-trial/>.
558 "Ping Lacson threatens to question Miriam Defensor-Santiago's fitness to serve on International Criminal Court", *Spot* (Manila), 15 February 2013, available at <http://www.spot.ph/the-feed/52894/ping-lacson-threatens-to-question-miriam-defensor-santiagos-fitness-to-serve-on-international-criminal-court>.
559 "Top Five Most Outrageous Things Senator Miriam Defensor Santiago Said About Senators", *The Manila Survival Guide*, blog, 24 June 2013, available at <http://manilarules.com/2013/06/24/top-ten-most-outrageous-things-senator-miriam-defensor-santiago-said-in-public/>.
560 "Santiago may let go ICC post", *Sun Star* (Manila), 16 August 2013, available at <http://www.sunstar.com.ph/breaking-news/2013/08/16/santiago-may-let-go-icc-post-298178>.
561 "Enter the Dragon-lady Senator-Judge Miriam Defensor Santiago", Philnews.com, 29 January 2012, available at <http://www.philnews.com/2012/06a.htm>.
562 See, "Sen. Miriam Santiago hit by online petition of Fil-Ams who want her out of International Criminal Court; They tag her 'psychologically unstable'", *Spot* (Manila), 12 March 2012, available at <http://www.spot.ph/the-feed/50660/sen-miriam-santiago-hit-by-online-petition-of-fil-ams-who-want-her-out-of-international-criminal-court>; and "International Court of Justice may cancel judgeship of Senator Merriam Santiago", June 2012, available at <http://pinoypolitikas.blogspot.co.uk/2012/06/international-court-of-justice-may.html>.

563 Amnesty International, "International Criminal Court Concerns at the Eighth Session of the Assembly of States Parties", London, October 2009, available at <http://www.amnesty.org/en/library/asset/IOR40/011/2009/en/fdf3fc92-6273-41a2-8dda-6771fcf49f11/ior400112009en.pdf>, p. 13.
564 Human Rights Watch, "Human Rights Watch Memorandum for the Eighth Session of the International Criminal Court Assembly of States Parties", November 2009, available at <http://www.hrw.org/sites/default/files/related_material/Memo%20for%20the%208th%20Session%20of%20the%20ASP%2011.09.09.pdf>.
565 *Selecting International Judges*, p. 84.
566 Interview T39, 11, p. 86.
567 Interview T39, 9, *op. cit.*, p. 43.
568 Interview T3, 8, *op. cit.*, p. 36.
569 Interview F22, 2, *op. cit.*, p. 36.
570 *Op. cit.*, p. 50.
571 Interview T56, 1-2, *op. cit.*, p. 75.
572 Interview T24, 12, *op. cit.*, p. 124.
573 Human Rights Watch, "Human Rights Watch Memorandum for the Tenth Session of the International Criminal Court Assembly of States Parties", November 2011, available at <http://www.hrw.org/sites/default/files/related_material/2011_Memo_tenth_%20session_ASP.pdf>.
574 *Ibid.*
575 For the Search Committee's terms of reference, see, Assembly of States Parties, "Bureau of the ASP, Search Committee for the position of the Prosecutor of the International Criminal Court, Terms of Reference" ("Terms of Reference"), ICC-ASP/9/INF.2, 6 December 2010, para. 6, available at <http://www.icccpi.int/iccdocs/asp_docs/Elections/EP2011/ICC-ASP-9-INF.2-ENG.pdf>.
576 Human Rights Watch, "Human Rights Watch Memorandum for the Tenth Session of the International Criminal Court Assembly of States Parties", *op. cit.*
577 "For ICC, France Offered to Support Unqualified Judge Quid Pro Quo for Cathala", *Inner City Press*, 29 October 2011, available at <http://www.innercitypress.com/icc1cathala102911.html>.
578 "Cosy club or sword of righteousness?", *The Economist*, 26 November 2011, available at <http://www.economist.com/node/21540230?zid=317&ah=8a47fc455a44945580198768fad0fa41>.
579 "For ICC, DR Gets In, Regional Solution Stalled on Mauritius & Cathala of France", *Inner City Press*, 15 December 2011, available at <http://www.innercitypress.com/icc5cathala121511.html>.
580 "Report on International Criminal Court Judicial Nominations 2011", Independent Panel on International Criminal Court Judicial Elections, New York, 26 October 2011, available at <http://www.iccindependentpanel.org/sites/default/files/Independent%20Panel%20on%20ICC%20Judicial%20Elections%20-%20Report%2026%20October%202011.pdf>.
581 ASP, "Letter to Permanent Representatives of States Parties to the Rome Statute of the International Criminal Court from Assembly of States Parties to the Rome Statute President Christian Wenaweser", reference: ASP/2011/056, 27 May 2011, available at <http://www.icc-cpi.int/iccdocs/asp_docs/Elections/EJ2011/ICC-ASP-2011-056-PASP-Letter-ENG.pdf, Annex II>.
582 "ICC judge elected president resigns", *Standard Digital* (Nairobi), 21 March 2013, available at <http://www.standardmedia.co.ke/?articleID=2000079827&story_title=Kenya-World:%20ICC%20judge%20resigns%20after%20being%20elected%20president>.
583 Frank Petit, "Interview: Claude Jorda, Judge at the International Criminal Court", *International Justice Tribune*, No. 38, 2005, p. 4.

584 Geoffrey Robertson, *Crimes Against Humanity. The Struggle for Global Justice*, op. cit., p. 551.
585 Human Rights Watch, "Human Rights Watch Memorandum for the Eighth Session of the International Criminal Court Assembly of States Parties", November 2009, available at <http://www.hrw.org/sites/default/files/related_material/Memo%20for%20the%208th%20Session%20of%20the%20ASP%2011.09.09.pdf>.
586 "ICC Shuffles the Deck", *Opinio Juris*, 24 March 2009, available at <http://iccobservers.wordpress.com/2009/03/24/icc-shuffles-the-deck-from-opinio-juris/>.
587 William Schabas, "The International Criminal Court: Struggling to Find its Way", in Antonio Cassese (editor), *Realizing Utopia: The Future of International Law*, Oxford University Press, Oxford, 2012, p. 254.
588 "Election shines light on war crimes court", *Financial Times*, 14 September 2011.
589 *Ibid*.
590 Human Rights Watch, "Human Rights Watch Memorandum for the Eleventh Session of the International Criminal Court Assembly of States Parties", 7 November 2012, available at <http://www.hrw.org/news/2012/11/07/human-rights-watch-memorandum-eleventh-session-international-criminal-court-assembly#2>.
591 "French Deal to Support Unqualified ICC Candidate for Cathala Nears Consummation", *Inner City Press*, 9 December 2011, available at <http://www.innercitypress.com/icc2cathala120911.html>.

Notes to Chapter Eight

592 Professor Mark Gibney, "The International Criminal Court", *Human Rights Human Welfare*, an online journal published through the Josef Korbel School of International Studies, University of Denver, 4 May 2009, available at <http://www.hrhw.org/2009/05/editors-introduction-may-2009.html>. Mark Gibney is the Belk Distinguished Professor at the University of North Carolina-Asheville. His publications include *International Human Rights Law: Returning to Universal Principles* (Rowman & Littlefield, 2008), the edited volume *The Age of Apology: Facing Up to the Past* (University of Pennsylvania Press, 2007); *The Politics of Human Rights* (Cambridge) (with Sabine Carey and Steve Poe); and an edited volume (with Sigrun Skogly) *Human Rights and Extraterritorial Obligations* (University of Pennsylvania Press).
593 Julie Flint and Alex de Waal, "Case Closed: A Prosecutor Without Borders", *World Affairs*, Spring 2009, available at <http://www.worldaffairsjournal.org/2009%20-%20Spring/full-DeWaalFlint.html>.
594 Sir Geoffrey Nice, "The Permanent International Criminal Court and Africa", Gresham College lectures, 31 October 2012, available at <http://www.gresham.ac.uk/lectures-and-events/the-permanent-international-criminal-court-%E2%80%93-the-icc-and-africa>.
595 ICC, "Situation in Libya, in the case of The Prosecutor v. Saif Al-Islam Gaddafi and Abdullah Al-Senussi", 12 June 2012, No. ICC-01/11-01/11 OA 3, p. 15, available at <http://www.icc-cpi.int/iccdocs/doc/doc1425502.pdf>.
596 Human Rights Watch, "Human Rights Watch Memorandum for the Tenth Session of the International Criminal Court Assembly of States Parties", November 2011, available at <http://www.hrw.org/sites/default/files/related_material/2011_Memo_tenth_%20session_ASP.pdf>.
597 Cited in David Kaye, "Who's Afraid of the International Criminal Court?", *Foreign Affairs*, May/June 2011, available at <http://www.foreignaffairs.com/articles/67768/david-kaye/whos-afraid-of-the-international-criminal-court>.
598 Benjamin Schiff, *Building the International Criminal Court*, op. cit., p. 127.

599 Cited in *Victims' Guide to the International Criminal Court*, Reporters without Borders, Paris, May 2003, p. 85, available at <http://www.rsf.org/IMG/pdf/doc-2255.pdf>.
600 Robertson, *Crimes Against Humanity. The Struggle for Global Justice, op. cit.*, p. 533.
601 Joshua Rozenburg, "Courting controversy", *The Law Gazette* (UK), 7 August 2008, available at <http://www.lawgazette.co.uk/opinion/columnists/courting-controversy>.
602 *Ibid.*
603 Jess Bravin, "Justice Delayed. For Global Court, Ugandan Rebels Prove Tough Test", *The Wall Street Journal*, 8 June 2006.
604 Editor's Introduction: "Annotation of 'Case Closed: A Prosecutor Without Borders'" by Julie Flint and Alex de Waal, World Affairs. Spring 2009", *Human Rights Human Welfare*, an online journal of the Josef Korbel School of International Studies, University of Denver, 4 May 2009, available at <http://www.hrhw.org/2009/05/editors-introduction-may-2009.html>.
605 "President's genocide trial tests reputation of international court", *Heraldscotland*, 28 February 2009, available at <http://www.heraldscotland.com/president-s-genocide-trial-tests-reputation-of-international-court-1.829023>.
606 "ICC's Ocampo Defends His Africa-Only Focus, His Strategy In Question", *Inner City Press*, 17 July 2008, available at <http://www.innercitypress.com/icc1africa071708.html>.
607 See, for example, Human Rights Watch, "Courting History. The Landmark International Criminal Court's First Years", New York, July 2008 available at < http://www.hrw.org/en/reports/2008/07/10/courting-history>, pp. 184–91.
608 See, for example, "Why the world's most powerful prosecutor should resign: Part 1 The International Criminal Court's first trial has been suspended because the prosecutor failed to disclose evidence that could have helped the defendant", *The Daily Telegraph* (London), 14 September 2008, available at <http://www.telegraph.co.uk/news/newstopics/lawreports/joshuarozenberg/2236288/Why-the-worlds-most-powerful-prosecutor-should-resign-Part-1.html>; "Why the world's most powerful prosecutor should resign: Part 2 Sexual misconduct allegations against Luis Moreno-Ocampo have been dismissed as manifestly unfounded but he is held personally responsible for a breach of due process," *The Daily Telegraph* (London), 14 September 2008, available at http://www.telegraph.co.uk/news/newstopics/lawreports/joshuarozenberg/2446064/Why-the-worlds-most-powerful-prosecutor-should-resign-Part-2.html; "Why the world's most powerful prosecutor should resign: Part 3 Luis Moreno-Ocampo wants the president of Sudan arrested for genocide. But the chances of a conviction are slim," *The Daily Telegraph* (London), 14 September 2008, available at <http://www.telegraph.co.uk/news/newstopics/lawreports/joshuarozenberg/2700862/Why-the-worlds-most-powerful-prosecutor-should-resign-Part-3.html>; "Why the world's most powerful prosecutor should resign: Part 4 In latest of four hard-hitting commentaries, Joshua Rozenberg argues that Luis Moreno-Ocampo still does not understand the concept of a fair trial," *The Daily Telegraph* (London), 14 September 2008, available at <http://www.telegraph.co.uk/news/newstopics/lawreports/joshuarozenberg/2700448/Why-the-worlds-most-powerful-prosecutor-should-resign-Part-4.html>; "International Criminal Court prosecutor under fire", Reuters, 19 August 2008.
609 Otto Triffterer (editor), "Commentary on the Rome Statute of the International Criminal Court" (second edition 2008), available at <http://article42-3.org/Triffterer3.pdf>.
610 Jess Bravin, "Justice Delayed. For Global Court, Ugandan Rebels Prove Tough Test", *op. cit.*
611 "ICC Hopes for Uganda Trial in 6 Months, Then Congo", Reuters, 26 January 2005, available at: <www.globalpolicy.org/intljustice/icc/2005/0126ugandatrial.htm>.
612 Conor Foley, "Darfur: a disaster for justice", *The Guardian*, 20 April 2009, available at <http://www.guardian.co.uk/commentisfree/2009/apr/20/sudan-war-crimes>. Conor Foley is a humanitarian aid worker. He has worked for a variety of human rights and

humanitarian aid organisations, including Liberty, Amnesty International and the UN High Commissioner for Refugees (UNHCR), in Kosovo, Afghanistan, Colombia, Sri Lanka, Indonesia and Bosnia-Herzegovina. He is a research fellow at the Human Rights Law Centre at the University of Nottingham. Foley's books include *The Thin Blue Line: How Humanitarianism Went to War* and *Combating Torture: a manual for judges and prosecutors* (2003), published by the Human Rights Centre at the University of Essex and the UK Foreign and Commonwealth Office.

613 "International court under fire for prosecution policy", NRC Handelsblad (the Netherlands), 20 November 2008, available at <http://www.nrc.nl/international/Features/article2067475.ece/International_court_under_fire_for_prosecution_policy>.

614 WikiLeaks, US government cable, "Subject: ICC: A cautious beginning with mixed signals from the Prosecutor", 15 July 2003, available at <http://cablegatesearch.wikileaks.org/cable.php?id=03THEHAGUE1806&q=court%20criminal%20international%20ocampo>.

615 International Criminal Court, "Criteria for Selection of Situations and Cases", OTP, draft policy paper on file with Human Rights Watch, June 2006, pp. 1–2.

616 Cited in Human Rights Watch, "Courting History. The Landmark International Criminal Court's First Years", New York, July 2008 available at <http://www.hrw.org/en/reports/2008/07/10/courting-history>.

617 Professor Rhona Smith, "International Criminal Justice Must Not Only Be Done, It Must Be Seen To Be Done", *Human Rights Human Welfare*, an online journal of the Josef Korbel School of International Studies, University of Denver, 4 May 2009, available at <http://www.hrhw.org/2009/05/international-criminal-justice-must-not>. Rhona Smith is Professor of International Human Rights at Northumbria University, Newcastle, UK. She is also the Raoul Wallenberg Institute of Human Rights (RWI) and Humanitarian Law Visiting Professor in Human Rights at Beijing University Law School in China. She has authored various texts on international human rights law and worked on human rights education capacity building projects particularly in China and Indonesia through RWI and the Norwegian Centre for Human Rights. She has taught human rights at universities in Canada, China, England and Scotland.

618 *Ibid.*

619 International Criminal Court, Prosecutor v. Lubanga, Case No. ICC-01/04-01/06, decision on the confirmation of charges (public redacted version), 29 January 2007, para. 370.

620 *Ibid.*, para. 44.

621 Human Rights Watch, "Human Rights Watch Memorandum for the Eleventh Session of the International Criminal Court Assembly of States Parties", 7 November 2012, available at <http://www.hrw.org/news/2012/11/07/human-rights-watch-memorandum-eleventh-session-international-criminal-court-assembly#2>.

622 Robertson, *Crimes Against Humanity. The Struggle for Global Justice, op. cit.*, p. 557.

623 *Ibid.*

624 Benjamin Schiff, *Building the International Criminal Court*, Cambridge University Press, New York, 2008, pp. 127–28.

625 Professor Chandra Lekha Sriram, "The Prosecutor of the ICC: Too Political, Not Political Enough, or Both?", *Human Rights Human Welfare*, an online journal of the Josef Korbel School of International Studies, University of Denver, 4 May 2009, available at <http://www.hrhw.org/2009/05/prosecutor-or-icc-too-political-not_04.html>. Chandra Lekha Sriram is Professor of Human Rights in the University of East London School of Law and founder and Director of the Centre on Human Rights in Conflict. She is author and co-editor of various books and journal articles on international relations, international law, human rights and conflict prevention and peace-building, including *Peace as Governance: Power-Sharing, Armed Groups, and Contemporary Peace Negotiations* (2008); a textbook (co-authored with Olga Martin-Ortega and Johanna Herman) *War, Conflict, and Human Rights: Theory and Practice*

(2009); (co-edited with John King, Julie Mertus, Olga Martin-Ortega, and Johanna Herman) *Surviving Field Research: Working in Violent and Difficult Situations* (2009); and (co-edited with Suren Pillay) *Peace vs Justice? The Dilemma of Transitional Justice in Africa* (2009).

626 William Schabas, "The International Criminal Court: Struggling to Find its Way", in Antonio Cassese (editor), *Realizing Utopia: The Future of International Law*, Oxford University Press, Oxford, 2012, p. 252.
627 *Ibid.*
628 *Ibid.*
629 ICC, "Draft Programme Budget for 2005", ICC-ASP/3/2, para. 159.
630 *Ibid.*, p. 49.
631 WikiLeaks, US government cable, "Subject: ICC's Ocampo Presses His Political Agenda", 4 June 2009, available at <http://cablegatesearch.wikileaks.org/cable.php?id=09USUNNEWYORK565&q=court%20criminal%20international%20ocampo>.
632 William Schabas, "The International Criminal Court: Struggling to Find its Way", *op. cit.*, p. 252.
633 *Ibid.*
634 *Ibid.*, p. 255.
635 ICC, *Prosecutorial Strategy 2009–12*, OTP, 1 February 2010, p. 2.
636 William Schabas, *Unimaginable Atrocities. Justice, Politics, and Rights at the War Crimes Tribunals*, Oxford University Press, Oxford, 2012, p. 92.
637 Cited in "As Indictment of Bashir Arises at UN, Moreno-Ocampo Accused of Ego and Errors", *Inner City Press*, 22 September 2008, <http://www.innercitypress.com/icc4ocampo092208.html>.
638 Professor Chandra Lekha Sriram, "The Prosecutor of the ICC: Too Political, Not Political Enough, or Both?", *op. cit.*
639 Cited in "African bloggers react to ICC charges against Sudanese President al-Bashir", available at <http://globalvoicesonline.org/2008/07/16/african-bloggers-reactions-to-charges-against-al-bashir/>.
640 Marlies Glasius, "What is global justice and who is it for? The ICC's first five years", Opendemocracy, 22 July 2008, available at <http://www.opendemocracy.net/article/globalisation/international_justice/the-iccs-first-five-years>.
641 Antonio Cassese, "Flawed International Justice for Sudan", Project Syndicate, available at <http://www.project-syndicate.org/commentary/cassese4short/English>. See, also, Antonio Cassese, "Flawed International Justice for Sudan", *The Daily Star*, 16 July 2008. The late Antonio Cassese was the first President of the International Criminal Tribunal for the Former Yugoslavia and later the Chairperson of the United Nations' International Commission of Inquiry on Darfur.
642 "President's genocide trial tests reputation of international court", *Heraldscotland*, 28 February 2009, available at <http://www.heraldscotland.com/president-s-genocide-trial-tests-reputation-of-international-court-1.829023>.
643 *Ibid.* Andrew T. Cayley, "The Prosecutor's Strategy in Seeking the Arrest of Sudanese President Al Bashir on Charges of Genocide", *Journal of International Criminal Justice*, Vol. 6, Issue 5 (2008), pp. 829–40, available at Social Science Research Network: <http://ssrn.com/abstract=1360573 or doi:mqn071>. Cayley was from February 2005 to July 2007 the ICC's Senior Prosecuting Counsel with regard to the Sudanese case. He supervised and provided legal direction on the ICC investigation into alleged human rights violations in Darfur. He oversaw a legal team of six lawyers and an investigative team of twenty investigators and analysts.
644 Dr. Christophe Fournier, "Punishment or Aid?", *The New York Times*, 27 March 2009, available at <http://www.nytimes.com/2009/03/28/opinion/28iht-edphelan.html?_r=1&emc=tnt&tntemail1=y>.

645   The Sudan Workers Trade Unions Federation (SWTUF) and the Sudan International Defence Group (SIDG). The SWTUF is the union of all trade unions of Sudan with affiliates from 25 state unions and 22 professional federations. Its affiliates include the State Trade Unions for the whole of Darfur. The SIDG is a non-governmental committee of Sudanese citizens established out of concern for the negative effects that ICC arrest warrants could have for the peace process in Sudan and for the ordinary people of this country. The aims and initiatives of the committee are supported by many Sudanese NGOs and by the association that co-ordinates Sudanese NGOs.

646   International Criminal Court, "Applicants, represented by Sir Geoffrey Nice QC and Rodney Dixon, Application on behalf of Citizens' Organisations of The Sudan in relation to the Prosecutor's Applications for Arrest Warrants of 14 July 2008 and 20 November 2008", ICC-02/05, 11 January 2009, available at <http://www2.icc-cpi.int/iccdocs/doc/doc616795.PDF>.

647   Luis Moreno Ocampo, "Now end this Darfur denial", *The Guardian*, 15 July 2010, available at <http://www.guardian.co.uk/commentisfree/libertycentral/2010/jul/15/world-cannot-ignore-darfur>.

648   "Report of the Secretary-General on the African Union-United Nations Hybrid Operation in Darfur (UNAMID)", UN document S/2010/213, April 2010.

649   William Schabas, "Inappropriate Comments from the Prosecutor of the International Criminal Court", PhD studies in human rights blog, 16 July 2010, available at <http://humanrightsdoctorate.blogspot.co.uk/2010/07/inappropriate-comments-from-prosecutor.html>.

650   *Ibid*.

651   Dapo Akande, "ICC Prosecutor's Inaccurate Statements about the Bashir Arrest Warrant Decision", blog of the *European Journal of International Law*, 19 July 2010, available at <http://www.ejiltalk.org/icc-prosecutors-inaccurate-statements-about-the-bashir-arrest-warrant-decision/>. Dapo Akande is Yamani Fellow and Tutor in Public International Law at Oxford University and a lecturer in public international law in the Oxford Law Faculty and Co-Director of the Oxford Institute for Ethics, Law and Armed Conflict (ELAC). He is the Convenor of the Oxford Law Faculty's Public International Law Group. In 2008/09 he was Visiting Associate Professor and Robinna Foundation International Fellow at Yale Law School.

652   *Ibid*.

653   *Ibid*.

654   William Schabas, "Inappropriate Comments from the Prosecutor of the International Criminal Court", *op. cit*.

655   "The Remarkable Arrogance of the ICC Prosecutor", *Opinio Juris*, 20 July 2010, available at <http://opiniojuris.org/2010/07/20/the-remarkable-arrogance-of-the-icc-prosecutor>.

656   "At UN, Ocampo Turns O-Kafka, Threatens Any Denier With ICC Prosecution, Sri Lanka Silence", *The Inner City Press*, 4 December 2009, available at <http://www.innercitypress.com/icc1okafka120409.html>. See, also, Luis Moreno Ocampo, "Statement to the United Nations Security Council on the situation in Darfur, the Sudan, pursuant to UNSCR 1593 (2005)", International Criminal Court, 4 December 2009, paragraph 44, available at <http://www2.icc-cpi.int/NR/rdonlyres/BA525867-5B58-4CDD-B6CF-8105181658D6/281343/UNSecurityCouncilStateFINAL.pdf>.

657   See, for example, "Ocampo threats. ICC prosecutor threatens to investigate Sudan UN ambassador", *Agence France-Presse*, 5 June 2012.

658   "Ocampo Says Speech Can Be Crime, Steps Back from Sri Lanka Mapping", *Inner City Press*, 5 June 2012, available at <http://www.innercitypress.com/ocampo1srispeech060512.html>.

659   *Ibid*.

660   Kevin Jon Heller, "Idle – and Ridiculous – Threats Courtesy of Moreno-Ocampo", *Opinio Juris*, 10 June 2012, available at <http://opiniojuris.org/2012/06/10/idle-and-ridiculous-

threats-courtesy-of-moreno-ocampo/>. Kevin Jon Heller is a senior lecturer at Melbourne Law School, where he teaches international criminal law and criminal law. His academic writing has appeared in a variety of journals, including the *European Journal of International Law*, the *American Journal of International Law*, the *Journal of International Criminal Justice*, the *Harvard International Law Journal*, the *Michigan Law Review*, the *Leiden Journal of International Law*, the *Journal of Criminal Law & Criminology*, *Criminal Law Forum*, and the *Georgetown International Environmental Law Review*. His book *The Nuremberg Military Tribunals and the Origins of International Criminal Law* was published by Oxford University Press in June 2011, and Stanford University Press published his edited book (with Markus Dubber), *The Handbook of Comparative Criminal Law* in February 2011. He is a permanent member of the international-law blog *Opinio Juris*.

661 "Sudan Dismisses Allegations Bashir has Billions Abroad", Reuters, 18 December 2010, available at <http://www.reuters.com/article/2010/12/18/us-sudan-bashir-wikileaks-idUSTRE6BH0P320101218>.

662 See, for example, House of Lords Hansard, 31 January 2011, Column WA233; and 28 February 2011, Column WA258.

663 "Susan Rice Denies Being Told Sudan's Bashir Stashed $9B, Despite WikiLeak", *Inner City Press*, 20 December 2010, available at <http://www.innercitypress.com/usun2bashir122010.html>.

664 "Once Ocampo Told Susan Rice of Bashir's $9 B in Lloyds, What Was Done?", *Inner City Press*, 20 December 2010, available at <http://www.innercitypress.com/usun1bashir122010.html>.

665 "Prosecutor Confirms Accusation Against Sudan Leader", *The New York Times*, 1 January 2011, available at <http://www.nytimes.com/2011/01/02/world/africa/02wikisudan.html?pagewanted=all&_r=0>.

666 Sir Geoffrey Nice, "The Permanent International Criminal Court and Africa", Gresham College Lectures, 31 October 2012, available at <http://www.gresham.ac.uk/lectures-and-events/the-permanent-international-criminal-court-%E2%80%93-the-icc-and-africa>.

667 *Ibid.*

668 Julie Flint and Alex de Waal, "Case Closed: A Prosecutor Without Borders", *World Affairs*, Spring 2009, available at <http://www.worldaffairsjournal.org/2009%20-%20Spring/full-DeWaalFlint.html>.

669 International Criminal Court, "Situation in Darfur", ICC, Case No. ICC-02/05, decision inviting observations in application of Rule 103 of the rules of procedure and evidence, 24 July 2006.

670 Human Rights Watch, "Courting History. The Landmark International Criminal Court's First Years", New York, July 2008 available at <http://www.hrw.org/en/reports/2008/07/10/courting-history>, pp. 23–24. For their submissions, see, International Criminal Court, "Situation in Darfur", Case No. ICC-02/05, "Observations of the United Nations High Commissioner for Human Rights invited in Application of Rule 103 of the Rules of Procedure and Evidence", 10 October 2006, paras. 64–80; International Criminal Court, "Situation in Darfur", Case No. ICC-02/05, "Observations on Issues Concerning the Protection of Victims and the Preservation of Evidence in the Proceedings on Darfur Pending Before the ICC", 31 August 2006, pp. 5–6, 10–11 ("Cassese Observations"). See also Heikelina Verrijn Stuart, "Arbour and Cassese Criticize the ICC in Darfur", *International Justice Tribune*, No. 55, 23 October 2006; Antonio Cassese, "Is the ICC Still Having Teething Problems?", *Journal of International Criminal Justice*, 2006; No. 4, pp. 434–41; and Franck Petit, "The Small Steps' Strategy of the ICC in Darfur", *International Justice Tribune*, No. 63, 5 March 2007.

671 Julie Flint and Alex de Waal, "Case Closed: A Prosecutor Without Borders", *op. cit.*

672 See International Criminal Court, "Third Report of the Prosecutor of the International Criminal Court to the UNSC Pursuant to UNSCR 1593 (2005)", OTP, 14 June 2006,

available at <http://www.icc-cpi.int/library/cases/OTP_ReportUNSC_3-Darfur_English.pdf>.
673 Julie Flint and Alex de Waal, "Case Closed: A Prosecutor Without Borders", *op. cit.* See, also, Antonio Cassese, International Criminal Court, "Observations on Issues Concerning the Protection of Victims and the Preservation of Evidence in the Proceedings on Darfur Pending Before the ICC", ICC-2/05, 25 August 2006; and Louise Arbour, "Observations of the United Nations High Commissioner for Human Rights invited in Application of Rule 103 of the Rules of Procedure and Evidence", ICC-02/05, 10 October 2006.
674 International Criminal Court, "Situation in Darfur", Case No. ICC-02/05, "Prosecutor's response to Arbour's observations of the United Nations High Commission for Human Rights invited in Application of Rule 103 of the Rules of Procedure and Evidence", 19 October 2006; "Situation in Darfur", Case No. ICC-02/05, "Prosecutor's Response to Cassese's Observation on Issues Concerning the Protection of Victims and the Preservation of Evidence into the Proceedings on Darfur Pending before the ICC", 11 September 2006.
675 "ICC Observers Exclusive Interview: William Schabas, Professor of Human Rights Law and Director of the Irish Centre for Human Rights at the National University of Ireland, Galway", ICC Observers, 26 March 2009, available at <http://iccobservers.wordpress.com/2009/03/26/icc-observers-exclusive-interview-william-schabas-professor-of-human-rights-law-and-director-of-the-irish-centre-for-human-rights-at-the-national-university-of-ireland-galway/>.
676 "International court under fire for prosecution policy", NRC Handelsblad (The Netherlands), 20 November 2008, available at <http://www.nrc.nl/international/Features/article2067475.ece/International_court_under_fire_for_prosecution_policy>.
677 Human Rights Watch, "Courting History. The Landmark International Criminal Court's First Years, New York", July 2008 available at < http://www.hrw.org/en/reports/2008/07/10/courting-history>.
678 "Dim prospects. The International Criminal Court loses credibility and co-operation in Africa", *The Economist*, 17 February 2011, available at <http://www.economist.com/node/18176088>.
679 Kevin Jon Heller, "The ICC Stays Lubanga's Prosecution – and May Let Him Walk", *Opinio Juris*, 16 June 2008, available at <http://opiniojuris.org/2008/06/16/the-icc-stays-lubangas-prosecution-and-may-let-him-walk/>.
680 International Criminal Court, "Decision on the consequences of non-disclosure of exculpatory materials covered by Article 54(3)(e) agreements and the application to stay the prosecution of the accused, together with certain other issues raised at the Status Conference on 10 June 2008", 13 June 2008.
681 "ICC's Ocampo Defends His Africa-Only Focus, His Strategy In Question", *Inner City Press*, 17 July 2008, available at <http://www.innercitypress.com/icc1africa071708.html>.
682 ICC, "Decision on the consequences of non-disclosure of exculpatory materials covered by Article 54(3)(e) agreements and the application to stay the prosecution of the accused, together with certain other issues raised at the Status Conference on 10 June 2008", ICC-01704-01/06, 13 June 2008, available at <http://www.haguejusticeportal.net/Docs/Court%20Documents/ICC/Lubanga_Decision-on-consequences-of-non-disclosure-of-evidence.pdf>.
683 "At UN, Doubts Grow Of ICC's Moreno-Ocampo, on Lubanga and Uganda Abuses", 16 September 2008, *Inner City Press*, available at <http://www.innercitypress.com/icc3ocampo091608.html>.
684 Robert Marquand, "Global court starts with a fumble. Warlord grins. Witness recants testimony during start of Congo militia leader Thomas Lubanga's trial", *Christian Science Monitor*, 30 January 2009, available at <http://www.csmonitor.com/2009/0130/p01s01-wogn.html>.

685 See, International Criminal Court, "Decision on the release of Thomas Lubanga Dyilo", 2 July 2008, and International Criminal Court, "Trial Chamber I ordered the release of Thomas Lubanga Dyilo – Implementation of the decision is pending", 16 June 2008.
686 See, International Criminal Court, "Stay of proceedings in the Lubanga case is lifted – trial provisionally scheduled for 26 January 2009", 18 November 2008; "Road cleared for start of ICC's long-delayed first trial", *Agence France-Presse*, 18 November 2008; "Allegations Against Prosecutor May Harm Bashir Genocide Case", *New York Sun*, available at <http://www.nysun.com/foreign/allegations-against-prosecutor-may-harm-bashir/82165/>; "The Controversial Actions of the ICC Prosecutor: a Crisis of Maturity?", available at <http://www.haguejusticeportal.net/eCache/DEF/9/763.TGFuZz1FTg.html>.
687 "New Group calls for police to investigate International Criminal Court Prosecutor", ICC Watch, 8 December 2008, available at <http://www.iccwatch.org/pressrelease_dec08.html>.
688 "Lubanga's lawyers denounce 'unfair' ICC trial", Radio Nederland Wereldomroep, 27 January 2009, available at <http://static.rnw.nl/migratie/www.rnw.nl/internationaljustice/icc/DRC/090127-lubanga-day2-redirected>.
689 Human Rights Watch, "Unfinished Business. Closing Gaps in the Selection of ICC Cases", September 2011, available at <http://www.hrw.org/sites/default/files/reports/icc0911webwcover.pdf>.
690 Human Rights Watch, "ICC: New Prosecutor Takes Reins Fatou Bensouda to be Sworn In as Second ICC Prosecutor for Nine-Year Term", 14 June 2012, available at <http://www.hrw.org/news/2012/06/13/icc-new-prosecutor-takes-reins>.
691 See, for example, Richard Ashby Wilson, *Writing History in International Criminal Trials*, Cambridge University Press, 2011, p. 198.
692 Benjamin Schiff, *Building the International Criminal Court*, *op. cit.*, pp. 142–43.
693 William Schabas, "The International Criminal Court: Struggling to Find its Way", in Antonio Cassese (editor), *Realizing Utopia: The Future of International Law*, Oxford University Press, Oxford, 2012, p. 251.
694 International Criminal Court, Assembly of States Parties, third session, "Report of the Committee on Budget and Finance", ICC-ASP/3/CBF.I/L4, 2004.
695 Benjamin Schiff, *Building the International Criminal Court*, *op. cit.*, p. 135.
696 *Ibid.*, p. 121.
697 *Ibid.*
698 WikiLeaks, US government cable, "Subject: ICC: Getting down to business?", 27 July 2004, available at <http://cablegatesearch.wikileaks.org/cable.php?id=04THEHAGUE1885&q=court%20criminal%20international%20ocampo>.
699 Benjamin Schiff, *Building the International Criminal Court*, *op. cit.*, p. 135.
700 ICC, "Report on Prosecutorial Strategy", OTP, 14 September 2006 available at <http://www.icc-cpi.int/library/organs/otp/OTP_Prosecutorial-Strategy-20060914_English.pdf>.
701 Text of the secret Human Rights Watch letter to the ICC OTP, 15 September 2008, available at <http://article42-3.org/Secret%20Human%20Rights%20Watch%20Letter.pdf>.
702 "International Criminal Court prosecutor under fire", Reuters, 19 August 2008.
703 Editor's introduction: "Case Closed: A Prosecutor Without Borders" by Julie Flint and Alex de Waal, World Affairs, Spring 2009, *Human Rights Human Welfare*, an online journal of the Josef Korbel School of International Studies, University of Denver, 4 May 2009, available at <http://www.hrhw.org/2009/05/editors-introduction-may-2009.html>.
704 Jess Bravin, "Justice Delayed. For Global Court, Ugandan Rebels Prove Tough Test", *The Wall Street Journal*, 8 June 2006.

705 "International court plagued by in-fighting", *NRC Handelsblad* (The Netherlands), 19 November 2008, available at <http://www.nrc.nl/international/Features/article2066177.ece>.
706 "Lubanga trial: another mishap", *The Daily Telegraph*, 17 December 2008, available at <http://www.telegraph.co.uk/news/newstopics/lawreports/joshuarozenberg/3816797/Lubanga-trial-another-mishap.html>.
707 See, Rome Statute, Rome Statute of the International Criminal Court (Rome Statute), A/CONF.183/9, 17 July 1998, entered into force 1 July 2002, Article 46.1(a); ICC Rules of Procedure and Evidence, Rule 24.1(a) and Rome Statute, Article 46.1(a); ICC Rules of Procedure and Evidence, Rule 24.1(b).
708 "Complaint against ICC Prosecutor Luis Moreno-Ocampo concerning serious misconduct", 20 October 2006. Palme's fifty-two page complaint is available at <http://www.innercitypress.com/ocampocomplaint.pdf>. See, also, "Top Prosecutor a 'Sex Molester'", *Mail & Guardian* (South Africa), 25 July 2008, available at <http://article42-3.org/Mail%20&%20Guardian%2025%20July%202008.pdf>.
709 "Complaint against ICC Prosecutor Luis Moreno-Ocampo concerning serious misconduct", *op. cit.*
710 *Palme v. ICC*, Judgment No. 2757, 105th Session, International Labour Organisation Administrative Tribunal, 9 July 2008, available at <http://www.haguejusticeportal.net/Docs/ICC/ILO_Palme_9-7-2008.pdf>.
711 "International court plagued by in-fighting", *NRC Handelsblad* (The Netherlands), 19 November 2008, available at <http://www.nrc.nl/international/Features/article2066177.ece>.
712 See, for example, "Lubbers quits over UN sex claims", BBC News, 20 February 2005. Lubbers was accused of sexual harassment. He defended himself by stating that "I ushered the lady out of the room with my hand on her back. And that was all. You could call it familiar but certainly not sexual harassment."
713 "Swede reported rape – was fired", Aftonbladet (Sweden), 29 August 2008.
714 Text of the secret Human Rights Watch letter to the ICC OTP, 15 September 2008, available at <http://article42-3.org/Secret%20Human%20Rights%20Watch%20Letter.pdf>.
715 "ICC's Moreno Ocampo Learned Nothing from Lubanga Case, Laughs at Retaliation Finding", *Inner City Press*, 3 December 2008, available at <http://www.innercitypress.com/icc5ocampo120308.html>.
716 "International court plagued by in-fighting", *NRC Handelsblad* (The Netherlands), 19 November 2008, available at <http://www.nrc.nl/international/Features/article2066177.ece>.
717 "Moreno Ocampo slammed for abuse of power; chief ICC prosecutor denies allegations", Radio Nederland Wereldomroep, 22 July 2009 available at <http://209.85.229.132/search?q=cache:rg0vsxAs5GoJ:www.rnw.nl/int-justice/article/moreno-ocampo-slammed-abuse-power-chief-icc-prosecutor-denies-allegations+ocampo+criticism&cd=3&hl=en&ct=clnk&gl=uk>.
718 "Why the world's most powerful prosecutor should resign: Part 2 Sexual misconduct allegations against Luis Moreno-Ocampo have been dismissed as manifestly unfounded but he is held personally responsible for a breach of due process", *The Daily Telegraph* (London), 14 September 2008, available at <http://www.telegraph.co.uk/news/newstopics/lawreports/joshuarozenberg/2446064/Why-the-worlds-most-powerful-prosecutor-should-resign-Part-2.html>.
719 "Gender Justice and the ICC Overview of Key Gender Issues – ASP 2008", Women's Initiatives for Gender Justice, available at <http://www.iccwomen.org/publications/resources/docs/Womens_Initiatives_PaperASP2008FIN.pdf>. The Women's Initiatives for Gender Justice is an international women's human rights organisation advocating for

gender-inclusive justice and working towards an effective and independent International Criminal Court.
720 The first well-known rendition case involving an airliner was one that involved the Palestinian activists who seized control of the *Achille Lauro* ocean liner in 1985, killing one passenger. Following the incident, while travelling on a commercial flight in international air space, they were forced by United States Navy fighter planes to land at the Naval Air Station Sigonella, an Italian military base in Sicily used by the US Navy and NATO, in an attempt to place them within judicial reach of United States government representatives for transport to and trial in the USA. This extraordinary rendition caused a considerable diplomatic row between the USA and Italy. Egypt demanded an apology from the USA for forcing the aeroplane off course. The Palestinians were subsequently brought to trial in Italy.
721 See, definition in Wikipedia, the free encyclopedia, available at <http://en.wikipedia.org/wiki/Extraordinary_rendition_by_the_United_States>.
722 "ICC bid to arrest Sudan suspect failed", Reuters, 7 June 2008.
723 Julian Ku, "The ICC's Foiled Extraordinary Rendition", *Opinio Juris*, available at <http://opiniojuris.org/2008/06/09/the-iccs-foiled-extraordinary-rendition/>.
724 "Darfur war crimes suspect denies attempt to travel abroad", *Sudan Tribune*, 8 June 2008.
725 "ICC counsel condemns plans to divert plane carrying Darfur suspect", *Sudan Tribune*, 16 June 2008.
726 See, for example, "EU endorses damning report on CIA", *BBC News*, 14 February 2007, available at <http://news.bbc.co.uk/1/hi/world/europe/6360817.stm>.
727 "ICC Prosecutor says international court needs more state help", Reuters, 31 January 2009.
728 See, for example, "Britain failing to make Bashir's arrest a priority, says ICC's chief prosecutor", *The Guardian*, 24 May 2009.
729 "Sudan expulsions 'confirm crimes'", Aljazeera, 21 March 2009.
730 Conor Foley, "Darfur: a disaster for justice", *The Guardian*, 20 April 2009, available at <http://www.guardian.co.uk/commentisfree/2009/apr/20/sudan-war-crimes>.
731 See, for example, "Waging Peace submitted more than 500 children's drawings of Darfur that were accepted by ICC as evidence in any trial", Sudan Watch, 4 March 2009, available at <http://sudanwatch.blogspot.com/2009/03/waging-peace-submitted-more-than-500.html>, and "One small step for the ICC, a giant step for Darfur", *The Times* (London), 5 March 2009.
732 See Sudaneseonline.com, 8 March 2009.
733 Julie Flint and Alex de Waal, "Case Closed: A Prosecutor Without Borders", *World Affairs*, Spring 2009, available at <http://www.worldaffairsjournal.org/2009%20-%20Spring/full-DeWaalFlint.html>.
734 "ICC's Moreno Ocampo Learned Nothing from Lubanga Case, Laughs at Retaliation Finding", *Inner City Press*, 3 December 2008, available at <http://www.innercitypress.com/icc5ocampo120308.html>.
735 "Justice for dictators. History rules", *The Economist*, 21 April 2012, available at <http://www.economist.com/node/21553010?zid=317&ah=8a47fc455a44945580198768fad0fa41>.
736 "A Lifelong Passion Is Now Put to Practice in The Hague", *New York Times*, 18 January 2013, available at <http://www.nytimes.com/2013/01/19/world/africa/challenging-start-for-bensouda-as-chief-prosecutor-in-the-hague.html?pagewanted=all&_r=0>.
737 *Ibid.*
738 "Kenya: ICC Under Fire Over Investigations", allAfrica.com, 25 March 2013, available at <http://allafrica.com/stories/201303260047.html?viewall=1>.
739 *Ibid.*

Notes to Chapter Nine

740 Geoffrey Robertson, *Crimes Against Humanity. The Struggle for Global Justice*, Penguin Books, fourth edition, 2012, p. 546.
741 William Schabas, *Unimaginable Atrocities. Justice, Politics, and Rights at the War Crimes Tribunals*, Oxford University Press, Oxford, 2012, p. 204.
742 "USA et al. v. Goering et al.", International Military Tribunal judgment, 30 September–1 October 1946, 1947, Vol. 41, *American Journal of International Law*, p. 186.
743 UN General Assembly Resolution 3314, of 14 December 1974, adopted without a vote. Ref: 3105(XXVIII), 2967(XXVII), 2781(XXVII), 2644(XXV), 2549(XXIV), 2420(XXIII), 2330(XXII), 1181(XII), 895(IX), 688(VII), 599(VI) at 2,319th plenary meeting, the following definition of aggression: Article I: Aggression is the use of armed force by a State against the sovereignty, territorial integrity or political independence of another State, or in any other manner inconsistent with the Charter of the United Nations, as set out in this Definition. Explanatory note: In this Definition the term "State": (a) Is used without prejudice to questions of recognition or to whether a State is a member of the United Nations; (b) Includes the concept of a "group of States" where appropriate. Article 2: The First use of armed force by a State in contravention of the Charter shall constitute prima facie evidence of an act of aggression although the Security Council may, in conformity with the Charter, conclude that a determination that an act of aggression has been committed would not be justified in the light of other relevant circumstances, including the fact that the acts concerned or their consequences are not of sufficient gravity. Article 3: Any of the following acts, regardless of a declaration of war, shall, subject to and in accordance with the provisions of article 2, qualify as an act of aggression: (a) The invasion or attack by the armed forces of a State of the territory of another State, or any military occupation, however temporary, resulting from such invasion or attack, or any annexation by the use of force of the territory of another State or part thereof, (b) Bombardment by the armed forces of a State against the territory of another State or the use of any weapons by a State against the territory of another State; (c) The blockade of the ports or coasts of a State by the armed forces of another State; (d) An attack by the armed forces of a State on the land, sea or air forces, or marine and air fleets of another State; (e) The use of armed forces of one State which are within the territory of another State with the agreement of the receiving State, in contravention of the conditions provided for in the agreement or any extension of their presence in such territory beyond the termination of the agreement; (f) The action of a State in allowing its territory, which it has placed at the disposal of another State, to be used by that other State for perpetrating an act of aggression against a third State; (g) The sending by or on behalf of a State of armed bands, groups, irregulars or mercenaries, which carry out acts of armed force against another State of such gravity as to amount to the acts listed above, or its substantial involvement therein. Article 4: The acts enumerated above are not exhaustive and the Security Council may determine that other acts constitute aggression under the provisions of the Charter. Article 5: 1. No consideration of whatever nature, whether political, economic, military or otherwise, may serve as a justification for aggression. 2. A war of aggression is a crime against international peace. Aggression gives rise to international responsibility. 3. No territorial acquisition or special advantage resulting from aggression is or shall be recognized as lawful. Article 6: Nothing in this Definition shall be construed as in any way enlarging or diminishing the scope of the Charter, including its provisions concerning cases in which the use of force is lawful. Article 7: Nothing in this Definition, and in particular article 3, could in any way prejudice the right to self-determination, freedom and independence, as derived from the Charter, of peoples forcibly deprived of that right and referred to in the Declaration on

Principles of International Law concerning Friendly Relations and Cooperation among States in accordance with the Charter of the United Nations, particularly peoples under colonial and racist regimes or other forms of alien domination: nor the right of these peoples to struggle to that end and to seek and receive support, in accordance with the principles of the Charter and in conformity with the above-mentioned Declaration. Article 8: In their interpretation and application the above provisions are interrelated and each provision should be construed in the context of the other provisions. See, also, J. Hogan-Doran and B. T. Van Ginkel, "Aggression as a Crime under International Law and the Prosecution of Individuals by the Proposed International Criminal Court", *Netherlands International Law Review*, Vol. 43 (1996), p. 321.

744   Robertson, *Crimes Against Humanity. The Struggle for Global Justice, op. cit.*, p. 286.
745   Loru Sinanyan, "The International Criminal Court: Why the United States should sign the statute (but perhaps wait to ratify)", *Southern California Law Review*, Vol. 73 (2000).
746   Geoffrey Robertson, *Crimes Against Humanity. The Struggle for Global Justice, op. cit.*, p. 521.
747   *Ibid.*, p. 287.
748   William Schabas, *Unimaginable Atrocities. Justice, Politics, and Rights at the War Crimes Tribunals, op. cit.*, p. 204.
749   Philippe Kirsch, "The Rome Conference on the International Criminal Court: A Comment", American Society of International Law *Newsletter*, November–December 1998.
750   *Ibid.*
751   *Ibid.*
752   *See* Rome Statute of the International Criminal Court, Article 121, paragraphs 5, 6.
753   William Schabas, *An Introduction to the International Criminal Court*, Cambridge University Press, 2001, p. 27. See, also, Lionel Lee, "The International Criminal Court and the Security Council: Articles 13 (b) and 16", in Roy Lee (editor), *The International Criminal Court: The Making of the Rome Statute, Issues, Negotiations, Results*, Kluwer Law International, 1999, pp. 143–52.
754   See Silvia A. Fernandez de Gurmendi, "The Working Group on Aggression at the Preparatory Commission for the International Criminal Court", *Fordham International Law Journal*, Vol. 25 (2002), pp. 589–90.
755   Herman von Hebel and Daryl Robinson, "Crimes Within the Jurisdiction of the Court", in Roy S. Lee (editor), *The International Criminal Court: The Making of the Rome Statute: Issues, Negotiations, Results*, 1999, p. 82.
756   Final Act of the United Nations Diplomatic Conference of Plenipotentiaries on the Establishment of an International Criminal Court, Rome, 15–17 July 1998, Resolution F, UN Doc., A/CONF.183/C.1/L.76/Add.14.
757   International Criminal Court, "Continuity of Work in Respect of the Crime of Aggression", Assembly of States Parties Res. ICC-ASP/l/Res.1, ICC Doc. ICC-ASP/l/3, 9 September 2002.
758   International Criminal Court, "The Crime of Aggression", Review Conf. Res. RC/Res.6, 2, ICC Doc. ICC-ASP-RC/lI, Annex I, 11 June 2010.
759   Schabas, *Unimaginable Atrocities. Justice, Politics, and Rights at the War Crimes Tribunals, op. cit.*, pp. 204–05.
760   Amnesty International, "International Criminal Court, Concerns at the seventh session of the Assembly of States Parties", October 2008, Index: IOR 40/022/2008, p. 22.
761   Human Rights Watch, "Memorandum for the Sixth Session of the Assembly of States Parties of the International Criminal Court", 2007.
762   Schabas, *Unimaginable Atrocities. Justice, Politics, and Rights at the War Crimes Tribunals, op. cit.*, p. 217.
763   "U.S. Engagement with the International Criminal Court and the Outcome of the recently concluded Review Conference", US Department of State, Washington DC, 15 June 2010.

764 Geoffrey Robertson, *Crimes Against Humanity. The Struggle for Global Justice, op. cit.*, p. 512.
765 *Ibid.*, p. 546.

Notes to Chapter Ten

766 Luis Moreno Ocampo, "Impunity No More", *The New York Times*, 1 July 2009, available at <http://www.nytimes.com/2009/07/02/opinion/02iht-edocampo.html>.
767 Human Rights Watch, *Unfinished Business. Closing Gaps in the Selection of ICC Cases*, September 2011.
768 Adam Branch, *Displacing Human Rights. War and Intervention in northern Uganda*, Oxford University Press, New York, 2011, p. 189.
769 See, "Impunity", *Merriam-Webster Online Dictionary*, Merriam-Webster Online. 22 November 2009, available at <http://www.merriam-webster.com/dictionary/IMPUNITY>.
770 See, "Immunity", The Free Dictionary, available at <http://www.thefreedictionary.com/immunity>.
771 Luis Moreno Ocampo, "Impunity No More", *The New York Times*, 1 July 2009, available at <http://www.nytimes.com/2009/07/02/opinion/02iht-edocampo.html>.
772 See, for example, International Criminal Court, *The ICC at a Glance*, 2012, available at <ICC-PIDS-FS-01-004/12_Eng>.
773 "ICC rules out immunity for Kenya's presidential aspirants", *Africa Review*, 22 October 2012, available at <http://www.africareview.com/News/ICC-rules-out-immunity-for-Kenya-presidential-aspirants/-/979180/1539172/-/iink30z/-/index.html>.
774 Mick Hume, "More to it than Milosevic", *Spiked*, 29 June 2001, available at <http://www.spiked-online.com/site/article/11454/>. Also cited in debates in the British House of Lords, House of Lords Hansard, 8 March 2001, column 385.
775 Courtenay Griffiths QC has been involved in some of the most high-profile and notable cases of the past two decades. He has a wide-ranging practice in domestic and international criminal law and is widely regarded as one of the most outstanding jury advocates of his generation. His criminal defence work emphasis is on terrorism and murder, some of the most note worthy cases being: The PC Blakelock murder trial, the Brighton bombing, the Harrods bombing, the Canary Wharf bombing, the Risley riot, the Dartmoor riot, the Damilola Taylor murder trial. He is a very established international criminal law specialist, providing representation in trials of genocide, crimes against humanity and other war crimes before international, internationalised and national courts. He is particularly noted for his work in the recent landmark case in The Hague defending the former President of Liberia, Charles Taylor. See, Tim Black, "'Let's teach these darkies about the rule of law': Courtenay Griffiths, lead counsel for ex-Liberian president Charles Taylor, tells spiked about the racial bias in international criminal justice", *Spiked*, 29 May 2012, available at <http://www.spiked-online.com/site/article/12494/>.
776 "The Politics Of International Criminal Law", *New African*, March 2012, available at <http://www.newafricanmagazine.com/special-reports/sector-reports/icc-vs-africa/the-politics-of-international-criminal-law>.
777 "Interview with Luis Moreno-Ocampo, Prosecutor for the International Criminal Court", UN News Service, 5 June 2009, available at <http://www0.un.org/apps/news/newsmakers.asp?NewsID=13>.
778 "Interview: Luis Moreno-Ocampo, ICC Prosecutor", *The Africa Report*, 21 September 2009, available at <http://www.theafricareport.com/index.php?option=com_content&view=article&id=3281793&catid=54>.
779 Luis Moreno Ocampo, "Impunity No More", *op. cit.*

780 International Court of Justice, "Case Concerning Armed Activities on the Territory of the Congo (Democratic Republic of the Congo v Uganda), Year 2005", General List No. 116, 19 December 2005, available at < http://www.icj-cij.org/docket/files/116/10455.pdf>.
781 Human Rights Watch, "Unfinished Business. Closing Gaps in the Selection of ICC Cases", September 2011. See, also, "Case Concerning Armed Activities on the Territory of the Congo (Democratic Republic of Congo v. Uganda)", International Court of Justice, Judgment, ICJ Reports 2005, available at <http://www.icj-cij.org/docket/files/116/10455.pdf>, pp. 13, 168, 239-45.
782 African Commission on Human and Peoples' Rights, "Democratic Republic of Congo v. Burundi, Rwanda and Uganda", Communication No. 227/99 (2003).
783 Human Rights Watch, "Ituri – 'Covered in Blood': Ethnically Targeted Violence in Northeastern DR Congo", Vol. 15, No. 11(A), July 2003, available at <http://hrw.org/reports/2003/ituri0703>, pp. 6–8.
784 Human Rights Watch, "Courting History. The Landmark International Criminal Court's First Years", New York, July 2008, available at <http://www.hrw.org/en/reports/2008/07/10/courting-history>.
785 Branch, *Displacing Human Rights. War and Intervention in northern Uganda*, *op. cit.*, p. 191.
786 *Ibid.*, p. 187.
787 *Ibid.*, p. 189.
788 Human Rights Watch, "'We Will Crush You': The Restriction of Political Space in the Democratic Republic of Congo", 25 November 2008, available at <http://www.hrw.org/en/reports/2008/11/25/we-will-crush-you>.
789 "UN in Congo May Face Indian Withdrawal, Rapes 'Happen,' Doss Says, Say Yes to Help Arrest Bosco, No Comment on Sudan", *Inner City Press*, 9 April 2009, available at <http://www.innercitypress.com/drc1doss040909.html>.
790 "On Congo, Obasanjo On Relocating Nkunda and FDLR, Bosco 'In Circulation' in Congo", *Inner City Press*, 30 June 2009, available at <http://www.innercitypress.com/icclra1egg071709.html>.
791 "Sudan Calls UK Ambassador an Amateur, of War Criminals in Congo Too", *Inner City Press*, 18 May 2009, available at <http://www.innercitypress.com/un9sc1africa051809.html>. See, also, "UN and Congolese War Criminal Bosco, No Pictures, Please, As Council Approaches", *Inner City Press*, 13 May 2009, available at <http://www.innercitypress.com/un2bosco051309.html>.
792 "International Criminal Court: Chronology", War Crimes Research Office, American University Washington College of Law, last updated 13 November 2009, available at <http://www.wcl.american.edu/warcrimes/about.cfm>.
793 "No arrest yet for ex-rebel leader Ntaganda: Kinshasa", *Agence France-Presse*, 10 November 2009.
794 Luis Moreno Ocampo, "Impunity No More", *op. cit.*
795 "Peace Before Justice, Congo Minister Tells ICC", *Agence France-Presse*, 12 February 2009.
796 "'Our Mission is To End Impunity' – Moreno Ocampo", Inter Press Service News Agency, 13 July 2009.
797 Human Rights Watch, "Unfinished Business. Closing Gaps in the Selection of ICC Cases", September 2011, available at <http://www.hrw.org/sites/default/files/reports/icc0911webwcover.pdf>, p. 16.
798 *Ibid.* Human Rights Watch points to interviews with representatives of civil society and community-based organisations whom it interviewed in Kampala and northern Uganda in March 2007. These groups "consistently criticized the ICC's failure to investigate and prosecute UDPF abuses or to explain why this was not being done". Human Rights Watch separate interviews with seven representatives of Ugandan civil society, Kampala, 27 February and 1 March, Gulu, 7 March, and Lira, 11 and 13 March 2007. For Human Rights Watch reports on large-scale human rights violations committed by Ugandan government

forces, see, "Uganda: Launch Independent Inquiry into Killings", Human Rights Watch news release, May 8, 2011, available at <http://www.hrw.org/news/2011/05/08/uganda-launch-independent-inquiry-killings>; "Violence Instead of Vigilance: Torture and Illegal Detention by Uganda's Rapid Response Unit", March 2011, available at <http://www.hrw.org/en/reports/2011/03/23/violence-instead-vigilance>; "Uganda: Investigate Use of Lethal Force during Riots", Human Rights Watch news release, 1 October 2009, available at <http://www.hrw.org/news/2009/10/01/uganda-troops-killed unarmed-people-riot-period>; "Open Secret: Illegal Detention and Torture by the Joint Anti-terrorism Task Force in Uganda", April 2009, available at <http://www.hrw.org/en/reports/2009/04/08/open-secret-0>; "Get the Gun: Human Rights Violations by Uganda's National Army in Law Enforcement Operations in Karamoja Region", September 2007, available at <http://www.hrw.org/en/reports/2007/09/10/get-gun>.

799 Human Rights Watch, "ICC: New Prosecutor Takes Reins Fatou Bensouda to be Sworn In as Second ICC Prosecutor for Nine-Year Term", 14 June 2012, available at <http://www.hrw.org/news/2012/06/13/icc-new-prosecutor-takes-reins>.

800 Human Rights Watch, "Unfinished Business. Closing Gaps in the Selection of ICC Cases", *op. cit.*

801 *Ibid.*, p. 28. See, also, Paul Amuro, "Local War Crimes Court Excludes UPDF from Trial", *The Monitor*, 18 September 2008, available at <http://allafrica.com/stories/200809180042.html>.

802 See, for example, Human Rights Watch, "Courting History. The Landmark International Criminal Court's First Years", 12 July 2008, available at <http://www.hrw.org/reports/2008/07/11/courting-history>, p. 42; Human Rights Watch, "Benchmarks for Justice for Serious Crimes in Northern Uganda", 2 September 2008, available at <http://www.hrw.org/en/news/2008/09/01/benchmarks-justice-serious-crimes-northernuganda>, pp. 24–25, 33, 44; Human Rights Watch, "Uprooted and Forgotten. Impunity and Human Rights Abuses in Northern Uganda", September 2005, available at <http://www.hrw.org/reports/2005/uganda0905/uganda0905.pdf>, p. 57.

803 See, for example, "Letter from the Representative of Canada to the UN President of the Security Council" (3 July 2002), UN Doc. S/2002/723, before the adoption of Resolution 2241: "[T]he issue is a potentially irreversible decision negatively affecting the integrity of the Rome Statute of the International Criminal Court, the integrity of treaty negotiations more generally, the credibility of the Security Council, the viability of international law with respect to the investigation and prosecution of grievous crimes, and the established responsibilities of States under international law to act on such crimes." Argentina, Brazil, Cameroon, China, Colombia, Costa Rica, Cuba, France, Germany, Guinea, Ireland, Islamic Republic of Iran, Jordan, Liechtenstein, Malaysia, Mauritius, Mexico, New Zealand, Samoa, South Africa, Switzerland, Syrian Arab Republic, UK, and Venezuela also voiced deep reservations. See, UN SCOR, fifty-seventh session, 4,568th meeting, UN Doc. S/PV.4568.

804 Neha Jain, "A Separate Law for Peacekeepers: The Clash between the Security Council and the International Criminal Court", *The European Journal of International Law*, Vol. 16, No. 2 (2005), pp. 239–54.

805 UN, "Security Council refers situation in Darfur, Sudan, to Prosecutor of International Criminal Court", press release SC/8351, 31 March 2005, available at <http://www.un.org/News/Press/docs/2005/sc8351.doc.htm>.

806 "Libya: African mercenaries 'immune from prosecution for war crimes'", *The Daily Telegraph*, 27 February 2011.

807 "ICC has fallen from high ideals of global justice, accountability", *Daily Nation* (Nairobi), 16 March 2013, available at <http://www.nation.co.ke/oped/Opinion/-/440808/1722100/-/k4rufnz/-/index.html>.

Notes to Chapter Eleven

808 Colonel Frederic L. Borch III, "Why Military Commissions Are the Proper Forum and Why Terrorists Will Have 'Full and Fair' Trials: A Rebuttal to Military Commissions: Trying American Justice", *The Army Lawyer*, Washington-DC, November 2003. Colonel Borch is the acting Chief Prosecutor within the Office of Military Commissions, Judge Advocate General's Corps, US Army.

809 The USA assumed territorial control over Guantánamo Bay in Cuba under the 1903 Cuban-American Treaty, which granted the USA a perpetual lease of the area.

810 Human Rights Watch interview with representative of local civil society, Bunia, 30 April 2007, cited in "Courting History. The Landmark International Criminal Court's First Years", *op. cit.*

811 George W. Bush, "Detention, treatment, and trial of certain non-citizens in the war against terrorism", Military Order, 13 November 2001, Section 1.

812 *Ibid.* Section 7(b). *Habeas corpus* is a legal action, or writ, through which a person can seek relief from the unlawful detention of himself or another person. It protects the individual from harming himself or from being harmed by the judicial system. Of English origin, the writ of *habeas corpus* has historically been an important instrument for the safeguarding of individual freedom against arbitrary state action.

813 See, J. Bybee, "Memorandum for Alberto R. Gonzales, Counsel to the President, and William J. Haynes II, General Counsel of the Department of Defense, Re: application of treaties and laws to al-Qaeda and Taliban detainees", US Department of Justice, Office of Legal Council, 22 January 2002; and P. F. Philbin, and J. Yoo, "Memorandum for William J. Haynes, General Counsel, Department of Defense, Re: possible habeas jurisdiction over aliens held in Guantanamo Bay, Cuba", 28 December 2001.

814 George W. Bush, "Detention, treatment, and trial of certain non-citizens in the war against terrorism", Military Order, 13 November 2001, Section 1(e).

815 See, "Military commission orders", US Department of Defense, 28 September 2005, available at <http://www.defenselink.mil/news/Aug2004/commissions_orders.html>; and, "Military commission instructions", US Department of Defense, 27 March 2006, available at <http://www.defenselink.mil/news/Aug2004/ commissions_instructions.html>.

816 "Procedures for Trials by Military Commissions of Certain Non-U.S. Citizens in the War Against Terrorism", 68 Fed. Reg. 39, pp. 374–99, 1 July 2003) (to be codified at 32 CFR pts. 10–17); "U.S, Dep't of Defense, Military Commission Instructions", 30 April 2003, available at <http://www.defenselink.mil/news/commissions.html>. The eight instructions were originally made available on the DOD website, but were later published in the Federal Register as part of a broader rule-making that included, along with the eight military commission instructions and the DOD's Military Commission Order No. 1 that had previously been issued on 21 March 2002, 68 Fed. Reg. 39, pp. 374–99; "U.S, Dep't of Defense, Military Commission Order No. 1", 21 March 2002, available at <http://www.defenselink.mil/news/commissions.html>; see "Establishment of New Subchapter B-Military Commissions", 68 Fed. Reg. 38, p. 609 (30 June 2003).

817 See S. L. Silliman, "On military commissions", *Case Western Reserve Journal of International Law*, Vol. 36, No. 2/3 (2004), pp. 529–40; and J. Prescott, and J. Eldridge, "Military commissions, past and future", *Military Review*, Vol. 83, No. 2 (2003), pp. 42–51.

818 US Supreme Court, Case No. 05-184, Hamdan vs. Rumsfeld et al., "Opinion of the Court", 29 June 2006, p. 25. Articles I and II of the US Constitution relate to the legislative branch and the presidency, respectively. The most recent amended version of the UCMJ can be found in the *Manual for Courts Martial United States*, US Army Publications Directorate, Washington DC, 2008.

819 See, for example, "Report and recommendations on military commissions", American Bar Association, Task Force on Terrorism and the Law, 4 January 2002, available at <http://www.abanet.org/leadership/military.pdf>, p. 3.
820 "Combatant Status Review Tribunal Summary", US Department of Defense, 2 November 2007, available at <http://www.defenselink.mil/news/Nov2007/CSRTUpdate-Nov2-07.pdf>.
821 Military Commissions Act of 2006, US Public Law 109-366.
822 "Bush Says Military Commissions Act Will Bring Justice", American Forces Press Service, Washington DC, 17 October 2006.
823 For a copy of the ruling, see "Supreme Court", available at <http://www.supremecourtus.gov/opinions/07pdf/06-1195.pdf>.
824 Colonel Frederic L. Borch III, "Why Military Commissions Are the Proper Forum and Why Terrorists Will Have 'Full and Fair' Trials: A Rebuttal to Military Commissions: Trying American Justice", *The Army Lawyer*, Washington DC, November 2003. Colonel Borch is the Acting Chief Prosecutor within the Office of Military Commissions, Judge Advocate General's Corps, US Army.
825 See, "Military commission orders", US Department of Defense, 28 September 2005, available at <http://www.defenselink.mil/news/Aug2004/commissions_orders.html>; and, "Military commission instructions", US Department of Defense, 27 March 2006, available at <http://www.defenselink.mil/news/Aug2004/ commissions_instructions.html>.
826 Rome Statute of the International Criminal Court, available at <http://untreaty.un.org/cod/icc/statute/romefra.htm>
827 See, Riddhi Dasgupta, "Would al-Bashir Get a Fair Trial? Lessons from Guantánamo for the ICC", Oxford Transitional Justice Research Working Papers, University of Oxford Centre for Socio-Legal Studies, 20 August 2008, available at <http://www.csls.ox.ac.uk/documents/Dasgupt.pdf>, and Riddhi Dasgupta, "Would Sudanese President Omar al-Bashir Get a Fair Trial? Lessons from the U.S. Military Commissions at Guantánamo Bay for the International Criminal Court (ICC)", paper presented at the annual meeting of the Midwest Political Science Association sixty-seventh Annual National Conference, the Palmer House Hilton, Chicago, USA, 22 May 2009, available at <http://www.allacademic.com/meta/p361363_index.html>.
828 *Ibid.*

Notes to Chapter Twelve

829 International Criminal Court, Letter from the OTP regarding Iraq, 9 February 2006, available at <http://www.icc-cpi.int/library/organs/otp/OTP_letter_to_senders_re_Iraq_9_February_2006.pdf>.
830 "Lawyer: 'Tens of thousands' of Iraqi abuse cases", ITV News, 29 January 2013, available at <http://www.itv.com/news/update/2013-01-29/lawyer-tens-of-thousands-of-iraqi-abuse-cases/>.
831 UNHCR-Iraq Fact Sheet June-July 2011, United Nations High Commissioner for Refugees, available at <http://www.iauiraq.org/documents/1462/FACT%20SHEET%20JUNE-JULY%202011.pdf>.
832 Gilbert Burnham, Riyadh Lafta, Shannon Doocy, and Les Roberts, "Mortality after the 2003 invasion of Iraq: a cross-sectional cluster sample survey", *Lancet*, 11 October 2006, available at <http://brusselstribunal.org/pdf/lancet111006.pdf>.
833 Other estimates for war-related mortality in Iraq include the following. Associated Press: 110,600 violent deaths March 2003 to April 2009; Iraq Body Count Project, 110,937–

        121,227 civilian deaths from violence, 172,907 civilian and combatant deaths, March 2003 to December 2012; Iraq Family Health Survey, 151,000 violent deaths March 2003 to June 2006; Opinion Research Business survey, 1,033,000 deaths as a result of the conflict March 2003 to August 2007; WikiLeaks Classified Iraq war logs, 109,032 deaths including 66,081 civilian deaths January 2004 to December 2009.

834   Gilbert Burnham, Riyadh Lafta, Shannon Doocy, and Les Roberts, "Mortality after the 2003 invasion of Iraq: a cross-sectional cluster sample survey", *Lancet*, *op. cit.*

835   *Ibid.*, p. 5.

836   Michael A. Newton and Michael Scharf, *Enemy of the State: The Trial and Execution of Saddam Hussein*, St Martin's Press, New York, 2008, p. 79.

837   "Prosecuting American 'War Crimes'", *The Wall Street Journal*, 26 November 2009.

838   Richard Norton-Taylor, "International court hears anti-war claims", *The Guardian* (London), 6 May 2005, available at <http://www.guardian.co.uk/print/0,3858,5187283-111289,00.html>.

839   International Criminal Court, letter from the OTP regarding Iraq, 9 February 2006, available at <http://www.icc-cpi.int/library/organs/otp/OTP_letter_to_senders_re_Iraq_9_February_2006.pdf>.

840   Alan Dershowitz, "For the International Criminal Court To Work, The Worst Must Come First", *The Huffington Post*, 10 February 2009, available at <http://www.huffingtonpost.com/alan-dershowitz/for-the-international-cri_b_165714.html?view=print>.

841   WikiLeaks, US government cable, "Subject: ICC: A cautious beginning with mixed signals from the Prosecutor", 15 July 2003, available at <http://cablegatesearch.wikileaks.org/cable.php?id=03THEHAGUE1806&q=court%20criminal%20international%20ocampo>.

842   It is also clear that British forces in Afghanistan are also acting in common purpose with the USA and other Western countries, and thereby also possibly accountable for alleged war crimes committed by American personnel. See President Obama's statement: "We have fought alongside Afghans, and close friends and allies from dozens of nations who have joined us in common purpose": "Obama: US Responsibly Ending Wars In Iraq, Afghanistan", Kuwait News Agency, 7 October 2011.

843   Nicholas Wood, *War Crime or Just War? The Iraq War 2003–2005. A Case for Indictment*, South Hill Press, London, 2005, p. 57.

844   "Lawyer: 'Tens of thousands' of Iraqi abuse cases", ITV News, *op. cit.*

845   "Iraqis claim British troops 'acted with brutality'", BBC News, 29 January 2013, available at <http://www.bbc.co.uk/news/uk-21241088>.

846   "Iraqi ex-prisoners call for inquiry into allegations of British military abuse. Lawyers for former detainees of British military in Iraq say only an inquiry can prevent systemic abuse and brutality in the future", *The Guardian* (London), 29 January 2013, available at <http://www.guardian.co.uk/world/2013/jan/29/iraqi-detainees-demand-uk-inquiry>.

847   "High Court hears of Iraqi girl 'shot dead by British'", London *Evening Standard*, 29 January 2013, <http://www.standard.co.uk/news/world/high-court-hears-of-iraqi-girl-shot-dead-by-british-8471268.html>.

848   "Is Britain guilty of systemic torture in Iraq? High court to hear shocking testimonies alleging sexual abuse and torture of Iraqi prisoners and their families by British armed forces between 2003 and 2008", *The Observer* (London), 19 January 2013, available at <http://www.guardian.co.uk/uk/2013/jan/19/britain-guilty-systemic-torture-iraq>.

849   *Ibid.*

850   "British soldier is first to admit war crime", *The Times* (London), 19 September 2006.

851   "UK soldier jailed over Iraq abuse", BBC News, 30 April 2007.

852   "A bloody epitaph to Blair's war", *Independent on Sunday* (London), 17 June 2007.

853   "Is Britain guilty of systemic torture in Iraq? High court to hear shocking testimonies alleging sexual abuse and torture of Iraqi prisoners and their families by British armed forces between 2003 and 2008", *op. cit.*

854 Ibid.
855 Ibid.
856 Schabas, *Unimaginable Atrocities. Justice, Politics, and Rights at the War Crimes Tribunals*, op. cit., p. 81.
857 See, for example, "About Us", Public Interest Lawyers, available at <http://www.publicinterestlawyers.co.uk/aboutus.php>.
858 Schabas, *Unimaginable Atrocities. Justice, Politics, and Rights at the War Crimes Tribunals*, op. cit., p. 84.
859 Ibid.
860 Ibid.
861 Ibid., p. 85.
862 Ibid., pp. 85–6.
863 Ibid., p. 89.
864 Ibid.
865 William Schabas, "The International Criminal Court: Struggling to Find its Way", in Antonio Cassese (editor), *Realizing Utopia: The Future of International Law*, Oxford University Press, Oxford, 2012, p. 258.
866 Schabas, *Unimaginable Atrocities. Justice, Politics, and Rights at the War Crimes Tribunals*, op. cit., p. 88.
867 "International court under fire for prosecution policy", *NRC Handelsblad* (The Netherlands), 20 November 2008, available at <http://www.nrc.nl/international/Features/article2067475.ece/International_court_under_fire_for_prosecution_policy>.
868 Professor Hans Köchler, "Global Justice or Global Revenge? The ICC and the Politicization of International Criminal Justice", lecture delivered at the World Conference for International Justice 'United against the politicization of justice', organized by the General Sudanese Students Union, Khartoum, Sudan, 6 April 2009, available at <http://www.i-p-o.org/IPO-Koechler-ICC-politicization-2009.htm>. See, also, Hans Köchler, "Law and Politics in the Global Order: The Problems and Pitfalls of Universal Jurisdiction", International Conference on the Emerging Trends in International Criminal Jurisprudence, Indian Society of International Law, souvenir and conference papers, New Delhi, 10–11 December 2005, pp. 28–30.
869 See, for example, "Ocampo threats. ICC prosecutor threatens to investigate Sudan UN ambassador", *Agence France-Presse*, 5 June 2012.

Notes to Chapter Thirteen

870 "Editorial: Obama in handcuffs", *The Washington Times*, 2 December 2009, available at <http://www.washingtontimes.com/news/2009/dec/02/obama-in-handcuffs/>.
871 Nadir Nadrey, Office of the Commissioner of Afghanistan Independent Human Rights Commission, electronic communication cited in Akbar Nasir Khan, "Afghanistan War Crimes: Government, ICC and NGOs", *Islamabad Policy Research Institute Journal*, Volume XII, No. 1 (Winter 2012).
872 In December 2001, the UN arranged for a conference of Afghan leaders to be held in the German city of Bonn to choose the leader of an Afghan interim authority. The conference chose Hamid Karzai, who was subsequently elected President in 2004. Karzai appointed many of his anti-Taliban allies and regional leaders to senior posts within the interim and provincial governments. The USA, Britain and other Western states pledged security assistance to the new administration. See, also, "Agreement on Provisional Arrangements in Afghanistan pending the re-establishment of Permanent Government Institutions", 5 December 2001, available at <http://www.washingtonpost.com/wp-srv/world/texts/bonnagreement.html>.

873 Schabas, *Unimaginable Atrocities. Justice, Politics, and Rights at the War Crimes Tribunals*, *op. cit.*, p. 81.
874 Philippe Sands, *Lawless World: The Whistle-Blowing Account of How Bush and Blair Are Taking the Law Into Their own Hands*, Penguin Books, 2005, p. 62.
875 "Editorial: Obama in handcuffs", *The Washington Times*, *op. cit.*
876 See, "'Bomber McNeill' reveals the 'Cheapness' of Afghan lives: the massacre in Haydarabad, Helmand", Cursor.org, 7 August 2007, available at <http://cursor.org/stories/archivistan.htm#3>.
877 "U.S. officials wash their hands of Farah massacre", Pslweb.org, 27 May 2009, available at <http://www2.pslweb.org/site/News2?page=NewsArticle&id=12061&printer_friendly=1>, Paul Anderson, "Calls Grow to Tackle Afghan War Crimes", BBC News, 14 February 2005, available at <http://news.bbc.co.uk/2/hi/programmes/from_our_own_correspondent/4258343.stm>.
878 "Alarm over Afghan civilian deaths", BBC News, 17 February 2009, available at <http://news.bbc.co.uk/1/hi/7894233.stm>. See, also, "Afghan Civilian Deaths Rose 40 Percent in 2008", *The New York Times*, 18 February 2009, available at <http://www.nytimes.com/2009/02/18/world/asia/18afghan.html?_r=1>; "Afghanistan civilian casualties: what are the real figures? Spiralling military deaths in Afghanistan have obscured catastrophic civilian casualties. How many people have died?", *The Guardian*, 19 November 2009, available at <http://www.guardian.co.uk/news/datablog/2009/nov/19/afghanistan-civilian-casualties-statistics-data>. See, for details of earlier civilian deaths, "'Troops in Contact'", Airstrikes and Civilian Deaths in Afghanistan", Human Rights Watch, 8 September 2008, available at <http://www.hrw.org/reports/2008/09/08/troops-contact-0#_Toc208224420>.
879 Akbar Nasir Khan, "Afghanistan War Crimes: Government, ICC and NGOs", *Islamabad Policy Research Institute Journal*, Volume XII, No. 1 (Winter 2012), pp. 88–118.
880 See, Emily Winterbothom, "The State of Transitional Justice in Afghanistan: Actors, Approaches and Challenges", discussion paper, Afghanistan Research and Evaluation Unit, April 2010; and Niamatullah Ibrahmi, "The Vacant Seat of Afghanistan at the ICC: A Short Report on the ICC Assembly of States Parties (ASP)", The Hague, Netherlands, November 2009, available at <http://www.watchafghanistan.org/article017.html>.
881 Akbar Nasir Khan, "Afghanistan War Crimes: Government, ICC and NGOs", *op. cit.*, pp. 39–48.
882 Aryn Baker, "Warlords of Afghanistan", *Time*, February 12, 2009, available at <http://www.time.com/time/magazine/article/0,9171,1879167,00.html>.
883 Philip Alston, "Report of the Special Rapporteur on Extrajudicial, Summary or Arbitrary Executions", UN, A/HRC/11/2/Add.4, 6 May 2009. See, also, Matt Glenn, "US Must Do More to Prevent War Crimes: UN Rapporteur Philip Alston", *Jurist*, 29 May 2009, available at <http://jurist.law.pitt.edu/paperchase/2009/05/us-must-do-more-to-prevent-war-crimes.php>.
884 See, "Afghan War Diary, 2004–2010", WikiLeaks, 25 July 2010, available at <http://wikileaks.org/wiki/Afghan_War_Diary,_2004-2010>. See, also, "'Evidence of War Crimes' in Afghan War Logs, White House Downplays Leak, Claiming 'No Broad New Revelations'", Democracy Now blog, comment posted 27 July 2010, <http://www.democracynow.org/2010/7/27/wikileaks_founder_says_afghan_war_logs>.
885 "WikiLeaks puts ICC credibility on the line", 15 November 2010, the One Click Group, available at <http://www.theoneclickgroup.co.uk/news.php?id=5537#newspost>.
886 *Ibid.*
887 "Ocampo to use leaked US cables as evidence", *Sunday Nation* (Nairobi), 11 July 2011, available at <http://www.nation.co.ke/News/politics/Ocampo-to-use-leaked-US-cables-as-evidence-/-/1064/1199130/-/15jnqmsz/-/index.html>.
888 "Ein deutsches Verbrechen", *Der Spiegel*, 1 February 2010, pp. 34–57.

889 "German court will examine Kunduz airstrike", *New Europe*, 18 April 2013, available at <http://www.neurope.eu/article/german-court-will-examine-kunduz-airstrike>.
890 Timo Noetzel, "The German politics of war: Kunduz and the war in Afghanistan", *International Affairs*, Volume 87, Issue 2 (2011), pp. 397–417. Timo Noetzel spent several years as a political advisor to the German Army at ISAF Regional Command North, HQ ISAF and Allied Joint Force Command Brunssum. He is a research group leader at the Centre of Excellence at Konstanz University. He is also a Fellow of the Stiftung Neue Verantwortung, Berlin and Senior Policy Advisor to the Chairman of the Munich Security Conference.
891 "The End of Innocence in Afghanistan: 'The German Air Strike Has Changed Everything'", *Der Spiegel*, 14 September 2009, available at <http://www.spiegel.de/international/world/the-end-of-innocence-in-afghanistan-the-german-air-strike-has-changed-everything-a-648925-4.html>.
892 *Ibid.*
893 "Ein deutsches Verbrechen", *Der Spiegel*, 1 February 2010, pp. 34–57.
894 "Dozens Dead in Afghanistan: UN Calls for Investigation into Air Strikes", *Der Spiegel*, 4 September 2009, available at <http://www.spiegel.de/international/world/dozens-dead-in-afghanistan-un-calls-for-investigation-into-air-strikes-a-647084.html>.
895 "Aftermath of Afghan Air Strike: Germany Pledges Full Probe as Pressure Mounts on Defense Minister, *Der Spiegel*, 7 September 2009, available at <http://www.spiegel.de/international/world/aftermath-of-afghan-air-strike-germany-pledges-full-probe-as-pressure-mounts-on-defense-minister-a-647398.html>.
896 "The End of Innocence in Afghanistan 'The German Air Strike Has Changed Everything'", *Der Spiegel, op. cit.*
897 *Ibid.*
898 "Germany Says No Civilians Died in NATO Afghanistan Air Strike", Bloomberg, 4 September 2009, available at <http://www.bloomberg.com/apps/news?pid=newsarchive&sid=aljxif.laYRg>.
899 *Ibid.*
900 "Aftermath of Afghan Air Strike: Germany Pledges Full Probe as Pressure Mounts on Defense Minister", *Der Spiegel, op. cit.*
901 "Deadly Afghanistan air strike killed 142: Top secret Bundeswehr bomb video – was the truth hidden? Defence Minister Guttenberg forces German general and secretary of state to resign", *Bild*, 27 November 2009, available at <http://www.bild.de/news/bild-english/news/top-secret-bundeswehr-bomb-video-jung-klein-10587654.bild.html>.
902 "NATO Says U.S. Airstrike in Kunduz Killed 30 Civilians", *The Wall Street Journal*, 17 September 2009.
903 Neta Crawford, *Accountability for Killing: Moral Responsibility for Collateral Damage in America's Post-9/11 Wars*, Oxford University Press USA, 2013, p. 107.
904 "NATO's Secret Findings. Kunduz Affair Report Puts German Defense Minister Under Pressure", *Der Spiegel*, 19 January 2010, available at <http://www.spiegel.de/international/germany/nato-s-secret-findings-kunduz-affair-report-puts-german-defense-minister-under-pressure-a-672468.html>.
905 *Ibid*
906 "German Minister Jung Quits on Afghan Air Strike", Bloomberg, 27 November 2009.
907 "German Minister Resigns over Afghan Airstrike", *The New York Times*, 27 November 2009, available at <http://www.nytimes.com/2009/11/28/world/europe/28germany.html>. For more details on the Kunduz air strike, see "NATO Strike Magnifies Divide on Afghan War", *The New York Times*, 4 September 2009, available at <http://www.nytimes.com/2009/09/05/world/asia/05afghan.html>.
908 Hans Monath, "Schneiderhan wirft Guttenberg Lüge vor", *Der Tagesspiegel*, 17 December 2009, available at <http://www.tagesspiegel.de/politik/deutschland/schneiderhan-wirft-guttenberg-luege-vor/1649374.html>.

909 "Deadly Afghanistan air strike killed 142: Top secret Bundeswehr bomb video – was the truth hidden? Defence Minister Guttenberg forces German general and secretary of state to resign", *Bild*, 27 November 2009, available at <http://www.bild.de/news/bild-english/news/top-secret-bundeswehr-bomb-video-jung-klein-10587654.bild.html>.

910 "One Year After the Kunduz Air Strike. No Sign of a Full Investigation", *Der Spiegel*, 30 August 2010, available at <http://www.spiegel.de/international/world/one-year-after-the-kunduz-air-strike-no-sign-of-a-full-investigation-a-714532.html>.

911 *Ibid.*

912 "Deadly Afghanistan air strike killed 142: Top secret Bundeswehr bomb video – was the truth hidden? Defence Minister Guttenberg forces German general and secretary of state to resign", *Bild*, *op. cit.*

913 "The World from Berlin: 'Allies Can't Conceal Schadenfreude' at Botched Air Strike", *Der Spiegel*, 7 September 2009, available at <http://www.spiegel.de/international/world/the-world-from-berlin-allies-can-t-conceal-schadenfreude-at-botched-air-strike-a-647446.html>.

914 "One Year After the Kunduz Air Strike. No Sign of a Full Investigation", *Der Spiegel*, 30 August 2010, available at <http://www.spiegel.de/international/world/one-year-after-the-kunduz-air-strike-no-sign-of-a-full-investigation-a-714532.html>.

915 *Ibid.*

916 "Kunduz Bombing in Afghanistan: German Defense Ministry Sought to Obscure the Truth", *Der Spiegel*, 18 March 2010, available at <http://www.spiegel.de/international/germany/kunduz-bombing-in-afghanistan-german-defense-ministry-sought-to-obscure-the-truth-a-684411.html>.

917 "Deadly Afghanistan air strike killed 142: Top secret Bundeswehr bomb video – was the truth hidden? Defence Minister Guttenberg forces German general and secretary of state to resign", *Bild*, *op. cit.*

918 Marcel Mettelsiefen and Christoph Reuter, *Kunduz, 4 September 2009: Eine Spurensuche*, Rogner und Bernhard Verlag, Berlin 2010.

919 Wolfgang Weber, "Munich exhibition documents German army atrocity in Afghanistan", World Socialist website, 8 February 2011, available at <http://www.wsws.org/en/articles/2011/02/kund-f08.html>.

920 *Ibid.*

921 *Ibid.*

922 "SPIEGEL Exclusive: How ISAF Sought to Play Down the German Air Strike", *Der Spiegel*, 16 December 2009, available at <http://www.spiegel.de/international/world/spiegel-exclusive-how-isaf-sought-to-play-down-the-german-air-strike-a-667476.html>.

923 *Ibid.*

924 Crawford, *Accountability for Killing: Moral Responsibility for Collateral Damage in America's Post-9/11 Wars*, *op. cit.*, p. 107. See, S. Carran, A. Ravindar, S. Y. Lau and J. Bohannon, Afghanistan Casualty Timeline (2008–2010), 11 March 2011, as referred to in J. Bohannon, "Counting the Dead in Afghanistan", *Science*, Vol. 331, 11 March 2011, p. 1256.

925 "NATO's Secret Findings: Kunduz Affair Report Puts German Defense Minister Under Pressure", *Der Spiegel*, 19 January 2010, available at <http://www.spiegel.de/international/germany/nato-s-secret-findings-kunduz-affair-report-puts-german-defense-minister-under-pressure-a-672468.html>.

926 "Letter from Berlin. Details on Afghanistan Bombing Have Merkel on the Defensive", *Der Spiegel*, 14 December 2009, available at <http://www.spiegel.de/international/germany/0,1518,667011,00.html>.

927 *Ibid.*

928 *Ibid.*

929 "Sole Informant Guided Decision On Afghan Strike", *Washington Post*, 6 September 2009, available at <http://www.washingtonpost.com/wp-dyn/content/article/2009/09/05/AR2009090502832.html>.
930 "The End of Innocence in Afghanistan 'The German Air Strike Has Changed Everything'", *Der Spiegel, op. cit.*
931 "Sole Informant Guided Decision On Afghan Strike", *Washington Post*, 6 September 2009, *op. cit.*
932 "Investigation in Afghanistan. New Allegations against German Officer who Ordered Kunduz Air Strike", *Der Spiegel*, 21 September 2009, available at <http://www.spiegel.de/international/world/investigation-in-afghanistan-new-allegations-against-german-officer-who-ordered-kunduz-air-strike-a-650200.html>.
933 "Deadly Bombing in Kunduz: German Army Withheld Information from US Pilots", *Der Spiegel*, 1 February 2010, available at <http://www.spiegel.de/international/germany/deadly-bombing-in-kunduz-german-army-withheld-information-from-us-pilots-a-675229.html>.
934 "Defense minister denies new accusations linked to Afghan airstrike", Deutsche Welle, 13 December 2009, available at <http://www.dw-world.de/dw/article/0,,5009573,00.html>.
935 "NATO's Secret Findings: Kunduz Affair Report Puts German Defense Minister Under Pressure", *Der Spiegel*, 19 January 2010, available at <http://www.spiegel.de/international/germany/nato-s-secret-findings-kunduz-affair-report-puts-german-defense-minister-under-pressure-a-672468.html>.
936 "Sole Informant Guided Decision On Afghan Strike", *Washington Post, op. cit.*
937 "NATO air strike a 'major error': Afghan president", Reuters, 7 September 2009.
938 "List of suspected civilian casualties in the NATO ordered airstrike on two fuel tankers in Kunduz, September 4th 2009", 30 October 2009, AI Index: ASA 11/016/2009, available at <http://www.amnesty.org/en/library/asset/ASA11/016/2009/en/989a091e-dafc-4fab-bda5-ad8bf4be0999/asa110162009en.pdf>.
939 "Afghanistan Kunduz victim families file Germany claim", *op. cit.*
940 "The End of Innocence in Afghanistan 'The German Air Strike Has Changed Everything'", *Der Spiegel*, 14 September 2009.
941 "Luftangriff von Kundus Rot-Kreuz-Bericht belastet Guttenberg", *Stern*, 9 December 2009, available at <http://www.stern.de/politik/deutschland/luftangriff-von-kundus-rot-kreuz-bericht-belastet-guttenberg-1527884.html>.
942 Popal owns a small law firm in the northern German city of Bremen. He specialises in asylum and immigration law. He was born in Afghanistan and raised in Kabul. His father was a governor and finance minister under the former Afghan king. Popal left Afghanistan for Germany after the communist coup in 1978. His research team included a former provincial member of parliament, a female gynaecologist, a mullah and the District Chief of Chahar Dara.
943 "Coverup of the German army's role in the Kunduz massacre continues", WSWS.org, 7 December 2009, available at <http://www.wsws.org/en/articles/2009/12/kund-d07.html>.
944 "Afghanistan: German government must investigate deadly Kunduz airstrikes", Amnesty International, 30 October 2009, available at <http://www.amnesty.org/en/news-and-updates/news/afghanistan-german-government-must-investigate-deadly-kunduz-airstrikes-20091030>.
945 "Aftermath of an Afghanistan Tragedy: Germany to Pay $500,000 for Civilian Bombing Victims", *Der Spiegel*, 6 August 2010, available at <http://www.spiegel.de/international/germany/aftermath-of-an-afghanistan-tragedy-germany-to-pay-500-000-for-civilian-bombing-victims-a-710439.html>.
946 "The faces of war *Stunned by the vagueness in the number of casualties reported in* Kunduz, two German journalists fill in the gap", *The Atlantic Times*, June 2010, available at <http://www.atlantic-times.com/archive_detail.php?recordID=2196>.

947 "Aftermath of an Afghanistan Tragedy Germany to Pay $500,000 for Civilian Bombing Victims", *Der Spiegel*, 6 August 2010, available at <http://www.spiegel.de/international/germany/0,1518,710439,00.html>.
948 "Afghanistan Kunduz victim families file Germany claim", BBC News, 28 December 2012, available at <http://www.bbc.co.uk/news/world-europe-20859920>.
949 "Deadly Bombing in Kunduz: German Army Withheld Information from US Pilots", *Der Spiegel*, 1 February 2010, available at <http://www.spiegel.de/international/germany/deadly-bombing-in-kunduz-german-army-withheld-information-from-us-pilots-a-675229.html>.
950 *Ibid.*
951 "Compensation for Bombing Victims: The Price of an Afghan Life", *Der Spiegel*, 8 October 2010, available at <http://www.spiegel.de/international/world/compensation-for-bombing-victims-the-price-of-an-afghan-life-a-710963-2.html>.
952 *Ibid.*
953 "Girl injured at birth awarded £11m in compensation", *The Guardian*, 30 April 2012, available at <http://www.theguardian.com/society/2012/apr/30/girl-injured-birth-compensation-nhs>.
954 "At the Bar; Lifting a briefcase can be a terrific strain. But a little cash can ease the pain", *New York Times*, 30 April 1993, available at <http://www.nytimes.com/1993/04/30/news/bar-lifting-briefcase-can-be-terrific-strain-but-little-cash-can-ease-pain.html>.
955 "$4 Million in Compensation Set for Man Left in D.E.A. Cell", *New York Times*, 31 July 2013, available at <http://www.nytimes.com/2013/08/01/us/4-million-set-for-man-left-in-dea-cell.html?_r=0>.
956 "The World from Berlin: 'New Evaluation on Afghanistan Long Overdue'", *Der Spiegel*, 11 February 2010, available at <http://www.spiegel.de/international/germany/the-world-from-berlin-new-evaluation-on-afghanistan-long-overdue-a-677289.html>.
957 "Aftermath of an Afghanistan Tragedy: Germany to Pay $500,000 for Civilian Bombing Victims", *Der Spiegel*, 6 August 2010, available at <http://www.spiegel.de/international/germany/aftermath-of-an-afghanistan-tragedy-germany-to-pay-500-000-for-civilian-bombing-victims-a-710439.html>.
958 "German prosecutors drop case against Kunduz airstrike colonel", Deutsche Welle, 19 April 2010, available at <http://www.dw.de/german-prosecutors-drop-case-against-kunduz-airstrike-colonel/a-5483181>.
959 "Germany to Pay $500,000 for Civilian Bombing Victims", *Der Spiegel*, 6 August 2010.
960 "Afghan politician calls German air strike payouts 'laughable'", *The Local*, 6 August 2010, available at <http://www.thelocal.de/national/20100806-28991.html#.URLqrmc2R7k>.
961 'Mord', § 211 *Strafgesetzbuch* (StGB). All references to the StGB are based on the English version found at <http://www.iuscomp.org/gla/statutes/StGB.htm#211>.
962 See Rudolf Rengier, *Strafrecht, Besonderer Teil II Delikte gegen die Person und die Allgemeinheit*, ninth edition, 2008, § 2 Rn. 1 ff.
963 *Ibid.*, "Totschlag", § 212 StGB.
964 Antje Pedain, "Intentional Killings: The German Law", in The Law Commission (editor), *The Law of Murder: Overseas Comparative Studies*, available at: <http://www.lawcom.gov.uk/docs/comparative_studies.pdf>.
965 Rudolf Rengier, *Strafrecht, Besonderer Teil II Delikte gegen die Person und die Allgemeinheit*, *op. cit.*, "Fahrlässige Tötung", § 222 StGB.
966 "Schwebebahn-Absturz: Wuppertal unter Schock", *Der Spiegel*, 13 April 1999, available at <http://www.spiegel.de/panorama/schwebebahn-absturz-wuppertal-unter-schock-a-16964.html>; "Four die as 'hanging train' crashes", *The Times*, 13 April 1999.
967 For details see *Landgericht* Wuppertal, Judgment, 29 September 2000 – 21 KLs 411 Js 533/99 – 2/00.

968 See *Rechtsprechung* BGHSt 47, 228, 26 April 2001, available at <http://dejure.org/dienste/vernetzung/rechtsprechung?Text=BGHSt%2047,%201>.
969 "NATO's Secret Findings: Kunduz Affair Report Puts German Defense Minister Under Pressure", *Der Spiegel*, 19 January 2010, available at <http://www.spiegel.de/international/germany/nato-s-secret-findings-kunduz-affair-report-puts-german-defense-minister-under-pressure-a-672468.html>; see, also, "Investigation in Afghanistan. New Allegations against German Officer who Ordered Kunduz Air Strike", *Der Spiegel*, 21 September 2009, available at <http://www.spiegel.de/international/world/investigation-in-afghanistan-new-allegations-against-german-officer-who-ordered-kunduz-air-strike-a-650200.html>.
970 "Fundamental Breaches of Procedure in Colonel Klein Case", European Centre for Constitutional and Human Rights, 4 May 2010, available at <http://www.ecchr.de/index.php/KUNDUZ_CASES/articles/fundamental-breaches-of-procedure-in-colonel-klein-case.html>.
971 "German prosecutors drop case against Kunduz airstrike colonel", Deutsche Welle, 19 April 2010, available at <http://www.dw.de/german-prosecutors-drop-case-against-kunduz-airstrike-colonel/a-5483181>.
972 "Investigations and Prosecution", European Centre for Constitutional and Human Rights, 31 August 2010, available at <http://www.ecchr.de/index.php/KUNDUZ_CASES/articles/investigations-and-prosecution.html>.
973 "Fundamental Breaches of Procedure in Colonel Klein Case", European Centre for Constitutional and Human Rights, *op. cit.*
974 "Kunduz: Constitutional Complaint Lodged", European Centre for Constitutional and Human Rights, 18 March 2011, available at <http://www.ecchr.de/index.php/KUNDUZ_CASES/articles/kunduz-constitutional-complaint-lodged.html>.
975 "Fundamental Breaches of Procedure in Colonel Klein Case", European Centre for Constitutional and Human Rights, *op. cit.*
976 *Ibid.*
977 "German military drops case against Kunduz airstrike colonel", Deutsche Welle, 19 August 2010, available at <http://www.dw.de/german-military-drops-case-against-kunduz-airstrike-colonel/a-5926249>.
978 "One Year After the Kunduz Air Strike. No Sign of a Full Investigation", *Der Spiegel*, 30 August 2010, available at <http://www.spiegel.de/international/world/one-year-after-the-kunduz-air-strike-no-sign-of-a-full-investigation-a-714532.html>.
979 See, "Once-maligned German officer promoted to general", Deutsche Welle, 8 August 2012, available at <http://www.dw.de/once-maligned-german-officer-promoted-to-general/a-16152501>.
980 "German court to rule on Kunduz airstrike", Deutsche Welle, 20 March 2013, available at <http://www.dw.de/german-court-to-rule-on-kunduz-airstrike/a-16680014>.
981 *Ibid.*
982 *Ibid.*
983 *Ibid.*
984 A political protest was broken up in the Guinean capital of Conakry on 28 September 2009. A number of deaths ensued. Some human rights groups claim that 157 people died in the violence; the government stated that about 57 people died, most of them having been trampled to death accidentally by people fleeing the scene. See, for example, "ICC investigates Guinea 'abuses'", BBC News, 15 October 2009, available at <http://news.bbc.co.uk/1/hi/8308420.stm>; "Timbuktu shrine destruction 'a war crime'", *The Daily Telegraph*, 2 July 2012, available at <http://www.telegraph.co.uk/news/worldnews/africaandindianocean/mali/9369271/Timbuktu-shrine-destruction-a-war-crime.html>.
985 UN, "Report of the International Criminal Court", A/67/308, 14 August 2012, p. 15,

available at <http://www.icc-cpi.int/en_menus/icc/reports%20on%20activities/court%20reports%20and%20statements/Documents/A67308EN.pdf>.

986 Louise Arbour, "The Rise and Fall of International Human Rights", lecture by Louise Arbour, President and CEO of the ICG, on the occasion of the Sir Joseph Hotung International Human Rights Lecture 2011, at the British Museum, 27 April 2011, available at <http://www.crisisgroup.org/en/publication-type/speeches/2011/the-rise-and-fall-of-international-human-rights.aspx>.

987 Crawford, *Accountability for Killing: Moral Responsibility for Collateral Damage in America's Post-9/11 Wars, op. cit.*, p. 183.

988 Article 8(2)(b)(iv) of the Rome Statute of the International Criminal Court.

989 See, ICC, The Prosecutor v. Mathieu Ngudjolo Chui, ICC-01/04-02/12, available at <http://www.icc-cpi.int/en_menus/icc/situations%20and%20cases/situations/situation%20icc%200104/related%20cases/ICC-01-04-02-12/Pages/default.aspx>; and ICC, "ICC, Combined Factsheet: Situation in the Democratic Republic of the Congo", Germain Katanga and Mathieu Ngudjolo Chui, 27 June 2008.

990 "DR Congo: Mathieu Ngudjolo Chui acquitted of war crimes by ICC", BBC News Africa, 18 December 2012, available at <http://www.bbc.co.uk/news/world-africa-20766597>.

991 "Testimony to Parliamentary Inquiry: German Officer Defends Controversial Afghanistan Air Strike", *Der Spiegel*, 10 February 2010, available at <http://www.spiegel.de/international/germany/a-677109.html>.

992 "Once-maligned German officer promoted to general", Deutsche Welle, 8 August 2012, available at <http://www.dw.de/once-maligned-german-officer-promoted-to-general/a-16152501>.

993 ICC, "Paper on some policy issues before the Office of the Prosecutor",.p. 2, available at <http://www.amicc.org/docs/OcampoPolicyPaper9_03.pdf>.

994 Sherard Cowper-Coles, *Cables from Kabul: The inside story of the West's Afghanistan campaign*, Harper Press, London, 2011.

995 *Ibid.*

996 "Karzai to decree ban on foreign air-strike assistance during Afghan ops", *The Guardian*, 16 February 2013.

997 "Afghanistan Bars Elite U.S. Troops From a Key Province", *New York Times*, 24 February 2013.

Notes to Chapter Fourteen

998 Nicholas Waddell and Phil Clark (editors), *Courting Conflict? Justice, Peace and the ICC in Africa*, Royal African Society, London, March 2008.

999 Eric Posner, "The Absurd International Criminal Court. After 10 years and hundreds of millions of dollars, it has completed precisely one trial", *The Wall Street Journal*, 10 June 2012, available at <http://online.wsj.com/article/SB10001424052702303753904577452122153205162.html>.

1000 Cited in "What's the ICC up to?", *New African*, 1 May 2009.

1001 Adam Branch, *Displacing Human Rights. War and Intervention in northern Uganda*, Oxford University Press, New York, 2011, p. 182. See, also, Makau wa Mutua, "Savages, Victims, and Saviors: The Metaphor of Human Rights", *Harvard International Law Journal*, Vol. 42, No. 1 (2001), pp. 201–45.

1002 See, Tim Black, "'Let's teach these darkies about the rule of law': Courtenay Griffiths, lead counsel for ex-Liberian president Charles Taylor, tells *Spiked* about the racial bias in international criminal justice", *Spiked*, 29 May 2012, available at <http://www.spiked-online.com/site/article/12494/>.

1003 "Is ICC recolonising Africa?", *The Southern Times*, 10 June 2013, available at <http://www.southerntimesafrica.com/news_article.php?id=8422&title=Is%20ICC%20recolonising%20Africa%20&type=81>.

1004 In his controversial "dissenting opinion" from the Charles Taylor verdict of the Special Court for Sierra Leone, alternative Justice Malick Sow confirmed Griffiths' viewpoint. He stated: "I disagree with the findings and conclusions of the other judges, because for me under any mode of liability, under any accepted standard of proof, the guilt of the accused from the evidence provided in this trial is not proved beyond reasonable doubt by the prosecution. And my only worry is that the whole system is not consistent with all the principles we know and love, and the system is not consistent with all the values of international criminal justice, and I'm afraid the whole system is under grave danger of just losing all credibility, and I'm afraid this whole thing is headed for failure." See, "Justice Sow: 'Charles Taylor Should Have Walked Free'", *New African*, 14 December 2012, available at <http://www.newafricanmagazine.com/features/interviews/justice-sow-charles-taylor-should-have-walked-free>. William Schabas noted that "[n]othing comparable has ever appeared in the history of international criminal justice." ("Judge Sow Interviewed on Taylor Trial", Ph.D studies in human rights, 23 November 2012, available at <http://humanrightsdoctorate.blogspot.co.uk/2012/11/judge-sow-interviewed-on-taylor-trial.html>.) Justice Malick Sow is the Chair-Rapporteur of the UN High Commission for Human Rights' Working Group on Arbitrary Detention. He served as a judge in Senegal for more than thirty years and is currently a judge of the Supreme Court of Senegal. He is also President of the National Commission on trafficking of persons in particular women and children in Senegal. He was the coordinator of the Senegalese Committee of Human Rights (the national human rights institution of Senegal) and chaired the Francophone Association of National Human Rights Commissions as its President between 2002 and 2007. Justice Sow is also a member of the Follow-up Committee on the Implementation of the Robben Island Guidelines.

1005 Tim Black, "'Let's teach these darkies about the rule of law': Courtenay Griffiths, lead counsel for ex-Liberian president Charles Taylor, tells spiked about the racial bias in international criminal justice", *Spiked*, *op. cit.*

1006 *Ibid.*

1007 "Nigeria attacks by Boko Haram could be crimes against humanity, says ICC Prosecutor", UN News Service, 5 August 2013, available at <http://reliefweb.int/report/nigeria/nigeria-attacks-boko-haram-could-be-crimes-against-humanity-says-icc-prosecutor>.

1008 "Nigeria: Call for ICC probe into Nigerian military", IRIN, 16 July 2013, available at <http://www.irinnews.org/report/98426/call-for-icc-probe-into-nigerian-military>.

1009 *Ibid.*

1010 "The West's contempt for Africa must end!", *New African*, 18 September 2013.

1011 Brendan O'Neill, "The International Criminal Court is, by any objective measurement, racist. So why do liberals love it?", *The Daily Telegraph*, 15 March 2012, available at <http://blogs.telegraph.co.uk/news/brendanoneill2/100144112/the-international-criminal-court-is-by-any-objective-measurement-racist-so-why-do-liberals-love-it/>.

1012 "5 things Fatou Bensouda should do at the ICC", *The Guardian*, 14 June 2012, available at <http://www.guardian.co.uk/law/2012/jun/14/fatou-bensouda-international-criminal-court1>.

1013 *Ibid.*

1014 Thomas Darnstädt, Helene Zuber and Jan Puhl, "A Dangerous Luxury. The International Criminal Court's Dream of Global Justice Part 2: 'A World Without Justice'", *Der Spiegel International*, 14 January 2009, available at <http://www.spiegel.de/international/world/0,1518,601258-2,00.html>.

1015 John Rosenthal, "A Lawless Global Court. How the International Criminal Court Undermines the U.N. System", *Policy Review*, Hoover Institution, February-March 2004.

1016 See, for example, American Society of International Law, Independent Task Force, "U.S. Policy Toward the International Criminal Court: Furthering Positive Engagement", March 2009, p. 18, at <http://www.asil.org/files/ASIL-08-DiscPaper2.pdf >, 31 July 2009, and International Criminal Court, OTP, "Communications, Referrals and Preliminary Analysis", available at <http://www2.icc-cpi.int/Menus/ICC/Structure+of+the+Court/Office+of+the+Prosecutor/Comm+and+Ref>, 31 July 2009.

1017 "Rape in Zimbabwe: Human rights lawyers build prosecution case", *Agence France-Presse*, 7 August 2008; Angus Shaw, "Nobel Peace Prize Winner Tutu Says Time Has Come for Threat of Force Against Zimbabwe's Leader", Associated Press, 24 December 2008; Michelle Faul, "Physicians: Corruption killing people in Zimbabwe", Associated Press, 13 January 2009.

1018 See, "International court charges Kenyan with bribing witnesses", Reuters, 2 October 2013, available at <http://uk.reuters.com/article/2013/10/02/uk-kenya-icc-bribes-idUKBRE9910BE20131002>.

1019 "ICC Observers Exclusive Interview: Eric Leonard, Professor of Political Science Shenandoah University", ICC Observers, 14 April 2009, available at <http://iccobservers.wordpress.com/2009/04/14/icc-observers-exclusive-interview-eric-leonard-professor-of-political-science-shenandoah-university/>.

1020 "5 things Fatou Bensouda should do at the ICC", *The Guardian, op. cit.*

1021 William Schabas, *Unimaginable Atrocities. Justice, Politics, and Rights at the War Crimes Tribunals*, Oxford University Press, Oxford, 2012, pp. 88–89.

1022 *Ibid.*, p. 89.

1023 "Africa and the International Criminal Court", Council on Foreign Relations, New York, 17 November 2006.

1024 WikiLeaks, US Government cable, "Subject: Abyei, Sudan on Knife's Edge, Warns Foreign Minister", 25 June 2008, available at <http://cablegatesearch.wikileaks.org/cable.php?id=08KHARTOUM941>.

1025 Human Rights Watch, "Courting History. The Landmark International Criminal Court's First Years", New York, July 2008 available at <http://www.hrw.org/en/reports/2008/07/10/courting-history>, p. 45. See, also, Marlise Simons, "Gambian Defends the International Criminal Court's Initial Focus on Africans", *New York Times*, 26 February 2007, available at <http://www.nytimes.com/2007/02/26/world/africa/26hague.html?_r=1&oref=slogin>.

1026 "Benin president expresses scepticism over ICC", *Sudan Tribune*, 27 September 2008, available at <http://www.sudantribune.com/spip.php?article28762>.

1027 Richard Goldstone: "The *Opinio Juris* Interview", 21 June 2005, available at <http://lawofnations.blogspot.com/2005/06/richard-goldstone-opinio-juris.html>.

1028 "Precedent set for ICC to target Mugabe, says former war crimes prosecutor", *The World Today*, 11 March 2009.

1029 See, UN Doc S/2008/481.

1030 AU, Doc. Assembly/AU-/Dec.221(XII).

1031 AU, Doc. Assembly/AU-/245(XIII) Rev. 1.

1032 Assembly of the African Union, "Decision on the Meeting of African States Parties to the Rome Statute of the International Criminal Court (ICC)", Assembly/AU/Dec.245 (XIII), Sirte, 3 July 2009, para. 10.

1033 AU, Doc. Assembly/AU/8(XIV).

1034 AU, Doc. Assembly/AU/10(XV).

1035 AU, Doc. Assembly/AU/334(XVI).

1036 AU, Assembly/AU/10(XV).

1037 Assembly of the African Union, "Decision on the Progress Report of the Commission on the Implementation of Decision Assembly/AU/Dec.270 (XIV) on the Second Ministerial Meeting on the Rome Statute of the International Criminal Court (ICC)", Assembly/AU/

Dec.296 (XV), Kampala, July 27, 2010, paras. 5, 8 and 9. See, also, "AU chief chides ICC prosecutor", News24.com, 23 July 2010, available at <http://www.news24.com/Africa/News/AUchief-chides-ICC-prosecutor-20100723>, "Africa: World Court Faces Charge of 'Judicial Imperialism'", allAfrica.com, 23 July 2010, available at <http://allafrica.com/stories/201007230728.html>; "Gaddafi elected AU head, Union backs Sudan in critique of ICC", *Rejoignez Votre Communauté*, 2 February 2009, available at <http://www.rfi.fr/actuen/articles/110/article_2786.asp>.

1038 AU, Assembly/AU/Dec.245 (XIII), Sirte, 3 July 2009, paras. 9, 10.
1039 AU, Assembly/AU/Dec. 296 (XV), Kampala, 27 July 2010, paras. 4, 5.
1040 AU, "On the decisions of Pre-Trial Chamber I of the International Criminal Court (ICC) pursuant to Article 87(7) of the Rome Statute on the alleged failure by the Republic of Chad and the Republic of Malawi to comply with the cooperation requests issued by the Court with respect to the arrest and surrender of President Omar Hassan Al Bashir of the Republic of the Sudan", Addis Ababa, 9 January 2012.
1041 *Ibid.*
1042 *Ibid.*
1043 AU, "On the decisions of Pre-Trial Chamber I of the International Criminal Court (ICC) pursuant to Article 87(7) of the Rome Statute on the alleged failure by the Republic of Chad and the Republic of Malawi to comply with the cooperation requests issued by the court with respect to the arrest and surrender of President Omar Hassan Al Bashir of the Republic of the Sudan", *op. cit.*
1044 *Ibid.*
1045 *Ibid.*
1046 AU, Assembly/AU/Dec.391-415(XVIII).
1047 AU, Assembly/AU/Dec.397(XVIII).
1048 Richard Dowden, "ICC in the Dock", *Prospect*, London, May 2007.
1049 *Ibid.*
1050 *Ibid.*
1051 "African Search for Peace Throws Court into Chaos", *The Guardian* (London), 9 January 2007.
1052 Louise Parrott, "The Role of the International Criminal Court in Uganda: Ensuring that the Pursuit of Justice does not come at the price of peace", *The Australian Journal of Peace Studies*, Vol. 1 (2006).
1053 Jack Snyder and Leslie Vinjamuri, "Trials and Errors: Principle and Pragmatism in Strategies of International Justice", *International Security*, Vol. 28, No. 3 (Winter 2003/04), pp. 5–44. Jack Snyder is the Robert and Renee Belfer Professor of International Relations in the political science department and the Saltzman Institute of War and Peace Studies at Columbia University. His books include *Electing to Fight: Why Emerging Democracies Go to War* (MIT Press, 2005), co-authored with Edward D. Mansfield; *From Voting to Violence: Democratization and Nationalist Conflict* (Norton Books, 2000); *Myths of Empire: Domestic Politics and International Ambition* (Cornell University Press, 1991); *The Ideology of the Offensive: Military Decision Making and the Disasters of 1914* (Cornell, 1984); and *Civil Wars, Insecurity, and Intervention*, co-editor with Barbara Walter (Columbia University Press, 1999). Dr. Leslie Vinjamuri is Convenor of General Diplomatic Studies and Practice at the Centre for International Studies and Diplomacy and a lecturer (Assistant Professor) in the Department of Politics and International Studies. She co-chairs the London Transitional Justice Workshop (together with the Centre on Human Rights in Conflict).
1054 John Bolton, "The United States and the International Criminal Court", remarks at the Aspen Institute, Berlin, Germany, 16 September 2002, available at <http://www.state.gov/t/us/rm/13538.htm>.

1055 "Kagame calls for equality in international justice", *The New Times* (Kigali), 24 September 2012.
1056 *Ibid.*
1057 *Ibid.*
1058 *Ibid.*
1059 "Mamdani Raps Bashir Indictment", *New Vision*, 26 August 2009, available at <http://allafrica.com/stories/printable/200908270286.html>.
1060 "Mamdani: Teenage Activists of 'Save Darfur' – Child Soldiers of the West", 19 May 2009, available at <http://209.85.229.132/search?q=cache:AlfIPYhgYSsJ:rubeneberlein.wordpress.com/2009/05/19/mamdani-save-darfur-child-soldiers/+mamdani+mozambique+peace&cd=6&hl=en&ct=clnk&gl=uk>.
1061 Cited in "World View", 11 January 2009, available at <http://209.85.229.132/search?q=cache:FqVaD5YBlc0J:ultrabrown.com/posts/world-view+mamdani+mozambique+peace&cd=16&hl=en&ct=clnk&gl=uk>.
1062 John Bolton, "The United States and the International Criminal Court", remarks at the Aspen Institute, Berlin, Germany, 16 September 2002, available at <http://www.state.gov/t/us/rm/13538.htm>.
1063 *Ibid.*
1064 "Abdoulaye Wade asks the International Criminal Court to freeze its Darfur investigation for a year", Radio Islam International, 17 July 2008.
1065 "World reaction: Bashir warrant", BBC News, 4 March 2009, available at <http://news.bbc.co.uk/1/hi/world/africa/7923797.stm>.
1066 "Outcry against arrest move from Arab, African countries, Russia, China", *Sudan Tribune*, 5 March 2009, available at <http://www.sudantribune.com/spip.php?article30380>.
1067 "Senegalese president urges ICC to drop genocide charges against Sudanese leader", Xinhua, 7 March 2009.
1068 See, UN, "Senegal. H. E. Mr. Abdoulaye Wade, President, 24 September 2010", statement summary, General Assembly, sixty-fifth session, available at <http://www.un.org/en/ga/65/meetings/generaldebate/View/SpeechView/tabid/85/smid/411/ArticleID/153/reftab/227/t/Senegal/Default.html>.
1069 "Burundi president meets Sudan's Bashir, calls ICC warrant 'harmful'", *Sudan Tribune*, 20 March 2009, available at <http://www.sudantribune.com/spip.php?article30575>.
1070 "Benin president expresses skepticism over ICC", *Sudan Tribune*, 27 September 2008, available at <http://www.sudantribune.com/spip.php?article28762>.
1071 "Former Nigerian president criticizes 'politicized' ICC", *Sudan Tribune*, 17 March 2009, available at <http://www.sudantribune.com/spip.php?article30564>.
1072 See, for example, "International Court Under Unusual Fire", *Washington Post*, 30 June 2009, available at <http://www.washingtonpost.com/wp-dyn/content/article/2009/06/29/AR2009062904322_pf.html>.
1073 See, for example, "Rwanda's Kagame says ICC Targeting Poor, African Countries", *Agence France-Presse*, 31 July 2008; "Rwandan President Dismisses ICC as Court Meant to 'Undermine' Africa", Rwanda Radio via BBC Monitoring, 1 August 2008.
1074 "African Backlash Against International Courts Rises", *Christian Science Monitor*, 6 October 2009, available at <http://www.globalpolicy.org/international-justice/the-international-criminal-court/general-documents-analysis-and-articles-on-the-icc/48267.html?Item=663>.
1075 *Ibid.*
1076 "African Union opposes President's trial at Hague", Reuters, 25 May 2013.
1077 "African Union accuses ICC of hunting Africans", BBC News Africa, 27 May 2013, available at <http://www.bbc.co.uk/news/world-africa-22681894>. See also, "International Criminal Court is 'hunting' Africans. The African Union has said that it will complain to the United

Nations about the International Criminal Court (ICC) 'hunting' Africans because of their race", *The Daily Telegraph*, 27 May 2013, available at <http://www.telegraph.co.uk/news/worldnews/africaandindianocean/10082819/International-Criminal-Court-is-hunting-Africans.html>, "Ethiopian leader accuses international court of racial bias", gmanetwork, 28 May 2013, available at <http://www.gmanetwork.com/news/story/310313/news/world/ethiopian-leader-accuses-international-court-of-racial-bias>, "International Criminal Court 'chases' Africans because of their race", *Voice of Russia*, 28 May 2013, available at <http://voiceofrussia.com/2013_05_28/International-Criminal-Court-chases-Africans-because-of-their-race-9403/> and "African Union accuses International Criminal Court of 'race hunting'", *Washington Times*, 27 May 2013, available at <http://www.washingtontimes.com/news/2013/may/27/african-union-accuses-international-criminal-court/>.

1078   "African Union accuses ICC of hunting Africans", BBC News Africa, 27 May 2013, available at <http://www.bbc.co.uk/news/world-africa-22681894>.
1079   "African political parties say ICC is targeted at African leaders", *Business Ghana*, 21 August 2013, available at <http://www.businessghana.com/portal/news/index.php?op=getNews&news_cat_id=&id=188970>.
1080   "Kabimba urges African countries to reject ICC, voices support for Kenya withdrawal", *Lusaka Times*, 9 September 2013.
1081   "Kenya African states in aggressive diplomatic efforts to halt ICC trials", *The East African* (Kenya), 16 September 2013, available at <http://www.afrika.no/Detailed/24185.html>.
1082   *Ibid*.
1083   *Ibid*.
1084   "Africa Halt ICC Cases, Give Kenyan Leaders Leeway – AU", Capital FM (Nairobi), 12 September 2013, available at <http://allafrica.com/stories/201309130202.html?aa_source=slideout>.
1085   *Ibid*.
1086   "African Union To Debate ICC Exit Amid Kenya Trial", Associated Press, 17 September 2013, available at <http://www.npr.org/templates/story/story.php?storyId=223370396>.
1087   "Museveni blasts ICC at UN General Assembly", *Sudan Tribune*, 26 September 2013, available at <http://www.sudantribune.com/spip.php?article48177>.
1088   "Africa: AU and the ICC – How They Voted", ThinkAfricaPress, 15 October 2013, available at <http://allafrica.com/stories/201310150876.html?viewall=1>.
1089   "African Union runs critical eye over ICC", Reuters, 11 October 2013.
1090   *Ibid*.
1091   "Africa: AU and the ICC – How They Voted", ThinkAfricaPress, 15 October 2013, available at <http://allafrica.com/stories/201310150876.html?viewall=1>.
1092   "Kenyan president Kenyatta's ICC trial set to be suspended", *The Daily Telegraph*, 13 October 2013.
1093   "Closing Remarks by H. E. Mr. Hailemariam Dessalegn, Prime Minister of the Federal Democratic Republic of Ethiopia and Chairperson of the African Union at the Extraordinary Summit of Heads of State and Government of the African Union", AU, Addis Ababa, 12 October 2013, available at <http://summits.au.int/en/icc/speeches/remarks-he-mr-hailemariam-dessalegn-prime-minister-federal-democratic-republic-ethiopia>.
1094   Jacqueline Geis and Alex Mundt, "When to Indict? The Impact of Timing International Criminal Indictments on Peace Processes and Humanitarian Action", the Brookings Institution-University of Bern Project on Internal Displacement, paper to the World Humanitarian Studies Conference, Groningen, Netherlands, February 2009, p. 18, available at <http://reliefweb.int/rw/RWFiles2009.nsf/FilesByRWDocUnidFilename/RWST-7RAQ9A-full_report.pdf/$File/full_report.pdf>.
1095   See, for example, Oraib Al Rantawi, "A Step Forward or Backward?", *Bitter Lemons*, 14 August 2008.

Notes to Chapter Fifteen

1096 "Interview: Luis Moreno-Ocampo", *The Africa Report*, 21 September 2009, available at <http://www.theafricareport.com/index.php?option=com_content&view=article&id=328 1793&catid=54>.
1097 "War Crimes Are Everywhere, UK Uses Karadzic to Say, African Focus of Ocampo's ICC Defended", *Inner City Press*, 22 July 2008, available at <http://www.innercitypress.com/uk1karadzic072208.html>.
1098 "Interview: Luis Moreno-Ocampo", "The Africa Report", 21 September 2009, *op. cit.*
1099 "Interview with Luis Moreno-Ocampo, Prosecutor for the International Criminal Court", UN News Service, 5 June 2009, available at <http://www0.un.org/apps/news/newsmakers.asp?NewsID=13>.
1100 William Schabas, *The International Criminal Court: A Commentary on the Rome Statute*, Oxford University Press, Oxford, 2010, p. 309.
1101 ICC, "Draft paper on some policy issues before the OTP, for discussion at the public hearing in The Hague on 17 and 18 June 2003", 2003, p. 5.
1102 Benjamin Schiff, *Building the International Criminal Court*, Cambridge University Press, New York, 2008, p. 116.
1103 Darryl Robinson, "The Controversy over Territorial State Referrals and Reflections on ICL Discourse", *Journal of International Criminal Justice*, Vol. 9, No. 2 (2011), pp. 355–84, available at <http://jicj.oxfordjournals.org/content/9/2/355.full.pdf+html>.
1104 William Schabas, "'Complementarity in Practice': Some Uncomplimentary Thoughts", *Criminal Law Forum*, Vol. 19, No. 1 (2009), p. 12.
1105 William Schabas, "Prosecutorial Discretion v. Judicial Activism at the International Criminal Court", *Journal of International Criminal Justice*, Vol. 6, No. 4 (2008), p. 751.
1106 *Ibid.*, p. 760.
1107 *Ibid.*, p. 761.
1108 Schabas, "'Complementarity in Practice': Some Uncomplimentary Thoughts", *op. cit.*, p. 33.
1109 Schabas, "The Rise and Fall of Complementarity", in C. Stahn and M. M. El Zeidy (editors), *The International Criminal Court and Complementarity: From Theory to Practice*, Cambridge University Press, Cambridge.
1110 Schabas, "Prosecutorial Discretion v. Judicial Activism at the International Criminal Court", *op. cit.*, p. 761.
1111 Schabas, "'Complementarity in Practice': Some Uncomplimentary Thoughts", *op. cit.*, p. 16.
1112 *Ibid.*, p. 13, see, also, Schabas, "Prosecutorial Discretion v. Judicial Activism at the International Criminal Court", *Journal of International Criminal Justice*, *op. cit.*, p. 751. Additionally, see the commentaries by Philippe Kirsch and Darryl Robinson, "Referral by States Parties" in Antonio Cassese, Paola Gaeta and John R. W. D. Jones (editors), *The Rome Statute of the International Criminal Court: A Commentary*, Oxford University Press, Oxford, 2002, pp. 619–25; and Antonio Archesi, "Referral of a situation by a State Party", in Otto Triffterer (editor), *Commentary on the Rome Statute of the International Criminal Court, Observers' Notes, Article by Article*, Nomos, Baden-Baden, 1999, pp. 353–58.
1113 Schabas, "'Complementarity in Practice': Some Uncomplimentary Thoughts", *op. cit.*, p. 7.
1114 Schabas, "'Complementarity in Practice': Some Uncomplimentary Thoughts", a presentation at the Twentieth Anniversary Conference of the International Society for the Reform of Criminal Law, Vancouver, 23 June 2007, available at <http://www.isrcl.org/Papers/2007/Schabas.pdf>.

1115 Andreas Muëller and Ignaz Stegmiller, "Self-Referrals on Trial: From Panacea to Patient", *Journal of International Criminal Justice*, Vol. 8, No. 5 (2010), p. 1269.
1116 Mahnoush Arsanjani and Michael Reisman, "Law-in-Action of the International Criminal Court", *American Journal of International Law*, Vol. 99, No. 2 (2005), pp. 386–87.
1117 Benjamin Schiff, *Building the International Criminal Court*, Cambridge University Press, New York, 2008, pp. 116–17.
1118 *Ibid.*, p. 117.
1119 Schabas, "Prosecutorial Discretion v. Judicial Activism at the International Criminal Court", *Journal of International Criminal Justice*, op. cit.
1120 Arsanjani and Reisman, "Law-in-Action of the International Criminal Court", *American Journal of International Law*, op. cit.
1121 *Ibid.*, p. 390.
1122 Andreas Muëller and Ignaz Stegmiller, "Self-Referrals on Trial: From Panacea to Patient", *Journal of International Criminal Justice*, op. cit., pp. 1293–94.
1123 Schabas, *Unimaginable Atrocities. Justice, Politics, and Rights at the War Crimes Tribunals*, op. cit., p.81.
1124 "Communications Received by the Office of the Prosecutor of the ICC", press release, 16 July 2003.
1125 "International Criminal Court prosecutor to 'follow closely' situation in the Democratic Republic of Congo; Of 499 communications, one situation to be examined for possible further action", M2 Presswire, 17 July 2003.
1126 "The Current Investigation by the ICC of the Situation in Northern Uganda", the American Non-Governmental Organizations Coalition for the International Criminal Court, a programme of the United Nations Association of the United States of America, 16 February 2006, available at <http://www.amicc.org/docs/Northern%20Uganda%20Fact%20Sheet.pdf>.
1127 "The Office of the Prosecutor of the International Criminal Court opens its first investigation", press release, ICC-OTP-20040623-59, ICC, 23 June 2004, available at < http://www.icc-cpi.int/menus/icc/press%20and%20media/press%20releases/2004/the%20office%20of%20the%20prosecutor%20of%20the%20international%20criminal%20court%20opens%20its%20first%20investigation?lan=en-GB>.
1128 "Farmers and Chickens. An interview with Luis Moreno Ocampo", *Guernica*, March 2009.
1129 Jess Bravin, "Justice Delayed. For Global Court, Ugandan Rebels Prove Tough Test", *The Wall Street Journal*, 8 June 2006.
1130 "International Criminal Court Cases in Africa: Status and Policy Issues", Congressional Research Service, Washington DC, 12 September 2008, p. 20, note 85, available at <https://www.policyarchive.org/bitstream/handle/10207/20071/RL34665_20080912.pdf?sequence=2>.
1131 Human Rights Watch, "Courting History. The Landmark International Criminal Court's First Years", New York, July 2008, available at < http://www.hrw.org/en/reports/2008/07/10/courting-history>, p. 41.
1132 "War Crimes Are Everywhere, UK Uses Karadzic to Say, African Focus of Ocampo's ICC Defended", *Inner City Press*, 22 July 2008, available at <http://www.innercitypress.com/uk1karadzic072208.html>.
1133 ICC, "Paper on some policy issues before the Office of the Prosecutor", p. 2, available at <http://www.amicc.org/docs/OcampoPolicyPaper9_03.pdf>.
1134 Phil Clark, "Law, Politics and Pragmatism: The ICC and Case Selection in the Democratic Republic of Congo and Uganda", in Nicholas Waddell and Phil Clark (editors), *Courting Conflict? Justice, Peace and the ICC in Africa*, Royal African Society, London, March 2008.
1135 *Ibid.*
1136 Robertson, *Crimes Against Humanity. The Struggle for Global Justice*, op. cit., p. 552.

1137 Schiff, *Building the ICC, op. cit.*, p.116.
1138 Government of Uganda, "Referral of the Situation Concerning the Lord's Resistance Army", Submitted by the Republic of Uganda, 16 December 2003, available at <http://www-rohan.sdsu.edu/~abranch/Current%20Projects/Uganda%20ICC%20Referral%202003.pdf>.
1139 Schiff, *Building the ICC, op. cit.*, p. 221. See, also, ICC Pre-Trial Chamber I, "Decision Concerning Pre-Trial Chamber I's Decision of 10 February 2006 and the Incorporation of Documents into the Record of the Case against Mr. Thomas Lubanga Dyilo, Annex 1: Decision on the Prosecutor's Application for a Warrant of Arrest, Article 58", 2006, para. 36.
1140 ICC, *The Prosecutor v. Thomas Lubanga Dyilo* (Case No. ICC-01/04-01/06-8), *Decision on the Prosecutor's Application for a Warrant of Arrest*, 10 February 2006, para. 36.
1141 Phil Clark, "Law, Politics and Pragmatism: The ICC and Case Selection in the Democratic Republic of Congo and Uganda", in *Courting Conflict? Justice, Peace and the ICC in Africa*.
1142 "A Poisoned Chalice? Just Justice? Civil Society, International Justice and the Search for Accountability in Africa", International Refugee Rights Initiative, Discussion Paper 1, October 2011, p. 5, available at <http://www.refugee-rights.org/Assets/PDFs/2012/PoisonChaliceFINAL.pdf>.
1143 Robertson, *Crimes Against Humanity. The Struggle for Global Justice*, Penguin Books, fourth edition, 2012, p. 553.
1144 Clark, "Law, Politics and Pragmatism: The ICC and Case Selection in the Democratic Republic of Congo and Uganda", *op. cit.*
1145 *Ibid.*
1146 *Ibid.*
1147 Sir Geoffrey Nice, "The Permanent International Criminal Court and Africa", Gresham College lectures, 31 October 2012, available at <http://www.gresham.ac.uk/lectures-and-events/the-permanent-international-criminal-court-%E2%80%93-the-icc-and-africa>.
1148 Schabas, "'Complementarity in Practice': Some Uncomplimentary Thoughts", *Criminal Law Forum, op. cit.*
1149 *Ibid.*, p. 16.
1150 Sir Geoffrey Nice, "The Permanent International Criminal Court and Africa", *op. cit.*
1151 Lucy Hovil, "Challenging International Justice: The Initial Years of the International Criminal Court's Intervention in Uganda", *Stability: International Journal of Security & Development*, Vol. 2, No. 1 (2013).
1152 Clark, "Law, Politics and Pragmatism: The ICC and Case Selection in the Democratic Republic of Congo and Uganda", *op. cit.*
1153 Schiff, *Building the ICC, op. cit.*, p. 199.
1154 Robertson,*Crimes Against Humanity. The Struggle for Global Justice, op. cit.*, p. 552.
1155 Schiff, *Building the ICC, op. cit.*, p. 212.
1156 "ICC has fallen from high ideals of global justice, accountability", *Daily Nation* (Nairobi), 16 March 2013, available at <http://www.nation.co.ke/oped/Opinion/-/440808/1722100/-/k4rufnz/-/index.html>.
1157 Darryl Robinson, "The Controversy over Territorial State Referrals and Reflections on ICL Discourse", *Journal of International Criminal Justice*, Vol. 9, No. 2 (2011), p. 370, note 75, available at <http://jicj.oxfordjournals.org/content/9/2/355.full.pdf+html>.
1158 Schabas, "Prosecutorial Discretion v. Judicial Activism at the International Criminal Court", *op. cit.*
1159 Andreas Mueller and Ignaz Stegmiller, "Self-Referrals on Trial: From Panacea to Patient", *Journal of International Criminal Justice*, Vol. 8, No. 5 (2010), p. 1285.
1160 "A Poisoned Chalice? Just Justice? Civil Society, International Justice and the Search for Accountability in Africa", International Refugee Rights Initiative, Discussion Paper 1, October 2011, pp. 8–9, available at <http://www.refugee-rights.org/Assets/PDFs/2012/PoisonChaliceFINAL.pdf>.

1161 Adam Branch, *Displacing Human Rights. War and Intervention in northern Uganda*, Oxford University Press, New York, 2011, p. 187.
1162 Benjamin Schiff, *Building the ICC, op. cit.*, p. 219.
1163 See, for example, "Mali asks Hague court to investigate rebel crimes", Reuters, 18 July 2012.
1164 William Schabas, "Mali Referral Poses Challenge for International Criminal Court", 19 July 2012, available at <http://humanrightsdoctorate.blogspot.nl/2012/07/mali-referral-poses-challenge-for.html>.
1165 Robinson, "The Controversy over Territorial State Referrals and Reflections on ICL Discourse", *op. cit.*
1166 Schabas, "Mali Referral Poses Challenge for International Criminal Court", *op. cit.*
1167 "Random Comments on the Mali Self-Referral to the ICC", Spreading The Jam, 20 July 2012, available at <http://dovjacobs.blogspot.co.uk/2012/07/random-comments-on-mali-self-referral.html>. Dov Jacobs is an assistant professor in international law and international criminal law at Leiden University.
1168 Mahnoush Arsanjani and Michael Reisman, "Law-in-Action of the International Criminal Court", *American Journal of International Law*, Vol. 99, No. 2 (2005), p. 392.
1169 William Schabas, "The Rise and Fall of Complementarity", in C. Stahn and M. M. El Zeidy (editors), *The International Criminal Court and Complementarity: From Theory to Practice*, Cambridge University Press, Cambridge, 2011.
1170 See, for example, "Mali crisis: ICC launches inquiry into 'atrocities'", BBC News, 8 July 2012, available at <http://www.bbc.co.uk/news/world-africa-18893233>.

Notes to Chapter Sixteen

1171 "The Reckoning: The Battle for the International Criminal Court. Q&A with Christine Chung", PBS, 14 July 2009, available at <http://www.pbs.org/pov/reckoning/christinechung.php>.
1172 House of Lords Hansard, 8 March 2001, Column 385.
1173 "Interview with Mr. Philippe Kirsch, President and Chief Judge of the ICC", Citizens for Global Solutions, updated 6 October 2005, available at <http://www.globalsolutions.org/publications/publications_phillipe_kirsch>.
1174 "The Reckoning: The Battle for the International Criminal Court. Q&A with Christine Chung", *op. cit.*
1175 "The Role of the ICC Prosecutor", 20 October 2007, available at <http://lawiscool.com/2007/10/20/the-role-of-the-icc-prosecutor/>.
1176 ICC, *The Prosecutor v. Thomas Lubanga Dyilo*, "Decision on the Prosecutor's Application for a Warrant of Arrest", ICC-01/04-01/06-8, 10 February 2006, para. 54.
1177 *Ibid.*, para. 60.
1178 Amnesty International, "ICC and rule of law help deter war crimes and genocide", The International Criminal Court, Fact Sheet No. 1, 2008, available at <http://www.amnestyusa.org/pdfs/IJA_Factsheet_1_International_Criminal_Court.pdf>.
1179 Nick Grono and Adam O'Brien, "Exorcising the Ghost of the ICC", *The Monitor* (Uganda), 31 October 2006, available at <http://www.crisisgroup.org/home/index.cfm?id=4483&l=1>.
1180 "Report of the International Criminal Court, United Nations", A/64/356, 17 September 2009, available at <http://www.icc-cpi.int/NR/rdonlyres/1BC01710-9C42-44AC-8B18-85EE2A8876EB/281210/A_64_356_ENG2.pdf>.
1181 ICC, "Proposed Programme Budget for 2010 of the International Criminal Court", ICC-ASP/8/10, The Hague, 18 November 2009.
1182 See, for example, Brian Urlacher, "The ICC: Deterring Atrocities or Deterring

Settlements?", paper presented at the annual meeting of the ISA's fiftieth Annual Convention "Exploring the Past, Anticipating the Future", New York Marriott Marquis, New York City, NY, USA, 15 February 2009, available at <http://www.allacademic.com/meta/p311371_index.html>, See, Pablo Castillo, "Rethinking Deterrence: The International Criminal Court in Sudan", Rutgers University, UNISCI Discussion Paper No 13, January 2007; Z. Lomo, "Why the International Criminal Court Must Withdraw Indictments against the Top LRA Leaders: A Legal Perspective", Refugee Law Project, August 2006; Helena Cobban, *Amnesty After Atrocity?: Healing Nations After Genocide and War Crimes*, Paradigm Publishers, Colorado, 2007; Adam Branch, "International Justice, Local Injustice", *Dissent*, Summer 2004, available at <http://dissentmagazine.org/article/?article=336>; and J. Ku and J. Nzelibe, "Do International Criminal Tribunals Deter or Exacerbate Humanitarian Atrocities?", *Washington University Law Quarterly*, Vol. 84 (2007); David Wippman, "Atrocities, Deterrence, and the Limits of International Justice", *Fordham International Law Journal*, Vol. 23 (1999); Michael L. Smidt, "The International Criminal Court: An Effective Means of Deterrence?", *Military Law Review*, Vol. 167 (2001); Tom J. Farer, "Restraining the Barbarians: Can International Criminal Law Help?", *Human Rights Quarterly*, Vol. 22 (2000); Payam Akhavan, "Beyond Impunity: Can International Criminal Justice Prevent Future Atrocities?", *American Journal of International Law*, Vol. 95, No. 1 (2001).

1183 See Helena Cobban, "Think Again: International Courts", *Foreign Policy*, February 2006, available at <http://www.foreignpolicy.com/articles/2006/02/17/think_again_international_courts>.
1184 *Ibid.*
1185 *Ibid.*
1186 Julian Ku and Jide Nzelibe, "Do International Criminal Tribunals deter or exacerbate humanitarian atrocities?, *Washington University Law Review*, Vol. 84, No. 4 (2006), p. 832.
1187 *Ibid.*, p. 783.
1188 Jacqueline Geis and Alex Mundt, "When to Indict? The Impact of Timing International Criminal Indictments on Peace Processes and Humanitarian Action", the Brookings Institution-University of Bern Project on Internal Displacement, paper to the World Humanitarian Studies Conference, Groningen, the Netherlands, February 2009, p. 18, available at <http://reliefweb.int/rw/RWFiles2009.nsf/FilesByRWDocUnidFilename/RWST-7RAQ9A-full_report.pdf/$File/full_report.pdf>.
1189 Nick Grono, "Sudan: 'Deterring Future Darfurs'", in Reuters, "The Great Debate", 4 March 2009, available at <http://www.crisisgroup.org/home/index.cfm?id=5966&l=1>. Grono is the Deputy President of the ICG.
1190 Gustavo Gallón, "Deterrence: A Difficult Challenge for the International Criminal Court", Working Paper No. 275, July 2000. This paper was prepared for the conference "The Permanent International Criminal Court: Will It Make a Difference for Peace and Human Rights?" organised by the Center for Civil and Human Rights (Notre Dame Law School), the Joan B. Kroc Institute for International Peace Studies (University of Notre Dame), and the Midwest Coalition for Human Rights, at the University of Notre Dame, 19–20 March 1999. Gustavo Gallón has been Director of the Colombian Commission of Jurists. Before and during his tenure at the Commission of Jurists he taught state theory and constitutional law at several Colombian universities. He served as an independent expert on special Colombian government commissions for peace (1991) and the reform of the military criminal code (1995) and as Special Representative of the United Nations Commission of Human Rights for Equatorial Guinea (1999–present). He is the recipient of the 1989 Human Rights Watch and the 1997 Lawyers Committee for Human Rights awards for international human-rights monitors.

1191 Paul van Zyl is the Country Programme Director at the International Center for Transitional Justice (ICTJ). He served as Executive Secretary of the Truth and Reconciliation Commission in South Africa, helping to establish the commission and develop its structure and modus operandi. He has also worked as a researcher for the Goldstone Commission and as a department head at the Centre for the Study of Violence and Reconciliation in Johannesburg. Van Zyl was recently Director of Columbia University Law School's Transitional Justice Program, and now teaches law at both Columbia and New York University Law Schools. See, "Rights and reconciliation in a new era of international law Part II", "Justice for a Lawless World? Rights and reconciliation in a new era of international law", IRIN, June 2006, p. 32, available at <http://www.irinnews.org/pdf/in-depth/RightsAndReconciliationPart2.pdf>.

1192 Michael Ignatieff, "We're So Exceptional", *The New York Review of Books*, 5 April 2012.

1193 Daniel Sutter, "The Deterrent Effects of the International Criminal Court", *Conferences on New Political Economy*, Vol. 23, No. 1 (2006), pp. 9–24.

1194 AU, "Conclusions de la Réunion Régionale Ministérielle sur l'Armée de Résistance du Seigneur", 14 October 2010.

1195 "African Union to Make Push Against Rebels", *New York Times*, 23 March 2012.

1196 US Government Open Source Center (OSC), "Central Africa - Poor Cooperation Hampering AU Initiative Against LRA", 15 March 2012.

1197 UN, "Security Council Press Statement on Lord's Resistance Army", Security Council, Department of Public Information, New York, 21 July 2011, SC/10335, AFR/2215, available at <http://www.un.org/News/Press/docs//2011/sc10335.doc.htm>.

1198 "African Union to Make Push Against Rebels", *New York Times*, 23 March 2012.

1199 David Lanz, "The ICC's Intervention in Northern Uganda: Beyond the Simplicity of Peace vs. Justice", the Fletcher School of Law and Diplomacy, May 2007, available at <http://reliefweb.int/sites/reliefweb.int/files/resources/EC66215A0071F156C12573910051D06D-Full_Report.pdf>.

1200 "Analysis: Jury still out on ICC trials in DRC", IRIN, 19 January 2011, available at <http://www.irinnews.org/Report/91672/Analysis-Jury-still-out-on-ICC-trials-in-DRC>.

1201 "Report of the International Criminal Court, United Nations", A/64/356, 17 September 2009, available at <http://www.icc-cpi.int/NR/rdonlyres/1BC01710-9C42-44AC-8B18-85EE2A8876EB/281210/A_64_356_ENG2.pdf>.

1202 Human Rights Watch, "Trail of Death. LRA Atrocities in Northeastern Congo", March 2010, 1-56432-614-4, available at <http://www.hrw.org/sites/default/files/reports/drc0310webwcover_0.pdf>.

1203 UN Office for the Coordination of Humanitarian Affairs statistics cited in "Trail of Death. LRA Atrocities in Northeastern Congo", Human Rights Watch, March 2010, 1-56432-614-4, available at <http://www.hrw.org/sites/default/files/reports/drc0310webwcover_0.pdf>.

1204 See "US/Central Africa: Protect Civilians from LRA Abuses", Human Rights Watch news release.

1205 Human Rights Watch, "Human Rights Watch Memorandum for the Eleventh Session of the International Criminal Court Assembly of States Parties", 7 November 2012, available at <http://www.hrw.org/news/2012/11/07/human-rights-watch-memorandum-eleventh-session-international-criminal-court-assembly#2>. See also, Human Rights Watch, "The Christmas Massacres: LRA attacks on Civilians in Northern Congo", February 2009, available at <http://www.hrw.org/sites/default/files/reports/drc0209webwcover_1.pdf>.

1206 "Fact Sheet: U.S. Support to Regional Efforts to Counter the Lord's Resistance Army", US Department of State, Washington DC, 14 October 2011.

1207 "LRA Regional Update: Central African Republic, DR Congo and South Sudan: January–December 2011", UN Office for the Coordination of Humanitarian Affairs, 2012.

1208 "DRC: ERC Amos calls for better security in LRA-affected areas", UN Office for the Coordination of Humanitarian Affairs, 10 March 2011 and "Fact Sheet: U.S. Support to Regional Efforts to Counter the Lord's Resistance Army", US Department of State, Washington DC, 14 October 2011.

1209 "Crisis Tracker: Reported attacks and abductions by LRA rebels double over last 12 months", *Resolve*, 1 August 2012, available at <http://www.theresolve.org/blog/archives/3071033490>.

1210 Adam Branch, *Displacing Human Rights. War and Intervention in northern Uganda*, Oxford University Press, New York, 2011, p. 190.

1211 "Congo's 'Terminator': Kabila calls for Ntaganda arrest", BBC News, 11 April 2012.

1212 Human Rights Watch, "DR Congo: M23 Rebels Committing War Crimes", 11 September 2012, available at <http://www.hrw.org/print/news/2012/09/11/dr-congo-m23-rebels-committing-war-crimes>.

1213 "Congo Rebels Seize Provincial Capital", *New York Times*, 20 November 2012.

1214 Human Rights Watch, "DR Congo: M23 Rebels Committing War Crimes", *op. cit.*

1215 "Congo: We did whatever we wanted, says soldier who raped 53 women. As the G8 discusses sexual violence in the DRC, perpetrators and victims speak out about mass rape in Minova", *The Guardian*, 11 April 2013.

1216 "UN Raises Minova Rape Count to 126, Ladsous Won't Name Units", *Inner City Press*, 18 December 2012, available at <http://www.innercitypress.com/minova4ladsous121812.html>.

1217 "Congo: We did whatever we wanted, says soldier who raped 53 women. As the G8 discusses sexual violence in the DRC, perpetrators and victims speak out about mass rape in Minova", *op. cit.*

1218 See MONUSCO report at <http://monusco.unmissions.org/LinkClick.aspx?fileticket=Pj7jOWjAxWo%3d&tabid=10662&language=en-US>.

1219 "Congo: We did whatever we wanted, says soldier who raped 53 women. As the G8 discusses sexual violence in the DRC, perpetrators and victims speak out about mass rape in Minova", *op. cit.*

1220 "Minova Rapes by DRC Army Raised to Minister & Kabila by UK & Power", *Inner City Press*, 5 October 2013, available at <http://www.innercitypress.com/unlakes1minova100513.html>.

1221 The UN human rights due diligence policy was explained by the UN Secretary-General's outgoing chief lawyer Patricia O'Brien at a 9 July 2013 meeting in New York: "First, the UN cannot provide support to non-UN security forces where there are substantial grounds for believing there is a real risk of those forces committing grave violations of international humanitarian, human rights or refugee law. Secondly, where grave violations are committed by non-UN security forces that are receiving support from the UN, the UN must intercede with a view to bringing those violations to an end. And thirdly, if, despite such intercession, the situation persists, the UN must suspend support to the offending forces." See, "Araud of France Tells ICP 391st is 'Best Unit' in DRC Army, Being 'Reassessed'", *Inner City Press*, 24 July 2013, available at <http://www.innercitypress.com/france1duedildrc072413.html>.

1222 See, "750 Congolese Soldiers Graduate from U.S.-led Military Training, Form Light Infantry Battalion", U.S. Africa Command, September 2010, available at <http://www.africom.mil/NEWSROOM/Article/7727/750-congolese-soldiers-graduate-from-us-led-milita>; and "US Trained 391 Battalion Comes Up at UN, US Comment, HRW Silence", *Inner City Press*, 22 July 2013, available at <http://www.innercitypress.com/drc1bat391usun072213.html>.

1223 "Araud of France Tells ICP 391st is 'Best Unit' in DRC Army, Being 'Reassessed'", *Inner City Press*, 24 July 2013, available at <http://www.innercitypress.com/france1duedildrc072413.html>.

1224 "DRC Army Unit Desecrating Corpses Aided by UN After Rapes, US Trained", *Inner City Press*, 20 July 2013, available at <http://www.innercitypress.com/drc1unabuseus072013.html>.

1225 See, for example, Human Rights Watch, "DR Congo: Bosco Ntaganda Recruits Children by Force", news release, 16 May 2012, available at <http://www.hrw.org/news/2012/05/15/dr-congo-bosco-ntaganda-recruits-children-force>; Human Rights Watch, "Bosco Ntaganda – Wanted for War Crimes", video, 13 April 2012, available at <http://www.hrw.org/video/2012/04/13/bosco-ntaganda-wanted-war-crimes>.

1226 See Human Rights Watch, "Democratic Republic of Congo – Killings in Kiwanja", 3 December 2008, pp 8–10.

1227 Human Rights Watch, "Human Rights Watch Memorandum for the Eleventh Session of the International Criminal Court Assembly of States Parties", 7 November 2012, available at <http://www.hrw.org/news/2012/11/07/human-rights-watch-memorandum-eleventh-session-international-criminal-court-assembly#2>. See, also, Human Rights Watch, "DR Congo: Rogue Leaders, Rebels Forcibly Recruit Youth", news release, 20 December 2010, available at <http://www.hrw.org/news/2010/12/20/dr-congo-rogue-leaders-rebels-forcibly-recruit-youth>.

1228 "Thomas Lubango Dyilo is sentenced to 14 years, as M23 advances on Goma", Armed Groups and International Law, 11 July 2012, available at< http://armedgroups-internationallaw.org/2012/07/11/thomas-lubango-dyilo-is-sentenced-to-14-years-as-m23-advances-on-goma/>.

1229 "Kenya: ICC Under Fire Over Investigations", allAfrica.com, 25 March 2013, available at <http://allafrica.com/stories/201303260047.html?viewall=1>.

Notes to Chapter Seventeen

1230 Human Rights Watch, "Unfinished Business". "Closing Gaps in the Selection of ICC Cases", September 2011, available at <http://www.hrw.org/sites/default/files/reports/icc0911webwcover.pdf>.

1231 ICC, "Victims and witnesses", available at <http://www2.icc-cpi.int/Menus/ICC/Structure+of+the+Court/Victims/>.

1232 "UN Secretary General Declares Overriding Interest of International Criminal Court Conference must be that of Victims and World Community as a Whole", UN press release, 15 June 1998, available at <http://www.un.org/icc/pressrel/lrom6r1.htm>, and cited in Luc Reydams, Jan Wouters and Cedric Ryngaert (editors), *International Prosecutors*, Oxford University Press, Oxford, 2012.

1233 ICC, "Decision on the applications for participation in the proceedings of VPRS 1–6", Pre-Trial Chamber I, 17 January 2006.

1234 Human Rights Watch, "Human Rights Watch Memorandum for the Eleventh Session of the International Criminal Court Assembly of States Parties", 7 November 2012, available at <http://www.hrw.org/news/2012/11/07/human-rights-watch-memorandum-eleventh-session-international-criminal-court-assembly#2>.

1235 ICC, "Prosecutorial Strategy 2009–2012", OTP, 1 February 2010, paras. 18–21, available at <http://www.icc-cpi.int/NR/rdonlyres/66A8DCDC-3650-4514-AA62-D229D1128F65/281506/OTPProsecutorialStrategy20092013.pdf>. See, also, "Unfinished Business", p. 7.

1236 *Ibid.*, para. 22.

1237 "5 things Fatou Bensouda should do at the ICC", *The Guardian*, 14 June 2012, available at <http://www.guardian.co.uk/law/2012/jun/14/fatou-bensouda-international-criminal-court1>.

1238 Human Rights Watch, "Human Rights Watch Memorandum for the Eleventh Session of the International Criminal Court Assembly of States Parties", *op. cit.*

1239 Julian Ku and Jide Nzelibe, "Do International Criminal Tribunals deter or exacerbate

humanitarian atrocities?, *Washington University Law Review*, Vol. 84, No. 4 (2006), p. 831.
1240 "'A Dangerous Luxury'. The International Criminal Court's Dream of Global Justice", *Der Spiegel*, 14 January 2009.
1241 *Ibid.*
1242 "The Impact of the Rome Statute System on Victims and Affected Communities", Victims' Rights Working Group, April 2010, available at <http://www.vrwg.org/VRWG_DOC/2010_Apr_VRWG_Impact_of_ICC_on_victims.pdf>.
1243 Katherine Southwick, "Investigating War in Northern Uganda: Dilemmas for the International Criminal Court", *Yale Journal of International Affairs*, Vol. 1 (2005), pp. 105–19, p. 113. Katherine Southwick has worked with Refugees International and the Refugee Law Project in Kampala, Uganda. She was a Robert L. Bernstein International Human Rights Fellow at the Orville H. Schell, Jr. Center for International Human Rights at Yale Law School. She has been employed as a senior program manager at the American Bar Association Rule of Law Initiative based in Washington DC.
1244 "Cosy club or sword of righteousness?", *The Economist*, 26 November 2011, available at <http://www.economist.com/node/21540230?zid=317&ah=8a47fc455a44945580198768fad0fa41>.
1245 "Kenya ICC Trials Have Done Little for Victims", Capital FM (Nairobi), 12 September 2013, available at <http://allafrica.com/stories/201309130205.html?aa_source=slideout>.
1246 "Justice for dictators. History rules", *The Economist*, 21 April 2012, available at <http://www.economist.com/node/21553010?zid=317&ah=8a47fc455a44945580198768fad0fa41>.
1247 "Did the ICC help Uhuru Kenyatta win Kenyan election?", BBC News, 11 March 2013, available at <http://www.bbc.co.uk/news/world-africa-21739347>.
1248 Human Rights Watch, "Courting History. The Landmark International Criminal Court's First Years", Human Rights Watch, New York, July 2008 available at < http://www.hrw.org/en/reports/2008/07/10/courting-history>, p. 5.
1249 Helena Cobban, "Think Again: International Courts", *Foreign Policy*, February 2006, available at <http://www.foreignpolicy.com/articles/2006/02/17/think_again_international_courts>.
1250 *Ibid.*
1251 Joshua Rozenberg, "Delay in Lubanga judgment demonstrates ICC weaknesses", *The Guardian*, 14 March 2012, available at <http://www.guardian.co.uk/law/2012/mar/14/delay-lubanga-weaknesses-icc-model>.

Notes to Chapter Eighteen

1252 Jacqueline Geis and Alex Mundt, "When to Indict? The Impact of Timing International Criminal Indictments on Peace Processes and Humanitarian Action", the Brookings Institution-University of Bern Project on Internal Displacement, paper to the World Humanitarian Studies Conference, Groningen, the Netherlands, February 2009, p. 19, available at <http://reliefweb.int/rw/RWFiles2009.nsf/FilesByRWDocUnidFilename/RWST-7RAQ9A-full_report.pdf/$File/full_report.pdf>.
1253 Phil Clark, "Law, Politics and Pragmatism: The ICC and Case Selection in the Democratic Republic of Congo and Uganda", in Nicholas Waddell and Phil Clark (editors), *Courting Conflict? Justice, Peace and the ICC in Africa*, Royal African Society, London, March 2008.
1254 ICC, "President of Uganda Refers Situation Concerning the Lord's Resistance Army (LRA) to the ICC", press release, OTP, 29 January 2004; see also Payam Akhavan, "The Lord's Resistance Army Case: Uganda's Submission of the First State Referral to the International Criminal Court", *The American Journal of International Law*, Vol. 99, No. 2 (2005), pp. 405–06.

1255 See, for example, "*Reports: Uganda, Conflict history*", ICG, 22 September 2004, available at http://www.crisisgroup.org/home/index.cfm?action=conflict_search&l=1&t=1&c_country=111. For more background on the LRA insurgency, see Crisis Group, "Northern Uganda: Understanding and Solving the Conflict", ICG, Africa Report No. 77, 14 April 2004; "Shock Therapy for Northern Uganda's Peace Process", ICG, Africa Briefings No. 23, 11 April 2005; No.22, "Peace in Northern Uganda: Decisive Weeks Ahead", 21 February 2005; and "Building a Comprehensive Peace Strategy for Northern Uganda", ICG, Africa Briefings No 27, 23 June 2005.
1256 Alexis Okeowo, "LRA and Ugandan Government Renew Truce", Institute for War & Peace Reporting, 24 May 2007, available at <http://www.globalpolicy.org/component/content/article/207/39833.html>.
1257 "LRA Leader Must Be Arrested, ICC Insists", Integrated Regional Information Networks, 5 July 2006, available at <http://www.globalpolicy.org/component/content/article/165/29603.html>.
1258 Mahnoush Arsanjani and Michael Reisman, "The Law-In-Action of the International Criminal Court", *American Journal of International Law*, No. 99, Vol. 5 (2005), p. 393.
1259 Ibid.
1260 Sarah Nouwen, *Complementarity in the Line of Fire: The Catalysing Effect of the International Criminal Court in Uganda and Sudan*, Cambridge University Press, 2013, p. 122.
1261 H. Abigail Moy, "The International Criminal Court's Arrest Warrants and Uganda's Lord's Resistance Army: Renewing the Debate over Amnesty and Complementarity", *Harvard Human Rights Journal*, Vol. 19 (2006).
1262 Clark, "Law, Politics and Pragmatism: The ICC and Case Selection in the Democratic Republic of Congo and Uganda", *op. cit.*
1263 Nick Grono and Adam O'Brien, "Justice in Conflict? The ICC and Peace Processes", in Nicholas Waddell and Phil Clark (editors), *Courting Conflict? Justice, Peace and the ICC in Africa*, Royal African Society, London, March 2008. Nick Grono is Vice President for Advocacy and Operations at the ICG. He has responsibility for the operation of all programmes and executive oversight of Crisis Group's operations, research unit, media and IT. He also coordinates the ICG's advocacy efforts worldwide and leads Crisis Group's work on ICC-related issues. Adam O'Brien was the ICG's Uganda analyst from 2006 to 2008. He previously worked with *Monitor* publications in Kampala. O'Brien has written widely on conflict and justice issues in northern Uganda. He is a graduate of the Temple University Beasley School of Law.
1264 Jess Bravin, "Justice Delayed. For Global Court, Ugandan Rebels Prove Tough Test", *The Wall Street Journal*, 8 June 2006.
1265 "ICC Hopes for Uganda Trial in 6 Months, Then Congo", Reuters, 26 January 2005, available at: <www.globalpolicy.org/intljustice/icc/2005/0126ugandatrial.htm>.
1266 Bravin, "Justice Delayed. For Global Court, Ugandan Rebels Prove Tough Test", *op. cit.*
1267 See "Joint Statement by ICC Chief Prosecutor and the visiting Delegation of Lango, Acholi, Iteso and Madi Community Leaders from Northern Uganda", The Hague, 16 April 2005, available at <http://www.icc-cpi.int/press/pressreleases/102.html>.
1268 Bravin, "Justice Delayed. For Global Court, Ugandan Rebels Prove Tough Test", *op. cit.*
1269 See, ICC, "Warrant of Arrest Unsealed Against Five LRA Commanders", press release, OTP, 14 October 2005, available at <http://www.icc-cpi.int/press/pressreleases/114.html>, ICC, "Pre-Trial Chamber II: Warrant of Arrest for Joseph Kony Issued On 8 July 2005 As Amended On 27 September 2005", available online at <http://www.icc-cpi.int/library/cases/ICC-02-04-01-05-53_English.pdf>; ICC, "Pre-Trial Chamber II: Warrant of Arrest for Raska Lukwiya", OTP, available online at <http://www.icc-cpi.int/library/cases/ICC-02-04-01-05-55_English.pdf>; ICC, "Pre-Trial Chamber II: Warrant of Arrest for Okot Odhiambo", OTP, available online at <http://www.icc-cpi.int/library/

cases/ICC-02-04-01-05-56_English.pdf>; OTP, ICC, "Pre-Trial Chamber II: Warrant of Arrest for Dominic Ongwen", OTP, available online at <http://www.icc-cpi.int/library/cases/ICC-02-04-01-05-57_English.pdf>. Kony is charged with twelve counts of crimes against humanity, including murder, enslavement, sexual enslavement, rape, and "inhumane acts", and twenty-one counts of war crimes, including murder, cruel treatment of civilians, directing an attack against a civilian population, pillaging, inducing rape, and the forced enlistment of children; the other LRA commanders are accused of crimes against humanity and war crimes, ranging from four to thirty-two counts. Lukwiya and Otti have reportedly been killed since the warrants were issued: See, Trial Watch, "Vincent Otti", available online at <http://www.trial-ch.org/en/trial-watch/profile/db/facts/vincent_otti_395.html>; and Trial Watch, "Raska Lukwiya", available online at <http://www.trial-ch.org/en/trial-watch/profile/db/facts/%20raska_lukwiya_396.html>.

1270 Jim Lobe, "Historic ICC Arrest Warrants Evoke Praise, Concern", Inter Press Service, 14 October 2005, available at <http://www.ipsnews.net/print.asp?idnews=30640>.
1271 Samuel Okiror Egadu, "International Justice Must Apply in Uganda", Institute for War & Peace Reporting, 28 August 2007, available at <http://www.globalpolicy.org/component/content/article/164/28643.html>.
1272 Bravin, "Justice Delayed. For Global Court, Ugandan Rebels Prove Tough Test", *op. cit.*
1273 *Ibid.*
1274 Paul Seils and Marieke Wierda, "The International Criminal Court and Conflict Mediation", the International Center for Transitional Justice, June 2005, available at <http://www.ictj.org/images/content/1/1/119.pdf>. See, also, Human Rights Watch, "Courting History. The Landmark International Criminal Court's First Years", New York, July 2008 available at < http://www.hrw.org/en/reports/2008/07/10/courting-history>, p.42.
1275 Michael Otim and Marieke Wierda, "Justice at Juba: International Obligations and Local Demands in Northern Uganda", in Nicholas Waddell and Phil Clark (editors), *Courting Conflict? Justice, Peace and the ICC in Africa*, Royal African Society, London, March 2008. See, also, concerns outlined in "Courting History. The Landmark International Criminal Court's First Years", Human Rights Watch, New York, July 2008 available at < http://www.hrw.org/en/reports/2008/07/10/courting-history>.
1276 Nick Grono and Adam O'Brien, "Exorcising the Ghost of the ICC", *The Monitor* (Uganda), 31 October 2006, available at <http://www.crisisgroup.org/home/index.cfm?id=4483&l=1>.
1277 See, for example, studies by Human Rights Watch, "Uganda: Launch Independent Inquiry into Killings", Human Rights Watch news release, May 8, 2011, available at <http://www.hrw.org/news/2011/05/08/uganda-launch-independent-inquiry-killings>; Human Rights Watch, "Violence Instead of Vigilance: Torture and Illegal Detention by Uganda's Rapid Response Unit", March 2011, available at <http://www.hrw.org/en/reports/2011/03/23/violence-instead-vigilance>; Human Rights Watch, "Uganda: Investigate Use of Lethal Force during Riots", news release, 1 October 2009, available at <http://www.hrw.org/news/2009/10/01/uganda-troops-killed unarmed-people-riot-period>; Human Rights Watch, "Open Secret: Illegal Detention and Torture by the Joint Anti-terrorism Task Force in Uganda", April 2009, available at <http://www.hrw.org/en/reports/2009/04/08/open-secret-0>; Human Rights Watch, "Get the Gun: Human Rights Violations by Uganda's National Army in Law Enforcement Operations in Karamoja Region", September 2007, available at <http://www.hrw.org/en/reports/2007/09/10/get-gun>.
1278 Clark, "Law, Politics and Pragmatism: The ICC and Case Selection in the Democratic Republic of Congo and Uganda", *op. cit.*
1279 Nick Grono and Adam O'Brien, "Justice in Conflict? The ICC and Peace Processes", in Nicholas Waddell and Phil Clark (editors), *Courting Conflict? Justice, Peace and the ICC in Africa*, Royal African Society, London, March 2008.

1280 H. Abigail Moy, "The International Criminal Court's Arrest Warrants and Uganda's Lord's Resistance Army: Renewing the Debate over Amnesty and Complementarity", *Harvard Human Rights Journal*, Vol. 19 (2006).
1281 Human Rights Watch pointed to "Armed Activities on the Territory of the Congo (Democratic Republic of Congo v. Uganda)", ICJ, judgment, ICJ reports 2005, p. 168, http://www.icj-cij.org/docket/files/116/10455.pdf, pp. 239–45, cited in "Unfinished Business. Closing Gaps in the Selection of ICC Cases", Human Rights Watch, September 2011, note 24, p. 13, available at <http://www.hrw.org/sites/default/files/reports/icc0911webwcover.pdf>.
1282 Human Rights Watch, "Unfinished Business. Closing Gaps in the Selection of ICC Cases", September 2011, available at <http://www.hrw.org/sites/default/files/reports/icc0911webwcover.pdf>. See, also. Human Rights Watch, *Uprooted and Forgotten*, pp. 13, 24–37, 62-71; see also Chris Dolan, *Social Torture, The Case of Northern Uganda 1986–2006*, Berghahn Books, New York, 2009; Sverker Finnstrom, *Living with bad surroundings: war, history, and everyday moments in northern Uganda*, Duke University Press, Durham, 2008.
1283 Jacqueline Geis and Alex Mundt, "When to Indict? The Impact of Timing International Criminal Indictments on Peace Processes and Humanitarian Action", *op. cit.*
1284 *Ibid.*
1285 Clark, "Law, Politics and Pragmatism: The ICC and Case Selection in the Democratic Republic of Congo and Uganda", *op. cit.*
1286 See, for example, Human Rights Watch, "Courting History", *op. cit.*, p. 42; *Benchmarks for Justice for Serious Crimes in Northern Uganda*, 2 September 2008, available at <http://www.hrw.org/en/news/2008/09/01/benchmarks-justice-serious-crimes-northernuganda>, pp. 24–25, 33, 44; *Uprooted and Forgotten*, p. 57.
1287 Human Rights Watch, "Unfinished Business. Closing Gaps in the Selection of ICC Cases", *op. cit.*
1288 *Ibid.*, p. 26.
1289 William Schabas, "'Complementarity in Practice': Some Uncomplimentary Thoughts", a presentation at the Twentieth Anniversary Conference of the International Society for the Reform of Criminal Law, Vancouver, 23 June 2007, available at <http://www.isrcl.org/Papers/2007/Schabas.pdf>.
1290 Human Rights Watch, "Unfinished Business. Closing Gaps in the Selection of ICC Cases", *op. cit.*, p. 26.
1291 Rebecca J. Hamilton, "Closing ICC Investigations: A second bite at the cherry for complementarity?", Research Working Paper Series, Human Rights Program, Harvard Law School, May 2012, available at <http://www.law.harvard.edu/programs/hrp/documents/Hamilton.pdf>.
1292 Nick Grono and Adam O'Brien, "Exorcising the Ghost of the ICC", *The Monitor* (Uganda), 31 October 2006, available at <http://www.crisisgroup.org/home/index.cfm?id=4483&l=1>.
1293 See, for example, "Why the ICC Must Stop Impeding Juba Process", *Daily Monitor* (Kampala), 27 July 2007.
1294 "Will ICC prosecutions threaten Ugandan peace process?", Institute for War & Peace Reporting, Africa Report Number 46, 16 November 2005.
1295 "Uganda: Give peace a chance, northern leaders tell ICC", News Integrated Regional Information Networks, UN Office for the Coordination of Humanitarian Affairs, Nairobi, 2 June 2006.
1296 "Uganda: ICC indictments to affect northern peace efforts, says mediator", Integrated Regional Information Networks, UN Office for the Coordination of Humanitarian Affairs, Nairobi, 10 October 2005.
1297 Josefine Volqvartz, "ICC Under Fire Over Uganda Probe", CNN, 23 February 2005, available at <http://www.cnn.com/2005/WORLD/africa/02/23/uganda>.

1298 Helma Chatlani, "Uganda: A Nation in Crisis", *California Western International Law Journal*, Vol. 37, No. 2 (2007), pp. 277–98.
1299 Bravin, "Justice Delayed. For Global Court, Ugandan Rebels Prove Tough Test", *op. cit.*
1300 "African Search for Peace Throws Court into Chaos", *The Guardian* (London), 9 January 2007.
1301 "Uganda's war victims prefer peace over punishment", Reuters, 30 April 2007.
1302 André-Michel Essoungou, "Uganda. Justice or Peace?", *The International Herald Tribune*, 21–22 April 2007.
1303 "Uganda's Government Wants Rebels Tried Locally", *Voice of America*, 12 September 2007.
1304 Cited in Tristan McConnell, "Uganda: Peace vs. Justice", openDemocracy, 14 September 2006, available at <http://www.opendemocracy.net/debates/article.jsp?id=3&debateId=130&articleId=3903>.
1305 Adam O'Brien, "The Impact of International Justice on Local Peace Initiatives: The Case of Northern Uganda", ICG, available at <www.crisisgroup.org/home/index.cfm?id=4927&l=1>.
1306 Michael Otim and Marieke Wierda, "Justice at Juba: International Obligations and Local Demands in Northern Uganda", in Nicholas Waddell and Phil Clark (editors), *Courting Conflict? Justice, Peace and the ICC in Africa*, Royal African Society, London, March 2008.
1307 See, for example, <http://www.amnesty.org.uk/news_details.asp?NewsID=17665> and <http://www.fidh.org/spip.php?article5256>.
1308 See Josephine Volqvartz, "ICC Under Fire over Uganda Probe", *op. cit.*
1309 Branch, *Displacing Human Rights. War and Intervention in northern Uganda*, *op. cit.*, pp. 191–92.
1310 *Ibid.*, p. 191.
1311 *Ibid.*, p. 198.
1312 "Whose Justice? Perceptions of Uganda's Amnesty Act 2000: The Potential for Conflict Resolution and long-term Reconciliation", Working Paper No. 15, Refugee Law Project, Kampala, Uganda, February 2005, available at <http://www.refugeelawproject.org/working_papers/RLP.WP15.pdf>.
1313 Katherine Southwick, "Investigating War in Northern Uganda: Dilemmas for the International Criminal Court", *Yale Journal of International Affairs*, Vol. 1 (2005), pp. 105–19, p. 113.
1314 Cited in Josefine Volqvartz, "ICC Under Fire Over Uganda Probe", Global Policy Forum, 23 February 2005.
1315 "Africa and the International Criminal Court", Council on Foreign Relations, New York, 17 November 2006.
1316 H. Abigail Moy, "The International Criminal Court's Arrest Warrants and Uganda's Lord's Resistance Army: Renewing the Debate over Amnesty and Complementarity", *Harvard Human Rights Journal*, Vol. 19 (2006).
1317 Nick Grono and Adam O'Brien, "Justice in Conflict? The ICC and Peace Processes", in Nicholas Waddell and Phil Clark (editors), *Courting Conflict? Justice, Peace and the ICC in Africa*, Royal African Society, London, March 2008.
1318 See Alex Atuhaire, "LRA Probe Still On, Says AI", *The Monitor* (Kampala), 20 November 2004. Amnesty International reported that the President made a statement encouraging LRA members to "engage in internal reconciliation mechanisms put in place by the Acholi community such as *mataput* or blood settlement", and mentioned the possibility of withdrawing his recommendation as an incentive for LRA cooperation, press release, Amnesty International, "Uganda: Government Cannot Prevent the International Criminal Court from Investigating Crimes", 16 November 2004, available at <http://web.amnesty.org/library/Index/ENGAFR590082004?open&of=ENG-385>.
1319 Alex K. Kriksciun, "Uganda's Response to International Criminal Court Arrest Warrants: A Misguided Approach?", Tulane Journal of International & Comparative Law, No. 1 (2007), pp. 213–14.

1320 "Might the Lord's Resisters Give Up?", The Economist, 15 March 2008.
1321 See press release, Amnesty International, "Uganda: Government Cannot Prevent the International Criminal Court from Investigating Crimes", 16 November 2004, available at <http://web.amnesty.org/library/Index/ENGAFR590082004?open&of=ENG-385>.
1322 Richard Goldstone, "The Future of International Justice, Notes for the UN Lecture", nd, available at <untreaty.un.org/cod/avl/pdf/ls/Goldstone_LectureNotes.pdf>.
1323 Summary report, "The Relationship Between International Criminal Justice and Conflict Resolution: Focus on the International Criminal Court", Joan B. Kroc Institute for Peace & Justice, University of San Diego, 12–13 December 2005, available online at <http://peace.sandiego.edu/documents/reports/ConferenceReports/wpm/2005/Report.pdf>.
1324 Nick Grono and Adam O'Brien, "Exorcising the Ghost of the ICC", *The Monitor* (Uganda), 31 October 2006, available at <http://www.crisisgroup.org/home/index.cfm?id=4483&l=1>.
1325 "Uganda defies war crimes court over indictments", *The Guardian*, 12 March 2008.
1326 Tom Ginsberg, "The Clash of Commitments at the International Criminal Court", *Chicago Journal of International Law*, Public Law Working Paper No. 251, Center on Law and Globalization Research Paper No. 09-03, University of Chicago, 18 November 2008.
1327 "Interview: Luis Moreno-Ocampo, ICC Prosecutor", *The Africa Report*, 21 September 2009, available at <http://www.theafricareport.com/index.php?option=com_content&view=article&id=3281793&catid=54>.

Notes to Chapter Nineteen

1328 Human Rights Watch, "Unfinished Business. Closing Gaps in the Selection of ICC Cases", September 2011, p. 21, available at <http://www.hrw.org/sites/default/files/reports/icc0911webwcover.pdf>.
1329 ICC, "Prosecutor Receives Referral of the Situation in the Democratic Republic of Congo", OTP, 19 April 2004.
1330 ICC, *The Prosecutor v. Thomas Lubanga Dyilo*, judgment pursuant to Article 74 of the statute, ICC-01/04-01/06-2842, T.Ch. I, 14 March 2012.
1331 Lubanga was arrested by Congolese authorities and charged with genocide, war crimes, and crimes against humanity, but had not been brought to trial when the ICC warrant was issued. See, "D. R. Congo: ICC Arrest First Step to Justice", Human Rights Watch, 17 March 2006.
1332 ICC, *The Prosecutor v. Thomas Lubanga Dyilo*, document containing the charges, Article 61(3)(a) (public redacted version), August 28, 2006.
1333 "Intermediaries" were organisations and individuals said to serve as a link between the Prosecutor and possible witnesses.
1334 Geoffrey Robertson, *Crimes Against Humanity. The Struggle for Global Justice*, op. cit., p. 551.
1335 ICC, "Situation in the Democratic Republic of the Congo in the case of the Prosecutor v Thomas Lubanga Dyilo", judgment pursuant to Article 74 of the statute, ICC-01/04-01/06, 14 March 2012, available at <http://www.icc-cpi.int/iccdocs/doc/doc1379838.pdf "Democratic Republic of the Congo – Lubanga case>.
1336 Kevin Jon Heller, "The ICC Stays Lubanga's Prosecution – and May Let Him Walk", *Opinio Juris*, 16 June 2008, available at <http://opiniojuris.org/2008/06/16/the-icc-stays-lubangas-prosecution-and-may-let-him-walk/>.
1337 ICC, "Decision on the consequences of non-disclosure of exculpatory materials covered by Article 54(3)(e) agreements and the application to stay the prosecution of the accused, together with certain other issues raised at the Status Conference on 10 June 2008", 13 June 2008.

1338 "ICC's Ocampo Defends His Africa-Only Focus, His Strategy In Question", *Inner City Press*, 17 July 2008, available at <http://www.innercitypress.com/icc1africa071708.html>.

1339 "At UN, Doubts Grow Of ICC's Moreno-Ocampo, on Lubanga and Uganda Abuses", *Inner City Press*, 16 September 2008, available at <http://www.innercitypress.com/icc3ocampo091608.html>.

1340 Robert Marquand, "Global court starts with a fumble. Warlord grins. Witness recants testimony during start of Congo militia leader Thomas Lubanga's trial", *Christian Science Monitor*, 30 January 2009, available at <http://www.csmonitor.com/2009/0130/p01s01-wogn.html>.

1341 See, ICC, "Decision on the release of Thomas Lubanga Dyilo", 2 July 2008; and ICC, "Trial Chamber I ordered the release of Thomas Lubanga Dyilo – Implementation of the decision is pending", 16 June 2008.

1342 See, ICC, "Stay of proceedings in the Lubanga case is lifted – trial provisionally scheduled for 26 January 2009", 18 November 2008; "Road cleared for start of ICC's long-delayed first trial", *Agence France-Presse*, 18 November 2008; "Allegations Against Prosecutor May Harm Bashir Genocide Case", *New York Sun*, available at <http://www.nysun.com/foreign/allegations-against-prosecutor-may-harm-bashir/82165/>; "The Controversial Actions of the ICC Prosecutor: a Crisis of Maturity?", available at <http://www.haguejusticeportal.net/eCache/DEF/9/763.TGFuZz1FTg.html>.

1343 Lisa Clifford, "Ocampo Underwhelms in Landmark Trial", Institute for War & Peace Reporting, 29 January 2009, available at <http://www.iwpr.net/?p=acr&s=f&o=349621&apc_state=heniacr2009>.

1344 "Lubanga's lawyers denounce 'unfair' ICC trial", Radio Nederland Wereldomroep, 27 January 2009, available at <http://static.rnw.nl/migratie/www.rnw.nl/internationaljustice/icc/DRC/090127-lubanga-day2-redirected>.

1345 Robert Marquand, "Global court starts with a fumble. Warlord grins. Witness recants testimony during start of Congo militia leader Thomas Lubanga's trial", *Christian Science Monitor*, 30 January 2009, available at <http://www.csmonitor.com/2009/0130/p01s01-wogn.html>.

1346 "Lubanga Trial, Week 1: Prosecutors Stumble out of the Gate", Lubanga trial at the ICC website, 30 January 2009, available at <http://www.lubangatrial.org/2009/01/30/lubanga-trial-week-1-prosecutors-stumble-out-of-the-gate/>.

1347 See, "Communications Strategy Trial of Thomas Lubanga" at <http://www2.icc-cpi.int/NR/rdonlyres/F8CB60B0-731D-41DB-9705-B45E20F0BE66/279608/Outreach_SP_Lubanga_ENGpdf.pdf>. See, ICC, "Communications Strategy Trial of Thomas Lubanga" at <http://www2.icc-cpi.int/NR/rdonlyres/F8CB60B0-731D-41DB-9705-B45E20F0BE66/279608/Outreach_SP_Lubanga_ENGpdf.pdf>.

1348 "First Challenges: An examination of recent landmark developments at the International Criminal Court", International Bar Association ICC monitoring and outreach programme, June 2009.

1349 Joshua Rozenberg, "Lubanga Trial: More Delays", *Standpoint*, 3 October 2009 available at <http://www.standpointmag.co.uk/node/2256>.

1350 These figures are taken from ICC document ICC-ASP/7/25, and were current as of 29 October 2008. However, consistent and accurate information on the numbers of victims applying and accepted to participate is not readily available. There are information gaps within and between the court's own documents and between the statistics for victims quoted by different sections of the court.

1351 See, "Report of the International Criminal Court", A/64/356, General Assembly, 17 September 2009, available at <http://www.icc-cpi.int/NR/rdonlyres/1BC01710-9C42-44AC-8B18-85EE2A8876EB/281210/A_64_356_ENG2.pdf>, and ICC, "17th Diplomatic Briefing of the International Criminal Court", remarks of Silvana Arbia, Registrar, ICC, The Hague, Wednesday 4 November 2009, available at <http://www.

icc-cpi.int/NR/rdonlyres/B2000A0D-2159-40E6-A24F-8952FF34D3B4/281190/Registrar_Statement_DB_03112009ENG.pdf>.

1352 Rachel Irwin, "Special Report: Lubanga Trial Transformed by Victims", Institute for War & Peace Reporting, AR No. 228, 4 September 2009, available at <http://www.iwpr.net/?p=acr&s=f&o=355616&apc_state=henpacr>.

1353 "Minority opinion on the 'Decision giving notice to the parties and participants that the legal characterisation of facts may be subject to change in accordance with Regulation 55(2) of the Regulations of the Court of 17 July 2009'", ICC, ICC-01/04-01/06, 31 July 2009, available at <http://www.icc-cpi.int/iccdocs/doc/doc718895.pdf>.

1354 "Lubanga defense case delayed", the Lubanga trial at the ICC website, 14 October 2009, available at <http://www.lubangatrial.org/2009/10/14/lubanga-defense-case-delayed/>.

1355 Irwin, "Special Report: Lubanga Trial Transformed by Victims", *op. cit.*

1356 "Bench-mark", *The Economist*, 14 March 2012, available at <http://www.economist.com/blogs/baobab/2012/03/international-criminal-court?zid=317&ah=8a47fc455a44945580198768fad0fa41>.

1357 Irwin, "Special Report: Lubanga Trial Transformed by Victims", *op. cit.*

1358 *Ibid.*

1359 Joshua Rozenberg, "Lubanga Trial: More Delays", *Standpoint*, 3 October 2009 available at <http://www.standpointmag.co.uk/node/2256>.

1360 Human Rights Watch, "Courting History. The Landmark International Criminal Court's First Years", New York, July 2008, available at <http://www.hrw.org/en/reports/2008/07/10/courting-history>, pp. 20–21. See, also, Human Rights Watch, "A Summary of Case Law of the International Criminal Court", March 2007, available at <http://hrw.org/backgrounder/ij/icc0307/icc0307web.pdf>.

1361 "First Challenges: An examination of recent landmark developments at the International Criminal Court", International Bar Association ICC monitoring and outreach programme, June 2009. See, also, Lubanga trial transcript 138, p. 21 lines 14–23 at <http://www.icc-cpi.int/iccdocs/doc/doc649086.pdf>.

1362 *Ibid.*

1363 ICC, "Redacted Decision on the Prosecution's Urgent Request for Variation of the Time-Limit to Disclose the Identity of Intermediary 143 or Alternatively to Stay Proceedings Pending Further Consultations with the VWU", 8 July 2010, ICC-01/04-01/06, available at <http://www.icc-cpi.int/iccdocs/doc/doc906146.pdf>.

1364 Ralph Henham and Mark Findlay, *Exploring the Boundaries of International Criminal Justice*, Ashgate, 2011, pp. 131–32.

1365 ICC, ICC-01/04-01/06-2434-Red2, para 2.

1366 Joshua Rozenberg, "Contempt for Court", *Standpoint*, November 2010, available at <http://standpointmag.co.uk/node/3520/full>.

1367 *Ibid.*

1368 ICC, Judgment on the appeal of the Prosecutor against the decision of Trial Chamber I of 8 July 2010 entitled "Decision on the Prosecution's Urgent Request for Variation of Time-Limit to Disclose the Identity of Intermediary 143 or Alternatively to Stay Proceedings Pending Further Consultations with the VWU", ICC-01/04-01/06-2582, 8 October 2010, available at <http://www.icc-cpi.int/iccdocs/doc/doc947768.pdf>. See also, <ICC-01/04-01/06-2690-Conf, ICC-01/04-01/06-2690-Red2>, 23 February 2011 (public redacted version on 7 March 2011), at <http://www.icc-cpi.int/iccdocs/doc/doc1036342.pdf>. See, also, Rachael Irwin, "Witness Admits to False Statements", <www.lubangatrial.org>, 19 June 2009; and "Defense Witnesses Claim ICC Agents Concocted Evidence", allafrica.com, 15 February 2010.

1369 ICC, judgment pursuant to Article 74 of the statute, ICC-01/04-01/06-2842, 14 March 2012, available at <http://www.icc-cpi.int/iccdocs/doc/doc1379838.pdf>.

1370 See, ICC, ICC-01/04-01/06-2433, 12 May 2010.
1371 ICC, ICC-01/04-01/06-2434-Red2, para. 25, citing ICC, ICC-01/04-01/06-T-236-CONF-ENG ET, p. 20, line 19 to p. 22, line 18.
1372 On 28 January 2009, the first prosecution witness, witness 298, recanted his testimony, stating "what he had said that morning did not come from him but from someone else". ICC, ICC-01/04-01/06-2434-Red2, para. 7, citing ICC, ICC-01/04-01/06-T-110-CONF-ENG, p. 40 line 10.
1373 ICC, ICC-01/04-01/06-2657.
1374 ICC, ICC-01/04-01/06-2690-Red2, para. 189.
1375 ICC, ICC-01/04-01/06-2842, paras. 124–77.
1376 See ICC, ICC-01/04-01/06-2434-Red2, para. 135; and ICC, ICC-01/04-01/06-2434-Red2, para. 146.
1377 ICC, ICC-01/04-01/06-Rule68Deposition-Red2-ENG, p. 14 lines 22–23; p. 15 lines 13–25; p. 16 lines 1–4.
1378 ICC, ICC-01/04-01/06-Rule68Deposition-Red2-ENG, p. 15 lines 1–12.
1379 ICC, ICC-01/04-01/06-2842, para. 144.
1380 ICC, ICC-01/04-01/06-2842, para. 147.
1381 ICC, ICC-01/04-01/06-2842, paras. 160–61.
1382 ICC, ICC-01/04-01/06-2842, para. 170.
1383 ICC, ICC-01/04-01/06-2842, para. 175.
1384 ICC, ICC-01/04-01/06-2842, para. 168.
1385 ICC, ICC-01/04-01/06-2842, para. 291.
1386 See, ICC, ICC-01/04-01/06-2517-Red, para. 8; and ICC, ICC-01/04-01/06-2517-Red, para. 31.
1387 On 28 January 2009, the prosecution's first witness, witness 298, recanted his testimony, stating "what he had said that morning did not come from him but from someone else". See, ICC, ICC-01/04-01/06-2434-Red2, para. 7, citing ICC, ICC-01/04-01/06-T-110-CONF-ENG, p. 40, line 10.
1388 See, ICC, ICC-01/04-01/06-2842, paras. 442–45; and ICC, ICC-01/04-01/06-2842, para. 483.
1389 Including alleged former child soldier witnesses 15 and 38, upon both of whose testimony the Trial Chamber relied in part. See, ICC, ICC-01/04-01/06-2842, paras. 295, 296.
1390 ICC, ICC-01/04-01/06-2842, para. 302.
1391 ICC, see ICC-01/04-01/06-2842, paras. 312–21.
1392 See ICC, ICC-01/04-01/06-2842, para. 369.
1393 ICC, ICC-01/04-01/06-2842, para. 374.
1394 ICC-01/04-01/06-2842, para. 482.
1395 In "Lubanga Judgement – the Prosecution's investigation and use of intermediaries", the Women's Initiatives for Gender Justice provided details of why the court dismissed almost all of witnesses presented by the prosecution. See, "Legal Eye on the ICC", special edition number 3, August 2012, available at <http://www.iccwomen.org/news/docs/WI-LegalEye8-12-FULL/LegalEye8-12.html>. Witness 7 – introduced to the OTP by intermediary 143; authorised to participate as a victim. He claimed to have been recruited into the UPC when under the age of fifteen, but gave contradictory evidence about his date of birth, name and the name of his father, and concerning information pertaining to his alleged service with the UPC. Documentary evidence contradicted his testimony regarding his school attendance, and the names of his family members. Witness 8 – introduced to the OTP by intermediary 143; authorised to participate as a victim. He claimed to have been recruited into the UPC when under the age of fifteen and to be the cousin of P-0007. He gave contradictory evidence about his date of birth and the names of his parents, and documentary evidence contradicted his testimony regarding his school attendance and the

names of his family members. The account of his military service was contradictory and "implausible". Witness 10 – introduced to the OTP by intermediary 143; authorised to participate as a victim. She claimed to have been recruited into the UPC when under the age of fifteen, but gave conflicting testimony as to her age and her service, including the name of the commander whom she served. Witness 11 – introduced to the OTP by intermediary 143; authorised to participate as a victim. He claimed to have been recruited into the UPC when under the age of fifteen. Substantial discrepancies arose concerning his name, date of birth, schooling, the alleged death of his mother (she is alive) and the dates and circumstances of his joining the UPC. His evidence was significantly contradicted by defence witness D-0024, a close family member. Witness 15 – introduced to the OTP by intermediary 316. At the outset of his testimony, he indicated he was instructed to lie by intermediary 316. He was recalled by the judges; and testified at great length about how intermediary 316 directed him to falsify his testimony. He stated that he did not serve as part of the UPC. Witness 157 – contact with this witness was re-established by intermediary 321. The chamber found his account of his military service, about which there was contradictory evidence, too vague to rely upon. Witness 213 – introduced to the OTP by intermediary 321. He gave inconsistent testimony concerning his name, schooling, alleged abduction and service with the UPC. Witness 293 – introduced to the OTP by intermediary 321. She is witness P-0294's mother, and testified concerning the year of his birth, which was contradicted by documentary evidence. Witness 294 – introduced to the OTP by intermediary 321. He gave inconsistent and incorrect testimony about his age, the centre with which he went through demobilisation and his mother's name. The chamber found that he used the details of his brother's military service to contribute to his own account. Witness 297 – introduced to the OTP by intermediary 321. He provided inconsistent and false testimony concerning his schooling, the name and alleged death of his mother (she is alive), his alleged military service and the age at which he allegedly served. Witness 298 – introduced to the OTP by intermediary 321; participated as a victim in the proceedings. He was the first witness called to give evidence, and began by stating that he had given false statements to the prosecution as he had been promised benefits for doing so by intermediary 321. He provided inconsistent testimony concerning his age and schooling. There were also inconsistencies in the testimonies of P-0298 and P-0299 (his father) over the death of his mother (she is still alive). The chamber found he had lied concerning his military service. Witness 299 – P-0298's father; participated as a victim in the proceedings. He testified concerning his son's age, military service and the fact that his mother is alive (although he stated that he told his son she was deceased). He indicated that his son did not take the initiative to demobilise, but, rather, was picked up off the street by an NGO. The chamber declined to rely on his testimony as it did not rely on his son's testimony. The chamber found witness 38 to be credible.

1396 ICC, ICC-01/04-01/06-2842, paras. 480, 481.
1397 See, for example, ICC, ICC-01/04-01/06-2842, paras. 243, 244, 262, 284, 365, 418, 435.
1398 "First Challenges: An examination of recent landmark developments at the International Criminal Court", IBA ICC Monitoring and Outreach Programme, June 2009. See, also, Lubanga trial transcript 138, p. 21, lines 14–23 at <http://www.icc-cpi.int/iccdocs/doc/doc649086.pdf>.
1399 *Ibid.*
1400 See, "Lubanga Trial Adjourned Over Transcription Problems", the Lubanga trial, 16 February 2010, available at <http://www.lubangatrial.org/2010/02/16/lubanga-trial-adjourned-over-transcription-problems/>, and "Lubanga Trial Suspended over Transcription Errors", <warcrimesreparations.info>, 16 February 2010, available at <http://warcrimesreparations.info/blog/2010/02/16/lubanga-trial-suspended-over-transcription-errors/>.

1401 Cited in David Bosco, "The International Criminal Court's first sentence", *Foreign Policy*, 10 July 2012, available at <http://bosco.foreignpolicy.com/posts/2012/07/10/the_international_criminal_courts_first_sentence>.
1402 "Thomas Lubango Dyilo is sentenced to 14 years, as M23 advances on Goma", Armed Groups and International Law, 11 July 2012, available at< http://armedgroups-internationallaw.org/2012/07/11/thomas-lubango-dyilo-is-sentenced-to-14-years-as-m23-advances-on-goma/>.
1403 ICC, "Combined Factsheet: Situation in the Democratic Republic of the Congo", Germain Katanga and Mathieu Ngudjolo Chui, 27 June 2008. Their cases were joined in March 2008.
1404 ICC, "Katanga and Ngudjolo Chui case: ICC Trial Chamber II severs charges; Verdict on Mathieu Ngudjolo Chui to be issued on 18 December 2012", press release, 21 November 2012, ICC-CPI-20121121-PR856, available at <http://icc-cpi.int/en_menus/icc/press%20 and%20media/press%20releases/news%20and%20highlights/Pages/pr856.aspx>.
1405 "DR Congo: Mathieu Ngudjolo Chui acquitted of war crimes by ICC", BBC News Africa, 18 December 2012, available at <http://www.bbc.co.uk/news/world-africa-20766597>.
1406 "Insight: International court's credibility in dock over failed prosecutions", Reuters, 19 March 2013, available at <http://news.yahoo.com/insight-international-courts-credibility-dock-over-failed-prosecutions-124740019.html>.
1407 *Ibid.*
1408 *Ibid.*
1409 See, *Prosecutor*, White Pine Pictures, 2010, available at <http://www.whitepinepictures.com/all-titles/ijd-the-prosecutor/>.
1410 Alex de Waal, "Moreno Ocampo's Coup de Théâtre", Making Sense of Darfur, 29 July 2008, available at <http://blogs.ssrc.org/darfur/2008/07/29/moreno-ocampos-coup-de-theatre/>.
1411 ICC, Pre-Trial Chamber I, "Decision on the confirmation of charges", ICC-01/04-01/10-465.
1412 ICC, Appeals Chamber, "Judgment on the appeal of the Prosecutor against the decision of Pre-Trial Chamber I of 16 December 2011 entitled 'Decision on the confirmation of charges'", ICC-01/04-01/10-514 (OA 4).
1413 ICC, the Prosecutor vs. Jean Bosco Ntaganda, Warrant of Arrest, 22 August 2006. The warrant states that Ntaganda is "believed to be" a Rwandan national.
1414 "Peace Before Justice, Congo Minister Tells ICC", *Agence France-Presse*, 12 February 2009.
1415 *Ibid.*
1416 *Inner City Press*, 5 June 2009, available at <http://www.innercitypress.com/icc7ocampo060509.html>.
1417 "At UN, Questions of Moreno Ocampo's Competence and Silence on Congo's Bosco", *Inner City Press*, 3 June 2009, available at <http://www.innercitypress.com/icc6ocampo060409.html>.
1418 "Congo's 'Terminator': Kabila calls for Ntaganda arrest", BBC News. 11 April 2012.
1419 Human Rights Watch, "DR Congo: M23 Rebels Committing War Crimes", 11 September 2012, available at <http://www.hrw.org/print/news/2012/09/11/dr-congo-m23-rebels-committing-war-crimes>.
1420 ICC, "Statement: ICC Prosecutor on New Applications for Warrants of Arrest, DRC Situation", 14 May 2012, available at <http://www.icc-cpi.int/menus/icc/situations%20 and%20cases/situations/situation%20icc%200104/press%20releases/otpstatement14052012>.
1421 ICC, ICC-01/04-613.
1422 ICC, ICC-01/04-613, para. 4.
1423 ICC, ICC-01/04-613, para. 4.
1424 ICC, ICC-01/04-616-Red2.
1425 ICC, ICC-01/04-01/12-1-Red.

1426 ICC, "Situation in the Democratic Republic of the Congo in the case of the Prosecutor v. Sylvestre Mudacumura, Public redacted version, Decision on the Prosecutor's Application under Article 58", 13 July 2012, ICC-01/04-01/12, available at <http://www2.icc-cpi.int/iccdocs/doc/doc1441410.pdf>.
1427 Phil Clark, "Law, Politics and Pragmatism: The ICC and Case Selection in the Democratic Republic of Congo and Uganda", in Nicholas Waddell and Phil Clark (editors), *Courting Conflict? Justice, Peace and the ICC in Africa*, Royal African Society, London, March 2008.
1428 *Ibid*.
1429 *Ibid*.
1430 *Ibid*.
1431 *Ibid*.
1432 "Lubanga Trial Cases doubt over ICC's capacity to provide fair trials", ICC Watch, London, 2 July 2009, available at <http://www.iccwatch.org/pressrelease_2july09.html>.
1433 Clark, "Law, Politics and Pragmatism: The ICC and Case Selection in the Democratic Republic of Congo and Uganda", *op. cit.*
1434 Human Rights Watch, *Courting History. The Landmark International Criminal Court's First Years*, *op. cit.*
1435 Marlies Glasius, "What is global justice and who is it for? The ICC's first five years", Opendemocracy, 22 July 2008, available at <http://www.opendemocracy.net/article/globalisation/international_justice/the-iccs-first-five-years>.
1436 "Africa and the International Criminal Court", Council on Foreign Relations, New York, 17 November 2006.
1437 *Ibid*.
1438 Human Rights Watch, *Courting History. The Landmark International Criminal Court's First Years*, *op. cit.*, p. 65.
1439 Human Rights Watch, "Unfinished Business. Closing Gaps in the Selection of ICC Cases", Human Rights Watch, September 2011, p. 11, available at <http://www.hrw.org/sites/default/files/reports/icc0911webwcover.pdf>.
1440 *Ibid*, p. 21.
1441 Pascal Kambale and Anna Rotman, "The International Criminal Court and Congo: Examining the Possibilities", Crimes of War Project, October 2004, available at <http://www.crimesofwar.org/africa-mag/afr_05_kambale.html>.
1442 ICC, Statement by Luis Moreno Ocampo, press conference in relation to the surrender to the court of Mr. Thomas Lubanga Dyilo, 18 March 2006.
1443 William Schabas, "'Complementarity in Practice': Some Uncomplimentary Thoughts", a presentation at the Twentieth Anniversary Conference of the International Society for the Reform of Criminal Law, Vancouver, 23 June 2007, available at <http://www.isrcl.org/Papers/2007/Schabas.pdf>.

Notes to Chapter Twenty

1444 Human Rights Watch, "Unfinished Business. Closing Gaps in the Selection of ICC Cases", September 2011, *op. cit.*
1445 ICC, "Prosecutor Receives Referral Concerning Central African Republic", OTP press release, 7 January 2005.
1446 ICC, "Prosecutor Opens Investigation in the Central African Republic", 22 May 2007, available at <http://www.icc-cpi.int/menus/icc/press%20and%20media/press%20releases/2007/prosecutor%20opens%20investigation%20in%20the%20central%20african%20republic?lan=en-GB>.

1447   See, Charles Onana, *Al-Bashir & Darfour, La Contre-Enquête, Menaces sur le Soudan et révélations sur le Procureur Ocampo,* Editions Duboiris, 2010, pp. 436–58.

1448   See, for example, International Federation for Human Rights, "War Crimes in the Central African Republic: When the Elephants Fight, the Grass Suffers", February 2003, and Marlies Glasius, "'We Ourselves, We Are Part of the Functioning': The ICC, Victims, and Civil Society in the Central African Republic" *African Affairs,* Vol. 108 (430), 2009, pp. 49–67.

1449   See Human Rights Watch, "ICC: Q&A on the Trial against Jean-Pierre Bemba", November 2010, available at <http://www.hrw.org/en/news/2010/11/18/bemba-qa#_Toc278190573>.

1450   Human Rights Watch, *Courting History. The Landmark International Criminal Court's First Years, op. cit.,* p. 134.

1451   Human Rights Watch, "Unfinished Business. Closing Gaps in the Selection of ICC Cases", *op. cit.*

1452   "Court Urged to Probe Officials: As it begins investigating the CAR conflict, the ICC is facing calls to adopt a more even-handed approach", AR No. 120, Institute for War & Peace Reporting, London, 4 July 2007, available at <http://www.iwpr.net/?p=acr&s=f&o=336779&apc_state=henpacr>.

1453   Human Rights Watch, "State of Anarchy: Rebellion and Abuses against Civilians", Vol. 19, No.14(A), September 2007, available at <http://hrw.org/reports/2007/car0907/.>.

1454   Human Rights Watch, *Courting History. The Landmark International Criminal Court's First Years, op. cit.*

1455   Katy Glassborow, "Court Urged to Probe Officials", Institute for War & Peace Reporting, 4 July 2007.

1456   Wakabi Wairagala, "Central African Probe Found Patassé And Bemba Culpable For Bangui Crimes", 8 April 2011, <www.bembatrial.org>, available at, <http://www.bembatrial.org/2011/04/central-african-probe-found-patasse-and-bemba-culpable-forbangui-crimes/>.

1457   See, for example, Katy Glassborow, "Locals Want Patassé to Face Justice", Institute for War & Peace Reporting, 18 May 2009, available at <http://iwpr.net/report-news/locals-want-patasse-face-justice>.

1458   Human Rights Watch, "Unfinished Business. Closing Gaps in the Selection of ICC Cases", September 2011.

1459   "Central African Republic", <internationalwarcrimesreport>, 4 June 2010, available at <http://internationalwarcrimesreport.wordpress.com/2010/06/04/central-african-republic/>.

1460   *Ibid.*

1461   "Rebels overthrow Central African Republic president, he flees capital as fighters seize palace", Associated Press, 24 March 2013 available at <http://globalnews.ca/news/411392/central-african-republic-president-flees-capital-rebels-seize-presidential-palace/>.

1462   "Coup leader declares himself president, defence minister of Central African Republic", Associated Press, 1 April 2013.

1463   "Raped, plundered, ignored: central Africa state where only killers thrive. The Central African Republic is all but lawless, with just 200 police to guard 4.6m people from rebel gangs who attack women, kill men and recruit children at will. Despite repeated warnings, the international community has done little, even as arms continue to flood into the country." *The Observer,* 27 July 2013, available at <http://www.theguardian.com/world/2013/jul/27/central-african-republic-rebels-seleka>.

1464   "Central African Republic's 'forgotten human rights crisis' worsening", Global News Canada, 16 October 2013, available at <http://globalnews.ca/news/906624/central-african-republics-forgotten-human-rights-crisis-worsening/>.

Notes to Chapter Twenty-one

1465 "A Losing Strategy on War Crimes", *The International Herald Tribune*, 12–13 February 2005. Stéphanie Giry was a legal adviser at the UN and also in private practice. She has written for *Foreign Affairs*, *The New York Times*, *The New Republic*, the *Washington Post*, the *Los Angeles Times*, *Legal Affairs* and Associated Press.
1466 Alex de Waal, "Moreno Ocampo's Coup de Théâtre", Making Sense of Darfur, 29 July 2008, available at <http://blogs.ssrc.org/darfur/2008/07/29/moreno-ocampos-coup-de-theatre/>.
1467 For more background, see, David Hoile, "Darfur: The Road to Peace", European-Sudanese Public Affairs Council, London 2008, available at <http://thesudanwire.com/PDF/DARFUR-road%20to%20peace.pdf>, or David Hoile, "Darfur in Perspective", European-Sudanese Public Affairs Council, London 2007, available at <http://www.darfurinperspective.com/>.
1468 "Darfur Governor Links Khartoum Plot with Rebels", Reuters, 26 September 2004. Ghazi Suleiman is Chairman of the Sudanese Human Rights Group. He has been arrested and detained by the Sudanese government on more than a dozen occasions. He became a SPLM Member of Parliament in 2005.
1469 "Sudan Islamists use Darfur as Battleground", Reuters, 22 September 2004.
1470 See, for example, "US envoy pledges to help Darfur rebels unite", *Agence France-Presse*, 22 August 2009, available at <http://www.google.com/hostednews/afp/article/ALeqM5jILxlz9OznDzPejjA8SQOxBBdqhA>.
1471 Alex de Waal, "Darfur and the failure of the responsibility to protect", *International Affairs*, Royal Institute of International Affairs, London, November 2007. Described by *The Observer* newspaper of London as a "world authority on the country", Dr. de Waal is a human rights advocate who has published widely on Sudan. De Waal is the leading international expert on Darfur. He has been an adviser to the AU during the Darfur peace talks from Abuja 2006 onwards. He is a programme director at the Social Science Research Council (SRRC), engaged in Emergencies and Humanitarian Action, HIV/AIDS and Social Transformation Projects. He is also a Fellow of the Global Equity Initiative at Harvard University, which is a partner in a consortium with the SSRC working on governance issues, and he is Director of Justice Africa, a human-rights organisation based in London. He is editor of the 'African Issues' series with James Currey Publishers. De Waal was a founder and Director of African Rights and Chairman of Mines Advisory Group 1993–98 (co-laureate of the 1997 Nobel Peace Prize). In his twenty-year career, de Waal has studied the social, political and health dimensions of famine, war, genocide and the HIV/AIDS epidemic, especially in the Horn of Africa and the Great Lakes. He has been at the forefront of mobilising African and international responses to these problems. De Waal's books include: *Famine that Kills: Darfur, Sudan, 1984–5* (Oxford University Press, 1989), *Facing Genocide: The Nuba of Sudan* (African Rights, 1995) *Who Fights? Who Cares? War and Humanitarian Action in Africa*, and *AIDS and Power: Why There is No Political Crisis Yet* (Zed, 2006). He is the editor of *War in Darfur and the Search for Peace*, Global Equity Initiative (Harvard and Justice Africa, 2007) and *Islam and Its Enemies in the Horn of Africa* (Indiana, 2004). De Waal earned his doctorate in social anthropology from Oxford University.
1472 Brendan O'Neill, "Darfur: Damned by Pity", *Spiked*, 21 September 2006, available at <http://www.spiked-online.com/index.php?/site/printable/1687/>.
1473 "Sudanese president Bashir charged with Darfur war crimes", *The Guardian*, 4 March 2009, available at <http://www.guardian.co.uk/world/2009/mar/04/omar-bashir-sudan-president-arrest>.
1474 "Death Rates Decline in Darfur", *Los Angeles Times*, 26 August 2007.
1475 Alex de Waal and Julie Flint, "In Darfur, From Genocide to Anarchy", *Washington Post*, 28 August 2007. Flint is another long-standing anti-Khartoum activist. She was a London-

based correspondent for *The Observer* from 1990 to 1992, focusing on the Middle East and the Horn of Africa. Since 1998, she has been a freelance journalist based in London and Beirut, concentrating since 2003 on Darfur.
1476 "Darfur's Outdated Script", *The International Herald Tribune*, 9 July 2007.
1477 "Death Rates Decline in Darfur", *op. cit.*
1478 "Unseen by western hysteria, Darfur edges closer to peace", *The Guardian* (London), 10 August 2007.
1479 "War in Sudan's Darfur 'is over'", BBC News online, 27 August 2009, available at <http://news.bbc.co.uk/1/hi/8224424.stm>.
1480 "Report of the International Commission of Inquiry on Darfur to the United Nations Secretary-General, pursuant to Security Council Resolution 1564 of 18 September 2004", UN, 25 January 2005, available at <http://www.un.org/News/dh/sudan/com_inq_darfur.pdf>. See, also, "Darfur killings not genocide, says UN group", *The Independent* (London), 31 January 2005, available at <http://www.independent.co.uk/news/world/africa/darfur-killings-not-genocide-says-un-group-488977.html>.
1481 Commission of Inquiry to Investigate Alleged Human Rights Violations Committed by Armed Groups in the Darfur States, Government of Sudan, Khartoum, January 2005. Also published as UN Document S/2005/80, 26 January 2005.
1482 "Only Sudanese judiciary can try Darfur war crimes – al-Bashir", *Sudan Tribune*, 19 February 2006 available at <http://www.sudantribune.com/article_impr.php3?id_article=14151>.
1483 "Decree Establishing the Special Criminal Court on the Events in Darfur", June 7, 2005, Article 5, reprinted in UN Doc.S/2005/403.
1484 Government of Sudan, "Decree on the Establishment of a Special Prosecution for Crimes against Humanity", 18 September 2005.
1485 Mark Oliver, "Sudan Rejects ICC Extradition Calls", *The Guardian*, 29 June 2005.
1486 Human Rights Watch, "Lack of Conviction. The Special Criminal Court on the Events in Darfur", a Human Rights Watch briefing paper, June 2006.
1487 See UN press release, "Security Council Refers Situation in Darfur, Sudan, to Prosecutor of International Criminal Court", SC/8351; and UN press release, "Secretary-General Welcomes Adoption of Security Council Resolution Referring Situation in Darfur, Sudan to International Criminal Court Prosecutor", March 31, 2005, SG/SM/9797-AFR/1132.
1488 See, UN Security Council Resolution 1593 (2005), 31 March 2005.
1489 Hans Köchler, "Sudan: double standards in international criminal justice. Security Council resolution violates Statute of International Criminal Court", International Progress Organization, P/RE/19140c-is, Vienna, 2 April 2005, available at <http://www.i-p-o.org/nr-sudan-icc-02apr05.htm>.
1490 Paragraph 648, "Report of the International Commission of Inquiry on Darfur to the United Nations Secretary-General", UN, January 2005.
1491 ICC, "Warrants of arrest for the Minister of State for Humanitarian Affairs of Sudan, and a leader of the Militia/Janjaweed", The Hague, ICC-20070502-214-En, 2 May 2007.
1492 "ICC judges issue arrest warrants for Darfur suspects", Reuters, 2 May 2007.
1493 See, ICC, *Public Redacted Version of the Prosecutor's Application under Article 58*, ICC-02/05, 14 July 2008, available at <http://www.icc-cpi.int/iccdocs/doc/doc559999.pdf>; and ICC, "ICC Prosecutor presents case against Sudanese President, Hassan Ahmad AL BASHIR, for genocide, crimes against humanity and war crimes in Darfur", 14 July 2008.
1494 Julie Flint and Alex de Waal, "Justice Off Course In Darfur", *Washington Post*, 28 June 2008, available at <http://www.washingtonpost.com/wp-dyn/content/article/2008/06/27/AR2008062702632_pf.html>.
1495 *Ibid.*
1496 See, ICC, "Situation in Darfur, the Sudan: Public Redacted Version of the Prosecutor's

Application under Article 58", OTP, ICC-02/05, 14 July 2008, available at <http://www.icc-cpi.int/iccdocs/doc/doc559999.pdf>.
1497 William Schabas, "What is Genocide? What are the Gaps in the Convention? How to Prevent Genocide?", *Foro Regional sobre Prevención del Genocidio*, Buenos Aires, 10–12 December 2008, available at <http://www.cancilleria.gov.ar/portal/dighu/docs/william_schabas.pdf>.
1498 "International Criminal Court prosecutor under fire", Reuters, 19 August 2008.
1499 Alex de Waal, "Moreno Ocampo's Coup de Théâtre", Making Sense of Darfur, 29 July 2008, available at <http://blogs.ssrc.org/darfur/2008/07/29/moreno-ocampos-coup-de-theatre/>.
1500 *Ibid.* See also, Julie Flint's comment that "Initial requests for the full application elicited the response that the names of confidential sources were being removed and the document would be made public, without them, in a matter of days – on 22 July, 'in theory'. As the delay has drawn out, however, ICC officials have admitted privately that the application submitted to the ICC judges a few minutes before Moreno Ocampo met the press was 'a mess', packed with errors – spelling, punctuation and the like – that would have to be painstakingly corrected before it could be made public. Some have suggested that there is a link between the timing of the public application and the ruling by the Administrative Tribunal of the International Labour Organisation in Geneva just 5 days earlier. Coverage of the ILO ruling in the mainstream media, which has been focused on the indictment of Bashir, has certainly been minimal," in Alex de Waal, "Moreno Ocampo's Coup de Théâtre", Making Sense of Darfur, 29 July 2008, available at <http://blogs.ssrc.org/darfur/2008/07/29/moreno-ocampos-coup-de-theatre/>.
1501 Alex de Waal, "A Critique of the Public Application by the Chief Prosecutor of the ICC for an Arrest Warrant against Sudanese President Omar al Bashir", Social Science Research Council, 25 January 2009, available at < http://blogs.ssrc.org/darfur/wp-content/uploads/2009/01/bashir-public-application-critique-d6-250109.pdf>.
1502 *Ibid.*
1503 *Ibid.*
1504 Conor Foley, "Darfur: a disaster for justice", *The Guardian*, 20 April 2009, available at <http://www.guardian.co.uk/commentisfree/2009/apr/20/sudan-war-crimes>.
1505 "Report of the International Commission of Inquiry on Darfur to the United Nations Secretary-General, pursuant to Security Council Resolution 1564 of 18 September 2004", S/2005/60, 25 January 2005, para. 518, available at <http://www.un.org/News/dh/sudan/com_inq_darfur.pdf>.
1506 Alex de Waal, "A Critique of the Public Application by the Chief Prosecutor of the ICC for an Arrest Warrant against Sudanese President Omar al Bashir", *op. cit.*
1507 Ali Haggar, "The Origins and Organization of the Janjawiid in Darfur", in Alex de Waal (editor), *War in Darfur and the Search for Peace*, Harvard University Press, 2007, p. 128.
1508 Julie Flint, "Darfur's Armed Movements", in Alex de Waal (editor), *War in Darfur and the Search for Peace*, Harvard University Press, 2007.
1509 "UK barrister Sir Geoffrey Nice disputes Sudan genocide", BBC Hardtalk, 4 September 2012, available at <http://news.bbc.co.uk/1/hi/programmes/hardtalk/9747719.stm>.
1510 Conor Foley, "Darfur: a disaster for justice", *op. cit.*
1511 Cited in "African bloggers react to ICC charges against Sudanese President al-Bashir", available at <http://globalvoicesonline.org/2008/07/16/african-bloggers-reactions-to-charges-against-al-bashir/>. Blattman is an assistant professor of political science and economics at Yale University. He is also a consultant and adviser to the World Bank (Human Development Group), the UN Peacebuilding Fund, Uganda's Office of the Prime Minister, and Liberia's Ministry of Internal Affairs.
1512 Alex de Waal, "Moreno Ocampo's Coup de Théâtre", *op. cit.*

1513   *Ibid.*
1514   Alex de Waal, "A Critique of the Public Application by the Chief Prosecutor of the ICC for an Arrest Warrant against Sudanese President Omar al Bashir", *op. cit.*
1515   Rony Brauman, "The ICC's Bashir Indictment: Law Against Peace", *World Politics Review*, 23 July 2008, available at <http://www.worldpoliticsreview.com/Article.aspx?id=2471>.
1516   *Ibid.*
1517   "Sudanese regime likened to Nazis", BBC News, 5 June 2008, available at <http://news.bbc.co.uk/1/hi/7436472.stm>.
1518   "Darfur warrant for Sudan's Bashir: ICC adds genocide", BBC News Africa, 12 July 2010, available at <http://www.bbc.co.uk/news/10603559>.
1519   Thijs Bouwknegt, "'Darfur genocide continues': ICC Prosecutor calls for arrests of war criminals", Radio Nederland Wereldomroep, 4 December 2008, available at <http://static.rnw.nl/migratie/www.rnw.nl/internationaljustice/icc/Sudan/081204-sudan-genocide-redirected>.
1520   "GI-Net End of 2008 Summary", Genocide Intervention Network, February 2009, <http://www.genocideintervention.net/files/u1/GINET_-_Year_End_Review_-_2008.pdf>. The GI-Net figure includes deaths resulting from JEM's attack on Omdurman, which do not figure in the UN data because they did not occur in Darfur.
1521   De Waal also observed for example that: "A particular issue in determining the numbers of civilian deaths is what status to accord the people killed in inter-tribal fighting. Based on the UNAMID dataset, I have coded these separately: 476 civilians and combatants killed in inter-tribal fighting among Arab tribes and a further 164 in other intra-tribal fights (e.g. Fellata and Gimir)." De Waal further pointed out that GI-Net's figures indicate between 359 and 720 civilian deaths. The range is due to the number of people whose identity was not specified. (The higher figure counts all those unidentified as civilians.) It indicates 279 combatants killed (on all sides). The UNAMID dataset indicates 496 civilians killed, of whom 60 were IDPs (38 killed in the 25 August incident at Kalma). Its figures indicate 416 combatants killed. For 107, identity was not indicated, and for a further 640 killed in inter-tribal fighting, the distinction between combatant and civilian was not clarified. See, Alex de Waal, "Data for Deaths in Darfur", Making Sense of Darfur, 26 February 2009, <http://blogs.ssrc.org/darfur/2009/02/26/data-for-deaths-in-darfur/>.
1522   AU, "Darfur The Quest for Peace, Justice and Reconciliation. Report of the African Union High Level Panel on Darfur (AUPD)", PSC/AHG/2(CCVII), 29 October 2009, available at <http://www.reliefweb.int/rw/RWFiles2009.nsf/FilesByRWDocUnidFilename/SKEA-7XFEKC-full_report.pdf/$File/full_report.pdf>. It should also be pointed out that of the ninety IDP deaths, thirty-eight were during a single armed clash in the Kalma camp in August 2008.
1523   "US embassy cables: UN asserts itself in Darfur", *The Guardian*, 17 December 2010, available at <http://www.guardian.co.uk/world/us-embassy-cables-documents/182294>.
1524   "Darfur 120-Day Plan Report September to December 2004", Office of the United Nations Resident and Humanitarian Co-ordinator for the Sudan, Khartoum, January 2005.
1525   "Darfur Humanitarian Profile", UN, Khartoum, September 2005, p. 9.
1526   "Uganda's IDP policy", *Forced Migration Review*, No. 27, Brookings-Bern Project on Internal Displacement, available at <http://www.fmreview.org/FMRpdfs/FMR27/53.pdf>.
1527   Presentation by the Rt. Rev. Macleord Baker Ochola II, retired Anglican Bishop of Kitgum Diocese, northern Uganda, to the Seventy-fifth General Convention of the Episcopal Church of the United States of America, 23 June 2006, Friends for Peace in Africa, available at <http://www.friendsforpeaceinafrica.org/analysis-op-ed/48-analysis/79-bishop-ocholas-response-and-convention-speech.html>.
1528   Francesco Checchi, "Humanitarian interventions in Northern Uganda: based on what evidence?", *Humanitarian Exchange Magazine*, Issue 36, Humanitarian Practice Network,

December 2006, available at <http://www.odihpn.org/report.asp?id=2856>. Francesco Checchi is an epidemiologist with several years' experience in tropical-disease research and health assessments in humanitarian emergencies. He coordinated the multi-agency health and mortality survey conducted in northern Uganda in 2005.
1529 See, for example, "Congo Crisis at a Glance", International Rescue Committee, available at <http://www.theirc.org/congo-crisis-glance>.
1530 See, also, "The Lancet Publishes IRC Mortality Study from DR Congo; 3.9 Million Have Died: 38,000 Die per Month", International Rescue Committee, 6 January 2006.
1531 ICC, "Public Redacted Version of the Prosecutor's Application under Article 58", ICC-02/05, 14 July 2008, para. 36, available at <http://www.icc-cpi.int/iccdocs/doc/doc559999.pdf>.
1532 *Ibid.*, para. 312.
1533 "Darfur 120-Day Plan Report September to December 2004", Office of the United Nations Resident and Humanitarian Co-ordinator for the Sudan, Khartoum, January 2005.
1534 *Darfur Humanitarian Profile*, UN, Khartoum, September 2005, p. 5.
1535 *Darfur Humanitarian Profile*, UN, Khartoum, January 2009, p. 6, available at <http://www.unsudanig.org/docs/090330%20DHP%2034%20narrative%201%20January%202009.pdf>.
1536 Marc Gustafson, "Activism, Genocide and Darfur", in *Collected Essays, 2008–2010: Debating International Justice in Africa*, the Foundation for Law, Justice and Society, in collaboration with the Centre for Socio-Legal Studies, University of Oxford, Oxford, 2010.
1537 "Powell Confronts Sudan on Genocide Allegations", National Public Radio, 30 June 2004, available at <http://www.npr.org/templates/story/story.php?storyId=3050059>.
1538 "Hearing of the Senate Foreign Relations Committee on the Current Situation in Sudan and Prospects for Peace, Testimony of Secretary of State Colin Powell", Federal News Service, 9 September 2004.
1539 Marc Gustafson, "Activism, Genocide and Darfur", in *Collected Essays, 2008–2010: Debating International Justice in Africa*, op. cit.
1540 See, "Never Again" BBC *Panorama* programme, 3 July 2005. See also, "Danforth Described Darfur as 'Genocide' to Please Christian Right", *The Independent* (London), 5 July 2005.
1541 "Zoellick reluctant to describe Darfur violence as genocide", *Financial Times*, 15 April 2005, available at <http://www.ft.com/cms/s/0/4bed5bba-ad4b-11d9-ad92-00000e2511c8.html>.
1542 Marc Gustafson, "Activism, Genocide and Darfur", in *Collected Essays, 2008–2010: Debating International Justice in Africa*, op. cit.
1543 Rony Brauman, "The ICC's Bashir Indictment: Law Against Peace", *World Politics Review*, 23 July 2008, available at <http://www.worldpoliticsreview.com/Article.aspx?id=2471>.
1544 "No Genocide in Sudan, Annan Says", Deutsche Presse-Agentur, 17 June 2004.
1545 AU, Communiqué of the Twelfth Meeting of the Peace and Security Council, the Peace and Security Council of the African Union, Meeting in its Twelfth Meeting, at ministerial level, PSC//MIN/Comm. (XII), para. 2, 4 July 2004.
1546 "Nigeria's Obasanjo Unconvinced on US Call of 'Genocide' in Darfur", *Agence France-Presse*, 3 December 2004.
1547 See, for example, "EU Mission Sees Abuses, But Not Genocide, in Darfur", Reuters, 9 August 2004; "EU Mission Finds No Evidence of Darfur Genocide", Al-Jazeera, 10 August 2004.
1548 See, for example, "Israel to turn away Darfur Refugees", Associated Press, 19 August 2007.
1549 See, for example, "Doctors Without Borders/Médecins Sans Frontières Challenges US Darfur Genocide Claims", Mediamonitors, 5 October 2004, available at <http://www.mediamonitors.net>.
1550 "Messages", Number 132, MSF, Paris, October-November 2004.
1551 *Ibid.*

1552 "Thousands Die as World Defines Genocide", *Financial Times* (London), 6 July 2004. See also, Bradol's views in "France Calls on Sudan to Forcibly Disarm Darfur Militias", *Agence France-Presse*, 7 July 2004.
1553 "Violence in the Sudan Displaces Nearly 1 Million. An Aid Worker Describes the Gravity of the Humanitarian Crisis", MSNBC, 16 April 2004.
1554 See, for example, MSF's own briefing: "Médecins Sans Frontières has been working in Darfur since December 2003. Today, 90 international volunteers and nearly 2,000 Sudanese staff provide medical and nutritional care in areas with more than 400,000 displaced people. Medical teams conduct medical consultations and hospitalisation, treat victims of violence, care for severely and moderately malnourished children, and provide water, blankets, feeding and other essential items in Mornay, Zalingei, Nyertiti, Kerenik, El Genina, Garsila, Deleig, Mukjar, Bindisi, and Um Kher in West Darfur State; Kalma Camp near Nyala and Kass in South Darfur State; and Kebkabiya in North Darfur State. MSF also continues to assess areas throughout Darfur. Additional teams provide assistance to Sudanese who have sought refuge in Chad in Adre, Birak and Tine, Iriba and Guereda," in "We are looking at a second catastrophe", MSF Australia Website, available at <http://www.msf.org.au/tw-feature/045twf.html>.
1555 MSF has received, among others, the following international awards for their activities: 1999, the Nobel Peace Prize; 1998, the Conrad Hilton Prize; 1997, *Prix International – Primo Levi*; 1997, *Prix International Sebetiater*; 1996, *Prix International pour la Paix et l'Action Humanitaire*; 1997, Indira Gandhi Prize; 1996, *Prix Seoul pour la Paix*; 1993, the European Parliament's *Prix pour la liberte de l'Esprit Prix Sakharov*, 1993, the United Nations High Commission for Refugees' Nansen Medal; 1992, the Council of Europe's *Prix Europeen des Droits de l'Homme*.
1556 "Messages", number 132, MSF, Paris, October-November 2004.
1557 "War Surgeon Gino Strada: 'Media Not Interested in Human Tragedies' of War", interview on DemocracyNow.org, 8 April 2005, available at <http://www.democracynow.org/article.pl?sid=05/04/08/1346222>.
1558 "'Elders' criticize West's response to situation in Darfur. Brahimi says West 'pampered' rebels, while Carter calls US's use of term 'genocide' to describe violence 'unhelpful'", *The Christian Science Monitor* (Boston), 6 October 2007, available at <http://www.csmonitor.com/2007/1005/p99s01-duts.html>.
1559 "Jimmy Carter confronts Sudan officials", Associated Press, 3 October 2007.
1560 Julie Flint and Alex de Waal, "Justice Off Course In Darfur", *Washington Post*, 28 June 2008, available at <http://www.washingtonpost.com/wp-dyn/content/article/2008/06/27/AR2008062702632_pf.html>.
1561 Jonathan Steele, "Darfur Wasn't Genocide and Sudan is not a Terrorist State", *The Guardian* (London), 6 October 2005. See, also, interview with Mahmood Mamdani, in "The Genocide Myth", *Guernica* magazine, May 2009, available at <http://www.guernicamag.com/interviews/1031/the_genocide_myth/>.
1562 "Why Genocide is Difficult to Prosecute", *The Christian Science Monitor*, 20 April 2007.
1563 Alex de Waal, "A Critique of the Public Application by the Chief Prosecutor of the ICC for an Arrest Warrant against Sudanese President Omar al Bashir", Social Science Research Council, 25 January 2009, available at < http://blogs.ssrc.org/darfur/wp-content/uploads/2009/01/bashir-public-application-critique-d6-250109.pdf>.
1564 See, Nicholas Kristof, "Driving Up the Price of Blood", *The New York Times*, 17 April 2007.
1565 See ICC, "Prosecutor v. Omar Al Bashir, Warrant of Arrest for Omar Hassan Ahmad Al Bashir", Case No. ICC-02/05-01/09, 4 March 2009, available at <http://www.icc-cpi.int/iccdocs/doc/doc639078.pdf>. See, also, "Warrant issued for Sudan's Bashir", BBC News, 4 March 2009.

1566 ICC, see "Prosecutor v. Omar Al Bashir, Decision on the Prosecution's Application for a Warrant of Arrest against Omar Hassan Ahmad Al Bashir", Case No. ICC-02/05-01/09, 4 March 2009, available at <http://www.icc-cpi.int/iccdocs/doc/doc639096.pdf>.
1567 "Sudan's Omar al-Bashir says ICC can 'eat' his arrest warrant", *The Daily Telegraph*, 4 March 2009, available at <http://www.telegraph.co.uk/news/worldnews/africaandindianocean/sudan/4933329/Sudans-Omar-al-Bashir-says-ICC-can-eat-his-arrest-warrant.html>.
1568 "Sudan expels 10 aid NGOs and dissolves 2 local groups", *Sudan Tribune*, 5 March 2009, available at <http://www.sudantribune.com/spip.php?article30382>.
1569 See, C.N.612.2008.TREATIES-6 [Depositary Notification], Rome Statute of the International Criminal Court, "Sudan: Notification".
1570 See the landmark International Court of Justice decision *Democratic Republic of Congo v. Belgium* (2002).
1571 *La Repubblica* (Rome), 5 March 2009. There was considerable controversy before and after the Prosecutor's application. See, for example, Julie Flint and Alex de Waal, "This Prosecution Will Endanger the People We Wish to Defend in Sudan", *The Observer*, 13 July 2008, available at <http://www.guardian.co.uk/world/2008/jul/13/sudan.humanrights> and "A Dilemma Over Darfur: Calculating the Consequences of Indicting Sudan's President, Omar al-Bashir, for Genocide and More", Economist.com, 15 July 2008, available at <http://www.economist.com/world/international/displaystory.cfm?story_id=11737170>.
1572 Professor Hans Köchler, "Global Justice or Global Revenge? The ICC and the Politicization of International Criminal Justice", lecture delivered at the World Conference for International Justice "United against the politicization of justice", organised by the General Sudanese Students Union, Khartoum, Sudan, 6 April 2009, available at <http://www.i-p-o.org/IPO-Koechler-ICC-politicization-2009.htm>.
1573 "Sudan Stages 'Million-man' March against UN War Crimes Trial", *Agence France-Presse*, 5 April 2005, available at <http://www.sudantribune.com/article.php3?id_article=8891>.
1574 "Sudan refuses questioning of top official over Darfur", *Agence France-Presse*, 26 March 2007.
1575 Max du Plessis and Christopher Gevers, "Darfur Goes to the International Criminal Court (Perhaps)", *African Security Review*, Vol. 14, No. 2 (2005).
1576 "A Losing Strategy on War Crimes", *The International Herald Tribune*, 12–13 February 2005.
1577 John Rosenthal, "A Lawless Global Court. How the International Criminal Court Undermines the U.N. System", *Policy Review*, Hoover Institution, February–March 2004.
1578 Max du Plessis and Christopher Gevers, "Darfur Goes to the International Criminal Court (Perhaps)", *op. cit.*
1579 Christopher Caldwell, "It is best to stay out of Darfur", *Financial Times* (London), 16 December 2006.
1580 Edward Thomas, "Against the Gathering Storm, Securing Sudan's Comprehensive Peace Agreement", Chatham House report, Royal Institute of International Affairs, London, 9 January 2009, p. 34, available at <http://www.chathamhouse.org.uk/files/12941_0109sudan_r.pdf>.
1581 Jacqueline Geis and Alex Mundt, "When to Indict? The Impact of Timing International Criminal Indictments on Peace Processes and Humanitarian Action", the Brookings Institution-University of Bern Project on Internal Displacement, paper to the World Humanitarian Studies Conference, Groningen, the Netherlands, February 2009, p. 11, available at <http://reliefweb.int/rw/RWFiles2009.nsf/FilesByRWDocUnidFilename/RWST-7RAQ9A-full_report.pdf/$File/full_report.pdf>.
1582 Mariam Bibi Jooma, "The International Criminal Court and Sudan – Opening a Pandora's Box", *ISS Today*, Institute for Security Studies, Tshwane (Pretoria), 6 March 2007.

1583 "Africa and the International Criminal Court", Council on Foreign Relations, New York, 17 November 2006.
1584 "UN concerned about staff security after ICC accuses Sudanese of war crimes", United Nations Radio, 28 February 2007.
1585 Rony Brauman, "The ICC's Bashir Indictment: Law Against Peace", *World Politics Review*, 23 July 2008, available at <http://www.worldpoliticsreview.com/Article.aspx?id=2471>.
1586 Ramesh Thakur, "Perks of the warring states", *The Japan Times*, 27 March 2009, available at <http://search.japantimes.co.jp/cgi-bin/eo20090327rt.html>.
1587 "Report of the Secretary-General on children and armed conflict in the Sudan", 09-23388 (E) 130209, UN, 10 February 2009. There are many other references to JEM and its forced recruitment of child soldiers. See, also, "Trafficking and Forced Recruitment of Child Soldiers on the Chad/Sudan Border", A Waging Peace Briefing, 6 June 2008, available at <http://www.wagingpeace.info/files/20080606_WagingPeaceReport_ChildrenSoldiers.pdf>.
1588 The ICC's own statute defines as a war crime "conscripting or enlisting children under the age of fifteen years into national armed forces or using them to participate actively in hostilities" (Article 8(2)(b)(xxvi)); and in the case of an internal armed conflict, "conscripting or enlisting children under the age of fifteen years into armed forces or groups or using them to participate actively in hostilities" (Article 8(2)(e)(vii)). The Additional Protocols to the four Geneva Conventions of 1949 (1977) set fifteen as the minimum age for recruitment or use in armed conflict. This minimum standard applies to all parties, both governmental and non-governmental, in both international and internal armed conflict. Article 4(3)(c) of the Additional Protocol II, applicable to non-international armed conflicts, states: Children who have not attained the age of fifteen years shall neither be recruited in the armed forces or groups nor allowed to take part in hostilities. The Convention on the Rights of the Child (1989) generally defines a child as any person under the age of eighteen, Article 38 uses the lower age of fifteen as the minimum for recruitment or participation in armed conflict. The Protocol to the Convention on the Rights of the Child on the involvement of children in armed conflict, adopted by the UN General Assembly on 25 May 2000 and which entered into force on 12 February 2002, sets eighteen as the minimum age for direct participation in hostilities, for recruitment into armed groups, and for compulsory recruitment by governments. Additional Protocols to the four Geneva Conventions of 1949.
1589 "ICC will not investigate JEM attack on Sudanese capital", *Sudan Tribune*, 23 November 2008.
1590 "Child Soldiers Recruited in Chad Still Held in Sudan, ICC's Lubanga Case Questioned", *Inner City Press*, 7 July 2008, available at <http://www.innercitypress.com/un1caac070708.html>.
1591 "ICC Prosecutor Accused of Child Soldier Hypocrisy", ICC Watch, 25 February 2009, available at <http://www.iccwatch.org/pdf/Press%20Release%2025Feb09.pdf>.
1592 Jacqueline Geis and Alex Mundt, *When to Indict? The Impact of Timing International Criminal Indictments on Peace Processes and Humanitarian Action*, op. cit., p. 12.
1593 Nancy Langar, "ICC Indictment of Sudan's al-Bashir Will Test Court's Relevancy", Henry L. Stimson Center, Washington DC, 14 August 2008.
1594 Alex de Waal, "A Critique of the Public Application by the Chief Prosecutor of the ICC for an Arrest Warrant against Sudanese President Omar al Bashir", *op. cit*.
1595 See, African Union Peace and Security Council, "Communiqué of the 142nd Meeting of the Peace and Security Council", PSC/MIN/Comm (CXLII), July 21, 2008, available at <http://www.iccnow.org/documents/AU_142-communique-eng.pdf>. See, also, "AU rejects Bashir Darfur charges", BBC News, 21 July 2008, available at <http://news.bbc.co.uk/1/hi/world/africa/7517393.stm>.

1596   "AU Statement", available at <http://invisiblecollege.weblog.leidenuniv.nl/2009/03/11/the-bashir-arrest-warrant-why-is-the-icc>.
1597   AU, "Decision on the Meeting of African States Parties to the Rome Statute of the International Criminal Court", Doc. Assembly/AU/13 (XIII), Assembly/AU/Dec.245(XIII), adopted by the Thirteenth Ordinary Session of the Assembly in Sirte, Great Socialist People's Libyan Arab Jamahiriya, available at: <http://www.africaunion.org/root/au/Conferences/2009/july/summit/decisions/ASSEMBLY%20AU%20DEC%20243%20-%20267%20(XIII)%20_E.PDF>. See, also, Andrew Heavens, "AU ruling means Bashir can travel in Africa: Sudan", Reuters, July 4, 2009, available at <http://www.reuters.com/article/worldNews/idUSTRE56315820090704>.
1598   "Africa fails to act on Bashir warrant", *Agence France-Presse*, 4 July 2009.
1599   See, "AU votes against cooperating with ICC arrest warrant for Bashir", *Agence France-Presse*, 3 July 2009, available at <http://www.france24.com/en/20090703-african-union-votes-end-cooperation-over-bashir-indictment-sudan-icc-darfur>. See, also, "Africa's leaders agree on no extradition for Al-Bashir", SABC News, 4 July 2009.
1600   "Darfur The Quest for Peace, Justice and Reconciliation. Report of the African Union High Level Panel on Darfur (AUPD)", PSC/AHG/2(CCVII), AU, 29 October 2009, available at <http://www.reliefweb.int/rw/RWFiles2009.nsf/FilesByRWDocUnidFilename/SKEA-7XFEKC-full_report.pdf/$File/full_report.pdf>.
1601   Alex de Waal, "Reading the AU Panel Report", Making Sense of Darfur, 30 October 2009, available at http://blogs.ssrc.org/darfur/2009/10/30/reading-the-au-panel-report/
1602   "Sudan will 'conditionally' accept hybrid courts for Darfur crimes", *Sudan Tribune*, 19 November 2009, available at <http://www.sudantribune.com/spip.php?article33172>.
1603   Mahmood Mamdani,, *Saviors and Survivors: Darfur, Politics, and the War on Terror*, Pantheon, 2009.
1604   "Sudan's coming elections How did it come to this? The man at the top of the International Criminal Court's most-wanted list is the favourite to be elected president, if elections take place at all", *The Economist*, 14 January 2010.
1605   "Darfur war crimes indictment threatens to split international community", *The Guardian*, 16 February 2009, available at <http://www.guardian.co.uk/world/2009/feb/16/sudan-war-crimes-split-international-community?INTCMP=SRCH>.
1606   "China against 'irresponsible' ICC move to arrest Sudan's Bashir", *Sudan Tribune*, 31 August 2008.
1607   "Outcry against arrest move from Arab, African countries, Russia, China", *Sudan Tribune*, 5 March 2009, available at <http://www.sudantribune.com/spip.php?article30380>. See, also, "Africa, Russia Blast Bashir Warrant", Islamonline, 4 March 2009, available at <http://www.islamonline.net/servlet/Satellite?c=Article_C&pagename=Zone-English-News/NWELayout&cid=1235628862974>.
1608   "Senegalese president urges ICC to drop genocide charges against Sudanese leader", Xinhua, 7 March 2009.
1609   "Often Split, Arab Leaders Unite for Sudan's Chief", *The New York Times*, 30 March 2009. See, also, for example, "Arab League Slams ICC Prosecutor for Seeking Sudan President Arrest", *Agence France-Presse*, 19 July 2008. "Arabs reject 'unbalanced' ICC request against Sudanese President", *Sudan Tribune*, 19 July 2008, available at <http://www.sudantribune.com/spip.php?article27945>; "Arab Gulf states criticize ICC move against Sudan president", *Sudan Tribune*, 30 December 2008, available at <http://www.sudantribune.com/spip.php?article29735>; "Arab leaders back 'wanted' Bashir", BBC News, 30 March 2009; "Arab league backs Sudan's Bashir against ICC indictments", *Sudan Tribune*, 16 September 2010, available at <http://www.sudantribune.com/spip.php?article36302>;

1610 See, WikiLeaks, US Government Cable, "Subject: Foreign Minister on Guantanamo, Western Sahara, Sudan", 18 April 2009, available at <http://wikileaks.org/cable/2009/04/09ALGIERS381.html>.
1611 WikiLeaks, US Government Cable, "El Bashir's Arrest Warrant Elicits Mixed Reactions", 8 March 2009, available at <http://wikileaks.org/cable/2009/03/09NOUAKCHOTT190.html>.
1612 "Gulf nations opposed to ICC 'double standards' against Sudan", Xinhua, 21 July 2008.
1613 "OIC backs Sudan's Bashir, slams ICC", Press TV, 28 March 2009, available at <http://www.presstv.ir/detail.aspx?id=89840&sectionid=351020504>. See, also, for example, "Islamic countries ask UN to defer ICC move against Sudan president", *Sudan Tribune*, 4 August 2008, available at <http://www.sudantribune.com/spip.php?article28159>.
1614 "Cambodia's Prime Minister says ICC's decision damages Sudan peace efforts", *Sudan Tribune*, 9 April 2009, available at <http://www.sudantribune.com/spip.php?article30818>.
1615 See, for example, "Sudan elected to chair Group of 77 at UN", *Sudan Tribune*, 27 September 2008, available at <http://www.sudantribune.com/spip.php?article28750>. The Group of seventy-seven aims to articulate and promote the collective economic interests and enhance the joint negotiating capacity of its member states during negotiations at the UN. There were originally 77 founding members of the organization, but the organisation has since expanded to 130 member countries. The group was founded on 15 June 1964 by the "Joint Declaration of the Seventy-Seven Countries", issued at the United Nations Conference on Trade and Development.
1616 "Hugo Chavez Backs Sudan's Al-bashir Against ICC", *Turkish Weekly*, 31 March 2009.
1617 Steven Fake and Kevin Funk, "Sudan: Justice or a poisoned chalice?", *Sudan Tribune*, 28 March 2009, available at <http://www.sudantribune.com/spip.php?article30684>. Fake and Funk are the co-authors of *The Scramble for Africa: Darfur-Intervention and the USA*. They maintain a website with their commentary at <http://www.scrambleforafrica.org>.
1618 "What does the ICC stand for?", *The Guardian. The Workers' Weekly*, Communist Party of Australia, 8 June 2011, available at <http://www.cpa.org.au/guardian/2011/1504/11-what-does.html>.
1619 *Ibid.*
1620 See, for example, "Sudan's Bashir visits Eritrea despite ICC warrant", Reuters, 23 March 2009; "Sudan's President Al-Bashir visits Egypt", *Sudan Tribune*, 25 March 2009; "Sudan's Bashir goes to Libya, defying ICC", Reuters, 26 March 2009; "Sudan's Bashir returns home after visits to Qatar and Saudi Arabia", *Sudan Tribune*, 2 April 2009.
1621 David Kaye, "Who's Afraid of the International Criminal Court?", *Foreign Affairs*, May/June 2011, available at <http://www.foreignaffairs.com/articles/67768/david-kaye/whos-afraid-of-the-international-criminal-court>.
1622 "Cosy club or sword of righteousness?", *The Economist*, 26 November 2011.
1623 See, for example, "Omar al-Bashir, Sudan President, Should Have Been Arrested in China: UN", *The Huffington Post*, 30 June 2011, available at <http://www.huffingtonpost.com/2011/06/30/omar-albashir-sudan-president-arrested-china-criticizedunited-nations_n_887611.html>, "Sudan's President to Tehran today for NAM summit", *Sudan Tribune*, 28 August 2012, available at <http://www.sudantribune.com/spip.php?iframe&page=imprimable&id_article=43736>; "Sudan's Bashir heads to Saudi for Pilgrimage", *Al Arabiya*, 1 April 2009, available at <http://www.alarabiya.net/articles/2009/04/01/69685.html>, "Defiant Bashir travels to Cairo", Aljazeera, 25 March 2009, available at <http://www.aljazeera.com/news/africa/2009/03/2009325135710312782.html>; "Sudanese President Omar al-Bashir to visit Egypt", *Egypt Independent*, 12 September 2012, available at <http://www.egyptindependent.com/news/sudanese-presidentomar-al-bashir-visit-egypt-sunday>; "President Al-Bashir thrilled by his three days Eritrea visit", *Tesfa News*, 29 May 2012, available at <http://www.tesfanews.net/

archives/8021>; "Sudan's Bashir offers to help Libya during criticised visit", BBC News, 7 January 2012, available at <http://www.bbc.co.uk/news/world-africa-16454493>; "Sudan's president to Tehran today for NAM summit", *Sudan Tribune*, 29 August 2012, available at <http://www.sudantribune.com/spip.php?iframe&page=imprimable&id_article=43736>; "Ban Ki-moon and Sudan's Bashir meet in Tehran", *Sudan Tribune*, 30 August 2012, available at <http://www.sudantribune.com/spip.php?article43758>; "UN: No meeting al-Bashir and Ban Ki-moon", Radio Dabanga, 3 September 2012, available at <http://www.radiodabanga.org/node/35283>; and "Are Bashir's visits to Qatar and Saudi Arabia a Signal to Bashar", *Gulf States Newsletter*, 22 March 2012, available at <http://www.gsn-online.com/arebashir%E2%80%99s-visits-to-qatar-and-saudi-arabia-asignal-to-bashar>.

1624 "Darfur rebel Abu Garda will not face ICC charges", BBC News, 8 February 2010, available at <http://news.bbc.co.uk/1/hi/world/africa/8505014.stm>.

1625 "Abu-Garda Takes Oath as Federal Minister of Health", Sudan Radio, 20 December 2011, available at <http://www.sudanradio.info/english/modules/news/article.php?storyid=3391>.

1626 "International Criminal Court terminates case against Sudanese", *News Afrique Informations*, 5 October 2013, available at <http://www.afriquejet.com/news/12386-international-criminal-court-terminates-case-against-sudanese.html>.

1627 See, for example, "Libya becomes first nation to receive Sudan defence minister after ICC warrant", *Sudan Tribune*, 12 March 2012; "Sudan defense minister in Saudi Arabia despite ICC warrant", *Sudan Tribune*, 24 February 2013.

1628 "Elisa Burchett: Sudan's Response to ICC Arrest Warrant", UN Observer and World Report, 5 March 2009, available at <http://www.unobserver.com/index.php?pagina=layout4.php&id=5719&blz=1>.

1629 Cited in Dayo Olopade, "Who's Afraid of the International Criminal Court? In Kenya, the answer is no one at all", *New Republic*, 9 March 2013, available at <http://www.newrepublic.com/article/112629/kenya-election-results-whos-afraid-icc#>.

1630 "Sudan: Former UN Rights Chief Says UNSC Referral of Darfur Case to ICC a 'Very Bad Idea'", AllAfrica.com, 22 July 2013, available at <http://allafrica.com/stories/201307221029.html?viewall=1>.

Notes to Chapter Twenty-two

1631 "Kenya: Kaul Insists Post-Election Violence Cases Don't Merit ICC Hearing", *The Star* (Nairobi), 8 October 2012, available at <http://allafrica.com/stories/201210090073.html>.

1632 See, ICC judge withdraws from Kenyan leaders' case. Christine Van Den Wyngaert criticises prosecutors for failing to disclose evidence against President Uhuru Kenyatta", Aljazeera, 27 April 2013, available at <http://www.aljazeera.com/news/africa/2013/04/2013427175150653880.html>.

1633 See, "Human Rights in Republic of Kenya", "Amnesty International Report 2009", Amnesty International, 2010, available at <http://www.amnesty.org/en/region/kenya/report-2009>.

1634 ICC, "Dissenting Opinion by Judge Hans-Peter Kaul to Pre-Trial Chamber II's 'Decision on the Prosecutor's Application for Summons to Appear for William Samoei Ruto, Henry Kiprono Kosgey and Joshua Arap Sang'", ICC-01/09-01/11, 15 March 2011, available at <http://www.icc-cpi.int/iccdocs/doc/doc1039488.pdf>.

1635 "Cosy club or sword of righteousness?", *The Economist*, 26 November 2011, available at <http://www.economist.com/node/21540230?zid=317&ah=8a47fc455a44945580198768fad0fa41>.

1636 See, ICC, "Decision on the Prosecutor's Application for Summons to Appear for William Samoei Ruto, Henry Kiprono Kosgey and Joshua Arap Sang", ICC-01/09-01/11, 8 March

2011, available at <http://www.icc-cpi.int/iccdocs/doc/doc1037044.pdf>; ICC, "Decision on the Prosecutor's Application for Summonses to Appear for Francis Kirimi Muthaura, Uhuru Muigai Kenyatta and Mohammed Hussein Ali", ICC-01/09-02/11, 8 March 2011, available at <http://www.icc-cpi.int/iccdocs/doc/doc1037052.pdf>.

1637 Ian Paisley Jr., "Peace Must Not Be the Victim of International Justice", *The New York Times*, 16 March 2012, available at <http://www.nytimes.com/2012/03/17/opinion/peace-must-not-be-the-victim-of-international-justice.html?_r=0>.

1638 ICC, "Application on behalf of the Government of the Republic of Kenya pursuant to Article 19 of the ICC Statute", ICC-01/09-01/11 and ICC-01/09-02/11, 31 March 2011, available at <http://www.icc-cpi.int/iccdocs/doc/doc1050005.pdf>.

1639 *Ibid.*

1640 "Parliament pulls Kenya from ICC treaty", *Daily Nation* (Nairobi), 22 December 2010.

1641 "MPs' vote sets stage for Kenya to cut ties with ICC", *Daily Nation* (Nairobi), 23 December 2010.

1642 Okiya Omtata Okoiti, "Our continued membership of the ICC is against the new Constitution", *Daily Nation* (Nairobi), 24 December 2010.

1643 ICC, "Decision on the Application by the Government of Kenya Challenging the Admissibility of the Case Pursuant to Article 19(2)(b) of the Statute", ICC-01/09-01/11, 30 May 2011, available at <http://www.icc-cpi.int/iccdocs/doc/doc1078822.pdf>.

1644 ICC, "Judgment on the appeal of the Republic of Kenya against the decision of Pre-Trial Chamber II of 30 May 2011 entitled 'Decision on the Application by the Government of Kenya Challenging the Admissibility of the Case Pursuant to Article 19(2)(b) of the Statute' Dissenting Opinion of Judge Anita Ušacka", No. ICC-01/09-02/11 OA, 20 September 2011, available at >http://www.worldcourts.com/icc/eng/decisions/2011.09.20_Prosecutor_v_Muthaura2.pdf>.

1645 See, In the Case of the Prosecutor v. William Samoei Ruto, Henry Kiprono Kosgey and Joshua Arap Sang, No. ICC-01/09-01/11, judgment on the appeal of the Republic of Kenya against the decision of Pre-Trial Chamber II of 30 May 2011 entitled "Decision on the Application by the Government of Kenya Challenging the Admissibility of the Case Pursuant to Article 19(2)(b) of the Statute", 30 August 2011; the Prosecutor v. Francis Kirimi Muthaura, Uhuru Muigai Kenyatta and Mohammed Hussein Ali, No. ICC-01/09-02/11, judgement on the appeal of the Republic of Kenya against the decision of Pre-Trial Chamber II of 30 May 2011 entitled "Decision on the Application by the Government of Kenya Challenging the Admissibility of the Case Pursuant to Article 19(2)(b) of the Statute", 30 August 2011.

1646 "African Union backs Kenya call to delay ICC case", BBC News, 1 February 2011, available at <http://www.bbc.co.uk/news/world-africa-12332563>.

1647 "ICC case against Kenya's deputy PM proceeds despite claim that witness lied", *The Guardian*, 7 February 2013, available at <http://www.guardian.co.uk/law/2013/feb/07/icc-case-kenya-deputy-pm>.

1648 "Did key Ocampo witness recant his testimony?", *Daily Nation* (Nairobi), 9 March 2012, available at <http://www.nation.co.ke/oped/Opinion/Did-key-Ocampo-witness-recant-his-testimony/-/440808/1363112/-/13amlrhz/-/index.html>.

1649 "Witness' bid to pull out could deal Hague cases a blow", *Business Daily*, 4 March 2012, available at <http://www.businessdailyafrica.com/Witness+bid+to+pull+out+could+deal+Hague+cases+a+blow+/-/539546/1359144/-/psrp5l/-/index.html>. For more details on witness 4, see, "Maina Kabutu, ICC Star Witness No. 4 – The Real story and why he counts", *Diaspora Messenger*, 7 February 2013, available at <http://diasporamessenger.com/maina-kabutu-icc-star-witness-no-4-the-real-story-and-why-he-counts/>.

1650 *Strategic Intelligence News*, 4 March 2012, available at <http://intelligencebriefs.com/?p=1829>.

1651 "ICC officials in Kenya to probe witness 'tampering'", Capital FM (Nairobi), 13 April 2012, available at <http://www.capitalfm.co.ke/news/2012/04/icc-officials-in-kenya-to-probe-witness-tampering/>.
1652 Ibid.
1653 Ibid.
1654 "Hague threatens Ugandan's arrest", The Star (Nairobi), 3 March 2012, available at <http://www.the-star.co.ke/news/article-27808/hague-threatens-ugandans-arrest>.
1655 "ICC case against Kenya's deputy PM proceeds despite claim that witness lied", The Guardian, 7 February 2013, available at <http://www.guardian.co.uk/law/2013/feb/07/icc-case-kenya-deputy-pm>.
1656 Ibid.
1657 "Kenya: ICC Claims 'Mere Gossip' Says Uhuru", The Star (Nairobi), 1 March 2013, <http://allafrica.com/stories/201303011286.html>.
1658 Ibid.
1659 Ibid.
1660 Courtenay Griffiths, "The International Criminal Court is hurting Africa", The Daily Telegraph, 3 July 2012, available at <http://www.telegraph.co.uk/news/worldnews/africaandindianocean/kenya/9373188/The-International-Criminal-Court-is-hurting-Africa.html>.
1661 Elliot Wilson, "A Political Trial at the ICC? Why, of Course!", The Huffington Post, 20 April 2012, available at <http://www.huffingtonpost.co.uk/elliot-wilson/a-political-trial-at-the-_b_1437224.html>.
1662 "ICC chief cites new challenges ahead of status hearing", Standard Digital, 14 February 2013, available at <http://www.standardmedia.co.ke/?articleID=2000077259&pageNo=1&story_title=Kenya-ICC-chief-cites-new-challenges-ahead-of-status-hearing>.
1663 "Tough battle shapes up at ICC over Witness 4", Daily Nation (Nairobi), 10 February 2013, available at <http://www.nation.co.ke/News/Tough-battle-shapes-up-at-ICC-over-Witness-4/-/1056/1689698/-/item/0/-/126xxnz/-/index.html>.
1664 "Muthaura Contests ICC Charges After Witness Fiasco", Capital FM (Nairobi), 8 February 2013, available at <http://allafrica.com/stories/201302080346.html>.
1665 "ICC's Long Shadow Over Impending Elections", New African, 8 January 2013, available at <http://www.newafricanmagazine.com/features/politics/iccs-long-shadow-over-impending-elections>.
1666 Ibid.
1667 "Did the ICC help Uhuru Kenyatta win Kenyan election?", BBC News, 11 March 2013, available at <http://www.bbc.co.uk/news/world-africa-21739347>.
1668 Gabrielle Lynch and Miša Zgonec-Rožej, The ICC Intervention in Kenya, Chatham House, February 2013, AFP/ILP 2013/01, available at <http://www.chathamhouse.org/sites/default/files/public/Research/Africa/0213pp_icc_kenya.pdf>.
1669 Ibid.
1670 Ibid.
1671 "ICC's Long Shadow Over Impending Elections", New African, 8 January 2013, available at <http://www.newafricanmagazine.com/features/politics/iccs-long-shadow-over-impending-elections>.
1672 Ibid.
1673 Cited in "The Return of President Kenyatta", New African, April 2013.
1674 "Kenya's Election: What Uhuru Kenyatta's Victory Means for Africa", Time, 9 March 2013, available at <http://world.time.com/2013/03/09/kenyas-election-what-uhuru-kenyattas-victory-means-for-africa/>.
1675 Cited in "The Return of President Kenyatta", New African, op. cit.
1676 Dayo Olopade, "Who's Afraid of the International Criminal Court? In Kenya, the answer is no one at all", op. cit.

1677 Before taking on her position in the Bush Administration, Frazer was Special Assistant to the President and Senior Director for African Affairs on the National Security Council and the first woman to serve as US Ambassador to South Africa.
1678 "Kenya's Election: What Uhuru Kenyatta's Victory Means for Africa", *Time*, 9 March 2013, available at <http://world.time.com/2013/03/09/kenyas-election-what-uhuru-kenyattas-victory-means-for-africa/>.
1679 "ICC has fallen from high ideals of global justice, accountability", *Daily Nation* (Nairobi), 16 March 2013, available at <http://www.nation.co.ke/oped/Opinion/-/440808/1722100/-/k4rufnz/-/index.html>.
1680 *Ibid.*
1681 "ICC's Long Shadow Over Impending Elections", *New African*, 8 January 2013, available at <http://www.newafricanmagazine.com/features/politics/iccs-long-shadow-over-impending-elections>.
1682 *Ibid.*
1683 *Ibid.*
1684 "ICC suspects officially registered to run for top seats in Kenya's March elections", Associated Press, 30 January 2013.
1685 "Kenya ICC trials postponed", Kenya Broadcasting Corporation, 26 February 2013, available at <http://www.kbc.co.ke/news.asp?nid=80264>.
1686 Mahmood Mamdani, "Mamdani, on why Raila lost", *Daily Monitor*, 10 March 2013, available at <http://www.monitor.co.ug/Magazines/ThoughtIdeas/Kenya-2013--The-ICC-election/-/689844/1715440/-/item/1/-/wh1tsgz/-/index.html>.
1687 *Ibid.*
1688 "Kenya must comply with International Criminal Court, European Union stresses", *Sabahi*, 12 February 2013, available at <http://sabahionline.com/en_GB/articles/hoa/articles/newsbriefs/2013/02/12/newsbrief-05>.
1689 Ian Paisley Jr., "Peace Must Not Be the Victim of International Justice", *op. cit.*
1690 Gabrielle Lynch and Miša Zgonec-Rožej, *The ICC Intervention in Kenya, op. cit.*
1691 *Ibid.* See, L. Muthoni Wanyeki, *The International Criminal Court's Cases in Kenya: Origin and Impact*, Institute for Security Studies, No. 237, August 2012.
1692 Dayo Olopade, "Who's Afraid of the International Criminal Court? In Kenya, the answer is no one at all", *op. cit.*
1693 *Ibid.*
1694 *Ibid.*
1695 "VIDEO: Uhuru Kenyatta's Interview on Al Jazeera – 'ICC Has the Wrong Guys'", Mwakilishi.com, 23 January 2013, available at <http://www.mwakilishi.com/content/articles/2013/01/23/video-uhuru-kenyattas-interview-on-al-jazeera-icc-has-the-wrong-guys.htm>.
1696 "Kenya's Election: What Uhuru Kenyatta's Victory Means for Africa", *Time*, 9 March 2013, available at <http://world.time.com/2013/03/09/kenyas-election-what-uhuru-kenyattas-victory-means-for-africa/>.
1697 Dayo Olopade, "Who's Afraid of the International Criminal Court? In Kenya, the answer is no one at all", *op. cit.*
1698 "Kenya election: Uhuru Kenyatta wins presidency", BBC News, 9 March 2013, available at <http://www.bbc.co.uk/news/world-africa-21723488>.
1699 *Ibid.*
1700 *Ibid.*
1701 "Another Failing Prosecution at the International Criminal Court", 7 March 2013, available at <http://humanrightsdoctorate.blogspot.co.uk/2013/03/another-failing-prosecution-at.html>.
1702 ICC, "The Prosecutor v. Francis Kirimi Muthaura and Uhuru Muigai Kenyatta, Public redacted version of the 25 February 2013 Consolidated Prosecution response to the Defence

applications under Article 64 of the Statue to refer the confirmation decision back to the Pre-Trial Chamber", 25 February 2013, ICC-01/09-02/11-664-Red2, available at <http://www.icc-cpi.int/iccdocs/doc/doc1557330.pdf>.

1703 ICC, "The Prosecutor v. Francis Kirimi Muthaura and Uhuru Muigai Kenyatta, Prosecution notification of withdrawal of the charges against Francis Kirimi Muthaura", 11 March 2013, ICC-01/09-02/11, available at <http://www.icc-cpi.int/iccdocs/doc/doc1565549.pdf>. See, also, "ICC drops charges against Kenyan leader", UPI, 11 March 2013, available at <http://www.upi.com/Top_News/Special/2013/03/11/ICC-drops-charges-against-Kenyan-leader/UPI-71711363016878/>.

1704 "Personal Statement of Ambassador Francis Kirimi Muthaura", Capital FM blog, 13 March 2013, available at <http://www.capitalfm.co.ke/eblog/2013/03/13/personal-statement-of-ambassador-francis-kirimi-muthaura/>.

1705 "ICC witness against Ruto steps down", *Standard Digital* (Nairobi), 18 March 2013, <http://www.standardmedia.co.ke/?articleID=2000079593&pageNo=2&story_title=Kenya:%20ICC%20witness%20against%20Ruto%20steps%20down>.

1706 *Ibid.*

1707 "Kenya: ICC Witness Who Recanted Ruto Accuses ICC Prosecutors of Harassment", *The Star* (Nairobi), 24 March 2013, available at <http://allafrica.com/stories/201303250588.html>.

1708 See, "Hard Talk Kenya", 26 March 2013, available at <https://hardtalkkenya.wordpress.com/2013/03/26/all-the-hype-that-luis-moreno-ocampo-and-his-prosecution-team-created-around-the-kenyan-icc-cases-is-falling-apart-what-kind-of-investigations-were-done-who-really-carried-out-those-investigations/>; and the *Sunday Nation*, 24 March 2013.

1709 'Three Witnesses Back Out of Uhuru ICC Case', Capital FM (Nairobi), 5 April 2013, available at <http://allafrica.com/stories/201304051483.html>.

1710 "Did the ICC help Uhuru Kenyatta win Kenyan election?", BBC News, 11 March 2013, available at <http://www.bbc.co.uk/news/world-africa-21739347>.

1711 Binyavanga Wainaina, "Kenyans elected a president we felt could bring peace", *The Guardian*, 10 March 2013, available at <http://www.guardian.co.uk/commentisfree/2013/mar/10/kenyans-peace-uhuru-kenyatta-defiant?INTCMP=ILCNETTXT3487>. Binyavanga Wainaina is the founding editor of the literary magazine *Kwani?* and won the Caine Prize for African Writing in 2002. He has written for *The New York Times*, *The Guardian* and *National Geographic*. He is the Director of the Chinua Achebe Center for African Writers and Artists at Bard College.

1712 Binyavanga Wainaina, "Kenyans elected a president we felt could bring peace", *op. cit.*

1713 *Ibid.*

1714 *Ibid.*

1715 See, "Hard Talk Kenya", 26 March 2013, *op. cit.*, and the *Sunday Nation*, 24 March 2013.

1716 See, "ICC judge withdraws from Kenyan leaders' case. Christine Van Den Wyngaert criticises prosecutors for failing to disclose evidence against President Uhuru Kenyatta", Aljazeera, 27 April 2013, available at <http://www.aljazeera.com/news/africa/2013/04/2013427175150653880.html>.

1717 Kevin Jon Heller, "Troubling Development in the Kenyatta Case (Updated) (Updated Again)", Opiniojuris, 27 May 2013, available at <http://opiniojuris.org/2013/04/27/troubling-development-in-the-kenyatta-case/>.

1718 *Ibid.*

1719 *Ibid.*

1720 See, "International court charges Kenyan with bribing witnesses", Reuters, 2 October 2013, available at <http://uk.reuters.com/article/2013/10/02/uk-kenya-icc-bribes-idUKBRE9910BE20131002>.

1721 "Kenya: Barasa Responds to ICC Arrest Warrant", *Sabahi* (Washington DC), 3 October 2013, available at <http://allafrica.com/stories/201310040128.html>.
1722 "Kenyan MPs vote to quit international criminal court", *The Guardian*, 5 September 2013, available at <http://www.theguardian.com/world/2013/sep/05/kenya-quit-international-criminal-court>.
1723 "Kenya National Assembly Passes Motion to Repeal Rome Statute", Capital FM (Nairobi), 5 September 2013.
1724 "Kenyan Senate Agrees to Withdraw From ICC", *Sabahi* (Washington DC), 12 September 2013, available at <http://allafrica.com/stories/201309130163.html>.
1725 "Africa vs Int'l Court: Quotes on the court as leaders meet before trial of Kenya's president", Associated Press, 11 October 2013, available at <http://articles.washingtonpost.com/2013-10-11/world/42913126_1_african-union-icc-kenyan-president-uhuru-kenyatta>.

Notes to Chapter Twenty-three

1726 See, "Ivory Coast: Gbagbo Appears Before the ICC. Laurent Gbagbo's confirmation of charges hearing at The Hague started today. However, the ICC runs the risk of producing one-sided justice", Think Africa Press, 19 February 2013, available at <http://thinkafricapress.com/ivory-coast/gbagbo-appears-icc>.
1727 Republic of Côte d'Ivoire, "Declaration Accepting the Jurisdiction of the International Criminal Court", 18 April 2003, available at <http://www.icc-cpi.int/NR/rdonlyres/9CFE32D1-2FCB-4EB4-ACA0-81C2343C5ECA/279844/ICDEENG7.pdf>.
1728 Republic of Côte d'Ivoire, "Letter reconfirming the acceptance of the ICC jurisdiction", 14 December 2010, available at <http://www.icc-cpi.int/NR/rdonlyres/498E8FEB-7A72-4005-A209-C14BA374804F/0/ReconCPI.pdf>.
1729 ICC, "Background information for the case The Prosecutor v. Laurent Gbagbo", available at <http://www.icc-cpi.int/en_menus/icc/situations%20and%20cases/situations/icc0211/related%20cases/icc02110111/background%20information/Pages/ginfo.aspx>.
1730 "Laurent Gbagbo and the right to 'difference'", *ResetDOC*, Reset-Dialogues on Civilizations, 30 January 2013, available at <http://www.resetdoc.org/page/00000000035>.
1731 See, for example, "3.1.2. No agreement was reached in the results announced by the president of the IEC as foreseen by the procedures; 3.1.3. The President of the IEC declared the results alone, in the absence of the other members of the IEC and therefore in violation of the provisions and procedures of the same IEC", Thabo Mbeki, *Le Rapport de Thabo Mbeki sur sa mediation en Côte d'Ivoire*, December 2010. Fagiolo points out that Mbeki recalls how the US Ambassador in Abidjan, Wanda L. Nesbitt, had already warned her government in 2009 that without some basic requirements fulfilled – a territorial and fiscal reunification of the country, the return of the national administration to the north, and especially the total disarmament of the rebellion, the *Forces Nouvelles*, implanted in the north since 2002 – no democratic elections could be held. See, Thabo Mbeki, "What the world got wrong in Côte d'Ivoire", *Foreign Policy*, 29 April 2011, available at <http://www.foreignpolicy.com/articles/2011/04/29/what_the_world_got_wrong_in_cote_d_ivoire>.
1732 "Laurent Gbagbo and the right to 'difference'", *op. cit*.
1733 Despite the fact that the call for the rebel pro-Ouattara forces, *Force Nouvelles*, to be demobilised, something repeated in eight peace agreements since 2003, this was never carried out. They remain active and are said to contribute to the climate of insecurity in which Côte d'Ivoire currently finds itself.
1734 "On Duekoue Massacre in Cote d'Ivoire, As Ouattara's Bamba Says Caritas is Pro-Gbagbo, UN Is Compromised", *Inner City Press*, 4 April 2011, available at <http://www.innercitypress.com/cote1duekoue040411.html>.

1735   "Analysis: A long road ahead for justice in Côte d'Ivoire", IRIN, 3 May 2013, available at <http://reliefweb.int/report/c%C3%B4te-divoire/analysis-long-road-ahead-justice-c%C3%B4te-divoire>.
1736   Nicoletta Fagiolo, "Orientalism in Africa? The ICC and the case of Laurent Gbagbo", *ResetDOC*, Reset-Dialogues on Civilizations, 30 May 2013, available at <http://www.resetdoc.org/story/00000022250>.
1737   ICC, "The Prosecutor v. Laurent Gbagbo Situation in the Republic of Côte d'Ivoire", Warrant of Arrest, 23 November 2011, ICC-02/11-01/11, available at <http://www.icc-cpi.int/iccdocs/doc/doc1276751.pdf>.
1738   ICC, *The Prosecutor v. Laurent Gbagbo*, "New suspect in the ICC's custody: Laurent Gbagbo arrived at the detention centre", press release, 30 November 2011, ICC-CPI-20111130-PR747, available at <http://www.icc-cpi.int/en_menus/icc/press%20and%20media/press%20releases/press%20releases%20%282011%29/Pages/pr747.aspx>.
1739   Tim Zwart and Alexander Knoops, "Who is persecuting Laurent Gbagbo?", *New African*, April 2013, p. 16.
1740   *Ibid.*
1741   See Laurent Gbagbo's pre-trial hearing speech, 28 February 2013. See, "CPI: le président Gbagbo vous parle (le 28 fev 2013)", YouTube, available at <http://www.youtube.com/watch?v=yN_ENjDTiYM>.
1742   See, for example, defence team submission, in *"Version publique expurgée des soumissions écrites de la défense portant sur un certain nombre de questions discutées lors de l'audience de confirmation des charges"*, the Prosecutor v. Laurent Gbagbo. Situation in the Republic of Côte d'Ivoire Public Court Records – Defence, ICC-02/11-01/11-429-Red, 3 April 2013, p. 10.
1743   Prosecution's submission on issues discussed during the confirmation hearing, the Prosecutor v. Laurent Gbagbo. Situation in the Republic of Côte d'Ivoire public court records, Office of the Prosecutor, ICC-02/11-01/11-420-Red, 14 March 2013, p. 12.
1744   Nicoletta Fagiolo, "Orientalism in Africa? The ICC and the case of Laurent Gbagbo", *ResetDOC*, Reset-Dialogues on Civilizations, 30 May 2013, available at <http://www.resetdoc.org/story/00000022250>.
1745   *Ibid.*
1746   Edward Said, *Orientalism*, Vintage books, New York, October 1979, p. 18.
1747   "Q&A: Laurent Gbagbo and the International Criminal Court", Human Rights Watch, 12 February 2013, available at <http://www.hrw.org/news/2013/02/12/qa-laurent-gbagbo-and-international-criminal-court#3>.
1748   "Laurent Gbagbo and the right to 'difference'", *ResetDOC*, Reset-Dialogues on Civilizations, 30 January 2013, available at <http://www.resetdoc.org/page/00000000035>.
1749   Nicoletta Fagiolo, "Orientalism in Africa? The ICC and the case of Laurent Gbagbo", *op. cit.*
1750   "Analysis: A long road ahead for justice in Côte d'Ivoire", IRIN, 3 May 2013, available at <http://reliefweb.int/report/c%C3%B4te-divoire/analysis-long-road-ahead-justice-c%C3%B4te-divoire>.
1751   "Random Comments on the Mali Self-Referral to the ICC", Spreading The Jam, 20 July 2012, available at <http://dovjacobs.blogspot.co.uk/2012/07/random-comments-on-mali-self-referral.html>.
1752   Tim Zwart and Alexander Knoops, "Who is persecuting Laurent Gbagbo?", *op. cit.*, p. 17.
1753   *Ibid.*
1754   "Ivory Coast: Gbagbo Appears Before the ICC. Laurent Gbagbo's confirmation of charges hearing at The Hague started today. However, the ICC runs the risk of producing one-sided justice", Think Africa Press, 19 February 2013, available at <http://thinkafricapress.com/ivory-coast/gbagbo-appears-icc>.

1755 "Turning Rhetoric Into Reality: Accountability for Serious International Crimes in Côte d'Ivoire", Human Rights Watch, New York, 4 April 2013, available at <http://www.hrw.org/node/114480>.
1756 Ibid.
1757 Ibid.
1758 See, for example, Théophile Kouamouo, *J'accuse Outtara, Pourquoi la place de cette homme et devant un juge*, Le Gri Gri, Paris, 2012.
1759 See, paragraph 35 in ICC, "*Decision on the 'Prosecution's provision of further information regarding potentially relevant crimes committed between 2002 and 2010*", 22 February 2012.
1760 "Laurent Gbagbo and the right to 'difference'", *ResetDOC*, Reset-Dialogues on Civilizations, 30 January 2013, available at <http://www.resetdoc.org/page/00000000035>.
1761 "ICC judges rule insufficient evidence for Gbagbo trial", Radio Netherlands Worldwide, 6 June 2013, available at <http://www.rnw.nl/africa/video/icc-judges-rule-insufficient-evidence-gbagbo-trial>.
1762 ICC, the Prosecutor v. Simone Gbagbo, Warrant of Arrest, ICC-02/11-01/12, 29 February 2012, available at <http://www.icc-cpi.int/iccdocs/doc/doc1344439.pdf>.
1763 "ICC unveils arrest warrant for Ivory Coast politician Ble Goude", Reuters, 1 October 2013, availble at <http://uk.reuters.com/article/2013/10/01/uk-ivorycoast-icc-idUKBRE9900H42013100112:24pm BST>.

Notes to Chapter Twenty-four

1764 Mark Kersten, "No winners in ICC-Libya standoff", *Foreign Policy*, 8 October 2012, available at <http://mideast.foreignpolicy.com/posts/2012/10/08/no_winners_in_icc_libya_standoff>.
1765 "Extradition of Abdullah al-Senussi is a blow to international justice", *The Guardian* (London), 5 September 2012, available at <http://www.guardian.co.uk/commentisfree/2012/sep/05/extradition-abdullah-al-senussi-justice>.
1766 See, for example, "Gaddafie Captured alive then Executed footage", Liveleak.com, 20 October 2011, available at <http://www.liveleak.com/view?i=598_1319129108>, "UN calls for probe into Gaddafi's death", Aljazeera, 22 October 2011 and "Pressure grows for Gaddafi death investigation", ABC News, 22 October 2011.
1767 UNSC, Security Council Resolution 1970 (2011), 26 February 2011, S/RES/1970 (2011), available at <http://www.unhcr.org/refworld/docid/4d6ce9742.html>.
1768 "Libya: African mercenaries 'immune from prosecution for war crimes'", *The Daily Telegraph*, 27 February 2011.
1769 "Due to US Libya ICC Loophole, Qatar, Ukraine & UAE Could Also Be Immune", *Inner City Press*, 23 March 2011.
1770 Sir Geoffrey Nice, "The Permanent International Criminal Court and Africa", Gresham College Lectures, 31 October 2012, available at <http://www.gresham.ac.uk/lectures-and-events/the-permanent-international-criminal-court-%E2%80%93-the-icc-and-africa>.
1771 "The ICC and the Security Council: Just Say No?", justiceinconflict.org, 29 February 2012, available at <http://justiceinconflict.org/2012/02/29/the-icc-and-the-security-council-just-say-no/>.
1772 UNSC, Security Council Resolution 1970 (2011), 26 February 2011, S/RES/1970 (2011), available at <http://www.unhcr.org/refworld/docid/4d6ce9742.html>.
1773 Michael Ignatieff, "We're So Exceptional", *The New York Review of Books*, 5 April 2012.
1774 "Indicting Gaddafi for War Crimes: Will It Help or Hurt?", *Time*, 4 May 2011.
1775 "Libya: Gaddafi continues to elude Nato's grasp", BBC, 21 June 2011.
1776 *Making Sense of Libya, op. cit.*

1777 "Libya Gaddafi continues to elude Nato's grasp", *op. cit.*
1778 "ICC prosecutor 'almost ready' for Libya abuse trial", *Agence France-Presse*, 15 May 2011.
1779 Mark Ierace, "Complexities in prosecuting international crimes: the ICC Libyan warrants", in Gideon Boas, William Schabas and Michael P. Scharf (editors), *International Criminal Justice: Legitimacy and Coherence*, Edward Elgar Publishing, 2012, p. 112. Mark Ierace, SC, is a visiting fellow in international criminal law at the University of New South Wales and a former prosecutor in the UN International Criminal Tribunal for the former Yugoslavia in The Hague.
1780 Louise Arbour, "The Rise and Fall of International Human Rights", Lecture by Louise Arbour, President and CEO of the ICG, on the occasion of the Sir Joseph Hotung International Human Rights Lecture 2011, at the British Museum, 27 April 2011, available at <http://www.crisisgroup.org/en/publication-type/speeches/2011/the-rise-and-fall-of-international-human-rights.aspx>.
1781 *Ibid.*
1782 Philippe Sands, "Referring Syria to the international criminal court is a justified gamble", *The Guardian*, 16 January 2013, available at <http://www.guardian.co.uk/commentisfree/2013/jan/16/syria-international-criminal-court-justified-gamble>.
1783 "ICC: Letter to Prosecutor-Elect Fatou Bensouda. Priorities for the New International Criminal Court Prosecutor", Human Rights Watch, 8 June 2012, available at <http://www.hrw.org/news/2012/06/08/icc-letter-prosecutor-elect-fatou-bensouda>.
1784 "Up to his eyeballs in murder...Gaddafi's fingernail-puller-in-chief", *Daily Mail*, 4 April 2011.
1785 Jody McIntyre, "'Revolutionaries' are not armed by the West", *The Independent*, 3 April 2011, <http://blogs.independent.co.uk/2011/04/03/%E2%80%98revolutionaries%E2%80%99-are-not-armed-by-the-west/>.
1786 David Ignatius, "In Libya a minefield of NATO miscues and tribal politics", *Washington Post*, 15 June 2011, available at <http://www.washingtonpost.com/opinions/in-libya-a-minefield-of-nato-miscues-and-tribal-politics/2011/06/14/AGRhlAVH_story.html>.
1787 See, "France: Gadhafi could possibly stay in Libya", Associated Press, 20 June 2011.
1788 "William Hague: Colonel Gaddafi 'could stay in Libya'", BBC News, 26 July 2011, available at <http://www.bbc.co.uk/news/uk-politics-14290213>.
1789 "Hague refuses to put timeline on operations in Libya", *The Independent*, 2 August 2011.
1790 "US looks on Libya as McDonald's – Gaddafi's son", *Russia Today*, 1 July 2011, available at <http://rt.com/news/interview-gaddafi-libya-usa/>.
1791 Seph Brown, "Four Questions NATO Must Answer on Libya", Huffpost Politics, 28 July 2011, available at <http://www.huffingtonpost.co.uk/seph-brown/four-questions-nato-must-_b_910564.html>.
1792 See, for example, "Gaddafi faces new ICC charges for using rape as weapon in conflict", *The Guardian*, 9 June 2011, and "Gaddafi ordered mass rapes in Libya, ICC prosecutor says", *Washington Post*, 9 June 2011.
1793 See, for example, "ICC: Evidence shows that Qaddafi ordered rape of hundreds", *The Christian Science Monitor*, 9 June 2011, "Libya mass rape claims: using Viagra would be a horrific first. Reports of the distribution of 'Viagra-type' pills to troops add an unprecedented element to Gaddafi's alleged war crimes", *The Guardian*, 9 June 2011.
1794 See "Libya rape claims 'hysteria' – investigator", *Agence France-Presse*, 10 June 2011, "UN investigator casts doubt over Libya mass rape claims", *Agence France Presse*, 9 June 2011.
1795 *Ibid.*
1796 "Libyan envoy accuses rebels, NATO of war crimes", *Arab News*, 9 June 2011, available at <http://www.arabnews.com/node/380255>.
1797 "Lies damn lies and reports of battlefield atrocities", *The Independent*, 19 June 2011, available at <http://www.independent.co.uk/opinion/commentators/patrick-cockburn-lies-damn-lies-and-reports-of-battlefield-atrocities-2299701.html>.

1798 "No evidence of Libya Viagra rape claims. But war crimes? Plenty", *Christian Science Monitor*, 24 June 2011, available at <http://www.csmonitor.com/World/Backchannels/2011/0624/No-evidence-of-Libya-Viagra-rape-claims.-But-war-crimes-Plenty>.
1799 "Amnesty questions claim that Gaddafi ordered rape as weapon of war", *The Independent*, 24 June 2011.
1800 *Ibid.*
1801 "Rape in Libya: The Crime That Dare Not Speak Its Name", *Time*, 9 June 2011.
1802 Diana Eltahawy is Amnesty International's Libya expert and was in the country throughout May, including in Misratah and Benghazi. She also visited the Libyan-Tunisian border area in April.
1803 "Lies damn lies and reports of battlefield atrocities", *The Independent, op. cit.*
1804 *Ibid.*
1805 "ICC to investigate reports of Viagra-fueled gang-rapes in Libya", CNN, 17 May 2011, available at <http://articles.cnn.com/2011-05-17/world/libya.rapes.icc_1_rapes-viagra-pills-libyan-leader-moammar-gadhafi?_s=PM:WORLD>. See, also, "Libya – Nato: Kadhafi used rape as weapon of war, Moreno-Ocampo claims", Radio France International, 9 June 2011, available at <http://mobile.english.rfi.fr/africa/20110609-kadhafi-used-rape-weapon-war-moreno-ocampo-claims>; "Kadhafi 'ordered mass rapes' in Libya: ICC", *Agence France-Presse*, 9 June 2011.
1806 "Libya rape claims 'hysteria' – investigator", *Agence France-Press*, 10 June 2011.
1807 "Amnesty questions claim that Gaddafi ordered rape as weapon of war", *The Independent*, 24 June 2011.
1808 "US intel: No evidence of Viagra as weapon in Libya. UN Ambassador Rice reportedly had said drug was being used in systematic rapes", NBC News and news services, 29 April 2011, available at <http://www.msnbc.msn.com/id/42824884/ns/world_news-mideastn_africa/#>.
1809 Russ Baker, "Did Qaddafi Really Order Mass Rapes? Or is the West Falling Victim to a Viagra-strength Scam?", 11 June 2011, Businessinsider.com, available at <http://www.businessinsider.com/did-qaddafi-really-order-mass-rapes-or-is-the-west-falling-victim-to-a-viagra-strength-scam-2011-6#ixzz1P2udSl58>.
1810 "Why women and truth are the first casualties of war", *Belfast Telegraph*, 15 June 2011, available at <http://www.belfasttelegraph.co.uk/opinion/columnists/eamon-mccann/why-women-and-truth-are-the-first-casualties-of-war-16011596.html#ixzz1PMTZ6ocY>.
1811 "No evidence of Libya Viagra rape claims. But war crimes? Plenty", *Christian Science Monitor, op. cit.*
1812 *Ibid.*
1813 Dr. Alan Huffman, *Here I Am: The Story of Tim Hetherington, War Photographer*, Grove Press, 2013, p. 174.
1814 "Libya: Behind the phony ICC 'rape' charges", *Workers World*, 15 June 2011, available at <http://www.workers.org/2011/world/libya_phony_rape_charges_0623/>.
1815 ICC, "Situation in the Libyan Arab Jamahiriya", ICC-01/11, 27 June 2011. See, also, ICC, "Statement ICC Prosecutor Press Conference on Libya", 16 May 2011.
1816 "Amnesty questions claim that Gaddafi ordered rape as weapon of war", *The Independent*, 24 June 2011.
1817 "Es fand eine regelrechte Jagd auf Migranten statt", *Der Standard* (Vienna), 6 July 2011, available at <http://derstandard.at/plink/1308680482845?sap=2&_pid=21929887>.
1818 "Libyan rebels accused of targeting blacks. Rights groups say African migrant workers and black Libyans face beatings and detention by rebel fighters who suspect them of being mercenaries hired by Moammar Kadafi to put down the rebellion", *Los Angeles Times*, 4 March 2011.
1819 *Ibid.*

1820	Annex I to Request for Disqualification, 3 May 2012, ICC-01/11-01/11-133-AnxI (OA 3), p. 2.
1821	"Amnesty questions claim that Gaddafi ordered rape as weapon of war", *The Independent*, 24 June 2011.
1822	"Making Sense of Libya", Middle East/North Africa Report No. 107, ICG, 6 June 2011.
1823	"Gadhafi's regime may be on the brink in Libya", Associated Press, 21 February 2011, cited in "Making Sense of Libya", Middle East/North Africa Report No107, ICG, 6 June 2011.
1824	"Head of the Executive Committee of the INC-Libya Mahmoud Jibril meets with the ICC Prosecutor", ICC, ICC-OTP-20110629-PR691, 29 June 2011.
1825	The courthouse incident was videoed and can be viewed on the internet. See, "Graffic Cannibalism In Libya War, Rape, Murder", Disclose.tv, available at <http://www.disclose.tv/action/viewvideo/75140/Graffic_Cannibalism_in_Libya_War_Rape_Murder/>.
1826	"Inferior Arms Hobble Rebels in Libya War", *The New York Times*, 20 April 2011.
1827	"Rebels-in-waiting: The children as young as SEVEN being trained to fight on the front lines against Gaddafi", *Daily Mail*, 13 July 2011, available at <http://www.dailymail.co.uk/news/article-2014236/Libya-Children-young-7-trained-fight-Gaddafi.html#>.
1828	See, for example, *The New York Times* at <http://www.nytimes.com/interactive/world/africa/2011-july-libya-slide-show.html#166>, *Los Angeles Times* at <http://latimesblogs.latimes.com/washington/2011/05/ticket-pic-of-the-week-libya-rebels.html>, *The Daily Telegraph* at <http://www.telegraph.co.uk/news/worldnews/africaandindianocean/libya/8414542/Wests-fears-over-spectre-of-al-Qaeda-among-rebels.html>, and Google at <https://sites.google.com/site/libyacivilcrisis1134/photos-from-libya-p>.
1829	See, for example, "Congo militia leader 'trained child soldiers to kill'", *The Guardian*, 26 January 2011, available at <http://www.guardian.co.uk/world/2009/jan/26/thomas-lubanga-international-criminal-court>.
1830	See, for example, "Libya: Saif al-Islam Gaddafi detained by rebels, ICC confirm", *The Daily Telegraph*, 22 August 2011, available at <http://www.telegraph.co.uk/news/worldnews/africaandindianocean/libya/8714931/Libya-Saif-al-Islam-Gaddafi-detained-by-rebels-ICC-confirm.html>, "Gaddafi's son Saif arrested in Libya: ICC", Reuters, 21 August 2011, available at <http://www.reuters.com/article/2011/08/21/us-libya-rebels-tripoli-idUSTRE77K2EX20110821>.
1831	"ICC in The Hague Holds Talks on Qaddafi's Son Saif Al-Islam", Bloomberg, 22 August 2011, available at <http://www.bloomberg.com/news/2011-08-22/icc-in-the-hague-holds-talks-on-qaddafi-s-son-saif-al-islam-1-.html>.
1832	Gaddafi was subsequently captured three months later. See, for example, "Muammar Qaddafi's Son Saif al-Islam Captured in Libya", Associated Press, 19 November 2011, available at <http://www.foxnews.com/world/2011/11/19/muammar-qaddafis-son-saif-al-islam-captured-in-libya/>.
1833	"Nick Clegg: only a matter of time before Gaddafi regime is defeated", *The Guardian*, 23 August 2011, available at <http://www.guardian.co.uk/world/2011/aug/23/libya-clegg-chairs-national-security-council>.
1834	"Libya says 1,100 dead in NATO 'war crimes'", *Deccan Herald*, 14 August 2011, available at <http://www.deccanherald.com/content/176140/libya-says-1100-dead-nato.html>.
1835	"Libya: NATO bombings killed 718 civilians", *Russia Today*, 1 June 2011, <http://rt.com/news/line/2011-06-01/#id11239>.
1836	"Nato strikes 'kill 354', says Gaddafi's spokesman", *The Independent* (London), 18 September 2011.
1837	"Libya accuses Nato over bombing of imams", *The Guardian*, 13 May 2011.
1838	See, for example, "France Says NATO Bombing Has Failed", Activist Post, 11 July 2011, available at <http://www.activistpost.com/2011/07/france-says-nato-bombing-has-failed.html>. See also, "NATO war crime: Libya water supply", *Pravda*, 23 July 2011; "Libya

blames NATO for raid on food warehouse", Aljazeera, 26 July 2011; "NATO war crimes, the murder of journalists", *Pravda*, 3 August 2011.

1839 "Nato accused of killing family in botched bombing raid", *The Daily Telegraph*, 4 August 2011.

1840 See, also, "NATO Strikes at Libyan State TV", *The New York Times*, 30 July 2011, and "NATO Planes Hit Libyan State TV Transmitters", Associated Press, 31 July 2011.

1841 "Media group slams NATO bombing of Libyan TV", IBNLive, 4 August 2011 available at <http://ibnlive.in.com/news/media-group-slams-nato-bombing-of-libyan-tv/172796-2.html>.

1842 "Islamists blamed for killing General Abdel Fattah Younes as Libya's rebels face up to enemy within", *The Daily Telegraph*, 30 July 2011.

1843 "Photographic Evidence of NATO War Crimes", *Pakistan Observer*, 11 August 2011.

1844 "Libya slams UN chief over civilian deaths comments", *Agence France-Presse*, 13 August 2011.

1845 "ICC's Ocampo Slow on Majer NATO Deaths, Duekoue in Cote d'Ivoire, 2 Stage Justice?", *Inner City Press*, 16 May 2012, available at <http://www.innercitypress.com/icc1majerciv051612.html>.

1846 "NATO backtracks on denials over killing of Libyan civilians", *The Australian* and *Agence France-Presse*, 22 June 2011, available <http://www.theaustralian.com.au/news/world/nato-backtracks-on-denials-over-killing-of-civilians/story-e6frg6so-1226079527332>. See also, "NATO denies new Libya claim of more civilian deaths in air strike", *The Australian*, 21 June 2011; "NATO takes blame for toddler deaths", *Herald Sun*, 21 June 2011; "NATO 'regrets' civilian deaths in Libya", *The Australian*, 21 June 2011. "Vatican: Airstrikes killed 40 civilians in Tripoli", *The Jerusalem Post*, 31 March 2011, available at <http://www.jpost.com/MiddleEast/Article.aspx?id=214560>; "Libya air raid 'killed civilians'", BBC News, 1 April 2011; "Libya: Coalition air strike near Brega kills rebels", BBC News, 2 April 2011; "Libya says NATO raids killed 718 civilians", Radio Netherlands Worldwide, 31 May 2011, available at <http://www.rnw.nl/english/bulletin/libya-says-nato-raids-killed-718-civilians>; "NATO Air Strikes Hit Residential House, Kill Seven Civilians", *Tripoli Post*, 19 June 2011, available at <http://tripolipost.com/articledetail.asp?c=1&i=6209>; "Libya says NATO strike kills nine civilians", Yahoo News, 19 June 2011, available at <http://news.yahoo.com/s/nm/us_libya>; "NATO Air Strikes in Tripoli Kill 19 Civilians: Libyan TV", Newsfrommiddleeast.com, 19 June 2011, available at <http://www.newsfrommiddleeast.com/?new=78030>; "Libya: Nato 'killed 15 civilians' in Sorman air strike", BBC News Online, 20 June 2011.

1847 "Moscow urges western nations to stop indiscriminate use of force in Libya", RIA Novosti, 20 March 2011, <http://en.rian.ru/russia/20110320/163108359.html>.

1848 UN, "Report of the International Commission of Inquiry on Libya", nineteenth session of the Human Rights Council, A/HRC/19/68, 2 March 2012.

1849 *Ibid.*

1850 Paul Salem and Amanda Kadlec, "Libya's Troubled Transition", Carnegie Paper, Carnegie Endowment, June 2012, available at <http://carnegieendowment.org/2012/06/14/libya-s-troubledtransition/cat5#>.

1851 Human Rights Watch, "Libya: Letter to the ICC Prosecutor on Libyan Amnesty Laws", 25 May 2012, available at <http://www.hrw.org/news/2012/05/25/libya-lettericc-prosecutor-libyan-amnesty-laws>.

1852 ICC, ICC-01/11-01/11-31 at para. 12.

1853 ICC, ICC-01/11-01/11-31, Annex F.

1854 "'Saif Al-Islam Could Be Tried in Libya' Says ICC Prosecutor", *The Guardian*, 22 November 2011. See also ICC, Annex D to ICC-01/11-01/11-31. It has to be pointed out that it can be presumed by virtue of the fact that the Prosecutor relied upon it in its submissions to the Pre-Trial Chamber that the Prosecutor does not dispute the accuracy of its reporting.

1855 ICC, ICC-01/11-01/11-34-Anx.
1856 ICC, ICC-01/11-01/11-72.
1857 ICC, ICC-01/11-01/11-82.
1858 "Hand over Gaddafi son, international criminal court tells Libya", *The Guardian*, 5 April 2012 (ICC, ICC-01/11-01/11, Annex C).
1859 "Hand over Saif Gadhafi, court tells Libya", CNN, 5 April 2012, available at <http://articles.cnn.com/2012-04-05/africa/world_africa_libya-saif-gadhafi_1_moammar-gadhafi-saif-al-islam-gadhafi-zintan?_s=PM:AFRICA>.
1860 ICC, ICC-01/11-01/11-113.
1861 ICC, ICC-01/11-01/11-115, 17 April 2012.
1862 See, "Libya insists on Gaddafi son trial as ICC visits", Reuters, 18 April 2012; "Moreno-Ocampo says ICC has not requested extradition of Senussi", *Libya Herald*, 18 April 2012.
1863 ICC, ICC-01/11-01/11-31, Annex F.
1864 ICC, "Situation in Libya, in the case of The Prosecutor v. Saif Al-Islam Gaddafi and Abdullah Al-Senussi. Public with Public Annex A OPCD. Application in Relation to Public Statements of the Prosecutor", the Office of Public Counsel for the Defence, ICC-01/11-01/11, 17 April 2012, available at <http://www.icc-cpi.int/iccdocs/doc/doc1396611.pdf>.
1865 ICC, "Situation in Libya, in the case of The Prosecutor v. Saif Al-Islam Gaddafi and Abdullah Al-Senussi. Public with Public Annex A OPCD. Application in Relation to Public Statements of the Prosecutor", *op. cit.*, p. 3
1866 *Ibid.*, pp. 8–9.
1867 ICC, "Situation in Libya, in the case of The Prosecutor v. Saif Al-Islam Gaddafi and Abdullah Al-Senussi. Public with Public Annex A OPCD. Application in Relation to Public Statements of the Prosecutor", *op. cit.*, p. 11.
1868 United Nations Human Rights Committee, General Comment 13, 13 April 1984, HRI/GEN/l/Rev.9 (Vol. I), para. 7; see also United Nations Human Rights Committee, "Communication No. 770/1997, *Gridin v. Russian Federation* (Views adopted on 20 July 2000, sixty ninth session)", 27 June 1996, GAOR, A/55/40 (part II), p. 176; African Commission on Human and Peoples' Rights, International PEN, Constitutional Rights Project, "Civil Liberties Organisation and Interights (on behalf of Ken Saro-Wiwa Jr.) v. Nigeria", 31 October 1998, 137/94-139/94-154/96-161/97, para. 96; African Commission on Human and Peoples' Rights, Law Office of Ghazi, *Suleiman v. Sudan*, 3 May 2003, 222/98-229/99, paras. 54–56; European Court of Human Rights, *Allenet de Ribemont v. France*, "Judgement", 10 February 1995, application no. 15175/89, paras. 39–41; European Court of Human Rights, *Butkevicius v. Lithuania*, "Judgement", 26 March 2002, application no. 48297/99, paras. 26–30, 49–54; European Court of Human Rights, *Fatullayev v. Azerbaijan*, "Judgement", 22 April 2010, application no. 40984/07, paras. 36–37, 157–163.
1869 *Daktaras v. Lithuania*, application no. 42095/98, 10 October 2000, para. 41. See also *Allenet de Ribemont v. France* judgment of 10 February 1995, Series A, no. 308, p. 16, § 35.
1870 M. Bergsmo and F. Harhoff, "Article 42", in O. Triffterer (editor) *Commentary on the Rome Statute of the International Criminal Court*, Hart Publishing, 2008, p. 977.
1871 ICC, ICC-02/05-01/09-76-Anx2, 19 March 2010, p. 5.
1872 See, R. Al-Shaeibi, "ICC: Libya has evidence of killing by Gadhafi son", Associated Press (Annex I) and Annex A, p. 4.
1873 ICC, Annex C.
1874 ICC, Annex I. As noted at para. 63 *infra*, the Prosecutor's assertion on this point was based on NTC evidence, which he subsequently claimed not to have seen.
1875 "Libya has 'great evidence' against Gadhafi's son, ICC prosecutor says", CNN, 19 April 2012 (and video insert) (Annex F1 and F2). See also "Libya building up case against Seif: ICC envoy", *Agence France-Presse*, 21 April 2012 (Annex G); and M. Gumuchian, "Libya

says building case against Gaddafi son – ICC prosecutor", 21 April 2012, Reuters (Annex H).
1876 ICC, Annex H.
1877 Special Court for Sierra Leone, *Prosecutor v. Sesay*, "Decision on Defence Motion Seeking the Disqualification of Justice Robertson from the Appeals Chamber", 13 May 2004, at para. 15.
1878 ICC, Annex A.
1879 ICC, Annex D to ICC-01/11-01/11-31.
1880 ICC, "Situation in Libya, in the case of *The Prosecutor v. Saif Al-Islam Gaddafi and Abdullah Al-Senussi*. With Public Annexes A to I. Request to Disqualify the Prosecutor from Participating in the Case Against Mr. Saif Al Islam Gaddafi", Defence, ICC-01/11-01/11, 3 May 2012.
1881 ICC, Annex D, ICC-01/11-01/11-31.
1882 ICC, ICC-01/11-01/11-115 at para. 18.
1883 ICC, Annex H, ICC-01/11-01/11.
1884 See for example, ICC, ICC-01/11-01/11-41-Anx2.
1885 ICC, ICC-01/09-01/11-127, at paras. 3 and 5.
1886 ICC, ICC-01/09-01/11-127, at paras. 9 and 10.
1887 ICC, ICC-01/09-80, 6 October 2011 at paras.8–10.
1888 ICC, ICC-01/09-80, at para. 24.
1889 ICC, ICC-01/09-80.
1890 ICC, Annex B.
1891 See, for example, "Commission of Inquiry Report", A/HRC/19/68 2 March 2012 at para. 41.
1892 ICC, "Situation in Libya, in the case of *The Prosecutor v. Saif Al-Islam Gaddafi and Abdullah Al-Senussi*. With Public Annexes A to I. Request to Disqualify the Prosecutor from Participating in the Case Against Mr. Saif Al Islam Gaddafi", Defence, ICC-01/11-01/11, 3 May 2012.
1893 ICC, "Situation in Libya, in the case of *The Prosecutor v. Saif Al-Islam Gaddafi and Abdullah Al-Senussi*. Public with Public Annex A OPCD. Application in Relation to Public Statements of the Prosecutor", the Office of Public Counsel for the Defence, ICC-01/11-01/11, 17 April 2012, available at <http://www.icc-cpi.int/iccdocs/doc/doc1396611.pdf>, p.15.
1894 See, ICC, ANNEX A PUBLIC, ICC-01/11-01/11-152-AnxA, 18 May 2012.
1895 Ronda Hauben, "Ocampo Misleads UNSC on Saif Al Islam Gaddafi's Detention", *Die Tageszeitung*, 25 May 2012, available at <http://blogs.taz.de/netizenblog/2012/05/25/ocampo-un-security-council-saif-al-islam/>.
1896 ICC, "Situation in Libya, in the case of *The Prosecutor v. Saif Al-Islam Gaddafi and Abdullah Al-Senussi*. With Public Annexes A to I. Request to Disqualify the Prosecutor from Participating in the Case Against Mr. Saif Al Islam Gaddafi, Defence", ICC-01/11-01/11, 3 May 2012.
1897 ICC, "Third Report of the Prosecutor of the International Criminal Court to the UN Security Council Pursuant to UNSCR 1970 (2011)". See also, ICC Prosecutor's briefing to the Security Council on Libya and state responses, 16 May 2012, <http://www.unmultimedia.org/tv/webcast/2012/05/security-council-meeting-the-situation-in-libya-english-6.html>.
1898 Ronda Hauben, "Ocampo Misleads UNSC on Saif Al Islam Gaddafi's Detention", *op. cit.*
1899 *Ibid.*
1900 *Ibid.*
1901 ICC, public redacted version of the "Defence Request", no. ICC-01/11-01/11, ICC, 18 May 2012.

1902 ICC, "Situation in Libya, in the case of *The Prosecutor v. Saif Al-Islam Gaddafi and Abdullah Al-Senussi*", 12 June 2012, no. ICC-01/11-01/11 OA 3, p. 17, available at <http://www.icc-cpi.int/iccdocs/doc/doc1425502.pdf>.
1903 *Ibid.*, p. 16.
1904 ICC, letter S/2012/440.
1905 "UPDATE 2-ICC team visit detained colleagues in Libya", Reuters, 12 June 2012, available at <http://www.reuters.com/article/2012/06/12/libya-icc-idAFL5E8HCI1C20120612?sp=true>.
1906 "Saif al-Islam will not get fair trial in Libya, says lawyer", BBC News Africa, 6 July 2012, available at <http://www.bbc.co.uk/news/world-africa-18734786>.
1907 See "Report of the International Commission of Inquiry on Libya", nineteenth session of the Human Rights Council, A/HRC/19/68,2 March 2012>, and "After the elections, what next for transitional justice in Libya?", No Peace Without Justice, 25 July 2012, available at <http://www.npwj.org/ICC/After-Elections-What-Next-Transitional-Justice-Libya.html>.
1908 "Libyan assembly votes Gaddafi opponent as president", Reuters, 9 August 2012, available at <http://www.reuters.com/article/2012/08/09/us-libya-assemblyidUSBRE8781ID20120809>.
1909 Ronda Hauben, "Ocampo Misleads UNSC on Saif Al Islam Gaddafi's Detention", *op. cit.*
1910 *Ibid.*
1911 Mark Kersten, "No winners in ICC-Libya standoff", *Foreign Policy*, 8 October 2012, available at <http://mideast.foreignpolicy.com/posts/2012/10/08/no_winners_in_icc_libya_standoff>.
1912 Geoffrey Robertson, *Crimes Against Humanity. The Struggle for Global Justice, op. cit.*, p. 779.
1913 *Ibid.*, p. 779.
1914 "Extradition of Abdullah al-Senussi is a blow to international justice", *The Guardian* (London), 5 September 2012, available at <http://www.guardian.co.uk/commentisfree/2012/sep/05/extradition-abdullah-al-senussi-justice>.
1915 *Ibid.*
1916 Richard Dicker, "The Court of Last Resort", *Foreign Policy*, 29 June 2012, available at <http://www.foreignpolicy.com/articles/2012/06/29/ICC_the_court_of_last_resort?page=full>.
1917 "Hague judges rule Gaddafi-era spy chief can face trial at home", Reuters, 11 October 2013.

Notes to Chapter Twenty-five

1918 "The ICC in Mali: Just Another ICC Intervention in Africa?", Justice in Conflict, 19 July 2012, available at <http://justiceinconflict.org/2012/07/19/the-icc-in-mali-just-another-icc-intervention-in-africa/>.
1919 "Mali", "Country Reports on Human Rights Practices for 2011", US Department of State, Washington DC, 2012, <http://www.state.gov/documents/organization/186428.pdf>.
1920 "The ICC in Mali: Just Another ICC Intervention in Africa?", *op. cit.*
1921 "Mali asks Hague court to investigate rebel crimes", Reuters, 18 July 2012, available at <http://www.reuters.com/article/2012/07/18/us-mali-crisis-warcrimes-idUSBRE86H0RA20120718>.
1922 "The ICC in Mali: Just Another ICC Intervention in Africa?", *op. cit.*
1923 William Schabas, "Mali Referral Poses Challenge for International Criminal Court", Ph.D studies in human rights blog, 19 July 2012, available at <http://humanrightsdoctorate.blogspot.co.uk/2012/07/mali-referral-poses-challenge-for.html>.
1924 "Mali", "Country Reports on Human Rights Practices for 2011", *op. cit.*
1925 "The ICC in Mali: Just Another ICC Intervention in Africa?", *op. cit.*

1926 "Mali", "Country Reports on Human Rights Practices for 2011", *op. cit.*
1927 Will Mali Be the First Bensouda-Era Investigation?, *Opinio Juris*, 18 July 2011, available at <http://opiniojuris.org/2012/07/18/will-mali-be-the-first-bensouda-era-investigation/?utm_source=rss&utm_medium=rss&utm_campaign=will-mali-be-the-first-bensouda-era-investigation>.
1928 ICC, "ICC Prosecutor opens investigation into war crimes in Mali: 'The legal requirements have been met. We will investigate'", 16 January 2013, statement, ICC-OTP-20130116-PR869, available at <http://www.icc-cpi.int/en_menus/icc/press%20and%20media/press%20releases/Pages/pr869.aspx>.
1929 ICC, "ICC Prosecutor opens investigation into war crimes in Mali: 'The legal requirements have been met. We will investigate'", *op. cit.*
1930 "Analysis: Cash-strapped ICC takes on Mali", IRIN, 29 January 2013, available at <http://reliefweb.int/report/mali/analysis-cash-strapped-icc-takes-mali>.
1931 "Mali: UN genocide adviser warns of reprisals against Tuareg and Arab populations", UN News Service, 1 February 2013, available at <http://reliefweb.int/report/mali/mali-un-genocide-adviser-warns-reprisals-against-tuareg-and-arab-populations>.
1932 "Analysis: Cash-strapped ICC takes on Mali", *op. cit.*
1933 "Tuaregs hole up to escape reprisal attacks in Mali", *Agence France-Presse*, 24 January 2013.
1934 "Mali: ICC urged to investigate possible war crimes", Amnesty International, 19 July 2012, available at <http://www.amnesty.org/en/news/icc-urged-make-prompt-decision-investigating-mali-war-crimes-2012-07-19>.
1935 "Prosecuting Mali's Extremists. As complex conflict runs on, does International Criminal Court have a role to play?", *ACR*, issue 338, Institute for War & Peace Reporting, 8 February 2013, available at <http://iwpr.net/report-news/prosecuting-malis-extremists>.

Notes to Chapter Twenty-six

1936 Julie Flint, 6 March 2009, "Making Sense of Darfur", available at <http://www.ssrc.org/blogs/darfur/2009/03/06/justice-and-hunger/>.
1937 Glenn Garvin, "The horrors of the Stasi's East Germany", *Reason*, January 2006.
1938 John O. Koehler, *Stasi: The Untold Story of the East German Secret Police*, Westview Press, 2000.
1939 *Ibid.*
1940 "The wall is gone, but the scars of Stasi brutality remain", *The Irish Times*, 14 November 2009. See, also, Mary Fulbrook, *Anatomy of a Dictatorship: Inside the GDR 1949–1989*, Oxford University Press, 1997; Anna Funder, *Stasiland: True Stories from Behind the Berlin Wall*, Granta, London; and Fana Hensel, *After the Wall: Confessions from an East German Childhood and the Life That Came Next*, Public Affairs, New York.
1941 "The Stasi: East Germany's enemy within", *Euronews*, 5 May 2009, available at <http://www.euronews.net/2009/05/05/the-stasi-east-germany-s-enemy-within/>.
1942 "The wall is gone, but the scars of Stasi brutality remain", *The Irish Times*, 14 November 2009.
1943 Koehler, *Stasi: The Untold Story of the East German Secret Police*, *op. cit.*
1944 *Ibid.*
1945 Barbara Miller, *The Stasi Files Unveiled: Guilt and Compliance in a Unified Germany*, Transaction Publishers, New Brunswick, 2004, p. 88.
1946 Koehler, *Stasi: The Untold Story of the East German Secret Police*, *op. cit.*
1947 *Ibid.*
1948 *Ibid.*
1949 *Ibid.*

1950 Steven Richard Ratner and Jason S. Abrams, *Accountability for Human Rights Atrocities in International Law: Beyond the Nuremberg Legacy*, Oxford University Press, 2001, pp. 171, 173.
1951 "East German victims lament lack of justice", *The Local* (Berlin), 5 November 2009, available at <http://www.thelocal.de/national/20091105-23067.html#.UWNIWlf46D4>.
1952 "The wall is gone, but the scars of Stasi brutality remain", *The Irish Times*, 14 November 2009.
1953 See, for example, "The Good Friday Agreement", BBC News, April 1998, <http://news.bbc.co.uk/hi/english/static/northern_ireland/understanding/events/good_friday.stm>.
1954 See, for example, "International Court issues arrest warrant for Sudanese president", CNN, 4 March 2009, available at <http://edition.cnn.com/2009/WORLD/africa/03/04/sudan.president.darfur.charges/>.
1955 See, for example, "Is the ICC Targeting Africa and the Third World Countries?", Modern Ghana.com, 17 March 2009, available at <http://www.modernghana.com/news/206812/1/is-the-icc-targeting-africa-and-the-third-world-co.html>.
1956 The partition of Ireland between the province of Northern Ireland, the north-eastern six counties of Ireland, and the rest of Ireland took place on 3 May 1921 under the *Government of Ireland Act 1920*. Northern Ireland remains part of the UK, while the remainder of Ireland is a sovereign state, known as the Republic of Ireland. Northern Ireland was a province consisting of a largely Protestant population loyal to the British state, governed by Protestant politicians. The minority community was Catholic and could be divided into nationalist and republican supporters, the latter not recognising the partition and seeking the reunification of Ireland as an Irish republic.
1957 The British Government, *We Will Remember Them: The Report of the Northern Ireland Victims Commissioner, Sir Kenneth Bloomfield*, HMSO, Belfast, 1998, p. 4.
1958 See M. T. Fay, M. Morrissey and M. Smyth, *Mapping Troubles-Related Deaths in Northern Ireland 1969–1999*, INCORE/United Nations University/University of Ulster, Londonderry, 1998, p. 44.
1959 See, for example, "Army 'colluded' with loyalist killers", BBC News, 17 April 2003, available at <http://news.bbc.co.uk/1/hi/northern_ireland/2955941.stm>; "Northern Ireland police colluded with killers", BBC News, 22 January 2007, available at <http://news.bbc.co.uk/1/hi/northern_ireland/6286695.stm>; "British security services 'colluded with Loyalists' in Ulster murders", *The Independent* (London), 4 May 1999; "Britain's political and military leaders worked hand in glove with unionist death squads", *An Phoblacht* (Dublin), 25 October 2007; "How Britain created Ulster's murder gangs", *Sunday Herald* (Glasgow), 20 January 2007, available at <http://www.sundayherald.com/news/heraldnews/display.var.1152814.0.how_britain_created_ulsters_murder_gangs.php>; "Police, Army and loyalists 'colluded in policy of murder'", *The Daily Telegraph* (London), 29 March 2003, available at <http://www.telegraph.co.uk/news/uknews/1426076/Police-Army-and-loyalists-colluded-in-policy-of-murder.html>; "How British state used death squads", *Socialist Worker*, 29 June 2002, available at <http://socialistworker.co.uk/art.php?id=5374>. For a legal perspective, see Bill Rolston, "'An effective mask for terror': Democracy, death squads and Northern Ireland", *Crime, Law and Social Change*, Vol. 44, No. 2 (2005), pp. 181–203.
1960 "Who Sanctioned Britain's Death Squads? Time for the truth", Sinn Fein, Dublin, 24 May 2003, available at <http://74.125.47.132/search?q=cache:H2hkqwY8ecgJ:www.sinnfein.ie/pdf/Collusion_Dossier.pdf+british+army+death+squads+ulster&cd=33&hl=en&ct=clnk&gl=uk>.
1961 "British army torture tactics are nothing new, says Adams", *Irish Democrat* (Dublin), available at <http://www.irishdemocrat.co.uk/features/ba-torture/>.
1962 Tom Hadden, "Flight", *Fortnight*, No. 25, 1 October 1971, pp. 8–9.

1963 See, for example, Philip Johnston, "Northern Ireland – ethnic cleansing and population movement", available at <http://www.philipjohnston.com/quot/ni_ethn.htm>.
1964 Displaced Darfurians overwhelmingly headed towards government-controlled towns within the province, actively choosing to place themselves under the protection of the government of Sudan and its institutions – this was before the influx of Western aid organisations. A very small percentage chose to cross the border into Chad. This phenomenon clearly belied the somewhat propagandistic claims that the government of Sudan was waging genocide on the people of Darfur. The victims of genocide rarely move towards those carrying out genocide. German Jews were actively fleeing from Germany in the 1930s, and 1940s, not moving towards Berlin or Munich.
1965 J. Darby and G. Morris, *Intimidation in housing*, Summary page c, Community Relations Commission, 1974.
1966 Julie Flint, 6 March 2009, available at <http://www.ssrc.org/blogs/darfur/2009/03/06/justice-and-hunger/>.
1967 Rob Crilly, "Saving Darfur: The International Criminal Court and the Language of Righting Wrongs", 9 February 2009, available at <http://www.fromthefrontline.co.uk/blogs/index.php?blog=14&title=saving_darfur_the_language_of_righting_w&more=1&c=1&tb=1&pb=1>. Martin McGuinness is a leading Irish nationalist figure within Northern Ireland. The "Good Friday Agreement" was the key peace agreement between the republican gunmen and the British government.
1968 Ian Paisley Jr., "Peace Must Not Be the Victim of International Justice", *op. cit.*
1969 House of Lords Hansard, 8 March 2001, Column 385.
1970 Alex de Waal, "The ICC, Sudan, and the Crisis of Human Rights", *African Arguments*, 5 March 2009, available at <http://africanarguments.org/2009/03/the-icc-sudan-and-the-crisis-of-human-rights/>.
1971 Ian Paisley Jr., "Peace Must Not Be the Victim of International Justice", *op. cit.*
1972 Ramesh Thakur, "Perks of the warring states", *The Japan Times*, 27 March 2009, available at <http://search.japantimes.co.jp/cgi-bin/eo20090327rt.html>.
1973 "Special Reports: UK 'breaking law' over CIA secret flights", *The Guardian*, 5 December 2005, available at <http://politics.guardian.co.uk/foreignaffairs/story/0,11538,1657737,00.html> and "British Tory MP Blasts Extraordinary Rendition, Says Britain Broke International Law and 'Complicit in Torture' if Flights Passed Through UK", *Democracy Now*, 5 December 2005, available at <http://www.democracynow.org/article.pl?sid=05/12/05/1455243>.
1974 "EU endorses damning report on CIA", BBC News, 14 February 2007, available at <http://news.bbc.co.uk/2/hi/europe/6360817.stm>.
1975 "EU rendition report: Key excerpts", BBC News, 14 February 2007, available at <http://news.bbc.co.uk/1/hi/world/europe/6361829.stm>.
1976 "U.N. Blasts Practice of Outsourcing Torture", Inter Press Service, 9 November 2007, available at <http://www.ipsnews.net/news.asp?idnews=30949>.
1977 Ramesh Thakur, "Perks of the warring states", *op. cit.*
1978 See, for example, Mallinder, *Amnesty, Human Rights and Political Transitions*, Hart Publishing, 2008; Mark Freeman, *Necessary Evils: Amnesties and the Search for Justice*, Cambridge University Press, Cambridge, 2009; Charles P. Trumbull IV, "Giving Amnesties a Second Chance", *Berkeley Journal of International Law*, Vol. 25, No. 2 (2007); and Tricia D. Olsen, Leigh A. Payne and Andrew G. Reiter, *Transitional Justice in Balance: Comparing Processes, Weighing Efficacy*, United States Institute of Peace Press, Washington DC, 2010. Dr. Louise Mallinder is a reader in human rights and international law at the Transitional Justice Institute (TJI). She is also TJI's "Dealing with the Past" Research Coordinator. Her doctoral thesis was published as *Amnesty, Human Rights and Political Transitions: Bridging the Peace and Justice Divide* (Hart Publishing, 2008), which was the 2009 Hart SLSA Early

Career Award and was a joint recipient of the 2009 British Society of Criminology Book Prize. Mallinder developed the amnesty law database, which currently contains information on over 520 amnesty laws in 138 countries since the end of World War Two. In addition, Mallinder also worked at Queen's University Belfast as a research fellow, with Professors Kieran McEvoy and Brice Dickson, on a two-year arts and humanities Research Council-funded research project entitled "Beyond Legalism: Amnesties, Transition and Conflict Transformation". This interdisciplinary, comparative study of amnesty laws in Argentina, Bosnia-Herzegovina, South Africa, Uganda and Uruguay, included fieldwork in these jurisdictions. She is Treasurer of the Committee on the Administration of Justice, a leading human-rights organisation in Northern Ireland and a co-vice chair of the American Society of International Law Working Group on Transitional Justice and the Rule of Law. She has also advised a range of policymakers and activists on transitional justice and rule of law internationally and in a number of countries.

1979 Louise Mallinder, "Amnesties' Challenge to the Global Accountability Norm? Interpreting Regional and International Trends in Amnesty Enactment", *op. cit*. For a more detailed discussion of this argument, see Louise Mallinder, "Peacebuilding, the Rule of Law and the Duty to Prosecute: What Role Remains for Amnesties?", in Faria Medjouba (editor), *Building Peace in Post-Conflict Situations*, British Institute of International and Comparative Law London, 2011.

1980 See Robert Parker, "Fighting the Siren's Song: The Problem of Amnesty in Historical and Contemporary Perspective", *Acta Juridica Hungaria*, Vol. 42, No. 1/2 (2001), pp. 69–89.

1981 House of Lords Hansard, 8 March 2001, Column 385.

1982 *Ibid*.

1983 See, "The Amnesty Law Database", available at <http://incore.incore.ulst.ac.uk/Amnesty/about.html>. The amnesty law database was created by Louise Mallinder and developed as part of the arts and humanities Research Council-funded Beyond Legalism project. The database was designed to collate and compare data on amnesty laws that have been introduced since the end of the Second World War. As of February 2010, the database contains information on over 500 amnesty laws in 138 countries that were introduced between 1945 and February 2010. For each amnesty process, where possible, the database contains information on how the amnesty was enacted, what its effects were, how it was implemented, what crimes it covered, whom it benefited, and whether there were conditions attached.

1984 Louise Mallinder, "Amnesties' Challenge to the Global Accountability Norm? Interpreting Regional and International Trends in Amnesty Enactment", *op. cit*.

1985 Uppsala University Department of Peace and Conflict Research, *Active Conflicts by Region (1946–2006)*, Conflict Data Program Uppsala, Sweden, 2007.

1986 Louise Mallinder, "Amnesties' Challenge to the Global Accountability Norm? Interpreting Regional and International Trends in Amnesty Enactment", *op. cit*.

1987 *Ibid*.

1988 See, for example, "Co-Chairs Of Sri Lanka Peace Process Urge Tamil Tigers To End Hostilities", RTT News, 3 February 2009; "Lay down arms, surrender – European Parliament tells LTTE", *The Colombo Times*, 6 February 2009; "U.N. Security Council Asks LTTE To Surrender", RTT News, 22 April 2009.

1989 Gordon Weiss, *The Cage: The Fight for Sri Lanka and the Last Days of the Tamil Tigers*, The Bodley Head, London, 2011, xxiv.

1990 *Ibid*., p. 2.

1991 *Ibid*., p. 80.

1992 *Ibid*., pp. 80–81.

1993 *Ibid*., p. 81.

1994 *Ibid*., p. 299.

1995 *Ibid*., xxii.

1996 "Truth and consequences. Nationalistic fury is good for the government, terrible for Sri Lanka", *The Economist*, 28 April 2011, available at <http://www.economist.com/node/18 620572?fsrc=nwl%7Cwwp%7C04-28-11%7Cpolitics_this_week>.
1997 "Taming the Tamil Tigers", Federal Bureau of Investigation, Washington DC, 2008, available at http://www.fbi.gov/news/stories/2008/january/tamil_tigers011008.
1998 See, *Blackstone's Counter-Terrorism Handbook*, Oxford University Press, 2009.
1999 "Statement on the Designation of 39 Organizations on the USA PATRIOT Act's 'Terrorist Exclusion List'", US Department of State, Washington DC, 6 December 2001. This list was mandated by the USA PATRIOT Act of 2001 (PL 107–56).
2000 "Obama Sends Troops Against Uganda Rebels", Bloomberg News, 14 October 2011.
2001 Louise Mallinder, "Amnesties' Challenge to the Global Accountability Norm? Interpreting Regional and International Trends in Amnesty Enactment", *op. cit*. See, William Schabas, *An Introduction to the International Criminal Court*, Cambridge University Press, Cambridge, third edition, 2007, p. 87.
2002 Michael Freeman, *Necessary Evils: Amnesties and the Search for Justice*, Cambridge University Press, Cambridge, 2011, p. 75.
2003 Protocol Additional to the Geneva Conventions of 12 August 1949, and relating to the Protection of Victims of Non-International Armed Conflicts, 8 June 1977, 1125 UNTS 609, Article 6(5).
2004 Yves Sandoz, Christophe Swinarski and Bruno Zimmerman (editor), *Commentary on the Additional Protocols of 8 June 1977 to the Geneva Conventions of 12 August 1949*, International Committee of the Red Cross, 1987, para. 4618.
2005 UNSC, "Report of the Secretary-General on the Rule of Law and Transitional Justice in Conflict and Post-Conflict Societies", UN, 2004, para. 46.
2006 Louise Mallinder, "Amnesties' Challenge to the Global Accountability Norm? Interpreting Regional and International Trends in Amnesty Enactment", *op. cit*.
2007 *Ibid*.
2008 Philippe Sands, *Lawless World: The Whistle-Blowing Account of How Bush and Blair Are Taking the Law Into Their own Hands*, Penguin Books, 2005, p. 58.

Notes to Chapter Twenty-seven

2009 Tim Black, "'Let's teach these darkies about the rule of law': Courtenay Griffiths, lead counsel for ex-Liberian president Charles Taylor, tells spiked about the racial bias in international criminal justice", *Spiked*, 29 May 2012, available at <http://www.spiked-online.com/site/article/12494/>.
2010 "Meron: International justice 'still selective'", BBC World News TV, 14 March 2013, available at <http://www.bbc.co.uk/news/world-radio-and-tv-21786810>.
2011 *Ibid*.
2012 Mahmood Mamdani,, "Mamdani, on why Raila lost", *Daily Monitor*, 10 March 2013, available at <http://www.monitor.co.ug/Magazines/ThoughtIdeas/Kenya-2013--The-ICC-election/-/689844/1715440/-/item/1/-/wh1tsgz/-/index.html>.
2013 Desmond Tutu, *No Future Without Forgiveness*, Rider, London, 1999, p. 51.
2014 AU, the Constitutive Act, available at <http://www.africa-union.org/root/au/aboutau/constitutive_act_en.htm>.
2015 Adopted by the Assembly of Heads of State and Government of the OAU in Ougoadougou, Burkina Faso, on 9 June 1998 OAU/LEG/MIN/AFCHPR/PROT (111). AU, Protocol to the African Charter on Human And Peoples' Rights on the Establishment of an African Court on Human and Peoples' Rights, available at <http://www.au.int/en/sites/default/files/PROTOCOL_AFRICAN_CHARTER_HUMAN_PEOPLES_RIGHTS_ESTABLISHMENT_AFRICAN_COURT_HUMAN_PEOPLES_RIGHTS_1.pdf>.

2016 Article 3 of the African Charter on Human and Peoples' Rights protocol.
2017 *Ibid*, Article 4.
2018 AU, Protocol on the *Statute of the African Court of Justice and Human Rights*, 2008, available at <http://www.africa-union.org/root/au/documents/treaties/text/Protocol%20on%20 the%20Merged%20Court%20-%20EN.pdf>.
2019 AU, Protocol of the Court of Justice of the African Union, available at <http://www. africa-union.org/root/au/Documents/Treaties/Text/Protocol%20to%20the%20African%20 Court%20of%20Justice%20-%20Maputo.pdf>.
2020 Article 2 of the Statute of the African Court of Justice and Human Rights.
2021 *Ibid*, Article 28.
2022 AU, Assembly/AU/Dec.213 (XII) of February 2009.
2023 Tim Black, "'Let's teach these darkies about the rule of law': Courtenay Griffiths, lead counsel for ex-Liberian president Charles Taylor, tells spiked about the racial bias in international criminal justice", *op. cit.*
2024 "The Politics Of International Criminal Law", *New African*, March 2012, available at <http://www.newafricanmagazine.com/special-reports/sector-reports/icc-vs-africa/the-politics-of-international-criminal-law>.
2025 See, "First Peace, then Justice: Dilemmas of Human Rights Enforcement in our Times", Royal Institute of International Affairs, 6 April 2009, available at <http://www. chathamhouse.org/sites/default/files/public/Research/Africa/060409_bereket_transcript. pdf>. Bereket Habte Selassie is a leading scholar on African law and government. He is William E. Leuchtenburg Professor of African and Afro-American Studies at University of North Carolina at Chapel Hill, and he also instructs at the University of North Carolina School of Law. Dr. Selassie is an activist for reform in Eritrea and a supporter of pan-Africanism. Professor Selassie graduated from the University of Perugia, and received his LL.B and Ph.D from the University of London. Dr. Selassie subsequently held numerous high-profile positions within Ethiopia, serving as Attorney General, Associate Justice of Ethiopia's Supreme Court and Vice Minister of Interior. For an overview of the *Gacaca* experience in Rwanda, see, C. Kirkby, "Rwanda's *Gacaca* Courts: A Preliminary Critique", *Journal of African Law*, Vol. 50 (2006); L. Waldorf, "Rwanda's Failing Experiment in Restorative Justice", in D. Sullivan and L. Tifft (editors), *Handbook of Restorative Justice: A Global Perspective*, Routledge, London, 2006; L. Waldorf, "Mass Justice for Mass Atrocity: Rethinking Local Justice as Transitional Justice", *Temple Law Review*), Vol. 79, No.1 (2006); J. E. Burnet, "The Injustice of Local Justice: Truth, Reconciliation, and Revenge in Rwanda", *Genocide Studies and Prevention*, Vol. 3 (2008); P. Clark, "Hybridity, Holism, and 'Traditional' Justice: The Case of the Gacaca Courts in Post-Genocide Rwanda", *George Washington International Law Review*, Vol. 39 (2008); P. Clark & Z. D. Kaufman (editors), *After Genocide: Transitional Justice, Post-Conflict Reconstruction and Reconciliation in Rwanda and Beyond*, Columbia University Press, 2008; J. H. Powell, "Amnesty, Reintegration, and Reconciliation in Rwanda", *Military Review*, Vol. 88 (2008); M. Sosnov, "The Adjudication of Genocide: Gacaca and the Road to Reconciliation in Rwanda", *Denver Journal of International Law and Policy*, Vol. 36 (2008); B. Oomen, "Justice Mechanisms and the Question of Legitimacy: The Example of Rwanda's Multi-layered Justice Mechanisms", in K. Ambos, J. Large & M. Wierda (editors), *Building a Future on Peace and Justice: Studies on Transitional Justice, Peace and Development*, Springer-Verlag, Berlin, 2009.
2026 William Burke-White, "Reframing Impunity: Applying Liberal International Law Theory to an Analysis of Amnesty Legislation", *Harvard International Law Journal*, Vol. 42 (2001), p. 467.
2027 Ian Paisley Jr., "Peace Must Not Be the Victim of International Justice", *op. cit.*
2028 *The Peace-Justice Dilemma and Amnesty in Peace Agreements*, Conflict Trends, Issue 3 (2007), African Centre for the Constructive Resolution of Disputes, South Africa, available at

<http://www.isn.ethz.ch/isn/Digital-Library/Publications/Detail/?ots591=0c54e3b3-1e9c-be1e-2c24-a6a8c7060233&lng=en&id=101969>.

2029 See, "First Peace, then Justice: Dilemmas of Human Rights Enforcement in our Times", Royal Institute of International Affairs, 6 April 2009, available at <http://www.chathamhouse.org/sites/default/files/public/Research/Africa/060409_bereket_transcript.pdf>.
2030 Barahona De Brito *et al.*, *The Politics of Memory: Transitional Justice in Democratizing Societies*, Oxford University Press, Oxford, 2001.
2031 Traggy Maepa, *The Truth and Reconciliation Commission as a Model of Restorative Justice*, Institute of Security Studies, Monograph No. 111, February 2005, available at <http://www.iss.co.za/pubs/Monographs/No111/Chap6.htm>.
2032 Andreas Follesdal, "Why the European Court of Human Rights might be democratically legitimate – A Modest Defense", *Nordic Journal of Human Rights*, Vol. 27, No. 2 (2009), pp. 289–303.
2033 *Ibid.* See, also, Jutta Limbach *et al.*, *Judicial Independence: Law and Practice of Appointments to the European Court of Human Rights*, Interrights, London, 2004.
2034 "Judge attacks human rights court", BBC News, 4 April 2009, available at <http://news.bbc.co.uk/1/hi/uk/7982785.stm>.
2035 "Lord Hoffmann's parting shot is aimed at European Court of Human Rights", *Solicitors Journal*, 14 April 2009, available at <http://www.solicitorsjournal.com/node/5870>.
2036 "President of Belgian Constitutional Court Criticizes European Court of Human Rights", Strasbourg Observers, 17 May 2010, available at <http://strasbourgobservers.com/2010/05/17/president-of-belgian-constitutional-court-criticizes-european-court-of-human-rights/>.
2037 "Europe's war on British justice: UK loses three out of four human rights cases, damning report reveals", *Daily Mail*, 11 January 2012, available at <http://www.dailymail.co.uk/news/article-2085420/Europes-war-British-justice-UK-loses-human-rights-cases-damning-report-reveals.html>.
2038 "Human rights court must ditch frivolous cases to avoid becoming 'small claims' arena, says Cameron", *Daily Mail*, 25 January 2012, available at <http://www.dailymail.co.uk/news/article-2091364/European-Court-Human-Rights-ditch-frivolous-cases-says-David-Cameron.html>.
2039 "Britain challenges power of human rights court", *The Daily Telegraph*, 21 January 2012, available at <http://www.telegraph.co.uk/news/politics/david-cameron/9030375/Britain-challenges-power-of-human-rights-court.html>.

Notes to Conclusion

2040 "The Politics Of International Criminal Law", *New African*, March 2012, available at <http://www.newafricanmagazine.com/special-reports/sector-reports/icc-vs-africa/the-politics-of-international-criminal-law>.
2041 Adam Branch, "International Justice, Local Injustice: The International Criminal Court in Northern Uganda", *Dissent*, Vol. 51, No. 3 (2004), pp. 22–26.
2042 Eric Posner, "The Absurd International Criminal Court. After 10 years and hundreds of millions of dollars, it has completed precisely one trial", *The Wall Street Journal*, 10 June 2012, available at <http://online.wsj.com/article/SB10001424052702303753904577452122153205162.html>. Posner is a professor at the University of Chicago Law School. He is the author of *The Perils of Global Legalism* (University of Chicago Press, 2009).
2043 Benjamin Schiff, *Building the International Criminal Court*, Cambridge University Press, New York, 2008, p. 2.

2044 ICC, "Statement made by Mr. Luis Moreno Ocampo at the ceremony for the solemn undertaking of the Chief Prosecutor of the ICC", 16 June 2003.
2045 Human Rights Watch, "Unfinished Business. Closing Gaps in the Selection of ICC Cases", September 2011, available at <http://www.hrw.org/sites/default/files/reports/icc0911webwcover.pdf>, p. 2.
2046 "Kenya mall attack may be setback for International Criminal Court: The ICC, already facing accusations of anti-African bias, could find its Kenyan cases – the first involving sitting leaders – even more difficult to prosecute", *Los Angeles Times*, 4 October 2013, available at <http://www.latimes.com/world/la-fg-africa-icc-20131004,0,4916252,full.story>.
2047 "On DRC Trip, Despite UN & French Blackout, ICC Debated, Opposition Ignored", *Inner City Press*, 4 October 2013, available at <http://www.innercitypress.com/unlakes1iccssr100413.html>.
2048 Joshua Rozenburg, "Courting controversy", *The Law Gazette* (UK), 7 August 2008, available at <http://www.lawgazette.co.uk/opinion/columnists/courting-controversy>.
2049 Robert M. Bohm, "'McJustice': On the McDonaldization of Criminal Justice", *Justice Quarterly*, Vol. 23, Issue 1, March 2006, pp. 127–46. Robert M. Bohm is Professor of Criminal Justice and Legal Studies at the University of Central Florida. He is a past president and fellow of ACJS as well as a recipient of its Founders Award. His research interests focus on criminal justice, criminological theory, and capital punishment. Bohm points out that the concept of McDonaldisation has been used to depict developments in a variety of different social institutions, including religion, education, the media, medicine, and leisure and travel.
2050 George Ritzer, *The McDonaldization of society*, Thousand Pine Forge Press, Oaks, Ca., 2004, p. 1. Ritzer points out that the theoretical basis for McDonaldization is Max Weber's theory of rationality and bureaucracy.
2051 *Ibid.*, p. 17.
2052 *Ibid.*, pp. 17, 134.
2053 *Ibid.*, p. 27.
2054 *Ibid.*, pp. 27, 66, 86.
2055 Bohm, *op. cit.*, p. 134.
2056 Ritzer, *op. cit.*, p. 27.
2057 *Ibid.*, p. 28.
2058 Bohm, *op. cit.*, p. 134.
2059 *Ibid.*, p. 141.
2060 See, for example, "Sudan elected to chair Group of 77 at UN", *Sudan Tribune*, 27 September 2008, available at <http://www.sudantribune.com/spip.php?article28750>.
2061 "International Court Under Unusual Fire. Africans Defend Sudan's Indicted Leader", *Washington Post*, 30 June 2009, available at <http://www.washingtonpost.com/wp-dyn/content/article/2009/06/29/AR2009062904322_pf.html>.
2062 Marlies Glasius, "What is global justice and who is it for? The ICC's first five years", Opendemocracy, 22 July 2008, available at <http://www.opendemocracy.net/article/globalisation/international_justice/the-iccs-first-five-years>.
2063 *Ibid.*
2064 Human Rights Watch, *Courting History. The Landmark International Criminal Court's First Years*, *op. cit.*, p. 5.
2065 Bolton declared in his memoirs, *Surrender Is Not an Option: Defending America at the United Nations and Abroad*, that "My happiest moment" at the US State Department "was personally 'unsigning' the Rome Statute" which set up the ICC, reversing the Clinton Administration's signature of the statute.
2066 John Bolton, "Courting Danger: What's Wrong With the International Criminal Court", *The National Interest*, Winter 1998/1999, p. 54.
2067 Luis Moreno Ocampo, ICC Prosecutor, address to international conference on "Building

	a Future on Peace and Justice", Nuremberg, 25 June 2007, available at <http://www.peace-justice-conference.info/download/speech%20moreno.pdf>.
2068	John Bolton, "The United States and the International Criminal Court", remarks at the Aspen Institute, Berlin, Germany, 16 September 2002, available at <http://www.state.gov/t/us/rm/13538.htm>.
2069	*Ibid.*
2070	Lanz, David, "The ICC's Intervention in Northern Uganda: Beyond the Simplicity of Peace vs. Justice", the Fletcher School of Law and Diplomacy, May 2007, available at <http://www.reliefweb.int/rw/RWFiles2007.nsf/FilesByRWDocUnidFilename/PANA-78VKGJ-full_report.pdf/$File/full_report.pdf>.
2071	Adam Branch, *Displacing Human Rights. War and Intervention in northern Uganda*, Oxford University Press, New York, 2011, p. 193.
2072	Ian Paisley Jr., "Peace Must Not Be the Victim of International Justice", *The New York Times*, 16 March 2012.
2073	"'A Dangerous Luxury'. The International Criminal Court's Dream of Global Justice", *Der Spiegel*, 14 January 2009.
2074	*Ibid.*
2075	Branch, *Displacing Human Rights. War and Intervention in northern Uganda*, op. cit., p. 215.

Index

A

Abd-Al-Rahman, Ali Muhammad Ali 282
Abrams, Jason 376, 590
Abubakar, Abdulsalami 304
Abu Ghraib 72, 157
Acana II, David Onen 242
Adada, Rodolphe 287
Adhanom, Tedros 216
African Studies Association of the United States 474
African Union 5, 6, 22, 52, 77, 122, 158, 200, 204, 205, 206, 207, 208, 209, 214, 215, 216, 217, 230, 231, 292, 298, 303, 304, 305, 319, 327, 369, 388, 390, 391, 409, 428, 429, 430, 431, 432, 539, 540, 542, 548, 564, 567, 568, 572, 593, 594
   and indictment of President al-Bashir 303, 304
Agence Nationale de Renseignement 263
Agwai, Martin 279
Akande, Dapo 125, 516
Akol, Lam 297
al-Assad, Bashar 59
Al-Attiya, Abdul Rahman
   and indictment of President al-Bashir 306
al-Bashir, Omar 6, 23, 31, 63, 65, 82, 113, 119, 121, 123, 124, 125, 126, 127, 128, 130, 141, 165, 166, 203, 204, 205, 206, 208, 209, 212, 213, 283, 284, 285, 286, 290, 295, 296, 297, 298, 299, 300, 302, 303, 304, 305, 306, 307, 308, 310, 354, 377, 380, 382, 400, 401, 407, 408, 409, 439, 473, 474, 475, 476, 477, 482, 489, 515, 516, 517, 519, 521, 528, 540, 541, 564, 565, 566, 567, 569, 570, 572, 573, 574
   and Darfur peace process 299, 300
   and the Comprehensive Peace Agreement 299
   arrest warrant for 283, 295
   indictment of 283

   the West's attitude to 299
Albright, Madeleine 70, 72
Alex, Julien 59
Ali, Muhammed Hussein 314
al-Mardi, Mohamed Ali 282
al-Qaddafi, Saif al-Islam. *See* Gaddafi, Saif al-Islam
al-Qaeda 73, 159, 160, 164, 527
al-Senussi, Abdullah 356, 357, 360, 364, 367, 368, 581, 586, 588
al-Zain, Ismat 284, 285
Amnesty International 8, 19, 20, 21, 52, 86, 109, 119, 179, 186, 187, 228, 242, 250, 276, 350, 351, 352, 353, 372, 403, 481, 482, 486, 487, 491, 511, 514, 523, 534, 546, 555, 556, 574, 583, 589
   and definition of the crime of aggression 148
   and Juba peace talks 248
   and the Kunduz bombing 187
Anderson, Kenneth 53, 87, 88, 96, 97, 492, 504, 507
Annan, Kofi 3, 7, 10, 115, 236, 292, 312, 313, 325, 474, 476, 477, 500, 568
Araud, Gerard 158, 234, 346
Arbour, Louise 7, 66, 129, 130, 195, 311, 347, 348, 498, 517, 518, 537, 582
Archer, Peter 32, 486, 487
Arsanjani, Mahnoush 220, 221, 227, 240, 544, 546, 552
Assembly of States Parties 14, 15, 16, 17, 18, 34, 38, 47, 50, 52, 62, 67, 79, 81, 94, 95, 98, 101, 102, 108, 109, 110, 111, 112, 113, 116, 126, 132, 140, 145, 146, 178, 206, 217, 237, 255, 385, 412, 432, 479, 480, 481, 488, 495, 496, 511, 512, 519, 523, 531
Axworthy, Lloyd 88

B

Bakayoko, Youssouf 336
Baker, Alan 85

Baker, Russ 351, 583
Ban Ki-moon 154, 155, 234, 574
Barasa, Walter Osapiri 333
Bassiouni, Cherif 350
Basu, Sudeshna 36, 42, 488, 489
Baudot, Caroline 101
Bellinger III, John B. 76
Bemba, Jean-Pierre 28, 123, 203, 274, 275, 276
  arrest 275
Benito, Elisabeth Odio 103, 106, 256
Bensouda, Fatou 116, 142, 143, 150, 215, 238, 256, 266, 320, 321, 322, 339, 371, 399, 400, 403, 519, 526, 538, 539, 550, 582
Bergsmo, Morten 65, 136, 358, 498, 586
Bertodano, Sylvia de 102, 508
Bethlehem, Daniel 111
Bigombe, Betty 241, 242
Bild 181, 182, 532, 533
bin Laden, Osama 73
bin Ra'ad Al-Hussein, Zeid 14, 101, 111
Biryabarema, Elias 289
Bitti, Gilbert 136
Blair, Tony 87, 200, 504, 531
Blattman, Chris 122, 285, 566
Blattmann, René 202, 256
Bohm, Robert 399, 596
Bolton, John 8, 71, 93, 210, 211, 212, 402, 403, 428, 500, 506, 540, 541, 596, 597
Bonomy, Iain 100, 107, 508, 509
Borch, Frederic 159, 163, 527, 528
Bork, Robert 96, 506
Börlin, Markus 14
Bossuyt, Marc 395
Bouckaert, Peter 352
Bourgi, Albert 57, 494
Bourguignon, Michael 35, 38, 45, 488, 489, 490
Bozizé, François 275, 277
Bradol, Jean-Hervé 293, 294, 569
  on the use of the term genocide 293
Brammertz, Serge 136, 262
Branch, Adam 7, 69, 75, 81, 82, 90, 150, 154, 199, 225, 233, 248, 249, 397, 403, 405, 499, 500, 501, 502, 505, 524, 525, 537, 546, 547, 549, 555, 595, 597
  and Ugandan peace process 248
Brauman, Rony 9, 286, 291, 300, 476, 567, 568, 571
Brockmann, Miguel D'Escoto 22

Brown, Bart 86
Brown, Malloch 204
Brugère, Anne-Laurence 192
Burns, Nicholas 76
Bush, George W. 71, 72, 73, 74, 75, 80, 81, 158, 159, 161, 162, 163, 291, 333, 494, 501, 503, 527, 528, 531
Buyoya, Pierre 304

C

Caldwell, Christopher 298, 570
Cameron, David 395, 595
Campbell, Menzies 354
Carbuccia, Olga V. Herrera 102
Carmona, Anthony T. A. 102, 112
Carnegie Endowment for International Peace 51
Carson, Johnnie 325
Carswell, Douglas 395
Carter, Jimmy 294
Carter Center and the ICC 294
  on the definition of genocide 294
Casey, Lee A. 2, 93, 94, 473, 492, 505, 506
Cassese, Antonio 7, 123, 129, 130, 280, 286, 296, 487, 498, 502, 503, 504, 512, 515, 517, 518, 519, 530, 543
Cathala, Bruno 111, 118, 135, 169, 511, 512
Cayley, Andrew 123, 136, 515
Chapman, Terrence 2, 473
Chaudoin, Stephen 2, 473
Chavez, Hugo 307, 573
Checchi, Francesco 289, 567, 568
Chirac, Jacques 202
Chomsky, Noam 75
Christian Science Monitor 132, 213, 255, 256, 351, 484, 518, 541, 557, 569, 582, 583
Chui, Mathieu Ngudjolo 134, 196, 203, 252, 266, 267, 270, 537, 561
Chung, Christine 136, 228, 546
Cissoko, Diango 370
Clapham, Andrew 85
Clark, Phil 7, 28, 133, 199, 221, 222, 223, 224, 225, 240, 241, 243, 244, 270, 271, 272, 372, 398, 484, 537, 544, 545, 551, 552, 553, 554, 555, 562, 594
Clifford, Lisa 256, 557
Clinton, Bill 71, 72, 117, 307, 333, 483, 484, 500
Clinton, Hillary 79, 81, 325
Coalition for the International Criminal Court 49, 50, 51, 52, 85, 86, 101, 102,

105, 112, 491
  and EU funding 51, 52
Cobban, Helena 229, 239, 547, 551
Cohen, William 72
Cold War 12, 210, 392
Cook, Robin 11, 25, 75, 424, 500
Coomaraswamy, Radhika 301
Corell, Hans 105, 509
Corona, Renato 108
Costa, Beth 355
Cotonou Agreement 39, 40, 41, 46, 489
Cotte, Bruno 266
Coulibaly, Malick 370
Council of Europe 6, 382
Cowper-Coles, Sherard 197, 537
Cox, Brendan 65
Crawford, Neta 181, 184, 195, 532, 533, 537
Crilly, Rob 380, 591

D

Daily Mail 349, 353, 582, 584, 595
Daily Telegraph, The 158, 346, 353, 355, 492, 501, 513, 520, 526, 536, 538, 542, 570, 576, 581, 584, 585, 590, 595
Danforth, John 77, 291
Danner, Allison 30, 485
Dasgupta, Riddhi 164, 165, 166, 528
d'Aspremont, Jean 96, 97, 506, 507
Davenport, David 13, 22, 85, 478, 482, 503
De Bito, Barahona 394
Defensor-Santiago, Miriam 102, 107, 108, 109, 114, 510
de Gurmendi, Silvia Fernandez 136, 523
Delay, Tom 73
del Ponte, Carla 103
De Poncins, Etienne 325
Dershowitz, Alan 169, 529
Desalegn, Hailemariam 214, 215, 216, 423
De Smedt, Michel 262
de Waal, Alex 7, 115, 117, 123, 129, 135, 141, 142, 267, 278, 279, 283, 284, 285, 286, 287, 295, 303, 304, 381, 475, 512, 513, 517, 518, 519, 521, 561, 564, 565, 566, 567, 569, 570, 571, 572, 591
Dicker, Richard 9, 40, 66, 72, 136, 268, 367, 497, 498, 500, 588
Dieng, Adama 372
Dienst, Christian 180
Dixon, Rodney 318
Djotodia, Michel 277
Dlamini-Zuma, Nkosazana 215, 423

Dobrinski, Reinhard 376
Dodd, Christopher 73, 79
Duale, Aden 333
Dunlap, Charles 2, 473

E

Eboe-Osuji, Chile 102
Economist, The 9, 19, 25, 29, 38, 65, 100, 112, 130, 238, 258, 308, 314, 385, 476, 481, 483, 485, 489, 498, 508, 511, 518, 521, 551, 556, 558, 572, 573, 574, 593
  and indictment of President al-Bashir 305
Egeland, Jan 247
  and Juba peace talks 247
Eide, Kai 197
El Sayed, Ahmed Maher 304
Eltahawy, Diana 350, 583
Emmerson, Ben 368
EU rapid reaction force 16
EU European Maritime Force 16
European Court of Human Rights 358, 359, 390, 394, 395
European Instrument for Democracy and Human Rights 49, 50, 51, 53, 86
European Parliament 49, 50, 54, 141, 382, 383, 491, 492, 569, 592
  and extraordinary rendition 141, 382
  policy on the ICC 54
European Union 3, 6, 12, 16, 17, 22, 33, 35, 36, 37, 38, 39, 40, 41, 42, 43, 44, 45, 46, 47, 48, 49, 50, 51, 52, 53, 54, 55, 59, 75, 86, 107, 151, 154, 204, 230, 270, 292, 298, 324, 326, 336, 376, 382, 383, 385, 391, 400, 410, 411, 412, 413, 414, 415, 416, 417, 425, 487, 488, 489, 490, 491, 492, 493, 500, 503, 521, 577, 591
  and amnesty in Sri Lanka 384
  and Bilateral Immunity Agreements 75
  and extraordinary rendition 382
  and justice in Côte d Ivoire 342
  and Kenya s internal affairs 326
  and law in Africa 374
  and the Coalition for the International Criminal Court 86
  and the Gbagbo government 336
  and the ICC 55
  and the Rome Statute 86
  contact with ICC indictees 325
  control over the ICC 324
EU funding of ICC 16

policy on the ICC 54
Evans-Pritchard, Blake 372

F

Fagiolo, Nicoletta 336, 339, 340, 343, 579, 580
Faizi, Aimal 198
Fake, Steven 307, 573
Farhang, Amin 189
Feindiro, Firmin 276
Ferrero-Waldner, Benita 40
Financial Times 26, 291, 476, 483, 492, 506, 507, 508, 509, 512, 568, 569, 570
Findlay, Mark 260, 558
Flint, Julie 117, 129, 135, 141, 142, 279, 283, 285, 295, 374, 380, 512, 513, 517, 518, 519, 521, 564, 565, 566, 569, 570, 589, 591
Flounders, Sara 351
Flynn, Mike 183
Foley, Conor 118, 142, 284, 285, 513, 514, 521, 566
Fordham, Michael 170
Fournier, Christophe 123, 515
Frantzman, Seth 38, 489
Frattini, Franco 355
Frazer, Jendayi 8, 76, 82, 83, 158, 225, 325, 502, 577
Freeman, Michael 385, 593
Fremr, Robert 102
Fulford, Adrian 134, 256, 257, 321
    and the Lubanga conviction 265
Funk, Kevin 307, 573
Funk, T. Markus 104, 509

G

Gaddafi, Muammar 56, 66, 120, 200, 203, 345, 346, 347, 349, 350, 352, 353, 356, 357, 362, 367, 398, 494, 581, 582, 583, 584
    death of 345
Gaddafi, Saif. *See* Gaddafi, Saif al-Islam
Gaddafi, Saif al-Islam 56, 63, 67, 203, 345, 349, 353, 354, 356, 357, 358, 359, 360, 361, 362, 363, 364, 365, 366, 367, 512, 584, 586, 587, 588
Gadhafi, Saif al-Islam. *See* Gaddafi, Saif al-Islam
Gage, William 171
Gallón, Gustavo 229, 547
García, Joel Hernández 111
García, María Solís 102

Garda, Abu 302, 308, 309, 574
Gbagbo, Laurent 202, 203, 335, 336, 337, 338, 339, 340, 341, 342, 343, 344, 579, 580, 581
    French political pressure on 343
Gbagbo, Simone 203, 343
Geis, Jacqueline 28, 32, 60, 218, 229, 240, 244, 299, 302, 485, 486, 496, 542, 547, 551, 554, 570, 571
Genocide Intervention-Net 5
Gerhart, Peter 97, 507
Gerntholtz, Liesel 350
Gibney, Mark 115
Gicheru, Paul 329, 330
Ginsberg, Tom 27, 251, 484, 486, 556
Giry, Stéphanie 297
Glasius, Marlies 50, 51, 85, 123, 272, 400, 401, 491, 492, 503, 515, 562, 563, 596
Glendening, Marc 271, 301
Global Action 50, 86
Goldstone, Richard 26, 28, 205, 209, 250, 483, 485, 539, 556
Goudé, Blé 337, 343
Griffiths, Courtenay 7, 35, 151, 199, 200, 322, 387, 392, 397, 524, 537, 538, 576, 593, 594
Grono, Nick 33, 229, 241, 243, 487, 497, 546, 547, 552, 553, 554, 555, 556
Grossman, Marc 95, 506
Guantánamo Bay 159, 160, 161, 163, 164, 166, 404, 527
    ICC as its European equivalent 1
    tribunals 1
Guardian, The 9, 30, 55, 99, 124, 126, 170, 201, 203, 234, 237, 239, 247, 250, 295, 305, 319, 320, 354, 382, 477, 478, 486, 493, 494, 507, 509, 513, 516, 521, 529, 531, 535, 537, 538, 539, 540, 549, 550, 551, 555, 556, 564, 565, 566, 567, 569, 572, 573, 575, 576, 578, 579, 581, 582, 584, 585, 586, 588, 591
Guariglia, Fabricio 136
Gustafson, Marc 291, 568

H

Hadden, Tom 379, 590
Haggar, Ali 285, 566
Hague, The 7, 9, 14, 15, 18, 33, 43, 48, 65, 79, 96, 107, 120, 133, 140, 141, 166, 214, 215, 225, 238, 239, 242, 247, 251, 256, 260, 268, 274, 275, 281, 305, 307, 318,

335, 338, 343, 349, 365, 366, 367, 373, 377, 380, 402, 403, 433, 475, 476, 480, 484, 488, 489, 498, 502, 503, 507, 524, 531, 543, 546, 552, 557, 565, 580, 584
  and false testimony 260
  compared with Guantánamo Bay 397
  tribunals 1
Hague, William 55, 349, 493, 494
Hall, Christopher 179
Hamilton, Rebecca 245, 554
Hansberry, Heidi 103, 508
Haram, Boko 200, 201
Haroun, Ahmed 124, 140, 282, 295, 297
Hart, H. L. A. 11, 477
Harvard Human Rights Journal 241, 250, 552, 554, 555
Hauben, Ronda 362, 363, 365, 587, 588
Heinsch, Robert 104, 509
Heller, Kevin Jon 126, 127, 200, 201, 257, 258, 332, 333, 369, 370, 371, 372, 516, 517, 518, 556, 578
Helms, Jesse 69, 70, 71, 72, 73, 499
Henham, Ralph 260, 558
Herold, Mark 177
Heusgen, Christoph 182
Honecker, Erich 374, 375, 376
Hooper, David 322
Houldey, Gemma 249
Hovil, Lucy 7, 90, 91, 97, 225, 505, 507, 545
Human Rights Watch 3, 8, 9, 28, 29, 30, 31, 41, 52, 61, 64, 66, 67, 72, 84, 99, 110, 111, 113, 114, 115, 117, 119, 120, 122, 129, 130, 133, 134, 135, 138, 150, 152, 153, 154, 155, 156, 157, 159, 204, 222, 232, 233, 234, 235, 236, 237, 238, 243, 244, 245, 252, 259, 268, 269, 271, 272, 273, 274, 275, 276, 281, 340, 341, 342, 348, 350, 352, 363, 367, 372, 398, 401, 403, 476, 484, 485, 486, 491, 492, 496, 499, 502, 503, 507, 511, 512, 513, 514, 517, 518, 519, 523, 524, 525, 526, 527, 531, 539, 544, 547, 548, 549, 550, 551, 553, 554, 556, 558, 561, 562, 563, 565, 580, 582, 585, 596
  and definition of the crime of aggression 149
  and justice in Côte d'Ivoire 342
  letter to Office of the Prosecutor 419
Hussein, Abdel Raheem Muhammad 310
Hussein, Saddam 73, 167

I

Ibrahim, Moussa 354
Ignatieff, Michael 9, 64, 70, 230, 347, 476, 477, 497, 499, 500, 548, 581
Ihsanoglu, Ekmeleddin
  and indictment of President al-Bashir 306
Independent, The 171, 349, 350, 565, 568, 582, 583, 584, 590
Institute for War & Peace Reporting 101, 143, 433
Intelmann, Tiina 14
International Bar Association 51, 106, 257, 258, 259, 272, 509, 557, 558, 560
International Commission of Jurists 51, 491
International Council of Médecins Sans Frontières 123
International Court of Justice 61, 119, 151, 152, 153, 207, 208, 244, 401
International Criminal Tribunal for Rwanda 12, 25, 33, 66, 116, 330, 387, 508
International Criminal Tribunal for the Former Yugoslavia 12, 18, 19, 25, 26, 33, 66, 95, 99, 103, 112, 116, 136, 229, 347, 383, 387, 480, 482, 508
International Crisis Group 9, 62, 229, 241, 243, 246, 247, 250, 347, 353, 498, 537, 547, 552, 555, 584
  and deterrence 228
International Monetary Fund 96
Irani, Paul 333

J

Jacobs, Dov 226, 341, 344, 546
Jain, Neha 157, 526
Jalil, Mustafa 357
Jamus, Saleh Mohammed Jerbo 309, 310
Jebril, Mahmoud 353, 584
Jeßberger, Florian 192
Jianping, Lu 22, 482, 483
Johnstone, Diana 9, 477
Jones, John 103
Jorda, Claude 112, 226, 511
Jung, Franz Josef 181, 182
Juppé, Alain 349

K

Kabando, Kabando Wa 333
Kabila, Joseph 154, 225, 233, 268, 270, 271, 275, 549, 561
Kabimba, Wynter 214

Kabutu, James Maina 319, 320, 321
Kagame, Paul 3, 142, 210, 211, 213, 392, 474, 541
Kagwanja, Peter 238
Kaiza, David 89
Kampala Review Conference 34, 145, 149, 205
Kanda, Ken 14
Kanu, Allieu Ibrahim 14
Karzai, Hamid 180, 198, 530, 537
Katanga, Germain 203, 252, 266, 267, 270, 271, 561
Kaul, Hans-Peter 17, 103, 312, 313, 314, 315, 404, 480, 574
Kaye, David 7, 8, 9, 63, 308, 476, 512, 573
Kay, Steven 319, 320, 321
Keïta, Xavier-Jean 357, 362
Kemmerer, Alexandra 48, 49, 491
Kennedy, Anthony 162
Kenyatta, Uhuru 6, 203, 214, 215, 216, 314, 315, 317, 318, 319, 320, 321, 322, 323, 324, 325, 326, 327, 328, 330, 331, 332, 333, 334, 431, 432, 475, 542, 551, 574, 575, 576, 577, 578
Kerry, John 79
Kersten, Mark 67, 345, 346, 366, 369, 370, 371, 498, 581, 588
  blog, justiceinconflict.org 433
Khan, Akbar Nasir 178, 531
Khan, Karim 322
Khan, Liaquat Ali 372
Khan, Omera 187
Khogyani, Attaullah 198
Kibaki, Mwai 312, 313, 314, 315, 319, 323, 426
Kilonzo, Mutula 315
Kimani, Dominic Wamugunda wa 331
Kindiki, Kithure 333
Kirsch, Philippe 102, 135, 145, 228, 523, 543, 546
Kissinger, Henry 8, 27, 483
Klaus, Vaclav 38, 489
Klein, Georg 179, 181, 182, 183, 184, 185, 186, 189, 190, 191, 192, 193, 194, 195, 196, 197
Knoops, Alexander 338, 341, 344, 580
Köchler, Hans 58, 59, 77, 78, 175, 281, 296, 494, 495, 530, 565, 570
Koehler, John 374, 375, 376, 589
Koh, Harold 79, 179, 501
Kony, Joseph 82, 203, 215, 223, 232, 240, 241, 242, 247, 250, 251, 385, 552, 553
Kosgey, Henry Kiprono 314, 574, 575

Kossendey, Thomas 182
Koterec, Miloš 111
Kouchner, Bernard 180, 204
Kristof, Nicholas 295, 569
Ku, Julian 229, 237, 521, 547, 550
Kusa, Musa 349
Kushayb, Ali 124, 203, 282, 295. *See* Abd-Al-Rahman, Ali Muhammad Ali
Kutesa, Sam 214

L

Lamamra, Ramtane 214
Lamont, Norman 380, 381, 383
Lanz, David 31, 231, 403, 486, 548, 597
Lavergne, Marc 295
Lavigne, Bernard 87, 136, 262
Lawfare Project 2, 473
le Frapper du Hellen, Béatrice 62, 81, 82, 139, 261
Leonard, Eric 27, 58, 203, 484, 494, 539
Lietzau, William 82
Lloyd, John 26
Lockerbie bombing 349
Lord's Resistance Army 26, 28, 30, 32, 62, 63, 81, 82, 89, 118, 157, 173, 215, 222, 223, 226, 230, 231, 232, 233, 237, 238, 240, 241, 242, 243, 244, 245, 246, 247, 248, 249, 250, 289, 370, 384, 385, 403, 404, 499, 547, 548, 551, 552, 553, 555
  and Juba peace talks 248
Los Angeles Times 279, 352, 353, 492, 564, 583, 584, 596
Losinu, Alex 231
Lubanga, Thomas 119, 120, 130, 131, 132, 133, 142, 143, 153, 174, 203, 223, 228, 252, 253, 254, 255, 256, 257, 258, 259, 260, 264, 265, 266, 268, 270, 271, 272, 273, 400, 402, 556, 557, 562
  and child soldiers 302
  arrest 130
  conviction of 265
Lubbers, Ruud 138
Lukwiya, Raska 242
Luzolo, Emmanuel-Janvier 268

M

Maalim, Farah 318
Mabille, Catherine 256, 258
Mackay, Alexander Murdoch 199
Mackenzie, Ruth 100
Madeira, Francisco 230

Index

Maepa, Traggy 394, 595
Magara, Omingo 238
Magarief, Mohammed 365
Malleson, Kate 100, 510
Mallinder, Louise 383, 384, 385, 386, 591, 592, 593
Mamdani, Mahmood 3, 5, 7, 10, 12, 26, 78, 211, 304, 326, 387, 474, 477, 478, 483, 501, 569, 572, 577, 593
Mandela, Nelson 394
Mao, Norbert 30, 247
Margelov, Mikhail 305
Martin, Guy 351
Martin, Penny 100
Martín, Vidal 35, 48, 49, 55
Marty, Dick 382
Matsanga, David 320
Mbarushimana, Callixte 267, 268, 269
Mbeki, Thabo 7, 201, 304, 336, 579
McCann, Eamonn 351
McChrystal, Stanley 183, 184, 185, 186
McGuinness, Martin 380, 591
McKinnon, Ronald 171
Médecins Sans Frontières 8, 9, 31, 122, 279, 286, 293, 294, 486, 568, 569
    as credible observer regarding allegations of genocide 293
    on allegations of genocide in Darfur 292
Medelci, Mourad 306
    and indictment of President al-Bashir 306
Merkel, Angela 182
Meron, Theodor 387, 593
Mettelsiefen, Marcel 183, 187, 533
Mettraux, Guénaël 18, 19, 480
Michel, Louis 273
Mielke, Erich 375, 376
Miliband, David 180
Miller, Barbara 375, 589
Milosevic, Slobodan 73, 95, 367, 402
Mission in Darfur 5
Mohamed, Amina 334
    BBC HARDtalk 434
Monageng, Sanji Mmasenono 102
Montas, Michele 155
Morris, Madeline 93, 94, 96, 372, 506
Morrison, Howard 102
Moscoso, Mireya 106
Mousa, Baha 171
    A Very British Killing 171
    inquiry 170, 171

Moustapha, Justin Kombo 277
Moy, H. Abigail 243, 552, 554, 555
Moyn, Samuel 56, 494
Mudacumura, Sylvestre 269
Muëller, Andreas 220, 221, 225, 544, 545
Mugabe, Robert 205, 216
Mugume, James 215
Muigai, Githu 318, 319, 325
Mumuni, Alhaji Muhammad 303
Mundt, Alex 28, 32, 60, 218, 229, 240, 244, 299, 302, 485, 486, 496, 542, 547, 551, 554, 570, 571
Murphy, Dan 351
Murungi, Kiraitu 318
Museveni, Yoweri 28, 30, 91, 136, 153, 154, 215, 216, 221, 222, 225, 240, 241, 243, 244, 246, 248, 249, 250, 251, 270, 271, 288, 403, 429, 485, 486, 542
Mushikiwabo, Louise 214
Musyoka, Kalonzo 326
Muthaura, Francis 314, 317, 318, 319, 322, 328, 329, 575, 576, 578
Mutunga, Willy 318, 326

N

Nankabirwa, Ruth 247
NATO 9, 56, 69, 74, 81, 151, 176, 177, 179, 181, 182, 183, 184, 185, 186, 187, 188, 190, 191, 194, 195, 196, 198, 307, 308, 345, 349, 352, 354, 355, 377, 383, 392, 399, 521, 532, 533, 534, 536, 582, 584, 585
    actions in Libya 345
    and the Gaddafi regime 348
    and the Kunduz bombing 184, 189, 190
    credibility of in Libya 355, 585
    UN mandate in Libya 355
Nethercutt, George 40
Newton, Michael 529
New York Times, The 142, 234, 306, 353, 486, 487, 492, 498, 501, 515, 517, 521, 524, 531, 532, 535, 537, 539, 548, 549, 564, 569, 572, 575, 578, 584, 585, 597
Nice, Geoffrey 7, 95, 103, 115, 123, 124, 129, 224, 225, 285, 318, 346, 434, 512, 516, 517, 545, 566, 581
    BBC HARDtalk 434
Niebel, Dirk 324
Nkurunziza, Pierre 212, 304
Noetzel, Timo 180, 532
Nourain, Abdallah Banda Abakaer 309
Nouwen, Sarah 241, 552

Nowak, Manfred 383
Ntaganda, Jean Bosco 155, 203, 226, 233, 235, 252, 268, 269, 525, 549, 550, 561
Nuremberg trials 3, 12
Nyachae, Charles 325
Nzelibe, Jide 229, 237, 547, 550

O

Obama, Barack 79, 80, 81, 82, 176, 177, 325, 489, 501, 502, 529, 530, 531, 593
    shared Luo background with Raila Odinga 324
Obasanjo, Olusegun 155, 213, 292, 525, 568
O'Brien, Adam 33, 241, 243, 487, 497, 546, 552, 553, 554, 555, 556
Observer, The 570
Ocampo, Luis Moreno 4, 5, 6, 9, 22, 27, 31, 32, 83, 84, 112, 115, 116, 117, 118, 119, 120, 121, 122, 123, 124, 125, 126, 127, 128, 129, 130, 131, 132, 133, 134, 135, 136, 137, 138, 139, 140, 141, 142, 150, 151, 153, 154, 155, 156, 167, 168, 169, 173, 174, 175, 204, 219, 220, 221, 222, 223, 228, 229, 237, 238, 241, 242, 243, 244, 251, 254, 255, 256, 257, 259, 260, 262, 265, 267, 268, 272, 282, 283, 284, 285, 286, 287, 288, 289, 290, 291, 292, 295, 303, 310, 318, 320, 321, 331, 337, 347, 349, 350, 351, 353, 355, 357, 358, 362, 363, 364, 398, 399, 400, 401, 402, 403, 404, 476, 482, 486, 513, 515, 516, 517, 518, 520, 521, 524, 525, 530, 531, 537, 543, 544, 556, 557, 561, 562, 564, 566, 583, 585, 586, 587, 588, 596
    and child soldiers 302
    and Darfur peace process 302
    and indictment of President al-Bashir 283, 302, 303
    and President al-Bashir 123
    and the Hema Lubanga 122
    and the Lubanga conviction 265
    credibility over genocide issue 291, 295
    Darfurian mortality claims 286
    methods critiqued by Alex de Wall 284
Ochola II, Macleord Baker 288, 289, 567
Ocora, Calvin 237, 238
Odama, John Baptist 246, 250
Odhiambo, Okot 242
Odinga, Raila 312, 313, 315, 322, 323, 326
    shared Luo background with Barack Obama 324
Odongo, Matthew 246
Office of the Prosecutor (OTP) 29, 30, 47, 48, 81, 84, 115, 116, 121, 122, 127, 129, 131, 133, 134, 135, 142, 143, 156, 157, 168, 173, 174, 175, 194, 197, 203, 219, 220, 221, 222, 225, 226, 228, 229, 237, 240, 241, 244, 245, 246, 253, 259, 261, 262, 263, 267, 269, 270, 271, 282, 284, 310, 320, 322, 329, 330, 333, 335, 338, 339, 341, 360, 362, 366, 370, 387, 415, 419, 420, 425, 485, 490, 502, 506, 514, 515, 517, 519, 520, 528, 529, 537, 539, 543, 544, 551, 552, 553, 556, 566, 580, 589
    and intermediaries 260, 267
Olopade, Dayo 327, 574, 576, 577
O'Malley, Patrick 79
Onega, Peter 246
O'Neill, Brendan 201
Ongeri, Sam 326
Ongwen, Dominic 242
Oryem, Okello 215
Osman, Daff-Alla Elhag Ali 127
Otim, Michael 243, 248, 553, 555
Otti, Vincent 62, 63, 203, 242, 553
Ouattara, Alassane 335, 336, 337, 340, 341, 342, 343, 344, 398
Ozaki, Kuniko 107

P

Pace, William 105, 122, 242, 492, 502, 503
Paisley Jr., Ian 33, 315, 380, 381, 393, 404, 487, 575, 577, 591, 594, 597
    and foreign involvement in Kenya s internal affairs 326
Palme, Christian 136, 137, 138, 139, 140, 520
Paolillo, Felipe 14
Parliamentarians for Global Action 51
Parrott, Louise 30, 61, 485, 496, 540
Parry, Emyr Jones
    and Ugandan peace process 248
Patassé, Ange-Félix 275, 276
Patten, Chris 35, 49, 86, 487, 491, 503
Paulus, Andreas 86, 87, 88, 503, 504
Payne, Donald 171
Pejic´, Jelena 65, 498
Perdomo, Claudia 243
Peskin, Victor 66, 498
Pillay, Navanethem 105
Ping, Jean 303

Popal, Karim 187, 193, 534
Posner, Eric 199, 398, 595
Powell, Colin 291
　and the Christian lobby 291
Prabakharan, Velupillai 384
Prosper, Pierre-Richard 77
Prunier, Gérard 7, 476

R

Rajao, Paulo 136
Rapp, Stephen J. 79, 80
Ratner, Steven 376, 590
Reisman, W. Michael 220, 221, 227, 240, 544, 546, 552
Reuter, Christoph 183, 187, 188
Rice, Condoleezza 76, 77
Rice, Susan 79, 127, 128, 517, 583
Rieff, David 53, 87, 88, 96, 97, 492, 504, 507
Ritzer, George 399, 596
Rivkin Jr., David B. 2, 93, 94, 473, 492, 505, 506
Robertson, Geoffrey 1, 7, 11, 13, 14, 56, 57, 68, 88, 100, 113, 116, 120, 144, 145, 149, 222, 223, 225, 254, 345, 366, 367, 473, 477, 478, 493, 494, 499, 504, 507, 512, 513, 514, 522, 523, 524, 544, 545, 556, 588
Robinson, Darryl 136, 220, 225, 226, 523, 543, 545, 546
Rome Conference 13, 23, 24, 36, 50, 51, 85, 105, 144, 145, 146, 224, 236, 385, 478, 523
　and Iraq War 168
　USA representation at 76
Rome Statute 2, 3, 6, 11, 12, 13, 14, 15, 16, 17, 18, 20, 21, 22, 23, 24, 27, 29, 36, 39, 41, 42, 43, 44, 45, 46, 47, 49, 50, 52, 54, 58, 59, 60, 61, 62, 63, 64, 66, 69, 71, 76, 77, 79, 80, 83, 86, 88, 93, 94, 95, 99, 101, 102, 103, 105, 112, 117, 119, 126, 145, 150, 157, 158, 164, 165, 169, 173, 174, 175, 176, 177, 178, 195, 196, 197, 205, 206, 207, 208, 209, 212, 213, 214, 215, 217, 218, 220, 221, 222, 228, 230, 236, 238, 239, 248, 249, 251, 252, 253, 266, 267, 268, 269, 282, 295, 296, 297, 303, 308, 309, 310, 312, 313, 314, 316, 318, 319, 322, 325, 329, 335, 338, 346, 347, 353, 356, 361, 362, 370, 371, 379, 381, 385, 394, 402, 407, 408, 409, 410, 411, 424, 432, 481, 489, 495, 498, 500, 504,
511, 520, 523, 526, 528, 537, 543, 579, 596
　African disillusionment with 400
　and definition of crime of aggression 145, 148
　and deterrence 228
　and selection of judges to the ICC 111
　and Sudan 77
　and the Bush Administration 71
　and the Clinton Administration 69, 70, 71
　and the European Union 86
　and the Obama Administration 80
　and the US Congress 70
　constitutionality of 318
　drafting of 88
　early history of 433
　Ivory Coast ratification of 335
　Mali's signing of 370
　motion to withdraw Kenya from 333
Rome Treaty 19, 36, 94, 95, 98, 296, 297, 428, 429, 500
　and the Clinton Administration 70
　and the US Congress 69
　US objections to 76
Rosenthal, John 8, 15, 17, 18, 21, 22, 27, 31, 35, 45, 202, 297, 480, 482, 484, 486, 487, 490, 538, 570
Rovera, Donatella 350, 352
Royal African Society 209, 487, 537, 551, 552, 553, 555, 562
Rozenberg, Joshua 107, 116, 117, 139, 257, 259, 260, 261, 399, 509, 513, 551, 557, 558, 596
Ruto, Isaac 318, 322
Ruto, William 214, 215, 216, 314, 317, 318, 323, 324, 325, 326, 327, 329, 330, 333, 334, 431, 432, 574, 575, 578

S

Sackur, Stephen 387
Said, Edward 339, 580
Saiga, Fumiko 47, 106, 107
Saleh, Salim 271
Samimi, Maghferat 178
Sands, Philippe 7, 12, 57, 76, 85, 99, 100, 105, 177, 348, 364, 386, 478, 494, 501, 503, 508, 510, 531, 582, 593
Sang, Joshua 203, 215, 314, 317, 324, 330
Sangqu, Baso 111
Sanogo, Amadou Haya 369

Sassòli, Marco 192
Sauer, Heiner 375
Schabas, William 7, 11, 27, 33, 34, 59, 61, 81, 85, 105, 113, 120, 121, 122, 125, 126, 130, 134, 135, 143, 144, 145, 148, 149, 172, 173, 174, 175, 177, 203, 219, 220, 221, 224, 225, 226, 227, 245, 266, 273, 283, 328, 370, 405, 433, 477, 478, 484, 487, 496, 498, 501, 503, 508, 509, 512, 515, 516, 518, 519, 522, 523, 530, 531, 538, 539, 543, 544, 545, 546, 554, 562, 566, 582, 588, 593
    blog, humanrightsdoctorate.blogspot.com 433
Schaefer, Brett D. 80, 501, 502
Scharf, Michael 168, 529, 582
Scheffer, David 70, 71, 72, 76, 78, 299, 499, 500, 501
Schiff, Benjamin 7, 52, 67, 85, 86, 89, 101, 102, 115, 120, 134, 135, 220, 222, 225, 398, 433, 492, 498, 503, 504, 595
Schneiderhan, Wolfgang 181
Scholz, Rupert 375
Schwarzenberger, Georg 11, 25, 397, 477
Sebire, Nicolas 262
Seils, Paul 136, 243, 553
Selassie, Bereket Habte 392, 393, 594
Sen, Hun
    and indictment of President al-Bashir 306
Shalluf, al-Hadi 140, 141
Shiner, Phil 170, 172, 173
Sidique, Safi 186
Simão, Leonardo 35
Sinanyan, Loru 144, 523
Singh, Param-Preet 342
Smith, Rhona 119, 514
Song, Sang-Hyun 36, 61, 102, 488, 496
Sonnenberger, Heinz 193, 194
Soro, Guillaume 341, 342, 343
Sorokobi, Yves 136, 137
Southwick, Katherine 238, 249, 551, 555
Spiegel, Der 180, 182, 183, 184, 185, 186, 187, 188, 189, 202, 237, 531, 532, 533, 534, 535, 536, 537, 551, 597
    and the Kunduz bombing 183, 184
Sriram, Chandra Lekha 120, 122, 514, 515
Starr, Kenneth 27, 483
Steele, Jonathan 279, 295, 569
Stegmiller, Ignaz 220, 221, 225, 544, 545
Stein, Eric 96, 97, 98, 505, 506, 507
Stern 183, 534
Stith, Charles 334
Strada, Gino 294, 569
Suleiman, Ghazi 278, 564
Suleiman, Issa Ibrahim 142
Sutter, Daniel 230, 548

T

Taliban 159, 163, 164, 176, 180, 181, 182, 184, 186, 197, 527, 530
Tarfusser, Cuno Jakob 102, 313
Taty, Mercedes 293
Taylor, Charles 524, 537, 538, 593, 594
Taylor, Melinda 357, 365
Teakle, Paddy 186
Thakur, Ramesh 3, 300, 382, 383, 474, 571, 591
Thomas, Edward 298, 570
Times, The 380
Tolbert, David 22, 58, 482, 494
Traoré, Dioncounda 369, 370
Trendafilova, Ekaterina 313
Turlan, Pascal 339
Turner, Christian 324, 325
Tutu, Desmond 388, 593
    and Ugandan peace process 248

U

Ušacka, Anita 113, 295, 318
United Nations 5, 7, 8, 12, 13, 16, 18, 19, 22, 32, 33, 39, 44, 51, 55, 58, 61, 62, 66, 67, 72, 73, 79, 80, 95, 102, 103, 105, 107, 111, 127, 130, 131, 142, 146, 155, 157, 158, 175, 177, 184, 213, 222, 232, 234, 235, 246, 250, 254, 267, 277, 284, 288, 290, 298, 299, 305, 307, 310, 336, 337, 341, 346, 347, 349, 350, 355, 370, 400, 404, 434, 475, 479
    and child soldiers 301
    and Darfur peace process 299
    and intermediaries 263
    and the Gbagbo government 336
    Sudanese confidence in 298
United Nations Security Council 1, 2, 5, 6, 12, 14, 20, 23, 24, 26, 33, 52, 54, 56, 57, 58, 61, 62, 64, 66, 71, 72, 75, 77, 78, 89, 94, 95, 98, 141, 145, 147, 157, 158, 176, 204, 206, 208, 209, 212, 214, 215, 217, 219, 234, 280, 281, 285, 286, 297, 298, 299, 303, 304, 310, 311, 312, 318, 345, 346, 363, 365, 366, 368, 370, 392, 398,

404, 408, 431, 432, 496, 497, 505, 581, 587, 588, 593
and definition of crime of aggression 146
and the Gaddafi regime 348

V
Vad, Erich 182
Valentine, Paul 97, 507
van der Borght, Erwin 372
van Zyl, Paul 230, 548
Vollmer, Jörg 183, 184

W
Waddell, Nicholas 28, 199, 484, 537, 544, 551, 552, 553, 555, 562
Wade, Abdoulaye 212, 541
Wainaina, Binyavanga 331, 578
Waki, Philip 313
Wall Street Journal, The 36, 96, 117, 118, 136, 222, 242, 473, 480, 488, 492, 502, 503, 504, 513, 519, 529, 532, 537, 544, 552, 595
Warlick, James B. 79
Washington Post 285, 349, 400, 492, 501, 506, 534, 541, 564, 565, 569, 582, 596
Weber, Max 399
Weiss, Gordon 384, 592
Weissman, Fabrice 31, 486
Wenaweser, Christian 67, 113, 114, 132, 255, 511
Westerwelle, Guido 188
Wichert, Peter 181
Wierda, Marieke 243, 553
Wiesenthal, Simon 374
WikiLeaks 65, 127, 173, 179, 476, 487, 496, 497, 498, 514, 515, 519, 529, 531, 539, 573
Will, George F. 35, 96, 487, 507
Williams, Andrew 171
Wilson, Elliot 321, 322, 576
Wilson, Richard Ashby 104, 134, 509, 519
Withopf, Ekkehard 136
Witteveen, Martin 136
Wolff, Alejandro 128
Wolpe, Howard 155
Wood, Nicholas 170, 529
World Bank 89, 96, 504
World Trade Organisation 96
Wouters, Jan 36, 42, 488, 489, 509, 550
Wyngaert, Christine Van den 312, 331, 332, 333, 387, 574, 578

Y
Yayi, Thomas Boni 212
Yee, Lionel 65, 498
Young-Jin, Choi 336

Z
Zhixiang, Wang 22, 482, 483
Zimmer, Mark 193
zu Guttenberg, Karl-Theodor 181, 191
Zwart, Tim 338, 341, 344, 580